BUSINESS ETHICS
Ethical Decision Making and Cases

TENTH EDITION

O. C. Ferrell
University of New Mexico

John Fraedrich
Southern Illinois University—Carbondale

Linda Ferrell
University of New Mexico

 CENGAGE
Learning·

Australia • Brazil • Japan • Korea • Mexico • Singapore • Spain • United Kingdom • United States

CENGAGE Learning

Business Ethics: Ethical Decision Making & Cases, 10e

O.C. Ferrell, John Fraedrich and Linda Ferrell

Senior Vice President, Global Product Management – Higher Ed: Jack W. Calhoun

Vice President, General Manager, Social Science & Qualitative Business: Erin Joyner

Product Director: Mike Schenk

Senior Product Manager: Mike Roche

Senior Content Developer: Julia Chase

Product Assistant: Tamara Grega

Senior Marketing Manager: Robin LeFevre

Market Development Manager: Emily Horowitz

Marketing Coordinator: Michael Saver

Art and Cover Direction, Production Management, and Composition: Integra Software Pvt. Ltd.

Senior Media Developer: Sally Nieman

Rights Acquisition Director: Audrey Pettengill

Rights Acquisition Specialist, Text and Image: Amber Hosea

Manufacturing Planner: Ron Montgomery

Cover Image(s): ©Dmitry Naumov/ shutterstock

For product information and technology assistance, contact us at **Cengage Learning Customer & Sales Support, 1-800-354-9706.**

For permission to use material from this text or product, submit all requests online at **www.cengage.com/permissions.** Further permissions questions can be emailed to **permissionrequest@cengage.com.**

Library of Congress Control Number: 2013948556

ISBN 13: 978-1-285-42371-5

ISBN 10: 1-285-42371-2

Cengage Learning
200 First Stamford Place, 4th Floor
Stamford, CT 06902
USA

Cengage Learning is a leading provider of customized learning solutions with office locations around the globe, including Singapore, the United Kingdom, Australia, Mexico, Brazil, and Japan. Locate your local office at **www.cengage.com/global.**

Cengage Learning products are represented in Canada by Nelson Education, Ltd.

To learn more about Cengage Learning Solutions, visit **www.cengage.com.**

Purchase any of our products at your local college store or at our preferred online store **www.cengagebrain.com.**

Printed in the United States of America
1 2 3 4 5 6 7 18 17 16 15 14 13

To James Collins Ferrell and
  George Collins Ferrell.

  —*O.C. Ferrell*

To Debbie FIBJ.

  —*John Fraedrich*

To Bruce and Becky Nafziger.

  —*Linda Ferrell*

BRIEF CONTENTS

CONTENTS

PART 5: CASES 380

PREFACE

This is the Tenth Edition of *Business Ethics: Ethical Decision Making* and Cases. Our text has become the most widely used business ethics book, with approximately one out of three business ethics courses in schools of business using our text. We were the first major business ethics textbook to use a managerial framework that integrates ethics into strategic decisions. Today in corporate America, ethics and compliance has become a major functional area that structures responsible managerial decision making. Now that ethics has been linked to financial performance, there is growing recognition that business ethics courses are as important as other functional areas such as marketing, accounting, finance, and management.

Our approach is to help students understand and participate in effective ethical decision making in organizations. We approach business ethics from an applied perspective, focusing on conceptual frameworks, risks, issues, and dilemmas that will be faced in the real world of business. We prepare students for the challenges they will face in understanding how organizational ethical decision making works. We describe how ethical decisions in an organization involve collaboration in groups, teams, and discussions with peers. Many decisions fall into grey areas where the right decision may not be clear and requires the use of organizational resources and the advice of others. Students will face many ethical challenges in their careers, and our approach helps them to understand risks and be prepared to address ethical dilemmas. One approach to business ethics education is to include only a theoretical foundation related to ethical reasoning. Our method is to provide a balanced approach that includes the concepts of ethical reasoning as well as the organizational environment that influences ethical decision making.

The Tenth Edition includes the most comprehensive changes we have made in any revision. Each chapter has been revised based on the latest research and knowledge available. Throughout the book, up-to-date examples are used to make foundational concepts come to life. There are 11 new cases, and the other nine cases have been revised with all major changes occurring through the middle of 2013. The most significant change is the inclusion of two new chapters that cover topics which were included in previous editions but that we now believe need separate chapters. First, chapter 11 focuses on ethical leadership. It is not enough to just make good ethical decisions; every employee has the responsibility and opportunity to lead others. Second, chapter 12 is dedicated to sustainability.

While sustainability is usually associated with social responsibility, ethical issues and decisions in this area are important to the long-term success of the organization.

Using a managerial framework, we explain how ethics can be integrated into strategic business decisions. This framework provides an *overview of the concepts, processes, mandatory, core,* and *voluntary business practices* associated with successful business ethics programs. Some approaches to business ethics are excellent as exercises in intellectual reasoning, but they cannot deal with the many actual issues and considerations that people in business organizations face. Our approach supports ethical reasoning and the value of individuals being able to face ethical challenges and voice their concerns about appropriate behavior. Employees in organizations are ultimately in charge of their own behavior and need to be skillful in making decisions in gray areas where the appropriate conduct is not always obvious.

We have been diligent in this revision to provide the most relevant examples of how the lack of business ethics has challenged our economic viability and entangled countries and companies around the world. This book remains the market leader because it *addresses the complex environment of ethical decision making in organizations and pragmatic, actual business concerns.* Every individual has unique personal principles and values, and every organization has its own set of values, rules, and organizational ethical culture. Business ethics must consider the organizational culture and interdependent relationships between the individual and other significant persons involved in organizational decision making. Without effective guidance, a businessperson cannot make ethical decisions while facing a short-term orientation, feeling organizational pressure to perform well and seeing rewards based on outcomes in a challenging competitive environment.

By focusing on individual issues and organizational environments, this book gives students the opportunity to see roles and responsibilities they will face in business. The past decade has reinforced the value of understanding the role of business ethics in the effective management of an organization. Widespread misconduct reported in the mass media every day demonstrates that businesses, governments, non-profits, and institutions of higher learning need to address business ethics.

Our primary goal has always been to enhance the awareness and the ethical decision-making skills that students will need to make business ethics decisions that contribute to responsible business conduct. By focusing on these concerns and issues of today's challenging business environment, we demonstrate that the study of business ethics is imperative to the long-term well-being of not only businesses, but also our economic system.

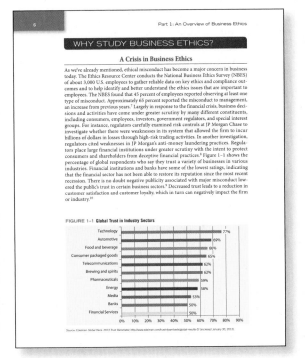

PHILOSOPHY OF THIS TEXT

Chapter 1: The Importance of Business Ethics   15

and respond to ethical issues. In our book the term *ethical culture* is acceptable behavior as defined by the company and industry. Ethical culture is the component of corporate culture that captures the values and norms an organization defines and is compared to by its industry as appropriate conduct. The goal of an ethical culture is to minimize the need for enforced compliance of rules and maximize the use of principles that contribute to ethical reasoning in difficult or new situations. Ethical culture is positively related to workplace confrontation over ethics issues, reports to management of observed misconduct, and the presence of ethics hotlines.³³ To develop better ethical corporate cultures, many businesses communicate core values to their employees by creating ethics programs and appointing ethics officers to oversee them. An ethical culture creates shared values and support for ethical decisions and is driven by top management.

Globally, businesses are working closely together to establish standards of acceptable behavior. We are already seeing collaborative efforts by a range of organizations to establish goals and mandate minimum levels of ethical behavior, from the European Union, the North American Free Trade Agreement (NAFTA), the Southern Common Market (MERCOSUR), and the World Trade Organization (WTO) to, more recently, the Council on Economic Priorities' Social Accountability 8000 (SA 8000), the Ethical Trading Initiative, and the U.S. Apparel Industry Partnership. Some companies refuse to do business with organizations that do not support and abide by these standards. Many companies demonstrate their commitment toward acceptable conduct by adopting globally recognized principles emphasizing human rights and social responsibility. For instance, in 2000 the United Nations launched the Global Compact, a set of 10 principles concerning human rights, labor, the environment, and anti-corruption. The purpose of the Global Compact is to create openness and alignment among business, government, society, labor, and the United Nations. Companies that adopt this code agree to integrate the ten principles into their business practices, publish their progress toward these objectives on an annual basis, and partner with others to advance broader objectives of the UN.³⁴ These 10 principles are covered in more detail in Chapter 10.

THE BENEFITS OF BUSINESS ETHICS

The field of business ethics continues to change rapidly as more firms recognize the benefits of improving ethical conduct and the link between business ethics and financial performance. Both research and examples from the business world demonstrate that building an ethical reputation among employees, customers, and the general public pays off. Figure 1–2 provides an overview of the relationship between business ethics and organizational performance. Although we believe there are many practical benefits to being ethical, many businesspeople make decisions because they believe a particular course of action is simply the right thing to do as responsible members of society. Granite Construction earned a place in *Ethisphere*'s "World's Most Ethical Companies" for four consecutive years as a result of its integration of ethics into the company culture. Granite formulated its ethics program to comply with the Federal Sentencing Guidelines for Organizations and helped inspire the Construction Industry Ethics and Compliance Initiative. To ensure all company employees are familiar with Granite's high ethical standards, the firm holds six mandatory training sessions annually, conducts ethics and compliance audits, and uses field compliance officers to make certain ethical conduct is taking place throughout the entire

---

The purpose of this book is to help students improve their ability to make ethical decisions in business by providing them with a framework that they can use to identify, analyze, and resolve ethical issues in business decision making. Individual values and ethics are important in this process. By studying business ethics, students begin to understand how to cope with conflicts between their personal values and those of the organization.

Many ethical decisions in business are close calls. It often takes years of experience in a particular industry to know what is acceptable. We do not, in this book, provide ethical answers but instead attempt to prepare students to make informed ethical decisions. First, we do not moralize by indicating what to do in a specific situation. Second, although we provide an overview of moral philosophies and decision-making processes, we do not prescribe any one philosophy or process as best or most ethical. Third, by itself, this book will not make students more ethical nor will it tell them how to judge the ethical behavior of others. Rather, its goal is to help students understand and use their current values and convictions in making business decisions and to encourage everyone to think about the effects of their decisions on business and society.

Many people believe that business ethics cannot be taught. Although we do not claim to teach ethics, we suggest that by studying business ethics a person can improve ethical decision making by identifying ethical issues and recognizing the approaches available to resolve them. An organization's reward system can reinforce appropriate behavior and help shape attitudes and beliefs about important issues. For example, the success of some campaigns to end racial or gender discrimination in the workplace provides evidence that attitudes and behavior can be changed with new information, awareness, and shared values.

CONTENT AND ORGANIZATION

In writing *Business Ethics*, Tenth Edition, we strived to be as informative, complete, accessible, and up-to-date as possible. Instead of focusing on one area of ethics, such as moral philosophy or social responsibility, we provide balanced coverage of all areas relevant to the current development and practice of ethical decision making. In short, we have tried to keep pace with new developments and current thinking in teaching and practices.

The first half of the text consists of 12 chapters, which provide a framework to identify, analyze, and understand how businesspeople make ethical decisions and deal with ethical issues. Several enhancements have been made to chapter content for this edition. Some of the most important are listed in the next paragraphs.

Part One, "An Overview of Business Ethics," includes two chapters that help provide a broader context for the study of business ethics. Chapter 1, "The Importance of Business Ethics," has been revised with many new examples and survey results to describe issues and concerns important to business ethics. Chapter 2, "Stakeholder Relationships, Social Responsibility, and Corporate Governance," has been significantly reorganized and updated with new examples and issues.

Part Two, "Ethical Issues and the Institutionalization of Business Ethics," consists of two chapters that provide the background that students need to identify ethical issues and understand how society, through the legal system, has attempted to hold organizations responsible for managing these issues. Chapter 3, "Emerging Business Ethics Issues," has been reorganized and updated and provides expanded coverage of business ethics issues. Chapter 4, "The Institutionalization of Business Ethics" examines key elements of core or best practices in corporate America today along with legislation and regulation requirements that support business ethics initiatives. The chapter is divided into three main areas: voluntary, mandated, and core boundaries.

Part Three, "The Decision-Making Process" consists of three chapters, which provide a framework to identify, analyze, and understand how businesspeople make ethical decisions and deal with ethical issues. Chapter 5, "Ethical Decision Making," has been revised and updated to reflect current research and understanding of ethical decision making and contains a new section on normative considerations in ethical decision making. Chapter 6, "Individual Factors: Moral Philosophies and Values," has been updated and revised to explore the role of moral philosophies and moral development as individual factors in the ethical decision-making process. Chapter 7, "Organizational Factors: The Role of Ethical Culture and Relationships," considers organizational influences on business decisions, such as role relationships, differential association, and other organizational pressures, as well as whistle-blowing.

Part Four, "Implementing Business Ethics in a Global Economy," looks at specific measures that companies can take to build an effective ethics program as well as how these programs may be affected by global issues, leadership, and sustainability issues. Chapter 8, "Developing an Effective Ethics Program," has been refined and updated with corporate best practices for developing effective ethics programs. Chapter 9, "Managing and Controlling Ethics Programs," offers a framework for auditing ethics initiatives as well as the importance of doing so. Such audits can help companies pinpoint problem areas, measure their progress in improving conduct, and even provide a "debriefing" opportunity after a crisis. Chapter 10, "Business Ethics in a Global Economy" has been updated to reflect the complex and dynamic events that occur in global business. This chapter will help students understand the major issues involved in making decisions in a global environment. Chapter 11 is a new chapter on ethical leadership. Reviewers indicated that they wanted more information provided on the importance of leadership to an ethical culture, and this chapter answers these requests. Finally, Chapter 12 is a new chapter on sustainability. It examines the ethical and social responsibility dimensions of sustainability.

Part Five consists of 20 cases in the text that bring reality into the learning process. Eleven of these cases are new to the tenth edition, and the remaining nine have been revised and updated. In addition, four shorter cases are available on the Instructor's Companion website:

- Toyota: Challenges in Maintaining Integrity
- The Container Store: An Employee-centric Retailer
- The Ethics Program at Eaton Corporation
- Barrett-Jackson Auction Company: Family, Fairness, and Philanthropy

The companies and situations portrayed in these cases are real; names and other facts are not disguised; and all cases include developments up to the end of 2013. By reading and analyzing these cases, students can gain insight into ethical decisions and the realities of making decisions in complex situations.

TEXT FEATURES

Many tools are available in this text to help both students and instructors in the quest to improve students' ability to make ethical business decisions.

- Each chapter opens with an outline and a list of learning objectives.
- Immediately following is "An Ethical Dilemma" that should provoke discussion about ethical issues related to the chapter. The short vignette describes a hypothetical incident involving an ethical conflict. Questions at the end of the "Ethical Dilemma" section focus discussion on how the dilemma could be resolved. All new ethical dilemmas have been provided for this edition.

CASE 1
Monsanto Attempts to Balance Stakeholder Interests

CASE 2
Starbucks' Mission: Social Responsibility and Brand Strength

CASE 3
Walmart Manages Ethics and Compliance Challenges

CASE 4
Sustainability Challenges in the Gas and Oil Industry

CASE 5
New Belgium Brewing: Ethical and Environmental Responsibility

CASE 6
National Collegiate Athletic Association Ethics and Compliance Program

CASE 7
Google: The Quest to Balance Privacy with Profits

CASE 8
Zappos: Delivering Customer Satisfaction

CASE 9
Enron: Questionable Accounting Leads to Collapse

CASE 10
Home Depot Implements Stakeholder Orientation

CASE 11
Frauds of the Century

CASE 12
Insider Trading at the Galleon Group

CASE 13
Whole Foods Strives to Be an Ethical Corporate Citizen

CASE 14
Apple Inc.'s Ethical Success and Challenges

CASE 15
PepsiCo's Journey Toward an Ethical and Socially Responsible Culture

CASE 16
Ethical Leadership at Cardinal IG: The Foundation of a Culture of Diversity

CASE 17
Better Business Bureau: Protecting Consumers and Dealing with Organizational Ethics Challenges

CASE 18
Managing the Risks of Global Bribery in Business

CASE 19
Mattel Responds to Ethical Challenges

CASE 20
Best Buy Fights Against Electronic Waste

- Each chapter has a contemporary real world debate issue. Many of these debate issues have been updated to reflect current ethical issues in business. These debate issues have been found to stimulate thoughtful discussion relating to content issues in the chapter. Topics of the debate issues include workplace privacy, the universal health care debate, the contribution of ethical conduct to financial performance, legislation concerning whistle-blowing, and the benefits of organic food.

- At the end of each chapter are a chapter summary and an important terms list, both of which are handy tools for review. Also included at the end of each chapter is a "Resolving Ethical Business Challenges" section. The vignette describes a realistic drama that helps students experience the process of ethical decision making. All new vignettes have been provided for this edition. The "Resolving Ethical Business Challenges" minicases presented in this text are hypothetical; any resemblance to real persons, companies, or situations is coincidental. Keep in mind that there are no right or wrong solutions to the minicases.

The ethical dilemmas and real-life situations provide an opportunity for students to use concepts in the chapter to resolve ethical issues.

Each chapter concludes with a series of questions that allow students to test their EQ (Ethics Quotient).

- Cases. In Part Five, following each real-world case are questions to guide students in recognizing and resolving ethical issues. For some cases, students can conduct additional research to determine recent developments because many ethical issues in companies take years to resolve.

EFFECTIVE TOOLS FOR TEACHING AND LEARNING

Instructor's Resource Website. You can find the following teaching tools on the pass word protected instructor site.

- **Instructor's Resource Manual.**   The *Instructor's Resource Manual* contains a wealth of information. Teaching notes for every chapter include a brief chapter summary, detailed lecture outline, and notes for using the "Ethical Dilemma" and "Resolving Ethical Business Challenges" sections. Detailed case notes point out the key issues involved and offer suggested answers to the questions. A separate section provides guidelines for using case analysis in teaching business ethics. Detailed notes are provided to guide the instructor in analyzing or grading the cases. Simulation role-play cases, as well as implementation suggestions, are included.

- **Role-Play Cases.**   The tenth edition provides six behavioral simulation role-play cases developed for use in the business ethics course. The role-play cases and implementation methods can be found in the *Instructor's Resource Manual* and on the website. Role-play cases may be used as a culminating experience to help students integrate concepts covered in the text. Alternatively, the cases may be used as an ongoing exercise to provide students with extensive opportunities for interacting and making ethical decisions.

  Role-play cases simulate a complex, realistic, and timely business ethics situation. Students form teams and make decisions based on an assigned role. The role-play case complements and enhances traditional approaches to business learning experiences because it (1) gives students the opportunity to practice making decisions that have business ethics consequences; (2) re-creates the power, pressures, and information that affect decision making at various levels of management; (3) provides students with a team-based experience that enriches their skills and understanding of group processes and dynamics; and (4) uses a feedback period to allow for the exploration of complex and controversial issues in business ethics decision making. The role-play cases can be used with classes of any size.

- **Cengage Learning Testing Powered by Cognero.**   This is a flexible, online system that allows you to author, edit, and manage test bank content from multiple Cengage Learning solutions; create multiple test versions in an instant; and deliver tests from your LMS, your classroom or wherever you want. Cengage Learning Testing Powered by Cognero works on any operating system or browser, no special installs or downloads needed. You can create tests from school, home, the coffee shop – anywhere with Internet access.

- **Video Segments.**   These brand new BBC video segments can be used across several chapters, and the Video Guide (which appears on the instructor website) contains a matrix intended to show the closest relationships between the videos and chapter topics. The Video Guide also includes summaries of each video as well as teaching guidelines and issues for discussion. Some topics include: Environmental waste reduction and Sony's efforts to reduce waste; The Rebuilding of the Starbucks Brand; BP Oil Spill and Risk Management ; PepsiCo's move into Russia; and many other timely and relevant segments.

CourseMate.   This unique student website makes course concepts come alive with interactive learning, study, and exam preparation tools supporting the printed text. CourseMate delivers what you need, including an interactive eBook, an interactive glossary, quizzes, videos, KnowNOW blogs, and more. The site contains links to companies and organizations highlighted in each chapter; links to association, industry, and company codes of conduct; case website links; company and organizational examples; and academic resources, including links to business ethics centers throughout the world and the opportunity to sign up for weekly abstracts of relevant *Wall Street Journal* articles. Four Ethical Leadership Challenge scenarios are available for each chapter. Training devices, including Lockheed Martin's Gray Matters ethics game, are also available. As well, a link to the Career Transitions site is provided for students where they can search for internships and career opportunities.

CengageNow.   This robust online course management system gives you more control in less time and delivers better student outcomes—NOW. CengageNow includes teaching and learning resources organized around lecturing, creating assignments, casework, quizzing, and gradework to track student progress and performance. The 20 end of book cases and questions appear in CengageNow. Multiple types of quizzes, including BBC video quizzes, multiple choice and essay questions for the chapter opening cases, closing cases, and "Check Your EQ" are assignable and gradable. Flexible assignments, automatic grading, and a gradebook option provide more control while saving you valuable time. A Personalized Study diagnostic tool empowers students to master concepts, prepare for exams, and become more involved in class.

Additional Teaching Resources.   O.C. Ferrell and Linda Ferrell are leading the Daniels Fund Ethics Initiative at the University of New Mexico. This initiative is part of a four-state initiative to develop teaching resources to support principle-based ethics education. Their publically accessible website contains original cases, debate issues, videos, interviews, and PowerPoint modules on select business ethics topics, as well as other resources such as articles on business ethics education. It is possible to access this website at http://danielsethics.mgt.unm.edu.

ACKNOWLEDGMENTS

A number of individuals provided reviews and suggestions that helped to improve this text. We sincerely appreciate their time and effort.

Donald Acker
Brown Mackie College

Donna Allen
Northwest Nazarene University

Suzanne Allen
Walsh University

Carolyn Ashe
University of Houston–Downtown

Laura Barelman
Wayne State College

Russell Bedard
Eastern Nazarene College

B. Barbara Boerner
Brevard College

Serena Breneman
University of Arkansas at Pine Bluff

Lance Brown
Miami Dade College

Judie Bucholz
Guilford College

Greg Buntz
University of the Pacific

Hoa Burrows
Miami Dade College

Julie Campbell
Adams State College

Robert Chandler
University of Central Florida

April Chatham-Carpenter
University of Northern Iowa

Leslie Connell
University of Central Florida

Peggy Cunningham
Dalhousie University

Carla Dando
Idaho State University

James E. Donovan
Detroit College of Business

Douglas Dow
University of Texas at Dallas

A. Charles Drubel
Muskingum College

Philip F. Esler
University of St. Andrews

Joseph M. Foster
*Indiana Vocational Technical College—
  Evansville*

Lynda Fuller
Wilmington University

Terry Gable
Truman State University

Robert Giacalone
University of Richmond

Suresh Gopalan
West Texas A&M University

Karen Gore
Ivy Technical College

Mark Hammer
Northwest Nazarene University

Charles E. Harris, Jr.
Texas A&M University

Kenneth A. Heischmidt
Southeast Missouri State University

Neil Herndon
Educational Consultant

Walter Hill
Green River Community College

Jack Hires
Valparaiso University

David Jacobs
American University

R. J. Johansen
Montana State University–Bozeman

Jeff Johnson
Athens State University

Edward Kimman
Vrije Universiteit

Janet Knight
Purdue North Central

Anita Leffel
University of Texas at San Antonio

Barbara Limbach
Chadron State College

Victor Lipe
Trident Tech

Nick Lockard
Texas Lutheran College

Terry Loe
Kennesaw State University

Nick Maddox
Stetson University

Isabelle Maignan
ING Bank

Phylis Mansfield
Pennsylvania State University–Erie

Robert Markus
Babson College

Therese Maskulka
Kutstown College

Randy McLeod
Harding University

Francy Milner
University of Colorado

Ali Mir
William Paterson University

Debi P. Mishra
Binghamton University, State University of New York

Patrick E. Murphy
University of Notre Dame

Lester Myers
University of San Francisco

Catherine Neal
Northern Kentucky University

Cynthia Nicola
Carlow College

Carol Nielsen
Bemidji State University

Sharon Palmitier
Grand Rapids Community College

Lee Richardson
University of Baltimore

James Salvucci
Curry College

William M. Sannwald
San Diego State University

Ruth Schaa
Black River Technical College

Zachary Shank
Albuquerque Technical Vocational Institute

Cynthia A. M. Simerly
Lakeland Community College

Karen Smith
Columbia Southern University

Filiz Tabak
Towson University

Debbie Thorne
Texas State University–San Marcos

Wanda V. Turner
Ferris State College

Gina Vega
Salem State College

William C. Ward
Mid-Continent University

David Wasieleski
Duquesne University

Jim Weber
Duquesne University

Ed Weiss
National-Louis University

Joseph W. Weiss
Bentley University

Jan Zahrly
University of North Dakota

We wish to acknowledge the many people who assisted us in writing this book. We are deeply grateful to Jennifer Sawayda for her work in organizing and managing the revision process. We would also like to thank Danielle Jolley and Michelle Urban for all their assistance in this edition. Finally, we express appreciation to the administration and to our colleagues at the University of New Mexico and Southern Illinois University at Carbondale for their support.

We invite your comments, questions, or criticisms. We want to do our best to provide teaching materials that enhance the study of business ethics. Your suggestions will be sincerely appreciated.

– O. C. Ferrell
– John Fraedrich
– Linda Ferrell

CHAPTER 1

THE IMPORTANCE OF BUSINESS ETHICS

CHAPTER OBJECTIVES

- Explore conceptualizations of business ethics from an organizational perspective
- Examine the historical foundations and evolution of business ethics
- Provide evidence that ethical value systems support business performance
- Gain insight into the extent of ethical misconduct in the workplace and the pressures for unethical behavior

CHAPTER OUTLINE

AN ETHICAL DILEMMA*

Sophie just completed a sales training course with one of the firm's most productive sales representatives, Emma. At the end of the first week, Sophie and Emma sat in a motel room filling out their expense vouchers for the week. Sophie casually remarked to Emma that the training course stressed the importance of accurately filling out expense vouchers.

Emma replied, "I'm glad you brought that up, Sophie. The company expense vouchers don't list the categories we need. I tried many times to explain to the accountants that there are more expenses than they have boxes for. The biggest complaint we, the salespeople, have is that there is no place to enter expenses for tipping waitresses, waiters, cab drivers, bell hops, airport baggage handlers, and the like. Even the government assumes tipping and taxes them as if they were getting an 18 percent tip. That's how service people actually survive on the lousy pay they get from their bosses. I tell you, it is embarrassing not to tip. One time I was at the airport and the skycap took my bags from me so I didn't have the hassle of checking them. He did all the paper work and after he was through, I said thank you. He looked at me in disbelief because he knew I was in sales. It took me a week to get that bag back."

"After that incident I went to the accounting department, and every week for five months I told them they needed to change the forms. I showed them the approximate amount the average salesperson pays in tips per week. Some of them were shocked at the amount. But would they change it or at least talk to the supervisor? No! So I went directly to him, and do you know what he said to me?"

"No, what?" asked Sophie.

"He told me that this is the way it has always been done, and it would stay that way. He also told me if I tried to go above him on this, I'd be looking for another job. I can't chance that now, especially in this economy. Then he had the nerve to tell me that salespeople are paid too much, and that's why we could eat the added expenses. We're the only ones who actually generate revenue and he tells me that I'm overpaid!"

"So what did you do?" inquired Sophie.

"I do what my supervisor told me years ago. I pad my account each week. For me, I tip 20 percent, so I make sure I write down when I tip and add that to my overall expense report."

"But that goes against company policy. Besides, how do you do it?" asked Sophie.

"It's easy. Every cab driver will give you blank receipts for cab fares. I usually put the added expenses there. We all do it," said Emma. "As long as everyone cooperates, the Vice President of Sales doesn't question the expense vouchers. I imagine she even did it when she was a lowly salesperson."

"What if people don't go along with this arrangement?" asked Sophie.

"In the past, we have had some who reported it like corporate wants us to. I remember there was a person who didn't report the same amounts as the co-worker traveling with her. Several months went by and the accountants came in, and she and all the salespeople that traveled together were investigated. After several months the one who ratted out the others was fired or quit, I can't remember. I do know she never worked in our industry again. Things like that get around. It's a small world for good salespeople, and everyone knows everyone."

"What happened to the other salespeople who were investigated?" Sophie asked.

"There were a lot of memos and even a thirty minute video as to the proper way to record expenses. All of them had conversations with the vice president, but no one was fired."

"No one was fired even though it went against policy?" Sophie asked Emma.

"At the time, my conversation with the VP went basically this way. She told me that corporate was not going to change the forms, and she acknowledged it was not fair or equitable to the salespeople. She hated the head accountant because he didn't want to accept the reality of a salesperson's life in the field. That was it. I left the office and as I walked past the Troll's office—that's what we call the head accountant—he just smiled at me."

This was Sophie's first real job out of school and Emma was her mentor. What should Sophie report on her expense report?

QUESTIONS | EXERCISES

1. Identify the issues Sophie has to resolve.
2. Discuss the alternatives for Sophie.
3. What should Sophie do if company policy appears to conflict with the firm's corporate culture?

*This case is strictly hypothetical; any resemblance to real persons, companies, or situations is coincidental.

The ability to recognize and deal with complex business ethics issues has become a significant priority in twenty-first–century companies. In recent years, a number of well-publicized scandals resulted in public outrage about deception and fraud in business and a subsequent demand for improved business ethics and greater corporate responsibility. The publicity and debate surrounding highly publicized legal and ethical lapses at a number of well-known firms highlight the need for businesses to integrate ethics and responsibility into all business decisions. On the other hand, the majority of ethical businesses with no or few ethical lapses are rarely recognized in the mass media for their conduct.

Highly visible business ethics issues influence the public's attitudes toward business and destroy trust. Ethical decisions are a part of everyday life for those who work in organizations. Ethics is a part of decision making at all levels of work and management. Business ethics is not just an isolated personal issue; codes, rules, and informal communications for responsible conduct are embedded in an organization's operations. This means ethical or unethical conduct is the province of everyone who works in an organizational environment.

Making good ethical decisions are just as important to business success as mastering management, marketing, finance, and accounting decisions. While education and training emphasize functional areas of business, business ethics is often viewed as easy to master, something that happens with little effort. The exact opposite is the case. Decisions with an ethical component are an everyday occurrence requiring people to identify issues and make quick decisions. Ethical behavior requires understanding and identifying issues, areas of risk, and approaches to making choices in an organizational environment. On the other hand, people can act unethically if they fail to identify an ethical issue. Ethical blindness results from individuals who fail to sense the nature and complexity of their decisions.[1] Some approaches to business ethics look only at the philosophical backgrounds of individuals and the social consequences of decisions. This approach fails to address the complex organizational environment of businesses and pragmatic business concerns. By contrast, our approach is managerial and incorporates real world decisions that impact the organization and stakeholders. Our book will help you better understand how business ethics is practiced in the business world.

It is important to learn how to make decisions in the internal environment of an organization to achieve goals and career advancement. But business does not exist in a vacuum. As stated, decisions in business have implications for shareholders, employees, customers, suppliers, and society. Ethical decisions must take these stakeholders into account, for unethical conduct can negatively affect society as a whole. Our approach focuses on the practical consequences of decisions and on positive outcomes that have the potential to contribute to both business success and society at large. The field of business ethics deals with questions about whether specific conduct and business practices are acceptable. For example, should a salesperson omit facts about a product's poor safety record in a sales presentation to a client? Should accountants report inaccuracies they discover in an audit of a client, knowing the auditing company will probably be fired by the client for doing so? Should an automobile tire manufacturer intentionally conceal safety concerns to avoid a massive and costly tire recall? Regardless of their legality, others will certainly judge the actions taken in such situations as right or wrong, ethical or unethical. By its very nature, the field of business ethics is controversial, and there is no universally accepted approach for resolving its dilemmas.

A cheating scandal at Harvard revealed what some see as a crisis in ethics. Approximately half of the students in a Harvard course allegedly collaborated on a take-home test despite directions from the professor not to do so. Some of the students were also accused of plagiarism when test answers were found to be similar or identical. Because these students are the business leaders of tomorrow, it is disturbing to see them at such a prestigious school acting unethically.[2] In addition to students, fraud among faculty has also been widely documented.[3] Cheating scandals are widespread in the academic community.

Before we get started, it is important to state our philosophies regarding this book. First, we do not moralize by telling you what is right or wrong in a specific situation, although we offer background on normative guidelines for appropriate conduct. Second, although we provide an overview of group and individual decision-making processes, we do not prescribe any one philosophy or process as the best or most ethical. However, we provide many examples of successful ethical decision making. Third, by itself, this book will not make you more ethical, nor will it tell you how to judge the ethical behavior of others. Rather, its goal is to help you understand, use, and improve your current values and convictions when making business decisions so you think about the effects of those decisions on business and society. In addition, this book will help you understand what businesses are doing to improve their ethical conduct. To this end, we aim to help you learn to recognize and resolve ethical issues within business organizations. As a manager, you will be responsible for your decisions and the ethical conduct of the employees you supervise. For this reason, we provide a chapter on ethical leadership. The framework we develop in this book focuses on how organizational ethical decisions are made and on ways companies can improve their ethical conduct. This process is more complex than you may think. People who believe they know how to make the "right" decision usually come away with more uncertainty about their own decision skills after learning about the complexity of ethical decision making. This is a normal occurrence, and our book will help you evaluate your own values as well as those of others. It also helps you to understand incentives found in the workplace that change the way you make decisions in business versus at home.

In this chapter, we first develop a definition of business ethics and discuss why it has become an important topic in business education. We also discuss why studying business ethics can be beneficial. Next, we examine the evolution of business ethics in North America. Then we explore the performance benefits of ethical decision making for businesses. Finally, we provide a brief overview of the framework we use for examining business ethics in this text.

BUSINESS ETHICS DEFINED

To understand business ethics, you must first recognize that most people do not have specific definitions they use to define ethics-related issues. The terms morals, principles, values, and ethics are often used interchangeably, and you will find this is true in companies as well. Consequently, there is much confusion regarding this topic. To help you understand these differences, we discuss these terms.

For our purposes, morals refer to a person's personal philosophies about what is right or wrong. The important point is that when one speaks of morals, it is personal or singular. Morals, your philosophies or sets of values of right and wrong, relate to you and you alone. You may use your personal moral convictions in making ethical decisions in any context. Business ethics comprises organizational principles, values, and norms that may originate from individuals, organizational statements, or from the legal system that primarily guide individual and group behavior in business. Principles are specific and pervasive boundaries for behavior that should not be violated. Principles often become the basis for rules. Some examples of principles could include human rights, freedom of speech, and fundamentals of justice. Values are enduring beliefs and ideals that are socially enforced. Several desirable or ethical values for business today are teamwork, trust, and integrity. Such values are often based on organizational or industry best practices. Investors, employees, customers, interest groups, the legal system, and the community often determine whether a specific action or standard is ethical or unethical. Although these groups influence the determination of what is ethical or unethical for business, they also can be at odds with one another. Even though this is the reality of business and such groups may not necessarily be right, their judgments influence society's acceptance or rejection of business practices.

Ethics is defined as behavior or decisions made within a group's values. In our case we are discussing decisions made in business by groups of people that represent the business organization. Because the Supreme Court defined companies as having limited individual rights,[4] it is logical such groups have an identity that includes core values. This is known as being part of a corporate culture. Within this culture there are rules and regulations both written and unwritten that determine what decisions employees consider right or wrong as it relates to the firm. Such right/wrong, good/bad evaluations are judgments by the organization and are defined as its ethics (or in this case their business ethics). One difference between an ordinary decision and an ethical one lies in "the point where the accepted rules no longer serve, and the decision maker is faced with the responsibility for weighing values and reaching a judgment in a situation which is not quite the same as any he or she has faced before."[5] Another difference relates to the amount of emphasis decision makers place on their own values and accepted practices within their company. Consequently, values and judgments play a critical role when we make ethical decisions.

Building on these definitions, we begin to develop a concept of business ethics. Most people agree that businesses should hire individuals with sound moral principles. However, some special aspects must be considered when applying ethics to business. First, to survive, businesses must earn a profit. If profits are realized through misconduct, however, the life of the organization may be shortened. Peregrine Financial Group collapsed after the firm used fraud to take more than $100 million from investors over a 20-year period and the CEO used fake financial statements to cover up the fraud.[6] Second, businesses must balance their desire for profits against the needs and desires of society. The good news is the world's most ethical companies often have superior stock performance. To address these unique aspects of the business world, society has developed rules—both legal and implicit—to guide businesses in their efforts to earn profits in ways that do not harm individuals or society and contribute to economic well-being.

WHY STUDY BUSINESS ETHICS?

A Crisis in Business Ethics

As we've already mentioned, ethical misconduct has become a major concern in business today. The Ethics Resource Center conducts the National Business Ethics Survey (NBES) of about 3,000 U.S. employees to gather reliable data on key ethics and compliance outcomes and to help identify and better understand the ethics issues that are important to employees. The NBES found that 45 percent of employees reported observing at least one type of misconduct. Approximately 65 percent reported the misconduct to management, an increase from previous years.[7] Largely in response to the financial crisis, business decisions and activities have come under greater scrutiny by many different constituents, including consumers, employees, investors, government regulators, and special interest groups. For instance, regulators carefully examined risk controls at JP Morgan Chase to investigate whether there were weaknesses in its system that allowed the firm to incur billions of dollars in losses through high-risk trading activities. In another investigation, regulators cited weaknesses in JP Morgan's anti-money laundering practices. Regulators place large financial institutions under greater scrutiny with the intent to protect consumers and shareholders from deceptive financial practices.[8] Figure 1–1 shows the percentage of global respondents who say they trust a variety of businesses in various industries. Financial institutions and banks have some of the lowest ratings, indicating that the financial sector has not been able to restore its reputation since the most recent recession. There is no doubt negative publicity associated with major misconduct lowered the public's trust in certain business sectors.[9] Decreased trust leads to a reduction in customer satisfaction and customer loyalty, which in turn can negatively impact the firm or industry.[10]

FIGURE 1–1 Global Trust in Industry Sectors

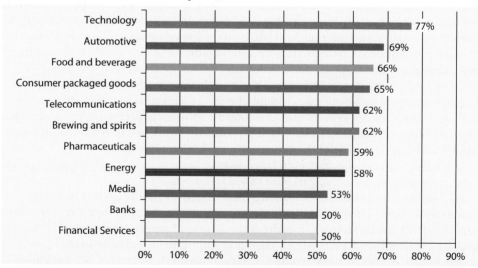

Source: Edelman *Global Deck: 2013 Trust Barometer,* http://www.edelman.com/trust-downloads/global-results-2/ (accessed January 30, 2013).

Specific Issues

Misuse of company resources, abusive behavior, harassment, accounting fraud, conflicts of interest, defective products, bribery, and employee theft are all problems cited as evidence of declining ethical standards. For example, Chesapeake Energy received negative publicity after it was revealed that CEO Aubrey McClendon had the unique perk of acquiring a small stake in every oil well that Chesapeake drilled. However, to pay for the costs, McClendon secured loans from firms, some of which were investors in Chesapeake. This represented a massive conflict of interest, and resulting criticism caused Chesapeake to eliminate the perk.[11] McClendon was later forced to resign.[12] Other ethical issues relate to recognizing the interest of communities and society. For instance, Whole Foods faced immense pressure when it took over the Latino-centered Hi-Lo market in Jamaica Plains, Massachusetts. Many residents of the community feared that the presence of an up-scale grocery chain would displace the lower-income residents of the community who could not afford Whole Foods' higher-priced grocery products. Opposition to Whole Foods continued even after the store was established when a neighborhood advisory committee suggested rejecting the store's request to add indoor and outdoor seating.[13] This demonstrates the community as a primary stakeholder. Although large companies like Whole Foods have significant power, pressures from the community still limit what they can do.

Ethics plays an important role in the public sector as well. In government, several politicians and high-ranking officials experienced significant negative publicity, and some resigned in disgrace over ethical indiscretions. Former Illinois governor Rod Blagojevich was sentenced to 14 years in prison for corruption while in office, including trying to "sell" the Illinois Senate seat vacated by Barack Obama when he became President.[14] The Blagojevich scandal demonstrates that ethical behavior must be proactively practiced at all levels of society.

Every organization has the potential for unethical behavior. For instance, Defense Secretary Leon Panetta ordered a review of military ethics after potential indiscretions were uncovered on the part of top military leaders. Investigations into improper relationships of top military personnel, including an extramarital affair by former Central Intelligence Director David Petraeus, have the potential to damage the reputation of the military. According to Panetta, senior officers in the military have a responsibility to do their jobs to the best of their abilities and also display high ethical standards in their personal behavior and in their handling of government resources.[15]

Even sports can be subject to ethical lapses. Well-known cyclist champion Lance Armstrong was stripped of his Tour de France titles after the U.S. Anti-Doping Agency found evidence that Armstrong participated in a large illicit drug scheme for more than a decade.[16] Another ethical dilemma in sports occurred when a number of lawsuits were filed against the National Football League (NFL) accusing them of hiding the risks and long-term harm that can occur from concussions sustained during games.[17]

Whether they are made in the realm of business, politics, science, or sports, most decisions are judged either right or wrong, ethical or unethical. Regardless of what an individual believes about a particular action, if society judges it to be unethical or wrong, new legislation usually follows. Whether correct or not, that judgment directly affects a company's ability to achieve its business goals. You should be aware that the public is more tolerant of questionable consumer practices than of similar business practices. Double standards are at least partly due to differences in wealth and the success between businesses and consumers. The more successful a company, the more the public is critical when misconduct occurs.[18] For this reason alone, it is important to understand business ethics and recognize ethical issues.

The Reasons for Studying Business Ethics

Studying business ethics is valuable for several reasons. Business ethics is not merely an extension of an individual's own personal ethics. Many people believe if a company hires good people with strong ethical values, then it will be a "good citizen" organization. But as we show throughout this text, an individual's personal moral values are only one factor in the ethical decision-making process. True, moral values can be applied to a variety of situations in life, and some people do not distinguish everyday ethical issues from business ones. Our concern, however, is with the application of principles, values, and standards in the business context. Many important issues are not related to a business context, although they remain complex moral dilemmas in a person's own life. For example, although abortion and human cloning are moral issues, they are not an issue in most business organizations.

Professionals in any field, including business, must deal with individuals' personal moral dilemmas because such dilemmas affect everyone's ability to function on the job. Normally, a business does not dictate a person's morals. Such policies would be illegal. Only when a person's morals influence his or her performance on the job does it involve a dimension within business ethics.

Just being a good person and having sound personal values may not be sufficient to handle the ethical issues that arise in a business organization. Although truthfulness, honesty, fairness, and openness are often assumed to be self-evident and accepted, business-strategy decisions involve complex and detailed discussions. For example, there is considerable debate over what constitutes antitrust, deceptive advertising, and violations of the Foreign Corrupt Practices Act. A high level of personal moral development may not prevent an individual from violating the law in a complicated organizational context where even experienced lawyers debate the exact meaning of the law. For instance, the Supreme Court struck down a ruling against a Thai student who was selling foreign textbooks in the United States at lower costs than books sold by the publishers. The student would purchase textbooks developed for foreign markets overseas and resell them in the United States. While normally people have the right to resell copyrighted items they have purchased legally, the courts found the Thai student's actions violated a law that prohibited the importation of copyrighted materials without the copyright holder's permission. However, the Supreme Court rejected the arguments and ruled in favor of the student.[19]

Some approaches to business ethics assume ethics training is for people whose personal moral development is unacceptable, but that is not the case. Because organizations are culturally diverse and personal morals must be respected, ensuring collective agreement on organizational ethics (that is, codes reasonably capable of preventing misconduct) is as vital as any other effort an organization's management may undertake.

Many people with limited business experience suddenly find themselves making decisions about product quality, advertising, pricing, sales techniques, hiring practices, and pollution control. The values they learned from family, religion, and school may not provide specific guidelines for these complex business decisions. In other words, a person's experiences and decisions at home, in school, and in the community may be quite different from his or her experiences and decisions at work. Many business ethics decisions are close calls. In addition, managerial responsibility for the conduct of others requires knowledge of ethics and compliance processes and systems. Years of experience in a particular industry may be required to know what is acceptable. For example, when are advertising claims more exaggeration than truth? When does such exaggeration become unethical? When Zale Corp. claimed that its Celebration Fire diamonds were the "most brilliant diamonds in the world," it automatically implied its competitors' diamonds are not as brilliant. Sterling Jeweler's Inc. filed a lawsuit claiming that Zale was engaging in false advertising. A judge refused to block Zale's advertising because there was not enough proof that the ads harmed Sterling's business in any way. This would seem to be an example of puffery, or an exaggerated claim that customers should not necessarily take seriously, rather than a serious attempt to mislead.[20]

Studying business ethics will help you begin to identify ethical issues when they arise and recognize the approaches available for resolving them. You will learn more about the ethical decision-making process and about ways to promote ethical behavior within your organization. By studying business ethics, you may also begin to understand how to cope with conflicts between your own personal values and those of the organization in which you work. As stated earlier, if after reading this book you feel a little more unsettled about potential decisions in business, your decisions will be more ethical and you will have knowledge within this area.

THE DEVELOPMENT OF BUSINESS ETHICS

The study of business ethics in North America has evolved through five distinct stages—(1) before 1960, (2) the 1960s, (3) the 1970s, (4) the 1980s, and (5) the 1990s—and continues to evolve in the twenty-first century (see Table 1–1).

Before 1960: Ethics in Business

Prior to 1960, the United States endured several agonizing phases of questioning the concept of capitalism. In the 1920s, the progressive movement attempted to provide citizens with a "living wage," defined as income sufficient for education, recreation, health, and retirement. Businesses were asked to check unwarranted price increases and any other practices that would hurt a family's living wage. In the 1930s came the New Deal that specifically blamed business for the country's economic woes. Business was asked to work more closely with the government to raise family income. By the 1950s, the New Deal evolved into President Harry S. Truman's Fair Deal, a program that defined such matters as civil rights and environmental responsibility as ethical issues that businesses had to address.

Until 1960, ethical issues related to business were often discussed within the domain of theology or philosophy or in the realm of legal and competitive relationships. Religious leaders raised questions about fair wages, labor practices, and the morality of capitalism. For example, Catholic social ethics, expressed in a series of papal encyclicals, included concern for morality in business, workers' rights, and living wages; for humanistic values rather than materialistic ones; and for improving the conditions of the poor. The Protestant work ethic encouraged individuals to be frugal, work hard, and attain success in the capitalistic system. Such religious traditions provided a foundation for the future field of business ethics.

The first book on business ethics was published in 1937 by Frank Chapman Sharp and Philip G. Fox. The authors separated their book into four sections: fair service, fair treatment of competitors, fair price, and moral progress in the business world. This early

TABLE 1–1 Timeline of Ethical and Socially Responsible Concerns

1960s	1970s	1980s	1990s	2000s
Environmental issues	Employee militancy	Bribes and illegal contracting practices	Sweatshops and unsafe working conditions in third-world countries	Cybercrime
Civil rights issues	Human rights issues	Influence peddling	Rising corporate liability for personal damages (for example, cigarette companies)	Financial misconduct
Increased employee-employer tension	Covering up rather than correcting issues	Deceptive advertising	Financial mismanagement and fraud	Global issues, Chinese product safety
Changing work ethic	Disadvantaged consumers	Financial fraud (for example, savings and loan scandal)	Organizational ethical misconduct	Sustainability
Rising drug use	Transparency issues			Intellectual property theft

Source: Adapted from "Business Ethics Timeline," *Ethics Resource Center*, http://www.ethics.org/resource/business-ethics-timeline (accessed June 13, 2013). Copyright © 2006, Ethics Resource Center (ERC). Used with permission of the ERC, 1747 Pennsylvania Ave. N.W., Suite 400, Washington, DC, 2006, www.ethics.org.

textbook discusses ethical ideas based largely upon economic theories and moral philosophies. However, the section's titles indicate the authors also take different stakeholders into account. Most notably, competitors and customers are the main stakeholders emphasized, but the text also identifies stockholders, employees, business partners such as suppliers, and government agencies.[21] Although the theory of stakeholder orientation would not evolve for many more years, this earliest business ethics textbook demonstrates the necessity of the ethical treatment of different stakeholders.

The 1960s: The Rise of Social Issues in Business

During the 1960s American society witnessed the development of an anti-business trend because many critics attacked the vested interests that controlled the economic and political aspects of society—the so-called military–industrial complex. The 1960s saw the decay of inner cities and the growth of ecological problems such as pollution and the disposal of toxic and nuclear wastes. This period also witnessed the rise of consumerism—activities undertaken by independent individuals, groups, and organizations to protect their rights as consumers. In 1962 President John F. Kennedy delivered a "Special Message on Protecting the Consumer Interest" that outlined four basic consumer rights: the right to safety, the right to be informed, the right to choose, and the right to be heard. These came to be known as the Consumers' Bill of Rights.

The modern consumer movement is generally considered to have begun in 1965 with the publication of Ralph Nader's *Unsafe at Any Speed* that criticized the auto industry as a whole, and General Motors Corporation (GM) in particular, for putting profit and style ahead of lives and safety. GM's Corvair was the main target of Nader's criticism. His consumer protection organization, popularly known as Nader's Raiders, fought successfully for legislation requiring automobile makers to equip cars with safety belts, padded dashboards, stronger door latches, head restraints, shatterproof windshields, and collapsible steering columns. Consumer activists also helped secure passage of consumer protection laws such as the Wholesome Meat Act of 1967, the Radiation Control for Health and Safety Act of 1968, the Clean Water Act of 1972, and the Toxic Substance Act of 1976.[22]

After Kennedy came President Lyndon B. Johnson and the "Great Society," a series of programs that extended national capitalism and told the business community the U.S. government's responsibility was to provide all citizens with some degree of economic stability, equality, and social justice. Activities that could destabilize the economy or discriminate against any class of citizens began to be viewed as unethical and unlawful.

The 1970s: Business Ethics as an Emerging Field

Business ethics began to develop as a field of study in the 1970s. Theologians and philosophers laid the groundwork by suggesting certain moral principles could be applied to business activities. Using this foundation, business professors began to teach and write about corporate social responsibility, an organization's obligation to maximize its positive impact on stakeholders and minimize its negative impact. Philosophers increased their involvement, applying ethical theory and philosophical analysis to structure the discipline of business ethics. Companies became more concerned with their public image, and as social demands grew, many businesses realized they needed to address ethical issues more directly. The Nixon administration's Watergate scandal focused public interest on the importance of ethics in government. Conferences were held to discuss the social responsibilities and ethical issues of business. Centers dealing with issues of business ethics were established. Interdisciplinary meetings brought together business professors, theologians, philosophers, and businesspeople. President Jimmy Carter attempted to focus on personal and administrative efforts to uphold ethical principles in government. The Foreign Corrupt Practices Act was passed during his administration, making it illegal for U.S. businesses to bribe government officials of other countries. Today this law is the highest priority of the U.S. Department of Justice.

By the end of the 1970s, a number of major ethical issues had emerged, including bribery, deceptive advertising, price collusion, product safety, and ecology. *Business ethics* became a common expression. Academic researchers sought to identify ethical issues and describe how businesspeople might choose to act in particular situations. However, only limited efforts were made to describe how the ethical decision-making process worked and to identify the many variables that influence this process in organizations.

The 1980s: Consolidation

In the 1980s, business academics and practitioners acknowledged business ethics as a field of study, and a growing and varied group of institutions with diverse interests promoted it. Centers for business ethics provided publications, courses, conferences, and seminars. R. Edward Freeman was among the first scholars to pioneer the concept of stakeholders as a foundational theory for business ethics decisions. Freeman defined stakeholders as "any group or individual who can affect or is affected by the achievement of the organization's objectives."[23] Freeman's defense of stakeholder theory had a major impact on strategic management and corporations' views of their responsibilities. Business ethics were also a prominent concern within leading companies such as General Electric, Hershey Foods, General Motors, IBM, Caterpillar, and S. C. Johnson & Son, Inc. Many of these firms established ethics and social policy committees to address ethical issues.

In the 1980s, the **Defense Industry Initiative on Business Ethics and Conduct** (DII) was developed to guide corporate support for ethical conduct. In 1986, 18 defense contractors drafted principles for guiding business ethics and conduct.[24] The organization has since grown to nearly 50 members. This effort established a method for discussing best practices and working tactics to link organizational practice and policy to successful ethical compliance. The DII includes six principles. First, the DII supports codes of conduct and their widespread distribution. These codes of conduct must be understandable and cover their more substantive areas in detail. Second, member companies are expected to provide ethics training for their employees as well as continuous support between training periods. Third, defense contractors must create an open atmosphere in which employees feel comfortable reporting violations without fear of retribution. Fourth, companies need to perform extensive internal audits and develop effective internal reporting and voluntary disclosure plans. Fifth, the DII insists member companies preserve the integrity of the defense industry. And sixth, member companies must adopt a philosophy of public accountability.[25]

The 1980s ushered in the Reagan–Bush era, with the accompanying belief that self-regulation, rather than regulation by government, was in the public's interest. Many tariffs and trade barriers were lifted and businesses merged and divested within an increasingly global atmosphere. Thus, while business schools were offering courses in business ethics, the rules of business were changing at a phenomenal rate because of less regulation. Corporations that once were nationally based began operating internationally and found themselves mired in value structures where accepted rules of business behavior no longer applied.

The 1990s: Institutionalization of Business Ethics

The administration of President Bill Clinton continued to support self-regulation and free trade. However, it also took unprecedented government action to deal with health-related social issues such as teenage smoking. Its proposals included restricting cigarette advertising, banning cigarette vending machine sales, and ending the use of cigarette logos in connection with sports events.[26] Clinton also appointed Arthur Levitt as chairman of the Securities and Exchange Commission in 1993. Levitt unsuccessfully pushed for many reforms that, if passed, could have prevented the accounting ethics scandals exemplified by Enron and WorldCom in the early twenty-first century.[27]

The **Federal Sentencing Guidelines for Organizations** (FSGO), approved by Congress in November 1991, set the tone for organizational ethical compliance programs in the 1990s. The guidelines, which were based on the six principles of the DII,[28] broke new ground by codifying into law incentives to reward organizations for taking action to prevent misconduct, such as developing effective internal legal and ethical compliance programs.[29] Provisions in the guidelines mitigate penalties for businesses striving to root out misconduct and establish high ethical and legal standards.[30] On the other hand, under FSGO, if a company lacks an effective ethical compliance program and its employees violate the law, it can incur severe penalties. The guidelines focus on firms taking action to prevent and detect business misconduct in cooperation with government regulation. At the heart of the FSGO is the carrot-and-stick approach; that is, by taking preventive action against misconduct, a company may avoid onerous penalties should a violation occur. A mechanical approach using legalistic logic will not suffice to avert serious penalties. The company must develop corporate values, enforce its own code of ethics, and strive to prevent misconduct. The law develops new amendments almost every year. We will provide more detail on the FSGO's role in business ethics programs in Chapters 4 and 8.

The Twenty-First Century of Business Ethics

Although business ethics appeared to become more institutionalized in the 1990s, new evidence emerged in the early 2000s that more than a few business executives and managers had not fully embraced the public's desire for high ethical standards. After George W. Bush became President in 2001, highly publicized corporate misconduct at Enron, WorldCom, Halliburton, and the accounting firm Arthur Andersen caused the government and the public to look for new ways to encourage ethical behavior.[31] Accounting scandals, especially falsifying financial reports, became part of the culture of many companies. Firms outside the United States, such as Royal Ahold in the Netherlands and Parmalat in Italy, became major examples of global accounting fraud. Although the Bush administration tried to minimize government regulation, there appeared to be no alternative to developing more regulatory oversight of business.

Such abuses increased public and political demands to improve ethical standards in business. To address the loss of confidence in financial reporting and corporate ethics, in 2002 Congress passed the **Sarbanes–Oxley Act**, the most far-reaching change in organizational control and accounting regulations since the Securities and Exchange Act of 1934. The new law made securities fraud a criminal offense and stiffened penalties for corporate fraud. It also created an accounting oversight board that requires corporations to establish codes of ethics for financial reporting and to develop greater transparency in financial reports to investors and other interested parties. Additionally, the law requires top executives to sign off on their firms' financial reports, and risk fines and long prison sentences if they misrepresent their companies' financial positions. The legislation further requires company executives to disclose stock sales immediately and prohibits companies from giving loans to top managers.[32]

Amendments to the FSGO require that a business's governing authority be well informed about its ethics program with respect to content, implementation, and effectiveness. This places the responsibility squarely on the shoulders of the firm's leadership, usually the board of directors. The board is required to provide resources to oversee the discovery of risks and to design, implement, and modify approaches to deal with those risks.

The Sarbanes–Oxley Act and the FSGO institutionalized the need to discover and address ethical and legal risk. Top management and the board of directors of a corporation are accountable for discovering risk associated with ethical conduct. Such specific industries as the public sector, energy and chemicals, health care, insurance, and retail have to discover the unique risks associated with their operations and develop ethics programs to prevent ethical misconduct before it creates a crisis. Most firms are developing formal and informal mechanisms that affect interactive communication and transparency about issues associated with the risk of misconduct. Business leaders should consider the greatest danger to their organizations lies in *not* discovering any serious misconduct or illegal activities that may be lurking. Unfortunately, most managers do not view the risk of an ethical disaster as being as important as the risk associated with fires, natural disasters, or technology failure. In fact, ethical disasters can be significantly more damaging to a company's reputation than risks managed through insurance and other methods. The great investor Warren Buffett stated it is impossible to eradicate all wrongdoing in a large organization and one can only hope the misconduct is small and is caught in time. Buffett's fears were realized in 2008 when the financial system collapsed because of pervasive, systemic use of instruments such as credit default swaps, risky debt such as subprime lending, and corruption in major corporations.

In 2009, Barack Obama became president in the middle of a great recession caused by a meltdown in the global financial industry. Many firms, such as AIG, Lehman Brothers, Merrill Lynch, and Countrywide Financial, engaged in ethical misconduct in developing and selling high-risk financial products. President Obama led the passage of legislation to provide a stimulus for recovery. His legislation to improve health care and provide more protection for consumers focused on social concerns. Congress passed legislation regarding credit card accountability, improper payments related to federal agencies, fraud and waste, and food safety. The **Dodd–Frank Wall Street Reform and Consumer Protection Act** addressed some of the issues related to the financial crisis and recession. The Dodd–Frank Act was the most sweeping financial legislation since the Sarbanes–Oxley Act and possibly since laws put into effect during the Great Depression. It was designed to make the financial services industry more ethical and responsible. This complex law required regulators to create hundreds of rules to promote financial stability, improve accountability and transparency, and protect consumers from abusive financial practices.

The basic assumptions of capitalism are under debate as countries around the world work to stabilize markets and question those who manage the money of individual corporations and nonprofits. The financial crisis caused many people to question government institutions that provide oversight and regulation. As societies work to create change for the better, they must address issues related to law, ethics, and the required level of compliance necessary for government and business to serve the public interest. Not since the Great Depression and President Franklin Delano Roosevelt has the United States seen such widespread government intervention and regulation—something most deem necessary, but is nevertheless worrisome to free market capitalists.

Future ethical issues revolve around the acquisition and sales of information. Cloud computing has begun a new paradigm. Businesses must no longer develop strategies based on past practices; they begin with petabytes of information and look for relationships and correlations to discover the new rules of business. What once was thought of as intrusive is now accepted and promoted. Only recently have people begun to ask whether the information collected by business is acceptable. Companies are becoming more sophisticated in understanding their customers by the use of predictive analytic technologies.

Is it acceptable for a business to review you on Facebook or other social networking services? When shopping, does the fact that Q codes and microchips give your information to businesses regarding where you are, what you are looking at, and what you have done in the last day (via cell phone tower triangulation) bother you? Should your non-professional life be subject to the ethics of the corporation when you are not at work? Finally, are you a citizen first and then an employee or an employee first and then a citizen? These are some of the business ethics issues in your future.

DEVELOPING AN ORGANIZATIONAL AND GLOBAL ETHICAL CULTURE

Compliance and ethics initiatives in organizations are designed to establish appropriate conduct and core values. The ethical component of a corporate culture relates to the values, beliefs, and established and enforced patterns of conduct employees use to identify and respond to ethical issues. In our book the term ethical culture is acceptable behavior as defined by the company and industry. Ethical culture is the component of corporate culture that captures the values and norms an organization defines and is compared to by its industry as appropriate conduct. The goal of an ethical culture is to minimize the need for enforced compliance of rules and maximize the use of principles that contribute to ethical reasoning in difficult or new situations. Ethical culture is positively related to workplace confrontation over ethics issues, reports to management of observed misconduct, and the presence of ethics hotlines.[33] To develop better ethical corporate cultures, many businesses communicate core values to their employees by creating ethics programs and appointing ethics officers to oversee them. An ethical culture creates shared values and support for ethical decisions and is driven by top management.

Globally, businesses are working closely together to establish standards of acceptable behavior. We are already seeing collaborative efforts by a range of organizations to establish goals and mandate minimum levels of ethical behavior, from the European Union, the North American Free Trade Agreement (NAFTA), the Southern Common Market (MERCOSUR), and the World Trade Organization (WTO) to, more recently, the Council on Economic Priorities' Social Accountability 8000 (SA 8000), the Ethical Trading Initiative, and the U.S. Apparel Industry Partnership. Some companies refuse to do business with organizations that do not support and abide by these standards. Many companies demonstrate their commitment toward acceptable conduct by adopting globally recognized principles emphasizing human rights and social responsibility. For instance, in 2000 the United Nations launched the Global Compact, a set of 10 principles concerning human rights, labor, the environment, and anti-corruption. The purpose of the Global Compact is to create openness and alignment among business, government, society, labor, and the United Nations. Companies that adopt this code agree to integrate the ten principles into their business practices, publish their progress toward these objectives on an annual basis, and partner with others to advance broader objectives of the UN.[34] These 10 principles are covered in more detail in Chapter 10.

THE BENEFITS OF BUSINESS ETHICS

The field of business ethics continues to change rapidly as more firms recognize the benefits of improving ethical conduct and the link between business ethics and financial performance. Both research and examples from the business world demonstrate that building an ethical reputation among employees, customers, and the general public pays off. Figure 1–2 provides an overview of the relationship between business ethics and organizational performance. Although we believe there are many practical benefits to being ethical, many businesspeople make decisions because they believe a particular course of action is simply the right thing to do as responsible members of society. Granite Construction earned a place in *Ethisphere*'s "World's Most Ethical Companies" for four consecutive years as a result of its integration of ethics into the company culture. Granite formulated its ethics program to comply with the Federal Sentencing Guidelines for Organizations and helped inspire the Construction Industry Ethics and Compliance Initiative. To ensure all company employees are familiar with Granite's high ethical standards, the firm holds six mandatory training sessions annually, conducts ethics and compliance audits, and uses field compliance officers to make certain ethical conduct is taking place throughout the entire

FIGURE 1–2 **The Role of Organizational Ethics in Performance**

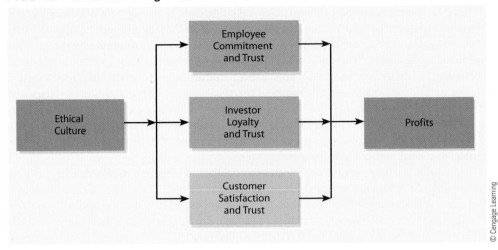

© Cengage Learning

organization.[35] Among the rewards for being more ethical and socially responsible in business are increased efficiency in daily operations, greater employee commitment, increased investor willingness to entrust funds, improved customer trust and satisfaction, and better financial performance. The reputation of a company has a major effect on its relationships with employees, investors, customers, and many other parties.

Ethics Contributes to Employee Commitment

Employee commitment comes from workers who believe their future is tied to that of the organization and from a willingness to make personal sacrifices for the organization.[36] The more a company is dedicated to taking care of its employees, the more likely the employees will take care of the organization. Issues that foster the development of an ethical culture for employees include the absence of abusive behavior, a safe work environment, competitive salaries, and the fulfillment of all contractual obligations toward employees. An ethics and compliance program can support values and appropriate conduct. Social programs improving the ethical culture range from work–family programs to stock ownership plans to community service. Home Depot associates, for example, participate in disaster-relief efforts after hurricanes and tornadoes, rebuilding roofs, repairing water damage, planting trees, and clearing roads in their communities. Because employees spend a considerable number of their waking hours at work, a commitment by an organization to goodwill and respect for its employees usually increases the employees' loyalty to the organization and their support of its objectives. The software company SAS topped *Fortune*'s "100 Best Places to Work For" list for eight years thanks to the way it values its employees. During the most recent recession, founder Charles Goodnight refused to lay off workers and instead asked his employees to offer ideas on how to reduce costs. By actively engaging employees in cost-cutting measures, SAS was able to cut expenses by 6 to 7 percent. SAS is also unusual in that its annual turnover rate is four percent, versus the 20 percent industry average. It also has an organic farm for the firm's four cafeterias.[37]

Employees' perceptions that their firm has an ethical culture lead to performance-enhancing outcomes within the organization.[38] A corporate culture that integrates strong ethical values and positive business practices has been found to increase group creativity and job satisfaction and decrease turnover.[39] For the sake of both productivity and teamwork, it is essential employees both within and among departments throughout an organization share a common vision of trust. The influence of higher levels of trust is greatest on relationships within departments or work groups, but trust is a significant factor in relationships among departments as well. Programs that create a trustworthy work environment make individuals more willing to rely and act on the decisions of their coworkers. In such a work environment, employees can reasonably expect to be treated with full respect and consideration by their coworkers and superiors. Trusting relationships between upper management and managers and their subordinates contribute to greater decision-making efficiencies. One survey found that when employees see values such as honesty, respect, and trust applied frequently in the workplace, they feel less pressure to compromise ethical standards, observe less misconduct, are more satisfied with their organizations overall, and feel more valued as employees.[40]

The ethical culture of a company matters to employees. According to a report on employee loyalty and work practices, companies viewed as highly ethical by their employees were six times more likely to keep their workers.[41] Also, employees who view their company as having a strong community involvement feel more loyal to their employers and positive about themselves.

Ethics Contributes to Investor Loyalty

Ethical conduct results in shareholder loyalty and contributes to success that supports even broader social causes and concerns. Investors today are increasingly concerned about the ethics and social responsibility that creates the reputation of companies in which they invest, and various socially responsible mutual funds and asset management firms help investors purchase stock in ethical companies. Investors also recognize that an ethical culture provides a foundation for efficiency, productivity, and profits. Investors know, too, that negative publicity, lawsuits, and fines can lower stock prices, diminish customer loyalty, and threaten a company's long-term viability. Many companies accused of misconduct experienced dramatic declines in the value of their stock when concerned investors divested. Warren Buffett and his company Berkshire Hathaway command significant respect from investors because of their track record of financial returns and the integrity of their organizations. Buffett says, "I want employees to ask themselves whether they are willing to have any contemplated act appear the next day on the front page of their local paper—to be read by their spouses, children and friends—with the reporting done by an informed and critical reporter."

When TIAA-CREF investor participants were asked if they would choose a financial services company with strong ethics or higher returns, surprisingly, 92 percent of respondents said they would choose ethics while only 5 percent chose higher returns.[42] Investors look at the bottom line for profits or the potential for increased stock prices or dividends, but they also look for any potential flaws in the company's performance, conduct, and financial reports. Therefore, gaining investors' trust and confidence is vital to sustaining the financial stability of the firm.

Ethics Contributes to Customer Satisfaction

It is generally accepted that customer satisfaction is one of the most important factors in a successful business strategy. Although a company continues to develop and adapt products to keep pace with customers' changing desires and preferences, it must also develop long-term relationships with its customers and stakeholders. As mentioned earlier, high levels

DEBATE ISSUE
TAKE A STAND

Does Being Ethical Result in Better Performance?

While research suggests ethical businesses have better performance, there is also an alternate view. Many businesspeople think ethics and social responsibility require resources that do not contribute to profits and time spent in ethics training could be better used for other business activities. One viewpoint is that when companies push the edge, pay minor fines for misconduct, or are not caught in wrongdoing, they may end up being more profitable than companies with a strong ethical culture. Many financial companies became extremely profitable when taking high-risk opportunities with limited transparency about the nature of the complex products they sold. To gain competitive advantage, a firm needs to be able to reach markets and make sales. If a firm is too ethical, it might lose competitive advantages. On the other hand, *Ethisphere's* World's Most Ethical Companies index indicates ethical companies have better financial performance.

1. Ethical businesses are the most profitable.
2. The most ethical businesses are not the most profitable.

of perceived corporate misconduct decreases customer trust.[43] On the other hand, companies viewed as socially responsible increase customer trust and satisfaction. Patagonia, Inc., engaged in a broad array of ecological, socially responsible, and ethical behaviors over many years to better connect with its target markets. The company donates 1 percent of its sales to environmental preservation and restoration. Employees can volunteer for environmental groups and earn up to one month's pay. The entire clothing line was sourced using organic cotton beginning in 1996. In addition, the company is currently creating the Patagonia National Park to protect ecosystems and biodiversity in Chile and Argentina. All new facilities are being built with LEED certification, demonstrating a commitment to green building and the environment.[44]

For most businesses, both repeat purchases and an enduring relationship of mutual respect and cooperation with customers are essential for success. By focusing on customer satisfaction, a company continually deepens the customer's dependence on the company, and as the customer's confidence grows, the firm gains a better understanding of how to serve the customer so the relationship may endure. Successful businesses provide an opportunity for customer feedback that engages the customer in cooperative problem solving. As is often pointed out, a happy customer will come back, but disgruntled customers will tell others about their dissatisfaction with a company and discourage friends from dealing with it.

Trust is essential to a good long-term relationship between a business and consumers. The perceived ethicality of a firm is positively related to brand trust, emotional identification with the brand, and brand loyalty.[45] A Nielsen survey revealed two-thirds of global consumer respondents stated they preferred companies that give back to society in a socially responsible manner.[46] As social responsibility becomes more important for companies, corporate social responsibility may be viewed as a sign of good management and may, according to one study, indicate good financial performance. However, another study indicates the reverse may be true, and companies who have good financial performance are able to spend more money on social responsibility.[47] Google would be an example of such a company. Google shows extreme care for its employees at its Googleplex headquarters in Mountain View, California. Investment in employee satisfaction and retention involves providing bicycles for efficient travel between meetings, lava lamps, massage chairs, shared work cubicles to allow for intellectual stimulation and idea generation, laptops for every employee, pool tables, volleyball courts, outdoor seating for brainstorming, snack rooms packed with various snacks and drinks, and more.[48]

When an organization has a strong ethical environment, it usually focuses on the core value of placing customers' interests first. However, putting customers first does not mean the interests of employees, investors, and local communities should be ignored. An ethical culture that focuses on customers incorporates the interests of all employees, suppliers, and other interested parties in decisions and actions. Employees working in an ethical environment support and contribute to the process of understanding customers' demands and concerns.

Ethics Contributes to Profits

A company cannot nurture and develop an ethical culture unless it has achieved adequate financial performance in terms of profits. Businesses with greater resources—regardless of their staff size—have the means to practice social responsibility while serving their customers, valuing their employees, and establishing trust with the public. Ethical conduct toward customers builds a strong competitive position shown to positively affect business performance and product innovation.[49] Zappos values the well-being of its employees and gives them the freedom to provide high-quality customer service to its customers. For instance, call-center employees are given the freedom to spend as much time as needed to answer customer concerns. This emphasis on the customer enables the firm to fulfill its goal of being able to "deliver WOW through customer service." It also made the firm widely successful, leading to its acquisition by Amazon.com in a $1.2 billion agreement.[50] Every day, business newspapers and magazines offer new examples of the consequences of business misconduct. It is worth noting, however, that most of these companies learned from their mistakes and recovered after they implemented programs to improve ethical and legal conduct.

Ample evidence shows being ethical pays off with better performance. As indicated earlier, companies perceived by their employees as having a high degree of honesty and integrity have a much higher average total return to shareholders than do companies perceived as having a low degree of honesty and integrity.[51] The World's Most Ethical Companies index was developed through methodology designed by a committee of leading attorneys, professors, and organization leaders. In a five-year period, the companies in this index outperformed the other indexes of publicly traded companies.[52] These results provide strong evidence that corporate concern for ethical conduct is becoming a part of strategic planning toward obtaining the outcome of higher profitability. Rather than being just a function of compliance, ethics is becoming an integral part of management's efforts to achieve competitive advantage.

OUR FRAMEWORK FOR STUDYING BUSINESS ETHICS

We developed a framework for this text to help you understand how people make ethical decisions and deal with ethical issues. Table 1–2 summarizes each element in the framework and describes where each topic is discussed in this book.

In Part One, we provide an overview of business ethics. This chapter defines the term *business ethics* and explore the development and importance of this critical business area.

In Chapter 2, we explore the role of various stakeholder groups in social responsibility and corporate governance.

Part Two focuses on ethical issues and the institutionalization of business ethics. In Chapter 3, we examine business issues that lead to ethical decision making in

TABLE 1–2 Our Framework for Studying Business Ethics

Chapter	Highlights
1. The Importance of Business Ethics	• Definitions
	• Reasons for studying business ethics
	• History
	• Benefits of business ethics
2. Stakeholder Relationships, Social Responsibility, and Corporate Governance	• Stakeholder relationships
	• Stakeholder influences in social responsibility
	• Corporate governance
3. Emerging Business Ethics Issues	• Recognizing an ethical issue
	• Honesty, fairness, and integrity
	• Ethical issues and dilemmas in business: abusive and disruptive behavior, lying, conflicts of interest, bribery, corporate intelligence, discrimination, sexual harassment, environmental issues, fraud, insider trading, intellectual property rights, and privacy
	• Determining an ethical issue in business
4. The Institutionalization of Business Ethics	• Mandatory requirements
	• Voluntary requirements
	• Core practices
	• Federal Sentencing Guidelines for Organizations
	• Sarbanes–Oxley Act
5. Ethical Decision Making	• Ethical issue intensity
	• Individual factors in decision making
	• Organizational factors in decision making
	• Opportunity in decision making
	• Business ethics evaluations and intentions
	• Normative considerations in ethical decision making
	• Role of institutions in normative decision making
	• Importance of principles and core values to ethical decision making

6. Individual Factors: Moral Philosophies and Values	• Moral philosophies, including teleological development philosophies and cognitive moral deontological, relativist, virtue ethics, and justice philosophies
	• Stages of cognitive moral development
7. Organizational Factors: The Role of Ethical Culture and Relationships	• Corporate culture
	• Interpersonal relationships
	• Whistle-blowing
	• Opportunity and conflict
8. Developing an Effective Ethics Program	• Ethics programs
	• Codes of ethics
	• Program responsibility
	• Communication of ethical standards
	• Systems to monitor and enforce ethical standards
	• Continuous improvement of ethics programs
9. Implementing and Auditing Ethics Programs	• Implementation programs
	• Ethics audits
10. Business Ethics in a Global Economy	• Global Culture and Cultural Relations
	• Economic Foundations of Business Ethics
	• Multinational Corporations
	• Global Cooperation
	• Global Ethics Issues
11. Ethical Leadership	• Requirements for Ethical Leadership
	• Managing Ethical Conflicts
	• Ethical Leadership Communication
	• Leader-Follower Relationships
12. Sustainability: Ethical and Social Responsibility Dimensions	• Sustainability and Ethical Decision Making
	• Global Environmental Issues
	• Business Response to Sustainability Issues
	• Strategic Implementation of Environmental Responsibility

organizations. In Chapter 4, we look at the institutionalization of business ethics, including both mandatory and voluntary societal concerns.

In Part Three, we delineate the ethical decision-making process and then look at both individual factors and organizational factors that influence decisions. Chapter 5 describes the ethical decision-making process from an organizational perspective. Chapter 6 explores individual factors that may influence ethical decisions in business, including moral philosophies and cognitive moral development. Chapter 7 focuses on organizational dimensions including corporate culture, relationships, and conflicts.

In Part Four, we explore systems and processes associated with implementing business ethics into global strategic planning. Chapter 8 discusses the development of an effective ethics program. In Chapter 9, we examine issues related to implementing and auditing ethics programs. Chapter 10 considers ethical issues in a global context. Chapter 11 examines ethical leadership and its importance in creating an ethical corporate culture. Finally, Chapter 12 discusses the ethical and social responsibility considerations of sustainability.

We hope that this framework helps you develop a balanced understanding of the various perspectives and alternatives available to you when making ethical business decisions. Regardless of your own personal values, the more you know about how individuals make decisions, the better prepared you will be to cope with difficult ethical decisions. Such knowledge will help you improve and control the ethical decision-making environment in which you work.

It is your job to make the final decision in an ethical situation that affects you. Sometimes that decision may be right; sometimes it may be wrong. It is always easy to look back with hindsight and know what you should have done in a particular situation. At the time, however, the choices might not have seemed so clear. To give you practice making ethical decisions, Part Five of this book contains a number of cases. In addition, each chapter begins with a vignette, "An Ethical Dilemma," and ends with a mini-case, "Resolving Ethical Business Challenges," that involves ethical problems. We hope these give you a better sense of the challenges of making ethical decisions in the business world.

SUMMARY

This chapter provided an overview of the field of business ethics and introduced the framework for the discussion of this subject. Business ethics comprises organizational principles, values, and norms that may originate from individuals, organizational statements, or from the legal system that primarily guide individual and group behavior in business. Investors, employees, customers, special interest groups, the legal system, and the community often determine whether a specific action is right or wrong, ethical or unethical.

Studying business ethics is important for many reasons. Recent incidents of unethical activity in business underscore the widespread need for a better understanding of the factors that contribute to ethical and unethical decisions. Individuals' personal moral philosophies and decision-making experience may not be sufficient to guide them in the business world. Studying business ethics helps you begin to identify ethical issues and recognize the approaches available to resolve them.

The study of business ethics evolved through five distinct stages. Before 1960, business ethics issues were discussed primarily from a religious perspective. The 1960s saw the emergence of many social issues involving business and the concept of social conscience as well as a rise in consumerism, which culminated with Kennedy's *Consumers' Bill of Rights*. Business ethics began to develop as an independent field of study in the 1970s, with academics and practitioners exploring ethical issues and attempting to understand how individuals and organizations make ethical decisions. These experts began to teach and write about the idea of corporate social responsibility, an organization's obligation to maximize its positive impact on stakeholders and minimize its negative impact. In the 1980s, centers of business ethics provided publications, courses, conferences, and seminars, and many companies established ethics committees and social policy committees. The Defense Industry Initiative on Business Ethics and Conduct was developed to guide corporate support for ethical conduct; its principles had a major impact on corporate ethics.

However, less government regulation and an increase in businesses with international operations raised new ethical issues. In the 1990s, government continued to support self-regulation. The FSGO sets the tone for organizational ethics programs by providing incentives for companies to take action to prevent organizational misconduct. The twenty-first century ushered in a new set of ethics scandals, suggesting many companies had not embraced the public's desire for higher ethical standards. The Sarbanes–Oxley Act stiffened penalties for corporate fraud and established an accounting oversight board. The Dodd–Frank Wall Street Reform and Consumer Protection Act was later passed to reform the financial system. The current trend is away from legally based ethical initiatives in organizations and toward cultural initiatives that make ethics a part of core organizational values. The ethical component of a corporate culture relates to the values, beliefs, and established and enforced patterns of conduct employees use to identify and respond to ethical issues. The term *ethical culture* describes the component of corporate culture that captures the rules and principles an organization defines as appropriate conduct. Ethical culture can be viewed as the character of the decision-making process employees use to determine whether their responses to ethical issues are right or wrong.

Research and anecdotes demonstrate building an ethical reputation among employees, customers, and the general public provides benefits that include increased efficiency in daily operations, greater employee commitment, increased investor willingness to entrust funds, improved customer trust and satisfaction, and better financial performance. The reputation of a company has a major effect on its relationships with employees, investors, customers, and many other parties, and thus has the potential to affect its bottom line.

Finally, this text introduces a framework for studying business ethics. Each chapter addresses some aspect of business ethics and decision making within a business context. The major concerns are ethical issues in business, stakeholder relationships, social responsibility and corporate governance, emerging business ethics issues, the institutionalization of business ethics, understanding the ethical decision-making process, moral philosophies and cognitive moral development, corporate culture, organizational relationships and conflicts, developing an effective ethics program, implementing and auditing the ethics program, global business ethics, ethical leadership, and sustainability.

IMPORTANT TERMS FOR REVIEW

business ethics 5

principles 5

values 5

Morals 5

Consumers' Bill of Rights 10

social responsibility 11

Defense Industry Initiative on Business Ethics and Conduct 12

Federal Sentencing Guidelines for Organizations 12

Sarbanes–Oxley Act 13

Dodd–Frank Wall Street Reform and Consumer Protection Act 14

ethical culture 15

RESOLVING ETHICAL BUSINESS CHALLENGES*

Lael was just hired by Best East Motels into their manager training program and was excited about the potential benefits after her graduation from Florida State University. Working part-time and going to school full-time was the norm for her, but the Best East job replaced her two part-time jobs. With this new job, she would be the one to assign work times. Her luck continued when she met her mentor Nikhil, who was the son of the owner. Best East Motels was a franchise motel chain in the United States. Owners bought into the chain with a $500,000 franchise fee and paid for the construction of the motel. In return for the fee, Best East gave each owner a comprehensive package of marketing, management, accounting, and financial materials to boost motel success rates to over 90 percent. In addition, Best East assisted each owner with groups of people that trained staff for every new job, from housekeeping to accounting. The new-hire training course for each type of employee was developed and based on the best practices within the industry. This particular motel had been in business for ten years and was seen as successful.

As Lael went through the manager training program, everything she heard was great. It sounded like Best East was a career path she would want to pursue long-term. Six months into her job, however, Lael started to hear strange rumors. For example, on the night shift she found there was heavy employee turnover and most were females. Lael began to investigate by scheduling herself onto several night shifts. One night, as she chatted with one of the front desk employees, she discovered the girl planned on quitting. She was seventeen and worked at this Best East motel for a year. "Why are you leaving?" asked Lael.

Her reply startled Lael. "I don't want trouble, just my last paycheck, a good letter of recommendation, and that's it."

As Lael pressed her for more information, the seventeen-year-old opened up. She spoke about Nikhil talking suggestively about her to other employees and how he made suggestive physical gestures when she was around. She told Lael about other female employees treated similarly, and this always occurred during night shifts when Nikhil was on duty.

Digging a little deeper, Lael spoke to several former employees. Most were fairly young female employees. They told her essentially the same thing. For example, Nikhil would routinely make suggestive comments to female employees. In one incident under Nikhil's watch, some male employees flirted with female employees, including undocumented workers. Nikhil reportedly sat there with a smile. They also told her Nikhil allowed customers at the motel to offer their room keys to female employees.

After a few weeks, Lael heard the same story from younger female employees and even some of the maids. Their responses to these situations were similar. They ranged from "Nikhil told me if I was older he would ask me out" to "I don't want to make a big deal out of this because it might appear I'm a tattle tale." Another common excuse for not reporting was that Nikhil assured them this was part of the motel business and was normal. Most employees were afraid to report on the boss's son and put their jobs on the line.

Lael reviewed the section of the franchise employee handbook. It clearly stated sexual harassment of any kind would not be tolerated and should be reported immediately to the proper manager. Lael could tell from the manual the allegations against Nikhil constituted sexual harassment. While the Best East Franchise Corporation had no ethics hotline, Lael thought this could be a legal issue.

She knew putting pressure on the female employees to report the behavior of the boss's son was problematic. Lael also felt that going to Nikhil personally about these allegations may not be a wise move. If the behavior was reported to the owner, it would become an official allegation and impact the motel's reputation and image in the community, and she would be responsible for it.

The things these women were saying had not personally happened to her yet.

QUESTIONS | EXERCISES

1. Why should Lael get involved in reporting if she has not experienced any of the allegations the other employees are making?

2. What are some of the characteristics of Best East's ethical culture that would create the current dilemma for Lael?

3. What should Lael do to resolve her concerns?

*This case is strictly hypothetical; any resemblance to real persons, companies, or situations is coincidental.

> > > CHECK YOUR EQ

Check your EQ, or Ethics Quotient, by completing the following. Assess your performance to evaluate your overall understanding of the chapter material.

1.	Business ethics focuses mostly on personal ethical issues.	Yes	No
2.	Business ethics deals with right or wrong behavior within a particular organization.	Yes	No
3.	An ethical culture is based upon the norms and values of the company.	Yes	No
4.	Business ethics contributes to investor loyalty.	Yes	No
5.	The trend is away from cultural or ethically based initiatives to legal initiatives in organizations.	Yes	No
6.	Investments in business ethics do not support the bottom line.	Yes	No

ANSWERS 1. **No.** Business ethics focuses on organizational concerns (legal and ethical—employees, customers, suppliers, society). 2. **Yes.** That stems from the basic definition. 3. **Yes.** Norms and values help create an organizational culture and are key in supporting or not supporting ethical conduct. 4. **Yes.** Many studies have shown that trust and ethical conduct contribute to investor loyalty. 5. **No.** Many businesses are communicating their core values to their employees by creating ethics programs and appointing ethics officers to oversee them. 6. **No.** Ethics initiatives create consumer, employee, and shareholder loyalty and positive behavior that contribute to the bottom line.

ENDNOTES

1. Guido Palazzo, Franciska Krings, and Ulrich Hoffrage, "Ethical Blindess," *Journal of Business Ethics 109* (2012), 323–338.

2. Kayla Webley, "Cheating Harvard," *Time*, September 17, 2012, 22.

3. Teressa L. Elliot, Linda M. Marquis, and Catherine S. Neal, "Business Ethics Perspectives: Faculty Plagiarism and Fraud," *Journal of Business Ethics 112* (2013), 91–99.

4. United v. Federal Election Commission, 558 U.S. 310 (2010), Accessed 2.5.13 http://www.supremecourt.gov/opinions/09pdf/08-205.pdf.

5. Wroe Alderson, *Dynamic Marketing Behavior* (Homewood, IL: Irwin, 1965), 320.

6. Tom Polansek, "Peregrine Financial ex-CEO expects life of fraud to end in jail," *Reuters*, January 30, 2013, http://www.reuters.com/article/2013/01/30/us-peregrine-financial-fate-idUSBRE90T1BL20130130 (accessed January 30, 2013).

7. Ethics Resource Center, *2011 National Business Ethics Survey* (Arlington, VA: Ethics Resource Center, 2012), 22–23.

8. Dan Fitzpatrick and Robin Sidel, "New J.P. Morgan Jam," *The Wall Street Journal*, November 16, 2012, C1–C2.

9. Edelman, *Global Deck: 2013 Trust Barometer*, http://www.edelman.com/trust-downloads/global-results-2/ (accessed January 30, 3013).

10. Leonidas C. Leonidou, Olga Kvasova, Constantinos N. Leonidou, and Simo Chari, "Business Unethicality as an Impediment to Consumer Trust: The Moderating Role of Demographic and Cultural Characteristics," *Journal of Business Ethics 112* (2013): 397–415.

11. Daniel Gilbert, "Chesapeake CEO McClendon to Exit," *The Wall Street Journal*, January 29, 2013, http://online.wsj.com/article/SB100014241278873243292045782272353396167988.html?mod=WSJ_business_whatsNews (accessed January 30, 2013).

12. Christopher Helman, "McClendon Out At Chesapeake-Is a Takeover Next?" *Forbes*, January 29, 2013, http://www.forbes.com/sites/christopherhelman/2013/01/29/aubrey-mcclendon-out-at-chesapeake-energy/ (accessed March 25, 2013).

13. Chris Helms,"Jamaica Plain Neighborhood Council Rejects Whole Foods Seating Proposal," *Jamaica Plain Patch*, April 25, 2012, http://jamaicaplain.patch.com/articles/jamaica-plain-neighborhood-council-rejects-whole-foods-seating-proposal (accessed February 1, 2013); John Ruch, "JP prof to head Whole Foods study," *Jamaica Plain Gazette*, April 27, 2012, http://jamaicaplaingazette.com/2012/04/27/jp-prof-to-head-whole-foods-study/ (accessed February 1, 2013).

14. The Associated Press, "Rod Blagojevich, convicted on corruption charges, begins serving 14-year prison sentence in Colorado," *New York Daily News*, http://www.nydailynews.com/news/national/rod-blagojevich-convicted-corruption-charges-begins-serving-14-year-prison-sentence-colorado-article-1.1040164 (accessed February 1, 2013).

15. Julian E. Barnes and James Hookway, "Military Ethics Review Is Ordered," *The Wall Street Journal*, November 16, 2012, A6.

16. Reed Albergotti, Vanessa O'Connell, and Suzanne Vranica, "Armstrong Gets Dumped," *The Wall Street Journal*, October 18, 2012, B1.

17. Ken Belson, "Concussion Liability Costs May Rise, and Not Just for N.F.L.," *The New York Times*, December 10, 2012, http://www.nytimes.com/2012/12/11/sports/football/insurance-liability-in-nfl-concussion-suits-may-have-costly-consequences.html?pagewanted=all&_r=0 (accessed February 1, 2013).

18. Tim De Bock, Iris Vermeir, and Patrick Van Kenhove, "'What's the Harm in Being Unethical? These Strangers are Rich Anyway!' Exploring Underlying Factors of Double Standards," *Journal of Business Ethics 112* (2013), 225–240.

19. Brent Kendall, "High Court Rules in Favor of Book Reseller," *The Wall Street Journal*, March 19, 2013, http://online.wsj.com/article/SB10001424127887324323904578370263406999592.html (accessed March 25, 2013); Brent Kendall and Wilawan Watcharasakwet, "High Court Dives into Resale Trade," October 29, 2012, *The Wall Street Journal*, http://online.wsj.com/article/SB10001424052970204789304578084730729110360.html (accessed March 25, 2013).

20. Ann Zimmerman, "Judge Refuses to Block Zale Diamond Ads," *The Wall Street Journal*, January 24, 2013, http://online.wsj.com/article/SB10001424127887324539304578262202669342698.html?KEYWORDS=zales (accessed February 1, 2013).

21. Frank Chapman Sharp and Philip G. Fox, *Business Ethics* (New York, NY: D. Appleton-Century Company Incorporated, 1937).

22. Archie B. Carroll and Ann K. Buchholtz, *Business and Society: Ethics and Stakeholder Management* (Cincinnati: South-Western, 2006), 452–455.

23. R. Edward Freeman, *Strategic Management: A Stakeholder Approach* (Boston: Pitman, 1984).

24. Alan R. Yuspeh, "Development of Corporate Compliance Programs: Lessons Learned from the DII Experience," in *Corporate Crime in America: Strengthening the "Good Citizenship" Corporation* (Washington, DC: U.S. Sentencing Commission, 1995), 71–79.

25. Eleanor Hill, "Coordinating Enforcement Under the Department of Defense Voluntary Disclosure Program," in *Corporate Crime in America: Strengthening the "Good Citizenship" Corporation* (Washington, DC: U.S. Sentencing Commission, 1995), 287–294.

26. "Huffing and Puffing in Washington: Can Clinton's Plan Curb Teen Smoking?" *Consumer Reports* 60 (1995): 637.

27. Arthur Levitt with Paula Dwyer, *Take on the Street* (New York: Pantheon Books, 2002).

28. Hill, "Coordinating Enforcement."

29. Richard P. Conaboy, "Corporate Crime in America: Strengthening the Good Citizen Corporation," in *Corporate Crime in America: Strengthening the "Good Citizenship" Corporation* (Washington, DC: U.S. Sentencing Commission, 1995), 1–2.

30. *United States Code Service* (Lawyers' Edition), 18 U.S.C.S. Appendix, Sentencing Guidelines for the United States Courts (Rochester, NY: Lawyers Cooperative Publishing, 1995), sec. 8A.1.

31. "Fraud Inc.," *CNN/Money*, http://money.cnn.com/news/specials/corruption/ (accessed February 5, 2002); "SEC Formalizes Investigation into Halliburton Accounting," *The Wall Street Journal* online, December 20, 2002, http://online.wsj.com; "WorldCom CEO Slaps Arthur Andersen," *CNN*, July 8, 2002, www.cnn.com.

32. "Corporate Reform Bill Passed," *CNN*, July 25, 2002, www.cnn.com.

33. Muel Kaptein, "From Inaction to External Whistleblowering: The Influence of the Ethical Culture of Organizations on Employee Responses to Observed Wrongdoing," *Journal of Business Ethics*, (2011) 98: 513–530.

34. United Nation, "Global Compact: Corporate Citizenship in the World Economy," http://www.unglobalcompact.org/docs/news_events/8.1/GC_brochure_FINAL.pdf (accessed February 15, 2011).

35. "The 2010 World's Most Ethical Companies—Company Profile: Granite Construction," *Ethisphere*, Q1, 33; "Granite Construction Named to *Ethisphere*'s 2011 "World's Most Ethical Companies" for 2nd Year in a Row," Granite, http://www.graniteconstruction.com/investor-relations/release_detail.cfm?printpage=1&Release ID=558348 (accessed April 27, 2011); Ethisphere Institute, "2012 World's Most Ethical Companies," http://www.ethisphere.com/wme/(accessed February 1, 2013).

36. Bernard J. Jaworski and Ajay K. Kohli, "Market Orientation: Antecedents and Consequences," *Journal of Marketing* 57 (1993): 53–70.

37. Michael Lee Stallard, "Has SAS Chairman Jim Goodnight Cracked the Code of Corporate Culture?" *The Economic Times*, June 18, 2010, http://economictimes.indiatimes.com/features/corporate-dossier/has-sas-chairman-jim-goodnight-cracked-the-code-of-corporate-culture/articleshow/6060110.cms (accessed February 15, 2011); "100 Best Companies to Work For: SAS," *CNNMoney*, http://money.cnn.com/magazines/fortune/bestcompanies/2011/snapshots/1.html (accessed February 15, 2011); "100 Best Companies to Work For: SAS," *CNNMoney*, http://money.cnn.com/magazines/fortune/best-companies/2013/snapshots/2.html?iid=bc_sp_list (accessed February 1, 2013).

38. Terry W. Loe, "The Role of Ethical Culture in Developing Trust, Market Orientation and Commitment to Quality" (PhD diss., University of Memphis, 1996).

39. Sean Valentine, Lynn Godkin, Gary M. Fleischman, and Rolan Kidwell, "Corporate Ethical Values, Group Creativity, Job Satisfaction and Turnover Intention: The Impact of Work Context on Work Response," *Journal of Business Ethics* (2011) 98: 353–572.

40. Ethics Resource Center, *2000 National Business Ethics Survey*, 5.

41. John Galvin, "The New Business Ethics," *SmartBusinessMag.com*, June 2000, 99.

42. "Investors Prefer Ethics over High Return," *USA Today*, January 16, 2006, B1.

43. Leonidas C. Leonidou, Olga Kvasova, Constantinos N. Leonidou, and Simo Chari, "Business Unethicality as an Impediment to Consumer Trust: The Moderating Role of Demographic and Cultural Characteristics," *Journal of Business Ethics* 112(2013): 397–415.

44. *Conservacion Patagonica*, http://www.conservacionpatagonica.org/index.htm (accessed February 16, 2011); *Patagonia Homepage*, http://www.patagonia.com/us/home (accessed February 16, 2011).

45. Jatinder J. Singh, Oriol Iglesias, and Joan Manel Batistia-Foguet, "Does Having an Ethical Brand Matter? The Influence of Consumer Perceived Ethicality on Trust, Affect and Loyalty," *Journal of Business Ethics* 111(2012): 541–549.

46. "The Global, Socially Conscious Consumer," *Nielsen Wire*, March 27, 2012, http://blog.nielsen.com/nielsenwire/consumer/the-global-socially-conscious-consumer/ (accessed February 1, 2013).

47. Marjorie Kelly, "Holy Grail Found. Absolute, Definitive Proof that Responsible Companies Perform Better Financially," *Business Ethics*, Winter 2004.

48. "Google's Corporate Culture," http://www.google.com/intl/en/corporate/culture.html (accessed February 1, 2013).

49. O. C. Ferrell, Isabelle Maignan, and Terry W. Loe, "The Relationship between Corporate Citizenship and Competitive Advantage," in *Rights, Relationships, and Responsibilities*, ed. O. C. Ferrell, Lou Pelton, and Sheb L. True (Kennesaw, GA: Kennesaw State University, 2003).

50. Simone Baribeau, "How Tony Hsieh Pivoted Zappos into a $1.2 Billion Amazon Acquisition," *Fast Company*, September 4, 2012, http://www.fastcompany.com/3000591/how-tony-hsieh-pivoted-zappos-12-billion-amazon-acquisition (accessed February 1, 2013); "Zappos Family Core Values," Zappos, http://about.zappos.com/our-unique-culture/zappos-core-values/deliver-wow-through-service (accessed February 1, 2013).

51. Galvin, "The New Business Ethics."

52. Ethisphere Institute, "2011 World's Most Ethical Companies," *Ethisphere*, http://ethisphere.com/2011-worlds-most-ethical-companies/ (accessed February 1, 2013).

CHAPTER 2

STAKEHOLDER RELATIONSHIPS, SOCIAL RESPONSIBILITY, AND CORPORATE GOVERNANCE

CHAPTER OBJECTIVES

- Identify stakeholders' roles in business ethics
- Define social responsibility
- Examine the relationship between stakeholder orientation and social responsibility
- Delineate a stakeholder orientation in creating corporate social responsibility
- Explore the role of corporate governance in structuring ethics and social responsibility in business
- List the steps involved in implementing a stakeholder perspective in social responsibility and business ethics

CHAPTER OUTLINE

AN ETHICAL DILEMMA*

After Megan Jones finished her BS degree in Management at The University of Rhode Island, she landed a great job with the "app" developing company Global App Creations (GAC). In her six months of training in Human Resources (HR) she faced challenges, but enjoyed working with people and solving their problems.

On Monday morning Megan's boss, Debbie, placed a 20-inch-thick personnel folder on her desk. "Megan, I want you to review these files and by Friday start the process of finding possible ethics violations. Some employees know this is coming, while others don't have a clue. It's your job to write them up for ethics violations and suggest whether you think some of them should go to legal as well. I will add my write-up to each one so you won't be the only one making the decisions. For now, I'll make the primary decisions, but sooner or later you'll be in charge of these tasks. If you have any questions, just stop by and we can talk."

That afternoon Megan began going through the files. Some were straightforward involving theft of office supplies, inappropriate remarks, and tardiness. GAC's code was straightforward on such matters. Yet other events appeared confusing. One salesperson was getting an official reprimand for using a company car for personal activities. This didn't make sense because all the salespeople drove company cars they took home after work. According to the file, the person visited a hospital ten miles away every evening for the past month. Megan realized every GAC car was equipped with a GPS device. While she didn't think it was illegal for companies to install tracking devices on items they owned, she heard having information about health or religion could become the basis of a lawsuit if the person's employment was terminated.

The most shocking file Megan reviewed was that of another employee being fired for sharing confidential information with a competitor. The file contained reports on computer activity, cell phone usage, GPS tracking, and included audio and video of personal conversations, dinners, and hotel rooms. On Tuesday Megan went to Jeremy, who worked for the company for several years, and asked him if he knew of employee tracking at the company.

Jeremy responded, "Well, I have heard rumors that managers want to keep track of employees and monitor whether they share confidential information with competitors. I've also heard they monitor where each employee goes through the GPS located in the company car."

Megan felt uneasy. "Jeremy, is what they are doing legal? Can they track and monitor our every move and conversation?"

Jeremy shrugged. "As far as I know it's legal, but I've never looked into the actual laws. I don't know why a company should track my personal time outside the office. But what are we supposed to do about it? We all need a job, and each one comes with a price."

On Thursday Megan met with Debbie and expressed her concerns about the information GAC collects through the employee tracking activities. After she finished, Debbie responded. "Don't be so naïve, Megan. You know as well as I do what employees do outside of work could legally hurt the company. It's also necessary to make sure employees aren't sharing confidential information with rivals. This is a competitive industry."

"But what about this employee using the company car to visit his daughter in the hospital? It was outside work hours and I heard his daughter is sick. What about an individual's right to privacy concerning medical records?"

Debbie brushed her concerns aside. "We don't have access to anybody's medical records. We got this from the GPS device in the company-owned car issued to him. We can't make exceptions for these types of things. Our reputation for ethics is excellent."

Then Debbie said, "I hope you haven't spoken to anyone about these cases because that violates confidentiality. Your job is to review the files and suggest appropriate action. All files and communications about the files are confidential."

QUESTIONS | EXERCISES

1. If tracking employees through technology is not illegal, why should Megan be concerned if she is not involved in any misconduct?

2. At this point, what are Megan's alternatives to resolve her current dilemma about her involvement and knowledge about GAC's tracking employees?

3. Who should have a stake or an interest in how GAC tracks and monitors its employees?

*This case is strictly hypothetical; any resemblance to real persons, companies, or situations is coincidental.

Business ethics issues, conflicts, and successes revolve around relationships. Building effective relationships is considered one of the most important areas of business today. Many companies consider business ethics as a team sport where each member performs and supports others. A business exists because of relationships between employees, customers, shareholders or investors, suppliers, and managers who develop strategies to attain success. In addition, an organization usually has a governing authority, often called a board of directors, that provides oversight and direction to assure the organization stays focused on its objectives in an ethical, legal, and socially responsible manner. When unethical acts are discovered in organizations, in most instances cooperation or complicity facilitated the acceptance and perpetuation of the unethical conduct.[1] Few decisions are made by one individual. Therefore, relationships are associated with organizational success and also organizational misconduct.

A stakeholder framework identifies the internal stakeholders (employees, boards of directors, and managers), and the external stakeholders (customers, special interest groups, regulators, and others) who agree, collaborate, and engage in confrontations on ethical issues. Most ethical issues exist because of conflicts in values and belief patterns about right and wrong among and within stakeholder groups. This framework allows an organization to identify, monitor, and respond to the needs, values, and expectations of different stakeholder groups.

The formal system of accountability and control of ethical and socially responsible behavior is corporate governance. In theory, the board of directors provides oversight for all decisions and use of resources. Ethical issues relate to the role of the board of directors, relationships with shareholders, internal control, risk management, and executive compensation. Ethical leadership is associated with appropriate corporate governance.

In this chapter, we first focus on the concept of stakeholders and examine how a stakeholder framework helps us understand organizational ethics. Then we identify stakeholders and the importance of a stakeholder orientation. Using the stakeholder framework, we explore the concept and dimensions of social responsibility. Next, we examine corporate governance as a dimension of social responsibility and ethical decision making to provide an understanding of the importance of stakeholder oversight. Finally, we provide the steps for implementing a stakeholder perspective on social responsibility and ethical decisions in business.

STAKEHOLDERS DEFINE ETHICAL ISSUES IN BUSINESS

In a business context, customers, investors and shareholders, employees, suppliers, government agencies, communities, and many others who have a "stake" or claim in some aspect of a company's products, operations, markets, industry, and outcomes are known as **stakeholders**. Business influences these groups, but these groups also have the ability to influence business; thus, the relationship between companies and their stakeholders is a two-way street.[2] Sometimes activities and negative press generated by special interest groups force a company to change its practices. For example, consumer groups have put pressure on government and business to decrease the amount of sodium, sugars, and other fatty ingredients in fast food and sodas. This increased pressure as well as the trend toward healthier food prompted Olive Garden, Red Lobster, and Carl's Jr. to reduce the amount of sodium in some menu items. Additionally, Boston Market removed salt shakers from tables in their restaurants.[3]

There are three approaches to stakeholder theory: normative, descriptive, and instrumental approaches.[4] The normative approach identifies ethical guidelines that dictate how firms should treat stakeholders. Principles and values provide direction for normative decisions. The descriptive approach focuses on the actual behavior of the firm and usually addresses how decisions and strategies are made for stakeholder relationships. The instrumental approach to stakeholder theory describes what happens if firms behave in a particular way.[5] This approach is useful because it examines relationships involved in the management of stakeholders including the processes, structures, and practices that implement stakeholder relationships within an organization. The survival and performance of any organization is a function of its ability to create value for all primary stakeholders and attempt to do this by not favoring one group over the others.[6]

Many firms experience conflicts with key stakeholders and consequently damage their reputations and shareholder confidence. While many threats to reputations stem from uncontrollable events such as economic conditions, ethical misconduct is more difficult to overcome than poor financial performance. Stakeholders most directly affected by negative events experience a corresponding shift in their perceptions of a firm's reputation. On the other hand, firms sometimes receive negative publicity for misconduct that destroys trust and tarnishes their reputations, making it more difficult to retain existing customers and attract new ones.[7] To maintain the trust and confidence of its stakeholders, CEOs and other top managers are expected to act in a transparent and responsible manner. Providing untruthful or deceptive information to stakeholders is, if not illegal, certainly unethical, and can result in a loss of trust. Brian Dunn, former CEO of Best Buy, was fired for having an inappropriate relationship with an employee. Richard Schulze, founder of Best Buy and former Chairman of the company, was also ousted when it was determined he knew about the relationship but failed to report it to the audit panel of the board.[8]

Ethical misconduct and decisions that damage stakeholders generally impacts the company's reputation in terms of both investor and consumer confidence. As investor perceptions and decisions begin to take their toll, shareholder value drops, exposing the company to consumer scrutiny that can increase the damage. According to a recent Edelman trust survey, three industries in terms of the lowest level of trust were the media, banks, and financial services; the most trusted industries were technology, automotive, and food and beverage.[9] Reputation is a factor in consumers' perceptions of product attributes and corporate image and can lead to consumer willingness to purchase goods and services at profitable prices. Perceived wrongdoing or questionable behavior may lead to boycotts and aggressive campaigns to dampen sales and earnings. When Apple decided to leave the green registry EPEAT, a government-backed registry that certifies products based on their sustainability, the company did not anticipate the backlash from governments. San Francisco announced it would boycott Apple by no longer purchasing Apple computers for its agencies. Under this pressure, Apple rejoined the registry.[10] New reforms intended to improve corporate accountability and transparency suggest that stakeholders, including regulatory agencies, local communities, attorneys, and public accounting firms play a major role in fostering responsible decision making.[11] Stakeholders apply their values and standards to diverse issues, including working conditions, consumer rights, environmental conservation, product safety, and proper information disclosure that may or may not directly affect an individual stakeholder's own welfare. We can assess the level of social responsibility an organization bears by scrutinizing its effects on the issues of concern to its stakeholders.[12]

Stakeholders provide resources critical to a firm's long-term success. These resources may be tangible and intangible. Shareholders, for example, supply capital; suppliers offer material resources or intangible knowledge; employees and managers grant expertise, leadership, and commitment; customers generate revenue and provide loyalty with word-of-mouth promotion; local communities provide infrastructure; and the media transmits positive corporate images. In a spirit of reciprocity, stakeholders should be fair, loyal, and treat the corporation in a responsible way.[13] When individual stakeholders share expectations about desirable business conduct, they may choose to establish or join formal communities dedicated to defining and advocating these values and expectations. Stakeholders' abilities to withdraw these needed resources gives them power over businesses.[14]

Identifying Stakeholders

We can identify two types of stakeholders. Primary stakeholders are those whose continued association is absolutely necessary for a firm's survival. These include employees, customers, investors, and shareholders, as well as the governments and communities that provide necessary infrastructure. Some firms take actions that damage relationships with primary stakeholders. Figure 2–1 indicates that strong ethical corporate cultures have decreased in recent years. Ethical corporate cultures are important because they are linked to positive relationships with stakeholders. By the same token, concern for stakeholders' needs and expectations is necessary to avoid ethical conflicts.

Secondary stakeholders do not typically engage in transactions with a company and are therefore not essential to its survival. These include the media, trade associations, and special interest groups like the American Association of Retired People (AARP), a special interest group working to support retirees' rights such as health care benefits. Both primary and secondary stakeholders embrace specific values and standards that dictate acceptable and unacceptable corporate behaviors. It is important for managers to recognize that

FIGURE 2–1 **Decline in the Strength of Ethical Cultures**

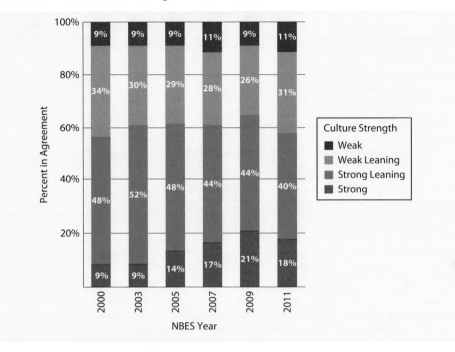

Note: Due to rounding, some numbers do not equal 100 percent.

Source: Ethics Resource Center, *2011 National Business Ethics Survey* (Arlington, VA: Ethics Resource Center, 2012), p. 19.

while primary groups may present more day-to-day concerns, secondary groups cannot be ignored or given less consideration in the ethical decision-making process.[15] Table 2–1 shows a select list of issues important to various stakeholder groups and identifies how corporations impact these issues.

Figure 2–2 offers a conceptualization of the relationship between businesses and stakeholders. In this **stakeholder interaction model**, there are reciprocal relationships between the firm and a host of stakeholders. In addition to the fundamental input of investors, employees, and suppliers, this approach recognizes other stakeholders and explicitly acknowledges that dialogue exists between a firm's internal and external environments. Corporate social responsibility actions that put employees at the center of activities gain the support of both external and internal stakeholders.[16]

A Stakeholder Orientation

The degree to which a firm understands and addresses stakeholder demands can be referred to as a **stakeholder orientation**. A stakeholder orientation involves "activities and processes within a system of social institutions that facilitate and maintain value through exchange relationships with multiple stakeholders."[17] This orientation comprises three sets of activities: (1) the organization-wide generation of data about stakeholder groups and assessment of the firm's effects on these groups; (2) the distribution of this information throughout the firm; and (3) the responsiveness of the organization as a whole to this information.[18]

TABLE 2-1 Examples of Stakeholder Issues and Associated Measures of Corporate Impacts

Stakeholder Groups and Issues	Potential Indicators of Corporate Impact on These Issues
Employees	
1. Compensation and benefits	• Ratio of lowest wage to national legal minimum or to local cost of living
2. Training and development	• Changes in average years of training of employees
3. Employee diversity	• Percentages of employees from different genders and races
4. Occupational health and safety	• Standard injury rates and absentee rates
5. Communications with management	• Availability of open-door policies or ombudsmen
Customers	
1. Product safety and quality	• Number of product recalls over time
2. Management of customer complaints	• Number of customer complaints and availability of procedures to answer them
3. Services to disabled customers	• Availability and nature of measures taken to ensure services to disabled customers
Investors	
1. Transparency of shareholder communications	• Availability of procedures to inform shareholders about corporate activities
2. Shareholder rights	• Frequency and type of litigation involving violations of shareholder rights
Suppliers	
1. Encouraging suppliers in developing countries	• Prices offered to suppliers in developed countries in comparison to countries' other suppliers
2. Encouraging minority suppliers	• Percentage of minority suppliers
Community	
1. Public health and safety protection	• Availability of emergency response plan
2. Conservation of energy and materials	• Data on reduction of waste produced and comparison to industry
3. Donations and support of local organizations	• Annual employee time spent in community service
Environmental Groups	
1. Minimizing the use of energy	• Amount of electricity purchased; percentage of "green" electricity
2. Minimizing emissions and waste	• Type, amount, and designation of waste generated
3. Minimizing adverse environmental effects of goods and services	• Percentage of product weight reclaimed after use

© Cengage Learning

FIGURE 2-2 **Interactions between a Company and Its Primary and Secondary Stakeholders**

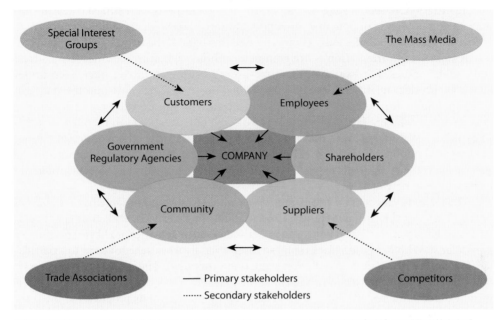

Source: Adapted from Isabelle Maignan, O. C. Ferrell, and Linda Ferrell, "A Stakeholder Model for Implementing Social Responsibility in Marketing."
European Journal of Marketing 39 (2005): 956–977. Used with permission.

Generating data about stakeholders begins with identifying the stakeholders relevant to the firm. Relevant stakeholder groups should be analyzed on the basis of the power each enjoys, as well as by the ties between them and the company. Next, the firm should characterize the concerns about the business's conduct each relevant stakeholder group shares. This information is derived from formal research, including surveys, focus groups, Internet searches, and press reviews. For example, Best Buy obtains input on social and environmental responsibility issues from company representatives, suppliers, customers, and community leaders. Shell has an online discussion forum that invites website visitors to express their opinions on the implications of the company's activities. Employees and managers also generate this information informally as they carry out their daily activities. For example, purchasing managers know about suppliers' demands, public relations executives are tuned into the media, legal counselors are aware of the regulatory environment, financial executives connect to investors, sales representatives are in touch with customers, and human resources advisers communicate directly with employees. Finally, companies should evaluate their impact on the issues of importance to the various stakeholders they identify.[19] While shareholders desire strong profitability and growth, societal stakeholders have needs extending beyond these two requirements.[20]

Given the variety of employees involved in the generation of information about stakeholders, it is essential the information gathered be circulated throughout the firm. The firm must facilitate the communication of information about the nature of relevant stakeholder communities, issues, and impact of the firm on these issues to all members of the organization. The dissemination of stakeholder intelligence can be formally organized through newsletters and internal information forums.[21] In particular, companies should use these activities to communicate the company's code of conduct to employees. Such communication informs employees about appropriate and inappropriate conduct within the organization. Research suggests employees in organizations with ethical codes of conduct are less accepting of potential misconduct toward stakeholders.[22] Ethical codes are of little use if they are not effectively communicated throughout the firm.

A stakeholder orientation is not complete without including activities that address stakeholder issues. For example, manufacturers in some countries have been under attack for product quality issues and safety violations. Walmart came into the spotlight when the public learned that a Bangladeshi factory with unsafe work conditions made goods for the retailer. This connection was discovered after a fire in the factory killed 112 workers. Walmart claimed some suppliers used the factory without approval. Even if Walmart did not have knowledge about the factory, as the most powerful member of the supply chain the company is expected to promote safety and workers' rights throughout its distribution network.[23]

The responsiveness of an organization as a whole to stakeholder intelligence consists of the initiatives the firm adopts to ensure it abides by or exceeds stakeholder expectations and has a positive impact on stakeholder issues. Such activities are likely specific to a particular stakeholder group (for example, family-friendly work schedules) or to a particular stakeholder issue (such as pollution reduction programs). These responsive processes typically involve participation of the concerned stakeholder groups. Kraft, for example, includes special interest groups and university representatives in its programs so the company is sensitized to present and future ethical issues.

A stakeholder orientation can be viewed as a continuum in that firms are likely to adopt the concept to varying degrees. To gauge a firm's stakeholder orientation, it is necessary to evaluate the extent the firm adopts behaviors that typify the generation and dissemination of stakeholder intelligence and the responsiveness to this intelligence. A given organization may generate and disseminate more intelligence about some stakeholder communities than others and respond accordingly.[24]

SOCIAL RESPONSIBILITY AND ETHICS

The terms *ethics* and *social responsibility* are often used interchangeably, but each has a distinct meaning. In Chapter 1, we defined *social responsibility* as an organization's obligation to maximize its positive impact on stakeholders and minimize its negative impact. For example, Google makes it a mission to become a zero-carbon company by investing in alternative energy, purchasing carbon offsets, and constructing more energy-efficient data centers.[25] Intuit matches employee donations and gives employees paid time off for volunteering in their communities.[26] SC Johnson gives 5 percent of pre-tax profits to corporate giving and is investing in wind turbines to power some of its manufacturing plants.[27] Conversely, one study found that a firm's sales margin will be damaged by the unethical treatment of stakeholders.[28] Many other businesses have tried to determine what relationships, obligations, and duties are appropriate between their organizations and various stakeholders. Social responsibility can be viewed as a contract with society, whereas business ethics involves carefully thought-out rules or heuristics of business conduct that guide decision making.

There are four levels of social responsibility—economic, legal, ethical, and philanthropic (see Figure 2–3).[29] At the most basic level, companies have a responsibility to be

FIGURE 2–3 **Steps of Social Responsibility**

Philanthropic: "giving back" to society

Ethical: following standards of acceptable behavior as judged by stakeholders

Legal: abiding by all laws and government regulations

Economic: maximizing stakeholder wealth and/or value

Source: Adapted from Archie B. Carroll, "The Pyramid of Corporate Social Responsibility: Toward the Moral Management of Organizational Stakeholders," *Business Horizons* (July–August 1991): 42, Fig. 3.

profitable at an acceptable level to meet the objectives of shareholders and create value. Of course, businesses are also expected to obey all relevant laws and regulations. For example, the European Union established an online privacy law going beyond what other countries require. Under the law individuals will be able to delete uploaded personal data if there are no legitimate grounds for retaining it. The law also addresses cookies, the common Internet files websites use to remember data about users that other firms collect to track users' online behavior. This means if a U.S. company such as Google wants to do business in the EU, it must obey the law or pay up to $1.4 million per violation.[30]

Business ethics, as previously defined, comprises principles and values that meet the expectations of stakeholders. Philanthropic responsibility refers to activities that are not required of businesses but that contribute to human welfare or goodwill. Ethics, then, is one dimension of social responsibility. Ethical decisions by individuals and groups drive appropriate decisions and are interrelated with all of the levels of social responsibility. For example, the economic level can have ethical consequences when making managerial decisions.

The term **corporate citizenship** is often used to express the extent to which businesses strategically meet the economic, legal, ethical, and philanthropic responsibilities placed on them by various stakeholders.[31] Corporate citizenship has four interrelated dimensions: strong sustained economic performance, rigorous compliance, ethical actions beyond what the law requires, and voluntary contributions that advance the reputation and stakeholder commitment of the organization. A firm's commitment to corporate citizenship indicates a strategic focus on fulfilling the social responsibilities its stakeholders expect. Corporate citizenship involves acting on the firm's commitment to corporate citizenship philosophy and measuring the extent to which it follows through by actually implementing citizenship initiatives. Table 2–2 lists some of the world's most ethical companies, all of which have demonstrated their commitment to stakeholders. As Chapter 1 demonstrated, many of these companies have superior financial performance compared to the indexes of other publically traded firms.

Reputation is one of an organization's greatest intangible assets with tangible value. The value of a positive reputation is difficult to quantify, but it is important. A single negative incident can influence perceptions of a corporation's image and reputation instantly and for years afterward. Corporate reputation, image, and brands are more important

TABLE 2–2 A Selection of the World's Most Ethical Companies

L'ORÉAL	Salesforce.com, Inc.
Xerox	T-Mobile USA
OfficeMax	Hasbro
Cummins, Inc.	Microsoft Corporation
Ford Motor Company	ARAMARK
General Electric	Eaton
PepsiCo	International Paper
Whole Foods Market	Time Warner, Inc.
Aflac	eBay
Petco	Intel Corporation
Kellogg Company	Gap
Starbucks	UPS
Target	Waste Management

Source: Ethisphere Institute, "2013 World's Most Ethical Companies," *Ethisphere*, http://m1.ethisphere.com/wme2013/index.html (accessed March 7, 2013).

than ever and are among the most critical aspects of sustaining relationships with constituents including investors, customers, employees, media, and regulators. Although an organization does not control its reputation in a direct sense, its actions, choices, behaviors, and consequences influence stakeholders' perceptions of it. For instance, employees are likely to perceive their firm's corporate social responsibility initiatives as authentic if the program appears to fit with the company's true identity and if they take a leadership role in these initiatives. Employees who feel their firms' corporate social responsibility programs are authentic are more likely to identify and connect with the organization.[32]

ISSUES IN SOCIAL RESPONSIBILITY

Social responsibility rests on a stakeholder orientation. The realities of global warming, obesity, consumer protection, and other issues are causing companies to look at a broader, more inclusive stakeholder orientation. In other words, a broader view of social responsibility looks beyond pragmatic and firm-centric interests and considers the long-term welfare of society. Each stakeholder is given due consideration. There needs to be a movement away from self-serving "co-optation" and a narrow focus on profit maximization.[33] In fact, there is strong evidence that an overemphasis on profit maximization is counter-productive. Long-term relationships with stakeholders develop trust, loyalty, and the performance necessary to maintain profitability. Issues generally associated with social responsibility can be separated into four general categories: social issues, consumer protection, sustainability, and corporate governance.

Social issues are associated with the common good. In other words, social issues deal with concerns affecting large segments of society and the welfare of the entire society. In terms of social responsibility, managers address social issues by examining the different groups to which they have an obligation. Marketers failing to meet these social obligations can create criticism and negative publicity for their organizations.

Social issues may encompass events such as jobs lost through outsourcing, abortion, gun rights, and poverty. While these issues may be indirectly related to business, there is a need to reflect on them in developing strategies in certain cases. Issues that directly relate to business include obesity, smoking, and exploiting vulnerable or impoverished populations, as well as a number of other issues. For example, marketers are increasingly targeting food advertising to children through Internet websites. One study found approximately 85 percent of food brands have websites with content targeted toward children.[34] With the childhood obesity epidemic increasing, marketers of foods perceived to be unhealthy are being pressured to change their strategies to account for this growing concern. In addition, some economic issues have ramifications to society such as antitrust, employee well-being, insider trading, and other issues that diminish competition and consumer choice.

Another major social issue gaining prominence involves Internet tracking and privacy for marketing purposes. Many consumers are shocked when they realize marketers are using cookies and other mechanisms to track their online activity. Internet privacy may soon become a consumer protection issue because the government is considering passing legislation limiting the types of tracking companies can perform over the Internet without users' permission. On the other hand, companies that develop signals on their websites reassuring consumers their information will be kept private are more likely to establish trust with consumers, which could help to build mutually beneficial online relationships.[35]

The second major issue is consumer protection, which often occurs in the form of laws passed to protect consumers from unfair and deceptive business practices. Issues involving consumer protection usually have an immediate impact on the consumer after a purchase. Major areas of concern include advertising, disclosure, financial practices, and product safety. Because consumers are less knowledgeable about certain products or business practices, it is the responsibility of companies to take precautions to prevent consumers from being harmed by their products. For instance, businesses marketing products that could potentially be harmful have responsibility to put warning labels on their products. The Federal Trade Commission and the Consumer Financial Protection Bureau are intent on enforcing consumer protection laws and pursuing violations.

Deceptive advertising has been a hot topic in the consumer protection area. For instance, covert marketing occurs when companies use promotional tools to make consumers believe the promotion is coming from an independent third party rather than from the company.[36] Often companies are forced to disclose to consumers if they are paying another entity to promote their products. However, as with many business ethics issues, some advertising practices skirt the line between ethical and questionable behavior. For instance, some believe promotions embedded into television programs without informing consumers are a type of covert marketing that warrants greater consumer protection.[37] Companies must be knowledgeable about consumer protection laws and recognize whether their practices could be construed as deceptive or unfair.

The third major issue is sustainability. We define sustainability as the potential for the long-term well-being of the natural environment, including all biological entities, as well as the mutually beneficial interactions among nature and individuals, organizations, and business strategies. With major environmental challenges such as global warming and the passage of new environmental legislation, businesses can no longer afford to ignore the natural environment as a stakeholder. Even industries traditionally considered high in pollution, such as the oil and gas industry, are investing in sustainable practices like alternative energy. Because sustainability is a major ethical issue, we cover this topic in more detail in Chapter 12.

Corporate governance is the fourth major issue of corporate social responsibility. Corporate governance involves the development of formal systems of accountability, oversight, and control. Strong corporate governance mechanisms remove the opportunity for employees to make unethical decisions. Research has shown that corporate governance has a positive relationship with social responsibility. For instance, one study revealed a positive correlation with corporate governance and corporate social responsibility engagement.[38] Additionally, firms with strong corporate governance mechanisms that prompt them to disclose their social responsibility initiatives can establish legitimacy and trust among their stakeholders.[39] We discuss corporate governance in more detail later in this chapter.

SOCIAL RESPONSIBILITY AND THE IMPORTANCE OF A STAKEHOLDER ORIENTATION

Many business people and scholars question the role of ethics and social responsibility in business. Legal and economic responsibilities are generally accepted as the most important determinants of performance. "If this is well done," say classical economic theorists, "profits are maximized more or less continuously and firms carry out their major responsibilities to society."[40] Some economists believe if companies address economic and legal issues they satisfy the demands of society, and trying to anticipate and meet additional needs would be almost impossible. Milton Friedman has been quoted as saying "the basic mission of business [is] ... to produce goods and services at a profit, and in doing this, business [is] making its maximum contribution to society and, in fact, being socially responsible."[41] Even with the business ethics scandals of the twenty-first century, Friedman suggests that although those individuals guilty of wrongdoing should be held accountable, the market is a better deterrent to wrongdoing than new laws and regulations.[42] Thus, Friedman would diminish the role of stakeholders such as the government and employees in requiring businesses to demonstrate responsible and ethical behavior. Friedman's capitalism is a far cry from Adam Smith, one of the founders of capitalism. Smith developed the concept of the invisible hand and explored the role of self-interest in economic systems; however, he went on to explain that the "common good is associated with six psychological motives and that each individual has to produce for the common good, with values such as

Propriety, Prudence, Reason, Sentiment and promoting the happiness of mankind."[43] These values correlate with the needs and concerns of stakeholders. Smith established normative expectations for motives and behaviors in his theories about the invisible hand. For instance, he distinguished justice as consisting of perfect or inalienable rights, such as the right to property, from beneficence, consisting of imperfect rights that *should* be performed but cannot be forced. A stakeholder orientation perspective would advocate managers take into account both the perfect and imperfect rights of stakeholders. Yet when tradeoffs are necessary, justice should be given priority over beneficence.[44]

Evidence suggests caring about the well-being of stakeholders leads to increased profits. One study found when firms were placed on a socially responsible index, stakeholders reacted positively.[46] Other studies also associate a stakeholder orientation with increased profits.[47] Therefore, although the purpose of a stakeholder orientation is to maximize positive outcomes that meet stakeholder needs,[48] the support stakeholders have for companies they perceive to be socially responsible also serve to enhance the firms' profitability. Table 2–3 lists *CR* Magazine's best companies in terms of corporate citizenship and social responsibility. Many of these firms are highly profitable, succeeding both ethically and financially.

DEBATE ISSUE
TAKE A STAND

Is It Acceptable to Promote a Socially Irresponsible but Legal Product to Stakeholders?

When you think of cheating, you may think of irresponsible behavior in the classroom. But Noel Biderman created a company called Avid Life Media (based in Toronto) that is dedicated to another form of cheating.

Avid Life Media is owner of six website brands, including Cougar Life and Hot or Not. One of its more controversial brands is Ashley Madison, the motto of which is "Life is Short. Have an Affair." The website has more than 8.5 million members. The company encourages married men and women to spend less than a minute to register on the largest website to openly promote infidelity. The company employs hundreds of programmers, designers, and marketers and has conducted a private placement for investors. While many stakeholders would say the purpose of the website is wrong, there is nothing illegal about this business. But the fact that the website helps people engage in cheating on their spouses—including providing an email address to which one's spouse would never have access—has many people concerned. They consider facilitating secrecy for socially questionable conduct to be wrong.[45]

1. There is nothing wrong in providing a legal service many people desire.
2. From a stakeholder perspective, it is wrong to provide socially irresponsible services.

CORPORATE GOVERNANCE PROVIDES FORMALIZED RESPONSIBILITY TO STAKEHOLDERS

Most businesses, and often many subjects taught in business schools, operate under the assumption that the purpose of business is to maximize profits for shareholders—an assumption manifest, for example, in the 1919 decision of the Michigan Supreme Court. In *Dodge v. Ford Motor Co.*[49] the court ruled that a business exists for the profit of shareholders, and the board of directors should focus on that objective. In contrast, the stakeholder

TABLE 2–3 CR's Best Corporate Citizens

1	Bristol-Myers Squibb
2	International Business Machines Corp.
3	Intel Corp.
4	Microsoft Corporation
5	Johnson Controls Inc.
6	Accenture plc
7	Spectra Energy Corp.
8	Campbell Soup Co.
9	Nike, Inc.
10	Freeport-McMoran Copper & Gold Inc.

Source: *CR's 100 Best Corporate Citizens 2012,* http://www.thecro.com/files/100Best2012_List_3.8.pdf
(accessed February 14, 2013).

model places the board of directors in the position of balancing the interests and conflicts of a company's various constituencies. External control of the corporation resides not only with government regulators but also with key stakeholders including employees, consumers, and communities, which exert pressure for responsible conduct. In fact, social responsibility activities have a positive impact on consumer identification with and attitude toward the brand.[50] Mandates for stakeholder interests have been institutionalized in legislation that provides incentives for responsible conduct. Shareholders have been pushing for more power in the boardroom, as many feel their interests have not been well represented in the resolution of issues such as executive compensation.

Today, the failure to balance stakeholder interests can result in a failure to maximize shareholders' wealth. Money managers sometimes engage in risky trading that leads to large losses, as evidenced in the conduct of traders at Citi. A trader at JP Morgan was nicknamed the London Whale for his risky trades. Eventually, these trades lost the company billions. Most firms are moving toward a more balanced stakeholder model as they see that this approach sustains the relationships necessary for long-term success.

Both directors and officers of corporations are fiduciaries for the shareholders. Fiduciaries are persons placed in positions of trust that act on behalf of the best interests of the organization. They have what is called a duty of care, or a *duty of diligence,* to make informed and prudent decisions.[51] Directors have a duty to avoid ethical misconduct and provide leadership in decisions to prevent ethical misconduct in the organization.

Directors are not generally held responsible for negative outcomes if they have been informed and diligent in their decision making. Board members have an obligation to request information, conduct research, use accountants and attorneys, and obtain the services of ethical compliance consultants to ensure the corporations in which they have an interest are run in an ethical manner. The National Association of Corporate Directors, a board of directors' trade group, has helped formulate a guide for boards to help them do a better job of governing corporate America.[52]

Directors share a *duty of loyalty,* which means all their decisions should be in the best interests of the corporation and its stakeholders. Conflicts of interest exist when a director uses the position to obtain personal gain, usually at the expense of the organization. For example, before the passage of the Sarbanes–Oxley Act in 2002, directors could give themselves and their officers interest-free loans. Scandals at Tyco, Kmart, and WorldCom are all associated with officers receiving personal loans that damaged the corporation.

Officer compensation packages present a challenge for directors, especially those on the board who are not independent. Directors have an opportunity to vote for others' compensation in return for their own increased compensation. Following the global financial crisis, many top executives at failed firms received multimillion dollar bonuses in spite of the fact their companies required huge government bailouts simply to stay afloat. This has led to a greater amount of shareholder activism regarding the issue of executive pay. Directors now find shareholders want to vote on executive officers' compensation, and although their votes are not binding, investor pressure has increased the shareholder role in deciding executive compensation. For instance, investors voted against the compensation plan proposed for Citigroup CEO Vikram Pandit because of dissatisfaction with company performance.[53]

Directors' knowledge about the investments, business ventures, and stock market information of a company creates issues that could violate their duty of loyalty. Insider trading of a firm's stock has specific rules, and violations should result in serious punishment. The obligations of directors and officers for legal and ethical responsibility interface and fit together based on their fiduciary relationships. Ethical values should guide decisions and buffer the possibility of illegal conduct. With increased pressure on directors to provide oversight for organizational ethics, there is a trend toward directors receiving training to increase their competency in ethics programs development, as well as other areas such as accounting. Automated systems to monitor and measure the occurrence of ethical issues within organizations are increasingly used in this oversight process.

Accountability is an important part of corporate governance. *Accountability* refers to how closely workplace decisions align with a firm's stated strategic direction and its compliance with ethical and legal considerations. *Oversight* provides a system of checks and balances that limit employees' and managers' opportunities to deviate from policies and strategies aimed at preventing unethical and illegal activities. *Control* is the process of

TABLE 2–4 Corporate Governance Topics

Executive Compensation
Enterprise-Wide Risk Management
Short- and Long-Term Strategies
Board Composition and Structure
Shareholder Relations
CEO Selection, Termination, and Succession Plans
Role of the CEO in Board Decisions
Auditing, Control, and Integrity of Financial Reporting
Compliance with Government Regulation and Reform
Organizational Ethics Programs

Source: "Corporate Alert: Top 10 Topics for Directors in 2011," December 6, 2010, http://www.corpgov.deloitte.com/binary/com.epicentric. contentmanagement.servlet.ContentDeliveryServlet/USEng/Documents/Board%20Governance/Top%2010%20Topics%20for%20Directors%20in %202011_Akin_120610.pdf (accessed February 15, 2011).

auditing and improving organizational decisions and actions. Table 2–4 lists examples of major corporate governance issues.

A clear delineation of accountability helps employees, customers, investors, government regulators, and other stakeholders understand why and how the organization identifies and achieves its goals. Corporate governance establishes fundamental systems and processes for preventing and detecting misconduct, for investigating and disciplining, and for recovery and continuous improvement. Effective corporate governance creates a compliance and ethics culture so employees feel integrity is at the core of competitiveness.[54] Even if a company adopts a consensus approach for decision making, there should be oversight and authority for delegating tasks, making difficult and sometimes controversial decisions, balancing power throughout the firm, and maintaining ethical compliance. Governance also provides mechanisms for identifying risks and planning for recovery when mistakes or problems occur.

The development of a stakeholder orientation should interface with the corporation's governance structure. Corporate governance also helps establish the integrity of all relationships. A governance system without checks and balances creates opportunities for top managers to indulge self-interest before those of important stakeholders. For example, while many people lost their investments during the recent financial crisis some CEOs actually made a profit from it. Some directors tweaked performance targets in order to make goals easier to achieve so they could receive more bonus money. Bonuses have become a contentious issue since they are the part of an executive's pay most tied to performance. Many people ask why executives receive bonuses as their companies fail; the fact is most executive bonuses are tied to targets other than stock prices.[55] Concerns about the need for greater corporate governance are not limited to the United States. Reforms in governance structures and issues are occurring all over the world.[56] Table 2–5 outlines some of the changes we have seen in corporate governance over the past 25 years.

Corporate governance normally involves strategic decisions and actions by boards of directors, business owners, top executives, and other managers with high levels of authority

TABLE 2-5 Changes in Corporate Governance

40% of boards split the CEO and Chair functions
Boards are getting smaller, with an average of 11 members (5:1 ratio independent: non-independent)
74% of boards have mandatory retirement rules for directors
Almost all boards conduct annual board performance evaluations
71% limit the time that board members can serve on outside boards
21% of new directors are women, although 10% of boards have no women directors
Over 50% of CEOs in the S&P 500 do not serve on outside boards
Important characteristics in directors: strong financial background, industry background, and international experience
Average board member retainer: $20,00 in 1986 ($40,000 in today's dollars) and $80,000 in 2010
Average total director compensation has risen to $215,000 in 2010

Source: Julie Hembrock Daum, "How Corporate Governance Changed from 1986–2010," *Business Week*, http://www.businessweek.com/managing/content/nov2010/ca2010118_316346.htm (accessed April 2, 2013).

and accountability. In the past these people have been relatively free from scrutiny, but changes in technology such as social media, consumer activism, as well as recent ethical scandals have brought new attention to communication and transparency. Corporate managers engage in dialogue with shareholder activists when the firm is large, responsive to stakeholders, the CEO is the board chair, and there are few large institutional investors that control significant shares of stock.[57]

Views of Corporate Governance

To better understand the role of corporate governance in business today, we must consider how it relates to fundamental beliefs about the purpose of business. Some organizations take the view that as long as they are maximizing shareholder wealth and profitability, they are fulfilling their core responsibilities. Other firms, however, believe that a business is an important member, even a citizen, of society, and therefore must assume broad responsibilities that include complying with social norms and expectations. From these assumptions, we can derive two major approaches to corporate governance: the shareholder model and the stakeholder model.[58]

The **shareholder model of corporate governance** is founded in classic economic precepts, including the goal of maximizing wealth for investors and owners. For publicly traded firms, corporate governance focuses on developing and improving the formal system for maintaining performance accountability between top management and the firm's shareholders.[59] Thus, a shareholder orientation should drive a firm's decisions toward serving the best interests of investors. Underlying these decisions is a classic agency problem, in which ownership (investors) and control (managers) are separate. Managers act as agents for investors, whose primary goal is increasing the value of the stock they own. However, investors and managers are distinct parties with unique insights, goals, and values with respect to the business. Managers, for example, may have motivations beyond stockholder value, such as market share, personal compensation, or attachment to particular products and projects. Because of these potential differences, corporate governance mechanisms are needed to align investor and management interests. The shareholder model has been criticized for its singular purpose and focus because there are other ways of "investing" in a business. Suppliers, creditors, customers, employees, business partners, the community, and others also invest their resources into the success of the firm.[60]

The **stakeholder model of corporate governance** adopts a broader view of the purpose of business. Although a company certainly has a responsibility for economic success and viability to satisfy its stockholders, it must also answer to other stakeholders, including employees, suppliers, government regulators, communities, and special interest groups with which it interacts. Because of limited resources, companies must determine which of their stakeholders are primary. Once the primary groups are identified, managers must implement the appropriate corporate governance mechanisms to promote the development of long-term relationships.[61] This approach entails creating governance systems that consider stakeholder welfare in tandem with corporate needs and interests. Patagonia, Yahoo!, and Google all use the stakeholder model of corporate governance to direct their business activities.

Although these two approaches represent the ends of a continuum, the reality is the shareholder model is a more restrictive precursor to the stakeholder orientation. Many businesses evolved into the stakeholder model as a result of government initiatives, consumer activism, industry activity, and other external forces.

The Role of Boards of Directors

For public corporations, boards of directors hold the ultimate responsibility for their firms' success or failure, as well as the ethics of their actions. This governing authority is held responsible by the 2004 and 2007 amendments to the Federal Sentencing Guidelines for Organizations (FSGO) for creating an ethical culture that provides leadership, values, and compliance. The members of a company's board of directors assume legal responsibility for the firm's resources and decisions, and they appoint its top executive officers. Board members have a fiduciary duty, meaning they have assumed a position of trust and confidence that entails certain responsibilities, including acting in the best interests of those they serve. Thus, board membership is not intended as a vehicle for personal financial gain; rather, it provides the intangible benefit of ensuring the success of both the organization and the people involved in the fiduciary arrangement. The role and expectations of boards of directors assumed greater significance after the accounting scandals of the early 2000s, and the global financial crisis motivated many stakeholders to demand greater accountability from boards.[62]

Despite this new emphasis on accountability for board members, many continue to believe current directors do not face serious consequences for corporate misconduct. Although directors may be sued by shareholders, the SEC does not usually pursue corporate directors for misconduct unless it can be proved they acted in bad faith. The traditional approach to directorship assumed board members managed the corporation's business, but research and practical observation show that boards of directors rarely, if ever, perform the management function.[63] Boards meet only a few times a year, which precludes them from managing effectively. In addition, the complexity of modern organizations mandates full attention on a daily basis. Therefore, boards of directors primarily concern themselves with monitoring the decisions made by executives on behalf of the company. This function includes choosing top executives, assessing their performance, helping to set strategic direction, and ensuring oversight, control, and accountability mechanisms are in place. Thus, board members assume ultimate authority for their organization's effectiveness and subsequent performance.

Perhaps one of the most challenging ethical issues boards of directors must deal with is compensation. When considering executive pay raises, directors may put their own self-interest above the interests of shareholders.[64] Another issue is the compensation the directors themselves receive. Trends show that director compensation is rising, with analysts predicting 50 percent of boards could see pay raises of up to 15 percent in a one-year period. Proponents argue that high compensation for part-time work is necessary because directors have a difficult job and good pay is needed to attract top-quality talent. On the other hand, critics believe this level of compensation causes a conflict of interest for directors. Some speculate compensation over $200,000 makes directors more complacent; they become less concerned with "rocking the boat" and more concerned with maintaining their high-paying positions.[65] Clearly, the debate over director accountability continues to rage.

Greater Demands for Accountability and Transparency

Just as improved ethical decision making requires more of employees and executives, boards of directors are also experiencing a greater demand for accountability and transparency. In the past, board members were often retired company executives or friends of current executives, but the trend today is toward "outside directors" who have little vested interest in the firm before assuming the director role. Inside directors are corporate officers, consultants, major shareholders, and others who benefit directly from the success of the organization. Directors today are increasingly chosen for their expertise, competence, and ability to bring diverse perspectives to strategic discussions. Outside directors are also thought to bring independence to the monitoring function because they are not bound by past allegiances, friendships, a current role in the company, or some other issue that creates a conflict of interest.

Many of the corporate scandals uncovered in recent years might not have occurred if the companies' boards of directors were better qualified, knowledgeable, and less biased. Diversity of board members, especially in age and gender, has been associated with improved social performance.[66] Shareholder involvement in changing the makeup of boards has always run into created difficulties. Most boards are not true democracies, and many shareholders have minimal impact on decision making because they are so dispersed. The concept of board members being linked to more than one company is known as interlocking directorate. The practice is not considered illegal unless it involves a direct competitor.[67] A survey by *USA Today* found that corporate boards have considerable overlap. More than 1,000 corporate board members sit on four or more boards, and of the nearly 2,000 boards of directors in the United States, more than 22,000 of their members are linked to boards of more than one company. For example, of the 1,000 largest companies, 20 percent share at least one board member with another top 1,000 firm. This overlap creates the opportunity for conflicts of interest in decision making and limits the independence of individual boards of directors. In some cases, it seems individuals earned placement on multiple boards of directors because they gained a reputation for going along with top management and never asking questions. Such a trend fosters a corporate culture that limits outside oversight of top managers' decisions.

Although labor and public pension fund activities waged hundreds of proxy battles in recent years, they rarely had much effect on the target companies. Now shareholder activists attack the process by which directors themselves are elected. Shareholders at Saks are not the only ones voting to change board election rules. Resolutions at hundreds of companies require candidates for director to gain a majority of votes before they can join the board. It is hoped this practice makes boards of directors more attentive and accountable.[68]

Executive Compensation

One of the biggest issues corporate boards of directors face is executive compensation. In fact, most boards spend more time deciding how much to compensate top executives than they do ensuring the integrity of the company's financial reporting systems.[69] How executives are compensated for their leadership, organizational service, and performance has become a controversial topic. After announcing that Hostess would go bankrupt, Hostess CEO Gregory Rayburn was highly criticized for cutting employee salaries but not cutting his own. Although he gave up his bonus, many stakeholders were unhappy he received such high compensation even though the company had failed.[70]

Many people believe no executive is worth millions of dollars in annual salary and stock options, even if he or she brings great financial return to investors. Their concerns often center on the relationship between the highest-paid executives and median employee wages in the company. If this ratio is perceived as too large, critics believe employees are not being compensated fairly or high executive salaries represent an improper use of company resources. According to the AFL-CIO, the average executive pay of an S&P 500 index company is nearly $13 million. Executive bonuses can reach into the hundreds of thousands of dollars.[71]

Understandably, many stakeholders are angry about this situation. The business press now supports high levels of executive compensation only when directly linked to strong company performance. Although the issue of executive compensation gained much attention in the media of late, some business owners long recognized its potential ill effects. In the early twentieth century, for example, JP Morgan implemented a policy limiting the pay of top managers in the businesses he owned to no more than 20 times the pay of any other employee.[72]

Other people argue that because executives assume so much risk on behalf of the company, they deserve the rewards that follow from strong company performance. In addition, many executives' personal and professional lives meld to the extent they are on call 24 hours a day. Because not everyone has the skill, experience, and desire to take on the pressure and responsibility of the executive lifestyle, market forces dictate a high level of compensation. When the pool of qualified individuals is limited, many corporate board members feel offering large compensation packages is the only way to attract and retain top executives, thus ensuring their firms maintain strong leadership. In an era when top executives are increasingly willing to "jump ship" for other firms offering higher pay, potentially lucrative stock options, bonuses, and other benefits, such thinking is not without merit.[73]

Executive compensation is a difficult but important issue for boards of directors and other stakeholders to consider because it receives much attention in the media, sparks shareholder concern, and is hotly debated in discussions of corporate governance. One area board members must consider is the extent executive compensation is linked to company performance. Plans basing compensation on the achievement of performance goals, including profits and revenues, are intended to align interests of owners with those of management. Amid rising complaints about excessive executive compensation, an increasing number of corporate boards impose performance targets on the stock and stock options they include in their CEOs' pay packages. Some boards also reduce executive compensation for corporate losses or misconduct. For example, CEO of JP Morgan Chase James Dimon had his compensation cut by half after a high-risk trading scandal cost the firm more than $6.2 billion in trading losses. As CEO he is responsible for noticing red flags that signal potential misconduct in the company.[74]

The SEC proposed companies disclose how they compensate lower-ranking employees as well as top executives. This proposal was part of a review of executive pay policies that addressed the belief that many financial corporations have historically taken on too much risk. The SEC believes compensation may be linked to excessive risk-taking.[75] Another issue is whether performance-linked compensation encourages executives to focus on short-term performance at the expense of long-term growth.[76] Shareholders today, however, may be growing more concerned about transparency and its impact on short-term performance and executive compensation. One study determined companies that divulge more details about their corporate governance practices generate higher shareholder returns than less transparent companies.[77]

IMPLEMENTING A STAKEHOLDER PERSPECTIVE

An organization that develops effective corporate governance and understands the importance of business ethics and social responsibility in achieving success should also develop processes for managing these important concerns. Although there are different approaches to this issue, we provide basic steps found effective in utilizing the stakeholder framework to manage responsibility and business ethics. The steps include (1) assessing the corporate culture, (2) identifying stakeholder groups, (3) identifying stakeholder issues, (4) assessing organizational commitment to social responsibility, (5) identifying resources and determining urgency, and (6) gaining stakeholder feedback. These steps include getting feedback from relevant stakeholders in formulating organizational strategy and implementation.

Step 1: Assessing the Corporate Culture

To enhance organizational fit, a social responsibility program must align with the corporate culture of the organization. The purpose of this first step is to identify the organizational mission, values, and norms likely to have implications for social responsibility. Relevant existing values and norms are those that specify the stakeholder groups and stakeholder issues deemed most important by the organization. Often, relevant organizational values and norms can be found in corporate documents such as the mission statement, annual reports, sales brochures, and websites. For example, REI states its mission is to "inspire, educate and outfit for a lifetime of outdoor adventure and stewardship." REI fulfills its mission by offering high-quality outdoor products, investing in green energy, and providing outdoor classes in areas such as rock climbing, cycling, and camping.[78]

Step 2: Identifying Stakeholder Groups

In managing this stage, it is important to recognize stakeholder needs, wants, and desires. Many important issues gain visibility because key constituencies such as consumer groups, regulators, or the media express an interest. When agreement, collaboration, or even confrontations exist, there is a need for a decision-making process such as a model of collaboration to overcome adversarial approaches to problem solving. Managers can identify relevant stakeholders who may be affected by or may influence the development of organizational policy.

Stakeholders have a level of power over a business because they are in the position to withhold organizational resources to some extent. Stakeholders have the most power when their own survival is not affected by the success of the organization and when they have access to vital organizational resources. For example, most consumers of shoes do not need to buy Nike shoes. Therefore, if they decide to boycott Nike, they endure only minor inconveniences. Nevertheless, consumer loyalty to Nike is vital to the continued success of the sport apparel giant. A proper assessment of the power held by a given stakeholder community includes an evaluation of the extent to which that community collaborates with others to pressure the firm.

Step 3: Identifying Stakeholder Issues

Together, steps 1 and 2 lead to the identification of the stakeholders who are both the most powerful and legitimate. The level of stakeholders' power and legitimacy determines the degree of urgency in addressing their needs. Step 3, then, consists of understanding the main issues of concern to these stakeholders. Conditions for collaboration exist when problems are so complex that multiple stakeholders are required to resolve the issue, and adversarial approaches to problem solving are clearly inadequate.

For example, obesity in children is becoming an issue across groups and stakeholders.[79] The United States is the most obese nation in the world with almost 40 percent of its population obese or overweight. This results in a huge rise in health problems. Additionally, while Americans have traditionally not supported government health care plans, increasing health care costs are causing some stakeholders to reconsider their stance. Job-based health insurance costs for families doubled in the past decade. Over 15 percent of Americans went without health insurance in 2011, although the number of uninsured decreased from the previous year.[80] Stakeholder concerns pushed the government into taking action on this important issue through the passage of the Affordable Care Act. The Affordable Care Act is estimated to extend health care coverage to 30 million Americans.[81]

Step 4: Assessing Organizational Commitment to Social Responsibility

Steps 1 through 3 are geared toward generating information about social responsibility among a variety of influences in and around an organization. Step 4 brings these three stages together to arrive at an understanding of social responsibility that specifically matches the organization of interest. This general definition will then be used to evaluate current practices and to select concrete social responsibility initiatives. Firms such as Starbucks selected activities that address stakeholder concerns. Starbucks formalized its initiatives in official documents such as annual reports, web pages, and company brochures. Starbucks is concerned with the environment and integrates policies and programs throughout all aspects of its operations to minimize its environmental impact. The company also has many community-building programs that help it to be a good neighbor and contribute positively to the communities where its partners and customers live, work, and play.[82]

Step 5: Identifying Resources and Determining Urgency

The prioritization of stakeholders and issues and the assessment of past performance lead to the allocation of resources. Two main criteria can be considered: the level of financial and organizational investments required by different actions, and the urgency when prioritizing social responsibility challenges. When the challenge under consideration is viewed as significant and stakeholder pressures on the issue can be expected, the challenge is considered urgent. For example, the Federal Trade Commission fined Google $22.5 million to settle charges it misled users about privacy settings on the Safari web browser. Although users were told they would be opted out of tracking, the company circumvented privacy settings and used cookies to track users for advertising purposes.[83] Internet privacy has become such an issue that regulators are proposing a "Do Not Track" list and a social networkers' bill of rights.[84]

Step 6: Gaining Stakeholder Feedback

Stakeholder feedback is generated through a variety of means. First, stakeholders' general assessment of a firm and its practices can be obtained through satisfaction or reputation surveys. Second, to gauge stakeholders' perceptions of a firm's contributions to specific issues, stakeholder-generated media such as blogs, websites, podcasts, and newsletters can be assessed. Third, more formal research may be conducted using focus groups, observation, and surveys. Many watchdog groups use the web to inform consumers and publicize their messages. For example, Consumer Watchdog, a California-based group that keeps an eye on everything from education to the oil industry, called for the new FTC chair to prioritize Internet privacy protection for consumers. This protection includes pressuring Congress to pass Do Not Track legislation, creating legislation to regulate data brokers, and developing a code to increase transparency regarding how mobile devices use data.[85]

CONTRIBUTIONS OF A STAKEHOLDER PERSPECTIVE

While we provide a framework for implementing a stakeholder perspective, balancing stakeholder interests requires good judgment. When businesses attempt to provide what consumers want, broader societal interests can create conflicts. Consider that the cheapest car in the world is the Tata Nano, made in India. The Nano has a starting price of $2,900, but it has only a small two-cylinder, 35-horsepower engine that could be suicidal on a modern expressway. Furthermore, the car has poor crash protection and no air bags. The Nano's manufacturer cuts many corners to be cheap, including using three lug nuts instead of four to hold the wheel to the axle. After launching the car, Tata beefed up the heat shield for the exhaust and added a fuse to the electrical system after several cars caught on fire. The company plans to export the Nano into the United States, but in order to successfully create an export market, the company must install more eco-friendly engines; this will drive up the price.[86] There are a number of ethical, social responsibility, and stakeholder issues with the Nano. Many consumers may only be able to afford a $2,900 car. On the other hand, stakeholders concerned with auto safety may object to a car that is potentially dangerous to drive. In the United States, regulatory authorities will prevent its sales as equipped in India. It is clear that balancing stakeholder interests can be a challenging process.

This chapter provides a good overview of the issues, conflicts, and opportunities of understanding more about stakeholder relationships. The stakeholder framework recognizes issues, identifies stakeholders, and examines the role of boards of directors and managers in promoting ethics and social responsibility. A stakeholder perspective creates a more ethical and reputable organization.

SUMMARY

Business ethics, issues, and conflicts revolve around relationships. Customers, investors and shareholders, employees, suppliers, government agencies, communities, and many others who have a stake or claim in an aspect of a company's products, operations, markets, industry, and outcomes are known as stakeholders. Stakeholders are influenced by and have the ability to affect businesses. Stakeholders provide both tangible and intangible resources that are critical to a firm's long-term success, and their relative ability to withdraw these resources gives them power. Stakeholders define significant ethical issues in business.

Primary stakeholders are those whose continued association is absolutely necessary for a firm's survival. Secondary stakeholders do not typically engage in transactions with a company and are not essential to its survival. The stakeholder interaction model suggests there are reciprocal relationships between a firm and a host of stakeholders. The degree to which a firm understands and addresses stakeholder demands is expressed as a stakeholder orientation and includes three sets of activities: (1) the generation of data about its stakeholder groups and the assessment of the firm's effects on these groups, (2) the distribution of this information throughout the company, and (3) the responsiveness of every level of the business to this intelligence. A stakeholder orientation can be viewed as a continuum in that firms are likely to adopt the concept to varying degrees.

Although the terms *ethics* and *social responsibility* are often used interchangeably, they have distinct meanings. Social responsibility in business refers to an organization's obligation to maximize its positive impact and minimize its negative impact on society. There are four levels of social responsibility—economic, legal, ethical, and philanthropic—and they can be viewed as a pyramid. The term *corporate citizenship* is used to communicate the extent businesses strategically meet the economic, legal, ethical, and philanthropic responsibilities placed on them by their stakeholders.

From a social responsibility perspective, business ethics embodies standards, norms, and expectations that reflect the concerns of major stakeholders including consumers, employees, shareholders, suppliers, competitors, and the community. Only if firms include ethical concerns in foundational values and incorporate ethics into business strategies can social responsibility as a value be embedded in daily decision making.

Issues in social responsibility include social issues, consumer protection issues, sustainability, and corporate governance. Social issues are associated with the common good and include such issues as childhood obesity and Internet privacy. Consumer protection often occurs in the form of laws passed to protect consumers from unfair and deceptive business practices. Sustainability is the potential for the long-term well-being of the natural environment, including all biological entities, as well as the mutually beneficial interactions among nature and individuals, organizations, and business strategies. Corporate governance involves the development of formal systems of accountability, oversight, and control.

Most businesses operate under the assumption that the main purpose of business is to maximize profits for shareholders. The stakeholder model places the board of directors in the position of balancing the interests and conflicts of various constituencies. Both directors and officers of corporations are fiduciaries for the shareholders. Directors have a duty to avoid ethical misconduct and provide leadership in decisions to prevent ethical misconduct in their organizations. To remove the opportunity for employees to make unethical decisions, most companies develop formal systems of accountability, oversight, and control known as corporate governance. Accountability refers to how closely workplace decisions are aligned with a firm's stated strategic direction and its compliance with ethical and legal considerations. Oversight provides a system of checks and balances that limit employees' and managers' opportunities to deviate from policies and strategies intended to prevent unethical and illegal activities. Control is the process of auditing and improving organizational decisions and actions.

There are two perceptions of corporate governance that can be viewed as a continuum. The shareholder model is founded in classic economic precepts, including the maximization of wealth for investors and owners. The stakeholder model adopts a broader view of the purpose of business that includes satisfying the concerns of other stakeholders, from employees, suppliers, and government regulators to communities and special interest groups.

Two major elements of corporate governance that relate to ethical decision making are the role of the board of directors and executive compensation. The members of a public corporation's board of directors assume legal responsibility for the firm's resources and decisions. Important issues related to boards of directors include accountability, transparency, and independence. Boards of directors are also responsible for appointing top executive officers and determining their compensation. Concerns about executive pay center on the often-disproportionate relationship between executive pay and median employee wages in the company.

An organization that develops effective corporate governance and understands the importance of business ethics and social responsibility in achieving success should develop a process for managing these important concerns. Although there are different approaches, steps have been identified that have been found effective in utilizing the stakeholder framework to manage responsibility and business ethics. These steps are: (1) assessing the corporate culture, (2) identifying stakeholder groups, (3) identifying stakeholder issues, (4) assessing organizational commitment to social responsibility, (5) identifying resources and determining urgency, and (6) gaining stakeholder feedback.

IMPORTANT TERMS FOR REVIEW

stakeholder 31

primary stakeholder 32

secondary stakeholder 32

stakeholder interaction model 33

stakeholder orientation 33

corporate citizenship 37

reputation 37

corporate governance 40

shareholder model of corporate governance 45

stakeholder model of corporate governance 45

interlocking directorate 47

executive compensation 47

RESOLVING ETHICAL BUSINESS CHALLENGES*

Demarco just graduated from Texas University and had been snatched up by Xeon Natural Resources Incorporated, one of the top natural resource extraction companies in the world. Because he was Brazilian, bi-lingual, and spoke several specific Brazilian dialects, his stationing in Brazil was a no-brainer. Xeon was deeply involved with a project within the Brazilian rain forests in mining an extremely valuable element called niobium. Niobium is a rare earth element essential for micro alloying steel as well as other products such as jet engines, rocket subassemblies, superconducting magnets, and super alloys. Brazil accounts for 92 percent of all niobium mined, and Xeon Natural mines much of the element in Brazil. Xeon discovered a large niobium deposit, and estimates the corporation could make an additional $5 billion in profits over the next two decades.

Demarco soon discovered he was one of several employees assigned to explain to the indigenous population that Xeon wanted to extract the niobium from the lands given to the tribes by the Brazilian government. The land was, by decree, compensation for native minorities. Having spent several months with various tribes, Demarco learned they were communities that had not been altered by western culture. It was obvious to Demarco if Xeon began strip mining the area, thousands of "outsiders" would be brought in and would impact the cultural heritage of the indigenous populations.

Demarco discussed this with his boss, Barbara. "Yes, I understand all you are saying, and I agree this will change their lives as well as their children and grandchildren's lives," Barbara said. "But think of it this way, their standard of living will be greatly enhanced. Schools will be built, hospitals will be available, and there will be more employment opportunities."

Demarco responded, "While the tribal leaders want a better life for their people, I feel they are being steamrolled into accepting something they don't understand." I've talked to some of the tribal leaders, and I am positive they have no idea of the impact this will have on their culture. We have many stakeholders involved in this decision, including Xeon's employees, the tribes, the Brazilian government, and even communities beyond the tribal lands. I think we need to reevaluate the impact on all of these stakeholders before proceeding.

Barbara sighed, "I think you make some good points, and I am concerned about these different stakeholders. But you should understand we already have buy-in from the key decision-makers, and our business depends upon being able to mine niobium. We've got to continue this project."

Demarco returned to the camp. The other specialists questioned him about Barbara's reaction. As he spoke, some of the specialists became concerned about their jobs. A few admitted they heard the local and national media were raising awareness about the negative impact mining this mineral could have on the indigenous populations.

A few days later, Demarco heard that some of the tribal leaders had new concerns about the project and were organizing meetings to obtain feedback from members. Demarco approached one of the mining specialists that studied the potential impact of strip mining the land. The specialist said that while he understood stakeholder interests, he felt the extraction methods Xeon used were environmentally friendly. While creating a temporary disruption in the ecosystem of the rainforest, Xeon's strip mining methods provided an opportunity for restoration. In fact, strip mining that was done in the United States before there were any regulations provides a good example of how the forest can recover and grow back to its original condition.

Demarco knew despite the potential benefits, there would still likely be opposition from the tribal community. Additionally, no method of strip mining is entirely environmentally-friendly. Demarco realized even with restoration, the lives of the indigenous tribes would be forever altered.

Demarco was to meet with tribal elders the next day to discuss their concerns. He understood that whatever the decision, it would negatively impact some stakeholders. On the one hand, the tribal members might compromise their traditional way of life and the environment would be harmed if the strip mining project began. On the other hand, Xeon's future and the future of its employees depended upon being able to mine the niobium. It could also benefit the tribes economically. He was not sure what he should tell the tribal leaders.

QUESTIONS | EXERCISES

1. How should Demarco approach this issue when he meets with the tribal leaders?
2. What should be the priorities in balancing the various stakeholder interests?
3. Can the CEO and board of directors of Xeon continue operations and maintain a stakeholder orientation?

*This case is strictly hypothetical; any resemblance to real persons, companies, or situations is coincidental.

> > > CHECK YOUR EQ

Check your EQ, or Ethics Quotient, by completing the following. Assess your performance to evaluate your overall understanding of the chapter material.

1. Social responsibility in business refers to maximizing the visibility of social involvement.   **Yes**   **No**

2. Stakeholders provide resources that are more or less critical to a firm's long-term success.   **Yes**   **No**

3. Three primary stakeholders are customers, special interest groups, and the media.   **Yes**   **No**

4. The most significant influence on ethical behavior in an organization is the opportunity to engage in unethical behavior.   **Yes**   **No**

5. The stakeholder perspective is useful in managing social responsibility and business ethics.   **Yes**   **No**

ANSWERS 1. **No.** Social responsibility refers to an organization's obligation to maximize its positive impact on society and minimize its negative impact. 2. **Yes.** These resources are both tangible and intangible. 3. **No.** Although customers are primary stakeholders, special interest groups and the media are usually considered secondary stakeholders. 4. **No.** Other influences such as corporate culture have more impact on ethical decisions within an organization. 5. **Yes.** The six steps to implement this approach were provided in this chapter.

ENDNOTES

1. Vikas Anand, Blake E. Ashforth, and Mahendra Joshi, "Business as Usual: The Acceptance and Perpetuation of Corruption in Organizations," *Academy of Management Executive* 18, no. 2 (2004): 39–53.

2. Debbie Thorne, O. C. Ferrell, and Linda Ferrell, *Business and Society* (Boston: Houghton Mifflin, 2003), 64–65.

3. Tiffany Hsu, "Boston Market removes salt from tables to help customers cut back," *Los Angeles Times*, August 22, 2012, http://articles.latimes.com/2012/aug/22/business/la-fi-mo-boston-market-salt-20120822 (accessed February 14, 2013).

4. T. Donaldson and L.E. Preston, "The stakeholder theory of the corporation: concepts, evidence, and implications," *Academy of Management Review 20*(1), 1995: 65–91.

5. T.M. Jones, "Instrumental stakeholder theory: A synthesis of ethics and economics," *Academy of Management Review* 20(2), 1995: 404–437.

6. M. Clarkson, "A stakeholder framework for analyzing and evaluating corporate social performance," *Academy of Management Review* 20(1): 92–117.

7. Lynn Brewer, Robert Chandler, and O. C. Ferrell, "Managing Risks for Corporate Integrity: How to Survive an Ethical Misconduct Disaster," (Mason, OH: Texere/Thomson, 2006), 11.

8. Miguel Bustillo, "Best Buy Chairman to Resign after Probe," *The Wall Street Journal*, May 15, 2012, http://online.wsj.com/article/SB10001424052702304192704577403922338506912.html (accessed February 14, 2013).

9. Edelman *Global Deck: 2013 Trust Barometer*, http://www.edelman.com/trust-downloads/global-results-2/ (accessed January 30, 3013).

10. Ian Sherr, "Apple Rejoins Green Registry," *The Wall Street Journal*, July 13, 2012, http://online.wsj.com/article/SB10001424052702304373804577525033302381546.html (accessed February 14, 2013); "San Francisco Boycotts Apple: Company's Withdrawal From Environmental Ratings Registry Sparks Anger," *The Huffington Post*, July 11, 2012, http://www.huffingtonpost.com/2012/07/11/san-francisco-boycotts-apple_n_1666562.html (accessed February 14, 2013).

11. Adapted from Isabelle Maignan, O. C. Ferrell, and Linda Ferrell, "A Stakeholder Model for Implementing Social Responsibility in Marketing," *European Journal of Marketing* 39 (2005): 956–977.

12. Ibid.

13. Yves Fassin, "Stakeholder Management, Reciprocity and Shareholder Responsibility," *Journal of Business Ethics* 109 (2012): 83–96.

14. Ibid.

15. Thorne, Ferrell, and Ferrell, *Business and Society*.

16. Sharon C. Bolton, Rebecca Chung-hee Kim, and Kevin D. O'Gorman, "Corporate Social Responsibility as a Dynamic Internal Organizational Process: A Case Study," *Journal of Business Ethics*, published online, January 7, 2011.

17. G. Tomas M. Hult, Jeannette A. Mena, O.C. Ferrell, and Linda Ferrell, "Stakeholder marketing: a definition and conceptual framework," *AMS Review 1*(2011): 44–65.

18. Isabelle Maignan and O. C. Ferrell, "Corporate Social Responsibility: Toward a Marketing Conceptualization," *Journal of the Academy of Marketing Science* 32 (2004): 3–19.

19. Ibid.

20. Wenlong Yuan, Yongjian Bao, and Alain Verbeke, "Integrating CSR Initiatives in Business: An Organizing Framework," *Journal of Business Ethics*, published online, January 8, 2011.

21. Ibid.

22. Joseph A. McKinney, Tisha L. Emerson, and Mitchell J. Neubert, "The Effects of Ethical Codes on Ethical Perceptions of Actions toward Stakeholders," *Journal of Business Ethics*, 97 (2010): 505–516.

23. Steven Greenhouse and Jim Yardley, "As Walmart Makes Safety Vows, It's Seen as an Obstacle to Change," *The New York Times*, December 28, 2012, http://www.nytimes.com/2012/12/29/world/asia/despite-vows-for-safety-walmart-seen-as-obstacle-to-change.html?pagewanted=all (accessed February 14, 2014).

24. Maignan and Ferrell, "Corporate Social Responsibility."

25. Brian Dumaine, "Google's Zero-carbon Quest," *Fortune Tech*, http://tech.fortune.cnn.com/2012/07/12/google-zero-carbon/ (accessed August 17, 2012); Bill Weihl, "Reducing Our Carbon Footprint" *Google*, May 6, 2009, http://googleblog.blogspot.com/2009/05/reducing-our-carbon-footprint.html#!/2009/05/reducing-our-carbon-footprint.html/ (accessed August 17, 2012)

26. Intuit, "Employee Giving and Volunteering," http://about.intuit.com/about_intuit/philanthropy/volunteer_about.jsp (accessed February 14, 2013).

27. PR Newswire, "SC Johnson Named as a 2011 Corporate Social Responsibility Company by Shanghai Pudong Government," February 22, 2012, http://www.prnewswire.com/news-releases/sc-johnson-named-as-a-2011-corporate-social-responsibility-company-by-shanghai-pudong-government-140024703.html (accessed February 14, 2013); SC Johnson, "Wind Energy to Power Windex®," June 21, 2012, http://www.scjohnson.com/en/press-room/press-releases/06-21-2012/Wind-Energy-to-Power-Windex%C2%AE.aspx (accessed February 14, 2013).

28. Les Coleman, "Losses from Failure of Stakeholder Sensitive Processes: Financial Consequences for Large U.S. Companies from Breakdowns in Product, Environmental, and Accounting Standards," *Journal of Business Ethics* 98 (2011): 247–258.

29. Archie B. Carroll, "The Pyramid of Corporate Social Responsibility: Toward the Moral Management of Organizational Stakeholders," *Business Horizons* 34 (1991): 42.

30. Frances Robinson, "EU Unveils Web-Privacy Rules," *The Wall Street Journal*, January 26, 2012, http://online.wsj.com/article/SB10001424052970203718504577182831566595316.html (accessed April 1, 2013).

31. Isabelle Maignan, O. C. Ferrell, and G. Tomas M. Hult, "Corporate Citizenship: Cultural Antecedents and Business Benefits," *Journal of the Academy of Marketing Science* 27 (1999): 457.

32. Lindsay McShane and Peggy Cunningham, "To Thine Own Self Be True? Employees' Judgments of the Authenticity of Their Organization's Corporate Social Responsibility Program," *Journal of Business Ethics* 108 (2012): 81–100.

33. Gene R. Laczniak and Patrick E. Murphy, "Stakeholder Theory and Marketing: Moving from a Firm-Centric to a Societal Perspective," *Journal of Public Policy & Marketing* 31 (2), Fall 2012: 284–292.

34. E. Moore and V.J. Rideout, "The Online Marketing of Food to Children: Is It Just Fun and Games?" *Journal of Public Policy & Marketing* 26 (2): 202–207.

35. Z. Tange, Y. Hu, and M.D. Smith, "Gaining Trust through Online Privacy Protection: Self-Regulation, Mandatory Standards, or *Caveat Emptor*," *Journal of Management Information Systems* 24 (4), 2008: 153–173.

36. R.D. Petty and J.C. Andrews, "Covert Marketing Unmasked: A Legal and Regulatory Guide for Practices that Mask Marketing Messages," *Journal of Public Policy & Marketing* 27 (1): 7–18.

37. R. M. Cain, "Embedded Advertising on Television: Disclosure, deception, and free speech rights," *Journal of Public Policy & Marketing* 30 (2), 2011: 226–238.

38. H. Jo and M.A. Harjoto, "The Causal Effect of Corporate Governance on Corporate Social Responsibility," *Journal of Business Ethics* 106 (2012): 53–72.

39. Arifur Khan, Mohammed Badrul Muttakin, and Javed Siddiqui, "Corporate Governance and Corporate Social Responsibility Disclosures: Evidence from an Emerging Economy," *Journal of Business Ethics*, http://link.springer.com/content/pdf/10.1007%2Fs10551-012-1336-0 (accessed March 28, 2013).

40. G. A. Steiner and J. F. Steiner, *Business, Government, and Society* (New York: Random House, 1988).

41. Milton Friedman, "Social Responsibility of Business Is to Increase Its Profits," *The New York Times Magazine*, September 13, 1970, 122–126.

42. "Business Leaders, Politicians and Academics Dub Corporate Irresponsibility 'An Attack on America from Within,'" *Business Wire*, November 7, 2002, via America Online.

43. Adam Smith, *The Theory of Moral Sentiments*, Vol. 2. (New York: Prometheus, 2000).

44. Jill A. Brown and William R. Forster, "CSR and Stakeholder Theory: A Tale of Adam Smith," *Journal of Business Ethics* 112 (2013): 301–312.

45. Sheelah Kolhatkar, "Cheating, Incorporated," *Bloomberg Businessweek*, February 14–February 20, 2011, 60–66; "Brands," *Avid Life Media*, http://www.avidlifemedia.com/brands.html (accessed February 21, 2011).

46. Iain Clacher and Jens Hagendorff, "Do Announcements about Corporate Social Responsibility Create or Destroy Shareholder Wealth? Evidence from the UK," *Journal of Business Ethics* 106 (2012): 253–266.

47. Isabelle Maignan, Tracy L. Gonzalez-Padron, G. Tomas M. Hult, and O.C. Ferrell, "Stakeholder orientation: development and testing of a framework for socially responsible marketing," *Journal of Strategic Marketing* 19 (4), 2011: 313–338.

48. Isabelle Maignan, Tracy L. Gonzalez-Padron, G. Tomas M. Hult, and O.C. Ferrell, "Stakeholder Orientation: Development and Testing of a Framework for Socially Responsible Marketing."

49. *Dodge v. Ford Motor Co.*, 204 Mich.459, 179 N.W. 668, 3 A.L.R. 413 (1919).

50. Yuan-Shuh Lii and Monle Lee, "Doing Right Leads to Doing Well: When the Type of CSR and Reputation Interact to Affect Consumer Evaluations of the Firm," *Journal of Business Ethics* 105 (2012): 69–81.

51. Alfred Marcus and Sheryl Kaiser, "Managing beyond Compliance: The Ethical and Legal Dimensions of Corporate Responsibility," *North Coast Publishers*, 2006, 79.

52. Joann S. Lublin, "Corporate Directors' Group Gives Repair Plan to Boards," *The Wall Street Journal*, March 24, 2009, http://online.wsj.com/article/SB123784649341118187.html (accessed April 14, 2011).

53. Donal Griffin and Bradley Keoun, "Citigroup Investors Reject Management Compensation Plan," *Bloomberg*, April 17, 2012, http://www.bloomberg.com/news/2012-04-17/citigroup-shareholders-reject-management-s-compensation-plan-1-.html (accessed February 14, 2013).

54. Ben W. Heineman, Jr., "Are You a Good Corporate Citizen?," *The Wall Street Journal*, June 28, 2005, B2.

55. Phred Dvorak, "Poor Year Doesn't Stop CEO Bonuses," *The Wall Street Journal*, March 18, 2009, http://online.wsj.com/article/SB123698866439126029.html (accessed April 14, 2011).

56. Darryl Reed, "Corporate Governance Reforms in Developing Countries," *Journal of Business Ethics* 37 (2002): 223–247.

57. Kathleen Rehbein, Jeanne M. Logsdon, and Harry J. Van Buren III, "Corporate Responses to Shareholder Activists: Considering the Dialogue Alternative," *Journal of Business Ethics* 112 (2013): 137–154.

58. Maria Maher and Thomas Anderson, *Corporate Governance: Effects on Firm Performance and Economic Growth* (Paris: Organization for Economic Co-operation and Development, 1999).

59. Demb and F. F. Neubauer, *The Corporate Board: Confronting the Paradoxes* (Oxford: Oxford University Press, 1992).

60. Maher and Anderson, *Corporate Governance*.

61. Organization for Economic Co-operation and Development, *The OECD Principles of Corporate Governance* (Paris: Organization for Economic Co-operation and Development, 1999).

62. Louis Lavelle, "The Best and Worst Boards," *BusinessWeek*, October 7, 2002, 104–114.

63. Melvin A. Eisenberg, "Corporate Governance: The Board of Directors and Internal Control," *Cordoza Law Review* 19 (1997): 237.

64. S. Trevis Certo, Catherine Dalton, Dan Dalton, and Richard Lester, "Boards of Directors' Self-Interest: Expanding for Pay in Corporate Acquisitions?," *Journal of Business Ethics* 77, no. 2 (January 2008): 219–230.

65. Gary Strauss, "$228, 000 for a part-time job? Apparently, that's not enough," *USA Today*, March 4–6, 2011, 1A.

66. Taïeb Hafsi and Gokhan Turgut, "Boardroom Diversity and its Effect on Social Performance: Conceptualization and Empirical Evidence," *Journal of Business Ethics* 112 (2013): 463–479.

67. Business Dictionary, http://www.businessdictionary.com/definition/interlocking-directorate.html, (accessed February 15, 2011).

68. Amy Borrus, "Should Directors Be Nervous?" *BusinessWeek* online, March 6, 2006 http://www.businessweek.com/magazine/content/06_10/b3974062.htm (accessed April 14, 2011).

69. John A. Byrne with Louis Lavelle, Nanette Byrnes, Marcia Vickers, and Amy Borrus, "How to Fix Corporate Governance," *BusinessWeek*, May 6, 2002, 69–78.

70. Kim Peterson, "Hostess CEO cuts everyone's pay but his," *MSN Money*, December 4, 2012, http://money.msn.com/now/post.aspx?post=f2d05306-bb26-4e35-9eb4-47f4b4902a56 (accessed February 14, 2013).

71. AFL-CIO, "Executive PayWatch," http://www.aflcio. org/Corporate-Watch/CEO-Pay-and-the-99 (accessed February 14, 2013).

72. Sarah Anderson, John Cavanagh, Ralph Estes, Chuck Collins, and Chris Hartman, *A Decade of Executive Excess: The 1990s Sixth Annual Executive.* Boston: United for a Fair Economy, 1999, online, June 30, 2006, http:// www.faireconomy.org/press_room/1999/a_decade_of_ executive_excess_the_1990s (accessed April 14, 2011).

73. Louis Lavelle, "CEO Pay, The More Things Change…," *BusinessWeek*, October 16, 2000, 106–108.

74. Christian Berthelsen, "Dimon's Pay Cut by 50%," *The Wall Street Journal*, January 16, 2013, http://online.wsj.com/ article/SB10001424127887323968304578245381734509580.html (accessed January 31, 2013).

75. Kara Scanell, "SEC Ready to Require More Pay Disclosures," *The Wall Street Journal*, June 3, 2009, http:// online.wsj.com/article/SB124397831899078781.html (accessed April 14, 2011).

76. Gary Strauss, "America's Corporate Meltdown," *USA Today*, June 27, 2002, 1A, 2A.

77. Li-Chiu Chi, "Do transparency and performance predict firm performance? Evidence from the Taiwan Market," *Expert Systems with Applications*, Vol. 36, Issue 8, October 2009, http://www.sciencedirect.com/ science?_ob=ArticleURL&_udi=B6V03-4VTVPW4-1&_ user=10&_rdoc=1&_fmt=&_orig=search&_sort=d&_ docanchor=&view=c&_acct=C000050221&_version=1&_ urlVersion=0&_userid=10&md5=3b7a30dbefb291c4c56f3a5f3a62d859 (accessed April 14, 2011).

78. REI, "REI's 2009 Stewardship Report Highlights Environmental Sustainability, Community Connections and Workplace Engagement," September 8, 2010, http:// www.rei.com/about-rei/newsroom/2010/10stewardship. html (accessed February 14, 2013); REI, "REI Outdoor School Classes and Outings," http://www.rei.com/ outdoorschool.html (accessed February 14, 2013).

79. "Obesity Issue Looms Large," Washington Wire, *The Wall Street Journal* online, March 3, 2006, http://blogs.wsj. com/washwire/2006/03/03/obesity-issue-looms-large/ (accessed April 14, 2011).

80. Jeffrey Young, "Census: Uninsured Rate Falls As Young Adults Gain Coverage And Government Programs Grow," *The Huffington Post*, September 12, 2012, http://www. huffingtonpost.com/2012/09/12/census-uninsured-young-adults_n_1876862.html (accessed February 14, 2013).

81. Ibid.

82. "Being a Responsible Company," http://www.starbucks. com/aboutus/csr.asp (accessed April 14, 2011).

83. Federal Trade Commission, "Google Will Pay $22.5 Million to Settle FTC Charges it Misrepresented Privacy Assurances to Users of Apple's Safari Internet Browser," August 9, 2012, http://ftc.gov/opa/2012/08/google.shtm (accessed February 14, 2013).

84. Jon Swartz, "Facebook changes its status in Washington," *USA Today*, January 13, 2011, 1B–2B; "Details of 100 Million Facebook Users Published Online," MSNBC.com, July 29, 2010, http://www.msnbc.msn.com/id/38463013/ ns/technology_and_science/?GT1=43001 (accessed April 14, 2011).

85. Consumer Watchdog, "As Leibowitz Steps Down, Consumer Watchdog Says Next FTC Chair Must Focus On Do Not Track Legislation, Data Brokers and 'Wild West' Of Mobile Devices," February 1, 2013, http://www.consumerwatchdog.org/newsrelease/ leibowitz-steps-down-consumer-watchdog-says-next-ftc-chair-must-focus-do-not-track-legis (accessed February 14, 2013).

86. Alex Taylor III, "Tata Takes on the World Building an Auto Empire in India," *Fortune*, May 2, 2011, 92; Fox News, "3,000 Tata Nano coming to U.S.," October 15, 2012, http://www.foxnews.com/leisure/2012/10/15/3000-car-coming-to-us/ (accessed February 14, 2013).

CHAPTER 3

EMERGING BUSINESS ETHICS ISSUES

AN ETHICAL DILEMMA*

Jayla just landed an internship with Acme Incorporated in the payroll department. She was excited because these internships usually turned into a full time job after graduation. Jayla was hired by Deon, the head of the Payroll Department. He told her about their policies and stressed the need for maintaining strict confidentiality regarding employee salaries and pay scales. "Several years ago we had an intern who violated the confidentiality policy and was given a negative internship summary," explained Deon.

"I understand, sir," Jayla responded.

Jayla was determined to learn as much as she could about the job. She made sure she was always on time, followed all of the policies and procedures, and got along well with her co-workers. She started to feel like she fit in at Acme and dreamed of the day when she worked there permanently. However, one day while studying the books, Jayla began to notice abnormalities in one of the salespeople's salary. Greg, one of the senior sales representatives, made three times as much as the next highest earning salesperson in the company. Jayla assumed he must be a spectacular salesperson and worked efficiently. She often overheard Mia, the General Manager, and Deon praise Greg for his sales numbers. She also noticed the three of them would often go to lunch together.

One morning, Deon handed a stack of client folders to Jayla. He explained, "These are the clients for the salespeople for the week. They will come to you when they need more work, and they are only to take the files on top of the pile. You are in charge of making sure the salespeople don't pick and choose the files. This is how we keep things fair among the sales force."

"I will make sure the files are distributed fairly," Jayla promised. She was excited to be trusted with this responsibility, and she made sure she did her best. Mary, one of the salespeople, came by to get files for the week. They made small talk as Mary looked into her files. She looked disappointed.

"You didn't get any good clients?" Jayla asked.

"Nope, not a one," replied Mary, "which is just my luck!" She threw down the files in exasperation. Jayla was concerned and asked, "What's the matter?"

"I'm sorry," she replied, "It's just that my sales have been slipping, and my paychecks are much smaller than they used to be. If my pay decreases much further, I may lose my health benefits. My daughter is asthmatic, and she has been in and out of the hospital over the last few months." Jayla looked at Mary sympathetically and tried her best to console her.

The next week, before the salespeople started coming into the office to pick from the pile, Jayla had some documents for Deon to sign. When she arrived at his office, the door was slightly open. She peeked in and saw Deon and Greg going through the stack of clients. Jayla watched as Greg rifled through the pile and picked out files.

"Thanks, Deon. These are the top clients for the week," Greg said.

"No problem, Greg," Deon responded "Anything for my favorite brother-in-law. Just keep up the good work."

Jayla stood there, mouth open. She turned to walk back toward her desk. She could not believe what she just saw. The boss was giving Deon all the good clients, while the rest of the salespeople had no choice in which they were assigned. Jayla knew this favoritism was a serious conflict of interest. Then she thought of Mary and her situation.

"What am I supposed to do?" Jayla wondered. "If I say something to Deon, he will give me a bad evaluation. If I say anything to Mia, I may get fired. And I definitely can't say anything to the other salespeople. There would be a riot." Saddened, she sat at her desk and wondered what to do.

QUESTIONS | EXERCISES

1. Discuss how this conflict of interest situation affects other salespeople, the organizational culture, and other stakeholders.
2. Describe the decision that Jayla must make. What are the potential ramifications of her choices?
3. Are there legal ramifications to this kind of behavior? If so, what are the potential consequences?

*This case is strictly hypothetical; any resemblance to real persons, companies, or situations is coincidental.

Stakeholders' concerns determine whether specific business actions and decisions are perceived as right or wrong, which drives what the company defines as ethical or unethical. In the case of the government, community, and society, what was merely an ethical issue can become a legal debate and eventually law. Ethical conflicts in which damages occur can turn into litigation. Additionally, stakeholders often raise issues when they exert pressure on businesses to make decisions that serve their particular agendas. Other stakeholders can exert different pressures as well. For example, some stakeholders believed Caterpillar acted unethically when it decided to close its plant in Canada and move production to the United States. Caterpillar had locked out employees who were protesting their wages. By moving to the United States, Caterpillar saved on labor costs since average pay for U.S. factory workers is less than Canadian factory workers. The move resulted in approximately 450 jobs lost. On the other hand, moving the plant to the United States benefited U.S. workers badly in need of jobs.[1]

People make ethical decisions only after they recognize a particular issue or situation has an ethical component; therefore, a first step toward understanding business ethics is to develop ethical issue awareness. Ethical issues typically arise because of conflicts among individuals' personal moral beliefs and values and the core values and culture of the organizations where they work. Institutions in society provide foundational principles and values that influence both individuals and organizations. The business environment presents many potential ethical conflicts. Organizational objectives can clash with its employees' attempts to fulfill their own personal goals. Similarly, consumers' need for safe and quality products may create a demand for consumer regulation. The desire of an oil company like BP or Chevron to create a profitable and dependable supply of oil and gas may conflict with the needs of many stakeholders. The fact BP possibly placed profits over the safety of employees and the environment culminated in the *Deepwater Horizon* explosion, which released 206.2 million gallons of oil into the Gulf of Mexico.[2]

In this chapter, we consider some of the ethical issues emerging in business today, including how they arise from the demands of specific stakeholder groups. In the first half of the chapter, we explain certain universal concepts that pervade business ethics, such as integrity, honesty, and fairness. The second half of the chapter explores a number of emerging ethical issues, including misuse of company time and resources, abusive and intimidating behavior, lying, conflicts of interest, bribery, corporate intelligence, discrimination, sexual harassment, fraud, financial misconduct, insider trading, intellectual property rights, and privacy. We also examine the challenge of determining decisions that have an ethical component for the firm to consider. Because of the rise of the multinational corporation as well as increased vertical systems competition, there are certain practices and products that become ethical and legal issues. It is important you understand that what was once a legal activity can become an ethical issue, resulting in well-known practices becoming illegal.

RECOGNIZING AN ETHICAL ISSUE (ETHICAL AWARENESS)

Although we have described a number of relationships and situations that may generate ethical issues, in practice it can be difficult to recognize them. Failure to acknowledge or be aware of ethical issues is a great danger in any organization. Some issues are difficult to recognize because they are gray areas that are hard to navigate. For example, when does a small gift become a bribe? Employees may engage in questionable behaviors because they are trying to achieve firm objectives related to sales or earnings. Our personal ethical issues are easier to define and control. The complexity of the work environment, however, makes it harder to define and reduce ethical issues.

Business decisions, like personal decisions, may involve a dilemma. In a dilemma all of the alternatives have negative consequences, so the less harmful choice is made. An ethical issue is simply a situation involving a group, a problem, or even an opportunity that requires thought, discussion, or investigation before a decision can be made. Because the business world is dynamic, new ethical issues emerge all the time. Table 3–1 defines specific ethical issues identified by employees in the National Business Ethics Survey (NBES). Misuse of company time, abusive behavior, and lying to employees are personal in nature, but are committed in the belief that the action is furthering organizational goals. Falsifying time or expenses, safety violations, and abuse of company resources are issues that directly relate to an ethical conflict that could damage the firm. The table compares the percentage of employees who observed specific types of misconduct over the past two National Business Ethics Surveys.

Employees could engage in more than one form of misconduct; therefore, each type of misconduct represents the percentage of employees who witnessed that particular act. Although it is impossible to list every conceivable ethical issue. Any type of manipulation or deceit, or even just the absence of transparency in decision making, can create harm to others. For example, collusion is a secret agreement between two or more parties for

TABLE 3–1 Specific Types of Observed Misconduct

Behavior	2011 (%)	2009 (%)
Misuse of company time	33	n/a
Abusive behavior	21	22
Lying to employees	20	19
Company resource abuse	20	23
Violating company Internet use policies	16	n/a
Discrimination	15	14
Conflicts of interest	15	16
Inappropriate social networking	14	n/a
Health or safety violations	13	11
Lying to outside stakeholders	12	12
Stealing	12	9
Falsifying time reports or hours worked	12	n/a
Employee benefit violations	12	11
Sexual harassment	11	7

Source: Ethics Resource Center, 2011 National Business Ethics Survey: Workplace Ethics in Transition (Arlington, VA: Ethics Resource Center, 2012), p. 39.

a fraudulent, illegal, or deceitful purpose. "Deceitful purpose" is the relevant phrase in regard to business ethics, as it suggests trickery, misrepresentation, or a strategy designed to lead others to believe something less than the whole truth. Collusion violates the general business value of honesty. Next, we examine three foundational values that are used to identify ethical issues.

FOUNDATIONAL VALUES FOR IDENTIFYING ETHICAL ISSUES

Integrity, honesty, and fairness are widely used values for evaluating activities that could become ethical issues. Ethical issues can emerge from almost any decision made in an organization. Understanding these foundational values can help identify and develop discussions and a constructive dialogue on appropriate conduct. It is just as important to emphasize appropriate conduct associated with these values as it is to discover inappropriate conduct.

Integrity

Integrity is one of the most important and oft-cited elements of virtue, and refers to being whole, sound, and in an unimpaired condition. Integrity is a value that relates to all business activities, not just ethical issues. Integrity relates to product quality, open communication, transparency, and relationships. Therefore, integrity is a foundational value for managers to build an internal organizational culture of trust. In an organization, it means uncompromising adherence to a set or group of values. Integrity is connected to acting ethically; in other words, there are substantive or normative constraints on what it means to act with integrity. An organization's integrity usually rests on its enduring values and unwillingness to deviate from standards of behavior as defined by the firm and industry.

At a minimum, businesses are expected to follow laws and regulations. In addition, organizations should not knowingly harm customers, clients, employees, or even other competitors through deception, misrepresentation, or coercion. Although they often act in their own economic self-interest, business relations should be grounded in values such as honesty, integrity, and fairness. Failure to live up to these expectations or abide by laws and standards destroys trust and makes it difficult, if not impossible, to continue business exchanges.[3] These values become the glue that holds business relationships together, making everything else more effective and efficient.

Honesty

Honesty refers to truthfulness or trustworthiness. To be honest is to tell the truth to the best of your knowledge without hiding anything. Confucius defined an honest person as *junzi*, or one who has the virtue *ren. Ren* can be loosely defined as one who has humanity. *Yi* is another honesty component and is related to what we should do according to our relationships with others. Another Confucian concept, *li*, relates to honesty but refers to the virtue of good manners or respect. Finally, *zhi* represents whether a person knows what to say and what to do as it relates to the honesty concept. The Confucian version of Kant's Golden Rule is to treat your inferiors as you would want your superiors to treat you. As a result, virtues such as familial honor and reputation for honesty become paramount.

Issues related to honesty also arise because business is sometimes regarded as a game governed by its own rules rather than those of society as a whole. Author Eric Beversluis suggests honesty is a problem because people often reason along these lines:

1. Business relationships are a subset of human relationships governed by their own rules that in a market society involve competition, profit maximization, and personal advancement within the organization.

2. Business can therefore be considered a game people play, comparable in certain respects to competitive sports such as basketball or boxing.

3. Ordinary ethics rules and morality do not hold in games like basketball or boxing. (What if a basketball player did unto others as he would have them do unto him? What if a boxer decided it was wrong to try to injure another person?)

4. Logically, then, if business is a game like basketball or boxing, ordinary ethical rules do not apply.[4]

This type of reasoning leads many to conclude that anything is acceptable in business. Indeed, several books have compared business to warfare—for example, *The Guerrilla Marketing Handbook* and *Sun Tsu: The Art of War for Managers*. The common theme is that surprise attacks, guerrilla warfare, and other warlike tactics are necessary to win the battle for consumer dollars. Larry Ellison, the CEO of Oracle, exemplified this when he sold PeopleSoft's technology and let most of its 8,000 employees go. PeopleSoft CEO Craig Conway stated, "Ellison has followed a page straight out of Genghis Khan." Ellison frequently quotes the thirteenth-century Mongol warlord, saying things such as, "It's not enough that we win; everyone else must lose."[5] Even when Ellison was ordered to donate $100 million to charity and $22 million to the attorneys who sued him for alleged stock-trading abuses, he argued he acted in good faith and in the best interests of Oracle and Oracle's shareholders.[6] This business-as-war mentality fosters the idea that honesty is unnecessary in business.

Many argue that because people are not economically self-sufficient, they cannot withdraw from the relationships of business. Therefore, business ethics must not only make clear what rules apply in business but also develop rules appropriate to the involuntary nature of its many participants. Such rules should contain the value of honesty.

The opposite of honesty is dishonesty. *Dishonesty* can be broadly defined as a lack of integrity, incomplete disclosure, and an unwillingness to tell the truth. Lying, cheating, and stealing are actions usually associated with dishonest conduct. The causes of dishonesty are complex and relate to both individual and organizational pressures. Many employees lie to help achieve performance objectives. For example, they may be asked to lie about when a customer will receive a purchase. Lying can be defined as (1) untruthful statements that result in damage or harm; (2) "white lies," which do not cause damage but instead function as excuses or a means of benefitting others; and (3) statements obviously meant to engage or entertain without malice. These definitions become important in the remainder of this chapter.

Fairness

Fairness is the quality of being just, equitable, and impartial. Fairness clearly overlaps with concepts of justice, equity, equality, and morality. There are three fundamental elements that motivate people to be fair: equality, reciprocity, and optimization. In business, **equality**

is about the distribution of benefits and resources. This distribution could be applied to stakeholders or the greater society.

Reciprocity is an interchange of giving and receiving in social relationships. Reciprocity occurs when an action that has an effect upon another is reciprocated with an action that has an approximately equal effect. Reciprocity is the return of favors approximately equal in value. For example, reciprocity implies workers be compensated with wages approximately equal to their effort. An ethical issue regarding reciprocity for business is the amount CEOs and other executives are paid in relation to their employees. Is a 380 to 1 pay ratio an example of ethical reciprocity? That is the wage differential between a CEO and an average worker in the United States.[7]

Optimization is the trade-off between equity (equality) and efficiency (maximum productivity). Discriminating on the basis of gender, race, or religion is generally considered unfair because these qualities have little bearing upon a person's ability to do a job. The optimal way to hire is to choose the employee who is the most talented, proficient, educated, and able. Ideas of fairness are sometimes shaped by vested interests. One or both parties in the relationship may view an action as unfair or unethical because the outcome was less beneficial than expected.

ETHICAL ISSUES AND DILEMMAS IN BUSINESS

As mentioned earlier, stakeholders and the firm define ethical issues. An **ethical issue** is a problem, situation, or opportunity that requires an individual, group, or organization to choose among several actions that must be evaluated as right or wrong, ethical or unethical. An **ethical dilemma** is a problem, situation, or opportunity that requires an individual, group, or organization to choose among several actions that have negative outcomes. There is not a right or ethical choice in a dilemma, only less unethical or illegal choices as perceived by any and all stakeholders.

A constructive next step toward identifying and resolving ethical issues is to classify the issues that are relevant to most business organizations. Table 3–2 reflects some pressing

TABLE 3–2 Shareholder Issues

1. Core values
2. Shareholder participation in electing directors
3. Executive compensation
4. Legal compliance
5. Lobbying and political activities
6. Reputation management
7. Integrity in collecting and managing data
8. Supply chain relationships and human rights

Source: Jaclyn Jaeger, Top Shareholder Issues for 2012 Proxy Season, Compliance Week, March 8, 2012, http://www.complianceweek.com/top-shareholder-issues-for-2012-proxy-season/article/231150/ (accessed April 17, 2013).

ethical issues to shareholders. Note some of these issues deal with the economic conditions and/or misconduct at firms from other countries. For instance, accounting irregularities at Chinese firms created concern among companies with Chinese-based partners or suppliers. Caterpillar Inc., for instance, was forced to write down its earnings due to fraud at a Chinese subsidiary.[8] In this section, we classify ethical issues in relation to misuse of company time and resources, abusive or intimidating behavior, lying, conflicts of interest, bribery, corporate intelligence, discrimination, sexual harassment, fraud, insider trading, intellectual property rights, and privacy issues.

Misuse of Company Time and Resources

Time theft can be difficult to measure but is estimated to cost companies hundreds of billions of dollars annually. It is widely believed the average employee "steals" 4.25 hours per week with late arrivals, leaving early, long lunch breaks, inappropriate sick days, excessive socializing, and engaging in personal activities such as online shopping and watching sports while on the job.[9]

Although companies have different viewpoints and policies, the misuse of time and resources has been identified by the Ethics Resource Center as a major form of observed misconduct in organizations. In the latest survey 33 percent of respondents observed others misusing company time, and 20 percent observed company resource abuse such as theft of office supplies. Therefore, over 50 percent noted misconduct related to resources issues. Often lax enforcement of company policies creates the impression among employees that they are entitled to certain company resources, including how they spend their time at work. Such misuse can range from unauthorized equipment usage to misuse of financial resources.

Using company computer software and Internet services for personal business is one of the most common ways employees misuse company resources. While it may not be acceptable for employees to sit in the lobby chatting with relatives or their stock brokers, these same employees go online and do the same thing, possibly unnoticed by others. Typical examples of using a computer to abuse company time include sending personal emails, shopping, downloading music, doing personal banking, surfing the Internet for information about sports or romance, or visiting social networking sites such as Facebook. It has been found that March Madness, the NCAA basketball tournament, is one of the most significant periods during which employees engage in time theft. Many firms block websites where employees can watch sports events.

Because misuse of company resources is such a widespread problem, many firms, such as Boeing, implemented policies delineating the acceptable use of such resources. Boeing's policy states resource use is acceptable when it does not result in "significant added costs, disruption of business processes, or any other disadvantage to the company." The policy further states use of company resources for non-company purposes is only acceptable when an employee receives explicit permission to do so.[10]

Abusive or Intimidating Behavior

Abusive or intimidating behavior is another common ethical problem for employees, but what does it mean to be abusive or intimidating? These terms refer to many things—physical threats, false accusations, being annoying, profanity, insults, yelling, harshness, ignoring someone, and unreasonableness—and their meaning differs from person to person. It is important to understand that within each term there is a continuum. For example, behavior one person might define as yelling could be another's definition of normal speech. The lack of civility in our society has been a concern, and it is as common in the workplace as elsewhere. The productivity level of many organizations has been damaged by time spent unraveling problematic relationships.

Is it abusive behavior to ask an employee to complete a project rather than be with a family member or relative in a crisis situation? What does it mean to speak profanely? Is profanity only related to specific words or terms that are, in fact, common in today's business world? If you are using words acceptable to you but that others consider profanity, have you just insulted, abused, or disrespected them?

Within abusive behavior or intimidation, intent should be a consideration. If the employee tries to convey a compliment, then he or she probably simply made a mistake. What if a male manager asks a female subordinate if she has a date because she is dressed nicely? When does the way a word is said (voice inflection) become important? There is also the problem of word meanings by age and within cultures. Is it okay to say "honey" to an employee, fellow employee, employee friend, and/or your superior, and does it depend on gender or location? For example, if you called a friend that worked with you "honey" in southern Illinois, Arkansas, or Kentucky, do you have the same acceptability factor as you would in northern Illinois, Michigan, or Minnesota? Does abusive behavior vary by gender? It is possible the term *honey* could be acceptable speech in some environments, and be construed as being abusive or intimidating in other situations. The fact that we live in a multicultural environment and do business and work with many different cultural groups and nationalities adds to the depth of the ethical and legal issues that may arise.

Bullying is associated with a hostile workplace where someone (or a group) considered a target is threatened, harassed, belittled, verbally abused, or overly criticized. Bullying creates what is referred to as a "hostile environment," but the concept of a hostile environment is generally associated instead with sexual harassment. Regardless, bullying can cause psychological damage that may result in health-endangering consequences to the target. For example, workplace bullying is strongly associated with sleep disturbances. The more frequent the bullying, the higher the risk of sleep disturbance. Other physical

DEBATE ISSUE
TAKE A STAND

Is Workplace Bullying Serious Enough to Warrant Legal Action?

Workplace bullying is abusive behavior used to assert one's power over another. One survey shows that 35 percent of employees claim to have been bullied at work, up from 27 percent the year before. In many cases, the bullies are the supervisors of the organization. Yet while some countries have laws against workplace bullying, the United States does not.

Many believe employees should be legally protected from workplace bullying because bullying is harmful to employee health. Victims of bullying suffer from symptoms including depression, anxiety, and low self-esteem. Bullying permeates the environment of the workplace, causing bystanders to feel its unpleasant effects and creating a toxic workplace. Others, however, believe anti-bullying laws would limit managers' ability to manage since they would constantly be afraid their management styles could be perceived as bullying. Also, critics of such a law argue that bullying is hard to define, making such a law difficult to enforce. Instead, they are in favor of internal ways to combat bullying, including conflict resolution, harassment awareness, and sensitivity trainings.[11]

1. Bullying in organizations can be harmful to employees and therefore warrants legal action.

2. Laws against bullying are not feasible as they are hard to define and have the potential to limit managers' ability to manage.

TABLE 3–3 Actions Associated with Bullies

1. Spreading rumors to damage others
2. Blocking others' communication in the workplace
3. Flaunting status or authority to take advantage of others
4. Discrediting others' ideas and opinions
5. Use of e-mails to demean others
6. Failing to communicate or return communication
7. Insults, yelling, and shouting
8. Using terminology to discriminate by gender, race, or age
9. Using eye or body language to hurt others or their reputations
10. Taking credit for others' work or ideas

Source: Based on Cathi McMahan, "Are You a Bully?" *Inside Seven*, California Department of Transportation Newsletter, June 1999, 6.

symptoms include depression, fatigue, increased sick days, and stomach problems.[12] As Table 3–3 indicates, bullies can use a mix of verbal, nonverbal, and manipulative threatening expressions to damage workplace productivity. Bullying happens more than people realize. One in three American workers has been the victim of bullying, and 20 percent of bullying is technically harassment, which is illegal. Additionally, corporate bullies often target employees who excel at their jobs and are popular with their coworkers.[13] If managers do not address bullying behaviors in the organization, then what starts out as one or two bullies may begin to spread. It has been found that employees who have been bullied are more likely to find it acceptable to bully others.[14]

There is currently no U.S. law prohibiting workplace bullying. However, 24 states have introduced the Healthy Workplace Bill to consider ways to combat bullying.[15] Workplace bullying is illegal in many other countries. Some suggest employers take the following steps to minimize workplace bullying:

- Create policies that place reprimand letters and/or dismissal for such behavior.
- Emphasize mutual respect in the employee handbook.
- Encourage employees who feel bullied to report the conduct via hotlines or other means.

In addition to the three items mentioned, firms are now helping employees understand what bullying is by the use of the following questions:

- Is your supervisor requiring impossible things from you without training?
- Does your supervisor always state that your completed work is never good enough?
- Are meetings to be attended called without your knowledge?
- Have others told you to stop working, talking, or socializing with them?
- Does someone never leave you alone to do your job without interference?
- Do people feel justified screaming or yelling at you in front of others, and are you punished if you scream back?

- Do human resources officials tell you that your harassment is legal and you must work it out between yourselves?
- Do many people verify that your torment is real, but do nothing about it?[16]

Bullying also occurs between companies that are in intense competition. Even respected companies such as Apple have been accused of monopolistic bullying. Former Palm CEO Edward Colligan accused the late Steve Jobs, former CEO of Apple, of anti-competitive behavior toward his firm. Jobs allegedly contacted Colligan to propose an agreement not to hire workers from each other's companies. According to the allegations, Jobs went on to state if Palm continued to poach Apple employees, it could expect a lawsuit from Apple accusing Palm of patent infringement. Five tech workers filed lawsuits against Apple, Google, and other tech firms regarding the existence of "no hire" agreements. If these agreements were made, they would most likely be considered anticompetitive because they place both employees and rival companies at a disadvantage.[17] In many cases, the alleged misconduct can have not only monetary and legal implications but can also threaten reputation, investor confidence, and customer loyalty.

Lying

Earlier in this chapter, we discussed the definitions of lying and how lying relates to distorting the truth. We mentioned three types of lies, one of which is joking without malice. The other two can become troublesome for businesses: lying by commission and lying by omission. *Commission lying* is creating a perception or belief by words that intentionally deceive the receiver of the message; for example, lying about being at work, expense reports, or carrying out work assignments. Commission lying also entails intentionally creating "noise" within the communication that knowingly confuses or deceives the receiver. *Noise* can be defined as technical explanations the communicator knows the receiver does not understand. It can be the intentional use of communication forms that make it difficult for the receiver to actually hear the true message. Using legal terms or terms relating to unfamiliar processes and systems to explain what was done in a work situation facilitate this type of lie.

Lying by commission can involve complex forms, procedures, contracts, words that are spelled the same but have different meanings, or refuting the truth with a false statement. Forms of commission lying include puffery in advertising. For example, saying a product is "homemade" when it is made in a factory is lying. "Made from scratch" in cooking technically means that all ingredients within the product were distinct and separate and were not combined prior to the beginning of the production process. One can lie by commission by showing a picture of the product that does not reflect the actual product. For example, many fast-food chains purchase iceberg lettuce for their products but use romaine lettuce in their advertising because they feel it is prettier and more appealing than shredded iceberg lettuce.

Omission lying is intentionally not informing others of any differences, problems, safety warnings, or negative issues relating to the product or company that significantly affect awareness, intention, or behavior. A classic example of omission lying was in the tobacco manufacturers' decades-long refusal to allow negative research about the effects of tobacco to appear on cigarettes and cigars. Another example is the behavior of FreeCreditReport.com, a company that promotes itself as a way for consumers to check their credit scores. Many customers do not realize that FreeCreditReport.com is a credit-monitoring service that costs $14.95 per month and they will be charged if they do not cancel the service within 30 days. When lying damages others, it can be the focus of a lawsuit. For example, prosecutors and civil lawsuits often reduce misconduct to lying about a fact, such as financial performance, that has the potential to damage others. CEOs at AIG, Lehman Brothers, Fannie Mae, and Freddie Mac were scrutinized to see if they told the truth about the financial conditions of their companies.

The point at which a lie becomes unethical in business is based on the *context* of the statement and its *intent* to distort the truth. A lie becomes illegal if it is determined by the courts to have damaged others. Some businesspeople may believe one must lie a little or that the occasional lie is sanctioned by the organization. The question you need to ask is whether lies are distorting openness and transparency and other values associated with ethical behavior.

Conflicts of Interest

A conflict of interest exists when an individual must choose whether to advance his or her own interests, those of the organization, or those of some other group. The three major bond rating agencies—Moody's, Standard & Poor's, and Fitch Ratings—analyze financial deals and assign letters (such as AAA, B, CC) to represent the quality of bonds and other investments. Prior to the financial meltdown, these rating agencies had significant conflicts of interest. The agencies earned as much as three times more for grading complex products than for corporate bonds. They also competed with each other for rating jobs, which contributed to lower rating standards. Additionally, the companies who wanted the ratings were the ones paying the agencies. Because the rating agencies were highly competitive, investment firms and banks would "shop" the different agencies for the best rating. Conflicts of interest were inevitable.

To avoid conflicts of interest, employees must be able to separate their private interests from their business dealings. Organizations must also avoid potential conflicts of interest when providing products. The U.S. General Accounting Office found conflicts of interest when the government awarded bids on defense contracts. Conflicts of interest usually relate to hiring friends, relatives, or retired military officers to enhance the probability of getting a contract.[18]

Bribery

Bribery is the practice of offering something (often money) in order to gain an illicit advantage from someone in authority. Gifts, entertainment, and travel can also be used as bribes. The key issue regarding whether or not something is considered bribery is whether it is used to gain an advantage in a relationship. Bribery can be defined as an unlawful act, but it can also be a business ethics issue in that a culture includes such fees as standard practice. Related to the ethics of bribery is the concept of active corruption or active bribery, meaning the person who promises or gives the bribe commits the offense. Passive bribery is an offense committed by the official who receives the bribe. It is not an offense, however, if the advantage was permitted or required by the written law or regulation of the foreign public official's country, including case law.

Small facilitation payments made to obtain or retain business or other improper advantages do not constitute bribery payments for U.S. companies in some situations. Such payments are often made to induce public officials to perform their functions, such as issuing licenses or permits. In the United Kingdom these facilitation payments were initially illegal. However, the U.K. government has decided to review this prohibition because it is often necessary in developing countries to pay low-level government officials small gratuities or tips for them to carry out their duties.[19] Ralph Lauren Corp. employees gave Argentine customs officials dresses, perfume, and cash to accelerate the passage of merchandise into the country. Over $580,000 was paid. This amount was not considered to be facilitation payments—they were considered to be bribes. When discovered, Ralph Lauren reported the bribery and cooperated with an investigation. As a result of their cooperativeness, they became the first company not to be prosecuted under the Foreign Corrupt Practices Act. However, they agreed to pay $1.6 million to resolve the investigation.[20]

In most developed countries, it is generally recognized that employees should not accept bribes, personal payments, gifts, or special favors from people who hope to influence the outcome of a decision. However, bribery is an accepted way of doing business in other countries, which creates challenging situations for global businesses. Bribes have been associated with the downfall of many managers, legislators, and government officials. The World Bank estimates that more than $1 trillion is paid annually in bribes.[21]

When a government official accepts a bribe, it is usually from a business that seeks some advantage, perhaps to obtain business or the opportunity to avoid regulation. Giving bribes to legislators or public officials is both a legal and a business ethics issue. It is a legal issue in the United States under the U.S. Foreign Corrupt Practices Act (FCPA). This act maintains it is illegal for individuals, firms, or third parties doing business in American markets to "make payments to foreign government officials to assist in obtaining or retaining business."[22] Companies have paid billions of dollars in fines to the Department of Justice for bribery violations. The law does not apply only to American firms, but to all firms transacting business with operations in the United States. This could also mean firms do not necessarily have to commit the bribery in the United States to be held accountable. For instance, Royal Philips Electronics NV paid $4.5 million to settle allegations that it had paid bribes in Poland to procure sales.[23]

Corporate Intelligence

Many issues related to corporate intelligence have surfaced in the last few years. Defined broadly, **corporate intelligence** is the collection and analysis of information on markets, technologies, customers, and competitors, as well as on socioeconomic and external political trends. There are three distinct types of intelligence models: a passive monitoring system for early warning, tactical field support, and support dedicated to top-management strategy.

Corporate intelligence (CI) involves an in-depth discovery of information from corporate records, court documents, regulatory filings, and press releases, as well as any other background information about a company or its executives. Corporate intelligence can be a legitimate inquiry into meaningful information used in staying competitive. For instance, it is legal for a software company to monitor its competitor's online activities such as blogs and Facebook posts. If the company learns from monitoring its competitor's public postings it is likely planning to launch a new product, the company could use this intelligence to release the product first and beat the competition. Such an activity is acceptable.

CI has its own set of procedures. For example, can you tell which of the following are acceptable strategies and practices in CI?

1. Develop an effective network of informants. Encourage staff members to gather competitive information as they interact with people outside the company.

2. Have every salesperson talk to those customers who are believed to have talked to competitors.

3. When interviewing job applicants from competitors, have Human Resources ask about critical information.

4. Have purchasers talk to suppliers to attempt to discover who is demanding what and when it is needed.

5. Interview every employee about his or her knowledge or expertise and leverage it for outside information about other firms within the industry.

6. When you interview consultants, ask them to share examples of their work.

7. Use press releases announcing new hires as an indicator of what type of talent companies are hiring.

8. Use web services to track all the changes anyone makes on a company's website, thus giving you an indication of which areas a competitor is thinking about and where it might be headed.

9. Use a proxy or other firm to act as a client for the competitor so as to ask about a company's pricing structure, how fast they ship, turnaround time, and number of employees. Ask for references and call those people as well.

All of these scenarios are legal and frequently used by corporate intelligence departments and firms.

However, corporate intelligence, like other areas in business, can be abused if due diligence is not taken to maintain legal and ethical methods of discovery. Computers, LANs (local-area networks), and the Internet have made the theft of trade secrets very easy. Proprietary information like secret formulas, manufacturing schematics, merger or acquisition plans, and marketing strategies all have tremendous value.[24] Theft of corporate trade secrets has been on the rise among technology companies such as Samsung. Corporate espionage is estimated to cost the American economy $13 billion annually, while German companies lose between $28 billion and $71 billion each year.[25] If discovered, corporate espionage can lead to heavy fines and prison sentences. For instance, former software engineer Hanjuan Jin was found guilty of stealing trade secrets from Motorola. She had in her possession more than 1,000 Motorola documents.[26] A lack of security and proper training allows a person to use a variety of techniques to gain access to a company's vital information. Some techniques for accessing valuable corporate information include physically removing hard drives and copying the information they contain to other machines, hacking, dumpster diving, social engineering, bribery, and hiring away key employees.

Hacking is considered one of the top three methods for obtaining trade secrets. Currently, there are thousands of websites that offer free downloadable and customizable hacking tools that require no in-depth knowledge of protocols or Internet protocol addresses. Hacking has three categories: system, remote, and physical. System hacking assumes the attacker already has access to a low-level, privileged-user account. Remote hacking involves attempting to remotely penetrate a system across the Internet. A remote hacker usually begins with no special privileges and tries to obtain higher level or administrative access.

Several forms of this type of hacking include unexpected input, buffer overflows, default configurations, and poor system administrator practices. Remote hacking activity against businesses and financial institutions is increasing, with hackers even penetrating the computer network of the company that runs the Nasdaq Stock Market.[27] **Physical hacking** requires the CI agent enter a facility personally. Once inside, he or she can find a vacant or unsecured workstation with an employee's login name and password. Next, the CI agent searches for memos or unused letterheads and inserts the documents into the corporate mail system. CI agents could also gain physical access to a server or telephone room, look for remote-access equipment, note any telephone numbers written on wall jacks, and place a protocol analyzer in a wiring closet to capture data, user names, and passwords.

Social engineering is another popular method of obtaining valuable corporate information. The basic goals are the same as hacking. **Social engineering** is the tricking of individuals into revealing their passwords or other valuable corporate information. Tactics include casual conversations with relatives of company executives and sending e-mails claiming to be a system administrator and asking for passwords under the guise of "important system administration work." Another common social engineering trick is **shoulder surfing**, in which someone simply looks over an employee's shoulder while he or she types in a password. **Password guessing** is another easy social engineering technique. If a person can find out personal things about someone, he or she might be able to use that information to guess a password. For example, a child's name, birthdays, anniversaries, and Social Security numbers are all common passwords and are easy to guess.

Dumpster diving is messy but successful for acquiring trade secrets. Once trash is discarded onto a public street or alley, it is considered fair game. Trash can provide a rich source of information for any CI agent. Phone books can give a hacker names and numbers of people to target and impersonate. Organizational charts contain information about people who are in positions of authority within the organization. Memos provide small amounts of useful information and assist in the creation of authentic-looking fake memos.

Whacking is wireless hacking. To eavesdrop on wireless networks, all a CI agent needs is the right kind of radio and to be within range of a wireless transmission. Once tapped into a wireless network, an intruder can easily access anything on both the wired and wireless networks because the data sent over networks are usually unencrypted. If a company is not using wireless networking, an attacker can pose as a janitor and insert a rogue wireless access node into a supposedly secure hard-wired network.

Phone eavesdropping is yet another tool for CI agents. A person with a digital recording device can monitor and record a fax line. By playing the recording back an intruder can reproduce an exact copy of a message without anyone's knowledge. Even without monitoring a fax line, a fax sent to a "communal" fax machine can be read or copied. By picking up an extension or by tapping a telephone, it is possible to record the tones that represent someone's account number and password using a tape recorder. The tape recording can then be replayed over the telephone to gain access to someone else's account.

Discrimination

Although a person's racial and sexual prejudices belong to the domain of individual ethics, racial and sexual discrimination in the workplace create ethical issues within the business world. **Discrimination** on the basis of race, color, religion, sex, marital status, sexual orientation, public assistance status, disability, age, national origin, or veteran status is illegal in the United States. Additionally, discrimination on the basis of political opinions or affiliation with a union is defined as harassment. Discrimination remains a significant ethical issue in business despite decades of legislation attempting to outlaw it.

A company in the United States can be sued if it (1) refuses to hire an individual, (2) maintains a system of employment that unreasonably excludes an individual from employment, (3) discharges an individual, or (4) discriminates against an individual with respect to hiring, employment terms, promotion, or privileges of employment as they relate to the definition of discrimination. More than 99,000 charges of discrimination were filed with the **Equal Employment Opportunity Commission** (EEOC) in 2012.[28]

Race, gender, and age discrimination are major sources of ethical and legal debate in the workplace. Once dominated by European American men, the U.S. workforce today includes significantly more women, African Americans, Hispanics, and other minorities, as well as disabled and older workers. These groups traditionally faced discrimination and higher unemployment rates and been denied opportunities to assume leadership roles in corporate America. For example, only somewhat more than one dozen Fortune 500 companies are led by African American CEOs. Although this is still highly disproportionate to the population, however, there are more African American CEOs than ever before.[29]

Another form of discrimination involves discriminating against individuals on the basis of age. The **Age Discrimination in Employment Act** specifically outlaws hiring practices that discriminate against people 40 years of age or older, as well as those that require employees to retire before the age of 70. The act prohibits employers with 20 or more employees from making employment decisions, including decisions regarding the termination of employment, on the basis of age or as a result of policies requiring retirement after the age of 40. Despite this legislation, charges of age discrimination persist in the workplace. Age discrimination accounts for approximately one-quarter of the complaints filed with the EEOC.[30] Given the fact that nearly one-third of the nation's workers will be 55 years old or over by 2016, many companies need to change their approach toward older workers.[31]

To help build workforces that reflect their customer base, many companies have initiated **affirmative action programs**, which involve efforts to recruit, hire, train, and promote qualified individuals from groups that have traditionally been discriminated against on the basis of race, gender, or other characteristics. Such initiatives may be imposed by federal law on an employer that contracts or subcontracts for business with the federal government, as part of a settlement agreement with a state or federal agency, or by court order.[32] For example, Safeway, a chain of supermarkets, established a program to expand opportunities for women in middle- and upper-level management after settling a sexual-discrimination lawsuit.[33] However, many companies voluntarily implement affirmative action plans in order to build a more diverse workforce. Although many people believe affirmative action requires the use of quotas to govern employment decisions, it is important to note two decades of Supreme Court rulings made it clear that affirmative action does not permit or require quotas, reverse discrimination, or favorable treatment of unqualified women or minorities. To ensure affirmative action programs are fair, the Supreme Court established standards to guide their implementation: (1) There must be a strong reason for developing an affirmative action program; (2) affirmative action programs must apply only to qualified candidates; and (3) affirmative action programs must be limited and temporary and therefore cannot include "rigid and inflexible quotas."[34]

Discrimination can also be an ethical issue in business when companies use race or other personal factors to discriminate against specific groups of customers. Many companies have been accused of using race, disabilities, gender, or age to deny service or to charge higher prices to certain ethnic groups. Employees have also been terminated or denied hire due to discrimination. Outback Steakhouse paid $65,000 to settle an EEOC lawsuit that an Arizona manager terminated a server due to a disability. The company stated it would revise its policies on discrimination regarding disabilities.[35]

Sexual Harassment

Sexual harassment is a form of sex discrimination that violates Title VII of the Civil Rights Act of 1964. Title VII applies to employers with 15 or more employees, including state and local governments. **Sexual harassment** can be defined as any repeated, unwanted behavior of a sexual nature perpetrated upon one individual by another. It may be verbal, visual, written, or physical and can occur between people of different genders or those of the same gender. Displaying sexually explicit materials "may create a hostile work environment or constitute harassment, even though the private possession, reading, and consensual sharing of such materials is protected under the Constitution."[36] The EEOC receives between 11,000 and 14,000 charges of sexual harassment annually.[37]

Even the United Nations, an organization whose mission is to protect human rights globally, has dealt with a series of sexual harassment cases. Many U.N. employees who have made or faced accusations claim the system is poorly equipped to handle complaints, resulting in unfair, slow, and arbitrary rulings. For example, one employee who claimed she was harassed for years in Gaza saw her superior cleared by one of his colleagues.[38]

To establish sexual harassment, an employee must understand the definition of a **hostile work environment**, for which three criteria must be met: the conduct was unwelcome; the conduct was severe, pervasive, and regarded by the claimant as so hostile or offensive as to alter his or her conditions of employment; and the conduct was such that a reasonable person would find it hostile or offensive. To assert a hostile work environment, an employee need not prove it seriously affected his or her psychological well-being or that it caused an injury; the decisive issue is whether the conduct interfered with the claimant's work performance.[39]

Sexual harassment includes unwanted sexual approaches (including touching, feeling, or groping) and/or repeated unpleasant, degrading, or sexist remarks directed toward an employee with the implied suggestion that the target's employment status, promotion, or favorable treatment depend on a positive response and/or cooperation. It can be regarded as a private nuisance, unfair labor practice, or, in some states, a civil wrong (tort) that may be the basis for a lawsuit against the individual who made the advances and against the employer who did not take steps to halt the harassment. The law is primarily concerned with the impact of the behavior and not its intent. An important facet of sexual harassment law is its focus on the victim's reasonable behaviors and expectations.[40] However, the definition of "reasonable" varies from state to state, as does the concept of expectations. In addition, an argument used by some in defense of what others term sexual harassment is the freedom of speech granted by the First Amendment.

The key ethical issues associated with sexual harassment are dual relationships and unethically intimate relationships. A **dual relationship** is defined as a personal, loving, and/ or sexual relationship with someone with whom you share professional responsibilities. **Unethical dual relationships** are those where the relationship could potentially cause a direct or indirect conflict of interest or a risk of impairment to professional judgment.[41] Another important factor in these cases is intent. If the sexual advances in any form are considered mutual, then consent is created. The problem is unless the employee or employer gets something in writing before the romantic action begins, consent can always be questioned, and when it comes to sexual harassment, the alleged perpetrator must prove mutual consent.

To avoid sexual misconduct or harassment charges a company should take at least the following steps:

1. *Establish a statement of policy* naming someone in the company as ultimately responsible for preventing harassment at the company.

2. *Establish a definition of sexual harassment* that includes unwelcome advances, requests for sexual favors, and any other verbal, visual, or physical conduct of a sexual nature; that provides examples of each; and reminds employees the list of examples is not all-inclusive.

3. *Establish a nonretaliation policy* that protects complainants and witnesses.

4. *Establish specific procedures for prevention* of such practices at early stages. However, if a company puts these procedures in writing, they are expected by law to train employees in accordance with them, measure their effects, and ensure the policies are enforced.

5. *Establish, enforce, and encourage* victims of sexual harassment to report the behavior to authorized individuals.

6. *Establish a reporting procedure.*

7. *Make sure the company has timely reporting requirements to the proper authorities.* Usually, there is a time limitation (ranging from six months to a year) to file a complaint for a formal administrative sexual charge. However, the failure to meet a shorter complaint period (for example, 60 to 90 days) so a rapid response and remediation may occur and to help ensure a harassment-free environment could be a company's defense against charges it was negligent.

Once these steps have been taken, a training program should identify and describe forms of sexual harassment and give examples, outline grievance procedures, explain how to use the procedures and discuss the importance of them, discuss the penalty for violation, and train employees about the essential need for a workplace free from harassment, offensive conduct, or intimidation. A corporation's training program should cover how to spot sexual harassment; how to investigate complaints, including proper documentation; what to do about observed sexual harassment, even when no complaint has been filed; how to keep the work environment as professional and non-hostile as possible; how to teach employees about the professional and legal consequences of sexual harassment; and how to train management to understand follow-up procedures on incidents.

Fraud

When individuals engage in intentional deceptive practices to advance their own interests over those of the organization or some other group, they are committing fraud. In general, **fraud** is any purposeful communication that deceives, manipulates, or conceals facts in order to harm others. Fraud can be a crime and convictions may result in fines, imprisonment, or both. Global fraud costs organizations more than $3.5 trillion a year; the average company loses about 5 percent of annual revenues to fraud.[42] Figure 3.1 indicates some of

FIGURE 3–1 Initial Detection of Operational Frauds

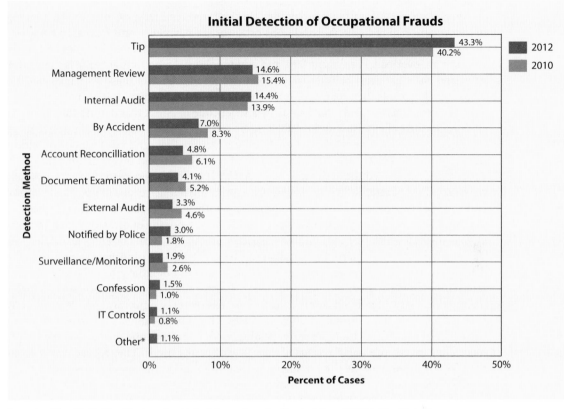

Source: Association of Certified Fraud Examiners, *Report to the Nations on Occupational Fraud and Abuse: 2012 Global Fraud Study*, 14.

the major ways fraud is detected. Note the majority of fraud detection occurs due to tips, thereby making reporting an important way of preventing and detecting wide-scale fraud. In recent years, accounting fraud has become a major ethical issue, but as we will see, fraud can also relate to marketing and consumer issues as well.

Accounting fraud usually involves a corporation's financial reports, in which companies provide important information on which investors and others base decisions involving millions of dollars. If the documents contain inaccurate information, whether intentionally or not, lawsuits and criminal penalties may result. Former AIG CEO Maurice Greenberg and other defendants agreed to pay AIG shareholders $115 million to resolve allegations charging them with misleading investors regarding an illegal bid-rigging arrangement in the insurance industry, as well as making misleading statements about a purported accounting fraud that took place at the firm years before.[43]

The field of accounting has changed dramatically over the last decade. The profession used to have a club-type mentality, and those who became certified public accountants (CPAs) were not concerned about competition. Now CPAs advertise their skills and short-term results in an environment where competition has increased and overall billable hours significantly decreased because of technological innovations. Additionally, accountants are permitted to charge performance-based fees rather than hourly rates, a rule change that encouraged some large accounting firms to promote tax-avoidance strategies for high-income individuals because the firms can charge 10 to 40 percent of the amount of taxes saved.[44]

Pressures on accountants today include time, reduced fees, client requests to alter opinions concerning financial conditions or lower tax payments, and increased competition. Other issues accountants face daily involve compliance with complex rules and regulations, data overload, contingent fees, and commissions. An accountant's life is filled with rules and data that must be interpreted correctly, and because of these pressures and the ethical predicaments they spawn, problems within the accounting industry are on the rise.

As a result, accountants must abide by a strict code of ethics that defines their responsibilities to their clients and to the public interest. The code also discusses the concepts of integrity, objectivity, independence, and due care. Despite the standards the code provides, the accounting industry has been the source of numerous fraud investigations in recent years. Congress passed the Sarbanes–Oxley Act in 2002 to address many of the issues that create conflicts of interest for accounting firms auditing public corporations. The law generally prohibits accounting firms from providing both auditing and consulting services to the same firm. Additionally, the law specifies corporate boards of directors must include outside directors with financial knowledge on the company's audit committee.

Marketing fraud—the process of dishonestly creating, distributing, promoting, and pricing products—is another business area that generates potential ethical issues. False or misleading marketing communications destroys customers' trust in a company. Lying, a major ethical issue involving communication, is a potentially significant problem. In both external and internal communications, it causes ethical predicaments because it destroys trust. The SEC charged two units at financial services firm Oppenheimer & Company with misleading investors about the value of their private equity funds. They agreed to pay more than $2.9 million to settle the lawsuit.[45] Misleading marketing can also cost consumers hard-earned money.

False or deceptive advertising is a key issue in marketing communications. One set of laws common to many countries concerns deceptive advertising—that is, advertisements not clearly labeled as advertisements. In the United States, Section 5 of the Federal Trade Commission (FTC) Act addresses deceptive advertising. Abuses in advertising range from exaggerated claims and concealed facts to outright lying, although improper categorization of advertising claims is the critical point. Courts place false or misleading advertisements into three categories: puffery, implied falsity, and literal falsity.

Puffery can be defined as exaggerated advertising, blustering, and boasting upon which no reasonable buyer would rely and is not actionable under the Lanham Act. For example, in a lawsuit between two shaving products companies, the defendant advertised the moisturizing strip on its shaving razor was "six times smoother" than its competitors' strips, while showing a man rubbing his hand down his face. The court rejected the defendant's argument that "six times smoother" implied that only the moisturizing strip on the razor's head was smoother. Instead, the court found the "six times smoother" advertising claim implied that the consumer would receive a smoother shave from the defendant's razor as a whole, a claim that was false.[46]

Implied falsity means the message has a tendency to mislead, confuse, or deceive the public. Advertising claims that use implied falsity are those that are literally true but imply another message that is false. In most cases, accusations of implied falsity can be proved only through time-consuming and expensive consumer surveys, the results of which are often inconclusive. An example of implied falsity might be a company's claim that its product has twice as much of an ingredient in its product, implying that it works twice as well, when in reality the extra quantity of the ingredient has no effect over performance. The characterization of an advertising claim as literally false can be divided into two subcategories: *tests prove* (*establishment claims*), when the advertisement cites a study or test that establishes the claim; and *bald assertions* (*nonestablishment claims*), when the advertisement makes a claim that cannot be substantiated, as when a commercial states a certain product is superior to any other on the market. Another form of advertising abuse involves making ambiguous statements; when the words are so weak or general that the viewer, reader, or listener must infer the advertiser's intended message. These "weasel words" are inherently vague and enable the advertiser to deny any intent to deceive. The verb *help* is a good example (as in expressions such as "helps prevent," "helps fight," "helps make you feel").[47] Consumers may view such advertisements as unethical because they fail to communicate all the information needed to make a good purchasing decision or because they deceive the consumer outright.

Labeling issues are even murkier. For example, Monster Beverage Corp. decided to change its label to indicate it is a beverage rather than a dietary supplement. Rather than putting "Supplement Facts" on its cans, the company will replace it with "Nutrition Facts." This may seem like a small change, but it is intended to stave off the increasing scrutiny of critics who believe that energy drink caffeine levels are unsafe. As part of the labeling change, Monster labels now display the drink's caffeine content.[48]

Advertising and direct sales communication can also mislead consumers by concealing the facts within the message. For instance, a salesperson anxious to sell a medical insurance policy might list a large number of illnesses covered by the policy but fail to mention it does not include some commonly covered illnesses. Indeed, the fastest-growing area of fraudulent activity is in direct marketing, which uses the telephone and impersonal media to communicate information to customers, who then purchase products via mail, telephone, or the Internet.

Consumer Fraud

Consumer fraud occurs when consumers attempt to deceive businesses for their own gain. Shoplifting is estimated to cost retailers approximately $30 billion annually.[49] Consumers engage in many other forms of fraud against businesses, including price tag switching, item switching, lying to obtain age-related and other discounts, and taking advantage of generous return policies by returning used items, especially clothing that has been worn (with the price tags still attached). Such behavior by consumers affects retail stores as well as other consumers who, for example, may unwittingly purchase new clothing that has actually been worn. Fraudulent merchandise returns are estimated to cost about $8.9 billion a year.[50]

Consumer fraud involves intentional deception to derive an unfair economic advantage by an individual or group over an organization. Examples of fraudulent activities include shoplifting, collusion or duplicity, and guile. *Collusion* typically involves an employee who assists the consumer in fraud. For example, a cashier may not ring up all merchandise or may give an unwarranted discount. *Duplicity* may involve a consumer staging an accident in a grocery store and then seeking damages against the store for its lack of attention to safety. A consumer may purchase, wear, and then return an item of clothing for a full refund. In other situations, a consumer may ask for a refund by claiming a defect. *Guile* is associated with a person who is crafty or understands right/wrong behavior but uses tricks to obtain an unfair advantage. The advantage is unfair because the person has the intent to go against the right behavior or result. Although some of these acts warrant legal prosecution, they can be difficult to prove, and many companies are reluctant to accuse patrons of a crime when there is no way to verify wrongdoing. Businesses that operate with the philosophy "the customer is always right" have found some consumers take advantage of this promise and have therefore modified return policies to curb unfair use.

Financial Misconduct

The failure to understand and manage ethical risks played a significant role in the financial crisis. The difference between bad business decisions and business misconduct can be hard to determine, and there is a thin line between the ethics of using only financial incentives to gauge performance and the use of holistic measures that include ethics, transparency, and responsibility to stakeholders. From CEOs to traders and brokers, all-too-tempting lucrative financial incentives existed for performance in the financial industry.

The most recent global recession was caused in part by a failure on the part of the financial industry to take appropriate responsibility for its decision to utilize risky and complex financial instruments. Loopholes in regulations and the failures of regulators were exploited. Corporate cultures were built on rewards for taking risks rather than rewards for creating value for stakeholders. Ethical decisions were based more on what was legal rather than what was the right thing to do. Unfortunately, most stakeholders, including the public, regulators, and the mass media, do not always understand the nature of the financial risks taken on by banks and other institutions to generate profits. The intangible nature of financial products makes it difficult to understand complex financial transactions. Problems in the subprime mortgage markets sounded the alarm for the most recent recession.

Ethics issues emerged early in subprime lending, with loan officers receiving commissions on securing loans from borrowers with no consequences if the borrower defaulted on the loan. "Liar loans" were soon developed to create more sales and higher personal compensation for lenders. Lenders encouraged subprime borrowers to provide false information on their loan applications in order to qualify for and secure the loans. Some appraisers provided inflated home values in order to increase loan amounts. In other instances consumers were asked to falsify their incomes to make the loans more attractive to the lending institutions. The opportunity for misconduct was widespread. Top managers and CEOs were complacent about the wrongdoing as long as profits were good. Congress and President Clinton encouraged Fannie Mae and Freddie Mac to support home ownership among low-income people by giving out home mortgages. Throughout the early 2000s, in an economy with rapidly increasing home values, the culture of unethical behavior was not apparent to most people. When home values started to decline and individuals were "upside down" on their loans (owing more than the equity of the home), the failures and unethical behavior of lending and borrowing institutions became obvious.

The top executives or CEOs are ultimately responsible for the repercussions of their employees' decisions. Top executives at Merrill Lynch awarded $3.6 billion in bonuses shortly before the company's merger with Bank of America in 2008.[51] A combined $121 million went to four top executives, in spite of the fact that Merrill Lynch had to be rescued from bankruptcy by the government. Two ethics issues are at play in this situation. First, paying out the bonuses at all; and second, rushing their distribution in order to complete the job before Bank of America's takeover. Risk management in the financial industry is a key concern, including paying bonuses to executives who failed in their duties. Unfortunately, at the same time the industry was focused on its own bottom line, regulatory agencies and Congress were not proactive in investigating early cases of financial misconduct and the systemic issues that led to the crisis. The legal and regulatory systems were more focused on individual misconduct rather than systemic ethical failures.

This widespread financial misconduct led to a call for financial reform. The U.S. Treasury Secretary, Timothy Geithner, is trying to change how the government goes about overseeing risk-taking in financial markets. He is pushing for stricter rules on financial management and controls on hedge funds and money market mutual funds. He believes the United States needs greater openness and transparency, greater oversight and enforcement, and clearer, more commonsense language in its financial system.[52] The Dodd–Frank Wall Street Reform and Consumer Protection Act was passed in 2010 to increase accountability and transparency in the financial industry and protect consumers from deceptive financial practices. The act established a Consumer Financial Protection Bureau (CFPB) to protect consumers from unsafe financial products. The CFPB was provided with supervisory power over the credit market. Its responsibility includes making financial products easier to understand, curtailing unfair lending and credit card practices, and ensuring the safety of financial products before their launch into the market. The Dodd–Frank Wall Street Reform and Consumer Protection Act also gives federal regulators more power over large companies and financial institutions to prevent them from engaging in risky practices, or becoming "too big to fail." The act also holds CEOs responsible for the behavior of their companies. Large financial firms must retain at least half of top executives' bonuses for at least three years. The goal is to tie compensation to the outcomes of the executives' decisions over time.[53] We will discuss the Dodd–Frank Act and the Consumer Financial Protection Bureau in detail in Chapter 4.

Insider Trading

An insider is any officer, director, or owner of 10 percent or more of a class of a company's securities. There are two types of insider trading: illegal and legal. *Illegal insider trading* is the buying or selling of stocks by insiders who possess information that is not yet public. This act, that puts insiders in breach of their fiduciary duty, can be committed by anyone who has access to nonpublic material, such as brokers, family, friends, and employees. In addition, someone caught "tipping" an outsider with nonpublic information can also be found liable. To determine if an insider gave a tip illegally the SEC uses the *Dirks test,* that states if a tipster breaches his or her trust with the company and understands that this was a breach, he or she is liable for insider trading.

Legal insider trading involves legally buying and selling stock in an insider's own company, but not all the time. Insiders are required to report their insider transactions within two business days of the date the transaction occurred. For example, if an insider sold 10,000 shares on Monday, June 12, he or she would have to report the sale to the SEC by Wednesday, June 14. To deter insider trading, insiders are prevented from buying and selling their company stock within a six-month period, thereby encouraging insiders to buy stock only when they feel the company will perform well over the long term.

Insider trading is often done in a secretive manner by an individual who seeks to take advantage of an opportunity to make quick gains in the market. The Justice Department has cracked down on insider trading in recent years, including recording phone calls of suspected insider traders to gather evidence. Galleon Group founder Raj Rajaratnam and former Goldman Sachs director Rajat Gupta were both sentenced after secretly videotaped phone conversations appeared to implicate them in an insider trading scheme. The government also used telephone conversation recordings to convict former hedge-fund manager Doug Whitman for trading on nonpublic information from Google and other firms.[54] Surveys revealed people who get involved in this type of activity often feel superior to others and are blind to the possibility of being discovered or facing consequences.[55]

Intellectual Property Rights

Intellectual property rights involve the legal protection of intellectual property such as music, books, and movies. Laws such as the Copyright Act of 1976, the Digital Millennium Copyright Act, and the Digital Theft Deterrence and Copyright Damages Improvement Act of 1999 were designed to protect the creators of intellectual property. However, with the advance of technology, ethical issues still abound for websites. For example, until it was sued for copyright infringement and subsequently changed its business model, Napster. com allowed individuals to download copyrighted music for personal use without providing compensation to the artists.

A decision by the Federal Copyright Office (FCO) helped lay the groundwork for intellectual property rules in a digital world. The FCO decided to make it illegal for web users to hack through barriers that copyright holders erect around material released online, allowing only two exceptions. The first exception was for software that blocks users from finding obscene or controversial material on the web, and the second was for people who want to bypass malfunctioning security features of software or other copyrighted goods they have purchased. This decision reflects the fact that copyright owners are typically being favored in digital copyright issues.[56]

However, digital copyrights continue to be a controversial issue in the United States and across the world, and existing laws are often difficult to enforce. Almost a quarter of all Internet traffic involves copyrighted material, including illegally downloaded or uploaded music, movies, and television shows.[57] As China grew into an economic powerhouse, the market for pirated goods of all types, from DVDs to pharmaceuticals and even cars, has become a multibillion dollar industry.[58] China's government has proven weak in protecting intellectual property, and the underground market for such pirated goods—which are sold all over the world—has grown at a rapid pace. Downloaders of illegal content are less concerned with the law than non-downloaders and are more likely to engage in other forms of illegal conduct such as shoplifting.[59]

While intellectual property rights infringement always poses a threat to companies that risk losing profits and reputation, it can also threaten the health and well-being of consumers. For example, illegally produced medications, when consumed by unknowing consumers, can cause sickness and even death. Research on software piracy has shown that high levels of economic well-being and an advanced technology sector are effective deterrents to software piracy.[60] However, as the number of patents filed in China increase, so are intellectual property lawsuits. It seems intellectual property theft is becoming a more important issue in China.[61] Perhaps as China's economy moves forward piracy will become less of a problem, but for now it poses a major threat.

Privacy Issues

Consumer advocates continue to warn consumers about new threats to their privacy, especially within the health care and Internet industries. As the number of people using the Internet increases, the areas of concern related to its use increase as well. Some **privacy issues** that must be addressed by businesses include the monitoring of employees' use of available technology and consumer privacy. Current research suggests that even when businesses use price discounts or personalized services, consumers remain suspicious. However, certain consumers are still willing to provide personal information despite the potential risks.[62]

A challenge for companies today is meeting their business needs while protecting employees' desire for privacy. There are few legal protections of an employee's right to privacy, which allows businesses a great deal of flexibility in establishing policies regarding employee privacy while using company equipment on company property. From computer monitoring and telephone taping to video surveillance and GPS satellite tracking, employers are using technology to manage their productivity and protect their resources. The ability to gather and use data about employee behavior creates an ethical issue related to trust and responsibility.

Electronic monitoring allows a company to determine whether productivity is being reduced because employees spend too much time on personal activities. Having this information enables the company to take steps to remedy the situation. Many employers have policies that govern personal phone and Internet use on company time. Additionally, some companies track everything from phone calls and Internet history to keystrokes and the time employees spend at their desks.[63] One study found that 42 percent of full-time employees with a company-assigned e-mail account "frequently use" it for personal communications, while another 29 percent "sometimes" do. Another survey found 89 percent of workers say they sent e-mail from work to an outside party that contained jokes, gossip, rumors, or disparaging remarks, while 14 percent sent messages that contained confidential or proprietary information, and 9 percent of respondents admitted to sending sexual, romantic, or pornographic text or images.[64] Instituting practices that show respect for employee privacy but do not abdicate the employer's responsibility helps create a climate of trust that promotes opportunities for resolving employee–employer disputes without lawsuits. On the other hand, if personal data is gathered that includes medical or religious information, it can result in litigation.

There are two dimensions to consumer privacy: consumer awareness of information collection and a growing lack of consumer control over how companies use the personal information they collect. For example, many are not aware that Google, Inc., reserves the right to track every time you click on a link from one of its searches.[65] Online purchases and even random web surfing can be tracked without a consumer's knowledge. A survey by the Progress and Freedom Foundation found 96 percent of popular commercial websites collect personally identifying information from visitors.[66]

Personal information about consumers is valuable not only to businesses but also criminals. It is estimated an identity is stolen once every three seconds.[67] Personal information is stolen and sold online. Although some of this information comes from sources such as social networking profiles, poorly protected corporate files are another major source. U.S. organizations report hundreds of security breaches annually.[68]

Companies are working to find ways to improve consumers' trust in their websites. For example, an increasing number of websites display an online seal from the Better Business Bureau, available only to sites that subscribe to certain standards. A similar seal is available through TRUSTe, a nonprofit global initiative that certifies those websites adhering to its principles. (Visit http://e-businessethics.com for more on Internet privacy.)

THE CHALLENGE OF DETERMINING AN ETHICAL ISSUE IN BUSINESS

Most ethical issues concerning a business will become visible through stakeholder concerns about an event, activity, or the results of a business decision. The mass media, special interest groups, and individuals, through the use of blogs, podcasts, and other individual-generated media, often generate discussion about the ethical nature of a decision. Another way to determine if a specific behavior or situation has an ethical component is to ask other individuals in the business how they feel about it and whether they view it as ethically challenging. Trade associations and business self-regulatory groups such as the Better Business Bureau often provide direction for companies in defining ethical issues. Finally, it is important to determine whether the organization adopted specific policies on the activity. An activity approved by most members of an organization, if it is also customary in the industry, is probably ethical. An issue, activity, or situation that can withstand open discussion between many stakeholders, both inside and outside the organization, probably does not pose ethical problems.

However, over time, problems can become ethical issues as a result of changing societal values. For instance, products manufactured by Kraft Foods, Inc., such as Kraft Macaroni and Cheese, Chips Ahoy! cookies, Lunchables, Kool-Aid, Fruity Pebbles, and Oreos, have been staples in almost every home in the United States for decades without becoming subjects of public debate; but when parents, schools, and politicians became more aware that the United States has the most overweight people in the world, things changed.[69] Additionally, since 1980 the rate of obesity in children and adolescents has more than tripled.[70] As a result, Congress proposed legislation focused on the advertising of unhealthy food products to children. Kraft faced an ethical situation regarding the advertising of many of its foods. Some consumer groups might perceive Kraft's advertising budget, which was primarily directed at children, as unethical. Because ignoring the situation could be potentially disastrous, Kraft decided to stop advertising some of its products to children and instead market healthier foods.

Once stakeholders trigger ethical issue awareness and individuals openly discuss it and ask for guidance and the opinions of others, one enters the ethical decision-making process, which we examine in Chapter 5.

SUMMARY

Stakeholders' concerns largely determine whether business actions and decisions are perceived as ethical or unethical. When government, communities, and society become involved, what was merely an ethical issue can quickly become a legal one. Shareholders can unwittingly complicate the ethical conduct of business by demanding managers make decisions to boost short-term earnings, thus maintaining or increasing the value of their stock.

A first step toward understanding business ethics is to develop ethical issue awareness; that is, to learn to identify which stakeholder issues contain an ethical component. Characteristics of the job, the corporate or local culture, and the society in which one does business can all create ethical issues. Recognizing an ethical issue is essential to understanding business ethics and therefore to create an effective ethics and compliance program that minimizes unethical behavior. Businesspeople must understand the universal moral constants of honesty, fairness, and integrity. Without embracing these concepts, running a business becomes difficult.

Fairness is the quality of being just, equitable, and impartial, and overlaps with concepts of *justice, equity, equality,* and *morality.* The three fundamental elements that motivate people to be fair are equality, reciprocity, and optimization. Equality relates to how wealth is distributed between employees within a company, country, or globally; reciprocity relates to the return of favors approximately equal in value; and integrity refers to a person's character and is made up of two basic parts, a formal relation one has to oneself and a person's set of terminal, or enduring, values from which he or she does not deviate.

An ethical issue is a problem, situation, or opportunity that requires an individual, group, or organization to choose among several actions that must be evaluated as right or wrong, ethical or unethical. By contrast, an ethical dilemma has no right or ethical solution.

Abusive or intimidating behavior includes physical threats, false accusations, being annoying, profanity, insults, yelling, harshness, ignoring someone, and unreasonableness. Bribery is the practice of offering something (usually money) in order to gain an illicit advantage. A conflict of interest occurs when individuals must choose whether to advance their own interests, those of the organization, or some other group. Corporate intelligence is the collection and analysis of information on markets, technologies, customers, and competitors, as well as on socioeconomic and external political trends. There are three intelligence models: passive, tactical, and top-management. The tools of corporate intelligence are many. One tool is hacking, accomplished through systemic, remote, and physical means; another is social engineering, in which someone is tricked into revealing valuable corporate information. Other techniques include dumpster diving, whacking, and phone eavesdropping.

Another ethical/legal issue is discrimination, which is illegal in the United States when it occurs on the basis of race, color, religion, sex, marital status, sexual orientation, public-assistance status, disability, age, national origin, or veteran status. Additionally, discrimination on the basis of political opinions or affiliation with a union is defined as harassment. Sexual harassment is a form of sex discrimination. To build workforces that reflect their customer base, many companies initiated affirmative action programs. In general, fraud is any purposeful communication that deceives, manipulates, or conceals facts in order to create a false impression. There are several types of fraud: accounting, marketing, and consumer.

An insider is any officer, director, or owner of 10 percent or more of a class of a company's securities. There are two types of insider trading: legal and illegal. Intellectual property rights involve the legal protection of intellectual property such as music, books, and movies. Consumer advocates continue to warn consumers about new threats to their privacy.

IMPORTANT TERMS FOR REVIEW

integrity 63

honesty 63

fairness 64

equality 64

reciprocity 65

optimization 65

ethical issue 65

ethical dilemma 65

abusive or intimidating behavior 66

lying 69

conflict of interest 70

bribery 70

active bribery 70

passive bribery 70

facilitation payment 70

corporate intelligence 71

hacking 72

system hacking 72

remote hacking 72

physical hacking 73

social engineering 73

shoulder surfing 73

password guessing 73

dumpster diving 73

whacking 73

phone eavesdropping 73

discrimination 73

Equal Employment Opportunity Commission 74

Age Discrimination in Employment Act 74

affirmative action program 74

sexual harassment 75

hostile work environment 75

dual relationship 75

unethical dual relationship 75

fraud 76

accounting fraud 77

marketing fraud 78

puffery 78

implied falsity 78

literally false 79

labeling issue 79

consumer fraud 79

insider trading 81

intellectual property rights 82

privacy issue 83

RESOLVING ETHICAL BUSINESS CHALLENGES*

Daniel just graduated from Michigan University and landed a job as a copywriter at Young, Olsen, Lindle, and Olson (YOLO) Advertising assigned to one of the subsidiary accounts of Delicious Uber Bacon Ingredients Extraordinaire Corporation. This conglomerate was primarily a food processing manufacturer beginning one hundred years ago with pork in the Midwest. Overall corporate sales of beef, chicken, pork, and seafood were more than $750 million each year. YOLO considered many advertising options and opted for a celebrity spokesperson. That meant Daniel would work with Gloria Kunies as the celebrity endorser. Ms. Kunies is a well-known, well-loved, young, and vibrant actress with a large younger following.

Chloe, President of YOLO, asked Daniel to step into her office. "Daniel, this new account is a good start for you. We usually don't let our new copywriters handle accounts by themselves, but you have proven to be a capable employee. Your job on this account is to write copy for the commercials using Ms. Kunies' product testimonials. The copy needs to be crafted as a testimonial, targeting the market of seventeen to thirty-year-olds. Ms. Kunies already signed an affidavit as to being a bona fide user of the product. The scripts should feature her testifying to the quality, value, and tastiness of the bacon. I want you to meet her tomorrow so you can start the writing process and understand her personality in order to script the messages. Spend the rest of the day immersing yourself in her biography and researching her on the Internet." As Daniel left Chloe's office he remembered a Facebook post about Ms. Kunies being a vegetarian.

The next day at their meeting, Daniel asked her if she had actually tasted the bacon. Ms. Kunies replied, "Why yes, technically and legally I have tried Uber. In fact, I've been a huge fan since I was a kid. Bacon is my favorite food. I've done several testimonials in the past and know the American Advertising Federation (AAF) rules. I know as long as my comments are based on verifiable personal use, the message cannot be challenged as deceptive. In fact, Uber bacon has been a favorite of mine since I was young. It wasn't until a month ago I became a vegetarian. Eating all that bacon for decades really did a number on my cholesterol."

"So, you feel comfortable about endorsing Uber even though you don't eat it now?" asked Daniel.

"No question about it. As far as bacon goes, Uber is second to none in taste. If people are going to eat bacon, why not eat the best? Even if it is a heart attack waiting to happen," Ms. Kunies joked.

The next day Chloe asked Daniel how it went. He explained their conversation and expressed concern over the fact Ms. Kunies is currently a vegetarian, and she attributed her high cholesterol to Uber bacon. Daniel felt relief when he saw the concern in Chloe's face, but soon realized her concern was about Ms. Kunies pulling out of the advertisement. Daniel reassured Chloe Ms. Kunies still wanted to promote the product, but it seemed like a contradiction to have a vegetarian promoting bacon. Chloe responded by saying as long as Ms. Kunies had eaten the bacon at some point in her life and thinks it is a good product, it makes no difference as to whether she currently eats the bacon. She continued, "Sometimes in advertising, you have to add a spin to the message you are communicating so it fits with the product you are selling. Not only are you selling a product, but more importantly, you are selling an experience, a feeling, an idea that appeals to consumers."

As Daniel walked home that evening, he wondered how he was going to write this advertisement. He did not want to begin his career in a dishonest manner, but he also wanted to produce work that pleased his boss. He tried to think of creative ways to mask the contradiction of the advertisement. Maybe with humor? He asked himself if this approach would still feel dishonest. The next morning Daniel was going to meet with both Ms. Kunies and Chloe about what he had written thus far.

QUESTIONS | EXERCISES

1. Describe the ethical issues that David is encountering.
2. Does this situation in any way violate the concepts of fairness, honesty, and integrity?

3. If the advertisement does not violate any laws, then why should Daniel be concerned? What are the possible consequences of the advertisement?

*This case is strictly hypothetical; any resemblance to real persons, companies, or situations is coincidental.

> > > CHECK YOUR EQ

Check your EQ, or Ethics Quotient, by completing the following. Assess your performance to evaluate your overall understanding of the chapter material.

1. Business can be considered a game people play, like basketball or boxing.	Yes	No
2. Key ethical issues in an organization relate to fraud, discrimination, honesty and fairness, conflicts of interest, and privacy.	Yes	No
3. Only 10 percent of employees observe abusive behavior in the workplace.	Yes	No
4. Fraud occurs when a false impression exists, which conceals facts.	Yes	No
5. Time theft is the most commonly observed type of misconduct.	Yes	No

ANSWERS 1. No. People are not economically self-sufficient and cannot withdraw from the game of business. 2. Yes. Fraud, discrimination, honesty and fairness, conflicts of interest, and privacy are some key ethical issues that businesses face. 3. No. According to Table 3–1, 21 percent of employees observe abusive behavior in the workplace. 4. No. Fraud must be purposeful rather than accidental, and exists when deception and manipulation of facts are concealed to create a false impression that causes harm. 5. Yes. The most observed form of misconduct in Table 3–1 is misuse of company time.

ENDNOTES

1. James R. Hagerty, "Caterpillar Closes Plant in Canada After Lockout," *The Wall Street Journal*, February 4, 2012, http://online.wsj.com/article/SB1000142405297020388990 4577200953014575964.html (accessed February 14, 2013).

2. Peter Elkind, David Whitford, and Doris Burke, "An Accident Waiting to Happen," *Fortune* February 7, 2011, 106–132.

3. Vernon R. Loucks, Jr., "A CEO Looks at Ethics," *Business Horizons* 30 (1987): 4.

4. Eric H. Beversluis, "Is There No Such Thing as Business Ethics?" *Journal of Business Ethics 6* (1987): 81–88. Reprinted with permission of Kluwer Academic Publishers, Dordrecht, Holland.

5. Carolyn Said, "Ellison Hones His 'Art of War' Tactics," *San Francisco Chronicle*, June 10, 2003, A1.

6. Michael Liedtke, "Oracle CO to Pay $122M to Settle Lawsuit," Associated Press, *USA Today* November 22, 2005, http://usatoday30.usatoday.com/tech/2005-11-22-ellison-oracle-stock-settlement_x.htm (accessed April 22, 2013).

7. Jennifer Liberto, "CEO pay is 380 times average worker's – AFL-CIO," *CNNMoney*, April 19, 2012, http://money. cnn.com/2012/04/19/news/economy/ceo-pay/index.htm (accessed March 21, 2013).

8. "Caterpillar Earnings Hit by China," *CNBC* January 28, 2013, http://www.cnbc.com/id/100408972 (accessed April 17, 2013); Jaclyn Jaeger, "Top Shareholder Issues for 2012 Proxy Season," *Compliance Week*, March 8, 2012, http://www. complianceweek.com/top-shareholder-issues-for-2012-proxy-season/article/231150/ (accessed April 17, 2013).

9. William Atkinson, "Stealing time," *BNet*, November 2006, http://findarticles.com/p/articles/mi_qa5332/ is_11_53/ai_n29304996/?tag=content;col1 (accessed February 17, 2011).

10. "Proper Use of Company, Customer, and Supplier Resources," Boeing, April 8, 2011, http://www.boeing. com/assets/pdf/companyoffices/aboutus/ethics/pro10.pdf (accessed April 22, 2013).

11. Adam Piore, "Kick Me or Don't," *Bloomberg Businessweek*, November 26–December 2, 2012 93–95. Melissa Korn, "Bullying is a Buzzkill for Collegues, Too," www.wsj.com, July 18, 2012, http://blogs.wsj. com/atwork/2012/07/18/bullying-is-a-buzzkill-for-colleagues-too/ (accessed December 13, 2012); Canadian Centre for Occupational Health and Safety, "Bullying in the Workplace," www.ccohs.ca, http://www.ccohs. ca/oshanswers/psychosocial/bullying.html (accessed January 31, 2013); Anita Bruzzese, Gannett, "On the Job: How to Battle Bullying at Work," www.usatoday. com, December 9, 2012, http://www.usatoday.com/ story/money/columnist/bruzzese/2012/12/05/on-the-job-bully-workplace/1749697/ (accessed December 13, 2012); Anita Bruzzese, "Workplace Becomes New Schoolyard for Bullies, www.usatoday.com, August 24, 2011, http://usatoday30.usatoday.com/money/ jobcenter/workplace/bruzzese/2011-08-24-bully-bosses-overtake-workplace_n.htm (accessed February 5, 2013); Emily Kimber. "Dealing with Workplace Bullies," www. canadianliving.com, *http://www.canadianliving.com/ life/work/dealing_with_workplace_bullies.php* (accessed February 5, 2013); Suzanne Lucas, "Why Workplace Bullying Should Be Legal," *Money Watch*, March 23,

2011, http://www.cbsnews.com/8301-505125_162-44941976/why-workplace-bullying-should-be-legal/ (accessedFebruary 5, 2013).

12. I. Niedhammer, S. David, S. Degioanni, A. Drummond, and P. Philip, "Workplace bullying and sleep disturbances: Findings from a large-scale cross-sectional survey in the French working population," *Sleep* (2009) 32 (9): 1211–1219.

13. Isiah Carey, "Corporate Bullying Affects 1 in 3: Stats," *Fox News Houston*, November 18, 2010, http://www. myfoxdetroit.com/dpp/news/national/corporate-bullying-affects-1-in-3-stats-20101118-wpms (accessed February 11, 2011).

14. M. Claybourn (2011). "Relationships Between Moral Disengagement, Work Characteristics and Workplace Harassment," *Journal of Business Ethics* 100, 283–301.

15. "Healthy Workplace Bill," http://www. healthyworkplacebill.org/index.php (accessed April 19, 2013).

16. Barbara Safani, "Bullying at Work a Growing Trend," *AOL Jobs* January 24, 2011, http://jobs.aol.com/ articles/2011/01/24/bullying-at-work-a-growing-trend/ (accessed April 27, 2011).

17. Edward Moyer, "Steve Jobs threatened Palm with patents in antitrust case, says court filing, *CBS News*, January 23, 2013, http://www.cbsnews.com/8301-205_162-57565377/ steve-jobs-threatened-palm-with-patents-in-antitrust-case-says-court-filing/ (accessed April 17, 2013).

18. "GAO Document B-295402," Lockheed Martin Corporation, February 18, 2005, http://www.gao.gov/ decisions/bidpro/295402.htm (accessed August 5, 2009).

19. Samuel Rubenfeld, "The Morning Risk Report: Bribery Act Review Considers Facilitation Payment Exception," *The Wall Street Journal*, May 31, 2013, http://blogs.wsj. com/riskandcompliance/2013/05/31/the-morning-risk-report-bribery-act-review-considers-facilitation-payment-exception/ (accessed June 14, 2013).

20. Chad Bray, "Ralph Lauren Corp. Settles Bribe Probe," *The Wall Street Journal*, April 22, 2013, http://online.wsj.com/ article/SB10001424127887324235304578438704093187288.html?mod=googlenews_wsj (accessed April 23, 2013).

21. Leslie Wayne, "Hits, and Misses, in a War on Bribery," *The New York Times*, March 10, 2012, http://www.nytimes. com/2012/03/11/business/corporate-bribery-war-has-hits-and-a-few-misses.html?pagewanted=all&_r=0 (accessed April 17, 2013).

22. United States Department of Justice, "Foreign Corrupt Practices Act Anti-bribery Provisions," http://www. justice.gov/criminal/fraud/fcpa/docs/lay-persons-guide. pdf (accessed February 17, 2011).

23. Maaike Noordhuis, "Philips Pays $4.5 Million to Settle Poland Bribery Case with SEC," *Bloomberg Businessweek*, April 9, 2013, http://www.businessweek.com/news/2013-04-09/philips-pays-4-dot-5-million-to-settle-poland-bribery-case-with-sec (accessed April 17, 2013).

24. Ira Winkler, *Corporate Espionage: What Is It, Why It's Happening in Your Company, What You Must Do about It* (New York: Prima, 1997).

25. Jun Yang and Kyunghee Park, "The Curious Case of Samsung's Missing TVs," *Bloomberg Businessweek*, December 3–December 9, 2012, 19–20.

26. Andrew Harris, "Ex-Motorola Worker Guilty of Trade Secret Theft, Judge Rules," *Bloomberg Businessweek*, February 13, 2012, http://www.businessweek.com/news/2012-02-13/ex-motorola-worker-guilty-of-trade-secret-theft-judge-rules.html (accessed April 17, 2013).

27. Develin Barrett, "Hackers Penetrate Nasdaq Computers," *The Wall Street Journal*, February 5, 2011, http://online.wsj.com/article/SB10001424052748704709304576124502351634690.html (accessed February 10, 2011).

28. U.S. Equal Employment Opportunity Commission, "Charge Statistics," http://eeoc.gov/eeoc/statistics/enforcement/charges.cfm (accessed April 17, 2013).

29. "Black millionaire: Fortune 500 CEOs," *Rolling Out*, http://rollingout.com/business/executive-suite/black-millionaire-fortune-500-ceos/ (accessed April 17, 2013).

30. Ann Brenoff, "Age Discrimination: Older Workers Worry about Hiring Bias," *The Huffington Post*, October 8, 2012, http://www.huffingtonpost.com/2012/10/08/ageism_n_1881619.html (accessed April 17, 2013).

31. "AARP Best Employers for Workers over 50: About the Program," *AARP* September 2009, http://www.aarp.org/work/employee-benefits/info-09-2009/about_the_best_employers_program.html (accessed February 18, 2011).

32. "What Is Affirmative Action?" *HR Content Library*, October 12, 2001, http://www.hrnext.com/content/view.cfm?articles_id=2007&subs_id=32 (accessed August 5, 2009).

33. "What Affirmative Action Is (and What It Is Not)," *National Partnership for Women & Families*, http://www.nationalpartnership.org/site/DocServer/AffirmativeActionFacts.pdf?docID=861 (accessed August 5, 2009).

34. Debbie M. Thorne, O. C. Ferrell, and Linda Ferrell, *Business and Society: A Strategic Approach to Social Responsibility and Ethics*, 4 th ed. (Mason, OH: South-Western Cengage Learning, 2011), 182.

35. U.S. Equal Employment Opportunity Commission, "Outback Steakhouse to Pay $65, 000 to Settle EEOC Disability Discrimination Lawsuit," March 22, 2013, http://www.eeoc.gov/eeoc/newsroom/release/3-22-13.cfm (accessed April 17, 2013).

36. Paula N. Rubin, "Civil Rights and Criminal Justice: Primer on Sexual Harassment Series: NIJ Research in Action," October 1995, http://www.ncjrs.org/txtfiles/harass.txt (accessed August 5, 2009).

37. U.S. Equal Employment Opportunity Commission, "Sexual Harassment Charges," http://www.eeoc.gov/eeoc/statistics/enforcement/sexual_harassment.cfm (accessed April 17, 2013).

38. Steve Stecklow, "Sexual Harassment Cases Plague UN," *The Wall Street Journal*, May 21, 2009, http://online.wsj.com/article/SB124233350385520879.html (accessed April 17, 2013).

39. *Zabkowicz v. West Bend Co.*, 589 F. Supp. 780, 784, 35 EPD Par.34, 766 (E.D. Wis.1984).

40. Iddo Landau, "The Law and Sexual Harassment," *Business Ethics Quarterly* 15, no. 2 (2005): 531–536.

41. "Enhancements and Justice: Problems in Determining the Requirements of Justice in a Genetically Transformed Society," *Kennedy Institute Ethics Journal* 15, no. 1 (2005): 3–38.

42. Association of Certified Fraud Examiners, *Report to the Nations on Occupational Fraud and Abuse: 2012 Global Fraud Study*, 4.

43. Nate Raymond, "NY judge approves $115 million AIG shareholder settlement," *Reuters*, April 10, 2013, http://www.reuters.com/article/2013/04/10/us-aig-settlement-idUSBRE93913H20130410 (accessed April 17, 2013).

44. Cassell Bryan-Low, "Accounting Firms Face Backlash over the Tax Shelters They Sold," *The Wall Street Journal* online, February 7, 2003, http://online.wsj.com/article/SB1044568358985594893.html?mod=googlewsj (accessed August 5, 2009).

45. U.S. Securities and Exchange Commission, "SEC Charges New York-Based Private Equity Fund Advisers With Misleading Investors About Valuation and Performance," March 11, 2013, http://www.sec.gov/news/press/2013/2013-38.htm (accessed April 17, 2013); Dan Primack, "Oppenheimer admits to misleading investors," *CNN*, March 11, 2013, http://finance.fortune.cnn.com/2013/03/11/sec-charges-oppenheimer-with-misleading-investors/ (accessed April 17, 2013).

46. *Gillette Co. v. Wilkinson Sword, Inc.*, 89-CV-3586, 1991 U.S. Dist. Lexis 21006, *6 (S.D.N.Y. January 9, 1991).

47. Archie B. Carroll, *Business and Society: Ethics and Stakeholder Management* (Cincinnati: South-Western, 1989), 228–230.

48. "Monster to label caffeine content on energy drinks," *CBS News* February 14, 2013, http://www.cbsnews.com/8301-204_162-57569470/monster-to-label-caffeine-content-on-energy-drinks/ (accessed April 17, 2013).

49. Pierre Thomas, "Shoplifting on the Rise as Thieves Swipe Small, Pricey Items for Resale," *ABC News*, October 26, 2012, http://abcnews.go.com/blogs/headlines/2012/10/shoplifting-on-the-rise-as-thieves-swipe-small-pricey-items-for-resale/ (accessed April 17, 2013).

50. Caroline Winter, "When Christmas Brings Retailers Many Unhappy Returns," *Bloomberg Businessweek*, December 30, 2012, http://www.businessweek.com/articles/2012-12-30/when-christmas-brings-retailers-many-unhappy-returns (accessed April 17, 2013).

51. Richard Esposito, "Thain Tells All on Merrill Lynch Bonuses," *ABC News*, February 25, 2009, http://abcnews.go.com/Blotter/WallStreet/story?id=6959962&page=1 (accessed February 21, 2011).

52. Damian Paletta, Maya Jackson Randall, and Michael R. Crittenden, "Geithner Calls for Tougher Standards on Risk," *The Wall Street Journal*, March 25, 2009, http://online.wsj.com/article/SB123807231255147603.html (accessed April 14, 2011).

53. Jennifer Liberto and David Ellis, "Wall Street reform: What's in the bill," *CNNMoney.com*, June 30, 2010, http://money.cnn.com/2010/06/25/news/economy/whats_in_the_reform_bill/index.htm (accessed February 14, 2011).

54. Chad Bray, "Former Hedge-Fund Manager Is Sentenced," *The Wall Street Journal*, January 25, 2013, C3.

55. Jason Zweig, "Insider Trading: Why We Can't Help Ourselves," *The Wall Street Journal*, April 2, 2011, http://online.wsj.com/article/SB10001424052748704530204576236922024758718.html (accessed April 27, 2011).

56. Anna Wilde Mathews, "Copyrights on Web Content Are Backed," *The Wall Street Journal*, October 27, 2000, B10.

57. Jennifer Martinez, "Report: One-fourth of web traffic is pirated content," Politico.com, February 21, 2011, http://hamptonroads.com/2011/02/report-onefourth-web-traffic-pirated-content (accessed February 21, 2011).

58. Roger Bate, "China's Bad Medicine," *The Wall Street Journal*, May 5, 2009, http://online.wsj.com/article/SB124146383501884323.html (accessed August 5, 2009); "Chinese Intellectual Property Violations," *Idea Buyer*, http://www.ideabuyer.com/news/chinese-intellectual-property-violations/ (accessedAugust 5, 2009).

59. Kirsten Robertson, Lisa McNeill, James Green, and Claire Roberts, "Illegal Downloading, Ethical Concern, and Illegal Behavior," *Journal of Business Ethics* 108 (2012), 215–227.

60. Deli Yang, Mahmut Sonmez, Derek Bosworth, and Gerald Fryzell, "Global Software Piracy: Searching for Further Explanations," *Journal of Business Ethics*, September 2008.

61. Still murky," *The Economist*, April 21, 2012, http://www.economist.com/node/21553040 (accessed April 19, 2013).

62. Nora J. Rifon, Robert LaRose, and Sejung Marina Choi, "Your Privacy Is Sealed: Effects of Web Privacy Seals on Trust and Personal Disclosures," *Journal of Consumer Affairs* 39, no. 2 (2002): 339–362.

63. "2005 Electronic Monitoring and Surveillance Survey: Many Companies Monitoring, Recording, Videotaping—and Firing—Employees," *The New York Times*, May 18, 2005, via http://www.amanet.org/press/amanews/ems05.htm (accessed August 5, 2009).

64. Ruth Mantell, "Watch Your E-mails. Your Boss Is," *The Wall Street Journal*, May 2, 2010, http://online.wsj.com/article/SB127277297445285515.html (accessed February 14, 2011).

65. Mitch Wagner, "Google's Pixie Dust," *InformationWeek*, Issue 1061 (2005): 98.

66. Stephenie Steitzer, "Commercial Web Sites Cut Back on Collections of Personal Data," *Wall Street Journal*, March 28, 2002, http://online.wsj.com/article/SB1017247161553469240.html?mod=googlewsj (accessed August 5, 2009).

67. Kate Rogers, "One New Identity Theft Victim Every 3 Seconds in 2012," *Fox Business*, February 20, 2013, http://www.foxbusiness.com/personal-finance/2013/02/20/one-new-identity-theft-victim-every-3-seconds-in-2012/ (accessed April 17, 2013).

68. Ben Worthen, "Hackers Aren't Only Threat to Privacy," *The Wall Street Journal*, June 22, 2010, http://online.wsj.com/article/SB10001424052748704122904575314703487356896.html (accessed February 14, 2011).

69. "Obesity and Overweight," *Centers for Disease Control*, June 18, 2010, http://www.cdc.gov/nchs/fastats/overwt.htm (accessed February 21, 2011).

70. Cynthia Ogden, Ph.D., and Margaret Carroll, M.S.P.H., "Prevalence of Obesity among Children and Adolescents: United States, Trends 1962–1965 through 2007–2008." *CDC Division of Health and Nutrition Examination Surveys*, June 2010, http://www.cdc.gov/nchs/data/hestat/obesity_child_07_08/obesity_child_07_08.pdf (accessed February 21, 2011).

CHAPTER 4

THE INSTITUTIONALIZATION OF BUSINESS ETHICS

CHAPTER OBJECTIVES

- Distinguish between the voluntary and mandated boundaries of ethical conduct
- Provide specific mandated requirements for legal compliance in specific subject matter areas related to competition, consumers, and safety
- Specifically address the requirements of the Sarbanes–Oxley legislation and implementation by the Securities and Exchange Commission
- Describe the passage of the Dodd–Frank Wall Street Reform and Consumer Protection Act along with some of its major provisions
- Provide an overview of regulatory efforts that provide incentives for ethical behavior
- Provide an overview of the recommendations and incentives for developing an ethical corporate culture contained in the Federal Sentencing Guidelines for Organizations
- Provide an overview of highly appropriate core practices and their relationship to social responsibility

AN ETHICAL DILEMMA*

One year out of the Pennsylvania university system, Randy was hired by Meeker, a medical warehouse that provides pharmaceutical products to various hospitals and clinics within a three state area. Meeker was the dominant company in the market. Equipped with his BS degree, Randy was eager to learn, get ahead, and begin his career. As a new employee, he was required to go through extensive training to learn about hospital and clinic regulations, laws, various system procedures, and software applications. The two-month training included descriptions of the usual type of emergencies experienced in clinics and hospitals and what the needs were concerning equipment and supplies. He learned how to use various products and equipment and to train others in these areas. Part of his training was working in all areas of the medical warehouse.

One day Randy's supervisor, Cheryl, brought him into her office to discuss his next assignment. She explained to him that several of the hospitals they serve were about to begin their annual inventory counts. When these inventory counts occur, a representative from Meeker must go into the hospitals and replace all expired supplies and equipment with new ones.

"One of the problems we've been having is the expiration dates on the products we supply are shorter than those of our competitors," Cheryl explained. "To keep our clients loyal, we offer a credit to our clients when we take back the expired products. Unfortunately, that's caused us to lose profits."

Cheryl paused for a moment, then continued. "We can't keep losing profits like this, so I've developed an idea for cutting costs and increasing our competitive advantage."

Cheryl handed several sheets of sticky labels to Randy. He looked them over and found they were exact replicas of the labels on their medical products for over-the-counter medications. The expiration dates on these labels were three months from the current date. Randy looked at Cheryl for more of an explanation.

Cheryl turned to Randy and told him to replace the old labels with the new ones and leave the inventory in the hospitals. Randy began to get uncomfortable.

"But Cheryl, couldn't this be dangerous if the hospital uses expired products?"

Cheryl shook her head. "You don't have to worry. Our competitors offer similar products with a longer expiration date, and there's really no harm in using these products after their expiration date. They are just a little less potent, but not more harmful in any way."

Randy took the labels and headed to the hospitals. As he drove, he went over the instructions in his head. Something about this made him feel uneasy, but he also understood there was no harm in changing the labels. In fact, there were times he remembered taking expired over-the-counter medication himself and it didn't hurt him in any way. Additionally, he would only be extending the date by three months, which is not a long time for medications.

On the other hand, he recalled a moment from his training when he was cautioned about expired medical products. Thinking back, Randy only recalled being cautioned against using expired prescription medications, not anything about over-the-counter medications. Randy also wondered if he would be questioned by the hospital administration staff when he asked for their signature on the inventory paperwork. He knew they would find it odd if there were no credits to their account for expired medications. How would he explain the "new policy" to them without being dishonest?

QUESTIONS | EXERCISES

1. How should Randy deal with the dilemma he is facing?
2. What are the implications of comparing Meeker's practices with those of its competitors?
3. What kind of responsibility does Randy have to the different stakeholders involved in this situation? Does his responsibility to Meeker differ from his responsibility to the hospitals?

*This case is strictly hypothetical; any resemblance to real persons, companies, or situations is coincidental.

To understand the institutionalization of business ethics, it is important to understand the voluntary and legally mandated dimensions of organizational practices. In addition, there are core practices, sometimes called best practices most responsible firms—those trying to achieve acceptable conduct—embrace and implement. The effective organizational practice of business ethics requires all three dimensions (legal, voluntary, and core practices) be integrated into an ethics and compliance program. This integration creates an ethical culture that effectively manages the risks of misconduct. Institutionalization relates to legal and societal forces that provide both rewards and punishment to organizations based on stakeholder evaluations of specific conduct. Institutionalization in business ethics relates to established laws, customs, and expected organizational programs considered normative in establishing reputation. This means deviations from expected conduct are often considered ethical issues and are therefore a concern to stakeholders. Institutions provide requirements, structure, and societal expectations that reward and sanction ethical decision making. For example, institutions such as federal regulatory agencies establish rules for appropriate conduct and even suggest core practices for ethical cultures.

In this chapter, we examine the boundaries of ethical conduct and focus on voluntary and core practices and mandated requirements for legal compliance—three important areas in developing an ethical culture. In particular, we concentrate on compliance in specific areas related to competition, consumers, and safety. We consider the requirements of the Sarbanes–Oxley legislation, its implementation by the Securities and Exchange Commission (SEC), and how its implementation has affected companies. We also examine the Dodd–Frank legislation and its rules affecting the finance industry. We provide an overview of the Federal Sentencing Guidelines for Organizations (FSGO), along with recommendations and incentives for developing an ethical corporate culture. The FSGO, the Sarbanes–Oxley Act and Dodd–Frank legislation, and industry trade associations, as well as societal expectations, support core practices. Finally, we examine voluntary responsibilities and look at how cause-related marketing and strategic philanthropy can be an important core competency in managing stakeholder relationships.

MANAGING ETHICAL RISK THROUGH MANDATED AND VOLUNTARY PROGRAMS

Table 4–1 provides an overview of the three dimensions of institutionalization. **Voluntary practices** include the beliefs, values, and voluntary contractual obligations of a business. All businesses engage in some level of commitment to voluntary activities to benefit both internal and external stakeholders. Google works hard to give its employees a positive work environment through its benefits package. In addition to being a famously great place to work, Google offices offer such amenities as swimming pools, gyms, volleyball courts, ping-pong tables, and dance classes. The company even allows employees to bring their dogs to work.[1] Most firms engage in **philanthropy**—giving back to communities and causes. There is strong evidence to suggest both the law and a sense of ethics increase voluntary corporate social responsibility practices. In addition, research has demonstrated that when both ethical and legal responsibilities are respected through core practices, economic performance benefits.[2]

TABLE 4-1 Voluntary Boundary, Core Practices, and Mandated Boundaries of Ethical Decisions

Voluntary boundary	A management-initiated boundary of conduct (beliefs, values, voluntary policies, and voluntary contractual obligations)
Core practice	A highly appropriate and common practice that helps ensure compliance with legal requirements, industry self-regulation, and societal expectations
Mandated boundary	An externally imposed boundary of conduct (laws, rules, regulations, and other requirements)

© Cengage Learning 2015

Source: Based on the "Open Compliance Ethics Group (OCEG) Foundation Guidelines," v1.0, Steering Committee Update, December 2005, Phoenix, AZ.

Core practices are documented best practices, often encouraged by legal and regulatory forces as well as industry trade associations. The Better Business Bureau is a leading self-regulatory body that provides directions for managing customer disputes and reviews advertising cases. Core practices are appropriate and common practices that ensure compliance with legal requirements and societal expectations. Although these practices are not enforced, there are consequences for not engaging in them when misconduct occurs. For example, the Federal Sentencing Guidelines for Organizations (FSGO) suggest the governing authority (board of directors) be responsible for and assess an organization's ethical and compliance activities. No reporting or investigation is required by government regulatory bodies, but there are incentives for the firms that effectively implement this recommendation. For example, if misconduct occurs, firms may have opportunities to avoid serious punishment. On the other hand, if the board has made no effort to oversee ethics and compliance, its failure could increase and compound the level of punishment the company suffers. In this way, in institutionalizing core practices the government provides organizations with the opportunity to structure their own approaches and only takes action if violations occur. Mandated boundaries are externally imposed boundaries of conduct, such as laws, rules, regulations, and other requirements. Antitrust and consumer protection laws create boundaries that must be respected by companies.

Organizations need to maintain an ethical culture and manage stakeholder expectations for appropriate conduct. They achieve these ends through corporate governance, compliance, risk management, and voluntary activities. The development of these drivers of an ethical culture has been institutionally supported by government initiatives and the demands of stakeholders. The compliance element represents areas that must conform to existing legal and regulatory requirements. Established laws and regulatory decisions leave limited flexibility to organizations in adhering to these standards. Corporate governance (as discussed in Chapter 2) is structured by a governing authority that provides oversight as well as checks and balances to make sure that the organization meets its goals and objectives for ethical performance. Risk management analyzes the probability or chance that misconduct could occur based on the nature of the business and its exposure to risky events. Voluntary activities often represent the values and responsibilities that firms accept in contributing to stakeholder needs and expectations.

Figure 4-1 depicts the key elements of an organizational culture. These elements include values, norms, artifacts, and behavior. An ethical culture creates an environment to structure behavior that is evaluated by stakeholders. As mentioned in previous chapters, values are broad and viewed as long-term enduring beliefs about issues such as integrity, trust,

FIGURE 4–1 **Elements of an Ethical Culture**

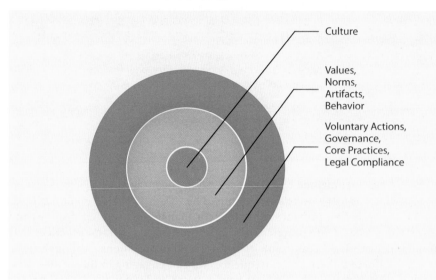

Culture

Values,
Norms,
Artifacts,
Behavior

Voluntary Actions,
Governance,
Core Practices,
Legal Compliance

openness, diversity, and individual respect and responsibility. Norms dictate and clarify desirable behaviors through principles, rules, policies, and procedures. For example, norms provide guiding principles for anti-bribery issues, sustainability, and conflicts of interest. Artifacts are visible, tangible external symbols of values and norms. Websites, codes of ethics, rituals, language, and physical settings are artifacts. These three elements have different impacts on behaviors. Organizational decisions on such issues as governance, codes of ethics, ethics training, and legal compliance are shaped by the ethical culture.

MANDATED REQUIREMENTS FOR LEGAL COMPLIANCE

Laws and regulations are established by governments to set minimum standards for responsible behavior—society's codification of what is right and wrong. Laws regulating business conduct are passed because some stakeholders believe business cannot be trusted to do what is right in certain areas, such as consumer safety and environmental protection. Because public policy is dynamic and often changes in response to business abuses and consumer demands for safety and equality, many laws have been passed to resolve specific problems and issues. But the opinions of society, as expressed in legislation, can change over time, and different courts and state legislatures may take diverging views. For example, the thrust of most business legislation can be summed up as follows: Any practice is permitted that does not substantially lessen or reduce competition or harm consumers or society. Courts differ, however, in their interpretations of what constitutes a "substantial" reduction of competition. Laws can help businesspeople determine what society believes at a certain time, but what is legally wrong today may be perceived as acceptable tomorrow, and vice versa.

Instructions to employees to "just obey the law" are meaningless without experience and effective training in dealing with specific legal risk areas. One area that illustrates the complexity of the law is patents. Large technology companies aggressively defend their patents in order to maintain their strategic advantages. Lawsuits among direct competitors in hardware and software have shifted to the mobile industry as technology companies fight to come out on top. For example, Motorola Mobility accused Apple, Inc., of using features on its iPhones that are protected under Motorola's patents.[3] Patent issues have become so important that some firms, such as IBM and Qualcomm, have created their own patent licensing businesses.[4]

Laws are categorized as either civil or criminal. Civil law defines the rights and duties of individuals and organizations (including businesses). Criminal law not only prohibits specific actions—such as fraud, theft, or securities trading violations—but also imposes fines or imprisonment as punishment for breaking the law. The primary difference between criminal and civil law is the state or nation enforces criminal laws, whereas individuals (generally, in court) enforce civil laws. Criminal and civil laws are derived from four sources: the U.S. Constitution (constitutional law), precedents established by judges (common law), federal and state laws or statutes (statutory law), and federal and state administrative agencies (administrative law). Federal administrative agencies established by Congress control and influence business by enforcing laws and regulations to encourage competition and to protect consumers, workers, and the environment. The Consumer Financial Protection Bureau was established after the latest financial crisis, which resulted in many consumers losing their homes. State and local laws and regulatory agencies also exist to achieve these objectives.

The primary method of resolving conflicts and serious business ethics disputes is through lawsuits, or when one individual or organization uses civil laws to take another individual or organization to court. However, businesses often want to avoid lawsuits if possible because of the high costs involved. For instance, Hon Hai Precision Industry Company signed a deal with Microsoft to license technology covered by Microsoft patents. Microsoft claims makers of Android devices have been using software elements Microsoft has already patented. By licensing Microsoft technology and paying royalties, Hon Hai reduces the risk of future litigation with Microsoft.[5] To avoid lawsuits and maintain the standards necessary to reduce risk and create an ethical culture, both legal and organizational standards must be enforced. When violations of organizational standards occur, the National Business Ethics Survey (NBES) notes many employees do not feel their company has a strong ethics program. On the other hand, effective ethics programs reduce misconduct. Figure 4–2 demonstrates how well-implemented ethics programs decrease ethical risks within an organization. It is therefore important for a company to have a functioning ethics program in place long before an ethical disaster strikes.

The role of laws is not so much to distinguish what is ethical or unethical as to determine the appropriateness of specific activities or situations. In other words, laws establish the basic ground rules for responsible business activities. Most of the laws and regulations that govern business activities fall into one of five groups: (1) regulation of competition, (2) protection of consumers, (3) promotion of equity and safety, (4) protection of the natural environment, and (5) incentives to encourage organizational compliance programs to deter misconduct that we will examine later.

Laws Regulating Competition

The issues surrounding the impact of competition on businesses' social responsibility arise from the rivalry among businesses for customers and profits. When businesses compete unfairly, legal and social responsibility issues can result. Intense competition sometimes

FIGURE 4–2 Well-Implemented Ethics Programs and Strong Cultures Reduce Risk

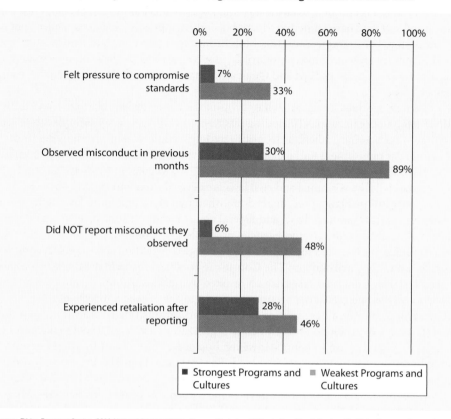

Source: Ethics Resource Center, *2011 National Business Ethics Survey: Workplace Ethics In Transition* (Arlington, VA: Ethics Resource Center, 2012), p. 35.

makes managers feel their company's survival is threatened. In these situations, managers may begin to see unacceptable alternatives as acceptable, and they begin engaging in questionable practices to ensure the survival of their organizations. Both Intel and Microsoft have been hit with fines amounting to billions of dollars for alleged antitrust activity in Europe. The European Union is famous for being tough on companies suspected of antitrust activities. For instance, Google came under investigation for allegedly manipulating search engine results so its paid services were favored over those of its rivals. This and other potential violations caused the EU to examine whether Google was competing fairly with its rivals. Google attempted to make changes to the look of its search engine to try and decrease fears it is unfairly harming competitors.[6] Being aware of antitrust laws is important for all large corporations around the world.

Size frequently gives some companies an advantage over others. Large firms can often generate economies of scale (for example, by forcing their suppliers to lower their prices) that allow them to put smaller firms out of business. Consequently, small companies and even whole communities may resist the efforts of firms like Walmart, Home Depot, and Best Buy to open stores in their vicinity. These firms' sheer size enables them to operate at such low costs that small, local firms often cannot compete. Some companies' competitive strategies may focus on weakening or destroying a competitor; that harms competition and ultimately reduces consumer choice. Many countries have laws restricting such anticompetitive behavior. For instance, China's economic planning agency is attempting to move closer toward international laws by creating new rules against price collusion that occurs when businesses get together and inflate prices above what they would be if each business priced its products independently.[7] Other examples of anticompetitive strategies include sustained price cuts, discriminatory pricing, and bribery. While the U.S. Justice Department aggressively enforces the Foreign Corrupt Practices Act prohibiting bribery of foreign government officials, the U.K. has even more sweeping anti-bribery laws. These laws apply to all companies doing business in Britain and prohibit bribes to foreign officials and private businesspeople. Other nations, including China, are taking a tougher stance on bribery and are prosecuting companies caught in the act.[8]

The primary objective of U.S. antitrust laws is to distinguish competitive strategies that enhance consumer welfare from those that reduce it. The difficulty of this task lies in determining whether the intent of a company's pricing policy is to weaken or even destroy a competitor.[9] President Obama took a strong position on antitrust violations, reversing the previous administration's policy that made it more difficult for the government to pursue antitrust violations. The former administration brought a historically low number of antitrust cases to trial.[10] President Obama attempted to follow Europe's model for antitrust cases, which marks a return to a historic norm after eight years of noninterventionism.[11]

Intense competition also leads companies to resort to corporate espionage. Corporate espionage is the act of illegally taking information from a corporation through computer hacking, theft, intimidation, sorting through trash, and impersonation of organizational members. Estimates show corporate espionage may cost companies nearly $50 billion annually. Unauthorized information collected includes patents in development, intellectual property, pricing strategies, customer information, unique manufacturing and technological operations, marketing plans, research and development, and future plans for market and customer expansion.[12] A former engineer at General Motors and her husband were found guilty of stealing GM trade secrets on hybrid technology and trying to sell the information to Chinese automakers. General Motors estimates the stolen trade secrets were valued at $40 million.[13] Determining an accurate amount for corporate espionage losses is difficult because most companies do not report such losses for fear the publicity will harm their stock price or encourage further break-ins. Espionage may be carried out by outsiders or employees—executives, programmers, network or computer auditors, engineers, or janitors who have legitimate reasons to access facilities, data, computers, or networks. They may use a variety of techniques for obtaining valuable information, such as dumpster diving, whacking, and hacking, as discussed in Chapter 3.

Laws have been passed to prevent the establishment of monopolies, inequitable pricing practices, and other practices that reduce or restrict competition among businesses. These laws are sometimes called **procompetitive legislation** because they were enacted to encourage competition and prevent activities that restrain trade (Table 4–2). The Sherman Antitrust Act of 1890, for example, prohibits organizations from holding monopolies in their industry, and the Robinson–Patman Act of 1936 bans price discrimination between retailers and wholesalers.

In law, however, there are always exceptions. Under the McCarran–Ferguson Act of 1944, Congress exempted the insurance industry from the Sherman Antitrust Act and other antitrust laws. Insurance companies joined together to set insurance premiums at specific industry-wide levels. However, even actions that take place under this legal

TABLE 4–2 Laws Regulating Competition

Sherman Antitrust Act, 1890	Prohibits monopolies
Clayton Act, 1914	Prohibits price discrimination, exclusive dealing, and other efforts to restrict competition
Federal Trade Commission Act, 1914	Created the Federal Trade Commission (FTC) to help enforce antitrust laws
Robinson–Patman Act, 1936	Bans price discrimination between retailers and wholesalers
Wheeler–Lea Act, 1938	Prohibits unfair and deceptive acts regardless of whether competition is injured
Lanham Act, 1946	Protects and regulates brand names, brand marks, trade names, and trademarks
Celler–Kefauver Act, 1950	Prohibits one corporation from controlling another where the effect is to lessen competition
Consumer Goods Pricing Act, 1975	Prohibits price maintenance agreements among manufacturers and resellers in interstate commerce
FTC Improvement Act, 1975	Gives the FTC more power to prohibit unfair industry practices
Antitrust Improvements Act, 1976	Strengthens earlier antitrust laws; gives Justice Department more investigative authority
Foreign Corrupt Practices Act, 1977	Makes it illegal to pay foreign government officials to facilitate business or to use third parties such as agents and consultants to provide bribes to such officials
Trademark Counterfeiting Act, 1980	Provides penalties for individuals dealing in counterfeit goods
Trademark Law Revision Act, 1988	Amends the Lanham Act to allow brands not yet introduced to be protected through patent and trademark registration
Federal Trademark Dilution Act, 1995	Gives trademark owners the right to protect trademarks and requires them to relinquish those that match or parallel existing trademarks
Digital Millennium Copyright Act, 1998	Refines copyright laws to protect digital versions of copyrighted materials, including music and movies
Controlling the Assault of Non-Solicited Pornography and Marketing Act (CAN-SPAM), 2003	Bans fraudulent or deceptive unsolicited commercial e-mail and requires senders to provide information on how recipients can opt out of receiving additional messages
Fraud Enforcement and Recovery Act, 2009	Strengthens provisions to improve the criminal enforcement of fraud laws, including mortgage fraud, securities fraud, financial institutions fraud, commodities fraud, and fraud related to the federal assistance and relief program

© Cengage Learning

"permission" could still be viewed as irresponsible and unethical if it neutralizes competition and if prices no longer reflect the true costs of insurance protection. What is legal is not always considered ethical by some interest groups. Major League Baseball has an antitrust exemption dating back to 1922. MLB is the only major sport with such a sweeping antitrust exemption, although the major effect it has on the game these days is that sports teams cannot relocate without MLB's permission.[14]

Laws Protecting Consumers

Laws that protect consumers require businesses to provide accurate information about their products and services and follow safety standards (Table 4–3). The first consumer protection law was passed in 1906, partly in response to a novel by Upton Sinclair. *The Jungle* describes, among other things, the atrocities and unsanitary conditions of the meatpacking industry in turn-of-the-century Chicago. The outraged public response to this book and other exposés

TABLE 4–3 Laws Protecting Consumers

Pure Food and Drug Act, 1906	Prohibits adulteration and mislabeling of foods and drugs sold in interstate commerce
Federal Hazardous Substances Labeling Act, 1960	Controls the labeling of hazardous substances for household use
Truth in Lending Act, 1968	Requires full disclosure of credit terms to purchasers
Consumer Product Safety Act, 1972	Created the Consumer Product Safety Commission to establish safety standards and regulations for consumer products
Fair Credit Billing Act, 1974	Requires accurate, up-to-date consumer credit records
Consumer Goods Pricing Act, 1975	Prohibits price maintenance agreements
Consumer Leasing Act, 1976	Requires accurate disclosure of leasing terms to consumers
Fair Debt Collection Practices Act, 1978	Defines permissible debt collection practices
Toy Safety Act, 1984	Gives the government the power to recall dangerous toys quickly
Nutritional Labeling and Education Act, 1990	Prohibits exaggerated health claims and requires all processed foods to have labels showing nutritional information
Telephone Consumer Protection Act, 1991	Establishes procedures for avoiding unwanted telephone solicitations
Children's Online Privacy Protection Act, 1998	Requires the FTC to formulate rules for collecting online information from children under age 13
Do Not Call Implementation Act, 2003	Directs the FCC and the FTC to coordinate so that their rules are consistent regarding telemarketing call practices including the Do Not Call Registry and other lists, as well as call abandonment
Credit Card Accountability Responsibility and Disclosure Act, 2009	Implemented strict rules on credit card companies regarding topics such as issuing credit to youth, terms disclosure, interest rates, and fees
Dodd–Frank Wall Street Reform and Consumer Protection Act (2010)	Promotes financial reform to increase accountability and transparency in the financial industry, protects consumers from deceptive financial practices, and establishes the Bureau of Consumer Financial Protection

© Cengage Learning

DEBATE ISSUE
TAKE A STAND

The Multilevel Marketing Controversy

Multilevel marketing (MLM) is a compensation method in direct selling when distributors earn income from their own sales of products as well as commissions from sales made by individuals they recruited. MLM creates internal consumption, involving purchasing products at a discount from the firm for the distributors' own use. MLM is controversial because there have been some accusations that it resembles a pyramid scheme. Pyramid schemes occur when there is no product to sell or when the product has no market value. Distributors pay a fee or make an investment when "recruited," generating money for the scheme. The scheme collapses when distributors cannot recruit anyone else. Those at the top benefit, while newer distributors lose out because the scheme is not based on selling products to consumers.

The three largest multilevel direct sellers are Avon, Amway, and Herbalife. MLM is legal because a legitimate product is sold and it is a sales compensation method. For example, Herbalife has 8 million U.S. customers that have purchased the product in three months, based on a Nielsen survey. It has 550,000 U.S, distributors, so most of its products are sold directly to consumers. Yet critics say distributors make more money from the sales of those they recruit than from selling products, although this concern has nothing to do with the implementation of a pyramid scheme. Many people enter the industry to purchase products and are not trying to earn a regular income. Oftentimes people become distributors because they enjoy using the product and often get discounts on purchases, as well as enjoying the social interaction.[19]

1. Multilevel marketing is a legitimate compensation method in direct selling.
2. Although legal, the multilevel compensation method is similar to a pyramid scheme.

of the industry resulted in the passage of the Pure Food and Drug Act. Similarly, Ralph Nader had a tremendous impact on consumer protection laws with his book *Unsafe at Any Speed.* His critique and attack on General Motors' Corvair had far-reaching effects on cars and other consumer products. Other consumer protection laws emerged from similar processes.

Large groups of people with specific vulnerabilities have been granted special levels of legal protection relative to the general population. For example, children and the elderly have received proportionately greater attention than other groups. American society responded to research and documentation showing young consumers and senior citizens encounter difficulties in the acquisition, consumption, and disposition of products. Special legal protection provided to vulnerable consumers is considered to be in the public interest.[15] For example, the Children's Online Privacy Protection Act (COPPA) requires commercial Internet sites to carry privacy policy statements, obtain parental consent before soliciting information from children under the age of 13, and provide an opportunity to remove any information provided by children using such sites. Critics of COPPA argue children aged 13 and older should not be treated as adults on the web. In a study of children ages 10 to 17, nearly half indicated they would give their name, address, and other demographic information in exchange for a gift worth $100 or more. Internet safety among children is another major topic of concern. Research shows filtering and age verification are not effective in making the Internet safer, and businesses, regulators, and parents are trying to decipher how to better protect children from dangers ranging from online predators to pornography.[16] Mobile technology also called for updates in the law. The FTC adopted changes to COPPA to account for mobile phone applications. Many standard mobile marketing practices, such as collecting location information and photos, are now considered to be personal information when applied to children under the age of 13.[17]

Seniors are another highly vulnerable demographic. New laws took aim at financial scams directed at seniors, such as free lunch seminars. The state of Arkansas took the lead on this issue, conducting police sweeps of suspected scams, increasing fines, and amending laws to impose increased penalties for those who prey on the elderly. Older people are the most vulnerable group for financial scams because they rely on their savings for retirement security.[18] The role of the FTC's Bureau of Consumer Protection is to protect consumers against unfair, deceptive, or fraudulent practices. The bureau, which enforces a variety of consumer protection laws, is divided into five divisions. The Division of Enforcement monitors compliance with and investigates violations of laws, including unfulfilled holiday delivery promises by online shopping sites, employment opportunities fraud, scholarship scams, misleading advertising for health care products, high-tech and telemarketing fraud, data security, and financial practices.

The Food and Drug Administration (FDA) regulates food safety, human drugs, tobacco, dietary supplements, vaccines, veterinary drugs, medical devices, cosmetics, products that give off radiation, and biological products. The FDA has the power to authorize the marketing of these products as well as to ban those deemed unsafe for the public.[20] For example, the FDA sent a warning to energy drink and supplement companies that use the stimulant dimethylamylamine (DMAA) in their products. The FDA found the stimulant is linked to serious health risks. Because it has not been sufficiently tested as an additive, the FDA is warning energy drink makers that products using this stimulant are illegal.[21]

Laws Promoting Equity and Safety

Laws promoting equity in the workplace were passed during the 1960s and 1970s to protect the rights of minorities, women, older persons, and persons with disabilities; other legislation sought to protect the safety of all workers (Table 4–4). Of these laws, probably the most important to business is Title VII of the Civil Rights Act, originally passed in 1964 and amended several times since. Title VII specifically prohibits discrimination in employment on the basis of race, sex, religion, color, or national origin. The Civil Rights Act also created the Equal Employment Opportunity Commission (EEOC) to enforce the provisions of Title VII. Among other things, the EEOC assists businesses in designing affirmative action programs. These programs aim to increase job opportunities for women and minorities by analyzing the present pool of employees, identifying areas where women and minorities are underrepresented, and establishing specific hiring and promotion goals, along with target dates for meeting those goals.

Other legislation addresses more specific employment practices. The Equal Pay Act of 1963 mandates that women and men who do equal work must receive equal pay. Wage differences are allowed only if they can be attributed to seniority, performance, or qualifications. The Americans with Disabilities Act of 1990 prohibits discrimination against people with disabilities. Despite these laws, inequities in the workplace still exist. Women earn an average of 77 to 82 cents for every dollar men earn.[22] The disparity in wages is higher for African American women (64 cents for every dollar a white man earns) and Hispanic women (55 cents for every dollar).[23]

Congress passed laws that seek to improve safety in the workplace. By far the most significant of these is the Occupational Safety and Health Act of 1970 that mandates employers provide safe and healthy working conditions for all workers. The Occupational Safety and Health Administration (OSHA) enforces the act and makes regular surprise inspections to ensure businesses maintain safe working environments.

TABLE 4–4 U.S. Laws Promoting Equity and Safety

Equal Pay Act of 1963	Prohibits discrimination in pay on the basis of sex
Equal Pay Act of 1963 (amended)	Prohibits sex-based discrimination in the rate of pay to men and women doing the same or similar jobs
Title VII of the Civil Rights Act of 1964 (amended in 1972)	Prohibits discrimination in employment on the basis of race, color, sex, religion, or national origin
Age Discrimination in Employment Act, 1967	Prohibits discrimination in employment against persons between the ages of 40 and 70
Occupational Safety and Health Act, 1970	Designed to ensure healthful and safe working conditions for all employees
Title IX of Education Amendments of 1972	Prohibits discrimination based on sex in education programs or activities that receive federal financial assistance
Vocational Rehabilitation Act, 1973	Prohibits discrimination in employment because of physical or mental handicaps
Vietnam Era Veterans Readjustment Act, 1974	Prohibits discrimination against disabled veterans and Vietnam War veterans
Pension Reform Act, 1974	Designed to prevent abuses in employee retirement, profit-sharing, thrift, and savings plans
Equal Credit Opportunity Act, 1974	Prohibits discrimination in credit on the basis of sex or marital status
Age Discrimination Act, 1975	Prohibits discrimination on the basis of age in federally assisted programs
Pregnancy Discrimination Act, 1978	Prohibits discrimination on the basis of pregnancy, childbirth, or related medical conditions
Immigration Reform and Control Act, 1986	Prohibits employers from knowingly hiring a person who is an unauthorized alien
Americans with Disabilities Act, 1990	Prohibits discrimination against people with disabilities and requires that they be given the same opportunities as people without disabilities
Civil Rights Act, 1991	Provides monetary damages in cases of intentional employment discrimination

© Cengage Learning

Even with the passage and enforcement of safety laws, many employees still work in unhealthy or dangerous environments. Safety experts suspect that companies underreport industrial accidents to avoid state and federal inspection and regulation. The current emphasis on increased productivity has been cited as the main reason for the growing number of such accidents. Competitive pressures are also believed to lie behind the increases in manufacturing injuries. Greater turnover in organizations due to downsizing means employees may have more responsibilities and less experience in their current positions, thus increasing the potential for accidents. Overworked employees are often cited as a primary factor in careless accidents, both in the United States and in other countries. For instance, cruise ship lawyers cite overworked employees as one of the major causes for the increase in cruise ship accidents. They state because cruise ship employees are no longer subject to the U.S. court system, but are directed to foreign arbitration when they have problems, they have experienced a deterioration in working conditions that has led to additional accidents.[24]

GATEKEEPERS AND STAKEHOLDERS

Trust is the glue that holds businesses and their stakeholders together. Trust creates confidence and helps to forge relationships of reliance between businesses and stakeholders. Trust also allows businesses to depend upon one another as they make transactions or exchange value. Ethics create the foundational trust between two parties in a transaction. Many people must trust and be trusted to make business work properly. Sometimes these parties are referred to as *gatekeepers*. Gatekeepers include accountants, who are essential to certifying the accuracy of financial information, as well as lawyers, financial rating agencies, and even financial reporting services. These groups are critical in providing information allowing stakeholders to gain an understanding of the financial position of an organization. Most of these gatekeepers operate with professional codes of ethics and face legal consequences, or even disbarment, if they fail to operate within agreed-upon principles of conduct. Therefore, there is a strong need for gatekeepers to uphold ethical standards and remain independent through using standard methods and procedures that can be audited by other gatekeepers, the regulatory system, and investors.

Accountants

Accountants measure and disclose financial information, with an assurance of accuracy, to the public. Managers, investors, tax authorities, and other stakeholders who make resource allocation decisions are all groups who use the information provided by accountants. Accountants make specific assumptions about their clients. One assumption is the corporation is an entity separate and distinct from its owners, and that it continues to operate as such in the future. Another assumption is a stable monetary system (such as the dollar) is in place and all necessary information concerning the business is available and presented in an understandable manner. Accountants have their own set of rules. One is that if there is a choice between equally acceptable accounting methods, they should use the one least likely to overstate or misdirect.

Some accountants have not adhered to their responsibilities to stakeholders. For example, Arthur Andersen was once a standard bearer for integrity. But at Andersen, growth became the priority, and its emphasis on recruiting and retaining big clients came at the expense of quality and independent audits. The company linked its consulting business in a joint cooperative relationship with its audit arm, which compromised its auditors' independence, a quality crucial to the execution of a credible audit. The firm's focus on growth generated a fundamental change in its corporate culture in that its high-profit consulting business was regarded as more important than providing objective auditing services. This situation presented a conflict of interest and posed a problem when partners decided how to treat questionable accounting practices discovered at some of Andersen's largest clients. Ultimately, Arthur Andersen dissolved because of its ties to the Enron scandal.

Risk Assessment

Another critical gatekeeper group are risk assessors of financial products. The top three companies in the world that independently assess financial risks are Standard & Poor's, Moody's, and Fitch. They express risk through letters ranging from "AAA," the highest grade, to "C," the lowest grade. Different rating services use the same letter grades, but use various combinations of upper- and lowercase letters to differentiate themselves.

As early as 2003, financial analysts and the three global rating firms suspected there were major problems with the way their models were assessing risk. In 2005 Standard & Poor's realized its algorithm for estimating the risks associated with debt packages was flawed. As a result, it asked for comments on improving its equations. In 2006–2007 many governmental regulators and others started to realize what the rating agencies knew for years: their ratings were not accurate. In 2008 during the financial crisis, bonds that credit agencies rated highly, with an estimated worth of $14 trillion, fell to "junk bond" status.[25] One report stated the high ratings given to debt were based on inadequate historical data and businesses were "ratings shopping" to obtain the best rating possible. Investment banks were among the worst offenders, paying for ratings and therefore causing conflicts of interest. The amount of revenue these three companies annually receive is approximately $5 billion.

Further investigations uncovered many disturbing problems. Moody's, Standard & Poor's, and Fitch all violated a code of conduct "that required analysts to consider only credit factors, not the potential impact on Moody's, or an issuer, an investor or other market participant."[26] These companies became overwhelmed by an increase in the volume and sophistication of the securities they were asked to review. Finally, faced with less time to perform the due diligence expected of them, analysts began to cut corners.

This failure to adequately account for risks is having consequences for financial credit-rating firms. New York's top prosecutor launched an investigation into the top three credit-rating firms to determine the objectivity of their ratings prior to the financial crisis. Additionally, the Justice Department filed a lawsuit against Standard & Poor's (S&P) due to the major losses federally-backed banks and credit unions suffered after depending upon the S&P's high ratings for mortgage-backed deals.[27]

Regulators believe more oversight for credit-rating firms is needed. Part of the problem, as former SEC Chairman Mary Schapiro saw it, is credit rating firms are paid by the securities they rank. This creates a conflict of interest problem and affects the reliability of the ratings.[28] No organization is exempt from criticism over its level of transparency. While large financial firms have been the target of the public's anger over risk taking and executive pay, even nonprofits are being scrutinized more carefully.[29]

THE SARBANES–OXLEY (SOX) ACT

In 2002, largely in response to widespread corporate accounting scandals, Congress passed the Sarbanes–Oxley Act to establish a system of federal oversight of corporate accounting practices. In addition to making fraudulent financial reporting a criminal offense and strengthening penalties for corporate fraud, the law requires corporations to establish codes of ethics for financial reporting and develop greater transparency in financial reporting to their investors and other stakeholders.

Supported by both Republicans and Democrats, the Sarbanes–Oxley Act was enacted to restore stakeholder confidence after accounting fraud at Enron, WorldCom, and hundreds of other companies resulted in investors and employees losing much of their savings. During the resulting investigations, the public learned hundreds of corporations failed to report their financial results accurately. Many stakeholders believed accounting firms, lawyers, top executives, and boards of directors developed a culture of deception to ensure investor approval and gain a competitive advantage. As a result of public outrage over the accounting scandals, the Sarbanes–Oxley Act garnered nearly unanimous support not only in Congress but also from government regulatory agencies, the president, and the general public. When President George W. Bush signed the Sarbanes–Oxley Act into law, he emphasized the need for new standards of ethical behavior in business, particularly among the top managers and boards of directors responsible for overseeing business decisions and activities.

At the heart of the Sarbanes–Oxley Act (SOX) is the **Public Company Accounting Oversight Board** that monitors accounting firms auditing public corporations and establishes standards and rules for auditors in accounting firms. The law gave the board investigatory and disciplinary power over auditors and securities analysts who issue reports about corporate performance and health. The law attempts to eliminate conflicts of interest by prohibiting accounting firms from providing both auditing and consulting services to the same client companies without special permission from the client firm's audit committee; it also places limits on the length of time lead auditors can serve a particular client. The Sarbanes–Oxley Act requires corporations to take greater responsibility for their decisions and to provide leadership based on ethical principles. Additionally, the law modifies the attorney–client relationship to require lawyers to report wrongdoing to top managers and/or the board of directors. It also provides protection for "whistle-blowing" employees who report illegal activity to authorities. This "whistle-blower" protection was strengthened with the passage of the Dodd–Frank Act several years later.

On the other hand, SOX raised a number of concerns. The complex law imposed additional requirements and costs on executives. Additionally, the new act caused many firms to restate their financial reports to avoid penalties. Big public companies spent thousands of hours and millions of dollars annually to make sure someone looked over the shoulder of key accounting personnel at every step of every business process, according to Financial Executives International. Perhaps the biggest complaint is in spite of Sarbanes–Oxley, financial executives discovered new loopholes that allowed them to engage in the misconduct that contributed to the global financial crisis.

A major change to Sarbanes-Oxley occurred with a new law in 2012. During 2012, the administration passed the Jumpstart Our Business Startups (JOBS) Act in an effort to jumpstart the economy. This act exempts what is termed as "emerging growth companies" from having to observe the auditor attestation requirements from Sarbanes–Oxley 404(b). The exemption can last a maximum of five years. The purpose of the law is to allow start-ups to easily attract funding and investors. One of the biggest provisions of this law is that qualified firms can raise funds in private and small public offerings without registering with the Securities and Exchange Commission, thus saving them money. In order to qualify, firms must have annual gross revenues of less than $1 billion and/or market capitalization of less than $700 million.[30] The JOBS Act is one way the government tries to lessen the burden of Sarbanes–Oxley on newer, smaller businesses and encourage entrepreneurship.

Public Company Accounting Oversight Board

SOX aims to promote transparency, reduce conflict of interest, and increase accountability. For instance, one provision called for the establishment of a board to oversee the audit of public companies in order to protect the interests of investors and further the public interest in the preparation of informative, accurate, and independent audit reports for companies. The Public Company Accounting Oversight Board faced several challenges throughout the years, including a lawsuit claiming the board was unconstitutional. The lawsuit passed to the Supreme Court. The court ruled in favor of the board. The board must also overcome obstacles with foreign auditing firms. Although Sarbanes–Oxley requires registration from all auditors listed on the U.S. public market including foreign auditors, several countries, such as the European Union and China, do not allow inspections of their auditing firms.[31]

Auditor and Analyst Independence

The Sarbanes–Oxley Act seeks to eliminate conflicts of interest among auditors, security analysts, brokers, dealers, and the public companies they serve in order to ensure enhanced financial disclosures of public companies' true conditions. To accomplish auditor independence, Section 201 prohibits registered public accounting firms from providing both non-audit and audit services to a public company. National securities exchanges and registered securities associations have adopted similar conflict-of-interest rules for security analysts, brokers, and dealers who recommend equities in research reports. Such independence enables the Sarbanes–Oxley Act to ensure compliance with the requirement for more detailed financial disclosures representing public companies' true condition. For example, registered public accounting firms are now required to identify all material correcting adjustments to reflect accurate financial statements. Also, all material off-balance-sheet transactions and other relationships with unconsolidated entities that affect current or future financial conditions of a public company must be disclosed in each annual and quarterly financial report. In addition, public companies must report "on a rapid and current basis" material changes in their financial condition or operations.

Whistle-Blower Protection

Employees of public companies and accounting firms are accountable to report unethical behavior. The Sarbanes–Oxley Act intends to motivate employees through whistle-blower protection that prohibits the employer from taking certain actions against employees who lawfully disclose private employer information to parties in a judicial proceeding involving a fraud claim, among others. Whistle-blowers are granted a remedy of special damages and attorneys' fees. Unfortunately, this law did not protect certain whistle-blowers from being penalized prior to the financial crisis. Whistle-blowers at Lehman Brothers, Madoff Securities, and Stanford Financial Group (that also operated a Ponzi scheme) warned auditors and government officials of misconduct at the companies. Some whistle-blowers were fired or, after losing lawsuits filed against the offending company, were forced to pay large sums in back pay and attorney's fees.[32] These cases prompted a provision for stronger whistle-blower protection in the Dodd–Frank Act, discussed in the next section.

Cost of Compliance

The national cost of compliance of the Sarbanes–Oxley Act can be extensive and includes internal costs, external costs, and auditor fees. For example, Section 404 requires companies to document both the results of financial transactions and the processes they used to generate them. A company may have thousands of processes that have never been written down. Writing down the processes is time consuming and costly.[33] Also, because the cost of compliance is so high for many small companies, some publicly traded companies even considered delisting themselves from the U.S. Stock Exchange.

However, studies show although compliance costs were high shortly after Sarbanes–Oxley was passed, they have declined over the years. Companies have reported their compliance costs decreased 50 percent from the level when the laws were put into effect. One reason why the costs may be decreasing is that companies have more experience with Sarbanes–Oxley and therefore require less time to complete the process.[34] Today, the costs of compliance with Sarbanes-Oxley range from between $100,000 and $500,000, depending upon the company's size.[35]

DODD–FRANK WALL STREET REFORM AND CONSUMER PROTECTION ACT

In 2010 President Obama signed into law the Dodd–Frank Wall Street Reform and Consumer Protection Act. It was heralded as "a sweeping overhaul of the financial regulatory system … on a scale not seen since the reforms that followed the Great Depression."[36] The new law seeks to improve financial regulation, increase oversight of the industry, and prevent the types of risk-taking, deceptive practices, and lack of oversight that led to the 2008–2009 financial crisis.[37] The Act contains sixteen provisions that include increasing the accountability and transparency of financial institutions, creating a bureau to educate consumers in financial literacy and protect them from deceptive financial practices, implementing additional incentives for whistle-blowers, increasing oversight of the financial industry, and regulating the use of complex derivatives.

Response to the law was split along party lines, with vocal opponents as well as proponents. Critics have several concerns, including claims the rules on derivatives are too burdensome, the belief such wide-scale changes will create chaos in the regulatory system, and the fear the government will gain too much power.[38] Other companies, such as JP Morgan, claim they support the law in general but oppose certain provisions.[39] The following sections describe some of the most notable provisions of the Dodd–Frank Act.

New Financial Agencies

One provision of the Dodd–Frank Act instituted the creation of two new financial agencies, the Office of Financial Research and the Financial Stability Oversight Council. The Office of Financial Research is charged with improving the quality of financial data available to government officials and creating a better system of analysis for the financial industry.[40] The Financial Stability Oversight Council (FSOC) is responsible for maintaining the stability of the financial system in the United States through monitoring the market, identifying threats, promoting market discipline among the public, and responding to major risks that threaten stability.[41] FSOC has the authority to limit or closely supervise financial risks, create stricter standards for banking and nonbanking financial institutions, and disband financial institutions that present a serious risk to market stability.[42] The addition of these two new agencies is intended not only to improve information collecting and oversight, but to close the types of loopholes that allowed financial industries to engage in risky and deceptive conduct prior to the financial crisis.

Consumer Financial Protection Bureau

Another agency the Dodd–Frank Act created was the Consumer Financial Protection Bureau (CFPB), an independent agency within the Federal Reserve System that "regulate[s] the offering and provision of consumer financial products or services under the Federal consumer financial laws."[43] One of the problems leading up to the 2008–2009 financial crisis was that average investors often did not understand the complex financial products they purchased. The CFPB aims to protect consumers from this problem in the future. The government granted the agency supervisory power over credit markets as well as the authority to monitor lenders and ensure they are in compliance with the law.[44] The CFPB also has the responsibility to curtail unfair lending and credit card practices, enforce consumer financial laws, and check the safety of financial products before their launch into the market.[45]

The CFPB is not without its critics. Several financial firms and legislators believe the bureau has too much power. Additionally, financial institutions are concerned the bureau's powers could lead to strict sanctions or burdensome regulations.[46] Goldman Sachs, for instance, limited its profitable practice of investing in its own private-equity funds to comply with the Volcker rule, part of the Dodd-Frank Act restricting financial institutions from using their own money to make large bets.[47] To protect against misconduct at all levels, the CFPB has oversight powers for institutions often accused of questionable dealings, such as payday lenders and debt collectors.[48] The goal of the CFPB is to create a more equitable and transparent financial environment for consumers.

Whistle-Blower Bounty Program

It is clear the whistle-blower provisions implemented in Sarbanes–Oxley were not enough to prevent the massive misconduct occurring at business institutions before the financial crisis. To encourage more employees to come forward when they witness misconduct, the Dodd–Frank law instituted a whistle-blower bounty program. Whistle-blowers who report financial fraud to the Securities and Exchange Commission and Commodities Exchange Commission are eligible to receive 10 percent to 30 percent of fines and settlements if their reports result in convictions of more than $1 million in penalties.[49]

While this will encourage more people to step forward, there are some challenges that need to be considered for the program to be a success. For instance, the SEC will certainly be flooded with tips, some of which will come from people who just want the money. Still, the SEC is optimistic half the tips it receives will result in payouts, suggesting the number of credible whistle-blower complaints will increase dramatically.[50] In 2012 the program provided its first payout of $50,000 to a whistleblower who helped regulators convict a company of fraud. The payout represented approximately 30 percent of the penalty levied against the company.[51]

LAWS THAT ENCOURAGE ETHICAL CONDUCT

Violations of the law usually begin when businesspeople stretch the limits of ethical standards, as defined by company or industry codes of conduct, and then choose to engage in schemes that either knowingly or unwittingly violate the law. In recent years, new laws and regulations have been passed to discourage such decisions—and to foster programs designed to improve business ethics and social responsibility (Table 4–5). The most important of these are the Federal Sentencing Guidelines for Organizations (FSGO), the Sarbanes–Oxley Act, and the Dodd–Frank Act. One of the goals of these acts is requiring employees to report observed misconduct. The development of reporting systems has advanced, with most companies having some method for employees to report observed misconduct. However, while reported misconduct is up, a sizable percentage of employees still do not report misconduct, as Figure 4–3 shows.

TABLE 4–5 Institutionalization of Ethics through the U.S. Sentencing Guidelines for Organizations

1991	*Law:* U.S. Sentencing Guidelines for Organizations created for federal prosecutions of organizations. These guidelines provide for just punishment, adequate deterrence, and incentives for organizations to prevent, detect, and report misconduct. Organizations need to have an effective ethics and compliance program to receive incentives in the case of misconduct.
2004	*Amendments:* The definition of an effective ethics program now includes the development of an ethical organizational culture. Executives and board members must assume the responsibility of identifying areas of risk, providing ethics training, creating reporting mechanisms, and designating an individual to oversee ethics programs.
2007–2008	*Additional definition of a compliance and ethics program:* Firms should focus on due diligence to detect and prevent misconduct and promote an organizational culture that encourages ethical conduct. More details are provided, encouraging the assessment of risk and outlining appropriate steps in designing, implementing, and modifying ethics programs and training that will include all employees, top management, and the board or governing authority. These modifications continue to reinforce the importance of an ethical culture in preventing misconduct.
2010	*Amendments for Reporting to the Board:* Chief compliance officers are directed to make their reports to their firm's board rather than to the general counsel. Companies are encouraged to create hotlines, perform self-audit programs, and adopt controls to detect misconduct internally. More specific language has been added to the word *prompt* in regards to what it means to promptly report misconduct. The amendment also extends operational responsibility to all personnel within a company's ethics and compliance program.
2012	*Amendments for Securities Fraud:* These amendments were developed to account for changes instituted by the 2010 passage of the Dodd-Frank Act. These amendments propose changes in how fraud losses are calculated, the sentencing of professionals guilty of insider trading, the determination of losses resulting from mortgage fraud, and different levels of offense for financial fraud.

Source: "U.S. Sentencing Guidelines Changes Become Effective November 1," FCPA Compliance and Ethics Blog, November 2, 2010, http://tfoxlaw. wordpress.com/2010/11/02/us-sentencing-guidelines-changes-become-effective-november-1/ (accessed April 18, 2013); United States Sentencing Commission, *Amendments to the Sentencing Guidelines*, April 30, 2012, http://www.ussc.gov/Legal/Amendments/Reader-Friendly/20120430_RF_ Amendments.pdf (accessed April 18, 2013).

FIGURE 4–3 **Employees Who Report Misconduct**

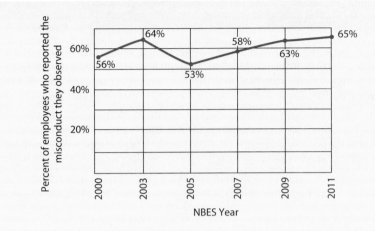

Source: Ethics Resource Center, 2011 *National Business Ethics Survey* (Arlington, VA: Ethics Resource Center, 2012), p. 22.

FEDERAL SENTENCING GUIDELINES FOR ORGANIZATIONS

As mentioned in Chapter 1, Congress passed the FSGO in 1991 to create an incentive for organizations to develop and implement programs designed to foster ethical and legal compliance. These guidelines, developed by the U.S. Sentencing Commission, apply to all felonies and class A misdemeanors committed by employees in association with their work. As an incentive, organizations that demonstrated due diligence in developing effective compliance programs to discourage unethical and illegal conduct may be subject to reduced organizational penalties if an employee commits a crime.[52] Overall, the government philosophy is that legal violations can be prevented through organizational values and a commitment to ethical conduct.

The commission delineated seven steps companies must implement to demonstrate due diligence:

1. A firm must develop and disseminate a code of conduct that communicates required standards and identifies key risk areas for the organization.

2. High-ranking personnel in the organization who are known to abide by the legal and ethical standards of the industry (such as an ethics officer, vice president of human resources, general counsel, and so forth) must have oversight over the program.

3. No one with a known propensity to engage in misconduct should be put in a position of authority.

4. A communications system for disseminating standards and procedures (ethics training) must also be put into place.

5. Organizational communications should include a way for employees to report misconduct without fearing retaliation, such as an anonymous toll-free hotline or an ombudsman. Monitoring and auditing systems designed to detect misconduct are also required.

6. If misconduct is detected, then the firm must take appropriate and fair disciplinary action. Individuals both directly and indirectly responsible for the offense should be disciplined. In addition, the sanctions should be appropriate for the offense.

7. After misconduct has been discovered, the organization must take steps to prevent similar offenses in the future. This usually involves making modifications to the ethical compliance program, conducting additional employee training, and issuing communications about specific types of conduct.

The government expects these seven steps for compliance programs to undergo continuous improvement and refinement.[53]

These steps are based on the commission's determination to emphasize compliance programs and to provide guidance for both organizations and courts regarding program effectiveness. Organizations have flexibility about the type of program they develop; the seven steps are not a checklist requiring legal procedures be followed to gain certification of an effective program. Organizations implement the guidelines through effective core practices appropriate for their firms. The programs they put into effect must be capable of reducing the opportunity employees have to engage in misconduct.

A 2004 amendment to the FSGO requires a business's governing authority be well informed about its ethics program with respect to content, implementation, and effectiveness. This places the responsibility squarely on the shoulders of the firm's leadership, usually the board of directors. The board must ensure there is a high-ranking manager accountable for the day-to-day operational oversight of the ethics program; provide for adequate authority, resources, and access to the board or an appropriate subcommittee of the board; and ensure there are confidential mechanisms available so the organization's employees and agents may report or seek guidance about potential or actual misconduct without fear of retaliation. Finally, the board is required to oversee the discovery of risks and to design, implement, and modify approaches to deal with those risks. Figure 4–4 demonstrates employees at companies with effective ethics programs are more likely to view their corporate cultures as ethical. If board members do not understand the nature, purpose, and methods available to implement an ethics program, the firm is at risk of inadequate oversight and ethical misconduct that may escalate into a scandal.[54]

FIGURE 4–4 Ethical Culture Perceptions of Employees Based Upon Ethics Program Implementation

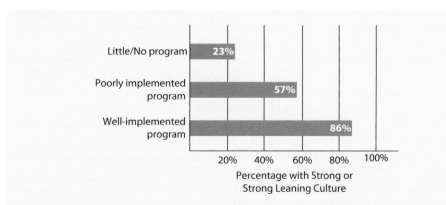

Source: Ethics Resource Center, *2011 National Business Ethics Survey* (Arlington, VA: Ethics Resource Center, 2012), p. 34.

A 2005 Supreme Court decision held that the federal sentencing guidelines were not mandatory but should serve only as recommendations for judges to use in their decisions. Some legal and business experts believe this decision might weaken the implementation of the FSGO, but most federal sentences remained in the same range as before the Supreme Court decision. The guidelines remain an important consideration in developing an effective ethics and compliance program.[55]

The 2007–2008 amendments to the FSGO extend the required ethics training to members of the board or governing authority, high-level personnel, employees, and the organizations' agents. This change applies not only oversight but mandatory training to all levels of the organization. Merely distributing a code of ethics does not meet the training requirements. The 2007 and 2008 amendments now require most governmental contractors to provide ethics and compliance training.

As new FSGO amendments are implemented, more explicit responsibility is being placed on organizations to improve and expand ethics and compliance provisions to include all employees and board members, as demonstrated in four amendments to the guidelines implemented in 2010. The first amendment concerned chief compliance officers who report misconduct to the general counsel. The guidelines recommend simplifying the complexity of reporting relationships by having the chief compliance officer make reports directly to the board or to a board committee. Companies are also encouraged to extend their internal ethical controls through hotlines, self-auditing programs, and other mechanisms so misconduct can be detected internally rather than externally. In the third amendment, the FSGO added more specific language of the word *prompt* to help employees recognize what it means to report an ethical violation promptly. Finally, the FSGO amended the extent of operational responsibility to apply to all personnel within a company's ethics and compliance program.[56]

In 2012 the Federal Sentencing Commission proposed new amendments to the Federal Sentencing Guidelines. While these amendments covered many topics, major emphasis was given to changes resulting from the Dodd-Frank Act. These new amendments proposed increased penalties for certain types of securities fraud. For instance, the amendments propose regulators differentiate between those who engage in frequent and deliberate insider trading and those who engage in this act due to the opportunity to make quick profits. The Federal Sentencing Commission recommended increasing sentences depending upon the money gained from the insider trading scheme as well as the willfulness of the offenders. The amendments also examined how to determine the value of collateral in cases of mortgage fraud. Additionally, the amendments listed four levels of offense for financial institution fraud: (1) whether the fraud caused the institution to become insolvent, (2) whether it forced the institution to reduce benefits to pensioners or the insured, (3) whether it caused the institution to become unable on demand to fully refund a deposit, payment, or investment, or (4) whether it depleted the assets of the institution to such an extent it was forced to merge with another institution. The amount of penalties can be increased depending upon the extent of the offense committed. Those found guilty of this type of fraud can have their sentences lengthened or reduced beyond the FSGO guidelines depending upon the amount of loss the fraud caused.[57]

The Department of Justice, through the Thompson Memo (Deputy Attorney General Larry Thompson's 2003 memo to U.S. Attorneys), advanced general principles to consider in cases involving corporate wrongdoing. This memo makes it clear ethics and compliance programs are important to detecting the types of misconduct most likely to occur in a particular corporation's line of business. If it does not have an effective ethics and compliance program in place to detect ethical and legal lapses, a firm found in violation should not be treated leniently. Additionally, the prosecutor generally has wide latitude in determining when, whom, and whether to prosecute violations of federal law. U.S. attorneys are directed that charging for even minor misconduct may be appropriate when the wrongdoing was perpetuated by a large number of employees in a particular role—for example, sales staff or procurement officers—or was condoned by upper management. Without an effective program to identify an isolated rogue employee involved in misconduct, a firm may suffer serious consequences in terms of regulatory issues, enforcement, and sentencing.[58] Therefore, there is general agreement both in law and administrative policy that an effective ethics and compliance program is necessary to prevent misconduct and reduce the legal consequences if it does occur.

HIGHLY APPROPRIATE CORE PRACTICES

The focus of core practices is on developing structurally sound organizational practices and integrity for financial and nonfinancial performance measures, rather than on an individual's morals. Although the Sarbanes–Oxley Act and the Dodd–Frank Act provide standards for financial performance, most ethical issues relate to non-financials such as marketing, human resource management, and customer relations. Abusive behavior, lying, and conflict of interest are still three significant issues.

A group called the Integrity Institute developed an integrated model to standardize the measurement of nonfinancial performance. Methodologies have been developed to assess communications, compensation, social responsibility, corporate culture, leadership, risk, and stakeholder perceptions, as well as the more subjective aspects of earnings, corporate governance, technology, and other important nonfinancial areas. The model exists to establish a standard that predicts the sustainability and success of an organization. The Integrity Institute uses measurement to an established standard as the basis for certification of integrity.[59] The Institute is one of the first to attempt such a model.

The majority of executives and board members want to measure nonfinancial performance, but no standards currently exist. The Open Compliance Ethics Group (oceg.org) developed benchmarking studies that are available to organizations wanting to conduct self-assessments to determine the elements of their ethics programs. Developing organizational systems and processes is a requirement of the regulatory environment, but organizations are given considerable freedom in developing these programs. Core practices exist and can be identified in every industry. Trade associations' self-regulatory groups and research studies often provide insights into the expected best core practices. An important priority is for each firm to assess its legal and ethical risk areas, and then develop structures to prevent, detect, and quickly correct any misconduct.

Consider Disney's approach concerning the childhood obesity epidemic. The company announced it will only advertise healthier foods to children on its Disney TV channels, radio shows, and website. All food manufacturers wanting to advertise with Disney must meet Disney's nutritional criteria. Those that meet said criteria can be certified with a

"Mickey Check" symbol. Additionally, Disney plans to offer more fruits and vegetables and reduce the amount of sodium in foods offered at its amusement park venues. Disney claims to be the first major media company to introduce these nutritional advertising standards.[60]

Voluntary Responsibilities

Voluntary responsibilities fall into the category of a business's contributions to its stakeholders. Businesses that address their voluntary responsibilities provide four major benefits to society:

1. Improve quality of life and make communities the places where people want to do business, raise families, and enjoy life. Thus, improving the quality of life in a community makes it easier to attract and retain employees and customers.

2. Reduce government involvement by providing assistance to stakeholders.

3. Develop employee leadership skills. Many firms, for example, use campaigns by the United Way and other community service organizations as leadership- and skill-building exercises for their employees.

4. Create an ethical culture and values that act as a buffer to organizational misconduct.[61]

The most common way businesses demonstrate their voluntary responsibilities is through donations to local and national charitable organizations. For example, Wells Fargo & Co. contributes around $315 million annually to nonprofit organizations and communities, and employees volunteer approximately 1.5 million hours to their local communities. The company also purchases green energy and has a website devoted to financial education.[62] Indeed, many companies are concerned about the quality of education in the United States after realizing the current pool of prospective employees lacks many basic work skills. Recognizing today's students are tomorrow's employees and customers, firms such as Kroger, Campbell Soup Co., American Express, Apple, Xerox, and Coca-Cola donate money, equipment, and employee time to improve schools in their communities and throughout the nation.

The Walmart Foundation, the charitable giving branch of Walmart Inc., donated $958.9 million in 2011 to charities and communities across the globe and is one of the largest corporate cash contributors in the nation. The money supports a variety of causes such as child development, education, the environment, and disaster relief. Walmart officials believe the company makes the greatest impact on communities by supporting issues and causes important to its customers and associates in their own neighborhoods. By supporting communities at the local level, Walmart encourages customer loyalty and goodwill.[63]

Cause-Related Marketing

The first attempts by organizations to coordinate organizational goals with philanthropic giving emerged with cause-related marketing in the early 1980s. **Cause-related marketing** ties an organization's product(s) directly to a social concern through a marketing program.

With cause-related marketing, a percentage of a product's sales is donated to a cause that appeals to the target market. Yoplait, for example, generates proceeds for the Susan G. Komen for the Cure cause with its Save Lids to Save Lives program. Susan G. Komen for the Cure is a nonprofit organization that raises funds to fight breast cancer. Yoplait created an annual philanthropic program that encourages consumers to send in pink Yoplait yogurt lids. For every lid sent in, Yoplait donates 10 cents to Susan G. Komen for the Cure, up to $2,500,000. Within 12 years, the program has resulted in more than $50 million in contributions.[64]

Cause-related marketing also affects buying patterns. For such a campaign to be successful, consumers must sympathize with the cause, the brand and cause must be perceived as a good fit, and consumers should be able to transfer their feelings about the cause to their brand perceptions and purchase intentions. Surveys reveal 85 percent of consumers view a brand more favorably if it contributes to a cause they care about, and 80 percent indicate their willingness to change to a brand that supports a worthwhile cause if its price and quality are equal to its competitors'.[65] When consumers identify with a cause, this identification leads to more positive evaluations of the campaign.[66] This finding lends support to the idea that cause-related marketing can bolster a firm's reputation.

Cause-related marketing has its weaknesses too. For instance, consumers may perceive a company's cause-related campaign as merely a publicity stunt, especially if they cannot understand the link between the campaign and the company's business practices. Also, cause-related campaigns are often of short duration, so consumers may not adequately associate the business with a particular cause. Strategic philanthropy is more holistic, as it ties the company's philanthropic giving to its overall strategy and objectives.

Strategic Philanthropy

Strategic philanthropy is the synergistic and mutually beneficial use of an organization's core competencies and resources to deal with key stakeholders so as to bring about organizational and societal benefits. It uses the profit motive, but argues that philanthropy must have at least a long-term positive impact. For example, Gentle Giant Moving Company, a U.S. moving company with offices in eight states, made it a priority to incorporate philanthropy and social responsibility into its business strategy. In addition to its goal to become the best movers in the industry, Gentle Giant values customer satisfaction so much it provides a 100 percent money-back guarantee if customers are not happy with its service. The company established a charitable foundation that supports youth leadership development, housing assistance and homeless prevention, and green initiatives to make its practices more eco-friendly. Founder Peter O'Toole also cares for his employees and works to instill in them the f values Gentle Giant embodies. The company's successful integration of strategic philanthropy into its organizational practices won it numerous awards, including a spot on *The Wall Street Journal*'s "Top Small Workplaces," a Better Business Bureau International Torch Award for Marketplace Ethics, and the Better Business Bureau Local Torch Award for Excellence (an honor won four times).[67]

Home Depot directs much of the money it spends on philanthropy toward affordable housing, at-risk youth, the environment, and disaster recovery. In 2011 Home Depot committed to working with nonprofit organizations to improve the homes of low-income veterans. The retailer has since donated $80 million to this cause. Since the creation of the Home Depot Foundation in 2002, the firm donated a total of $300 million in assistance to local homes and communities.[68] These organizations demonstrate how companies successfully incorporate voluntary responsibilities into their business strategies.

THE IMPORTANCE OF INSTITUTIONALIZATION IN BUSINESS ETHICS

Institutionalization involves embedding values, norms, and artifacts in organizations, industries, and society. In the United States and many other countries, institutionalization involves legislation often finalized through Supreme Court decisions. This chapter provides an overview of legal as well as cultural institutions that work both outside and inside the organizational environment to support and control ethical decision making in organizations.

As discussed in Chapter 2, those in charge of corporate governance should be especially mindful of the institutions, including mandated requirements for legal compliance as well as core practices and voluntary actions that support ethics and social responsibility. While voluntary conduct, including philanthropic activities, is not required to run a business, the failure to understand highly appropriate and common practices, referred to as core practices, provides the opportunity for unethical conduct.

It is important to recognize the institutionalization of business ethics has advanced rapidly over the last 20 years as stakeholders recognized the need to improve business ethics. The government stepped in when scandals and misconduct damaged consumers, investors, and other key constituents important for businesses. More recently, gatekeepers such as lawyers, financial rating agencies, and financial reporting services have been questioned because some of their decisions contributed to major scandals. Legislation and amendments related to the Federal Sentencing Guidelines for Organizations, the Sarbanes–Oxley Act, and the Dodd–Frank Act attempted to develop and enforce ethical practices that support trust in business.

SUMMARY

To understand the institutionalization of business ethics, it is important to understand the voluntary and legally mandated dimensions of organizational practices. Core practices are documented best practices, often encouraged by legal and regulatory forces as well as by industry trade associations. The effective organizational practice of business ethics requires three dimensions to be integrated into an ethics and compliance program. This integration creates an ethical culture that effectively manages the risks of misconduct. Institutionalization in business ethics relates to established laws, customs, and the expectations of organizational ethics programs considered a requirement in establishing reputation. Institutions reward and sanction ethical decision making by providing structure and reinforcing societal expectations. In this way, society as a whole institutionalizes core practices and provides organizations with the opportunity to take their own approach, only taking action if there are violations.

Laws and regulations established by governments set minimum standards for responsible behavior—society's codification of what is right and wrong. Civil and criminal laws regulating business conduct are passed because society—including consumers, interest groups, competitors, and legislators—believes business must comply with society's standards. Such laws regulate competition, protect consumers, promote safety and equity in the workplace, and provide incentives for preventing misconduct.

In 2002, largely in response to widespread corporate accounting scandals, Congress passed the Sarbanes–Oxley Act to establish a system of federal oversight of corporate accounting practices. In addition to making fraudulent financial reporting a criminal offense and strengthening penalties for corporate fraud, the law requires corporations to establish codes of ethics for financial reporting and develop greater transparency in financial reporting to investors and other stakeholders. The Sarbanes–Oxley Act requires corporations to take greater responsibility for their decisions and provide leadership based on ethical principles. For instance, the law requires top managers to certify their firms' financial reports are complete and accurate, making CEOs and CFOs personally accountable for the credibility and accuracy of their companies' financial statements. The act establishes an oversight board to oversee the audit of public companies. The oversight board aims to protect the interests of investors and further the public interest in the preparation of informative, accurate, and independent audit reports for companies.

In 2010, largely in response to the widespread misconduct leading to the global recession, the Dodd–Frank Wall Street Reform and Consumer Protection Act was passed. The purpose of the Dodd–Frank Act is to prevent future misconduct in the financial sector, protect consumers from complex financial instruments, oversee market stability, and create transparency in the financial sector. The Act created two financial agencies, the Financial Stability Oversight Council and the Office of Financial Research. It also created the Consumer Financial Protection Bureau to regulate the industry and ensure consumers are protected against overly complex and/or deceptive financial practices. Whistle-blower protection was extended to include a whistle-blower bounty program whereby whistle-blowers who report corporate misconduct to the SEC may receive 10 to 30 percent of settlement money if their reports result in a conviction of more than $1 million in penalties.

Congress passed the Federal Sentencing Guidelines for Organizations (FSGO) in 1991 to create an incentive for organizations to develop and implement programs designed to foster ethical and legal compliance. These guidelines, developed by the U.S. Sentencing Commission, apply to all felonies and class A misdemeanors committed by employees in association with their work. As an incentive, organizations that have demonstrated due diligence in developing effective compliance programs that discourage unethical and illegal conduct may be subject to reduced organizational penalties if an employee commits a crime. Overall, the government philosophy is that legal violations can be prevented through organizational values and a commitment to ethical conduct. A 2004 amendment to the FSGO requires a business's governing authority be well-informed about its ethics program with respect to content, implementation, and effectiveness. This places the responsibility squarely on the shoulders of the firm's leadership, usually the board of directors. The board must ensure there is a high-ranking manager accountable for the day-to-day operational oversight of the ethics program. The board must provide adequate authority, resources, and access to the board or an appropriate subcommittee of the board. The board must also ensure there are confidential mechanisms available so the organization's employees and agents report or seek guidance about potential or actual misconduct without fear of retaliation. A 2010 amendment to the FSGO directs chief compliance officers to make their reports to the board rather than to e general counsel. In 2012 new amendments were passed to deal with changes resulting from the Dodd-Frank Act.

The FSGO and the Sarbanes–Oxley Act provide incentives for developing core practices that ensure ethical and legal compliance. Core practices move the emphasis from a focus on the individual's moral capability to a focus on developing structurally sound organizational core practices and integrity for both financial and nonfinancial performance.

The Integrity Institute developed an integrated model to standardize the measurement of nonfinancial performance. The group developed methodologies to assess communications, compensation, social responsibility, corporate culture, leadership, risk, and stakeholder perceptions, as well as the more subjective aspects of earnings, corporate governance, technology, and other important nonfinancial areas.

Voluntary responsibilities touch on businesses' social responsibility insofar as they contribute to the local community and society as a whole. Voluntary responsibilities provide four major benefits to society: improving the quality of life, reducing government involvement by providing assistance to stakeholders, developing staff leadership skills, and building staff morale. Companies contribute significant amounts of money to education, the arts, environmental causes, and the disadvantaged by supporting local and national charitable organizations. Cause-related marketing ties an organization's product(s) directly to a social concern through a marketing program. Strategic philanthropy involves linking core business competencies to societal and community needs.

IMPORTANT TERMS FOR REVIEW

voluntary practices 94

philanthropy 94

core practices 95

Better Business Bureau 95

mandated boundaries 95

civil law 97

criminal law 97

procompetitive legislation 99

consumer protection law 101

Occupational Safety and
Health Administration 103

Public Company Accounting
Oversight Board 107

Consumer Financial
Protection Bureau 110

cause-related marketing 116

strategic philanthropy 117

RESOLVING ETHICAL BUSINESS CHALLENGES*

Like most students at Arizona University, Ahmed was a student and spent twenty hours each week working at the university library. He liked the library because it was quiet and he could study some of the time. One interesting aspect of the library was the access to incredible databases, some of which were only for the professors. As a student worker he was privy to all the database codes, and soon discovered large amounts of materials for almost every class on campus.

Bill, one of Ahmed's fellow library student workers, was constantly talking about doing weird stunts and antics to put on YouTube. He was a nice person to be around but sometimes he was a little overbearing. One evening when Ahmed started work, Bill was talking about the many ways to download pirated music, movies, and books from the library's system. "It is very easy and untraceable. I just route my requests to a professor's IP address, then send it to several other faculty IP addresses so it is difficult to trace. I then go to one of the library computers, log in as someone else, put in a CD or Blu-Ray DVD, and burn what I want. The people's computers I route through get a message that someone logged into their account, but the IT guys just tell them it's no big deal and it happens all the time. IT never really looks into it because of the many systems and IP addresses on campus. Do you want me to get you any movies or CDs?" Ahmed politely refused, knowing full well this could get a person expelled from the university.

Several months passed and Bill became more popular. Every day someone stopped by the library desk where he worked and talked to Bill. The person walked to one of the library's computers, stuck in a disk, and several minutes later was gone. Ahmed looked at Bill and shook his head. Bill responded with a smile. One day, Ahmed found an envelope with his name on it when he went to his usual desk. When he opened it, there was five hundred dollars with a note saying, "Enjoy." He started to ask people about the money, but then saw Bill smiling. At that moment, Ahmed knew the money was from Bill. He tried to give it back, but Bill refused to take it or admit he had given it to Ahmed in the first place.

Ahmed became increasingly uncomfortable with Bill's behavior. He knew what Bill did was wrong and possibly illegal. He didn't want to be involved with it in any way, but he also didn't want to become a snitch. Now he was receiving money for his involvement. Ahmed felt the situation was escalating and he should say something to his supervisor before something really bad happened, but he didn't want to be the one to get Bill in trouble. Ahmed knew Bill could be expelled for something like this, which could potentially damage his entire future. Then again, Ahmed had his own future to worry about. Could he be expelled just for knowing what kind of activities Bill was involved in? What should he do with the money Bill gave him? What might happen if he doesn't blow the whistle?

QUESTIONS | EXERCISES

1. Describe the stakeholders involved in this ethical dilemma. What stake do they have in the situation?
2. Are Bill's actions an ethical issue, a legal issue, or both? Explain your reasoning.
3. What are some of the risks Ahmed faces if he becomes a whistleblower? What are the risks if he remains silent?

*This case is strictly hypothetical; any resemblance to real persons, companies, or situations is coincidental.

> > > CHECK YOUR EQ

Check your EQ, or Ethics Quotient, by completing the following. Assess your performance to evaluate your overall understanding of the chapter material.

1. Voluntary practices include documented best practices.   **Yes**   **No**

2. The primary method for resolving business ethics disputes is through the criminal court system.   **Yes**   **No**

3. The FSGO provides an incentive for organizations to conscientiously develop and implement ethics programs.   **Yes**   **No**

4. The Sarbanes–Oxley Act encourages CEOs and CFOs to report their financial statements accurately.   **Yes**   **No**

5. Strategic philanthropy represents a new direction in corporate giving that maximizes the benefit to societal or community needs and relates to business objectives.   **Yes**   **No**

ANSWERS **1. No.** Core practices are documented best practices. **2. No.** Civil litigation is the primary way in which business ethics disputes are resolved. **3. Yes.** Well-designed ethics and compliance programs can minimize legal liability when organizational misconduct is detected. **4. No.** The Sarbanes–Oxley Act *requires* CEOs and CFOs to accurately report their financial statements to a federal oversight committee; they must sign the document and are held personally liable for any inaccuracies. **5. Yes.** Strategic philanthropy helps both society and the organization.

ENDNOTES

1. Corporate Information: Corporate Culture," *Google*, http://www.google.com/corporate/culture.html (accessed April 18, 2013).

2. Paul K. Shum and Sharon L. Yam, "Ethics and Law: Guiding the Invisible Hand to Correct Corporate Social Responsibility Externalities," *Journal of Business Ethics* 98 (2011): 549–571.

3. Susan Decker, "Google's Motorola Files New Patent Case Against Apple," *Bloomberg Businessweek*, August 18, 2012, http://www.businessweek.com/news/2012-08-17/google-s-motorola-files-new-patent-case-against-apple-at-itc (accessed April 18, 2013).

4. Don Clark and Shayndi Raice, "Tech Firms Intensify Clashes over Patents," *The Wall Street Journal*, October 4, 2010, B3.

5. Lorraine Luk, "Microsoft and Hon Hai Reach Agreement on Patent Licensing," *The Wall Street Journal*, April 17, 2013, http://online.wsj.com/article/SB100014241278873 23309604578426808060135990.html (accessed April 18, 2013).

6. Amir Efrati, "Google Proposes Settlement Terms to EU Regulators," *The Wall Street Journal*, April 13, 2013, http://online.wsj.com/article/SB10001424127887324240804578 421043011099914.html (accessed April 18, 2013).

7. Aaron Back, "China Acts to Prevent Collusion on Prices," *The Wall Street Journal*, January 5, 2011, http://online.wsj.com/article/SB1000142405274870472310457606116062 0783364.html (accessed April 18, 2013).

8. Dionne Searcey, "U.K. Laws on Bribes Has Firms In a Sweat," *The Wall Street Journal*, December 28, 2010, B1.

9. Gregory T. Gundlach, "Price Predation: Legal Limits and Antitrust Considerations," *Journal of Public Policy & Marketing* 14 (1995): 278.

10. David Goldman, "Obama Vows Antitrust Crackdown," *CNN Money*, May 11, 2009, http://money.cnn.com/2009/05/11/news/economy/antitrust/index.htm (accessed April 18, 2013).

11. Steve Lohr, "High-Tech Antitrust Cases: The Road Ahead," *The New York Times*, May 13, 2009, http://bits.blogs.nytimes.com/2009/05/13/high-tech-antitrust-the-road-ahead/?scp=1&sq=high-tech%20antitrust&st=cse (accessed April 18, 2013).

12. "10 Ways to Combat Corporate Espionage," *Data Destruction News*, http://www.imakenews.com/accushred/e_article001225805.cfm?x=bdtNVCP, bbGvRs5c, w (accessed April 18, 2013).

13. Margaret Cronin Fisk and Steve Raphael, "Ex-GM Engineer, Husband Guilty of Trade Secrets Theft," *Bloomberg*, November 30, 2012, http://www.bloomberg.com/news/2012-11-30/ex-gm-engineer-husband-found-guilty-of-trade-secrets-theft-1-.html (accessed April 18, 2013).

14. "Baseball's Antitrust Exemption: Q&A," *ESPN*, December 5, 2001, http://sports.espn.go.com/espn/print?id=1290707&type=story (accessed April 18, 2013).

15. "A Child Shall Lead the Way: Marketing to Youths," *Credit Union Executive*, May–June 1993, 6–8.

16. Julia Angwin, "How to Keep Kids Safe Online," *The Wall Street Journal*, January 22, 2009, http://online.wsj.com/article/SB123238632055894993.html (accessed April 18, 2013).

17. Anton Troianovski, "Developers Brace for New Rules on Kids' Apps," *The Wall Street Journal*, April 5, 2013, B1.

18. Jennifer Levitz, "Laws Take on Financial Scams against Seniors," *The Wall Street Journal*, May 19, 2009, http://online.wsj.com/article/SB124269210323932723.html (accessed April 18, 2013).

19. Gerald Albaum and Robert A. Peterson, "Multilevel (Network) Marketing: An Objective View," *The Marketing Review*, Volume 11, Number 4, 2011, 347–361. Daniel B. Ravicher. "Might Other Companies Be Liable If Herbalife Is A Pyramid Scheme?" *Seeking Alpha*, February 5, 2013, http://seekingalpha.com/article/1157581-might-other-companies-be-liable-if-herbalife-is-a-pyramid, (accessed February 5, 2013). Karen E. Klein. "A Charm Offensive by Direct Sellers," *Bloomberg Businessweek*, June 25–July 1, 2012, 52–54; Duane Stanford. "Bill Ackman's Crusade Against Herbalife," *Bloomberg Businessweek*, January 14–20, 2012, 40; Gerald Albaum, "Multi-level Marketing and Pyramid Scheme: Myth versus Reality," *AMS Quarterly*, November 2008, 10; Business Wire, "Herbalife announces Results of Study on Distributors and End Users in the U.S., Yahoo! Finance, June 11, 2013, http://finance.yahoo.com/news/herbalife-announces-results-study-distributors-214500826.html (accessed June 17, 2013).

20. "What We Do," *U.S. Food and Drug Administration*, http://www.fda.gov/AboutFDA/WhatWeDo/default.htm (accessed April 18, 2013).

21. Deborah Kotz, "Energy drinks: FDAA warns against DMAA," *The Boston Globe*, April 15, 2013, http://bostonglobe.com/lifestyle/health-wellness/2013/04/14/energy-drinks-fda-warns-against-dmaa/dqcTK77PuB0EizVIeMrlTP/story.html (accessed April 18, 2013).

22. Latifa Lyles, "Closing the Equal Pay Gap: 50 Years and Counting," *United States Department of Labor*, April 9, 2013, http://social.dol.gov/blog/closing-the-equal-pay-gap-50-years-and-counting/ (accessed April 18, 2013).

23. Cynthia Bell, "'Our Journey is Not Complete' – Equal Pay Requires Passage of Paycheck Fairness Act," *ACLU*, January 29, 2013, http://www.aclu.org/blog/womens-rights-lgbt-rights-religion-belief/our-journey-not-complete-equal-pay-requires-passage (accessed April 18, 2013).

24. Business Wire, "Cruise Lawyers to Senator Rockefeller: Overworked Cruise Employees Denied," *Bloomberg*, April 11, 2013, http://www.bloomberg.com/article/2013-04-11/amJSvA8pDWGk.html (accessed April 18, 2013).

25. Steven Scalet and Thomas F. Kelly, "The Ethics of Credit Rating Agencies: What Happened and the Way Forward," *Journal of Business Ethics* 111(2012): 477–490.

26. VikasBajas, "At Moody's, Some Debt was Rated Incorrectly," *The New York Times*, July 2, 2008, http://query.nytimes.com/gst/fullpage.html?res=9505E3DB 173DF931A35754C0A96E9C8B63 (accessed April 18, 2013).

27. Jeannette Neymann, "New York Looks at Ratings Firms," *The Wall Street Journal*, February 8, 2013, C1–C2.

28. Sarah Lynch, "Schapiro: More Oversight Needed for Credit-Rating Firms," *The Wall Street Examiner*, April 15, 2009, http://forums.wallstreetexaminer.com/index. php?showtopic=807630 (accessed March 15, 2011).

29. Mike Spector and Shelly Banjo, "Pay at Nonprofits Gets a Closer Look," *The Wall Street Journal*, March 27, 2009, http://online.wsj.com/article/SB123811160845153093. html (accessed April 18, 2013).

30. Protiviti, 2012 Sarbanes-Oxley Compliance Survey, 2012, http://www.protiviti.com/en-US/Documents/ Surveys/2012-SOX-Compliance-Survey-Protiviti.pdf (accessed April 18, 2013).

31. Floyd Norris and Adam Liptak, "Justices Uphold Sarbanes-Oxley Act," *The New York Times*, June 28, 2010, http://www.nytimes.com/2010/06/29/ business/29accounting.html?pagewanted=1&_r=1 (accessed April 18, 2013).

32. Tim Elfrink, "The Rise and Fall of the Stanford Financial Group," *Houston Press*, April 9, 2009, http://www. houstonpress.com/content/printVersion/1173931/ (accessed April 18, 2013); Shira Ovide, "Lehman Brothers Whistle-blower Matthew Lee Again in Spotlight," *The Wall Street Journal*, December 21, 2010, http://blogs.wsj. com/deals/2010/12/21/lehman-brothers-whistleblower- matthew-lee-again-in-spotlight/ / (accessed April 18, 2013).

33. Tricia Bisoux, "The Sarbanes–Oxley Effect," *BizEd*, July/ August 2005, 24–29.

34. 2010 *Sarbanes-Oxley Compliance Survey*, http:// www.auditnet.org/articles/KL201010.pdf (accessed February 22, 2011).

35. Protiviti, 2012 Sarbanes-Oxley Compliance Survey, 2012, http://www.protiviti.com/en-US/Documents/ Surveys/2012-SOX-Compliance-Survey-Protiviti.pdf (accessed April 18, 2013).

36. President Barack Obama, "Remarks by the President on 21st Century Financial Regulatory Reform," The White House, June 17, 2009, http://www.whitehouse.gov/the_ press_office/Remarks-of-the-President-on-Regulatory- Reform/ (accessed April 18, 2013).

37. Ibid.

38. Joshua Gallu, "Dodd-Frank May Cost $6.5 Billion and 5,000 Workers," *Bloomberg*, February 14, 2011, http:// www.bloomberg.com/news/2011-02-14/dodd-frank- s-implementation-calls-for-6-5-billion-5-000-staff- in-budget.html (accessed April 18, 2013); Binyamin Appelbaum and Brady Dennis, "Dodd's overhaul goes well beyond other plans," *The Washington Post*, November 11, 2009, http://www.washingtonpost.com/ wp-dyn/content/article/2009/11/09/AR2009110901935. html?hpid=topnews&sid=ST2009111003729 (accessed April 18, 2013).

39. Maria Bartiromo, "JPMorgan CEO Jamie Dimon sees good times in 2011," *USA Today*, February 21, 2011, http://www.usatoday.com/money/companies/ management/bartiromo/2011-02-21-bartiromo21_ CV_N.htm (accessed April 18, 2013).

40. "Office of Financial Research," *U.S. Department of Treasury*, http://www.treasury.gov/initiatives/Pages/ofr. aspx (accessed April 18, 2013).

41. "Initiatives: Financial Stability Oversight Council," *U.S. Department of Treasury*, http://www.treasury.gov/ initiatives/Pages/FSOC-index.aspx (accessed April 18, 2013).

42. Financial Stability Oversight Council Created Under the Dodd-Frank Wall Street Reform and Consumer Protection Act: Frequently Asked Questions, October 2010, http://www.treasury.gov/initiatives/wsr/ Documents/FAQs%20-%20Financial%20Stability%20 Oversight%20Council%20-%20October%202010%20 FINAL%20v2.pdf (accessed April 18, 2013).

43. "Subtitle A—Bureau of Consumer Financial Protection," *One Hundred Eleventh Congress of the United States of America*, 589.

44. "Wall Street Reform: Bureau of Consumer Financial Protection (CFPB)," U.S. Treasury, http://www.treasury. gov/initiatives/Pages/cfpb.aspx (accessed April 18, 2013).

45. "Wall Street Reform: Bureau of Consumer Financial Protection (CFPB)," *U.S. Treasury*, http://www.treasury. gov/initiatives/Pages/cfpb.aspx (accessed April 18, 2013); Sudeep Reddy, "Elizabeth Warren's Early Words on a Consumer Financial Protection Bureau," *The Wall Street Journal*, September 17, 2010, http://blogs.wsj.com/ economics/2010/09/17/elizabeth-warrens-early-words- on-a-consumer-financial-protection-bureau/ (accessed April 18, 2013); Jennifer Liberto & David Ellis, "Wall Street reform: What's in the bill," *CNN*, June 30, 2010); http://money.cnn.com/2010/06/25/news/economy/ whats_in_the_reform_bill/index.htm (accessed April 18, 2013).

46. Jean Eaglesham, "Warning Shot on Financial Protection," *The Wall Street Journal*, February 9, 2011, http://online. wsj.com/article/SB1000142405274870350780457613 0370862263258.html?mod=googlenews_wsj (accessed April 18, 2013).

47. Liz Rappaport, Liz Moyer, and Anupreeta Das, "Goldman Sets Funds for 'Volcker'," *The Wall Street Journal*, February 8, 2013, C1–C2.

48. Jean Eaglesham, "Warning Shot on Financial Protection."

49. Jean Eaglesham and Ashby Jones, "Whistle-blower Bounties Pose Challenges," *The Wall Street Journal*, December 13, 2010, C1, C3.

50. Ibid.

51. "SEC announces first whistleblower payout under Dodd- Frank bounty program," *Compliance Corner*, August 2012, http://compliancecorner.wnj.com/?p=177 (accessed April 18, 2013).

52. Win Swenson, "The Organizational Guidelines' 'Carrot and Stick' Philosophy, and Their Focus on 'Effective' Compliance," in Corporate Crime in America: Strengthening the "Good Citizenship"-Corporation (Washington, DC: U.S. Sentencing Commission, 1995), 17–26.

53. United States Code Service (Lawyers' Edition), 18 U.S.C.S. Appendix, Sentencing Guidelines for the United States Courts (Rochester, NY: Lawyers Cooperative Publishing, 1995), sec. 8A.1.

54. O. C Ferrell and Linda Ferrell, "Current Developments in Managing Organizational Ethics and Compliance Initiatives," University of Wyoming, white paper, Bill Daniels Business Ethics Initiative 2006.

55. Open Compliance Ethics Group 2005 Benchmarking Study Key Findings, http://www.oceg.org/view/Benchmarking2005 (accessed June 12, 2009).

56. "US Sentences Guidelines Changes Become Effective November 1," *FCPA Compliance and Ethics Blog*, November 2, 2010, http://tfoxlaw.wordpress.com/2010/11/02/us-sentencing-guidelines-changes-become-effective-november-1/ (accessed April 18, 2013).

57. United States Sentencing Commission, *Amendments to the Sentencing Guidelines*, April 30, 2012, http://www.ussc.gov/Legal/Amendments/Reader-Friendly/20120430_RF_Amendments.pdf (accessed April 18, 2013); "U.S. Sentencing Commission Promulgates Amendment to the Federal Sentencing Guidelines Responding to the Dodd-Frank Act," April 13, 2012, http://www.ussc.gov/Legislative_and_Public_Affairs/Newsroom/Press_Releases/20120413_Press_Release.pdf (accessed April 18, 2013); "Sentencing Panel Amends Guidelines for Mortgage Fraud," Crime in the Suites, May 11, 2012, http://crimeinthesuites.com/sentencing-panel-amends-guidelines-mortgage-fraud/ (accessed April 18, 2013); David Debold and Matthew Benjamin, "U.S. Sentencing Commission Approves Increased Penalties for Certain Fraud Offenses," FindLaw, August 28, 2012, http://corporate.findlaw.com/litigation-disputes/u-s-sentencing-commission-approves-increased-penalties-for-certa.html (accessed April 18, 2013).

58. Ferrell and Ferrell, "Current Developments in Managing Organizational Ethics and Compliance Initiatives."

59. Lynn Brewer, "Capitalizing on the Value of Integrity: An Integrated Model to Standardize the Measure of Non-financial Performance as an Assessment of Corporate Integrity," in Managing Risks for Corporate Integrity.

How to Survive an Ethical Misconduct Disaster, ed. Lynn Brewer, Robert Chandler, and O. C. Ferrell (Mason, OH: Thomson/Texere, 2006), 233–277.

60. Nanci Hellmich, "Disney cuts junk from its ad diet," *USA Today*, June 5, 2012, 1B.

61. Ingrid MurroBotero, "Charitable Giving Has 4 Big Benefits," *Business Journal of Phoenix*, online, January 1, 1999, www.bizjournals.com/phoenix/stories/1999/01/04/smallb3.html (accessed April 18, 2013).

62. Wells Fargo, Corporate Social Responsibility Interim Report 2012, https://www.wellsfargo.com/downloads/pdf/about/csr/reports/2012-social-responsibility-interim.pdf (accessed April 18, 2013).

63. Walmart, "Community Giving," http://foundation.walmart.com/ (accessed April 18, 2013).

64. Susan G. Komen for the Cure, http://ww5.komen.org/AboutUs/AboutUs.html (accessed April 18, 2013); "Save Lids to Save Lives®," Yoplait, https://savelidstosavelives.com (accessed April 18, 2013).

65. "Even as Cause Marketing Grows, 83 Percent of Consumers Still Want to See More," Cone, http://www.coneinc.com/cause-grows-consumers-want-more (accessed February 23, 2011).

66. Joëlle Vanhamme, Adam Lindgreen, Jon Reast, and Nathalie van Popering, "To Do Well by Doing Good: Improving Corporate Image Through Cause-Related Marketing," *Journal of Business Ethics* 109 (2012): 259–274.

67. Leigh Buchanan, "More Than a Moving Company," Inc., December 1, 2010, www.inc.com/magazine/20101201/more-than-a-moving-company.html (accessed April 18, 2013); Gentle Giant Movers website, www.gentlegiant.com (accessed April 17, 2013).

68. The Home Depot, "Living our Values," http://careers.homedepot.com/our-culture/community-involvement.html (accessed April 16, 2013).

CHAPTER 5

ETHICAL DECISION MAKING

AN ETHICAL DILEMMA*

Steven, a junior at Texas University, just started working part-time at a local fast food restaurant chain. Although not his dream job, it paid for tuition and books, and the restaurant gave him the flexible schedule he needed for school. After a few months, Steven found he got along well with all of his co-workers, but it was apparent they did not respect the company or the management. The employees made fun of their bosses and treated the work area like a playground. In some respects, Steven thought it was a fun environment to work in, especially after hours when management was gone for the day. They played their music loudly, laughed, and talked with one another during the down times instead of cleaning up their work areas like they were supposed to. Despite the fact there were ethical policies telling employees how they were expected to act in the workplace, these policies never seemed to be enforced.

One day, while working with his co-worker Julie on the food assembly table, Steven saw Julie accidentally drop a meat patty on the floor. Without so much as a flinch, she bent down, picked up the patty, stuck it back on the bun, and wrapped it up. It happened so fast that Steven wasn't even sure he had seen right—especially since Julie had done it so casually. Steven watched in dismay as another worker took the hamburger out to the customer.

Over the next few weeks, Steven saw others, including the shift supervisor, do the same thing with burgers and other products. Once, an entire cheeseburger hit the greasy floor, was picked up, and was taken to the customer. This time the customer complained the burger tasted funny and sent it back. Steven noticed other unsanitary practices such as employees not washing their hands between handling meat and vegetables and not washing utensils between uses. Obviously, such practices were against company policies and, if reported, the supervisors in charge could get in trouble and the restaurant would face investigations from the health department. However, there was ample opportunity for things like this to occur. There was no one watching them, and the shift supervisor also engaged in these activities. Steven felt it was the company's responsibility to hire good people, so they were to blame if these things happened.

One day, Steven approached Julie and asked, "Why do so many people here serve food that has fallen on the floor to customers?"

Julie thought about it briefly as though she had never considered it before and replied, "I guess it's because it would take too much time to get another beef patty out of the freezer, cook it, and serve it to the customer. This is a fast food restaurant, after all, and I'm not interested in hearing customers complain about the time it takes for them to get their food. Besides, the restaurants with the fastest service get a bonus from corporate headquarters. Last year the supervisors rewarded us with some extra money for doing our jobs so quickly."

Steven was somewhat taken aback by the honest reply and asked, "Wouldn't you be disgusted if you were served dirty food at a restaurant?"

This time Julie's response was quick. She said, "What I don't know won't hurt me." She walked off.

Several weeks went by and the same practices continued. Steven became more and more concerned about the consequences that could happen in an environment so laid back and unconcerned about safety and health. It seemed like the more time that passed, the worse everyone's attitude became.

One day, at the beginning of his shift, Steven noticed the walk-in freezer had been left open. As he went to shut the door, he discovered a smell of rotten meat. It almost made him vomit. "How could this happen?" he wondered. He threw away the rotten meat without asking anyone because he was afraid of what the answer might be.

After Steven threw out the spoiled meat, he began to wonder how the culture of the restaurant got to the point of supporting such practices. He realized the seemingly minor unsanitary practices allowed major issues to arise that could possibly hurt someone. Steven felt he should say or do something, but to whom? He sat down and pondered what he should do.

QUESTIONS | EXERCISES

1. Describe the nature of the organizational culture in the restaurant. What kind of opportunities are there for unethical behavior to occur? Are there any opportunities for ethical behavior?

2. What are some of the incentives employees might have to engage in this type of behavior?

3. If the organizational culture of the restaurant does not change, what are some likely outcomes and consequences?

*This case is strictly hypothetical; any resemblance to real persons, companies, or situations is coincidental.

To improve ethical decision making in business, you must first understand how individuals make decisions in an organization. Too often it is assumed people in organizations make ethical decisions in the same way they make them at home, in their families, or in their personal lives. Within the context of an organizational work group, however, few individuals have the freedom to personally decide ethical issues independent of the organization and its stakeholders.

This chapter summarizes our current knowledge of ethical decision making in business and provides a model so you may better visualize the ethical decision making process. Although it is impossible to describe exactly how any one individual or work group might make ethical decisions, we can offer generalizations about average or typical behavior patterns within organizations. These generalizations are based on many studies and at least six ethical decision models that have been widely accepted by academics and practitioners.[1] Based on this research, we present a model for understanding ethical decision making in the context of business organizations. The model integrates concepts from philosophy, psychology, sociology, and organizational behavior. This framework should be helpful in understanding organizational ethics and developing ethical programs. Additionally, we describe some normative considerations that prescribe how organizational decision making should approach ethical issues. Principles and values are used by organizations as a foundation for establishing core values to provide enduring beliefs about appropriate conduct. Therefore, we provide both a descriptive understanding of how ethical decisions are made as well as the normative framework to determine how decisions ought to be made.

A FRAMEWORK FOR ETHICAL DECISION MAKING IN BUSINESS

As Figure 5–1 shows, our model of the ethical decision making process in business includes ethical issue intensity, individual factors, and organizational factors such as corporate culture and opportunity. All of these interrelated factors influence the evaluations of and intentions behind the decisions that produce ethical or unethical behavior. This model does not describe how to make ethical decisions, but it does help you to understand the factors and processes related to ethical decision making.

Ethical Issue Intensity

The first step in ethical decision making is to recognize that an ethical issue requires an individual or work group to choose among several actions that various stakeholders inside or outside the firm will ultimately evaluate as right or wrong. The first step

FIGURE 5-1 Framework for Understanding Ethical Decision Making in Business

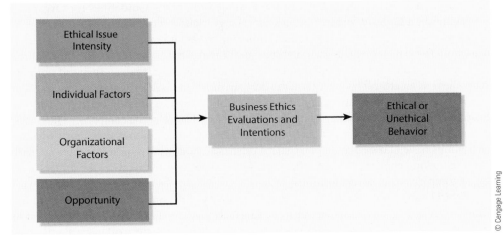

is becoming aware that an ethical issue exists. **Ethical awareness** is the ability to perceive whether a situation or decision has an ethical dimension. Costly problems can be avoided if employees are able to first recognize whether a situation has an ethical component. However, ethical awareness can be difficult in an environment when employees work in their own areas of expertise with the same types of people. It is easier to overlook certain issues requiring an ethical decision, particularly if the decision becomes a routine part of the job. This makes it important for organizations to train employees how to recognize the potential ethical ramifications of their decisions. Familiarizing employees with company values and training them to recognize common ethical scenarios can help them develop ethical awareness.

The intensity of an ethical issue relates to its perceived importance to the decision maker.[2] **Ethical issue intensity** can be defined as the relevance or importance of an event or decision in the eyes of the individual, work group, and/or organization. It is personal and temporal in character to accommodate values, beliefs, needs, perceptions, the special characteristics of the situation, and the personal pressures prevailing at a particular place and time.[3] Senior employees and those with administrative authority contribute significantly to ethical issue intensity because they typically dictate an organization's stance on ethical issues. For instance, greenhouse gas emissions are an important global topic. The Environmental Protection Agency (EPA) collects and publishes data on carbon dioxide due to its negative impact on the environment. Although the EPA can fine or sanction firms that go above carbon dioxide standards, industry groups have filed numerous lawsuits. As a result of the controversy, power plant companies like Scherer and Martin Lake have labeled this an ethical issue.[4] Additionally, insider trading is considered a serious ethical issue by the government because the intent is to take advantage of information not available to the public. Therefore, it is an ethical issue of high intensity for regulators and government officials. This often puts them at odds with financial companies such as hedge funds. A survey of hedge fund companies revealed 35 percent of respondents feel pressured to break the rules.[5] Because of their greater ability to gather financial information from the market—some of which might not be public information—hedge funds and other financial institutions have often come under increased scrutiny by the federal government.

Under current law, managers can be held liable for the unethical and illegal actions of subordinates. In the United States, the Federal Sentencing Guidelines for Organizations contain a liability formula judges use as a guideline regarding illegal activities of corporations. For example, many of the Enron employees and managers aware of the firm's use of off-the-balance-sheet partnerships—that turned out to be the major cause of the energy firm's collapse—were advised these partnerships were legal, so they did not perceive them as an ethical issue. Although such partnerships were legal at that time, the way Enron officials designed them and the methods they used to provide collateral (that is, Enron stock) created a scheme that brought about the collapse of the company.[6] Thus, ethical issue intensity involves individuals' cognitive state of concern about an issue, or whether or not they have knowledge that an issue is unethical, that in turn indicates their involvement in making choices. The identification of ethical issues often requires the understanding of complex business relationships.

Ethical issue intensity reflects the ethical sensitivity of the individual and/or work group facing the ethical decision-making process. Research suggests that individuals are subject to six "spheres of influence" when confronted with ethical choices—the workplace, family, religion, legal system, community, and profession—and the level of importance of each of these influences varies depending on how important the decision maker perceives the issue to be.[7] Additionally, individuals' moral intensity increases their perceptiveness of potential ethical problems, which in turn reduces their intention to act unethically.[8] **Moral intensity** relates to individuals' perceptions of social pressure and the harm they believe their decisions will have on others.[9] All other factors in Figure 5–1, including individual factors, organizational factors, and intentions, determine why different individuals perceive ethical issues differently. Unless individuals in an organization share common concerns about ethical issues, the stage is set for ethical conflict. The perception of ethical issue intensity can be influenced by management's use of rewards and punishments, corporate policies, and corporate values to sensitize employees. In other words, managers can affect the degree to which employees perceive the importance of an ethical issue through positive and/or negative incentives.[10]

For some employees, ethical issues may not reach the critical awareness level if managers fail to identify and educate them about specific problem areas. One study found that more than a third of the unethical situations that lower and middle-level managers face come from internal pressures and ambiguity surrounding internal organizational rules. Many employees fail to anticipate these issues before they arise.[11] This lack of preparedness makes it difficult for employees to respond appropriately when they encounter an ethics issue. One field recognized as having insufficient ethics training is science. A panel of experts found young scientists tend to lack knowledge about ethical frameworks to navigate ethical gray areas. They therefore tend to be unprepared when faced with an ethical issue.[12] Organizations that consist of employees with diverse values and backgrounds must train workers in the way the firm wants specific ethical issues handled. Identifying the ethical issues and risks employees might encounter is a significant step toward developing their ability to make ethical decisions. Many ethical issues are identified by industry groups or through general information available to a firm. Flagging certain issues as high in ethical importance could trigger increases in employees' ethical issue intensity. The perceived importance of an ethical issue has shown a strong influence on both employees' ethical judgment and their behavioral intention. In other words, the more likely individuals perceive an ethical issue as important, the less likely they are to engage in questionable or unethical behavior.[13] Therefore, ethical issue intensity should be considered a key factor in the ethical decision-making process.

Individual Factors

When people need to resolve issues in their daily lives, they often base their decisions on their own values and principles of right or wrong. They generally learn these values and principles through the socialization process with family members, social groups, religion, and in their formal education. Good personal values have been found to decrease unethical practices and increase positive work behavior. The moral philosophies of individuals, discussed in more detail in Chapter 6, provide principles and rules people use to decide what is right or wrong from a moral and personal perspective. Values of individuals can be derived from moral philosophies to apply to daily decisions. However, values are subjective and vary a great deal across different cultures. For example, some individuals might place greater importance on keeping their promises and commitments than others would. Values could also relate to negative rationalizations, such as "Everyone does it," or "We have to do what it takes to get the business."[14] Research demonstrates that individuals with destructive personalities who violate basic core values can cause a work group to suffer a performance loss of 30 percent to 40 percent compared to groups with no "bad apples."[15] The actions of specific individuals in scandal-plagued financial companies such as Goldman Sachs and JP Morgan often raise questions about those individuals' personal character and integrity. They appear to operate in their own self-interest or in total disregard for the law and the interests of society.

Although an individual's intention to engage in ethical behavior relates to individual values, organizational and social forces also play a vital role. An individual's attitudes as well as social norms help create behavioral intentions that shape his or her decision-making process. While an individual may intend to do the right thing, organizational or social forces can alter this intent. For example, an individual may intend to report the misconduct of a coworker, but when faced with the social consequences of doing so, may decide to remain complacent. In this case, social forces overcome a person's individual values when it comes to taking appropriate action.[16] At the same time, individual values strongly influence how people assume ethical responsibilities in the work environment. In turn, individual decisions can be heavily dependent on company policy and the corporate culture.

The way the public perceives business ethics generally varies according to the profession in question. Telemarketers, car salespersons, advertising practitioners, stockbrokers, and real estate brokers are often perceived as having the lowest ethics. Research regarding individual factors that affect ethical awareness, judgment, intent, and behavior include gender, education, work experience, nationality, age, and locus of control.

Extensive research has been done regarding the link between **gender** and ethical decision making. The research shows that in many aspects there are no differences between men and women, but when differences are found, women are generally more ethical than men.[17] By "more ethical," we mean women seem to be more sensitive to ethical scenarios and less tolerant of unethical actions. One study found that women and men had different foundations for making ethical decisions: women rely on relationships; men rely on justice or equity.[18] In another study on gender and intentions for fraudulent financial reporting, females reported higher intentions to report them than male participants.[19] As more and more women work in managerial positions, these findings may become increasingly significant.

Education is also a significant factor in the ethical decision-making process. The important thing to remember about education is that it does not reflect experience. Work experience is defined as the number of years in a specific job, occupation, and/or industry.

Generally, the more education or work experience people have, the better they are at making ethical decisions. The type of education someone receives has little or no effect on ethics. For example, it doesn't matter if you are a business student or a liberal arts student—you are pretty much the same in terms of ethical decision making. Current research, however, shows students are less ethical than businesspeople, which is likely because businesspeople have been exposed to more ethically challenging situations than students.[20]

Nationality is the legal relationship between a person and the country in which he or she is born. In the twenty-first century, nationality is redefined by regional economic integration such as the European Union (EU). When European students are asked their nationality, they are less likely to state where they were born than where they currently live. The same thing is happening in the United States, as people born in Florida living in New York might consider themselves to be New Yorkers. Research about nationality and ethics appears to be significant in how it affects ethical decision making; however, just how nationality affects ethics is somewhat hard to interpret.[21] Because of cultural differences, it is impossible to state that ethical decision making in an organizational context will differ significantly among individuals of different nationalities. The reality of today is that multinational companies look for businesspeople that make decisions regardless of nationality. Perhaps in 20 years, nationality will no longer be an issue because the multinational individual's culture will replace national status as the most significant factor in ethical decision making.

Age is another individual factor researched within business ethics. Several decades ago, we believed age was positively correlated with ethical decision making. In other words, the older you are, the more ethical you are. However, recent research suggests there is probably a more complex relationship between ethics and age.[22] We believe older employees with more experience have greater knowledge to deal with complex industry-specific ethical issues. Younger managers are far more influenced by organizational culture than are older managers.[23]

Locus of control relates to individual differences in relation to a generalized belief about how you are affected by internal versus external events or reinforcements. In other words, the concept relates to how people view themselves in relation to power. Those who believe in **external control** (externals) see themselves as going with the flow because that is all they can do. They believe the events in their lives are due to uncontrollable forces. They consider what they want to achieve depends on luck, chance, and powerful people in their company. In addition, they believe the probability of being able to control their lives by their own actions and efforts is low. Conversely, those who believe in **internal control** (internals) believe they control the events in their lives by their own effort and skill, viewing themselves as masters of their destinies and trusting in their capacity to influence their environment.

Current research suggests we still cannot be sure how significant locus of control is in terms of ethical decision making. One study that found a relationship between locus of control and ethical decision making concluded that internals were positively correlated whereas externals were negatively correlated.[24] In other words, those who believe they formed their own destiny were more ethical than those who believed their fate was in the hands of others.

Organizational Factors

Although people can and do make individual ethical choices in business situations, no one operates in a vacuum. Indeed, research established that in the workplace, the organization's values often have greater influence on decisions than a person's own values.[25] Ethical choices in business are most often made jointly, in work groups and committees, or in conversations and discussions with coworkers. Employees approach ethical issues on the basis of what they learned not only from their own backgrounds, but also from others in the organization. The outcome of this learning process depends on the strength of personal values, the opportunities to behave unethically, and the exposure to others who behave ethically or unethically. An alignment between a person's own values and the values of the organization help create positive work attitudes and organizational outcomes. Research has further demonstrated that congruence in personal and organizational values is related to commitment, satisfaction, motivation, ethics, work stress, and anxiety.[26] Although people outside the organization such as family members and friends also influence decision makers, the organization develops a personality that helps determine what is and is not ethical. Just as a family guides an individual, specific industries give behavioral cues to firms. Within the family develops what is called a culture and so too in an organization.

Corporate culture can be defined as a set of values, norms, and artifacts, including ways of solving problems that members (employees) of an organization share. As time passes, stakeholders come to view the company or organization as a living organism with a mind and will of its own. The Walt Disney Co., for example, requires all new employees to take a course in the traditions and history of Disneyland and Walt Disney, including the ethical dimensions of the company. The corporate culture at American Express stresses that employees help customers out of difficult situations whenever possible. This attitude is reinforced through numerous company legends of employees who have gone above and beyond the call of duty to help customers. This strong tradition of customer loyalty might encourage an American Express employee to take unorthodox steps to help a customer who encounters a problem while traveling overseas. Employees learn they can take some risks in helping customers. Such strong traditions and values have become a driving force in many companies, including Starbucks, IBM, Procter & Gamble, Southwest Airlines, and Hershey Foods.

One way organizations can determine the ethicalness and authenticity of their corporate cultures is having organizations go back to their mission statement or goals and objectives. These goals and objectives are often developed by various stakeholders, such as investors, employees, customers, and suppliers. Comparing the firm's activities with its mission statement, goals, and objectives helps the organization understand whether it is staying true to its values. Additionally, most industries have trade associations that disperse guidelines developed over time from others in the industry. These rules help guide the decision making process as well. The interaction between the company's internal rules and regulations and industry guidelines form the basis of whether a business is making ethical or unethical decisions. It also gives an organization an idea of how an ethical or unethical culture may look.

An important component of corporate or organizational culture is the company's ethical conduct. Corporate culture involves values and norms that prescribe a wide range of behavior for organizational members, while **ethical culture** reflects the integrity of decisions made and is a function of many factors, including corporate policies, top management's leadership on ethical issues, the influence of coworkers, and the opportunity for unethical behavior. Communication is also important in the creation of an effective ethical culture. There is a positive correlation between effective communication and empowerment and the development of an organizational ethical climate.[27] Within the organization as a whole, subcultures can develop in individual departments or work groups, but these are influenced by the strength of the firm's overall ethical culture, as well as the function of the department and the stakeholders it serves.[28] The more employees perceive an organization's ethical culture to be, the less likely they are to make unethical decisions.

Corporate culture and ethical culture are closely associated with the idea that significant others within the organization help determine ethical decisions within that organization. Research indicates the ethical values embodied in an organization's culture are positively correlated to employees' commitment to the firm and their sense that they fit into the company. These findings suggest companies should develop and promote ethical values to enhance employees' experiences in the workplace.[29]

Those who have influence in a work group, including peers, managers, coworkers, and subordinates, are referred to as **significant others**. They help workers on a daily basis with unfamiliar tasks and provide advice and information in both formal and informal ways. Coworkers, for instance, can offer help in the comments they make in discussions over lunch or when the boss is away. Likewise, a manager may provide directives about certain types of activities employees perform on the job. Indeed, an employee's supervisor can play a central role in helping employees develop and fit in socially in the workplace.[30] Numerous studies conducted over the years confirm that significant others within an organization may have more impact on a worker's decisions on a daily basis than any other factor.[31]

Obedience to authority is another aspect of the influence significant others can exercise. Obedience to authority helps explain why many employees resolve business ethics issues by simply following the directives of a superior. In organizations that emphasize respect for superiors, employees may feel they are expected to carry out orders by a supervisor even if those orders are contrary to the employees' sense of right and wrong. Later, if the employee's decision is judged to be wrong, he or she is likely to say, "I was only carrying out orders," or "My boss told me to do it this way." In addition, research shows the type of industry and size of the organization were found to be relevant factors, with bigger companies at greater risk for unethical activities.[32]

Opportunity

Opportunity describes the conditions in an organization that limit or permit ethical or unethical behavior. Opportunity results from conditions that either provide rewards, whether internal or external, or fail to erect barriers against unethical behavior. Examples of internal rewards include feelings of goodness and personal worth generated by performing altruistic acts. External rewards refer to what an individual expects to receive from others in the social environment in terms of social approval, status, and esteem.

An example of a condition that fails to erect barriers against unethical behavior is a company policy that does not punish employees who accept large gifts from clients. The absence of punishment essentially provides an opportunity for unethical behavior because it allows individuals to engage in such behavior without fear of consequences. The prospect of a reward for unethical behavior can also create an opportunity for questionable decisions. For example, a salesperson given public recognition and a large bonus for making a valuable sale obtained through unethical tactics will probably be motivated to use such tactics again, even if such behavior goes against the salesperson's personal value system. If ten percent of employees observe others at the workplace abusing drugs or alcohol and nobody reports or responds to this conduct, then the opportunity for others to engage in these activities exists.[33]

Opportunity relates to individuals' immediate job context—where they work, whom they work with, and the nature of the work. The immediate job context includes the motivational "carrots and sticks" superiors use to influence employee behavior. Pay raises, bonuses, and public recognition act as carrots, or positive reinforcements, whereas demotions, firings, reprimands, and pay penalties act as sticks, or negative reinforcements. One survey reports more than two-thirds of employees steal from their workplaces, and most do so repeatedly.[34] As Table 5–1 shows, many office supplies, particularly smaller ones, tend to "disappear" from the workplace. Small supplies such as Post-It notes, copier paper, staples, and pens appear to be the more commonly pilfered items, but some office theft sometimes reaches more serious proportions. One employee was indicted for stealing more than $376,000 in ink toner from a law firm and selling it on the black market over a two-year period.[35] The retail industry is particularly hard hit—total losses from employee theft are often greater than shoplifting at retail chains.[36] If there is no policy against this practice, one concern is employees will not learn where to draw the line and get into the habit of taking more expensive items for personal use.

The opportunities that employees have for unethical behavior in an organization can be eliminated through formal codes, policies, and rules adequately enforced by

TABLE 5–1 Most Common Office Supplies Stolen by Employees

1	Post-It notes
2	Tape
3	Scissors
4	Toilet paper
5	Copier paper
6	USB memory sticks
7	Notepads
8	Pens
9	Staplers
10	Highlighters

Source: "Top Office Supplies that Are Stolen and the Average Value of Contents In A Woman's Purse!" *KMLE*, May 16, 2012, http://kmle1079.cbslocal.com/2012/05/16/top-office-supplies-that-are-stolen/ (accessed April 12, 2013).

management. For instance, the American Economic Association adopted new conflict-of-interest rules to help academic economists become more transparent about their relationships with hedge funds, banks, and financial institutions. These rules responded to the criticisms levied against academic economists over the consulting services and derivative risk models they provided to financial companies such as Lehman Brothers—services that have been partially blamed for the U.S. financial crisis.[37] Financial companies—such as banks, savings and loan associations, and securities companies—developed elaborate sets of rules and procedures to avoid creating opportunities for individual employees to manipulate or take advantage of their trusted positions. In banks, one such rule requires most employees to take a vacation and stay out of the bank a certain number of days every year so they cannot be physically present to cover up embezzlement or other diversions of funds. This rule prevents the opportunity for inappropriate conduct.

Despite the existence of rules, misconduct can still occur without proper oversight. News Corp. received a blow when an investigation revealed its most popular tabloid in the United Kingdom, *News of the World*, engaged in wide-scale phone hacking to secure leads. Resulting backlash led to the closure of the tabloid and the arrest of more than 100 News Corp. officials. How did the tabloid manage to get away with this misconduct for years? Investigators believe the company paid off police officers to look the other way. Many officers and other public officials were arrested in connection with the hacking and alleged bribery scheme.[38] To avoid similar situations, there must be checks and balances that create transparency.

Opportunity also comes from knowledge. A major type of misconduct observed among employees in the workplace is lying to employees, customers, vendors, or the public or withholding needed information from them.[39] A person with expertise or information about the competition has the opportunity to exploit this knowledge. Individuals can be a source of information because they are familiar with the organization. Individuals employed by one organization for many years become "gatekeepers" of its culture and often have the opportunity to make decisions related to unwritten traditions and rules. They socialize newer employees to abide by the rules and norms of the company's internal and external ways of doing business, as well as understanding when the opportunity exists to cross the line. They function as mentors or supervise managers in training. Like drill sergeants in the army, these trainers mold the new recruits into what the company wants. Their training can contribute to either ethical or unethical conduct.

The opportunity for unethical behavior cannot be eliminated without aggressive enforcement of codes and rules. A national jewelry store chain president explained to us how he dealt with a jewelry buyer in one of his stores who took a bribe from a supplier. There was an explicit company policy against taking incentive payments to deal with a specific supplier. When the president of the firm learned about the accepted bribe, he immediately traveled to the office of the buyer in question and terminated his employment. He then traveled to the supplier (manufacturer) selling jewelry to his stores and terminated his relationship with the firm. The message was clear: Taking a bribe is unacceptable for the store's buyers, and salespeople from supplying companies could cost their firm significant sales by offering bribes. This type of policy enforcement illustrates how the opportunity to commit unethical acts can be eliminated or at least significantly reduced.

As defined previously, stakeholders are those directly and indirectly involved with a company and can include investors, customers, employees, channel members, communities, and special interest groups. Each stakeholder has goals and objectives that somewhat align with other stakeholders and the company. It is the diverging of goals that causes friction between and within stakeholders and the corporation. Most stakeholders understand firms must generate revenues and profit to exist, but not all. Special interest groups or communities may actively seek the destruction of the corporation because of perceived or actual harm to themselves or those things held important to them. The employee is also affected by such stakeholders, usually in an indirect way. Depending upon the perceived threat level to the firm, employees may act independently or in groups to perpetrate unethical or illegal behaviors. For example, one author knew of a newspaper firm that had been losing circulation to one of its competitors and the loss was putting people at the firm out of work. The projection was if the newspaper could not turn subscriptions around they would be closed within a year. As a result of the announcement employees started pulling up newspaper receptacles and damaging the competition's automatic newspaper dispensers. Both activities were illegal, yet the employees felt justified because they believed they were helping the company survive.

Business Ethics Intentions, Behavior, and Evaluations

Ethical dilemmas involve problem-solving situations when the rules governing decisions are often vague or in conflict. The results of an ethical decision are often uncertain; it is not always immediately clear whether or not we made the right decision. There are no magic formulas, nor is there computer software that ethical dilemmas can be plugged into to get a solution. Even if they mean well, most businesspeople make ethical mistakes. Therefore, there is no substitute for critical thinking and the ability to take responsibility for our own decisions.

Individuals' intentions and the final decision regarding what action they take are the last steps in the ethical decision-making process. When intentions and behavior are inconsistent with their ethical judgment, people may feel guilty. For example, when an advertising account executive is asked by her client to create an advertisement she perceives as misleading, she has two alternatives: to comply or refuse. If she refuses, she stands to lose business from that client and possibly her job. Other factors—such as pressure from the client, the need to keep her job to pay her debts and living expenses, and the possibility of a raise if she develops the advertisement successfully—may influence her resolution of this ethical dilemma. Because of these factors, she may decide to act unethically and develop the advertisement even though she believes it to be inaccurate. In this example her actions are inconsistent with her ethical judgment, meaning she will probably feel guilty about her decision.

Guilt or uneasiness is the first sign an unethical decision has occurred. The next step is changing the behavior to reduce such feelings. This change can reflect a person's values shifting to fit the decision or the person changing his or her decision type the next time a similar situation occurs. You can eliminate some of the problematic situational factors by resigning your position. For those who begin the value shift, the following are the usual justifications that reduce and finally eliminate guilt:

1. I need the paycheck and can't afford to quit right now.
2. Those around me are doing it, so why shouldn't I? They believe it's okay.
3. If I don't do this, I might not be able to get a good reference from my boss or company when I leave.
4. This is not such a big deal, given the potential benefits.
5. Business is business with a different set of rules.
6. If not me, someone else would do it and get rewarded.

The road to success depends on how the businessperson defines *success*. The success concept drives intentions and behavior in business either implicitly or explicitly. Money, security, family, power, wealth, and personal or group gratification are all types of success measures people use. The list described is not comprehensive, and in the next chapter, you will understand more about how success can be defined. Another concept that affects behavior is the probability of rewards and punishments, an issue explained further in Chapter 6.

USING THE ETHICAL DECISION-MAKING MODEL TO IMPROVE ETHICAL DECISIONS

The ethical decision-making model presented in this chapter cannot tell you if a business decision is ethical or unethical. It bears repeating that it is impossible to tell you what is right or wrong; instead, we attempt to prepare you to make informed ethical decisions. Although this chapter does not moralize by telling you what to do in a specific situation, it does provide an overview of typical decision-making processes and factors that influence ethical decisions. The model is not a guide for how to make decisions, but is intended to provide you with insights and knowledge about typical ethical decision-making processes in business organizations.

Business ethics scholars developing descriptive models have focused on regularities in decision making and the various phenomena that interact in a dynamic environment to produce predictable behavioral patterns. Furthermore, it is unlikely an organization's ethical problems will be solved strictly by having a thorough knowledge about how ethical decisions are made. By its very nature, business ethics involves value judgments and collective agreement about acceptable patterns of behavior. In the next section, we discuss normative concepts that describe appropriate ethical conduct.

We propose gaining an understanding of the factors that make up ethical decision making in business will sensitize you concerning whether the business problem is an ethical issue or dilemma. It will help you know what the degree of moral intensity may be for you and others as well as how individual factors such as gender, moral philosophy, education level, and religion within you and others affect the process. We hope you remember the organizational factors that impact the ethics of business decisions and what to look for in a firm's code of ethics, culture, opportunity, and the significance of other employees and how they sway some people's intentions and behaviors. You now know non-business factors such as friends, family, and the economic reality of an employee's situation can lead to unethical business decisions. Finally, we hope you remember the type of industry, the competition, and stakeholders are all factors that can push some employees into making unethical decisions. In later chapters we delve deeper into different aspects of the ethical decision making process so ultimately you can make better, more informed decisions and help your company do the right things for the right reasons.

One important conclusion that should be taken into account is that ethical decision making within an organization does not rely strictly on the personal values and morals of individuals. Knowledge of moral philosophies or values must be balanced with business knowledge and an understanding of the complexities of the dilemma requiring a decision. For example, a manager who embraces honesty, fairness, and equity must understand the diverse risks associated with a complex financial instrument such as options or derivatives. Business competence must exist, along with personal accountability, in ethical decisions.

Organizations take on a culture of their own, with managers and coworkers exerting a significant influence on ethical decisions. While formal codes, rules, and compliance are essential in organizations, an organization built on informal relationships is more likely to develop a high level of integrity within an organization's culture.[40]

NORMATIVE CONSIDERATIONS IN ETHICAL DECISION MAKING

In the first part of the chapter, we described how ethical decision making occurs in an organization. This descriptive approach provides an understanding of the role of individuals in an organizational context for making ethical decisions. Understanding what influences the ethical decision making process is important in sensitizing you to the intensity of issues and dilemmas as well as the management of ethics in an organization.

However, understanding how ethical decisions are made is different from determining what should guide decisions. A normative approach to business ethics examines what ought to occur in ethical decision making. The word "normative" is equivalent to an ideal standard. Therefore, when we discuss **normative approaches**, we are talking about how organizational decision makers *should* approach an issue. This is different from a descriptive approach that examines *how* organizational decision makers approach ethical decision making. A normative approach in business ethics revolves around the standards of behavior within the firm as well as within the industry. These normative rules and standards are based on individual moral values as well as the collective values of the organization. The normative approach for business ethics is concerned with general ethical values implemented into business. Concepts like fairness and justice are highly important in a normative structure. Strong normative structures in organizations are positively related to ethical decision making. Normative considerations also tend to deal with moral philosophies such as utilitarianism and deontology that we will explore in more detail in the next chapter.

Most organizations develop a set of core values to provide enduring beliefs about appropriate conduct. Core values are central to an organization and provide directions for action. For most firms, the selection of core values relates directly to stakeholder management of relationships. These values include an understanding of the descriptive approaches we covered in the first part of this chapter. It also includes instrumental elements that justify the adoption of core values. An instrumental concern focuses on positive outcomes, including firm profitability and benefits to society. Normative business dimensions are rooted in social, political, and economic institutions as well as the recognition of stakeholder claims.

By incorporating stakeholder objectives into corporate core values, companies begin to view stakeholders as significant. Each stakeholder has goals and objectives that somewhat align with other stakeholders and the company. The diverging of goals causes friction between and within stakeholders and the corporation. Ethical obligations are established for both internal stakeholders such as employees as well as external stakeholders such as the community.[41] For instance, 3M recognizes it has societal obligations as well as obligations to its employees and customers. 3M donates millions in time and money to charitable causes, including higher education, disaster relief, and nonprofit institutes.[42] Ethical decisions are often embedded in many organizational decisions—both managerial and societal—so it is necessary to recognize the importance of core values in providing ideals for appropriate conduct.

Institutions as the Foundation for Normative Values

Institutions are important in establishing a foundation for normative values. According to institutional theory, organizations operate according to taken-for-granted institutional norms and rules. For instance, government, religion, and education are institutions that influence the creation of values, norms, and conventions that both organizations and individuals should adhere.[43] Indeed, many researchers argue that normative values largely originate from family, friends, and more institutional affiliations such as religion and government.[44] In other words, organizations face certain normative pressures from different institutions to act a certain way. These pressures can take place internally (inside the organization itself) and/or externally (from the government or other institutions).[45] For our purposes, we sort institutions into three categories: political, economic, and social.

Consider for a moment how political institutions influence the development of values. If you live in country with a democratic form of government, you likely consider freedom of speech and the right to own property as important ideals. Organizations must comply with these types of institutional norms and belief systems in order to succeed—to do otherwise would result in the failure of the organization.[46] Companies such as IBM should recognize that using bribery to gain a competitive advantage is inappropriate according to U.S. and U.K. bribery laws. Political influences can also take place within the organization. An ethical organization has policies and rules in place to determine appropriate behavior. This is often the compliance component of the firm's organizational culture. Failure to abide by these rules results in disciplinary action. For instance, engineering and construction company Fluor Corporation's code of conduct states that it is every employee's duty to report unsafe conduct in the workplace. Those who fail to report can be subject to disciplinary procedures.[47]

Normative business ethics takes into account the political realities outside the legal realm in the form of industry standards. Different types of industries have different standards and policies which either increase or decrease the ethicality and legality of their decisions. Legal issues such as price fixing, antitrust issues, and consumer protection are important in maintaining a fair and equitable marketplace. Antitrust regulators tend to scrutinize mergers and acquisitions between large firms to make sure these companies do not gain so much power they place competitors at a major disadvantage. Price-fixing is illegal because it often creates unfair prices for buyers. For instance, seven retailers sued DuPont and three other manufacturers for allegedly manipulating the prices of a pigment used in white paint. They claimed the price fixing agreement caused them to pay inflated prices for the pigment.[48] Because of their impact on the economy, these issues must be major considerations for businesses when making ethical decisions.

Competition is also important to economic institutions and ethical decision making. The nature of competition can be shaped by the economic system. The economic system helps determine how a particular country or society distributes its resources in the production of products. Basic economic systems such as communism, socialism, and capitalism influence the nature of competition. Competition affects how a company operates as well as the risks employees take for the good of the firm. The amount of competition in an industry can be determined and described according to the following: 1) barriers to entry into the industry, 2) available substitutes for the products produced by the industry rivals, 3) the power of the industry rivals over their customers, and 4) the power of the industry rivals' suppliers over the industry rivals. An example of a highly competitive industry is smartphone manufacturing, whereas the vacuum cleaning manufacturing industry is competitively low. High levels of competition create a higher probability that firms cut corners because margins are usually low. Competitors aggressively seek differential advantages from others so as to increase market share, profitability, and growth. When taken to extremes, unethical and illegal activities can become normal. To cut health care, Michelin North America charges as much as $1,000 more for healthcare coverage if an employee's waist is more than forty inches or if they have high blood pressure. They are also requiring employees to share personal health information such as body-mass index and weight and blood-sugar levels. Employee-rights advocates say the penalties are akin to "legal discrimination" while the company calls them wellness incentives.[49]

Social institutions impact a firm's normative values as well. Social institutions include religion, education, and individuals such as the family unit. There are laws meant to ensure an organization acts fairly, but there is no law saying people should do to others as they would prefer to have done to them. Yet many cultures adopted this rule that has been institutionalized into businesses with standards on competing fairly, being transparent with consumers, and treating employees with respect. These social institutions help individuals form their personal values and the moral philosophies they bring into the workplace. From an organizational context, societal trends influence which values to adopt as well as when to adapt decisions to take into account new concerns. For instance, because of the changing socio cultural concerns over obesity, Walmart decided to support an initiative to sell healthier foods.

While we might not consider stakeholders to be institutions, it should now be clear that many stakeholders actually act as institutions in terms of values. Stakeholders closely align with institutions. The regulatory system aligns with political institutions, competition relates to economic institutions, and personal values and norms derive from social institutions. There is therefore a clear link between institutional theory and the stakeholder orientation of management.

As we reiterated, an organization uses rules dictated by its institutional environment to measure the appropriateness of its behavior.[50] Organizations facing the same environmental norms or rules (e.g. those in the same industry) become isomorphic, or institutionalized.[51] Although organizations in a particular industry might differ, most share certain values that characterize the industry. Additionally, institutional factors often overlap in ethical decision making. For example, General Motors began releasing more fuel-efficient vehicles such as the Chevrolet Volt. We could characterize this decision as having political, economic, and social considerations. Politically, new laws are requiring automobile companies to increase the fuel efficiency of their vehicles. General Motors competes against rival vehicles such as the Toyota Prius, the Nissan Leaf, and the Fusion Hybrid. GM's investment in greater fuel efficiency also results from society's increasing demands for more sustainable vehicles.

While industry shared values promote organizational effectiveness when linked to goals, it can also hinder effectiveness if more efficient means of organization and structure are avoided in exchange for stability.[52] There is a risk that organizations might sacrifice new ideas or methodologies in order to be more acceptable.[53] This can limit innovativeness and productivity. On the other hand, it is important that an organization does not stray so far from industry norms and values that it creates stakeholder concerns. A company known for selling environmentally friendly apparel would not likely succeed in selling a new clothing line made of animal fur. From both an ethical and managerial standpoint, knowing which institutional norms to comply with and when it would be more beneficial to explore new norms and values is important for organizations to consider.

How does this fit with ethical theory? Institutions directly impact a firm's norms, values, and behavior as well as "the long-run survival of the organization."[54] When Galleon Group's founder Raj Rajaratnam and other major employees were found guilty of insider trading, the firm floundered. In this case, the government was the major institution involved. By violating the law, the organization did not have the ability to bounce back from this type of misconduct. The firm did not have normative values in place to dictate appropriate (and in this case legal) behavior.

Conversely, when values from political, economic, and social institutions are embedded into the organizational culture to provide incentives for appropriate behavior, firms tend to act more socially responsible.[55] If incentives such as organizational rewards align with the organization's normative values and society's cultural institutions, employees—and therefore the organization as a whole—are more likely to act in a socially responsible manner. Many organizations provide employees with a certain amount of time off to volunteer in their communities. This incentive matches the normative institutional value of giving back to the community. If incentives do not align with institutional normative values or if they contradict these values, then misconduct is likely. While Enron and Countrywide Financial outwardly supported ethical conduct, in reality the company culture rewarded those who took risks even if they violated normative values.

Implementing Principles and Core Values in Ethical Decision Making

Political, economic, and social institutions help organizations determine principles and values for appropriate conduct. Principles and values are important normative considerations in ethical decision making. We learned from Chapter 1 that principles are specific and pervasive boundaries for behavior that should not be violated. Principles are important in preventing organizations from "bending the rules." Values are enduring beliefs and ideals that are socially enforced. Together, principles and values set an ideal standard for the organization. Figure 5–2 demonstrates some of the similarities and differences between principles and values.

John Rawls was one of the most influential philosophers in his research on how principles support the concept of justice.[56] Rawls believed justice principles were beliefs that everyone could accept—a key element in our own definition of principles. According to our definition, principles are beliefs that are universal in nature. For instance, most cultures agree that honesty and fairness are essential to a well-functioning society, although there may be differences on how to implement this principle in daily living.

In his experiments, Rawls used what he called the *veil of ignorance*, a thought experiment that examined how individuals would formulate principles if they did not know what their future position in society would be. A person might emerge from the veil of ignorance as a rich person or as a beggar. While individuals might formulate different values based on their position in society, Rawls believed that because principles were universally accepted both the rich person and the beggar would agree upon them. Thus, using the veil of ignorance, Rawls identified principles that were not biased by one's social position.[57]

Rawls' work led him to develop two main principles of justice: the liberty principle and the difference principle. The liberty principle, also known as the equality principle, states that each person has basic rights that are compatible to the basic liberties of others. This is similar to the U.S. Constitution's statement that everyone has certain inalienable rights such as life,

FIGURE 5–2 **Principles and Values**

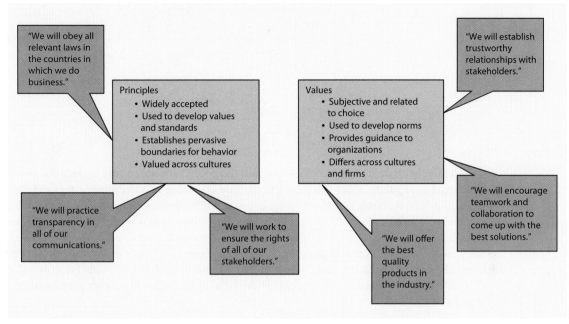

liberty, and the pursuit of happiness. The difference principle states that economic and social equalities (or inequalities) should be arranged to provide the most benefit to the least-advantaged members of society. This means the most ethical course of action is one that increases the benefits of those that are the least well-off. Actions that harm disadvantaged members of society should be avoided.[58] It is important to note that the difference principle does not advocate for the complete elimination of inequalities in society, but that the most ethical decision seeks to benefit and not harm disadvantaged populations. In the corporate world, organizations operating according to the difference principle would not take actions that could create economic and social harm to the least advantaged members of society. For example, a firm might avoid accepting business from a foreign country with a record of human rights abuses because the country supports the exploitation of disadvantaged groups.[59] Both of Rawls' justice principles relate to political, economic, and social institutions.

While organizations might agree that they should behave honestly, transparently, and responsibly toward stakeholders, they might differ on how to implement these principles. Companies take basic principles and translate them into core values. Core values provide the abstract ideals that are distinct from individual values and daily operational procedures. Value practices evolve and are translated into normative definitions of ethical or unethical. Value practices become the end results and are distinct from organizational practices driven by technical or efficiency considerations.[60]

Individual and organizational values can differ significantly[61] because of ethical diversity among individuals. To join an organization, members need to accept that some values are superior and deal with the organizational need to develop collective agreement. This results in possible tensions that must be worked out between individual and organizational values.[62] Instead of individuals just accepting core values from top management, there needs to be group discussions, negotiations, and adjustments to determine how core values are implemented.[63]

TABLE 5–2 Core Values of Marriott

1. Put People First
2. Pursue Excellence
3. Embrace Change
4. Act with Integrity
5. Serve Our World

Source: Marriott, *2011 Annual Report*, http://investor.shareholder
.com/mar/marriottAR11/index.html (accessed April 19, 2013).

Remember that leaders, stakeholders, and the organizational culture impact the development of core values. Core values might include operating in a sustainable manner, collaboration and teamwork, and avoiding bribery. Unlike principles, values are shaped by company specific, industry specific, country specific and global specific factors.[64] Firms from countries that stress individualism encourage the ability to work independently, whereas firms from more collectivist nations place more value on teamwork. Additionally, core values differ depending upon the industry. For example, although safety is a core value of many firms, it is more likely to be emphasized as a core value in a factory environment than in an office environment.

A firm's core values provide a blueprint into the firm's purpose as well as how it views ethical decision making and prioritizes stakeholders. Table 5–2 provides an example of the core values of Marriot International. How Marriot organized its core values provides a snapshot of what the firm considers important. For instance, its first value, to put people first, provides guidance for all of the firm's stakeholder relationships. From its other core values you can determine that Marriot strives to deliver excellent customer service and operate with the highest forms of integrity. All five of Marriott's values reinforce its vision "to be the #1 hospitality company in the world."[65] Organizational core values such as these are essential to ethical decision making in organizations. Organizations that have ethics programs based on a values orientation are found to make a greater contribution than those based simply on compliance, or obeying laws and regulations.[66]

UNDERSTANDING ETHICAL DECISION MAKING

Our ethical decision-making framework demonstrates the many factors that influence ethical decisions. Ethical issue intensity, individual factors, organizational factors, and opportunity result in business ethics evaluations and decisions. An organizational ethical culture is shaped by effective leadership. Without top level support for ethical behavior, the opportunity for employees to engage in their own personal approaches to ethical decision making will evolve. An ethical corporate culture needs shared values along with proper oversight to monitor the complex ethical decisions being made by employees. It requires the establishment of a strong ethics program to educate and develop compliance policies. Consider the ethics program at construction and engineering company Bechtel Corporation. Top managers at Bechtel show strong support for ethical conduct, with the chief ethics officer and vice chairman speaking at events such as the European Business Ethics Forum and the

Ethics and Compliance Officer Association meeting to share best industry practices. Every year the company holds an ethics awareness workshop for its employees to discuss ethical scenarios and how best to resolve them.[67]

On the other hand, some companies with a strong reputation for ethical conduct sometimes fail to maintain their ethical culture. Johnson and Johnson's (J&J) quick action during the Tylenol murders secured its reputation for putting customer safety first. However, J&J experienced several quality control issues that put its reputation as an ethical company in jeopardy. Additionally, many criticized the way J&J handled these issues and began to question whether J&J lost its standing as a gold standard for values-based ethics.[68] Despite these setbacks, J&J continues to be ranked among the top ten in Harris Interactive's reputation quotient ratings.[69] To continue maintaining credibility among stakeholders, J&J must learn from its mistakes and return to the values in its credo that made it a role model for ethical conduct.

Normative dimensions are also important to ethical decision making. Normative perspectives set forth ideal goals that organizations should aspire. Normative considerations also provide the foundation needed to develop organizational principles and values, the building blocks of a firm's ethical culture. Without this foundation, companies will not be able to develop an ethical culture or have the basis to make ethical decisions. The Ford Pinto case is an interesting example of how normative considerations can be easily ignored. Ford recognized that its Pintos had a design flaw that made it easier for explosions to occur in accidents. However, it refused to initiate a recall. This led to needless deaths. It is interesting to note that in one class discussing the Ford Pinto case students tended to point out the monetary and reputational impact of Ford's actions, but only later did a student state that Ford should not have knowingly sold a dangerous car that could harm people.[70] Normative frameworks are largely influenced by political, economic, and social institutions. However, a normative perspective also recognizes the existence of universal ethical behaviors, such as honesty and justice. Total, a French oil and gas company, lists human rights, financial transparency, and respect for people as being among its main principles.[71]

Finally, the more you know about ethical decision making in business, the more likely you will make good decisions. There are many challenges in organizations beyond the control of any one individual. On the other hand, as you move to higher levels of the organization, there is the opportunity for ethical leadership to become a role model for good ethics. The descriptive framework of ethical decision making in this chapter provides many insights into the relationships that contribute to an ethical culture.

SUMMARY

The key components of the ethical decision-making framework include ethical issue intensity, individual factors, organizational factors, and opportunity. These factors are interrelated and influence business ethics evaluations and intentions that result in ethical or unethical behavior.

The first step in ethical decision making is to recognize an ethical issue requires an individual or work group to choose among several actions that will ultimately be evaluated as ethical or unethical by various stakeholders. Ethical issue intensity is the perceived relevance or importance of an ethical issue to an individual or work group. It reflects the ethical sensitivity of the individual or work group that triggers the ethical decision-making process. Other factors in our ethical decision-making framework influence this sensitivity, and therefore different individuals often perceive ethical issues differently.

Individual factors such as gender, education, nationality, age, and locus of control affect the ethical decision-making process, with some factors being more important than others. Organizational factors such as an organization's values often have greater influence on an individual's decisions than that person's own values. In addition, decisions in business are most often made jointly, in work groups and committees, or in conversations and discussions with coworkers. Corporate cultures and structures operate through the ability of individual relationships among the organization's members to influence those members' ethical decisions. A corporate culture is a set of values, beliefs, goals, norms, and ways of solving problems that members (employees) of an organization share. Corporate culture involves norms that prescribe a wide range of behavior for the organization's members. The ethical culture of an organization indicates whether it has an ethical conscience. Significant others—including peers, managers, coworkers, and subordinates—who influence the work group have more daily impact on an employee's decisions than any other factor in the decision-making framework. Obedience to authority may explain why many business ethics issues are resolved simply by following the directives of a superior.

Ethical opportunity results from conditions that provide rewards, whether internal or external, or limit barriers to ethical or unethical behavior. Included in opportunity is a person's immediate job context that includes the motivational techniques superiors use to influence employee behavior. The opportunity employees have for unethical behavior in an organization can be eliminated through formal codes, policies, and rules that are adequately enforced by management.

The ethical decision-making framework is not a guide for making decisions. It is intended to provide insights and knowledge about typical ethical decision-making processes in business organizations. Ethical decision making within organizations does not rely strictly on the personal values and morals of employees. Organizations have cultures of their own that when combined with corporate governance mechanisms may significantly influence business ethics.

Normative approaches describe how organizational decision makers *should* approach an ethical issue. Institutional theory is an important normative concept that states that organizations operate according to taken-for-granted institutional norms and rules. Political, economic, and social institutions help organizations determine principles and values for appropriate conduct. Principles are important in preventing organizations from "bending the rules." Philosopher John Rawls contributed important work on principles, particularly principles of justice. Core values are enduring beliefs about appropriate conduct and provide guidance for the ethical direction of the firm.

IMPORTANT TERMS FOR REVIEW

ethical awareness 129	age 132	significant other 134
ethical issue intensity 129	locus of control 132	obedience to authority 134
moral intensity 130	external control 132	opportunity 134
gender 131	internal control 132	immediate job context 135
education 131	corporate culture 133	normative approach 139
nationality 132	ethical culture 134	

RESOLVING ETHICAL BUSINESS CHALLENGES*

CrudeOil, a subsidiary of a major energy multinational that manufactures oil drilling parts around the world, experienced a lag in sales. The board of directors brought in a new manager to revamp the company. They recommended Jim Stone as the new manager because he had an impeccable reputation for achieving results, and top managers in the industry liked him because of his west Texas demeanor. After eighteen months passed, Jim was successful in increasing the company's sales and profits. He began his tenure as manager by laying off several salespeople who had not performed according to his high standards. This made those who stayed with the company uneasy and they responded in different ways. Some tried to get on Jim's good side, while others focused on achieving their sales goals and avoiding any type of interaction with him.

The problem was Jim's managing style was harsh and unpredictable. For example, when a mistake was made, he blamed salespeople he disliked even if it was not their fault. On one occasion, Marjorie, one of the newest salespeople, brought in an unusually big sale. Rather than giving her positive feedback, Jim acted like it was a normal occurrence. What was ironic was the company's most important value was to treat everyone with respect. It was considered so significant it was printed on a banner and hung at the front of the office for all to see. When Jim lost his temper, it often happened while he stood in front of all the employees underneath the banner.

His personality really came out when he got angry. At several meetings he would randomly pick out salespeople and engage in intimidating behaviors such as staring at them for long periods of time, discounting their ideas, or simply ignoring them. Jim treated all of the employees with intimidating behavior, even the ones he claimed to like. Every so often Jim picked out an employee and make snide comments over the course of several days. He made no excuses about it.

One day, when one of the employees finally broached Jim about the matter, Jim announced to the entire office, "I pick out the employees who are underperforming. I am the boss, and I need to make sure you people make as many sales as possible." He paused and looked at the expressions on the employees' faces. He then continued, "Actually, you should make more sales than that!" Jim turned toward his office, laughing as he shut the door. The employee who spoke up was given the subsidiary's lesser sales accounts.

Madison, who hired in as a salesperson a few months before Jim took control of the company, was continuously in Jim's crosshairs. He told her even though she made her sales quota, it was not satisfactory. Furthermore, he took credit for her performance at meetings. When her numbers exceeded the quota, he spread rumors suggesting she wasn't meeting her goals because of problems in her personal life.

One day Peter, another salesperson, approached Madison and asked her how she was doing. Madison looked at him confusedly, and responded, "I'm as fine as anyone else here. Why?"

Peter answered, "Jim told me you had been in the hospital lately and you might be suffering from a serious illness." Madison was taken aback. "Peter, Jim is just saying that because my sales numbers were low this last quarter. Believe me, I am fine." Madison sat there infuriated that Jim would be spreading rumors about her.

Madison knew initiating a conversation with Jim would not be the way to resolve this issue. She felt she would be fired if she confronted him about his behavior or demoted like the other employee. She tried talking to others Jim had bullied, but many feared for their jobs and preferred to remain silent. She also considered speaking with the board of directors, but she did not know any one of them well and she knew they had a good relationship with Jim. Some kind of action had to take place because Madison could not work in an environment like that much longer. Besides, other employees' tolerance would wear out soon and the company as a whole could suffer lasting consequences. As Madison walked toward the front door at the end of the day, she avoided looking at the banner featuring CrudeOil's most important value.

QUESTIONS | EXERCISES

1. Describe the organizational culture at CrudeOil. How does it contribute to the current situation?

2. How is CrudeOil violating its core value of treating others with respect? What are some ways it could reincorporate this core value into its organizational culture?

3. If Madison cannot report her problems to her immediate supervisor, what are some other ways she can handle the situation?

*This case is strictly hypothetical; any resemblance to real persons, companies, or situations is coincidental.

> > > CHECK YOUR EQ

Check your EQ, or Ethics Quotient, by completing the following. Assess your performance to evaluate your overall understanding of the chapter material.

1. The first step in ethical decision making is to understand the individual factors that influence the process.   Yes   No

2. "Opportunity" describes the conditions within an organization that limit or permit ethical or unethical behavior.   Yes   No

3. Core values are enduring beliefs about appropriate conduct.   Yes   No

4. The most significant influence on ethical behavior in an organization is the opportunity to engage in (un)ethical behavior.   Yes   No

5. Obedience to authority relates to the influence of corporate culture.   Yes   No

ANSWERS 1. No. The first step is to become more aware that an ethical issue exists and to consider its relevance to the individual or work group. 2. Yes. Opportunity results from conditions that provide rewards or fail to erect barriers against unethical behavior. 3. Yes. Core values are enduring beliefs about appropriate conduct. 4. No. Significant others have more impact on ethical decisions within an organization. 5. No. Obedience to authority relates to the influence of significant others and supervisors.

ENDNOTES

1. Thomas M. Jones, "Ethical Decision Making by Individuals in Organizations: An Issue-Contingent Model," *Academy of Management Review*, 16 (February 1991): 366–395; O. C. Ferrell and Larry G. Gresham, "A Contingency Framework for Understanding Ethical Decision Making in Marketing," *Journal of Marketing* 49 (Summer 1985): 87–96; O. C. Ferrell, Larry G. Gresham, and John Fraedrich, "A Synthesis of Ethical Decision Models for Marketing," *Journal of Macromarketing* 9 (Fall 1989): 55–64; Shelby D. Hunt and Scott Vitell, "A General Theory of Marketing Ethics," *Journal of Macromarketing* 6 (Spring 1986): 5–16; William A. Kahn, "Toward an Agenda for Business Ethics Research," *Academy of Management Review* 15 (April 1990): 311–328; Linda K. Trevino, "Ethical Decision Making in Organizations: A Person-Situation Interactionist Model," *Academy of Management Review* 11 (March 1986): 601–617.

2. Jones, "Ethical Decision Making," 367–372.

3. Donald P. Robin, R. Eric Reidenbach, and P. J. Forrest, "The Perceived Importance of an Ethical Issue as an Influence on the Ethical Decision Making of Ad Managers," *Journal of Business Research* 35 (January 1996): 17.

4. David Doniger, "New EPA Study Shows Largest Greenhouse Gas Emitters—Are They In Your Backyard?" *Eco Watch*, February 6, 2013, http://ecowatch.com/2013/epa-greenhouse-gas-emitters/ (accessed April 22, 2013); John M. Broder, "E.P.A. Will Delay Rule Limiting Carbon Emissions at New Power Plants," *The New York Times*, April 12, 2013, http://www.nytimes.com/2013/04/13/science/earth/epa-to-delay-emissions-rule-at-new-power-plants.html?_r=1& (accessed June 17, 2013).

5. Andrew Tangel, "Many at hedge funds still feel pressure to break rules, survey finds," *Los Angeles Times*, April 4, 2013, http://www.latimes.com/business/money/la-fi-mo-wall-street-insider-trading-survey-20130404,0,7610072.story (accessed April 12, 2013).

6. Jack Beatty, "The Enron Ponzi Scheme," *The Atlantic Monthly*, March 13, 2002, http://www.theatlantic.com/doc/200203u/pp2002-03-13 (accessed August 17, 2009).

7. Roselie McDevitt and Joan Van Hise, "Influences in Ethical Dilemmas of Increasing Intensity," *Journal of Business Ethics* 40 (October 2002): 261–274.

8. Anusorn Singhapakdi, Scott J. Vitell, and George R. Franke, "Antecedents, Consequences, and Mediating Effects of Perceived Moral Intensity and Personal Moral Philosophies," *Journal of the Academy of Marketing Science* 27 (Winter 1999): 19.

9. Ibid.

10. Ibid.

11. Kathy Lund Dean, Jeri Mullins Beggs, and Timothy P. Keane, "Mid-level Managers, Organizational Context, and (Un)ethical Encounters," *Journal of Business Ethics* 97 (2010): 51–69.

12. Beryl Benderly, "Inadequate Ethics Training Leaves Young Scientists Unprepared for "Ethical Emergencies," *Science Careers Blog*, July 14, 2012, http://blogs.sciencemag.org/sciencecareers/2012/07/difficult-ethic.html (accessed April 12, 2013).

13. Singhapakdi, Vitell, and Franke, 17.

14. Damodar Suar and Rooplekha Khuntia, "Influence of Personal Values and Value Congruence on Unethical Practices and Work Behavior," *Journal of Business Ethics* 97 (2010): 443–460.

15. "Lead the Way," *Spirit*, February 2011, 41.

16. B. Elango, Karen Paul, Sumit K. Kundu, and Shishir K. Paudel, "Organizational Ethics, Individual Ethics, and Ethical Intentions in International Decision-Making," *Journal of Business Ethics* 97 (2010): 543–561.

17. T. W. Loe, L. Ferrell, and P. Mansfield, "A Review of Empirical Studies Assessing Ethical Decision Making in Business," *Journal of Business Ethics* 25 (2000): 185–204.

18. C. Gilligan, "In a Different Voice: Women's Conceptions of Self and Morality," *Harvard Educational Review*, 47(4), 1977, 481–517.

19. Steven Kaplan, Kurt Pany, Janet Samuels, and Jian Zhang, "An Examination of the Association between Gender and Reporting Intentions for Fraudulent Financial Reporting," *Journal of Business Ethics* 87, No. 1 (June 2009): 15–30.

20. Michael J. O'Fallon and Kenneth D. Butterfield, "A Review of the Empirical Ethical Decision-Making Literature: 1996–2003," *Journal of Business Ethics* 59 (July 2005): 375–413; P. M. J. Christie, J. I. G. Kwon, P. A. Stoeberl, and R. Baumhart, "A Cross-Cultural Comparison of Ethical Attitudes of Business Managers: India, Korea and the United States," *Journal of Business Ethics* 46 (September 2003): 263–287; G. Fleischman and S. Valentine, "Professionals' Tax Liability and Ethical Evaluations in an Equitable Relief Innocent Spouse Case," *Journal of Business Ethics* 42 (January 2003): 27–44; A. Singhapakdi, K. Karande, C. P. Rao, and S. J. Vitell, "How Important Are Ethics and Social Responsibility? A Multinational Study of Marketing Professionals," *European Journal of Marketing* 35 (2001): 133–152.

21. R. W. Armstrong, "The Relationship between Culture and Perception of Ethical Problems in International Marketing," *Journal of Business Ethics* 15 (November 1996): 1199–1208; J. Cherry, M. Lee, and C. S. Chien, "A Cross-Cultural Application of a Theoretical Model of Business Ethics: Bridging the Gap between Theory and Data," *Journal of Business Ethics* 44 (June 2003): 359–376; B. Kracher, A. Chatterjee, and A. R. Lundquist, "Factors Related to the Cognitive Moral Development of Business Students and Business Professionals in India and the United States: Nationality, Education, Sex and Gender," *Journal of Business Ethics* 35 (February 2002): 255–268.

22. J. M. Larkin, "The Ability of Internal Auditors to Identify Ethical Dilemmas," *Journal of Business Ethics* 23 (February 2000): 401–409; D. Peterson, A. Rhoads, and B. C. Vaught, "Ethical Beliefs of Business Professionals: A Study of Gender, Age and External Factors," *Journal of Business Ethics* 31 (June 2001): 225–232; M. A. Razzaque and T. P. Hwee, "Ethics and Purchasing Dilemma: A Singaporean View," *Journal of Business Ethics* 35 (February 2002): 307–326.

23. B. Elango, Karen Paul, Sumit K. Kundu, Shishir K. Paudel, "Organizational Ethics, Individual Ethics, and Ethical Intentions in International Decision-Making," *Journal of Business Ethics* 97 (2010): 543–561.

24. J. Cherry and J. Fraedrich, "An Empirical Investigation of Locus of Control and the Structure of Moral Reasoning: Examining the Ethical Decision-Making Processes of Sales Managers," *Journal of Personal Selling and Sales Management* 20 (Summer 2000): 173–188; M. C. Reiss and K. Mitra, "The Effects of Individual Difference Factors on the Acceptability of Ethical and Unethical Workplace Behaviors," *Journal of Business Ethics* 17 (October 1998): 1581–1593.

25. O. C. Ferrell and Linda Ferrell, "Role of Ethical Leadership in Organizational Performance," *Journal of Management Systems* 13 (2001): 64–78.

26. Barry Z. Posner, "Another Look at the Impact of Personal and Organizational Values Congruency," *Journal of Business Ethics* 97 (2010): 535–541.

27. K. Praveen Parboteeah, Hsien Chun Chen, Ying-Tzu Lin, I-Heng Chen, Amber Y-P Lee, and Anyi Chung, "Establishing Organizational Ethical Climates: How Do Managerial Practices Work?" *Journal of Business Ethics* 97 (2010): 599–611.

28. James Weber and Julie E. Seger, "Influences upon Organizational Ethical Subclimates: A Replication Study of a Single Firm at Two Points in Time," *Journal of Business Ethics* 41 (November 2002): 69–84.

29. Sean Valentine, Lynn Godkin, and Margaret Lucero, "Ethical Context, Organizational Commitment, and Person-Organization Fit," *Journal of Business Ethics* 41 (December 2002): 349–360.

30. Bruce H. Drake, Mark Meckler, and Debra Stephens, "Transitional Ethics: Responsibilities of Supervisors for Supporting Employee Development," *Journal of Business Ethics* 38 (June 2002): 141–155.

31. Ferrell and Gresham, "A Contingency Framework," 87–96.

32. R. C. Ford and W. D. Richardson, "Ethical Decision Making: A Review of the Empirical Literature," *Journal of Business Ethics* 13 (March 1994): 205–221; Loe, Ferrell, and Mansfield, "A Review of Empirical Studies."

33. National Business Ethics Survey, *How Employees Perceive Ethics at Work* (Washington, DC: Ethics Resource Center, 2000), 30.

34. "Top Office Suppliers That Are Stolen & The Average Value of Contents In A Woman's Purse," *KMLE*, May 16, 2012, http://kmle1079.cbslocal.com/2012/05/16/top-office-supplies-that-are-stolen/ (accessed April 12, 2013).

35. Marc Santora, "For a Thief in This Office, Paper Clips Wouldn't Do," *The New York Times*, January 15, 2013, http://www.nytimes.com/2013/01/16/nyregion/man-charged-in-theft-of-copy-toner-worth-over-376000.html accessed April 12, 2013).

36. National Retail Federation, "Retail Theft Decreased in 2011, According to Preliminary National Retail Security Survey Findings," June 22, 2012, http://www.nrf.com/modules.php?name=News&op=viewlive&sp_id=1389 (accessed April 12, 2013).

37. Ben Casselman, "Economists Set Rules on Ethics," *The Wall Street Journal*, January 9, 2012, http://online.wsj.com/article/SB10001424052970203436904577148940410667970.html (accessed April 12, 2013).

38. "100 Arrests In News Corp. Scandal Over Phone, Computer Hacking, Corrupt Payments To Public Officials," *The Huffington Post*, February 12, 2013, http://www.huffingtonpost.com/2013/02/12/100-people-arrested_n_2669111.html (accessed April 12, 2013).

39. National Business Ethics Survey, 30.

40. Peter Verhezen, "Giving Voice in a Culture of Silence: From a Culture of Compliance to a Culture of Integrity," *Journal of Business Ethics* 96 (2010): 187–206.

41. Gene R. Laczniak and Patrick E. Murphy, "Stakeholder Theory and Marketing: Moving from a Firm-Centric to a Societal Perspective," *Journal of Public Policy & Marketing* 31 (2): 284–292.

42. 3M, "Community Giving," http://solutions.3m.com/wps/portal/3M/en_US/3M-Sustainability/Global/Stakeholders/Giving/ (accessed April 12, 2013).

43. R.L. Jepperson, "Institutions, institutional effects, and institutionalism," In Walter W. Powell and Paul J. DiMaggio (eds.), *The new institutionalism in organizational analysis* (Chicago, IL: University of Chicago Press, 1991).

44. Patrick E. Murphy, Gene R. Laczniak, G. R., and Andrea Prothero, *Ethics in Marketing: International Cases and Perspectives* (New York, NY: Routledge, 2012).

45. Lynn G. Zucker, "The Role of Institutionalization in Cultural Persistence," *American Sociological Review* 42(5), October 1977, 726–743.

46. Paul J. DiMaggio and Walter W. Powell, "The Iron Cage Revisited: Institutionalized Isomorphism and Collective Rationality in Organizational Fields," *American Sociological Review*, 48 (April 1983): 147–60; John W. Meyer and Brian Rowan, "Institutionalized Organization: Formal Structure as Myth and Ceremony," *American Journal of Sociology* 83 (2), September 1977, 340–363.

47. Fluor Corporation, *The Code of Business Conduct and Ethics*, February 2011.

48. Karen Gallo, "DuPont Sued by Retailers on Price-Fixing Claim for Pigment," *Bloomberg*, March 16, 2013, http://www.bloomberg.com/news/2013-03-16/dupont-sued-by-retailers-alleging-pigment-price-fixing-1-.html (accessed April 19, 2013).

49. Leslie Kwohm, "When Your Boss Makes You Pay for Being Fat," *The Wall Street Journal*, http://online.wsj.com/article/SB10001424127887324600704578402784123334550.html (accessed April 23, 2013).

50. Walter W. Powell and Paul J. DiMaggio (eds.), *The new institutionalism in organizational analysis* (Chicago, IL: University of Chicago Press, 1991).

51. Tina M. Dacin, "Isomorphism in Context: The Power and Prescription of Institutional Norms," *Academy of Management Journal*, 40 (February 1997), 46–81.

52. Lynn G. Zucker, "The Role of Institutionalization in Cultural Persistence," *American Sociological Review* 42(5), October 1977, 726–743.

53. John W. Meyer and Brian Rowan, "Institutionalized Organization: Formal Structure as Myth and Ceremony," *American Journal of Sociology* 83 (2), September 1977, 340–363.

54. Jay M. Handelman and Stephen J. Arnold, "The Rule of Marketing Actions with a Social Dimension," *Journal of Marketing* 63 (1999): 33–48.

55. John L. Campbell, "Why Would Corporations Behave in Socially Responsible Ways? An Institutional Theory of Corporate Social Responsibility," *Academy of Management Review* 32(3), 2007, 946–967; J. Galaskiewicz, "Making corporate actors accountable: Institution-building in Minneapolis-St. Paul," In W. W. Powell & P. J. DiMaggio (Eds.), *The new institutionalism in organizational analysis*, 293–310 (Chicago: University of Chicago Press, 1991).

56. Bart Victor and Carroll Underwood Stephens, "Business Ethics: A Synthesis of Normative Philosophy and Empirical Social Science," *Business Ethics Quarterly* 4(2), 1994, 145–155.

57. John Rawls, *A Theory of Justice*, Cambridge, MA: Harvard University Press, 1971.

58. Ibid.

59. Patrick E. Murphy, Gene R. Laczniak, G. R., and Andrea Prothero, *Ethics in Marketing: International Cases and Perspectives* (New York, NY: Routledge, 2012).

60. Joel Gehman, Linda K. Treviño, and Raghu Garud, "Values Work: A Process Study of the Emergence and Performance of Organizational Values Practices," *Academy of Management Journal* 56(1), 2013, 84–112.

61. Shalom H. Schwartz, "Cultural value differences: Some implications for work," *Applied Psychology: An International Review,* 48(1999): 23–47.

62. M. Callon, P. Lascoumes, and Y. Barthe, *Acting in an uncertain world: An essay on technical democracy* (Cambridge, MA: MIT Press, 2009).

63. Joel Gehman, Linda K. Treviño, and Raghu Garud, "Values Work: A Process Study of the Emergence and Performance of Organizational Values Practices," *Academy of Management Journal* 56(1), 2013, 84–112.

64. Bert Scholtens and Lammertjan Dam, "Cultural Values and International Differences in Business Ethics," *Journal of Business Ethics* 75 (2007): 273–284.

65. Marriott, *2011 Annual Report*, http://www. wholefoodsmarket.com/mission-values/core-values (accessed April 19, 2013).

66. Gary R. Weaver and Linda K. Trevino, "Compliance and Values Oriented Ethics Programs: Influences on Employees' Attitudes and Behavior," *Business Ethics Quarterly* 9 (2), 1999, 315–335.

67. Bechtel Corporation, "Bechtel's approach to ethics training," YouTube, January 24, 2013, http://www. youtube.com/watch?v=EG9qWOloLR0 (accessed April 12, 2013); Bechtel Corporation, "Ethics," http://www.bechtel.com/ethics.html (accessed April 12, 2013); Bechtel Corporation, "Bechtel's Chief Ethics and Compliance Officer Shares Best Practices at European Ethics Conference," January 24, 2013, http://www.bechtel.com/2013-01-24.html (accessed April 12, 2013).

68. "Patients versus Profits at Johnson & Johnson: Has the Company Lost its Way?" Knowledge@Wharton, February 15, 2012, http://knowledge.wharton.upenn.edu/article. cfm?articleid=2943 (accessed April 12, 2013).

69. Harris Interactive, *The Harris Poll 2013 RQ® Summary Report*, http://www.harrisinteractive.com/vault/2013%20 RQ%20Summary%20Report%20FINAL.pdf (accessed April 12, 2013).

70. Mark. D. Promislo and Robert A. Giacalone, "Sick about Unethical Business," *BizEd*, January/February 2013, 20–26.

71. Total, "Our Code of Conduct," http://www.total.com/en/ about-total/group-presentation/our-ethical-principles-and-practices/code-of-conduct-940521.html (accessed April 12, 2013).

CHAPTER 6

INDIVIDUAL FACTORS: MORAL PHILOSOPHIES AND VALUES

AN ETHICAL DILEMMA*

Connor graduated from Illinois University with a B.S. in operations and logistics after he came back from his tour in the army. His work in the army prepared him well as a manager in operations and logistics, and it showed when he was hired at AlumaArc, a manufacturing facility that produced various tank parts for the U.S. Army. Connor's co-workers and fellow managers at his company respected him for the proficiency he showed in his work. Within eighteen months he became the key person in the logistics department, and a few months after that Connor became one of twenty managers in charge of the third shift. Above him were two Assistant General Managers (GMs) and the General Manager. The plant employed two thousand general workers and several hundred specialists.

Recently, the U.S. Army asked AlumaArc to step up production. This meant adding another shift with existing personnel and a number of incentives for increased productivity. At first, Connor was happy with the new business AlumaArc was getting. However, as he began examining the amount of output required to meet the army's expectations, he grew concerned. Even with overtime, the plant would still find it difficult to meet output goals running at maximum capacity. He also noticed many of the workers appeared worn out.

Because the plant had heavy equipment that required workers to take several safety precautions, it was standard procedure for workers to fill out a checklist marking off the different safety requirements before they began operating the machinery. One day Connor noticed the checklist for his shift hadn't been filled out. He asked Joe, one of the employees, about why it hadn't been done.

"Oh, we've been so busy lately trying to meet our production quota that George told us we could just skip it," Joe explained. George was one of the Assistant GMs.

"But these checklists are used to make sure you're operating everything safely," Connor responded.

Joe looked grim. "Well, if we filled them out, we'd just be lying anyway." He informed Conner that to save time, the workers were encouraged to bypass standard safety procedures. Additionally, Connor was horrified to realize many of the workers were not taking their required breaks in order to get rewarded for increasing their output.

Later that day, Connor confronted George. "George, these incentives are encouraging careless and unsafe behaviors. Employees are skipping safety procedures and breaks to get the work done. It's only a matter of time before someone gets seriously hurt."

George looked firmly at Connor. "I realize there are potential risks, but we can't afford to hire additional workers right now. If we can just meet this output, it'll increase our business tenfold. We'll be able to hire new workers and pay our current employees more."

Connor was stunned. "But these are people we are putting at risk!"

George sighed. "Connor, each worker has a choice whether or not they take advantage of these incentives. They are not being forced to do anything they don't want to do. Besides, these are not my rules. The GM put these incentives in place. It's really out of my control. Just think about it…we're doing it for the greater good of our company and our employees."

Connor replied, "But if they refuse, they are probably afraid they'll lose their jobs. And even if they do feel the risks are worth it, isn't it our job to make sure they have safe work conditions?"

Although George continued to reassure him, Connor left George's office determined to enforce all safety protocols and force his employees to take their required breaks. He figured if top management would not consider the well-being of the employees, he would do what he could to protect those who fell under his authority.

Later that week, George came up to Connor and said, "I'm sorry to tell you this, but your shift is not meeting the required output levels. We need to meet these deadlines quickly and accurately, and your shift has always been our fastest. Without you we're never going get the work done on time. That means we'll have to start laying off employees who aren't performing up to expectations." Connor recognized George's veiled threat but refused to compromise his workers' safety. Meanwhile, he began hearing stories of employees getting injured on other shifts.

Connor decided to talk to Wendy Smith, the General Manager. He knew she probably was not pleased with him, but he felt it necessary to try to persuade her about the dangers of what the company was doing. Connor wondered how he should approach Wendy. If he was not careful, she could fire him. He did not want to be disrespectful, but he also didn't want to be a part of a company that knowingly put their employees in harm's way.

QUESTIONS | EXERCISES

1. Describe Conner's moral beliefs and values.
2. In AlumaArc's reasoning, the benefits of increasing production outweigh the risks of potential injuries. How could this approach potentially backfire?
3. How should Connor approach this issue?

*This case is strictly hypothetical; any resemblance to real persons, companies, or situations is coincidental.

Most discussions of business ethics address the moral philosophies of the individual in ethical decision making, and the model we provided in Chapter 5 identifies individual moral perspectives as a central component of ethical decision making. In this chapter, we provide a detailed description and analysis of how individuals' backgrounds and philosophies influence their decisions. People often use their individual moral philosophies to justify decisions or explain their actions. To understand how people make ethical decisions, it is useful to have a grasp of the major types of moral philosophies. In this chapter, we discuss the stages of cognitive development as they relate to these moral philosophies. We also explain why cognitive moral development theory may not explain as much as we thought. Additionally, we examine white-collar crime as it relates to moral philosophies and personal values.

MORAL PHILOSOPHY DEFINED

When people talk about philosophy, they usually refer to the general system of values by which they live. **Moral philosophy**, on the other hand, refers to the specific principles or values people use to decide what is right and wrong. It is important to understand the distinction between moral philosophies and business ethics. Moral philosophies are person-specific, while business ethics is based on decisions made by groups or when carrying out tasks to meet business objectives. A moral philosophy is a person's principles and values. In the context of business, ethics refers to what the group, firm, or organization defines as right or wrong actions that pertain to its business operations and the objective of profits, earnings per share, or some other financial measure of success. For example, a production manager may be guided by a general philosophy of management that emphasizes encouraging workers to get to know as much as possible about the product they are manufacturing. However, the manager's moral philosophy comes into play when he must make decisions such as whether to notify employees in advance of upcoming layoffs. Although workers prefer advance warning, issuing that warning could jeopardize the quality and quantity of production. Such decisions require a person to evaluate the "rightness," or morality of choices in terms of his or her own principles and values.

Moral philosophies present guidelines for "determining how conflicts in human interests are to be settled and for optimizing mutual benefit of people living together in groups."[1] These philosophies direct people as they formulate business strategies and resolve specific ethical issues. However, there is no single moral philosophy everyone accepts. Moral philosophies are often used to defend a particular type of economic system and individuals' behavior within these systems.

Adam Smith is considered the father of free-market capitalism. He was a professor of logic and moral philosophy and wrote the treatise "The Theory of Moral Sentiments" (1759) and the book *Inquiry into the Nature and Causes of the Wealth of Nations* (1776). Smith believed business was and should be guided by the morals of good people. But in the eighteenth century, Smith could not imagine the complexity of modern markets, the size of multinationals, or the fact that four or five companies could gain control of the vast majority of the resources of the world. His ideas did not envision the full force of democracy, or the immense wealth and power some firms could wield within countries.

Under capitalism, some managers view profit as the ultimate goal of an enterprise and may not be concerned about the impact of their firms' decisions on society. The economist Milton Friedman supports this viewpoint, contending the market will reward or punish companies for unethical conduct without the need for government regulation.[2] The emergence of this Friedman-type capitalism as the dominant and most widely accepted economic system created market-driven societies around the world. Even China's communist government adapted capitalism and free enterprise to help it become a leading economic power.

The United States exported the idea that the invisible hand of free-market capitalism can solve the troubles of mankind and guide societies toward greater happiness and prosperity as a result of the increased availability of products and services. Marketing helps consumers understand, compare, and obtain these products, thereby increasing the efficiency and effectiveness of the exchange. However, free markets will not solve all problems. For example, excessive consumption has negative effects on the environment and can be psychologically, spiritually, and physically unhealthy.[3] More is not necessarily best in every situation.

Economic systems not only allocate resources and products within a society but also influence, and are influenced by, the actions and beliefs of individuals (morals) and of society (laws) as a whole. The success of an economic system depends on both its philosophical framework and on the individuals within the system who maintain moral philosophies that bring people together in a cooperative, efficient, and productive marketplace. There is a long Western tradition going back to Aristotle of questioning whether a market economy and individual moral behavior are compatible. Individuals in today's society exist within a framework of social, political, and economic institutions.

People facing ethical issues often base their decisions on their own values and principles of right or wrong, most of which they learned through the socialization process with the help of family members, social groups, religions, and formal education. Individual factors that influence decision making include personal moral philosophies. Ethical dilemmas arise in problem-solving situations when the rules governing decision making are vague or in conflict. In real-life situations, there is no substitute for an individual's own critical thinking and ability to accept responsibility for his or her decisions.

Moral philosophies are ideal moral perspectives that provide individuals with abstract principles for guiding their social existence. For example, a person's decision to recycle waste or to purchase or sell recycled or recyclable products is influenced by moral philosophies and individual attitudes toward recycling.[4] It is often difficult to implement an individual moral philosophy within the complex environment of a business organization. On the other hand, our economic system depends on individuals coming together and sharing philosophies to create the values, trust, and expectations that allow the system to work. Most employees within a business organization do not think about the particular moral philosophy they are using when confronted with an ethical issue.

Many theories associated with moral philosophies refer to a value orientation and concepts such as economics, idealism, and relativism. The concept of the **economic value orientation** is associated with values quantified by monetary means; according to this theory, if an act produces more value for its effort, then it should be accepted as ethical. **Idealism**, on the other hand, is a moral philosophy that places special value on ideas and ideals as products of the mind. The term refers to the efforts required to account for all objects in nature and experience and to assign to them a higher order of existence. Studies uncovered a positive correlation between idealistic thinking and ethical decision making. **Realism** is the view that an external world exists independent of our perceptions. Realists assume humankind is not naturally benevolent and kind, but instead inherently self-centered and competitive. According to realists, each person is ultimately guided by his or her own self-interest. Research shows a negative correlation between realistic thinking and ethical decision making. The belief that all actions are ultimately self-motivated seems to lead to a tendency toward unethical decision making.

MORAL PHILOSOPHIES

There are many moral philosophies, but because a detailed study of all of them is beyond the scope of this book, we will limit our discussion to those that are most applicable to the study of business ethics. Our approach focuses on the most basic concepts needed to help you understand the ethical decision-making process in business. We do not prescribe the use of any particular moral philosophy, for there is no one correct way to resolve ethical issues in business.

To help you understand how the moral philosophies discussed in this chapter may be applied in decision making, we use a hypothetical situation as an illustration. Suppose that Sam Colt, a sales representative, is preparing a sales presentation for his firm, Midwest Hardware, which manufactures nuts and bolts. Sam hopes to obtain a large sale from a construction firm that is building a bridge across the Mississippi River near St. Louis, Missouri. The bolts manufactured by Midwest Hardware have a 3 percent defect rate, which, although acceptable in the industry, makes them unsuitable for use in certain types of projects, such as those that may be subject to sudden, severe stress. The new bridge will be located near the New Madrid Fault line, the source of the United States' greatest earthquake in 1811. The epicenter of that earthquake, which caused extensive damage and altered the flow of the Mississippi, is less than 200 miles from the new bridge site. Earthquake experts believe there is a 50 percent chance that an earthquake with a magnitude greater than 7 will occur somewhere along the New Madrid Fault by the year 2030. Bridge construction in the area is not regulated by earthquake codes, however. If Sam wins the sale, he will earn a commission of $25,000 on top of his regular salary. But if he tells the contractor about the defect rate, Midwest may lose the sale to a competitor that markets bolts with a lower defect rate. Sam's ethical issue is whether to point out to the bridge contractor that, in the event of an earthquake, some Midwest bolts could fail, possibly resulting in the collapse of the bridge.

We will come back to this illustration as we discuss particular moral philosophies, asking how Sam Colt might use each philosophy to resolve his ethical issue. We don't judge the quality of Sam's decision, and we do not advocate any one moral philosophy; in fact, this illustration and Sam's decision rationales are necessarily simplistic as well as hypothetical. In reality, the decision maker would probably have many more factors to consider in making his or her choice and thus might reach a different decision. With that note of caution, we introduce the concept of goodness and several types of moral philosophy: teleology, deontology, the relativist perspective, virtue ethics, and justice (see Table 6–1).

Instrumental and Intrinsic Goodness

To appreciate moral philosophy, you must understand the different perspectives on the notion of goodness. Is there a clear and unwavering line between "good" and "bad"? What is the relationship between the ends and the means in generating "good" and "bad" outcomes? Is there some way to determine if the ends can be identified independently as good or bad? Because the answers can be complex and confusing, we have simplified the discussion. Aristotle, for example, argued that happiness is an intrinsically good end and that its goodness is natural and universal, without relativity. On the other hand, the philosopher Immanuel Kant argued that goodwill, seriously applied toward accomplishment, is the only thing good in itself.

Two basic concepts of goodness are monism and pluralism. Monists believe only one thing is intrinsically good, and pluralists believe two or more things are intrinsically good. Monists are often characterized by hedonism—the idea that pleasure is the ultimate good, or the best moral end involves the greatest balance of pleasure over pain. Hedonism defines right or acceptable behavior as that which maximizes personal pleasure. Moral philosophers describe those who believe more pleasure is better as quantitative hedonists and those who believe it is possible to get too much of a good thing (such as pleasure) as qualitative hedonists.

TABLE 6–1 A Comparison of the Philosophies Used in Business Decisions

Teleology	Stipulates acts are morally right or acceptable if they produce some desired result, such as realization of self-interest or utility
Egoism	Defines right or acceptable actions as those that maximize a particular person's self-interest as defined by the individual
Utilitarianism	Defines right or acceptable actions as those that maximize total utility, or the greatest good for the greatest number of people
Deontology	Focuses on the preservation of individual rights and on the intentions associated with a particular behavior rather than on its consequences
Relativist	Evaluates ethicalness subjectively on the basis of individual and group experiences
Virtue ethics	Assumes what is moral in a given situation is not only what conventional morality requires but also what the mature person with a "good" moral character deems appropriate
Justice	Evaluates ethicalness on the basis of fairness: distributive, procedural, and interactional

© Cengage Learning

Pluralists, often referred to as non-hedonists, take the opposite position that no *one* thing is intrinsically good. For example, a pluralist might view beauty, aesthetic experience, knowledge, and personal affection as ultimate goods. Plato argued that the good life is a mixture of (1) moderation and fitness, (2) proportion and beauty, (3) intelligence and wisdom, (4) sciences and arts, and (5) pure pleasures of the soul.

Although all pluralists are non-hedonists, all monists are not necessarily hedonists. An individual can believe in a single intrinsic good other than pleasure; Machiavelli and Nietzsche held power to be the sole good, for example, and Kant's belief in the single virtue of goodwill classifies him as a monistic non-hedonist.

A more modern view is expressed in the instrumentalist position. Sometimes called pragmatists, **instrumentalists** reject the ideas that (1) ends can be separated from the means that produce them and (2) ends, purposes, or outcomes are intrinsically good in and of themselves. The philosopher John Dewey argued that the difference between ends and means is merely a matter of the individual's perspective; thus, almost any action can be an end or a mean. Dewey gives the example that people eat to be able to work, and they work to be able to eat. From a practical standpoint, an end is only a remote mean, and the means are but a series of acts viewed from an earlier stage. From this conclusion it follows there is no such thing as a single, universal end.

A discussion of moral value often revolves around the nature of goodness, but theories of moral obligation change the question to "What makes an action right or obligatory?" **Goodness theories** typically focus on the *end result* of actions and the goodness or happiness created by them. **Obligation theories** emphasize the *means* and *motives* by which actions are justified, and are divided into the categories of teleology and deontology.

Teleology

Teleology (from the Greek word for "end" or "purpose") refers to moral philosophies in which an act is considered morally right or acceptable if it produces some desired result, such as pleasure, knowledge, career growth, the realization of self-interest, utility, wealth, or even fame. Teleological philosophies assess the moral worth of a behavior by looking at its consequences, and thus moral philosophers today often refer to these theories as **consequentialism**. Two important teleological philosophies that often guide decision making in individual business decisions are egoism and utilitarianism.

Egoism defines right or acceptable behavior in terms of its consequences for the individual. Egoists believe they should make decisions that maximize their own self-interest, which is defined differently by each individual. Depending on the egoist, self-interest may be construed as physical well-being, power, pleasure, fame, a satisfying career, a good family life, wealth, or something else. In an ethical decision-making situation, an egoist will probably choose the alternative that contributes most to his or her self-interest. Many believe egoistic people and companies are inherently unethical, short-term oriented, and willing to take advantage of any opportunity for gain. Some telemarketers demonstrate egoism when they prey on elderly consumers who may be vulnerable because of loneliness or fear of losing their financial independence. Thousands of senior citizens fall victim to fraudulent telemarketers every year, in many cases losing all their savings and sometimes even their homes.

However, there also is **enlightened egoism**. Enlightened egoists take a long-range perspective and allow for the well-being of others although their own self-interest remains paramount. An example of enlightened egoism is a person helping a turtle across a highway because if it were killed the person would feel distressed.[5] Enlightened egoists may abide by professional codes of ethics, control pollution, avoid cheating on taxes, help create jobs, and support community projects not because these actions benefit others but because they help achieve some ultimate individual goal, such as advancement within their firms. An enlightened egoist might call management's attention to a coworker who is making false accounting reports, but only to safeguard the company's reputation and thus the egoist's own job security. In addition, an enlightened egoist could become a whistleblower and report misconduct to a regulatory agency to receive a reward for exposing misconduct.

Let's return to the hypothetical case of Sam Colt, who must decide whether to warn the bridge contractor that 3 percent of Midwest Hardware's bolts are likely to be defective. If he is an egoist, he will choose the alternative that maximizes his own self-interest. If he defines his self-interest in terms of personal wealth, his personal moral philosophy may lead him to value a $25,000 commission more than a chance to reduce the risk of a bridge collapse. As a result, an egoist might well resolve this ethical dilemma by keeping quiet about the bolts' defect rate, hoping to win the sale and the $25,000 commission. He may rationalize that there is a slim chance of an earthquake, that bolts would not be a factor in a major earthquake, and even if defective bolts were a factor, no one would actually be able to prove they caused the bridge to collapse.

Like egoism, utilitarianism is concerned with consequences, but unlike the egoist, the utilitarian seeks the greatest good for the greatest number of people. Utilitarians believe they should make decisions that result in the greatest total *utility,* or the greatest benefit for all those affected by a decision. For instance, one might use a utilitarianism perspective to argue for companies who legally sell harmful products, such as tobacco, guns, or alcohol. It has been argued that despite their drawbacks, allowing them to be sold legally is less harmful than having them sold illegally and unregulated.[6] Such an approach influenced similar forms of legislation, such as the recent laws in Colorado and Washington permitting the regulated sale of recreational marijuana. Utilitarian decision making relies on a systematic comparison of the costs and benefits to all affected parties. Using such a cost–benefit analysis, a utilitarian decision maker calculates the utility of the consequences of all possible alternatives and then selects the one that results in the greatest benefit. For example, the U.S. Supreme Court ruled that supervisors are responsible for the sexual misconduct of employees, even if the employers knew nothing about the behavior, a decision that established a strict standard for harassment on the job. One of the justices wrote that the burden on the employer to prevent harassment is "one of the costs of doing business."[7] The Court decided the greatest utility to society would result from forcing businesses to prevent harassment.

In evaluating an action's consequences, utilitarians must consider all of the potential costs and benefits for all of the people affected by a decision. For example, Baxter Pharmaceuticals sells an anticoagulant drug called heparin, and for a time Baxter's suppliers in China were deliberately cutting their raw heparin batches with a counterfeit product to reduce costs. The U.S. Food and Drug Administration (FDA) discovered problems with heparin from China when patients reported difficulty breathing, vomiting, excessive sweating, rapidly falling blood pressure, and even death.[8] The Chinese contamination crisis was linked to 81 deaths, and the FDA identified the chemical contaminant deliberately added to unrefined heparin to stretch its supply and increase its potency.[9] If Baxter Pharmaceuticals' suppliers had done a utilitarian analysis and included the costs associated with losing Baxter as a client and the legal sanctions from both the U.S. and China, they might have chosen to avoid using the counterfeit product. Zheng Xiaoyu, former head of China's State Food and Drug Administration, was found guilty of corruption related to this situation and other cases of deaths from tainted pharmaceuticals. He was convicted and executed for taking bribes and for dereliction of duty.[10]

Utilitarians use various criteria to evaluate the morality of an action. Some utilitarian philosophers argue that general rules should be followed to decide which action is best.[11] These **rule utilitarians** determine behavior on the basis of principles or rules designed to promote the greatest utility, rather than on individual examinations of each situation they encounter. One such rule might be "Bribery is wrong." If people felt free to offer bribes whenever they might be useful, the world would become chaotic; therefore, a rule prohibiting bribery would increase utility. A rule utilitarian would not bribe an official, even to preserve workers' jobs, but instead would adhere strictly to the rule. Rule utilitarians do not automatically accept conventional moral rules, however; if they determined an alternative rule would promote greater utility, they would advocate its use instead.

Other utilitarian philosophers have argued that the rightness of each individual action must be evaluated to determine whether it produces the greatest utility for the greatest number of people.[12] These **act utilitarians** examine specific actions, rather than the general rules governing them, to assess whether they will result in the greatest utility. Rules such as "Bribery is wrong" serve only as general guidelines for act utilitarians. They would likely agree that bribery is generally wrong, not because there is anything inherently wrong with bribery, but because the total amount of utility decreases when one person's interests are placed ahead of those of society. In a particular case, however, an act utilitarian might argue that bribery is acceptable. For example, sales managers might believe their firm will not win a construction contract unless a local government official gets a bribe, and if the firm does not obtain the contract, it will have to lay off 100 workers. The manager might therefore argue that bribery is justified because saving 100 jobs creates more utility than obeying a law. For example, Pfizer paid $60 million to settle charges of bribery; according to the SEC, the firm bribed foreign officials in Bulgaria, China, Croatia, the Czech Republic, Italy, Kazakhstan, Russia and Serbia in order to obtain business and gain approvals.[13] These Pfizer employees may have decided winning the contracts generated the most utility for the company.

Now suppose that Sam Colt, the bolt salesperson, is a utilitarian. Before making his decision, he would conduct a cost–benefit analysis to assess which alternative would create the greatest utility. On the one hand, building the bridge would improve roadways and allow more people to cross the Mississippi River to reach jobs in St. Louis. The project would create hundreds of jobs, enhance the local economy, and unite communities on both sides of the river. Additionally, it would increase the revenues of Midwest Hardware, allowing the firm to invest more in research to lower the defect rate of the bolts it produces in the future. On the other hand, a bridge collapse could kill or injure as many as 100 people. But the bolts have only a 3 percent defect rate, there is only a 50 percent probability of an earthquake *somewhere* along the fault line, and there might be only a few cars on the bridge at the time of a disaster.

After analyzing the costs and benefits of the situation, Sam might rationalize that building the bridge with his company's bolts would create more utility (jobs, unity, economic growth, and company growth) than telling the bridge contractor the bolts might fail in an earthquake. If so, a utilitarian would probably not alert the bridge contractor to the defect rate of the bolts.

Deontology

Deontology (from the Greek word for "ethics") refers to moral philosophies that focus on the rights of individuals and the intentions associated with a particular behavior rather than its consequences. Fundamental to deontological theory is the idea that equal respect must be given to all persons. Unlike utilitarians, deontologists argue that there are some things we should *not* do, even to maximize utility. For example, deontologists would consider it wrong to kill an innocent person or commit a serious injustice against someone, no matter how much greater social utility might result from doing so, because such an action would infringe on individual rights. The utilitarian, however, might consider an action resulting in a person's death acceptable if that action lead to some greater benefit. Deontological philosophies regard certain behaviors as inherently right, and the determination of this rightness focuses on the individual actor, not on society. Therefore these perspectives are sometimes referred to as **nonconsequentialism**, a system of ethics based on *respect for persons.*

Contemporary deontology has been greatly influenced by the German philosopher Immanuel Kant, who developed the so-called **categorical imperative**: "Act as if the maxim of thy action were to become by thy will a universal law of nature."[14] Simply put, if you feel comfortable allowing everyone in the world to see you commit an act and if your rationale for acting in a particular manner is suitable to become a universal principle guiding behavior, then committing that act is ethical. People who borrow money and promise to return it with no intention of keeping that promise cannot "universalize" their act. If everyone borrowed money without the intention of returning it, no one would take such promises seriously, and all lending would cease.[15] The rationale for the action would not be a suitable universal principle, and the act could not be considered ethical.

The term *nature* is crucial for deontologists. In general, deontologists regard the nature of moral principles as permanent and stable, and they believe compliance with these principles define ethicalness. Deontologists believe individuals have certain absolute rights, including freedom of conscience, freedom of consent, freedom of privacy, freedom of speech, and due process.[16]

To decide if a behavior is ethical, deontologists look for conformity to moral principles. For example, if a manufacturing worker becomes ill or dies as a result of conditions in the workplace, a deontologist might argue that the company must modify its production processes to correct the condition, no matter what the cost—even if it means bankrupting the company and thus causing all workers to lose their jobs. In contrast, a utilitarian would analyze all the costs and benefits of modifying production processes and make a decision on that basis. This example is greatly oversimplified, of course, but it helps to clarify the difference between teleology and deontology. In short, teleological philosophies consider the *ends* associated with an action, whereas deontological philosophies consider the *means*.

Returning again to our bolt salesperson, let's consider a deontological Sam Colt. He would probably feel obligated to tell the bridge contractor about the defect rate because of the potential loss of life that might result from an earthquake-caused bridge collapse. Even though constructing the bridge would benefit residents and earn Sam a substantial commission, the failure of the bolts during an earthquake would infringe on the rights of any person crossing the bridge at the time of the collapse. Thus, the deontological Sam would likely inform the bridge contractor about the defect rate and point out the earthquake risk, even though he would probably lose the sale as a result.

As with utilitarians, deontologists may be divided into those who focus on moral rules and those who focus on the nature of the acts themselves. **Rule deontologists** believe conformity to general moral principles based on logic determines ethicalness. Examples include Kant's categorical imperative and the Golden Rule of the Judeo-Christian tradition: "Do unto others as you would have them do unto you." Such rules, or principles, guiding ethical behavior override the imperatives that emerge from a specific context. One could argue that Jeffery Wigand—who exposed the underside of the tobacco industry when he blew the whistle on his employer, Brown & Williamson Tobacco—was such a rule deontologist. Although it cost him financially and socially, Wigand testified to Congress about the realities of marketing cigarettes and their effects on society.[17]

Rule deontology is determined by the relationship between the basic rights of the individual and a set of rules governing conduct. For example, a video store owner accused of distributing obscene materials could argue from a rule deontological perspective that the basic right to freedom of speech overrides the indecent or pornographic aspects of his business. Indeed, the free-speech argument has held up in many U.S. courts. Kant and rule deontologists would support a process of discovery to identify the moral issues relevant to a firm's mission and objectives. Then they would follow a process of justifying that mission or those objectives based on rules.[18] An example of a rule deontologist is JetBlue's former CEO David Neeleman. Because of a severe snowstorm, several JetBlue flights were delayed for as many as nine hours on the runway, and passengers were kept in their seats. After the incident, Neeleman issued a public apology for his company's mismanagement of the situation, introduced a "Customer Bill of Rights,"[19] and offered $40 million in compensation to the affected passengers. He was replaced as CEO by David Barger. Despite the disaster, some criticized the ousting of Neeleman as he was considered to be a visionary who appeared to care deeply about customer service.[20]

Act deontologists, in contrast, hold that actions are the proper basis to judge morality or ethicalness. Act deontology requires a person use equity, fairness, and impartiality when making and enforcing decisions.[21] For act deontologists, past experiences are more important than rules; rules serve only as guidelines in the decision-making process. In effect, act deontologists suggest people simply *know* that certain acts are right or wrong, regardless of their consequences. In addition, act deontologists consider the unique characteristics of a particular act or moment in time take precedence over any rule. For example, many people view data collection by Internet sites as a violation of personal privacy; regardless of any website's stated rules or policies, many Internet users want to be left alone unless they provide permission to be tracked while online. Privacy has become such an issue that the government is considering regulation to protect online users.[22] Research suggests that rule and act deontological principles play a larger role in a person's decision than teleological philosophies.[23]

As we have seen, ethical issues can be evaluated from many different perspectives. Each type of philosophy discussed here provides a clear basis for deciding whether a particular action was right or wrong. Adherents of different personal moral philosophies may disagree in their evaluations of a given action, yet all are behaving ethically *according to their own standards*. The relativist perspective may be helpful in understanding how people make such decisions in practice.

Relativist Perspective

From the **relativist perspective**, definitions of ethical behavior are derived subjectively from the experiences of individuals and groups. Relativists use themselves or the people around them as their basis for defining ethical standards, and the various forms of relativism include descriptive, meta-ethical, and normative.[24] **Descriptive relativism** relates to observations of other cultures. Different cultures exhibit different norms, customs, and values, but these observations say nothing about the higher questions of ethical justification. At this point meta-ethical relativism comes into play. **Meta-ethical relativism** proposes that people naturally see situations from their own perspectives, and there is no objective way of resolving ethical disputes between different value systems and individuals. Simply put, one culture's moral philosophy cannot logically be preferred to another's because no meaningful basis for comparison exists. Because ethical rules are embedded in a specific culture, the values and behaviors of people in one culture do not generally influence the behaviors of people in another culture.[25] Finally, at the individual level of reasoning, we have **normative relativism**. Normative relativists assume one person's opinion is as good as another's.[26]

Basic relativism acknowledges that we live in a world in which people have many different views and bases from which to justify decisions as right or wrong. The relativist looks to the interacting groups and tries to determine probable solutions based on group consensus. When formulating business strategies and plans, for example, a relativist would try to anticipate the conflicts that might arise between the different philosophies held by members of the organization, suppliers, customers, and the community at large.

The relativist observes the actions of members of an involved group and attempts to determine that group's consensus on a given behavior. A positive consensus signifies that the group considers the action to be ethical. However, such judgments may not remain valid forever. As circumstances evolve or the makeup of the group changes, a formerly accepted behavior may come to be viewed as wrong or unethical, or vice versa. Within the accounting profession, for example, it was traditionally considered unethical to advertise. However, advertising has now gained acceptance among accountants. This shift in ethical views may be the result of the increase in the number of accountants that led to greater competition. Moreover, the federal government investigated the restrictions accounting groups placed on their members and concluded that they inhibited free competition. Consequently, advertising is now acceptable because of the informal consensus that emerged on this issue in the accounting industry.

One problem with relativism is it emphasizes peoples' differences while ignoring their basic similarities. Similarities across different people and cultures—such as beliefs against incest, murder, and theft, or beliefs that reciprocity and respect for the elderly are good—may be hard to explain from the relativist perspective. Additionally, studies suggest relativism is negatively correlated to a person's sensitivity to ethical issues. Thus, if someone is a relativist, he or she will be less likely to detect issues with an ethical component.[27] On the other hand, managers with high relativism may show more commitment to completing a project. This indicates that relativism is associated with dedication to group values and objectives, leading to less independent ethical decision making.[28]

If Midwest Hardware salesperson Sam Colt was a relativist, he would attempt to determine consensus before deciding whether to tell his prospective customer about the bolts' defect rate. The relativist Sam Colt would look at his company's policy and at the general industry standards for disclosure. He might also informally survey his colleagues and superiors as well as consult industry trade journals and codes of ethics. Such investigations would help him determine the group consensus that should reflect a variety of moral philosophies. If he learns company policy and industry practice suggest discussing defect rates with those customers for whom faulty bolts may cause serious problems, he may infer there is a consensus on the matter. As a relativist, he probably would inform the bridge contractor that some of the bolts may fail, perhaps leading to a bridge collapse in the event of an earthquake. Conversely, if he determines that the normal practice in his company and the industry is not to inform customers about defect rates, he would probably not discuss the bolt defect rate with the bridge contractor.

Virtue Ethics

Virtue ethics argues that ethical behavior involves not only adhering to conventional moral standards but also considering what a mature person with a "good" moral character would deem appropriate in a given situation. A moral virtue represents an acquired disposition valued as a part of an individual's character. As individuals develop socially, they come to behave in ways they consider to be moral.[29] A person with the character trait of honesty will be disposed to tell the truth because it is considered to be the right approach in terms of human communication.

A virtue is considered praiseworthy because it is an achievement that an individual developed through practice and commitment.[30] Proponents of virtue ethics often list basic goods and virtues that are presented as positive and useful mental habits or cultivated character traits. Aristotle named loyalty, courage, wit, community, and judgment as "excellences" society requires. While listing the most important virtues is a popular theoretical task, the philosopher John Dewey cautions that virtues should not be looked at separately, and points out that examining interactions between virtues actually provides the best idea of a person's integrity of character.

The virtue ethics approach to business can be summarized as follows:

1. Good corporate ethics programs encourage individual virtue and integrity.
2. By the employee's role in the community (organization), these virtues form a good person.
3. An individual's ultimate purpose is to serve society's demands and the public good and be rewarded in his or her career.
4. The well-being of the community goes hand in hand with individual excellence.[31]

The difference between deontology, teleology, and virtue ethics is the first two are applied *deductively* to problems, whereas virtue ethics is applied *inductively*. Virtue ethics assumes societal moral rules form the foundation of virtue. Our political, social, and economic systems depend upon the presence of certain virtues among citizens in order to function successfully.[32]

Indeed, virtue ethics could be thought of as a dynamic theory of how to conduct business activities. The virtue ethicist believes a successful market economy depends upon social institutions such as family, school, church, and community where virtues can be nurtured. These virtues, including honesty, trust, tolerance, and restraint, create obligations that make cooperation possible. In a market economy based on virtues, individuals have powerful incentives to conform to prevailing standards of behavior. Some philosophers think social virtues may be eroded by the market, but virtue ethicists believe economic institutions are in balance with and support other social institutions.[33] Some of the virtues that could be seen as driving a market economy are listed in Table 6–2. Although not comprehensive, the list provides examples of the types of virtues that support the conduct of business.

The elements of virtue most important to business transactions are trust, self-control, empathy, fairness, and truthfulness. Non-virtuous characteristics include lying, cheating,

TABLE 6–2 Virtues That Support Business Transactions

Trust: The predisposition to place confidence in the behavior of others while taking the risk that the expected behavior will not be performed	Eliminates the need for and associated cost of monitoring compliance with agreements, contracts, and reciprocal agreements, as there is the expectation a promise or agreement can be relied on
Self-control: The disposition to pass up an immediate advantage or gratification; the ability to avoid exploiting a known opportunity for personal gain	Gives up short-term self-interest for long-term benefits
Empathy: The ability to share the feelings or emotions of others	Promotes civility because success in the market depends on the courteous treatment of people who have the option of going to competitors; the ability to anticipate needs and satisfy customers and employees contributes to a firm's economic success
Fairness: The disposition to deal equitably with the perceived injustices of others	Often relates to doing the right thing with respect to small matters in order to cultivate a long-term business relationship
Truthfulness: The disposition to provide the facts or correct information as known to the individual	Involves avoiding deception and contributes to trust in business relationships
Learning: The disposition to constantly acquire knowledge internal and external to the firm, whether about an industry, corporate culture, or other societies	Gaining knowledge to make better, more informed decisions
Gratitude: A sign of maturity that is the foundation of civility and decency	The recognition that people do not succeed alone
Civility: The disposition or essence of courtesy, politeness, respect, and consideration for others	Relates to the process of doing business in a culturally correct way, thus decreasing communication errors and increasing trust
Moral leadership: Strength of character, peace of mind and heart, leading to happiness in life	A trait of leaders who follow a consistent pattern of behavior based on virtues

Source: Adapted from Ian Maitland, "Virtuous Markets: The Market as School of the Virtues," *Business Ethics Quarterly* (January 1997): 97; and Gordon B. Hinckley, *Standing for Something: 10 Neglected Virtues that Will Heal Our Hearts and Homes* (New York: Three Rivers Press, 2001).

fraud, and corruption. In their broadest sense, concepts of virtue appear across all cultures. The problem of virtue ethics comes in its implementation within and between cultures. If a company tacitly approves of corruption, the employee who adheres to the virtues of trust and truthfulness would consider it wrong to sell unneeded repair parts despite the organization's approval of such acts. Other employees might view this truthful employee as highly ethical; however, in order to rationalize their own behavior, they may judge his or her ethics as going beyond what is required by the job or society. Critics of virtue ethics argue that true virtue is an unattainable goal, but to virtue ethicists, this relativistic argument is meaningless because they believe in the universality of the elements of virtue.

If bolt salesperson Sam Colt was a virtue ethicist, he would consider the elements of virtue (such as honesty and trust) and tell the prospective customer about the defect rate and his concerns regarding the building of the bridge. Sam would not resort to puffery to explain the product or its risks, and might even suggest alternative products or companies that would lower the probability of the bridge collapsing.

Justice

Justice is fair treatment and due reward in accordance with ethical or legal standards, including the disposition to deal with perceived injustices of others. The justice of a situation is based on the perceived rights of individuals and on the intentions of the people involved in a business interaction. In other words, justice relates to the issue of what individuals feel they are due based on their rights and performance in the workplace. For this reason, justice is more likely to be based on deontological moral philosophies than on teleological or utilitarian philosophies.

Three types of justice provide a framework for evaluating different situations (see Table 6–3). Distributive justice is based on the evaluation of the outcomes or results of a business relationship. If some employees feel they are paid less than their coworkers for the same work, they have concerns about distributive justice. Distributive justice is difficult to effect when one member of the business exchange intends to take advantage of the relationship. A boss who forces his employees to do more work so he can take more time off would be unjust because he is taking advantage of his position. Situations such as this cause an imbalance in distributive justice.

Procedural justice considers the processes and activities that produce a particular outcome. A climate that emphasizes procedural justice positively influences employees' attitudes and behaviors toward work-group cohesion. The visibility of supervisors and the work group's perceptions of its own cohesiveness are products of a climate of procedural justice.[34] When there is strong employee support for decisions, decision makers, organizations, and outcomes, procedural justice is less important to the individual. In contrast, when employees' support for decisions, decision makers, organizations, or outcomes is not very strong, then procedural justice becomes more important.[35] For example, Nugget Market in Woodland, California, has a corporate culture that focuses on employees, who create policies for each store. Because of the economy and as a result of employee comments, Nugget Market gives employees cards good for 10 percent discounts on $500 worth of groceries every month, and at one employee-appreciation event, the executive team members washed the cars of all the associates.[36] Thus, Nugget Market uses methods of procedural justice to establish positive stakeholder relationships by promoting understanding and inclusion in the decision-making process. The United Nations consumer protection guidelines adopt a highly procedural justice outlook with its concerns for safety, the right to be

TABLE 6–3 Types of Justice

Justice Type	Areas of Emphasis
Distributive justice: Based on the evaluation of *outcomes* or *results* of the business relationship	Benefits derived Equity in rewards
Procedural justice: Based on the *processes* and *activities* that produce the outcome or results	Decision-making process Level of access, openness, and participation
Interactional justice: Based on *relationships* and the *treatment* of others	Accuracy of information Truthfulness, respect, and courtesy in the process

© Cengage Learning

heard, and the right to privacy.[37] Evaluations of performance not consistently developed and applied can lead to problems with procedural justice. For instance, employees' concerns about unequal compensation relate to their perceptions that the processes of justice in their company are inconsistent.

Interactional justice is based on the relationships between organizational members, including the way employees and management treat one another. Interactional justice is linked to fairness within member interactions. It often involves an individual's relationship with the accuracy of the information a business organization provides. Although interactional justice often refers to how managers treat their subordinates, employees can also be guilty in creating interactional justice disputes. For example, many employees admit they stay home when they are not really sick if they feel they can get away with it. Such workplace absenteeism costs businesses millions of dollars each year.

All three types of justice—distributive, procedural, and interactional—could be used to measure a single business situation and the fairness of the organization and individuals involved. In general, justice evaluations result in restitution seeking, relationship building, and evaluations of fairness in business relationships. Using the example of Sam Colt, Sam would feel obligated to tell all affected parties about the bolt defect rate and the possible consequences in order to create a fair transaction process.

APPLYING MORAL PHILOSOPHY TO ETHICAL DECISION MAKING

Individuals use different moral philosophies depending on whether they make a personal decision or a work-related decision.[38] Two things may explain this behavior. First, in the business arena, some goals and pressures for success differ from the goals and pressures in a person's life outside of work. As a result, an employee might view a specific action as good in the business sector but unacceptable outside the work environment. Some suggest business managers are morally different from other people. In a way, this is correct, in that business contains one variable that is absent from other situations: the profit motive. The various factors that make up a person's moral philosophy are weighted differently in a business (profit) situation. The comment "It's not personal, it's just business" demonstrates the conflict businesspeople can experience when their personal values do not align with utilitarian or profit-oriented decisions. The reality is if firms do not make a profit, they will fail. However, this fact should not be a justification for seeking excessive profits or executive pay, issues that are now being questioned by stakeholders.

The second reason people change moral philosophies is the corporate culture where they work. When children enter school, they learn certain rules, such as raising their hands to speak or asking permission to use the restroom. So it is with a new employee. Rules, personalities, and precedents exert pressure on the employee to conform to the firm's culture. As this process occurs, the individual's moral philosophy may change to become compatible with the work environment. Many people are acquainted with those who are respected for their goodness at home or in their communities but make unethical decisions in the workplace. Even Bernard Madoff, the perpetrator of the largest Ponzi scheme in history, had a reputation as an upstanding citizen before his fraud was uncovered.

Obviously, the concept of a moral philosophy is inexact. For that reason, moral philosophies must be assessed on a continuum rather than as static entities. Each philosophy states an ideal perspective, and most individuals shift between different moral philosophies as they experience and interpret ethical dilemmas. In other words, implementing moral philosophies from an individual perspective requires individuals to apply their own accepted value systems to real-world situations. Individuals make judgments about what they believe to be right or wrong, but in their business lives they make decisions that take into consideration how to generate the greatest benefits with the least harm. Such decisions should respect fundamental moral rights as well as perspectives on fairness, justice, and the common good, but these issues become complicated in the real world.

Problems arise when employees encounter ethical situations they cannot resolve. Sometimes gaining a better understanding of their decision rationale helps employees choose the right solutions. For instance, to decide whether they should offer bribes to potential customers to secure a large contract, salespeople need to understand their own personal moral philosophies as well as their firm's core values and the relevant laws. If complying with company policy or legal requirements is an important motivation to the individual, he or she is less likely to offer a bribe. On the other hand, if the salesperson's ultimate goal is a successful career and if offering a bribe seems likely to result in a promotion, then bribery might not be inconsistent with that person's moral philosophy of acceptable business behavior. Even though bribery is illegal under U.S. law, the employee may rationalize that bribery is necessary "because everyone else does it."

The virtue approach to business ethics, as discussed earlier, assumes there are certain ideals and values everyone should strive for in order to achieve the maximum welfare and happiness of society.[39] Aspects of these ideals and values are expressed through individuals' specific moral philosophies. Every day in the workplace, employees must decide what is right or wrong and act accordingly. At the same time, as members of a larger organization, employees cannot simply enforce their own personal perspectives, especially if they adhere narrowly to a single moral philosophy. Because individuals cannot control most of the decisions in their work environment, they rarely have the power (especially in entry-level and middle-management positions) to impose their own personal moral perspectives on others. In fact, although they are always responsible for their own actions, a new employee is not likely to have the freedom to make independent decisions on a variety of job responsibilities.

Sometimes a company makes questionable decisions from the perspective of individual customers' values and moral philosophies. For example, some stakeholders might consider a brewery or a distributor of sexually explicit movies unethical, based on their personal perspectives. A company's core values will determine how it makes decisions in which moral philosophies are in conflict. Most businesses have developed a mission statement, a corporate culture, and a set of core values that express how they want to relate to their stakeholders, including customers, employees, the legal system, and society. It is usually impossible to please all stakeholders at once.

COGNITIVE MORAL DEVELOPMENT AND ITS PROBLEMS

Many people believe individuals advance through stages of moral development as their knowledge and socialization progress. In this section, we examine a model that describes this cognitive moral development process. Cognitive moral processing is based on a body of literature in psychology that focuses on the study of children and their cognitive development.[40] However, cognitive moral processing is also an element in ethical decision making, and many models attempt to explain, predict, and control individuals' ethical behavior.

Psychologist Lawrence Kohlberg developed a six-stage model of cognitive development. Although not specifically designed for business contexts, this model provides an interesting perspective on the issue of moral philosophy in business. According to **Kohlberg's model of cognitive moral development (CMD)**, people make different decisions in similar ethical situations because they are in different moral development stages. The six stages identified by Kohlberg are as follows:

1. *The stage of punishment and obedience.* An individual in Kohlberg's first stage defines *right* as literal obedience to rules and authority. A person in this stage responds to rules and labels of "good" and "bad" in terms of the physical power of those who determine such rules. Right and wrong are not connected with any higher order or philosophy but rather with a person who has power. Stage 1 is usually associated with small children, but signs of stage 1 development are also evident in adult behavior. For example, some companies forbid their buyers to accept gifts from salespeople. A buyer in stage 1 might justify a refusal to accept gifts from salespeople by referring to the company's rule, or the buyer may accept the gift if he or she believes there is no chance of being caught and punished.

2. *The stage of individual instrumental purpose and exchange.* An individual in stage 2 defines *right* as what serves his or her own needs. In this stage, individuals no longer make moral decisions solely on the basis of specific rules or authority figures; they evaluate behavior on the basis of its fairness to them. For example, a sales representative in stage 2 doing business for the first time in a foreign country may be expected by custom to give customers gifts. Although gift giving may be against company policy in the United States, the salesperson may decide certain company rules designed for operating in the United States do not apply overseas. In the cultures of some foreign countries, gifts may be considered part of a person's pay. So, in this instance, not giving a gift might put the salesperson at a disadvantage. Some refer to stage 2 as the stage of reciprocity because from a practical standpoint, ethical decisions are based on an agreement of "you scratch my back and I'll scratch yours" instead of on principles of loyalty, gratitude, or justice.

3. *The stage of mutual interpersonal expectations, relationships, and conformity.* Individuals in stage 3 emphasize the interests of others rather than simply those of themselves, although ethical motivation is still derived from obedience to rules. A production manager in this stage might obey upper management's order to speed up an assembly line if he or she believed doing so would generate more profit for the company and thus save employee jobs. These managers not only consider their own well-being in deciding to follow the order but also put themselves in upper management's and fellow employees' shoes. Thus, stage 3 differs from stage 2 in that fairness to others is one of the individual's ethical motives.

4. *The stage of social system and conscience maintenance.* Individuals in stage 4 determines what is right by considering their duty to society, not just to certain other people. Duty, respect for authority, and the maintenance of the social order become the focal points at this stage. For example, some managers consider it a duty to society to protect privacy and therefore refrain from monitoring employee conversations.

5. *The stage of prior rights, social contract, or utility.* In stage 5, individuals are concerned with upholding the basic rights, values, and legal contracts of society. Individuals in this stage feel a sense of obligation or commitment to other groups—they feel, in other words, that they are part of a social contract—and recognize in some cases legal and moral points of view may conflict. To reduce such conflict, stage 5 individuals base their decisions on a rational calculation of overall utility. For example, the president of a firm may decide to establish an ethics program because it provides a buffer against legal problems and the firm will be perceived as a responsible contributor to society.

6. *The stage of universal ethical principles.* A person in this stage believes right is determined by universal ethical principles everyone should follow. Stage 6 individuals believe certain inalienable rights exist that are universal in nature and consequence. These rights, laws, or social agreements are valid not because of a particular society's laws or customs, but because they rest on the premise of universality. Justice and equality are examples of principles some individuals and societies deem universal in nature. A person in this stage may be more concerned with social ethical issues and therefore not rely on the business organization for ethical direction. For example, a businessperson at this stage might argue for discontinuing a product that has caused death and injury because the inalienable right to life makes killing wrong, regardless of the reason. Therefore, company profits are not a justification for the continued sale of the product.[41]

Kohlberg's six stages can be reduced to three levels of ethical concern. At the first level, a person is concerned with his or her own immediate interests and with external rewards and punishments. At the second level, an individual equates *right* with conformity to the expectations of good behavior of the larger society or some other significant reference group. Finally, at the third or "principled," level, an individual sees beyond the norms, laws, and authority of groups or individuals. Employees at this level make ethical decisions regardless of negative external pressures. However, research shows most workers' abilities to identify and resolve moral dilemmas do not reside at this third level and their motives are often a mixture of selflessness, self-interest, and selfishness.

Kohlberg suggests people continue to change their decision-making priorities after their formative years, and as a result of time, education, and experience, they may change their values and ethical behavior. In the context of business, an individual's moral development can be influenced by corporate culture, especially ethics training. Ethics training and education have been shown to improve managers' cognitive development scores.[42] Because of corporate reform, most employees in *Fortune* 1000 companies today receive some type of ethics training. Training is also a requirement of the Federal Sentencing Guidelines for Organizations.

Some experts believe experience in resolving moral conflicts accelerates an individual's progress in moral development. A manager who relies on a specific set of values or rules may eventually come across a situation that these rules do not apply. Suppose Sarah is a manager whose policy is to fire any employee whose productivity declines for four consecutive months. Sarah has an employee, George, whose productivity suffered because of depression, but George's coworkers tell Sarah George will recover and soon become a top performer again. Because of the circumstances and the perceived value of the employee, Sarah may bend the rule and keep George. Managers in the highest stages of the moral development process seem to be more democratic than autocratic, and they are more likely than those at lower stages to consider the ethical views of the other people involved in an ethical decision-making situation.

Several problems with CMD relate back to its origins. These problems have been termed the three hit theory. Kohlberg's original work of CMD came from psychologist and philosopher Jean Piaget's research with children about the nature and development of intelligence. When Kohlberg transferred Piaget's theory to adults he did not take into account the full functioning and development of the adult brain (Strike One). From a philosophical perspective CMD argues for a hierarchical or step-like progression of moral philosophies starting from the lowest and going to the highest. This contradicts basic moral philosophy because there is no hierarchy. Each moral philosophy should be equal to the others (Strike Two). Finally, research suggests that CMD has a high reliability but not validity. For example, if a person shoots at a target and the shots are all close together, you can state there is high reliability. However, if the shots are all down and to the right, and the goal was to hit the center, then you have low validity (Strike Three). As a result, it is important to be cautious when using CMD to explain why good people make bad decisions.

WHITE-COLLAR CRIME

For many people, the terms *crime* and *criminal* tend to evoke thoughts of rape, arson, armed robbery, or murder. These violent crimes are devastating, but they are no less destructive than crimes perpetrated every year by nonviolent business criminals. So-called white-collar crime (WCC) does more damage in monetary and emotional loss in one year than violent crimes do over several years combined.[43]

White-collar criminals tend to be highly educated people in positions of power, trust, respectability and responsibility within a business or organization. They commit illegal acts for personal and/or organizational gains by abusing the trust and authority normally associated with their positions. The victims of WCC are often trusting consumers who believe businesses are legitimate.

At first glance, deciding what constitutes a white-collar crime seems fairly simple. According to the U.S. Department of Justice, a WCC is a "non-violent criminal act involving deceit, concealment, subterfuge and other fraudulent activity." The corporate executive who manipulates the stock market, the tax cheat, or the doctor who falsely bills Medicaid are all obvious white collar criminals. But a government official who accepts illegal payments is also a white-collar criminal, and guilty of official corruption. Additionally, a corporate executive who approves the illegal disposal of toxic waste is a white-collar criminal guilty of violating environmental regulations.

Online white-collar crime is a growing problem around the world. Because many companies rely on advanced technology systems, anyone with the ability to hack into a system can access the highly sensitive information necessary to commit WCC. WCCs previously originating at the top of organizations now occur at any level of a firm. Common online white-collar crimes include non-delivery of merchandise or payment, FBI-related scams, and identity theft (see Figure 6–1).

White-collar crime is a major problem in the financial world. For instance, financier R. Allen Stanford operated a Ponzi scheme that cost investors billions. He used his Southern Baptist roots as a springboard to promote his financial scheme, using passages such as Proverbs 13:11: "Wealth from get-rich-quick schemes quickly disappears; wealth from hard work grows." Former employees stated that a mix of religious faith, personal ties, and Stanford's leadership created a culture that supported hard work and the promotion of the bank's certificates of deposits—and that also indirectly promoted Stanford's $8 billion

FIGURE 6–1 Top 5 Reported Internet Crimes

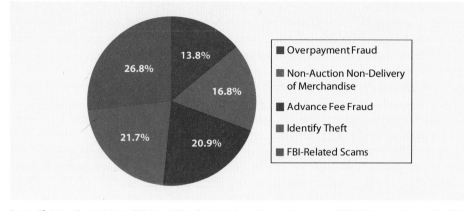

Source: IC³, *Internet Complaint Center 2011 Internet Crime Report*, http://www.ic3.gov/media/annualreport/2011_ic3report.pdf (accessed April 25, 2013).

Ponzi scheme. The company was also characterized by family ties, because several employees were related to key executives in the firm.[44] Stanford was later convicted and received a 110-year sentence.[45]

Another case of white-collar crime also involves a well-known financier. Russell Wasendorf Sr., CEO of futures brokerage firm Peregrine Financial Group, stated how he felt he had no other alternative than to falsify financial records so he could sustain his firm and lifestyle. His personal lifestyle included a personal four-star chef, $6.9 million life insurance policy, Hawker Beechcraft 400A jet, and $20 million office building. Wassendorf was sentenced to fifty years in prison for stealing $215.5 million over a twenty-year time span.[46] While many in business feel such stiff sentences are excessive due to the permanent damage done to reputations and that these are non-violent crimes, others argue that being robbed at gunpoint is less devastating than working and saving for a life time only to discover the sacrifices made were meaningless.

White-collar crime is increasing steadily (see Table 6–4). In 2012 consumers lost more than $1.4 billion due to fraud.[47] A few common white-collar offenses include antitrust violations, computer and Internet fraud, credit card fraud, bankruptcy fraud, health care fraud, tax evasion, violating environmental laws, insider trading, bribery, kickbacks, money laundering, and theft of trade secrets.

In response to the surge in white-collar crime, the U.S. government stepped up efforts to combat it. The government is concerned about the destabilizing effect WCC has on U.S. households and the economy in general. The government can charge individuals and corporations for WCC offenses. The penalties include fines, home detention, paying for

TABLE 6–4 U.S. Consumer Fraud Complaints

Year	Complaints Received	Amount Paid
2012	818,239	$1,491,656,241
2011	1,038,966	$1,544,849,568
2010	818,239	$1,729,567,228

Source: Federal Trade Commission, *Consumer Sentinel Network Datab Book*, February 2013, http://www.ftc.gov/sentinel/reports/sentinel-annual-reports/sentinel-cy2012.pdf (accessed April 25, 2013).

the cost of prosecution, forfeitures, and prison time. However, sanctions are often reduced if the defendant takes responsibility for the crime and assists the authorities in their investigation. Many people do not feel the government is devoting enough resources to combat WCC.

Why do individuals commit white-collar crimes? Advocates of the organizational deviance perspective argue that a corporation is a living, breathing organism that can collectively become deviant. When companies have lives separate and distinct from biological persons, the corporate culture of the company transcends the individuals who occupy these positions. With time, patterns of activities become institutionalized within the organization, and these patterns sometimes encourage unethical behaviors.

Another common cause of WCC is the views and behaviors of an individual's acquaintances within an organization. Employees, at least in part, self-select the people with whom they associate within an organization. For companies with a high number of ethical or unethical employees, people who are undecided about their behavior (about 40 percent of businesspeople) are more likely go along with their coworkers.

Additionally, the incidence of WCCs tends to increase in the years following economic recessions. When companies downsize, the stressful business climate may anger some employees and force others to act out of desperation. Furthermore, as businesses begin to expand and grow, fraudsters find gaps in corporate processes and exploit growth opportunities.[49]

Finally, as with criminals in the general population, there is the possibility some businesspeople may have inherently criminal personalities.[50] Corporate psychopaths, or managers who are nonviolent, selfish, and remorseless, exist in many large corporations. Corporate

DEBATE ISSUE
TAKE A STAND

Why Do People Engage in White-Collar Crime?

White-collar crime occurs when highly trusted and educated individuals commit criminal misconduct. Two examples of white-collar criminals are Bernard Madoff, who developed one of the largest Ponzi schemes ever, and R. Allen Stanford, who developed an $8 billion certificate of deposit program promising unrealistically high interest rates. Different theories exist why individuals become white-collar criminals. Research shows one percent of business executives may be corporate psychopaths with a predisposition to lie, cheat, and take any other measures necessary to come out ahead. This possibility may account for the fact that many white-collar criminals become entrepreneurs, thus putting themselves in a position to control others. This theory might account for rogue individuals such as Bernard Madoff.

Many believe white-collar crime evolves when corporate cultures do not have effective oversight and control over individuals' behavior. Such toxic organizational cultures occur when unethical activities are overlooked or even encouraged. For instance, many employees engaged in liar loans at Countrywide Financial because they received rewards for bringing in additional profits. It seems unlikely they all had psychological maladies.[48]

1. White-collar criminals tend to have psychological disorders that encourage misconduct as a route to success.

2. White-collar crime occurs as a result of organizational cultures that do not effectively control organizational behavior.

psychopaths may be more likely to use moral disengagement, in which they reframe the individuals or actions of a particular situation to convince themselves certain ethical standards to not apply.[51] Employees of corporate psychopaths are less likely to believe that their organization is socially responsible, the organization shows commitment to employees, or they receive recognition for their work.[52] Some organizations use personality tests to predict behavior, but such tests presuppose individual values and philosophies are constant; therefore, they seem to be ineffective in understanding the motivations of white-collar criminals.[53]

TABLE 6–5   Common Justifications for White-Collar Crime

1. Denial of responsibility. (Everyone can, with varying degrees of plausibility, point the finger at someone else.)

2. Denial of injury. (White-collar criminals often never meet or interact with those who are harmed by their actions.)

3. Denial of the victim. (The offender is playing tit-for-tat and claims to be responding to a prior offense inflicted by the supposed victim.)

4. Condemnation of the condemners. (Executives dispute the legitimacy of the laws under which they are charged, or impugn the motives of the prosecutors who enforce them.)

5. Appeal to a higher authority. ("I did it for my family" remains a popular excuse.)

6. Everyone else is doing it. (Because of the highly competitive marketplace, certain pressures exist to perform that may drive people to break the law.)

7. Entitlement. (Criminals simply deny the authority of the laws they have broken.)

Source: Based on Daniel J. Curran and Claire M. Renzetti, *Theories of Crime* (Needham Heights, MA: Allyn & Bacon, 1994).

The reasons for the increases in WCC are not easy to pinpoint because many variables may cause good people to make bad decisions. Businesspeople must make a profit on revenue to exist, a fact that slants their orientation toward teleology and creates a culture in which white-collar crimes can become normalized. Table 6–5 lists top justifications given by perpetrators of white-collar crimes. The Federal Sentencing Guidelines for Organizations state that all organizations should develop effective ethics and compliance programs as well as internal controls to prevent WCC.

INDIVIDUAL FACTORS IN BUSINESS ETHICS

Of course, not everyone agrees on the roles of collective moral philosophies in ethical decision making within an organization. Unfortunately, many people believe individual values are the main driver of ethical behavior in business. This belief can be a stumbling block in assessing ethical risk and preventing misconduct in an organizational context. The moral values learned within the family and through religion and education are certainly key factors that influence decision making, but as indicated in the models in Chapter 5, these values are only one factor. Many business schools focus mainly on personal character or moral development in their programs, reinforcing the notion that employees can control their work environments. Although a personal moral compass is important, it is not sufficient to prevent ethical misconduct in an organizational context. According to ethics consultant David Gebler, "Most unethical behavior is not done for personal gain, it's done to meet performance goals."[54] The rewards for meeting performance goals and the corporate culture in general have been found to be the most important drivers of ethical decision making, especially for coworkers and managers.[55]

The development of strong abilities in ethical reasoning will probably lead to more ethical business decisions in the future than individualized character education for each employee.[56] Equipping employees with intellectual skills that allow them to understand

and resolve the complex ethical dilemmas they encounter in complex corporate cultures will help them make the right decisions. This approach will hopefully keep employees from being negatively influenced by peer pressure and lulled by unethical managers.[57] The West Point model for character development focuses on the fact that competence and character must be developed simultaneously. This model assumes ethical reasoning has to be approached in the context of a specific profession. The military has been effective in teaching skills and developing principles and values that can be used in most of the situations a soldier encounters. In a similar manner, accountants, managers, and marketers need to develop ethical reasoning in the context of their jobs.

SUMMARY

Moral philosophy refers to the set of principles or rules people use to decide what is right or wrong. These principles or rules provide guidelines for resolving conflicts and for optimizing the mutual benefit of people living in groups. Businesspeople are guided by moral philosophies as they formulate business strategies and resolve specific ethical issues, even if they may not realize it.

Teleological, or consequentialist, philosophies stipulate that acts are morally right or acceptable if they produce some desired result such as the realization of self-interest or utility. Egoism defines right or acceptable behavior in terms of the consequences for the individual. In an ethical decision-making situation, the egoist chooses the alternative that contributes most to his or her own self-interest. Egoism can be further divided into hedonism and enlightened egoism. Utilitarianism is concerned with maximizing total utility, or providing the greatest benefit for the greatest number of people. In making ethical decisions, utilitarians often conduct cost–benefit analyses that consider the costs and benefits to all affected parties. Rule utilitarians determine behavior on the basis of rules designed to promote the greatest utility rather than by examining particular situations. Act utilitarians examine the action itself rather than the rules governing the action, to determine if it results in the greatest utility.

Deontological, or nonconsequentialist, philosophies focus on the rights of individuals and the intentions behind an individual's particular behavior rather than its consequences. In general, deontologists regard the nature of moral principles as permanent and stable and believe compliance with these principles defines ethical behavior. Deontologists believe individuals have certain absolute rights that must be respected. Rule deontologists believe conformity to general moral principles determines ethical behavior. Act deontologists hold that actions are the proper basis to judge morality or ethicalness and that rules serve only as guidelines.

According to the relativist perspective, definitions of ethical behavior derive subjectively from the experiences of individuals and groups. The relativist observes behavior within a relevant group and attempts to determine what consensus group members reach on the issue in question.

Virtue ethics states what is moral in a given situation is not only what is required by conventional morality or current social definitions, however justified, but by what a person with a "good" moral character would deem appropriate. Those who profess virtue ethics do not believe the end justifies the means in any situation.

The concept of justice in business relates to fair treatment and due reward in accordance with ethical or legal standards. Distributive justice is based on the evaluation of the outcome or results of a business relationship. Procedural justice is based on the processes and activities that produce outcomes or results. Interactional justice is based on an evaluation of the communication process in business.

The concept of a moral philosophy is not exact; moral philosophies can only be assessed on a continuum. Individuals use different moral philosophies depending on whether they are making a personal or a workplace decision.

According to Kohlberg's model of cognitive moral development, individuals may make different decisions in similar ethical situations because they are in a different stage of moral development. In Kohlberg's model, people progress through six stages of moral development: (1) punishment and obedience; (2) individual instrumental purpose and exchange; (3) mutual interpersonal expectations, relationships, and conformity; (4) social system and conscience maintenance; (5) prior rights, social contract, or utility; and (6) universal ethical principles. Kohlberg's six stages can be further reduced to three levels of ethical concern: immediate self-interest, social expectations, and general ethical principles. Cognitive moral development may not explain as much as people once believed.

White-collar crime occurs when an educated individual who is in a position of power, trust, respectability, and responsibility commits an illegal act in relation to his or her employment, and who abuses the trust and authority normally associated with the position for personal and/or organizational gains. White-collar crime is not heavily researched because this type of behavior does not normally come to mind when people think of crime; the offender (or organization) is in a position of trust and respectability; criminology and criminal justice systems look at white-collar crime differently than average crimes; and many researchers have not moved past the definitional issues. New developments in technology seem to be increasing the opportunity to commit white-collar crime with less risk.

Individual factors such as religion, moral intensity, and a person's professional affiliations can influence an employee's decision-making process. The impacts of ethical awareness, biases, conflict, personality type, and intelligence on ethical behavior remain unclear. One thing we do know is that the interrelationships among moral philosophies, values, and business are extremely complex.

IMPORTANT TERMS FOR REVIEW

moral philosophy 154	teleology 158	relativist perspective 162
economic value orientation 156	consequentialism 158	descriptive relativism 162
idealism 156	egoism 158	meta-ethical relativism 163
realism 156	enlightened egoism 158	normative relativism 163
monist 157	utilitarianism 159	virtue ethics 164
hedonism 157	rule utilitarian 160	justice 166
quantitative hedonist 157	act utilitarian 160	distributive justice 166
qualitative hedonist 157	deontology 161	procedural justice 166
pluralist 158	nonconsequentialism 161	interactional justice 167
instrumentalist 158	categorical imperative 161	Kohlberg's model of cognitive
goodness theory 158	rule deontologist 161	moral development (CMD) 169
obligation theory 158	act deontologist 162	white-collar crime 171

RESOLVING ETHICAL BUSINESS CHALLENGES*

Dr. Robert Smith owned his family practice for over 20 years. He came from a family of success. His father was a brain surgeon and his mother a well-known author. His younger brother, Saul, owned his own accounting firm for several years, but came to work with Dr. Smith after he sold it for a modest amount.

After graduating at the top of his class from Johns Hopkins University, Dr. Smith was awarded a cardiothoracic surgery fellowship in New York. He spent a few years there and was well on his way to fulfilling his dream of becoming a heart surgeon. During this time, however, his father became ill. Dr. Smith decided to return to his hometown of Zoar, Ohio, to take care of him. Under Dr. Smith's care, his father started showing signs of improvement. He was glad not only for his father, but that he could go back and continue his pursuit of becoming a heart surgeon. On the day he was set to leave, his mother became ill and died a few days later from a rare form of cancer that showed no symptoms. The devastation hit the family hard. Saul was still in college, and Dr. Smith's father needed someone to be with him at all times. Dr. Smith decided to stay in Zoar to take care of his father. He opened up a family practice in the town, thus putting his dream of becoming a heart surgeon on hold indefinitely.

Over the years, Dr. Smith sometimes felt regret that he never achieved his dream, but his job as the town doctor had been fulfilling. Now Saul was working with him, helping with the business. This made things significantly easier for Dr. Smith, who haphazardly kept his own books and patient files. One day, as Saul organized Dr. Smith's piles of paperwork, he noticed there were charges to Medicaid that must be a mistake. While most of the population of Zoar, Ohio, was considered low-level income and qualified for Medicaid, this was not the case for all patients. There were several elderly middle- and higher-income families who regularly visited the office and usually paid with a check or cash. Saul assumed his brother's administrative office skills were poor and aimed to fix it. However, as Saul organized the paperwork and checked files, these charges to Medicaid appeared to increase, dating back at least five years.

Saul approached his brother. "Robert, are you aware you charged Medicaid for Mr. and Mrs. Bennett's visits?"

"Hmmm. Let me see the paperwork," Dr. Smith asked. Saul handed it to him. Dr. Smith glanced at the document and said, "Yes, they are over age 65, so I made a bill for Medicaid."

"But we have records they paid you with cash," Saul replied. He handed Dr. Smith an old receipt. "And there are similar instances with some of your other patients. Besides, Medicaid is for low-income patients, not the elderly. Mr. and Mrs. Bennett are clearly not low-income."

Looking a little bit flustered, Dr. Smith replied, "Saul, you know how I am with details. I'm no good at it. That's why I hired you. Thanks for catching my mistake." Dr. Smith walked back into his office and shut the door, leaving Saul standing in the hallway with a stack of files.

Saul knew what his brother gave up for their family and the good he did for the families in this small town, but he was convinced these charges were not accidental. There were too many of them and the amount of money charged exceeded $75,000.

"What happened to all that money?" Saul wondered. He also wondered how to handle the situation. He thought to himself, "How can I report this without sending Robert to jail? If I don't report it and Medicaid finds out, I could go to jail and lose my accounting license. This is such a small town. If anybody finds out, we'll never live it down." At that moment, the phone rang, and Saul was the only one there to answer it.

QUESTIONS | EXERCISES

1. Describe Saul's ethical dilemma.
2. Why would Medicare fraud be a white-collar crime?
3. How should Saul approach the situation?

*This case is strictly hypothetical; any resemblance to real persons, companies, or situations is coincidental.

> > > CHECK YOUR EQ

Check your EQ, or Ethics Quotient, by completing the following. Assess your performance to evaluate your overall understanding of the chapter material.

1. Teleology defines right or acceptable behavior in terms of its consequences for the individual.   **Yes**   **No**

2. A relativist looks at an ethical situation and considers the individuals and groups involved.   **Yes**   **No**

3. A utilitarian is most concerned with bottom-line benefits.   **Yes**   **No**

4. Act deontology requires a person use equity, fairness, and impartiality in making decisions and evaluating actions.   **Yes**   **No**

5. Virtues supporting business transactions include trust, fairness, truthfulness, competitiveness, and focus.   **Yes**   **No**

ANSWERS **1. No.** That's egoism. **2. Yes.** Relativists look at themselves and those around them to determine ethical standards. **3. Yes.** Utilitarians look for the greatest good for the greatest number of people and use a cost–benefit approach. **4. Yes.** The rules serve only as guidelines, and past experience weighs more heavily than the rules. **5. No.** The characteristics include trust, self-control, empathy, fairness, and truthfulness—not competitiveness and focus.

ENDNOTES

1. James R. Rest, *Moral Development Advances in Research and Theory* (New York: Praeger, 1986), 1.

2. "Business Leaders, Politicians and Academics Dub Corporate Irresponsibility 'An Attack on America from Within,'" *Business Wire*, November 7, 2002, via The Free Library, http://www.thefreelibrary.com/Business+Leaders,+ Politicians+and+Academics+Dub+Corporate...-a094631434 (accessed April 25, 2013).

3. A. C. Ahuvia, "If Money Doesn't Make Us Happy, Why Do We Act as If It Does?" *Journal of Economic Psychology* 29 (2008): 491–507.

4. Abhijit Biswas, Jane W. Licata, Daryl McKee, Chris Pullig, and Christopher Daughtridge, "The Recycling Cycle: An Empirical Examination of Consumer Waste Recycling and Recycling Shopping Behaviors," *Journal of Public Policy & Marketing* 19 (2000): 93; Miguel Bastons, "The Role of Virtues in the Framing of Decisions," *Journal of Business Ethics* (2008): 395.

5. Miquel Bastons, "The Role of Virtues in the Framing of Decisions," *Journal of Business Ethics* (2008): 395.

6. Margaret Lindorff, Elizabeth Prior Jonson, and Linda McGuire, "Strategic Corporate Social Responsibility in Controversial Industry Sectors: The Social Value of Harm Minimization," *Journal of Business Ethics* 110 (4), 2012, 457–467.

7. "Court Says Businesses Liable for Harassing on the Job," *Commercial Appeal*, June 27, 1998, A1; Richard Brandt, *Ethical Theory* (Englewood Cliffs, NJ: Prentice-Hall, 1959), 253–254.

8. Gardiner Harris and Walt Bogdanich, "Drug tied to China had contaminant, FDA says," *The New York Times*, March 6, 2008, http://www.nytimes.com/2008/03/06/ health/06heparin.html (accessed April 25, 2013).

9. Brandon Wirtz, "Poison Baxter's Heparin From China Triggers Class-Action Lawsuit," XYHD.tv, http://www. xyhd.tv/2008/12/random-news/legal-issues/poison-baxters-heparin-from-china-triggers-class-action-suit/ (accessed April 25, 2013); "Heparin Contamination leads to Two Heparin Recalls," LawyersandSettlements.com, August 6, 202, http://www.lawyersandsettlements.com/ lawsuit/heparin.html#.UXbuM8otLp (accessed April 25, 2013).

10. "Consolidation of China's SFDA Grants Agency More Prestige, Power," RF, March 11, 2013, http://www.raps. org/focus-online/news/news-article-view/article/2993/ consolidation-of-chinas-sfda-grants-agency-more-prestige-power.aspx (accessed April 25, 2013).

11. J. J. C. Smart and B. Williams, *Utilitarianism: For and Against* (Cambridge, UK: Cambridge University Press, 1973), 4.

12. C. E. Harris, Jr., *Applying Moral Theories* (Belmont, CA: Wadsworth, 1986), 127–128.

13. James O'Toole, "Pfizer settles foreign bribery charges," *CNNMoney*, August 7, 2012, http://money.cnn. com/2012/08/07/news/companies/pfizer-bribery-charges/ index.htm (accessed April 25, 2013).

14. Example adapted from Harris, *Applying Moral Theories*, 128–129.

15. Gerald F. Cavanaugh, Dennis J. Moberg, and Manuel Velasquez, "The Ethics of Organizational Politics," *Academy of Management Review* 6 (1981): 363–374; U.S.

Bill of Rights, http://www.law.cornell.edu/constitution/ constitution.billofrights.html (accessed April 25, 2013).

16. U.S. Bill of Rights, http://www.law.cornell.edu/constitution/ constitution.billofrights.html (accessed April 25, 2013).

17. Marie Brenner, "The Man Who Knew Too Much," *Vanity Fair*, May 1996, available at http://www.jeffreywigand. com/vanityfair.php (accessed April 25, 2013).

18. Norman E. Bowie and Thomas W. Dunfee, "Confronting Morality in Markets," *Journal of Business Ethics* 38 (2002): 381–393.

19. "JetBlue cancels flights, to present 'Bill of Rights,'" CNN, February 19, 2007, http://money.cnn.com/2007/02/19/ news/companies/jetblue/index.htm?postversion=2007021 917&iid=EL (accessed April 25, 2013).

20. Adam Hanft, *Fast Company*, "Firing Neeleman; JetBlue Just Blew It," *Fast Company*, http://www.fastcompany. com/660116/firing-neeleman-jetblue-just-blew-it (accessed April 25, 2013).

21. Immanuel Kant, "Fundamental Principles," 229.

22. Thomas E. Weber, "To Opt In or Opt Out: That Is the Question When Mulling Privacy," *The Wall Street Journal*, October 23, 2000, B1.

23. R. Bateman, J. P. Fraedrich, and R. Iyer, "The Integration and Testing of the Janus-Headed Model within Marketing," *Journal of Business Research* 56 (2003): 587–596; J. B. DeConinck and W. F. Lewis, "The Influence of Deontological and Teleological Considerations and Ethical Culture on Sales Managers' Intentions to Reward or Punish Sales Force Behavior," *Journal of Business Ethics* 16 (1997): 497–506; J. Kujala, "A Multidimensional Approach to Finnish Managers' Moral Decision Making," *Journal of Business Ethics* 34 (2001): 231–254; K. C. Rallapalli, S. J. Vitell, and J. H. Barnes, "The Influence of Norms on Ethical Judgments and Intentions: An Empirical Study of Marketing Professionals," *Journal of Business Research* 43 (1998): 157–168; M. Shapeero, H. C. Koh, and L. N. Killough, "Underreporting and Premature Sign-Off in Public Accounting," *Managerial Auditing Journal* 18 (2003): 478–489.

24. William K. Frankena, *Ethics* (Englewood Cliffs: Prentice-Hall, 1963).

25. R. E. Reidenbach and D. P. Robin, "Toward the Development of a Multidimensional Scale for Improving Evaluations of Business Ethics," *Journal of Business Ethics* 9, no. 8 (1980): 639–653.

26. Patrick E. Murphy and Gene R. Laczniak, "Emerging Ethical Issues Facing Marketing Researchers," *Marketing Research* 4, no. 2 (1992): 6–11.

27. T. K. Bass and Barnett G. Brown, "Religiosity, Ethical Ideology, and Intentions to Report a Peer's Wrongdoing," *Journal of Business Ethics* 15, no. 11 (1996): 1161–1174; R. Z. Elias, "Determinants of Earnings Management Ethics among Accountants," *Journal of Business Ethics* 40, no. 1 (2002): 33–45; Y. Kim, "Ethical Standards and Ideology among Korean Public Relations Practitioners," *Journal of Business Ethics* 42, no. 3 (2003): 209–223; E. Sivadas, S. B. Kleiser, J. Kellaris, and R. Dahlstrom, "Moral Philosophy, Ethical Evaluations, and Sales Manager Hiring Intentions," *Journal of Personal Selling & Sales Management* 23, no. 1 (2003): 7–21.

28. Cheng-Li Huang and Bau-Guang Chang, "The Effects of Managers' Moral Philosophy on Project Decision under Agency Problem Conditions," *Journal of Business Ethics* 94 (2010): 595–611.

29. Manuel G. Velasquez, *Business Ethics Concepts and Cases,* 5th ed. (Upper Saddle River, NJ: Prentice-Hall, 2002), 135–136.

30. Ibid.

31. Adapted from Robert C. Solomon, "Victims of Circumstances? A Defense of Virtue Ethics in Business," *Business Ethics Quarterly* 13, no. 1 (2003): 43–62.

32. Ian Maitland, "Virtuous Markets: The Market as School of the Virtues," *Business Ethics Quarterly* (January 1997): 97.

33. Ibid.

34. Stefanie E. Naumann and Nathan Bennett, "A Case for Procedural Justice Climate: Development and Test of a Multilevel Model," *Academy of Management Journal* 43 (2000): 881–889.

35. Joel Brockner, "Making Sense of Procedural Fairness: How High Procedural Fairness Can Reduce or Heighten the Influence of Outcome Favorability," *Academy of Management Review* 27 (2002): 58–76.

36. "Nugget Markets Named #8 in *Fortune* Magazine's "100 Best Companies to Work for," January 20, 2011, http://www.nuggetmarket.com/press-release/100 (accessed April 25, 2013); "100 Best Companies to Work for 2010," Fortune, http://money.cnn.com/magazines/fortune/bestcompanies/2010/snapshots/5.html (accessed April 25, 2013); "100 Best Companies to Work for," *CNNMoney,* 2011, http://money.cnn.com/magazines/fortune/bestcompanies/2011/snapshots/8.html (accessed April 25, 2013).

37. Gretchen Larsen and Rob Lawson, "Consumer Rights: An Assessment of Justice," *Journal of Business Ethics* 112 (2013): 515–528.

38. John Fraedrich and O. C. Ferrell, "Cognitive Consistency of Marketing Managers in Ethical Situations," *Journal of the Academy of Marketing Science* 20 (1992): 245–252.

39. Manuel Velasquez, Claire Andre, Thomas Shanks, S. J. and Michael J. Meyer, "Thinking Ethically: A Framework for Moral Decision Making," *Issues in Ethics* (Winter 1996): 2–5.

40. Lawrence Kohlberg, "Stage and Sequence: The Cognitive Developmental Approach to Socialization," in *Handbook of Socialization Theory and Research*, ed. D. A. Goslin (Chicago: Rand McNally, 1969), 347–480.

41. Adapted from Kohlberg, "Stage and Sequence."

42. Clare M. Pennino, "Is Decision Style Related to Moral Development among Managers in the U.S.?" *Journal of Business Ethics* 41 (2002): 337–347.

43. K. M. Au and D. S. N. Wong, "The Impact of Guanxi on the Ethical Decision-Making Process of Auditors: An Exploratory Study on Chinese CPA's in Hong Kong," *Journal of Business Ethics* 28, no. 1 (2000): 87–93; D. P. Robin, G. Gordon, C. Jordan, and E. Reidenback, "The Empirical Performance of Cognitive Moral Development in Predicating Behavioral Intent," *Business Ethics Quarterly* 6, no. 4 (1996): 493–515; M. Shapeero, H. C. Koh, and L. N. Killough, "Underreporting and Premature Sign-Off in Public Accounting," *Managerial Auditing Journal* 18, no. 6 (1996): 478–489; N. Uddin and P. R. Gillett, "The Effects of Moral Reasoning and Self-Monitoring on CFO Intentions to Report Fraudulently on Financial Statements," *Journal of Business Ethics* 40, no. 1 (2002): 15–32.

44. Michael Forsythe and Alison Fitzgerald, "Stanford Prayer with Dying Man Pumped Agents in Alleged Fraud," *Bloomberg,* March 9, 2009, "http://www.bloomberg.com/apps/news?pid=washingtonstory&sid=aw1dZUb28Qc8 (accessed April 25, 2013).

45. Daniel Gilbert and Jean Eaglesham, "Stanford Hit with 110 Years," *The Wall Street Journal,* June 14, 2012, http://online.wsj.com/article/SB10001424052702303734204577466634068417466.html (accessed April 25, 2013).

46. Jacob Bunge, "Peregrine Founder Hit With 50 Years," *The Wall Street Journal,* February 1, 2013, C1.

47. Federal Trade Commission, Consumer Sentinel Network Data Book, February 2013, http://www.ftc.gov/sentinel/reports/sentinel-annual-reports/sentinel-cy2012.pdf (accessed April 25, 2013).

48. "The Influence of Corporate Psychopaths on Corporate Social Responsibility and Organizational Commitment to Employees," *Journal of Business Ethics* 97 (2010): 1–19; Clive R. Boddy, Richard K. Ladyshewsley, and Peter Galvin, "The Implications of Corporate Psychopaths for Business and Society: An Initial Examination and a Call to Arms," AJBBS 1, no.2 (2005): 30–40, http://www.mtpinnacle.com/pdfs/Psychopath.pdf (accessed May 3, 2011).

49. KPMG, "Fraud contagion shows no sign of abating," *Fraud Barometer,* June 2010, http://www.zurich.com/NR/rdonlyres/61135D66-3194-4362-A9D3-07AC64C40B54/0/KPMGAUFraudBarometerFindingsAustAug2010.pdf (accessed April 25, 2013).

50. Eysenck, "Personality and Crime: Where Do We Stand?" *Psychology, Crime & Law* 2, no. 3 (1996): 143–152; Shelley Johnson Listwan, *Personality and Criminal Behavior: Reconsidering the Individual,* University of Cincinnati, Division of Criminal Justice, 2001, http://cech.uc.edu/content/dam/cech/programs/criminaljustice/docs/phd_dissertations/2001/ShelleyJohnson.pdf (accessed April 25, 2013).

51. Gregory W. Stevens, Jacqueline K. Deuling, and Achilles A. Armenakis, "Successful Psychopaths: Are They Unethical Decision-Makers and Why?" *Journal of Business Ethics* 105 (2012): 139–149.

52. "The Influence of Corporate Psychopaths on Corporate Social Responsibility and Organizational Commitment to Employees," *Journal of Business Ethics.*

53. J. M. Rayburn and L. G. Rayburn, "Relationship between Machiavellianism and Type A Personality and Ethical-Orientation," *Journal of Business Ethics* 15, no. 11 (1996): 1209–1219.

54. Quoted in Marjorie Kelly, "The Ethics Revolution," *Business Ethics* (Summer 2005): 6.

55. O. C. Ferrell and Larry G. Gresham, "A Contingency Framework for Understanding Ethical Decision Making in Marketing," *Journal of Marketing* 49 (2002): 261–274.

56. Thomas I. White, "Character Development and Business Ethics Education," in *Fulfilling Our Obligation: Perspectives on Teaching Business Ethics,* ed. Sheb L. True, Linda Ferrell, and O. C. Ferrell (Kennesaw, GA: Kennesaw State University Press, 2005), 165.

57. Ibid., 165–166.

CHAPTER 7

ORGANIZATIONAL FACTORS: THE ROLE OF ETHICAL CULTURE AND RELATIONSHIPS

CHAPTER OBJECTIVES

- Understand the concept of corporate culture
- Examine the influence of corporate culture on business ethics
- Determine how leadership, power, and motivation relate to ethical decision making in organizations
- Assess organizational structure and its relationship to business ethics
- Explore how the work group influences ethical decisions
- Discuss the relationship between individual and group ethical decision making

AN ETHICAL DILEMMA*

When Jim began working in the human resources department at KR Electronics, he was impressed with the number of advancement opportunities the job offered. His first task was to monitor reports that came in from employees through the company's ethics hotline. It was a simple job but one Jim felt would lead him to a higher position in the HR department. He spent two days learning about the company's ethical policies and values, such as the importance of integrity and confidentiality. Jim felt reassured he chose a great company in which to start a career.

KR Electronics was a competitive company, and every six years employees were evaluated for performance. While the highest performers received substantial bonuses, the lowest 15 percent were consistently fired. This didn't bother Jim too much. He knew many other well-known companies had a similar system in place.

What bothered Jim was the way the supervisors treated employees who did not perform highly. Several employees approached Jim and told him of an abusive manager who often yelled at employees in front of other co-workers. Jim heard reports that the supervisor would make comments such as "I can't wait till the year is up and I can tell you to get lost. It'll be nice to actually get someone in this job with half a brain."

When Jim approached David, the human resources manager of his department, about what he heard, David shrugged off Jim's concerns. "You've got to understand, Jim," David explained. "We operate in a highly competitive field. Employees have to work quickly and efficiently in order to maintain our business. This often requires supervisors to get tough. Besides, this supervisor's unit is one of our highest performers. Apparently, whatever he's doing is working." This remark made Jim feel uncomfortable, but he did not want to argue with his boss about it.

One day Jim got a call from a woman in the company's sales department. She informed him that many of the firm's salespeople made exaggerated claims about the quality of their electronics. He also learned salespeople were making guarantees about products that were not true, such as how long the product would last.

"The salespeople are given substantial bonuses for exceeding their quotas, so many promise whatever it takes to increase their sales," the woman explained.

Although it was not required to provide a name when reporting, the person talking to Jim gave her name as Sarah Jones. She asked Jim to make sure her sales manager Rick Martin did not find out she called the hotline. Jim gave the report to his supervisor for further investigation.

Two weeks later Jim heard that Sarah Jones had been fired for poor performance. He approached David to ask him about the situation and was horrified to find out the sales manager of Sarah's division had been told about her report.

"But David, this is a violation of our confidentiality code! I promised Sarah we would keep her name anonymous when investigating this matter. What if Rick fired her out of retaliation?" Jim asked.

David looked at Jim in exasperation. "Jim, you are making too big of a deal out of this. Nobody forced Sarah to give her name to us over the hotline. And trust me, Rick's a good man. He wouldn't fire someone simply to get back at them for reporting. It seems to me that these reports didn't have credibility, anyway. It's likely that Sarah made up these allegations to hide her poor performance."

Jim left David's office upset. Even if Sarah was a poor performer, he did not feel that it was right that her sales manager was told about her report when she expressly requested otherwise. As he went back to his desk, he remembered hearing that the sales manager and David were good friends and often went out together for lunch.

QUESTIONS | EXERCISES

1. How does the company's organizational culture appear to conflict with its ethical policies?
2. What are the options for Sarah if this was retaliation?
3. What should Jim do next?

*This case is strictly hypothetical; any resemblance to real persons, companies, or situations is coincidental.

Companies are much more than structures in which we work. Although they are not alive, we attribute human characteristics to them. When times are good, we say the company is "well"; when times are bad, we may try to "save" the company. Understandably, people have strong feelings about the place that provides them with income and benefits, challenges, satisfaction, self-esteem, and often lifelong friendships. In fact, excluding time spent sleeping, almost 50 percent of our lives are spent in this second "home" with our second "family." It is important to examine how the culture and structure of these organizations influence the ethical decisions made within them.

In the ethical decision-making framework described in Chapter 5, we introduced the concept that organizational factors and interpersonal relationships influence the ethical decision-making process. We also describe the normative foundation of ethical decision making, such as organizational core values. In this chapter, we take a closer look at corporate culture and the ways a company's values and traditions can affect employees' ethical behavior. We also discuss the role of power in influencing ethical behavior within a company. Next we describe two organizational structures and examine how they may influence ethical decisions. We discuss new organizational structures created to address the organization's corporate responsibility to employees and other stakeholders. Then we consider the impact of groups within organizations. Finally, we examine the implications of organizational relationships for ethical decision making.

DEFINING CORPORATE CULTURE

Culture is a word people generally use in relation to country of origin, language and the way people speak, the types of food they eat, and other customs. Many define culture as nationality or citizenship. Values, norms, artifacts, and rituals all play a role in culture. Chapter 5 defined corporate culture as a set of values, norms, and artifacts, including ways of solving problems that members (employees) of an organization share. Corporate culture is also "the shared beliefs top managers in a company have about how they should manage themselves and other employees, and how they should conduct their business(es)."[1] Mutual of Omaha considers its corporate culture in its mission statement. Its intent is to "back our products with fair and timely service, and pursue operational excellence at every level. Above all, we will maintain the highest degree of integrity in all our interactions."[2] Mutual of Omaha's executives believe the company's corporate culture provides the foundation for its work and objectives such that the organization has adopted a set of core values called "Values for Success." Mutual of Omaha feels these core values form the foundation for a corporate culture that helps the organization realize its vision and achieve its goals. Corporate culture is exhibited through the behavioral patterns, concepts, documents such as codes of ethics, and rituals that emerge in an organization.[3] This culture gives the members of the organization a sense of meaning and purpose and familiarizes them with the organization's internal rules of behavior.[4]

Southwest Airlines has a strong and friendly, fun-loving organizational culture that dates back to the days of its key founder Herb Kelleher. Kelleher became legendary for appearing in a dress and feather boa and joining baggage handlers on Southwest flights. He organized an awards ceremony for employees that many felt rivaled the Academy Awards. He treated his employees like family. Today, Southwest continues that legacy. Pilots willingly and enthusiastically support the "Adopt a Pilot" program. Students in classrooms around the country adopt a Southwest pilot for a four-week educational and mentoring program. The pilots volunteer in the students' classrooms and send e-mails and postcards to a variety of destinations. Southwest's culture allows it to attract some of the best talent in the industry.[5] Values, beliefs, customs, rules, and ceremonies that are accepted, shared, and circulated throughout an organization represent its culture. All organizations, not just corporations, have some sort of culture, and therefore we use the terms *organizational culture* and *corporate culture* interchangeably.

A company's history and unwritten rules are a part of its culture. For many years, IBM salespeople adhered to a series of unwritten standards for dealing with clients. The history or stories passed down from generation to generation within an organization are like the traditions perpetuated within society at large. Henry Ford, the founder of Ford Motor Co., left a legacy that emphasized the importance of the individual employee. Henry Ford pioneered the then-unheard-of high wage of $5 a day in the early years of the twentieth century, and current company chairman William Clay Ford, Jr., continues to affirm that positive employee relationships create a sustainable competitive advantage for the company.[6] William Ford maintained his grandfather's legacy by taking a leadership role in improving vehicle fuel efficiency while reducing emissions. Ford is trying to become an industry leader in sustainability through initiatives such as its Go Green Dealership Program. This voluntary program offers dealers the chance to receive energy assessments from Ford's sustainability experts with the intent of increasing their energy efficiency. Dealers that wish to sell the Ford Focus Electric need to enroll in Ford's Go Green program as well as install at least two EV charging stations at their dealerships. For dealers that choose to make changes, Ford experts provide guidance on sustainable product selections and state and federal tax incentives.[7]

Leaders are responsible for the actions of their subordinates, and corporations should have ethical corporate cultures. For this reason, the definition and measurement of a corporate culture is important. It is defined in the Sarbanes–Oxley Act, enacted after the Enron, Tyco International, Adelphia, Peregrine Systems, and WorldCom scandals. The characteristics of an ethical corporate culture were codified within the Sarbanes–Oxley 404 compliance section. This section includes a requirement that management assess the effectiveness of the organization's internal controls and commission an audit of these controls by an external auditor in conjunction with the audit of its financial statements. Section 404 requires firms to adopt a set of values that forms a portion of the company's culture. The evaluation of corporate culture it mandates is meant to provide insight into the character of an organization, its ethics, and transparency.

Compliance with Sarbanes–Oxley 404 requires not merely changes in accounting but a change in corporate culture. The intent is to expose mismanagement, fraud, theft, abuse, and to sustain a corporate culture that does not allow these conditions and actions to exist. Many consultants that filled the need of companies wanting to comply with Sarbanes-Oxley lacked understanding of what "culture" means in this case. These consultants sought to provide direction and criteria for improving an organization's ability to manage risk, not its ethics. In many firms, an ethical corporate culture is measured in the following ways:

- Management and the board demonstrate their commitment to strong controls and core values through their communications and actions.

- Every employee is encouraged and required to have hands-on involvement in compliance, especially internal control systems.

- Every employee is encouraged and empowered to report policy exceptions.

- Employees are expected to be in the communication loop through resolutions and corrective actions.
- Employees have the ability to report policy exceptions anonymously to any member of the organization, including the CEO, other members of management, and the board of directors.[8]

The problem with these measurement standards is they evaluate merely risk and compliance. They are not a complete measure of the aspects of a company that make up its ethical culture. Yet many assume the four aforementioned items define an ethical corporate culture. Since values, norms, and artifacts are the three major components of culture, all of these elements are important in measuring an ethical culture.

In the past 50 years, scholars developed at least 164 distinct definitions of culture. More recent reviews indicate the number of definitions has been increasing.[9] While these definitions of culture vary greatly, they share three common elements: (1) "culture is shared among individuals belonging to a group or society," (2) "culture is formed over a relatively long period of time," and (3) "culture is relatively stable."[10]

Different models of culture, and consequently different instruments for measuring it, focus on various levels (national, organizational, individual) and aspects (values, practices, observable artifacts and rituals, underlying implicit assumptions). Geert Hofstede researched IBM's corporate culture and described it as an onion with many layers representing different levels within the corporation.[11] Today, IBM describes its culture as one of trust. The company adopted IBM Business Conduct Guidelines that describe ethics and compliance issues in-depth and provide direction for employees dealing with observed misconduct. The company also created an online reporting system that allows employees worldwide to raise issues and report concerns. These measures serve to advance IBM's goal of ensuring its relationships with stakeholders "are truly built on trust."[12] Many in business define ethics as what society considers right or wrong and develop measures that manage the risk of misconduct. Managing risk is not the same as understanding what makes up a firm's culture. We know for certain that culture has a significant effect on the ethical decision-making process of those in business. Ethical audits, ethical compliance, and risk culture surveys may be good tools, but in and of themselves they are not useful in defining organizational culture or in explaining what makes a particular organizational culture more ethical or unethical.

THE ROLE OF CORPORATE CULTURE IN ETHICAL DECISION MAKING

Corporate culture has been associated with a company's success or failure. Some cultures are so strong that to outsiders they come to represent the character of the entire organization. For example, Levi Strauss, Ben & Jerry's Homemade Ice Cream, and Hershey Foods are widely perceived as casual organizations with strong ethical cultures, whereas Lockheed Martin, Procter & Gamble, and Texas Instruments are seen as having more formal ethical cultures. The culture of an organization may be explicitly articulated or left unspoken.

Explicit statements of values, beliefs, and customs usually come from upper management. Memos, written codes of conduct, handbooks, manuals, forms, and ceremonies are formal expressions of an organization's culture. Many of these statements can be found on company websites, like that of U.S. Bank (Table 7–1).

TABLE 7–1 U.S. Bank's Principles for Integrity

- Being a role model for ethical behavior
- Promoting our culture of integrity
- Fostering open communication
- Recognizing behavior that exemplifies our ethical principles and values
- Responding to misconduct and reporting violations

Source: U.S. Bank, *Do the Right Thing: Code of Ethics and Business Conduct,* https://www.usbank.com/hr/docs/policies/coeHandbook.pdf (accessed March 8, 2011).

Corporate culture is often expressed informally through statements, both direct and indirect, that communicate the wishes of management. In some companies, shared values are expressed by instituting informal dress codes, working late, and participating in extra-curricular activities. Corporate culture can be expressed through gestures, looks, labels, promotions, programs, and legends (or the lack thereof). Many catastrophic events stem from ethical deficiencies resulting in a lack of human value judgments and actions influenced by different corporate cultures. Conversely, Phil Knight, Nike co-founder and sports icon, created a strong and appealing organizational culture. Knight seeks out new employees on one of their first few days on the job to "borrow $20 for lunch." The unsuspecting new employees are astounded Knight spoke to them. Knight uses that tactic as a subtle way to let new employees know they are on his radar. Interestingly, Knight has never paid back any of the employees. Most employees know what is happening and have fun with the new employee initiation. This ritual becomes a source of camaraderie among employees. It has contributed to building trust and commitment, and differentiates Nike's organizational culture from that of its competitors.

The "tone at the top" is a determining factor in the creation of a high-integrity organization. When leaders are perceived as trustworthy, employee trust increases; leaders are seen as ethical and as honoring a higher level of duties.[13] In a survey of chief financial officers (Figure 7–1), CFOs were asked what traits they look for when training future leaders of their organizations. The most popular answer was integrity. It is interesting to note that integrity was listed as more important than business savvy or the ability to motivate others. In fact, integrity is included more than any other core value by organizations.

Ethical Frameworks and Evaluations of Corporate Culture

Corporate culture has been conceptualized in many ways. For example, N. K. Sethia and Mary Ann Von Glinow proposed two basic dimensions to describe an organization's culture: (1) concern for people—the organization's efforts to care for its employees' well-being, and (2) concern for performance—the organization's efforts to focus on output and employee productivity.[14] Figure 7–2 provides examples of companies that display elements of these four organizational cultures.

As Figure 7–2 shows, the four organizational cultures can be classified as apathetic, caring, exacting, and integrative. An apathetic culture shows minimal concern for either people or performance. In this culture, individuals focus on their own self-interest. Apathetic tendencies can occur in almost any organization. Steel companies and airlines were among the first to freeze employee pensions to keep their businesses operating. Sweeping changes

FIGURE 7–1 **Traits to Look for in Future Leaders**

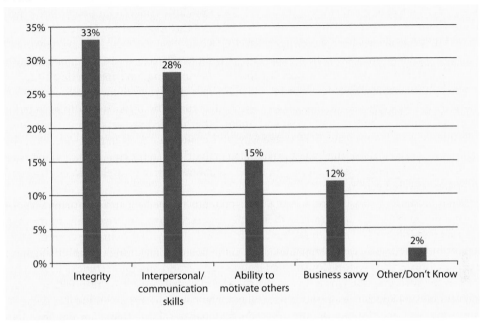

Note: Survey based upon responses from more than 1,400 telephone interviews with CFOs from U.S. companies with 20 or more employees.

Source: "Robert Half Management Resources Survey: CFOs Cite Integrity as Most Important Trait for Future Leaders," PR Newswire, September 30, http://www.prnewswire.com/news-releases/robert-half-management-resources-survey-cfos-cite-integrity-as-most-important-trait-for-future-leaders-104072008.html (accessed April 26, 2013).

in corporate America affect employee compensation and retirement plans. Simple gestures of appreciation, such as anniversary watches, rings, dinners, or birthday cards for family members, are being dropped. Many companies view long-serving employees as dead wood and do not take into account past performance. This attitude demonstrates the companies' apathetic culture.

A caring culture exhibits high concern for people but minimal concern for performance issues. From an ethical standpoint, the caring culture seems appealing. However,

FIGURE 7–2 **Company Examples of the Four Organizational Cultures**

Ben & Jerry's—A Caring Culture
Ben & Jerry's embraces community causes, treats its employees fairly, and expends numerous resources to enhance the well-being of its customers.

Starbucks—An Integrative Culture
Starbucks always looks for ways to expand and improve performance. It also exhibits a high concern for people through community causes, sustainability, and employee health care.

Countrywide Financial—An Apathetic Culture
Countrywide seemed to show little concern for employees and customers. The company's culture appeared to encourage unethical conduct in exchange for profits.

United Parcel Systems—An Exacting Culture
Employees are held to high standards to ensure maximum performance, consistency of delivery, and efficiency.

© Cengage Learning

it is difficult to find nationally recognizable companies that maintain little or no concern for performance. In contrast, an exacting culture shows little concern for people but a high concern for performance; it focuses on the interests of the organization. United Parcel Service (UPS) has always been exacting. With over 8.8 million daily customers in over 220 countries, UPS knows exactly how many employees it needs to move 16.3 million packages and documents per day worldwide.[15] To combat the uncaring, unsympathetic attitude of many of its managers, UPS developed a community service program for employees. Global Volunteer Week gives UPS employees around the world the opportunity to help paint schools, renovate shelters, and assist with many other needed projects within their communities. An early innovator, UPS tested ways to use alternate fuels in the 1930s. Now the company operates one of the largest private alternative fleets in the transportation industry with over 2,500 compressed natural gas, liquefied natural gas, hybrid-electric, electric, and propane-powered vehicles.[16]

An integrative culture combines a high concern for people and performance. An organization becomes integrative when superiors recognize employees are more than interchangeable parts—employees have an ineffable quality that helps the firm meet its performance criteria. Many companies, such as the Boston Consulting Group (BCG), have such a culture. The Boston Consulting Group rated second among *Fortune*'s "Best Companies to Work for." BCG is a financially successful global consulting firm with a strong reputation that specializes in business strategy. The company values employees and creates significant mentorship opportunities and extensive training that allow employees to develop rapidly. It also has what it calls "red flag reports" to signal when employees are working too many long weeks. New consultants to the company can receive $10,000 for volunteering at a nonprofit organization.[17]

Companies can classify their corporate culture and identify its specific values, norms, beliefs, and customs by conducting a cultural audit. A cultural audit is an assessment of an organization's values. The audit is usually conducted by outside consultants but may be performed internally as well. Communication about ethical expectations and support from top management help to identify a corporate culture that encourages ethical conduct or leads to ethical conflict.[18]

Ethics as a Component of Corporate Culture

As indicated in the framework presented in Chapter 5, ethical culture—the ethical component of corporate culture—is a significant factor in ethical decision making. If a firm's culture encourages or rewards unethical behavior, the employees may act unethically. If the culture dictates hiring people with specific, similar values and if those values are perceived as unethical by society, society will view the organization and its members as unethical. Such a pattern often occurs in certain areas of marketing. Salespeople sometimes use aggressive selling tactics to get customers to buy things based on emotional response to appeals. If a company's primary objective is to make as much profit as possible through whatever means, its culture may foster behavior that conflicts with stakeholders' ethical values. After the *Deepwater Horizon* disaster, the culture of BP, with its emphasis on financial performance, became the focus of criticism. BP has a history of accidents, explosions, and other events over the past six years. The year after the disaster, BP was accused of criminal negligence regarding previous oil spills in Alaska. These events lead to questions about how BP's culture views the prevention of accidents and environmental damage.[19]

On the other hand, if an organization values ethical behaviors, it rewards them. It is important to handle recognition and awards for appropriate behavior in a consistent and balanced manner. All employees should be eligible for recognition. All performance at the threshold level should be acknowledged, and praise or rewards given as close to the performance as possible.[20] FedEx's Bravo Zulu award is one example of company recognition. The award is given to employees who demonstrate exceptional performance above and beyond job expectations. Rewards for recipients can include cash bonuses, theater tickets, gift certificates, and more. By rewarding employees who go above their normal duties, FedEx provides motivation for other workers to strive for excellent work conduct.[21]

Management's sense of an organization's culture may not be in line with the values and ethical beliefs that actually guide a firm's employees. Table 7–2 provides an example of a corporate culture ethics audit. Companies interested in assessing their culture can use this tool and benchmark against previous years' results to measure organizational improvements. Ethical issues may arise because of conflicts between the cultural values perceived by management and those actually at work in the organization. For example, managers may believe their firm's organizational culture encourages respect for peers and subordinates. On the basis of the rewards or sanctions associated with various behaviors, the firm's employees may believe the company encourages competition among organizational members. A competitive orientation may result in a less ethical corporate culture. This was the case at Enron when the employees in the lowest 20 percent for performance were fired.

On the other hand, employees appreciate working in an environment designed to enhance workplace experiences through goals that encompass more than just maximizing profits.[22] Therefore, it is important for top managers to determine their organization's culture and monitor its values, traditions, and beliefs to ensure they represent the desired culture. It is also important to note that if corporate communication to improve corporate social responsibility (CSR) and ethics is reactive or focused on avoiding negative consequences, it may not make a significant contribution to creating an ethical culture. Reactive communication without commitment therefore fails to improve business ethics.[23] On the other hand, by placing high emphasis upon ethics and CSR, organizations are able to foster positive relationships with employees and enhance job satisfaction while gaining a good business image. Along with implementing CSR within the organization, the alternative benefit for some organizations is an ability to charge a premium price for their product.[24]

The rewards and punishments imposed by an organization must reflect the culture those at the top wish to create. Two business ethics experts observed, "Employees will value and use as guidelines those activities for which they will be rewarded. When a behavior that is rewarded comes into conflict with an unstated and unmonitored ethical value, usually the rewarded behavior wins out."[25] For example, if the most important and rewarded value is sales performance, then activities to achieve performance will be given top priority.

Compliance versus Values-Based Ethical Cultures

During the latter part of the twentieth century a distinction evolved between types of corporate cultures. The traditional ethics-based culture focused on compliance. The accounting professional model of rules created a compliance culture organized around risk. Compliance-based cultures use a legalistic approach to ethics. They use laws and regulatory rules to create codes and requirements. Codes of conduct are established with compliance as their focus, with rules and policies enforced by management. Instead of revolving around an ethical culture, the company revolves around risk management. The compliance

TABLE 7–2 Corporate Culture Ethics Audit

		Answer Yes or No to each of the following questions*
Yes	No	Has the founder or top management of the company left an ethical legacy to the organization?
Yes	No	Does the company have methods for detecting ethical concerns both within the organization and outside it?
Yes	No	Is there a shared value system and understanding of what constitutes appropriate behavior within the organization?
Yes	No	Are stories and myths embedded in daily conversations about appropriate ethical conduct?
Yes	No	Are codes of ethics or ethical policies communicated to employees?
Yes	No	Are there ethical rules or procedures in training manuals or other company publications?
Yes	No	Are penalties for ethical transgressions publicly discussed?
Yes	No	Are there rewards for good ethical decisions even if they don't always result in a profit?
Yes	No	Does the company recognize the importance of creating a culture concerned about people and their investment in the business?
Yes	No	Does the company have a value system of fair play and honesty toward customers?
Yes	No	Do employees treat each other with respect, honesty, and fairness?
Yes	No	Do employees spend their time working in a cohesive way on what is valued by the organization?
Yes	No	Are there ethically based beliefs and values about how to succeed in the company?
Yes	No	Are there heroes or stars in the organization who communicate a common understanding about which positive ethical values are important?
Yes	No	Are there day-to-day rituals or behavior patterns that create direction and prevent confusion or mixed signals on ethics matters?
Yes	No	Is the firm more focused on the long run than on the short run?
Yes	No	Are employees satisfied or happy, and is employee turnover low?
Yes	No	Do the dress, speech, and physical aspects of the work setting contribute to a sense of consistency about what is right?
Yes	No	Are emotional outbursts about role conflict and ambiguity rare?
Yes	No	Has discrimination and/or sexual harassment been eliminated?
Yes	No	Is there an absence of open hostility and severe conflict?
Yes	No	Do people act on the job in a way consistent with what they say is ethical?
Yes	No	Is the firm more externally focused on customers, the environment, and the welfare of society than on its own profits?
Yes	No	Is there open communication between superiors and subordinates about ethical dilemmas?
Yes	No	Have employees ever received advice on how to improve ethical behavior or been disciplined for committing unethical acts?

*Add up the number of "Yes" answers. The greater the number of "Yes" answers, the less likely ethical conflict is in your organization.

© Cengage Learning

approach is good in the short term because it helps management, stakeholders, and legal agencies ensure laws, rules, and the intent of compliance are fulfilled. A problem with the compliance approach, however, is its lack of long-term focus on values and integrity. In addition, it does not teach employees to navigate ethical gray areas.

There has been a shift from an approach focused on compliance to a values-based approach. A **values-based ethics culture** approach to ethical corporate cultures relies upon an explicit mission statement that defines the core values of the firm and how customers and employees should be treated. The board of directors as well as upper management might add to the general value statements by formulating specific value statements for its strategic business units (SBU), which can be organized by product, geography, or function within the firm's management structure. Certain areas may have rules associated with stated values, enabling employees to understand the relationship between the two. The focus of this type of corporate culture is on values such as trust, transparency, and respect to help employees identify and deal with ethical issues. It is important when using a values-based approach to explain why rules exist, what the penalties are if rules are violated, and how employees can help improve the ethics of the company. The crux of any ethical culture is top-down integrity with shared values, norms that provide guides for behavior, and visible artifacts such as codes of ethics that provide a standard of conduct. In developing a values-based ethical culture, a compliance element is also necessary because every organization has employees who will try to take advantage if the risk of being caught is low.

Ikea represents a values-based culture, with a mission "to create a better everyday life for the many." The company maintains a strong commitment to best business practices, ethical behavior, and environmental initiatives. Not only does Ikea sell eco-friendly products and use alternative energy to power its stores, it also supports numerous causes such as Save the Children and American Forests.[26]

Differential Association

Differential association is the idea that people learn ethical or unethical behavior while interacting with others who are part of their role-sets or belong to other intimate personal groups.[27] The learning process is more likely to result in unethical behavior if the individual associates primarily with persons who behave unethically. Associating with others who are unethical, combined with the opportunity to act unethically, is a major influence on ethical decision making, as described in the decision-making framework in Chapter 5.[28]

Consider a company in which salespeople incur travel expenses each week. When new salespeople are hired, experienced salespeople encourage the new hires to pad their expense accounts because some expenses cannot be charged to the company. The new employee is shown how to pad the expense account and is told that failure to engage in this conduct makes others' reports look too high. In other words, the new employee is pressured to engage in misconduct.

A variety of studies support the notion that differential association influences ethical decision making and superiors in particular have a strong influence on the ethics of their subordinates. The actions of Mark Hernandez, who worked at NASA's Michoud Assembly Facility applying insulating foam to the space shuttles' external fuel tanks, provide an example of how coworker influence can produce tragic results. Within a few weeks on the job, coworkers taught Hernandez to repair scratches in the insulation without reporting the repairs. Supervisors encouraged the workers not to complete the required paperwork on the repairs so they could meet the space shuttle program's tight production schedules.

DEBATE ISSUE
TAKE A STAND

Is Government Support for External Whistle-Blowing Effective?

A number of laws have been enacted to encourage members of organizations to report misconduct. While most firms support internal reporting of misconduct through anonymous hotlines, many organizations are concerned about employees going public or reporting misconduct to the government. Whistle-blowers are protected through the Sarbanes–Oxley Act and a number of other government agencies that deal with fraud, stock trading, and corrupt practices. In 2010 the Dodd–Frank Act gave additional incentives for whistle-blowers. Whistle-blowers are encouraged to turn themselves in if they were part of a team or group that engaged in misconduct, and doing so could result in monetary rewards. Despite these incentives, whistle-blowers in general do not get good treatment and often have trouble finding employment after they report misconduct. It has also been found that companies with good internal reporting systems have fewer whistle-blowers that report externally in an attempt to obtain rewards. This could be because employees feel that their concerns will be taken seriously and misconduct will be halted before it becomes a major problem.

1. Government support through financial incentives for reporting misconduct in organizations is effective and benefits society.
2. Government support of whistle-blowing should be redirected toward stronger incentives for internal reporting of misconduct, not external whistle-blowing that could be harmful to the individual.

After the shuttle *Columbia* broke up on reentry, killing all seven astronauts, investigators found that a piece of foam falling off a fuel tank during liftoff had irreparably damaged the shuttle.[29]

Several research studies found that employees, especially young managers, tend to go along with their superiors' moral judgments to demonstrate loyalty. In one study, an experiment was conducted to determine how a hypothetical board of directors would respond to the marketing of one of its company's most profitable drugs that resulted in 14 to 22 unnecessary deaths a year. When the imaginary board learned that a competitor's drug was coming into the market with no side effects, more than 80 percent supported continuing to market the drug and taking legal and political action to prevent a ban. When asked their personal view on this situation, 97 percent believed that continuing to market the drug was irresponsible.[30] We have made it clear that *how* people typically make ethical decisions is not necessarily the way they *should* make these decisions. We believe you will improve your own ethical decision making once you understand potential influences of your interactions with others in your intimate work groups.

Whistle-Blowing

Interpersonal conflict occurs when employees think they know the right course of action in a situation, yet their work group or company promotes or requires a different, unethical decision. In such cases, employees may choose to follow their own values and refuse to participate in unethical or illegal conduct. If they conclude that they cannot discuss what they are doing or what should be done with coworkers or immediate supervisors, and if there is no method of protection for anonymous reporting, these employees may go outside the organization to publicize and correct the unethical situation. A number of laws exist to protect whistle-blowers.

Whistle-blowing means exposing an employer's wrongdoing to outsiders such as the media or government regulatory agencies. The term *whistle-blowing* is sometimes used to refer to internal reporting of misconduct to management, especially through anonymous reporting mechanisms, often called hotlines. Legal protection for whistle-blowers exists to encourage reporting of misconduct. Whistle-blower laws have provisions against retaliation and are enforced by a number of government agencies. Under the Sarbanes–Oxley Act, the

U.S. Department of Labor (DOL) directly protects whistle-blowers who report violations of the law and refuse to engage in any action made unlawful. The Corporate and Criminal Fraud Accountability (CCFA) Act protects employees of publicly traded firms from retaliation if they report violations of any rule or regulation of the Securities and Exchange Commission, or any provision of federal law relating to fraud against shareholders. It also requires attorneys to become internal whistle-blowers as well.

The 2010 passage of the Dodd–Frank Act proposed additional incentives for whistle-blowers. Under the new rules, whistle-blowers who provide information that aids in the recovery of over $1 million could receive 10 to 30 percent of that amount. The belief is that monetary incentives will prompt observers of corporate misconduct to come forward, which could prevent future scandals like those leading up to the 2008–2009 financial crisis. One major concern with this new provision is it may cause whistle-blowers to go external with the information rather than internal. Because of the potential for monetary rewards, whistle-blowers might be tempted to go straight to the Securities and Exchange Commission with reports rather than reporting the misconduct to the company's internal compliance officers.[31]

The Sarbanes–Oxley Act and the Federal Sentencing Guidelines for Organizations (FSGO) institutionalized internal whistle-blowing to encourage discovery of organizational misconduct. For example, billionaire R. Allen Stanford's worst enemies may be former employees turned whistle-blowers who once worked for his company Stanford Financial Group. One lawsuit alleges that an employee hired to edit the firm's corporate magazine objected and raised concerns about firm practices he believed violated federal and state laws. He was later fired. Others who filed industry arbitration claims alleged they were forced out of the fast-growing firm after questioning the ability of Stanford International Bank to justify high CD rates. In the Stanford case, whistle-blowers provided pivotal evidence documenting corporate malfeasance at a number of companies.[32] Historically, the fortunes of external whistle-blowers have not been positive; most were labeled traitors and many lost their jobs. Even Sherron Watkins was a potential candidate for firing as the Enron investigation unfolded, with law firms assessing the implications of terminating her in light of her ethical and legal concerns about Enron.[33] The cost of inaction by regulatory institutions after a whistle-blowing claim is made can be high. Harry Markopolos attempted to alert the SEC about the Bernie Madoff "Ponzi" scheme for years. The scheme resulted in a loss to investors of about $50 billion. Listening to these whistle-blower claims might have prevented major losses to investors if addressed sooner.[34]

A study of 300 whistle-blowers by researchers at the University of Pennsylvania found that 69 percent lost their jobs or were forced to retire after exposing their companies' misdeeds.[35] For example, the whistle-blower who exposed Walmart chairman Thomas Coughlin for defrauding the company was terminated about a week after Coughlin resigned. Jared Bowen, a former vice president for Walmart Stores, Inc., claims he was terminated for his exposure of Coughlin, in violation of a provision of the Sarbanes–Oxley Act protecting whistle-blowers.[36] Another whistle-blower who was terminated was Linda Almonte who alerted her bosses at JP Morgan Chase about a potentially fraudulent deal she was helping to close. Almonte was fired after alerting her boss and was essentially blacklisted from the banking industry.[37] If an employee provides information to the government about a company's wrongdoing under the Federal False Claims Act, the whistle-blower is known as a *qui tam relator*. Upon investigation of the matter by the U.S. Department of Justice, the whistle-blower can receive between 15 and 25 percent of the recovered funds, depending upon how instrumental his or her claims were in holding the firm accountable

TABLE 7–3 Questions to Ask before Engaging in External Whistle-Blowing

1. Have I exhausted internal anonymous reporting opportunities within the organization?
2. Have I examined company policies and codes that outline acceptable behavior and violations of standards?
3. Is this a personal issue that should be resolved through other means?
4. Can I manage the stress that may result from exposing potential wrongdoing in the organization?
5. Can I deal with the consequences of resolving an ethical or legal conflict within the organization?

© Cengage Learning

for its wrongdoing.[38] Although most whistle-blowers do not receive positive recognition for pointing out corporate misconduct, some turned to the courts and obtained substantial settlements. However, whistle-blowers have traditionally had a difficult time winning their cases. During the Clinton and Bush administrations, less than 5 percent of whistle blowers won settlements.[39]

To be truly effective, whistle-blowing requires that the individual have adequate knowledge of wrongdoing that could damage society. It is important to minimize risk to the whistle-blower while dealing with ethical issues.[40] Table 7–3 provides a checklist of questions an employee should ask before going to external sources. Figure 7–3 shows the increase in retaliation whistle-blowers have faced in recent years. About 22 percent of respondents to the National Business Ethics Survey indicated they experienced some form of retaliation after reporting misconduct, an all-time high.[41]

If whistle-blowers present an accurate picture of organizational misconduct, they should not fear for their jobs. Indeed, Sarbanes–Oxley and Dodd–Frank make it illegal to "discharge, demote, suspend, threaten, harass, or in any manner discriminate against" a whistle-blower and set penalties of up to 10 years in jail for executives who retaliate against whistle-blowers. The law requires publicly traded companies to implement an anonymous reporting mechanism that allows employees to question actions they believe may indicate fraud or other misconduct.[42] In addition, the FSGO provides rewards for companies that systematically detect and address unethical or illegal activities. Within the federal

FIGURE 7–3 Percentage of Employees Who Experience Retaliation after Reporting Misconduct

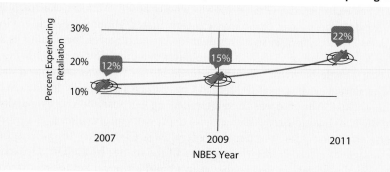

Source: Ethics Resource Center, *2011 National Business Ethics Survey: Workplace Ethics in Transition* (Arlington, VA: Ethics Resource Center, 2012), p. 15.

stimulus funds, new whistle-blower protection was supported for state and local government employees and contractors, subcontractors, and grantees. The new law provides specific protections including the right to seek investigation and review by federal Inspectors General for "adverse actions" such as termination or demotions.[43]

Most public companies are creating computer systems that encourage internal whistle-blowing. With over 2,000 employees, Marvin Windows (one of the world's largest custom manufacturers of wood windows and doors) wants employees to feel comfortable reporting violations of safety conditions, bad management, fraud, or theft. The system is anonymous and allows reporting in employees' native languages. This system is used to alert management to potential problems in the organization and facilitate investigations.[44] Marvin Windows is noted for its culture of caring for employees. The company did not lay off any workers during the most recent recession and was able to offer its employees profit-sharing checks at the end of 2012.[45]

Even before the passage of the Sarbanes–Oxley Act, an increasing number of companies set up anonymous reporting services. Through toll-free numbers, employees could report suspected violations or seek input on how to proceed when encountering ambiguous situations. These internal reporting services are perceived to be most effective when managed by an outside organization that specializes in maintaining ethics hotlines.

Figure 7–4 reveals that the majority of employees report misconduct to their immediate supervisors. However, the presence of hotlines and other mechanisms helps employees who feel uncomfortable reporting to their superiors. The results of a study show that three internal actions—confrontation, reporting to management, and calling the company ethics hotline—were positively correlated to several dimensions of an ethical culture. Conversely,

FIGURE 7–4 How Employees Report Observed Misconduct

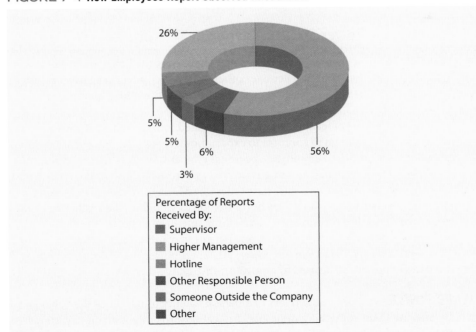

Percentage of Reports
Received By:
■ Supervisor
■ Higher Management
■ Hotline
■ Other Responsible Person
■ Someone Outside the Company
■ Other

Source: Ethics Resource Center, *2011 National Business Ethics Survey: Workplace Ethics in Transition* (Arlington, VA: Ethics Resource Center, 2012), p. 21.

inaction and external whistle-blowing were negatively correlated to several dimensions of an ethical culture. External whistle-blowing generally reflects a weakness in the ethical culture.[46] The extent to which employees feel there will be no corrective action or there will be retaliation as a result of their actions is a leading factor influencing their decisions not to report observed misconduct.

LEADERS INFLUENCE CORPORATE CULTURE

Organizational leaders can shape and influence corporate culture, resulting in ethical or unethical leadership. Leaders need to be effective and ethical. An effective leader is one who does well for the stakeholders of the corporation. Effective leaders get followers to their common goals or objectives in the most effective and efficient way. Ken Lay and Jeffery Skilling were effective in transforming Enron from a small oil and gas pipeline firm into one of the largest entities in the industry. They were inspirational, imaginative, creative, and motivated their personnel to achieve goals. Because they failed to create an ethical culture, however, they were detrimental to the company in the long term. According to Alan Yuspeh, Senior Vice President and Chief Ethics and Compliance Officer of Hospital Corporation of America (HCA), ethical companies and leadership should possess "aspirations that are higher than observing the law." The CEO of HCA and its board of directors empowered Yuspeh to provide leadership and supporting values to help employees appropriately respond to difficult ethical situations.[47] Consistency is also important for successful leaders. We discuss leadership in more detail in Chapter 11. The next section discusses how leaders use different types of power to influence corporate culture.

Power Shapes Corporate Culture

Power refers to the influence leaders and managers have over the behavior and decisions of subordinates. Individuals have power over others when their presence causes others to behave differently. Exerting power is one way to influence the ethical decision-making framework described in Chapter 5.

The status and power of leaders is directly correlated to the amount of pressure they exert on employees to get them to conform to expectations. A superior can put strong pressure on employees, even when employees' personal ethical values conflict with the superior's wishes. For example, a manager might say to a subordinate, "I want the confidential information about our competitor's sales on my desk by Monday morning, and I don't care how you get it." A subordinate who values his or her job or who does not realize the ethical questions involved may feel pressure to do something unethical to obtain the data.

There are five power bases from which one person may influence another: (1) reward power, (2) coercive power, (3) legitimate power, (4) expert power, and (5) referent power.[48] These five bases of power can be used to motivate individuals either ethically or unethically.

REWARD POWER **Reward power** refers to a person's ability to influence the behavior of others by offering them something desirable. Typical rewards might be money, status, or promotion. Consider, for example, an auto salesperson that has two cars (a Toyota and a Kia) for sale. Let's assume the Toyota is rated higher in quality than the Kia but is priced the same. In the absence of any form of reward power, the salesperson logically attempts to sell the Toyota. However, if the Kia had a higher rate of commission, he would probably focus his efforts on selling the Kia. Such "carrot dangling" and incentives have been shown to be effective in getting people to change their behavior in the long run. Therefore, rewards could encourage individuals to act in their own self-interest, not necessarily in the interest of stakeholders. In the short run, reward power is not as effective as coercive power.

COERCIVE POWER   Coercive power is essentially the opposite of reward power. Instead of rewarding a person for doing something, coercive power penalizes actions or behavior. As an example, suppose a valuable client asks an industrial salesperson for a bribe and insinuates he will take his business elsewhere if his demands are not met. Although the salesperson believes bribery is unethical, her boss tells her she must keep the client happy or lose her chance for promotion. The boss imposes a negative sanction if certain actions are not performed. Many companies use a system whereby they systematically fire the lowest performing employees in their organization on an annual basis. Enron called it "rank and yank" and annually fired the lowest 20 percent. Motorola, Dow Chemical, and Microsoft use similar systems for firing employees. Coercive power relies on fear to change behavior. For this reason, it has been found to be more effective in changing behavior in the short run than in the long run. Coercion is often employed in situations where there is an extreme imbalance of power. However, people continually subjected to coercion may seek a counterbalance and align themselves with other, more powerful persons or leave the organization. In firms using coercive power, relationships usually break down in the long run. Power is an ethical issue not only for individuals but also for work groups that establish policy for large corporations.

LEGITIMATE POWER   Legitimate power stems from the belief that a certain person has the right to exert influence and certain others have an obligation to accept it. The titles and positions of authority organizations bestow on individuals appeals to this traditional view of power. Many people readily acquiesce to those wielding legitimate power, sometimes committing acts contrary to their beliefs and values. Betty Vinson, an accountant at WorldCom, objected to her supervisor's requests to produce improper accounting entries in an effort to conceal WorldCom's deteriorating financial condition. She finally gave in, however, accepting that this was the only way to save the company. She and other WorldCom accountants eventually pled guilty to conspiracy and fraud. She was sentenced to five months in prison and five months of house arrest.[49]

Such loyalty to authority figures can be seen in corporations that have strong charismatic leaders and centralized structures. In business, if a superior tells an employee to increase sales "no matter what it takes" and that employee has a strong affiliation to legitimate power, the employee may try anything to fulfill that order. Dysfunctional leaders that are abusive and treat employees with contempt and disrespect can use legitimate power to pressure subordinates into unethical conduct. In these situations, employees may not voice their concerns or may use anonymous reporting systems to deal with the dysfunctional leader.[50]

EXPERT POWER   Expert power is derived from a person's knowledge (or a perception that a person possesses knowledge). Expert power usually stems from a superior's credibility with subordinates. Credibility, and thus expert power, is positively correlated to the number of years a person worked in a firm or industry, education, and honors he or she has received for performance. The perception that a person is an expert on a specific topic can also confer expert power on him or her. A relatively low-level secretary may have expert power because he or she knows specific details about how the business operates and can even make suggestions on how to inflate revenue through expense reimbursements.

Expert power may cause ethical problems when used to manipulate others or gain an unfair advantage. Physicians, lawyers, and consultants can take unfair advantage of unknowing clients, for example. Accounting firms may gain extra income by ignoring concerns about the accuracy of financial data they examine in an audit.

REFERENT POWER   Referent power may exist when one person perceives that his or her goals or objectives are similar to another's. The second person may attempt to influence the first to take actions that allows both to achieve their objectives. Because they share the same goals, the first person perceives the other's use of referent power as beneficial. For this power relationship to be effective, some sort of empathy must exist between the individuals. Identification with others helps boost the decision maker's confidence, thus increasing the referent power.

Consider the following situation: Lisa Jones, a manager in the accounting department of a manufacturing firm, is pressured to increase the rate of processing sales. She asked Michael Wong, a salesperson, to speed up the delivery of sales contracts, and, if possible, encourage advanced sales with delayed delivery. Michael protests that he does not want to push customers for future sales. Lisa makes use of referent power. She invites Michael to lunch and they discuss their work concerns, including the problem of increasing sales for accounting purposes. They agree if document processing can be done through advanced sales, both will benefit. Lisa then suggests that Michael start sending sales contracts for the *next* quarter. He agrees to give it a try and within several weeks the contracts are moving faster and sales increase for the next quarter. Lisa's job is made easier, and Michael gets his commission checks a little sooner. On the other hand, this may be the start of channel stuffing, or inflating the sales and income in the current quarter.

The five bases of power are not mutually exclusive. People typically use several power bases to effect change in others. Although power in itself is neither ethical nor unethical, its use can raise ethical issues. Sometimes a leader uses power to manipulate a situation or a person's values in a way that creates a conflict with the person's value structure. For example, a manager who forces an employee to choose between staying home with a sick child and keeping a job is using coercive power and creating a direct conflict with the employee's values. In business, titles and salary signify power, but power and wealth often breed arrogance and are easily abused.

Motivating Ethical Behavior

A leader's ability to motivate subordinates plays a key role in maintaining an ethical organization. Motivation is a force within the individual that focuses his or her behavior toward achieving a goal. Job performance is considered to be a function of ability and motivation and can be represented by the equation (job performance = ability × motivation). This equation shows that employees can be motivated to accomplish things, but resources and know-how are also needed to get a job done. To create motivation, an organization offers incentives that encourage employees to work toward organizational objectives. Understanding motivation is important to effective management and helps explain employees' ethical behavior. For example, a person who aspires to higher positions in an organization may sabotage a coworker's project to make that person look bad. This unethical behavior is directly related to the first employee's ambition (motivation) to rise in the organization. Employees want to feel they are a good fit with their organization, have a clear understanding of job expectations, are supported in their role, and are valued and inspired to perform well. If an organization has shared values and an ethical culture, employees should be highly engaged and motivated because of their trust in others.

As businesspeople move into middle management and beyond, higher-order needs (social connections, esteem, and recognition) tend to become more important than lower-order needs (salary, safety, and job security). Research shows an individual's career stage, age, organization size, and geographic location affect the relative priority given to satisfying respect, self-esteem, and basic physiological needs. An individual's hierarchy of needs may influence his or her motivation and ethical behavior. After basic needs such as food, working conditions (existence needs), and survival are satisfied, relatedness needs and growth needs become important. **Relatedness needs** are satisfied by social and interpersonal relationships, and **growth needs** by creative or productive activities.[51]

From an ethics perspective, needs or goals may change as a person progresses through the ranks of the company. This shift may cause or help solve problems depending on the person's current ethical status relative to the company or society. For example, junior executives might inflate purchase or sales orders, overbill time worked on projects, or accept cash gratuities if they are worried about providing for their families' basic physical necessities. As they continue up the ladder and are able to fulfill these needs, such concerns may become less important. Consequently, these managers may go back to obeying company policy or conforming to organizational culture and be more concerned with internal recognition and achievement than their families' physical needs. Younger employees tend to rely on organizational culture for guidance, but older employees have been found to improve ethical performance.

Examining the role motivation plays in ethics offers a way to relate business ethics to the broader social context in which workers live and the moral assumptions on which society depends. Workers are individuals and will be motivated by a variety of personal interests. Although we emphasize that managers are positioned to exert pressure and force individuals' compliance on ethically related issues, we also acknowledge an individual's personal ethics and needs will significantly affect his or her ethical decisions.

Organizational Structure and Business Ethics

An organization's structure is important to the study of business ethics because the various roles and job descriptions that comprise that structure can create opportunities for unethical behavior. The structure of organizations can be described in many ways. For simplicity's sake, we discuss two broad categories of organizational structures—centralized and decentralized. These are not mutually exclusive structures; in the real world, organizational structures exist on a continuum. Table 7–4 compares strengths and weaknesses of centralized and decentralized structures.

In a **centralized organization**, decision-making authority is concentrated in the hands of top-level managers, and little authority is delegated to lower levels. Responsibility, both internal and external, rests with top-level managers. This structure is especially suited to organizations that make high-risk decisions and have lower-level managers not highly skilled in decision making. It is also suitable for organizations when production processes are routine and efficiency is of primary importance. These organizations are usually

TABLE 7–4 Structural Comparison of Organizational Types Emphasis

Characteristic	Centralized	Decentralized
Hierarchy of authority	Centralized	Decentralized
Flexibility	Low	High
Adaptability	Low	High
Problem recognition	Low	High
Implementation	High	Low
Dealing with changes	Poor environmental complexity	Good
Rules and procedures	Many and formal	Few and informal
Division of labor	Clear-cut	Ambiguous
Span of control	Many employees	Few employees
Use of managerial techniques	Extensive	Minimal
Coordination and control	Formal and impersonal	Informal and personal

© Cengage Learning

bureaucratic, and the division of labor is typically well defined. All workers know their job and what is expected; each has a clear understanding of how to carry out assigned tasks. Centralized organizations stress formal rules, policies, and procedures backed up with elaborate control systems. Codes of ethics may specify the techniques used for decision making. General Motors, the Internal Revenue Service, and the U.S. Army are examples of centralized organizations.

Because of the top-down approach and distance between managers and decision makers, centralized organizational structures can lead to unethical acts. If formal rules and policies are unfairly executed, they lose their validity or efficacy. To some extent, rules can be deactivated even if they are formally in force.[52] If the centralized organization is bureaucratic, some employees may behave according to the letter of the law rather than the spirit. A centralized organization can have a policy about bribes that does not include wording about donating to a client's favorite charity before or after a sale. Such donations can be construed as a tacit bribe because the employee buyer could be swayed by the donation, or gift, to act in a less than favorable way or not act in the best interests of the firm.

Other ethical concerns may arise in centralized structures because they typically have little upward communication. Top-level managers may not be aware of problems and unethical activity. Some companies' use of sweatshop labor may be one manifestation of this lack of upward communication. Sweatshops produce products such as clothing by employing laborers, sometimes through forced immigrant labor, who often work 12- to 16-hour shifts for little or no pay. The UN International Labor Office says 21 million people are victims of forced labor in the form of children enslaved in sweatshops, migrant laborers working on farms and building homes, illegal immigrants subservient to their smugglers, and other forms of coercion. Asia is home to more than 50 percent of all forced labor workers in the world. Industries that benefit the most from this cheap labor include electronics, automobiles, textiles, construction, fishing, and agriculture.[53] Another ethical issue that may arise in centralized organizations is blame shifting, or scapegoating. People may try to transfer blame for their actions to others who are not responsible. The specialization and rigid division of labor in centralized organizations can also create ethical problems. Employees may not understand how their actions affect the overall organization because they work with only one piece of a much larger puzzle. This lack of connectedness can lead employees to engage in unethical behavior because they fail to understand the overall ramifications of their behavior.

In a **decentralized organization**, decision-making authority is delegated as far down the chain of command as possible. Such organizations have relatively few formal rules, and coordination and control are usually informal and personal. They focus instead on increasing the flow of information. As a result, one of the main strengths of decentralized organizations is their adaptability and early recognition of external change. With greater flexibility, managers can react quickly to changes in their ethical environment. Google is known for being decentralized and empowering its employees. A parallel weakness of decentralized organizations is the difficulty in responding quickly to changes in policy and procedures established by top management. In addition, independent profit centers within a decentralized organization may deviate from organizational objectives. Decentralized firms may have fewer internal controls and use shared values for their ethical standards. If a firm depends on abstract values without specific rules of conduct, there may be more variation in behavior. Also, it may be harder to control rogue employees engaging in misconduct. Table 7–5 gives examples of centralized versus decentralized organizations and describes their different corporate cultures.

Because of the strict formalization and implementation of ethics policies and procedures in centralized organizations, they tend to be more ethical in their practices than decentralized organizations. Centralized organizations may also exert more influence on their employees because they have a central core of policies and codes of ethical conduct. Decentralized organizations give employees extensive decision-making autonomy because management empowers the employees. Ambiguity in the letter versus the spirit of rules can create ethical challenges, especially for newer managers.[54] However, it is also true that decentralized organizations may avoid ethical dilemmas through the use of effective codes of conduct and ethics. If widely shared values and effective ethics programs are in place in decentralized organizations, there may be less need for excessive compliance systems. However, different units in the company may evolve with diverse value systems and approaches to ethical decision making. A high-tech defense firm like Lockheed Martin might cope with different decisions on the same ethical issue if it did not have a centralized ethics program. Boeing has become more centralized since the entrance of CEO W. James

TABLE 7–5 Examples of Centralized and Decentralized Corporate Cultures

Company	Organizational Culture	Characterized by
Nike	Decentralized	Creativity, freedom, informality
Southwest Airlines	Decentralized	Fun, teamwork orientation, loyalty
General Motors	Centralized	Unions, adherence to task assignments, structured
Microsoft	Decentralized	Creative, investigative, fast paced
Procter & Gamble	Centralized	Experienced, dependable, a rich history and tradition of products, powerful

© Cengage Learning

McNerney, Jr., and the exit of CEO Harry Stonecipher, who carried on a relationship with a female vice president of the company. Before McNerney stepped in, Boeing went through several years of ethics and legal difficulties. These include the jailing of the former CFO for illegal job negotiations with Pentagon officials, indictment of a manager for stealing 25,000 pages of proprietary documents, abuse of attorney-client privilege to cover up internal studies showing pay inequities, and other scandals.[55]

Unethical behavior is possible in centralized or decentralized structures when specific corporate cultures permit or encourage workers to deviate from accepted standards or ignore corporate legal and ethical responsibilities. Centralized firms may have a more difficult time uprooting unethical activity than decentralized organizations as the latter has a more fluid structure in which changes may affect only a small portion of the company. Often, when a centralized firm uncovers unethical activity and it appears to be pervasive, the leadership is removed so the old unethical culture is uprooted and replaced with a more ethical one. For example, Mitsubishi Motors suggested significant management changes after it was discovered a cover-up of auto defects had gone on for more than two decades.

GROUP DIMENSIONS OF CORPORATE STRUCTURE AND CULTURE

When discussing corporate culture, we tend to focus on the organization as a whole. But corporate values, beliefs, patterns, and rules are often expressed through smaller groups within the organization. Moreover, individual groups within organizations often adopt their own rules and values.

Types of Groups

Two categories of groups affect ethical behavior in business. A **formal group** is defined as an assembly of individuals with an organized structure that is explicitly accepted by the group. An **informal group** is defined as two or more individuals with a common interest but without an explicit organizational structure.

FORMAL GROUPS   Formal groups can be divided into committees, work groups, and teams.

A *committee* is a formal group of individuals assigned to a specific task. Often a single manager could not complete the task, or management may believe a committee can better represent different constituencies and improve the coordination and implementation of decisions. Committees may meet regularly to review performance, develop plans, or make decisions. Most formal committees in organizations operate on an ongoing basis, but their membership may change over time. A committee is an excellent example of a situation that coworkers and significant others within the organization can influence ethical decisions. Committee decisions are legitimized in part by agreement or majority rule. In this respect, minority views on issues such as ethics can be pushed aside through the majority's authority. Committees bring diverse personal moral values to the ethical decision-making process and may expand the number of alternatives considered. Also inherent in the committee structure is a lack of individual responsibility. Because of the diverse composition of the group, members may not be committed or willing to assume responsibility for the group decision. Groupthink may emerge, enabling the majority to explain ethical considerations away.

Although many organizations have financial, diversity, personnel, or social responsibility committees, only a few organizations have committees devoted exclusively to ethics. An ethics committee might raise ethical concerns, resolve ethical dilemmas in the organization, and create or update the company's code of ethics. Motorola, for example, maintains a Business Ethics Compliance Committee that interprets, classifies, communicates, and enforces the company's code and ethics initiatives. An ethics committee can gather information on functional areas of the business and examine manufacturing practices, personnel policies, dealings with suppliers, financial reporting, and sales techniques to determine if the company's practices are ethical. Though much of a corporation's culture operates informally, an ethics committee is an example of a highly formalized approach for dealing with ethical issues.

Work groups are used to subdivide duties within specific functional areas of a company. For example, on an automotive assembly line, one work group might install the seats and interior design elements of the vehicle while another group installs all the dashboard instruments. This enables production supervisors to specialize in a specific area and provide expert advice to work groups.

While work groups operate within a single functional area, *teams* bring together the expertise of employees from several different areas of the organization—such as finance, marketing, and production—on a single project, like developing a new product. Many manufacturing firms, including General Motors, Westinghouse, and Procter & Gamble, use the team concept to improve participative management. Ethical conflicts may arise because team members come from different functional areas. Each member of the team has a particular role to play and probably had limited interaction with other members of the team. Conflicts often occur when members of different organizational groups interact. However, airing viewpoints representative of all the functional areas provides more options from which to choose.

Work groups and teams provide the organizational structure for group decision making. One of the reasons individuals cannot implement their own personal ethical beliefs in organizations is that work groups collectively reach so many decisions. However, those who have legitimate power are in a position to influence ethics-related activities. The work group and team often sanction certain activities as ethical or define others as unethical.

INFORMAL GROUPS   In addition to the groups businesses formally organize and recognize—such as committees, work groups, and teams—most organizations contain a number of informal groups. These groups are usually composed of individuals, often from the same department, who have similar interests and band together for companionship or for purposes that may or may not be relevant to the goals of the organization. For example, four or five people with similar tastes in outdoor activities and music may discuss their interests while working and may meet outside work for dinner, concerts, sports events, or other activities. Other informal groups may evolve to form a union, improve working conditions or benefits, get a manager fired, or protest work practices they view as unfair. Informal groups may generate disagreement and conflict, or enhance morale and job satisfaction.

Informal groups help develop informal channels of communication, sometimes called the grapevine, that are important in every organization. Informal communication flows up, down, diagonally, and horizontally, not necessarily following the communication lines on a company's organizational chart. Information passed along the grapevine may relate to the job, the organization, an ethical issue, or it may simply be gossip and rumors. The grapevine can act as an early warning system for employees. If employees learn informally that the company may be sold or a particular action will be condemned as unethical by top management or the community, they have time to think how they will respond. Because gossip is not uncommon in an organization, the information passed along the grapevine is not always accurate, but managers who understand how the grapevine works can use it to reinforce acceptable values and beliefs.

The grapevine is an important source of information for individuals to assess ethical behavior within their organization. One way an employee can determine acceptable behavior is to ask friends and peers in informal groups about the consequences of certain actions such as lying to a customer about a product-safety issue. The corporate culture may provide employees with a general understanding of the patterns and rules that govern behavior, but informal groups make this culture come alive and provide direction for employees' daily choices. For example, if new employees learn anecdotally through the grapevine that the organization does not punish ethical violations, they may seize the next opportunity for unethical behavior if it accomplishes the organization's objectives. There is a general tendency to discipline top sales performers more leniently than poor sales performers for engaging in identical forms of unethical selling behavior. A superior sales record appears to induce more lenient forms of discipline despite organizational policies that state otherwise.[56] In this case, the grapevine has clearly communicated that the organization rewards those who break the ethical rules to achieve desirable objectives.

Group Norms

Group norms are standards of behavior groups expect of their members. Just as corporate culture establishes behavior guidelines for an organization's members, group norms help define acceptable and unacceptable behavior within a group. In particular, group norms define the limit allowed on deviations from group expectations. Norms provide explicit ethical directions. For example, there may be a behavioral expectation that personal cell phones cannot be brought into the work place. Many group norms relate directly to managerial decisions. There may be the expectation that all advertising claims are truthful. Salespersons may be required to never lie to a customer.

Most work organizations develop norms that govern group rates of production and communication with management, as well as provide a general understanding of behavior considered right or wrong, ethical or unethical, within the group. For example, group members may punish an employee who reports to a supervisor that a coworker has covered up a serious production error. Other members of the group may glare at the informant, and refuse to talk to or sit next to him or her.

Norms have the power to enforce a strong degree of conformity among group members. At the same time, norms define the different roles for various positions within the organization. A low-ranking member of a group may be expected to carry out an unpleasant task such as accepting responsibility for someone else's ethical mistake. Abusive behavior toward new or lower-ranking employees could be a norm in an informal group.

Sometimes group norms conflict with the values and rules prescribed by the organization's culture. The organization may have policies prohibiting the use of personal social networking sites during work hours and use rewards and punishments to encourage this culture. In a particular informal group, norms may accept using personal social networking sites during work hours and try to avoid management's attention. Issues of equity may arise in this situation if other groups believe they are unfairly forced to follow policies that are not enforced on the other group. These employees may complain to management or the offending group. If they believe management is not taking corrective action they, too, may begin to use social networking for personal use, thus hurting the organization's productivity. For this reason, management must carefully monitor not only the corporate culture but also the norms of all the various groups within the organization. Sanctions may be necessary to bring in line a group whose norms deviate sharply from the overall culture.

VARIATION IN EMPLOYEE CONDUCT

Although a corporation is required to take responsibility for conducting its business ethically, a substantial amount of research indicates significant differences exist in individual employees' values and philosophies and therefore in how they deal with ethical issues.[57] Because people are culturally diverse and have different values, they interpret situations differently and the ethical decisions they make on the same issue will vary.

Table 7–6 shows approximately 10 percent of employees take advantage of situations to further their own personal interests. These individuals are more likely to manipulate, cheat, or act in a self-serving manner when the benefits gained from doing so are greater than the penalties for the misconduct. Such employees may choose to take office supplies from work for personal use if the only penalty they suffer is paying for the supplies. The lower the risk of being caught is, the higher the likelihood that the 10 percent most likely to take advantage of the company will be involved in unethical activities.

Another 40 percent of workers go along with the work group on most matters. These employees are most concerned about the social implications of their actions and want to fit into the organization. Although they have personal opinions, they are easily influenced by what the people around them are doing. These individuals may know using office supplies for personal use is improper, yet they view it as acceptable because their coworkers do so. These employees rationalize their actions by saying the use of office supplies is a benefit of working at their particular company and it must be acceptable because the company does not enforce a policy prohibiting the behavior. Coupled with this philosophy is the belief that no one will get into trouble for doing what everybody else is doing.

About 40 percent of a company's employees, as shown in Table 7–6, always try to follow company policies and rules. These workers not only have a strong grasp of their corporate culture's definition of acceptable behavior, but also attempt to comply with codes of ethics, ethics training, and other communications about appropriate conduct. If the

TABLE 7–6 Variation in Employee Conduct*

10%	40%	40%	10%
Follow their own values and beliefs; believe that their values are superior to those of others in the company	Always try to follow company policies	Go along with the work group	Take advantage of situations if the penalty is less than the benefit and the risk of being caught is low

© Cengage Learning

*Estimates based on the author's research and reports from ethics and compliance officers from many industries.

company has a policy prohibiting taking office supplies from work, these employees probably will observe it. However, they are not likely to speak out about the 40 percent who choose to go along with the work group, for these employees prefer to focus on their jobs and steer clear of any organizational misconduct. If the company fails to communicate standards of appropriate behavior, members of this group will devise their own.

The final 10 percent of employees try to maintain formal ethical standards that focus on rights, duties, and rules. They embrace values that assert certain inalienable rights and actions, which they perceive to be always ethically correct. In general, members of this group believe that their values are right and superior to the values of others in the company, or even to the company's value system, when an ethical conflict arises. These individuals have a tendency to report the misconduct of others or to speak out when they view activities within the company as unethical. Consequently, members of this group will probably report colleagues who take office supplies.

The significance of this variation in the way individuals behave ethically is simply the fact that employees use different approaches when making ethical decisions. Because of the probability that a large percentage of any work group will either take advantage of a situation or at least go along with the work group, it is vital companies provide communication and control mechanisms to maintain an ethical culture. Companies that fail to monitor activities and enforce ethics policies provide a low-risk environment for those employees inclined to take advantage of situations to accomplish their personal, and sometimes unethical, objectives.

Good business practices and concern for the law require organizations to recognize this variation in employees' desire to be ethical. The percentages cited in Table 7–6 are only estimates, and the actual percentages of each type of employee may vary widely across organizations based on individuals and corporate culture. The specific percentages are less important than the fact our research has identified these variations as existing within most organizations. Organizations should focus particular attention on managers who oversee the day-to-day operations of employees within the company. They should also provide training and communication to ensure the business operates ethically, it does not become the victim of fraud or theft, and employees, customers, and other stakeholders are not abused through the misconduct of people who have a pattern of unethical behavior.

As seen throughout this book, examples can be cited of employees and managers with no concern for ethical conduct but who are nonetheless hired and placed in positions of trust. Some corporations continue to support executives who ignore environmental concerns, poor working conditions, or defective products, or engage in accounting fraud. Executives who get results, meaning profits, regardless of the consequences, are often admired and lauded, especially in the business press. When their unethical or even illegal actions become public knowledge, however, they risk more than the loss of their positions.

CAN PEOPLE CONTROL THEIR ACTIONS WITHIN A CORPORATE CULTURE?

Many people find it hard to believe an organization's culture can exert so strong an influence on individuals' behavior within the organization. In our society, we want to believe individuals control their own destinies. A popular way of viewing business ethics is to see it as a reflection of the alternative moral philosophies individuals use to resolve their personal moral dilemmas. As this chapter shows, ethical decisions within organizations are often made by committees and formal and informal groups, not by individuals. Decisions related to financial reporting, advertising, product design, sales practices, and pollution-control issues are often beyond the influence of individuals alone. In addition, these decisions are frequently based on business rather than personal goals.

Most new employees in highly bureaucratic organizations have limited input into the basic operating rules and procedures for getting things done. Along with learning sales tactics and accounting procedures, employees may be taught to ignore a design flaw in a product that could be dangerous to users. Although many personal ethics issues may seem straightforward and easy to resolve, individuals entering business usually need several years of experience within a specific industry to understand how to resolve ethical close calls. Both individual and organizational ethics have an impact on an employee's ethical intention. If there is congruence between individual ethics and the organizational ethical culture, there is an increase in the potential for making ethical choices in organizational decision making. Younger managers may need more support and guidance from the organization because of their limited experience in dealing with complex issues.[58] Research also indicates congruence between individual and organizational values is greater in the private sector. On the other hand, age and organizational type aside, personal values appear to be a strong factor in decreasing unethical practices and increasing appropriate work behavior as compared to congruence in personal and organizational values.[59]

It is not our purpose to suggest you should go along with management or the group on business ethics issues. Honesty and open discussions of ethical issues are important to successful ethical decision making. We believe most companies and businesspeople try to make ethical decisions. However, because there is so much difference among individuals, ethical conflict is inevitable. If you manage and supervise others, it will be necessary to maintain ethical policies for your organization and report misconduct that occurs. Ethics is not just a personal matter.

Regardless of how a person or organization views the acceptability of a particular activity, if society judges it to be wrong or unethical, then this larger view directly affects the organization's ability to achieve its goals. Not all activities deemed unethical by society are illegal, but if public opinion decries or consumers protest against a particular activity, the result may be legislation that restricts or bans a specific business practice. For instance, concern about promoting unhealthy products to children has prompted some governments to take action.

If people believe that their personal ethics severely conflict with the ethics of the work group and those of superiors in an organization, that person's only alternative may be to leave the organization. In the highly competitive employment market of the twenty-first century, quitting a job because of an ethical conflict requires courage and, possibly, the ability to survive without a job. Obviously, there are no easy answers for resolving ethical conflicts between the organization and the individual. Our goal is not to tell you what you should do. But we do believe that the more you know about how ethical decision making occurs within organizations, the more opportunity you have to influence decisions positively and help resolve ethical conflicts more effectively.

SUMMARY

Corporate culture refers to the set of values, beliefs, goals, norms, and ways of solving problems that members (employees) of an organization share. These shared values may be formally expressed or unspoken. Corporate cultures can be classified in several ways, and a cultural audit identifies an organization's culture. If an organization's culture rewards unethical behavior, people within the company are more likely to act unethically. A company's failure to monitor or manage its culture may foster questionable behavior.

Leadership has a significant impact on the ethical decision-making process because leaders have the power to motivate others and enforce both the organization's rules and policies and their own viewpoints. A leader must not only gain the respect of his or her followers but also provide a standard of ethical conduct. Leaders exert power to influence the behaviors and decisions of subordinates. There are five power bases from which a leader may influence ethical behavior: reward power, coercive power, legitimate power, expert power, and referent power. Leaders attempt to motivate subordinates; motivation is an internal force that focuses an individual's behavior toward achieving a goal. It can be created by the incentives an organization offers employees.

The structure of an organization may create opportunities to engage in unethical behavior. In a centralized organization, decision-making authority is concentrated in the hands of top managers, and little authority is delegated to lower levels. In a decentralized organization, decision-making authority is delegated as far down the chain of command as possible. Centralized organizations tend to be more ethical than decentralized ones because they enforce more rigid controls, such as codes of ethics and corporate policies, on ethical practices. However, unethical conduct can occur in both types of structures.

In addition to the values and customs that represent the culture of an organization, individual groups within the organization often adopt their own rules and values and even create subcultures. The main types of groups are formal groups—which include committees, work groups, and teams—and informal groups. Informal groups often feed an informal channel of communication called the grapevine. Group norms are standards of behavior groups expect of their members. They help define acceptable and unacceptable behavior within a group and especially the limits on deviating from group expectations. Sometimes group norms conflict with the values and rules prescribed by the organization's culture.

Sometimes an employee's personal ethical standards conflict with what is expected of him or her as a member of an organization and its corporate culture. This is especially true given that an organization's ethical decisions are often resolved by committees, formal groups, and informal groups rather than by individuals. When such ethical conflict is severe, the individual may have to decide whether to leave the organization.

IMPORTANT TERMS FOR REVIEW

RESOLVING ETHICAL BUSINESS CHALLENGES*

Candace always tried to do the right thing, but did not know what to do in this dilemma. She knew someone would get hurt. All because of an overzealous supervisor, she thought sadly.

Two years ago Candace took a job at ABCO Corporation in its public relations division. Although new to the corporate world, Candace quickly learned the ropes of the highly bureaucratic organization and excelled at many of her projects. As a result, her bosses assigned her more lucrative responsibilities.

The only downside to the job Candace could see was many people appeared to be promoted based more upon their relationships with their superiors than their merit. While Candice knew her work was excellent, she could not help but wonder whether her friendly repertoire with her immediate supervisors had anything to do with her success so far.

A few months ago, Candace learned her division would be getting a new supervisor. Britney transferred to her division from a similar position in another subsidiary of the company because of her proven talent for organizing and improving the efficiency of operations there. A no-nonsense type of manager, Britney was experienced and determined to be successful in this assignment as well. Candace knew from Britney's reputation that her success had everything to do with hard work and a commitment to make sure everyone else was working just as hard.

On the day Britney assumed her responsibilities as the new division manager, the company held a reception for her to meet the employees. At the reception, Britney circulated throughout the room, introducing herself to people and asking each of them if they had any suggestions that would make the section a better place to work. When she approached Candace, Candace decided to let her know what was bothering her.

"I don't want to make waves or anything, but one thing I've noticed happening recently is some people seem to gain promotions and are given opportunities to work overtime based on who likes them and not on the quality of their work,"

Candace told her. She quickly continued. "It's not that people here don't work hard or anything. It's just that I noticed there might some favoritism going on in some of the major personnel decisions."

Britney looked concerned, but smiled at Candace. "Thank you for telling me, Candace. I assure you I will do everything in my power to make sure this problem does not continue. This kind of thing has no place in the team I'm going to lead."

The next day, Britney requested Candace meet with her. As Candace entered Britney's office for the meeting, Britney looked her straight in the face and said, "I will not tolerate individuals in this organization who are not team players. Yesterday afternoon you led me to believe there are people in this office who are not acting in the best interests of the company, and I want to know who. These people have no place in this division."

Candace was stunned. She did not want to hurt anyone. She just wanted to express her concerns in the hopes certain practices would change.

When she did not answer right away, Britney looked at her with annoyance. "Look," she said, "I want you to tell me the names of the managers you were referring to now, and keep me informed if you see anyone hurting this company, or I've got to think maybe you're part of the problems around here."

Candace tried to explain. "I'm sorry," she said. "I didn't want to implicate anyone in particular. I just wanted to alert you to some concerns I've been having…"

Britney cut Candace off before she could continue. "Candace, you seem like a smart person. I'm trying to create an example here. There are no shortcuts in this job. You work hard, or you get out. I've got no room for slackers. Now once again, who are the managers you were talking about?"

Candace's heart raced in her chest and she felt close to tears. Britney noticed because she sighed exasperatedly. "Fine. Here's what I'll do. We'll set up another meeting tomorrow and talk then. That'll give you time to think about where your priorities lie."

Candace sat at her desk, her work forgotten. She could not believe the mess she had gotten herself into. If she told Britney what she wanted, certain managers would get disciplined or perhaps even fired. Of course, it would be her word against theirs, so Candace knew she faced the risk of being thought of as someone who was just trying to make trouble. At the very least, the managers she named would dislike her for reporting them. But if she refused Britney, she risked the ire of her new boss.

QUESTIONS | EXERCISES

1. Describe the organizational structure of ABCO Corporation.
2. Which type of leadership power is Britney using? Do you feel it is effective in this situation?
3. Does Candace have any other alternatives than the two that she is considering?

*This case is strictly hypothetical; any resemblance to real persons, companies, or situations is coincidental.

> > > CHECK YOUR EQ

Check your EQ, or Ethics Quotient, by completing the following. Assess your performance to evaluate your overall understanding of the chapter material.

1.	Decentralized organizations tend to put the blame for unethical behavior on lower-level personnel.	**Yes**	**No**
2.	Decentralized organizations give employees extensive decision-making autonomy.	**Yes**	**No**
3.	Corporate culture provides rules that govern behavior within the organization.	**Yes**	**No**
4.	An integrative culture shows high concern for performance and little concern for people.	**Yes**	**No**
5.	Coercive power works in the same manner as reward power.	**Yes**	**No**

ANSWERS **1. No.** This is more likely to occur in centralized organizations. **2. Yes.** This is known as empowerment. **3. Yes.** Values, beliefs, customs, and ceremonies represent what is acceptable and unacceptable in the organization. **4. No.** This describes an exacting culture. An integrative culture combines a high concern for people with a high concern for production. **5. No.** Coercive power is the opposite of reward power. One offers rewards and the other responds with punishment to encourage appropriate behavior.

ENDNOTES

1. J. W. Lorsch, "Managing Culture: The Invisible Barrier to Strategic Change," *California Management Review* 28 (1986): 95–109.

2. Mutual of Omaha, *Our Mutual Commitment: Mutual of Omaha's Code of Ethics and Business Conduct*, http://www.mutualofomaha.com/documents/about/m27710.pdf (accessed April 26, 2013).

3. Richard L. Daft, *Organizational Theory and Design* (Cincinnati: South-Western, 2007).

4. Stanley M. Davis, quoted in Alyse Lynn Booth, "Who Are We?" *Public Relations Journal* (July 1985): 13–18.

5. Southwest Airlines, "Welcome to Adopt-A-Pilot," http://www.southwest.com/adoptapilot/ (accessed April 26, 2013).

6. "A Study of the Ford Motor Co. Turnaround 2010," *Business Value Group LLC*, September 2010, http://www.bvgintl.com/wp-content/uploads/2010/10/FordMotorCoWhitePaperI.pdf (accessed April 26, 2013); "GM and Ford: Roadmaps for Recovery," *BusinessWeek* online, March 14, 2006, GM and Ford: Roadmaps for Recovery (accessed April 26, 2013).

7. Ariel Schwartz, "Ford Gives Dealers a Blueprint for Sustainability," *Fast Company*, February 16, 2010, http://www.fastc, 2013ompany.com/1551705/ford-gives-dealerships-a-blueprint-for-sustainability (accessed April); Andrew Munchbach, "Dealers wanting to sell Ford's first all-electric car must Focus on the environment," *engadget*, April 30, 2012, http://www.engadget.com/2012/04/30/dealers-wanting-to-sell-fords-first-all-electric-car-must-focus/ (accessed April 26, 2013).

8. Abstracted from "Enhancing Compliance with Sarbanes–Oxley 404," *Quantisoft*, http://www.quantisoft.com/Industries/Ethics.htm (accessed April 26, 2013).

9. Taras Vasyl, Julie Rowney, and Piers Steel, "Half a Century of Measuring Culture: Approaches, Challenges, Limitations, and Suggestions Based on the Analysis of 121 Instruments for Quantifying Culture," white paper, 2008, Haskayne School of Business, University of Calgary, http://www.ucalgary.ca/~taras/_private/Half_a_Century_of_Measuring_Culture.pdf (accessed April 26, 2013).

10. Ibid.

11. Geert Hofstede, Bram Neuijen, Denise Daval Ohayv, and Geert Sanders, "Measuring Organizational Cultures: A Qualitative and Quantitative Study across Twenty Cases," *Administrative Science Quarterly* 35, no. 2 (1990): 286–316.

12. "Culture of trust," *IBM*, http://www.ibm.com/ibm/responsibility/trust.shtml (accessed April 26, 2013); IBM, *Basic Conduct Guidelines*, http://www.ibm.com/investor/pdf/BCG_Feb_2011_English_CE.pdf (accessed April 26, 2013).

13. Cam Caldwell, Linda A. Hayes, and Do Tien Long, "Leadership, Trustworthiness, and Ethical Stewardship," *Journal of Business Ethics* 96 (2010): 497–512.

14. N. K. Sethia and M. A. Von Glinow, "Arriving at Four Cultures by Managing the Reward System," in *Gaining Control of the Corporate Culture* (San Francisco: Jossey-Bass, 1985), 409.

15. "UPS Fact Sheet," *UPS*, http://www.pressroom.ups.com/Fact+Sheets/UPS+Fact+Sheet (accessed May 1, 2013).

16. "UPS Global Volunteer Month Fact Sheet," *UPS*, http://pressroom.ups.com/Fact+Sheets/UPS+Global+Volunteer+Month+Fact+Sheet (accessed May 1, 2013); "Alternative Fuel Fleet," *UPS*, http://www.ups.com/content/us/en/bussol/browse/leadership-afvfleet.html (accessed May 1, 2013).

17. "100 Best Companies to Work for" *Fortune*, February 7, 2011, 91–101; *Fortune* Magazine, "100 Best Companies to Work for" *CNNMoney*, 2013, http://money.cnn.com/magazines/fortune/best-companies/2013/snapshots/4.html?iid=bc_sp_list (accessed May 1, 2013).

18. *2005 National Business Ethics Survey: How Employees Perceive Ethics at Work*, 20. Copyright © 2006, Ethics Resource Center (ERC), Used with permission of the ERC, 1747 Pennsylvania Ave. NW, Suite 400, Washington, DC 2006, www.ethics.org.

19. Cassandra Sweet and Guy Chazan, "BP Faces New Hit over Spill in Alaska," *The Wall Street Journal*, November 20–21, 2011, B1.

20. Susan M. Heathfield, "Five Tips for Effective Employee Recognition," http://humanresources.about.com/od/rewardrecognition/a/recognition_tip.htm (accessed May 1, 2013).

21. "Recognition Programs," *FedEx*, http://about.van.fedex.com/recognition-programs (accessed May 1, 2013).

22. Isabelle Maignan, O. C. Ferrell, and Thomas Hult, "Corporate Citizenship, Cultural Antecedents and Business Benefit," *Journal of the Academy of Marketing Science* 27 (1999): 455–469.

23. Susanne Arvidsson, "Communication of Corporate Social Responsibility: A Study of the Views of Management Teams in Large Companies," *Journal of Business Ethics* 96 (2010): 339–354.

24. Kub Chieh-Peng, Yehuda Barch, and Wei-Chi Shih, "Corporate Social Responsibility and Team Performance: The Mediating Role of Team Efficacy and Team Self-Esteem," *Journal of Business Ethics* 108 (2012): 167–180.

25. R. Eric Reidenbach and Donald P. Robin, *Ethics and Profits* (Englewood Cliffs, NJ: Prentice-Hall, 1989), 92.

26. "IKEA Named as One of the 'World's Most Ethical Companies' for Fourth Consecutive Year in 2010," PRNewswire, March 29, 2010, http://www.prnewswire.com/news-releases/ikea-named-as-one-of-the-worlds-most-ethical-companies-for-fourth-consecutive-year-in-2010-89384407.html (accessed May 1, 2013); "IKEA U.S. Community Relations guidelines," http://www.ikea.com/ms/en_US/ikea_near_you/woodbridge/new_wood_app.pdf (accessed May 1, 2013).

27. E. Sutherland and D. R. Cressey, *Principles of Criminology*, 8th ed. (Chicago: Lippincott, 1970), 114.

28. O. C. Ferrell and Larry G. Gresham, "A Contingency Framework for Understanding Ethical Decision Making in Marketing," *Journal of Marketing* 49 (1985): 90–91.

29. Edward Wong, "Some at Shuttle Fuel Tank Plant See Quality Control Problems," *The New York Times*, February 18, 2003, http://www.nytimes.com/2003/02/18/national/nationalspecial/18ORLE.html (accessed May 1, 2013); *Columbia Crew Survival Investigation Report*, NASA, http://www.nasa.gov/pdf/298870main_SP-2008-565.pdf (accessed May 1, 2013).

30. "Ethics and Nonprofits," *Stanford Social Innovation Review* (Summer 2009), http://www.ssireview.org/articles/entry/ethics_and_nonprofits (accessed May 1, 2013).

31. "Whistle-blower Debate Heats up," *CFO*, February 11, 2011, http://www.cfo.com/article.cfm/14554934/c_14556017 (accessed May 1, 2013).

32. Matthew Goldstein, "Ex-Employees at Heart of Stanford Financial Probe," *BusinessWeek*, February 13, 2009, http://www.businessweek.com/bwdaily/dnflash/content/feb2009/db20090213_848258.htm (accessed May 1, 2013).

33. Thomas S. Mulligan, "Whistle-Blower Recounts Enron Tale," *The Los Angeles Times*, March 16, 2006, via http://www.whistleblowers.org/storage/whistleblowers/documents/whistle_blower_-_la_times.pdf (accessed May 1, 2013).

34. Nielsen P Richard, "Whistle-Blowing Methods for Navigating Within and Helping Reform Regulatory Institutions," *Journal of Business Ethics* 112 (2013): 385–395.

35. John W. Schoen, "Split CEO-Chairman Job, Says Panel," *NBC News*, http://www.nbcnews.com/id/3073028/t/split-ceo-chairman-job-says-panel/#.UYGd1fUmx8E (accessed May 1, 2013).

36. Michael Barbaro, "Walmart Says Official Misused Company Funds," *The Washington Post*, July 15, 2005, http://www.washingtonpost.com/wp-dyn/content/article/2005/07/14/AR2005071402055.html (accessed May 1, 2013).

37. Loren Berlin, "JP Morgan Chase Whistleblower: 'Essentially Suicide' To Stand Up To Bank," *Huffington Post, May, 7, 2012*, http://www.huffingtonpost.com/2012/05/07/linda-almonte-jpmorgan-chase-whistleblower_n_1478268.html (accessed April 15, 2013)

38. "Qui Tam Tips: How to File a Whistle-blower Complaint," http://www.jameshoyer.com/practice_qui_tam.html?se=Overture (accessed May 1, 2013).

39. James Sandler, "The war on whistle-blowers," *Salon*, November 1, 2007, http://www.salon.com/news/feature/2007/11/01/whistleblowers (accessed May 1. 2013).

40. Wim Vandekerckhove, and Eva E. Tsahuridu, Risky Rescues and the Duty to Blow the Whistle," *Journal of Business Ethics* 97 (2010): 365–380.

41. Ethics Resource Center, *2011 National Business Ethics Survey: Workplace Ethics in Transition* (Arlington, VA: Ethics Resource Center, 2012), 15.

42. Paula Dwyer and Dan Carney, with Amy Borrus, Lorraine Woellert, and Christopher Palmeri, "Year of the Whistle-blower," *BusinessWeek*, December 16, 2002, 106–110.

43. Paula J. Desiom, "Federal Whistle-blower Rights Increase under the Stimulus Law," *Ethics Today*, February 18, 2009, http://www.ethics.org/ethics-today/0209/policy-report3.html (accessed May 1, 2013).

44. Darren Dahl, "Learning to Love Whistle-blowers," *Inc.*, March 2006, 21–23; Andrew Martin, "Housing Slump Forces Cuts at a Company Town," *The New York Times*, September 24, 2011, http://www.nytimes.com/2011/09/25/business/economy/housing-slump-forces-cuts-at-a-small-town-company.html?pagewanted=all (accessed May 1, 2013).

45. Andrew Martin, "No Lay-Off Company Now Writes Profit-Sharing Checks," *The New York Times*, December 21, 2012, http://www.nytimes.com/2012/12/22/business/marvin-windows-and-doors-offers-workers-profit-sharing-checks.html?_r=0 (accessed May 1, 2013).

46. Muel Kaptein, "From Inaction to External Whistle-blowing: The Influence of the Ethical Culture of Organizations on Employee Responses to Observed Wrongdoing," *Journal of Business Ethics* 98 (2011): 513–530.

47. Alan Yuspeh, "Speaking up: Letter from the Editor," *Ethisphere*, Q1, 2010, 6.

48. John R. P. French and Bertram Ravin, "The Bases of Social Power," in *Group Dynamics: Research and Theory*, ed. Dorwin Cartwright (Evanston, IL: Row, Peterson, 1962), 607–623.

49. Jennifer Bayot and Roben Farzad, "Ex-WorldCom CFO Gets Five Years for Role in Accounting Fraud," *The New York Times*, August 12, 2005, http://www.nytimes.com/2005/08/12/business/12worldcom.html?pagewanted=all (accessed May 1, 2013); "Ordered to Commit Fraud, A Staffer Balked, Then Caved," *The Wall Street Journal*, June 23, 2003, http://online.wsj.com/article/0,SB105631811322355600,00.html (accessed May 1, 2013).

50. Cam Caldwell and Mayra Canuto-Carranco, "'Organizational Terrorism' and Moral Choices: Exercising Voice When the Leader Is the Problem," *Journal of Business Ethics* 97 (2010): 159–171.

51. Clayton Alderfer, *Existence, Relatedness, and Growth* (New York: Free Press, 1972), 42–44.

52. Pablo Zoghbi-Manrique-de-Lara, "Do Unfair Procedures Predict Employees' Ethical Behavior by Deactivating Formal Regulations?" *Journal of Business Ethics* 94 (2010): 411–425.

53. International Labor Conference, *The cost of coercion: Global Report under the follow-up to the ILO Declaration on Fundamental Principles and Rights at Work*, 98th session, Report I(B) (Geneva: International Labor Office, 2009), 42; International Labor Organization, "21 million people are now victims of forced labor, ILO says," June 1, 2012, http://www.ilo.org/global/about-the-ilo/newsroom/news/WCMS_181961/lang—en/index.htm (accessed May 1, 2013).

54. Kathy Lund Dean, Jeri Mullins Beggs, and Timothy P. Keane, "Mid-level Managers, Organizational Context, and (Un)ethical Encounters," *Journal of Business Ethics* 97 (2010): 51–69.

55. Stanley Holmes, "Cleaning up Boeing," *BusinessWeek* online, March 13, 2006, http://www.businessweek.com/stories/2006-03-12/cleaning-up-boeing (accessed May 1, 2013).

56. Joseph A. Belizzi and Ronald W. Hasty, "Supervising Unethical Sales Force Behavior: How Strong Is the Tendency to Treat Top Sales Performers Leniently?" *Journal of Business Ethics* 43 (2003): 337–351.

57. John Fraedrich and O. C. Ferrell, "Cognitive Consistency of Marketing Managers in Ethical Situations," *Journal of the Academy of Marketing Science* 20 (1992), 243–252.

58. B. Elango, Karen Paul, Sumit K. Kundu, and Shishir K. Paudel, "Organizational Ethics, Individual Ethics, and Ethical Intentions in International Decision Making," *Journal of Business Ethics* 97 (2010), 543–561.

59. Damodar Suar and Rooplekha Khuntia, "Influence of Personal Values and Value Congruence on Unethical Practices and Work Behavior," *Journal of Business Ethics* 97 (2010): 443–460.

CHAPTER 8

DEVELOPING AN EFFECTIVE ETHICS PROGRAM

CHAPTER OBJECTIVES

- Understand the responsibility of the corporation to be a moral agent
- Understand why businesses need to develop ethics programs
- List the minimum requirements for an ethics program
- Describe the role of codes of ethics in identifying key risk areas for an organization
- Identify the keys to successful ethics training, including program types and goals
- Examine the ways that ethical standards are monitored, audited, and enforced, and to understand the need for continuous improvement

CHAPTER OUTLINE

The Responsibility of the Corporation as a Moral Agent

The Need for Organizational Ethics Programs

An Effective Ethics Program

An Ethics Program Can Help Avoid Legal Problems

Values Versus Compliance Programs

Codes of Conduct

Ethics Officers

Ethics Training and Communication

Systems to Monitor and Enforce Ethical Standards

Continuous Improvement of an Ethics Program

Common Mistakes in Designing and Implementing an Ethics Program

AN ETHICAL DILEMMA*

Even though Todd had just graduated from Indiana University, he interned with Jennings Department Store for two summers. This experience helped him get promoted to Section Manager once he graduated. Although Todd was young and most of the people he managed were older, they respected him because of his expertise and ability to form good relationships with his co-workers and customers.

Several weeks ago, Todd began to hear rumors about one of the unit managers, Zara. He checked Zara's past financial reports and verified she was one of his better managers. Her unit posted the highest sales volume and growth, received positive customer feedback, and showed excellent cost control. The unit's people also did consistently well on inspections. In fact, Zara consistently rated higher than all the other managers for the last two years. Todd wondered why she hadn't been promoted. He knew upper management went over the financials with a magnifying glass. Todd decided to investigate further.

Over the next few weeks Todd began talking informally to those that knew Zara. He heard the same story over and over again. Zara was kind, firm, great with the customers, and looked out for her employees. Zara even had a dedicated following of customers that came in to ask questions about fashion and accessories. She had a client list that followed her tweets and made her department the cash cow of the store. Even though Zara had not graduated from college, she took night classes and was about a year away from her management degree.

Next, Todd spoke to some of her retail clients. The comments made him realize just how much he needed to learn about retailing. They spoke of Zara's advice on shoes, dresses, and jewelry. Some told him they routinely came in to give Zara Christmas gifts. He discovered the store was doing so well in large part because this one employee cared about her clients and workers.

Yet as he questioned more clients, Todd found something rather odd. Some of the customers told him that for small items they handed Zara cash and told her to keep the change. Todd soon discovered these sales were not rung up. Next, he checked the store's shrinkage measures or items that may have been stolen or damaged. The records indicated some shrinkage but nothing significantly "excessive."

After a few weeks of investigation Todd discovered Zara used the money or cash as unrecorded payments to her retail staff. She gave the money in the form of performance bonuses, overtime incentives, and off-hours work. He knew this was in violation of company procedures, yet he couldn't definitively prove Zara was actually taking the shrinkage money and using it to achieve the high performance that had become her trademark. It wasn't as if the employees were being over paid, compared to top management's 700:1 income disparity ratio. Most employees just scraped by, as was evident by the company's high employee turnover rates. But Zara's turnover rate had always been low.

Todd could not definitively say whether Zara was stealing. He did know there were some cash purchases that were not recorded properly. However Zara was officially getting the money, whether through theft or simply by "keeping the change" the customers gave her for purchases, he knew that because the funds were not listed as income, the extra "wages" to Zara's employees meant no payroll taxes were being withheld. This meant Jennings was at risk for a tax liability action by the IRS.

Todd thought about what to do. He looked through the company's ethics code, but found the guidelines vague. The code itself only spanned two pages and did not provide any contact information for him to ask questions. Todd murmured under his breath, "Why did I start this mess? I should have left things alone." He knew nothing at a company is secret for long and his questions would soon alert others to start asking questions. On the other hand, he knew this had gone on for quite some time. Why had nobody noticed before?

QUESTIONS | EXERCISES

1. Describe some of the weaknesses in Jennings' ethics program.
2. Discuss the alternatives for Todd.
3. How has Zara been given the opportunity to engage in misconduct?

*This case is strictly hypothetical; any resemblance to real persons, companies, or situations is coincidental.

Programs designed to foster ethical decision making in business are controversial today because much unethical and illegal business conduct continues to occur even in organizations that have adopted such programs. Enron, BP, and JP Morgan are examples of organizations with codes of ethics that experienced ethical disasters. Many business leaders believe ethics initiatives should arise naturally from a company's corporate culture and that simply hiring good employees limits unethical conduct. Moreover, business executives and board members often do not understand how organizational ethics can be systematically implemented. In business, many ethical issues are complex and require organizations to reach a consensus on appropriate action. Top executives and boards of directors must provide the leadership and a system to resolve these issues. Legislation and regulatory rules require leadership to create and implement effective ethics programs. These requirements come into play when misconduct is investigated by the government. We believe customized ethics and compliance programs assist businesses to provide guidance so employees from diverse backgrounds understand what behaviors are acceptable (and unacceptable) within the organization.

Business ethics programs have the potential to help top managers establish an ethical culture and eliminate the opportunity for unethical conduct. This chapter provides a framework for developing an ethics program consistent with research, best practices, and the decision-making process described in Chapter 5, as well as with the Federal Sentencing Guidelines for Organizations (FSGO), the Sarbanes–Oxley Act, and the Dodd–Frank Act described in Chapter 4. These legislative reforms require executives and boards of directors to assume responsibility and ensure ethical standards are properly implemented on a daily basis.

In this chapter, we first examine the corporation as a social entity, then provide an overview of why businesses need to develop organizational ethics programs. Next, we consider the factors that must be incorporated in such a program: a code of conduct, an ethics officer and the appropriate delegation of authority, an effective ethics-training program, a system for monitoring and supporting ethical compliance, and continual efforts to improve the ethics program. Finally, we consider common mistakes in designing and implementing ethics programs.

THE RESPONSIBILITY OF THE CORPORATION AS A MORAL AGENT

Increasingly, corporations are viewed not merely as profit-making entities but also as moral agents accountable for their conduct to their stakeholders, including employees, investors, suppliers, governments, and customers. Companies are more than the sum of their parts or participants. Because corporations are chartered as citizens of a state and/or nation, they generally have the same rights and responsibilities as individuals. Through legislation and court precedents, society holds companies accountable for the conduct of their employees as well as for their decisions and the consequences of those decisions. Coverage in the news media of specific issues such as employee benefits, executive compensation, defective products, competitive practices, and financial reporting contributes to a firm's reputation as a moral agent.

As moral agents, companies are required to obey the laws and regulations that define acceptable business conduct. However, it is important to acknowledge they are not human beings who can think through moral issues. Because companies are not human, laws and

FIGURE 8–1 Most Common Employee Observed Forms of Misconduct at Fortune 500© Companies

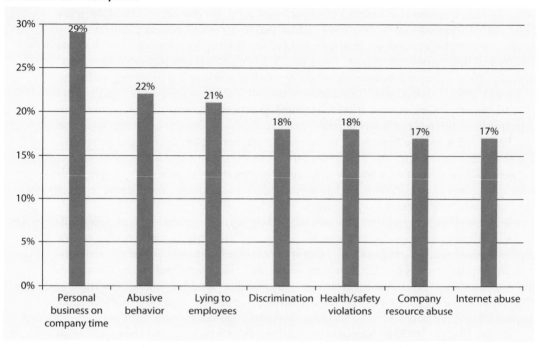

Source: Ethics Resource Center, *National Business Ethics Survey®* of Fortune *500®* Employees: An Investigation into the State of Ethics at America's Most Powerful Companies (Arlington, VA: Ethics Resource Center, 2012).

regulations are necessary to provide formal structural restraints and guidance. Employees have a moral obligation to responsibly think through complex ethical issues to contribute to the ethical conduct of the corporation as a whole.[1] Figure 8–1 illustrates the most commonly observed forms of misconduct at Fortune 500® corporations. The key reason why people seem to engage in misconduct is they feel pressured to do "whatever it takes to meet business targets."

Though obviously not a person, a corporation can be considered a moral agent in society created to perform specific social functions. It is therefore responsible to society for its actions. Because corporations have characteristics of agents, responsibility for ethical behavior is assigned to them as legal entities, as well as to individuals or work groups they employ. A corporate culture without values and appropriate communication about ethics can facilitate individual misconduct. Some corporate outcomes cannot be tied to one individual or group, and misconduct can be the result of a collective pattern of decisions supported by a corporate culture. Therefore, corporations can be held accountable when they are found to be operating in a manner inconsistent with major legal requirements. Large fines and negative publicity have put many companies out of business. On the other hand, companies selected as top corporate citizens, including American Express, Salesforce.com, Kellogg Company, and Kimberly-Clark, receive awards and recognition for being responsible moral agents.[2]

In many cases, a coherent ethical corporate culture does not evolve through independent individual and interpersonal relationships. Although ethics is often viewed as an individual matter, many believe the best way to develop an ethical corporate culture is to provide character education to existing employees or hire individuals with good character and sensitize them to ethical issues. This theory assumes ethical conduct develops through company-wide agreement and consensus. Although these assumptions are laudable and contain some truth, companies that are responsible for most of the economic activity in the world employ thousands of culturally diverse individuals who will never reach agreement on all ethical issues. Many ethical business issues are complex close calls, and the only way to ensure consistent decisions that represent the interests of all stakeholders is to require ethical policies. This chapter provides support for the idea that implementing a centralized corporate ethics program can provide a cohesive, internally consistent set of statements and policies representing the corporation as a moral agent.

THE NEED FOR ORGANIZATIONAL ETHICS PROGRAMS

To understand why companies need to develop ethics programs, judge whether each of the following actions is unethical versus illegal.

- You want to skip work to go to a baseball game, but you need a doctor's excuse. You make up symptoms so that your insurance company pays for the doctor's visit. (unethical, illegal)

- While having a latte at a local café, you run into an acquaintance who works as a salesperson for a competing firm. You wind up chatting about future product prices. When you get back to your office, you tell your supervisor what you heard. (unethical, illegal)

- You are fired from your company, but before leaving for a position with another company, you copy a confidential list of client names and telephone numbers you compiled for your former employer. (unethical, illegal)

- You receive a loan from your parents to make the down payment on your first home, but when describing the source of the down payment on the mortgage application, you characterize it as a gift. (unethical, illegal)

- Your manager asks you to book some sales revenue from the next quarter into this quarter's sales report to help the firm reach target sales figures. You agree to do so. (unethical, illegal)

You probably labeled one or more of these five scenarios as unethical rather than illegal. The reality is all of them have the potential to be illegal. You may have chosen incorrectly because it is nearly impossible to know every detail of the highly complex laws relevant to these situations. Consider that there are 10,000 laws and regulations associated with the processing and selling of a single hamburger. Unless you are a lawyer specializing in a particular area, it is difficult to know every law associated with your job. However, you can become more sensitized to what might be unethical or, in these cases, illegal. One reason ethics programs are required in one form or another is to sensitize employees to the potential legal and ethical issues within their work environments. Studies show ethics programs can increase employees' ethical awareness, participation in ethical decision making, and ethical behavior.[3]

As previously discussed, ethics scandals in U.S. businesses have destroyed employees' trust in top management and significantly lowered the public's trust of business. Even highly respected individuals such as government officials or doctors have seen trust diminish. The Department of Justice alleged GlaxoSmithKline (GSK) paid celebrity physician Dr. Drew, who at the time hosted his own radio show, $275,000 to talk about the drug Wellbutrin. It is not illegal for a doctor to endorse a product, but the endorser must disclose the relationship. GSK paid $3 billion to resolve allegations it used paid experts to market pharmaceuticals for purposes not approved by the Food and Drug Administration.[4]

Pepsi CEO Indra Nooyi believes all businesses are challenged to restore consumer confidence and trust. She stated that rebuilding trust will "require all companies to think again about what they do to build trust, and to think again about how they make, give, and add value."[5] Understanding the factors that influence the ethical decision-making process, as discussed in Chapter 5, can help companies encourage ethical behavior and discourage undesirable conduct. Fostering ethical decision making within an organization requires terminating unethical employees and improving the firm's ethical standards. Consider the "bad apple–bad barrel" analogy. Some people are simply "bad apples" who will always do things in their self-interest regardless of their organization's goals or accepted standards of conduct.[6] For example, Raj Rajaratnam, co-founder of the hedge fund Galleon Group, allegedly used a "corrupt network" of consultants to make illegal profits. According to prosecutors, Rajaratnam and employees at Galleon Group engaged in insider trading on over 35 stocks, generating $45 million in profits. The corporate culture at Galleon Group appears to have promoted illegal behavior simply as a way of doing business.[7] Eliminating bad apples through screening techniques and enforcement of a firm's ethical standards can improve the firm's overall behavior.[8]

Organizations can also become "bad barrels," not because individuals are bad, but the pressures to succeed create opportunities that reward unethical decisions. In the case of bad barrels, firms must redesign their image and culture to conform to industry and social standards of acceptable behavior.[9] Most companies attempt to improve ethical decision making by establishing and implementing a strategic approach to improving their organizations' ethics. Companies as diverse as Texas Instruments, Starbucks, Ford Motor Co., and Whole Foods have adopted a strategic approach to organizational ethics. They continuously monitor their programs and make adjustments when problems occur.

To promote legal and ethical conduct, an organization should develop a program by establishing, communicating, and monitoring the ethical values and legal requirements that characterize its history, culture, industry, and operating environment. Without such programs, uniform standards, and policies of conduct, it is difficult for employees to determine what behaviors are acceptable within a company. As discussed in Chapter 6 and 7, in the absence of such programs and standards, employees generally make decisions based on their own observations of how their coworkers and superiors behave. A strong ethics program includes a written code of conduct; an ethics officer to oversee the program; careful delegation of authority; formal ethics training; and rigorous auditing, monitoring, enforcement, and revision of program standards. Without a strong program, problems are likely to occur. For example, despite laws protecting intellectual property in China, weak compliance programs have created piracy problems for businesses. Microsoft and other companies in the Business Software Alliance estimate almost 80 percent of software for personal computers in China is pirated material. However, top officials in China's government in charge of combating copyright violations claim this number is distorted.[10]

Although there are no universal standards that can be applied to organizational ethics programs, most companies develop codes, values, or policies to provide guidance on business conduct. The American Institute of CPAs Professional Code of Conduct, for instance, is more than 400 pages and covers areas such as accounting principles, responsibilities to different stakeholders, and principles for professional conduct.[11] It would be naïve to think simply having a code of ethics solves all the ethical dilemmas a company might face.[12] Indeed, most of the companies that have experienced ethical and legal difficulties in recent years had formal ethics codes and programs. The problem is top managers have not integrated these codes, values, and standards into their firms' corporate cultures where they can provide effective guidance for daily decision making. High-status officials may be more inclined to engage in unethical organizational conduct because social isolation can create insensitivity and a lower motivation to regulate ethical decision making.[13] Top managers tend to focus on financial performance because their jobs and personal identities are often intimately connected to their firms' quarterly returns. A culture of short-term performance as a company's highest priority can diminish ethical decision making. On the other hand, Warren Buffett's Berkshire Hathaway corporations, such as Burlington Northern Santa Fe and GEICO, are not subject to Wall Street's quarterly returns and can focus on an unusual commitment to long-run performance and responsible conduct.[14]

If a company's leadership fails to provide the vision and support needed for ethical conduct, then an ethics program will not be effective. Ethics is not something to be delegated to lower-level employees. To satisfy the public's escalating demands for ethical decision making companies need to develop plans and structures for addressing ethical considerations. Some directions for improving ethics are mandated through regulations, but companies must be willing to put in place a system for implementing values and ethics that exceeds the minimum requirements.

AN EFFECTIVE ETHICS PROGRAM

Throughout this book, we emphasize that ethical issues are at the forefront of organizational concerns as managers and employees face increasingly complex decisions. These decisions are often made in a group environment composed of different value systems, competitive pressures, and political concerns that contribute to the opportunity for misconduct. The more misconduct occurs at a company, the less trust employees feel toward the organization—and the greater the turnover will likely be. A Deloitte LLP Ethics & Workplace survey indicated 48 percent of employee respondents who were looking for a new job cited a loss of workplace trust as the primary reason for their departure. About 40 percent indicated unethical treatment as the reason.[15] When opportunities to engage in unethical conduct abound, companies are vulnerable to ethical problems and legal violations if their employees do not know how to make the right decisions.

A company must have an effective ethics program to ensure all employees understand its values and comply with the policies and codes of conduct. If the culture encourages unethical conduct, then misconduct is likely to occur even if the company has ethical guidelines in place. Consider that a French court sentenced a Société Générale trader to three years in prison for his role in one of the world's biggest trading scandals. The trader and his lawyers claimed the company ignored red flags because the trader made the company so much money. Even the bank admitted it shared some of the responsibility for the misconduct.[16]

Because we come from diverse business, educational, and family backgrounds, it cannot be assumed we know how to behave appropriately when we enter a new organization or job. The pharmaceutical company Merck requires all employees to be responsible for supporting its Code of Business Conduct that is available in 26 languages. Employees take classes in ethics to help them understand how to resolve ethical dilemmas in the workplace, as well as receiving online training to raise their awareness of ethical issues and assist them in maintaining an ethical organizational culture.[17] According to a fraud survey, 66 percent of executives feel inadequate ethics and compliance programs are the reason for much of the unchecked misconduct in business.[18] It would therefore appear that the creation of effective ethics programs like Merck's Code of Business Conduct acts as important deterrents to organizational misconduct.

An Ethics Program Can Help Avoid Legal Problems

As mentioned in Chapter 7, some corporate cultures provide opportunities for or reward unethical conduct because management is not sufficiently concerned about ethics or the company failed to comply with the minimum requirements of the Federal Sentencing Guidelines for Organizations (FSGO) (Table 8–1). Companies may face penalties and the loss of public confidence if one of their employees breaks the law. The FSGO encourages companies to assess their key risk areas and customize a compliance program to address these risks and satisfy key effectiveness criteria. An effective risk assessment involves not only examining legal issues but also environmental, health and safety, and other risk areas. Companies should prioritize and weigh these risks based on their potential impact on the organization. Firms can then use these risk assessments to change or update internal control mechanisms. It is also important to monitor and weigh the risks of third-party suppliers and/or business partners since a company can be damaged by misconduct that occurs in the supply chain.

Guidelines also hold companies responsible for the misconduct of their employees. Indeed, an Ernst & Young global survey of 1,758 CFOs and heads of internal audit, legal, and compliance divisions in major corporations revealed that while instances of fraud are rising in some regions, reported fraud in the United States has been decreasing. Figure 8–2 shows the percentage of CFOs who find it acceptable for their companies to engage in questionable practices to retain or procure business. About 39 percent of global respondents stated that corruption occurs frequently in their countries. Another 52 percent of respondents believe that boards of directors should have a better understanding of the business if they are to adequately prepare against corruption and other ethical risks.[19] Ethics programs that provide guidelines outlining board responsibilities encourage compliance at the highest levels of the organization.

At the heart of the FSGO is a "carrot-and-stick" philosophy. Companies that act to prevent misconduct by establishing and enforcing ethical and legal compliance programs may receive a "carrot" and avoid penalties should a violation occur. The ultimate

TABLE 8–1 Minimum Requirements for Ethics and Compliance Programs

1. Standards and procedures, such as codes of ethics, that are reasonably capable of detecting and preventing misconduct

2. High-level personnel who are responsible for an ethics and compliance program

3. No substantial discretionary authority given to individuals with a propensity for misconduct

4. Standards and procedures communicated effectively via ethics training programs

5. Systems to monitor, audit, and report misconduct

6. Consistent enforcement of standards, codes, and punishment

7. Continuous improvement of the ethics and compliance program

Source: Based on U.S. Sentencing Commission, *Federal Sentencing Guidelines Manual*, effective November 1, 2004 (St. Paul, MN: West, 2008).

"stick" is the possibility of being fined or put on probation if convicted of a crime. Organizational probation involves using on-site consultants to observe and monitor a company's legal compliance efforts as well as to report the company's progress toward avoiding misconduct to the U.S. Sentencing Commission. Table 8–2 shows the fines the Securities and Exchange Commission has levied against well-known firms for corporate misconduct. Conversely, it is important for organizations to consider incentives for employees who do act according to ethical standards. Recently updated Foreign

FIGURE 8–2 Which, If Any, of the Following do Global CFOs Feel Justified if They Help a Business Survive an Economic Downturn?

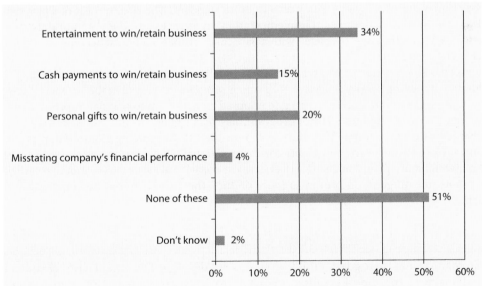

Source: Ernst & Young, *Growing Beyond: a place for integrity—12th Global Fraud Survey*, http://www.ey.com/Publication/vwLUAssets/Global-Fraud-Survey-a-place-for-integrity-12th-Global-Fraud-Survey/$FILE/EY-12th-GLOBAL-FRAUD-SURVEY.pdf (accessed May 6, 2013).

TABLE 8-2 Penalties for Corporate Misconduct

Company	Penalty	Reason
WorldCom	$750 million	Accounting fraud
Goldman Sachs	$550 million	Misleading investors
Fannie Mae	$400 million	Accounting fraud
Time Warner	$300 million	Accounting fraud
J.P. Morgan Securities	$296.9 million	Misleading investors
Qwest	$250 million	Accounting fraud
Charles Schwab	$118 million	Misleading investors
Bank of America	$150 million	Misleading investors

Source: Matt Phillips, "SEC's Greatest Hits: Biggest Penalties. Ever." *The Wall Street Journal*, July 16, 2010, http://blogs.wsj.com/marketbeat/2010/07/16/secs-greatest-hits-some-of-the-other-biggest-penalties/(accessed May 6, 2013); Melanie Waddell, "SEC's 16 Biggest Penalties Since Financial Crisis," *AdvisorOne*, January 24, 2013, http://www.advisorone.com/2013/01/24/secs-16-biggest-penalties-since-financial-crisis?t=risk-management&page=2 (accessed May 6, 2013).

Corrupt Practices Act guidelines recommend incorporating incentives into the firm's corporate culture to encourage ethical behavior.[20]

The FSGO encourages federal judges to increase fines for organizations that continually tolerate misconduct and to reduce or eliminate fines for firms with extensive compliance programs that make due diligence attempts to abide by legal and ethical standards. Until the guidelines were formulated, courts were inconsistent in holding corporations responsible for employee misconduct. There was no incentive to build effective programs to encourage employees to make ethical and legal decisions. Now companies earn credit for creating ethics programs that meet a rigorous standard. The effectiveness of a program is determined by its design and implementation. In other words, the program must deal effectively with the risks associated with a particular business and must become part of the corporate culture.

An ethics program can help a firm avoid civil liability, but the company still bears the burden of proving it has an effective program. A program developed in the absence of misconduct will be more effective than one imposed as a reaction to scandal or prosecution. A legal test of a company's ethics program may occur when an individual employee is charged with misconduct. The court system or the U.S. Sentencing Commission evaluates the organization's responsibility for the individual's behavior during the process of an investigation. If the courts find the company contributed to the misconduct or failed to show due diligence in preventing misconduct, then the firm may be convicted and sentenced.

Values Versus Compliance Programs

No matter what their goals, ethics programs are developed as organizational control systems, with the aim of creating predictability in employee behavior. Two types of control systems can be created. A compliance orientation creates order by requiring employees identify with and commit to specific required conduct. It uses legal terms, statutes, and contracts that teach employees the rules and penalties for noncompliance. The other system is a **values orientation**, which strives to develop shared values. Although penalties are attached, the focus is more on an abstract core of ideals such as accountability and commitment. Studies found that when personal and organizational values are compatible with one another, it tends to positively influence workplace ethics.[21]

The advantage of a values orientation is it gives employees a clearly defined basis on which to make decisions, one in which fairness, compassion, respect, and transparency is paramount. At the same time, diversity in employees' experience and personal values requires explicit communication and training on subject matter areas such as financial reporting, use of company resources, and intellectual property. Establishing compliance standards helps employees understand rules of conduct when there are identified risks. For example, rules on the recruiting and hiring of new employees will help enforce company policy and prevent legal violations. When there are new, unexpected, or ambiguous issues with no compliance requirements, values may help the employee navigate through the ethical issues at hand.

Research into compliance- and values-based approaches reveals both types of programs can interact or work toward the same end but a values orientation has the added benefit of sparking ethical reasoning among employees. Values-based programs increase employees' awareness of ethics at work, integrity, willingness to deliver information to supervisors, use of reporting mechanisms, and perception that ethical decisions are being made. Compliance-based programs are linked to employees' awareness of ethical risks at work and a clear understanding of rules and expectations that facilitates decision making. In the final analysis, both orientations can be used to help employees and managers; however, a values-based program is the foundation of an organizational ethical culture.

CODES OF CONDUCT

The perception of business accountability has changed over the years; expectations for organizational codes of ethics have grown. Today, society expects to see employees adhere to ethical principles and standards specified through company ethics programs.[22] Most companies begin the process of establishing organizational ethics programs by developing **codes of conduct**, or formal statements that describe what an organization expects of its employees. Such statements may take three different forms: a code of ethics, a code of conduct, and a statement of values. A **code of ethics** is the most comprehensive and consists of general statements, sometimes altruistic or inspirational, that serve as principles and as the basis for rules of conduct. A code of ethics generally specifies methods for reporting violations, disciplinary action for violations, and a structure of due process. Table 8–3 describes some benefits of having a comprehensive code of conduct. A code of conduct is a written document that may contain some inspirational statements but mainly specifies acceptable and unacceptable types of behavior. A code of conduct is more akin to a regulatory set of rules and, as such, tends to elicit less debate about specific actions. Some of the key reasons that codes of ethics fail are (1) the code is not promoted and employees do not read it; (2) the code is not easily accessible; (3) the code is written too legalistically and therefore is not understandable by average employees; (4) the code is

DEBATE ISSUE
TAKE A STAND

Examining Banking and Insurance Companies' Codes of Conduct

The financial industry has been involved with significant misconduct. Much recent regulation, including the Dodd-Frank Act, is focused on protecting consumers and avoiding misconduct. Codes of conduct, sometimes referred to as codes of ethics, should provide behavioral expectations an organization maintains for its managers, employees, and agents. Section 406 of the Sarbanes-Oxley Act requires a code of ethics for financial officers. Recent research shows companies with a code of ethics for financial officers are more likely to restate their earnings voluntarily. The Ethisphere Institute developed a grade methodology for evaluating codes of conduct, using the criteria of public availability, tone from the top, readability and tone, non-retaliation and reporting, values and commitments, risk topics, comprehension aids, and presentation and style. Of the 25 companies evaluated in the banking industry, only two banks received a relatively high ranking. In the insurance industry, only two companies received above a C rating. It is interesting that in the banking industry, 19 of the 25 companies received an F for tone at the top, indicating a lack of communication from the CEO or Chairman of the Board. This seems to suggest that misconduct tends to occur more frequently in organizations with badly written codes of conduct.[24]

1. The Ethisphere Institute's analysis of banking and insurance codes of conduct explains why widespread misconduct has been so prevalent in the financial industry.

2. Written codes of conduct are only a small part of the ethical culture of a company and cannot by themselves explain why misconduct has been so widespread in the financial industry.

written too vaguely, providing no accurate direction; and (5) top management never refers to the code in body or spirit.[23]

The final type of ethical statement is a statement of values that serves the general public and also addresses distinct groups such as stakeholders. Values statements are conceived by management and are fully developed with input from all stakeholders. Despite the distinction made in this book between a code of ethics and a values statement, it is important to recognize these terms are often used interchangeably.

Regardless of its degree of comprehensiveness, a code of ethics should reflect upper managers' desires for compliance with the values, rules, and policies that support an ethical culture. The development of a code of ethics should involve the president, board of directors, and chief executive officers who will implement the code. Legal staff should also be called on to ensure the code has correctly assessed key areas of risk and provides buffers for potential legal problems. A code of ethics that does not address specific high-risk activities within the scope of daily operations is inadequate for maintaining standards that prevent misconduct. Table 8–4 shows factors to consider when developing and implementing a code of ethics.

Codes of ethics may address a variety of situations, from internal operations to sales presentations and financial disclosure practices. Research found that corporate codes of ethics often contain about six core values or principles in addition to more detailed descriptions and examples of appropriate conduct.[25] The six values that have been suggested as being desirable for codes of ethics are (1) trustworthiness, (2) respect, (3) responsibility, (4) fairness, (5) caring, and (6) citizenship.[26] These values will not be effective without distribution, training, and the support of top management in making these values a part of the corporate culture. A study of 75 U.S. firms revealed that their codes of ethics were similar in content and the content was often vague.[27] This emphasizes the need for companies to develop codes that address issues common to their particular field or industry. Employees need specific examples of how these values can be implemented.

TABLE 8–3 Benefits of Having an Ethics Code

A Comprehensive Code of Conduct Can...
1. Guide employees in situations where the ethical course of action is not immediately obvious.
2. Help the company reinforce—and acquaint new employees with—its culture and values. A code can help create a climate of integrity and excellence.
3. Help the company communicate its expectations for its staff to suppliers, vendors, and customers.
4. Minimize subjective and inconsistent management standards.
5. Help a company remain in compliance with complex government regulations.
6. Build public trust and enhance business reputations.
7. Offer protection in preempting or defending against lawsuits.
8. Enhance morale, employee pride, loyalty, and the recruitment of outstanding employees.
9. Promote constructive social change by raising awareness of the community's needs and encouraging employees and other stakeholders to help.
10. Promote market efficiency, especially in areas where laws are weak or inefficient, by rewarding the best and most ethical producers of goods and services.

Source: "Ten Benefits of Having an Ethics Code," Josephson Institute Center for Business Ethics, http://josephsoninstitute.org/business/blog/2010/11/ten-benefits-of-having-an-ethics-code/(accessed March 14, 2010). Originally adapted from *Good Ideas for Creating a More Ethical and Effective Workplace.*

Research demonstrates that employees at organizations with effective ethical codes of conduct tend to be less tolerant of unethical behavior toward stakeholders than those at companies without ethical codes.[28] Codes of conduct will not resolve every ethical issue encountered in daily operations, but they help employees and managers deal with ethical dilemmas by prescribing or limiting specific activities. Many companies have a code of ethics, but it is not communicated effectively. A code placed on a website or in a training manual is useless if it is not reinforced every day. By communicating to employees both what is expected of them and what punishments they face if they violate the rules, codes of conduct curtail opportunities for unethical behavior and thereby improve ethical decision making. For example, the American Society for Civil Engineers' code of ethics

TABLE 8–4 Developing and Implementing a Code of Ethics

1. Consider areas of risk and state the values as well as conduct necessary to comply with laws and regulations. Values are an important buffer in preventing serious misconduct.
2. Identify values that specifically address current ethical issues.
3. Consider values that link the organization to a stakeholder orientation. Attempt to find overlaps in organizational and stakeholder values.
4. Make the code understandable by providing examples that reflect values.
5. Communicate the code frequently and in language that employees can understand.
6. Revise the code every year with input from organizational members and stakeholders.

© Cengage Learning

specifies that engineers must act with zero tolerance toward bribery, fraud, and corruption in all engineering and construction projects in which they are engaged.[29] Codes of conduct do not have to be so detailed they take into account every situation, but they should provide guidelines and principles capable of helping employees achieve organizational ethical objectives and address risks in an accepted way.

In Japan, Kao Corporation has gained recognition for its leading ethics programs. The company won numerous ethics awards as well as the Environmental Technology Award from the Japan Chemical Industry Association. Kao is also the only Japanese company included on *Ethisphere*'s World's Most Ethical Companies list for seven consecutive years. Kao is extremely focused on ethics and integrity. The company ensures its employees are provided with training in ethics and in the characteristics and cultures of other countries. Kao also created new ecofriendly products that save resources and are well-suited to areas like China, where water is scarce.[30] Ethics programs are essential in large corporations such as Kao Corporation. However, it is not only large companies that need to develop an ethics and compliance program; small companies need to do so as well.

ETHICS OFFICERS

Organizational ethics programs must have oversight by high-ranking persons known to respect legal and ethical standards. These individuals—often referred to as **ethics officers**— are responsible for managing their organizations' ethics and legal compliance programs. They are usually responsible for (1) assessing the needs and risks an organization-wide ethics program must address, (2) developing and distributing a code of conduct or ethics, (3) conducting training programs for employees, (4) establishing and maintaining a confidential service to answer employees' questions about ethical issues, (5) making sure the company is in compliance with government regulation, (6) monitoring and auditing ethical conduct, (7) taking action on possible violations of the company's code, and (8) reviewing and updating the code. Ethics officers are also responsible for knowing thousands of pages of relevant regulations as well as communicating and reinforcing values that build an ethical corporate culture. The Ethics Resource Center reports that having a comprehensive ethics program in place, one that includes an ethics officer, helps companies reduce incidences of misconduct by as much as 75 percent.[31] Corporate wrongdoings and scandal-grabbing headlines have a profound negative impact on public trust. To ensure compliance with state and federal regulations, many corporations are now appointing chief compliance officers and ethics and business conduct professionals to develop and oversee corporate compliance programs.[32]

The Ethics and Compliance Officer Association (ECOA) has over 1,200 members who are frontline managers of ethics programs in over 30 countries.[33] Ethics officers often move into their position from other jobs in their companies. Ethics and compliance officers have backgrounds in law, finance, and human resource management. Sarbanes–Oxley and the amendments to the FSGO increased the responsibility ethics officers and boards of directors have for oversight of financial reporting. Ethics officers' positions are still relatively new and somewhat ill-defined. Although tough economic times call all expenditures into question, economic uncertainty brings about the greatest need for an investment in and formalization of the ethics and compliance roles within an organization. Times of economic distress tend to generate significant organizational and individual wrongdoing.[34]

Although recommended as best practice, it is not common for ethics officers to report directly to the board of directors. Ethics officers often report directly to the chief executive officer and may have some access to the board. In a survey of chief financial officers, more than 30 percent indicated their operations had been impacted or disrupted by unexpected circumstances in the past year. Oversight, monitoring, and review of operating procedures and outcomes by the ethics and compliance function can prevent such surprises.[35]

ETHICS TRAINING AND COMMUNICATION

A major step in developing an effective ethics program is implementing a training program and communication system to educate employees about the firm's ethical standards. The National Business Ethics Survey looked at 18 dimensions of ethical culture and formal programs and found companies with strong ethical cultures and formal ethics programs were 36 percentage points less likely to observe misconduct than employees in organizations with weak cultures and ethics programs.[36] A significant number of employees report they frequently find such training useful. Training can educate employees about the firm's policies and expectations, relevant laws and regulations, and general social standards. Training programs can also make employees aware of available resources, support systems, and designated personnel who can assist them with ethical and legal advice. Training can empower employees to ask tough questions and make ethical decisions. Many organizations are now incorporating ethics training into their employee and management development training efforts. The American Bar Association adopted six new proposals for its Model Rules of Professional Conduct dealing with issues such as client confidentiality protection when using technology and outsourcing.[37] Governments often mandate training for officials as well. For example, employees working for the National Institutes of Health must undergo annual ethics training.[38]

As we emphasized in Chapters 5 and 7, ethical decision making is influenced by corporate culture, coworkers and supervisors, and the opportunities available to engage in unethical behavior. Ethics training can impact all three types of influence. Full awareness of a company's philosophy of management, rules, and procedures can strengthen both the corporate culture and the ethical stance of peers and supervisors. Such awareness, too, arms employees against opportunities for unethical behavior and lessens the likelihood of misconduct. Thus, the existence and enforcement of company rules and procedures limit unethical practices in the organization. If adequately and thoughtfully designed, ethics training can make employees aware of ethical issues, increase the importance of ethics training to employees, and increase employees' confidence they can make the correct decision when faced with an ethical dilemma.[39] If ethics training is to be effective, it must start with a theoretical foundation based on values, a code of ethics, procedures for airing ethical concerns, line and staff involvements, and clear executive priorities on ethics, all of which must be communicated to employees. Managers from every department must be involved in the development of an ethics training program. Training and communication initiatives should reflect the unique characteristics of an organization: its size, culture, values, management style, and employee base. To be successful, business ethics programs should educate employees about formal ethical frameworks and models for analyzing business ethics issues. Then employees can base ethical decisions on their knowledge of choices rather than on emotions.

A key component of managing an effective and efficient ethics and compliance program is a firm grasp of techniques that clearly communicate the company's values, culture, and policies for dealing with ethical issues to employees. Many feel "hands on" training when employees are forced to confront actual or hypothetical ethical dilemmas helps them understand how their organization would like them to deal with potential problems. Lockheed Martin, for example, developed training games that include dilemmas that can be resolved in teams. Each team member offers his or her perspective, thereby helping other team members fully understand the ramifications of a decision for coworkers and the organization.

Another training device is the behavioral simulation, which gives participants a short, hypothetical ethical issue situation to review. Each participant is assigned a role within a hypothetical organization and provided with varying levels of information about the scenario. Participants must then interact to develop recommended courses of action representing short-term, mid-term, and long-term considerations. Such simulations recreate the complexities of organizational relationships as well as the realities of having to address difficult situations with incomplete information. These exercises help participants gain awareness of the ethical, legal, and social dimensions of business decision making; develop analytical skills for resolving ethical issues; and gain exposure to the complexity of ethical decision making in organizations. Research indicates "the simulation not only instructs on the importance of ethics but on the processes for managing ethical concerns and conflict."[40]

Top executives must communicate with managers at the operations level (in production, sales, and finance, for instance) and enforce overall ethical standards within the organization. Table 8–5 lists the goals for successful ethics training. Making employees aware of the key risk areas for their occupation or profession is of major importance in any ethics training program. In addition, employees need to know whom to contact for guidance when they encounter gray areas in the organization's values, rules, policies, and training that do not provide adequate direction. On the other hand, firms that provide employees with the ability to voice their opinions but do not take their recommendations seriously can increase intra-group conflict.[41] It is therefore necessary for companies to display a strong commitment for communication and feedback mechanisms within the organization.

TABLE 8–5 Key Goals of Successful Ethics Training Programs

1. Identify key risk areas employees will face.

2. Provide experience in dealing with hypothetical or disguised ethical issues within the industry through mini-cases, online challenges, DVDs, or other experiential learning opportunities.

3. Let employees know wrongdoing will never be supported in the organization and employee evaluations will take their conduct in this area into consideration.

4. Let employees know they are individually accountable for their behavior.

5. Align employee conduct with organizational reputation and branding.

6. Provide ongoing feedback to employees about how they are handling ethical issues.

7. Allow a mechanism for employees to voice their concerns that is anonymous, but provides answers to key questions (24-hour hotlines).

8. Provide a hierarchy of leadership for employees to contact when they are faced with an ethical dilemma they do not know how to resolve.

Although training and communication should reinforce values and provide employees with opportunities to learn about rules, they represent just one aspect of an effective ethics program. Moreover, ethics training will be ineffective if conducted solely because it is required or because it is something competing firms are doing. Enron had an ethics program in place. However, unethical executives knew they had the support of Arthur Andersen, the firm's auditing and accounting consulting partner, as well as that of law firms, investment analysts, and in some cases, government regulators. Enron's top managers therefore probably believed that efforts to hide debt in off-balance-sheet partnerships would not be exposed.

When measuring the effectiveness of an ethics program, it is important to get input from employees. Employee surveys and the incorporation of ethics measurements in performance appraisal systems are two ways to help determine the effectiveness of a firm's ethics training. If ethical performance is not a part of regular performance appraisals, employees get the message that ethics is not an important component of decision making in their company. For ethics training to make a difference, employees must understand why it is conducted, how it fits into the organization, and what their own role in implementing it is.

SYSTEMS TO MONITOR AND ENFORCE ETHICAL STANDARDS

An effective ethics program employs a variety of resources to monitor ethical conduct and measure the program's effectiveness. Observing employees, conducting internal audits and investigations, circulating surveys, and instituting reporting systems are ways a company can assess compliance with its ethical code and standards. An external audit and review of company activities may sometimes be helpful in developing benchmarks of compliance. (We examine the process of ethical auditing in Chapter 9.)

To determine if a person is performing his or her job adequately and ethically, observers might focus on how the employee handles an ethically charged situation. Many businesses employ role-playing exercises when they train salespeople and managers. Ethical issues can be introduced into the discussion, and the results can be videotaped so participants and their superiors can evaluate the outcome of the ethics dilemma.

Questionnaires can serve as benchmarks in an ongoing assessment of ethical performance by measuring employees' ethical perceptions of their company, their superiors, their coworkers, and themselves, as well as serving as a means of developing ratings of ethical or unethical practices within their firm and industry. Then, if unethical conduct appears to be increasing, management will have a better understanding of what types of unethical practices may be occurring and why. A change in the company's ethics training may then be necessary.

The existence of an internal system that allows employees to report misconduct is especially useful for monitoring and evaluating ethical performance. Many companies set up ethics assistance lines, also known as hotlines, to provide support and give employees the opportunity to ask questions or report concerns. The most effective ethics hotlines operate on an anonymous basis and are supported 24 hours a day, 365 days a year. Approximately 50 percent of hotline calls occur at night or on the weekends. Many times troubling ethical issues can cause people to lose sleep and occupy their thoughts during their free time.[42] Although there is always some concern employees may misreport a situation or abuse a hotline to retaliate against a coworker, hotlines have become widespread and employees do use them. An easy-to-use hotline or help desk can serve as a safety net that increases the chance of detecting and responding to unethical conduct in a timely manner. Hotlines serve as a central contact point where critical comments, dilemmas, and advice can be assigned to the person most appropriate for handling a specific case.[43] Employees often prefer to deal with ethical issues through their supervisors or managers or resolve the matter directly before using an anonymous reporting system such as a hotline.[44]

Companies are increasingly using consultants that provide professional case-management services and software. Software is becoming popular because it provides reports of employee concerns, complaints, or observations of misconduct that can be tracked and managed. Thus the company can track investigations, analysis, resolutions, and documentation of misconduct reports. This system helps prevent lawsuits and helps a company learn about and analyze ethical lapses. However, it is important for companies to choose the right software for their needs. Although only 10 to 15 percent of companies currently use some type of compliance management tool, many companies are moving toward the automated process technology and software provide.

If a company is not making progress toward creating and maintaining an ethical culture, it needs to determine why and take corrective action, either by enforcing current standards more strictly or setting higher standards. Corrective action may involve rewarding employees who comply with company policies and standards and punishing those who do not. When employees abide by organizational standards, their efforts should be acknowledged through public recognition, bonuses, raises, or some other means. On the other hand, when employees violate organizational standards, they must be reprimanded, transferred, docked, suspended, or even fired. If a firm fails to take corrective action against unethical or illegal behavior, the inappropriate behavior is likely to continue. In the Ethics Resource Center Survey, the biggest reason employees gave for not reporting observed misconduct was they were skeptical their report would make a difference. The second most common reason was fear of retaliation.[45] However, new laws and court rulings are making it more difficult for businesses to engage in retaliation. The Supreme Court ruled an employee can sue if a close associate or relative is fired by an employer in retaliation for reporting misconduct such as discrimination.[46]

Consistent enforcement and necessary disciplinary action are essential to a functional ethics or compliance program. The ethics officer is usually responsible for implementing all disciplinary actions for violations of the firm's ethical standards. Many companies are including ethical compliance in employee performance evaluations. During performance evaluations, employees may be asked to sign an acknowledgment that they have read the company's current ethics guidelines. The company must also promptly investigate any known or suspected misconduct. The appropriate company official, usually the ethics officer, needs to make a recommendation to senior management on how to deal with a particular ethical infraction. In some cases, a company may be required to report substantiated misconduct to a designated government or regulatory agency so as to receive credit. Under the FSGO, such credit for having an effective compliance program can reduce fines.[47]

Efforts to deter unethical behavior are important to companies' long-term relationships with their employees, customers, and community. If the code of ethics is aggressively enforced and becomes part of the corporate culture, it can effectively improve ethical behavior within an organization. If a code is not properly enforced, however, it becomes mere window dressing and will accomplish little toward improving ethical behavior and decision making.

Continuous Improvement of an Ethics Program

Improving a system that encourages employees to make more ethical decisions differs little from implementing any other type of business strategy. Implementation requires designing activities to achieve organizational objectives using available resources and given existing constraints. Implementation translates a plan for action into operational terms and establishes a means by which an organization's ethical performance will be monitored, controlled, and improved. Figure 8–3 indicates global organizations are more likely to engage in corporate responsibility reporting as they grow larger. This fact is in part due to increased resources, but also undoubtedly to increased stakeholder responsibilities and liabilities.

A firm's ability to plan and implement ethical business standards depends in part on how it structures resources and activities to achieve its ethical objectives. People's attitudes and behavior must be guided by a shared commitment to the business rather than by mere obedience to traditional managerial authority. Encouraging diversity of perspectives, disagreement, and the empowerment of people helps align the company's leadership with its employees.

If a company determines its ethical performance has been less than satisfactory, executives may want to change how certain kinds of decisions are made. For example, a decentralized organization may need to centralize key decisions, at least for a time, so upper managers can ensure these decisions are made in an ethical manner. Centralization may reduce the opportunities lower-level managers and employees have to make unethical decisions. Executives can then focus on initiatives for improving the corporate culture and infusing more ethical values throughout the firm by rewarding positive behavior and sanctioning negative behavior. In other companies, decentralizing important decisions may be a better way to attack ethical problems so lower-level managers who are familiar with the local business environment and local culture and values can make more decisions.

FIGURE 8–3 **Larger Companies Engage More in Corporate Responsibility Reporting**

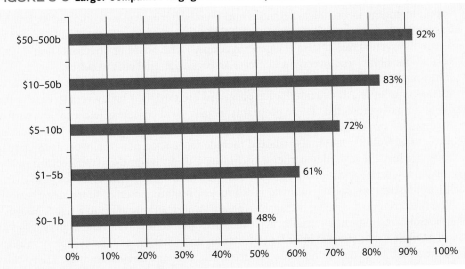

Research performed on 3,400 global companies, including the world's largest 250 companies

Source: KPMG International Corporate Responsibility Reporting Survey, 2011, http://www.kpmg.com/Global/en/IssuesAndInsights/ArticlesPublications/corporate-responsibility/Documents/2011-survey.pdf (accessed May 6, 2013).

Whether the ethics function is centralized or decentralized, the key need is to delegate authority in such a way that the organization can achieve ethical performance.

Common Mistakes in Designing and Implementing an Ethics Program

Many business leaders recognize they need to have an ethics program, but few take the time to answer fundamental questions about the goals of such a program. As we mentioned previously, some of the most common program objectives are to deter and detect unethical behavior as well as violations of the law; to gain competitive advantages through improved relationships with customers, suppliers, and employees; and, especially for multinational corporations, to link employees through a unifying and shared corporate culture. Failure to understand and appreciate these goals is the first mistake many firms make when designing ethics programs.

A second mistake is not setting realistic and measurable program objectives. Once a consensus on objectives is reached, companies should solicit input through interviews, focus groups, and survey instruments. Finding out how employees might react in a particular situation can help companies better understand how to correct unethical or illegal behavior either reactively or proactively. Research suggests employees and senior managers often know they are doing something unethical but rationalize their behavior as being "for the good of the company." As a result, ethics program objectives should contain some elements that are measurable.[48]

The third mistake is senior management's failure to take ownership of the ethics program. Maintaining an ethical culture may be impossible if CEOs and other top officers do not support an ethical culture. As discussed earlier in this chapter, upper-level managers, including chief financial officers and chief marketing officers, may have greater insensitivity to the needs of all stakeholders because of the pressure they feel for financial performance. Top managers may be more vulnerable to pressures placed on them to push employees to engage in unethical activities and thereby become more competitive. It is for this reason that recent amendments to the FSGO suggest ethics officers should report to the board of directors rather than the general counsel. The board of directors should have ultimate responsibility and oversight to create an organizational ethical culture.

The fourth mistake is developing program materials that do not address the needs of the average employee. Many compliance programs are designed by lawyers to ensure the company is legally protected. These programs usually yield complex "legalese" few within the organization can understand. To avoid this problem, ethics programs—including codes of conduct and training materials—should include feedback from employees from across the firm, not just the legal department. Including a question-and-answer section in the program; referencing additional resources for guidance on key ethical issues; and using checklists, illustrations, and even cartoons can make program materials more user-friendly.

The fifth common mistake is transferring an "American" program to a firm's international operations. In multinational firms, executives should involve overseas personnel as early as possible in the process in order to foster an understanding of the company's values and to minimize potential for misconduct stemming from misunderstandings. These aims can be accomplished by developing an inventory of common global management practices and processes and examining the corporation's standards of conduct in light of these international standards.

A final common mistake is designing an ethics program that is little more than a series of lectures. In such cases, participants typically recall less than 15 percent the day after the training. A more practical solution is to allow employees to practice the skills they learn through case studies or small-group exercises.

A firm cannot succeed solely by taking a legalistic compliance approach to ethics. Top managers must seek to develop high ethical standards that serve as barriers to illegal conduct. Although an ethics program should help reduce the possibility of penalties and negative public reaction to misconduct, a company must want to be a good corporate citizen and recognize the importance of ethics to success in business.

SUMMARY

Ethics programs help sensitize employees to potential legal and ethical issues within their work environments. To promote ethical and legal conduct, organizations should develop ethics programs, establishing, communicating, and monitoring ethical values and legal requirements that characterize the firms' history, culture, industry, and operating environment. Without such programs and uniform standards and policies of conduct, it is difficult for employees to determine what behaviors a company deems acceptable.

A company must have an effective ethics program to ensure employees understand its values and comply with its policies and codes of conduct. An ethics program should help reduce the possibility of legally enforced penalties and negative public reaction to misconduct. The main objective of the Federal Sentencing Guidelines for Organizations is to encourage companies to assess risk and then self-monitor and aggressively work to deter unethical acts and punish unethical employees. Ethics programs are organizational control systems that create predictability in employee behavior. These control systems may have a compliance orientation, which uses legal terms, statutes, and contracts that teach employees the rules and the penalties for noncompliance, or a values orientation that consists of developing shared values.

Most companies begin the process of establishing organizational ethics programs by developing codes of conduct, or formal statements that describe what an organization expects of its employees. Codes of conduct include a company's code of ethics and/or its statement of values. A code of ethics must be developed as part of senior management's desire to ensure the company complies with values, rules, and policies that support an ethical culture. Without uniform policies and standards, employees have difficulty determining what qualifies as acceptable behavior in the company.

Having a high-level manager or committee responsible for an ethical compliance program can significantly enhance its administration and oversight. Such ethics officers are usually responsible for assessing the needs and risks to be addressed in an organization-wide ethics program, developing and distributing a code of conduct or ethics, conducting training programs for employees, establishing and maintaining a confidential service to answer questions about ethical issues, making sure the company is complying with government regulations, monitoring and auditing ethical conduct, taking action on possible violations of the company's code, and reviewing and updating the code.

Successful ethics training is important in helping employees identify ethical issues and in providing them with the means to address and resolve such issues. Training can educate employees about the firm's policies and expectations, available resources, support systems, and designated ethics personnel, as well as relevant laws and regulations and general social standards. Top executives must communicate with managers at the operations level and enforce overall ethical standards within the organization.

An effective ethics program employs a variety of resources to monitor ethical conduct and measure the program's effectiveness. Compliance with the company's ethical code and standards can be assessed by observing employees, performing internal audits and surveys, instituting reporting systems, and conducting investigations, as well as through external audits and review, as needed. Corrective action involves rewarding employees who comply with company policies and standards and punishing those who do not. Consistent enforcement and disciplinary action are necessary for a functioning ethical compliance program.

Ethical compliance can be ensured by designing activities that achieve organizational objectives using available resources and given existing constraints. A firm's ability to plan and implement ethical business standards depends in part on its ability to structure resources and activities to achieve its objectives effectively and efficiently.

In implementing ethics and compliance programs many firms make common mistakes, including failing to answer fundamental questions about the goals of such programs, not setting realistic and measurable program objectives, failing to have senior management take ownership of the ethics program, developing program materials that do not address the needs of the average employee, transferring an "American" program to a firm's international operations, and designing an ethics program that is little more than a series of lectures. Although an ethics program should help reduce the possibility of penalties and negative public reaction to misconduct, a company must want to be a good corporate citizen and recognize the importance of ethics to successful business activities.

IMPORTANT TERMS FOR REVIEW

compliance orientation 222	code of conduct 223	statement of values 224
values orientation 223	code of ethics 223	ethics officers 226

RESOLVING ETHICAL BUSINESS CHALLENGES*

Mary, a recent college graduate from Stanford University, works for JSYK Incorporated, a realty company that represents clients interested in either buying or selling businesses. As a "business broker," Mary's job is to arrange sales just like a normal realtor. On the outskirts of town, a small building used for manufacturing sat idle for over a year. The realtors called it Moby Dick because no one could find a buyer for it; either the price was too high or the building did not quite match the buyer's needs. Dozens of potential buyers had come and gone. It did not help that the building was owned by Ted St. Clair, a 65-year-old miser that lived in the town all his life. The man had a reputation for hoarding every last dime. Ted made Dickens' Scrooge look saintly. While JSYK Incorporated told Ted more than once he needed to lower the price if he wanted to sell the building, Ted always refused.

One hot afternoon Reverend Smith, a retired minister, contacted JSYK and asked if he could look at the property. Because Mary was in the office it was given to her. While they inspected the building, the conversation came around to what Reverend Smith would do with the building. He had recently formed a nonprofit corporation to aid troubled youths and wanted to convert the building into a recreation center. Mary knew Reverend Smith because she formerly attended his church. She knew of his honesty and integrity as well as his decades of serving.

When Mary returned to the office, the Reverend was seriously talking about the building and how it could be refitted for his purposes. As they talked, the Reverend asked about the machinery still in the building. Some of the machines at the manufacturing plant were in poor condition and required an estimated $100,000 to repair. Reverend Smith had no use for them and would have them removed.

After preliminary discussions, Mary said she would contact the owner. "Reverend, I believe the seller is asking for a $250,000 down payment on this $1,000,000 sale."

"I can't afford that much," replied the Reverend. "I've been saving donations for a number of years and I only have $150,000."

"If I may ask," asked Mary, "How are you going to pay the balance?"

"Well, I've spoken to some older church members, and they told me that if I could make the down payment, they would cover the rest."

"I'll try to work with you on this. Give me a few days and I'll call you," said Mary.

As Reverend Smith left, George, the owner and CEO of JSYK, came into the office. "What did Reverend Smith want?" asked George.

"He's actually interested in Moby Dick, and I believe it matches his needs perfectly."

"That's great!" George replied. Then he noticed Mary's face. "So what's the problem?"

"You and I both know Ted will not come down on the price." Mary quickly explained the situation, with George listening intently. After she was done, George said, "Mary, this is what you are going to do. I want you to convince Ted that repairing those machines is important to the buyer. DO NOT tell him who it is. Tell Ted the buyer wants the machines, but the repair estimate he calculated is $150,000. Tell Ted you know you can get the buyer to buy if the down payment was reduced to $150,000 and the asking price to $950,000. Finally, tell Ted he would be making an additional $50,000 for not having to do the repairs."

"I don't know about this," said Mary. "It doesn't feel honest, and besides Reverend Smith has not approved the deal, nor do I believe he would want me to lie on his behalf."

George replied, "Mary, the Reverend is going to do something good with that building. You and I both know Ted will never get more than this. We're just helping him make the best deal possible."

Mary still was not certain. Although Ted was a miser, it did not feel right to lie. Besides, she wondered what Ted would do after he found out the Reverend had no use for the machines.

QUESTIONS | EXERCISES

1. How is top management supporting a culture of ethical or unethical behavior?
2. Discuss the alternatives and duties Mary has as a representative for both the buyer and seller.

3. If realtors have a code of ethics that requires truthful and transparent information, what should Mary tell George, the owner of JSKY?

*This case is strictly hypothetical; any resemblance to real persons, companies, or situations is coincidental.

> > > CHECK YOUR EQ

Check your EQ, or Ethics Quotient, by completing the following. Assess your performance to evaluate your overall understanding of the chapter material.

1. A compliance program should be deemed effective if it addresses the seven minimum requirements for ethical compliance programs. **Yes**   **No**

2. The accountability and responsibility for appropriate business conduct rests with top management. **Yes**   **No**

3. Ethical compliance can be measured by observing employees as well as through investigating and reporting mechanisms. **Yes**   **No**

4. The key goal of ethics training is to help employees identify ethical issues. **Yes**   **No**

5. An ethical compliance audit is designed to determine the effectiveness of ethics initiatives. **Yes**   **No**

ANSWERS 1. **No.** An effective compliance program has the seven elements of a compliance program in place and goes beyond those minimum requirements to determine what will work in a particular organization. 2. **Yes.** Executives in an organization determine the culture and initiatives that support ethical behavior. 3. **Yes.** Sometimes external monitoring is necessary, but internal monitoring and evaluation are the norm. 4. **No.** It is much more than that—it involves not only recognition but also an understanding of the values, culture, and rules in an organization as well as the impact of ethical decisions on the company. 5. **Yes.** It helps in establishing the code and in making program improvements.

ENDNOTES

1. Bob Lewis, "Survival Guide: The Moral Compass—Corporations Aren't Moral Agents, Creating Interesting Dilemmas for Business Leaders," *ACCESSmyLIBRARY*, March 11, 2002, http://www.accessmylibrary.com/article-1G1-84072220/survival-guide-moral-compass.html (accessed May 6, 2013).

2. Ethisphere Institute, "2013 World's Most Ethical Companies," *Ethisphere*, 2013, http://m1.ethisphere.com/wme2013/index.html (accessed May 6, 2013).

3. Itai Beeri, Rachel Dayan, Eran Vigoda-Gadot, and Simcha B. Werner, "Advancing Ethics in Public Organizations: The Impact of an Ethics Program on Employees' Perceptions and Behaviors in a Regional Council," *Journal of Business Ethics* 112 (2013): 59–78.

4. Matthew Herper, "Feds Say Dr. Drew Was Paid By Glaxo To Talk Up Antidepressant," *Forbes*, July 2, 2012, http://www.forbes.com/sites/matthewherper/2012/07/02/feds-say-dr-drew-was-paid-by-glaxo-to-talk-up-antidepressant/ (accessed May 6, 2013).

5. Indra Nooyi, "Business Has a Job to Do: Rebuild Trust," April 22, 2009, http://www.money.cnn.tv/2009/04/19/news/companies/nooyi.fortune/index.htm (accessed May 6, 2013).

6. Linda K. Trevino and Stuart Youngblood, "Bad Apples in Bad Barrels: Causal Analysis of Ethical Decision Making Behavior," *Journal of Applied Psychology* 75 (1990): 378–385.

7. Caroline Winter, David Glovin, and Jennifer Daniel, "A Guide to the Galleon Case," *Bloomberg Businessweek*, March 10, 2011, http://www.businessweek.com/magazine/content/11_12/b4220079522428.htm (accessed May 6, 2013); Ashby Jones, "Raj Opening Statements: 'Tomorrow's Trades Today' vs. 'Shoe-Leather Research,'" *The Wall Street Journal*, March 9, 2011, http://blogs.wsj.com/law/2011/03/09/raj-opening-statements-tomorrows-trades-today-vs-shoe-leather-research/?KEYWORDS=rajaratnam (accessed May 6, 2013).

8. Trevino and Youngblood, "Bad Apples in Bad Barrels."

9. Ibid.

10. Ben Blanchard, "China slams 'distorted' view of copyright piracy problem," *Reuters*, November 11, 2012, http://www.reuters.com/article/2012/11/11/us-china-congress-piracy-idUSBRE8AA04620121111 (accessed May 6, 2013).

11. AICPA Professional Code of Conduct, http://www.aicpa.org/Research/Standards/CodeofConduct/Pages/default.aspx (accessed April 25, 2013).

12. Constance E. Bagley, "The Ethical Leader's Decision Tree," *Harvard Business Review* (February 2003), 18–19.

13. Bella L. Galperin, Rebecca J. Bennett, and Karl Aquino, "Status Differentiation and the Protean Self: A Social-Cognitive Model of Unethical Behavior in Organizations," *Journal of Business Ethics* 98 (2011): 407–424.

14. "Warren Buffett's Berkshire Hathaway Letter to Shareholders," http://www.berkshirehathaway.com/letters/2010ltr.pdf (accessed May 6, 2013).

15. "Trust in the workplace: 2010 Ethics & Workplace Survey," Deloitte, http://www.deloitte.com/assets/Dcom-UnitedStates/Local%20Assets/Documents/us_2010_Ethics_and_Workplace_Survey_report_071910.pdf (accessed May 6, 2013).

16. David Gauthier-Villars, "Rogue French Trader Sentenced to Three Years," *The Wall Street Journal*, October 6, 2010, A1.

17. "Conducting Ourselves Ethically and Transparently," *Merck*, http://www.merck.com/corporate-responsibility/business-ethics-transparency/approach.html (accessed May 6, 2013); Merck, "Merck Code of Conduct," http://www.merckresponsibility.com/focus-areas/ethics-and-transparency/office-of-ethics/merck-code-of-conduct/home.html (accessed May 6, 2013).

18. "Limiting Exposure to Fraud and Corporate Wastage with Next Generation GRC Applications," *OCEG*, http://www.oceg.org/event/limiting-exposure-fraud-and-corporate-wastage-next-generation-grc-applications (accessed May 6, 2013).

19. Ernst & Young, *Growing Beyond: a place for integrity—12th Global Fraud Survey*, http://www.ey.com/Publication/vwLUAssets/Global-Fraud-Survey-a-place-for-integrity-12th-Global-Fraud-Survey/$FILE/EY-12th-GLOBAL-FRAUD-SURVEY.pdf (accessed May 6, 2013).

20. Criminal Division of the U.S. Department of Justice and the Enforcement Division of the U.S. Securities and Exchange Commission, *FCPA: A Resource Guide to the U.S. Foreign Corrupt Practices Act* (Washington, D.C.: U.S. Department of Justice and U.S. Securities & Exchange Commission, 2012).

21. Barry Z. Posner, "Another Look at the Impact of Personal and Organizational Values Congruency," *Journal of Business Ethics* 97 (2010): 535–541.

22. Frances Chua and Asheq Rahman, "Institutional Pressures and Ethical Reckoning by Business Corporations," *Journal of Business Ethics* 98 (2011): 307–329.

23. KPMG Forensic Integrity Survey 2008–2009, http://www.kpmg.com.br/publicacoes/forensic/Integrity_Survey_2008_2009.pdf (accessed May 6, 2013).

24. Christopher Sindik, "50 Banking & Insurance Industries Companies," *Ethisphere*, Q4, 15–17.

25. Mark S. Schwartz, "A Code of Ethics for Corporate Code of Ethics," *Journal of Business Ethics* 41 (2002): 37.

26. Ibid.

27. Lori Holder-Webb and Jeffrey Cohen, "The Cut and Paste Society: Isomorphism in Codes of Ethics," *Journal of Business Ethics* 107 (2012): 485–509.

28. Joseph A. McKinney, Tisha L. Emerson, and Mitchell J. Neubert, "The Effects of Ethical Codes on Ethical Perceptions of Actions toward Stakeholders," *Journal of Business Ethics* 97 (2010): 505–516.

29. "Code of Ethics," American Society of Civil Engineers, http://www.asce.org/Leadership-and-Management/Ethics/Code-of-Ethics/ (accessed May 6, 2013).

30. "Kao Named One of the 'World's Most Ethical Companies' for Four Consecutive Years," *Kao*, March 23, 2010, http://www.kao.com/jp/en/corp_news/2010/20100323_001.html (accessed May 6, 2013); "Kao receives Environmental Technology Award from JCIA," *Kao*, http://www.kao.com/jp/en/corp_csr/topics/eco_activities_20090617_001.html (accessed May 6, 2013); "Special Advertising Section—Japan 3.0: Serving the Global Community," *Fortune*, S15–S15; The Ethisphere Institute "2013 World's Most Ethical

Companies," *Ethisphere*, http://m1.ethisphere.com/
wme2013/index.html (accessed May 6, 2013).

31. *National Business Ethics Survey 2007*, 39.

32. "USSC Commissioner John Steer Joins with Compliance
and Ethics Executives from Leading U.S. Companies
to Address Key Compliance, Business Conduct and
Governance Issues," *Society for Corporate Compliance and
Ethics*, PR Newswire, October 31, 2005.

33. "The Power of ECOA Membership," *Ethics & Compliance
Officer Association*, http://www.theecoa.org/imis15/
Documents/ECOA-Global-Membership-2010.pdf
(accessed May 6, 2013).

34. Jim Nortz, "Compliance and Ethics Officers: A Survival
Guide for the Economic Downturn," March 10, 2009,
http://www.corporatecomplianceinsights.com/2010/
compliance-and-ethics-officers-surviving-economic-
downturn/ (accessed May 6, 2013).

35. Anne M. Simmons, "Want to Avoid Unpleasant
Compliance Surprises? Embrace a Strong Whistle-
Blowing Policy," January 8, 2009, http://ethisphere.com/
want-to-avoid-unpleasant-compliance-surprises-embrace-
a-strong-whistle-blowing-policy/ (accessed May 6, 2013).

36. "Combat Fraud of Almost $1 Trillion," April 17, 2009,
http://ethicaladvocate.blogspot.com/2009_04_01_archive.
html (accessed May 6, 2013).

37. "Ethics 20/20 Rule Changes Approved by ABA
Delegates With Little Opposition," *Bloomberg BNA*,
August 15, 2012, http://www.bna.com/ethics-2020-
rule-n12884911245/ (accessed May 6, 2013).

38. National Institutes of Health, "Ethics Training," http://
ethics.od.nih.gov/training.htm (accessed May 6, 2013).

39. Linda Ferrell and O. C. Ferrell, *Ethical Business* (DK
Essential Managers Series, May 4, 2009): 1–72.

40. Debbie Thorne LeClair and Linda Ferrell, "Innovation in
Experiential Business Ethics Training," *Journal of Business
Ethics* 23 (2000), 313–322.

41. Gerdien de Vries, Karen A. Jehn, Bart W. Terwel,
"When Employees Stop Talking and Start Fighting: The
Detrimental Effects of Pseudo Voice in Organizations,"
Journal of Business Ethics 105 (2012), 221–230.

42. David Slovin, "The Case for Anonymous Hotlines,"
Risk & Insurance, April 15, 2007, FindArticles, http://
findarticles.com/p/articles/mi_m0BJK/is_5_18/ai_
n27221119/ (accessed March 15, 2011).

43. Mael Kaptein, "Guidelines for the Development of an
Ethics Safety Net," *Journal of Business Ethics* 41 (2002): 217.

44. Ethics Resource Center, *Research Brief from the 2009
NBES*, 15.

45. *National Business Ethics Survey, 2007*, 6.

46. Jess Bravin, "Justices Extend Protection over Workplace
Retaliation," *The Wall Street Journal*, January 25, 2011, B1.

47. Curt S. Jordan, "Lessons in Organizational Compliance:
A Survey of Government-Imposed Compliance
Programs," *Preventive Law Reporter* (Winter 1994): 7.

48. Lori T. Martens and Kristen Day, "Five Common
Mistakes in Designing and Implementing a Business
Ethics Program," *Business and Society Review* 104 (1999):
163–170.

CHAPTER 9

MANAGING AND CONTROLLING ETHICS PROGRAMS

CHAPTER OBJECTIVES

- Define ethics auditing
- Identify the benefits and limitations of ethics auditing
- Examine the challenges of measuring nonfinancial performance
- Explore the stages of the ethics-auditing process
- Understand the strategic role of the ethics audit

CHAPTER OUTLINE

AN ETHICAL DILEMMA*

Mei-li stared at the code of ethics she received when she first began to consult with Business Equipment Corporation (BEC). Right there, under the heading "Competition," it stated, "BEC strongly believes in the competitive process. While we are dedicated to selling the best products, we have a strong commitment toward competing fairly and honestly." Mei-li wondered if there was any way to do her assignment without going against this core value.

Mei-li's first consulting assignment after graduating from UCLA was to work with Kyle, an engineer at BEC. Their assignment was to help develop and produce a new copy machine. Last year BEC discovered a new technology that would enable them to manufacture a copy machine with a copy quality far superior to anything else on the market. Mei-li and Kyle are both sure they have a winning product.

"I am especially excited about this. My kids are going to be so proud," said Kyle. "I've been promised a promotion and a doubling of my salary if the new product launch is successful."

Several months went by, and one morning Kyle came in, panic stricken. "Have you read the news?" Kyle asked Mei-li. "The industry reporter says that our competitor Hiyota plans to launch a new high-quality copier machine within the next month! If the Hiyota machine is as good as this article says, I'm dead," said Kyle.

"What do we do?" asked Mei-li. Kyle thought for a while and then replied, "Mei-li, we have to do this quickly before they roll out their machine. We need to make sure ours is better. I want you to pretend to be a potential customer and call Hiyota. Tell him you'll meet at the Hilton in one of the conference rooms. When the salesperson starts up, make sure you ask about copy quality, get samples, and learn as much as possible about novel product features, pricing, advertising strategy, etc. If we can get this information this week, we can help the plant people modify our machine so that it kills Hiyota."

Mei-li replied, "Kyle, I'm not comfortable with pretending to be a buyer. What if Hiyota finds out?

What about me wasting the time of this salesperson? I don't want the firm to get a reputation for this sort of thing."

Kyle replied, "This isn't a big deal. It's not illegal because we're not stealing trade secrets. If the salesperson is telling clients about the product, then it can't be illegal. Getting competitive product information takes place all the time, and it's Hiyota's responsibility to develop security procedures to prevent information from slipping out before the product hits the market. As far as the sales representative's time, you know that many of them have nonproductive sales calls. We can't afford to wait, Mei-li!"

As Mei-li left the office, she decided to ask Bob, their boss, about Kyle's proposal. As she discussed the information with Bob, he replied, "Unofficially, I'd say unless you can come up with some valid reasons to reject Kyle's plan, you should call Hiyota. Officially, I would say that BEC does not condone such practices and considers them unethical according to our code of ethics. Finally, unofficially, you need to know, Mei-li, that if Kyle doesn't pull this one out of the fire, he won't be here for very long."

"Have you ever done something like this, Bob?" asked Mei-li.

"I know this type of thing happens frequently, and I know some of the justifications for it. For example, it's common to state that the person had no choice or try to deny responsibility. Or they have a family to support, or everyone else does it. Those are the justifications I hear the most. However you want to justify it, it happens. Sometimes people get caught and sometimes they don't."

"You didn't answer my question, Bob. Have you ever done something like this?"

"Mei-li, I just answered your question." With those words, Bob excused himself and left.

That was Tuesday. Now Mei-li was sitting at her desk two days later staring at the code of conduct. She did not know what to do. It seemed like Kyle's job hung on the line. She heard footsteps and looked up as Kyle approached her.

"Have you set up the appointment?" Kyle asked.

QUESTIONS | EXERCISES

1. Discuss whether Kyle's proposal would violate BEC's code of ethics.

2. Identify the organizational pressures that Mei-li is facing to call Hiyota?

3. How should Mei-li handle the situation?

*This case is strictly hypothetical; any resemblance to real persons, companies, or situations is coincidental.

Chapter 8 introduces the idea of ethics programs as a way for organizations to improve ethical decision making and conduct in business. To properly implement these programs and ensure their effectiveness, companies need to measure their impact. Increasingly, companies are applying the principles of auditing to ascertain whether their ethics codes, policies, and corporate values are having a positive impact on the firm's ethical conduct. These audits can help companies identify risks and areas of noncompliance with laws and company policies as well as other areas that need improvement. An audit should provide a systematic and objective survey of the firm's ethical culture and values.

We begin this chapter by examining some of the requirements of a successful ethics program. We then discuss the concept of an ethics audit as a way to execute such a program. We define the term *ethics audit* and explore its relationship to a social audit. Next, we examine the benefits and limitations of this implementation tool, especially with regard to avoiding a management crisis. We consider the challenges of measuring nonfinancial ethical performance, and review evolving standards from AA100 and the Open Compliance Ethics Group. We then describe our framework for the steps of an ethics audit, including securing the commitment of directors and top managers; establishing a committee to oversee the audit; defining the scope of the audit process; reviewing the firm's mission, values, goals, and policies and defining ethical priorities; collecting and analyzing relevant information; and verifying and reporting the results. Finally, we consider the strategic importance of ethics auditing.

IMPLEMENTING ETHICS PROGRAMS

Developing an effective business ethics program requires organizations to cope with the realities of implementing such a program. Implementation requires executing specific actions that ensure the achievement of business ethics objectives. The organization must have ways of managing, evaluating, and controlling business ethics programs. Five items in particular have a significant impact on whether an ethics program is successful: (1) the content of the company's code of ethics, (2) the frequency of communication regarding the ethical code and program, (3) the quality of communication, (4) senior management's ability to successfully incorporate ethics into the organization, (5) and local management's ability to do the same.[1] If an organization has a culture more focused on planning than on implementation, employees may come to view unethical conduct as acceptable behavior. Without proper controls in place, lying to customers, manipulating prices, abusive behavior, and misuse of organizational resources can become a part of some employees' conduct.

Viewing a business ethics program as a part of strategic planning and management activities is critical to the success of any firm. Some companies still do not understand that ethics is a critical aspect of business strategy in action. This misunderstanding stems from a belief that the ethics of employees is primarily an individual matter, and not the responsibility of managers. The nature of ethics programs in corporate America is to determine risks, develop policies and codes of conduct, and require specific standards of conduct. However, in order to do the right thing and know when to say no or ask for assistance in gray areas, employees must have a strong sense of personal ethics.

Shared values among employees are the glue of successful management as well as of business ethics programs. When business ethics programs align and direct employees' activities toward an ethical culture, employees feel a commitment to the long-term ethical progress of the firm. Johnson Controls is a business recognized for its emphasis on ethical conduct. It has consistently earned a place in *Ethisphere*'s "World's Most Ethical Companies."[2] Johnson Controls adopted a model consisting of what it calls four spheres of ethical behavior based upon a stakeholder orientation: 1) Employees and other team members, 2) Company and shareholders, 3) Customers, competitors, and suppliers, and 4) Public and communities. At the center of its model is integrity, symbolizing that the company must operate with integrity in each of these "spheres."[3]

Formal controls for business ethics include input controls such as proper selection of employees, effective ethics training, and strong structural systems (including communication systems). Chapter 8 discussed internal control systems whereby employees can report misconduct. Ethics assistance lines, sometimes called hotlines, provide support and give employees the opportunity to get assistance, ask questions, or report concerns. Another internal control system that can improve ethical assistance is an ethics help desk. An ethics help desk is a point of contact within an organization where employees and managers can bring their concerns and receive assistance from the most appropriate person in the firm to handle the situation. For this model to be successful, the help desk must be supportive of employees, be easily accessible, and have simple procedures for employees to follow when they express concerns.[4]

Process controls include management's commitment to the ethics program and the methods or system for ethics evaluation. These methods might involve daily coaching for managers and employee reminders regarding appropriate ethical conduct. The best way to provide leadership on ethics is to set a good example, and there are many examples of effective corporate leaders who promote ethics from the top. Jeffrey Swartz, the CEO of Timberland, won recognition as a strong and ethical corporate leader. Swartz expanded Timberline's Green Index—a measurement that shows the product's environmental impact based on climate impact, chemicals used, and resource consumption—to include its entire footwear collection. Swartz exhibits good leadership qualities in the care he shows his employees and his willingness to take responsibility for past mistakes.[5]

Output controls involve comparing standards with actual behavior. One of the most popular methods of evaluating ethical performance is an ethics audit. The primary purpose of an ethics audit is to identify the risks and problems in outgoing activities and plan the necessary steps to adjust, correct, or eliminate these ethical concerns. Regardless of the complexity of a firm's ethics program, an ethics audit is critical to the program's success; therefore, a major part of this chapter focuses on how such audits should be conducted. The Federal Sentencing Guidelines for Organizations' amendment suggests that the results of an ethics audit be reported directly to the board of directors. Such direct reporting would prevent the CEO or another top officer from covering up misconduct.

This chapter will help complete your understanding of how organizational ethics is managed and controlled to create an effective program. Although you may never be in charge of such a program, as a manager or employee you will be part of it. The more you understand the role and function of the various parts of the program, the more effective you will be in engaging and guiding others to make ethical decisions. Business ethics in an organization is not simply a personal matter based on your individual values. You will be responsible, both ethically and legally, for engaging in ethical conduct and reporting the unethical conduct of others in your organization.

THE ETHICS AUDIT

An **ethics audit** is a systematic evaluation of an organization's ethics program and performance to determine whether it is effective. A major component of the ethics program described in Chapter 8, the ethics audit includes "regular, complete, and documented measurements of compliance with the company's published policies and procedures."[6] As such, the audit provides an opportunity to measure conformity to the firm's desired ethical standards. An audit can be a precursor to setting up an ethics program, as it identifies the firm's ethical standards as well as its existing policies and risk areas. Recent legislation and FSGO amendments encourage greater ethics auditing as companies attempt to demonstrate to various stakeholders that they are abiding by the law and have established programs to improve ethical decision making. While companies are not required to report the results of their audits to the public, some firms, such as New Belgium Brewing, do report the results of audits in areas such as employment practices, sustainability efforts, and community outreach.

The concept of ethics auditing emerged from the movement to evaluate and report on companies' broader social responsibility initiatives, particularly with regard to sustainability. An increasing number of companies are auditing their social responsibility programs and reporting the results to document their efforts to be more responsible to various interested stakeholder groups. A **social audit** is the process of assessing and reporting on a business's performance in fulfilling the economic, legal, ethical, and philanthropic responsibilities expected of it by its stakeholders.[7] Social reports often discuss issues related to a firm's performance in the four dimensions of social responsibility as well as specific social responsibility and ethical issues such as employment issues, community economic development, volunteerism, and environmental impact.[8] In contrast, ethics audits focus more narrowly on a firm's ethical and legal conduct. However, an ethics audit can be a component of a social audit; indeed, many companies include ethical issues in their social audits. Walmart, for example, includes ethical performance in its Global Responsibility Report.[9]

Regardless of the breadth of the audit, ethics auditing is a tool companies can employ to identify and measure their ethical commitment to stakeholders. Employees, customers, investors, suppliers, community members, activists, the media, and regulators increasingly demand companies act ethical and accountable for their conduct. In response, businesses are working to incorporate accountability into their actions, from long-term planning, everyday decision making, and rethinking processes for corporate governance and financial reporting to hiring, retaining, and promoting employees and building relationships with customers. The ethics audit provides an objective method for demonstrating a company's commitment to improving strategic planning, including its compliance with legal and ethical standards and standards of social responsibility. The auditing process is important to business because it can improve a firm's performance and effectiveness, increase its attractiveness to investors, improve its relationships with stakeholders, identify potential risks, and decrease the risk of misconduct and adverse publicity that could harm its reputation.[10] As we discussed earlier, the "World's Most Ethical Companies" have often shown better financial performance than the firms in the general stock indexes.

Ethics auditing employs procedures and processes similar to those found in financial auditing to create an objective report of a company's performance. As in an accounting audit, someone with expertise from outside the organization may be chosen to conduct an ethics audit. Although the standards used in financial auditing can be adapted to provide an objective foundation for ethics reporting, there are significant differences between the two types of audits. Whereas financial auditing focuses on all systems related to money flow and on financial assessments of value for tax purposes and managerial accountability, ethics auditing deals with the internal and broad external impact of an organization's ethical performance. Another significant difference is that ethics auditing is not usually associated with regulatory requirements, while financial audits are required of public companies that issue securities. Because ethics and social audits are voluntary, there are fewer standards a company can apply with regard to reporting frequency, disclosure requirements, and remedial actions that it should take in response to results. This may change as more companies develop ethics programs in the current regulatory environment, in which regulatory agencies support requiring boards of directors to oversee corporate ethics. If boards are to track the effectiveness of ethics programs, audits will be required. In addition, nonfinancial auditing standards are developing, with data available for benchmarking and comparing a firm's nonfinancial ethical performance with its own past performance and with the performance of other firms.

BENEFITS OF ETHICS AUDITING

There are many reasons why companies choose to analyze, report on, and improve their ethical conduct. Assessment of an organization's ethical culture is necessary to improve ethical performance and to document in legal proceedings that a firm has an effective ethics program. Companies can use ethical audits to detect misconduct before it becomes a major problem, and audits provide evidence of a firm's attempts to identify and deal with major ethical risks. For instance, companies that prove they had corporate ethics and compliance programs and report misconduct when discovered can often receive deferred prosecution agreements (DPAs), in which the company can resolve criminal charges without having to admit guilt. Under a typical DPA, companies admit wrongdoing (but not guilt), pay a fine, cooperate with the Justice Department, and agree to meet certain terms within a certain time frame. After the compliance deadline, if the Justice Department acknowledges the company met all of the terms, the charges against the firm will be dropped.[11] This provides significant encouragement for companies to account more for their actions in a wide range of areas, including corporate governance, ethics programs, customer relationships, employee relations, environmental policies, and community involvement.

One company may want to achieve the most ethical performance possible, whereas another may use an ethics audit merely to project a good image to hide its corrupt culture. Top managers might use an ethics audit to identify ethical problems in their companies, but identification alone does not mean they will take steps to correct these lapses through punishments or sanctions.[12] Without appropriate action on the part of management, an ethics audit is mere lip service intended to enhance the firm's reputation without actually improving its ethical conduct. Other firms might conduct audits in an attempt to comply with the Federal Sentencing Guidelines for Organizations' (FSGO) requirement that the board of directors oversee the discovery of ethical risk, design and implement an ethics program, and evaluate performance. Some companies view the auditing process as tied to continuous improvement that is closely related to improved financial performance. Companies' reasons for supporting the FSGO are complex and diverse. For example, it is common for firms to conduct audits of business practices with legal ramifications such as employee safety, environmental impact, and financial reporting. Although these practices are important to a firm's ethics and social responsibility, they are also legally required and therefore constitute the minimum level of commitment. However, because stakeholders are demanding increased transparency and taking a more active role through external organizations representing their interests, government regulators are calling on companies to improve their ethical conduct and make more decisions based on principles rather than on laws alone.

Measuring the ethical work climate of an organization is one way to learn about its ethical culture. While most measurements of ethical climate are conducted by academic researchers, some firms become proactive by working with consultants to measure their ethical climate. Measures of ethical climate include collective ethical sensitivity (empathetic concern and awareness), collective character, collective judgment (focus on others and focus on self), and collective moral motivation.[13] These measures can help evaluate changes in a firm's ethical culture after the development of ethics programs.

The auditing process can highlight trends, improve organizational learning, and facilitate communication and working relationships.[14] Auditing can also help companies assess the effectiveness of their programs and policies, which often improves their operating efficiencies and reduces costs. Information from audits and reports can allow a company to ensure it achieves the greatest possible impact with available resources.[15] The process of ethics auditing also helps an organization identify potential risks and liabilities and improve its compliance with the law. Furthermore, the audit report may help document a firm's compliance with legal requirements as well as demonstrate its progress in areas where it previously failed to comply—for example, by describing the systems it is implementing to reduce the likelihood of a recurrence of misconduct.[16]

For organizations, one of the greatest benefits of the auditing process is improved relationships with stakeholders who desire greater transparency. Many stakeholders have become wary of corporate public relations campaigns. Verbal assurances by corporate management are no longer sufficient to gain stakeholders' trust. An ethics audit could have saved Countrywide Financial if liar loans and the manipulation of borrowers' financial data had been identified earlier. When companies and their employees, suppliers, and investors trust each other, the costs of monitoring and managing these relationships are lower. Companies experience less conflict with these stakeholders, resulting in a heightened capacity for innovation and collaboration.

Because of these benefits shareholders and investors have welcomed the increased disclosure that comes with corporate accountability. Table 9–1 indicates the top challenges CEOs face. Issues such as trust, sustainability, and customer relationships are among the top ten challenges. These issues can be considered risks associated with managing and controlling ethics programs. Therefore, they represent key areas important in an ethics

TABLE 9–1 Top Challenges for CEOs

1. Human capital
2. Operational excellence
3. Innovation
4. Customer relationships
5. Global political/economic risk
6. Government regulation
7. Global expansion
8. Corporate brand and reputation
9. Sustainability
10. Trust in business

N = 729 total responses. Response rate varied for each challenge.

Source: The Conference Board, *CEO Challenge® 2013 Summary Report*, 2013.

audit. A growing number of investors are considering nonfinancial measures—such as the existence of ethics programs, legal compliance, board diversity and independence, and other corporate governance issues like CEO compensation—when they analyze the quality of current and potential investments. Research suggests investors may be willing to pay higher prices for the stock of companies they deem accountable,[17] such as stock from *Fortune*'s "World's Most Admired Companies," including Samsung, Cisco, Berkshire Hathaway, Southwest Airlines, Marriott International, Procter & Gamble, 3M, Deere, UPS, and BMW, who have generally avoided major ethical disasters.[18]

However, even companies that experienced legal issues or had their ethics questioned can make a comeback. One of the most famous ethical turnaround stories is Nike. When it was revealed that some of Nike's suppliers were using child labor in Asian factories, there was a public outcry against Nike and the company lost much business. In response the firm adopted a number of auditing tools to ensure factory compliance and was the first company to respond to stakeholder requests to publicly disclose the names and locations of its contracted factories. Many of Nike's reports on its factories can be accessed on the Fair Labor Association website. Nike appears to have learned the important lesson of taking stakeholder demands seriously. For instance, when Greenpeace objected to Nike and Adidas suppliers releasing toxic waste into waterways, Nike responded within a few weeks with a plan to become more transparent about chemicals being released from its contracted factories as well as making a commitment toward eliminating toxic chemicals from its supply chain by 2020.[19]

Regular audits permit shareholders and investors to judge whether a firm is achieving the goals it established, and whether it abides by the values that it specified as important. Moreover, it permits stakeholders to influence the organization's behavior.[20] Increasingly, a broad range of stakeholder groups are seeking specific, often quantifiable, information from companies. These stakeholders expect companies to take a deeper look at the nature of their operations and to publicly disclose their progress and problems in addressing these issues. Some investors use their rights as stockholders to encourage companies to modify their plans and policies to address specific ethical issues. On a broader scale, the Obama administration sought to impose limits on executive compensation of those firms seeking government financial support. The 2010 passage of the Dodd–Frank Wall Street Reform and Consumer Protection Act implemented new regulations for executive compensation. Under these new provisions, shareholders of public companies can cast advisory votes on whether they approve of the compensation awarded to top executives. While the shareholder vote is non-binding, it does place pressure on boards when determining compensation packages. Additionally, top executives must provide more disclosure on how their compensation aligns with the company's financial performance.[21]

Ethical Crisis Management and Recovery

A significant benefit of ethics auditing is that it may prevent crises resulting from ethical or legal misconduct, crises that can potentially be more devastating than natural disasters or technological disruptions. Just as companies develop crisis management plans to respond to and recover from natural disasters, they should also prepare for ethical disasters that can result in substantial legal and financial costs and disrupt routine operations, paralyze employees, reduce productivity, destroy organizational reputation, and erode stakeholder confidence. Ethical and legal crises have resulted in the demise or acquisition of a number of well-known companies including Lehman Brothers, Merrill Lynch, and Washington Mutual. Many other companies—HealthSouth, Firestone, Waste Management, Rite Aid, U.S. Foodservice, Qwest, Kmart, Mitsubishi Motors, and Archer Daniels Midland, for example—have survived ethical and legal crises but paid a high price both financially and in terms of compromised reputation and diminished stakeholder trust. In recent years, companies have spent up to $7 million a month on outside legal counsel to defend against alleged organizational wrongdoing. One study found that publicity about unethical corporate behavior lowers stock prices for at least six months.[22] Bribery allegations and an internal probe at Avon Products, Inc., temporarily lowered its share prices because of fears that a scandal could harm operations.[23]

Organizational members engaging in questionable or illegal conduct are guilty of ethical misconduct, and these employees can threaten the overall integrity of the organization. Top leaders in particular can magnify ethical misconduct to disastrous proportions. The misconduct of Raj Rajaratnam at the Galleon Group, Andrew Fastow at Enron, Dennis Kozlowski at Tyco, and Bernie Ebbers at WorldCom caused financial disasters on both organizational and global levels.[24] An ethics audit can uncover rogue employees who violate the firm's ethical standards and policies or laws and regulations.

Ethical disasters follow recognizable phases of escalation, from ethical issue recognition and the decision to act unethically to the organization's discovery of and response to the act. Appropriate anticipation and intervention during these situations can stave off major problems. Such contingency planning assesses risks, plans for eventualities, and provides ready tools for responding to ethical crises. The process of ethical disaster-recovery planning involves assessing an organization's values, developing an ethics program, performing an ethics audit, and developing contingency plans for potential ethical disasters. The ethics audit itself provides the key to preventing ethical disasters.

Formal mechanisms should be in place to discover risk as a part of evaluating compliance and the effectiveness of ethics programs. The greatest fear of most corporate leaders is discovering misconduct or illegal activity that could be reported by the mass media, used by competitors, or prosecuted by the government. Yet this process is extremely important to the long-term well-being of an organization. While risks such as earthquakes, fires, hurricanes, and other natural disasters cannot always be determined, companies can plan for these types of disasters. Unfortunately, ethical risks are often given the lowest priority. However, it is worth noting that many common risks, such as reputational, product quality, litigation, and more have an ethical component. Indeed, ethical risks can be just as damaging as natural disaster risks because a firm that gains a reputation for being unethical will likely lose investors, customers, and employees. It can take many years for a firm to recover from a misconduct disaster.

Ernst & Young conducted an investigation into some of the ways Chief Risk Officers of global companies manage risks and used their insight to help develop a list of recommendations for managing business risk. Table 9–2 lists five recommendations for improving risk management. For instance, asset managers have begun to create what Ernst & Young terms Regulatory Reform Project Risk Management Offices with the intent to monitor and identify the potential for new regulation with wide-reaching global impact, such as the provisions in the Dodd-Frank Act or the United Kingdom Bribery Act.[25] By understanding new and potential legislation in different areas of the world, businesses can determine how to best meet these regulations and minimize their risks of violating the laws of a specific country.

Measuring Nonfinancial Ethical Performance

Although much of the regulation of corporate ethics and compliance focuses on financial measures, to truly have integrity, an organization must also focus on nonfinancial areas of performance. The word *integrity* in this context implies a balanced organization that not only makes ethical financial decisions but also is ethical in the more subjective aspects of its corporate culture. The Sarbanes–Oxley Act focused on questionable accounting and the metrics that destroy shareholder value, but other models have been developed—such as Six Sigma, the Balanced Scorecard, and the triple bottom Line—to capture structural and behavioral organizational ethical performance. Six Sigma is a methodology designed to manage process variations that cause defects, defined as unacceptable deviations from the mean or target, and to systematically work toward managing variation to eliminate those defects. The objective of Six Sigma is to deliver world-class performance, reliability, and value to the end customer. The Balanced Scorecard is a management system that focuses

TABLE 9–2 Improving Organizational Risk Management

1. Create a Regulatory Reform Project Management Office with the appropriate governance to direct business and operating models and manage risks proportionately.

2. Chief Risk Officers should report to Group CROs or board members.

3. Involve risk and compliance at the beginning of the product development cycle.

4. Improve independent controls by setting appropriate governance frameworks with which portfolio managers need to comply.

5. Manage and optimize the use of capital.

Source: Ernst & Young, *Risk Management for Asset Management: Ernst & Young Survey 2012*, 6–7, http://www.ey.com/Publication/vwLUAssets/2012_EMEIA_asset_management_risk_survey/$FILE/Risk_Management_for_AM_EY_Survey_2012.pdf (accessed May 14, 2013).

on all the elements that contribute to organizational performance and success, including financial, customer, market, and internal processes. The goal is to develop a broader perspective on performance factors and to foster a culture of learning and growth that improves all organizational communication. The triple bottom line provides a perspective that takes into account the social, environmental, and financial impacts of decisions made within an organization. When making an increased commitment to social responsibility, sustainability, or ethics, companies consider implementing triple bottom line reporting as a way to confirm their investments and initiatives support their organization's values and overall success. Table 9–3 provides additional detail on these three measurement tools. The purpose of a variety of measures of performance and goal achievement is to determine the quality and effectiveness of environmental, social, and ethics initiatives. Many believe that an inherent gain is realized by companies with strong ethical cultures and environmental commitments, paid in customer commitment and in avoiding the negative publicity and costs associated with wrongdoing.

The Global Reporting Initiative (GRI) has become a prominent framework that companies have adopted to report their social and sustainability progress.[26] The GRI advances sustainability reporting, which incorporates the triple bottom line factors of economic, social, and environmental indicators. The primary goal of the GRI is "the mainstreaming of disclosure on environmental, social, and governance performance."[27] Businesses can use the GRI to develop a more standardized method of reporting nonfinancial results in a way users of the reports can understand. Companies benefit because the GRI provides tools for improving their implementation of the triple bottom line, as well as assisting with the

TABLE 9–3 Description of Measurement Tools

Measurement Systems	Description
Balanced Scorecard	Developed by Drs. Robert Kaplan and David Norton, the Balanced Scorecard incorporates nonfinancial performance indicators into the evaluation system to provide a more "balanced" view of organizational performance. The system uses four metrics—financial, internal business processes, learning and growth, and customer—to measure the overall performance of the firm.
Six Sigma	Six Sigma focuses on improving existing processes that do not meet quality specifications or that need to be improved as well as developing new processes that meet Six Sigma standards. To meet Six Sigma specifications, the process must not produce more than 3.4 defects per million opportunities.
Triple Bottom Line	This approach to measuring social, financial, and environmental factors (or people, places, and planet) recognizes that business has a responsibility to positively influence a variety of stakeholders, including customers, employees, shareholders, community, and the natural environment. The challenge is how to evaluate a business' social and environmental impacts, since there are no universally standard forms of measuring these criteria.

Source: "Balanced Scorecard Basics,"Balanced Scorecard Institute, http://www.balancedscorecard.org/BSCResources/AbouttheBalancedScorecard/tabid/55/Default.aspx (accessed May 14, 2013); "What is Six Sigma," iSix Sigma, http://www.isixsigma.com/index.php?option=com_k2&view=item&id=1463:what-is-six-sigma?&Itemid=155 (accessed May 14, 2013); "Triple bottom line," The Economist, November 17, 2009, http://www.economist.com/node/14301663?story_id=14301663 (accessed May 14, 2013).

disclosure of their progress in this area. These tools give them the ability to compare their sustainability efforts with those of other companies and the chance to enhance their reputation in the eyes of stakeholders. Users benefit because this standardized sustainability reporting gives them a point of comparison with other companies' sustainability initiatives.[28] GRI continually revises its framework to ensure it remains relevant and encourages multiple stakeholders from global business, civil society, labor, and academic sectors to participate in the process.[29]

AccountAbility is an international membership organization committed to enhancing the performance of organizations, and to develop the competencies of individuals in social and ethical accountability and sustainable development. Figure 9–1 illustrates the AccountAbility AA1000 framework for ethics and social responsibility. The AA1000 process standards link the definition and embedding of an organization's values to the development of performance targets and the assessment and communication of organizational performance. Through this process, focused around the organization's engagement with stakeholders, AA1000 ties social and ethical issues into the organization's strategic management and operations. AA1000 recognizes these different traditions. It combines the terms *social* and *ethical* to refer to the systems and individual behavior within an organization, as well as to the *direct* and *indirect* impact of an organization's activities on stakeholders. *Social* and *ethical issues* (relating to systems, behavior, and impacts) are defined by an organization's values and aims, as shaped by the influence of the interests and expectations

FIGURE 9–1 AA1000 Framework for Ethics and Social Accountability

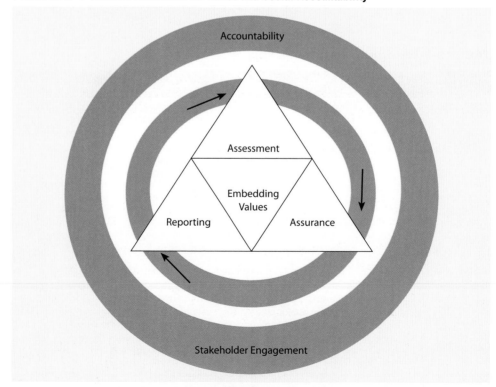

Source: Adapted from AccountAbility AA1000 Series of Standards, http://www.accountability21.net/aa1000series (accessed March 12, 2009). Reprinted with permission of The Institute of Social and Ethical Accountability.

of its stakeholders and by societal norms and expectations. *Assessment* means measuring organizational responsiveness or the extent to which an organization takes action on the basis of stakeholder engagement. This is followed by *assurance,* including control mechanisms, and then reporting to document the process. The *embedding* of an organization's values to assure performance is a continuous process.

Figure 9–2 shows the Open Compliance Ethics Group's functions of governance, risk, and compliance framework. The Open Compliance Ethics Group (OCEG) (http://www.oceg.org) worked with more than 100 companies to create a universal framework for compliance and ethics management. The OCEG focuses on nonfinancial compliance and the more qualitative elements of internal controls. The OCEG framework deals with complex issues of compliance and solutions to address the development of organizational ethics. By establishing guidelines rather than standards, OCEG provides a tool for each company to use as it sees fit, given its size, scope, structure, industry, and other factors that create individualized needs. The OCEG guidelines and benchmarking studies can be valuable to a firm conducting an ethics audit. Most significant is the opportunity to compare an organization's activities to those of other organizations. To this end, the OCEG created tools and certification procedures to help businesses, such as the Burgundy Book, that assists in assessing "the design and operation of government, risk management, and compliance processes."[30] Additionally, the organization awards certification to companies and individuals that demonstrate to stakeholders they operate at the highest standards regarding governance, risk management, and compliance.[31]

Risks and Requirements in Ethics Auditing

Although ethics audits provide many benefits for individual companies and their stakeholders, they have the potential to create risks. For example, a firm may uncover a serious ethical problem it would prefer not to disclose until it has remedied the situation. It may find one or more of its stakeholders' criticisms cannot be easily addressed. Occasionally, the process of conducting an ethics audit may foster stakeholder dissatisfaction rather than

FIGURE 9–2 Roles and Functions of Risk, Management, and Compliance

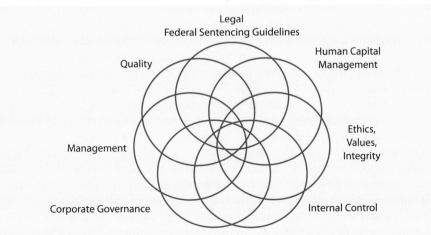

Source: The Open Compliance Ethics Group Framework Overview, http://www.oceg.org/framework.asp (accessed April 4, 2006). Reprinted with permission.

stifle it. Moreover, the auditing process imposes burdens (especially with regard to record keeping) and costs for firms that undertake it. Auditing, although a prudent measure, provides no assurance that ethical risks and challenges can be avoided. Another challenge is in assessing risk and identifying standards of comparison. How can a company sufficiently analyze and manage its risks? What goals for improvement should it develop? Some initiatives to benchmark risk assessment and best practices have begun to emerge, but this process is in its early stages.

Many companies suspected of misconduct respond to public scrutiny of their practices by conducting an ethics audit to show their concern and respond appropriately to weaknesses in their programs. As a result of questionable conduct or legal violations, companies such as JP Morgan, Fannie Mae, Freddie Mac, and Merrill Lynch should conduct audits to demonstrate their visible commitment to improving decision making and business conduct.

Research suggests that generating ethics and corporate social responsibility auditing procedures can be tricky because of a lack of standardization and widely accepted measures.[32] Although ethics and social responsibility are defined and perceived differently by various stakeholders, a core of minimum standards for ethical performance is evolving. These standards represent a fundamental step in the development of minimum ethics requirements that are specific, measurable, achievable, and meaningful to a business' impact on all stakeholders. Standards help companies set measurable and achievable targets for improvement, and they form an objective foundation for reporting the firm's efforts to all direct stakeholders. Disagreements may still arise over key issues, but overall these standards should enable companies to make progress in meeting their goals. The FSGO's seven steps for effective ethical compliance, discussed in Chapters 3 and 8, as well as the Sarbanes–Oxley Act and the Dodd–Frank Act, provide standards organizations can use in ethics auditing.

THE AUDITING PROCESS

Many considerations are addressed when conducting an audit, such as the depth and width of the audit, application of the standards of performance, the frequency of audits, how the results are reported to stakeholders, and what actions should be taken in response to audit results.[33] Therefore, corporate approaches to ethics audits are as varied as their approaches to ethics programs and their responses to improving social responsibility.

An ethics audit should be unique to each company, reflecting its size, industry, corporate culture, and identified risks as well as the regulatory environment in which it operates. Thus, an ethics audit for a bank will differ from one for an automobile manufacturer or a food processor. Each company has different regulatory concerns and unique risks stemming from the nature of its business. For this reason, Table 9–4 maps out a framework that is somewhat generic and which most companies can expand on when conducting their own ethics audits. The steps in the framework can be applied to broader social audits that include specific ethical issues as well as other economic, legal, and philanthropic concerns of interest to various stakeholders. As with any new initiative, companies may choose to begin their effort with smaller, less formal audits and work up to more comprehensive social audits. For example, a firm may choose to focus on primary stakeholders in its initial audit year and then expand to secondary groups in subsequent audits.

TABLE 9–4 Framework for an Ethics Audit

- Secure the commitment of top managers and board of directors

- Establish a committee to oversee the ethics audit

- Define the scope of the audit process, including subject matter areas important to the ethics audit

- Review the organization's mission, policies, goals, and objectives and define its ethical priorities

- Collect and analyze relevant information in each designated subject matter area

- Have the results verified by an independent agent

- Report the findings to the audit committee and, if approved, to managers and stakeholders

Sources: These steps are compatible with the social auditing methods prescribed by Warren Dow and Roy Crowe in *What Social Auditing Can Do for Voluntary Organizations* (Vancouver: Volunteer Vancouver, July 1999), and Sandra Waddock and Neil Smith in "Corporate Responsibility Audits: Doing Well by Doing Good," *Sloan Management Review* 41 (2000), 79.

The framework encompasses a wide range of business responsibilities and relationships. The audit entails an individualized process and outcomes for a particular firm, since it requires a careful consideration of the unique issues that face a particular organization. For example, the auditing process at Coca-Cola must consider several specific factors. To ensure an effective internal audit, Coca-Cola's board of directors appoints an audit committee whose responsibilities include a review of the company's financial statements as well as an assessment of its risk management, internal and disclosure controls, complaints procedures, and compliance programs (including the Company's Code of Business Conduct). The committee's statement of purpose is as follows:

> The Committee will represent and assist the Board in fulfilling its oversight responsibility to the shareowners and others relating to the integrity of the Company's financial statements and the financial reporting process, the systems of internal accounting and financial controls, the internal audit function, the annual independent audit of the Company's financial statements, the Company's compliance with legal and regulatory requirements, and its ethics programs as established by management and the Board, including the Company's Code of Business Conduct. The Committee shall also oversee the independent auditors' qualifications and independence. The Committee will evaluate the performance of the Company's internal audit function (responsibilities, budget and staffing) and the Company's independent auditors, including a review and evaluation of the engagement partner and coordinating partner. In so doing, it is the responsibility of the Committee to act independently while maintaining free and open communication between the Committee, the independent auditors, the internal auditors and management of the Company. The Committee is also responsible for producing an annual report for inclusion in the Company's proxy statement.[34]

Figure 9–3 provides a fictional example of how a corporate social responsibility structure might be organized within a well-known company. Notice that the 2010 amendments to the Federal Sentencing Guidelines for Organizations recommend that chief ethics and compliance officers report directly to the board of directors. Although this chapter presents a structure and recommendations for both general social and ethics-specific audits, there is no generic approach that will satisfy every firm's circumstances. Nevertheless, the benefits and limitations companies derive from auditing are relatively consistent.

FIGURE 9–3 **Model Corporate Social Responsibility Structure**

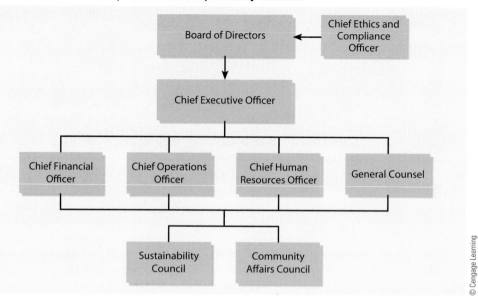

© Cengage Learning

Secure Commitment of Top Managers and Board of Directors

The first step in conducting any audit is securing the commitment of the firm's top management and, if it is a public corporation, its board of directors. Indeed, the push for an ethics audit may come directly from the board itself in response to specific stakeholder concerns or corporate governance reforms related to the Sarbanes–Oxley Act, which suggests that boards of directors provide oversight for *all* auditing activities. In addition, court decisions related to the FSGO hold board members responsible for the ethical and legal compliance programs of the firms they oversee. Rules and regulations associated with the Sarbanes–Oxley Act require that boards include members who are knowledgeable and qualified to oversee accounting and other types of audits to ensure these reports are accurate and include all material information. Although a board's financial audit committee will examine ethical standards throughout the organization as they relate to financial matters, it also deals with the implementation of codes of ethics for top financial officers. Many of those issues relate to corporate governance issues such as compensation, stock options, and conflicts of interest. An ethics audit can demonstrate that a firm has taken steps to prevent misconduct and is useful in cases where civil lawsuits blame the firm and its directors for the actions of a rogue employee.

Pressure for an audit can also come from top managers looking for ways to track and improve ethical performance and perhaps give their firm an advantage over competitors that face questions about their ethical conduct. Additionally, under the Sarbanes–Oxley Act, CEOs and CFOs may be criminally prosecuted if they knowingly certify misleading financial statements. They may request an ethics audit as a tool to improve the confidence in their firm's reporting processes. Some companies established a high-level ethics office in conjunction with an ethics program, and the ethics officer may campaign for an audit as a measure of the effectiveness of the firm's program. Regardless of the impetus for an audit, its success hinges on the full support of top management, particularly the CEO and the board of directors. Without this support, an audit will not improve the ethics program or the corporate culture.

Establish a Committee to Oversee the Ethics Audit

The next step in the framework is to establish a committee or team to oversee the audit process. Ideally, the board of directors' financial audit committee oversees the audit, but this does not happen in most companies. In most firms, managers or ethics officers do not always report to the board of directors when conducting social and ethics auditing. In any case, this team should include employees knowledgeable about the nature and role of ethics audits, and those people should come from various departments within the firm. The team may recruit individuals in-house or hire outside consultants to coordinate the audit and report the results directly to the board of directors. The Ethics Resource Center, a nonprofit organization engaged in supporting ethical conduct in the public and private sector, assists companies with assessments and audits.[35] As with a financial audit, an external auditor should not have conflict-of-interest relationships with top managers or board members. Based on the best practices of corporate governance, audits should be monitored by an independent board of directors' committee, as recommended by the Sarbanes–Oxley Act.

Define the Scope of the Audit Process

The ethics audit committee should establish the scope of the audit and monitor its progress to ensure it stays on track. The scope of an audit depends on the type of business, the risks it faces, and the opportunities it has to manage ethics. This step includes defining the key subject matter or risk areas important to the audit (for example, sustainability, discrimination, product liability, employee rights, privacy, fraud, financial reporting, and/or legal compliance) as well as the bases on which these areas are assessed. Assessments can be based on direct consultation, observation, surveys, or focus groups.[36] Table 9–5 lists sample subject matter areas and the audit items for each.

Review Organizational Mission, Values, Goals, and Policies and Define Ethical Priorities

Because ethics audits generally involve comparing an organization's ethical performance to its goals, values, and policies, the audit process should include a review of the mission statement and strategic objectives. A company's overall mission may incorporate ethics objectives, but these may be located in separate documents, including those that focus on social responsibility. For example, a firm's ethics statement or statement of values may offer guidance for managing transactions and human relationships that support the firm's reputation, thereby fostering the confidence of the firm's external stakeholders.[37] Franklin Energy specifies the five core values it uses in managing its business which contributes to its success: ingenuity, results orientation, frugality, integrity, and environmental stewardship.[38]

This review should include an examination of all formal documents that make explicit commitments to ethical, legal, or social responsibility, as well as less formal documents.

TABLE 9–5 The Ethics Audit

Organizational Issues*		
Yes	No	1. Does the company have a code of ethics that is reasonably capable of preventing misconduct?
Yes	No	2. Does the board of directors participate in the development and evaluation of the ethics program?
Yes	No	3. Is there a person with high managerial authority responsible for the ethics program?
Yes	No	4. Are there mechanisms in place to prevent the delegation of authority to individuals with a propensity for misconduct?
Yes	No	5. Does the organization effectively communicate standards and procedures to its employees via ethics training programs?
Yes	No	6. Does the organization communicate its ethical standards to suppliers, customers, and significant others that have a relationship with the organization?
Yes	No	7. Do the company's manuals and written documents guiding operations contain messages about appropriate behavior?
Yes	No	8. Is there formal or informal communication within the organization about procedures and activities that are considered acceptable ethical behavior?
Yes	No	9. Does top management have a mechanism in place to detect ethical issues relating to employees, customers, the community, and society?
Yes	No	10. Is there a system in place for employees to report unethical behavior?
Yes	No	11. Is there consistent enforcement of standards and punishments in the organization?
Yes	No	12. Is there a committee, department, team, or group that deals with ethical issues in the organization?
Yes	No	13. Does the organization make a continuous effort to improve its ethical compliance program?
Yes	No	14. Does the firm perform an ethics audit?
Examples of Specific Issues That Could Be Monitored in an Ethics Audit†		
Yes	No	1. Are there any systems or operational procedures in place to safeguard individual employees' ethical behavior?
Yes	No	2. Is it necessary for employees to break the company's ethical rules to get the job done?
Yes	No	3. Is there an environment of deception, repression, and cover-ups concerning events that would embarrass the company?
Yes	No	4. Are there any participatory management practices that allow ethical issues to be discussed?
Yes	No	5. Are compensation systems totally dependent on performance?
Yes	No	6. Does sexual harassment occur?

Yes	No	7. Does any form of discrimination—race, sex, or age—occur in hiring, promotion, or compensation?
Yes	No	8. Are the only standards about environmental impact those that are legally required?
Yes	No	9. Do the firm's activities show any concern for the ethical value systems of the community?
Yes	No	10. Are there deceptive and misleading messages in promotion?
Yes	No	11. Are products described in misleading or negative ways or without communicating their limitations to customers?
Yes	No	12. Are the documents and copyrighted materials of other companies used in unauthorized ways?
Yes	No	13. Are expense accounts inflated?
Yes	No	14. Are customers overcharged?
Yes	No	15. Does unauthorized copying of computer software occur?

© Cengage Learning

*A high number of "Yes" answers indicate ethical control mechanisms and procedures are in place within the organization.

†The number of "Yes" answers indicates the number of possible ethical issues to address.

Informal documents include marketing materials, workplace policies, ethics policies, and standards for suppliers or vendors. This review may reveal a need to create additional statements to fill the identified gaps or create a new comprehensive mission statement or ethical policy that addresses any deficiencies.[39]

It is important to examine all of the firm's policies and practices with respect to the specific areas covered by the audit. In an audit that scrutinizes discrimination issues, this review step would consider the company's goals and objectives as well as its policies related to discrimination. It would consider the means available for communicating the firm's policies and assess their effectiveness. Such an evaluation should look at whether and how managers are rewarded for meeting their goals and the systems employees have to give and receive feedback. An effective ethics audit reviews all these systems and assesses their strengths and weaknesses.[40]

Concurrent with this step in the auditing process, the firm should define its ethical priorities. Determining these priorities is a balancing act because identifying the needs and assessing the priorities of each stakeholder can be difficult. Because there are no legal requirements for ethical priorities, it is up to management's strategic planning processes to determine risks, designate appropriate standards, and outline processes of communication with stakeholders. It is important to articulate the firm's ethical priorities and values as a set of parameters or performance indicators that can be objectively and quantitatively assessed. Because the ethics audit is a structured report with quantitative and descriptive assessments, actions should be measurable by quantitative indicators. However, it is sometimes not possible to go beyond description.[41]

At some point, a firm must demonstrate action-oriented responsiveness to ethics issues of top priority. Electricity and gas company National Grid has a long history of minimizing damage to the environment. The firm adopted the international standard for environmental management systems, ISO 14001, and the guidelines that require external auditing by a certified auditor. Additionally, National Grid has a global Corporate Responsibility Summary Report on its website.[42]

Collect and Analyze Relevant Information

The next step in the ethical audit framework is to identify the tools or methods for measuring a firm's progress to improve employees' ethical decisions and conduct. The firm should collect relevant information for each subject matter area. To understand employee issues, for example, the auditing committee should work with the firm's human resource department to gather employee survey information and other statistics and feedback. A thorough ethics audit reviews all relevant reports, including external documents sent to government agencies and others. Measuring a firm's sustainability strategy often depends upon a company's own reports and secondary data.[43] The information collected should help determine baseline levels of compliance as well as the internal and external expectations of the company. This step also identifies where the company has, or has not, met its commitments, including those dictated by its mission statement and other policy documents. The documents reviewed in this process vary from company to company based on size, type of industry, and scope of the audit.[44] At Green Mountain Coffee, the audit committee of the board of directors is responsible for providing oversight of reporting procedures and audits. Green Mountain's code of ethics, described in Table 9–6, establishes a framework for the principles that are the backbone of the ethics audit.[45]

Some techniques for collecting evidence might involve examining both internal and external documents, observing the data-collection process, and confirming information in the organization's accounting records. Auditors may also employ ratio analysis of relevant indicators to identify any inconsistencies or unexpected patterns. Objective measurement is the key consideration of the ethics auditor.[46]

Stakeholder involvement is another component in the successful implementation of an ethics audit since they yield significant insights. In one study examining reporting

TABLE 9–6 Green Mountain Coffee's Code of Ethics

- Respect the rights and the property of others

- Maintain accurate records and report unethical behavior

- Comply with all laws, rules, and regulatory requirements

- Avoid conflicts of interest and any appearance of impropriety

- Be responsible stewards in the use, protection, and management of GMCR's assets and resources

- Understand antitrust laws and uphold fair competitive practices

- Share GMCR's story while following the Media Relations guidelines on consistent communications

- Act with integrity while maintaining the confidentiality of GMCR information

- Support GMCR's Purpose, Principles, Policies, and Procedures and encourage GMCR's business partners to do so as well

Source: Adapted from GMC's Code of Ethics, http://investor.gmcr.com/documentdisplay.cfm?DocumentID=7206 (accessed May 14, 2013).

channels, employees were asked to whom they would "feel comfortable" reporting misconduct if they suspected or became aware of it. Supervisors and local managers received the most favorable responses, suggesting the need for organizations to ensure front-line managers are equipped to respond appropriately to allegations. Personnel primarily charged with taking action in response to alleged misconduct (legal, internal audit, and board or audit committee functions) were cited among the least likely channels employees would feel comfortable using to report allegations. A company's ethical culture also determines whether those who report misconduct experience retaliation—and could determine how often employees report misconduct. Figure 9–4 shows that misconduct occurs more often in weak ethical cultures. It is essential for management to create a strong ethical culture so employees are encouraged to report observed misconduct.

Because integrating stakeholder feedback in the ethics audit process is so crucial, these stakeholders must be defined and interviewed during the data-collection stage. For most companies, stakeholders include employees, customers, investors, suppliers, community groups, regulators, nongovernment organizations, and the media. Both social and ethics audits typically interview and conduct focus groups with these stakeholders to gain an understanding of their perception of the company. The Chris Hani Baragwanath Hospital (CHBH) in Johannesburg, South Africa, conducted an audit that included focus groups with the hospital's management, doctors, nurses, related health professionals, support staff, and patients. Using the trends uncovered in these focus groups, CHBH developed an ethics survey questionnaire that it administered to a larger group of individual stakeholders.[47] The more stakeholders auditors include in this measurement stage, the more time and resources the audit consumes. However, a larger sample of stakeholders yields a useful variety of opinions about the company. Multinational corporations must decide whether to include in the audit only the main office or all facilities around the globe.[48]

FIGURE 9–4 Where Cultures are Weaker, Misconduct is More Prevalent

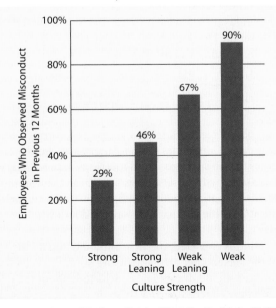

Source: Ethics Resource Center, *2011 National Business Ethics Survey: Workplace Ethics in Transition* (Arlington, VA: Ethics Resource Center, 2012), p. 20.

Because employees carry out a business' operations, understanding employee issues is vital to a successful audit. Useful indicators include staff turnover and employee satisfaction. High turnover rates could indicate poor working conditions, an unethical culture, inadequate compensation, or general employee dissatisfaction. Companies can analyze these factors to determine key areas for improvement.[49] Questionnaires that survey employees' perceptions of the ethics of their company serve as benchmarks in an ongoing assessment of ethical performance. Then, if unethical behavior increases, management will better understand what types of unethical practices may be occurring and why. The CHBH ethics survey asked employees about corporate culture and values, their work space, human resource issues, misconduct, standards of patient care, and problems and sources of stress.[50] Most organizations recognize employees behave in ways that lead to recognition and rewards and avoid behavior resulting in punishment. Therefore, companies can design and implement human resource policies and procedures for recruiting, hiring, promoting, compensating, and rewarding employees that encourage ethical behavior.[51]

Customers are another primary stakeholder group because their patronage and loyalty determines a company's financial success. Providing meaningful feedback is critical to creating and maintaining customer satisfaction. Through surveys and customer-initiated communication systems such as response cards, online social networks, e-mail, and toll-free numbers, organizations can monitor and respond to customer issues and its perceived social performance. Procter & Gamble uses online social networking sites like Facebook to determine what social issues consumers are passionate about, as well as to gain insights into consumers' product needs and reactions to products.

A growing number of investors seek to include in their investment portfolios the stocks of companies that conduct ethics and social audits. Investors are more aware of the financial benefits that stem from socially responsible management systems—as well as the negative consequences of a lack of responsibility. President Obama praised City National Bancshares CEO Leonard Abess for distributing his $60 million bonus to employees. On the other hand, former hostess CEO Gregory Rayburn was criticized by many stakeholders for taking his full salary when other employees were forced to take an 8 percent pay cut while the company prepared for bankruptcy. Rayburn stated that his role was never meant to be permanent and he was not on the Hostess payroll. He did, however, give up his bonus.[52]

Even the hint of wrongdoing can affect a company's relations with investors. Many investors simply do not want to invest in companies engaging in unfavorable business practices, such as the use of sweatshops or child labor. It is therefore critical that companies understand the issues of this important group of stakeholders and their expectations, both financially and socially.

Organizations can obtain feedback from stakeholders through standardized surveys, interviews, and focus groups. Companies can encourage stakeholder exchanges by inviting specific groups together for discussions. Such meetings may include an office or facility tour or a field trip by company representatives to sites in the community. Regardless of how companies collect information about stakeholders' views, the primary objective is to generate opinions about how the company is perceived and whether it is fulfilling stakeholders' expectations.[53]

Once this information is collected, the firm should compare the internal perceptions to those identified in the stakeholder assessment and summarize its findings. During this phase, the audit committee should draw some conclusions about the information obtained in the previous stages. These conclusions may include descriptive assessments of the findings, such as the costs and benefits of the company's ethics program, the strengths and weaknesses of the firm's policies and practices, the nature of feedback from stakeholders, and issues to be addressed in future audits. In some cases, it may be appropriate to see how the findings fit with standards identified earlier, both quantitatively and qualitatively.[54]

Data analysis should include an examination of other organizations in the industry and their performance in the designated subject areas. The audit committee can investigate the successes of another firm considered the best in a particular area and compare that company's performance to their own. Some common benchmarks available from corporate ethics audits are employee or customer satisfaction, community groups' perceptions, and the impact of the company's philanthropy. For example, the Ethics and Compliance Officer Association (ECOA) conducts research on legal and ethical issues in the workplace. These studies allow ECOA members to compare their responses to the aggregate results obtained through the study.[55] Such comparisons can assist the audit committee to identify best practices for a particular industry or establish a baseline for minimum ethics requirements. A wide variety of standards are emerging that apply to ethics accountability. The aim of these standards is to create a tool for benchmarking and a framework for businesses to follow.

Verify the Results

The next step is to have an independent party—such as a social/ethics audit consultant, a financial accounting firm offering social auditing services (such as KPMG), or a nonprofit special interest group with auditing experience (for example, the New Economics Foundation)—verify the results of the data analysis. Business for Social Responsibility, a nonprofit organization supporting social responsibility initiatives and reporting, defined *verification* as an independent assessment of the quality, accuracy, and completeness of a company's social report. Independent verification offers a company, its stakeholders, and the general public a measure of assurance that the company reported its ethical performance fairly and honestly, as well as providing an assessment of the company's social and environmental reporting systems.[56] Verification also lends an audit report credibility and objectivity.[57] However, a survey conducted by one of the Big Four accounting firms found only a few social reports contained any form of external verification.

This lack of third-party assurance may have contributed to the criticism that social and ethics auditing and reporting have more to do with public relations than genuine change. But though the independent validation of ethics audits is not required, the number of independently verified reports is increasing.[58] Many public policy experts believe an independent, objective audit can be provided only if the auditor plays no role in the reporting process—in other words, consulting and auditing should be distinctly separate roles. The Sarbanes–Oxley Act essentially legalized this belief.

Verification of the results of an audit should involve standard procedures that control the reliability and validity of the information. As with a financial audit, auditors can apply substantive tests to detect material misstatements in the audit data and analysis. The tests commonly used in financial audits—confirmation, observation, tracing, vouching, analytical procedures, inquiry, and re-computing—can be used in ethics and social audits as well. For example, positive confirmations can be requested from the participants of a stakeholder focus group to verify that the reported results are consistent with the results the focus group believed it found. Likewise, an ethics auditor can observe a company's procedures for handling ethical disputes to verify statements made in the report. Just as a financial auditor follows supporting documents to financial statements to test their completeness, an ethics auditor or verifier examines employee complaints about an ethics issue to check whether the reporting of such complaints was complete. An auditor can also employ analytical procedures by examining plausible relationships such as the prior year's employee turnover ratio or the average turnover rate commonly reported within the industry. With the reporting firm's permission, an auditor can contact the company's legal counsel to inquire about pending litigation that may shed light on ethical and legal issues currently facing the firm.[59]

Additionally, a financial auditor may be asked to provide a letter to the company's board of directors and senior managers to highlight inconsistencies in the reporting process. The auditor may request that management reply to particular points in the letter to indicate the actions it intends to take to address problems or weaknesses. The financial auditor must report to the board of directors' financial audit committee (or equivalent) significant adjustments or difficulties encountered during the audit as well as any disagreements with management. Ethics auditors should be required to report to the board of directors' audit committee the same issues a financial auditor would report.[60] Green Mountain Coffee uses this method.

DEBATE ISSUE
TAKE A STAND

Which Ethics Audit Process Works Better for Smaller Companies?

ABC Specialty Marketing, Inc. is considering a formal ethics audit. The company has 200 employees, including 50 salespeople that sell promotional printing products. Recent ethical issues have raised concerns within the company, causing the board of directors to think about implementing an audit. During the meeting, one of the board members who examined the auditing process represented in Table 9.5 indicated that for a small company, this approach looked too formal. He felt the Better Business Bureau Torch Award Criteria for ethical companies was a more practical approach to auditing ethical risks and conduct. Another member pointed out that the BBB criteria were more for judging than for understanding the risk areas and ethics program implementation concerns. This led to a discussion about how to implement an ethics audit in a small company with a fairly limited ethics program. The meeting ended without a clear decision on which approach to use.

1. The Better Business Bureau Torch Award Criteria is the best method for conducting a formal ethics audit in a smaller company.

2. The auditing process represented in Table 9.5 offers a better way to understand a small company's ethical risks and conduct.

Report the Findings

The final step in the framework is issuing the ethics audit report. This involves reporting audit findings through a formal report to the board of directors and top executives and, if approved, to external stakeholders. Although some companies prefer not to release the results of their audits to the public, more companies are choosing to make their reports available to stakeholders. Some companies, including the U.K.-based Co-operative Bank and the British newspaper *The Guardian,* integrate the results of their social audits with their annual financial reports and other important information. Many other companies, including Johnson and Johnson, Shell, and Green Mountain Coffee, make audit reports available on their corporate websites.[61]

Based on the guidelines established by the Global Reporting Initiative and AccountAbility, the report should spell out the purpose and scope of the audit, the methods used in the audit process (evidence gathering and evaluation), the role of the (preferably independent) auditor, auditing guidelines followed by the auditor, and any reporting guidelines followed by the company.[62] The ethics audit of Johannesburg's Chris Hani Baragwanath Hospital followed these guidelines.[63] The report is more meaningful if integrated with other organizational information available, such as financial reports, employee surveys, regulatory filings, and customer feedback. The firm might want to include in the ethics audit a section on best industry practices and how it compares to other companies in its field. Such a comparison can help a firm identify its weaknesses and develop suggestions for improvement. The use of information such as the OCEG Benchmarking Study pinpoints key elements of corporate and ethics programs that help assess best practices across the industry.[64]

As mentioned earlier, ethics audits may resemble financial audits, but they take quite different forms. In a financial audit, the Statement of Auditing Standards dictates literally every word found in a financial audit report in terms of content and placement. Based on the auditor's findings, the report issued can take one of the following four forms, among other variations. An *unqualified opinion* states that the financial statements are fairly stated. A *qualified opinion* asserts that although the auditor believes the financial statements are fairly stated, an unqualified opinion is not possible either because of limitations placed on the auditor or because of minor issues involving disclosure or accounting principles. An *adverse opinion* states that the financial statements are not fairly presented. Finally, a *disclaimer of opinion* states that the auditor did not have full access to records or discovered a conflict of interest. These different opinions each have enormous consequences for companies.

THE STRATEGIC IMPORTANCE OF ETHICS AUDITING

Although the concept of auditing implies an official examination of ethical performance, many organizations audit performance informally. Any attempt to verify outcomes and compare them with standards is considered an auditing activity. Many small firms might not use the word *audit,* but they still perform auditing activities. Organizations such as the Better Business Bureau (BBB) provide awards and assessment tools to help any organization evaluate its ethical performance. Companies with fewer resources may wish to use the judging criteria from the BBB's Torch Award Criteria for Ethical Companies (Table 9–7) as benchmarks for informal self-audits. Recent winners of this award included Ford Motor Company, Barney & Barney LLC, and Rockwell Automation, Inc.[65] The award criteria even provide a category for companies with less than 10 employees.

An ethics audit should be conducted regularly rather than in response to problems or questions about a firm's priorities and conduct. The ethics audit is not a control process to be used during a crisis, although it can pinpoint potential problem areas and generate solutions in a crisis situation. As mentioned earlier, an audit may be comprehensive and encompass all the ethics and social responsibility areas of a business, or it can be specific and focus on one or two areas. One specialized audit could be an environmental impact audit in which specific environmental issues, such as proper waste disposal, are analyzed. According to the KPMG International Survey of Corporate Responsibility Reporting, 95 percent of the 250 largest companies report on their corporate social responsibility activities.[66] Examples of other specialized audits include diversity, employee benefits, and conflicts of interest. Ethics audits can present several problems. They can be expensive and time consuming, and selecting the auditors may be difficult if objective, qualified personnel are not available. Employees sometimes fear comprehensive evaluations, especially by outsiders, and in such cases audits can be extremely disruptive.

TABLE 9–7 Better Business Bureau's Torch Award Criteria for Ethical Companies

A business should demonstrate its superior commitment to exceptional standards that benefit its customers, employees, suppliers, shareholders and surrounding communities. The business must provide supporting documentation in four areas for consideration in the Marketplace Excellence category. While examples from all four areas must be provided, the bullet points below are only suggestions and not all bullet points are required to be addressed in order for a business to compete in this category.

Management Practices Note: Owners of companies with no employees must explain how a personal commitment to exceptional standards is applied in business practices.

- Pertinent sections from an employee handbook, business manual or training program (formal or informal) showing how the business's commitment to exceptional standards are communicated to and implemented by employees

- A vision, mission or core values statement describing the business's commitment to exceptional standards that benefit its customers, employees, suppliers, shareholders and surrounding communities

- Formal training and/or procedures used to address concerns an employee may have in dealing with ethical issues

- Management practices and policies that foster positive employee relations

- Employee benefits and/or workplace practices contributing to the quality of family life

- Actions taken to assess and mitigate risks, and prevent workplace injury

- Examples of sound environmental practices

- Examples of operational practices focused on security and privacy issues—on and offline

- Illustrations of your business's commitment to standards that build trust in the marketplace (i.e., customer service program, employee relation policy or practice, vendor/supplier relationship, etc.)

Community/Investor/Stakeholder Relations

- Examples of the business's vision, mission and/or core values statement in action—describing how the business's beliefs have been leveraged for the benefit of consumers, employees, suppliers, shareholders, and surrounding communities

- Business policies and practices that demonstrate accountability and responsibility to communities, investors and other stakeholder audiences

- Corporate governance practices address accountability and responsibility to shareholders

- Complimentary feedback from customers, vendors, suppliers and/or community leaders

- Actions taken by the business demonstrating service "beyond the call of duty"

- Brief case study examples of circumstances in which the business made tough decisions that had negative short-term consequences, but created long-term value and benefits

- Examples of, and results produced by, pro bono work

- Examples of the business working closely within the community and making a positive social impact—and any recognition for charitable and/or community service projects.

Communications and Marketing Practices

- Descriptions of methods the business uses to ensure all sales, promotional materials and advertisements are truthful and accurate

- Sales training policies and/or codes of ethics used by sales personnel that ensure all transactions are made in a transparent, honest manner

- Crisis communications efforts and associated marketing actions that educated audiences, prevented negative outcomes and restored trust and confidence in the business, its products and services

- Examples of internal communications practices benefiting employees and contributing to overall business effectiveness and efficiency

Industry Reputation

- Media coverage reflecting the business's industry and community reputation as a trustworthy business

- Awards, recognition and/or complimentary letters from within the business's industry, trade group or community

Source: "International Torch Award Judging Criteria," Better Business Bureau, http://www.bbb.org/international-torch-awards/critera.html (accessed May 14, 2013).

Despite these problems, however, auditing ethical performance can generate many benefits, as you have seen throughout this chapter. The ethics audit provides an assessment of a company's overall ethical performance as compared to its core values, ethics policy, internal operating practices, management systems, and most importantly, key stakeholder expectations.[67] As such, ethics and social audit reports are a useful management tool for helping companies identify and define their impacts and facilitate important improvements.[68] This assessment can be used to reallocate resources and activities as well as focus on new opportunities. The audit process can also help companies fulfill their mission statements in ways that boost profits and reduce risks.[69] More specifically, a company may seek continual improvement in its employment practices, its customer and community relations, and the ethical soundness of its general business practices.[70] An audit can pinpoint areas where improving operating practices can improve bottom-line profits and stakeholder relationships.[71]

Most managers view profitability, ethics, and social responsibility as a trade-off. This "either/or" mindset prevents them from taking a more proactive "both/and" approach.[72] But the auditing process can demonstrate the positive impact of ethical conduct and social responsibility initiatives on the firm's bottom line, convincing managers—and other primary stakeholders—of the value of adopting more ethical and socially responsible business practices.[73]

SUMMARY

Viewing a business ethics program as a part of strategic planning and management activities is critical to the success of any firm. However, for such programs to be successful, firms must put controls and systems in place to ensure they are being executed effectively. Controls include input, output, and process controls. Input controls are concerned with providing necessary tools and resources to the organization, such as good employees and effective ethics training and structural systems. Process controls include managerial commitment to an ethics program and the methods or system for the evaluation of ethics. Output controls involve comparing standards with actual behavior. One of the most popular methods of evaluating ethical performance is an ethics audit.

An ethics audit is a systematic evaluation of an organization's ethics program and/or its ethical performance. Such audits provide an opportunity to measure conformity with the firm's desired ethical standards. The concept of ethics auditing emerged from the movement toward auditing and reporting on companies' broader social responsibility initiatives. Social auditing is the process of assessing and reporting a business' performance in fulfilling the economic, legal, ethical, and philanthropic social responsibilities expected of it by its stakeholders. An ethics audit may be conducted as a component of a social audit. Auditing is a tool companies can use to identify and measure their ethical commitment to stakeholders and demonstrate their commitment to improving strategic planning, including their compliance with legal, ethical, and social responsibility standards.

The auditing process can highlight trends, improve organizational learning, and facilitate communication and working relationships. Audits help companies assess the effectiveness of their programs and policies, identify potential risks and liabilities, improve compliance with the law, and demonstrate progress in areas of previous noncompliance. One of the greatest benefits of these audits is improved relationships with stakeholders. Ethics auditing may help prevent public relations crises associated with ethical or legal misconduct. Although ethics audits provide benefits for companies and their stakeholders, they have the potential to expose risks; the process of auditing cannot guarantee a firm will not face challenges. Additionally, there are few common standards for judging disclosure and effectiveness or for making comparisons within an industry.

An ethics audit should be unique to each company based on its size, industry, corporate culture, identified risks, and the regulatory environment in which it operates. This chapter offers a framework for conducting an ethics audit that can also be used for a broader social audit.

The first step in conducting an audit is securing the commitment of the firm's top management and/or its board of directors. The push for an ethics audit may come directly from the board of directors in response to specific stakeholder concerns, corporate governance reforms, or top managers looking for ways to track and improve ethical performance. Whatever the source of the audit, its success hinges on the full support of top management.

The second step is establishing a committee or team to oversee the audit process. Ideally the board of directors' financial audit committee would oversee the ethics audit, but in most firms, managers or ethics officers conduct auditing. This committee recruits an individual from within the firm or hires an outside consultant to coordinate the audit and report the results.

The third step is establishing the scope of the audit, which depends on the type of business, the risks faced by the firm, and available opportunities to manage ethics. This step includes defining the key subject matter or risk areas important to the ethics audit.

The fourth step is a review of the firm's mission, values, goals, and policies. This step includes an examination of formal documents that make explicit commitments with regard to ethical, legal, or social responsibility issues, and informal documents including marketing materials, workplace policies, ethics policies, and standards for suppliers or vendors. During this step, the firm should define its ethical priorities and articulate them as a set of parameters or performance indicators that can be objectively and quantitatively assessed.

The fifth step is identifying the tools or methods used to measure the firm's progress, and collecting and analyzing the relevant information. Evidence-collection techniques include examining internal and external documents, observing the data-collection process (such as discussions with stakeholders), and confirming the information in the organization's accounting records. During this step, a company's stakeholders need to be defined and interviewed to understand how they perceive the company. This is accomplished through standardized surveys, interviews, and focus groups. Once information is collected, it should be analyzed and summarized. Analysis should include an examination of how other organizations in the industry are performing in the designated subject matter areas.

The sixth step is having an independent party—such as a social/ethics audit consultant, a financial accounting firm that offers social auditing services, or a nonprofit special interest group with auditing experience—verify the results of the data analysis. Verification is an independent assessment of the quality, accuracy, and completeness of a company's audit process. Such verification gives stakeholders confidence in a company's ethics audit and lends the audit report credibility and objectivity. The verification of the results of an audit should involve standard procedures that control the reliability and validity of the information.

The final step in the audit process is reporting the audit findings to the board of directors and top executives and, if approved, to external stakeholders. The report should spell out the purpose and scope of the audit, methods used in the audit process (evidence gathering and evaluation), the role of the (preferably independent) auditor, any auditing guidelines followed by the auditor, and any reporting guidelines followed by the company.

Although the concept of auditing implies an official examination of ethical performance, many organizations audit informally. Ethics audits should be conducted regularly. Although social auditing may present problems, it can also generate many benefits. Through the auditing process, a firm can demonstrate the positive impact of ethical conduct and social responsibility initiatives on its bottom line, which may convince stakeholders of the value of adopting more ethical and socially responsible business practices.

IMPORTANT TERMS FOR REVIEW

RESOLVING ETHICAL BUSINESS CHALLENGES*

Charles worked at Butterfly Corporation for two years after graduating from the University of Texas. He liked his job but the firm was going through some rough times. Because the firm was losing money, Douglas, the CEO, set increasingly rigorous performance goals. Charles noticed a lot of employees were grumbling about these unrealistic expectations. He also heard rumors of quality control incidents and other problems.

One day Charles was called into Douglas' office. "Hello, Doug. You wanted to see me?" Charles asked.

"Yes, Charles. Come in." Doug looked grim. After Charles sat down, he began to speak. "Look, you know about the tough times we are in. We are losing money left and right. So far I've been able to keep this company afloat by drastically making cuts and speeding up production. I guess in all this cost-cutting, there have been problems that have come up. A lot of people have called the hotline to complain about ethical problems, such as employees cutting corners to make their quotas. Now I've got the board on my back."

"I'm really sorry, Doug. How can I help?" Charles asked.

"Well, the board requested we perform an ethics audit to make sure everyone is complying with company regulations. As if we don't have enough to worry about. This is only going to increase our costs. Anyway, I want you to lead the audit."

Charles was stunned. "Me? But Doug, I've only been here two years. Shouldn't you choose a more experienced manager to lead this?"

Doug shook his head. "We need all our managers to continue doing their jobs. I don't have the time to pull one of them away from their responsibilities just because the board wants us to do an ethics audit."

Charles agreed to lead the audit process. That night he researched how to conduct an ethics audit. He promised to have a rudimentary plan outlining how the ethics audit should be conducted on Doug's desk for approval the next day.

As he researched on the Internet, he became more excited. He spent hours forming objectives for the audit, determining the audit's scope, and defining what he thought should be the firm's ethical priorities. He created a plan for using focus groups of employees to see what the greatest concerns were. If time permitted, he wanted to get other stakeholders involved as well, especially their customers. Charles was interested in assessing the overall corporate culture of the firm. Because Charles knew his data analysis skills were not good, he recommended bringing in a committee of competent coworkers who had been in the organization for years and knew the system inside and out. He also developed a list of organizations Butterfly could hire to verify the results once data was collected and analyzed.

The next day, Charles turned in his report and waited while Doug read through it. When finished, he looked up at Charles and frowned.

"Charles, I can see you put a lot of work into this. However, what you have recommended is not going to suit our needs."

"What do you mean?" Charles asked.

"First off, I already told you, I don't want to remove people from their jobs to work on this. We're behind schedule as it is. Also, focus groups of employees and customer feedback? That's going to take up time and resources we can't afford to lose. You also propose hiring an independent third-party? We're supposed to be cutting costs, not throwing money at some organization simply to check our results."

"So what would you like me to do then?" Charles asked.

Doug sighed. "That's why I made you the person in charge of the project. You make the decisions. Just make sure it's something that won't cost a lot of money. I want this process to go as quickly as possible so we satisfy the board and get back to work. Maybe you could survey a few employees and get it over with. Just remember to make us look good."

Doug handed back Charles' proposal. "Revise this and bring it back to me tomorrow," he said.

QUESTIONS | EXERCISES

1. What is a key component of a successful auditing process missing from this situation?

2. How would you describe the corporate culture of Butterfly?

3. What steps would you recommend Charles take?

*This case is strictly hypothetical; any resemblance to real persons, companies, or situations is coincidental.

> > > CHECK YOUR EQ

Check your EQ, or Ethics Quotient, by completing the following. Assess your performance to evaluate your overall understanding of the chapter material.

1. Ethics audits are required by the Sarbanes–Oxley Act of 2002.	**Yes**	**No**
2. In public corporations, the results of ethics audits should be reported to the board of directors.	**Yes**	**No**
3. An ethics audit helps identify risks and rogue employees.	**Yes**	**No**
4. The scope of an ethics audit depends on the type of risks and the opportunities to manage them.	**Yes**	**No**
5. Smaller companies can skip the step of verifying the results of an ethics audit.	**Yes**	**No**

ANSWERS **1. No.** Financial audits are required, and these may address some ethical issues. **2. Yes.** This is consistent with good corporate governance but not required. **3. Yes.** This is the main benefit of an ethics audit. **4. Yes.** The scope determines the risks unique to the organization. **5. No.** Verification is necessary to maintain integrity and accuracy.

ENDNOTES

1. Muel Kaptein, Toward Effective Codes: Testing the Relationship with Unethical Behavior," *Journal of Business Ethics* 99 (2011): 233–251.

2. The Ethisphere Institute, "2013 World's Most Ethical Companies," *Ethisphere*, http://m1.ethisphere.com/wme2013/index.html (accessed May 14, 2013).

3. Johnson Controls, *Ethics Policy: Integrity Every Day*, http://www.johnsoncontrols.com/content/dam/WWW/jci/corporate/our_corporate_governance/ethics_policies/ENG_EthicsPolicy.pdf (accessed May 14, 2013).

4. Muel Kaptein, "Guidelines for the Development of an Ethics Safety Net," *Journal of Business Ethics* 41 (2002): 217–234.

5. "The 100 Most Influential People in Business Ethics," *Ethisphere*, 2010, Q4, 37; "Green Index," *Timberland*, http://community.timberland.com/Earthkeeping/Green-Index (accessed May 14, 2013); Andrew Clark, "Timberland boss Jeffrey Swartz puts the boot in—over his own failures," guardian.co.uk, March 18, 2010, http://www.guardian.co.uk/business/2010/mar/18/jeffrey-swartz-timberland (accessed May 14, 2013).

6. John Rosthorn, "Business Ethics Auditing—More Than a Stakeholder's Toy," *Journal of Business Ethics* 27 (2000): 9–19.

7. Debbie Thorne, O. C. Ferrell, and Linda Ferrell, *Business and Society: A Strategic Approach to Corporate Citizenship*, 3rd ed. (Boston: Houghton Mifflin, 2008).

8. Rosthorn, "Business Ethics Auditing."

9. *2013 Global Responsibility Report*, http://az204679.vo.msecnd.net/media/documents/updated-2013-global-responsibility-report_130113953638624649.pdf (accessed May 14, 2013).

10. "Accountability," *Business for Social Responsibility*, http://www.bsr.org/BSRResources/WhitePaperDetail.cfm?DocumentID=259 (accessed February 13, 2003).

11. Christopher M. Matthews, "The Morning Risk Report: Much Ado About DPAs," *The Wall Street Journal*, May 6, 2013, http://blogs.wsj.com/riskandcompliance/2013/05/06/the-morning-risk-report-much-ado-about-dpas-deferred-prosecution-agreements/ (accessed May 14, 2013).

12. Marcus Selart and Svein Tvedt Johansen, "Ethical Decision Making in Organizations: The Role of Leadership Stress," *Journal of Business Ethics* 99 (2011): 129–143.

13. Anke Arnaud, "Conceptualizing and Measuring Ethical Work Climate," *Business & Society* 49 (2010): 345–358.

14. Kevin J. Sobnosky, "The Value-Added Benefits of Environmental Auditing," *Environmental Quality Management* 9 (1999): 25–32.

15. "Accountability," Business for Social Responsibility.

16. Trey Buchholz, "Auditing Social Responsibility Reports: The Application of Financial Auditing Standards," Colorado State University, professional paper, November 28, 2000, 3.

17. "Accountability," Business for Social Responsibility.

18. *Fortune*, "World's Most Admired Companies," *CNNMoney*, 2013, http://money.cnn.com/magazines/fortune/most-admired/2013/list/ (accessed May 14, 2013).

19. Simon Birch, "How activism forced Nike to change its ethical game," *The Guardian*, July 6, 2012, http://www.guardian.co.uk/environment/green-living-blog/2012/jul/06/activism-nike (accessed May 14, 2013); "Nike commits to champion a toxic-free future," *Greenpeace*, August 17, 2011, http://www.greenpeace.org/international/en/news/features/Nike-vs-adidas/ (accessed May 14, 2013); Clare Delaney, "Nike and Puma Say No More Hazardous Chemicals (Video)," EcoExpert Blog, http://www.ecofriendlylink.com/blog/nike-and-puma-hazardous-chemical-free-video/#.UZKl0MoauSo (accessed May 14, 2013).

20. John Pearce, *Measuring Social Wealth* (London: New Economics Foundation, 1996), as reported in Warren Dow and Roy Crowe, *What Social Auditing Can Do for Voluntary Organizations* (Vancouver: Volunteer Vancouver, July 1999), 8.

21. Colin Barr, "Obama Talks Tough on CEO Pay," February 4, 2009, http://money.cnn.com/2009/02/04/news/obama.exec.pay.fortune/index.htm (accessed May 14, 2013); "Executive Comp and Governance Provisions of Dodd–Frank Act," *Business Ethics*, July 22, 2010, http://business-ethics.com/2010/07/22/1640-executive-compensation-and-corporate-governance-provisions-of-the-dodd-frank-act/ (accessed May 14, 2013).

22. "The Effect of Published Reports of Unethical Conduct on Stock Prices," reported in "Business Ethics," *Business for Social Responsibility*, http://www.bsr.org/BSRResources/WhitePaperDetail.cfm?DocumentID=270 (accessed March 5, 2003).

23. Ellen Byron and Joann S. Lublin, "Probe Fears Hit Avon Shares," *The Wall Street Journal*, April 14, 2010, http://online.wsj.com/article/SB10001424052702304604204575182402303199376.html (accessed May 14, 2013).

24. Penelope Patsuris, "The Corporate Accounting Scandal Sheet," *Forbes* online, August 26, 2002, www.forbes.com/2002/07/25/accountingtracker.html (accessed May 14, 2013).

25. Ernst & Young, *Risk Management for Asset Management: Ernst & Young Survey 2012*, 6–7, http://www.ey.com/Publication/vwLUAssets/2012_EMEIA_asset_management_risk_survey/$FILE/Risk_Management_for_AM_EY_Survey_2012.pdf (accessed May 14, 2013).

26. David L. Levy, Halina Szejnwald Brown, and Martin de Jong, "The Contested Politics of Corporate Governance: The Case of the Global Reporting Initiative," *Business & Society* 49 (March 2010): 88–115.

27. "About GRI," *Global Reporting Initiative*, https://www.globalreporting.org/Information/about-gri/Pages/default.aspx (accessed May 14, 2013).

28. "FAQs: About GRI," https://www.globalreporting.org/information/FAQs/Pages/About-GRI.aspx (accessed May 14, 2013).

29. "About GRI," Global Reporting Initiative.

30. "Burgundy Book (GRC Assessment Tools)," *OCEG*, http://www.oceg.org/resource/burgundy-book-grc-evaluation-tool (accessed March 23, 2011).

31. "Certification of Capabilities and Individuals," *OCEG*, http://www.oceg.org/certification (accessed March 23, 2011).

32. Risako Morimoto, John Ash, and Chris Hope, "Corporate Social Responsibility Audit: From Theory to Practice," *Journal of Business Ethics* 62 (2005): 315–325.

33. The methodology in this section was adapted from Thorne, Ferrell, and Ferrell, *Business and Society.*

34. The Coca-Cola Company, "Audit Committee Charter," http://www.coca-colacompany.com/investors/audit-committee-charter (accessed May 14, 2013).

35. Ethics Resource Center, "Mission and Values," http://www.ethics.org/page/erc-mission-and-values (accessed September 3, 2009).

36. "Verification," *Business for Social Responsibility*, http://www.bsr.org/BSRResources/White PaperDetail.cfm?DocumentID=440 (accessed February 13, 2003).

37. "Ethical Statement," Social Audit, *SocialAudit.org*, http://www.socialaudit.org/pages/ethical.htm (accessed March 4, 2003).

38. "Our Five Core Values," *Franklin Energy*, http://www.franklinenergy.com/corevalues.html (accessed May 14, 2013).

39. "Verification," Business for Social Responsibility.

40. "Audit and Evaluation," *Open Compliance and Ethics Group*, http://www.oceg.org/view/15839 (accessed September 3, 2009).

41. "Ethical Statement," Social Audit.

42. National Grid, *National Grid and the Environment: Environment policy April 2009*, http://www.nationalgridus.com/non_html/shared_env_policy.pdf (accessed May 14, 2013).

43. Judith L. Walls, Phillip H. Phan, and Pascual Berrone, "Measuring Environmental Strategy: Construct Development, Reliability, and Validity," *Business & Society* 50 (2011): 71–115.

44. "Verification," Business for Social Responsibility.

45. Green Mountain Coffee, http://www.greenmountaincoffee.com (accessed May 14, 2013).

46. Buchholz, "Auditing Social Responsibility Reports," 15.

47. Willem Landman, Johann Mouton, and Khanyisa Nevhutalu, "Chris Hani Baragwanath Hospital Ethics Audit," *Ethics Institute of South Africa*, 2001, http://ethicssa.intoweb.co.za/UserFiles/ethicssa.intoweb.co.za//CHBHFinalReport.pdf (accessed September 3, 2009).

48. "Verification," Business for Social Responsibility.

49. "Introduction to Corporate Social Responsibility," *Business for Social Responsibility*, http://www.bsr.org/BSRResources/WhitePaperDetail.cfm?Document ID=138 (accessed March 5, 2003).

50. Landman, Mouton, and Nevhutalu, "Chris Hani Baragwanath Hospital Ethics Audit."

51. "Introduction to Corporate Social Responsibility," Business for Social Responsibility.

52. Kim Peterson, "Hostess CEO cuts everyone's pay but his," *MSN Money*, December 4, 2012, http://money.msn.com/now/post.aspx?post=f2d05306-bb26-4e35-9eb4-47f4b4902a56 (accessed May 14, 2013).

53. "Accountability," Business for Social Responsibility.

54. Ibid.

55. Ethics and Compliance Officer Association, http://www.theecoa.org (accessed June 18, 2009).

56. "Verification," Business for Social Responsibility.

57. Ibid.

58. Nicole Dando and Tracey Swift, "From Methods to Ideologies," *Journal of Corporate Citizenship*, December 2002, via http://goliath.ecnext.com/coms2/gi_0199-1001798/From-methods-to-ideologies-closing.html (accessed March 24, 2011), 81.

59. Buchholz, "Auditing Social Responsibility Reports," 16–18.

60. Ibid., 19–20.

61. "Accountability," Business for Social Responsibility.

62. Buchholz, "Auditing Social Responsibility Reports," 19–20.

63. Mouton, "Chris Hani Baragwanath Hospital Ethics Audit."

64. "OCEG 2005 Benchmarking Study Key Findings," *Open Compliance Ethics Group*, http://www.oceg.org/Details/18594 (accessed September 3, 2009).

65. Better Business Bureau, "BBB Celebrates 100th Anniversary with Awards to Business and Consumer Leaders," September 20, 2012, http://www.bbb.org/us/article/bbb-celebrates-100th-anniversary-with-awards-to-business-and-consumer-leaders-37065 (accessed May 14, 2013).

66. KPMG, *KPMG International Corporate Responsibility 2011*, http://www.kpmg.com/Global/en/IssuesAndInsights/ArticlesPublications/corporate-responsibility/Documents/2011-survey.pdf accessed May 14, 2013).

67. KPMG, *KPMG International Survey of Corporate Responsibility Reporting 2008*, http://www.kpmg.com/EU/en/Documents/KPMG_International_survey_Corporate_responsibility_Survey_Reporting_2008.pdf (accessed May 14, 2013).

68. Buchholz, "Auditing Social Responsibility Reports," 1.

69. Sandra Waddock and Neil Smith, "Corporate Responsibility Audits: Doing Well by Doing Good," *Sloan Management Review* 41 (2000): 75–83.

70. Buchholz, "Auditing Social Responsibility Reports," 1.

71. Waddock and Smith, "Corporate Responsibility Audits"

72. J. C. Collins and J. I. Porras, *Built to Last: Successful Habits of Visionary Companies* (New York: HarperCollins, 1997).

73. Waddock and Smith, "Corporate Responsibility Audits."

CHAPTER 10

GLOBALIZATION OF ETHICAL DECISION-MAKING

CHAPTER OBJECTIVES

- Discuss global values, goals, and business practices within ethics
- Understand the role of capitalism and economics as factors in business ethics
- Assess the role of multinational corporations in business ethics
- Assess the role of the International Monetary Fund in business ethics
- Assess the role of the United Nations Global Compact in business ethics
- Assess the role of the World Trade Organization in business ethics
- Explore and discuss common global business practices
- Gain awareness of global ethical issues

CHAPTER OUTLINE

AN ETHICAL DILEMMA*

Dun and Ready (D&R) Company is a retail firm that started out in the United Kingdom. It recently expanded into Mexico. D&R management are excited about the expansion because they anticipate a large market for their goods in Latin America. They hired Raul to negotiate contracts for getting the necessary permissions to begin building retail stores in Mexico City. Although Raul graduated from Cornell University, he spent his childhood in Mexico and knew the country well. Raul's manager, Ian Menkin, stressed to Raul the importance of getting the new locations approved as soon as possible so the company could begin building their stores.

Unfortunately, Raul ran into some difficulties receiving permissions in the required time frame. Due to unforeseen circumstances, the permissions process took longer than originally thought. When Raul explained to Ian that the building process would likely be delayed due to these problems, Ian was not pleased. "Look, Raul. We have a schedule to keep. The people here at headquarters will not take kindly to any delays."

"But what should I do, Ian?" Raul asked.

"Just do whatever it takes to get those permits approved," Ian said before hanging up the phone.

Raul called up Pedro, his main government contact that worked on approving zoning permits. Raul explained the situation, but Pedro would not budge.

"I'm sorry, Raul. But I can't make the process go any faster."

Raul, knowing his job could be on the line, begged Pedro to reconsider. Finally, Pedro agreed to meet with Raul to "talk things through."

Later that day, the two men met. Raul again presented his case. Pedro listened and finally spoke. "I understand your predicament. And although it's against policy, I believe I can help you get those permits approved. However, I'm going to need 6,000 pesos to complete the job."

Raul was uncomfortable with the idea. Again, he called up Ian in London. Raul explained the situation. "Unfortunately, this is really going to be the only way to get this process done quickly."

Ian was quiet for a little while. Then he spoke. "The money isn't that important. It only amounts to a little more than £300. Go ahead and pay him."

"But Ian, what if anyone at the company finds out?"

Ian replied, "It's our policy to respect the different cultures in which we do business. It is one of our core values. If giving small payments is the only way to get things done quickly, then that's what we have to do."

Raul agreed and paid Pedro the money. The permits were approved, and the first store was built. The success of the store convinced the company to expand to more locations in the area. Unfortunately, Raul ran into the same problem. Management at D&R wanted their building permits to be approved in a reasonable time period. Raul explained that gaining approval could be a long process in Mexico, but D&R assumed since he had gotten approval quickly once before, he could do it again. Raul was in a bind. So whenever Pedro offered to speed up the process in exchange for a small amount of money, Raul agreed.

As a result of Raul's success, he was promoted and relocated to the United Kingdom to the corporate offices. His pay tripled since from when he had first started. Raul enjoyed London and loved his new job responsibilities. Everything seemed to be going well.

Then one day Raul got a frantic call from Ian. "We have a problem. Somehow someone figured out about the payments made to secure building permits in Mexico. They are launching an investigation."

Although Raul was nervous, he could not understand Ian's panic. "But the payments we made were not extensive. It's just the way things work in Mexico. You said everything would be fine."

Ian's voice was sharp. "You fool! It doesn't matter whether the payments were small! Any type of bribery can be prosecuted under the U.K. Bribery Act. It doesn't matter whether the bribery took place in Mexico—any company with operations in the U.K. can be held liable."

Raul swallowed. "So what do we do?" he asked.

"Listen carefully to what I'm telling you," Ian said. "I want you to find any documentation that might be incriminating and destroy it. If anyone comes asking, deny any payments. Also, contact the person you made the payments to. Do what it takes to make sure he denies that D&R made any improper payments to him."

Raul hung up the phone. He knew if found out the company could face massive fines. Perhaps he and Ian could get into legal trouble. However, he also knew covering up the bribery would make it worse for everyone if discovered. On the other hand, Raul thought there was a good probability that the payments would not be noticed. He knew that almost all companies have to make these payments to get transactions done in different countries, and many have not been caught.

QUESTIONS | EXERCISES

1. What are the ethical issues in this situation?
2. Identify the pressures that caused the ethical issues to develop.
3. Discuss the advantages and disadvantages of each decision Raul could make.

*This case is strictly hypothetical; any resemblance to real persons, companies, or situations is coincidental.

Advances in communication, technology, and transportation have minimized the world's borders, creating a new global economy in which more and more countries are industrializing and competing internationally. These transactions across national boundaries define global business, a practice that brings together people from countries with different cultures, values, laws, and ethical standards. Therefore, international businesspersons must understand the values, culture, and ethical standards of their own countries and also be sensitive to those of other cultures.

In this chapter, we explore the ethical complexities and challenges facing businesses that operate internationally. We help you understand how global business ethics has more complexity than domestic business. The global business environment, if not understood, can destroy the trust companies need to be successful. To transition from one well-understood culture or country to the global arena requires additional knowledge. Our goal in this chapter is to help you become aware of or avoid the ethical quagmires that lurk in this domain. To help you become ethically sensitive to the global environment of business ethics, we start with discussing global values and cultural dimensions used by companies to modify their business practices to different countries. Next, we examine the economic foundations of business ethics. In addition, we help you understand there are global entities that do not necessarily conform to your country's view of the world or the way to do business. In this chapter we examine multinational corporations and the ethical problems they face. We then discuss the International Monetary Fund, the United Nations Global Compact, and the World Trade Organization. We conclude with an analysis of current and future ethical problems facing global businesses, including global ethical risks, bribery, antitrust activity, Internet security and privacy, human rights, health care, labor and right to work issues, compensation, and consumerism. Our goal is to help you understand how international business activities can create ethical conflicts and help you improve your ethical decision-making ability.

GLOBAL CULTURE, VALUES, AND PRACTICES

A nation's culture consists of values that are subjective, based on social and economic institutions, and used to develop norms that are socially and legally enforced. Because institutions such as government and religion affect the development of norms, conventions, and other aspects of culture, values can be specific to countries, regions, sects, or groups. **National culture** is a much broader concept than organizational culture and includes everything in our surroundings made by people—both tangible items, such as artifacts, and intangible entities, such as concepts and values. Language, law, politics, technology, education, social organizations, general values, and ethical standards are all included within this definition. Each nation contains unique cultures and distinctive beliefs about what business activities are acceptable or unethical. Subcultures also exist within many nations, ethnic groups, and religious groups. Therefore, when transacting international business, individuals encounter values, beliefs, and ideas that may diverge from their own. When someone from another culture mentions "integrity" or "democracy," many Americans might feel confident that these are familiar concepts. However, these concepts mean different things to different people, depending on their culture. Moreover, you must keep in mind that organizational culture is different from national culture, though often organizational cultures are derived from—and influenced by—national cultures.

Most cultures need auditors, directors, or other entities associated with corporate governance to provide independent oversight of the operations of an organization. Yet even with such a simple concept as "independent oversight," culture can come into play. For example, in the Japanese banking system, the concept of "independent oversight" is blurred because retired Japanese bureaucrats often become auditors and directors. They are trusted simply because of their status. When those providing oversight also have relationships within and/or a vested interest in the success of the company, a truly independent relationship does not exist and could create conflicts of interest or corporate governance oversight failure.

Different cultural values and how they affect business have intrigued management experts for years. Many have developed frameworks for classifying cultural behavior patterns that can help businesspeople who work in different countries. One of the most well-known frameworks was proposed by Dutch management professor Geert Hofstede. Hofstede identified four cultural dimensions that can have a profound impact on the business environment: individualism/collectivism, power distance, uncertainty avoidance, and masculinity/femininity.[1] We will discuss the first three in the following paragraphs.

The individualism/collectivism dimension of culture refers to how self-oriented members of a culture are in their behavior. Individualist cultures place high value on individual achievement and self-interest. The United States exemplifies an individualistic culture. Collectivist cultures value working toward collective goals and group harmony. Mexico and several countries in Asia adhere to more collectivistic principles. Collectivist cultures tend to avoid public confrontations and disagreements.[2] In Thailand, for instance, negatives such as "no" tend to be avoided in business settings. By understanding this cultural dimension, you are more likely to maneuver correctly within different cultural business settings.

The power distance dimension refers to the power inequality between superiors and subordinates. The United States has elements of both a higher and a lower power distance culture. Over the years, the U.S. business environment adopted forms of management, such as participative management, that place supervisors and subordinates on a more equal footing. In some businesses, employees address their superiors by their first names and have the power to make decisions normally reserved for management. Arab countries score higher on the power distance dimension. Cultures with high power distance tend to be more hierarchal, and respect for (or fear of) supervisors may be so great that managerial misconduct could be hard to pinpoint.[3]

Uncertainty avoidance refers to how members of a society respond to uncertainty or ambiguity. Cultures scoring high on the uncertainty avoidance dimension, such as Great Britain, tend to avoid risk-taking. Organizations within these cultures may have more rules in place to ensure employees do not deviate from accepted standards. Cultures with low levels of uncertainty avoidance, such as Canada, believe risk-taking and innovation are important in achieving successful outcomes.[4] Businesses from either culture need to be aware of how a particular culture views uncertainty avoidance. For instance, if a business-person from the United States gives a sales presentation to a business in Uruguay—a culture with higher uncertainty avoidance—the American businessperson might reassure the Uruguayan company by mitigating the risks involved.

As Hofstede's dimensions suggest, businesspeople traveling to other countries quickly perceive other business cultures have different modes of operation. Interestingly, research shows that consumers who score high on collectivism and uncertainty avoidance and low on masculinity and power distance tend to avoid engaging in more questionable activities than those scoring the exact opposite. This has important implications for international managers when dealing with consumers in different countries.[5]

The perception exists that American companies differ from those in other countries, and some view U.S. companies as superior to their foreign counterparts. This implied perspective of ethical superiority—"us" versus "them"—is also common in other countries. Figure 10–1 indicates the countries that businesspeople, risk analysts, and the general public perceive as the most and least corrupt.

In business, the idea that "we" differ from "them" is called the self-reference criterion (SRC). The SRC is an unconscious reference to one's own cultural values, experiences, and knowledge. When confronted with a situation, we react on the basis of knowledge we accumulated over a lifetime, usually grounded in our culture of origin. Our reactions are based on meanings, values, and symbols that relate in a certain way to our culture but may not have the same relevance to people of other cultures.

Yahoo!'s clash with the French government is one example of how the SRC can cause problems. The International League against Racism and Anti-Semitism (LICRA) claimed Yahoo! violated French law by displaying Nazi memorabilia on its auction sites. Yahoo! was asked to remove the memorabilia or block the auctions from being accessed by France and its territories. Yahoo! refused to comply, stating doing so would create a large financial burden for the company and Yahoo! had the right to display these items under the First Amendment of the U.S. Constitution guaranteeing freedom of speech. Nevertheless, French courts found Yahoo! violated the law. While Yahoo! appealed in the United

FIGURE 10–1 Perceived Levels of Public Sector Corruption

Source: Transparency International, *Corruptions Perceptions Index 2012* (Berlin: Transparency International, 2012).

States, and criminal charges against Yahoo! in France were later dismissed, the U.S. Ninth Circuit Court of Appeals eventually ruled that Yahoo! could not use the First Amendment to break French law. Critics believe Yahoo! failed to execute corporate social responsibility by assuming U.S. law enabled them to use the Internet to display items considered illegal in other countries.[6] This example demonstrates that despite the global nature of the Internet, Internet firms must understand relevant laws in the countries where they do business.

One of the critical ethical business issues linked to cultural differences is the question of whose values and ethical standards take precedence during international negotiations and business transactions. When conducting business outside their home country, should businesspeople impose their own values, ethical standards, and laws on members of other cultures? Should they adapt to the values, ethical standards, and laws of the countries where they are doing business? This was the issue Yahoo! faced in its conflict with French law. As with many ethical issues, there are no easy answers to these questions.

"When in Rome, do as the Romans do," or "you must adapt to the cultural practices of the country where you operate" are rationalizations businesspeople sometimes offer for straying from their own ethical values when doing business abroad. By defending the payment of bribes or "greasing the wheels of business" and other questionable practices in this fashion, they are resorting to **cultural relativism**, the concept that morality varies from one culture to another and that "right" and "wrong" are defined differently.

Despite the various differences in values between countries, there are certain values broadly accepted worldwide. These **global common values** are shared across most cultures. Most laws are directly or indirectly the result of values derived from the major religions of Hinduism, Buddhism, Confucianism, Judaism, Islam, and Christianity. Although most of these religions have similar core virtues, the importance placed on these virtues may vary. For instance, predominately Hindu cultures value nonviolence, mind and sense control, and austerity;[7] traditional Chinese cultures honor respect, righteousness, and loyalty; Islamic cultures value wisdom, tolerance, self-restraint, and mercy;[8] Judaism promotes the virtues of kindness, peace, and hospitality; predominately Christian cultures cherish forgiveness, mercy, and faith;[9] and Buddhist cultures place high importance on the "four immeasurables" of equanimity, joy, loving-kindness, and generosity.[10] By understanding a particular culture's values, global businesses have a better chance of forming relationships with individuals and organizations in that culture. They may also avoid conduct offensive to citizens of certain countries (e.g., shaking with the left hand in Islamic nations). It is beyond our scope to explain all nuances, but there seems to be a consensus on the following desirable and undesirable common values.[11]

- Desirable common values: Integrity, family and community unity, equality, honesty, fidelity, sharing, and unselfishness
- Undesirable common values: Ignorance, pride and egoism, selfish desires, lust, greed, adultery, theft, deceit, lying, murder, hypocrisy, slander, and addiction

ECONOMIC FOUNDATIONS OF BUSINESS ETHICS

Economic and political events as well as natural disasters reflect and affect the environment for global ethical decision making. We first examine how recent developments influenced global systems that structure the business world.

The last economic recession highlighted the fact that firms were taking extreme risks, bending rules, and engaging in unethical activity. A major part of the problem was the excessive focus on rewards and the bottom line that pervaded the global financial industry. The global financial market is a highly interconnected system that can exhibit a lack of transparency in decision making, accountability, and accounting methods. This system, combined with rampant leveraging and the widespread use of highly complex financial computer models many experts did not fully understand, resulted in a global financial meltdown.

Our financial system is complex, and this complexity provides ample opportunity to take excessive risks and manipulate various stakeholders. Many who should have known about such risks were ignorant because of risk compartmentalization. **Risk compartmentalization** occurs when profit centers within corporations are unaware of the overall consequences of their actions on the firm as a whole. As a result, no one person, company, or agency should be blamed—the problems were systemic. Before the financial meltdown, most companies remained in compliance with legal systems, while others looked for legal loopholes and unregulated means of maximizing profits and financial rewards. Many companies tried to be ethical, yet the complex nature of the global economy prevented them from seeing the impending disaster because everyone was focused on their bottom lines.

Economic and social disasters and conflicts have intensified the risks and challenges global businesses encounter. For instance, widespread changes are occurring in the Middle East. While democracy becomes more of a possibility, instability within these regions has led to an exodus of foreign businesspeople.[12] Attempts to oust the Syrian president and overthrow the ruling party led to a civil war wherein thousands of people have died. The instability of Middle Eastern governments and their views toward global commerce could strain business relations. In fact, the Eurasia Group, a global political risk research and consulting firm, listed the Arab Summer as one of the top risks of 2013.[13] Although it is possible this upheaval could lead to positive long-term change, the economies of these countries may take time to stabilize. Economic stability is affected by the supply and commodity price fluctuations caused by such political events. Changes in governments result in the necessity for new social and legal processes, processes that support ethical and legal systems that fit into the global economy.

National disasters can also destabilize economies and affect the economic system. The devastating 2011 earthquake and tsunami in Japan resulted in the destabilization of the economic and social institutions within that country. Japan also faced the challenge of a nuclear meltdown after the tsunami breached the seawall around the Fukushima Daiichi complex and damaged the reactors. The combined crises caused the Tokyo Stock Exchange to lose $700 billion within a three-day period.[14] Later that year flooding in Thailand—the site of many of the world's automotive and technology supply chains—cost businesses such as Honda and JPMorgan millions of dollars.[15]

Many ethical issues emerge while coping with crises. The disruption of necessities and global supply chains creates opportunities for individuals and organizations to engage in exploitation. An unethical organization might charge exorbitant prices during a time of crisis because the people are dependent upon its products for survival. Conversely, the global community is expected to engage in aid and philanthropic efforts to help countries recover from disasters. Corporations, particularly multinationals, are often expected to help in recovery efforts since many have profited from doing business within the affected countries.

Finally, the world is still coping with the aftereffects of the last global recession that caused public distrust of the stability of governmental institutions as well as those charged with managing the money of individuals, corporations, and countries. Some countries, such as Iceland, Zimbabwe, Hungary, Ukraine, and Serbia, declared a form of bankruptcy as a result of the recession.[16] The European Union is still struggling to recover since Portugal, Ireland, Greece, and Spain all required bailouts to stay afloat. Greece defaulted on its debt. As a lack of trust, honesty, and fairness caused major investors to question the competence of regulatory institutions, which in turn caused instability and public mistrust in the entire financial system, many questioned the foundations of capitalism and the policies needed to make it function. Today, people are discussing and even revising fundamental concepts and assumptions of capitalism. Because you will enter this new reality, we will briefly explain the global economic debate.

Economic Systems

To understand capitalism—and the types of businesses that operate in different economies—you must understand basic economic systems. Economic systems have a significant impact on business ethics because they determine the role of governments in business, the types of laws that regulate businesses, and the amount of freedom companies have in their activities. The main forms of capitalism and socialism are derived from the works of Adam Smith, John Maynard Keynes, and Milton Friedman.

Adam Smith was a professor of logic and moral philosophy during the late eighteenth century, as noted earlier, and he developed critical economic ideas still considered important today. Smith observed the supply and demand, contractual efficiency, and division of labor of various companies within England and wrote about what he saw. His idea of laissez-faire, or the "invisible hand," is critical to capitalism because it assumes the market, through its own inherent mechanisms, keeps commerce in equilibrium. Smith also believed businesses must be guided by ethical people for the market to work properly.

The second form of capitalism gained support at the beginning of the Great Depression. During the 1930s John Maynard Keynes argued that the state could stimulate economic growth and improve stability in the private sector through, for example, controlling interest rates, taxation, and public projects.[17] Keynes argued that government policies could be used to increase aggregate demand, thus increasing economic activity and reducing unemployment and deflation. He believed the solution was to stimulate the economy through some combination of a reduction in interest rates and government investment in infrastructure. President Franklin D. Roosevelt employed Keynesian economic theories during his time in office when he sought to pull the United States out of the Great Depression.

The third and most recent form of capitalism is associated with Milton Friedman, and represents a swing to the right of the political spectrum. Friedman lived through the Great Depression but rejected the Keynesian conclusion that markets sometimes need intervention to function efficiently. He believed deregulation could reach equilibrium without government intervention.[18] Friedman's ideas were the guiding principles for government policy making in the United States, and increasingly throughout the world, starting in the second half of the twentieth century.

Both Keynes and Friedman agreed that "(1) People have rational preferences among outcomes that can be identified and associated with a value; (2) Individuals maximize utility and firms maximize profits; (3) People act independently on the basis of full and relevant information."[19] Today, however, these assumptions are being questioned.

Socialism refers to economic theories advocating the creation of a society when wealth and power are shared and distributed evenly based on the amount of work expended in production. Modern socialism originated in the late nineteenth century and was a working-class political movement that criticized the effects of industrialization and private ownership. Karl Marx was one of socialism's most famous and strongest advocates. Marxism was Marx's own interpretation of socialism, and it was transformed into communism in countries such as the Soviet Union and Cuba. History has shown that communism, strictly interpreted, causes economies to fail. For example, Cuba traditionally held an antagonistic view toward capitalism and private enterprise. As a result, most of the population was employed in the public sector. However, during the most recent recession, the Cuban government realized it could not support so many workers. In an attempt to save its struggling economy, the government took the unprecedented step of laying off half a million state workers to make room for private sector jobs.[20] In the 1940s forms of social democracy emerged. Social democracy allows private ownership of property and also features a large government equipped to offer such services as education and health care to its citizens. Social democracies take on such problems as disease, ignorance, squalor, and idleness, and advocate governmental intervention. The Scandinavian countries such as Denmark, Sweden, and Finland are examples of social democracies. Studies indicate that the populations of these small European democratic nations are some of the happiest in the world.[21]

Past economists could not imagine the multinational corporation, or that the world's energy resources would be concentrated under the control of a handful of corporations. Our world has grown increasingly bimodal in wealth distribution. Bimodal wealth distribution occurs when the middle class shrinks, resulting in highly concentrated wealth among the rich and increased numbers of poor people with few resources. This is not a desirable scenario and can result in instability. The size and power of today's multinational corporations are immense. For instance, companies can pit one government against another for strategic advantages. You can see the same strategy by country group in trade blocs such as NAFTA (North American Free Trade Agreement), the EU (European Union), and ASEAN (Association of Southeast Asian Nations). These trade blocs give economic leverage to country groups and use the same economic principles as multinationals. To understand the future global perspective, we next discuss the difference between rational and behavioral economics.

Rational economics is based on the assumption that people are predictable and will maximize the utility of their choices relative to their needs and wants. For example, if you are hungry and have $10 to spend, rational economics suggests you will spend the money on food that satisfies your hunger needs and wants. However, people are not always rational. No one wants to go to jail. Even those who stole millions admit the reward was probably not worth the punishment. Yet this does not stop individuals from engaging in crimes to secure short-term gains. Barry Minkow, former pastor, businessman, and fraud investigator, pleaded guilty to securities fraud as a result of manipulating the stock of Lennar Corp. Minkow already served seven years in prison after being convicted in 1988 of operating a Ponzi scheme through his business.[22] He clearly did not act in a rational manner when he decided to commit another instance of securities fraud.

The second assumption is that people act independently on the basis of full and relevant information. Normally, we might assume that a criminal did not have full or relevant information concerning his/her actions. However, Minkow already experienced prison time and, as a fraud investigator, likely knew the penalties he faced should he get caught. His example illustrates that some individuals will act irrationally even when they have a clear idea of the consequences of their actions. There are many individuals and organizations willing to take risks to achieve their objectives. This high-risk approach often results in manipulation and misconduct.

Behavioral economics assumes humans act irrationally because of genetics, emotions, learned behavior, and heuristics, or rules of thumb. Heuristics are based upon past experiences and do not always yield the most rational response. Behavioral economics assumes economic decisions are influenced by human behavior. Figure 10–2 depicts where countries may be in the process of developing economic philosophies, and helps to understand where they may want to go. China, Sweden, and the former Soviet Union are in the lower left quadrant, representing socialism as a society with behavioral economics as the vehicle to happiness. As we mentioned, each of these country's definitions of happiness is derived from social democratic goals. They are behavioral because they believe very little in laissez-faire. The dates presented are important, because they show countries can change their positions over time. In the upper right quadrant, the graphic shows how certain countries' economies define happiness and the government's role. Finally, in the upper left quadrant are the United States and (again) Sweden, representing Sweden's shift to capitalism and more laissez-faire economics, and the United States' shift to a less laissez-faire economy.

The conflict between capitalism and socialism stems partly from the Cold War. Many in the United States perceive socialism as Marxism; it is not. Outside the United States, socialism is often perceived as group-oriented as it relates to social problems. Socialism argues for the good of the community, with government helping people

FIGURE 10–2 The Economic Capitalism Country Differential

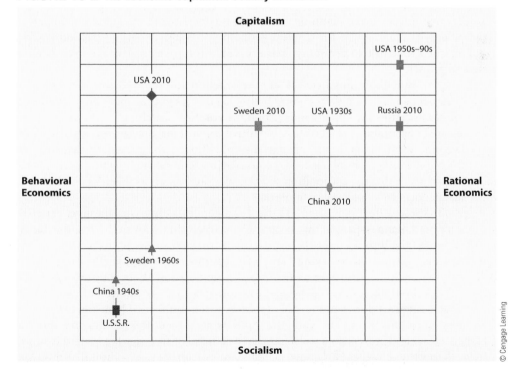

© Cengage Learning

through manipulation of the economy. The American form of capitalism is grounded in individualism, where government is perceived as a hindrance in the pursuit of happiness.

Today, capitalism is one of the United States' many cultural exports. But while the United States practices one kind of capitalism, there are many other forms. The success of the U.S. model of capitalism during the 1990s and 2000s led many businesses and countries to champion it as the premier economic model. However, the last recession, combined with the collapse of some of the world's largest financial firms, dampened global enthusiasm for this model. It is likely that in the future, more attention will be directed toward other forms of capitalism.[23]

Sweden was one of the poorest countries in Western Europe in the 1880s. During the 1890s, it became more worker-friendly. From 1918 to 1970, Sweden's standard of living rose faster than most countries'.[24] After 1970 the country changed worker policies to become more corporate friendly and continues to enjoy one of the highest standards of living in the world.

India and China have introduced the free market into their systems, although their models are different. China's large communist government blurs the lines between organizations, businesses, and government because organizations must comply with government mandates. India, on the other hand, is democratic with a lively civil society that is often empowered to stand up against the government and capitalism. These two countries represent about one-third of the world's population and are considered rising powers—yet their forms of capitalism are radically dissimilar. China's government involvement in business, combined with the rapid growth of its economy, may cause us to question the notion that large governments stand in the way of business success—in fact, the government often appears to be the premier entrepreneur.[25] In 2010 China superseded Japan to become the world's second largest economy.[26] More recently, the Chinese government began planning for private businesses and open markets to play a larger role in its economy. As the Chinese economy slowed in 2013, Chinese leaders felt reducing the state's role in economic matters would improve creativity, entrepreneurship, and growth.[27]

Is capitalism with minimal government interaction and the free flow of goods and services across national boundaries best? Or should governments be more protectionist in giving local businesses the upper hand? Economists are still searching for the answer. On the one hand, corporations can create competitive barriers via government legislation or by collusion to form oligopolies for managed competition. The argument is that without government intervention, local businesses could decline. On the other hand, certain forms of capitalism argue that the corporation should pay shareholders as much as possible and other stakeholders are of secondary importance.

Despite these differing viewpoints there is a general consensus amongst experts, academics, and businesspeople that corporations operating with social responsibility in mind must take into account the norms and mores of the societies in which they operate. Corporations take varying views of corporate social responsibility (CSR).[28] A broad view includes thinking about the consequences of their actions on a wide range of stakeholders and using the corporation as a tool for public policy, while a narrow view involves, for example, only looking at the number of jobs created. These are ethical questions businesses and governments need to address as they operate on a globalized scale. There is no agreement that one form of free-market system is more ethical than others. Ethical business systems are not restricted to capitalist models;

socialist countries also develop ethical businesses. Countries, institutions, social systems, technology, and other cultural factors have a major effect on organizational ethics. To understand global ethics, we examine ethical dimensions surrounding multinational firms.

MULTINATIONAL CORPORATION

Multinational corporations (MNCs) are public companies that operate on a global scale without significant ties to any one nation or region. MNCs represent the highest level of international business commitment and are characterized by a global strategy focusing on opportunities throughout the world. Examples of U.S.–based multinational corporations include Nike, Monsanto, and Cisco Systems. Some of these firms have grown so large that they generate higher revenues than the gross domestic product (GDP)—the sum of all the goods and services produced in a country during one year—of some of the countries where they do business, as shown in Table 10–1.

Based on revenues versus GDP, Royal Dutch Shell is greater than the economies of Greece, Denmark, Taiwan, Argentina, and Iran. Because of their size and financial power, MNCs are the subject of much ethical debate, and their impact on countries where they do business is controversial. Both American and European labor unions argue it is unfair for MNCs to transfer jobs overseas where wage rates are lower. Other critics charge that multinationals use labor-saving devices that increase unemployment in countries where they manufacture. MNCs have been accused of increasing the gap between rich and poor

TABLE 10–1 A Comparison Between Countries and Corporations Based on Gross Domestic Products and Revenues

Country	GDP (millions $ U.S.)*	Company	Revenues (millions $ U.S.)
United States	15,650,000	Royal Dutch Shell	484,489.0
China*	12,380,000	Exxon Mobil	452,926
Japan	5,984,000	Walmart	446,950
Germany	3,367,000	BP	386,463
India	1,947,000	Sinopec Group	375,214
Iran	483,800	China National Petroleum	352,338
Argentina	474,800	State Grid	259,142
Taiwan	474,100	Chevron	245,621
Denmark	309,200	ConocoPhillips	237,272
Greece	255,000	Toyota Motor	235,364

Note: Because China bases its exchange rate on the fiat, purchasing power parity was used to get a better comparison of its GDP compared to other countries.

Source: Based on "Global 500: Fortune's Annual Ranking of the World's Largest Corporations," *CNNMoney*, http://money.cnn.com/magazines/fortune/global500/2012/full_list/(accessed May 16, 2013). CIA *World Fact Book*, https://www.cia.gov/library/publications/the-world-factbook/fields/2195.html (accessed May 16, 2013).

nations and of misusing and misallocating scarce resources. Their size and financial clout enable them to control money, supplies, employment, and even the economic well-being of less-developed countries. For example, IKEA, the Swedish furniture company, dealt with the consequences of questionable labor practices that occurred over 30 years ago in Germany. The allegation is that under the Communist regime, East German political prisoners were forced to produce various parts of furniture for the company. If the inmates did not meet the given expectations of production, they were severely punished. IKEA has closely monitored its supply chain since 2000 to ensure forced labor is not a part of the production process. However, these claims from the past have shown that top management knew about the forced labor and did little to deal with the issue. Some praise IKEA for taking responsibility for the company's past actions, but others see it as a blight on the company's reputation.[29]

Critics believe the size and power of MNCs create ethical issues involving the exploitation of both natural and human resources. One question is whether MNCs should be able to pay a low price for the right to remove minerals, timber, oil, and other natural resources, and then sell products made from those resources for a much higher price. In many instances, only a fraction of the ultimate sale price of such resources comes back to benefit the country of origin. This complaint led many oil-producing countries to form the Organization of Petroleum Exporting Countries (OPEC) in the 1960s to gain control over the revenues from oil produced in those lands.

Critics also accuse MNCs of exploiting the labor markets of host countries. As noted earlier, MNCs have been accused of paying inadequate wages. Sometimes MNCs pay higher wages than local employers can afford to match; then local businesses complain the most productive and skilled workers go to work for multinationals. Measures have been taken to curtail such practices. For example, host governments levy import taxes that increase the prices MNCs charge for their products and reduce their profits. Import taxes are meant to favor local industry as supply sources for an MNC operating in the host country. If a tax raises the MNC's costs, it might lead the MNC to charge higher prices or accept lower profits, but such effects are not the fundamental goal of the law. Host governments have also imposed export taxes on MNCs to force them to share more of their profits.

The activities of MNCs also raise issues of unfair competition. Because of their diversified nature, MNCs can borrow money from local capital markets in much higher volume than smaller local firms. MNCs have also been accused of failing to carry an appropriate share of the cost of social development. They frequently apply advanced, high-productivity technologies that local companies cannot afford or implement because they lack qualified workers. The MNCs thus become more productive and can afford to pay higher wages to workers. Because of their technology, however, they require fewer employees than local firms would hire to produce the same product. Additionally, given their economies of scale, MNCs can also negotiate lower tax rates. By manipulating transfer payments among their affiliates, they pay fewer taxes. All these advantages explain why some claim MNCs compete unfairly.

Sometimes countries refuse outright to allow MNCs into their countries. For example, heavy-equipment companies from industrialized nations argue that their equipment will make it possible to complete infrastructure projects sooner, which could help boost the economies of less-developed countries. However, countries such as India believe it is better in the long run to hire laborers to do construction work since this practice provides much-needed employment and keeps currency within the local economy. Therefore, they often choose to use local laborers instead of purchasing equipment from foreign countries.

Although it is usually MNCs' unethical or illegal conduct that grabs world headlines, many MNCs strive to be good global citizens with strong ethical values. Texas Instruments (TI) adopted a three-tiered global approach to ethical integrity that asks: "(1) Are we complying with all legal requirements on a local level? (2) Are there business practices or requirements at the local level that affect how we interact with co-workers in other parts of the world? (3) Do some of our practices need to be adapted based on the local laws and customs of a specific locale? On what basis do we define the universal standards that apply to TI employees everywhere?"[30] One of the ways Texas Instruments puts this approach into practice is specifying rules on excessive gift giving. Since what is considered to be "excessive" varies depending on country, Texas Instruments adopted an approach that forbids gift-giving "in a way that exerts undue pressure to win business or implies a quid-pro-quo [sic]."[31]

Many companies, including Coca-Cola, DuPont, Hewlett-Packard, Levi Strauss & Co., and Walmart, endorse following responsible business practices abroad. These companies support a globally based resource system called **Business for Social Responsibility** (BSR). BSR tracks emerging issues and trends, provides information on corporate leadership and best practices, conducts educational workshops and training, and assists organizations in developing practical business ethics tools. It addresses issues such as community investment, corporate social responsibility, the environment, governance, and accountability. BSR also established formal partnerships with other organizations that focus on corporate responsibility in Brazil, Israel, the United Kingdom, Chile, and Panama.[32]

Although MNCs are not inherently unethical, their size and power often seems threatening to people and businesses in less-developed countries. The ethical problems MNCs face arise from the opposing viewpoints intrinsic to multicultural situations. Differences in cultural perspectives may be as important as differences in economic interests. Because of their size and power, MNCs must take extra care to make ethical decisions that not only achieve their own objectives, but also benefit the countries where they manufacture or market their products. Even the most respected MNCs sometimes find themselves in ethical conflict and face liability as a result.

The U.S. model of the MNC is fading as developing countries such as China, India, Brazil, and South Korea form MNCs as alliances, joint ventures, and wholly owned subsidiaries.[33] The turn away from the American model does not mean less concern for ethics and social responsibility. As corporations expand internationally, ethics and social responsibility are important firm-specific capabilities that can be a resource and lend a company an advantage for growth and profit. The development of trust and corporate citizenship is a necessary capability, much like technology or marketing. A number of Chinese businesses have learned that long-term success cannot be achieved by selling products that are unsafe or of inferior quality. Ethical and responsible business conduct is a requirement for long-term success in global business. With the increasing globalization of companies has come a growing intolerance toward opportunistic business activities driven by profit and a greater acceptance for multinationals able to contribute toward economic and social improvement.[34] As a result, several global organizations have formed to support cooperation and responsible business practices.

GLOBAL COOPERATION TO SUPPORT RESPONSIBLE BUSINESS

International Monetary Fund

The International Monetary Fund (IMF) originated from the Bretton Woods agreement of July 1944 when a group of international leaders decided the primary responsibility for the regulation of monetary relationships among national economies should rest in an international body, the IMF. The IMF makes short-term loans to member countries with deficits and provides foreign currencies for its members. The IMF also provides information about countries that might default on their debts. Member states provide resources to fund the IMF through a system of quotas proportional to the size of their respective economies. Member states also receive IMF voting power relative to these quota contributions. Under this rule, the United States has just under one-fifth of the votes. The IMF has become the international coordinator of regulatory policy for the world.

Although the IMF's main function is to regulate monetary relationships between national economies, the organization has taken steps to promote responsible global business conduct. For instance, the IMF suggested governments adopt a "binding code of conduct across nations" to determine the conditions necessary for interceding in troubled firms, and how to share losses from financial institutions operating across multiple borders. The IMF also recommended new regulations for large firms posing the biggest "systemic risk."[35] The concept of risk and IMF bailouts took on significant importance during the last global recession. Because of a massive amount of debt, the European countries of Greece, Ireland, Portugal, and Spain required major bailout packages from the IMF. These bailouts caused a negative economic impact felt throughout the European Union.[36]

United Nations Global Compact

The United Nations (UN) was founded in 1945 by 51 nations. Its goals are to promote worldwide peace, establish beneficial relationships between countries, and support the creation of better standards and human rights on a global scale. Today, the UN includes 193 member states from across the world. Although the United Nations is generally thought of as a peacekeeping organization, this coalition of diverse countries also focuses extensively on sustainable development, human rights and gender equality, global environmental issues, and more.[37] Another major concern for the UN is business development. Recognizing that business is "a primary driver in globalization," the UN views business as a way to increase the economic outlook of countries, create equality with fair labor practices, combat corruption, and promote environmental sustainability.[38] Conversely, unethical businesses that go global to take advantage of favorable factors such as cheap labor could have the opposite effect.

To support business as a driver for positive change, the UN created the United Nations Global Compact, a set of 10 principles that promote human rights, sustainability, and the eradication of corruption. Table 10–2 gives a brief description of these principles. Above all, the UN hopes the Global Compact creates a collaborative arrangement among businesses, governments, nongovernmental organizations, societies, and the United Nations to overcome challenges and advocate positive economic, social, and political change.

TABLE 10–2 United Nations Global Compact

Human Rights
- Principle 1: Businesses should support and respect the protection of internationally proclaimed human rights; and
- Principle 2: make sure that they are not complicit in human rights abuses.

Labour
- Principle 3: Businesses should uphold the freedom of association and the effective recognition of the right to collective bargaining;
- Principle 4: the elimination of all forms of forced and compulsory labour;
- Principle 5: the effective abolition of child labour; and
- Principle 6: the elimination of discrimination in respect of employment and occupation.

Environment
- Principle 7: Businesses should support a precautionary approach to environmental challenges;
- Principle 8: undertake initiatives to promote greater environmental responsibility; and
- Principle 9: encourage the development and diffusion of environmentally friendly technologies.

Anti-Corruption
- Principle 10: Businesses should work against corruption in all its forms, including extortion and bribery.

Source: "The Ten Principles," United Nations Global Compact, http://www.unglobalcompact.org/AboutTheGC/TheTenPrinciples/index.html (accessed May 16, 2013).

The Global Compact is voluntary for organizations. Those that join are held accountable, and are required to annually post the organization's progress toward Global Compact goals and show commitment to UN guiding principles. Global members are expected to cooperate with the UN on social projects within developing nations where they do business. More than 10,000 entities participate in the UN Global Compact.[39]

While global business ethics is essential knowledge for companies, it is critical knowledge for business students. The Association to Advance Collegiate Schools of Business (AACSB) International, an organization that represents about 1,350 members, joined with groups such as the UN Global Compact to inspire a set of six principles for business schools. These principles fall under the title "Principles for Responsible Management Education."[40] The first principle encourages students to become future leaders in creating sustainable value for business, society, and the global economy. Other principles include incorporating global social responsibility into curricula; creating educational materials that cultivate responsible leaders; and encouraging dialogue among educators, students, businesses, and other stakeholders to address social responsibility and sustainability issues. The Principles for Responsible Management Education are powerfully influenced by the idea of sustainable development and corporate social responsibility.[41]

World Trade Organization (WTO)

The World Trade Organization (WTO) was established in 1995 at the Uruguay round of negotiations of the General Agreement on Tariffs and Trade (GATT). Today, the WTO has 159 member and observer nations. On behalf of its membership, the WTO administers its own trade agreements, facilitates trade negotiations, settles trade disputes, and monitors the trade policies of member nations. The WTO addresses economic and social issues involving agriculture, textiles and clothing, banking, telecommunications, government purchases, industrial standards, food sanitation regulations, services, and intellectual property. It also provides legally binding ground rules for international commerce and trade policy. The organization attempts to reduce barriers to trade between and within nations and settle trade disputes. For instance, the WTO often rules on situations involving allegations of dumping. **Dumping** is the practice of charging high prices for products in domestic markets while selling the same products in foreign markets at low prices, often at below cost. It places local firms at a disadvantage and is therefore illegal in many countries. Two U.S. honey processors were fined after they allegedly imported Chinese sweeteners to avoid antidumping duties. One of the major reasons provided for fining the firms was the fact that the scheme placed legitimate importers and other firms in the honey industry at a disadvantage.[42]

Not all countries agree with the WTO's particular stance on free trade. In the past, import tariffs increased on Asian plastic bags in Europe; oil in South Korea; Chinese steel pipes in the United States; and all imports in Ukraine. According to the WTO, shoes, cars, and steel are among the goods most vulnerable to protectionism, or trade restrictions among countries.[43] During global downturns, countries tend to restrict trading. However, many firms find ways to get around tariffs. If a company wants instant free trade access to the United States, for instance, it can manufacture in Israel. If the company wants free trade access for low-tech products to the EU, the company can manufacture in the African country of Senegal because of its free trade agreement with France. Companies with the right knowledge can find a number of ways to bypasses tariffs, particularly as trading blocs such as the EU continue to grow.[44]

GLOBAL ETHICS ISSUES

In this section we focus on issues that have a dramatic impact on global business, including global ethical risks, bribery, antitrust activities, Internet security, and privacy. We also discuss fundamental rights such as human rights, health care, labor, and compensation, as well as the issue of consumerism. Bribery and antitrust issues are among the most targeted areas of concern for governments worldwide. Human and labor rights are some of the more commonly abused in global business environments.

Global Ethical Risks

Although globalization has many benefits, it is not without risks. Risk creates ethical issues for global companies to manage. The organization known as the Eurasia Group recently identified 10 key areas of international risk. Many of these risks require organizations conducting business globally to make ethical business decisions. Some of these risks are described below.

- Emerging markets offer many opportunities for investors but are not without significant risks. Political instability, imbalances in power, social discontent, and faltering economies represent major risks for foreign investment

- Chinese leadership has been encouraging more nationalism, which could threaten relationships with other countries, particularly the United States and countries in Southeast Asia. Tension between China and Japan appears to be rising; attacks on Japanese businesses in several Chinese cities demonstrates this heightened conflict. Additionally, the growing influence of the Internet and the proliferation of information available to citizens could potentially lead to more crackdowns or attempts at censorship.

- The economic outlook for many countries in the Euro zone continues to remain weak. While policies for financial reform have been recommended, opposition is likely to be fierce.[45]

Corporations worldwide have become more global in their compliance actions. Table 10–3 represents a compilation of important compliance issues of global companies based in the United States and in the European Union. Global competition laws, anti-bribery requirements, ethics and values, and export controls are considered more relevant by the EU than confidentiality, records management, and labor and employment laws. These differences give us clues as to the types of laws governments will formulate in the future.

Bribery

Bribery is a difficult topic because its acceptance varies from country to country. While bribery between businesses is illegal in countries such as the United States, it is an

TABLE 10–3 Global Business Ethics and Legal Issues

U.S. Ranking	European Ranking	Important Issues
1	1	Code of Conduct
2	5	U.S. Antitrust
3	3	Mutual Respect
4	7	U.S. Foreign Corrupt Practices Act (FCPA)
5	4	Conflicts of Interest and Gifts
6	9	Proper Use of Computers
7		Insider Trading
8	6	Financial Integrity
9		Confidentiality
10		Records Management
11		Labor and Employment Law
12	8	Intellectual Property
	2	Global Competition Law
	10	Global Anti-bribery Requirements
	11	Ethics and Values
	12	Export Controls

Source: Based on Integrity Interactive Corporation, "Top Compliance Concerns of Global Companies," http://www.i2c.com (accessed May 16, 2013).

accepted way of doing business in other countries. It is not unusual for managers in BRIC countries (Brazil, Russia, India, and China) to offer favors in order to attain business goals. Because these "favors" are of minimal value and are not considered to be bribery within these countries, their use is generally considered to be ethical in these cultures.[46] Today, most developed countries recognize that bribery is not a responsible or fair way of conducting business because of the potential to damage consumers and competition. However, companies must determine what constitutes a bribe. In Japan it is considered courteous to present a small gift before doing business. Are such gifts bribes or merely acts of gratitude? Without clear guidelines, the topic of bribery remains ambiguous enough for misconduct to occur. For this reason, both the United States and the United Kingdom passed regulations defining bribery and set legal precedents for businesses that encounter these situations.

U.S. FOREIGN CORRUPT PRACTICES ACT (FCPA)   The U.S. Foreign Corrupt Practices Act (FCPA) prohibits American companies from making payments to foreign officials for the purpose of obtaining or retaining business. In 1988 Congress became concerned that American companies operated at a disadvantage compared to foreign companies whose governments allowed bribes. In 1998 the United States and 33 other countries signed an agreement intended to combat the practice of bribing foreign public officials in international business transactions, with an exception for payments made to facilitate or expedite routine governmental actions (known as facilitation or "grease" payments). Prosecution of bribery has increased, with the U.S. Justice Department making violations of the FCPA a top priority.

Bribery has become a problem for some major corporations. IBM, Daimler AG, and Monsanto were charged for violating the FCPA and paid heavy fines. Walmart is under investigation for alleged bribes in Mexico. Although sometimes bribery is done with the full compliance of top management, larger companies with multiple branches, global operations, and many employees have a harder time detecting such misconduct. The FCPA was modified recently and now provides a "best practices" guide for companies. The change was prompted by two major cases. RAE Systems Chinese joint ventures paid about $400,000 to Chinese officials in exchange for contracts worth $3 million. The company's sales force used cash advances to fund the bribes. The SEC claimed RAE lacked solid internal controls and failed to respond to red flags. The other case related to the company Panalpina and also involved bribery.[47] The resulting settlements led to the creation of guidelines used by the U.S. Department of Justice and the Securities and Exchange Commission in assessing FCPA compliance. The guidelines can be helpful to ensure companies comply with the Foreign Corrupt Practices Act. These guidelines are outlined in Table 10–4.

Violations of the act can result in individual fines of $100,000 and jail time. Penalties for companies can reach into the millions.[48] Some FCPA violations are easier to detect than others. Some of the riskiest practices include payment for airline tickets, hotel and meal expenses of traveling foreign officials, the wiring of payments to accounts in offshore tax havens, and the hiring of agents recommended by government officials to perform "consulting" services.[49] Current enforcement agencies are targeting these third-party bribery payments.

U.K. BRIBERY ACT   Many nations, including China and European nations, are taking a tougher stance against bribery. The United Kingdom instituted perhaps the most

TABLE 10–4 FCPA "Best Practices" for Compliance Guidelines

The development of clear policies against FCPA violations
Support by senior management for the company's compliance policy
The development of standards and policies relating to the acceptance of gifts, hospitality, entertainment, expenses, customer travel, political contributions, charitable donations and sponsorships, facilitation payments, solicitation, and extortion
The development of compliance procedures that include risk assessment and internal controls
Annual reviews of compliance procedures and updates when needed
The development of appropriate financial and accounting procedures
The implementation of policies to properly communicate procedures to directors, officers, employees, and other appropriate stakeholders
The establishment of a system that provides legal guidance to appropriate stakeholders
Disciplinary procedures for violations of anticorruption rules
The exercise of due diligence to ensure compliance with anticorruption policies
The inclusion of anticorruption provisions in agreements and contracts with suppliers, agents, and other partners
Periodic reviews of codes and procedures to ensure they measure up to FCPA regulations
Prompt reporting of violations to the SEC

Source: Based on "U.S. Securities and Exchange Commission and Department of Justice Clarify 'Best Practices' for FCPA Compliance," *Mayer Brown*, January 11, 2011.

sweeping anti-bribery legislation to date.[50] The U.K.'s Bribery Act will likely cause companies doing business in the U.K. to dramatically change their compliance reports. While the act overlaps with the U.S. Foreign Corrupt Practices Act, it takes further steps to curb bribery. Under the law British residents and businesses, as well as foreign companies with operations in the U.K., can be held liable for bribery, no matter where the offense is committed or who in the company commits the act, even if the bribe itself has no connection with the U.K. Unlike under the FCPA, companies are not required to have explicit knowledge of a bribe to be held criminally liable.[51] Additionally, the law classifies bribes between private businesspeople as illegal. Initially, the law did not make provisions allowing for "grease payments" to speed up services that otherwise would be delayed, although this part of the law is being reconsidered. The law also requires corporations to determine if their subsidiaries or joint-venture partners are involved in bribery at any level.[52] The act increased the maximum jail time for bribery from seven to 10 years.[53]

Such encompassing provisions against bribery created concern for businesses that operate in the United Kingdom. Some fear something as simple as taking a client out to dinner will be considered a bribe under U.K. law. However, U.K. officials and legal experts state that acts of hospitality will not be considered illegal. Additionally, businesses can protect themselves from heavy penalties by instituting an effective compliance program that management supports. Managers should set the correct tone at the top along with implementing proper reporting procedures, periodic reviews of the company's code of conduct and compliance programs, risk assessments, and other policies discussed in this book and outlined in the U.S. Federal Sentencing Guidelines.[54] Legal experts question if the Serious Fraud Office in the U.K. will choose to prosecute cases that deal with small "grease" payments or prosecute cases that occur outside the United Kingdom.[55]

Antitrust Activity

Fair competition is viewed favorably in many countries, with the belief that competition yields the best products at the best prices. This basic concept of capitalism has begun to change, however. During the nineteenth and early twentieth centuries, U.S. corporations began using what today would be considered anticompetitive practices, creating high barriers of entry for competitors in an attempt to dominate markets. These practices led to higher prices and fewer options for consumers. In 1890 the United States passed the Sherman Antitrust Act to prevent such anticompetitive behavior. Other countries have similar laws. Issues of competition become more complicated when companies do business in countries with differing laws. For instance, the EU has stricter antitrust laws than does the United States, making it harder for some MNCs to compete in Europe. EU antitrust probes have been launched against Google, Microsoft, and IBM, among other companies.

Because large MNCs create economies of scale and barriers to entry, they tend to reduce overall competition and can put smaller companies out of business. If these firms remain unregulated, they could engage in a vertical systems approach to become monopolies. A **vertical system** is created when a channel member (manufacturer, wholesaler, distributor, or retailer) has control of the entire business system, via ownership or contract, or through its purchasing ability. Vertical systems create inertia, causing channel members to stay with their various retailers and distributors even though competitors may have better products and prices. Sometimes MNCs use their size to coerce other companies to do business exclusively with them. The EU charged Intel $1.45 billion for anticompetitive behavior. Intel allegedly provided rebates to retailers if they bought only its computer chips, as well as paying manufacturers for delaying or restricting the distribution of products from its main rival, Advanced Micro Devices (AMD).[56]

Internet Security and Privacy

Today's computer hackers can use tools like the Internet and computer viruses to commit corporate espionage, launch cyber attacks against government infrastructures, and steal confidential information.[57] Until recently, Internet security has not been a significant part of business ethics. However, serious Internet crimes have brought this issue to the public's attention. Computer hackers became particularly problematic in the United States and China. Several cyber attacks in the United States have been traced back to a Chinese hacker group that accessed trillions of terabytes of highly sensitive information. Not only are the attacks directed toward businesses and their trade secrets, but more alarmingly, they are directed at the country's power grid systems, financial systems, and military information systems. The United States admits to cyber hacking as a form of national security, as does China. However, one report suggests that a Chinese hacker group that stole American trade secrets is linked with the Chinese armed forces. China vehemently denies these claims. Because of the economic and national security threats, the United States considered implementing trade sanctions against China. This illuminates another complexity between perceptions of right and wrong between countries and cultures.[58]

Hacking, Trojan horses (devices that look desirable but steal information once installed), and worms are not necessarily illegal in some countries. However, the global community has begun to classify such practices as unethical, arguing they should become illegal. Although companies develop software to track down viruses and malware and keep them from infecting computers, hackers constantly create new ways to bypass these systems. Many companies use questionable Internet practices that may not be illegal but could be construed as unethical. For instance, many websites install cookies, or small iden-tifying strings of text, onto users' computers. This allows the website to identify the user's computer when he or she revisits the site. These companies use cookies as a way to tailor their offerings to specific users. For example, Amazon.com uses cookies to make product recommendations to users. Despite the consumer convenience and competitive advantages of cookies, being able to identify users without their consent or direct knowledge creates an ethical issue: privacy.

While some Internet privacy violations, such as breaking into users' accounts and stealing their financial information are clearly unethical, many other situations present more challenging ethical issues. For instance, mobile advertising networks face privacy issues for the way they display advertisements to mobile application users. Businesses hire ad networks to post their advertisements on Internet pages and mobile applications. The businesses buy a certain amount of space on the mobile or website page and do not always know how the ad networks display their ads. The ad networks started using tracking methods within the mobile devices to determine the user's location and preferences in order to display ads relevant to each individual. Apple, after discovering their methods, has prohibited ad networks from using personal information for advertising. The ad networks claim people are identified by a random set of numbers that cannot be traced back to anyone's personal identity, but others claim this information is stored in specific profiles that could eventually be traced to personal identifying characteristics. There is no current legislation on this issue, but the Federal Trade Commission is investigating the matter to determine if it is a violation of consumer privacy.[59]

Another ethical dilemma regarding privacy is the use of personal information by com-panies. Facebook, the most popular social networking site worldwide, has been criticized for lax privacy policies and making member information too public. Privacy has become such a concern that governments have begun considering new legislation to regulate infor-mation collection on the Internet. The United States government is debating whether to regulate the Internet to limit the types of information websites track.[60]

In countries such as Saudi Arabia and China, Internet privacy is not just a cor-porate issue. Governments take an active role in censoring citizens' use of the Internet. Saudi Arabia nearly banned BlackBerry smartphones because BlackBerrys use overseas routing. Overseas routing gives the government less control and Saudi Arabia feared it would allow third parties outside the country to gain access to encrypted messages. The Saudi government also censors websites and provides users with online messages telling them they have been denied access to a particular site.[61] The Chinese government rou-tinely uses an Internet-filtering system called the "Great Firewall" to censor Internet sites. It often does not tell its citizens when materials are censored. Instead, the filtering looks like a technical glitch. Networks such as YouTube and Facebook are blocked completely. This makes it difficult for foreign businesses such as Google, which adheres to a "Don't Be Evil" policy, to justify doing business with China. Google experienced repeated clashes with the Chinese government over censorship, including accusations that the government disrupted the company's email services among its Chinese users.[62] These scenarios demonstrate the types of ethical issues companies encounter when conducting business globally.

Human Rights

The meaning of the term human rights is codified in a UN document, and is defined as an inherent dignity with equal and inalienable rights and the foundation of freedom, justice, and peace in the world. The concept of human rights is not new in business. It was established decades ago, but few companies took it into consideration until recently. Table 10–5 presents three articles from the UN Human Rights Declaration. Their implementation in the world of business has serious ethical ramifications. Article 18 concerns freedom of religion. From a Western perspective this is straightforward. However, how should firms respond to employees from countries where it is acceptable to have multiple wives? Should they all be granted health insurance? In response to such challenges, Ford Motor Co. started the Ford Interfaith Network to educate employees about different religions and foster respect for the beliefs of its diverse employees across the world.[63] On the other hand, research on FTSE 100 firms demonstrates that while many large corporations have basic human rights policies listed in their documents, including non-discrimination and the right to join unions, other rights in the UN Human Rights Declaration such as right to privacy, right to work, and equal pay are mentioned far less.[64]

Health Care

Another ethical issue gaining in importance is health care. Globally, a billion people lack access to health care systems, and about 11 million children under the age of five die from malnutrition and preventable diseases each year.[65] As a result, global concern about the priorities of pharmaceutical companies is on the rise. This ethical dilemma involves profits versus health care. Those who believe pharmaceutical companies are inherently unethical suggest the quest for profits led these companies to research drugs aimed at markets that can afford luxuries, such as cures for baldness or impotence, rather than focusing on cures for widespread deadly diseases like malaria, HIV, and AIDS.

Patents are another challenging issue. Since patents give pharmaceutical companies exclusive rights to their products for a certain period, the companies can charge higher prices—prices those in emerging economies cannot often afford. In a major decision, the Indian supreme court ruled against a drug patent for Novartis for the cancer drug Glivec.

TABLE 10–5 Selected Articles from the UN Human Rights Declaration

Article 18. Freedom of thought, conscience and religion … either alone or in community … in public or private …
Article 23. The right to work … to just and favorable conditions of work and to protection against unemployment … equal pay for equal work … ensuring for himself and his family an existence worthy of human dignity … right to form and to join trade unions …
Article 25. Right to a standard of living adequate for the health and well-being … Motherhood and childhood are entitled to special care and assistance.

Source: United Nations, "The Universal Declaration of Human Rights," https://www.un.org/en/documents/udhr/ (accessed May 16, 2013).

Novartis argued that because it made improvements to the drug, it should be awarded patent protection. The Indian supreme court disagreed, ruling the changes were not enough to warrant a patent for something already out on the market. While this ruling has major implications for lower-income people's ability to afford the medication, Novartis claims the ruling discourages innovation and taught the company to be cautious when investing in the country.[66] Pharmaceutical companies such as Novartis argue that high prices are needed to recoup the costs of creating the drugs, and without profits their companies would not be able to function. Another argument is that since other firms are allowed to patent their products, pharmaceutical companies should be allowed the same privileges. Yet when the issue is one of life or death, businesses must find ways to balance profitability with human need.

A related issue affecting both developing and developed countries is the affordability of health care. Rising health care costs continue to pose a critical challenge, particularly in the United States, where millions of people remain uninsured. Studies have revealed that the United States spends more per capita on health care than other industrialized countries—but without better results for the investment. Prices of health care products and procedures can vary greatly within the country.[67] When health care becomes too costly, businesses tend to either drop health care packages offered to employees or downgrade to less expensive—and less inclusive—packages. For instance, some unions, companies, and insurers have begun dropping mental health care plans due to a law that states mental health care, if offered, must be as "robust" as the rest of the medical benefits. Rather than offer the more costly mental health benefits, some companies are choosing to drop them entirely.[68]

Global health care fraud is a serious ethics issue, costing businesses and governments millions and depriving individuals of funds needed for critical care. One estimate places the losses from global health care fraud at $260 billion annually.[69] Fraud includes providing less medicine in packages for the same price, filing false Medicare claims, and providing kickbacks for referrals, and fraud can be committed by individuals, companies, doctors, and pharmacists. A jury convicted the supervisor of mental health care company Health Care Solutions Network with spearheading a $63 million fraud that crossed state lines. The fraud took place in the form of falsified statements to Medicare and Medicaid.[70]

DEBATE ISSUE
TAKE A STAND

Is Health Care a Right or a Privilege?

The Universal Declaration of Human Rights, adopted by the United Nations in 1948, proclaims "everyone has the right to a standard of living adequate for the health and well-being of oneself and one's family, including food, clothing, housing, and medical care." Hard work and healthy living does not assure being healthy. With the high costs of health care, many consumers cannot afford health insurance. The U.S. government is following other industrialized nations in adopting universal health care.

Critics argue it is the individual's responsibility, not the government's, to ensure personal health. Many health problems, such as obesity and diabetes, can often be prevented by individuals choosing to live healthier lifestyles. Another concern involves the cost of health care. Critics believe universal health insurance will increase costs because more people will depend upon the government for health care. This in turn might cause costs to be passed onto the consumers and prompt the government to limit certain types of care. Guaranteeing health care for all may lead people to make riskier decisions because they know if they get hurt, they are guaranteed health care coverage.

1. Because health care protects life, it is a fundamental right and should therefore be ensured by the federal government.

2. Health care is a privilege and should not be provided by the government because of the high costs involved.

The fundamental issue leading some businesses into ethical and legal trouble around the world is the question of whether health care is a right or a privilege. Many people in the United States see health care as a privilege, not a right; thus, it is the responsibility of individuals to provide for themselves. People in other countries, such as Germany, consider it a right. German employees have been guaranteed access to high-quality, comprehensive health care since 1883.[71] Many countries believe health care is important because it increases productivity; therefore, governments should provide it. As health care costs continue to increase, the burden for providing it falls on companies, countries, employees, or all three.

Labor and the Right to Work

Another global issue businesses encounter is labor. Today, many people live and work in a country other than their homeland. In the European Union, workers can carry benefits across countries within the EU without any reductions or changes. Many workers therefore ask the question, "Am I a multinational employee first and then a citizen of a country, or am I a citizen first and an employee second?" Because businesses must make a profit, there are increasing occasions when nationality no longer is a deciding factor. In business, we are becoming global citizens. As a result, firms need to understand that certain employee issues, once country-specific, have become global.

One example of a global labor issue involves gender pay inequality. This debate has spread throughout the globe, in both developing and industrialized countries. In the European Union women are estimated to earn on average 16 percent less than their male counterparts per hour.[72] Despite these disparities, equal pay is recognized as a fundamental right by the UN Human Rights Declaration, and gender pay inequality is illegal in many countries. Businesses, particularly multinationals, must consider this issue carefully. Failure to do so could lead to lawsuits or reputational damages. Walmart spent years fighting a class-action lawsuit from hundreds of female employees claiming they were discriminated against in pay and promotions. Companies working to eliminate gender pay inequalities within their organizations will be acting ethically and protecting themselves legally as well.

In addition to equal pay, Article 23 of the UN Human Rights Declaration discusses the right to work and join trade unions. Within the European Union, trade unions are accepted, but in many other countries, including Burma, North Korea, Cuba, and Iran, trade unionists risk imprisonment. China and Syria allow only one trade union.[73] European companies with employees in these countries face many ethically charged decisions. Trade unions are an issue in the United States, too. McDonald's and Walmart have discouraged attempts to unionize in the United States, but they acquiesced to their workers in China and allowed them to unionize. Both companies have unions in all of their Chinese facilities, yet they continue to fight against unions in their home countries.[74]

Article 25 of the UN Human Rights Declaration mentions a standard of living and special rights related to pregnancy. The United States lags behind other industrialized nations in its treatment of pregnant women and new mothers. While other countries allow female employees a specific amount of paid maternity leave, the United States guarantees only 12 weeks of unpaid leave.[75] Some countries have argued for allowing men to take off the same amount of leave (either paid or unpaid). This debate never takes place in Sweden because Swedish parents get 480 paid days off that can be split between parents at 100 percent pay.[76]

Compensation

The last global recession set off a spark prompting employees worldwide to question their compensation relative to those of others. Employees, particularly those in places without strong employee protections, began questioning why high-level executives get so many benefits while their incomes have stayed the same or fallen. These questions highlight two wage issues having a profound effect on business: the living wage and executive compensation.

A LIVING WAGE A living wage refers to the minimum wage workers require to meet basic needs. Many countries have passed minimum wage laws to provide employees with a living wage (whether the "minimum wage" is actually enough to meet a worker's basic needs is highly debatable). These laws vary from country to country. While the United States has a federal minimum wage law of $7.25 per hour, Australia's minimum wage is $15.37 per hour, while the United Kingdom's minimum wage equals $9.57 per hour for workers 21 or older.[77] Regions within these countries may adopt higher regional minimum wage laws to account for higher costs of living. The issue of a living wage is a controversial topic for MNCs. Because laws of industrialized countries dictate employers must pay a minimum wage, some MNCs choose to outsource their labor to other countries where no minimum wage exists. While not necessarily unethical in and of itself, this practice becomes a significant ethical dilemma when the public perceives the organization as paying foreign laborers unfair wages. The problem multinationals face is finding a solution that balances the interests of the company as a whole with those of its employees and other interested stakeholders. Nike continues to be criticized for the wages paid to factory workers in other countries. While Nike claims it pays workers in these countries higher than the mandated minimum wage laws of the country, critics point out the amount is not suitable to cover living expenses of workers or their families. Nike contends that a "fair" wage is hard to determine when dealing with other countries, a statement with which many multinationals would likely agree.[78] However, the concept of a living wage is a challenge companies must acknowledge if they hope to successfully do business in the global environment.

EXECUTIVE COMPENSATION The issue of executive pay came to the forefront during the last global recession. In the United States the government felt it necessary to bail out firms that would go bankrupt otherwise. However, when companies that received taxpayer money such as American International Group and Merrill Lynch subsequently paid their executives millions in compensation, the public was outraged. These types of incidents led to a global demand for better alignment between managerial performance and compensation.

The Swiss government, after bailing out several organizations, recently passed a referendum called "say-on-pay" that requires a yearly shareholder vote determining executive pay.[79] Another referendum called "1:12 Initiative for Fair Pay," which limits executive pay to no more than twelve times the company's lowest paid employee, is receiving Swiss support and is expected to pass into law. This kind of mentality on executive pay, often called "shareholder activism," is spreading to American companies as well.[80] Meanwhile, the Chinese government ruled the disparity between the country's executives and its workers was too great. It therefore cut the salaries of top executives at state-owned banks and insurers.[81] The gap between executive and worker compensation will likely remain a major business ethics issue until stakeholders are satisfied that executives earn their compensation.

Consumerism

Consumerism is the belief that the interests of consumers, rather than those of producers, should dictate the economic structure of a society. It refers to the theory that consumption of goods at an ever-increasing rate is economically desirable, and equates personal happiness with the purchase and consumption of material possessions. However, over the past 50 years consumption placed significant strains on the environment. Many scientists argue that human factors (such as the increase in fossil fuel emissions from industrialization and development and deforestation), have caused global warming. Many countries contend that consumer choices are moral choices, that choosing a high rate of consumption affects vulnerable groups such as the poor, and the world will be less habitable if people refuse to change their behaviors.[82]

As nations increase their wealth, consumers increase their quality of living with luxury items and technological innovations that improve the comfort, convenience, and efficiency of their lives. Such consumption beyond basic needs is not necessarily a bad thing; however, as more people engage in this type of behavior, waste and pollution increase. Some important issues must be addressed in relation to consumerism. For example:

- What are the impacts of production on the environment, society, and individuals?
- What are the impacts of certain forms of consumption on the environment, society, and individuals?
- Who influences consumption, and how and why are goods and services produced?
- What goods are necessities, and what are luxuries?
- How much of what we consume is influenced by corporations rather than by our needs?
- What is the impact on poorer nations of the consumption patterns of wealthier nations?[83]

China's rise to dominance in manufacturing and world trade caused it to outpace the United States as a consumer. It now leads the United States in consumption of basic goods such as grain, meat, coal, and steel. China also surpassed the United States in greenhouse gas emissions. Some fear China's newfound consumerism will drive up global prices for goods, as well as speed up global warming, even as other nations take measures to stop it. Chinese consumers are pushing for more cars, appliances, and technology like never before. With 1.3 billion consumers, this causes a major strain on the environment. China has taken steps to curb its negative environmental impact, such as becoming the largest investor in wind turbines in the world. Unfortunately, most of China's energy needs are still produced by fossil fuels that cause its carbon dioxide emissions to increase.[84]

India, with its 1.1 billion people, is following China and the West on the consumerist path. India has the world's fastest-growing information technology market, creating skilled, high-wage jobs for software engineers, business process experts, and call-center workers. The country is well-situated to weather global recessions because much of the country's demand for goods is domestic. India has the second-largest domestic market for goods in the world.[85] While this demand has fueled growth, it has also led to an enormous increase in greenhouse gas emissions. India is now the third largest emitter of greenhouse gases.[86]

The ethics of these consumerism issues are many. Large emerging economies are the profit-making centers of the future. Most in business understand it is in the best interests of the firm that consumer needs and desires are never completely or permanently fulfilled, so consumers can repeat the consumption process and buy more products. For example, made-to-break, or planned obsolescence, products are better for business since they keep consumers returning to buy more. It also is profitable to make products part of a continuously changing fashion market. Thus, items still in good condition and that last for many years are deemed in need of constant replacement to keep up with fashion trends. In this way, steady profits are assured—as well as waste. The top 20 percent of consumers in the highest-income countries comprise 86 percent of global consumption expenditures, whereas the poorest 20 percent comprise 1.3 percent of consumption expenditures. The richest 20 percent also consume 58 percent of the total energy used on the planet.[87]

One ethical question being asked by more people and countries is, "Does consumerism lead to happiness?" Consumer detractors are gaining ground globally, and the United States is their example of non-sustainable consumption. They note that while the United States comprises 4.6 percent of the world's population, it consumes 33 percent of the world's resources. The world's poorest 2.3 billion people consume 3 percent of the world's resources. The average American generates twice as much waste per person per year as the average European.[88]

These consumption statistics point to a different lifestyle for the future, and global business will drive it. The moral conflict between countries, especially between the United States and the developing world, will increase, with corresponding ethical challenges for business. The future may be one filled with international violence, to which business must respond, or it may be characterized by a lifestyle that global business creates and markets to avoid civil and global war. It is up to you and others to decide.

THE IMPORTANCE OF ETHICAL DECISION MAKING IN GLOBAL BUSINESS

Ethical decision making is essential if a company is to operate successfully within a global business context. Without a clear understanding of the complexities of global ethics, companies will face a variety of legal and political snares that could result in disaster. It is important to realize that many of the same issues we discussed in this chapter can be applied to domestic markets as well. Internet security, for instance, can be just as much of an ethical issue domestically as it is in companies operating internationally. As such, businesses should incorporate both global and domestic ethical issues into their risk management strategies.

For companies looking to expand globally, the multitude of ethical issues to consider seems daunting. Many companies choose to adopt global business codes of ethics to provide guidelines for their international operations. To this end, several organizations created ethics and social responsibility frameworks businesses can adopt in formulating their own global ethics codes. The International Organization for Standardization has developed ISO 26000 and ISO 14000, among other guidelines, to address issues such as ethics, sustainability, and social responsibility. Another set of global principles were developed by Reverend Leon Sullivan as a way to rise above the discrimination and struggles in post-apartheid South Africa. Reverend Sullivan worked with the UN Secretary General to revise the principles to meet global needs. Since then, both large and small companies have agreed to abide by the Global Sullivan Principles that encourage social responsibility throughout the world. The Global Sullivan Principles, the UN Global Compact, the UN Human Rights Declaration, as well as others promote foundational principles of conduct for global businesses. Table 10–6 provides a synthesis of typical foundational statements.

For multinational corporations, risk management and global ethics are so integral to the stability of their overseas operations that they have created special officers or

TABLE 10–6 Global Principles for Ethical Business Conduct

Global principles are integrity statements about foundational beliefs that should remain constant as businesses operate globally. These principles address issues such as accountability, transparency, trust, natural environment, safety, treatment of employees, human rights, importance of property rights, and adhering to all legal requirements. The principles are designed to focus on areas that may present challenges to the ethical conduct of global business.

1. **Require accountability and transparency in all relationships.** Accountability requires accurate reporting to stakeholders, and transparency requires openness and truthfulness in all transactions and operations.

2. **Comply with the spirit and intent of all laws.** Laws, standards, and regulations must be respected in all countries as well as global conventions and agreements developed among nations.

3. **Build trust in all stakeholder relationships through a commitment to ethical conduct.** Trust is required to build the foundation for high integrity relationships. This requires organizational members to avoid major international risks such as bribery and conflicts of interest. Laws supporting this principle include the U.S. Foreign Corrupt Practices Act, the U.K. Anti-bribery Act, OECD Convention, and UN Convention Against Corruption.

4. **Be mindful and responsible in relating to communities where there are operations.** The communities where businesses operate should be supported and improved as much as possible to benefit employees, suppliers, customers, and the community overall.

5. **Engage in sustainable practices to protect the natural environment.** This requires the protection of the long-term well-being of the natural environment including all biological entities as well as the interaction among nature, individuals, organizations, and business strategies.

6. **Provide equal opportunity, safety, and fair compensation for employees.** Employees should be treated fairly, not exploited or taken advantage of, especially in developing countries. Laws supporting this principle include equal opportunity legislation throughout the world.

7. **Provide safe products and create value for customers.** Product safety is a global issue as various governments and legal systems sometimes provide opportunities for firms to cut corners on safety. All products should provide their represented value and performance.

8. **Respect human rights as defined in the UN Global Compact.** Human rights are a major concern of the UN Global Compact and most other respected principles statements of international business.

9. **Support the economic viability of all stakeholders.** Economic viability supports all participants in business operations. Concerns such as fair trade and payment of a living wage are embedded in this principle.

10. **Respect the property of others.** Respect for property and those who own it is a broad concept that is an ethical foundation for the operation of economic systems. Property includes physical assets as well as the protection of intellectual property.

committees to oversee global compliance issues. Walmart created a global ethics office to communicate company values and encourage ethical decision making throughout its global stores.[89] General Motors' Board Audit Committee created the Global Ethics and Compliance Department after revisions were implemented to the U.S. Federal Sentencing Guidelines. GM not only wanted to comply with these guidelines, it also wanted to create a centralized system of compliance that would be used at all GM locations worldwide.[90]

The successful implementation of a global ethics program requires more than just a global ethics committee. It also requires extensive training for employees. As this chapter demonstrated, various differences exist between cultures and businesses from different countries. Employees of global companies should be trained to understand and respect these differences, particularly those employees directly involved in global operations. Ford Motor Co. has an online global ethics training program for employees available in 13 languages. The company also offers hotlines for employees in 24 countries and trains its Office of the General Counsel how to handle global complaints.[91] Codes of global ethical conduct, global ethics training, and global channels for employees to communicate misconduct are important mechanisms in creating a culture of globalized ethical decision making.

A global firm cannot succeed simply by applying its domestic ethical programs to other global environments. Although ethical issues such as honesty and integrity are common to most countries, differences in laws, political systems, and cultures require a more targeted approach to ethical decision making. Global ethics is not a "one size fits all" concept. With that said, it is important for companies to act with integrity even if they are doing business in a country with lax laws on certain ethical subjects. Those companies who incorporate globalized ethical decision making throughout their international operations not only enhance their reputations, but also demonstrate a respect for their employees and cultures—as well as avoid the costly litigation that often accompanies misconduct.

SUMMARY

In this chapter we tried to sensitize you to the important topic of ethical decision making in an international context. We began by looking at values and culture. A country's values are influenced by ethnic groups, social organizations, and other cultural aspects. Hofstede identified four cultural dimensions that can have a profound impact on the business environment: individualism/collectivism, power distance, uncertainty avoidance, and masculinity/femininity. The self-reference criterion is the unconscious reference to one's own cultural values, experiences, and knowledge and is a common stumbling block for organizations. Another approach organizations tend to take is that of cultural relativism, or the idea that morality varies from one culture to another and business practices are defined as right or wrong differently.

Risk compartmentalization is an important ethical issue and occurs when various profit centers within corporations become unaware of the overall consequences of their actions on the firm as a whole. The last financial meltdown was in part the result of risk compartmentalization. Understanding rational economics and systems is an important foundation for understanding business ethics. Rational economics assumes people make decisions rationally based upon utility, value, profit maximization, and relevant information. Capitalism bases its models on these assumptions. Behavioral economics, by contrast, argues that humans may not act in a rational way as a result of genetics, learned behavior, emotions, framing and heuristics, or rules of thumb. Social democracy, a form of socialism, allows private ownership of property and features a large government equipped to offer services such as education and health care to its citizens. Sweden, Denmark, and Finland are social democracies.

Multinational corporations are public companies that operate on a global scale without significant ties to any one nation or region. MNCs contributed to the growth of global economies but are by no means immune to criticism. The International Monetary Fund makes short-term loans to member countries that have deficits and provides foreign currencies for its members. The UN Global Compact is a set of 10 principles that promote human rights, sustainability, and the eradication of corruption, while the World Trade Organization administers its own trade agreements, facilitates trade negotiations, settles trade disputes, and monitors the trade policies of member nations.

There are several critical ethics issues that global businesses should be aware. Global risks create ethical issues for global companies to manage. Bribery is a major ethical issue, prompting legislation such as the U.S. Foreign Corrupt Practices Act and the U.K. Bribery Act. Antitrust activities are illegal in most industrialized countries and are pursued even more ardently in the European Union than in the United States. Internet security is an ethical issue, and hacking and privacy violations are on the rise. The United Nations codified human rights as a function of inherent human dignity and includes equal and inalienable rights such as the foundation of freedom, justice, and peace in the world. Health care and labor issues are important ethical issues but tend to vary by country. Wage issues such as a living wage and executive compensation are controversial topics that affect a variety of global stakeholders. Consumerism is the belief that the interests of consumers should dictate the economic structure of a society, rather than the interests of producers; it refers to the theory that an increasing consumption of goods is economically desirable, and equates personal happiness with the purchase and consumption of material possessions.

IMPORTANT TERMS FOR REVIEW

global business 274

consumerism 298

made-to-break 299

self-reference criterion 276

cultural relativism 277

national culture 275

risk 278

compartmentalization 278

global common values 277

John Maynard Keynes 279

Adam Smith 279

laissez-faire 279

social democracy 280

Milton Friedman 279

Socialism 280

behavioral economics 281

bimodal wealth distribution 280

rational economics 280

Business for Social Responsibility 285

International Monetary Fund 286

multinational corporation 283

Dumping 288

United Nations Global Compact 286

World Trade Organization 287

vertical system 292

human rights 294

RESOLVING ETHICAL BUSINESS CHALLENGES*

After graduating from college and working a few years at a small technology firm, Preet scored a high-level job in the logistics department at Amex Corporation. Amex sells high-quality electronic products that are extremely popular among technical savvy young adults. Part of Preet's job involves working with a team to oversee Amex's contractors in China. Amex contracts with factories across Asia to build components for the company's electronics. Preet's team was to ensure the shipments were as orderly as possible. Preet's team had innovative people, and they performed so well the company began giving them more responsibility, including solving major challenges that arouse within the factories.

One day Preet was to visit the factory in the Shandong province of China. Shipments were falling behind schedule, and there seemed to be more accidents occurring there. Preet was to observe the factory and meet with management to determine where the problems occurred. Preet looked forward to her first trip to China and to actually visit a factory to learn more about the manufacturing process.

When Preet arrived at the airport, the managers of the factory greeted her and showed her around. When she got to the factory, all of the employees were hard at work. One group of workers cleaned the components using special chemicals. Preet noticed they did not wear protective face masks, even though she knew the chemicals could be harmful if inhaled. When Preet asked about this, she was told that face masks were recommended but not required because the chances of getting sick from the chemicals were low.

As Preet spent time at the factory, she noticed more things wrong. She discovered employees, on average, worked at least 12 hours per day, sometimes with no breaks. She knew company policy mandated an eight-hour work day. Sometimes employees would put in as much as 18-hour shifts. Preet spoke with one of the employees who told her on condition of anonymity that they were denied sick leave. Any perceived idleness on the employee's part resulted in reduced pay. He also

informed her there had been several suicides at the plant from overworked employees. When Preet asked the supervisor why the factory did not hire more workers, he replied they did not have the money.

When Preet returned to the United States, she wrote a list of recommendations for improving the factory. Later that month, her team met with the company's top managers in the logistics department. They expressed concern about Preet's findings but offered no recommendations for how to fix them. Afterward, Preet complained to members on her team.

"Of course they aren't going to do anything," said Jim, who had been working in the logistics department for 12 years. "Why should they? As long as the company gets their shipments, they aren't going to disrupt the process by requiring major changes."

Dawn, who had only been working for six months, chimed in. "But Jim, they have to do something. From what Preet said, the workers have terrible working conditions."

Jim sighed. "Dawn, you haven't been in this business long enough to see how things work. The factory in Shandong really isn't that bad compared to many other factories in China. It's not unusual for factory workers to work longer hours. Besides, you might think the employees there don't make much for the amount that they work, but it's a lot better than what people get in other factories. For better pay people are willing to work in less than ideal conditions."

Preet spoke up. "Just because that's normal in the culture doesn't necessarily make it right. Many of these problems could be avoided if the factory ensured their workers wore appropriate safety gear and hired more employees."

"The factory probably can't hire more workers," Jim said. "Where are they going to get the money?"

"Well, maybe Amex should begin paying them more," Dawn replied. "That would translate into higher wages and the ability to hire more staff."

"You've got to be kidding!" Jim said. "The whole reason why Amex is there in the first place is because labor costs are so cheap. Besides, being able to keep costs low is the only way to price our products reasonably. Consumers want low-priced products."

"But consumers also care about how workers are treated, don't they?" Preet asked.

"They might show some concern," Jim replied. "But if it's between higher-priced products or better working conditions, I guarantee customers will choose the latter."

QUESTIONS | EXERCISES

1. Discuss some of the choices of the firm and the advantages and disadvantages of each.
2. Describe how Jim takes a cultural relativism approach to the problem.
3. Since Amex does not own the Chinese factory, are they still accountable for the working conditions of its suppliers? Why or why not?

*This case is strictly hypothetical; any resemblance to real persons, companies, or situations is coincidental.

> > > CHECK YOUR EQ

Check your EQ, or Ethics Quotient, by completing the following. Assess your performance to evaluate your overall understanding of the chapter material.

1.	Most countries have a strong orientation toward ethical and legal compliance.	Yes	No
2.	The self-reference criterion is an unconscious reference to one's own cultural values, experience, and knowledge.	Yes	No
3.	One of the critical ethical business issues linked to cultural differences is the question of whose values and ethical standards take precedence during international negotiations and business transactions.	Yes	No
4.	Multinational corporations have identifiable home countries but operate globally.	Yes	No
5.	Certain facilitating payments are acceptable under the Foreign Corrupt Practices Act.	Yes	No

ANSWERS 1. **No.** That's an ethnocentric perspective; in other countries laws may be viewed more situationally. 2. **Yes.** We react based on what we have experienced over our lifetimes. 3. **Yes.** Ethical standards and values differ from culture to culture, and this can be a critical point in effective business negotiations. Some people believe in cultural relativism, which means that the standards of the host country hold sway. However, many MNCs are legally bound to adhere to the standards of the host country. 4. **No.** Multinational corporations have no significant ties to any nation or region. 5. **Yes.** A violation of the FCPA occurs when the payments are excessive or are used to persuade the recipients to perform other than normal duties.

ENDNOTES

1. Philip R. Cateora, Mary C. Gilly, and John L. Graham, *International Marketing*, 15th ed. (New York: McGraw-Hill Irwin, 2011), 109–110.

2. Linda K. Trevino and Katherine A. Nelson, *Managing Business Ethics*, 3rd ed. (Hoboken, NJ: John Wiley & Sons, Inc., 2004), 319.

3. Cateora, Gilly, and Graham, *International Marketing*, 110–111.

4. Ibid.

5. Zaid Swaidan, "Culture and Consumer Ethics," *Journal of Business Ethics* 108 (2012): 201–213.

6. Raphel Cohen-Almagor, "Freedom of Expression, Internet Responsibility, and Business Ethics: The Yahoo! Saga and Its Implications," *Journal of Business Ethics* 106 (2012), 353–365; Matthew Lasar, "Nazi hunting: How France first 'civilized' the Internet," *ars technica*, June 22, 2011, http://arstechnica.com/tech-policy/2011/06/how-france-proved-that-the-internet-is-not-global/ (accessed May 16, 2013).

7. The Heart of Hinduism website, http://hinduism.iskcon.org/ (accessed May 17, 2013).

8. Mecca Centric Dawa Group, "Islamic virtues from the Quran," *Muslim Internet Directory*, http://www.2muslims.com/directory/Detailed/224066.shtml (accessed May 17, 2013).

9. Gordon B. Hinckley, *Standing for Something: Ten Neglected Virtues That Will Heal Our Hearts and Homes*, 1st ed. (New York: Times Books, 2000).

10. "Unit Six: The Four Immeasurables," Buddhist Studies," http://www.buddhanet.net/e-learning/buddhism/bs-s15.htm (accessed May 17, 2013).

11. John (Jack) Ruhe and Monle Lee, "Teaching Ethics in International Business Courses: The Impacts of Religions," *Journal of Teaching in International Business* 19, no. 4 (2008); Andrew Wilson, editor, *World Scripture: A Comparative Anthology of Sacred Texts*, A project of the international religious foundation (Paragon House: New York, 1995).

12. "Briefing after Mubarak," *The Economist*, February 19–25, 2011, 47–53.

13. Eurasia Group, *Top Risks 2013* (New York, NY: Eurasia Group, 2013).

14. Nancy Gibbs, "The Day the Earth Moved," *Time*, March 28, 2011, 26; Hannah Beech, "How Japan Will Reawaken," *Time*, March 28, 2011, 42–47.

15. The Economist Staff, "Counting the cost of calamities," *The Economist*, January 14, 2012, http://www.economist.com/node/21542755 (accessed May 16, 2013).

16. "What Happens When Countries Go Bankrupt?" *TimeTurk: English*, November 5, 2008, http://en.timeturk.com/What-Happens-when-Countries-Go-Bankrupt-10871-haberi.html (accessed June 13, 2009).

17. Alan S. Blinder, *Keynesian Economics*, Library of Economics and Liberty, http://www.econlib.org/library/Enc/KeynesianEconomics.html (accessed May 17, 2013).

18. Robert L. Formaini, "Milton Friedman—Economist as Public Intellectual," *Economic Insights* 7, no. 2 (Dallas, TX: Federal Reserve Bank of Dallas, 2002).

19. E. Roy Wientraub, "Neoclassical Economics," *Library of Economics and Liberty*, http://www.econlib.org/library/Enc1/NeoclassicalEconomics.html (accessed May 17, 2013).

20. Jose De Cordoba and Nicholas Casey, "Cuba Unveils Huge Layoffs in Tilt toward Free Market," *The Wall Street Journal*, September 14, 2010, A1, A15.

21. David G. Blanchflower and Andrew J. Oswald, "International Happiness: A New View on the Measure of Performance," *The Academy of Management Perspectives* 25 (February 2011): 6–22.

22. Robbie Whelan, "Barry Minkow Charged in Fraud against Lennar," *The Wall Street Journal*, March 25, 2011, http://online.wsj.com/article/SB1000142405274870443810457621966279505634.html (accessed May 17, 2013).

23. Richard Whitely, "U.S. Capitalism: A Tarnished Model?" *The Academy of Management Perspectives* (May 2009): 11–22.

24. Thayer Watkins, "The Economy and the Economic History of Sweden," *San Jose State University Department of Economics*, http://www.sjsu.edu/faculty/watkins/sweden.htm (accessed May 17, 2013).

25. Tarun Khana, "Learning from Economic Experiments in China and India," *The Academy of Management Perspectives* (May 2009): 36–43.

26. Andrew Monahan, "China Overtakes Japan as World's No. 2 Economy," *The Wall Street Journal*, February 14, 2011, http://online.wsj.com/article/SB10001424052748703361904576142832741439402.html (accessed May 17, 2013).

27. David Barboza and Chris Buckley, "China Plan Cuts the State's Role in the Economy," *The New York Times*, May 25, 2013, A1.

28. Timothy M. Devinney, "Is the Socially Responsible Corporation a Myth? The Good, the Bad, and the Ugly of Corporate Social Responsibility," *The Academy of Management Perspectives* (May 2009): 44–56.

29. James Angelos, "IKEA Rues Using Prison Labor," *The Wall Street Journal*, November 19, 2012, B7; Kate Connolly, "Ikea Says Sorry to East German Political Prisoners Forced to Make its Furniture," *The Guardian*, http://www.guardian.co.uk/business/2012/nov/16/ikea-regrets-forced-labour-germany (accessed March 28, 2013).

30. "Ethics in the global market: 2009 Corporate Citizenship Report," *Texas Instruments*, http://www.ti.com/corp/docs/csr/corpgov/ethics/global_market.shtml (accessed May 16, 2013).

31. "Ethics in TI," *Texas Instruments*, http://actrav.itcilo.org/actrav-english/telearn/global/ilo/code/texas.htm (accessed May 16, 2013).

32. Business for Social Responsibility, http://www.bsr.org (accessed May 17, 2013).

33. Mauro F. Guillén and Esteban García-Canal, "The American Model of the Multinational Firm and the "New" Multinationals From Emerging Economies," *The Academy of Management Perspectives* (May 2009): 23–25.

34. Roland Bardy, Stephen Drew, and Tumenta F. Kennedy, "Foreign Investment and Ethics: How to Contribute to Social Responsibility by Doing Business in Less-Developed Countries," *Journal of Business Ethics* 106 (2012), 267–282.

35. "Global Roundup," *International Business Ethics Review* (Spring/Summer 2005), 17.

36. Abigail Moses, "Greek Contagion Concern Spurs European Sovereign Default Risk to Record," *Bloomberg*,

April 26, 2010, http://www.bloomberg.com/news/2010-04-26/greek-contagion-concern-spurs-european-sovereign-default-risk-to-record.html (accessed May 17, 2013); James G. Neuger and Joe Brennan, "Ireland Weighs Aid as EU Spars over Debt-Crisis Remedy," *Bloomberg*, http://www.bloomberg.com/news/2010-11-16/ireland-discusses-financial-bailout-as-eu-struggles-to-defuse-debt-crisis.html (accessed May 17, 2013).

37. "UN at a Glance," *UN*, http://www.un.org/en/aboutun/index.shtml (accessed May 16, 2013).

38. "Overview of the UN Global Compact," *United Nations Global Compact*, http://www.unglobalcompact.org/AboutTheGC/index.html (accessed May 16, 2013).

39. Ibid.

40. "About AACSB," *AACSB International*, http://www.aacsb.edu/about/ (accessed May 16, 2013); Principles for Responsible Management Education home page, April 7, 2007, http://www.unprme.org/ (accessed May 16, 2013).

41. "The Principles for Responsible Business Education," *PRME*, http://www.unprme.org/the-6-principles/index.php (accessed May 16, 2013).

42. Mark Peters, "U.S. Firms Settle on Honey Case," *The Wall Street Journal*, February 21, 2013, B8.

43. John W. Miller, "WTO Details Rising Protectionism, Pushes Countries to Reverse Course," *The Wall Street Journal*, March 26, 2009, http://online.wsj.com/article/SB123808014186248481.html (accessed May 17, 2013).

44. "Global Village Investment Club," *Earthlink*, http://home.earthlink.net/~beowulfinvestments/globalvillageinvestmentclubwelcome/id25.html (accessed May 17, 2013).

45. Eurasia Group, *Top Risks 2013* (New York, NY: Eurasia Group, 2013).

46. Daniel J. McCarthy, Sheila M. Puffer, Denise R. Dunlap, and Alfred M. Jaeger, "A Stakeholder Approach to the Ethicality of BRIC-firm Managers' Use of Favors," *Journal of Business Ethics* 109 (2012): 27–38.

47. "U.S. Securities and Exchange Commission and Department of Justice Clarify 'Best Practices' for FCPA Compliance," *Mayer Brown*, January 11, 2011, 1; Mike Koehler, "RAE Systems Held Liable for the Acts of Its Subsidiaries' Joint Venture Partners," *Corporate Compliance Insights*, December 13, 2010, http://www.corporatecomplianceinsights.com/2010/rae-systems-held-liable-for-the-acts-of-its-subsidiaries-joint-venture-partners/ (accessed May 17, 2013).

48. "Foreign Corrupt Practices Act's Antibribery Provisions," *The 'Lectric Law Library*, Excerpted from U.S. Commerce Dept., May 10, 1994, http://www.lectlaw.com/files/bur21.htm (accessed May 17, 2013).

49. "Global Fact Gathering," James Mintz Group, June 2009, http://www.mintzgroup.com/pdf/GFG-Issue4.pdf (accessed March 28, 2011).

50. Dionne Searcey, "U.K. Law on Bribes Has Firms in a Sweat," *The Wall Street Journal*, December 28, 2010, B1.

51. Julius Melnitzer, "U.K. enacts 'far-reaching' antibribery act," *Law Times*, February 13. 2011, http://www.lawtimesnews.com/201102148245/Headline-News/UK-enacts-far-reaching-anti-bribery-act (accessed May 17, 2013).

52. Searcey, "U.K. Law on Bribes Has Firms in a Sweat"; Melnitzer, "U.K. enacts 'far-reaching' anti-bribery act."

53. Searcey, "U.K. Law on Bribes Has Firms in a Sweat."

54. Melnitzer, "U.K. enacts 'far-reaching' anti-bribery act."

55. Michael Volkov, "The U.K. Antibribery Act: Let's Cool Down the Hysteria," http://www.fcpablog.com/blog/2011/1/18/the-uk-anti-bribery-act-lets-cool-down-the-hysteria.html (accessed May 17, 2013).

56. James Kanter, "Europe Fines Intel $1.45 Billion in Antitrust Case," *The New York Times*, May 13, 2009, http://www.nytimes.com/2009/05/14/business/global/14compete.html (accessed May 17, 2013).

57. "Cyber Security," *Business Exchange*, http://bx.businessweek.com/cyber-security/jobs/ (accessed May 17, 2013).

58. The Economist staff, "Getting Ugly," *The Economist*, February 23, 2013, http://www.economist.com/news/leaders/21572200-if-china-wants-respect-abroad-it-must-rein-its-hackers-getting-ugly (accessed March 21, 2013); G.F., "How to Steal a Trillion," *The Economist*, February 19, 2013, http://www.economist.com/blogs/babbage/2013/02/chinese-cyber-attacks (accessed March 21, 2013); Siobhan Gorman and Jared A. Favole, "U.S. Ups Ante for Spying On Firms," *The Wall Street Journal*, February 21, 2013, A1, A16.

59. Joel Schectman and Jessica E. Vascellaro, "Ad Networks Get Around iPhone Privacy Rules," *The Wall Street Journal*, June 5, 2012, B4.

60. Jon Swartz, "Facebook changes its status in Washington," *USA Today*, January 13, 2011, 1B–2B.

61. Summer Said, "Pact Keeps BlackBerrys Running," *The Wall Street Journal*, August 9, 2010, B3; Loretta Chao and Jason Dean, "China's internet censors thrive by confusing web users," *The Wall Street Journal*, April 1, 2010, A10.

62. Chao and Dean, "China's internet censors thrive by confusing web users"; "China rejects Google accusation on email," *Bloomberg Businessweek*, March 22, 2011, http://www.businessweek.com/ap/financialnews/D9M46A3G0.htm (accessed May 17, 2013).

63. Matt Villano, "The Separation of Church and Job," *The New York Times*, February 5, 2006, http://www.nytimes.com/2006/02/05/business/yourmoney/05advi.html (accessed May 17, 2013).

64. Lutz Preuss and Donna Brown, "Business Policies on Human Rights: An Analysis of Their Content and Prevalence Among FTSE 100 Firms," *Journal of Business Ethics* 109 (2012): 289–299.

65. Anup Shah, "Health Issues," *Global Issues*, October 27, 2008, http://www.globalissues.org/issue/587/health-issues (accessed May 17, 2013).

66. Sarah Boseley, "Novartis denied cancer drug patent in landmark Indian case," *The Guardian*, April 1, 2013, http://www.guardian.co.uk/world/2013/apr/01/novartis-denied-cancer-drug-patent-india (accessed May 16, 2013).

67. Katherine Hobson, "Two Surveys Spotlight Health Care Cost Variations," *The Wall Street Journal*, November 22, 2010, http://blogs.wsj.com/health/2010/11/22/two-surveys-spotlight-health-care-cost-variations/ (accessed May 17, 2013).

68. "Law Prompts Some Health Care Plans to Drop Mental-Health Benefits," *The Wall Street Journal*, December 23, 2010, http://online.wsj.com/article/SB10001424052748703395904576025410628499574.html (accessed May 17, 2013).

69. Kate Kelland, January 18, 2010, "Global healthcare fraud costs put at $260 billion," *Reuters*, http://www.

reuters.com/article/2010/01/18/us-healthcare-fraud-idUSTRE60H01620100118?pageNumber=1 (accessed May 17, 2013).

70. U.S. Department of Justice, "Supervisor of $63 Million Health Care Fraud Scheme Convicted," *The Federal Bureau of Investigation*, April 25, 2013, http://www.fbi.gov/miami/press-releases/2013/supervisor-of-63-million-health-care-fraud-scheme-convicted (accessed May 16, 2013),

71. "Germany: Development of the Health Care System," Country Database, http://www.country-data.com/cgi-bin/query/r-4924.html (accessed May 17, 2013).

72. European Commission, "Gender pay gap," http://ec.europa.eu/justice/gender-equality/gender-pay-gap/index_en.htm (accessed May 16, 2013).

73. "Annual survey of violations of trade union rights," *ITUC*, http://survey.ituc-csi.org/+-Whole-World-+.html (accessed May 17, 2013).

74. David Barboza, "McDonald's in China Agrees to Unions," *The New York Times*, April 10, 2007, http://query.nytimes.com/gst/fullpage.html?res=9D00E6DC153FF933A25757C0A9619C8B63&n=Top/Reference/Times%20Topics/Subjects/F/Fringe%20Benefits (accessed May 17, 2013).

75. Lisa Belkin, "The Fight for Paid Maternity Leave," *The New York Times*, February 1, 2010, http://parenting.blogs.nytimes.com/2010/02/01/the-fight-for-paid-maternity-leave/ (accessed May 17, 2013).

76. "Paternity Leave: International Comparisons," *emplaw.co.uk*, http://www.emplaw.co.uk/lawguide?startpage=data/20033221.htm (accessed May 17, 2013).

77. "Wages," United States Department of Labor, http://www.dol.gov/dol/topic/wages/minimumwage.htm (accessed May 17, 2013); "The National Minimum Wage Rates," Directgov, http://www.direct.gov.uk/en/Employment/Employees/TheNationalMinimumWage/DG_10027201 (accessed May 17, 2013); Ben Schneiders, "Minimum wage lifted to $570 a week," *The Sydney Morning Herald*, June 3, 2010, http://www.smh.com.au/business/minimum-wage-lifted-to-570-a-week-20100603-x1by.html (accessed May 17, 2013).

78. "Corporate Social Responsibility: Companies in the News," Mallenbaker.net, http://www.mallenbaker.net/csr/CSRfiles/nike.html (accessed May 17, 2013).

79. Carol Matlack, "Swiss Limits on Executive Pay: Less Than Meets the Eye," *Bloomberg Businessweek*, March 4, 2013, http://www.businessweek.com/articles/2013-03-04/swiss-limits-on-executive-pay-less-than-meets-the-eye (accessed May 17, 2013).

80. John Revill, "Swiss Expected to Vote on More Pay Limits," *The Wall Street Journal*, March 21, 2013, B6.

81. "China bosses told to cut salaries," *BBC News*, April 09, 2009, http://news.bbc.co.uk/2/hi/7993377.stm (accessed May 17, 2013).

82. Anup Shah, "Consumption and Consumerism," *Global Issues*, September 3, 2008, http://www.globalissues.org/issue/235/consumption-and-consumerism (accessed May 17, 2013).

83. Ibid.

84. Keith Bradsher, "China Fears Consumer Impact on Global Warming," *The New York Times*, July 4, 2010, http://www.nytimes.com/2010/07/05/business/global/05warm.html?_r=1&ref=business (accessed May 17, 2013).

85. Subhash Agrawal, "India's Premature Exuberance," *The Wall Street Journal*, June 16, 2009, http://online.wsj.com/article/SB124513568534118169.html (accessed May 17, 2013).

86. "Greenhouse gas emission list: India 3rd," *Financial Express*, August 4, 2011, http://www.financialexpress.com/news/greenhouse-gas-emission-list-india-3rd/827084 (accessed May 16, 2013).

87. Sarita Agrawal, "Globalisation, consumption and green consumerism," *HighBeam Research*, originally published in *Political Economy Journal of India*, January 1, 2010, http://www.highbeam.com/doc/1G1-227797569.html (May 17, 2013).

88. "How Much of the World's Resource Consumption Occurs in Rich Countries?" *Earth Trends*, http://earthtrends.wri.org/updates/node/236 (accessed April 1, 2011); "The Global Sustainability Challenge," http://www.globalsustainabilitychallenge.com/ (accessed April 1, 2011).

89. "Global Ethics Office," Walmart Corporate, http://walmartstores.com/aboutus/280.aspx (accessed May 17, 2013).

90. "As GM Struggles, Its Ethics and Compliance Office Moves On," *Ethikos and Corporate Conduct Quarterly*, September/October 2008, http://www.ethikospublication.com/html/generalmotors.html (accessed May 17, 2013).

91. Mary Swanton, "Combating Corruption: GCs Aim to Establish Global Ethics Codes," *InsideCounsel*, January 1, 2011, http://www.insidecounsel.com/Issues/2011/January/Pages/Combating-Corruption-GCs-Aim-to-Establish-Global-Ethics-Codes.aspx?page=3 (accessed May 17, 2013).

CHAPTER 11

ETHICAL LEADERSHIP

CHAPTER OBJECTIVES

- Define ethical leadership
- Examine requirements for ethical leadership
- Realize the benefits that come from effective ethical leadership
- Understand how ethical leadership impacts organizational culture
- Learn about the different styles of conflict management
- Understand how employees can be empowered to take on responsibilities in ethical leadership
- Examine leader–follower relationships in communication
- Learn about leadership styles and how they influence ethical leadership
- Use the RADAR model to determine how ethical leaders handle misconduct situations

CHAPTER OUTLINE

AN ETHICAL DILEMMA*

Stacy, a recently hired employee of a growing local CPA firm called Dewey, Cheatume, and Howe, just passed all four parts of the CPA exam. The University of Virginia prepped her well for her new job, and the partners had high expectations for Stacy because she scored near the top of her graduating class. As a result, Stacy was fast tracked and performed at an advanced level on some jobs. This was due, in part, to her excellent skill set but also because of heavy firm turnover at the senior level.

Because of the long hours and her inexperience, Stacy started to make simple errors such as not meeting time budgets. She began working off the clock because she did not want management to know she had a hard time handling the workload. After a few months, she casually mentioned the extra hours to a co-worker, who told her working off the clock is considered unethical and the company has strict policies against it. Stacy was embarrassed but also upset that the company never made this known to her—particularly since she knew her immediate supervisor knew full well what she was doing. Stacy stopped working off the clock and began to work more quickly to get things done in the expected time frame.

A few weeks ago, Stacy learned her recent work on a tax return had to be redone; Stacy mistakenly charged the wrong client for the return. Doug, one of the partners, publicly reprimanded her by saying, "Next time it's coming out of your paycheck." Later that same week, as Stacy helped interview a candidate for one of the open accounting positions, she accidentally chipped the glass table in the conference room. When Doug heard about it, he said, "I hope your personal insurance covers the table. You'll need to speak to the secretary and get this replaced."

Over the following months, the firm continued having more resignations. It became so problematic that the Senior Board requested a psychologist interview all staff members. When Stacy was interviewed, she described the poor treatment of employees and unreasonable expectations. Apparently, other employees had the same complaint. The resulting report from the consultant pointed toward numerous management problems at the company. Shortly thereafter, the partners responded in a way the staff did not expect: they took the report personally. As a result, rumors began to surface that the firm was going to go up for sale. Still, the interviews for staff positions continued. One Monday morning a memo surfaced stating that all staff doing interviews for new hires were to "present the firm in a positive and favorable manner." Stacy was one of those staff members doing the interviews.

Stacy did not know how to portray the firm in a positive manner when she was so miserable. She particularly disliked Doug. It seemed to Stacy that Doug made it his mission to torment her by criticizing her every move. He hovered around her desk and made comments about making sure not to mess up again.

After getting advice from one of her co-workers, Stacy decided to approach Doug about his behavior. He did not take it well.

"Look, if you think I'm being too hard on you, then maybe you should just leave," Doug responded. "It's obvious you were not cut out for this business." Doug continued to berate Stacy for her "shoddy" work until she was close to tears.

"If you want to make it in this business, honey, you got to realize when to pick your fights. Me, I'm not in the habit of losing." Doug walked off in a huff.

The next day Stacy was to interview someone for a lower-level accounting position. As she walked down the hallway, Doug approached her.

"I hear you're going to be interviewing a new candidate today. Just remember, make this company look good. No whining about your bad work experience."

Stacy contained her anger when she entered the room and sat down in front of the candidate. She did her best to act professional and stifle her emotions. The real dilemma came when the candidate asked about the firm's culture and how Stacy personally liked working there. She swallowed. She did not know how to sugarcoat her answer without making it an outright lie.

QUESTIONS | EXERCISES

1. Describe the deficiencies in ethical leadership at Stacy's firm.
2. What type of conflict management style does Doug have? Are there more constructive ways for him to handle conflicts with employees?
3. Describe the alternatives Stacy has answering the candidate's question and the advantages and disadvantages of each.

*This case is strictly hypothetical; any resemblance to real persons, companies, or situations is coincidental.

Leadership is a basic requirement for developing an ethical corporate culture and reinforcing ethical decision making among employees. For this reason, we devote an entire chapter to the leadership qualities that support ethical conduct in business. While it is important to have a CEO and board of directors committed to ethical decision making, it is equally important all employees understand their roles in becoming ethical leaders. There are many examples of ethical leadership failures, resulting in ethical and legal crises that damage firms. The former CEO of Diamond Foods led the company on a massive acquisition spree using debt to finance the purchases. In order to make its financial statements look better, the company used improper accounting methods to artificially inflate earnings. As a result of this misconduct, the CEO left the firm, Diamond Foods' reputation suffered, and its share price dropped 37 percent.[1] On the other hand, companies such as IBM, Procter & Gamble, and Zappos may have minor ethical transgressions; however, their leadership keeps them on the right course in responding appropriately and recovering from ethical issues. Many companies founded by ethical leaders such as Milton Hershey, founder of Hershey Foods, experienced few ethical crises over the years.

This chapter demonstrates the importance of leadership in creating an ethical culture. We first provide a definition of ethical leadership and explore its relationship to ethical decision making. Next, requirements of ethical leadership are provided, followed by how ethical leadership benefits the company. The relationship between ethical leadership and organizational culture is examined, as well as ways ethical leaders can manage conflict. Managing conflict appropriately identifies potential issues and reinforces a firm's ethical climate. An important part of leadership is the implementation of employee-centered leadership. Employee-centered leadership recognizes that while not everyone will be a manager, every employee can and should practice leadership skills to support ethical decision making. An essential component of employee-centered leadership is communication. Without communication all attempts at maintaining an ethical culture fail. We describe common ethical leadership styles proven effective in building an ethical corporate culture. Finally, we conclude with a model to address ethical issues and misconduct disasters. Leaders can use this model to guide the firm's ethical culture, detect ethical risk areas before they become problematic, and develop methods of recovery if an unethical decision or disaster occurs.

It should be obvious that ethical companies are not 100 percent misconduct free. There will always be employees or managers that push the boundaries of acceptable conduct as well as situations not anticipated in an ethics, compliance, or risk assessment programs. Recall the 10-40-40-10 rule; people are motivated by different values, resulting in ethical diversity. Additionally, ethics programs can always be improved, making it important to periodically audit the program to uncover weaknesses. Similarly, ethical leaders have weaknesses and are not free from mistakes, or lapses and blind spots, in oversight.

What separates them from unethical leaders is how they respond to ethical issues, interact with stakeholders, and learn from their mistakes. All managers and most employees will witness misconduct at some point in their careers. What is important is how they respond to it.

DEFINING ETHICAL LEADERSHIP

Leadership is the ability or authority to guide and direct others toward a goal. Most people agree that effective leadership is essential for a company. Ethical decisions are one dimension of leadership. Successful companies develop based upon the leadership and creative abilities of their founders. Without the leadership capabilities of entrepreneurs such as Steve Jobs of Apple, Bill Gates of Microsoft, Sam Walton of Walmart, and Mark Zuckerberg of Facebook, the most successful companies today would be greatly diminished, or nonexistent. However, a strong founder is only one part of a company's success. Strong ethical leadership must be demonstrated through successors, other managers, and employees to continue the firm's success. The ethical leadership skills of Tim Cook of Apple, Steve Balmer of Microsoft, and Sheryl Sandberg, COO of Facebook, are as important as problem solving, planning, delegation, internal communications, and meeting management for the continued success of the company.

Ethical leadership creates an ethical culture. Top managers provide a blueprint for a firm's corporate culture.[2] If these leaders fail to express desired ethical behaviors and goals, a corporate culture evolves on its own to reflect the values and norms of the company. Consider the fate of one highly profitable and successful accounting company. The founder of the company was known for his integrity—so much so that he refused to make an improper accounting entry for a major client despite the consequences. That man was Arthur E. Andersen, who went on to found Arthur Andersen, one of the top five accounting firms in the United States.[3] Yet despite the ethical integrity of its founder, Arthur Andersen strayed from its original values. Successive leaders appeared to stress business over integrity, leading the firm to inaccurately audit companies later found guilty of accounting misconduct, most notably Enron. Arthur Andersen, which started out with such strong ethical leadership, was destroyed. Thus, it is not enough to have strong ethical leaders and corporate values initially—an ethical corporate culture must be maintained through effective leadership at all times during the firm's existence. Table 11–1 provides a snapshot of leaders admired for their ethical conduct.

Leadership has a significant impact on ethical decision making because leaders have the power to motivate others and enforce the organization's norms, policies, and viewpoints. Ethical leaders ensure these goals are met in an ethical manner. Leaders are central to influencing an organization's corporate culture and ethical posture. Ethical leadership is not simply allowing employees to follow their own moral codes; it is about helping to implement and reinforce shared ethical values to promote an ethical culture, as well as assume responsibility to model ethical conduct for employees.[4] Ethical leadership has a positive relationship with the organizational citizenship of employees and a negative relationship with deviance, or misconduct. In other words, ethical business leaders are more likely to have employees that follow their example and less likely to have deviants that create trouble in the company.[5]

Although we often think of CEOs and other managers as the most important leaders in an organization, the corporate governance reforms discussed in Chapter 4 make it clear

TABLE 11-1 Leaders Admired for Ethical Conduct

Leaders	Company	Ethical Leadership Activities
Warren Buffett	Berkshire Hathaway	• Promotes ethical conduct as a necessity of business • Shares responsibility and decision making with managers of various companies
Howard Schultz	Starbucks	• Offers healthcare to part-time workers; • Developed Create Jobs for USA program to fund small businesses in America
Tony Hsieh	Zappos	• Creates a fun work environment for employees; encourages employees to make decisions • Stresses an environment of quality customer service
Kenneth Chenault	American Express	• Used his strong work ethic to turn around the struggling company • Noted for ensuring that stranded cardholders found a way home during the September 11th attacks and approved of a $1 million donation to the families of American Express employees lost in the tragedy
Kip Tindell	The Container Store	• Creates a corporate culture in which employees feel appreciated and motivated to perform beyond expectations • Employees are provided with better pay and more training than competing retailers

Source: "10 Most Ethical CEOs in America," Online MBA, March 28, 2012, http://www.onlinemba.com/blog/10-most-ethical-ceos-in-corporate-america/ (accessed April 25, 2013).

a firm's board of directors is also an important leadership component. Indeed, directors have a legal obligation to manage companies "for the best interests of the corporation." To determine what is in the best interest of the firm, directors must consider the effects a decision has not only on shareholders and employees but other important stakeholders as well.[6] Ethical leadership is not limited to management or board members. In many situations the actions of co-workers profoundly impacts the ethical decisions of employees.[7] Therefore, it is important to realize that although ethical leadership is often discussed in terms of corporate directors and top executives, even lower-level employees exhibit ethical leadership traits. All responsible employees must engage in ethical decision-making and exhibit ethical leadership characteristics.

Many CEOs articulate the firm's core values but fail to exhibit ethical leadership. Unfortunately, some CEOs and other managers intentionally deceive stakeholders. In the presence of competing stakeholder expectations, CEOs may "muddle through," depending on the degree of consensus among managers and their reactions to stakeholder demands.[8] Managers that muddle through are not consistent to core values. However, other CEOs are genuine in their commitment to stakeholder engagement and balance interests as well as prioritize initiatives. For ethical leadership to exist, CEOs must go beyond initiatives such as sponsorships and other activities seen as simply good public relations.[9]

In the long run, if stakeholders are unsatisfied with a company's leader, he or she will not retain that position. A leader must have followers' respect and also provide a standard of conduct. For example, former CEO candidate Christopher Kubasik of Lockheed Martin resigned after an internal audit revealed he had an inappropriate relationship with an employee.[10] Such relationships do not demonstrate appropriate behavior for employees to follow. Failure to demonstrate effective leadership qualities at the top creates the perception that managers either do not care about the company's ethics program or they feel they are above ethics and compliance requirements.

REQUIREMENTS FOR ETHICAL LEADERSHIP

While ethical leaders need good character, they also require skills to lead and guide others. Ethical leadership skills develop through years of training, experience, and learning other best practices of leadership. In pinpointing what makes someone a "good" leader, experts remain divided; leadership qualities differ for each situation. However, a number of requirements have been identified. For instance, ethical leaders must model organizational values, place what is best for the organization over their own interests, train and develop employees throughout their careers, establish reporting mechanisms, understand employee values and perceptions, and recognize the limits of organizational rules and values.[11] These characteristics can be developed through proper training. Most importantly, ethical leaders should not turn a blind eye to observed misconduct.

Ethical leaders never operate in a silo of decision making. They seek to encourage the development of other leaders within the organization. The strength of ethical leaders involves recognizing their own weaknesses and relying on others to help them. Ethical leaders encourage employees to reach their full potential and emphasize their role as important co-creators of value.[12] They also try to develop policies and procedures that provide incentives to those who train new leaders.[13] Developing leaders should be a cyclical, or never-ending, process in the organization.

We have researched many books on leadership and have discovered that a good example within business ethics is Archie Carroll's "7 Habits of Highly Moral Leaders" based on Stephen Covey's *The 7 Habits of Highly Effective People*.[14] We adapted Carroll's "7 Habits of Highly Moral Leaders"[15] to create "Seven Habits of Strong Ethical Leaders" (Table 11–2). In particular, we believe ethical leadership is based on holistic thinking that embraces the complex and challenging issues companies face on a daily basis. Ethical leaders need knowledge and experience to make the right decisions. Strong ethical leaders have the knowledge, wisdom, and courage to pull the pertinent information together so the best or most ethical decisions are made. This is no easy task because of various stakeholders

TABLE 11–2 Seven Habits of Strong Ethical Leaders

1. Ethical leaders have strong personal character.
2. Ethical leaders have a passion to do right.
3. Ethical leaders are proactive.
4. Ethical leaders consider all stakeholders' interests.
5. Ethical leaders are role models for the organization's values.
6. Ethical leaders are transparent and actively involved in decision making.
7. Ethical leaders take a holistic view of the firm's ethical culture.

© Cengage Learning

and the subsequent conflicts in objectives. This means ethical leaders must stick to their principles and, if necessary, leave the organization if its corporate governance system is so flawed that it is impossible to make the right choice.

Finally, strong ethical leaders are those passionate about the organization and act in the organization's best interests.[16] By promoting shared values, leaders are able to align employees behind a common vision.[17] We discuss some of these habits in more detail in the following paragraphs.

Many corporate founders—including Sam Walton, Bill Gates, Milton Hershey, Michael Dell, Steve Jobs, and Ben Cohen and Jerry Greenfield—left their ethical stamp on their companies. Their conduct set the tone, making them role models for desired conduct in the early growth of their respective corporations. For instance, Milton Hershey's legacy endures, and Hershey Foods continues to be a role model for an ethical corporate culture. In the case of Sam Walton, Walmart embarked on a course of rapid growth after his death and became involved in numerous conflicts with various stakeholder groups, especially employees, regulators, competitors, and communities. Despite the ethical foundation left by Sam Walton, Walmart, like most large corporations, deals with hundreds of reported ethical lapses every month.[18] As mentioned earlier, ethical leaders must maintain and build upon an ethical firm's culture to maintain the stamp of the original founders through successive generations.

There is general agreement that ethical leadership is highly unlikely without a strong personal character. The question is how to teach or develop a moral person in a corporate environment. Thomas I. White, a leading authority on character development, believes the focus should be developing "ethical reasoning" rather than being a "moral person." According to White, the ability to resolve the complex ethical dilemmas encountered in a corporate culture requires intellectual skills.[19] For example, when Lawrence S. Benjamin took over as president of U.S. Food Service after a major ethical disaster, he initiated an ethics and compliance program to promote transparency and teach employees how to make difficult ethical choices. A fundamental problem in traditional character development is that specific values and virtues are used to teach a belief or philosophy. This approach becomes muddled in a business environment where cultural diversity, privacy, and the profit motive must be respected. On the other hand, teaching individuals who want to do the right thing regarding corporate values and ethical codes, and equipping these individuals with the intellectual skills to address the complexities of business decisions with ethical/ unethical results, is the correct approach.

Ethical leaders do not wait for ethical problems to arise. They anticipate, plan, and act proactively to avoid potential crises.[20] One way to be proactive is to take a leadership role in developing effective programs that provide employees with guidance and support for making more ethical choices, even in the face of considerable pressure to do otherwise. Ethical leaders who are proactive understand social needs and apply or develop the best practices of ethical leadership that exist in their industry. One of *Fortune* magazine's "Best Companies to Work for" includes data storage company NetApp, which takes a proactive stance toward ethical conduct. Vice Chairman Tom Mendoza encourages managers to report when an employee is "doing something right." He then calls the employees personally to thank them. Mendoza makes approximately 10 to 20 calls per day.[21] Such strong leadership is crucial in maintaining impressive ethical credentials over the long term.

Additionally, ethical leaders must model the organization's values. If leaders do not actively serve as role models for the organization's core values, then those values become nothing more than lip service. According to behavioral scientist Brent Smith, as role

TABLE 11-3 Whole Food's Core Values

- Selling the highest quality natural and organic products
- Satisfying and delighting our customers
- Supporting team member happiness and excellence
- Creating wealth through profits and growth
- Caring about our communities and our environment
- Creating ongoing win-win partnerships with our suppliers
- Promoting the health of our stakeholders through healthy eating education

Source: "Our Core Values," Whole Foods Markets, www.wholefoodsmarket.com/company/corevalues.php (accessed April 25, 2013).

models, leaders are the primary influence on individual ethical behavior. Leaders whose decisions and actions are contrary to the firm's values send a signal that the values are trivial or irrelevant.[22] Consider Whole Foods, the world's largest organic and natural grocer. Since its 1980 conception in Austin, Texas, Whole Foods demonstrated a commitment to social responsibility and strong core values (see Table 11-3). In addition to providing consumers with fresh, healthy foods, Whole Foods cares for its employees by creating a transparent and friendly work environment. The company encourages a sense of teamwork by imposing a salary cap for top executives. The company also supports growers and the environment through sourcing from sustainable growers and supporting efforts such as recycling and reducing energy. At each store, Whole Foods donates a minimum of 5 percent of profits to local communities. Many people are drawn to Whole Foods because of its high quality standards, educational initiatives, and close relationships with suppliers.[23]

BENEFITS OF ETHICAL LEADERSHIP

Ethical leadership creates many benefits for an organization. Most importantly, ethical leadership has a direct impact on the corporate culture of the firm. For instance, ethical leaders communicate and monitor an organization's values, ensuring that employees are familiar with the company's purpose and beliefs.[24] They also provide cultural motivations for ethical behavior, such as reward systems for ethical conduct and decision making. This reinforcement is positively correlated with ethical employee behavior patterns.[25] Thus, ethical leadership encourages employees to act in an ethical manner in their day-to-day work environment. It is a well-known fact that a firm is only as good as its employees, so instilling employees with a strong sense of integrity is crucial to creating an ethical organization.

Ethical leadership can also lead to higher employee satisfaction and employee commitment.[26] Research shows that employees like to work for ethical companies and are less likely to leave ethical organizations.[27] These factors translate into significant cost savings for the firm and serve to increase employee productivity. At The Container Store, for instance, employees are given first priority. They receive 263 hours of training, higher pay than comparable retailers, and are treated to special appreciation events such as We Love Our Employees Day. The purpose of this employee-centered corporate culture is to increase employee productivity and the quality of customer service. As a result, The Container Store's turnover rate is 10 percent (compared to 100 percent for other retailers in the industry) and customer loyalty is high (many employees originated as loyal customers of the company).[28]

While ethical leadership can create competitive advantages through employee satisfaction and productivity, it also creates strong relationships with external stakeholders. For instance, customers are willing to pay higher prices for products from ethical companies.[29] As consumer trust for businesses continues to recover after the financial crisis and recession, consumers are more likely to do business with companies they consider to be trustworthy.

Ethical leadership is a foundational requirement for impacting the long-term market valuation of the firm. There is a positive association between the ethical commitment of employees and a firm's valuation on the stock market.[30] A firm's reputation for corporate social responsibility also impacts investor decisions. Corporate social responsibility is negatively related to ethical risks in the long-term, and investors view risk as a factor when determining whether to invest in the firm.[31] The ethical reputation of the company can therefore assure them about the short and long-term sustainability of the company. Finally, as demonstrated in Chapter 4, the Federal Sentencing Guidelines for Organizations mandates that public firms have ethics programs in place to detect organizational misconduct. Those companies that demonstrate they have strong ethics programs are more likely to see their fines reduced if misconduct occurs.[32] Through the creation of favorable relationships with employees, customers, investors, and regulators, ethical leaders create significant competitive advantages and value for their companies.

ETHICAL LEADERSHIP AND ORGANIZATIONAL CULTURE

Organizational culture emerges whether or not there is effective leadership. The ethical dimension is dependent on how the company's leaders influence the culture. In organizations where leaders are tolerant or indifferent toward misconduct, a culture will likely develop in which employees cut corners and/or take excessive risks to advance their careers. On the other hand, ethical leaders recognize that organizational culture will directly impact employee conduct and make a greater effort to promote a culture of ethics and compliance. Leaders help set the tone for such a culture through shared values, attitudes, and ethical practices.

Ethical leaders generally adopt one of two approaches to leadership: a compliance-based approach or an integrity-based approach. These approaches are similar to the compliance orientation and values orientation discussed in Chapter 8. Leaders that adopt a compliance-based approach emphasize obedience to rules and regulations and sets processes in place to ensure compliance. Such an approach deters illegal conduct and stresses a culture of avoidance. Corporate annual reports may give clues as to the type of approach a company chooses to adopt. If those in charge of ethics are called compliance officers or risk managers, then it is highly likely the firm is more compliance-based. Also, if those in charge of the ethics and compliance program are mostly accountants and legal professionals, the firm tends to be more compliance-based. Some see this as achieving the bare minimum to avoid getting in trouble with the law.

An integrity-based approach views ethics as an opportunity to implement core values. Leaders who adopt an integrity-based approach take responsibility for the firm's ethical culture and hold employees accountable for practicing ethical behaviors and core practices.[33] Integrity-based approaches usually have chief officers, human resource managers, and board member committees involved with the ethics and compliance program. This type of approach not only empowers employees but helps them integrate ethical values and principles established by the firm. Finally, it helps the firm understand where questionable practices are occurring and where possible new ethical issues are arising. Remember, business is not static; it is dynamic. While it might seem that an integrity-based approach is preferable, many ethical leaders use a combination of the two approaches. Without compliance to laws and basic rules and regulations the company and industry have set, an organization will not survive in the long-term.

Another way to classify leader types includes the following categories: the unethical leader, the apathetic leader, and the ethical leader. Each of these types influences the development of an organizational culture, whether positive or negative. While we use this classification typology, the reality is that each leader type falls on a continuum or line and not a box. We use this classification to analyze the most desirable type of leader.

The unethical leader is usually ego-centric and often does whatever it takes to achieve the organization's objectives and his/her own. This leader looks at laws as guidelines to be fitted to the goals of the firm. If the laws go against the company, then the leader attempts to shift the laws. Unethical leaders perceive ethics codes, compliance regulations, and industry standards as optional. The justification used for breaking laws or rules is usually that doing so serves a greater good. An example of an unethical leader is A. Alfred Taubman. After acquiring the legendary auction house Sotheby's, Taubman conspired with rival Christie's to raise commission fees without regard for the future of the company or for stakeholders. He was later convicted of price fixing, spent a year in prison, and paid a $7.5 million fine.[34]

Another type of unethical leader is known as a psychopathic leader, or corporate psychopath. We discussed this briefly in Chapter 6. Research suggests that 1 percent of the population could qualify as a corporate psychopath. These leaders are characterized as having superficial charm, no conscience, grandiose self-worth, little or no empathy, and enjoy flouting the rules. Companies with such leaders usually experience increases in the following problems: heightened level of conflict, lower employee commitment, higher organizational constraints, heavier workloads, poor levels of training, lower job satisfaction, and an increase in employee absenteeism. Research suggests these leaders are disproportionately at higher levels within an organization, possibly because their tendencies are to be in a position of control.[35]

Apathetic leaders are not necessarily unethical, but they care little for ethics within the company.[36] This leader does not listen to employees and does not communicate well.[37] Apathetic leaders display no passion for the firm or the mission of the organization.[38] Employees do not see the sacrifices in them that other managers or leaders display.[39] One possible example of this leader type might be Tony Hayward, former BP CEO. As the oil spill in the Gulf of Mexico leaked over 172 million gallons of oil into the ocean, Mr. Hayward attended a yacht race and allegedly directed employees to downplay the disaster to keep stock prices afloat. At the same time he complained, "I'd like my life back."[40] He later resigned, and BP pled guilty to eleven counts of manslaughter and agreed to pay $4 billion to the Justice Department.

Ethical leaders include ethics at every operational level and stage of the decision making process.[41] There will always be ethical lapses in any organization, but ethical leaders address issues as soon as they appear. Oftentimes ethical leaders try to create participative organizational cultures to which employees are encouraged to provide input. Ethical leaders view such employee collaboration as an important resource. In this type of organizational culture, employees are seen as major co-contributors of value.[42] Leaders must therefore establish strong systems of communication to inform employees of company activities and encourage them to report concerns to company leaders.[43] To ensure employees are on the same page, ethical leaders must also communicate the company's guiding values and principles and display competence and credibility in ethical decision making. Above all, ethical leaders must model the ethical values they promote.[44] Hence, ethical leadership is a requirement for building a culture where ethical decisions occur daily.

MANAGING ETHICAL CONFLICTS

Ethical conflicts occur when there are two or more positions on an ethical decision. Sometimes ethical conflicts emerge because employees feel uncomfortable about their own or their co-workers' decisions. One benefit of ethical conflict is it helps pinpoint ethical issues. Ethical decision making does not occur unless an ethical issue is identified and needs to be resolved. For example, suppose the board of directors of a major company discovered that the CEO embellished his résumé. The company had gone through a succession of CEOs and must make the choice whether to fire another one. Even if the CEO is fired, the company receives a blow to its reputation for not vetting its CEO candidates appropriately. The board has an ethical conflict it must resolve. This situation occurred at Yahoo!, and the CEO was pressured to resign.[45] While leaders cannot totally avoid ethical conflict, they can maintain an ethical corporate culture through appropriate conflict management.

Before describing ethical conflict management styles, note that ethical conflict issues will not be brought to management's attention without effective mechanisms for transparent communication. It is common for companies to have some means for employees to express concerns or give suggestions, such as hotlines, feedback forms, or suggestion boxes. Indeed, these mechanisms for communication establish a participative organizational culture. However, failure to act on employee concerns or suggestions can do more harm than good. Employees who believe that their concerns are ignored feel deceived and are likely to experience more group conflict.[46] Instead, leaders must take an authentic, proactive approach to communication. This not only involves listening to employee input but attempts to identify ethical issues before they lead to conflict.[47] Bringing ethical issues into the open may lead to ethical conflict, but it enables ethical leaders to manage that conflict and bring it closer to resolution.

Employees themselves should be trained to handle conflict situations. Training employees to recognize and resolve conflict can prevent employees from being the victims of questionable conduct such as bullying.[48] Employees may choose to approach a conflict situation in one of five ways: ignore the issue, confront the other person, report the conflict to management, use a hotline, or engage in external whistle blowing. Employees who feel their leaders are ethical and willing to listen to their concerns are more likely to approach the other person or report the conflict internally.[49]

Conflict Management Styles

There are many instances in the workplace when a leader must step in to resolve an ethical conflict. How a leader approaches conflict situations determines which strategy he or she adopts when resolving conflicts. We categorize conflict management into five styles: competing, avoiding, accommodating, collaborating, and compromising. These styles are based on two dimensions: assertiveness and cooperativeness. Assertiveness is acting in one's own best interests, while cooperativeness means working toward the best interests of the other person.[50] Figure 11–1 provides a visual representation of these five conflict management styles based on levels of assertiveness and cooperativeness. In developing conflict management styles to resolve ethical issues, a leader may need to adjust the style to fit a particular ethical dilemma.

In the upper left quadrant is a competing conflict style of management. Leaders having a competing conflict management style are highly assertive and not very cooperative. Competing leaders believe in winning at any cost and measure success by how much the other side loses.[51] Al Dunlap, former CEO of Sunbeam, had a competing style. He did what it took to "win" even when it meant firing thousands of employees. This contributed to his nickname "Chainsaw Al." These leaders are usually not considered to be ethical because their conflict style makes them less likely to consider the concerns of employees and other stakeholders. Managers with this style are likely to be more power-oriented and even narcissistic. While leaders should exhibit competing characteristics in certain situations, firms must be careful they do not hire leaders willing to win so much that ethical values and the company's well-being are ignored. However, high assertiveness is not always a problem. For instance, leaders enforce compliance with rules when compromise is impossible. Ethical leaders should never cooperate in misconduct or in behavior that goes against the firm's ethical principles and values.

In the lower left quadrant is an avoiding style of conflict management. Leaders with this approach are not effective because they avoid conflict at any costs—even if it leads to misconduct. They are uncooperative and non-assertive. Even if they are aware of

FIGURE 11–1 Conflict Management Styles

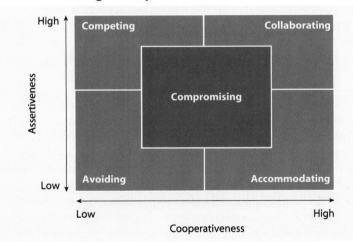

Source: Adapted from Kenneth W. Thomas and Ralph H. Kilmann (March 2, 2010). *Thomas-Kilmann Conflict Mode Instrument: Profile and Interpretative Report.* © CPP, Inc.

misconduct, they have no desire to manage it. Chairman Ken Lay and CEO Jeff Skilling of Enron appeared to adopt this style. They were aggressive in terms of managing the operations of the business, but they were ethically passive as Enron became increasingly complacent toward misconduct. Leaders who adopt this style automatically assume that conflict is always undesirable. However, conflict provides the organization with the ability to explore new points of view and consider the most ethical choice from a variety of options.[52] Ethical conflict also alerts leaders to ethical issues within the company that they might not have noticed otherwise. The avoiding leader has commonly been associated with ethical crises that have destroyed the reputations of organizations. Enron collapsed because of its ethical complacency and the adoption of an avoiding style toward ethical conflict.

In the lower right quadrant is the accommodating style of conflict management. Leaders who adopt this style are highly cooperative but non-assertive. Individuals with this approach to conflict give in to the other side even if it means sacrificing their own interests and values.[53] When a leader accommodates those engaging in misconduct, the result can be an ethical disaster. For instance, a sales manager who knows her salespeople engage in bribery and kickbacks to sell products but allows the misconduct to continue because of their high performance has an accommodating style of conflict management. An accommodating style makes it increasingly hard to compete in a business environment. Because it is necessary to remain competitive in order to survive, businesses must be assertive to keep an edge over the competition. Although you might not consider an accommodating leader unethical, sacrificing the company's principles and values to accommodate the other side is a serious breach of an ethical leader's responsibility.

In the middle is a compromising style of conflict management. Leaders who adopt this management style are in between the assertiveness and cooperativeness dimensions. They believe the best approach to resolving conflicts is for each side to give something up in order to gain something of value.[54] Compromising leaders are still able to receive part of what they want, and that makes it different from an accommodating style of conflict management. On the other hand, they allow the other side a partial victory that prevents them from assuming a competing style of conflict management. This management style is useful in resolving ethical dilemmas when all solutions have disadvantages. Compromising chooses a solution that is the most beneficial to all participants. While there are advantages to compromising in a conflict situation, leaders who overly use this style may find that their rivals will expect them to compromise even when doing so would harm the firm. Also, the parties involved likely experience less commitment since each gave something up.[55] However, an ethical culture is built on participants sharing, compromising, and in some cases, accommodating on issues once they become aware of the consequences.

In the upper right quadrant is the collaborating style of conflict management. The collaborating style is the most advantageous. Leaders who adopt a collaborating style to conflict management are cooperative and assertive. Rather than immediately compromising, collaborative leaders collaborate with others to find a creative way to obtain a beneficial solution. Collaborative leaders desire to meet the needs of stakeholders. However, they also strongly adhere to organizational values and principles. Collaboration requires both parties to concentrate on the conflict at hand. Leaders with collaborative styles are flexible because they can be both assertive and cooperative, depending upon the situation. They are careful to make sure they do not abuse their power and consider the needs of their rivals in the conflict.[56] Because a collaborative style of conflict management is most in sync with ethical leadership, it is the role of the ethical leader to foster, model, and facilitate a collaborative conflict style. A collaborative style works particularly well in gray areas requiring the need to listen, learn, and share in coming up with the best solution.

While we have separated conflict management into five styles, in reality effective leaders can use different styles depending upon the situation. For instance, while a collaborative style might normally be the most ethical means of managing conflict, it would be ethically questionable to collaborate with an employee caught committing serious misconduct, such as fraud or embezzlement. Compromise may be the best solution when two parties reach an impasse. Companies might choose to avoid an issue if pursuing action would take up too much time and resources.[57]

Ethical leaders should also have the ability to identify the conflict management styles of others. Understanding how other stakeholders manage conflicts can help ethical leaders determine whether their own style should be adapted. This is the heart of ethical leadership. Observing and understanding others' styles of conflict management is important in making the best decision.[58] For instance, if you assume the other person will always be accommodating, you might choose to adopt a competing approach in the next conflict. If both sides to a conflict have competing styles of conflict management, than an outside mediator may be required to assist. This form of organizational learning is important and can lead toward a solution that is most beneficial to both parties. An effective leader must therefore have enough knowledge and emotional intelligence to determine the style of others involved in an ethical conflict.

Additionally, an ethical leader must know which style of conflict management to apply to a particular issue. An ethical leader is not someone who always avoids risks or continuously seeks to beat his or her opponent. Rather, an ethical leader engages in ethical decision making to determine when to be assertive, when to compromise, and when to accommodate or avoid. However, an ethical leader should never attempt to compromise an organization's ethical values. The organization's ethical values can be used as a benchmark to determine the right course of action for conflict resolution. While ethical conflict management is not an easy process, knowledge of the firm's ethical principles, values, and culture helps leaders determine the appropriate course of action.

ETHICAL LEADERS EMPOWER EMPLOYEES

Ethical leaders within an organization cannot make every ethical decision by themselves. In fact, many of the day-to-day decisions will not be made by management, but by employees. Employees constantly face organizational pressures and opportunities in the workplace to engage in ethical conduct or misconduct. Because employee decisions have wide ranging repercussions on an organization, ethical leaders must empower employees to make ethical decisions and take responsibility for their conduct. Employees at all levels of the organization should have an opportunity to develop and employ ethical leadership skills.

Employee empowerment is an essential component of a values-based organizational culture. A values-based culture encourages employees to express concerns, bring up ethical issues, and take a proactive approach toward resolving conflicts. Easy access to ethical codes and policies assists employees when making ethical decisions. Creating an open communication culture where discussion of ethics topics is commonplace encourages employees to come forward with concerns.[59] Periodic feedback between leaders and followers can bring ethical issues into the light and allow the firm to identify and work toward resolving these issues before they become major problems.

Organizations are increasingly realizing the advantages of empowering employees to become ethical leaders. For instance, managers at Wegmans supermarket stated that the secret to its success is employee empowerment. Wegmans provides employees with the opportunity to make decisions on how to best meet customer needs. This empowerment increased employee satisfaction and also made Wegmans well-known for exemplary customer service.[60] However, there is still disagreement between company leaders and employees regarding how this process is implemented. For instance, in one study managers were eight times more likely than employees to believe their firms' corporate cultures were based upon values. Employees, on the other hand, were much more likely to view their companies' corporate cultures as more command-and-control based, in that organizational leaders make all the decisions.[61] Organizational leaders may therefore misjudge their firms' corporate cultures. For this reason, it is important organizational leaders solicit constant feedback from employees and encourage their input.

Ethical leadership training for both managers and employees is helpful. Training for employees should include ethical decision making, teamwork, and conflict resolution skills. Managers should be trained how to create a participative organizational culture that encourages employees to engage in ethical decision making.[62] To reiterate to employees on the importance of ethical conduct, a firm might choose to make ethics a part of annual employee performance evaluations.[63]

Employee empowerment is important in creating employee-centered ethical leadership. Managers still have many ethical responsibilities that employees do not have. For instance, they are responsible for making the final decision and for overseeing the firm's corporate culture to ensure ethics and compliance. However, employees can contribute to the firm's ethical culture by reporting questionable activities, providing suggestions to improve the firm's culture, and modeling the firm's values to new employees. A firm's ethical culture relies not simply on documents such as a code of ethics, but on how employees embody the principles of integrity that the organization's values.

ETHICAL LEADERSHIP COMMUNICATION

The way an ethical leader communicates to employees has just as much impact on the firm's ethical culture. A narcissistic leader, for instance, is highly controlling and does not tolerate any criticism of his or her leadership decisions. Consider other leaders who tell employees they do not care how they get a task done as long as they do it. This type of communication signals to employees that they need to get their work done at any cost. Ethical leaders, on the other hand, communicate with employees regularly regarding expectations and progress toward company goals. Table 11–4 describes some of the ways leaders can use communication to improve their leadership skills.

Transparency and reporting are two major dimensions of ethical communication. Ethical leaders create transparency by developing a culture where ethics is frequently discussed. Openness and leader accessibility are important in addressing and resolving ethical issues. Reporting is a two-way process in which the communicator communicates with superiors and subordinates. While it is common practice to report to superiors, it is less

TABLE 11–4 Communication for Becoming a Better Leader

1. Have the tough conversations that you've been meaning to have, including telling people what they need (and not necessarily want) to hear.

2. Stop talking and listen more.

3. Pick up the phone or walk down the hall to actually talk with someone rather than relying on more impersonal emails.

4. Communicate bad news in the same way, with the same zest, as good news.

5. Share performance feedback with others regularly so that others know how they can improve.

6. Be purposeful and thoughtful in how you communicate.

7. Ask for feedback so you can improve your skills.

8. Work on your blind spots in your leadership abilities.

Source: Adapted from David K. Grossman, "13 Ways to Become a Better Leader," *The Public Relations Strategist*, Winter 2012, pp. 12–13.

common to feel a responsibility to report to one's subordinates. Yet ethical leaders hold themselves accountable for reporting to their employees, because they recognize that employees have an important stake in the ethical success of the organization.

Reporting can be a formal or informal process. Formal reporting happens in environments such as meetings and conferences. Formal processes of reporting also include anonymous reporting systems. Informal reporting occurs when leaders interact among employees, keeping them informed about company decisions, policies, and ethical expectations.[64] Ethical issues are often identified through these types of casual conversations, especially as employees are often more aware of questionable conduct in the workplace. An ethical leader should engage in both formal and informal systems of reporting to create an open communication culture where employees feel comfortable stepping forward with concerns or suggestions.

Ethical leadership is not possible without effective communication. How a leader communicates provides employees with a clear idea of company roles and expectations. For instance, communication about ethics topics demonstrates that the leader cares enough about the ethical culture and employee participation to communicate goals and values among employees. Secondly, it increases employee morale. Employees are made aware that their contributions and ability to make ethical decisions are important to the firm. Next, it shows employees they can bring up issues without fears of retaliation. Finally, ethical communication creates leader–follower relationships that can lead to mutually beneficial relationships between the firm and employees. Leaders who want to encourage ethical organizational conduct must make ethical communication skills a major consideration.

Ethical Leadership Communication Skills

Much like ethical leadership skills, ethical communication skills do not come easily. While some might be better communicators than others, these communication skills take practice. A well-intentioned leader might not be a good communicator, and each individual communicates differently. However, with proper training an individual can learn how to effectively and ethically communicate with other stakeholders. Organizational

FIGURE 11–2 **Four Categories of Communication**

- *Interpersonal Communication*
- *Small Group Communication*
- *Nonverbal Communication*
- *Listening*

© Cengage Learning 2015

communication is separated into four categories: interpersonal communication, small group communication, nonverbal communication, and listening. Figure 11–2 lists the four categories of communication.

Interpersonal communication is the most well-known form of communication and occurs when two or more people interact with one another.[65] Interpersonal communication provides an intimate opportunity for the ethical leader to receive or dispense information. It also provides an opportunity to coach employees when potential ethical issues arise. How to communicate effectively can be a difficult skill to master. An ethical method of communicating treats the other person with respect—even when leaders are forced to discipline employees. Respectful interpersonal communication does not involve placating the other person and never involves condoning misconduct. However, appreciating the dignity of another person even during disciplinary procedures is an important way to maintain ethical interpersonal communication. Ideally, civil interpersonal communication in these situations leads to positive behavioral changes.

It is often difficult to communicate to a superior. Differences in power status and fears that their concerns will be rebuffed makes employees more hesitant to approach organizational leaders.[66] An ethical leader must work to reassure employees by balancing the interests of all relevant stakeholders.[67] While power distance cannot be completely eliminated between a superior and subordinate—and in many cases should not be—exchanging respect and openness for judgmental language makes employees feel comfortable enough to speak up about their concerns.[68]

Like everything else, communication has gray areas. Lying to employees or consumers would generally be considered wrong. However, some find small white lies that do not damage stakeholders permissible. Sometimes communication takes on more serious dimensions. For instance, is discussing the nonpublic financial situation of your firm with a friend to use in his trades merely doing him a favor, or does your communication constitute insider trading? Former CEO of McKinsey Company Rajat Gupta told his hedge fund friend Raj Rajaratnam nonpublic financial information about Goldman Sachs. He was a board member, and did not know his personal conversation was monitored by the government. While Gupta might publicly argue this information was merely a simple business discussion with an old friend, the government saw it as insider trading. Top managers have many situations where they must consider the ethical implications of their communication and look toward the interests of all relevant stakeholders.

Collaboration and assessing the issue are good approaches to ethical interpersonal communication. Interacting with employees and maintaining strong relationships is essential to communicating the firm's values and positively influencing its ethical culture. Leaders who make an effort to maintain ethical interpersonal communication can create employee empowerment while also exercising their responsibility in carrying out organizational ethics.

Small group communication is growing in organizations. As such, this type of communication becomes increasingly important to ethical decision making.[69] Today many of an organization's ethical decisions are made in teams, and these decisions impact the ethical success of the firm. Ethical decision making in small groups is beneficial because it allows a number of individuals to collaborate and spread out responsibilities. It also empowers employees to engage in greater decision making responsibilities.

There are advantages and disadvantages to small group communication. Small groups can increase collaboration and generate a variety of different perspectives and opinions on a particular issue. However, engaging in repetitive or routine decision making can cause small groups to overlook certain ethical issues. It is difficult to anticipate all the repercussions of the group's ethical decisions. Groupthink and group polarization are common negative side effects. Groupthink occurs when one or more group members feel pressured to conform to the group's decision even if they personally disagree. Group polarization refers to the fact that a group is more likely to move toward a more extreme position than the group members might have done individually.[70] As a result, groups have been known to make riskier decisions than an average individual member from the group would have made.

Group decision making can, however, yield ethical outcomes. The diversity of opinions and discussions can result in better solutions than what would occur individually. If members are encouraged to speak up and create checks and balances in the team, then they are better able to hold other group members accountable. To ensure all group members are empowered to contribute, everyone should be familiar with the firm's ethical values and principles, trained in ethical communication techniques and how to listen to other member's input, attempt to understand the other person's point of view, show a willingness to seek common ground, explore different options, and commit to finding the most ethical solution.[71] Additionally, the ethical leader should make sure anonymous mechanisms are in place so team members can seek support if necessary. Table 11–5 provides a seven-step process for eliminating groupthink in small groups.

TABLE 11–5 Ways to Avoid Groupthink in Small-Group Decision Making

1) Emphasize to each team member that he or she is a "critical evaluator" with the responsibility to express opinions and objections freely
2) Eliminate leadership biases by refusing to express an opinion when assigning tasks to a group
3) Set up a number of independent groups to work on the same issue
4) Encourage each team member to express the group's ideas with someone he or she can trust from outside the group
5) Express the need to examine all alternatives
6) Invite outside experts into group meetings, and allow members to interact with these experts
7) Assign one person to be "Devil's advocate."

Source: Irving L. Janis (1972). *Victims of Groupthink: a Psychological Study of Foreign-Policy Decisions and Fiascos.* Boston, MS: Houghton-Mifflin.

So far we have only covered spoken communication. However, non-spoken communication is just as important to ethical leadership. Nonverbal communication is communication expressed through actions, body language, expressions, or other forms of communication not written or oral. Nonverbal communication provides major clues about an individual's emotional state.[72] In fact, some researchers believe nonverbal communication makes up about half of the communication process.[73] Nonverbal communication includes gestures, facial expressions, proximity, time, dress, and paralanguage. Paralanguage is the way we talk, such as volume, inflection, tone, and rhythm.[74] Paralanguage provides important indicators of the person's emotional status. For instance, we can tell whether another person is angry based on loudness and inflection of voice, as well as other nonverbal cues such as frowning and redness of face. These nonverbal indicators can tell us what a person really feels even if the person's language indicates otherwise.

Often a person's nonverbal cues are deemed more reliable than what he or she states verbally. This is because unlike speaking, nonverbal communication is often subconscious. It is hard for people to control what they are communicating nonverbally. Nonverbal communication is also helpful in clarifying language that might be ambiguous or confusing. Leaders should pay close attention to the nonverbal behaviors of employees. Additionally, they should show respect to others in the organization both verbally through language and nonverbal behaviors. Those who take the time to learn how to interact with those they work with can make great strides in communicating in a way that employees understand.

Listening involves paying attention to both verbal and nonverbal behavior.[75] Listening is just as important as speaking. If one of the parties to a dialogue does not listen, communication becomes ineffective. From an ethical perspective, leaders with poor listening skills or who fail to listen to concerns often overlook ethical issues. Listening is also important to employee morale. Employees cite the failure to take their concerns seriously as one of the top complaints in the workplace.[76] Failing to listen limits leaders' decision-making capacity because they cannot get the information they need to make ethical decisions. Because employee reporting is one of the primary ways leaders discover ethical concerns, failing to listen to employee reports causes them to miss key information.

However, ethical leaders developing good listening skills tend to establish credibility and trustworthiness with employees.[77] Leaders who encourage employees to provide input and assure them their concerns are taken seriously support an open communication culture. Companies with strong communication methods identify strengths and weaknesses within the firm. Additionally, leaders who spend time listening to their employees encourage employees to reciprocate in kind, further promoting the adoption and acceptance of ethical principles and values.

LEADER–FOLLOWER RELATIONSHIPS IN COMMUNICATION

Communication is essential for reducing leader isolation and creating leader–follower congruence. Leader–follower congruence occurs when leaders and followers share the same vision, ethical expectations, and objectives for the company. Although each individual has their own personal goals and personalities, it is important for a company to get leaders and followers to adopt shared values and work toward goals for the organization. If followers feel disconnected from the leader, they will not likely be committed toward promoting the firm's vision and goals.

The leader–exchange theory claims that leaders form unique relationships with followers through social interactions. Therefore, a leader who is socially isolated from employees will have a tenuous relationship because employees are left to make their own decisions. On the other hand, micromanaging employees make them feel stifled and believe leaders do not trust them. Micromanaged employees often have lower morale, productivity, and greater willingness to leave the company.[78] Conversely, leaders that have positive and respectful relationships with employees can increase job satisfaction and commitment to the firm.[79]

Because organizational leaders often occupy a managerial position, their job responsibilities are likely to differ from lower-level employees. This creates a greater tendency for the leader to be isolated. To decrease this social isolation, it is important for ethical leaders to frequently communicate and interact with employees. Communication that incorporates respect, listening, and feedback can create mutually beneficial relationships. Leaders must take a proactive stance toward the communication of ethical values, expectations, and concerns. This is particularly important because ethical issues and questionable behavior are difficult for many employees to discuss.[80] An ethical leader must therefore use communication to reassure employees that their concerns will be taken seriously.

Should the CFO be the key leader to deal with ethical risks?

In many public companies the chief financial officer (CFO) is the leader in assessing risks. Many ethical risks relate to the financial area. The Sarbanes-Oxley Act requires the CFO to abide by a code of ethics. The top concerns of CFOs are the ability to maintain margins, costs (especially health care), and forecasts of results, as well as working capital management. Therefore, some firms put the CFO as the key leader in managing risks.

However, CFOs may not define ethical risks the right way. For instance, they tend to focus on insurance coverage, regulatory compliance, and operational risks. Another viewpoint is based on a consulting firm's findings that more shareholder value is lost through strategic and ethical risks. Therefore, ethical leadership should be companywide rather than left to one person. The entire senior leadership team should self-assess their divisions of the business and report their top risks. According to this argument, risk management becomes a part of the organizational culture, and ethics is woven through all key decisions.[81]

1. To prevent financial misconduct and operational risks, the CFO should be the key leader.

2. Companywide ethical risk management is the best approach to manage financial and operational risks.

Ethics Programs and Communication

Perhaps one of the most observable ways of communicating ethical values to employees is through codes of ethics and training in how to make ethical decisions. Codes of ethics provide important guidelines for employees on how to act in different situations. Although it is impossible for any code to discuss every potential ethical issue an employee may face, effective codes should familiarize employees with the firm's values, make them aware of some of the more common ethical and legal issues they will likely face, and reinforce the firm's ethical corporate culture. For a code to be truly effective, it should be accessible and supported by every level of the company. Ethical training is another important way values are communicated. While codes provide employees with basic ethical guidelines, training allows employees to practice these guidelines. Effective ethical training programs teach employees how to apply the firm's values to some of the organization's most common ethical risk areas.

Interpersonal communication that is both formal and informal is also important between leaders and followers. Leader–follower communication connects followers with those in the company who are most familiar with the firm's ethical values. One survey found 97 percent of executives polled believed transparent communication is the key method for building trust with employees.[82] Bringing awareness to ethical topics in the workplace not only makes employees feel comfortable discussing them, but also demonstrates a commitment toward ethical conduct on the part of organizational leaders. Raytheon attempts to create an open communication culture by sending out four videos annually to each employee. The videos feature ethical dilemmas and encourage employees to work out these dilemmas and discuss ethics in the workplace.[83]

Power Differences and Workplace Politics

While there will likely be power differences between supervisors and employees within the organization, it is important that ethical leaders attempt to reduce these differences when ethical communication is involved. Some leaders occupying positions of authority within the organization might have the tendency to view information from employees as unimportant.[84] Such a perspective is detrimental to the ethical health of the company. Employees who feel their concerns are not taken seriously are less likely to bring them up—and more likely to ignore observed misconduct in the workplace. Additionally, employees who feel intimidated by the power differences might try to avoid communication with the organizational leader.

Ethical leaders can mitigate power differences through frequent communication with workers. Ethical leaders should move among employees and listen to their feedback and concerns. The point of this interaction is to create more beneficial relationships with employees and also reduce perceived power differences between these groups.

Workplace politics can be another detriment to communication in the workplace. Organizational politics is often perceived as trying to achieve one's own ends even if it means harming others in the organization. Gossip, manipulation, playing favorites, and taking credit for another's work are all examples commonly associated with workplace politics. In a highly politicized environment, employees are encouraged to compete rather than collaborate in order to win the leader's favor.[85] This leads to lower morale, higher turnover, and negative behaviors by employees who feel they are treated unfairly.[86] Ethical leaders should try to avoid having such a workplace environment.

On the other hand, there is a difference between having a high degree of office politics and having good political skills. Ethical leaders should avoid the former but adopt the latter. Political skills can be used to promote organizational goals and help rather than hinder other employees. Ethical leaders with good political skills are able to navigate difficult situations, reduce uncertainty, and advocate for positive change.[87] An ethical leader leads employees through challenges while avoiding office politics by distributing rewards fairly and communicating the firm's corporate values.

Feedback

Most companies recognize the need for organizational leaders to provide feedback to employees. Feedback can occur through informal methods like a simple conversation or through more formal systems such as employee performance evaluations. Ethical leaders understand the importance of both positive and negative feedback for employees. Negative feedback, while sometimes difficult to convey, is important to inform employees of weaknesses and provide constructive ways for improving them. However, it is important for leaders to recognize that positive feedback is just as necessary as negative feedback. Leaders who only provide negative feedback may create the perception that the organization is characterized by weaknesses, which in turn can lower employee morale. It also does not allow employees to identify and improve upon their strengths. Reinforcing the positive behavior and ethical decisions of employees is important for both the development of an ethical culture and the overall success of the firm.

While most companies understand the need for leader-to-follower feedback, not as many recognize the need for organizational leaders to get feedback from their employees. It is important to remember that while leaders might implement an ethics program, employees will be responsible for applying the company's principles and values into their daily decisions. Additionally, because they often observe conduct that leaders do not, developing feedback mechanisms for employees is crucial for identifying ethical issues. Finally, it is helpful to incorporate feedback when measuring the effectiveness of the company's ethics program.

Employee feedback can be generated in many different ways, including interviews, anonymous surveys, ethical audits, and websites. Encouraging employees to provide feedback is important in making employees feel involved in developing the firm's corporate culture. U.K. supermarket chain Sainsbury developed a strong feedback loop to address concerns and recommendations. The firm's managers are available to address employee concerns, and employees have the ability to provide feedback through other mechanisms as well. Sainsbury has received over 30,000 messages from employees offering feedback.[88] Feedback remains one of the most vital means of testing the effectiveness of a firm's ethical culture and decision making abilities.

LEADERSHIP STYLES INFLUENCE ETHICAL DECISIONS

Leadership styles influence many aspects of organizational behavior, including employees' acceptance of and adherence to organizational norms and values. Styles that focus on building strong organizational values among employees contribute to shared standards of conduct. They also influence the organization's transmission and monitoring of values, norms, and codes of ethics.[89] In short, the leadership style of an organization influences how its employees act. The challenge for leaders is in gaining the trust and commitment of organizational members, which is essential if organizational leaders are to steer their companies toward success. Those leaders recognized as trustworthy are more likely to be perceived as ethical stewards.[90] Studying a firm's leadership styles and attitudes also helps to pinpoint where future ethical issues may arise. Even for actions that may be against the law, employees often look to their organizational leaders to determine how to respond.

Ethical leadership by a CEO requires an understanding of his or her firm's vision and values, as well as of the challenges of responsibility and the risks involved in achieving organizational objectives. Lapses in ethical leadership can occur in people who possess strong ethical character, especially if they view the organization's ethical culture as being outside the realm of decision making that exists in the home, family, and community. This phenomenon has been observed in countless cases of so-called good community citizens engaging in unethical business activities. For example, Robin Szeliga, former CFO of Qwest, who pleaded guilty for insider trading, was an excellent community leader, even serving on a business college advisory board.

Ethical leaders need both knowledge and experience to make decisions. Strong ethical leaders must have the right kind of moral integrity. Such integrity must be transparent; in other words, they must "do in private as if it were always public." The ethical leader must balance current issues with potential future issues. Such a person must be concerned with shareholders as well as the lowest-paid employees. Experience shows that no leader can always be right or judged ethical by stakeholders in every case. The acknowledgment of this fact may be perceived as a weakness, but in reality it supports integrity and increases the debate exchange of views on ethics and openness.

The most effective ethical leaders possess the ability to manage themselves and their relationships with others effectively, a skill known as **emotional intelligence**. Emotionally intelligent leaders are skilled in self-awareness, self-control, and relationship building. They are outward directed and have a vision about achieving "something greater than themselves."[91] Warren Buffett is an example of an emotionally intelligent leader able to align employees behind a common vision and provide them with the motivation to make decisions and contribute. Emotional intelligence has many positive effects on corporate culture. Because emotionally intelligent leaders exhibit self-control and self-awareness, they handle stressful situations better. Additionally, employees tend to view leaders with high emotional intelligence as effective leaders because of their ability to motivate and make employees feel like an important part of the organization.[92] Because of the increased importance of emotional intelligence to productivity and leadership, many employers view emotional intelligence as more important than IQ when recruiting new employees.[93]

Six leadership styles that are based on emotional intelligence have been identified by Daniel Goleman.[94]

1. The coercive leader demands instantaneous obedience and focuses on achievement, initiative, and self-control. Although this style can be very effective during times of crisis or during a turnaround, it otherwise creates a negative climate for organizational performance.

2. The authoritative leader—considered to be one of the most effective styles—inspires employees to follow a vision, facilitates change, and creates a strongly positive performance climate.

3. The affiliative leader values people, their emotions, and their needs and relies on friendship and trust to promote flexibility, innovation, and risk taking.

4. The democratic leader relies on participation and teamwork to reach collaborative decisions. This style focuses on communication and creates a positive climate for achieving results.

5. The pacesetting leader can create a negative climate because of the high standards that he or she sets. This style works best for attaining quick results from highly motivated individuals who value achievement and take the initiative.

6. The coaching leader builds a positive climate by developing skills to foster long-term success, delegating responsibility, and skillfully issuing challenging assignments.

Richard Boyatzis and Annie McKee adapted Goleman's work on emotional intelligence to describe what they call a resonant leader. Resonant leaders demonstrate mindfulness of themselves and their own emotions, a belief that goals can be met, and a caring attitude toward others within the organization. These abilities create resonance within the organization, enabling employees to work toward common goals.[95] Resonant leaders create an ethical corporate culture as well as leader–follower congruence.

The most successful leaders do not rely on one style, but alter their techniques based on the characteristics of the situation. Different styles are effective in developing an ethical culture depending on the leader's assessment of risks and the desire to achieve a positive climate for organizational performance. Additionally, many emotional intelligence characteristics can be taught. Starbucks, for instance, has their new employees go through a training program called the "Latte Method" where employees learn to recognize negative emotions from their customers and respond appropriately.[96]

Another way to consider leadership styles is to classify them as transactional or transformational. **Transactional leaders** attempt to create employee satisfaction through negotiating, or "bartering," for desired behaviors or levels of performance. **Transformational leaders** strive to raise employees' level of commitment and foster trust and motivation.[97] Both transformational and transactional leaders can positively influence the corporate culture.

Transformational leaders communicate a sense of mission, stimulate new ways of thinking, and enhance as well as generate new learning experiences. These leaders consider employee needs and aspirations in conjunction with organizational needs. They also build commitment and respect for values that promote effective responses to ethical issues. Thus, transformational leaders strive to promote activities and behavior through a shared vision and common learning experience. As a result, they have a stronger influence on coworker support for ethical decisions and for building an ethical culture than transactional leaders. Transformational ethical leadership is best suited for organizations that have higher levels of ethical commitment among employees and strong stakeholder support for an ethical culture. A number of industry trade associations—including the American Institute of Certified Public Accountants, Defense Industry Initiative on Business Ethics and Conduct, Ethics and Compliance Officer Association, and Mortgage Bankers Association of America—are helping companies provide transformational leadership.[98]

In contrast, transactional leaders focus on ensuring required conduct and procedures are implemented. Their negotiations to achieve desired outcomes result in a dynamic relationship with subordinates where reactions, conflict, and crisis influence the relationship more than ethical concerns. Transactional leaders produce employees who achieve a negotiated level of performance, including compliance with ethical and legal standards. As long as employees and leaders both find this exchange mutually rewarding, the relationship is likely to be successful. However, transactional leadership is best suited for rapidly changing situations, including those that require responses to ethical problems or issues. For example, when Eric Pillmore took over as senior vice president of corporate governance at Tyco after a major scandal involving CEO Dennis Kozlowski, the company needed transitional leadership. To turn the company around, many ethics and corporate governance decisions needed to be made quickly. The company also required cross-functional leadership, improved accountability, and empowered leaders to improve corporate culture. Pillmore helped install a new ethics program that changed leadership policies and allowed him direct communications with the board of directors in order to implement the leadership transition.[99] Research indicates that companies characterized by transformational leadership are more likely to be involved in corporate social responsibility (CSR) activities. No link was found between transactional leadership and CSR activities.[100]

Finally, another leadership style gaining attention recently is known as authentic leadership. **Authentic leaders** are passionate about the company, live out corporate values daily in their behavior in the workplace, and form long-term relationships with employees and other stakeholders. Kim Jordan, CEO of craft brewery New Belgium Brewing (NBB), is an authentic leader who constantly strives to live NBB's mission to "operate a profitable company which makes our love and talent manifest."[101] As a role model for other employees, Jordan aligned them toward a common vision of providing high quality products and adopting a stakeholder orientation.

Authentic leaders do not mimic other leaders, but they do learn by observing them.[102] Authentic leaders display principle-centered power, because they are able to effectively handle difficult situations and display a strong commitment to their organizations.[103] Notice the similarity between principle-centered power and the self-control exhibited by emotionally intelligent leaders. Finally, authentic leaders demonstrate core values and integrate these values into the operation of the firm. Authentic leadership should be a goal for any leader who wants to create a strong ethical company.

THE RADAR MODEL

We mentioned earlier that ethical leaders must be proactive and cannot just wait for problems to arrive. Rather, they must interact with employees and have systems in place to recognize or detect ethical issues before they arise. The best way of handling misconduct is to avoid it completely. However, even the best organizations suffer from ethical risks. For instance, Warren Buffett, considered to be one of the most ethical and highly respected CEOs, faced an ethical issue after one of his managers was accused of engaging in questionable stock trades based on confidential information inside the organization. Buffett accepted the manager's resignation. When ethical misconduct or issues arise, the leader should have plans in place to answer stakeholder concerns and recover from misconduct. We adopted the acronym RADAR to describe an ethical leader's duty to *recognize* ethical issues, *avoid* misconduct whenever possible, *discover* ethical risk areas, *answer* stakeholder concerns when an ethical issue comes to light, and *recover* from a misconduct disaster by improving upon weaknesses in the ethics program.

The first step to prevent misconduct is recognizing the firm's ethical risk areas. Ethical leaders must determine what issues the firm is most likely to face so controls can be implemented to limit the opportunity for misconduct. A good way to create recognition is to teach employees about common types of ethical issues through ethical training programs. It is important that all employees recognize their responsibility to identify ethical issues before they become major problems. Additionally, part of the recognition process should include plans for how to address ethical issues once identified and whether disciplinary action is warranted. For instance, when the board of Best Buy realized its CEO had

FIGURE 11–3 The RADAR Model

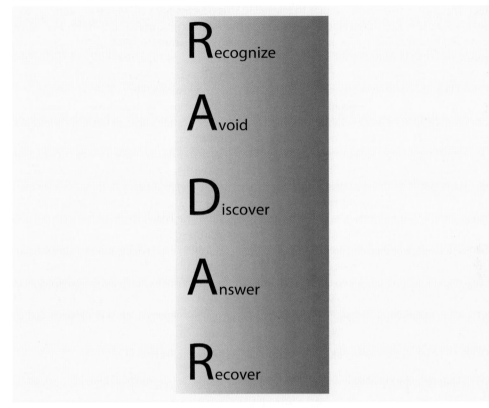

© Cengage Learning 2015

engaged in a romantic relationship with an employee, an investigation into the relationship determined it had a negative impact on the workplace. After recognizing it as an ethical violation, the CEO was forced to resign.[104] Recognizing and identifying ethical issues helps leaders develop internal controls to limit certain types of conduct and/or have plans in place to handle misconduct should it occur.

After identifying ethical risk areas, ethical leaders should develop policies and procedures for detecting and avoiding misconduct. This process is an important part of risk management. While companies might adopt risk management plans to deal with economic, marketing, technology, and environmental risks, they are less likely to consider ethical risks as a major area of concern. However, as seen throughout this text, some of the biggest dangers to a company are internal to the organization. For this reason, ethical leaders should engage in ethics continuity planning. Ethics continuity planning involves the identification of risk areas and the development of a response plan to deal with major issues. By imagining worst case scenarios, leaders brainstorm with others in the firm on the best way to avoid them. Ethics continuity planning also considers the ethical goals the firm wishes to accomplish.[105] Nike, for instance, developed supplier codes of conduct as well as auditing tools to monitor whether their suppliers adhere to the firm's ethical expectations. Nike's actions seek to avoid misconduct disasters in the supply chain and also provide directions for the firm to take if suppliers are found in violation of corporate policies.

Discovery involves proactively uncovering ethical risk areas that could lead to misconduct. Many managers are reluctant to engage in this process because they fear doing so will uncover questionable conduct that could put the firm in an unfavorable light. However, ignoring risk areas makes it much harder to resolve ethical issues when they do occur. Instead, ethical leaders engage in an assessment process to evaluate the firm's ethical weaknesses so the firm can address them. Ethics audits are a good assessment tool to discover ethical issues. While discovery is often thought of as the responsibility of management, it is important that all employees have the ability to discover ethical issues before they snowball into a misconduct disaster. Table 11–6 describes some questions ethical leaders should ask in assessing the firm's ethics program and corporate culture.

The last two steps of the process occur when a firm is faced with an ethical conflict or dilemma. It is not a question of *if* a firm is faced with an ethical dilemma, but *when*. Answering involves responding to the discovery of an ethical dilemma through communication both internally and externally. When an ethical issue is detected, a leader should communicate with employees so everyone is aware of the issue, its importance, and the necessity for resolving it. Codes of ethics, ethics training, and hotlines are just a few of the ways leaders and employees communicate internally.[106] Externally, leaders should also answer stakeholder concerns and reassure them that actions will be taken to resolve the issue. Remaining silent can be one of the biggest public relations blunders a firm makes after a disaster. Research in Motion encountered this situation after a global outage of services on its Blackberry devices. While the company's leaders eventually responded to

TABLE 11–6 Questions to Ask for Discovery and Assessment Processes

- *Does the company have a written code of conduct?*

- *Have individuals from high-level positions in the organization been assigned overall responsibility to oversee compliance with standards and procedures?*

- *What are the processes or other means by which ethics are integrated into any or all manufacturing, marketing, distribution, electronic commerce, and general corporate strategy decisions?*

- *Is there a review process whereby legal, ethical, and business practice considerations are presented, reviewed, or otherwise considered by the board of directors?*

- *What steps has the company taken to communicate its standards, procedures, and policies to all employees through training programs or publications that describe company expectations?*

- *Has the organization taken reasonable steps to achieve compliance by utilizing, monitoring, and auditing systems designed to detect misconduct and by providing a reporting system whereby employees can report without fear of retribution?*

- *Is adherence to, and implementation of, the code of ethics one of the standards by which the corporate culture can be linked directly to performance measures?*

- *Has the organization used due care not to delegate substantial responsibility to individuals that it knows does not have the ability to implement organization wide risk-reduction processes?*

- *Have the standards been sufficiently enforced through appropriate methods, such as discipline of employees who violated ethical policies?*

Source: Based on Lynn Brewer, Robert Chandler, and O.C. Ferrell (2006). *Managing Risks for Corporate Integrity* (Mason, OH: Thomson), 76–84.

stakeholder concerns, the company was criticized for waiting too long in responding to the crisis.[107]

Recovery occurs when a firm begins to rebuild its reputation. From an ethical standpoint, leaders should use this period to fix any weaknesses in the ethics program and develop improved ways of detecting misconduct. Recovery involves a four step process: 1) take corrective action; 2) compensate stakeholders harmed by the misconduct; 3) express regret for the misconduct; and 4) reinforce the firm's reputation with positive messages.[108] By improving the company's internal controls and addressing areas of ethical weakness, firms can sometimes emerge from a disaster stronger than they were before.[109] For instance, a major fraud disaster at Hospital Corporation of America provided the impetus for the development of a strong ethics and compliance program that in turn helped restore the firm's reputation as an ethical company.

SUMMARY

Leadership is the ability or authority to guide and direct others toward a goal. Ethical decisions should be one dimension of leadership. Ethical leadership has a significant impact on ethical decision making because leaders have the power to motivate others and enforce the organization's norms and policies.

Ethical leadership skills are developed through years of training, experience, and learning from other best practices of leadership. Ethical leadership involves modeling organizational values, placing what is best for the organization over the leader's own interests, training and developing employees throughout their careers, establishing reporting mechanisms, understanding employee values and perceptions, and recognizing the limits of organizational rules and values. Ethical leaders have strong personal characters, a passion to do what is right, are proactive, consider all stakeholders' interests, are role models for the organization's values, are transparent and actively involved in decision making, and take a holistic view of the firm's ethical culture.

There are many benefits to ethical leadership. Ethical leadership encourages employees to act in an ethical manner in their daily work environment. Ethical leadership can also lead to higher employee satisfaction and employee commitment. Customers are often willing to pay higher prices for products from ethical companies. Ethical leadership can also impact the long-term market valuation of the firm. Finally, companies that demonstrate they have strong ethics programs are more likely to see their fines reduced if misconduct should occur.

Ethical leaders generally adopt one of two approaches to leadership: a compliance-based approach or an integrity-based approach. A compliance approach is more focused upon risks, while an integrity approach views ethics more as an opportunity. Leaders can be classified as an unethical leader, apathetic leader, and ethical leader. The unethical leader is usually ego-centric and will often do whatever it takes to achieve the organization's objectives and his/her own. A small proportion may even be classified as psychopathic, in which they have no conscience and little or no empathy toward others. This type of leader does not try to learn about best practices for ethics and compliance. Apathetic leaders are not necessarily unethical, but they care little for ethics within the company. Ethical leaders include ethics at every operational level and stage of the decision making process.

Ethical leaders are skilled at conflict management. Ethical conflicts occur when there are two or more positions on an ethical decision. Sometimes ethical conflicts emerge because employees feel uncomfortable about their own or their co-workers' decisions. There are five types of conflict management styles: competitive, avoidance, accommodating, compromising, and collaborating. However, an ethical leader should be able to adapt his or her style depending on the situation. Additionally, ethical leaders are often skilled at recognizing the conflict management styles of others and adapting their styles accordingly.

While we tend to focus on top managers when discussing ethical leadership, ethical leadership is not limited to managers or supervisors. Employee empowerment is an essential component of a values-based organizational culture. Employees can contribute to the firm's ethical culture by reporting questionable activities, providing suggestions to improve the firm's culture, and modeling the firm's values to new employees. A firm's ethical culture relies not simply on documents such as a code of ethics, but on how employees embody the principles of integrity the organization values.

Communication is an important part of ethical leadership. Four types of communication include interpersonal communication, small group communication, nonverbal communication, and listening. Communication is essential for reducing leader isolation and creating leader–follower congruence. Leader–follower congruence occurs when leaders and followers share the same vision, ethical expectations, and objectives for the company. An important way of communicating ethical values to employees is through codes of ethics and training on how to make ethical decisions. Minimizing power differences and workplace politics and encouraging feedback from employees are also ways to create leader–follower congruence to support an ethical organizational culture.

As teams become increasingly important, particularly in organizations requiring complex problem solving, knowing how to manage teams has taken on a significant role for organizational leaders. Ethical leaders can increase the effectiveness of teams by supporting the team's ability to make decisions, initiating the structure of the team, and assigning tasks if needed. Team members should be trained in effective team building skills to help them arrive at more ethical decisions while avoiding common pitfalls such as groupthink.

Leadership styles influence many aspects of organizational behavior, including employees' acceptance of and adherence to organizational values. The most effective ethical leaders possess the ability to manage themselves and their relationships with others effectively, a skill known as emotional intelligence. Resonant leaders are emotionally intelligent leaders who demonstrate mindfulness of themselves and their own emotions, a belief that goals can be met, and a caring attitude toward others within the organization. Transactional leaders attempt to create employee satisfaction through negotiating, or "bartering," for desired behaviors or levels of performance. Transformational leaders strive to raise employees' level of commitment and to foster trust and motivation. Another leadership style gaining attention is authentic leadership. Authentic leaders are passionate about the company, live out corporate values daily in their behavior in the workplace, and form long-term relationships with employees.

The RADAR model stands for Recognize, Avoid, Discover, Answer, and Recover. An ethical leader can use this model to identify ethical risk areas, respond to ethical issues, and, if necessary, help the organization recover from ethical mishaps. First, an ethical leader must be able to identify or recognize issues having an ethical component. Next, the leader should seek to avoid having the ethical risk areas turn into ethical disasters by putting systems and controls in place to limit the opportunity for misconduct. Discovery involves proactively uncovering ethical risk areas that could lead to misconduct. Ethical audits are a good discovery tool. When an ethical issue or a misconduct disaster occurs, answering involves responding to the discovery of an ethical dilemma through communication both internally and externally. Finally, recovery involves fixing any weaknesses in the ethics program and developing improved ways of detecting misconduct.

IMPORTANT TERMS FOR REVIEW

Leadership 311

ethical conflict 318

leader–follower
congruence 326

emotional intelligence 330

transactional leader 331

transformational leader 331

authentic leader 332

RESOLVING ETHICAL BUSINESS CHALLENGES*

David Hannigan had come far since he started working at a subsidiary of Emper Corp., a manufacturer of automobile parts. He began as a line manager after graduating from UCLA four years ago. His skills at maintaining efficiency, his leadership, and his repartee with the factory workers soon gained the attention of management. Even the lowest factory workers seemed to respect David for his caring attitude and his ability to empathize with employees. While he made it clear he expected hard work, David had the ability to make every member of the factory floor feel like their contributions mattered. He shot up through the ranks and was recently promoted to Director of Personnel of this subsidiary when the previous director retired. In the entire history of the firm, nobody had moved through the ranks so quickly. David even received a letter of congratulations from the CEO of Emper Corp. after his promotion was announced. David was confident that within a few more years, he would be able to secure a high-level job at the corporate headquarters in Chicago.

A few months into his new position, David had lunch with a few key personnel from the company. One of them included Vice President Stanley Martin. Stan began the lunch meeting by praising all of them for their success. Later into his talk, he said, "You all know Emper Corp. wants to increase revenues and give big bonuses to as many employees as possible, but we need to become more efficient. That said, corporate decided the amount of automation in some of our factories, namely this one, needs to be increased."

Jane Newton from the accounting department replied, "But the cost and accounting analyses we sent to headquarters showed it wouldn't be profitable to make changes like that in this particular plant. Why did they pick this one?"

"Apparently," replied Stan, "Top management wants to test robots and all the high-tech gadgets at one factory to see if they increase product quality and pay for themselves. They think that in the long run, stockholders will benefit from automation. Anyway, the decision has been made, and it's our job to make it work. We're going to have to sell the work force and the community on the decision."

David knew what this meant. He replied, "That won't be easy. Hundreds of people are going to lose their jobs, and we are the largest source of employment for this town."

Stan's reply was pleasant, yet forceful. "Some of the factory people will be able to stay on if they get additional training. We can convince the workers and the people in town that the decision was necessary, if we can show them accounting and cost information to justify the decision. If they see good, sound reasoning for the action, they'll be less likely to resist and cause trouble. We all need to maintain productivity and efficiency until the new equipment is here. I want the accountants to work on a cost summary we can release to the employees and the town newspaper that shows why automation is a good idea."

Jane spoke up once more. "But Stan, I already told you. The net present value and other analyses I did earlier show this plant would benefit from staying the way it is."

Stan countered, "Jane, when you were working on the analyses, you said yourself that the benefits of automation are hard to identify and assign numbers to. You had to make several assumptions in order to do those analyses. If you change some of your assumptions, you can make the numbers look better. Try a longer useful life for the new equipment, or change some of the projected cost information. As soon as you have the new numbers, bring them to me to look at."

He stood up and addressed each member at the table and said, "Remember, if you can pull this off, your yearly bonuses will triple your annual salaries." Stan walked out of the room.

David felt uncomfortable about the situation. He could not understand why one of the company's top leaders would advocate for such a massive change when the numbers clearly stated that automating the factory would cause more harm than good. He remembered hearing a rumor that Stan was under serious consideration as a candidate for a prestigious position at corporate headquarters.

He wondered if Stan was trying to gain favor with those at corporate. Then again, this was mere speculation on his part. What David really worried about was what he was going to tell the employees.

QUESTIONS | EXERCISES

1. Compare and contrast the leadership characteristics of Stan and David.

2. Discuss whether David has any alternatives than implementing Stan's orders.

3. Even if the automation is successful at increasing productivity, what might be some other consequences of Stan's decision that could negatively impact the firm?

*This case is strictly hypothetical; any resemblance to real persons, companies, or situations is coincidental.

> > > CHECK YOUR EQ

Check your EQ, or Ethics Quotient, by completing the following. Assess your performance to evaluate your overall understanding of the chapter material.

1. Ethical leadership is solely the concern of top management.	Yes	No
2. Ethical conflicts occur when there are two or more positions on an ethical decision.	Yes	No
3. The four types of communication are interpersonal, small group, nonverbal, and listening.	Yes	No
4. Transactional leadership strives to raise employees' level of commitment and to foster trust and motivation	Yes	No
5. Discovery in the RADAR model involves proactively trying to uncover ethical risk areas that could lead to misconduct.	Yes	No

ANSWERS 1. **No.** While we often discuss ethical leadership in the context of top managers, all employees should be encouraged to practice ethical leadership. 2. **Yes.** Ethical conflicts occur when there are two or more positions on an ethical decision. 3. **Yes.** The four types of communication an ethical leader should master are interpersonal communication, small group communication, nonverbal communication, and listening. 4. **No.** Transformational leadership strives to raise employees' level of commitment and to foster trust and motivation. Transactional leaders attempt to create employee satisfaction through negotiating, or "bartering," for desired behaviors or levels of performance. 5. **Yes.** Discovery involves proactively trying to uncover ethical risk areas that could lead to misconduct. Ethics audits are a good tool to use in the discovery process.

ENDNOTES

1. Nanette Brynes, P. J. Huffstutter, & Mihir Dalal, "Diamond Foods Accounting Scandal Seeds Sown Years Ago," *Huffington Post*, March 19, 2012, http://www.huffingtonpost.com/2012/03/19/diamond-foods-accounting-scandal_n_1361234.html (accessed June 7, 2012); Andrew S. Ross, "Michael Mendes' dream for Diamond Foods shattered," *San Francisco Chronicle*, February 12, 2012, http://www.sfgate.com/cgi-bin/article.cgi?f=/c/a/2012/02/11/BUAE1N5CQM.DTL (accessed June 7, 2012).

2. R. Eric Reidenbach and Donald P. Robin, *Ethics and Profits* (Englewood Cliffs, NJ: Prentice-Hall, 1989), 92.

3. Chris Golis, "Emotional Intelligence: Did Meyers-Brigg Destroy Arthur Andersen?" *CBS*, April 16, 2011, http://www.cbsnews.com/8301-505125_162-31147296/emotional-intelligence-did-myers-briggs-destroy-arthur-andersen/ (accessed March 15, 2013).

4. R. Edward Freeman & Lisa Stewart, "Developing Ethical Leadership," *Business Roundtable Institute for Corporate Ethics*, 2006, www.corporate-ethics.org.

5. James B. Avey, Michael E. Palanski, and Fred O. Walumbwa, "When Leadership Goes Unnoticed: The Moderating Role of Follower Self-Esteem on the Relationship between Ethical Leadership and Follower Behavior," *Journal of Business Ethics* 98 (2011): 573–582.

6. Constance E. Bagley, "The Ethical Leader's Decision Tree," *Harvard Business Review*, January–February 2003, 18.

7. O.C. Ferrell & Larry G. Gresham, "A Contingency Framework for Understanding Ethical Decision Making in Marketing," *Journal of Marketing*, 49 (1985): 90–91.

8. Donal Crilly, Morten T. Hansen, and Maurizio Zollo, "Faking It Or Muddling Through? Understanding Decoupling In Response To Stakeholder Pressures," *Academy of Management Journal* 55(6), 2012, 1429–1448.

9. Patrick E. Murphy, Magdalena Öberseder, and Gene R. Laczniak, "Corporate Societal Responsibility in Marketing: Normatively Broadening the Concept," *AMS Review 3*(2).

10. "Christopher Kubasik, "Lockheed Exec Ousted Over Inappropriate Relationship, To Receive $3.5 Million," November 12, 2012, http://www.huffingtonpost.com/2012/11/12/christopher-kubasik-separation-package_n_2117840.html (accessed March 13, 2013).

11. R. Edward Freeman & Lisa Stewart, "Developing Ethical Leadership. *Business Roundtable Institute for Corporate Ethics*, 2006, www.corporate-ethics.org.

12. J.M. Burns, *Leadership* (New York, NY: Harper & Row, 1985).

13. John P. Kotter, "What Leaders Really Do." *Harvard Business Review*, December 2001, http://fs.ncaa.org/Docs/DIII/What%20Leaders%20Really%20Do.pdf (accessed June 4, 2012).

14. Stephen R. Covey, *The 7 Habits of Highly Effective People* (New York: Simon & Schuster, 1989).

15. Archie B. Carroll, "Ethical Leadership: From Moral Managers to Moral Leaders," in *Rights, Relationships and Responsibilities*, Vol. 1, ed. O. C. Ferrell, Sheb True, and Lou Pelton (Kennesaw, GA: Kennesaw State University, 2003), 7–17.

16. Jim Collins, "Leadership Lessons," *Leadership Excellence* 29(2), February 2012, 10.

17. John P. Kotter, "What Leaders Really Do," *Harvard Business Review*, December 2001, http://fs.ncaa.org/Docs/DIII/What%20Leaders%20Really%20Do.pdf (accessed June 4, 2012).

18. Andy Serwer, "Walmart: Bruised in Bentonville," *Fortune* online, April 4, 2005, http://money.cnn.com/magazines/fortune/fortune_archive/2005/04/18/8257005/index.htm (accessed August 17, 2009).

19. Thomas I. White, "Character Development and Business Ethics Education," in *Rights, Relationships and Responsibilities*, Vol. 1, ed. O. C. Ferrell, Sheb True, and Lou Pelton (Kennesaw, GA: Kennesaw State University, 2003), 137–166.

20. Carroll, "Ethical Leadership," 11.

21. Fortune, "100 Best Companies to Work for: NetApp," *CNNMoney*, 2013, http://money.cnn.com/magazines/fortune/best-companies/2013/snapshots/6.html?iid=bc_fl_list (accessed March 13, 2013).

22. Brent Smith, Michael W. Grojean, Christian Resick, and Marcus Dickson, "Leaders, Values and Organizational Climate: Examining Leadership Strategies for Establishing an Organizational Climate Regarding Ethics," *Journal of Business Ethics*, as reported at "Research @ Rice: Lessons from Enron—Ethical Conduct Begins at the Top," Rice University, June 15, 2005, www.explore.rice.edu/explore/NewsBot.asp?MODE=VIEW&ID=7478&SnID=878108660 (accessed August 17, 2009).

23. Whole Foods, "Our Core Values," http://www.wholefoodsmarket.com/company/corevalues.php (accessed March 13, 2013).

24. Daniel J. Brass, Kenneth D Butterfield, and Bruce C. Skaggs, "Relationship and Unethical Behavior: A Social Science Perspective," *Academy of Management Review 23* (January 1998): 14–31.

25. Linda Klebe Trevino, Gary R. Weaver, David G. Gibson, and Barbara Lay Toffler, "Managing Ethics and Legal Compliance: What Works and What Hurts," *California Management Review 41* (1999): 131–151; Michael E. Brown and Linda K. Trevino, "Ethical Leadership: A review and future directions," *The Leadership Quarterly 17* (6), December 2006, 595–616.

26. Mitchell J. Neubert, Dawn S. Carlson, K. Michele Kacmar, James A. Roberts, and Lawrence B. Chonko, "The Virtuous Influence of Ethical Leadership Behavior: Evidence from the Field," *Journal of Business Ethics* 90 (2009): 157–170.

27. Sean Valentine, Lynn Godkin, Gary M. Fleischman, Roland E. Kidwell, & Karen Page (2011). "Corporate Ethical Values, Group Creativity, Job Satisfaction and Turnover Intention: The Impact of Work Context on Work Response." *Journal of Business Ethics* 98, 353–372.

28. Fortune, "100 Best Companies to Work For 2009," *CNNMoney*, http://money.cnn.com/magazines/fortune/bestcompanies/2009/snapshots/32.html (accessed March 7, 2011); "The Container Store: An Employee-Centric Retailer," UNM Daniels Fund Business Ethics Initiative, http://danielsethics.mgt.unm.edu/pdf/Container%20Store%20Case.pdf (accessed July 30, 2012).

29. Remi Trudel and June Cotte, "Does It Pay to Be Good?" *MIT Sloan Management Review* 50 (2), 2009, 60–68.

30. Tae Hee Choi and Jinchul Jung, "Ethical Commitment, Financial Performance, and Valuation: An Empirical Investigation of Korean Companies," *Journal of Business Ethics* 81 (2): 447–463.

31. Jin-Woo Kim, "Assessing the long-term financial performance of ethical companies," *Journal of Targeting, Measurement and Analysis for Marketing* 18 (3/4), 2010, 199–208.

32. Win Swenson, "The Organizational Guidelines' 'Carrot and Stick' Philosophy, and Their Focus on 'Effective' Compliance," In *Corporate Crime in America: Strengthening the "Good Citizenship" Corporation*, 17–26, 1995, Washington, D.C.: U.S. Sentencing Commission.

33. Lynn Sharp Paine (1994), "Managing for Organizational Integrity." *Harvard Business Review*, 105–117.

34. "Ex-Chairman of Sotheby's Gets Jail Time," *The New York Times*, April 23, 2002, http://www.nytimes.com/2002/04/23/nyregion/ex-chairman-of-sotheby-s-gets-jail-time.html (accessed April 25, 2013).

35. Clive R. Boddy, (2011), "*Corporate Psychopaths: Organizational Destroyers*, Basingstroke, UK: Palgrave Macmillan, 2011, 23–25.William D. Cohan, "Did Psychopaths Take Over Wall Street Asylum," *Bloomberg*, January 2, 2012, http://www.bloomberg.com/news/2012-01-03/did-psychopaths-take-over-wall-street-asylum-commentary-by-william-cohan.html (accessed April 25, 2013).

36. Adapted from Archie B. Carroll (2003), "Ethical Leadership: From Moral Manager to Moral Leader," In O.C. Ferrell, Sheb L. True, and Lou E. Pelton, 7–17), *Rights, Relationships, & Responsibilities 1* (Kennesaw, GA: Kennesaw State University).

37. Michael Cole, "Become the leader followers want to follow," *Supervision*, Oct. 72 (10), 2011, 24–26.

38. Kenneth R. Williams, "An Assessment of Moral and Character Education in Initial Entry Training (IET)," *Journal of Military Ethics*, Mar. 9 (1), 2010, 41–56.

39. Jim Kouzes and Barry Posner, "Five Best Practices," *Leadership Excellence*, Jul. 26 (7), 2009, 3–4.

40. The Associated Press, "Former BP CEO Hayward makes brief appearance at oil spill trial," *CBC News*, February 27, 2013, http://www.cbc.ca/news/business/story/2013/02/27/bp-gulf-spill-trial.html (accessed April 25, 2013).

41. Adapted from Archie B. Carroll (2003), "Ethical Leadership: From Moral Manager to Moral Leader," In O.C. Ferrell, Sheb L. True, and Lou E. Pelton, 7–17), *Rights, Relationships, & Responsibilities 1*, (Kennesaw, GA: Kennesaw State University).

42. R. Edward Freeman & Lisa Stewart, "Developing Ethical Leadership," *Business Roundtable Institute for Corporate Ethics*, 2006, www.corporate-ethics.org.

43. Quantisoft (n.d.). "Enhancing Compliance With Sarbanes–Oxley 404." http://www.quantisoft.com/Industries/Ethics.htm (accessed June 26, 2012).

44. Lynn Sharp Paine, "Managing for Organizational Integrity," *Harvard Business Review*, 1994, 105–117.

45. Julianne Pepitone, "Yahoo confirms CEO is out after resume scandal," *CNNMoney*, May 14, 2012, http://money.cnn.com/2012/05/13/technology/yahoo-ceo-out/index.htm (accessed March 14, 2013); Abram Brown,

"Yahoo CEO Apologizes For Resume Scandal But Refuses To Leave," *Forbes*, May 8, 2012, http://www.forbes.com/sites/abrambrown/2012/05/08/yahoo-ceo-apologies-for-resume-deception-but-refuses-to-leave/ (accessed March 14, 2013).

46. Gerdien de Vries, Karen A. Jehn, and Bart W. Terwel, "When Employees Stop Talking and Start Fighting: The Detrimental Effects of Pseudo Voice in Organizations," *Journal of Business Ethics* 105 (2012): 221–230.

47. Susanne Arvidsson, "Communication of Corporate Social Responsibility: A Study of the Views of Management Teams in Large Companies," *Journal of Business Ethics* 96 (2010): 339–354.

48. Al-Karim Samnani, The Early Stages of Workplace Bullying and How It Becomes Prolonged: The Role of Culture in Predicting Target Responses. *Journal of Business Ethics*, 2012, http://www.springerlink.com/content/d482276876363471/fulltext.pdf (accessed March 14, 2013).

49. Muel Kaptein, (2011), "From Inaction to External Whistleblowing: The Influence of the Ethical Culture of Organizations on Employee Responses to Observed Wrongdoing," *Journal of Business Ethics* 98, 513–530.

50. Kenneth W. Thomas and Ralph H. Kilmann (March 2, 2010). *Thomas-Kilmann Conflict Mode Instrument: Profile and Interpretative Report*. © CPP, Inc.

51. Ibid.

52. Deborah Harrington-Mackin, *Team Building Tool Kit: Tips, Tactics, and Rules for Effective Workplace Teams* (Nashville, TN: New Direction Management Services, Inc., 1994), 21.

53. Kenneth W. Thomas and Ralph H. Kilmann, *Thomas-Kilmann Conflict Mode Instrument: Profile and Interpretative Report*, March 2, 2010. © CPP, Inc.

54. MindToolsTM, "Conflict Resolution," http://www.mindtools.com/pages/article/newLDR_81.htm (accessed July 3, 2012).

55. Joseph P. Folger, Marshall Scott Poole, and Randall K. Stutman, *Working through Conflict: Strategies for Relationships, Groups, and Organizations*, 6th ed. (Upper Saddle River, NJ: Pearson Education Inc., 2009).

56. Ibid.

57. Kenneth W. Thomas and Ralph H. Kilmann, *Thomas-Kilmann Conflict Mode Instrument: Profile and Interpretative Report*, March 2, 2010. © CPP, Inc.

58. Joseph P. Folger, Marshall Scott Poole, and Randall K. Stutman, *Working through Conflict: Strategies for Relationships, Groups, and Organizations*, 6th ed. (Upper Saddle River, NJ: Pearson Education Inc., 2009).

59. N. Leila Trapp, "Staff Attitudes to Talking Openly About Ethical Dilemmas: The Role of Business Ethics Conceptions and Trust," *Journal of Business Ethics*, 103 (2011): 543–552.

60. "How Wegmans, Apple Store and Ritz-Carlton empower employees to offer best-in-class service," December 27, 2012, http://www.retailcustomerexperience.com/article/205849/How-Wegmans-Apple-Store-and-Ritz-Carlton-empower-employees-to-offer-best-in-class-service (accessed March 14, 2013).

61. "The view from the top, and bottom," *The Economist*, September 24, 2011, http://www.economist.com/node/21530171 (accessed March 14, 2013).

62. C.L. Pearce and C.C. Manz, "*The New Silver Bullets of Leadership*: The Importance of Self- and Shared Leadership in Knowledge Work," *Organizational Dynamics* 34 (2), 2005, 130–140.

63. M.E. Brown and L.K. Treviño (2006). "Ethical leadership: A review and future directions." *The Leadership Quarterly* 17, 595–616.

64. Gary T. Hunt, *Communication Skills in the Organization*, Upper Saddle-River, NJ: Prentice-Hall, February 1989).

65. Ibid.

66. Robert Gatewood, Robert Taylor, and O.C. Ferrell, *Management* (Homewood, IL: Richard D. Irwin, Inc., 1995).

67. Sally Planalp and Julie Fitness, "Interpersonal Communication Ethics," In George Cheney, Steve May, and Debashish Munshi, *The Handbook of Communication Ethics*, 135–147. New York, NY: Taylor and Francis, 2011).

68. Jack R. Gibb, "Defensive Communication," *Journal of Communication* 11 (September 1961): 141–148.

69. Gary T. Hunt, *Communication Skills in the Organization* (Upper Saddle-River, NJ: Prentice-Hall, 1989).

70. Cass R. Sunstein, "The Law of Group Polarization," John M. Olin Law & Economics Working Paper No. 91(1999) (2D Series), http://www.law.uchicago.edu/files/files/91. CRS_.Polarization.pdf (accessed July 10, 2012).

71. Mary Ellen Guffey, Kathleen Rhodes, and Patricia Rogen, *Business Communication: Process and Product* (Toronto, Canada: Nelson Education Ltd., 2010).

72. Robert Gatewood, Robert Taylor, and O.C. Ferrell, *Management* (Homewood, IL: Richard D. Irwin, Inc., 1995), 530.

73. Jeff Thompson, "Is Nonverbal Communication a Numbers Game?" *Psychology Today*, September 20, 2011, http://www.psychologytoday.com/blog/beyond-words/201109/is-nonverbal-communication-numbers-game (accessed July 10, 2012).

74. Cynthia Burgraff Torppa, *Nonverbal Communication: Teaching Your Child the Skills of Social Success*, 2009, http://ohioline.osu.edu/flm03/FS10.pdf (accessed March 21, 2013).

75. Gary T. Hunt, *Communication Skills in the Organization* (Upper Saddle-River, NJ: Prentice-Hall, 1989).

76. Susan M. Heathfield, "Top Ten Employee Complaints," About.com, http://humanresources.about.com/od/retention/a/emplo_complaint.htm (accessed July 10, 2012).

77. Ibid.

78. SK Collins and KS Collins, "Micromanagement—A costly management style," *Radiology Management* 24 (6), 2002, 32–35.

79. G. Yukl, "Managerial Leadership: A Review of Theory and Research," *Journal of Management* 15 (June 1989): 251–289.

80. Ryan S. Bisel, Katherine M. Kelley, Nicole A. Ploeger, and Jake Messersmith, "Workers' Moral Mum Effect: On Facework and Unethical Behavior in the Workplace," *Communication Studies* 62 (2), 2011, 153–170.

81. Kate O'Sullivan, "Business Outlook Survey: Proceeding with Caution," *CFO*, January/February 2012, 37–42; Alix Stuart, "How to Direct a Risk Team," *CFO*, April 2012, 46–53.

82. Deloitte, *Trust in the workplace: 2010 Ethics and Workplace Survey*, 2010, http://www.deloitte.com/assets/Dcom-UnitedStates/Local%20Assets/Documents/us_2010_Ethics_and_Workplace_Survey_report_071910.pdf (accessed July 10, 2012).

83. Steve Watkins, "Regular Ethics Training Keeps Employees Talking," Investor.com, March 15, 2012, http://news.investors.com/article/604453/201203151416/ethics-education-keeps-company-on-right-path.htm?p=full (accessed July 10, 2012).

84. Robert Gatewood, Robert Taylor, and O.C. Ferrell, *Management* (Homewood, IL: Richard D. Irwin, Inc., 1995).

85. K. Michele Kacmar, Martha C. Andrews, Kenneth J. Harris, and Bennett J. Tepper, "Ethical Leadership and Subordinate Outcomes: The Mediating Role of Organizational Politics and the Moderating Role of Political Skill," *Journal of Business Ethics*, June 16, 2012, http://www.springerlink.com/content/yu5570k436347857/ (accessed July 11, 2012).

86. C. Chang, C.C. Rosen, and P.E. Levy, "The relationship between perceptions of organizational politics and employee attitudes, strain, and behavior: A meta-analytic examination," *Academy of Management Journal* 52(4), 2009, 779–801; K. Michele Kacmar, Martha C. Andrews, Kenneth J. Harris, and Bennett J. Tepper, "Ethical Leadership and Subordinate Outcomes: The Mediating Role of Organizational Politics and the Moderating Role of Political Skill," *Journal of Business Ethics*, June 16, 2012, http://www.springerlink.com/content/yu5570k436347857/ (accessed July 11, 2012).

87. J. Pfeffer, "Understanding power in organizations," *California Management Review* 34 (1992): 29–5; K. Michele Kacmar, Martha C. Andrews, Kenneth J. Harris, and Bennett J. Tepper, "Ethical Leadership and Subordinate Outcomes: The Mediating Role of Organizational Politics and the Moderating Role of Political Skill," *Journal of Business Ethics*, June 16, 2012, http://www.springerlink.com/content/yu5570k436347857/ (accessed July 11, 2012).

88. Katie Allen, "Companies that put employee engagement policy into practice," *Inc.*, August 21, 2010, http://www.guardian.co.uk/business/2010/aug/22/top-companies-employee-engagement (accessed July 11, 2012).

89. Daniel J. Brass, Kenneth D. Butterfield, and Bruce C. Skaggs, "Relationship and Unethical Behavior: A Social Science Perspective," *Academy of Management Review* 23(January 1998), 14–31.

90. Cam Caldwell, Linda A. Hayes, and Do Tien Long, "Leadership, Trustworthiness, and Ethical Stewardship," *Journal of Business Ethics* 96 (2010): 497–512.

91. Jim Collins, "Be Great Now." *Inc.*, June 2012, 72–73.

92. Robert Kerr, John Garvin, Norma Heaton, and Emily Boyle, "Emotional intelligence and leadership effectiveness," *Leadership & Organizational Development Journal* 27 (4), 2006, 265–279.

93. "Seventy-One Percent of Employers Say They Value Emotional Intelligence over IQ, According to CareerBuilder Survey," CareerBuilder, August 18, 2011, http://www.careerbuilder.com/share/aboutus/pressreleasesdetail.aspx?id=pr652&sd=8/18/2011&ed=8/18/2099 (accessed March 21, 2013).

94. Lynn Brewer, Robert Chandler, and O.C. Ferrell, *Managing Risks for Corporate Integrity: How to Survive an Ethical Misconduct Disaster* (Mason, OH: Thomson, 2006).

95. Richard Boyatzis and Annie McKee, *Resonant Leadership: Renewing Yourself and Connecting with Others Through Mindfulness, Hope and Compassion*, 2005, Boston, MA: Harvard Business Review Press; Bruce Rosenstein, "Resonant leader is one in tune with himself, others," *USA Today*, November 27, 2005, http://usatoday30.usatoday.com/money/books/reviews/2005-11-27-resonant-book-usat_x.htm (accessed March 21, 2013).

96. Peter Ubel, "Do Starbucks Employees Have More Emotional Intelligence than Your Physician?" *Forbes,* November 2, 2012, http://www.forbes.com/sites/peterubel/2012/11/02/do-starbucks-employees-have-more-emotional-intelligence-than-your-physician/ (accessed March 21, 2013).

97. J. M. Burns, *Leadership* (New York: Harper & Row, 1985).

98. Royston Greenwood, Roy Suddaby, and C. R. Hinings, "Theorizing Change: The Role of Professional Associations in the Transformation of Institutionalized Fields," *Academy of Management Journal* 45 (January 2002): 58–80.

99. Eric Pillmore, "How Tyco International Remade its Corporate Governance," speech at Wharton Business School, September 2006.

100. Shuili Du, Valérie Swaen, Adam Lindgreen, and Sankar Sen, "The Roles of Leadership Styles in Corporate Social Responsibility," *Journal of Business Ethics 114*(2013): 155–169.

101. New Belgium Brewing, "Culture," http://www.newbelgium.com/culture/our-story.aspx (accessed July 31, 2012).

102. Bill George, Peter Sims, Andrew M. McLean, and Diana Mayer, "Discovering Your Authentic Leadership," *Harvard Business Review*, February 2007, http://hbr.org/2007/02/discovering-your-authentic-leadership/ar/1 (accessed June 22, 2012).

103. Stephen R. Covey, *Principle-Centered Leadership* (New York, NY: Franklin Covey Co., 1991), 102–105.

104. Miguel Bustillo, "Best Buy CEO Quits in Probe," *The Wall Street Journal*, April 10, 2012, http://online.wsj.com/article/SB100014240527023038154045773355517 94808074.html (accessed March 27, 2013).

105. Lynn Brewer, Robert Chandler, and O.C. Ferrell, *Managing Risks for Corporate Integrity: How to Survive an Ethical Misconduct Disaster* (Mason, OH: Thomson, 2006).

106. O.C. Ferrell, John Fraedrich, Linda Ferrell, *Business Ethics: Ethical Decision Making and Cases*, 9th ed. (Mason, OH: South-Western Cengage Learning, 2013).

107. Daniel Tencer, "BlackBerry Outage: Can RIM's Reputation Survive This PR Disaster?" *The Huffington Post*, October 13, 2011, http://www.huffingtonpost.ca/2011/10/13/blackberry-outage-rim-pr-disaster_n_1009766.html (accessed March 27, 2013).

108. Robert C. Chandler, J.D. Wallace, and D.P. Ferguson, "Corporate Reconciliation with Critical Stakeholders through Communication: An Empirical Assessment of Efficacy, Ethicality, and Utilization Likelihood of Benoit's Image Restoration Strategies in Crisis Management Situational Contingencies," July 2002, unpublished manuscript presented at the International Communication Association, Seoul, Republic of Korea.

109. Open Compliance and Ethics Group, *GRC 360˚: Perspectives on Governance, Risk, Compliance & Culture*, Fall 2005, 13.

CHAPTER 12

SUSTAINABILITY: ETHICAL AND SOCIAL RESPONSIBILITY DIMENSIONS

AN ETHICAL DILEMMA*

Jared worked for Darwin Chemical Company (DCC) for four years. DCC is a multinational corporation with subsidiaries in eight countries. About six months ago Jared was offered a job as a plant manager for its Chinese subsidiary.

"We don't usually offer this opportunity to someone who has only been with the company for a few years," said Jonathon, Jared's supervisor. "But in the short time you've been with the firm, we feel you've shown a lot of management potential. We also see from your resume you spent a semester abroad in China as part of your MBA program. We believe this makes you a better fit than other candidates since you are more familiar with the culture." Jared saw this promotion as a stepping stone to a much higher position within the company. He agreed to the promotion and arrived in China a few months later.

Jared found the transition in dealing with another culture challenging, but rewarding. He especially appreciated his assistant manager Bojing, who helped him learn the ropes and communicate with the employees. DCC gave Jared free rein in running the plant. Its main measure of performance is the bottom line, and employees are well aware of this fact.

A few weeks ago Jared noticed something odd about the plant's waste disposal procedures of one of its more popular chemicals. Developing this particular chemical involves a complex process, and every liter of water used results in half a liter of chemical waste. Company procedures stated this waste had to be disposed of safely. The problem was the paperwork employees were required to submit and file with corporate detailing how they performed the procedure was missing. In fact, Jared could not find any record paperwork had ever been filed.

Jared approached Bojing about the issue. "The paperwork is more of a formality," Bojing replied. "Nobody seems to follow up on it."

"That's beside the point," Jared said. "We need to have these systems in place to make sure we are disposing of waste properly."

After more questions, Bojing finally confessed that while they usually tried to dispose of the waste properly, in a time crunch the entire process took too long. This resulted in employees sometimes dumping the waste in the local river.

Jared was shocked. The local river was not large, and many of the rural villagers in the area used it for drinking water. "But this is a toxic chemical! How long has this been going on?"

"Several years now," Bojing stated. "However, the previous plant manager told us not to worry. He said when mixed with water the chemical byproduct loses its potency. You would need to consume a lot for it to be harmful."

Jared immediately took action. He ordered a halt to the operations to investigate the matter further. He called the employees of the plant together and stated that from then on they would be following all procedures for disposing of waste properly. He also reported the situation to his supervisor Jonathon back home and told him about the previous plant manager's knowledge and noncompliance with proper waste disposal.

When Jared called Jonathon, he detailed all of the changes he made and was planning to make. Jonathon congratulated him on detecting and immediately putting a stop to the improper disposal practices. Then Jared started to discuss how the company should report the situation to the Chinese authorities and discuss cleanup methods.

Jonathon was quiet for a while. "Look, Jared, you must understand that in China, water pollution and improper disposal of waste is more accepted than it is here. I'm not sure we should be worried about cleaning up the river, particularly as other companies in the area likely use the river to get rid of waste. We are not the only factory around there, after all."

"But Jonathon, people who use the river for drinking water might get sick," Jared replied.

"I don't know, Jared. A cleanup would cost millions of dollars, and we'd probably be cleaning up the mess of other factories in the area. Additionally, we would probably be given heavy fines since we're a foreign company. Besides, you said yourself people would have to consume a lot of this chemical waste before they got sick."

Jared hung up the phone, more confused than ever. He thought perhaps Jonathon was right.

Maybe he was overreacting. However, later that day some reports he requested showed up. The reports stated that local fishing in the area had decreased dramatically in the past few years, and some of the fish were deformed or sickly. Jared was worried the chemicals could be impacting the fish population in the river. If this was the case, what kind of an impact might it have on the rural villagers using the river as drinking water?

QUESTIONS | EXERCISES

1. Describe the ethical dilemma Jared faces.
2. How does Jonathon rationalize his reasons for not reporting the pollution?
3. How might the water pollution impact different stakeholders?

*This case is strictly hypothetical; any resemblance to real persons, companies, or situations is coincidental.

Environmental responsibility and sustainability have become mainstream for businesses. Many consumers are willing to buy sustainable products, especially when there is no increase in price, and other consumers are willing to pay more for sustainable products. The reality is, we live in a world with limited resources being used up by more than seven billion people. These global environmental issues have numerous consequences for business. The collective participation of employees in making sustainable decisions can result in business success and at the same time contribute to finding positive solutions to questions about the use of natural resources and the well-being of society.

Our focus is how ethics can be integrated into strategic business decisions. In most firms' guiding principles, values, and norms create an ethical culture that shapes decisions. Artifacts of ethical decision making reflecting the ethical culture include statements and strategic plans such as policies about sustainability initiatives. While most decisions can have ethical implications, organizations must be mindful that inaction concerning the natural environment creates a host of ethical issues. Using non-renewable natural resources can inflict damage on consumers, communities, and society at large. The BP *Deepwater Horizon* oil spill, the second largest oil spill in the world, destroyed not only marine life but also put the livelihoods of fisherman and other industries relying on the Gulf of Mexico on hold, resulting in massive losses for the regions bordering the Gulf. Sustainability claims in marketing activities will be evaluated by relevant stakeholders, and all organizations are expected to make accurate and truthful disclosures.

Our purpose is to outline key issues and risks in making business decisions that impact the natural environment. This is not a chapter on the scientific evaluation of environmental ethical decisions. Identifying issues and risks provides opportunities for responsible individual and organizational responses to promote sustainability. We examine the concept of sustainability and the concerns of various stakeholders about our future. Next, we look at some of the major issues that relate to sustainability. We then examine some of the major environmental agencies and legislation that impact business sustainability practices. We look at businesses' responses to sustainability issues, including green marketing and greenwashing. Finally, we link sustainability to a stakeholder orientation that considers the ethical and financial performance of organizations. Firms that adopt a stakeholder orientation in their sustainability initiatives need to conduct stakeholder assessments and environmental audits to ensure they meet stakeholder needs while not overlooking financial performance.

DEFINING SUSTAINABILITY

Sustainability from a strategic business perspective is the potential for the long-term well-being of the natural environment, including all biological entities, as well as mutually beneficial interactions among nature and individuals, organizations, and business strategies. Sustainability includes the assessment and improvement of business strategies, economic sectors, work practices, technologies, and lifestyles while maintaining the natural environment. It meets the needs of the present without compromising the ability of future generations to meet their own needs. Before going any further, you should note that sustainability can have different definitions, particularly in different cultures. In Europe, for example, sustainability includes both environmental and economic connotations. In the United States, sustainability is associated more with environmental concerns. Others believe the term environment is itself too broad, and sustainability in business should focus on human sustainability with a customer focus.[1] Indeed, these differing definitions make it complex for businesses to determine what to evaluate when investigating ways to increase the sustainable impact of their organizations. For the purposes of this chapter, we reiterate our earlier definition of sustainability in terms of the long-term well-being of the natural environment and the mutually beneficial interactions among nature, individuals, organizations, and business strategies.

HOW SUSTAINABILITY RELATES TO ETHICAL DECISION MAKING AND SOCIAL RESPONSIBILITY

Sustainability falls into the social responsibility domain of maximizing positive and minimizing negative impacts on stakeholders. As a result, sustainability issues fit into our stakeholder model addressed in Chapter 2. Because most stakeholders have concerns about some aspects of the natural environment, organizations should respond to those issues in their strategies, policies, and operations. Decisions in this area relate to assessing risks, monitoring legal compliance, and avoiding misconduct within the environment.

A corporate culture that includes a sustainability agenda can create long term favorable stakeholder responses.[2] In addition, corporate social responsibility performance can increase employees' company identification and commitment.[3] Values are an important part of an ethical culture and support an organization's sustainability agenda.[4] Research indicates employees' exposure to sustainability activities increases the ability to implement sustainability programs as well as economic benefits.[5] Many firms use sustainable business practices to demonstrate their social commitment through such activities as sponsoring cleanup events, recycling, modifying manufacturing processes to reduce waste and pollution, using more alternative energy sources, and generally reevaluating the effects of their products on the natural environment. Table 12–1 provides a list of some of the world's most sustainable companies. Some companies are even becoming involved politically. For example, Exxon Mobil's CEO Rex Tillerson encouraged the U.S. Congress to enact a tax on greenhouse gas emissions in order to fight global warming.[6] Companies that do not recognize the potential impact of green programs on future profits and corporate reputation may pay later.

TABLE 12–1 World's Most Sustainable Companies

Company	Industry	Country
Umicore	Materials	Belgium
Natura Cosmeticos	Consumer Staples	Brazil
Statoil	Energy	Norway
Neste Oil	Energy	Finland
Novo Nordisk	Health care	Denmark
Storebrand	Financials	Norway
Koninklijke Philips Electronics	Industrials	Netherlands
Biogen Idec	Health care	United States
Dassault Systems	Information Technology	France
Westpac Banking	Financials	Australia

Source: Jacquelyn Smith, "The World's Most Sustainable Companies," *Forbes*, January 23, 2013, http://www.forbes.com/sites/jacquelynsmith/2013/01/23/the-worlds-most-sustainable-companies/ (accessed March 15, 2013).

Sustainability, social responsibility, and ethics should not be used interchangeably. Some take the approach that if an organization is sustainable then it is also ethical. However, an organization cannot ignore basic principles, values, and legal obligations to society. For instance, Walmart made a name for itself in sustainability with its attempt to sell more organic food, develop more environmentally-friendly supply chain practices, and invest in other green alternatives. Yet allegations it used bribery to conduct business in Mexico demonstrates that although it has made great strides in sustainability, it has experienced lapses in other areas of ethical decision making. Because ethical decisions relate to specific conduct and relationships in the decision making process, it becomes clear that sustainability is only one aspect of ethical decision making.

Additionally, social responsibility is a much broader area than sustainability. Examples of social responsibility topics relating to various stakeholders include consumer protection, corporate governance, employee well-being, and more. All of these social responsibility areas have an ethical decision making dimension. Figure 12–1 describes how ethical decisions impact sustainability as a component of corporate social responsibility (CSR).

The concept of CSR—and by relation sustainability—has become a major initiative because of stakeholder expectations. Common questions asked of companies might include how they use energy resources, how they control for pollution, whether they recycle, and how pure their food products might be. This prompted organizations like Best Buy to release corporate social responsibility reports to answer these questions. In the United States such reports are optional, whereas in the European Union they are mandatory for publicly held corporations.

There are four reasons social responsibility became such an issue for organizations. First, socially responsible activities such as sustainable business practices can create competitive advantages. Consumers' buying behavior, the interaction of stakeholders with representatives of the organization, advertising practices, and participation in social media can help a firm stay on top of market knowledge and create beneficial relationships

FIGURE 12–1 **Ethical Decisions Affect Sustainability as a Component of Social Responsibility**

Examples of Social Responsibility Concerns

Ethical Issue Awareness → Social Issues / Employee Well-Being / Legal Responsibilities / **Sustainability** / Philanthropy / Consumer Protection / Corporate Governance → Decisions

Stakeholder Evaluations

© Cengage Learning 2015

with stakeholders. Second, both positive and negative information about products and organizations became more available. Therefore, consumers and other stakeholders gained power and can influence the economic success of the company.[7] Third, organizations can use their products and brand identity to create social value, quality, and consumer loyalty. Finally, in this interconnected society, companies use their sustainable and socially responsible decisions to differentiate their firms and promote their products. Patagonia, for instance, uses organic cotton in its apparel. As a result of these reasons, social responsibility is becoming part of the budget, and sustainability is becoming a tool for ethical decision making and financial performance.[8] Positive stakeholder evaluations about sustainability are viewed as a valuable resource that contributes to competitive advantages. By responding to multiple stakeholders, the firm taps into valuable resources and provides a means to forge enduring relationships of strategic importance.[9]

Entire industries, often encouraged by regulation and consumer demands, are responding to stakeholder concerns about sustainability. It might be surprising to learn companies in the oil and gas industry are some of the largest investors in alternative clean energy sources. Within a ten-year period, the industry claims it invested about $71 billion into sustainable and renewable energy technologies, more than the U.S. government. While some of these investments are the result of new regulations, the industry recognizes the positive publicity that arises from investing in cleaner energy. Additionally, if the trend toward clean energy sources continues, companies in the industry will not want to be left behind.[10] Even companies generally thought to be unsustainable are recognizing the need for sustainability investments for the continued success of their business operations.

GLOBAL ENVIRONMENTAL ISSUES

The protection of air, water, land, biodiversity, and renewable natural resources emerged as a major issue in the twentieth century in the face of increasing evidence that mankind was putting pressure on the long-term sustainability of these resources. As the environmental movement sounded the alarm over these issues, governments responded with environmental protection laws during the 1970s. In recent years, companies are increasingly incorporating these issues into their overall business strategies. Most of these issues are the focus of concerned citizens as well as government and corporate efforts. Some nonprofit organizations have stepped forward to provide leadership in gaining the cooperation of diverse groups in responsible business activities. For example, the Coalition for Environmentally Responsible Economies (CERES), a union of businesses, consumer groups, environmentalists, and other stakeholders, established a set of goals for environmental performance. By being proactive in addressing these issues, companies can reduce their environmental impact and generate a reputation as an eco-responsible company.

In the following sections, we examine some of the most significant environmental issues facing business and society today, including air pollution, acid rain, global warming, water pollution and water quantity, land pollution, waste management, deforestation, urban sprawl, biodiversity, and genetically modified foods.

Atmospheric

Among the most far-reaching and controversial environmental issues are those that relate to the air we breathe. These include air pollution, acid rain, and global warming.

AIR POLLUTION   As emerging economies become more industrialized, air pollution is an increasingly serious issue. Air pollution typically arises from three different sources: stationary sources such as factories and power plants; mobile sources such as cars, trucks, planes, and trains; and natural sources such as windblown dust and volcanic eruptions.[11] These sources discharge gases, as well as particulates, that can be carried long distances by surface winds or linger when air stagnation occurs. Air pollution can cause markedly shorter life spans, along with chronic respiratory problems (e.g., asthma, bronchitis, and allergies) in humans and animals. The most susceptible people are children, seniors and endurance athletes. Some of the toxic chemicals associated with air pollution contribute to birth defects, cancer, and brain, nerve, and respiratory system damage. Air pollution harms plants, animals, and bodies of water. Ozone creates a haze that reduces visibility and interferes with traveling.[12]

Recently, another air pollution concern emerged with the increased use of hydraulic fracturing, or fracking. Fracking occurs when water, chemicals, and sand are pumped into a well at high pressure. This process fractures the rock layers deep in the ground, allowing natural gas to be extracted. Because the United States has a great amount of shale, fracking can increase the country's energy independence. Combustion of natural gas is more carbon efficient—it releases about half the particulates and gaseous emissions of oil and coal.[13] The advantages of fracking and the financial opportunities prompted many energy companies to invest in such wells. However, fracking also releases fast-moving flammable gases such as methane that is flared (burned) without proper control equipment. For this reason, the Environmental Protection Agency passed legislation that fracking wells must have pollution-control equipment to catch the released gas by 2015.[14]

ACID RAIN   In addition to the health risks posed by air pollution, when nitrous oxides and sulfur dioxides are emitted from manufacturing facilities, the compounds are exposed to air and rain and form new compounds, resulting in what is commonly called acid rain. This phenomenon contributes to the deaths of many valuable forests and lakes in North America and Europe. Acid rain corrodes paint and deteriorates stone, leaving automobiles, buildings, and cultural resources such as architecture and outside art vulnerable.[15] Cleaning up emissions from factories and cars is one way to reduce acid rain. Acid rain legislation in the United States appears effective. Research shows sulfates in rain (a major contributor to acid rain) in the northeastern United States have decreased 40 percent.[16]

Unfortunately, Canada's Sudbury plant is one of the largest emitters of sulfur dioxide and impacts acid rain levels in the United States.

GLOBAL WARMING   When carbon dioxide and other gases collect in Earth's atmosphere, they trap the sun's heat like a greenhouse and prevent Earth's surface from cooling. Without this process, the planet becomes too cold to sustain life. However, during the twentieth century, the burning of fossil fuels—gasoline, natural gas, oil, and coal—accelerated dramatically, increasing the concentration of "greenhouse" gases (carbon dioxide, methane, nitrogen oxides and fluorinated gases) in Earth's atmosphere. At the same time, chlorofluorocarbons—from refrigerants, coolants, and aerosol cans—are believed to be the cause of a giant hole in the Earth's atmospheric ozone layer. The ozone layer filters out the sun's harmful ultraviolet light. To further complicate things, while the United States and China give off the most greenhouse gases, developing nations like India are going to make up an increasing percentage of overall emissions. Emerging economies are also more likely to use coal, which is the dirtiest of all fossil fuels in terms of emissions and the most expensive to control. Because controlling the levels of pollutants is costly, businesses have to decide whether to take action and spend resources to control these gases or take a wait-and-see approach.

Global warming remains a hotly debated issue, especially between scientists, politicians, environmental groups, and industries. Scientific proof of global warming can be difficult as the test tube for global warming is the Earth and its atmosphere. The Earth goes through natural heating and cooling cycles. However, many scientists believe that concentrations of greenhouse gases in the atmosphere accelerate global warming. Greenhouse gas accumulations increased dramatically in the past century, causing some of the hottest years on record within the last two decades. The accumulation of five gases increased average temperatures by over 1° Fahrenheit over the last century. This is sufficient to increase the rate of polar ice sheet melting. For the first time in thousands of years, ships are able to cross through areas of the North Pole previously covered with ice. Climate change also affects weather. For instance, climate change is blamed for making northern countries more prone to flooding and southern countries more drought-ridden. As the polar icecaps melt, scientists fear rising sea levels will flood many coastal areas and submerge low-lying island nations. The Arctic is warming twice as fast as the rest of the planet, resulting in increased melting and habitat loss for Arctic animals such as the polar bear. However, the melting Arctic also provides the ability for ships once blocked by ice to travel more efficiently. Geologists believe the arctic region holds huge oil and gas reserves. For this reason, countries bordering the Arctic are eager to use these new passages for oil and gas exploration.[17]

One attempt at addressing global warming is the **Kyoto Protocol** created in 1997. This protocol is an international treaty meant to curb global greenhouse gas emissions by having countries voluntarily reduce national outputs. The United States did not ratify the treaty and therefore is not bound to it. Since 1997 the Kyoto Protocol has been highly unpopular among polluting multinational corporations. Signing the treaty required slashing their level of greenhouse gas emissions by 6 percent of their 1990 levels. U.S. leaders feared compliance would jeopardize U.S. businesses and the economy.[18] The treaty went into effect in 2005, and by 2006 the number of signatory nations topped 150.

In 2010 most of the world's nations agreed to a package of climate initiatives called the Cancun Package. The agreement called for industrialized countries to cut greenhouse gas emissions and pay into a $100 billion a year green fund to help poorer countries.

The goal was to limit global warming to less than 3.6° Fahrenheit above pre-industrial levels. The United States, China, Japan, and India did not agree to a binding climate treaty but did discuss emissions reductions.[19] Two years later there was another attempt to develop a universal, legally binding international agreement to cut greenhouse gas emissions called the Doha Gateway Agreement. The agreement calls for both developed and developing countries to reduce greenhouse gas emissions. The global agreement is expected to be signed in 2015 and be implemented in 2020.[20]

Coal is another area of contention among different countries and is one of the dirtiest forms of energy. Burning coal contributes to air pollution by releasing large amounts of gaseous and particulate emissions into the atmosphere. Some countries are combating coal usage by implementing cap-and-trade programs. A cap-and-trade program sets carbon emissions limits (caps) for businesses, countries, or individuals. Companies are given a certain amount of carbon they are allowed to emit, and to legally emit anything beyond the limit a company must purchase carbon credits from another company that does not pollute as much. The EU, which has been at the forefront of emissions reductions, mandated and implemented a cap-and-trade program on carbon emissions, known as the European Union Emission Trading Scheme. However, efforts to create a cap-and-trade program in the United States have met with much criticism. Most states in the United States, however, have a form of cap-and-trade. Any new source that emits more than 100 tons of emissions a year must offset their emissions. Capping carbon emissions cost businesses money and can lead to job losses within the coal industry. Coal burning is also the main source of electricity in many Asian nations. Coal plants are used to generate more than four-fifths of China's electricity and 70 percent of India's. The problem is that coal is less expensive compared to renewable energy.[21] This represents a major dilemma between the well-being of the environment and humanity.

Water

Water is emerging as the most important and contested resource of the Twenty First century. Nothing is more important to human survival, yet fresh water is being polluted and consumed at an unprecedented rate. A 2012 report on drinking water and sanitation found that more than 780 million people lack access to improved or uncontaminated water sources; more than 2.5 billion people live without basic sanitation; and only half of rural populations have access to improved sanitation facilities, versus 80 percent of those living in urban areas.[22] In order to remain viable, all businesses must think about water conservation, purification, and allocation.

WATER POLLUTION   Water pollution is one of the biggest contributors to illnesses in developing countries. Chemicals found in commonly used fertilizers and pesticides can drain into water supplies with each rainfall. Mercury, a common chemical found in batteries and some household products, is another concern as it contaminates oceans and therefore human food supplies. Even in the United States, which has one of the safest drinking water supplies in the world, pollution remains a problem. Pollutants come from a wide variety of sources in today's industrialized world, and many of them have unknown side effects on people and wildlife. Water pollution associated with fracking is also a major issue. Chemicals and methane have been released into water sources from fracking operations, a serious concern for consumers and governments.[23] In addition, waste liquids from fracking are re-injected into the wells. The waste stream causes pollution in aquifers and can increase the number of earthquakes in the area. Ohio has had earthquakes thought to be a result of fracking activities. These concerns led France to abolish hydraulic fracturing.[24] Table 12–2 lists common causes of global water pollution.

For some corporations the sustainability of water has become a major consideration. For example, Unilever is developing products that require 50 percent less water associated with the consumer usage.[25] General Motors designed an assembly plant in San Luis Potosi, Mexico, with a zero percent waste water discharge. All water is treated on-site and reused, reducing water consumption by 20 million gallons per year.[26] Finally, Talisman Energy partnered with environmental non-governmental organizations to assess water-related shale operations with the goal to improve the process, reuse, and storage of fluids.[27]

While environmental groups in the United States criticize U.S. water policy, special interests make it even more difficult to regulate water pollution in other parts of the world. Tougher regulations are needed globally to address pollution from activities such as the dumping of waste into the ocean, large animal-feeding operations, logging sites, public roads, parking lots, oil spills, and industrial waste created by production operations.

WATER QUANTITY In addition to concerns about the quality of water, some parts of the globe are increasingly worried about its quantity. Water use has increased dramatically in the last two decades, creating serious consequences for the global water supply and

TABLE 12–2 Facts about Water Pollution

1. Up to 90% of wastewater in developing countries flow untreated into rivers, lakes and coastal zones.
2. Many industries such as leather and chemicals are moving from high-income countries to emerging market economies where pollution laws are not enforced.
3. Every day, 2 million tons of untreated human waste is put into some water source.
4. In developing countries, 70 percent of industrial waste is dumped untreated into water sources.
5. Projected increases in fertilizer use for food production and in wastewater effluents over the next three decades suggest there will be a 10% to 20% global increase in nitrogen water contamination.
6. Common organic water pollutants include detergents, disinfection by-products (chloroform), food processing waste (fats/grease), insecticides and herbicides, petroleum hydrocarbons (gasoline, diesel fuel, jet fuels, fuel oil, motor oil), Volatile organic compounds (VOCs), chlorinated solvents (DNAPLs), polychlorinated biphenyl (PCBs), trichloroethylene, and perchlorate
7. Common inorganic water pollutants include acidity caused by industrial discharges (especially sulfur dioxide from power plants), ammonia from food processing waste, chemical waste as industrial byproducts, fertilizers containing nutrients (nitrates and phosphates), heavy metals from motor vehicles, and acid mine drainage
8. Macroscopic pollution (large visible items polluting the water) include urban storm water, marine debris, trash or garbage, nurdles (small ubiquitous waterborne plastic pellets), shipwrecks, and large derelict ships.

Sources: 2012 UN Water Statistics, http://www.unwater.org/statistics.html; Allen Burton, Jr., and Robert Pitt, *Stormwater Effects Handbook: A Toolbox for Watershed Managers, Scientists, and Engineers*, New York: CRC/Lewis Publishers, 2001; Thomas R. Schueler, "Cars Are Leading Source of Metal Loads in California," Reprinted in *The Practice of Watershed Protection*, Ellicott City, MD: Center for Watershed Protection, 2000.

for business. For instance, Coca-Cola met with hostility in many areas of India over concerns that its beverage production draws excessively on already strained water tables.[28] It is estimated that by 2030, almost half of the world's population will live in areas with major water stress.

Proactive companies are facing this reality and coming forward with solutions. For instance, Starbucks installed a new, manually operated pump faucet to replace regular turn-on fixtures in their stores, estimated to save approximately 100 gallons of water per store each day. Volkswagen has also set a target to reduce its water consumption by 25 percent by 2018. To reach its goal, the company studied its water usage to gain a broader understanding of its corporate impact so as to target water reduction activities more effectively.

Land

Land sustainability issues include everything from pollution and waste to loss of biodiversity and genetically modified food. These ethical issues are decreasing the use of viable land for human and animal habitation. Because businesses generate waste, contribute to urban sprawl, and often require the use of hard-to-restore natural resources, they have an ethical responsibility to minimize their harmful impact on the land.

LAND POLLUTION   Land pollution results from the dumping of residential and industrial wastes, strip mining, and poor forest conservation. Such pollution causes health problems in humans, jeopardizes wildlife habitats, causes erosion, alters watercourses (leading to flooding), and can eventually poison groundwater supplies. China is at the epicenter of a debate over pollution. Chinese officials revealed that soil pollution is a serious problem, perhaps more so than air and water pollution. Much of the soil contamination in China comes from arsenic, a byproduct from mining operations.[29] On the one hand, mining creates many jobs for the Chinese economy. While soil pollution may not be as much of a problem in other countries, balancing the needs of stakeholders, including consumers, businesses, the environment, and society at large, is an important ethical consideration. In order to reduce pollution around the planet, all businesses must become aware of and accept responsibility for the problem of pollution.

However, trying to pinpoint who is responsible for environmental degradation is not always easy, especially when it involves different countries. For example, an Ecuadorian judge ordered the gas giant Chevron to pay $9.5 billion to clean up oil pollution in the Ecuadorian rainforest. The original lawsuit was filed in 1993 by 30,000 plaintiffs against Texaco, which was acquired by Chevron in 2001. This could mean Chevron is liable for the damages, but Chevron claims a 1998 agreement that Texaco signed with Ecuador absolves it of liability. Additionally, Chevron officials cried foul, claiming the government colluded with the plaintiffs in the ruling.[30] At this point, Chevron has not had to pay the settlement, and an arbitration decision was in favor of Chevron blocking the plaintiffs' attempts to collect the money.

WASTE MANAGEMENT   One of the biggest factors in land pollution is the dumping of waste into landfills. American consumers are by far the world's biggest wasters. The nation has up to 40,000 abandoned landfills that are often left untreated and are filled with plastics and other materials that can take 1,000 years to degrade. San Francisco, Portland, the Indian state of Himachal, the United Arab Emirates, and Bangladesh have all banned plastic grocery bags, and Ireland and Washington D.C. charge grocery-goers for plastic bags.[31]

Some stores such as Whole Foods banned plastic bags voluntarily and other companies offer incentives for consumers to use more recyclable materials such as canvas grocery bags. Starbucks, for instance, gives a small discount to those who bring in their own Starbucks mugs. The United States and the United Kingdom recycle 10 percent and 11 percent of their household waste. Swiss households recycle about 56 percent of their waste, while Austria, Germany, and the Netherlands have recycling rates of more than 45 percent.[32]

Electronic waste is becoming a big problem since it can release harmful toxins into the air and water. Increasingly, electronics firms are pressured to take back used electronics for recycling. Large chains such as Best Buy now offer e-cycling to keep this waste out of landfills. 3M voluntarily stopped making Scotchguard, a successful product for 40 years with $300 million in sales, after tests showed it did not decompose in the environment.[33] Other organizations like Terracycle organized a business around turning trash into sellable products. Many stakeholders believe companies that produce the goods should be responsible for their proper disposal and recycling. Companies, on the other hand, argue this practice would be too expensive and argue for greater responsibility on the part of individuals. Perhaps a more suitable solution would be to balance environmental responsibility between companies, governments, and individuals.

One solid-waste problem is the result of rapid innovations in computer hardware, which render machines obsolete after just 18 months. Today, hundreds of millions of computers have reached obsolescence and tens of millions are expected to end up in landfills. Cell phones are another problem, with billions destined for landfills. Computers and cell phones contain such toxic substances as lead, mercury, and polyvinyl chloride, which leach into the soil and contaminate groundwater when disposed of improperly. The Environmental Protection Agency hosts its own electronics recycling program, stores like Staples and Best Buy offer limited recycling programs, and companies like Dell and Samsung are all seeking to extend the availability of recycling for their products.[34] Laws are also changing how consumers discard their old electronics. Seventeen states, including Minnesota, Connecticut, North Carolina, and New Jersey, banned e-waste from landfills. Instead, it must be recycled properly.[35]

DEFORESTATION The world's forests are being destroyed at a rate of nearly 50,000 square miles annually.[36] The reasons for this wide-scale destruction are varied. Because of the boom in biofuels, Southeast Asia and the Pacific regions cut down trees to make room for palm oil plantations. Brazil cuts down the Amazon rain forests for farming or raising sugarcane. On a more optimistic note, in 2012 deforestation of the Brazilian rainforest hit its lowest rate in 22 years. The Brazilian government credits improved oversight and police monitoring for the reduction in deforestation and hopes to reach its goal of decreasing deforestation to 5,000 square kilometers (1,930.5 miles) per year by 2017.[37]

A competitive global economy drives the need for money in economically challenged tropical countries. In the short term, logging and converting forestlands to other uses seems the profitable thing to do. However, the profits from deforestation for farmers are usually short-lived since rainforest soil is poor quality. This prompts low-income farmers to destroy more forest to eke out a living. Unless this cycle of poverty is stopped, the destruction of forests is likely to continue. Ecuador has posed a potential solution to the problem: if the world wants it to avoid cutting down its rainforests, then it must compensate Ecuador for the lost revenue it could obtain drilling for oil where the rainforest now stands. Although some might feel the Ecuadorian government is engaging in a strange type of blackmail, it also poses the idea that the entire world should be responsible for preserving and paying for the maintenance of the world's rainforests, not just the countries where they are located.[38]

Companies are adopting designations like one granted by the Forest Stewardship Council, a nonprofit organization comprised of loggers, environmentalists, and sociologists. The FSC seeks to coordinate forest management around the world and develop a uniform set of standards. Being FSC-certified helps companies indicate to consumers and stakeholders they are committed to preserving forest resources, they are socially responsible, and they take a long-term view of environmental management. Home Depot sells more FSC-certified wood products than any other retailer in the United States.[39]

URBAN SPRAWL   Urban sprawl began in the United States with the post–World War II building boom. This boom transformed the nation from primarily low-density communities designed to accommodate one-car households, bicyclists, and pedestrians to large-scale suburban developments at the edges of established towns and cities. Downtowns and inner cities deteriorated as shopping malls, office parks, corporate campuses, and residential developments sprang up on what was once forest, prairie, or farmland. As the places where people live, work, and shop grew further apart, people began spending more time in automobiles driving greater distances. Urban sprawl consumed wildlife habitat, wetlands, and farmland, but has also contributed to land, water, and especially air pollution. Lack of urban planning means these places grow without reason. In an age of erratic gas prices, traffic congestion, and obesity, it becomes increasingly expensive in terms of dollars and health to live in sprawling cities. Walmart as well as other big-box stores have been accused of contributing to urban sprawl.

Some urban areas fight to limit sprawl. Portland, Oregon, for example, established an Urban Growth Boundary to restrict growth and preserve open space and rural land around the city. Adding to the appeal of returning to cities is a movement to increase urban parks. Rather than allowing loggers to profit from forests, more cities are buying forested land to convert to park space. Stemming sprawl preserves natural spaces outside the city. People also realize that living near their place of employment is more convenient, cheaper, and better for their health. Although limiting urban sprawl creates disadvantages for car and oil companies, many businesses can benefit from urban renewal movements that reduce sprawl.

BIODIVERSITY   Deforestation, pollution, development, and urban sprawl put increasing pressure on wildlife, plants, and their habitats. Many plants and animals became extinct, and thousands more are threatened. The Yangtze River Dolphin is a recent extinction, and thousands more animals, including the Florida panther, tigers, frog species, and most lemurs, face the same fate.

Experts fear overutilization of natural resources will cause catastrophic imbalances in the environment. Because each biological species plays a unique role in its ecosystem and is part of a complex chain of events, the loss of any of them may threaten the entire ecosystem. Pollinators, for example, play a significant role in the growth of fruits and vegetables by spreading pollen from plant to plant. Increasing development and widespread use of pesticides reduced the populations of bees, insects, and bats needed to help plants reproduce. Without these species, the world's food supply would be seriously jeopardized. People and businesses must use resources more carefully in order to maintain a livable world for many generations to come.

GENETICALLY MODIFIED ORGANISMS Depending on whom you ask, genetically modified foods are going to save impoverished areas from starvation and revolutionize agriculture, or destroy biodiversity and make us all sick. **Genetically modified (GM) organisms** are created through manipulating plant and animal DNA to produce a desired effect like resistance to pests and viruses, drought resistance, or high crop yield. This process generally involves transferring genes from one organism to another in a way that would never occur naturally, in order to create a new life form with unique traits. Companies like Monsanto and DuPont develop genetically modified corn, soybeans, potatoes, canola oil seeds, and cotton plants they claim are more weed and insecticide resistant and provide higher yields. Many people fear these unnatural genes will have negative effects on nature, somewhat like how invader species of plants and animals can wipe out native ones. People are afraid that GM food will have negative effects on humans. Also, because GM seeds are patented, farmers cannot keep any of the seed themselves but must purchase seeds each year from companies such as Monsanto. Even so, interest in GM products remains high. In countries where malnutrition is a problem, the idea of higher yields is appealing, even if the seed itself is more expensive. Monsanto, the world's largest agricultural biotechnology company, is experimenting with genetically-modified seeds that can withstand drought, which could make a major difference in drought-prevalent countries.

However, the long-term impact of this genetic tinkering is not known, although the Food and Drug Administration deemed GM food safe to consume. Today, as much as 75 percent of all processed food contains GM ingredients—and the United States does not require these products to be labeled as such. This causes many consumers to turn toward organic foods, creating a market opportunity for organic and all-natural grocery chains like Whole Foods. Other parts of the world boycott products made from GM crops. For instance, it is illegal to grow GM crops in Thailand. In addition, studies show that certain GM crops are losing their effectiveness as insects become increasingly resistant. More farmers have reverted to using pesticides, which also damages the environment.[40]

As with GM plants, the problem with the genetic engineering of animals or animal products is that the long-run effects are unknown. Large numbers of genetically altered animals

DEBATE ISSUE
TAKE A STAND

The benefits of organic food

Organic food has become a profitable industry in the past decade. Consumers who purchase organic feel confident they are buying more natural food without the health risks of genetically modified (GM) organisms.

However, consumer perceptions of organic food are not always accurate. For instance, the Food and Drug Administration has not found organic food any healthier than non-organic. Additionally, many consumers mistakenly assume organic food is completely pesticide-free. In reality, to be certified organic, any pesticides used on the produce must be made from natural materials. Many farmers use organic pesticides on their produce to protect from bugs and other pests.

On the other hand, consumers should not rule out the benefits of organic food. Supporters claim that although GM food is not considered to have health risks, its relative newness makes it questionable. Organic food is also more environmentally-friendly, and consumers might still believe organic pesticides derived from natural sources are safer than synthetic pesticides.

1. Organic food is a healthier alternative to genetically-modified products.

2. Consumers are misled about the benefits of organic food.[41]

could upset the balance in relationships among various species with undetermined effects, such as the ability to reproduce or fight diseases and pests. Additionally, if genetically modified plant seeds are carried by wind or pollinators to areas with native plants, it is possible genetic contamination could take place among native plants, thus reducing biological diversity. Further research is needed to address public concerns about the safety and long-term environmental effects of these technologies.

ENVIRONMENTAL LEGISLATION

Until the 1970s, environmental concerns were of little importance to many organizations. However, with the first Earth Day, increasing stakeholder awareness of environmental concerns and the creation of the Environmental Protection Agency brought sustainability to the forefront. As the world's resources become increasingly depleted, the costs to business and consumers simultaneously increase.[42] As such, it is no longer acceptable for businesses to continue their day-to-day business operations without concern for how their activities impact the environment. Laws such as the Clean Air Act and the Environmental Protection Act are meant to protect the environment by limiting activities that create damage or harm to the planet. Organizations found to be in violation of these laws can receive severe penalties. However, while some companies adopt sustainability initiatives simply to avoid getting in trouble with the law, more companies are recognizing that all of their activities either directly or indirectly affect the planet—and thereby the lives and well-being of its inhabitants.[43] For these companies, sustainability is not merely a legal issue but a significant ethical issue that must be addressed. Recognizing the finiteness of the world's resources and the changing preferences of consumers, many firms are adapting their marketing activities and operational areas toward a more sustainable framework.[44]

The United States, like most other nations, passed numerous laws and established regulatory agencies to address environmental issues. Most of these efforts focused on the activities of businesses, government agencies, and other organizations that use natural resources in providing goods and services.

Environmental Protection Agency (EPA)

The most influential regulatory agency that deals with environmental issues and enforces environmental legislation in the United States is the Environmental Protection Agency (EPA). The EPA was created in 1970 to coordinate environmental agencies involved in conducting environmental research, providing assistance in fighting pollution, and enforcing the nation's environmental laws. Establishing the EPA was the culmination of a decade of growing protests over the deterioration of environmental quality. This movement reached a significant climax with the publication of Rachel Carson's *Silent Spring,* an attack on the indiscriminate use of pesticides, which rallied scientists, activists, and citizens from around the country to crusade to protect the environment from abuses of the time. President Nixon responded with the establishment of the EPA. The agency is charged with ensuring the following:

- Protecting Americans from significant health and environmental risks.
- Managing environmental risks based on empirical information.

- Ensuring the fairness and effectiveness of laws protecting human health and the environment.

- Ensuring environmental protection is an integral consideration in U.S. policies.

- Making available access to accurate information that allows participation in managing health and environmental risks.

- Making sure environmental legislation contributes to diverse, sustainable, and economically productive communities and ecosystems.[45]

To fulfill its mission, the EPA established five strategic goals to define its planning, budgeting, analysis, and accountability processes (see Table 12–3). These goals reflect public priorities in the form of statutes and regulations designed to achieve clean air and water, proper waste management, and other important concerns.[46]

The EPA can file civil charges against companies that violate the law. For instance, the EPA fined Scotts Miracle-Gro Co. for placing insecticides into its wild bird food that was lethal to certain birds. The company was forced to pay a total of $12.5 million. Even though employees warned management about the pesticide dangers and more than 70 million units were sold, it was the actions of a few employees that created the situation.[47]

Environmental Legislation

A significant number of laws have been promulgated to address both general and specific environmental issues, including public health, threatened species, toxic substances, clean air and water, and natural resources. For instance, leaded gasoline was phased out during the 1990s because catalytic converters, used to reduce pollution caused by automobile emissions and required by law on most vehicles, do not work properly with leaded gasoline. In addition, lead exposure harms people, particularly children. Increased Corporate Average Fuel Economy (or CAFE) standards are forcing the automobile industry to determine methods to increase gas mileage. For instance, automobiles must get 35.5 miles per gallon (mpg) by 2016 and 54.5 mpg by 2025.[48] This has led car makers to look for alternative ways of building their cars to get better gas mileage, such as incorporating lighter materials like aluminum.[49] Strategies include increased production and sales of hybrid vehicles, as well as improving electric cars and hydrogen fuel-cell technology. Table 12–4 summarizes significant laws related to environmental protection.

TABLE 12–3 Goals of the Environmental Protection Agency

Goal	Long-term Outcome
1	Taking Action on Climate Change and Improving Air Quality
2	Protecting America's Water
3	Cleaning Up Communities and Advancing Sustainable Development
4	Ensuring the Safety of Chemicals and Preventing Pollution
5	Better waste management, restoration of contaminated waste sites, and emergency response

Source: Environmental Protection Agency, "EPA Strategic Plan," February 15, 2013, http://www.epa.gov/planandbudget/strategicplan.html (accessed February 22, 2013).

TABLE 12–4 Laws Protecting the Environment

Clean Air Act, 1970	Established air-quality standards; requires approved state plans for implementation of the standards
National Environmental Policy Act, 1970	Established broad policy goals for all federal agencies; created the Council on Environmental Quality as a monitoring agency
Coastal Zone Management Act, 1972	Provides financial resources to the states to protect coastal zones from overpopulation
Federal Water Pollution Control Act, 1972	Designed to prevent, reduce, or eliminate water pollution
Noise Pollution Control Act, 1972	Designed to control the noise emission of certain manufactured items
Federal Insecticide, Fungicide and Rodenticide Act, 1972	Provides federal control of pesticide distribution, sale, and use
Endangered Species Act, 1973	Provides a program for the conservation of threatened and endangered plants and animals and the habitats in which they are found
Safe Drinking Water Act, 1974	Established to protect the quality of drinking water in the United States; focuses on all waters actually or potentially designed for drinking use, whether from above ground or underground sources; establishes safe standards of purity and requires all owners or operators of public water systems to comply with primary (health-related) standards
Energy Policy and Conservation Act, 1975	Requires auto dealers to have "gas mileage guides" in their showrooms
Toxic Substances Control Act, 1976	Requires testing and restricts use of certain chemical substances to protect human health and the environment
Resource Conservation and Recovery Act, 1976	Gives the EPA authority to control hazardous waste from the "cradle to grave"; includes the generation, transportation, treatment, storage, and disposal of hazardous waste, as well as a framework for the management of nonhazardous waste
Comprehensive Environmental Response, Compensation, and Liability Act, 1980	Created a tax on chemical and petroleum industries and provides broad federal authority to respond directly to releases or threatened releases of hazardous substances that may endanger public health or the environment
Emergency Planning and Community Right-to-Know Act, 1986	The national legislation on community safety, designed to help local communities protect public health, safety, and the environment from chemical hazards
Oil Pollution Act, 1990	Streamlined and strengthened the EPA's ability to prevent and respond to catastrophic oil spills; a trust fund financed by a tax on oil is available to clean up spills when the responsible party is incapable of doing so or unwilling to do so
Pollution Prevention Act, 1990	Focuses industry, government, and public attention on reducing the amount of pollution through cost-effective changes in production, operation, and raw materials use

Food Quality Protection Act, 1996	Amended the Federal Insecticide, Fungicide and Rodenticide Act and the Federal Food Drug and Cosmetic Act; the requirements include a new safety standard—reasonable certainty of no harm—that must be applied to all pesticides used on foods
Energy Policy Act, 2005	Addresses the way energy is produced in the United States in terms of energy efficiency, renewable energy, oil and gas, coal, Tribal energy, nuclear matters and security, vehicles and motor fuels, hydrogen, electricity, energy tax incentives, hydropower and geothermal energy, and climate change technology
Energy Independence and Security Act, 2007	Established a plan for moving the United States toward a more sustainable future, with steps that include the phasing out of the incandescent light bulb

© Cengage Learning

CLEAN AIR ACT   The Clean Air Act (CAA) is a comprehensive federal law that regulates atmospheric emissions from a variety of sources.[50] The law established national air quality standards as well as standards for significant new pollution sources emitting hazardous substances. These maximum pollutant standards, called National Ambient Air Quality Standards (NAAQS), were federally mandated to protect public health and the environment. Individual states were directed to develop state implementation plans (SIPs) to meet the NAAQS by restricting emissions of criteria pollutants from stationary sources (industries) within the state.

Under the Clean Air Act, states are responsible for the quality of their air and cannot negatively impact the air quality in bordering states. The EPA continues to develop stricter standards to address this issue. However, the general populace overwhelmingly agrees with the purpose of the Clean Air Act; a survey from the American Lung Association showed that 75 percent of respondents thought clean air was very or extremely important.[51] This has important implications for businesses and their relationships with consumers, particularly those in industries that have a greater tendency to contribute to air pollution.

ENDANGERED SPECIES ACT   The Endangered Species Act established a program to protect threatened and endangered species as well as the habitats in which they live.[52] An endangered species is one in danger of extinction, whereas a threatened species is one that may become endangered without protection. The U.S. Fish and Wildlife Service of the Department of the Interior maintains the list of endangered and threatened species, which currently includes more than 2,000 endangered and threatened species, including the bald eagle, American bison, and Ozark big-eared bat.[53] The Endangered Species Act prohibits any action that results in the harm to or death of a listed species or that adversely affects endangered species habitat. It also makes the import, export, interstate, and foreign commerce of listed species illegal. Protected species may include birds, insects, fish, reptiles, mammals, crustaceans, flowers, grasses, cacti, and trees.

The Endangered Species Act is highly controversial. In some cases, threatened or endangered species deemed a nuisance by ranchers and farmers, for example, have been harmed or killed by landowners seeking to avoid the hassle or expense of compliance. For instance, both the Gray wolf and the Red wolf are endangered in the United States, and livestock owners would like to eliminate them. Concerns about the restrictions and costs associated with the law are not entirely unfounded. There have been cases where consumers bought land only to be told they could not use it because it was home to an endangered species. This becomes a business ethics issue when the Endangered Species Act impacts firms.

TOXIC SUBSTANCES CONTROL ACT   Congress passed the Toxic Substances Control Act (TSCA) to empower the EPA with the ability to track the 75,000 industrial chemicals currently produced or imported into the United States. The agency repeatedly screens these chemicals and requires reporting or testing of those that pose an environmental or human health hazard. It can also ban the manufacture and import of chemicals that pose an unreasonable risk. The EPA tracks thousands of new chemicals developed each year with either unknown or dangerous characteristics. The agency can control these chemicals as necessary to protect human health and the environment.[54] For instance, the Environmental Protection Agency considered using the Toxic Substances Control Act to decide upon new rules for bisphenol A (BPA), a toxic chemical found in some plastics. Not only is this chemical deemed to have a negative impact on the environment, but it can also be harmful for humans who consume it. BPA has been used in plastic baby bottles as well as food packaging.[55]

CLEAN WATER ACT   In 1977, Congress amended the Federal Water Pollution Control Act of 1972 as the Clean Water Act (CWA). This law granted the EPA the authority to establish effluent standards on an industry basis and continued the earlier law's requirements to set water quality limits for all contaminants in surface waters. The Clean Water Act makes it illegal for anyone to discharge any pollutant from a point source directly into navigable waters without a permit.[56] This rule also requires industrial companies to draft plans to prevent storm water run-off. Arch Coal Inc. paid $4 million in fines for violating the Clean Water Act. Charges against the company maintained the firm improperly discharged pollutants into water sources, including large amounts of the mineral selenium, iron, manganese, and other pollutants that harm aquatic wildlife. Arch Coal also had to agree to increase inspecting, auditing, and tracking of its treatment systems.[57]

POLLUTION PREVENTION ACT   The Pollution Prevention Act focuses on reducing pollution through cost-effective changes in production, operation, and raw materials use. Practices include recycling, source reduction, sustainable agriculture, and other practices that increase efficiency in the use of energy, water, or other natural resources and protect resources through conservation.[58]

One common method for reducing pollution has been designing buildings to be more environmentally-friendly. Buildings are rarely considered major pollution sources. Yet 33 percent of major U.S. energy consumption, 33 percent of major greenhouse gas emissions, and 30 percent of raw material use are the result of buildings.[59] Two competitive certification groups authorize schools, houses, and commercial buildings as "green." These two rival groups, Green Globes and Leadership in Energy and Environmental Design (LEED), are vying for leadership in government adoption of environmental rules to determine whether a building can be labeled green. Green Globes is led by a former timber company executive and received much of its seed money from timber and wood products companies. LEED is a nonprofit organization with fewer ties to business interests. Already two states, Maryland and Arkansas, have adopted Green Globes as an alternative to LEED, giving officials an alternative for government-funded construction. The Clinton Presidential

Library in Little Rock as well as 7 World Trade Center, the first tower rebuilt near Ground Zero in New York, were certified by Green Globes.[60]

FOOD QUALITY PROTECTION ACT In 1996, the Food Quality Protection Act amended the Federal Insecticide, Fungicide, and Rodenticide Act and the Federal Food, Drug, and Cosmetic Act to fundamentally change the way the EPA regulates pesticides. The law included a new safety standard—reasonable certainty of no harm—that must be applied to all pesticides used on foods.[61] The legislation establishes a consistent, science-based regulatory environment and mandates a single health-based standard for all pesticides in all foods. The law also provides special protections for infants and children, expedites approval of safer pesticides, provides incentives for the development and maintenance of effective crop protection tools for farmers, and requires periodic reevaluation of pesticide registrations and tolerances to ensure they are up-to-date and based on good science.

ENERGY POLICY ACT Signed into law in 2005, the Energy Policy Act's focus is on promoting alternative forms of energy in the desire to lessen U.S. dependence on foreign oil. The bill gives tax breaks and loan guarantees to alternative energy companies like nuclear power plants, solar, and wind energy and requires utilities to comply with federal reliability standards for the electricity grid. Additionally, the bill provides tax benefits to consumers who purchase hybrid gasoline-electric cars and take other energy-saving measures. These benefits lasted from 2006 until 2010. Tax credits were provided for plug-in electric drive conversion kits.[62] In addition, the bill extends daylight savings time by one month to save energy.[63]

ALTERNATIVE ENERGY SOURCES

Alternative energy sources already have a major impact on many stakeholders. In some cases, they significantly decreased the carbon footprint of communities, cities, and even countries. Figure 12–2 provides a sustainability map of the world's different countries.

FIGURE 12–2 Sustainability Index Based on Consumer Choice

Note: The higher the index score, the greater the choice sustainability.

Source: "Greendex," *National Geographic*, http://environment.nationalgeographic.com/environment/greendex/ (accessed June 3, 2013).

Businesses such as New Belgium Brewing incorporated alternative energy sources into their operations, decreasing their carbon emissions as well as their energy costs. The following section will describe some of the more popular forms of alternative energy sources being explored.

Wind Power

Wind power holds great promise for the United States and has already taken off in many countries. For instance, one-fifth of Denmark's electricity needs are supplied by wind farms.[64] Because the United States is home to the Great Plains—one of the greatest sources of wind energy in the world—experts believe wind energy could meet as much as 20 percent of the nation's energy needs. However, restructuring the nation's power grids to efficiently transmit wind-generated power will take huge investments. Widespread adoption of wind power is slowed by the high cost of the turbines as well as limitations on an outdated national power grid. Despite these roadblocks, many people believe the United States will be a wind power hot spot in the future. Wind power also offers opportunities for businesses, even those for whom alternative energy might otherwise be perceived as a threat. BP, for example, invested in several wind farms in North America and in other parts of the globe.

Geothermal Power

Geothermal power has significant advantages and disadvantages that either advance or limit its adoption. On the one hand, geothermal energy provides a constant source of heat. It is subsequently a more dependable energy source than some other forms of alternative energy. Geothermal plants also emit fewer carbon emissions than coal power plants. On the other hand, geothermal energy is expensive, and geothermal drilling sites are not readily available everywhere. However, in spite of these initial costs, those who use geothermal energy reported a savings in overall energy costs. Due to its reliability, geothermal power could be a good substitute for natural gas in powering buildings and homes. Some IKEA stores as well as Lipscomb University started to use geothermal power to meet their energy needs.

Solar Power

Solar power is 100 percent renewable energy that can be converted into electricity through the use of either photovoltaic cells (solar cells) on homes and other structures or solar power plants. The major disadvantages of solar power are the technology remains expensive and inefficient compared to traditional fossil fuel-generated energy, and the infrastructure for mass production of solar panels is not in place in many locations. However, cloudy days are not necessarily a problem as the UV rays needed to generate power filter through clouds.

Given the strong sunshine in places like the U.S. Southwest and California, solar power gained a lot of support in the United States. The administration is attempting to lead by example. For instance, the Obama administration approved 17 zones of public land for solar energy development projects.[65] Solar power was implemented at the White House during the Bush administration to heat the pool and power a maintenance building on the grounds.[66] These actions at the top levels of government might spur more businesses and individuals to invest in alternative energy like solar power. Dell, Whole Foods, Intel, Johnson & Johnson, and Kohl's already use solar power at some of their locations.[67]

Nuclear Power

Countries throughout Europe managed to greatly reduce their emissions through the implementation of nuclear power plants, yet this form of power remains controversial. Because of the danger associated with nuclear meltdowns and radioactive waste disposal, nuclear power earned a bad reputation in the United States. On the one hand, nuclear power is pollution-free and cost-competitive. Uranium is abundant enough that generating even 60 times more energy than what is produced today would not be a problem. Nuclear energy is France's main source of power and reduced the country's nitrogen oxide and other emissions by 70 percent.[68] With careful oversight, nuclear energy could change the world's dependence on oil.

On the other hand, critics are concerned with the safety of nuclear power plants and the disposal of waste. Since production of nuclear power gives off radiation, the safety of workers and the transport of nuclear waste is a prime concern. The Chernobyl nuclear disaster in the Ukraine, which resulted in deaths, sicknesses, and birth defects, made this a viable concern. The crisis that occurred in Japan after nuclear reactors were damaged in the 2011 earthquake and tsunami further decreased support for nuclear energy.

Biofuels

Perhaps the most controversial form of alternative energy after nuclear power is ethanol. Critics argue manufacturing ethanol takes a lot of energy and is not much more sustainable than oil. Carmakers said the models they currently manufacture are not calibrated to handle greater amounts of ethanol. Because ethanol in the United States is made from corn, opponents believe it decreases the world's food supply and increases food prices. One study showed expanding ethanol production in the United States cost net corn importing countries an additional $11.6 billion in prices for corn. With 870 million people who go hungry worldwide, higher prices for a common food staple could become a problem.[69] This prompted some companies to begin looking at alternatives to corn ethanol.

However, ethanol has taken off in countries like Brazil, leading to legal mandates to incorporate biofuels as a substitute for fossil fuels. In 1976, for example, the Brazilian government made it a requirement to blend gasoline with ethanol. As a result, Brazil currently is the largest exporter of bioethanol. Biofuel production in countries like the Philippines has been criticized because it has contributed to rapid deforestation of ecologically sensitive areas—companies in a rush to create profits from the popularity of biofuels installed plantations on former jungle land, for example.

To solve these problems and take advantage of the benefits of ethanol, scientists are researching alternative sources for this fuel. Algae and nonedible plants such as grasses are currently being explored. Since grass and algae are not food sources and do not require the destruction of trees, ethanol proponents are excited to see whether these alternatives will be adopted.

Hydropower

Throughout history, people used water as a power source and means of transportation. From the water-powered mills of centuries past to modern hydroelectric dams, water is a powerful renewable energy source. Although in the United States, hydroelectric power provides only 7 percent of total output, hydroelectric provides 19 percent of total electricity production worldwide, making it the largest form of renewable energy.[70] The Three Gorges Dam in China resulted in reducing greenhouse gases for the country, although there are other environmental issues associated with the dam.[71]

As with all other forms of energy production, hydropower has benefits and downsides. One of the major downsides is the destruction of wildlife and human habitats when valleys are flooded using dams. Hydroelectricity also disrupts the lifecycles of aquatic life. However, hydroelectric power decreases greenhouse gas emissions and air pollution. To be a suitable and sustainable alternative to fossil fuels, hydroelectric facilities should be built to minimize negative environmental impacts.

BUSINESS RESPONSE TO SUSTAINABILITY ISSUES

Many businesses responded to sustainability by adopting a triple-bottom line approach. This approach takes into consideration social and environmental performance variables in addition to economic performance. Many firms are learning that being environmentally friendly and sustainable has numerous benefits—including increased goodwill from stakeholders and money savings from being more efficient and less wasteful. Several companies have a vice president of environmental affairs, like Staples, Disney, and Hyatt Hotels & Resorts. This position is designed to help firms achieve their business goals in an environmentally responsible manner. Businesses like Walmart and IBM developed environmental scorecards for their suppliers.[72] Corporate efforts to respond to environmental issues focus on green marketing, recycling, emissions reductions, and socially responsible buying.

Yet despite the importance of the environment, companies are in business to make a profit. Economic performance is still a necessary bottom line. Studies suggest improving a company's environmental performance can in fact increase revenues and reduce costs. Figure 12–3 suggests mechanisms through which this can occur.

As shown in the figure, better environmental performance can increase revenue in three ways: through better access to certain markets, differentiation of products, and the sale of pollution-control technology. A firm's innovation in sustainability can be based on applying existing knowledge and technology or creating a completely new approach. Improving a firm's reputation for environmental stewardship helps companies capture a growing market niche. Large companies like Walmart are requiring their suppliers to be more environmentally friendly, and improving a supply chain's environmental performance may be key to attracting more business from the retail industry. "Greening" a company's supply chain is particularly important because it is an often overlooked part of improving a company's sustainability. In one study, 42 percent of responding companies stated they do not include supply chain members when considering their environmental footprint.[73] This suggests companies tend to focus more on their own efforts as a distinct unit rather than on the entire supply chain.[74] Recognizing the interconnectedness of firms regarding sustainability could be a major step in improving corporate environmental impact.

Going green may help firms differentiate their products from competitors. Whole Foods, a natural foods retailer, made being environmentally friendly part of its image from the start. Method built an entire business around green cleaning products. Finally, going green opened up a new industry referred to as the eco-industry, where some firms actually discovered pollution-control technology and are now able to sell this technology to other

FIGURE 12-3 Positive Links Between Environmental and Economic Performance

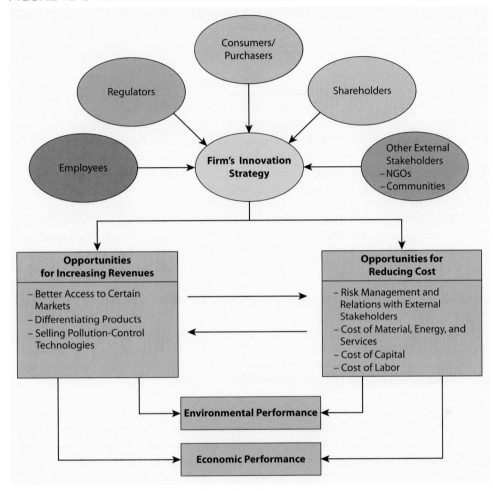

Source: "Stefan Ambec and Paul Lanoie, "Does It Pay to Be Green? A Systematic Overview," *The Academy of Management Perspectives*, **22** (4), November 2008, p. 47

firms. Siemens now generates 40 percent of its products from eco-friendly technologies.[75] The company developed technology that helped firms decrease water usage, reduce carbon emissions, and reduce traffic congestion.[76]

Better environmental performance can reduce costs by improving risk management and stakeholder relationships, reducing the amount of materials and energy used, and reducing capital and labor costs. Improved environmental standards should prevent major environmental disasters in the future. For those disasters that cannot be avoided, the firm can at least show it applied due diligence with its environmental performance, which may reduce the company's culpability in the public's eye. Companies can decrease the costs of compliance with governmental regulations and reduce fines if they become more energy efficient.

Today's greener firms may find they have better access to capital. Banks often have environmental experts evaluate the environmental performance of potential borrowers to determine whether to grant bank loans. Banks recognize poor environmental management as an increased liability. Finally, labor surveys show that workers care about the environmental impact of the firms for whom they work. Clearly, company environmental performance is ceasing to be just an environmental matter; it also influences the bottom line.

Green Marketing

Green marketing is a strategic process involving stakeholder assessment to create meaningful long-term relationships with customers, while maintaining, supporting, and enhancing the natural environment. Two of the largest craft brewers are known for their commitment to sustainability. Sierra Nevada gets 20 percent of its energy from solar power and 40 percent from hydrogen fuel cells.[77] New Belgium Brewing gets 100 percent of its energy from wind power, its facilities use natural lighting, and it provides its employees with bikes so they can travel to work and reduce fossil fuel usage. Some real estate developers are attempting to integrate environmental concerns into new communities to protect the land. As environmental mandates on emissions and waste become stricter, real estate developers can cut costs and increase compliance by using green technology and materials as much as possible.

Firms that want to become leaders in sustainability should embed sustainability into its values, norms, and beliefs.[78] For instance, UPS made it a goal to increase the sustainability of its business practices, particularly its delivery services. The company tests the use of lighter trucks that use less fuel. While these trucks might be healthier for the environment, UPS also believes they might help the firm increase efficiency and save on fuel costs.[79] By investing in more fuel efficient delivery, UPS aligns its sustainability agenda with strategic goals of efficiency and cost effectiveness.

Many products are certified as "green" by environmental organizations such as Green Seal and carry a special logo identifying them as such. In Europe, companies can voluntarily apply for an Eco-label to indicate their product is less harmful to the environment than competing products, based on scientifically determined criteria. The European Union supports the Eco-label program, which has been used in product categories as diverse as refrigerators, mattresses, vacuum cleaners, footwear, and televisions.[80]

Greenwashing

As green products become more popular, greenwashing increasingly becomes an ethical issue. Greenwashing involves misleading a consumer into thinking a product or service is more environmentally friendly than it really is. Greenwashing ranges from making environmental claims required by law and are therefore irrelevant (CFC-free) to puffery (exaggerating environmental claims) to fraud. Researchers compared claims on products sold in ten countries, including the United States, to the labeling guidelines established by the International Organization for Standardization (ISO), which prohibits vague, misleading and unverifiable claims such as "environmentally friendly" and "nonpolluting." The study found many products' claims are too vague or misleading to meet the ISO standards.[81] For example, some products are labeled "chemical-free," when the fact is everything contains chemicals, including plants and animals. Products with the highest number of misleading or unverifiable claims were laundry detergents, household cleaners, and paints. Environmental advocates agree there is still a long way to go to ensure shoppers are adequately informed about the environmental impact of the products they buy.[82]

The most common reason for greenwashing is to attract environmentally-conscious consumers. Many consumers do not find out about the false claims until after the purchase.[83] Therefore, greenwashing may increase sales in the short-term. However, while greenwashing might make a company appear sustainable, this strategy can seriously backfire when consumers find out they are being deceived. Greenwashing is negatively related to financial performance; therefore, companies that engage in greenwashing can expect to receive criticism and decreased sales in the long-run.[84] On the other hand, because the term "green" and "sustainability" can be hard to define, some greenwashing might not be intentional. Is a product green if one component is environmentally-friendly, even if the other components are not? Often stakeholders look at the product itself but may not consider the sustainability practices throughout the rest of the supply chain. To reduce this ambiguity, the Federal Trade Commission released green guidelines to help marketers determine the truthfulness of "green" claims.[85]

Another challenge with greenwashing is determining if companies are actually engaging in deception. Consumers often perceive certain practices as being more sustainable or healthier even when marketers never make claims to support this assumption. For instance, it has long been an assumption that locally grown food is more eco-friendly. New research suggests local food may not be much more environmentally-friendly than non-local.[86] Using certain colors on products can lead consumers to believe the products are sustainable. Consumers associate the color brown with recycled materials, leading firms like Dunkin' Donuts to use brown recycled napkins in their stores.[87] While these may be good cues for consumers to pinpoint more "eco-friendly" items, it also leads to the possibility that marketers could use consumer perceptions to market products without actually changing their content. Research indicates greenwashing destroys consumer trust and creates consumer confusion and perceived risk associated with green products.[88]

Although environmentalists and businesses are often at odds, there is growing agreement between them that companies should work to protect and preserve sustainability by implementing a number of goals. First, companies should strive to eliminate waste. Because pollution and waste stems from inefficiency, the issue should not be what to do with waste, but how to make things more efficiently so no waste is produced. Second, companies should rethink the concept of a product. Products are classified as consumables, that are eaten or biodegradable; durable goods, such as cars, televisions, computers, and refrigerators; and unsalables, including undesirable byproducts such as radioactive materials, heavy metals, and toxins. The design of durable goods should use a closed loop system of manufacture and use, and a return to the manufacturing process that allows products and resources to be disassembled and recycled while minimizing the disposal of unsalables. Third, the price of products should reflect their true costs, including the costs of replenishing natural resources used or damaged during the production process. Finally, businesses should seek ways to make their commitment to the environment profitable.[89]

STRATEGIC IMPLEMENTATION OF ENVIRONMENTAL RESPONSIBILITY

Businesses have responded to the opportunities and threats created by environmental issues with varying levels of commitment. Some companies, like New Belgium Brewing, consider sustainability a core component of the business. Other companies engage in greenwashing and do not actively seek to be more sustainable. A low-commitment business attempts to avoid dealing with environmental issues and hopes nothing bad happens or no one ever finds out about an environmental accident or abuse. Such firms may try to protect themselves against lawsuits. After the *Deepwater Horizon* oil leak in the Gulf of Mexico, BP faced a number of lawsuits, including one filed by the U.S. Justice Department because of the environmental damage. Other firms are proactive in anticipating risks and environmental issues. Such firms develop strategic management programs that view the environment as an opportunity for advancing organizational interests. These companies respond to stakeholder interests, assess risks, and develop a comprehensive environmental strategy.

Recycling Initiatives

Many organizations engage in **recycling**. Recycling is the reprocessing of materials, especially steel, aluminum, paper, glass, rubber, and some plastics, for reuse. In fact, recycling is one of the country's greatest sustainability success stories. Paper consists of one-third of the recyclables in the United States.[90] More than 50 percent of all products sold in stores are packed in recycled paperboard.

Paper is not the only material that is recyclable, however. Gills, the largest onion processor in the country, uses onion waste to make 600 kilowatts of electricity and cattle feed. Starbucks makes coffee grounds available free to those who wish to use them for compost to add nutrition to their gardens. Additionally, more than 2,000 organizations are part of a group called WasteWise that aims to reduce municipal solid waste and industrial waste.[91] Groups like this help companies save money through reducing waste, receive positive publicity, and track how they reduce waste over time.

Companies and local and regional governments are finding ways to recycle water to avoid discharging chemicals into rivers and streams and preserve diminishing water supplies. Companies such as Coca-Cola took steps to reduce water use. These types of

FIGURE 12–4 **Strategic Approaches to Environmental Issues**

Low Commitment	Medium Commitment	High Commitment
Deals only with existing problems	Attempts to comply with environmental laws	Has strategic programs to address environmental issues
Makes only limited plans for anticipated problems	Deals with issues that could cause public relations problems	Views environment as an opportunity to advance the business strategy
Fails to consider stakeholder environmental issues	Views environmental issues from a tactical, not a strategic, perspective	Consults with stakeholders about their environmental concerns
Operates without concern for long-term environmental impact	Views environment as more of a threat than an opportunity	Conducts an environmental audit to assess performance and adopts international standards

© Cengage Learning

concerns and efforts led to the formation of the Beverage Industry Environmental Round-table, developed by 18 companies in 2006 to investigate water conservation, energy use, and other issues that impact the industry. Since its creation, companies partnered with environmental groups and cities to enhance water conservation and bring water to consumers living in low-income countries. As part of the initiative, Dr Pepper Snapple Group is working with the Nature Conservancy on a $1.1 million project to conserve Texas watersheds.[92]

Stakeholder Assessment

Stakeholder assessment is an important part of a high-commitment approach to environmental issues. This process requires acknowledging and actively monitoring the environmental concerns of all legitimate stakeholders. Thus, a company must have a process in place for identifying and prioritizing the many claims and stakes on its business and for dealing with trade-offs related to the impact on different stakeholders. Although no company satisfies every claim, all risk-related claims should be evaluated before a firm takes action or ignores a particular issue. To make accurate assumptions about stakeholder interests, managers need to conduct research, assess risks, and communicate with stakeholders about their respective concerns.

However, not all stakeholders are equal. There are specific regulations and legal requirements that govern some aspects of stakeholder relationships, such as air and water quality. A business cannot knowingly harm the water quality of other stakeholders in order to generate a profit. Additionally, some special-interest groups take extreme positions that, if adopted, would undermine the economic base of many other stakeholders (e.g., fishing rights, logging, and hunting). Regardless of the final decision a company makes with regard to particular environmental issues, information should be communicated consistently across all stakeholders. This is especially important when a company faces a crisis or negative publicity about a decision. Another aspect of strong relationships with stakeholders is the willingness to acknowledge and openly address potential conflicts. Some degree of negotiation and conciliation is necessary to align a company's decisions and strategies with stakeholder interests.

Risk Analysis

The next step in a high-commitment response to environmental concerns is assessing risk. Through industry and government research, an organization can usually identify environmental issues that relate to manufacturing, marketing, and consumption and use patterns associated with its products. Through risk analysis, it is possible to assess the environmental risks associated with business decisions. The real difficulty is measuring the costs and benefits of environmental decisions, especially in the eyes of interested stakeholders. Research studies often conflict, adding to the confusion and controversy over sustainability.

Debate surrounding environmental issues force corporate decision makers to weigh evidence and take some risks in final decisions. The important point for high-commitment organizations is to continue to evaluate the latest information and maintain communication with all stakeholders. For example, if the millions of sport utility vehicles (SUVs) on U.S. roads today were replaced with fuel-efficient electric-powered cars and trucks, there would be a tremendous reduction of greenhouse gas emissions. However, the cooperation and commitment needed to gain the support of government, manufacturers, consumers, and other stakeholders to accomplish this would be almost impossible to achieve. Although

SUVs may harm the environment, many of their owners have prioritized other concerns, such as protection in case of an accident. A compromise might be to increase the use of mass transit to limit the use of those SUVs. Urban sprawl makes this an unattractive option.

Additionally, it is important that companies remain competitive. Container-shipping company Maersk Liner has been using low-sulfur fuel when leaving Hong Kong to reduce the city's pollution problem. Despite government incentives to use the fuel, Maersk states using the fuel is too costly compared to competitors. As a result, the company stated it would stop using the cleaner fuel unless its competitors were forced to use the fuel as well.[93]

This issue illustrates that many environmental decisions involve trade-offs for various stakeholders' risks. Through risk management, it is possible to quantify the trade-offs to determine whether to accept or reject environmentally-related activities and programs. Usually, the key decision is between the amount of investment required to reduce the risk of damage and the amount of risk acceptable in stakeholder relationships. A company should assess these relationships on an ongoing basis. Both formal and informal methods are used to get feedback from stakeholders. For example, the employees of a firm can use formal methods such as exit interviews, an open-door policy, and toll-free telephone hot lines. Conversations between employees could provide informal feedback. But it is ultimately the responsibility of the organization's management to make the best decision possible after processing all available research and information. Then, if it is later discovered a mistake was made, change is still possible through open disclosure and thoughtful reasoning. Finally, a high-commitment organization will incorporate new information and insights into the strategic planning process.

The Strategic Environmental Audit

Organizations highly committed to environmental responsibility may conduct an audit of their efforts and report the results to all interested stakeholders. Table 12–5 provides a starting point for examining environmental sensitivity. Such organizations may use globally accepted standards, such as ISO 14000, as benchmarks in a strategic environmental audit. The International Organization for Standardization developed ISO 14000 as a comprehensive set of environmental standards that encourage a cleaner, safer, and healthier world. Currently, there is considerable variation among the environmental laws and regulations of nations and regions, making it difficult for high-commitment organizations to find acceptable solutions on a global scale. The goal of the ISO 14000 standard is to promote a common approach to environmental management and help companies attain and measure improvements in environmental performance. Companies that choose to abide by the ISO standards must review their environmental management systems periodically and identify all aspects of their operations that could impact the environment.[94] Other performance benchmarks available for use in environmental audits come from nonprofit organizations such as CERES, which has also developed standards for reporting information about environmental performance to interested stakeholders.

As this chapter demonstrated, social responsibility entails responding to stakeholder concerns about the environment, and many firms are finding creative ways to address environmental challenges. Although many of the companies mentioned in this chapter chose to implement strategic environmental initiatives to capitalize on opportunities and achieve greater efficiency and cost savings, most also believe responding to stakeholders' concerns about environmental issues will improve relationships with stakeholders and make the world a better place.

TABLE 12-5   Strategic Sustainability Audit

Yes	No	Checklist
O	O	Does the organization show a high commitment to a strategic environmental policy?
O	O	Do employees know the environmental compliance policies of the organization?
O	O	Do suppliers and customers recognize the organization's stand on environmental issues?
O	O	Are managers familiar with the environmental strategies of other organizations in the industry?
O	O	Has the organization compared its environmental initiatives with those of other firms?
O	O	Is the company aware of the best practices in environmental management regardless of industry?
O	O	Has the organization developed measurable performance standards for environmental compliance?
O	O	Does the firm reconcile the need for consistent responsible values with the needs of various stakeholders?
O	O	Do the organization's philanthropic efforts consider environmental issues?
O	O	Does the organization comply with all laws and regulations that relate to environmental impact?

© Cengage Learning

SUMMARY

Sustainability from a strategic business perspective is the potential for the long-term well-being of the natural environment, including all biological entities, as well as the mutually beneficial interactions among nature and individuals, organizations, and business strategies. Sustainability includes the assessment and improvement of business strategies, economic sectors, work practices, technologies, and lifestyles while maintaining the natural environment. Sustainability falls into the social responsibility domain of maximizing positive and minimizing negative impacts on stakeholders.

The protection of air, water, land, biodiversity, and renewable natural resources emerged as a major issue in the twentieth century in the face of increasing evidence that mankind was putting pressure on the long-term sustainability of these resources. Global sustainability topics include atmospheric issues, including air pollution, acid rain, and global warming; water issues, including water pollution and water depletion; and land issues, including land pollution, waste management, deforestation, urban sprawl, biodiversity, and genetically modified organisms. By being proactive in addressing these issues, companies can reduce their environmental impact and generate a reputation as an eco-responsible company.

The most influential regulatory agency that deals with environmental issues and enforces environmental legislation in the United States is the Environmental Protection

Agency (EPA). The EPA was created in 1970 to coordinate environmental agencies involved in conducting environmental research, providing assistance in reducing pollution, and enforcing the nation's environmental laws. A significant number of laws were promulgated to address both general and specific environmental issues, including public health, threatened species, toxic substances, clean air and water, and natural resources. Some of the most important environmental laws include the Clean Air Act, the Endangered Species Act, the Toxic Substances Control Act, the Clean Water Act, the Pollution Prevention Act, the Food Quality Protection Act, and the Energy Policy Act. Alternative energy sources also have a major impact on many stakeholders. Some of the major alternative forms of energy include wind, geothermal, solar, nuclear, biofuels, and hydropower.

Better environmental performance can increase revenue in three ways: through better access to certain markets, differentiation of products, and the sale of pollution-control technology. Good environmental performance also reduces costs by improving risk management and stakeholder relationships, reducing the amount of materials and energy used, and reducing capital and labor costs.

Green marketing is a strategic process involving stakeholder assessment to create meaningful long-term relationships with customers while maintaining, supporting, and enhancing the natural environment. However, some companies desire to obtain the benefits of green marketing without the investment. Greenwashing involves misleading a consumer into thinking a product or service is more environmentally friendly than it really is. While it might seem to be helpful to a firm, companies discovered engaging in greenwashing may suffer reputational damage.

Businesses have responded to the opportunities and threats created by environmental issues with varying levels of commitment. Those firms proactive in anticipating risks and environmental issues develop strategic management programs that view the environment as an opportunity for advancing organizational interests. Many organizations engage in recycling, the reprocessing of materials, especially steel, aluminum, paper, glass, rubber, and some plastics, for reuse. Additionally, stakeholder assessment, risk analysis, and the strategic environmental audit are important parts of a high-commitment approach to environmental issues. Stakeholder assessment is a process that acknowledges and actively monitors the environmental concerns of all legitimate stakeholders. Through risk analysis, it is possible to assess the environmental risks associated with business decisions. Organizations highly committed to environmental responsibility may conduct an audit of their efforts using standards such as ISO 14000 and report the results to all interested stakeholders.

IMPORTANT TERMS FOR REVIEW

Sustainability 347

Kyoto Protocol 351

Genetically Modified (GM) Organisms 357

Environmental Protection Agency (EPA) 358

Green Marketing 368

Greenwashing 368

Recycling 370

RESOLVING ETHICAL BUSINESS CHALLENGES*

After graduating from Ohio State, Keisha got a job in the marketing and public relations department at a small soda company called Smith's Sodas. Smith's Sodas specializes in high-quality fruit-flavored soft drinks with unique flavors such as pomegranate, raspberry, blueberry, and coconut. The company had great plans for the future. In ten years Smith's Sodas wanted to become a competitor to its larger rivals, Pepsi and Coca-Cola. The company sold sodas with lower calories than its rivals and offered them in a variety of flavors. However, the product was only half the battle. The rest was up to the marketing department to promote the sodas as being superior to the competition.

Recently, Keisha was called into her supervisor's office and assigned a new project. She would take the lead in a marketing initiative that promoted a new feature meant to appeal to the eco-conscious consumer: biodegradable packaging. One of the company's suppliers came up with a soda bottle made with a new biodegradable plastic manufactured with plant materials. Keisha was told the supplier struggled to develop this plastic for years and Smith's Sodas was staking much of its credibility on developing an image as an environmentally-friendly organization.

Keisha immediately began learning about the plastic and writing up press releases to send to local news stations. She put in long hours working on a marketing campaign touting the product's sustainability and how much better it is for the environment. She stressed the fact that the plastic should be composted rather than simply thrown in the trash to biodegrade properly.

A few days ago Keisha received a call from a local reporter. "I've heard all of the hype concerning these biodegradable bottles your company is using. I wanted to test just how biodegradable this plastic really is. I contacted scientists at the local university to test its biodegradability. They tested the bottle under ten different conditions with different types of soil. Only four out of the ten tests resulted in the plastic degrading to any major extent."

When Keisha hung up the phone, she decided to investigate whether the reporter's claims were accurate. After two days of phone calls, she finally contacted someone who had been involved in the actual development of the plastic.

"Yes, it's true the plastic only degrades under certain conditions," he informed her. "But that's still better than a lot of other plastics."

Keisha approached her manager, Louis, to discuss the issue. Louis did not understand Keisha's concern. "I don't see what the problem is, Keisha, other than the fact that this reporter is trying to cause trouble. As long as the plastic biodegrades under certain natural conditions, then we are fine."

"Yes, but Louis, our claims made it seem the bottles degrade fairly easily, when in reality people must compost them. Even then they only degrade under certain conditions. Isn't this a type of greenwashing?"

Louis frowned at the mention of *greenwashing*. "Keisha, the term biodegradable is vague. We have a supplier, and it is not our responsibility to prove the packaging is biodegradable. We are not being deceitful, and it is up to the consumer to know how to dispose of the package so it degrades properly. We can't control what happens to the product after the consumer buys it. Many may simply toss it into the garbage."

"What happens if the reporter publishes her findings?" Keisha asked.

Louis looked adamant. "We are not lying when we say the plastic is biodegradable. Besides, most companies have to rely on supplier claims. I don't see any reason why we need to change our marketing claims."

QUESTIONS | EXERCISES

1. Are Smith's Sodas' marketing claims accurate and truthful?
2. Discuss the justifications Louis uses to argue for the truthfulness of the company's marketing claims.
3. Assume there is a news story questioning the sustainability of Smith's Sodas packaging. How should Keisha respond?

*This case is strictly hypothetical; any resemblance to real persons, companies, or situations is coincidental.

> > > CHECK YOUR EQ

Check your EQ, or Ethics Quotient, by completing the following. Assess your performance to evaluate your overall understanding of the chapter material.

1. Sustainability is the potential for the long-term well-being of the natural environment, including all biological entities, as well as the mutually beneficial interactions among nature and individuals, organizations, and business strategies.   **Yes**   **No**

2. The Environmental Protection Agency (EPA) deals with environmental issues and enforces environmental legislation in the United States.   **Yes**   **No**

3. Ethanol, fracking, and hydropower are all forms of alternative energy.   **Yes**   **No**

4. Greenwashing is a strategic process involving stakeholder assessment to create meaningful long-term relationships with customers, while maintaining, supporting, and enhancing the natural environment.   **Yes**   **No**

5. Stakeholder assessment is an important part of a high-commitment approach to environmental issues.   **Yes**   **No**

ANSWERS **1. Yes.** Sustainability is the potential for the long-term well-being of the natural environment, including all biological entities, as well as the mutually beneficial interactions among nature and individuals, organizations, and business strategies. **2. Yes.** The Environmental Protection Agency deals with environmental issues and enforces environmental legislation in the United States. **3. No.** Fracking is not a form of alternative energy. **4. No.** Green marketing is a strategic process involving stakeholder assessment to create meaningful long-term relationships with customers, while maintaining, supporting, and enhancing the natural environment. **5. Yes.** Stakeholder assessment is an important part of a high-commitment approach to environmental issues.

ENDNOTES

1. Kevin Gibson, "Stakeholders and Sustainability: An Evolving Theory," *Journal of Business Ethics 109*(1), 2012, 15–25.

2. Sean Valentine, Lynn Godkin, Gary M. Fleischman, and Roland Kidwell, "Corporate Ethical Values, Group Creativity, Job Satisfaction and Turnover Intention: The Impact of Work Context on Work Response," *Journal of Business Ethics* 98 (2011): 353–372.

3. Hae-Ryong Kim, Moonkyu Lee, Hyoung-Tark Lee, and Na-Min Kim, "Corporate Social Responsibility and Employee-Company Identification," *Journal of Business Ethics* 95 (2010): 557–569.

4. Liviu Florea, Yu Ha Cheung, and Neil C. Herndon, "For All Good Reasons: Role of Values in Organizational Sustainability," *Journal of Business Ethics 114*(3), 2013, 393–408.

5. Marcus Wagner, "'Green Human Resource Benefits: Do they Matter as Determinants of Environmental Management System Implementation?" *Journal of Business Ethics 114*(3), 2013, 443–456.

6. Russell Gold and Ian Talley, "Exxon CEO Advocates Emissions Tax," *The Wall Street Journal*, January 9, 2009, http://online.wsj.com/article/SB123146091530566335.html (accessed March 15, 2013).

7. Patrick E. Murphy, Magdalena Öberseder, and Gene R. Laczniak (2013), "Corporate Societal Responsibility in Marketing: Normatively Broadening the Concept," *AMS Review 3*(2).

8. Ibid.

9. Alain Verbeke and Vincent Tung, "The Future of Stakeholder Management Theory: A Temporal Perspective," *Journal of Business Ethics* 112, 529–543.

10. Ken Wells, "Green Giants," *Bloomberg Businessweek*, May 14–May 20, 2012, 57–58.

11. "Air Quality," Office of Air Quality Planning and Standards, *Environmental Protection Agency*, www.epa.gov/oar/oaqps/cleanair.html (accessed March 15, 2013).

12. "The Plain English Guide to the Clean Air Act," Office of Air Quality Planning and Standards, *Environmental Protection Agency*, http://www.epa.gov/air/caa/peg/ (accessed March 15, 2013).

13. Bryan Walsh, "The Gas Dilemma," *Time*, April 11, 2011, pp. 40–48; Jim Efstathiou Jr. and Kim Chipman, "The Great Shale Gas Rush," *Bloomberg BusinessWeek*, March 7–13, 2011, pp. 25–28.

14. Tennille Tracy, "Firms Given Time on Fracking," *The Wall Street Journal*, April 19, 2012, A3.

15. "The Effects of Acid Rain," *Environmental Protection Agency*, http://www.epa.gov/acidrain/effects/index.html (accessed February 2, 2013).

16. Bill Chameides, "U.S. Acid Rain Regulations: Did They Work?" *The Huffington Post*, May 10, 2012, http://www.huffingtonpost.com/bill-chameides/us-acid-rain-regulations_b_1507392.html (accessed February 2, 2013).

17. Economist Staff, "The melting north," Special Report, *The Economist*, June 16, 2012.

18. Mark Alpert, "Protections for the Earth's Climate," *Scientific American*, 293 (December 2005): 55.

19. Cassandra Sweet, Casandra (2010), "Nations Approve Cancun Climate Package", *The Wall Street Journal*, December 11, 2010, http://online.wsj.com/article/SB1000142405274870351860457601292225436 6218.html?KEYWORDS=global+warming+initiatives (accessed May 17, 2013).

20. Fiona Harvey, "Doha climate gateway: the reaction," *The Guardian*, December 10, 2012, http://www.guardian.co.uk/environment/2012/dec/10/doha-climate-gateway-reaction (accessed May 20, 2013); "Conference leaders hail Doha Gateway agreement," Doha 2012 *COP18*. CMP8, December 8, 2012, http://www.cop18.qa/news/singlestory.aspx?id=296 (accessed May 17, 2013).

21. The Economist Staff, "Banyan: Old king coal," *The Economist*, http://www.economist.com/node/21548237 (accessed February 22, 2013).

22. UNICEF and World Health Organization, *Progress on Drinking Water and Sanitation 2012 Update*, 2012, http://www.unicef.org/media/files/JMPreport2012.pdf (accessed May 20, 2013).

23. Bryan Walsh, "The Gas Dilemma," *Time,* April 11, 2011, pp. 40–48; Jim Efstathiou Jr. and Kim Chipman, "The Great Shale Gas Rush," *Bloomberg BusinessWeek*, March 7–13, 2011, 25–28.

24. Tara Patel, "The French Say No to 'Le Fracking,'" *Bloomberg BusinessWeek*, April 4–10, 2011, 60–62.

25. Carbon Disclosure Project: Collective responses to rising water challenges: CDP Global Water Report 2012 by Deloitte. Available upon written request to Paul Simpson, CEO.

26. Ibid.

27. Ibid.

28. Amit Srivasteva, "Communities Reject Coca-Cola in India," *Crop Watch*, July 10, 2003, http://www.corpwatch.org/article.php?id=7508 (accessed March 15, 2013).

29. Jonathan Watts, "The clean-up begins on China dirty secret – soil pollution," *The Guardian*, June 12, 2012, http://www.guardian.co.uk/environment/2012/jun/12/china-soil-pollution-bonn-challenge (accessed February 22, 2013).

30. Associated Press, "Chevron asks court to block $9.5B Ecuadorian award," *The Wall Street Journal*, February 18, 2011, http://online.wsj.com/article/AP9feedefd566647f98c76c9c2111578f3.html?KEYWORDS=Chevron+Ecuador (accessed February 24, 2011); Ben Casselman, Isabel Ordonez, and Angel Gonzalez, "Chevron Hit with Record Judgment," *The Wall Street Journal*, February 15, 2011, A1, A2.

31. Baldev Chauhan, "Indian state outlaws plastic bags," *BBC News*, August 7, 2003, http://news.bbc.co.uk/2/hi/south_asia/3132387.stm (accessed February 22, 2013); Beth Slovic, "Portland adopts ban on plastic bags that takes effect Oct. 15," July 21, 2011, *The Oregonian*, http://www.oregonlive.com/portland/index.ssf/2011/07/portland_adopts_ban_on_plastic.html (accessed February 22, 2013); "Should Cities Ban Plastic Bags?" *The Wall Street Journal*, October 8, 2012, http://online.wsj.com/article/SB10000872396390444165804578006832478712400.html (accessed February 22, 2013).

32. Jessica Williams, "Americans discard 2.5 million plastic bottles every hour. That's enough bottles to reach all the way to the moon every three weeks," *50 Facts that should Change the World 2.0* (New York, NY: Disinformation Company Ltd., 2007), p. 316; "Tackling Britain's 'waste mountain'," *BBC*, July 11, 2002, http://news.bbc.co.uk/2/hi/uk_news/2121882.stm (accessed July 15, 2013).

33. Michael Arndt, Wendy Zellner, and Peter Coy, "Too Much Corporate Power," *BusinessWeek*, September 11, 2000, 149.

34. "Electronics Recycling Is Making Gains, Says EPA," *PC World*, January 8, 2009, http://www.pcworld.com/businesscenter/article/156721/article.html?tk=nl_bnxnws (accessed March 15, 2011).

35. Wendy Koch, "More states ban disposal of electronics in landfills," *USA Today*, December 18, 2011, http://usatoday30.usatoday.com/tech/news/story/2011-12-18/electronics-recycling/52055158/1 (accessed February 22, 2013).

36. Food and Agriculture Organization of the United Nations, "World deforestation decreases, but remains alarming in many countries," March 25, 2010, http://www.fao.org/news/story/en/item/40893/icode/ (accessed February 28, 2013).

37. "Brazil: Amazon deforestation falls to new low," *BBC*, December 1, 2010, http://www.bbc.co.uk/news/world-latin-america-11888875 (accessed March 3, 2011); Kenneth Rapoza, "Deforestation Slows in Brazil's Amazon," November 27, 2012, http://www.forbes.com/sites/kenrapoza/2012/11/27/deforestation-slows-in-brazils-amazon/ (accessed February 22, 2013).

38. Bryan Walsh, "Rain Forest for Ransom," *TIME*, February 6, 2012, 36–39.

39. Home Depot, "Frequently Asked Questions," https://corporate.homedepot.com/CorporateResponsibility/Environment/WoodPurchasing/Pages/FAQs.aspx (accessed June 3, 2013).

40. Ian Berry, "Pesticides Make a Comeback," *The Wall Street Journal*, May 21, 2013, http://online.wsj.com/article/SB10001424127887323463704578496923254944066.html (accessed June 3, 2013).

41. David Biello, "Is Organic Really Better?" *Scientific American*, http://www.scientificamerican.com/podcast/episode.cfm?id=is-organic-really-better-09-05-28 (accessed March 8, 2013); "Organic Pesticides Not Always Greener Choice," *Science Daily*, June 23, 2010, http://www.sciencedaily.com/releases/2010/06/100622175510.htm (accessed March 8, 2013).

42. Patrick Penfield, "Sustainability Within the Supply Chain," March 2008, *e-Journal USA*, US Department of State.

43. Victoria L. Crittenden, William F. Crittenden, Linda K. Ferrell, O.C. Ferrell, and Christopher Pinney, "Market-oriented sustainability: a conceptual framework and propositions," *Journal of the Academy of Marketing Science* 39(2011), 71–85.

44. Philip Kotler, "Reinventing Marketing to Manage the Environmental Imperative," *Journal of Marketing 75*(4), 2012, 132–135.

45. Environmental Protection Agency, "Our Mission," http://www.epa.gov/aboutepa/whatwedo.html (accessed February 22, 2013).

46. "About EPA," http://www.epa.gov/epahome/aboutepa.htm (accessed July 14, 2009).

47. Kristin Jones, "Scotts Miracle-Gro to Pay $12.5 Million for Improper Pesticide Use," *Wall Street Journal*, 2012, Section 2.

48. James R. Healey, "The Big Squeeze Has Begun," *USA Today*, August 29, 2012, 1B-2B.

49. Chris Woodyard and James Healey, "Ford looking to aluminum for pickups?" *USA Today*, July 26, 2012, http://www.usatoday.com/money/autos/story/2012-07-26/aluminum-ford-f-150/56515524/1 (accessed August 30, 2012).

50. "The Plain English Guide to the Clean Air Act," http://www.epa.gov/air/caa/peg/ (accessed July 14, 2009).

51. The Economist Staff, "Breathing room," *The Economist*, September 8, 2012, http://www.economist.com/node/21562248 (accessed February 22, 2013).

52. "Summary of the Endangered Species Act," Environmental Protection Agency, http://www.epa.gov/regulations/laws/esa.html, accessed July 14, 2009.

53. U.S. Fish & Wildlife Service, "Summary of Listed Species Listed Populations and Recovery Plans as of Thu, 28 Feb. 2013," *U.S. Fish and Wildlife Services Species Report*, http://ecos.fws.gov/tess_public/TESSBoxscore (accessed February 28, 2013).

54. "Summary of the Toxic Substances Control Act," Environmental Protection Agency, http://www.epa.gov/regulations/laws/tsca.html, accessed July 14, 2009.

55. Environmental Protection Agency, "Bisphenol A (BPA) Action Plan Summary," 2012, http://www.epa.gov/opptintr/existingchemicals/pubs/actionplans/bpa.html (accessed June 3, 2013); Laura Blue, "Are Plastic Baby Bottles Harmful?" *Time*, February 8, 2008, http://www.time.com/time/health/article/0,8599,1711398,00.html (accessed June 3, 2013).

56. "Summary of the Clean Water Act," *Environmental Protection Agency*, http://www.epa.gov/regulations/laws/cwa.html (accessed July 14, 2009).

57. The United States Department of Justice, "Arch Coal to Pay $4 Million to Settle Clean Water Act Violations in Appalachian Mining Operations," March 1, 2011, http://www.justice.gov/opa/pr/2011/March/11-enrd-257.html (accessed February 28, 2013).

58. "Summary of the Pollution Prevention Act," Environmental Protection Agency, http://www.epa.gov/regulations/laws/ppa.html, accessed July 15, 2009.

59. Alex Frangos, "Timber Backs a New 'Green' Standard," *The Wall Street Journal*, March 29, 2006, B6.

60. Ibid.

61. "Food Quality Protection Act (FQPA)," Environmental Protection Agency, http://www.epa.gov/agriculture/lqpa.html, accessed July 15, 2009.

62. Nicolas Loris and David W. Kreutzer, "Economic Realities of the Electric Car," *The Heritage Foundation*, January 24, 2011, http://www.heritage.org/research/reports/2011/01/economic-realities-of-the-electric-car (accessed June 3, 2013).

63. Associated Press, "Bush signs $12.3 billion energy bill into law," *MSNBC*, August 8, 2005, http://www.msnbc.msn.com/id/8870039 (accessed June 22, 2009).

64. Bertrand d'Armagnac, "Danish wind farms show sustainable attitude toward renewable energy," *guardian.co.uk*, August 10, 2010, http://www.guardian.co.uk/world/2010/aug/10/denmark-renewable-wind-farm-energy (accessed March 15, 2013).

65. Ehren Goossens, "U.S. Creates 17 Zones for 'Faster' Solar-Farm Development," *Bloomberg*, July 24, 2012, http://www.bloomberg.com/news/2012-07-24/u-s-creates-17-zones-for-faster-solar-farm-development.html (accessed March 15, 2013).

66. Wendy Koch, "Here comes the sun: White House to install solar panels," *USA Today*, October 6, 2010, 10A.

67. Nate Lew, "The Top Five Fortune 500 Companies Using Solar Power," SolarEnergy.net, May 13, 2010, http://www.solarenergy.net/News/2010051301-the-top-five-fortune-500-companies-using-solar-power.aspx (accessed February 28, 2013).

68. Ami Cholia, "Top Ten Green Countries," *The Huffington Post*, August 21, 2009, http://www.huffingtonpost.com/2009/07/21/top-10-green-countries-ph_n_241867.html?slidenumber=7 (accessed January 25, 2011).

69. Louise Lucas, "Enough to go round but millions still starve," *Financial Times*, November 21, 2012, 1–2.

70. "Hydroelectric power water use," *USGS*, http://ga.water.usgs.gov/edu/wuhy.html (accessed March 15, 2013).

71. Chen Jialu, "Three Gorges Dam champions clean energy program," *China Daily*, February 23, 2010, http://www.chinadaily.com.cn/cndy/2010-02/23/content_9486733.htm (accessed March 15, 2013).

72. Stefan Ambec and Paul Lanoie, "Does It Pay to Be Green? A Systematic Overview," *The Academy of Management Perspectives* 22 (4), November 2008, 45–62.

73. Environmental Leader, "Study reveals companies lack supply chain sustainability," 2009, http://www.environmentalleader.com/2009/07/18/study-reveals-companieslack-supply-chain-sustainability/ (accessed January 2, 2010).

74. Bill Schneiderman, "Supply chain and sustainability—will this marriage last?" *Supply Demand Executive*, March 23, 2009, http://www.sdcexec.com/article/10269461/supply-chain-and-sustainability-will-this-marriage-last (accessed March 4, 2013).

75. John O'Mahoney, "Taking Sustainability to the People," Special Advertising Section, *Bloomberg Businessweek*, S1–S3.

76. Siemens, "Sustainable Cities," http://www.usa.siemens.com/sustainable-cities/ (accessed March 5, 2013).

77. Sierra Nevada, "Sustainability: Energy," http://www.sierranevada.com/brewery/about-us/sustainability#/energy (accessed June 3, 2013).

78. Victoria L. Crittenden, William F. Crittenden, Linda K. Ferrell, O.C. Ferrell, and Christopher C. Pinney, *Journal of the Academy of Marketing Science* 39(2011): 71–85.

79. Ariel Schwartz, "The Unbearable Lightness of UPS's Plastic Trucks," *Fast Company*, http://www.fastcoexist.com/1678059/the-unbearable-lightness-of-upss-plastic-trucks (accessed March 8, 2013).

80. "The EU Eco-label," http://www.eco-label.com/default.htm (accessed July 15, 2009).

81. "The Seven Sins of Greenwashing," Terra Choice, http://sinsofgreenwashing.org/ (accessed February 22, 2013).

82. "Eco-Friendly Product Claims Often Misleading," *NPR*, November 30, 2007, http://www.npr.org/templates/story/story.php?storyId=16754919 (accessed February 22, 2013).

83. Timothy N. Carson and Lata Gangadharan, "Environmental Labeling and Incomplete Consumer Information in Laboratory Markets," *Journal of Environmental Economics and Management 43*(1), January 2002, 113–134.

84. Kent Walker and Fang Wan, "The Harm of Symbolic Actions and Green-Washing: Corporate Actions and Communications on Environmental Performance and Their Financial Implications," *Journal of Business Ethics 109*(2012), 227–242.

85. Amy Westervelt, "FTC Finalizes Green Guides," *Forbes*, October 1, 2012, http://www.forbes.com/sites/amywestervelt/2012/10/01/ftc-finalizes-green-guides-puts-greenwashers-on-notice/ (accessed March 4, 2013).

86. Wendy Koch, "Local food may be trendy, but is it really more eco-friendly?" *USA Today*, August 9, 2012, 7B.

87. Sarah Nassauer, "To Scream Green, Dyeing Paper a Light Brown," *The Wall Street Journal*, January 25, 2012, D3.

88. Yu-Shan Chen and Ching-Hsun Chang, "Greenwash and Green Trust," The Mediation Effects of Green Consumer Confusion and Green Perceived Risk," *Journal of Business Ethics 114*(3), 2013, 489–500.

89. Paul Hawken and William McDonough, "Seven Steps to Doing Good Business," *Inc.*, November 1993, 79–90, www.inc.com/magazine/19931101/3770.html (March 15, 2013).

90. Environmental Protection Agency, "Frequent Questions," http://www.epa.gov/osw/conserve/materials/paper/faqs.htm (accessed March 8, 2013).

91. "About WasteWise," http://www.epa.gov/osw/conserve/materials/paper/faqs.htm (accessed March 8, 2013).

92. Ramit Plushnick-Masti, "Beverage companies pay millions to conserve water," *USA Today*, August 8, 2012, http://usatoday30.usatoday.com/money/industries/environment/story/2012-08-11/beverage-companies-water-conservation/56875526/1 (accessed March 8, 2013).

93. Jasmine Wang, Kyunghee Park, and Natasha Khan, "Does Green Shipping Cost Too Much Green?" *Bloomberg Businessweek*, January 14–January 20, 2013, 20–21.

94. "Voluntary Environmental Management Systems/ISO 14001: Frequently Asked Questions," *United States Environmental Protection Agency*, http://www.epa.gov/OWM/iso14001/isofaq.htm (accessed February 22, 2013).

Cases

CASE 1

Monsanto Attempts to Balance Stakeholder Interests*

When you think of Monsanto, the phrase *genetically modified* likely comes to mind. The Monsanto Company is the world's largest seed company, with sales of over $11.8 billion. It specializes in biotechnology, or the genetic manipulation of organisms. Monsanto scientists have spent the last few decades modifying crops, often by inserting new genes or adapting existing genes within plant seeds, to meet certain aims, such as higher crop yields or insect resistance. Monsanto produces plants that can survive weeks of drought, ward off weeds, and kill invasive insects. Monsanto's genetically modified (GM) seeds have increased the quantity and availability of crops, helping farmers worldwide increase food production and revenues.

Today, 90 percent of the world's GM seeds are sold by Monsanto or companies that use Monsanto genes. Monsanto also holds a 70 to 100 percent market share on certain crops. Yet Monsanto has met its share of criticism from sources as diverse as governments, farmers, activists, and advocacy groups. Monsanto supporters say the company creates solutions to world hunger by generating higher crop yields and hardier plants. Critics accuse the multinational giant of attempting to take over the world's food supply and destroying biodiversity. Since biotechnology is relatively new, critics also express concerns about the possibility of negative health and environmental effects from biotech food. However, these criticisms have not kept Monsanto from becoming one of the world's most successful companies.

This analysis first looks at the history of Monsanto as it progressed from a chemical company to an organization focused on biotechnology, then examines Monsanto's current focus on developing genetically modified seeds, including stakeholder concerns regarding the safety and environmental effects of these seeds. Next, we discuss key ethical concerns, including organizational misconduct and patent issues. We also look at Monsanto's corporate responsibility initiatives. We conclude by examining the challenges and opportunities that Monsanto may face in the future.

HISTORY: FROM CHEMICALS TO FOOD

Monsanto was founded by John F. Queeny in 1901 in St. Louis, Missouri. He named the company after his wife, Olga Monsanto Queeny. The company's first product was the artificial sweetener saccharine, which it sold to Coca-Cola. Monsanto also sold Coca-Cola

*This case was prepared by Jennifer Sawayda and Danielle Jolley for and under the direction of O. C. Ferrell and Linda Ferrell. It was prepared for classroom discussion rather than to illustrate either effective or ineffective handling of an administrative, ethical, or legal decision by management. All sources used for this case were obtained through publicly available material.

caffeine extract and vanillin, an artificial vanilla flavoring. At the start of World War I, company leaders realized the growth opportunities in the industrial chemicals industry and renamed the company The Monsanto Chemical Company. The company began specializing in plastics, its own agricultural chemicals, and synthetic rubbers.

Due to its expanding product lines, the company's name was changed back to the Monsanto Company in 1964. By this time, Monsanto was producing such diverse products as petroleum, fibers, and packaging. A few years later, Monsanto created its first Roundup herbicide, a successful product that propelled the company even more into the spotlight.

However, during the 1970s, Monsanto encountered a major legal obstacle. The company had produced a chemical known as Agent Orange, which was used during the Vietnam War to quickly deforest the thick Vietnamese jungles. Agent Orange contained dioxin, a chemical that caused a legal nightmare for Monsanto. Dioxin was found to be extremely carcinogenic, and in 1979, a lawsuit was filed against Monsanto on behalf of hundreds of veterans who claimed they were harmed by the chemical. Monsanto and several other manufacturers agreed to settle for $180 million, but the repercussions of dioxin continued to plague the company for decades.

In 1981 Monsanto leaders determined that biotechnology would be the company's new strategic focus. The quest for biotechnology was on, and in 1994 Monsanto introduced the first biotechnology product to win regulatory approval. Soon the company was selling soybean, cotton, and canola seeds engineered to be tolerant to Monsanto's Roundup Ready herbicide. Many other herbicides killed good plants as well as the bad ones. Roundup Ready seeds allowed farmers to use the herbicide to eliminate weeds while sparing the crop.

In 1997 Monsanto spun off its chemical business as Solutia, and in 2000 the company entered into a merger and changed its name to the Pharmacia Corporation. Two years later, a new Monsanto, focused entirely on agriculture, broke off from Pharmacia, and the companies became two legally separate entities. The company before 2000 is often referred to as "old Monsanto," while today's company is known as "new Monsanto."

The emergence of new Monsanto was tainted by disturbing news about the company's conduct. For nearly forty years the Monsanto Company had released toxic waste into a creek in the Alabama town of Anniston. The company had also disposed of polychlorinated biphenyls (PCBs), a highly toxic chemical, in open-pit landfills in the area. The results were catastrophic. Fish from the creek were deformed, and the population had elevated PCB levels that astounded environmental health experts. A paper trail showed that Monsanto leaders had known about the pollution since the 1960s, but had not stopped the dumping. Once the cover-up was discovered, thousands of plaintiffs from the city filed a lawsuit against the company. In 2003 Monsanto and Solutia agreed to pay a settlement of $700 million to more than 20,000 Anniston residents.

When current CEO Hugh Grant took over in 2003, scandals and stakeholder uncertainty over Monsanto's GM products had tarnished the company's reputation. The price of Monsanto's stock had fallen by almost 50 percent, down to $8 a share. The company had lost $1.7 billion the previous year. Grant knew the company was fragile and decided to shift its strategic focus. Through a strong strategic focus on GM foods, the company has recovered and is now prospering.

In spite of their controversial nature, GM foods have become popular in developed and developing countries. Monsanto became so successful with its GM seeds it acquired Seminis, Inc., a leader in the fruit and vegetable seed industry. The acquisition transformed Monsanto into a global leader in the seed industry. Today, Monsanto employs approximately 21,000 people in 160 countries. It is recognized as a top employer in Brazil, India, and Canada and was ranked number 16 in *Forbes'* list of the world's most innovative companies.

MONSANTO'S EMPHASIS ON BIOTECHNOLOGY

While the original Monsanto made a name for itself through the manufacturing of chemicals, the new Monsanto took quite a different turn. It changed its emphasis from chemicals to food. Today's Monsanto owes its $11.8 billion in sales to biotechnology, specifically to its sales of genetically modified (GM) plant seeds. These seeds have revolutionized the agriculture industry.

Throughout history, weeds, insects, and drought have been the bane of the farmer's existence. In the twentieth century, synthetic chemical herbicides and pesticides were invented to ward off pests. Yet applying these chemicals to an entire crop was both costly and time consuming. Then Monsanto scientists, through their work in biotechnology, were able to implant seeds with genes that make the plants themselves kill bugs. They also created seeds containing the herbicide Roundup, an herbicide that kills weeds but spares the crops.

Since then Monsanto has used technology to create many innovative products, such as drought-tolerant seeds for dry areas like Africa. The company also utilizes its technological prowess to gain the support of stakeholders. For example, Monsanto has a laboratory in St. Louis that gives tours to farmers. One of the technologies the company shows farmers is a machine known as the corn chipper, which picks up seeds and removes genetic material from them. That material is analyzed to see how well the seed will grow if planted. The "best" seeds are the ones Monsanto sells for planting. Impressing farmers with its technology and the promise of better yields is one way Monsanto attracts potential customers.

However, genetically modified crops are not without critics. Opponents believe influencing the gene pools of the plants we eat could result in negative health consequences. Others worry about the health effects on beneficial insects and plants, fearing that pollinating GM plants could affect nearby insects and non-GM plants. CEO Hugh Grant decided to curtail the tide of criticism by focusing biotechnology on products not directly placed on the dinner plate, but on seeds that produce goods like animal feed and corn syrup. In this way, Grant reduced some of the opposition. The company invests largely in four crops: corn, cotton, soybeans, and canola. Monsanto owes much of its revenue to its work on GM seeds, and today more than half of U.S. crops, including most soybeans and 88 percent of corn, are genetically modified.

Farmers who purchase GM seeds can grow more crops on less land and with less left to chance. GM crops have saved farmers billions by preventing loss and increasing crop yields. For example, in 1970 the average corn harvest yielded approximately 70 bushels an acre. With the introduction of biotech crops, the average corn harvest increased to roughly 150 bushels an acre. Monsanto predicts even higher yields in the future, possibly up to 300 bushels an acre by 2030. According to Monsanto CEO Hugh Grant, this increase in productivity will increase crop yields without taking up more land, helping to meet the world's growing agricultural needs.

As a result of higher yields, the revenues of farmers in developing countries have increased. According to company statistics, the cotton yield of Indian farmers rose by 50 percent, doubling their income in one year. Additionally, the company claims that insect-resistant corn has increased crop yields in the Philippines by 24 percent. Critics argue that these numbers are inflated; they say the cost of GM seeds is dramatically higher than traditional seeds, and therefore actually reduce farmers' take-home profits.

Monsanto's GM seeds have not been accepted everywhere. Attempts to introduce them into Europe met with consumer backlash. The European Union banned most Monsanto crops except for one variety of corn. Consumers have gone so far as to destroy fields of GM crops and arrange sit-ins. Greenpeace has fought Monsanto for years, especially in the company's efforts to promote GM crops in developing countries. Even India has banned a variety of genetically modified eggplant because of concerns over safety. This animosity toward Monsanto's products is generated by two main concerns: the safety of GM food and the environmental effects of genetic modification.

Concerns about the Safety of GM Food

Of great concern to many stakeholders are the moral and safety implications of GM food. Many skeptics see biotech crops as unnatural, with the Monsanto scientist essentially "playing God" by controlling what goes into the seed. Because GM crops are relatively new, critics maintain that the health implications of biotech food may not be known for years to come. They also contend that effective standards have not been created to determine the safety of biotech crops. Some geneticists believe the splicing of these genes into seeds could create small changes that might negatively impact the health of humans and animals that eat them. Also, even though the Food and Drug Administration has declared biotech crops safe, critics say they have not been around long enough to gauge their long-term effects.

One concern is toxicity, particularly considering that many Monsanto seeds are equipped with a gene to allow them to produce their own Roundup herbicide. Could ingesting this herbicide, even in small amounts, cause detrimental effects on consumers? Some stakeholders say yes, and point to statistics on glyphosate, Roundup's chief ingredient, for support. According to an ecology center fact sheet, glyphosate exposure is the third most commonly reported illness among California agriculture workers, and glyphosate residues can last for a year. Yet the Environmental Protection Agency (EPA) lists glyphosate as having low skin and oral toxicity, and a study from the New York Medical College states that Roundup does not create a health risk for humans.

In March 2013 over 250,000 people signed a petition in response to President Barack Obama's signing of H.R. 933 into law. The new law, called the Agricultural Appropriations Bill of 2013, contains a provision that protects genetically modified organisms and genetically engineered seeds from litigation concerning their health risks. In other words, courts cannot bar the sale of GM food even if future health risks are revealed. Critics of the provision claim the provision was slipped in at the last moment and that many members of Congress were not aware of it. For consumers, questions pertaining to the health risks associated with GM crops have gone unanswered and are the primary reason the petition was started. Many people have called this bill the "Monsanto Protection Act" and believe it will help protect the survival of biotech corporations. Critics also say that the continuing resolution spending bill will no longer allow the court system to protect consumers, which could create a further disconnect between consumers and producers.

Despite consumer concerns, the Food and Drug Administration (FDA) and the American Association for the Advancement of Science have proclaimed that GM food is safe to consume. The European Commission examined more than 130 studies and concluded that GM food does not appear to be riskier than crops grown by conventional methods. As a result of its research, the FDA has determined that Americans do not need to know when they are consuming GM products. Therefore, this information is not placed on labels in the United States, although other countries, notably those in the European Union, do require GM food products to state this fact in their labeling.

Concerns about Environmental Effects of Monsanto Products

Some studies have supported the premise that Roundup herbicide, used in conjunction with the GM seeds called "Roundup Ready," can be harmful to birds, insects, and particularly amphibians. Such studies revealed that small concentrations of Roundup may be deadly to tadpoles. Other studies suggest that Roundup might have a detrimental effect on human cells, especially embryonic, umbilical, and placental cells. Monsanto has countered these claims by questioning the methodology used in the studies. The Environmental Protection Agency maintains glyphosate is not dangerous at recommended doses.

Another concern with GM seeds in general is the threat of environmental contamination. Bees, other insects, and wind can carry a crop's seeds to other areas, sometimes to fields containing non-GM crops. These seeds and pollens might then mix with the farmer's crops. Organic farmers have complained that genetically modified seeds from nearby farms have "contaminated" their crops. This environmental contamination could pose a serious threat. Some scientists fear that GM seeds spread to native plants may cause those plants to adopt the GM trait, thus creating new genetic variations of those plants that could negatively influence (through genetic advantages) the surrounding ecosystem. The topic has taken on particular significance in Mexico. For eleven years, Mexico had a moratorium on genetically modified corn. It lifted the moratorium in 2005, enabling Monsanto to begin testing its genetically modified corn in northern Mexico. Monsanto is seeking authorization to begin the pre-commercial stage in Mexico and expand its growing area to approximately 500 acres. However, consumers are putting up a fight. Believing that GM corn could contaminate their more than 60 maize varieties, Mexicans have staged protests and formed groups to keep GM corn out of the country. These protests have delayed approval of the GM corn for large-scale commercialization.

Another controversy involves the discovery of a field in Oregon filled with an experimental form of Monsanto's genetically modified wheat. The wheat was not approved by the United States Department of Agriculture. The discovery raised concerns over whether it could have contaminated U.S. wheat supplies. As a result, Japan temporarily instituted a ban on U.S. wheat. Initial investigations revealed the wheat had been stored in a Colorado facility but were unable to provide an explanation for how it showed up in an Oregon field. Monsanto denied involvement and stated that it suspected someone had covertly obtained the GM wheat and planted it. The company also claims that this incident was an isolated occurrence. The altered wheat was not believed to have caused any damage, and Japan lifted the ban. However, some farmers have filed lawsuits against Monsanto seeking class-action status.

Monsanto took action in addressing environmental and health concerns. The company maintains that the environmental impact of everything it creates has been studied by the EPA and approved. Monsanto officials claim that glyphosate in Roundup rarely ends up in ground water, and when it does contaminate ground water, it is soluble and will not have much effect on aquatic species. The firm has stated that it will not file lawsuits against farmers if GM crops accidentally mix with organic. Monsanto has also partnered with Conservation International in an effort to conserve biodiversity. Stakeholders are left to make their own decisions regarding genetically modified crops.

Crop Resistance to Pesticides and Herbicides

Another environmental problem that has emerged is the possibility of weed and insect resistance to the herbicides and pesticides on Monsanto crops. On the one hand, it is estimated that GM crops have prevented the use of 965 million pounds of pesticides. On the other hand, critics fear that continual use of the chemicals could result in "super weeds" and "super bugs," much like the overuse of antibiotics in humans has resulted in drug-resistant bacteria. The company's Roundup line, in particular, has come under attack. Genetically modified plants labeled Roundup Ready are engineered to withstand large doses of the herbicide Roundup. Because Roundup is used more frequently, weeds have started to develop a resistance to this popular herbicide. Significant numbers of Roundup resistant weeds had been found in the United States and Australia. One study conducted internationally found the potential health effects of using corn that is Roundup tolerant can potentially be dangerous. The study found that rats that consumed GM products developed tumors and died 2-3 times more than those not consuming the GM product. The study concluded that further long-term testing should be completed to evaluate the toxicity in GM products and determine potential toxic effects.

To combat "super bugs," the government requires farmers using Monsanto's GM products to create "refuges," in which they plant 20 percent of their fields with a non-genetically modified crop. The theory is that this allows nonresistant bugs to mate with those that are resistant, preventing a new race of super bugs. To prevent resistance to the Roundup herbicide, farmers are required to vary herbicide use and practice crop rotations. However, since Roundup is so easy to use, particularly in conjunction with Roundup Ready seeds, some farmers do not take the time to institute these preventative measures. When they do rotate their crops, some will rotate one Roundup Ready crop with another. As a result, agricultural pests such as rootworm are becoming resistant to genes in GM crops intended to kill them. This resistance is causing some farmers to turn toward more traditional herbicides and pesticides. Resistance is of particular concern in Latin America, Africa, and Asia, where farmers may not be as informed of the risks of herbicide and pesticide overuse.

DEALING WITH ORGANIZATIONAL ETHICAL ISSUES

In addition to concerns over the safety of GM seeds and environmental issues, Monsanto has dealt with concerns about organizational conduct. Organizations face significant risks from strategies and employees striving for high performance standards. Such pressure sometimes encourages employees to engage in illegal or unethical conduct. All firms have these concerns, and in the case of Monsanto, bribes and patents have resulted in legal, ethical, and reputational consequences.

Bribery Issues

Bribery presents a dilemma to multinational corporations because different countries have different perspectives. While bribery is illegal in the United States, other countries allow it. Monsanto faced this problem in Indonesia, and its actions resulted in the company being fined a large sum.

In 2002 a Monsanto manager instructed an Indonesian consulting firm to pay a bribe of $50,000 to an official in the country's environment ministry. The official accepted the bribe in exchange for bypassing an environmental study. It was later revealed that such bribery was not an isolated event; the company had paid off many officials between 1997 and 2002. Monsanto headquarters became aware of the problem after discovering irregularities at its Indonesian subsidiary in 2001. As a result, the company launched an internal investigation and reported the bribery to the U.S. Department of Justice (DOJ) and the Securities and Exchange Commission (SEC). Monsanto accepted full responsibility for its employees' behavior and agreed to pay $1 million to the DOJ and $500,000 to the SEC. It also agreed to three years of close monitoring of its activities by American authorities.

Patent Issues

As bioengineered creations of the Monsanto Company, Monsanto's seeds are protected under patent law. Under the terms of the patent, farmers using Monsanto seeds are not allowed to harvest seeds from the plants for use in upcoming seasons. Instead, they must purchase new Monsanto seeds each season. By issuing new seeds each year, Monsanto ensures it secures a profit as well as maintains control over its property. This patent protection has become a controversial subject among farmers and has led to numerous litigation battles for Monsanto.

Throughout agricultural history, farmers have collected and saved seeds from previous harvests to plant the following year's crops. Critics argue that requiring farmers to suddenly purchase new seeds year after year puts an undue financial burden on them and gives Monsanto too much power. However, the law protects Monsanto's right to have exclusive control over its creations, and farmers must abide by these laws. When they are found guilty of using Monsanto seeds from previous seasons, either deliberately or out of ignorance, they are often fined.

Since it is fairly easy for farmers to violate the patent, Monsanto has found it necessary to employ investigators from law firms to investigate suspected violations. The resulting investigations are a source of contention between Monsanto and accused farmers. According to Monsanto, investigators deal with farmers in a respectful manner. They approach the farmers suspected of patent infringement and ask them questions. The company claims that investigators practice transparency with the farmers and tell them why they are there and who they represent. If after the initial interview is completed and suspicions still exist, the investigators may pull the farmer's records. They may bring in a sampling team, with the farmer's permission, to test the farmer's fields. If found guilty the farmer must often pay Monsanto. However, some farmers tell a different story about Monsanto and its seed investigators. They claim that Monsanto investigators have used unethical practices to get them to cooperate. They call the investigators the "seed police" and say they behave like a "Gestapo" or "mafia."

In 2007 Monsanto sued Vernon Bowman, an Indiana farmer who Monsanto claims used second generation Monsanto seeds to plant soybeans. Monsanto claimed their patent protection reaches past first-generation seeds and Mr. Bowman infringed upon their patent. In 2009 the court ruled in favor of Monsanto and ordered Bowman to pay $84,000 in damages. Mr. Bowman did not accept defeat, and in 2013 brought his case before the Supreme Court. The Supreme Court ruled in favor of Monsanto, representing a great victory for biotechnology companies.

Monsanto does not limit its investigations to farmers. It filed a lawsuit against DuPont, the world's second-largest seed maker, for combining DuPont technology with Roundup Ready. Monsanto won that lawsuit, but was countersued by DuPont for anticompetitive practices. These accusations of anticompetitive practices garnered the attention of federal antitrust lawyers. With increased pressure coming from different areas, Monsanto agreed to allow patents to expire on its seeds starting in 2014. This will allow other companies to create less expensive versions of Monsanto seeds. However, Monsanto announced it would continue to strictly enforce patents for new versions of its products, such as Roundup Ready 2 soybeans.

Legal Issues

Many major companies have government and legal forces to deal with, and Monsanto is no exception. The government has begun to examine Monsanto's practices more closely. In 1980 the Supreme Court allowed living organisms to be patented for the first time, giving Monsanto the ability to patent its seeds. Despite this victory, Monsanto came to the attention of the American Antitrust Institute for alleged anticompetitive activities. The institute suggested that Monsanto hinders competition, exerting too much power over the transgenic seed industry and limiting seed innovation. When Monsanto acquired DeKalb and Delta Land and Pine, it had to obtain the approval of antitrust authorities, and gained that approval after agreeing to certain concessions. As a result of complaints, the Department of Justice began a civil investigation into Monsanto's practices. Although the DOJ eventually dropped the antitrust probe, concerns over Monsanto's power continue. Monsanto must be careful to ensure that its activities cannot be seen as anticompetitive.

In early 2013, Monsanto settled with local residents in Nitro, West Virginia, after claims of health problems became persistent in a now-closed Agent Orange plant. The company agreed to spend up to $93 million on medical testing and local cleanup of as many as 4,500 homes. It also agreed to establish a medical monitoring program and will make additional money available to continue the program's operation for 30 years.

The most talked about litigation involving Monsanto is their constant battle with competitor DuPont. In the past, DuPont has filed multiple lawsuits against Monsanto. One lawsuit claimed Monsanto used its power and licenses to block DuPont products. In March 2013, the battle for dominance between these two companies was settled. A patent-licensing deal was reached and DuPont agreed to pay Monsanto at least $1.75 billion over the next 10 years. This payment enables DuPont to have rights and access to technology for genetically engineered soybeans that resist herbicides. DuPont will also obtain rights to combine patented genes from Monsanto with other genes to develop multiple crop traits. On the opposing side, Monsanto is given access to DuPont patents for corn defoliation and crop-disease resistance techniques. This settlement will hopefully create positive results for farmers and enable the development of technologies that will aide in higher crop yields for years to come.

CORPORATE RESPONSIBILITY AT MONSANTO

Today the public generally expects multinational corporations to advance the interests and well-being of the people in the countries where they do business. Monsanto has given millions of dollars in programs to improve communities in developing countries. In fact, *Corporate Responsibility Magazine* ranked Monsanto number 36 on its 100 Best Corporate Citizens list of 2013. This is the fourth time Monsanto has been included in the magazine's ranking of corporate responsibility performance.

Monsanto created a Code of Business Conduct to provide guidance on the firm's ethical expectations and is concerned with maintaining integrity among its many different stakeholders. In 2003 the company adopted an additional Code of Conduct for its chief executives and financial officers and a Human Rights Policy in 2006 to ensure the rights of Monsanto employees and those in its supply chain. The company's Business Conduct Office is responsible for investigating cases of alleged misconduct as well as maintaining the company's anonymous hotline.

As part of Monsanto's culture, the company wrote a pledge informing stakeholders about what it sees as its ethical commitments. According to Monsanto, the pledge "helps us to convert our values into actions, and to make clear who we are and what we champion." Table 1 provides the values Monsanto pledges to uphold, including integrity, dialogue, transparency, sharing, benefits, respect, acting as owners to achieve results, and creating a great place to work.

As an agricultural company, Monsanto must address the grim reality that the world's population is increasing fast, and the amount of land and water available for agriculture is decreasing. Some experts believe our planet must produce more food in the next 50 years to feed the world's population than what has grown in the past 10,000 years, requiring us to double our food output. As a multinational corporation dedicated to agriculture, Monsanto is expected to address these problems. The company has developed a three-tiered commitment policy: (1) produce more yield in crops, (2) conserve more resources, and (3) improve the lives of farmers.

The company hopes to achieve these goals through initiatives in sustainable agriculture.

Sustainable Agriculture

Monsanto CEO Hugh Grant has said, "Agriculture intersects the toughest challenges we all face on the planet. Together, we must meet the needs for increased food, fiber, and energy while protecting the environment. In short, the world needs to produce more and conserve smarter." Monsanto is quick to point out that its biotech products added more than 100 million tons to worldwide agricultural production in a ten-year period, and the company estimates that this has increased farmers' incomes by $33.8 billion. Monsanto also created partnerships between nonprofit organizations across the world to enrich the lives of farmers in developing countries. The company's goal is to double its core crop yields by 2030. Monsanto intends to achieve this goal through new product innovations such as drought-tolerant seeds and better technology. Two regions Monsanto is now focusing on are India and Africa.

TABLE 1 The Monsanto Pledge

Integrity
Integrity is the foundation for all that we do. Integrity includes honesty, decency, consistency, and courage. Building on those values, we are committed to:

Dialogue
We will listen carefully to diverse points of view and engage in thoughtful dialogue. We will broaden our understanding of issues in order to better address the needs and concerns of society and each other.

Transparency
We will ensure that information is available, accessible, and understandable.

Sharing
We will share knowledge and technology to advance scientific understanding, to improve agriculture and the environment, to improve crops, and to help farmers in developing countries.

Benefits
We will use sound and innovative science and thoughtful and effective stewardship to deliver high-quality products that are beneficial to our customers and to the environment.

Respect
We will respect the religious, cultural, and ethical concerns of people throughout the world. The safety of our employees, the communities where we operate, our customers, consumers, and the environment will be our highest priorities.

Act as owners to achieve results
We will create clarity of direction, roles, and accountability; build strong relationships with our customers and external partners; make wise decisions; steward our company resources; and take responsibility for achieving agreed-upon results.

Create a great place to work
We will ensure diversity of people and thought; foster innovation, creativity and learning; practice inclusive teamwork; and reward and recognize our people.

Source: Monsanto Corporation, *Monsanto Code of Business Conduct*, http://www.monsanto.com/SiteCollectionDocuments/Code-of-Business-Conduct-PDFs/code_of_conduct_english.pdf (accessed May 8, 2013).

The need for better agriculture is apparent in India, where the population is estimated to hit 1.3 billion by 2017. Biotech crops have helped improve the size of yields in India, allowing biotech farmers to increase their yields by as much as 50 percent. Monsanto estimates that cotton farmers in India using biotech crops earn approximately $176 more in revenues per acre than their non-biotech contemporaries. Monsanto launched Project SHARE, a sustainable yield initiative created in conjunction with the nonprofit Indian Society of Agribusiness, to improve the lives of 10,000 cotton farmers in 1,100 villages.

In Africa, Monsanto partnered with the African Agricultural Technology Foundation, scientists, and philanthropists to embark on the Water Efficient Maize for Africa (WEMA) initiative. During this five-year project, Monsanto developed drought-tolerant maize seeds; small-scale African farmers did not have to pay Monsanto royalties for their use. As CEO Hugh Grant writes, "This initiative isn't simply altruistic; we see it as a unique business proposition that rewards farmers and shareowners." But not all view Monsanto's presence in Africa as an outreach in corporate responsibility. Some see it as another way for Monsanto to improve its bottom line. Critics see the company as trying to take control of African agriculture and destroy African agricultural practices that have lasted for thousands of years.

Charitable Giving

In 1964 the Monsanto Company established the Monsanto Fund. This fund contributes to educational opportunities and the needs of communities across the world. One recipient of the Monsanto Fund is Nanmeng Village in China. The company is helping to train farmers in the area about ways to improve agricultural methods and infrastructure development. The Monsanto Company also committed $10 million to provide fellowship opportunities for Ph.D. students seeking to get their degree in rice or wheat plant breeding.

Another program implemented by the company is the Matching Gifts Program. This program matches employee contributions to charitable and educational organizations, dollar-for-dollar, by the Monsanto Fund. The program matches a maximum of $5,000 per employee every year and includes organizations supporting the environment, arts and culture, and disaster relief, among many others.

In the first decade of the twenty-first century, Monsanto supported youth programs and donated nearly $1.5 million in scholarships to students wanting to pursue agriculture-related degrees. The company supports 4-H programs and the program Farm Safety 4 Just Kids, a program that teaches rural children about safety while working on farms. Monsanto also partnered with the organization Agriculture Future of America (AFA), providing more than $100,000 in scholarships to youth in eight states who want to pursue agricultural careers.

THE FUTURE OF MONSANTO

Monsanto faces challenges that it must address, including lingering concerns over the safety and the environmental impact of its products. The company needs to enforce its code of conduct effectively to avoid organizational misconduct (such as bribery) in the future. Monsanto also faces increased competition from other companies. The seed company Pioneer Hi-Bred International, Inc., uses pricing strategies and seed sampling to attract price-conscious customers. Chinese companies are formidable rivals for Monsanto since their weed killers began eating into some of Monsanto's Roundup profits. As a result, Monsanto announced plans to restructure the Roundup area of the business.

Yet despite the onslaught of criticism from Monsanto detractors and the challenge of increased competition from other companies, Monsanto has numerous opportunities to thrive in the future. The company is currently working on new innovations that could increase its competitive edge as well as benefit farmers worldwide, and after a plunge in Roundup sales, Monsanto's profits are bouncing back. The company is preparing several biotech products for commercialization. Additionally, Monsanto sees major opportunities for expansion into places like China. The company has discussed a possible deal with chemicals conglomerate Sinochem Corp., which has been tasked with ensuring food security for China's large population. If Monsanto enters into the largely untapped Chinese market for genetically modified foods, perhaps through a joint venture or by acquiring a stake in a Chinese company, it might be able to gain access to an additional 1.34 billion consumers.

Although Monsanto has made ethical errors in the past, it is trying to portray itself as a socially responsible company dedicated to improving agriculture. As noted, the company still has problems. The predictions from Monsanto critics about biotech food have not yet come true, but that has not eradicated the fears among stakeholders. Faced with the increasing popularity of organic food and staunch criticism from opponents, Monsanto needs to continue working with stakeholders to promote its technological innovations and eliminate fears concerning its industry.

QUESTIONS

1. Does Monsanto maintain an ethical culture that effectively responds to various stakeholders?
2. Compare the benefits of growing GM seeds for crops with the potential negative consequences of using them.
3. How should Monsanto manage the potential harm to plant and animal life from using products such as Roundup?

SOURCES

"$700 Million Settlement in Alabama PCB Lawsuit," *The New York Times*, August 21, 2001, http://www.nytimes.com/2003/08/21/business/700-million-settlement-in-alabama-pcb-lawsuit.html (accessed May 8, 2013); David Alire Garcia and Adriana Barrera, "Mexico postpones approval of large-scale GM corn fields," *Reuters*, November 22, 2012, http://www.reuters.com/article/2012/11/23/us-mexico-corn-idUSBRE8AM00O20121123 (accessed May 1, 2013); Associated Press, "Another wheat lawsuit," *The Kansas City Star*, July 8, 2013, http://www.kansascity.com/2013/07/08/4334882/another-wheat-lawsuit-filed-against.html (accessed July 8, 2013); Donald L. Barlett and James B. Steele, "Monsanto's Harvest of Fear," *Vanity Fair*, May 5, 2008, http://www.vanityfair.com/politics/features/2008/05/monsanto200805 (accessed May 8, 2013); Dennis K. Berman, Gina Chon, and Scott Kilman, "Monsanto Pushes Deeper Into China," *The Wall Street Journal*, July 11, 2011, B1–B2; Ian Berry, "The Future of Patent Law Rest in a Farmer's Hands," *Wall Street Journal*, February 15, 2013, B1; Ian Berry, "Monsanto's Seeds Sow a Profit," *The Wall Street Journal*, January 7, 2011, B3; Ian Berry, "Pesticides Make a Comeback," *The Wall Street Journal*, May 21, 2013, http://online.wsj.com/article/SB10001424127887323463704578496923254944066.html (accessed May 28, 2013); Lindsey Boerma, "Critics Slam Obama for protecting Monsanto." *CBS NEWS*, March 28, 2013, http://www.cbsnews.com/8301-250_162-57576835/critics-slam-obama-for-protecting-monsanto/ (accessed April 22, 2013); "CR's 100 Best Corporate Citizens 2013,"*CR*, http://www.thecro.com/files/100Best2013_web.pdf (accessed May 8, 2013); "DuPont and Monsanto Agree to End Lawsuits." *Bloomberg*, March, 26, 2013, http://www.bloomberg.com/news/2013-03-26/dupont-monsanto-agree-to-end-lawsuits.html (accessed April 22, 2013); Nina Easton, "Why the March on Genetically Modified Food Hurts the Hungry," *Fortune*, June 10, 2013, 64; EPA, "R.E.D. Facts." EPA, September 1993, http://www.epa.gov/oppsrrd1/REDs/factsheets/0178fact.pdf (accessed May 8, 2013); "Even Small Doses of Popular Weed Killer Fatal to Frogs, Scientist Finds." *ScienceDaily*, August 5, 2005, http://www.sciencedaily.com/releases/2005/08/050804053212.htm (accessed May 8, 2013); Fortune Magazine, "Monsanto—Fortune 500," *CNNMoney*, http://money.cnn.com/magazines/fortune/fortune500/2012/snapshots/11092.html (accessed April 30, 2013); E. Freeman, "Seed Police?" Monsanto, http://www.monsanto.com/newsviews/Pages/Seed-Police-Part-4.aspx (accessed May 8, 2013); Crystal Gammon and Environmental Health News, "Weed-Whacking Herbicide Proves Deadly to Human Cells," *Scientific American*, June 23, 2009, http://www.scientificamerican.com/article.cfm?id=weed-whacking-herbicide-p&page=3 (accessed May 8, 2013); Ellen Gibson, "Monsanto," *BusinessWeek*, December 22, 2008, 51; Carey Gillam, "UPDATE 1-Monsanto unapproved GMO wheat stored in Colorado through '11," *Reuters*, June 28, 2013, "http://www.reuters.com/article/2013/06/28/monsanto-wheat-idUSL2N0F4oQR20130628 (accessed July 8, 2013); Seralini Gilles-Eric, Emilie Clair, Robin Mesnage, Steeve Gress, Nicolas Defarage, Manuela

Malatesta, Didier Hennequin, Joel Spiroux de Vendomois, "Long term toxicity of a Roundup herbicide and a Roundup-tolerant genetically modified maize," *Food and Chemical Toxicology.* Vol 57. (March 2013), 476–483; "GMOs under a Microscope," Science and Technology in Congress, October 1999, http://www.aaas.org/spp/cstc/ pne/pubs/stc/bulletin/articles/10-99/GMOs.htm (accessed March 25, 2009); Michael Grunwald, "Monsanto Hid Decades of Pollution," *The Washington Post*, January 1, 2002, A1; Jean Guerrero, "Altered Corn Advances Slowly in Mexico," *The Wall Street Journal*, December 9, 2010, B8; Georgina Gustin, "Justice department ends Monsanto antitrust probe," *St. Louis Post-Dispatch*, November 19, 2012, http://www.stltoday.com/business/local/justice-department-ends-monsanto-antitrust-probe/article_667ceab6-e568-57c8-a110-3d99efc31c4c.html (accessed May 8, 2013). Brian Hindo, "Monsanto: Winning the Ground War," *BusinessWeek*, 35–41; "India's Green Counter-Revolution," *The Wall Street*, February 13, 2010, http://online.wsj.com/article/SB10001424052748704140104575505838 3515565108.html (accessed May 1, 2013); Jack Kaskey, "Monsanto Says Rogue Wheat in Oregon May Be Sabotage," *Bloomberg*, June 5, 2013, http://www.bloomberg.com/news/2013-06-05/monsanto-says-rogue-wheat-didn-t-contaminate-oregon-seed.html (accessed July 8, 2013); Jack Kaskey, "Monsanto Sets a Soybean Free," *Bloomberg Businessweek*, February 1– 8, 2010, 19; Jack Kaskey, "Monsanto 'Warrior' Grant Fights Antitrust Accusations, Critics," *Bloomberg Businessweek*, March 4, 2010, http://www.bloomberg.com/apps/news?pid=newsarchive&sid=axVdNmPt Sgts (accessed May 8, 2013); Margie Kelly, "Top 7 Genetically Modified Crops," *The Huffington Post*, October 30, 2012, http://www.huffingtonpost.com/margie-kelly/genetically-modified-food_b_2039455.html (accessed May 1, 2013); Scott Kilman, "Monsanto's Net Profit Declines by 45%," *The Wall Street Journal*, July 1, 2010, B7; Mark Memmot, "Supreme Court Rules for Monsanto In Case Against Farmer," *NPR*, May 13, 2013, http://www.npr.org/ blogs/thetwo-way/2013/05/13/183603368/supreme-court-rules-for-monsanto-in-case-against-farmer (accessed May 13, 2013); John W. Miller, "Monsanto Loses Case in Europe over Seeds," *The Wall Street Journal*, July 7, 2010, B1; Monsanto Company, "Backgrounder: Glyphosate and Environmental Fate Studies." http://www.monsanto.com/ products/Documents/glyphosate-background-materials/gly_efate_bkg.pdf (accessed May 8, 2013); Monsanto Company, "Biotech Cotton Improving Lives of Farmers, Villages in India," http://www.monsanto.com/ responsibility/sustainable-ag/biotech_cotton_india.asp (accessed March 31, 2009); Monsanto Company, "Code of Ethics for Chief Executives and Senior Financial Officers," February 19, 2003, http://www.monsanto.com/whoweare/ Pages/code-of-ethics.aspx (accessed May 8, 2013); "Monsanto Company—Company Profile, Information, Business Description, History, Background Information on Monsanto Company," http://www.referenceforbusiness.com/ history2/92/Monsanto-Company.html (accessed May 8, 2013); Monsanto Company, "Corporate Profile," http:// www.monsanto.com/investors/Pages/corporate-profile.aspx (accessed May 8, 2013); Monsanto Company, "Do GM Crops Increase Yields?" http://www.monsanto.com/newsviews/Pages/do-gm-crops-increase-yield.aspx (accessed May 1, 2013); Monsanto Company, "Drought-Tolerant Corn Promises to Aid Sub-Sahara African Farmers," http:// www.monsanto.com/ourcommitments/Pages/water-efficient-maize-for-africa.aspx (accessed February 14, 2011); Monsanto Company, "Great Place to Work," http://www.monsanto.com/careers/culture/great_place.asp (accessed April 2009); Monsanto Company, *Monsanto Code of Business Conduct*, http://www.monsanto.com/ SiteCollectionDocuments/Code-of-Business-Conduct-PDFs/code_of_conduct_english.pdf (accessed May 8, 2013); "Monsanto Fined $1.5M for Bribery," *BBC News*, January 7, 2005, http://news.bbc.co.uk/2/hi/business/4153635.stm (accessed May 8, 2013); The Monsanto Fund website, http://www.monsantofund.org/ (accessed May 8, 2013); Monsanto Company, "What Is Monsanto Doing To Help?" http://www.monsanto.com/improvingagriculture/Pages/ what-is-monsanto-doing-to-help.aspx (accessed July 8, 2013); Monsanto Company, "Youth and Education," http:// www.monsanto.com/whoweare/Pages/youth-and-education.aspx (accessed May 8, 2013); "Monsanto Mania: The Seed of Profits," *iStockAnalyst*, http://www.istockanalyst.com/article/viewarticle.aspx?articleid=1235584&zoneid=H ome (accessed May 8, 2013); Claire Oxborrow, Becky Price, and Peter Riley, "Breaking Free," *Ecologist* 38, no. 9 (November 2008), 35–36; "The parable of the sower," *The Economist*, November 21, 2009, 71–73; "The Perils of Always Ignoring the Bright Side," *The Wall Street Journal*, http://online.wsj.com/article/SB100008723963904440047 04578030340322277954.html (accessed May 28, 2013); Mark Peters and Kris Maher, "Monsanto Settles Lawsuits." *The Wall Street Journal*, February 25–26, 2012, B3; Andrew Pollack, "So What's the Problem with Roundup?" *Ecology Center*, January 14, 2003, http://www.ecologycenter.org/factsheets/roundup.html (accessed March 25, 2009);

Andrew Pollack, "Widely Used Crop Herbicide Is Losing Weed Resistance," *The New York Times*, January 14, 2003, http://www.nytimes.com/2003/01/14/business/widely-used-crop-herbicide-is-losing-weed-resistance.html (accessed May 8, 2013); Michael Pollan, "Playing God in the Garden," *The New York Times Magazine*, October 25, 1998, http://www.michaelpollan.com/article.php?id=73 (accessed May 8, 2013); Connor Adam Sheets, "Farmers and food safety advocates lead Monsanto backlash," *Salon*, March 27, 2013, http://www.salon.com/2013/03/27/farmers_and_food_safety_advocates_lead_monsanto_backlash_partner/ (accessed May 8, 2013); G. M. Williams, R. Kroes, and I. C. Monro, "Safety Evaluation and Risk Assessment of the Herbicide Roundup and Its Active Ingredient, Glyphosate, for Humans," *NCBI*, April 2000, http://www.ncbi.nlm.nih.gov/pubmed/10854122 (accessed May 8, 2013); World Health Organization, "Food Security," http://www.who.int/trade/glossary/story028/en/ (accessed May 8, 2013); "The World's Most Innovative Companies," *Forbes*, http://www.forbes.com/innovative-companies/list/ (accessed May 6, 2013).

CASE 2

Starbucks' Mission: Social Responsibility and Brand Strength*

Howard Schultz joined Starbucks in 1982 as director of retail operations and marketing. Returning from a trip to Milan, Italy, with its 1,500 coffee bars, Schultz recognized an opportunity to develop a similar retail coffee-bar culture in Seattle.

In 1985 the company tested the first downtown Seattle coffeehouse, served the first Starbucks café latté, and introduced its Christmas Blend. Since then, Starbucks has expanded across the United States and around the world, now operating over 20,000 stores in 63 countries. Historically, Starbucks grew at a rate of about three stores a day, although the company cut back on expansion in recent years. The company serves millions of customers a week and has net revenues of approximately $13 billion a year. It has become the third largest chain restaurant in the United States.

Starbucks locates its retail stores in high-traffic, high-visibility locations. The stores are designed to provide an inviting coffee-bar environment that is an important part of the Starbucks product and experience. It was the intention of Howard Schulz to make Starbucks into "the third place" for consumers to frequent, after home and work. Because the company is flexible regarding size and format, it locates stores in or near a variety of settings, including office buildings, bookstores, and university campuses. It also situates retail stores in select rural and off-highway locations to serve a broader array of customers outside major metropolitan markets and further expand brand awareness. To provide a greater degree of access and convenience for non-pedestrian customers, the company increased the development of stores with drive-thru lanes. Starbucks has announced that 60 percent of all new stores built in the next five years will be drive-thrus.

In addition to selling products through retail outlets, Starbucks sells coffee and tea products and licenses its trademark through other channels and its partners. For instance, its Frappuccino coffee drinks, Starbucks Doubleshot espresso drinks, super-premium ice creams, and VIA coffees can be purchased in grocery stores and through retailers like Walmart and Target. Starbucks partnered with Courtesy Products to create single-cup Starbucks packets marketed toward hotel rooms. Starbucks also partnered with Green Mountain Coffee Roasters to introduce Starbucks-branded coffee and tea pods to the market. These pods target consumers who own Keurig single-cup brewing machines. Although the two businesses would normally be rivals, this partnership is beneficial for both Green Mountain and Starbucks. Since Green Mountain owns Keurig's single-serve

---

*This case was prepared by Michelle Urban and Jennifer Sawayda for and under the direction of Linda Ferrell, O. C. Ferrell, and Jennifer Jackson. Ben Siltman and Melanie Drever contributed to previous editions of this case. It was prepared for classroom discussion rather than to illustrate either effective or ineffective handling of an administrative, ethical, or legal decision by management. All sources used for this case were obtained through publicly available material and the Starbucks website.

machines, the partnership enables Starbucks to access this technology to market a new product. Green Mountain benefits because the partnership generates new users of Keurig single-cup brewing machines attracted to the Starbucks name. Starbucks and Green Mountain announced that they were extending their strategic partnership with an eye toward expanding Keurig machines beyond North America.

This partnership between Green Mountain and Starbucks did not stop Starbucks from launching its own line of single-serve machines. In 2012 Starbucks introduced its Verismo 580 Brewer, which allows consumers to brew a cup of Starbucks coffee in their own homes. The coffee has the strong, bold flavor of a cup purchased in any Starbucks retail location. Starbucks offers a limited assortment of coffees to emphasize quality rather than quantity. Not to be outdone, Green Mountain released another type of single-serve coffee brewer called the Rivo. Unlike the Verismo, which uses powdered milk pods, the Rivo uses fresh milk. The race to conquer the single-serve coffee market is intensifying between the two companies.

A common criticism of Starbucks is the company's strategy for location and expansion. Its "clustering" strategy, placing a Starbucks literally on every corner in some cases, forced many smaller coffee shops out of business. This strategy was so dominant for most of the 1990s and 2000s that Starbucks became the butt of jokes. Many people began to wonder whether we really needed two Starbucks directly across the street from each other. The recent global recession brought a change in policy, however. Starbucks pulled back on expansion, closed hundreds of stores around the United States, and focused more on international markets.

NEW PRODUCT OFFERINGS

Starbucks has introduced a number of new products over the years to remain competitive. In 2008 Starbucks decided to return to its essentials with the introduction of its Pike Place Blend, which the company hoped would return Starbucks to its roots of distinctive, expertly blended coffee. In order to get the flavor perfect, Starbucks enlisted the input of 1,000 customers over 1,500 hours. To kick off the new choice, Starbucks held the largest nationwide coffee tasting in history. To make the brew even more appealing, Starbucks joined forces with Conservation International to ensure the beans were sustainably harvested. After feedback revealed many of its customers desired a lighter blend, Starbucks introduced Blonde Roast blend in 2011.

Starbucks executives believe the experience customers have in the stores should be consistent. Therefore, Starbucks began to refocus on the customer experience as one of the key competitive advantages of the Starbucks brand. To enhance the European coffee shop experience for which Starbucks is known, shops are replacing their old espresso machines with new, high-tech ones and some are changing over to Clover Brand single-cup brewing machines so each customer receives a freshly brewed cup of coffee made to his or her specifications. To keep the drink-making operation running efficiently, Starbucks mandated that baristas can make no more than two drinks at the same time. The company hopes this reduces errors and increases product quality.

Additionally, Starbucks fosters brand loyalty by increasing repeat business. One of the ways it accomplishes this is through the Starbucks Card, a reloadable card introduced in 2001. For the tech-savvy visitor, Starbucks partnered with the mobile payments company

Square and introduced the Square Wallet application for mobile devices. The "app" enables customers to store their debit, credit, or Starbucks card information. When they order their coffee, they merely scan their phone for payment. This mobile app can be used at approximately 7,000 company-owned Starbucks stores, along with Starbucks Card eGifts sent to friends through the Internet.

In 2013 Starbucks announced that it would label calorie information on its menu boards in its U.S. stores. This greater transparency will help Starbucks customers make more informed decisions regarding wellness. During the summer Starbucks also introduced wholesome salad bowls with less than 450 calories. With increasing demands for healthier food, consumers are likely to see these actions as a positive response to their concerns.

STARBUCKS CULTURE

In 1990 Starbucks' senior executive team created a mission statement that specified the guiding principles for the company. They hoped the principles included in the mission statement would help their partners determine the appropriateness of later decisions and actions. After drafting the mission statement, the executive team asked all Starbucks partners to review and comment on the document. Based on their feedback, the final statement put "people first and profits last." In fact, the number one guiding principle in Starbucks' mission statement is to create a great and respectable work environment for its employees.

Starbucks has done three things to keep the mission and guiding principles alive over the decades. First, it distributes the mission statement and comment cards for feedback during orientation to all new partners. Second, Starbucks continually relates decisions back to the guiding principle or principles it supports. And finally, the company formed a "Mission Review" system so partners can comment on a decision or action relative to its consistency with one of the six principles. These guiding principles and values have become the cornerstone of a strong ethical culture of predominately young and educated workers.

Starbucks founder and chair Howard Schultz has long been a public advocate for increased awareness of ethics in business. In a 2007 speech at Notre Dame, he spoke to students about the importance of balancing "profitability and social consciousness." Schultz is a true believer that ethical companies do better in the long run, something that has been confirmed by research. Schultz maintains that, while it can be difficult to do the right thing at all times, in the long term it is better for a company to take short-term losses than lose sight of its core values.

Because of its strong corporate culture, for nearly a decade Starbucks has been ranked one of *Fortune*'s "100 Best Companies to Work For." In 2012 the company ranked 73rd out of 100 companies. Despite the challenges of the recession, Starbucks has been praised for not cutting back employee health care costs. The care the company shows its employees is a large part of what sets it apart. Starbucks offers all employees who work more than 20 hours per week a comprehensive benefits package that includes stock options as well as medical, dental, and vision benefits. In 2013 it was voted "World's Most Ethical Company" in the *Ethisphere* ranking for the seventh consecutive year.

Another key part of the Starbucks image involves its commitment to ethics and sustainability. To address concerns related to these issues, Starbucks launched the Shared Planet website. Shared Planet has three main goals: to achieve ethical sourcing, environmental stewardship, and greater community involvement. The website is a means of keeping customers current on initiatives within the company. It describes how well Starbucks fares on achieving its social responsibility goals, and it provides a means for customers to learn things like the nutrition data of Starbucks' offerings and other concerns related to Starbucks products.

Starbucks actively partners with nonprofits around the globe. In 2011, Starbucks became one of the largest buyers of Fair Trade Certified coffee at 34.3 million pounds. It also purchased 9.6 million pounds of certified organic coffee. Another organization Starbucks partnered with is the Foodservice Packaging Institute/Paper Recovery Alliance. The partnership addresses the issue of responsible foodservice packaging in terms of its use, recovery, and processing. Additionally, Starbucks makes $14.5 million in loans to poor farmers around the world and plans to increase that number to $20 million by 2015.

Conservation International joined with Starbucks in 1998 to promote sustainable agricultural practices, namely shade-grown coffee, and help prevent deforestation in endangered regions around the globe. The results of the partnership proved to be positive for both the environment and farmers. For example, in Chiapas, Mexico, shade-grown coffee acreage (that reduces the need to cut down trees for coffee plantations) increased well over 220 percent, while farmers receive a price premium above the market price. Starbucks increased awareness of its company while simultaneously building goodwill through a charity initiative with Foursquare. For every Starbucks check-in on Foursquare, Starbucks donates $1 to the Global Fund for RED, an organization that works to fight AIDS.

Starbucks works with many other organizations as well, including the African Wildlife Foundation and Business for Social Responsibility. The company's efforts at transparency, the treatment of its workers, and its dozens of philanthropic commitments demonstrate how genuine Starbucks is in its mission to be an ethical and socially responsible company.

CORPORATE SOCIAL MISSION

Although Starbucks has supported responsible business practices virtually since its inception, as the company has grown, so has the importance of defending its image. At the end of 1999 Starbucks created a Corporate Social Responsibility department, now known as the Global Responsibility Department. Global Responsibility releases an annual report in order for shareholders to keep track of its performance, and can be accessed through the Shared Planet website. Starbucks is concerned about the environment, its employees, suppliers, customers, and its communities.

Environment

In 1992, long before it became trendy to be "green," Starbucks developed an environmental mission statement to clearly articulate the company's environmental priorities and goals. This initiative created the Environmental Starbucks Coffee Company Affairs team, the purpose of which was to develop environmentally responsible policies and minimize the company's "footprint." As part of this effort, Starbucks began using environmental purchasing guidelines to reduce waste through recycling, conserving energy, and educating partners through the company's "Green Team" initiatives. Concerned stakeholders can now track the company's progress through its Shared Planet website, which clearly outlines Starbucks' environmental goals and how the company fares in living up to those goals.

Recently Starbucks hosted a series of Cup Summits, inviting various thinkers to develop a new way of producing the traditional Starbucks disposable cup so it is entirely decomposable. As a result, Starbucks began offering a $1 plastic cup for purchase—offered in tall, grande, and venti sizes—that is good for a recommended 30 uses. This is an attempt by Starbucks to reduce the 4 billion cups globally deposited into the environment.

Employees

Growing up poor with a father whose life was nearly ruined by an unsympathetic employer who did not offer health benefits, Howard Schultz always considered the creation of a good work environment a top priority. He believes companies should value their workers. When forming Starbucks, he decided to build a company that provided opportunities his father did not have. The result is one of the best health care programs in the coffee shop industry. Schultz's key to maintaining a strong business is developing a shared vision among employees as well as an environment where they can actively contribute. Understanding how vital employees are, Shultz is the first to admit his company centers on personal interactions: "We are not in the coffee business serving people, but in the people business serving coffee."

However, being a great employer does take its toll on the company. In 2008 Starbucks decided to close 10 percent of stores in order to continue to provide employees with health insurance. This decision, based on its guiding principle of "people first, profits last," shows how much the company values its employees. As a way to improve employee health, Starbucks established a program for employees called "Thrive Wellness" that offers various resources aimed at assisting employees in incorporating wellness into their lives. The program offers resources such as smoking cessation, weight loss, and exercise.

Suppliers

Even though it is one of the largest coffee brands in the world, Starbucks maintains a good reputation for social responsibility and business ethics throughout the international community of coffee growers. It builds positive relationships with small coffee suppliers while also working with governments and nonprofits wherever it operates. Starbucks practices conservation as well as Starbucks Coffee and Farmer Equity Practices (C.A.F.E.), a set of socially responsible coffee buying guidelines that ensure preferential buying status for participants that receive high scores in best practices. Starbucks pays coffee farmers premium prices to help them make profits and support their families. About 87 percent of total coffee purchases are C.A.F.E. verified.

The company is also involved in social development programs, investing in programs to build schools and health clinics, as well as other projects that benefit coffee-growing communities. Starbucks collaborates directly with some of its growers through Farmer Support Centers, located in Costa Rica, Rwanda, Tanzania, South America, and China. Farmer Support Centers provide technical support and training to ensure high-quality coffee into the future. Starbucks has donated approximately $70 million for loans and farmer support programs. It is a major purchaser of Fair Trade Certified, shade-grown, and certified organic beans, which further supports environmental and economic efforts. In 2013 the firm bought its first coffee farm, located in Costa Rica and employing about 70 people. The purchase is one step toward Starbucks' goal of increasing its ethically sourced coffee to 100 percent by 2015.

In 1991 Starbucks began contributing to CARE, a worldwide relief and development foundation, as a way to give back to coffee-origin countries. Starbucks' donations help with projects like clean water systems, health and sanitation training, and literacy efforts. Starbucks continues its long-term relationship with CARE, making Pike Place Blend its first CARE-certified brew.

Customers

Strengthening its brand and customer satisfaction is more important than ever as Starbucks seeks to regroup after the global economic crisis forced the company to rethink its strategy. Starbucks refocused the brand by upgrading its coffee-brewing machines, introducing new food and drink items for health and budget-conscious consumers, and refocusing on its core product. Recognizing the concern over the obesity epidemic, Starbucks ensures all of its menu items are under 500 calories and is involved in two sodium reduction programs: the National Salt Reduction Initiative in New York and the UK Food Standards Agency Salt Campaign. The company focuses more on the quality of the coffee, the atmosphere of the coffee shops, and the overall Starbucks experience, rather than continuing its rapid expansion of stores and products. Enhancing the customer experience in its stores also became a high priority. As a way to encourage people to relax and spend time there, Starbucks offers free wireless Internet access in all its U.S. stores.

Communities

Starbucks coffee shops have long sought to become the "instant gathering spot" wherever they locate, a "place that draws people together." To enhance the local, community-oriented feel of Starbucks shops, store managers are encouraged to donate to local causes. For example, one Seattle store donated more than $500,000 to Zion Preparatory Academy, an African American school for inner-city youth. Howard Schultz believes literacy has the power to improve lives and to give hope to underprivileged children. Schultz even used the advance and ongoing royalties from his book, *Pour Your Heart into It,* to create the Starbucks Foundation, which provides opportunity grants to nonprofit literacy groups, sponsors young writers' programs, and partners with Jumpstart, an organization helping children prepare developmentally for school.

Additionally, Starbucks takes a proactive approach to addressing unemployment in America. In light of the high unemployment rate, the company partnered with the Opportunity Finance Network to establish a program called Create Jobs for the USA. This initiative provides funds to Community Development Financial Institutions, which in turn finances small businesses, community centers, and housing projects. Starbucks donated $5 million to this initiative.

BRAND EVOLUTION

Although Starbucks has achieved massive success in the last 40 years, the company realizes it must modify its brand to appeal to changing consumer tastes. All established companies, no matter how successful, must learn to adapt their products and image to appeal to the shifting demands of their target markets. Starbucks is no exception. The company is mostly associated with premium coffee beverages, an association that served it well over the years. However, as competition in specialty coffee drinks increases, Starbucks recognized the need to expand its brand in the eyes of consumers.

One way it is doing this is adopting more products. In addition to coffee, Starbucks stores now sell coffee accessories, teas, muffins, CDs, water, grab-and-go products, Starbuck Petites, and upscale food items. Food sales make up 20 percent of Starbucks' revenue. With coffee prices projected to increase in the near future, an expansion into consumer packaged goods will protect Starbucks against the risks of relying solely on coffee. In order to remain competitive, Starbucks made a series of acquisitions to increase the value of its brand, including Bay Bread (a small artisan bakery), La Boulange (a bakery brand), and Evolution Fresh (a juice brand). This allowed Starbucks to offer high quality breakfast sandwiches as well as Paninis and wraps for lunch.

To symbolize this shift into the consumer packaged goods business, Starbucks gave its logo a new look. Previously, the company's circular logo featured a mermaid with the words "Starbucks Coffee" encircling it. In 2011 Starbucks announced it was removing the words and enlarging the mermaid to signal to consumers that Starbucks is more than just the average coffee retailer.

SUCCESS AND CHALLENGES

For decades, Starbucks has been revolutionizing our leisure time. Starbucks is not only the most prominent brand of high-end coffee in the world, but it is also one of the defining brands of our time. In most large cities, it is impossible to walk more than a few blocks without seeing the familiar mermaid logo.

In nearly two decades, Starbucks achieved amazing levels of growth, creating financial success for shareholders. Starbucks' reputation is built on product quality, stakeholder concern, and a balanced approach to all of its business activities. Of course, Starbucks does receive criticism for putting other coffee shops out of business and creating a uniform retail culture in many cities. Yet the company excels in its relationship with its employees and is a role model for the fast-food industry in employee benefits. In addition, in an age of shifts in supply chain power, Starbucks is as concerned about its suppliers and meeting their needs as it is about any other primary stakeholder.

In spite of Starbucks' efforts to support sustainability and maintain high ethical standards, the company garnered harsh criticism in the past on issues such as a lack of fair trade coffee, hormone-added milk, and Howard Shultz's alleged financial links to the Israeli government. In an attempt to counter these criticisms, in 2002 Starbucks began offering Fair Trade Certified coffee, a menu item that was quickly made permanent. In Ireland and the U.K., all Starbucks Espresso is now 100 percent Fair Trade certified, although this is not yet true for the United States.

Starting in late 2008, Starbucks had something new to worry about. A global recession caused the market to bottom out for expensive coffee drinks. The company responded by slowing its global growth plans after years of expanding at a nonstop pace and instead refocused on strengthening its brand, satisfying customers, and building consumer loyalty. After Starbucks stock started to plummet, Howard Schultz returned as CEO to try to return the company to its former glory.

Schultz was successful, and Starbucks rebounded from the effects of the recession. The company is once again looking toward possibilities in international markets. This represents both new opportunities and challenges. For instance, although Starbucks owes its existence to Schultz's trip to Italy, there are no Starbucks retailers in that country. The coffee culture within Italy is different from the United States, and although Schultz wants to expand into Italy eventually, the company will need to adapt to target Italian coffee drinkers.

When attempting to break into the U.K. market, Starbucks met with serious resistance. Realizing that the homogenization of its stores did not work as well in the United Kingdom, Starbucks began to remodel its stores to take on a more local feel. At the end of 2012, Starbucks came under public scrutiny for allegedly not paying taxes for the last 14 of the 15 years the company was established in the United Kingdom. A protest group called UK Uncut began "sitting in" at the stores, encouraging coffee drinkers to buy their coffee elsewhere. Starbucks claims it did not pay taxes because it did not make a profit. However, the company said it would stop using certain accounting techniques that showed their profits overseas. Starbucks also agreed to pay 20 million pounds over the next two years, whether or not it makes a profit.

Starbucks is also looking to China for expansion. The company currently operates 700 stores in China, with plans to open hundreds more. Effectively tapping into the Chinese market will require Starbucks to overcome unexpected obstacles and adapt its strategy to attract Chinese consumers. For example, in 2007 Starbucks was forced to close a retail operation in the Forbidden City because it was viewed as an oddity near such an important Chinese cultural location. People were concerned that the presence of the Western staple undermined the history and experience of visiting the Forbidden City. Despite these potential challenges, however, Starbucks announced it intends for China to become its biggest market.

Another challenge Starbucks must address is the fact that, despite the company's emphasis on sustainability, an estimated 4 billion disposable Starbucks cups are thrown into landfills each year. Only 5 percent of its stores recycle the cups. Although Starbucks has taken initiatives to make the cups more ecofriendly, such as changing from polyethylene No. 1 to the more ecofriendly polypropylene No. 5, the cup represents a serious waste problem for Starbucks. Starbucks encourages consumers to bring in reusables (such as the Starbucks tumblers it sells) for a 10-cent rebate, yet these account for less than 2 percent of drinks served. The company hopes to achieve less cup waste with its new $1 reusable cup. In 2010 Starbucks held a two-day "Cup Summit," inviting outside participants to brainstorm how to create a more sustainable cup. It is unclear whether Starbucks will achieve its goal of total recyclability in the short term.

Despite the setbacks it experienced during the recession, the future looks bright for Starbucks. The company continues to expand globally into markets such as Mumbai, India; San Jose, Costa Rica; Oslo, Norway; and Ho Chi Minh City, Vietnam. The challenges the company experienced and will continue to experience in the future convinced the firm to focus on its strengths and embrace the opportunity to emphasize community involvement, outreach work, and its overall image and offerings. The company must continue to apply the balanced stakeholder orientation so crucial to its success.

QUESTIONS

1. Why do you think Starbucks has been so concerned with social responsibility in its overall corporate strategy?
2. Is Starbucks unique in being able to provide a high level of benefits to its employees?
3. Do you think Starbucks has grown rapidly because of its ethical and socially responsible activities or because it provides products and an environment customers want?

SOURCES

Vikas Bajaj, "Starbucks Opens in India With Pomp and Tempered Ambition," *New York Times*, October 19, 2012, http://india.blogs.nytimes.com/2012/10/19/starbucks-opens-in-india-with-pomp-and-tempered-ambition/ (accessed January 22, 2013); Chris Barth, "Green Mountain Hopes To Beat Starbucks In The U.S. With One Simple Ingredient," *Forbes*, November 9, 2012, http://www.forbes.com/sites/chrisbarth/2012/11/09/green-mountain-hopes-to-beat-starbucks-in-the-u-s-with-one-simple-ingredient/ (accessed January 22, 2013); Susan Berfield, "Starbucks' Food Fight," *Businessweek*, June 12, 2012, http://www.businessweek.com/articles/2012-06-12/starbucks-food-fight (accessed January 22, 2013); Laurie Burkitt, "Starbuck Menu Expands in China," *The Wall Street Journal*, March 9, 2011, B7; Business Wire, "Starbucks Introduces Caloric Menu Board Labeling Nationwide," *The New York Times*, June 18, 2013, http://markets.on.nytimes.com/research/stocks/news/press_release.asp?docTag= 201306180900BIZWIRE_USPRX____BW5416&feedID=600&press_symbol=248911 (accessed July 9, 2013); Peter Campbell, "Starbucks caves in to pressure and promises to hand the taxman £20m after public outcry," *dailymail. co.uk*, December 6, 2012, http://www.dailymail.co.uk/news/article-2244100/Starbucks-caves-pressure-promises-pay-20m-corporation-tax-2-years.html (accessed January 22, 2013); CC, "Starbucks Brings Imported Coffee to a Land of Exported Coffee," *Fast Company*, May 2012, 30; CNN, "The 100 Best Companies To Work For," 2012, http://money.cnn.com/magazines/fortune/best-companies/2012/full_list/ (accessed January 15, 2013); "Coffee deal has stocks soaring," *USA Today*, March 11, 2011, 5B; "Coffee and Farmer Equity (C.A.F.E.) Practices," Conservation International, 2013, http://www.conservation.org/campaigns/starbucks/Pages/CAFE_Practices_ Results.aspx (accessed January 22, 2013); Eartheasy.com, "Shade Grown Coffee," http://www.eartheasy.com/eat_ shadegrown_coffee.htm (accessed May 7, 2009); Eatocracy editors, "Starbucks Introduces $1 Reusable Cup to Cut Down on Waste," *Eatocracy*, January 3, 2013, http://eatocracy.cnn.com/2013/01/03/starbucks-introduces-1-reusable-cup-to-cut-down-on-waste/, (accessed January 22, 2013); Roxanne Escobales and Tracy McVeigh, "Starbucks hit by UK Uncut protests as tax row boils over," *guardian.co.uk*, December 8, 2012, http://www.guardian.co.uk/business/2012/dec/08/starbucks-uk-stores-protests-tax (accessed January 22, 2013); Ethisphere Institute, "2012 World's Most Ethical Companies," *Ethisphere*, 2012, http://www.ethisphere.com/wme/ (accessed January 15, 2013); Stephan Faris, "Ground Zero: A Starbucks-Free Italy," *Bloomberg Businessweek*, February 9, 2012, http://www.businessweek.com/magazine/grounds-zero-a-starbucksfree-italy-02092012.html#p1 (accessed July 12, 2013). Bobbie Gossage, "Howard Schultz, on Getting a Second Shot," *Inc.*, April 2011, 52–54; Jason Groves and Peter Campbell, "Starbucks set to cave in and pay more tax after threats of boycott at its 'immoral' financial dealings," *dailymail.co.uk*, December 3, 2012, http://www.dailymail.co.uk/news/article-2242596/Starbucks-pay-tax-public-outcry-financial-dealings.html (accessed January 22, 2013); Bruce Horovitz, "Starbucks Aims beyond Lattes to Extend Brand to Films, Music and Books," *USA Today*, May 19, 2006, A1, A2; Bruce Horovitz, "Starbucks remakes its future," *USA Today*, October 18, 2010, 1B–2B; Bruce Horovitz, "Starbucks sales pass BK, Wendy's," *USA Today*, April 27, 2011, 1A. Bruce Horovitz, "Starbucks Shells Out Bread for Bakery," *USA Today*, June 5, 2012, Page 1B; Bruce Horovitz, "Starbucks Unveils Menu Deal to Halt Slide," *USA Today*, February 8, 2009, www. usatoday.com/money/industries/food2009-02-08-value-menu-starbucks_N.htm (accessed May 5, 2009); Bruce Horovitz and Howard Schultz, "Starbucks Hits 40 Feeling Perky," *USA Today*, March 7, 2011, 1B, 3B. "How Many Starbucks are There?" *www.loxcel.com*, November 16, 2012, http://www.loxcel.com/sbux-faq.html (accessed January 10, 2013); John Jannarone, "Green Mountain Eclipses Starbucks," *The Wall Street Journal*, March 9, 2011, C14; John Jannarone, "Grounds for Concern at Starbucks," *The Wall Street Journal*, May 3, 2011, C10; Julie Jargon, "At Starbucks, Baristas Told No More than Two Drinks," *The Wall Street Journal*, October 13, 2010, http://online. wsj.com/article/SB10001424052748704164004575548403514060736.html (accessed February 10, 2011); Julie Jargon, "Coffee Talk: Starbucks Chief on Prices, McDonald's Rivalry," *The Wall Street Journal*, March 7, 2011, B6; Julie Jargon, "Starbucks Logo Loses 'Coffee,' Expands Mermaid as Firm Moves to Build Packaged-Goods Business," *The Wall Street Journal*, January 6, 2011, B4; Julie Jargon, "Starbucks in Pod Pact," *The Wall Street Journal*, March 11, 2011, B4; Sarah Jones, "Starbucks Shows that Healthcare isn't a Job Killer by Adding 1, 500 Cafes," *PoliticusUSA*, December 6, 2012, http://www.politicususa.com/healthcare-providing-starbucks-expanding-1500-cafes.html

(accessed January 17, 2013); Anya Kamenetz, "'What are you going to do about this damn cup?'" *Fast Company*, November 2010, www.fastcompany.com/magazine/150/a-story-of-starbucks-and-the-limits-of-corporate-sustainability.html (accessed December 20, 2010); Beth Kowitt, "Coffee Shop, Contained," *Fortune*, May 20, 2013, 24; Paul R. La Monica, "Starbucks at 40: No mid-life crisis for stock," *CNNMoney*, March 8, 2011, http://money.cnn.com/2011/03/08/news/companies/thebuzz/index.htm (accessed March 10, 2011); Kate McClelland, "Starbucks Founder Speaks on Ethics," *Notre Dame Observer*, March 30, 2007, http://media.www.ndsmcobserver.com/media/storage/paper660/news/2007/03/30/News/Starbucks.Founder.Speaks.On.Ethics-2814792.shtml (accessed September 1, 2009); Sona Makker, "Foursquare and Starbucks Get in on Virtual Charity," *article-3*, June 6, 2012, http://www.article-3.com/foursquare-and-starbucks-get-in-on-virtual-charity-97564 (accessed January 17, 2013); MSNBC.com, "Health Care Takes Its Toll on Starbucks," http://www.msnbc.msn.com/id/9344634/, September 14, 2005 (accessed May 5, 2009); Reuters, "Starbucks to open first outlet in Vietnam in early February," *Economic Times*, January 3, 2013, http://articles.economictimes.indiatimes.com/2013-01-03/news/36130785_1_starbucks-china-john-culver-china-and-asia-pacific (accessed January 22, 2013); Mariko Sanchanta, "Starbucks Plans Big Expansion in China," *The Wall Street Journal*, April 14, 2010, B10; David Schorn, "Howard Schultz: The Star of Starbucks," *60 Minutes*, http://www.cbsnews.com/stories/2006/04/21/60minutes/main1532246.shtml (accessed February 10, 2011); E.J. Schultz, "How VIA Steamed up the Instant Coffee Category," *Advertising Age*, January 24, 2011, http://adage.com/article?article_id=148403 (accessed February 10, 2011); Starbucks, "2008 Annual Report." http://media.corporate-ir.net/media_files/irol/99/99518/AR2008.pdf (accessed April 1, 2009); "Starbucks: A farm of its own," *Bloomberg Businessweek*, March 25-March 31, 2013, 23; Starbucks. "C.A.F.E. Practices (Coffee and Farmer Equity Practices)," http://www.starbucks.ca/en-ca/_Social+Responsibility/C.A.F.E.+Practices.htm (accessed May 7, 2009); Starbucks, "Create Jobs for USA," http://www.starbucks.com/responsibility/community/create-jobs-for-usa-program (accessed January 22, 2013); Starbucks, "Coffee Purchasing," http://www.starbucks.com/responsibility/learn-more/goals-and-progress/coffee-purchasing (accessed February 10, 2011); Starbucks, "Create Jobs for America," http://www.starbucks.com/responsibility/community/create-jobs-for-usa-program, (accessed January 22, 2013); Starbucks, "Food," http://www.starbucks.com/menu/food (accessed January 22, 2013); Starbucks, "Goals & Progress: Coffee Purchasing," http://www.starbucks.com/responsibility/global-report/ethical-sourcing/coffee-purchasing, (accessed January 17, 2013); Starbucks, "Introducing Starbucks Card eGifts," http://www.starbucks.com/blog/introducing-starbucks-card-egifts, January 25, 2011 (accessed March 10, 2011); Starbucks, "Farmer Loans," http://www.starbucks.com/responsibility/learn-more/goals-and-progress/farmer-loans (accessed February 10, 2011; Starbucks, "Mobile Applications," http://www.starbucks.com/coffeehouse/mobile-apps (accessed February 10, 2011); Starbucks, "The Proof Is in the Cup: Starbucks Launched Historic New Pike Place Roast™," http://news.starbucks.com/article_display.cfm?article_id=51, April 7, 2008 (accessed May 4, 2009); Starbucks, "Recycling & Reducing Waste," http://www.starbucks.com/responsibility/environment/recycling, (accessed January 17, 2013); Starbucks, "Responsibly Grown Coffee," http://www.starbucks.com/responsibility/sourcing/coffee (accessed February 10, 2011); Starbucks, "Supporting Farmers and Their Communities," http://www.starbucks.com/responsibility/sourcing/farmer-support (accessed January 17, 2013); Starbucks, "Starbucks Company Profile," http://assets.starbucks.com/assets/aboutuscompanyprofileq12011final13111.pdf (accessed February 10, 2011); Starbucks, "Starbucks Company Fact Sheet," http://www.starbucks.com/aboutus/Company_Factsheet.pdf (accessed May 5, 2009); "Starbucks to Enter China's Tea Drinks Market," *China Retail News*, March 11, 2010, www.chinaretailnews.com/2010/03/11/3423-starbucks-to-enter-chinas-tea-drinks-market (accessed June 14, 2010); "Starbucks unveils minimalist new logo," *USA Today*, January 6, 2011, 11B; Starbucks, "Wellness," http://www.starbucks.com/responsibility/wellness (accessed January 17, 2013); Starbucks, "When you care about what you do, it shows," http://www.starbuckscoffee.co.uk/when-you-care-about-what-you-do-it-shows/, February 10, 2010 (accessed February 10, 2011); "Starbucks Corp.," Market Watch, http://www.marketwatch.com/investing/stock/sbux/financials (accessed January 22, 2013); Starbucks Newsroom, "Starbucks and Green Mountain Coffee Roasters Enter Into Expanded, Long-Term Strategic Partnership," May 8, 2013, http://news.starbucks.com/article_display.cfm?article_id=779 (accessed July 9, 2013); John D. Stoll, "Starbucks Aims to Invade Nordic

Region," *The Wall Street Journal*, Thursday, September 27, 2012, http://online.wsj.com/article/SB100008723963904 43507204578020553998689868.html (accessed January 22, 2013); David Teather, David, "Starbucks legend delivers recovery by thinking smaller," *The Guardian*, January 21, 2010, www.guardian.co.uk/business/2010/jan/21/ starbucks-howard-schultz (accessed June 12, 2010); Rachel Tepper, "Starbucks: Square Mobile Payment System Now Live at 7, 000 Locations," *The Huffington Post*, November 9, 2012, http://www.huffingtonpost.com/2012/11/09/ starbucks-square-mobile-payment_n_2101791.html (accessed January 15, 2013); Jorge Velasquez, "Starbucks Debuts $1 Reusable Cup," *KRCA*, January 3, 2013, http://www.kcra.com/news/Starbucks-debuts-1-reusable-cup/-/11797728/17994788/-/5dbclr/-/index.html, (accessed January 22, 2013); Nicole Wakelin, "The New Starbucks Verismo Single-Serve Home Coffee Brewer," *Wired*, November 18, 2012, http://www.wired.com/geekmom/2012/11/ starbucks-verismo/ (accessed January 22, 2013); Jonathan Watts, "Starbucks faces eviction from the Forbidden City," *www.guardian.co.uk*, January 18, 2007, http://www.guardian.co.uk/world/2007/jan/18/china.jonathanwatts (accessed January 22, 2013); Dan Welch, "Fairtrade beans do not mean a cup of coffee is entirely ethical," *guardian. co.uk*, February 28, 2011, http://www.guardian.co.uk/environment/green-living-blog/2011/feb/28/coffee-chains-ethical (accessed July 11, 2011).

CASE 3

Walmart Manages Ethics and Compliance Challenges*

Walmart Stores, Inc., is an icon of American business. From small-town business to multinational corporation, from a hugely controversial company to a leader in renewable energy, Walmart has long been a lightning rod for news and criticism. With 2012 net sales of more than $443 billion and more than 2 million employees, the world's second largest public corporation must carefully manage many stakeholder relationships. It is a challenge that has sparked significant debate.

While Walmart's mission is to help people save money and live better, the company has received plenty of criticism regarding its treatment of employees, suppliers, and economic impacts on communities. Walmart has the potential to save families hundreds of dollars a year, according to some studies. At the same time, however, research shows that communities can be negatively affected by Walmart's arrival in their areas. Moreover, feminists, activists, and labor union leaders have all voiced their belief that Walmart has engaged in misconduct. Walmart has attempted to turn over a new leaf with emphases on diversity, charitable giving, support for nutrition, and sustainability, all of which have contributed to a revitalized image for Walmart. In fiscal year 2012, the company, along with its Walmart Foundation, donated more than $1 billion in cash and in-kind contributions. However, more recent scandals such as bribery accusations in Mexico have created significant ethics and compliance challenges that Walmart must address in its quest to become a socially responsible retailer.

This analysis begins by briefly examining the growth of Walmart; next, it discusses the company's various relationships with stakeholders, including competitors, suppliers, and employees. The ethical issues concerning these stakeholders include accusations of discrimination, leadership misconduct, bribery, and safety. We discuss how Walmart deals with these concerns, as well as recent endeavors in sustainability and social responsibility. The analysis concludes by examining what Walmart is currently doing to increase its competitive advantage and repair its reputation.

HISTORY: THE GROWTH OF WALMART

The story of Walmart begins in 1962, when founder Sam Walton opened the first Walmart Discount Store in Rogers, Arkansas. Although it got off to a slow start, over the next 40 years the company grew from a small chain to more than 8,000 facilities in 27 countries.

---

*This case was prepared by O.C. Ferrell, Jennifer Sawayda, and Michelle Urban. Jennifer Jackson made significant contributions to previous editions of this case. It was prepared for classroom discussion rather than to illustrate either effective or ineffective handling of an administrative, ethical, or legal decision by management. All sources used for this case were obtained through publicly available material and the Walmart website.

The company now serves more than 200 million customers weekly. Much of the success Walmart experienced can be attributed to its founder. A shrewd businessman, Walton believed in customer satisfaction and hard work. He convinced many of his associates to abide by the "10-foot rule," whereby employees pledged that whenever they got within 10 feet of a customer, they would look the customer in the eye, greet him or her, and ask if he or she needed help with anything. Walton's famous mantra, known as the "sundown rule," was: "Why put off until tomorrow what you can do today?" Due to this staunch work ethic and dedication to customer care, Walmart claimed early on that a formal ethics program was unnecessary because the company had Mr. Sam's ethics to follow.

In 2002 Walmart officially became the largest grocery chain, topping the *Fortune* 500. *Fortune* named Walmart the "most admired company in America" in 2003 and 2004. Although it has slipped since then, it remains high on the list. In 2012 *Fortune* ranked Walmart as the 24th most admired company in the world.

Effects on Competitive Stakeholders

Possibly the greatest complaint against Walmart is it puts other companies out of business. With its low prices, Walmart makes it harder for local stores to compete. Walmart is often accused of being responsible for the downward pressure on wages and benefits in towns where the company locates. Some businesses have filed lawsuits against Walmart, claiming the company uses predatory pricing to put competing stores out of business. Walmart countered by defending its pricing, asserting that its purpose is to provide quality, low-cost products to the average consumer. Yet although Walmart has saved consumers millions of dollars and is a popular shopping spot for many, there is no denying that many competing stores go out of business once Walmart comes to town.

In order to compete against the retail giant, other stores must reduce wages. Studies show that overall payroll wages, including Walmart wages, are reduced by 5 percent after Walmart enters a new market. As a result, some activist groups and citizens have refused to allow Walmart to take up residence in their areas. This in turn brings up another social responsibility issue. While it is acceptable for stakeholder activists to protest the building of a Walmart store in their area, other actions may be questionable, especially when the government gets involved. When Walmart announced plans to open stores in Washington D.C., for instance, a chairman of the D.C. City Council attempted to pass a law that would require stores occupying more than 75,000 square feet to pay their employees a minimum of $11.75 per hour—despite the city's minimum wage of $8.25 an hour. While supporters of the law state that it is difficult to live on a wage of $8.25 an hour, critics state that this gives employees at large retailers more of an advantage than those working at small retailers. Perhaps the most scathing criticism is that Walmart and other big-box retailers are being unfairly targeted by government bodies. As with most issues, determining the most socially responsible decision that benefits the most stakeholders is a complex issue not easily resolved.

Relationships with Supplier Stakeholders

Walmart achieves its "everyday low prices" (EDLPs) by streamlining the company. Well-known for operational excellence in its ability to handle, move, and track merchandise, Walmart expects its suppliers to continually improve their systems as well. Walmart typically works with suppliers to reduce costs of packaging and shipping, which lessens costs for consumers. Since 2009 the company has worked with The Sustainability Consortium to develop a measurement and reporting system known as the Sustainability Index. Among its many goals, Walmart desires to use the Sustainability Index to increase the sustainability of its products and create a more efficient, sustainable supply chain.

In 2008 Walmart introduced its "Global Responsible Sourcing Initiative," a list providing details of the policies and requirements included in new supplier agreements. In 2012 CEO Mike Duke expanded upon these initiatives to set improved goals for increasing the sustainability of the company's supply chain. He highlighted four main sustainability goals: (1) purchase 70 percent of merchandise sold in U.S. Walmart stores and Sam's Clubs from global suppliers that use the Sustainability Index to assess and share information about their products by 2017; (2) use the Sustainability Index as a model for U.S. private brands; (3) apply new evaluative criteria for key sourcing merchants to encourage sustainability to become a more important consideration in buyers' daily jobs; and (4) donate $2 million to fund The Sustainability Consortium.[1] If fully achieved, these goals will increase the sustainability of Walmart suppliers significantly. Some critics, however, believe pressures to achieve these standards will shift more of a cost burden onto suppliers. When suppliers do not meet its demands, Walmart may cease to carry the supplier's product or, often, will find another supplier for the product at the desired price.

Walmart's power centers around its size and the volume of products it requires. Many companies depend on Walmart for much of their business. This type of relationship allows Walmart to influence terms with its vendors, and indeed, there are benefits to being a Walmart supplier; as suppliers become more efficient and streamlined for Walmart, they help other customers as well. Numerous companies believe supplying Walmart has been the best thing for their businesses.

However, many others found the amount of power Walmart wields to be disconcerting. The constant drive by Walmart for lower prices can negatively affect suppliers. Many have been forced to move production from the United States to less expensive locations in Asia. Companies such as Master Lock, Fruit of the Loom, and Levi's, as well as many other Walmart suppliers, moved production overseas at the expense of U.S. jobs.

This was not founder Sam Walton's original intention. In the 1980s, after learning his stores were putting other American companies out of business, Walton started his "Buy American" campaign. However, the quest to maintain low prices has pushed many Walmart suppliers overseas, and some experts now estimate as much as 80 percent of Walmart's global suppliers are stationed in China. The challenges and ethical issues associated with managing a vast network of overseas suppliers will be discussed later in this case.

Ethical Issues Involving Employee Stakeholders

EMPLOYEE BENEFITS   Much of the Walmart controversy over the years has focused on the way the company treats its employees, or "associates" as Walmart refers to them. Although Walmart is the largest retail employer in the world, it has been roundly criticized for low wages and benefits. Walmart has been accused of failing to provide health insurance for more than 60 percent of its employees. In a memo sent to the board of directors by Susan Chambers, Walmart's executive vice-president for benefits, she encouraged the hiring of more part-time workers while also encouraging the hiring of "healthier, more

---

[1]Walmart, "Walmart Announces New Commitments to Drive Sustainability Deeper into the Company's Global Supply Chain," October 25, 2012, http://news.walmart.com/news-archive/2012/10/25/walmart-announces-new-commitments-to-drive-sustainability-deeper-into-the-companys-global-supply-chain (accessed April 19, 2013).

productive employees." After this bad publicity, between 2000 and 2005 Walmart's stock decreased 27 percent.

As a result of the deluge of bad press, Walmart took action to improve relations with its employee stakeholders. In 2006 Walmart raised pay tied to performance in about one-third of its stores. The company also improved its health benefits package by offering lower deductibles and implementing a generic prescription plan estimated to save employees $25 million. Walmart estimates over three-fourths of its employees have insurance (though not always through Walmart). Walmart is quick to point out that the company offers health care benefits competitive in the retail industry.

Despite these improvements, a new Walmart policy eliminates healthcare coverage for new hires working less than 30 hours a week. Walmart also states that it reserves the right to cut healthcare coverage of workers whose work week goes below 30 hours. Some analysts claim that Walmart might be attempting to shift the burden of healthcare coverage onto the federal government, as some employees would make so little that they would qualify for Medicaid under the new healthcare law. It is important to note that Walmart is not alone in this practice; many other firms are moving their workforces to part-time to avoid having to pay healthcare costs. However, as such a large employer, Walmart's actions are expected to have more of a ripple effect on the economy.

Another criticism levied against Walmart is that it decreased its workforce at the same time it expanded. In the United States Walmart decreased its workforce by 1.4 percent while increasing its retail stores by 13 percent. Employee dissatisfaction often translates to customer dissatisfaction. With fewer employees it is harder to provide quality customer service. This led some customers to complain of longer lines and fewer items on shelves. In the American Customer Satisfaction Index, Walmart placed the lowest among discount stores and department stores on customer satisfaction. On the other hand, Walmart claims the dissatisfaction expressed by some customers is not reflective of the overall shopping experience of customers as a whole.

WALMART'S STANCE ON UNIONS   Some critics believe workers' benefits could improve if workers become unionized. Unions have been discouraged since Walmart's foundation; Sam Walton believed they were a divisive force and might render the company uncompetitive. Walmart maintains that it is not against unions in general, but it sees no need for unions to come between workers and managers. The company says it supports an "open-door policy" in which associates can bring problems to managers without resorting to third parties. Walmart associates have voted against unions in the past.

Although the company officially states that it is not opposed to unions, Walmart often seems to fight against them. Critics claim that when the word "union" surfaces at a Walmart location, the top dogs in Bentonville are called in. In 2000 seven of ten Walmart butchers in Jacksonville, Texas, voted to join the United Food Workers Union. Walmart responded by announcing it would only sell precut meat in its Supercenters, getting rid of its meat-cutting department entirely. Although Walmart offers justifications for actions such as this, many see the company as aggressively working to prevent unionization in its stores.

However, Walmart's stance against unions has not always held up in foreign countries. In China, Walmart faced a similar decision regarding unions. To grow in China, it appeared necessary to accept a union. Poor working conditions and low wages generated social unrest, and the government attempted to craft a new set of labor laws giving employees greater protection and giving the All-China Federation of Trade Unions (ACFTU) more power. In 2004 the Chinese Labor Federation pushed Walmart to allow the formation of unions. As a result, Walmart technically allowed this, but critics claimed Walmart made it increasingly difficult for workers to join a union. In 2006 a district union announced the first formation of a Walmart union at a store in China, and within a week, four more branches announced their formations of unions. Walmart initially reacted to these announcements by stating it would not renew the contracts of unionized workers. However, the pressure mounted, and later that year Walmart signed a memorandum with the ACFTU allowing unions in stores. Walmart also negotiates with unions in Brazil, Chile, Mexico, Argentina, the United Kingdom, and South Africa.

WORKPLACE CONDITIONS AND DISCRIMINATION   Despite accusations of low employee benefits and a strong stance against unions, Walmart remains the largest nongovernment employer in the United States, Mexico, and Canada. It provides jobs to millions of people and is a mainstay of *Fortune*'s "Most Admired Companies" list since the start of the twenty-first century. However, in December 2005, Walmart was ordered to pay $172 million to more than 100,000 California employees in a class-action lawsuit claiming that Walmart routinely denied meal breaks. The California employees also alleged that they were denied rest breaks and Walmart managers deliberately altered time cards to prevent overtime. Similar accusations began to pop up in other states as well. Walmart denied the allegations and filed an appeal in 2007. In 2008 Walmart agreed to pay up to $640 million to settle sixty-three such lawsuits.

Walmart has also been accused of discrimination by employees. Although women account for more than two-thirds of all Walmart employees, they make up less than 10 percent of store management. Walmart insists it trains and promotes women fairly, but in 2001 an internal study showed the company paid female store managers less than males in the same positions. In 2004 a federal judge in San Francisco granted class-action status to a sex-discrimination lawsuit against Walmart involving 1.6 million current and former female Walmart employees. The plaintiffs claimed Walmart discriminated against them in regard to promotions, pay, training, and job assignments. Walmart argued against the class-action suit, claiming promotions were made on an individual basis by each store. Walmart took the case to the Supreme Court, claiming the suit violates the company's right of due process. The Supreme Court determined that the women in the lawsuit do not have enough in common to classify for class-action status. Although the women can sue Walmart individually, the impact on the company will be far less than if a class-action lawsuit had been allowed to proceed.

In 2010 dissatisfied employees at Walmart started the Organization United Respect Walmart, or OUR Walmart. Although not a labor union, OUR Walmart receives much of its funding from the United Food and Commercial Workers International Union (UFCW). According to OUR Walmart, it has 5,000 members who desire to change working conditions at Walmart. Their grievances against Walmart include raising the number of hours needed for part-time workers to qualify for benefits, capping the wages of some long-time workers, and using its work-scheduling systems to decrease hours for employees so they will not qualify for benefits. OUR Walmart arranged protests and picketing at Walmart stores for six months, with a major protest scheduled for the 2012 Thanksgiving holiday. Walmart complained to the National Labor Relations Board and accused the UFCW of anti-labor practices. According to Walmart, OUR Walmart violated rules because, since it is not a union, it is allowed to protest only 30 days before gathering signatures for an employee vote. While the protests did occur, not as many Walmart employees participated as anticipated. Walmart claims this demonstrates that the movement is not as popular as it tries to appear. Walmart filed a lawsuit against the UFCW and others who protested around its Florida stores for illegal trespassing and disrupting customers.

Ethical Leadership Issues

Aside from Sam Walton, other distinguished people have been associated with Walmart. One of them is Hillary Clinton, who served on Walmart's board for six years before her husband assumed the presidency. However, the company has not been immune from scandal at the top. In March 2005, board vice chair Thomas Coughlin was forced to resign because he stole as much as $500,000 from Walmart in the form of bogus expenses, reimbursements, and the unauthorized use of gift cards. Coughlin, a protégé and hunting buddy of Sam Walton, was a legend at Walmart. He often spent time on the road with Walton expanding the Sam's Club aspect of the business. At one time, he was the second highest-ranking Walmart executive and a candidate for CEO.

In January 2006 Coughlin agreed to plead guilty to federal wire-fraud and tax-evasion charges. Although he took home millions of dollars in compensation, Coughlin secretly used Walmart funds to pay for a range of personal expenses including hunting vacations, a $2,590 dog enclosure at his home, and a pair of handmade alligator boots. Coughlin's deceit was discovered when he asked a subordinate to approve $2,000 in expense payments without receipts. Walmart rescinded Coughlin's retirement agreement, worth more than $10 million. For his crimes, he was sentenced to 27 months of home confinement, $440,000 in fines, and 1,500 hours of community service.

Although confidence in Walmart's leadership rose after CEO Lee Scott became CEO, it waned once more after a bribery scandal was discovered in Mexico. In 2012 a significant percentage of Walmart's non-family shareholders voted against the reelection of CEO Mike Duke to the board. They also voted against the reelection of other board members, including former CEO Lee Scott and Robert Walton. While this did not prevent these board members from being reelected, it did signal the disappointment and lack of confidence in the leadership for not preventing the store from getting involved in misconduct. In order to reassure investors, it is essential for Walmart's leadership to demonstrate a renewed commitment toward ensuring the company adheres to ethics and compliance standards.

Problems with Environmental Stakeholders

Like many large corporations, Walmart has been targeted as a violator of safe environmental practices. In 2005 Walmart received a grand jury subpoena from the U.S. Attorney's Office in Los Angeles, California, seeking documents and information relating to the company's receipt, transportation, handling, identification, recycling, treatment, storage, and disposal of certain merchandise constituting hazardous material. In 2013 the retailer pled guilty to criminal charges for dumping hazardous waste materials. It agreed to pay $81 million to settle the charges. Walmart admits that it failed to train its employees adequately on how to properly dispose of these materials.

However, the greatest environmental concern associated with Walmart has been urban sprawl. The construction of a Walmart can stress a city's infrastructure of roads, parking, and traffic flow. There have been concerns about the number of acres of city green space devoured by Walmart construction (Walmart Supercenters occupy about twenty to thirty acres of land). Another issue is the number of abandoned stores, deserted when the company outgrows locations. Walmart allegedly goes out of its way to prevent other retail companies from buying its abandoned stores.

Walmart's large stores have put it at a disadvantage when trying to expand into urban areas. In places like New York City where space is a significant issue, there is less room for Walmart stores. As a result, Walmart began testing smaller stores consisting of about 15,000 square feet in urban and rural areas. This strategy of smaller stores is already showing promise, with Chicago's zoning committee finally approving a Walmart on its south side. However, not all big cities are eager to embrace Walmart. Walmart experienced a verbal backlash from officials and citizens of New York City at the mere suggestion of Walmart entering the city. To break into urban areas, the company needs to work on changing how Walmart is perceived among these stakeholders. It may also be difficult for Walmart to open smaller stores in high-income areas such as major cities and still offer its everyday low priced items. As a result, the company is taking a careful approach and is opening these "minimarts" at a slower pace.

Bribery Scandal

The biggest blow to Walmart's reputation in recent years is the discovery of an alleged large-scale bribery ring among its Mexican arm, Walmex. It has been claimed that Walmex executives paid millions in bribes to obtain licensing and zoning permits for store locations. The Mexican approval process for zoning licenses often takes longer than in the United States; therefore, paying bribes to speed up the process is advantageous for Walmart but places competing retailers who do not offer bribes at a disadvantage. The Walmex executives covered their tracks with fraudulent reporting methods.

In the last few years, bribery has become a hot button issue for the U.S. government, which has levied its largest convictions against firms found guilty of bribery. It is not unusual for large firms with operations in many countries to face bribery allegations at some point. On the other hand, the bribery scandal in Mexico was exacerbated by two major considerations: top executives at Walmart appeared to turn a blind eye to the bribery, and bribery among Walmart stores in foreign countries may be more widespread than originally thought.

Walmart first reported to the U.S. Justice Department that it was launching an internal investigation of suspected bribery at its Mexico stores in December 2011. However, the report to the U.S. Justice Department did not arrive until after an investigation by *The New York Times* revealed that top leaders at Walmart were alerted to the possibility of bribery as early as 2005. That year Walmart received an email discussing the bribery and providing the company with names, dates, and other information. Walmart sent investigators to Mexico City, where they discovered approximately $24 million in bribes had been paid to public officials to get necessary building permits. Mexican executives and the company's Mexican general counsel were implicated in the scheme. Yet it has been suggested that when they were informed of the bribery evidence, top executives at Walmart, including then-CEO Lee Scott, were reluctant to report the bribery because they knew it would be a serious blow to the firm's reputation. Additionally, Walmart has been successful in Mexico; business in Mexico currently accounts for approximately one-fourth of the company's sales. Revealing bribery could have negative repercussions in this profitable area of growth.

The investigation was turned over to the Mexican general counsel even though it was believed the general counsel had approved of the scheme. This move was against the advice of one of Walmart's top lawyers, who recommended an independent third party investigator. The general counsel cleared the Mexican executives accused of bribery from wrongdoing, and the investigation was closed without anyone being disciplined. It did not reopen until after *The New York Times* began its own investigation.

Such allegations are serious if leaders at Walmart knew of the bribery. It is believed that former CEO Lee Scott and current CEO Michael Duke, who at the time was in charge of Walmart International, may have had knowledge of the bribery. Under the Foreign Corrupt Practices Act (FCPA), it is illegal to bribe foreign officials. Walmart can face millions in fines, and its executives could lose their jobs or face prison time if it is revealed they helped cover up knowledge of the bribery.

The impact on Walmart after the bribery scandal became public was significant. Shortly after the announcement, the stock lost $1 billion in value, and shareholders began filing lawsuits against the company and its executives. Additionally, Walmart has had to pay for its own internal probe, which has already cost it $99 million. Its probe revealed even greater possibilities of bribery in other countries. Walmart expanded its bribery probe to China, India, and Brazil.

The bribery probe has taken on particular interest in India. Walmart's Indian joint venture with Bharti Enterprises suspended some of its key executives believed to have engaged in bribery. This investigation halted Walmart's expansion in the country. Indian authorities began investigating Walmart and Bharti to determine if they attempted to circumvent foreign investment laws. Foreign retailers like Walmart are allowed to partner with local businesses and open stores in the country as long as they do not own a majority stake in the venture (less than 51 percent ownership). It is alleged that Walmart offered Bharti an interest-free, $100 million loan that would later enable it to gain a majority stake in the company. Both companies deny they tried to violate foreign investment rules.

Such allegations not only have serious consequences for Walmart, but also for other foreign retailers in the country. Many political officials in India were against allowing foreign retailers to open stores in India. This potential misconduct has added fuel for the opposition. Hence, the operation of other foreign retailers may be threatened. This situation demonstrates how the misconduct of one or two companies impacts entire businesses or industries.

Many shareholders are demanding disciplinary action and compensation cuts against those involved in the bribery scandal. Shareholders are demanding that the leaders of Walmart improve transparency and compliance standards. As part of its compliance overhaul, Walmart announced it would tie some executive compensation to compliance efforts.

Safety Issues

Using overseas suppliers has also caused trouble for Walmart. Many of its suppliers, both inside the United States and in other countries, employ subcontractors to manufacture certain products. This makes the supply chain complex, and retailers like Walmart are forced to exert more oversight to ensure its suppliers meet compliance standards. Citing safety concerns or telling a supplier not to work with a certain subcontractor is not enough without enforcement. Walmart learned this the hard way after a Bangladeshi factory fire killed 112 workers.

The factory, Tazreen Fashions Ltd., has several assembly lines devoted to Walmart apparel. At least one of Walmart's suppliers used the factory to subcontract work for Walmart, but Walmart claims the supplier was unauthorized to do so. Walmart states it removed Tazreen Fashions from its list of approved suppliers months before the incident. It has since terminated its relationship with the supplier that subcontracted the work to Tazreen Fashion. Previous inspections at Tazreen showed many fire dangers, including blocked stairwells and a lack of firefighting equipment. In November 2012 a fire broke out in the factory that burned down the building and killed 112 employees, some of whom jumped to their deaths.

Many were outraged that Walmart did not do a better job to ensure the safety of the factory workers. While Walmart does have auditing and approval mechanisms, third parties usually perform the audits. Suppliers often pay for the inspection processes as well. This limits the amount of information that actually gets to the parent company. Critics have also accused Walmart of advocating against equipping factories with better fire protection due to the costs involved. Walmart claims it takes fire dangers and worker safety seriously.

Walmart has also faced criticism on its home front. Workers at warehouses in the United States doing business with Walmart have complained about harsh working conditions and violations of labor laws. Safety violations are also a common complaint. The situation is complex because these workers are hired by staffing agencies or third-party contractors, making it harder for Walmart to assess working conditions. Walmart has argued that these third-party contractors are responsible for working conditions. Yet as the firm hiring the contractors, Walmart has the responsibility to ensure their contractors and subcontractors obey proper labor laws.

The Bangladeshi fire and worker complaints have increased the pressure on Walmart to improve its oversight and auditing mechanisms. Previously, Walmart employed a three-strike policy for suppliers and subcontractors who violated its ethical standards. However, after the Bangladeshi fire Walmart changed its policy to adopt a zero-tolerance approach. Whereas before, suppliers that violated sourcing policies had three chances to rectify problems, now Walmart exerts the right to terminate relationships with suppliers immediately after discovering a violation. Walmart also requires all suppliers to have an independent agency assess the electrical and building safety conditions of their factories. To address domestic complaints, Walmart applies the same monitoring system to U.S. suppliers. Walmart announced it will make unannounced visits to U.S. third-party operated warehouses by independent auditors to check whether they adhere to the firm's ethical standards. Walmart hopes these stricter measures improve compliance at its suppliers as well as reiterate the company's commitment toward ethical sourcing practices. Yet these measures have failed to appease some critics, who believe that Walmart cannot truly be held accountable until the results of its factory audits are made public.

The controversy of worker safety in Bangladesh intensified after a factory collapsed and killed 1,127 workers. The tragedy has caused retailers like Walmart to consider new safety plans. European retailers, worker safety groups, and labor unions agreed to a five-year legally binding pact that would improve worker safety in Bangladesh. However, Walmart declined to sign the pact and instead devised its own safety plan for its Bangladesh factories. Its plan includes hiring an independent auditor to inspect Bangladeshi factories, requiring factories deemed to be unsafe to improve safety standards, publishing the audit results of more than 250 factories that have been revoked, and developing an independent call center for workers to report unsafe factory conditions.

RESPONDING TO STAKEHOLDER CONCERNS

Walmart has suffered significantly from these recent scandals. Studies reveal that between 2011 and 2012, consumer interest, customer loyalty, and other factors important to a brand's value diminished 50 percent among college-educated adults. Being a large multinational corporation brings many global risks, including bribery and supplier issues. In response to the allegations of bribery, Walmart replaced the general counsel in Mexico and is conducting an investigation into the allegations. In addition, CEO Mike Duke assured the public that the company is re-evaluating its global compliance program with assistance from auditing firm KPMG LLP and law firm Greenberg Traurig LLP.

At a pep rally held in May of 2012, Mike Duke emphasized integrity in operations and employee behavior at all levels, and rewarded 11 employees for "leading with integrity." In highlighting the actions of these select employees, he reiterated the firm's ethics hotline and open-door policy. He assured employees and other stakeholders that the company is cooperating with the U.S. Department of Justice in order to get to the bottom of the bribery allegations. Mike Duke acknowledged that there were ethical issues in some of the stores and stated that he plans to slow expansion plans so the company can improve on these issues.

As a form of damage control, Walmart released an advertising campaign to frame the company as an "American success story." After market research revealed Walmart's brand image lost traction among college-educated adults, Walmart developed a multi-million advertising campaign called "The Real Walmart." The advertisements feature customers, truck drivers, and employees sharing their happy experiences with the company. Walmart particularly wants to target opinion leaders so they can convince others of the company's value and brand image. The ads were first released during the Kentucky Derby and also featured on Sunday news shows. Walmart's former executive Vice-President of Corporate Affairs, Leslie Dach, who left Walmart in 2013, also emphasized the company's commitment to healthier food alternatives to fight the obesity epidemic. This advertising campaign is similar to those released by other companies attempting to restore their images, such as Toyota during the recall crisis and BP after the *Deepwater Horizon* disaster. It remains to be seen whether Walmart's advertising efforts and its renewed commitment to corporate responsibility will prove successful toward improving its brand image.

Sustainability Leadership

Among Walmart's sustainability goals are its intentions to be supplied entirely by renewable energy, create no waste, and sell products that sustain people and the environment. In order to achieve these ambitious goals, Walmart has built relationships with influential people in supplier companies, government, NGOs, and academia. Together they have created Sustainable Value Networks (SVN) serving to integrate and evaluate efforts in renewable energy and practices. This approach has served them well. By 2012 Walmart had 115 onsite rooftop solar installations in seven countries providing 71 million annual kilowatt hours of electricity. They completed 26 fuel cell installations in the United States, providing 65 million kilowatt hours of annual electricity, and are testing micro-wind and solar water heating projects in various locations. Walmart's company value of everyday low cost translates to their renewable energy endeavors through the signing of long-term contracts with renewable energy providers. These contracts finance utility-scale projects in renewable sources, allowing these options to be offered at lower costs not only to Walmart but also to other clients of these providers.

Walmart has also financed its own renewable energy projects. In addition to the company's rooftop solar and fuel cell installations, Walmart has more than 180 projects underway, including micro-wind installations in parking lots and biodiesel generator sets. Taken together, these projects provide 22 percent of Walmart's electricity needs. Nearly 350 Mexico stores have reduced emissions by 137,000 tons annually through wind power, and the 14 stores in Northern Ireland are powered by wind energy. The Environmental Protection Agency's Green Power Partnership Program ranks Walmart as the second largest purchaser of green power among its U.S. retail competitors and third largest purchaser in the Fortune 500. It is the second largest onsite green power generator in the United Sates.

To reduce energy consumption, Walmart facilities conserve energy in two major ways. First, most new stores include a "daylighting" feature enabling stores to dim or turn off lights as daylight increases and enters through skylights, thereby reducing the demand for electricity during peak hours. Second, Walmart manages energy consumption by centrally controlling the heating and cooling of U.S. Walmart stores. The company is opening U.S. stores with LED lighting and is in the process of replacing their open freezers with secondary loop refrigeration systems. This is to meet their goal of reducing greenhouse gas emissions by 20 million metric tons globally by 2015. Walmart is attempting to reduce fossil fuel use and sell more "green" products. Through the use of its networks, Walmart is able to ship more products while traveling fewer miles, resulting in a reduction of carbon emissions of 41,000 tons.

The retailer has also begun selling more products made from sustainable or recycled materials and has taken efforts to reduce packaging. For example, the firm is selling preschool toys made from wood that is Forest Stewardship Council-certified. Walmart also started a program to sell more local produce (produce grown and sold in the same state). At the end of 2012, they increased sales of locally grown produce by 97 percent. Walmart is also investing in medium and smaller-sized farms, particularly in emerging economies.

To measure the sustainability of its products and suppliers, Walmart has launched its Sustainability Index. This index consists of three parts, each with its own goal. The first goal creates a more transparent supply chain in terms of sustainability. As part of the first step to achieving this goal, Walmart surveyed suppliers about their companies' sustainability. The second step involves forming a consortium of universities, suppliers, NGOs, government officials, and retailers to create a database on product life cycles, enabling Walmart and other companies to understand more about the sustainability of their products. The third step involves conveying this information to consumers to help them make informed decisions.

In line with their zero waste goals, Walmart Mexico has been successful in converting 1.2 million pounds of used cooking oil into biodiesel, soap, and supplements for cattle feed as well as composting over 1,900 metric tons of organic waste. The company has also been testing recycling methods, which it aims to incorporate into all of its stores over the next three years. Walmart's recycling efforts have allowed the company to reduce its global plastic bag waste by 35 percent since 2007. The company has been able to keep 80 percent of its U.S. operational waste out of landfills.

Although Walmart's environmental overhaul is a step in the right direction, some are skeptical as to whether it can accomplish its goals. Suppliers are worried that products receiving higher "sustainability" rankings might be given preferential treatment over their own. Also, the concept of "being green" is subjective, since not everyone agrees on how it is defined or whether one environmentally friendly practice is more beneficial than another. Despite these obstacles, Walmart has achieved some success in this area because of its dedication to its goals and the strength of its partnerships.

WHAT IS WALMART DOING TO IMPROVE ETHICS AND SOCIAL RESPONSIBILITY?

Walmart is working to improve its ethical reputation along with its reputation for sustainability and corporate governance. In 2004 Walmart formed its Global Ethics Office and released a revised Global Statement of Ethics. The intent of the Global Ethics Office is to spread an ethical corporate culture among its global stakeholders. The Global Ethics Office provides guidance on ethical decision making based on the Global Statement of Ethics and an ethics helpline. The helpline is an anonymous and confidential way for associates to contact the company regarding ethical issues. Additionally, Walmart has an Ethical Standards Team to monitor the compliance of supplier factories with the company's "Standards for Suppliers" and local laws. Walmart claims that in a period of several months the firm interviewed 1,000 market personnel in various countries, dedicated $35 million to new processes and procedures, and developed ethical training sessions for more than 19,000 associates.

Walmart has also contributed significantly to disaster management projects, economic empowerment for women, and supplier development. The company donated over $1.5 million in aid for the victims of Hurricane Sandy, including money, food, and goods. Walmart allocates $2 million in grants for associates whose homes are damaged and created a toll-free number for associates needing help. In terms of increasing opportunities for women, Walmart made a commitment in partnering with 150 factories and 60,000 women to teach women valuable skills to help them escape poverty. Additionally, Walmart created the Supplier Development Program, a partnership that works with 100 suppliers annually with the intent to improve their factories' productivity and working conditions.

The company has also recently embarked on a health initiative to address the growing problem of obesity in America. Walmart U.S. President Bill Simon met with First Lady Michelle Obama to discuss the issue. Walmart announced it would lower the prices of its fruits and vegetables and reduce the amounts of fats, sugars, and salts in the foods it sells. Specifically, the company formulated goals that include cutting sodium by 25 percent and sugars by 10 percent in food under its Great Value brand over a five-year period. By putting its weight behind solving the obesity epidemic, the world's largest retailer might be able to create significant change toward healthier eating habits.

Walmart Today

Walmart remains the preferred shopping destination of many consumers, particularly after the financial meltdown of 2008–2009. Although Walmart prospered during the recession while other retailers suffered, the company's U.S. sales have begun to decline. Walmart itself acknowledged that it strayed from Sam Walton's original vision of everyday low prices in order to court higher-income customers. Several initiatives, such as Walmart's adoption of organic food and trendy clothes, did not achieve much success with discount shoppers. Walmart also underwent a renovation effort that cut certain products, such as fishing tackle, from its stores. These actions alienated Walmart's original customer base. Households earning less than $70,000 annually defected to discounters like Dollar Tree and Family Dollar. Analysts believe Walmart's mistake was trying to be everything to everyone, along with copying its more "chic" rivals like Target. Because of these blunders, Walmart's domestic sales are experiencing a slump. As a result, Walmart is returning to Sam Walton's original vision and returning to its "everyday low prices" mantra. The company unleashed a new campaign, "It's Back," to signal the return of the merchandise it removed. Walmart executives are encouraging store managers to compare prices with competitors to ensure Walmart offers the lowest prices.

In spite of these problems at its domestic stores, Walmart's revenues are on the rise thanks to its international stores. While domestic sales remain flat, the company continues to expand internationally to make up for lower growth in the home market. This strategy requires Walmart to adapt to different social, cultural, regulatory, economic, and political factors. Walmart is known for its ability to adapt quickly to different environments, but even this large-scale retailer has experienced trouble. For instance, it closed its stores in Germany and South Korea after failing to interest the local population. The more Walmart expands internationally, the more the company must decide what concessions it is willing to make to enter certain markets.

Despite the difficulties of operating globally, Walmart has achieved a number of successes. After years of struggling in the Japanese market, for example, Walmart began turning a profit in 2008 through its acquisition of Japanese retailer Seiyu Ltd. Walmart is investing heavily in its Canadian operations and acquired a majority stake in South African firm Massmart Holdings Ltd. Though the company will likely experience several bumps in the road, its international markets appear to offer strong growth potential.

The Future of Walmart

Walmart can be viewed through two very different lenses. Some think the company represents all that is wrong with America, while others love it. In response to criticism, and in an attempt to initiate goodwill with consumers, the company has continued to improve stakeholder relationships and made efforts to demonstrate it is an ethically responsible company. Although it has faced controversy regarding competition, suppliers, employees, and global corruption, it has also demonstrated concern for sustainability initiatives and social responsibility. Its goals of decreasing its waste and carbon emissions extend to all facets of its operations, including suppliers. These efforts demonstrate Walmart's desire (whether through genuine concern for the environment or for its own bottom-line profits) to become a more sustainable company.

Similarly, Walmart's creation of an ethics and compliance program shows it has come a long way since its beginning, when formal ethics programs were deemed unnecessary. However, without strong monitoring systems and a commitment from top management to enforce the company's ethical policies, such efforts will prove fruitless. Overseas bribery scandals and employee discontent has tarnished Walmart's reputation. As a result, the company is working to improve internal control mechanisms and supplier auditing. Both critics and supporters of Walmart alike are waiting to see whether Walmart's efforts will position the company as a large retailer dedicated to social responsibility.

QUESTIONS

1. Do you think Walmart is doing enough to become more sustainable?
2. What are the ethical issues Walmart has faced?
3. How is Walmart attempting to answer concerns regarding misconduct?

SOURCES

James Arkin, "D.C. Council panel hears testimony on 'living wage' bill targeting large retailers," *The Washington Post*, March 20, 2013, http://articles.washingtonpost.com/2013-03-20/local/37864098_1_minimum-wage-retailers-outlets (accessed May 13, 2013); Associated Press, "Ex-Wal-Mart Vice Chairman Pleads Guilty in Fraud Case," *The Wall Street Journal*, January 31, 2006; The Associated Press, "Wal-Mart at-a-glance," *The Wall Street Journal*, February 5, 2011, http://online.wsj.com/article/AP34bbe45fa23c495983e16f1a72669698.html (accessed February 6, 2011); Vikas Bajaj, "India Unit of Wal-Mart Suspends Employees," *The New York Times*, November 23, 2012, http://www.nytimes.com/2012/11/24/business/global/wal-marts-india-venture-suspends-executives-as-part-of-bribery-inquiry.html?_r=0 (accessed April 19, 2013); James Bandler, "Former No. 2 at Wal-Mart Set to Plead Guilty," *The Wall Street Journal*, January 7, 2006, A1; James Bandler and Ann Zimmerman, "A Wal-Mart Legend's Trail of Deceit," *The Wall Street Journal*, April 8, 2005, A10; Shelly Banjo, "Can Wal-Mart Think Small," *The Wall Street Journal*, May 17, 2012, http://online.wsj.com/article/SB10001424052702303879604577408540682212740.html (accessed April 19, 2013); Shelly Banjo, "Wal-Mart Ads Tout 'American Success Story'," *The Wall Street Journal*, May 3, 2013, http://online.wsj.com/article/SB10001424127887324582004578460973584445016.html (accessed May 8, 2013); Shelly Banjo, "Wal-Mart Cheer: I-n-t-e-g-r-i-t-y," *The Wall Street Journal*, May 31, 2012, B3; Shelly Banjo, "Wal-Mart to Monitor Warehouses," *The Wall Street Journal*, December 28, 2012, B4; Shelly Banjo, "Wal-Mart Toughens Supplier Policies," *The Wall Street Journal*, February 22, 2013, B1, B7.Shelly Banjo, "Wal-Mart Will Tie Executive Pay to Compliance Overhaul," *The Wall Street Journal*, April 23, 2013, B8; Shelly Banjo and Ann Zimmerman, "Protestors Wage Campaign Against Wal-Mart," *The Wall Street Journal*, November 23, 2012, http://online.wsj.com/article/SB10001424127887323713104578136992890118444.html (accessed April 19, 2013); Shelly Banjo, Ann Zimmerman, and Suzanne Kapner, "Wal-Mart Crafts Own Bangladesh Safety Plan," *The Wall Street Journal*, May 15, 2013, B1-B2; Michael Barbaro, "Image Effort by Wal-Mart Takes a Turn," *The New York Times*, May 12, 2006, C1, C4; David Barstow, "Vast Mexico Bribery Case Hushed Up by Wal-Mart After Top-Level Struggle," *The New York Times*, April 21, 2012, http://www.nytimes.com/2012/04/22/business/at-wal-mart-in-mexico-a-bribe-inquiry-silenced.html?pagewanted=all (accessed April 19, 2013); Susan Berfield, "Walmart vs. Walmart," *Bloomberg Businesweek*, December 13, 2012, pp. 53-60; Ira Boudway, "Labor Disputes, the Walmart Way," *Bloomberg Businessweek*, December 13, 202, http://www.businessweek.com/articles/2012-12-13/labor-disputes-the-walmart-way (accessed April 19, 2013); Abram Brown, "Wal-Mart Bribery Probe Expands Past Mexico To Brazil, China, And India," *Forbes*, November 15, 2012, http://www.forbes.com/sites/abrambrown/2012/11/15/probe-into-wal-mart-bribery-past-mexico-to-brazil-china-and-india/ (accessed April 19, 2013); Chris Burritt, "Wal-Mart Overseas Expansion to Accelerate, CEO Says (Update5)," *Bloomberg Businessweek*, June 2, 2010, http://www.businessweek.com/news/2010-06-02/wal-mart-overseas-expansion-to-accelerate-ceo-says-update5-.html (accessed February 8, 2011); Miguel Bustillo and Timothy W. Martin, "Beyond the Big Box: Wal-Mart Thinks Smaller," *The Wall Street Journal*, April 28, 2010, B1; Miguel Bustillo, "Wal-Mart Faces Risk in Mexican Bribe Probe," *The Wall Street Journal*, April 23, 2012, http://online.wsj.com/article/SB10001424052702303978104577360283629622556.html (accessed April 19, 2013); Miguel Bustillo, "Wal-Mart Pledges to Promote Healthier Foods," *The Wall Street Journal*, January 20, 2011, http://online.wsj.com/article/SB10001424052748704881304576093872178374258.html (accessed May 8, 2013); Miguel Bustillo, "Wal-Mart to Assign New 'Green Ratings'," *The Wall Street Journal*, July 16, 2009, http://online.wsj.com/article/SB124766892562645475.html (accessed May 8, 2013); Miguel Bustillo, Miguel, "Wal-Mart Merchandise Goes Back to Basics," *The Wall Street Journal*, April 11, 2011, B3; Miguel Bustillo, "Wal-Mart Tries to Recapture Mr. Sam's Winning Formula," *The Wall Street Journal*, February 22, 2011, A1, A11; Miguel Bustillo, "With Sales Flabby, Wal-Mart Turns to Its Core," *The Wall Street Journal*, March 21, 2011, B1, B8; Stephanie Clifford, "More Dissent Is Expected Over a Wal-Mart Scandal," *The New York Times*, June 6, 2013, http://www.nytimes.com/2013/06/07/business/more-dissent-is-in-store-over-wal-mart-scandal.html?pagewanted=all&_r=1& (accessed July 9, 2013); Stephanie Clifford, "Wal-Mart Gains in Its Wooing of Chicago," June 24, 2010, *The New*

York Times, www.nytimes.com/2010/06/25/business/25walmart.html (accessed May 8, 2013); Stephanie Clifford, "Wal-Mart to Buy More Local Produce," *The New York Times*, October 14, 2010, http://www.nytimes.com/2010/10/15/business/15walmart.html (accessed May 8, 2013); Andrew Clark, "Wal-Mart, the U.S. retailer, taking over the world by stealth," guardian.co.uk, http://www.guardian.co.uk/business/2010/jan/12/walmart-companies-to-shape-the-decade (accessed April 19, 2013); Lauren Coleman-Lochner, "Independent Look at Wal-Mart Shows Both Good and Bad: With Savings and Jobs Come Falling Wages and Rising Medicaid Costs," *The San Antonio Express-News*, November 5, 2005, 4D; Anne d'Innocenzio, "Wal-Mart executive Leslie Dach to leave June," *Yahoo! News*, March 8, 2013, http://news.yahoo.com/wal-mart-executive-leslie-dach-162826265.html (accessed May 8, 2013); Renee Dudley, "Customers Flee Wal-Mart Empty Shelves for Target, Costco," *Bloomberg*, March 26, 2013, http://www.bloomberg.com/news/2013-03-26/customers-flee-wal-mart-empty-shelves-for-target-costco.html (accessed April 19, 2013); Lauren Etter, "Gauging the Wal-Mart Effect," *The Wall Street Journal*, December 3–4, 2005, A9; Charles Fishman, "The Wal-Mart You Don't Know: Why Low Prices Have a High Cost," *Fast Company*, December 2003, 68–80; Mei Fong and Ann Zimmerman, "China's Union Push Leaves Wal-Mart with Hard Choice," *The Wall Street Journal*, May 13–14, 2006, A1, A6; Fortune, "World's Most Admired Company," *CNNMoney*, http://money.cnn.com/magazines/fortune/most-admired/2012/full_list/ (accessed April 19, 2013). Emily Jane Fox, "Wal-Mart Toughens Regulations After Bangladesh Fire," *CNNMoney*, January 22, 2013, http://money.cnn.com/2013/01/22/news/companies/walmart-supplier-regulations/index.html (accessed April 19, 2013); Global Insight, "Global Insight Releases New Study on the Impact of Wal-Mart on the U.S. Economy," http://www.globalinsight.com/MultiClientStudy/MultiClientStudyDetail2438.htm (accessed January 23, 2005); Steven Greenhouse, "Documents Indicate Wal-Mart Blocked Safety Push," *The New York Times*, December 5, 2012, http://www.nytimes.com/2012/12/06/world/asia/3-walmart-suppliers-made-goods-in-bangladeshi-factory-where-112-died-in-fire.html (accessed April 19, 2013); Steven Greenhouse and Stephanie Clifford, "Wal-Mart steps up efforts to supress strike," *The New York Times*, November 20, 2012, 15; Alice Hines, "Walmart's New Health Policy Shifts Burden to Medicaid, Obamacare," *The Huffington Post*, December 1, 2012, http://www.huffingtonpost.com/2012/12/01/walmart-health-care-policy-medicaid-obamacare_n_2220152.html (accessed April 19, 2013); John Jannarone, "Wal-Mart's Tough Work Experience," *The Wall Street Journal*, February 23, 2011, C 14; Marcus Kabel, "Wal-Mart at War: Retailer Faces Bruised Image, Makes Fixes," *Marketing News*, January 15, 2006, 25; Hadley Malcolm, "Scraping by at Walmart," *USA Today*, June 7, 2012, http://usatoday30.usatoday.com/MONEY/usaedition/2012-06-08-Walmart-workers-strugglenew--_CV_U.htm (accessed April 19, 2013); Sagar Malviya, "Anti-Bribery Saga in India: Walmart puts new outlets in freezer," *The Economic Times*, March 13, 2013, http://articles.economictimes.indiatimes.com/2013-03-13/news/37683765_1_bharti-walmart-new-stores-new-outlets (accessed April 19, 2013); Devon Maylie, "Africa Learns the Wal-Mart Way," *The Wall Street Journal*, September 6, 2012, http://online.wsj.com/article/SB10000872396390443517104577574551277530954.html (accessed April 19, 2013); Daniel McGinn, "Wal-Mart Hits the Wall." *Newsweek*, November 14, 2005, 44–46; Kimberly Morrison, "Coughlin's Sentence Will Stand: U.S. Attorney Will Not Appeal," NWA Online, March 28, 2008, http://www.nwaonline.net/articles/2008/03/29/news/032908wzcoughlinappeal.txt (accessed February 21, 2009); *Newser*, "Wal-Mart Will Pay \$640M to Settle Wage Lawsuits," http://www.newser.com/story/46142/wal-mart-will-pay-640m-to-settle-wage-lawsuits.html?utm_source=ssp&utm_medium=cpc&utm_campaign=story, December 23, 2008 (accessed April 19, 2013); Al Norman, "The Case against Wal-Mart," Raphel Marketing, 2004; Karen Olsson, "Up against Wal-Mart," *Mother Jones*, March/April 2003, http://www.motherjones.com/politics/2003/03/against-wal-mart (accessed April 19, 2013); Jayne O'Donnell, "Wal-Mart guilty of dumping hazardous waste," *USA Today*, May 29, 2013, 2B; Reuters, "Ex-Wal-Mart Exec Pleads Guilty to Fraud Case, Tax Evasion," *Fox News*, January 31, 2006, http://www.foxnews.com/story/0, 2933, 183341, 00.html (accessed April 19, 2013); Margaret Rhodes, "Mini-(Wal)mart vs. Micro-Target: Inside the Battle for the Next Frontier of Big-Box Retail," *Fast Company*, January 12, 2011, 32; Steve Quinn, "Wal-Mart Green with Energy," *The Fort Collins Coloradoan*, July 24, 2005, E1–E2; Kate Rockwood, "Will Wal-Mart's 'Sustainability Index' Actually Work?" *Fast Company*, February 1, 2010, http://www.fastcompany.

com/magazine/142/attention-walmart-shoppers-clean-up-in-aisle-nine.html (accessed May 8, 2013); Mariko Sanchanta, "Wal-Mart Bargain Shops for Japanese Stores to Buy," *The Wall Street Journal*, November 14, 2010, http://online.wsj.com/article/SB10001424052748704327704575613861567263350.html (accessed May 8, 2013); Kyle Smith, "You Won't Believe The Stupidity Of The Latest Attack On Walmart," *Forbes*, March 21, 2013, http://www.forbes.com/sites/kylesmith/2013/03/21/you-wont-believe-the-stupidity-of-the-latest-attack-on-walmart/ (accessed May 13, 2013); Robert Smith, "New York City Officials to Wal-Mart: Keep Out," *NPR*, February 4, 2011, http://www.npr.org/2011/02/04/133483848/new-york-city-officials-to-walmart-keep-out (accessed April 19, 2013); Greg Stohr, "Wal-Mart vs. a Million Angry Women," *Bloomberg Businessweek*, November 22–28, 2010, 39–40; "Top companies: Biggest," *CNN*, http://money.cnn.com/magazines/fortune/fortune500/2011/performers/companies/biggest/employees.html (accessed April 19, 2013); Rick Ungar, "Walmart Pays Workers Poorly and Sinks while Costco Pays Workers Well and Sails—Proof that You Get What You Pay For," *Forbes*, April 17, 2013, walmart-pays-workers-poorly-and-sinks-while-costco-pays-workers-well-and-sails-proof-that-you-get-what-you-pay-for (accessed April 19, 2013); United States Security and Exchange Commission, "Wal-Mart Stores, Inc.," January 31, 2008, http://msnmoney.brand.edgar-online.com/EFX_dll/EDGARpro.dll?FetchFilingHTML1?ID=5835838&SessionID=5Rgc WZDBP11rCl9 (accessed May 8, 2013); Walmart, *Beyond 50 years: Building a sustainable future*, 2012 Global Sustainability Report, http://www.walmartstores.com/sites/responsibility-report/2012/pdf/WMT_2012_GRR.pdf (accessed May 8, 2013); Walmart, "Environmental Sustainability," http://walmartstores.com/Sustainability/7785.aspx (accessed May 8, 2013); Walmart, "Five-Year Financial Summary," http://www.walmartstores.com/sites/annual-report/2012/WalMart_Financials.pdf (accessed April 19, 2013); Walmart, "Frequently Asked Questions," http://stock.walmart.com/investor-faqs (accessed April 19, 2013); Wal-Mart, "Global Ethics Office," https://www.walmartethics.com/ (accessed May 8, 2013); Walmart, "Hurricane Disaster Response," http://news.walmart.com/disaster-response (accessed May 8, 2013); Walmart, "Our Initiatives," http://corporate.walmart.com/global-responsibility/ethical-sourcing/our-initiatives (accessed May 8, 2013); Walmart, "Sustainability Index," http://corporate.walmart.com/global-responsibility/environment-sustainability/sustainability-index (accessed April 19, 2013). Walmart, "Walmart Announces New Commitments to Drive Sustainability Deeper into the Company's Global Supply Chain," October 25, 2012, http://news.walmart.com/news-archive/2012/10/25/walmart-announces-new-commitments-to-drive-sustainability-deeper-into-the-companys-global-supply-chain (accessed April 19, 2013); Walmart, "The Wal-Mart Foundation," http://walmartstores.com/CommunityGiving/203.aspx (accessed May 8, 2013); Walmart, "Walmart Giving in Last Fiscal Year Exceeds $1 Billion for the First Time," April 22, 2013, http://news.walmart.com/news-archive/2013/04/22/walmart-giving-in-last-fiscal-year-exceeds-1-billion-for-the-first-time (accessed May 13, 2012). Walmart, "Walmart Statement in Response to December 17 New York Times Article About Allegations of Corruption in Mexico," http://news.walmart.com/news-archive/2012/12/17/walmart-statement-in-response-to-new-york-times-article-about-allegations-of-corruption-in-mexico (accessed May 8, 2013); Walmart, "Wal-Mart's Healthcare Benefits Are Competitive in the Retail Sector," February 8, 2011, http://walmartstores.com/pressroom/news/5575.aspx (accessed May 8, 2013); "Wal-Mart Concedes China Can Make Unions," *China Daily*, November 23, 2004, http://www.chinadaily.com.cn/english/doc/2004-11/23/content_394129.htm (accessed May 8, 2013); Wal-Mart Watch, "Event Highlights the Wal-Mart Health Care Crisis: New Study Declares Wal-Mart in Critical Condition," Making Change at Walmart, November 16, 2005, http://makingchangeatwalmart.org/2005/11/16/the-wal-mart-health-care-crisis-new-study-declares-wal-mart-in-critical-condition/ (accessed May 8, 2013); Wal-Mart Watch, "Is Wal-Mart Really a 'Green' Company?" http://walmartwatch.com/img/blog/environmental_fact_sheet.pdf (accessed May 8, 2013); "Walmart's Mexican morass," *The Economist*, April 28, 2012, 71; Jack and Suzy Welch, "Whistleblowers: Why You Should Heed Their Warnings," *Fortune*, June 11, 2012, 86; Stuart Weinberg and Phred Dvorak, "Wal-Mart's New Hot Spot: Canada," *The Wall Street Journal*, January 27, 2010, B3; Jessica Wohl, "'No' votes jump against Wal-Mart CEO, directors," *Reuters*, June 4, 2012, http://www.reuters.com/article/2012/06/04/us-walmart-vote-idUSBRE8530IR20120604 (accessed April 19, 2013). Jessica Wohl, "Walmart Sues Grocery Workers Union, Others Who Have Protested at Florida

Stores," *The Huffington Post*, March 25, 2013, http://www.huffingtonpost.com/2013/03/25/walmart-sues-protesters-florida-stores_n_2950992.html (accessed April 19, 2013); Syed Zain Al-Mahmood, Tripti Lahiri, and Dana Mattioli, "Fire Warnings Went Unheard," *The Wall Street Journal*, December 11, 2012, B1, B9; Ann Zimmerman, Anne. "Federal Officials Asked to Probe Wal-Mart Firing," Wake Up Wal-Mart, April 28, 2005, http://www.wakeupwalmart.com/news/20050428-wsj.html (accessed May 8, 2013).

CASE 4

Sustainability Challenges in the Gas and Oil Industry*

Despite the many controversies surrounding the economic and environmental effects of drilling for oil and gas, there is no denying the world's dependence on these commodities. It is estimated that total global demand for natural gas will reach over 4 trillion cubic meters by 2017. Global crude oil demand is already at 90 million barrels per day. While petroleum products are most often associated with machines or factories, they are also used to produce commercial products including plastic, pesticides, fertilizers, and even certain pharmaceuticals.

Unfortunately, the world's dependence on oil and gas has created significant challenges. The demand for oil depletes the world's oil reserves at an alarming rate; while there appears to be little agreement on when the world's oil reserves will be completely depleted, fears that demand is quickly outstripping supply have increased the drive toward investigating alternative energy sources. Additionally, the oil and gas industry has many risks. Safety is a large concern, and major accidents have caused the gas and oil industry to be highly criticized.

However, one of the greatest concerns of the oil and gas industry is the environmental risks associated with it. Drilling operations are accused of contributing to water pollution and the release of air contaminants into the atmosphere. These greenhouse gases in turn contribute to the warming of the Earth's atmosphere, leading to greater risks of polar ice cap melting, flooding, and other environmental damages. Yet what attracts the most attention are when oil and gas companies experience major disasters leading to massive environmental damage—namely, oil spills. Because many of the world's oil reserves are located beneath the ocean—requiring petroleum companies to use drilling rigs to extract the oil from beneath the surface of the ocean floor—any leak has the potential to create serious harm in a quick amount of time. Petroleum companies must guard against these industry-specific risks.

As a result of these risks, the oil and gas industry adopted safety procedures and processes meant to reduce their environmental impact and prevent these disasters from occurring. However, ethical lapses on the part of these companies have led to major environmental mishaps. The first oil spill that gained widespread attention in the United States was the *Exxon-Valdez* spill, important not only for its environmental impact but also for increasing the liability and responsibility oil companies have for cleanup and restoration. Despite the lessons learned from the *Exxon-Valdez* spill, two decades later an accident on

---

*This case was prepared by Jennifer Sawayda for and under the direction of O. C. Ferrell and Linda Ferrell. The case was prepared for classroom discussion rather than to illustrate either effective or ineffective handling of an administrative, ethical, or legal decision by management. All sources used for this case were obtained through publicly available material.

the *Deepwater Horizon* oil rig managed by BP led to the worst oil spill in U.S. history to date. Both disasters took place as a result of the companies ignoring ethical risk areas and, in some cases, taking risks that directly led to the disasters.

This analysis highlights the environmental risks of the oil industry by examining specific cases that have impacted stakeholder views on the industry's responsibility for sustainability. We begin by examining the *Exxon-Valdez* oil spill and the negligence that caused the disaster. Next, we describe some of the risks and causes of the BP *Deepwater Horizon* oil spill in 2010. However, our analysis would not be complete without considering the sustainability concerns of an emerging industry quickly gaining traction within the United States: hydraulic fracturing, or fracking, for shale gas. We conclude by emphasizing how oil and gas companies need to improve their safeguards to protect against environmental catastrophes. Ethical leadership and ethical responsibility at all management levels is needed to manage the risks of the industry.

THE WRECK OF THE EXXON VALDEZ

On March 24, 1989, the *Exxon Valdez* was under the command of Third Mate Gregory Cousins, who was not licensed to pilot the vessel through the waters of Prince William Sound. The ship's captain, Joseph Hazelwood, slept below deck. In an effort to dodge floating ice in the sound, Cousins performed what officials later described as an unusual series of right turns. The ship ran aground on Bligh Reef, spilling much of its cargo through the ruptured hull. According to the transcripts of radio conversations between Captain Hazelwood and the Coast Guard immediately after the accident, the captain tried for an hour to rock the tanker free from the reef. The Coast Guard claims that Hazelwood ignored their warnings that rocking the ship might make the oil spill much worse. The spill spread rapidly during the next few days, killing thousands of sea birds, sea otters, and other wildlife; covering the coastline with oil; and closing the fishing season in the sound for several years.

The Prince William Sound area was home to abundant wildlife. More than 200 species of birds had been reported there, including one-fifth of the world's trumpeter swans. The fishing industry derived annual sales of $100 million from the sound's abundant fish species, as well as crabs and shrimp. The world's largest concentration of killer whales and about one-fourth of the total U.S. sea otter population inhabited the sound at the time of the wreck. Later tests revealed Captain Hazelwood had a blood-alcohol content of 0.061, although it is a violation of Coast Guard regulations for a person operating a ship to have a blood-alcohol level in excess of 0.04. Exxon officials later admitted they knew the captain went through an alcohol detoxification program, yet they still gave him command of the *Exxon Valdez*, Exxon's largest tanker.

Response to the Disaster

From the onset the situation went from bad to worse. Alyeska Pipeline Service Co., one of the companies that operated the Trans-Alaska pipeline and the shipping terminal in Valdez, Alaska, was supposed to arrive shortly after the disaster to help contain the spill. After being notified of the accident, Alyeska Pipeline Service sent an observation tug to the scene and began to assemble its oil-spill containment equipment, much of which was in disarray. It loaded containment boom and lightering equipment (emergency pumps to suction oil from the *Exxon Valdez* onto other vessels) onto a damaged barge. The Coast Guard decided the barge was too slow and the need for the lightering equipment more urgent, so Alyeska crews reloaded the lightering equipment onto a tugboat, losing still more time.

The first Alyeska containment equipment did not arrive at the scene until hours after the disaster; the rest of the equipment came the next morning. Neither Alyeska nor Exxon had enough containment booms and chemical dispersants to fight the spill. They were not ready to test the effectiveness of the dispersants until 18 hours after the spill, and they conducted the test by tossing buckets of chemicals out the door of a helicopter. The helicopter's rotor dispersed the chemicals, and they missed their target. Moreover, the skimmer boats used to scoop oil out of the sea kept breaking down. The skimmers filled up rapidly and had to be emptied into nearby barges, taking them out of action for long periods of time. Cleanup efforts were further hampered by communication breakdowns between coordinators on shore and crews at the scene because of technical problems and limited range. In addition, although a fleet of private fishing boats stood by ready to assist with the containment and cleanup, Exxon and Alyeska failed to mobilize them. Because of inclement weather and other problems, by the end of the week the oil slick had spread to cover 2,600 miles of coastline and sea.

Some of the problems could have resulted from cutting safety corners. For instance, Alyeska convinced the Coast Guard that certain additional safety features were not needed on tankers. Its contingency plan underestimated the time needed for containing the spill, and it lacked equipment needed to contain the spill. Overall, Alyeska gave the impression that it was unprepared for a major disaster.

Exxon received blame as well. For instance, it saved $22 million by not building the *Exxon Valdez* with a second hull. At the time of the spill, Chairman Lawrence Rawl did not comment on the spill for nearly six days, and then he did so from New York. Although Rawl personally apologized for the spill, crisis-management experts say it is important for the chief executive to be present at the site of an emergency. Perhaps most damaging was Exxon's insistence that it would stop all cleanup operations on September 15, 1989, regardless of how much shoreline remained to be cleaned. In a memorandum released in July 1989, the September deadline was said to be "not negotiable." After much public and government protest, however, the company's president promised Exxon would return in the spring of 1990 if the Coast Guard determined further cleanup was warranted. Exxon returned that spring and for the next four years for further cleanup efforts.

The Aftermath

During the period of the oil spill, Exxon spent more than $2.2 billion for cleanup and reimbursements to the federal, state, and local governments. The company faced numerous lawsuits, including a lawsuit from the state of Alaska for mismanaging the response to the oil spill. In a civil settlement with the state of Alaska and the federal government, Exxon agreed to make ten annual payments totaling $900 million, for injuries to natural resources and services and the restoration and replacement of natural resources. In addition, $5 billion was awarded in punitive damages, to be divided evenly among the 14,000 commercial fishermen, natives, business owners, landowners, and native corporations that were part of the class-action suit. By 2009, that amount was reduced to $507 million.

In a criminal plea agreement, Exxon was fined $150 million, of which $125 million was remitted in recognition of its cooperation in cleaning up the spill and paying private claims. In addition, Exxon agreed to pay restitution of $50 million to the United States and $50 million to the state of Alaska.

Exxon, now called ExxonMobil, insists the area has completely recovered. However, a study by the National Marine Fisheries Service found toxins leaching from *Exxon Valdez* oil remaining on the beaches continued to harm sea life more than a decade after the disaster. Most of the oil is now subsurface and hardened into a semi-solid layer underwater, which poses less of a threat to plants and animals than liquid oil. Twenty acres of Prince William Sound shoreline are still contaminated, and there are several "pits" of oil and sludge in the area.

The one positive from the *Exxon Valdez* disaster is the industry has better response time to oil spills. However, has the oil industry learned from the mistakes of the *Exxon Valdez*? The 2010 *Deepwater Horizon* oil spill in the Gulf of Mexico suggests oil and gas companies still engage in risky behavior to increase profits.

DEEPWATER HORIZON OIL SPILL

For some years BP tried to change its image. After a series of major scandals, including a Texas refinery explosion that killed 15 employees, the firm expressed a renewed commitment to make safety and sustainability top priorities. For instance, the company changed its name to BP and then tried to rebrand itself as Beyond Petroleum. This rebranding signaled to stakeholders that it was focused on sustainability and the need to move beyond nonrenewable energy sources. It adopted an extensive code of conduct and invested heavily in alternative energy sources. BP was the first oil company to acknowledge global warming. But when a company tries to reposition itself as socially responsible and sustainable, it has an obligation to live up to its promises. BP's failures to do so became tragically clear when the *Deepwater Horizon* oil rig, operated under the oversight of BP, exploded in the Gulf of Mexico.

BP had subcontracted an oil rig from Transocean, Ltd. to tap into a new, highly profitable oil reservoir in the Gulf of Mexico. On April 20, 2010, an explosion rocked the rig, killing 11 employees. The burning rig sank two days later. A damaged oil well was leaking thousands of gallons of crude oil into the Gulf of Mexico, quickly creating an environmental catastrophe.

BP immediately started drilling other holes in the hopes they would relieve pressure on the damaged well, but these and other efforts proved unsuccessful. Soon as much as 2.5 million gallons of oil was pouring into the Gulf of Mexico daily. Oil washed up on the coasts of Louisiana, Texas, Alabama, Mississippi, and Florida, wreaking havoc on the livelihoods of fishermen and others dependent on the Gulf for income.

While the ocean rig had safety systems in place, these systems were not as safe as they could have been. For instance, the rig did not have a remote-control shut-off switch that could have been used as a last resort in a major spill (such a switch was not required by law). Investigations revealed BP's contingency plan in case of disaster was inadequate and contained many inaccuracies. One of the wildlife experts listed as an emergency responder had been dead since 2005. The contingency plan also estimated that should a spill occur, the company could recover about 500,000 barrels of oil per day. In reality, it took BP months to contain the leak, at a spill rate much less than that listed in the contingency plan. The inaccuracies in BP's contingency plan highlight how unprepared the company was for a disaster like the *Deepwater Horizon* spill.

What Caused the Explosion?

The explosion was likely caused by a number of events. Investigations suggest that actions on BP's part made the well more vulnerable. One investigation implies BP cut short procedures and quality testing of the pipe—tests meant to detect gas in the well. Some experts hypothesize that one of the final steps in installing the pipe, which involved cementing the steel pipe in place, could have been the catalyst for the explosion. The cement was not able to hold back the surging oil and gas that led to the explosion. In addition, BP decided to use a less costly well design that some Congressional investigators deemed "risky." Installation of this design is easier and costs are lower. However, it provides a better path for gas to rise outside the pipe. Although BP did not break any laws by using such a design, it ignored safer alternatives that might have prevented, or at least hindered, the accident.

Another reason why the spill became such a wide-scale disaster is likely due to a faulty blowout preventer. Instead of sealing the pipe completely, the blowout preventer blades stuck in the pipe, leaving enough space for oil to leak out. BP filed lawsuits against the manufacturer of the blowout preventer, Cameron International Corp. There is also some speculation that BP engineers ignored warning signs from safety tests conducted on the rig hours before the explosion. Two BP engineers who conducted negative pressure tests on the drilling rig recorded results they found to be confusing. However, after talking with others on the rig, one of the engineers gave the go-ahead. At the time there were no federal rules that clarified the test procedures.

Repercussions of the Disaster

The BP oil spill has wide-ranging repercussions for BP and the entire industry. An immediate consequence of the disaster was the resignation of BP CEO Tony Hayward. Despite an impressive track record, Hayward became the face of the worst oil spill in U.S. history. Additionally, the firm spent or will spend $36.5 billion on cleanup costs. In a lawsuit from the Justice Department, BP was ordered to pay a record $4.5 billion in fines and faced 14 counts of criminal acts, including felony manslaughter.

Drilling contractors and oil service companies also suffered from the spill because of plummeting stock values. The Obama administration issued a six-month moratorium on deepwater and oil gas drilling in the Gulf of Mexico, which shut down 33 deepwater rigs. With one-third of America's oil coming from the Gulf, the repercussions stemming from the spill will be felt for years to come.

The Aftermath

It took nearly three months to contain the oil leaking into the Gulf. In the interim, thousands of marine animals died in the oily waters, oil turned beaches black, and hundreds of people depending on the Gulf of Mexico lost part or all of their income. By the time the leak was sealed in August 2010, more than 640 miles of shoreline across several states were "tarred" with oil. The Gulf had suffered a massive loss of wildlife and was left with a tremendous amount of oil lurking beneath the water's surface. Scientists are finding evidence that oil has settled across several thousand square miles of seafloor, posing a potential threat to coral reefs and other marine life.

In an attempt to compensate stakeholders that depend on the Gulf, BP set aside $20 billion in an escrow fund, and a government-appointed administrator is overseeing the claims. Another issue that concerns the public is safety. Many worry about the safety of consuming seafood along the Gulf coast. It is largely unknown whether the oil and chemicals will have long-term effects on the quality of seafood. This situation demonstrates that it is often not enough for global companies involved in an ethical crisis to pay only for immediate costs like compensation; often they must pay for testing, additional safeguards, and environmental degradation in both the short and long term.

Such efforts are already underway. After the ousting of CEO Tony Hayward, Bob Dudley took over operations. While BP originally downplayed the disaster, Dudley freely admitted the incident was a "catastrophe" and the company was committed to the cleanup. BP hired former Federal Emergency Management Agency chief James Lee Witt and his public safety and crisis management consulting firm to help manage the incident and establish plans for long-term recovery. BP also created a safety organization given authority to stop operations whenever danger is detected.

Fracking: More Beneficial or Harmful to the Environment?

Hydraulic fracturing, or fracking, occurs when water, sand, or chemicals are pumped into shale rock to force natural gas to rise to the surface. Fracking has been around for approximately 60 years. However, only recently has this type of drilling attracted wide-scale media attention. One reason is the recent discovery of large shale gas reserves in the United States. Some scientists estimate that these reserves will last for more than 100 years. New hydraulic fracking techniques made it possible to drill for this gas, which increased 45 percent in a one-year period. This has created an energy boom that could lead the United States to energy independence. It also created more jobs in areas where wells are located, such as Pennsylvania and North Dakota. The Marcellus shale range in Pennsylvania is believed to have gas equivalent to 86 billion barrels of oil.

In addition to the economic benefits of fracking, proponents claim fracking results in greater sustainability than other traditional energy sources. Natural gas releases half the carbon emissions of oil and coal. Supporters claim natural gas is cleaner than coal because it releases less sulfur dioxide, nitrogen oxide, and mercury into the atmosphere. The benefits convinced supporters that fracking represents a revolutionary opportunity to reduce emissions and import natural gas to other countries. While fracking uses chemicals, it is estimated that fracking chemicals only consist of 0.5 percent of drilling fluid.

However, fracking carries significant risks as well. Fracking has been accused of releasing chemicals and methane into water near the drilling sites. Fracking also releases fast-moving gases such as methane into the atmosphere. There have even been accusations that fracking causes small seismic shifts in the area. Fracking also requires large amounts of water, from two to five million gallons per well. This means that while drilling fluid might only contain 0.5 percent of chemicals, the millions of gallons used per well results in a significant amount of chemicals used. While some of these chemicals are harmless, others, including benzene, diesel, and hydrochloric acid, have carcinogenic properties.

Critics also claim that hydraulic fracking is exempt from certain federal regulations that normally apply to drilling activities.

Proponents of fracking are quick to point out that proper procedures can greatly reduce the environmental risk. Ensuring the well-shafts are properly sealed can act as a strong deterrent against water contamination. This requires wells to be properly cemented. Fracking companies can attempt to reduce the amount of water used by recycling or reusing the water. The Environmental Protection Agency also determined that methane contaminating ground water might not be as serious as it appears. In one study of a town with high methane levels in its drinking water, the EPA found that the methane did not come from the fracking operations in the area.

However, the environmental risks of fracking are not to be taken lightly. New York and Vermont banned fracking activities, as well as certain countries such as France. Additionally, individuals have complained of environmental damage as a result of drilling activities. For instance, one couple reported that drilling blowouts on their land released chemicals into a creek, turning it white and igniting the water if lit. Health and safety is also a major concern. Randy Moyer, a worker for a hydraulic fracturing company who would climb into the vats and clean out the fracking fluid, was allegedly not told that the drilling mud is toxic and radioactive. He claims that he has suffered for more than a year from inflammation, migraines, trouble breathing, as well as many trips to the emergency room. Another couple claims the animals on their farm, which were previously healthy, began dying after they allowed drilling on their land. The couple themselves claims to suffer from headaches, nosebleeds, fatigue, and cirrhosis of the liver. Fracking has also lowered the values of homes; many people with fracking on their land have not been able to sell their houses. Unlike the *Exxon Valdez* and *Deepwater Horizon* disasters, fracking complaints are less on a massive scale and more from individuals living close to the drilling fields. Yet any type of major fracking disaster can have significant safety implications, since many fields are located close to highly populated areas.

Concerns also remain over the methane gas released from fracking activities. While methane's lifetime in the Earth's atmosphere is shorter than carbon emissions, its effects in trapping radiation are estimated to be 20 times greater. To combat these emissions, the EPA mandated that wells have pollution-control equipment to catch methane and other volatile gases such as benzene by 2015. New rules will limit the amount of methane emissions from fracking. There have also been promises from leaders of fracking organizations to increase the safety and sustainability of their activities. The CEO of company Tamboran, for instance, committed to stop using chemicals in the firm's Irish fracking operations. While the benefits of fracking seem promising, natural gas companies must take the time to analyze the environmental and safety impacts of their operations to avoid the risks of environmental degradation.

CONCLUSION

Developing an ethical organizational culture requires an examination of the risks to various stakeholders. In the case of the oil and gas industry, several companies failed to put in the safeguards necessary to protect employees, local communities, suppliers, and the viability of many industries. After the *Exxon-Valdez* disaster, there should have been a heightened awareness of the risks of offshore drilling and a mandate to implement every safeguard necessary to protect the environment. Yet BP appeared to assume that such a disaster would not happen to them, despite previous safety issues at the firm. Much like in the *Exxon Valdez* disaster, BP failed to implement certain safeguards that might have prevented or lessened the scope of the disaster.

This corporate culture of risk taking must stop in order for the oil and gas industry to restore its reputation. This requires ethical leadership and effective ethics and compliance programs that reach all employees. Employees need to be educated that they are responsible for displaying leadership to avoid misconduct that could create an accident. While the nature of the industry makes certain risks inevitable, firms can develop improved safety measures and contingency plans to contain the disaster should things go wrong. Many actions occur when risks are present and there is a failure to observe existing ethical codes and policies. Companies involved in the lucrative field of hydraulic fracking can use the lessons from its predecessors to develop a culture that makes safety and environmental consideration top priorities during the drilling process. The industry has a new responsibility to provide leadership in safety and sustainability. The reputation of the oil and gas industry is dependent on its ability to commit to a socially responsible approach and stakeholder engagement.

QUESTIONS

1. How does managing ethical risk in the oil and gas industry relate to reducing accidents?
2. Compare the risks that BP, Exxon, and the fracking industry continue to face in providing an adequate supply of energy?
3. How can ethical leadership help the oil and gas industry to manage risk?

SOURCES

American Petroleum Institute, "Oil Spill Prevention and Response: It's in Everyone's Best Interest," http://www.api.org/resources/valdez/ (accessed Jun. 14, 1999); Jeffrey Ball, "BP Spill's Next Major Phase: Wrangling over Toll on Gulf," *The Wall Street Journal*, April 13, 2011, http://online.wsj.com/article/SB1000142405274870401360457624853153 0234442.html (accessed May 15, 2013); Jeffrey Ball, "Strong Evidence Emerges of BP Oil on Seafloor," *The Wall Street Journal*, December 9, 2010, A20; Jeffrey Ball, Stephen Power, and Russell Gold, "Oil Agency Draws Fire," *The Wall Street Journal*, May 4, 2010, A1; Kathy Barks Hoffman, "Oil Spill's Cleanup Costs Exceed $1.3B," *USA Today*, Jul. 25, 1989, B1; Wayne Beissert, "In *Valdez*'s Wake, Uncertainty," *USA Today*, Jul. 28, 19893 A; Joel K. Bourne, Jr. "The Deep Dilemma." *National Geographic*, October 2010, 40–53; Ellen Cantarow, "Fracking ourselves to death in Pennyslvania," *Grist*, http://grist.org/climate-energy/fracking-ourselves-to-death-in-pennsylvania/ (accessed May 23, 2013); Ben Casselman and Russell Gold, "BP Decisions Set Stage for Disaster." *The Wall Street Journal*, May 27, 2010, http://online.wsj.com/article/SB10001424052748704026204575266560930780190.html (accessed May 15, 2013); CBS News, "BP's Spill Contingency Plans Vastly Inadequate," June 9, 2010, http://www.cbsnews.com/stories/2010/06/09/national/main6563631.shtml (accessed May 15, 2013); Guy Chazan, "BP's Worsening Spill Crisis Undermines CEO's Reforms." *The Wall Street Journal*, May 3, 2010, A1; Ryan Dezember and Matt Day, "Oil-Drilling Boom Under Way," *The Wall Street Journal*, February 10, 2011, http://online.wsj.com/article/SB100014240 5274870485840457613455399056775o.html (accessed May 15, 2013); Carrie Dolan, "Exxon to Bolster Oil-Cleanup Effort After Criticism," *The Wall Street Journal*, May 11, 1989, A10; The Economist staff, "Shale of the century," *The Economist*, July 2, 2012, http://www.economist.com/node/21556242 (accessed May 15, 2013); Jim Efstathiou Jr. and

Kim Chipman, "The Great Shale Gas Rush", *Bloomberg BusinessWeek*, March 7-13, 2011, 25–28; Peter Elkind, David Whitford, and Doris Burke, "'An Accident Waiting to Happen'," *Fortune*, February 7, 2011, 107–132; Yousef Gamal El-Din, "US Energy Boom Is Great, Unless You're the Saudis," *CNBC*, May 15, 2013, http://www.cnbc.com/ id/100739228 (accessed May 15, 2013); Stuart Elliot, "Public Angry at Slow Action on Oil Spill," *USA Today*, Apr. 21, 1989 B1; Environmental Protection Agency, "Overview of Greenhouse Gases," http://epa.gov/climatechange/ ghgemissions/gases/ch4.html (accessed May 15, 2013); "Exxon Valdez Disaster Haunts Alaska 14 Years On," *Sydney Morning Herald*, Jan. 16, 2003, http://www.smh.com.au/articles/2003/01/15/1042520672374.html (accessed May 15, 2013); "Exxon Will Pay $3.5 Million to Settle Claims in Phase Four of *Valdez* Case," *BNA State Environment Daily*, Jan. 19, 1996; Tom Fowler, "BP Slapped With Record Fine," *The Wall Street Journal*, November 16, 2013, A1, A6; Tom Fowler and Russell Gold, "Engineers Deny Charges in BP Spill," *The Wall Street Journal*, November 19, 2012, A6; William Glasgall and Vicky Cahan, "Questions That Keep Surfacing After the Spill," *Business Week*, Apr. 17, 1989, 18; Russell Gold and Tom McGinty, "BP Relied on Cheaper Wells," *The Wall Street Journal*, June 19, 2010, http://online.wsj.com/article/NA_WSJ_PUB: SB10001424052748704289504575313010283981200.html (accessed May 15, 2013); Russell Gold, "BP Sues Maker of Blowout Preventer," *The Wall Street Journal*, April 21, 2011, B1; Angel Gonzalez and Brian Baskin, "'Static Kill' Begins, Raising New Hopes," *The Wall Street Journal*, August 4, 2010, http://online.wsj.com/article/SB10001424052748703545604575407251664344386.html (accessed May 15, 2013); Dan Harris, Claudia Acosta and Christina Ng, Lasting Effects of Exxon Valdez and the Future of the Gulf," *ABC World News*, July 18, 2010, http://abcnews.go.com/WN/exxon-valdez-lessons-bp-spill-gulf-mexico/ story?id=11194132&page=1 (accessed May 15, 2013); Kevin A. Hassett and Aparna Mathur, "Benefits of hydraulic fracturing," *American Enterprise Institute*, April 4, 2013, http://www.aei.org/article/economics/benefits-of-hydraulic-fracking (accessed May 15, 2013); Siobhan Hughes, "BP Deposits $3 Billion in Spill Fund," *The Wall Street Journal*, August 9, 2010, http://online.wsj.com/article/SB10001424052748704388504575419281620436778. html (accessed May 15, 2013); *Institute for Crisis Management Newsletter*, 4 (March 1995), 3; Neil King, Jr., "BP Claims Chief Faces Knotty Task," *The Wall Street Journal*, July 17–18, 2010, A5; Robert Jackson, "Expert answers your questions on fracking," *USA Today*,. April 24, 2013, http://content.usatoday.com/communities/sciencefair/ post/2012/04/expert-answers-your-questions-on-fracking/1#.UZP2gvUmx8E (accessed May 15, 2013); Rick Jervis, "New hurdles await survivors of drilling moratorium," *USA Today*, January 18, 2011, 3A; "Judge Cuts Exxon Valdez Punitive Damage Award," *Alaska Journal*, Dec. 16, 2002, http://www.alaskajournal.com/stories/121602/ loc_20021216003.shtml; Monica Langley, "U.S. Drills Deep into BP as Spill Drama Drags on," *The Wall Street Journal*, July 21, 2010, A1, A14; David Leonhardt, "Spillonomics: Underestimating Risk," *The New York Times*, May 31, 2010, http://www.nytimes.com/2010/06/06/magazine/06fob-wwln-t.html (accessed May 15, 2013); Charles McCoy and Ken Wells, "Alaska, U.S. Knew of Flaws in Oil-Spill Response Plans," *The Wall Street Journal*, Apr, 7,1989, A3; Peter Nulty, "The Future of Big Oil," *Fortune*, May 8, 1989, 46–49; Bruce Orwall, Monica Langley, and James Herron, "Embattled BP Chief to Exit," *The Wall Street Journal*, July 26, 2010, A1, A6; Tara Patel, "The French Say No to 'Le Fracking,'" *Bloomberg BusinessWeek*, April 4-10, 2011, 60–62; Natalie Phillips, "$3.5 Million Settles Exxon Spill Suit," *Anchorage Daily News*, Jan. 18, 1996, 113; Byron Pitts, "Exxon Valdez Oil Spill: 20 Years Later," CBS Evening News, February 2, 2009, http://www.cbsnews.com/stories/2009/02/02/eveningnews/ main4769329.shtml (accessed May 15, 2013); Jim Polson, BP Oil Is Biodegrading, Easing Threat to East Coast," *BusinessWeek*, July 28, 2010, http://www.businessweek.com/news/2010-07-28/bp-oil-is-biodegrading-easing-threat-to-east-coast.html (accessed May 11, 2011); Stephen Power and Ben Casselman, "White House Probe Blames BP, Industry in Gulf Blast," *The Wall Street Journal*, January 6, 2011, A2; Lawrence G. Rawl, letter to Exxon shareholders, Apr. 14, 1989; "Recordings Reveal Exxon Captain Rocked Tanker to Free It from Reef," [Texas A&M University] *Battalion*, Apr. 26, 1989, 1; Jim Roth, "The Shale Gas Revolution," *China Brief*, March 2012, pp. 14–15; Michael Satchell, with Steve Lindbeck, "Tug of War over Oil Drilling," *U.S. News & World Report*, Apr. 10, 1989, 47–48; Richard B. Schmitt, "Exxon, Alyeska May Be Exposed on Damages," *The Wall Street Journal*, Apr. 10, 1989, A8; Stratford P. Sherman,"Smart Way to Handle the Press," *Fortune*, Jun. 19, 1989, 69–75; Rich Smith, "Big Oil Isn't as Profitable as Everyone Thinks," *Daily Finance*, October 20, 2012, http://www.dailyfinance.com/2012/10/20/big-oil-isnt-as-profitable-as-everyone-thinks/ (accessed May 15, 2013); Jeff Short, Stanley Rice, and Mandy Lindeberg,

'The *Exxon Valdez* Oil Spill: How Much Oil Remains?" Alaska Fisheries Science Center, 2001, http://www.afsc. noaa.gov/Quarterly/jas2001/feature_jas01.htm (accessed May 15, 2013); "Status of Injured Resources & Services," *Exxon Valdez* Oil Spill Trustee Council, 2010, http://www.evostc.state.ak.us/recovery/status.cfm (accessed May 15, 2013); Allanna Sullivan and Amanda Bennett, "Critics Fault Chief Executive of Exxon on Handling of Recent Alaskan Oil Spill," *The Wall Street Journal*, Mar. 31, 1989, B1; Cassandra Sweet, "BP Will Pay Fine in Spills," *The Wall Street Journal*, May 4, 2011, B3; Tennille Tracy, "Firms Given Time on Fracking," *The Wall Street Journal*, April 19, 2012, A3; Bryan Walsh, "The Gas Dilemma," *Time*, April 11, 2011, 40–48; Vivienne Walt, "Can BP Ever Rebuild Its Reputation?" *Time*, July 19, 2010, http://www.time.com/time/business/article/0, 8599, 2004701-2, 00. html (accessed May 15, 2013); Harry R. Weber, and Greg Bluestein, "Dudley: Time for 'Scaleback' in BP Cleanup." *Time*, July 30, 2010, http://content.usatoday.com/communities/greenhouse/post/2010/07/bp-hayward-gulf-oil-spill/1#.UZQAk_Umx8E (accessed May 15, 2013); Jonathon Weisman, "In Western Pennsylvania, an Energy Boom Not Visibly Stifled," *The New York Times*, June 20, 2012, http://www.nytimes.com/2012/06/21/us/an-energy-boom-in-western-pennsylvania.html?pagewanted=all&_r=0 (accessed May 23, 2013); Ken Wells, "Alaska Begins Criminal Inquiry of Valdez Spill," *The Wall Street Journal*, Mar. 30, 1989, A4; Ken Wells, "Blood-Alcohol Level of Captain of Exxon Tanker Exceeded Limits," *The Wall Street Journal*, Mar. 31, 1989, A4; Ken Wells, "For Exxon, Cleanup Costs May Be Just the Beginning," *The Wall Street Journal*, Apr. 14, 1989, B1, B2; Ken Wells and Marilyn Chase, "Paradise Lost: Heartbreaking Scenes of Beauty Disfigured Follow Alaska Oil Spill," *The Wall Street Journal*, Mar. 31, 1989, A1, A4; Ken Wells and Charles McCoy, "How Unpreparedness Turned the Alaska Spill into Ecological Debacle," *The Wall Street Journal*, Apr. 3, 1989, A1, A4; Selina Williams, "For BP, the Cleanup Isn't Entirely Over," *The Wall Street Journal*, February 4, 2013, B2; Ben Wolfgang, "Methane study, EPA debunk claims of water pollution, climate change from fracking," *The Washington Times*, April 29, 2013, http://www. washingtontimes.com/news/2013/apr/29/pa-environment-agency-debunks-fracking-water-claim/?page=all (accessed May 15, 2013).

CASE 5

New Belgium Brewing: Ethical and Environmental Responsibility

Although most of the companies frequently cited as examples of ethical and socially responsible firms are large corporations, it is the social responsibility initiatives of small businesses that often have the greatest impact on local communities. These businesses create jobs and provide goods and services for customers in smaller markets that larger corporations are often not interested in serving. Moreover, they also contribute money, resources, and volunteer time to local causes. Their owners often serve as community leaders, and many choose to apply their skills and resources to tackling local problems and issues to benefit the whole community. Managers and employees become role models for ethical and socially responsible actions. One such small business is the New Belgium Brewing Company, Inc., based in Fort Collins, Colorado.

HISTORY OF THE NEW BELGIUM BREWING COMPANY

The idea for the New Belgium Brewing Company began with a bicycling trip through Belgium. Belgium is arguably the home of some of the world's finest ales, some of which have been brewed for centuries in the country's monasteries. As Jeff Lebesch, an American electrical engineer, cruised around Belgium on his mountain bike, he wondered if he could produce such high-quality beers back home in Colorado. After acquiring the special strain of yeast used to brew Belgian-style ales, Lebesch returned home and began to experiment in his Colorado basement. When his beers earned thumbs up from friends, Lebesch decided to market them.

The New Belgium Brewing Company (NBB) opened for business in 1991 as a tiny basement operation in Lebesch's home in Fort Collins. Lebesch's wife at the time, Kim Jordan, became the firm's marketing director. They named their first brew Fat Tire Amber Ale in honor of Lebesch's bike ride through Belgium. Initially, getting New Belgium beer onto store shelves was not easy. Jordan often delivered the beer to stores in the back of her Toyota station wagon. However, New Belgium beers quickly developed a small but devoted customer base, first in Fort Collins and then throughout Colorado. The brewery soon outgrew the couple's basement and moved into an old railroad depot before settling into its present custom-built facility in 1995. The brewery includes two brew houses, four quality assurance labs, a wastewater treatment facility, canning and bottling line, and numerous technological innovations for which New Belgium has become nationally recognized as a "paradigm of environmental efficiencies."

Under the leadership of Kim Jordan, who has since become CEO, New Belgium Brewing Company offers a variety of permanent and seasonal ales and pilsners. The company's standard line includes Sunshine Wheat, Blue Paddle, 1554, Ranger IPA, Abby, Trippel, and the original Fat Tire Amber Ale, still the firm's bestseller. Some customers refer to the company as the Fat Tire Brewery. The brewery also has seasonal ales Dig and Rolle Bolle (a summer ale). In addition, the firm started a Lips of Faith program, where small batch brews like La Folie, Biere de Mars, and Chocolate Stout are created for internal celebrations or landmark events. New Belgium works in collaboration (or colla-BEER-ation) with other craft brewers to come up with new products. Through this, they hope to create better efficiency and experimentation along with taking collaborative strides toward the future of American craft beer making. Products resulting from these collaborations are Ranger IPA and Biere de Garde.

NBB's most effective form of advertising is word of mouth. Indeed, before New Belgium beers were widely distributed throughout Colorado, one liquor-store owner in Telluride purportedly offered people gas money if they would stop by and pick up New Belgium beer on their way through Fort Collins. Although New Belgium expanded distribution to a good portion of the U.S. market, the brewery receives numerous e-mails and phone calls every day inquiring when its beers will be available in other parts of the country.

Although still a small brewery when compared to many beer companies, like fellow Coloradan Coors, NBB has consistently experienced strong growth with estimated sales of more than $100 million (because New Belgium is a private firm, detailed sales and revenue numbers are not available). It now has its own blog, Twitter, and Facebook pages. The organization sells more than 700,000 barrels of beer per year and has many opportunities for continued growth. For instance, while total beer consumption has remained flat, the market share of the craft beer industry is now at 6 percent. Growth for craft beer is likely to continue since new generations of beer drinkers appear to favor locally brewed beers.

Currently, New Belgium's products are distributed in 30 states plus the District of Columbia, with plans to begin distributing in Florida. Beer connoisseurs that appreciate the high quality of NBB's products, as well as the company's environmental and ethical business practices drove this growth. For example, when the company began distribution in Minnesota, the beers were so popular a liquor store opened early and made other accommodations for the large amount of customers. The store sold 400 cases of Fat Tire in the first hour it was open.

With expanding distribution the brewery recognized a need to increase its opportunities for reaching its far-flung customers. It hired Dr. Douglas Holt, an Oxford professor and cultural branding expert. After studying the company, Holt, together with former Marketing Director Greg Owsley, drafted a 70-page "manifesto" describing the brand's attributes, character, cultural relevancy, and promise. In particular, Holt identified in New Belgium an ethos of pursuing creative activities simply for the joy of doing them well and in harmony with the natural environment.

With the brand defined, New Belgium worked with New York advertising agency Amalgamated to create a $10 million advertising campaign. The campaign targeted high-end beer drinkers, men ages 25 to 44, and highlighted the brewery's down-to-earth image. The grainy ads focused on a man, Charles the Tinkerer, rebuilding a cruiser bike out of used parts and then riding it along pastoral country roads. The product appeared in just five seconds of each ad between the tag lines, "Follow Your Folly ... Ours Is Beer." With nostalgic music playing in the background, the ads positioned the growing brand as whimsical, thoughtful, and reflective. NBB later re-released its Tinkerer commercial during the U.S. Pro Challenge. The re-released commercial had an additional scene with the Tinkerer riding part way next to a professional cyclist contestant, with music from songwriter and Tour de Fat enthusiast Sean Hayes. The commercial was featured on NBC.

In addition to the ad campaign, the company maintains its strategy of promotion through event sponsorships and digital media. To launch its Ranger IPA beer, New Belgium created a microsite and an online video of its NBB sales force dressed as rangers performing a hip-hop number to promote the beer. Instead of horses, the NBB rangers rode bicycles. The purpose of the video was to create a hip, fun brand image for its new beer, with the campaign theme "To Protect. To Pour. To Partake."

NEW BELGIUM ETHICAL CULTURE

According to New Belgium, the company places great importance on the ethical culture of the brand. The company is aware that if it embraces citizenship in the communities it serves, it can forge enduring bonds with customers. More than ever before, what a brand says and what a company does must be synchronized. NBB believes that as the mandate for corporate social responsibility gains momentum, business managers must realize business ethics is not so much about the installation of compliance codes and standards as it is about the spirit in which such codes and standards are integrated. The modern-day brand steward—usually the most externally focused of the business management team—must be the internal champion of the bottom-line necessity for ethical, values-driven company behavior.

At New Belgium, a synergy of brand and values occurred naturally because the firm's ethical culture (in the form of core values and beliefs) was in place long before NBB had a marketing department. Back in early 1991, when New Belgium was just a fledgling home-brewed business, Jeff Lebesch and Kim Jordan took a hike into Rocky Mountain National Park armed with a pen and a notebook. There they took their first stab at what the company's core purpose would be. If they were going forward with this venture, what were their aspirations beyond profitability? What was at the heart of their dream? What they wrote down that spring day, give or take a little editing, are the core values and beliefs you can read on the NBB website today.

From the start, NBB adopted a triple bottom line (TBL) approach to business. Whereas the traditional bottom line approach for measuring business success is economic, TBL incorporates economic, social, and environmental factors. In other words, rather than just looking at financial data to evaluate company success, NBB looks at its impact on profits, people, and the planet. One way it is advancing the TBL approach is through the creation of a high-involvement corporate culture. All employees at NBB are expected to contribute to the company vision, and accountability is spread throughout the organization. Just about any New Belgium worker can list many, if not all, of these shared values. For NBB, branding strategies are rooted in its company values.

NEW BELGIUM'S PURPOSE AND CORE BELIEFS

New Belgium's dedication to quality, the environment, its employees, and its customers is expressed in its mission statement: "To operate a profitable brewery which makes our love and talent manifest." The company's stated core values and beliefs about its role as an environmentally concerned and socially responsible brewer include the following:

1. Remembering that we are incredibly lucky to create something fine that enhances people's lives while surpassing our consumers' expectations

2. Producing world-class beers

3. Promoting beer culture and the responsible enjoyment of beer

4. Kindling social, environmental, and cultural change as a business role model

5. Environmental stewardship: minimizing resource consumption, maximizing energy efficiency, and recycling

6. Cultivating potential through learning, participative management, and the pursuit of opportunities

7. Balancing the myriad needs of the company, staff, and their families

8. Trusting each other and committing ourselves to authentic relationships, communications, and promises

9. Continuous, innovative quality and efficiency improvements

10. Having Fun

Employees believe these statements communicate to customers and other stakeholders what New Belgium, as a company, is about. These simple values developed roughly 20 years ago are just as meaningful to the company and its customers today, even though there has been much growth.

EMPLOYEE CONCERNS

Recognizing employees' role in the company's success, New Belgium provides generous benefits for its employees. In addition to the usual paid health and dental insurance and retirement plans, employees get a catered lunch every month to celebrate employees' birthdays as well as a free massage once a year and they can bring their children and dogs to work. Employees who stay with the company for five years earn an all-expenses paid trip to Belgium to "study beer culture." Employees are also reimbursed one hour of paid time off for every two hours of volunteer work they perform. Perhaps most importantly, employees also earn stock in the privately held corporation that grants them a vote in company decisions. Employees currently own 100 percent of company stock. Open book management allows employees to see the financial costs and performance of the company. Employees are provided with financial training so they can understand the books and ask questions about the numbers.

New Belgium tries to get its employees involved not only in the company but in its sustainability efforts as well. To help their own sustainability efforts, employees are given a fat-tired cruiser bike after one year's employment so they can ride to work instead of drive. An onsite recycling center is also provided for employees. Additionally, each summer New Belgium hosts the Tour de Fat, where employees can dress in costumes and lead locals on a bike tour. Other company perks include inexpensive yoga classes, free beer at quitting time, and a climbing wall. To ensure workers' voices are heard, NBB has a democratically-elected group of co-workers called POSSE. POSSE acts as a liaison between the board, managers, and employees.

SUSTAINABILITY CONCERNS

New Belgium's marketing strategy involves linking the quality of its products, as well as its brand, with the company's philosophy of environmental friendliness. From leading-edge environmental gadgets and high-tech industry advancements to employee-ownership programs and a strong belief in giving back to the community, New Belgium demonstrates its desire to create a living, learning community. For consumers curious about where NBB gets its ingredients for its beers, the company provides a map showing the different states where it sources its materials.

NBB strives for cost-efficient energy-saving alternatives to conduct its business and reduce its impact on the environment. In staying true to the company's core values and beliefs, the brewery's employee–owners unanimously agreed to invest in a wind turbine, making New Belgium the first fully wind-powered brewery in the United States. NBB invested in the following energy-saving technologies:

- A smart grid installation that allows NBB to communicate with its electricity provider to conserve energy. For example, the smart grid alerts NBB to non-essential operational functions, allowing the company to turn them off and save power.

- The installation of a 20 kW photovoltaic array on top of the packaging hall. The array produces three percent of the company's electricity.

- A brew kettle, the second of its kind installed in the nation, that heats wort sheets instead of the whole kettle at once. This kettle heating method conserves energy more than standard kettles do.

- Sun tubes that provide natural daytime lighting throughout the brew house all year long.

- A system to capture waste water and extract methane from it. This can contribute up to 15 percent of the brewery's power needs while reducing the strain on the local municipal water treatment facility.

- A steam condenser that captures and reuses the hot water that boils the barley and hops in the production process to start the next brew. The steam is redirected to heat the floor tiles and de-ice the loading docks in cold weather.

New Belgium also strives to reduce waste through recycling and creative reuse strategies. The company diverts over 94 percent of its waste away from landfills. The company strives to recycle as many supplies as possible, including cardboard boxes, keg caps, office materials, and the amber glass used in bottling. The brewery also stores spent barley and hop grains in an on-premise silo and invites local farmers to pick up the grains, free of charge, to feed their pigs. Going further down the road to produce products for the food chain, NBB works with partners to take the same bacteria that creates methane from NBB wastewater and converts them into a harvestable, high-protein fish food. NBB also buys recycled products when it can, and encourages employees to reduce air pollution by using alternative transportation. Reduce, Reuse, Recycle—the three R's of environmental stewardship—are taken seriously at NBB. Figure 5.1 depicts New Belgium's 2011 recycling efforts:

Additionally, New Belgium has been a long-time participant in green building techniques. With each expansion of the facility, it incorporated new technologies and learned

FIGURE 5–1 **New Belgium's Recycling Efforts**

Information obtained from the New Belgium Brewing website, (http://www.newbelgium.com/sustainability/Environmental-Metrics.aspx) (accessed April 18, 2013).

a few lessons along the way. In 2002, NBB agreed to participate in the United States Green Building Council's Leadership in Energy and Environmental Design for Existing Buildings (LEED-EB) pilot program. From sun tubes and day lighting throughout the facility to reusing heat in the brew house, NBB continues to search for new ways to close loops and conserve resources.

New Belgium has made significant achievements in sustainability, particularly compared to other companies in the industry. For instance, New Belgium uses only 4.2 gallons of water to make 1 gallon of beer and intends to reduce this amount to 3.5 by 2015. The company is attempting to create a closed-loop system for their wastewater with its own Process Water Treatment Plant, where microbes are used to clean the wastewater. Today 100 percent of the brewery's electricity comes from renewables, and the company intends to reduce its energy intensity by 10 percent between 2008 and 2018. Despite these achievements, New Belgium has no intention of halting its sustainability efforts. By 2015, the company hopes to reduce the amount of water used to make beer by 10 percent through better production processes and decrease its carbon footprint by 25 percent per barrel. To encourage sustainability throughout the supply chain, NBB adopted Sustainable Purchasing

Guidelines. The Guidelines allow them to pinpoint eco-friendly suppliers and work with them closely to create sustainability throughout the entire value chain.

SOCIAL CONCERNS

Beyond its use of environmentally friendly technologies and innovations, New Belgium strives to improve communities and enhance people's lives through corporate giving, event sponsorship, and philanthropic involvement. Since its inception, NBB has donated more than $2.5 million to philanthropic causes. For every barrel of beer sold the prior year, NBB donates $1 to philanthropic causes within their distribution territories. The donations are divided between states in proportion to their percentage of overall sales. This is the company's way of staying local and giving back to the communities that support and purchase NBB products. NBB also participates in 1 Percent for the Planet, a philanthropic network to which the company donates 1 percent of its profits.

Funding decisions are made by New Belgium's Philanthropy Committee, comprised of employees throughout the brewery, including owners, employee–owners, area leaders, and production workers. New Belgium looks for nonprofit organizations that demonstrate creativity, diversity, and an innovative approach to their mission and objectives. The Philanthropy Committee also looks for groups that involve the community to reach their goals.

Additionally, NBB maintains a community bulletin board in its facility, where it posts an array of community involvement activities and proposals. This community board allows tourists and employees to see the different ways they can help out in the community, and it gives nonprofit organizations a chance to make their needs known. Organizations can apply for grants through the NBB website, with a link designated for this purpose. The company donates to causes with emphasis on water conservation, sensible transportation and bike advocacy, sustainable agriculture, and youth environmental education, among other areas.

NBB also sponsors a number of events, with a special focus on those involving "human-powered" sports that cause minimal damage to the natural environment. Through event sponsorships, such as the Tour de Fat, NBB supports various environmental, social, and cycling nonprofit organizations. In the Tour de Fat, one participant hands over his or her car keys and vehicle title in exchange for an NBB commuter bike and trailer. The participant is then filmed for the world to see as he or she promotes sustainable transportation over driving. New Belgium also partners with nonprofit organizations to support Skinny Dip for a Cause, a campaign where skinny dipping is used to raise awareness of water issues and conservation. In the course of one year, New Belgium can be found at 150 to 200 festivals and events across the nation.

ORGANIZATIONAL SUCCESS

New Belgium Brewing Company's efforts to live up to its own high standards have paid off with a loyal following—in fact, the company recently expanded the number of tours it offers at its facilities because of high demand. The company has been the recipient of numerous awards. Past awards for NBB include the *Business Ethics* Magazine's Business Ethics Award for its "dedication to environmental excellence in every part of its innovative brewing process," its inclusion in *The Wall Street Journal's* 15 best small workplaces, and the award for best mid-sized brewing company of the year and best mid-sized brewmaster at the Great American Beer Festival. New Belgium took home medals for three different brews: Abbey Belgian Style Ale, Blue Paddle Pilsner, and La Folie specialty ale.

According to David Edgar, former director of the Institute for Brewing Studies at the Brewers Association in Boulder, Colorado, "They've created a very positive image for their company in the beer-consuming public with smart decision-making." Although some members of society do not believe a company whose major product is alcohol can be socially responsible, New Belgium set out to prove that for those who make a choice to drink responsibly, the company will do everything possible to contribute to society. New Belgium also promotes the responsible appreciation of beer through its participation in and support of the culinary arts. For instance, it frequently hosts New Belgium Beer Dinners, in which every course of the meal is served with a complementary culinary treat.

Although New Belgium made great strides in creating a socially responsible brand image, its work is not done. New Belgium must continually reexamine its ethical, social, and environmental responsibilities. In 2004, New Belgium received the Environmental Protection Agency's regional Environmental Achievement Award. The award was both an honor and a motivator for the company to continue its socially responsible goals. After all, there are still many ways for NBB to improve as a corporate citizen. For example, although all electric power comes from renewable sources, the plant is still heated in part by using natural gas. There will always be a need for public dialogue on avoiding alcohol abuse. Additionally, continued expansion requires longer distances to travel for distributing the product, which increases the use of fossil fuels. As a way to deal with these longer distances, New Belgium announced it would open a second brewery in Asheville, North Carolina, to expand NBB's capacity. The new brewery is set to open in 2015. Practically speaking, the company has a never-ending to-do list.

NBB executives acknowledge that as its annual sales increase, so do the challenges to remain on a human scale and continue to be culturally authentic. How to boldly grow the brand while maintaining its humble feel has always been a challenge. Reducing waste to an even greater extent takes lots of work on behalf of both managers and employees, creating the need for a collaborative process that requires the dedication of both parties toward sustainability.

New Belgium faces increased competition from other craft breweries. It lags behind Boston Beer Co. (maker of Sam Adams beer) and Sierra Nevada in market share. Like New Belgium, Boston Beer Co. and Sierra Nevada plan to expand, with Boston Beer allocating $35 million for capital investment projects at breweries in Massachusetts, Pennsylvania, and Ohio in 2012. New Belgium competes against craft beer alternatives released by traditional breweries, such as MillerCoor's New Moon Belgian White. New Belgium must constantly engage in environmental scanning and competitive analysis to compete in this increasingly competitive environment.

Every six-pack of New Belgium Beer displays the phrase, "In this box is our labor of love. We feel incredibly lucky to be creating something fine that enhances people's lives." Although Jeff Lebesch and Kim Jordan divorced and Lebesch left the company to focus on other interests, the founders of New Belgium hope this statement captures the spirit of the company. According to employee Dave Kemp, NBB's social responsibilities give the company a competitive advantage because consumers want to believe in and feel good about the products they purchase. NBB's most important asset is its image—a corporate brand that stands for quality, responsibility, and concern for society. Defining itself as more than a beer company, the brewer also sees itself as a caring organization concerned for all stakeholders.

QUESTIONS

1. What environmental issues does the New Belgium Brewing Company work to address? How has NBB taken a strategic approach to addressing these issues? Why do you think the company has taken such a strong stance toward sustainability?
2. Do you agree that New Belgium's focus on social responsibility provides a key competitive advantage for the company? Why or why not?
3. Some segments of society contend that companies that sell alcoholic beverages and tobacco products cannot be socially responsible organizations because of the nature of their primary products. Do you believe New Belgium's actions and initiatives are indicative of a socially responsible corporation? Why or why not?

SOURCES

The facts of this case are from Peter Asmus, "Goodbye Coal, Hello Wind," *Business Ethics*, 13 (July/August 1999), 10–11; "A Tour of the New Belgium Brewery—Act One," *LiveGreen* blog, April 9, 2007, http://www.livegreensd.com/2007/04/tour-of-new-belgium-brewery-act-one.html (accessed April 13, 2012); Robert Baun, "What's in a Name? Ask the Makers of Fat Tire," [Fort Collins] *Coloradoan.com*, October 8, 2000, E1, E3; Robert F. Dwyer and John F. Tanner, Jr., *Business Marketing* (Irwin McGraw-Hill, 1999), 104; "Four Businesses Honored with Prestigious International Award for Outstanding Marketplace Ethics," *Better Business Bureau*, press release, September 23, 2002 http://www.bbb.org/alerts/2002torchwinners.asp; Julie Gordon, "Lebesch Balances Interests in Business, Community," *Coloradoan.com*, February 26, 2003; Del I. Hawkins, Roger J. Best, and Kenneth A. Coney, *Consumer Behavior: Building Marketing Strategy*, 8th ed. (Irwin McGraw-Hill, 2001); David Kemp, Tour Connoisseur, New Belgium Brewing Company, personal interview by Nikole Haiar, November 21, 2000; Steve Raabe, "New Belgium Brewing Turns to Cans," *Denver Post*, May 15, 2008, http://www.denverpost.com/breakingnews/ci_9262005 (accessed April 16, 2013); "New Belgium Brewing Wins Ethics Award," *Denver Business Journal*, January 2, 2003, http://www.bizjournals.com/denver/stories/2002/12/30/daily21.html (accessed April 16, 2013); New Belgium Brewing website, http://www.newbelgium.com (accessed April 16, 2013); Greg Owsley, "The Necessity For Aligning Brand with Corporate Ethics," in Sheb L. True, Linda Ferrell, O. C. Ferrell, *Fulfilling Our Obligation, Perspectiveson Teaching Business Ethics* (Atlanta, GA: Kennesaw State University Press, 2005), 128–132; Bryan Simpson, "New Belgium Brewing: Brand Building Through Advertising and Public Relations," *eBusiness Ethics*, http://e-businessethics.com/NewBelgiumCases/newbelgiumbrewing.pdf (accessed May 13, 2009); Kelly K. Spors, "Top Small Workplaces 2008," *The Wall Street Journal*, February 22, 2009 http://online.wsj.com/article/SB122347733961315417.html (accessed April 16, 2013); "Craft Beer industry continues to grow," *PJ Star*, March 26, 2012, Norman Miller http://www.pjstar.com/community/blogs/beer-nut/x140148153/Craft-Beer-industry-continues-to-grow (accessed April 16, 2013); "COLLABEERATIONS," *Elysian Brewing Company*, http://www.elysianbrewing.com/beer/collabeerations.html (accessed March 27, 2012); Devin Leonard, "New Belgium and the Battle of the Microbrews," *Bloomberg Businessweek*, December 1, 2011, http://www.businessweek.com/magazine/new-belgium-and-the-battle-of-the-microbrews-12012011.html (accessed March 27, 2012); *Corporate Sustainability Report*, New Belgium Brewing website, http://www.newbelgium.com/culture/alternatively_empowered/sustainable-business-story.aspx (accessed April 13, 2012); Dick Kreck, "Strange Brewing standing out," *Denver Post*, June 2, 2010, http://www.denverpost.com/lifestyles/ci_15198853 (accessed April 16, 2013); Karlene Lukovitz, "New

Belgium Brewing Gets 'Hopped Up,'" *Media Post News*, http://www.mediapost.com/publications/?fa=Articles. showArticle&art_aid=121806 (accessed March 4, 2011); "New Belgium Brewing Company, Inc.," *Businessweek*, http://investing.businessweek.com/research/stocks/private/snapshot.asp?privcapId=919332 (accessed April 16, 2013); "Tour de New Belgium," *Brew Public*, November 23, 2010, http://brewpublic.com/places-to-drink-beer/tour-de-new-belgium/ (accessed April 16, 2013); Steve Raabe, "Plans Brewing for New Belgium Facility on East Coast," *Denver Post*, December 22, 2011, http://www.denverpost.com/business/ci_19597528 (accessed April 16, 2013); Mike Esterl, "Craft Brewers Tap Big Expansion," *The Wall Street Journal*, December 28, 2011, http://online.wsj.com/article/SB10001424052970203862045771142917216610070.html (accessed February 18, 2012); "Industry Profile: Breweries," *First Research*, October 17, 2011, http://www.firstresearch .com (accessed February 17, 2012); New Belgium Brewing, *New Belgium Brewing: Follow Your Folly*, May 9, 2007, http://www.newbelgium.com/Files/NBB_student-info-packet.pdf (accessed April 17, 2012); "New Belgium Brewing Announces Asheville as Site for Second Brewery," *Denver Post*, April 5, 2012, http://marketwire.denverpost.com/client/denver_post/release.jsp?actionFor=1595119 (accessed April 19, 2012); "The 2011 World's Most Ethical Companies," *Ethisphere*, Q1 2011, 37–43; Chris Furnari, "New Belgium Brewing to Expand Distribution Into Three New States," *Brewbound*, February 8, 2013, http://www.brewbound.com/news/new-belgium-brewing-to-expand-distribution-into-three-new-states (accessed April 16, 2013); "How New Belgium Brewing is positioning itself to remain independent," *Denver Post*, January 15, 2013, http://blogs.denverpost.com/beer/2013/01/15/new-belgium-positio/7872/ (accessed April 16, 2013); Garrett Ellison, "New Belgium's Biere de Garde, a collaboration with Brewery Vivant of Grand Rapids, hits shelves," *Michigan Live*, December 10, 2012, http://www.mlive.com/business/west-michigan/index.ssf/2012/12/new_belgiums_biere_de_garde_a.html (accessed April 16, 2013); NBB Films, "NBBspotsonNBC," NBB Films, *YouTube*, http://www.youtube.com/watch?v=KCnzyX-x-WQ (accessed April 16, 2013).

CASE 6

National Collegiate Athletic Association Ethics and Compliance Program*

INTRODUCTION

Perhaps no sport at American colleges is as popular, or as lucrative, as college football. College football often has a significant impact on the school's culture. This is especially true for the more successful and prolific football programs, such as Texas A&M or Notre Dame. Football has increasingly become a big money maker for many colleges, with a significant amount of sports revenue coming from their football programs. Within the past two years, the sports channel *ESPN* made deals with certain teams to gain rights to air more games than usual. Because of this influx of revenue, the duties of coaches have evolved beyond just coaching. In many ways, they became the face of the team. Programs that show positive returns have coaches working hard to fill seats on game day and encourage college alumni to donate to the school. The more successful the football team, the more visibility it is given in the media. This visibility leads to greater awareness of the college or university among the public, and schools with the best football programs can see a greater influx of applications.

The collegiate football programs have an intangible influence within and outside their immediate surroundings. This is mainly seen in their fan base, composed of current students, alumni, staff, faculty, and local businesses. For example, when the University of Alabama won its 15th national championship, the victory was celebrated by an enormous crowd, fireworks, and a parade. Texas A&M University is one example of a football program that generates not only profits but also a sense of loyalty among its fans. Approximately 70,000 football fans pile into Texas A&M's Kyle Field stadium at every home game to show their support for the team and the university. Table 1 shows the value of some of the most successful college-football programs. These games also help local businesses generate more revenues.

Because of the financial support and widespread influence of the football program, the players, coaches, and football administrators have to deal with a lot of pressure to fundraise, sell tickets, and win games. These pressures open up opportunities for misconduct to occur, and it is increasingly important that university administrators and football program officials directly acknowledge opportunities for misconduct. While the university is ultimately responsible for the operation of each department and the behavior of its employees, it can be difficult for the administrators to have an objective view of incidents that occur, especially when it involves a successful football program that benefits the entire

*This case was prepared by Michelle Urban, Kathleen Dubyk, Ben Skaer, and Bethany Buchner for and under the direction of O.C. and Linda Ferrell. It was prepared for classroom discussion rather than to illustrate either effective or ineffective handling of an administrative, ethical, or legal decision by management. All sources used for this case were obtained through publicly available material.

TABLE 1 Value of major-conference college-football programs, plus Notre Dame and BYU (in millions)

Rank	School	Value	Rank	School	Value	Rank	School	Value	Rank	School	Value
1	Texas	$761.7	19	Oregon	$264.6	37	Virginia	$146.3	55	Mississippi St.	$99.3
2	Michigan	$731.9	20	Washington	$259.9	38	Purdue	$145.1	56	Maryland	$96.0
3	Florida	$599.7	21	Michigan St.	$224.8	39	N.C. State	$143.0	57	California	$92.6
4	Notre Dame	$597.4	22	Texas Tech	$211.0	40	Indiana	$142.7	58	Syracuse	$91.4
5	Ohio St.	$586.6	23	Oklahoma St.	$209.1	41	Iowa St.	$140.3	59	Texas Christian	$76.6
6	Auburn	$508.1	24	Kansas St.	$207.1	42	Minnesota	$139.7	60	Louisville	$75.4
7	Georgia	$481.8	25	Colorado	$202.9	43	BYU	$136.1	61	Washington St.	$73.4
8	Alabama	$476.0	26	Kentucky	$202.7	44	Arizona	$126.8	62	Baylor	$71.3
9	LSU	$471.7	27	Clemson	$201.8	45	UCLA	$125.8	63	Rutgers	$64.1
10	Oklahoma	$454.7	28	USC	$197.8	46	Utah	$119.7	64	Duke	$62.0
11	Iowa	$384.4	29	Georgia Tech	$188.4	47	Oregon St.	$118.8	65	Pittsburgh	$59.6
12	Tennessee	$364.6	30	Virginia Tech	$171.5	48	Illinois	$117.3	66	Vanderbilt	$57.3
13	Nebraska	$360.1	31	Arizona St.	$164.6	49	Mississippi	$111.7	67	Missouri	$56.4
14	Arkansas	$332.0	32	West Virginia	$159.4	50	Boston College	$110.2	68	Cincinnati	$48.9
15	S.Carolina	$311.9	33	Florida St.	$159.0	51	Kansas	$103.4	69	Temple	$46.9
16	Penn St.	$300.8	34	Miami (Fla.)	$157.7	52	Connecticut	$101.8			
17	Wisconsin	$296.1	35	Northwestern	$148.8	53	South Florida	$101.2			
18	Texas A&M	$278.5	36	Stanford	$148.7	54	North Carolina	$99.8			

Source: Ryan Brewer, Indiana University-Purdue University Columbus

Note: Excludes Wake Forest

university. The university administrators are often subject to the same pressures as those in the football program to increase the level of revenue and reputation. This led to the development of a more objective institution to set and enforce rules and standards: the National Collegiate Athletic Association (NCAA). The NCAA views ethical conduct as a crucial component to a college football program and works to promote leadership and excellence among student–athletes and the universities to which they belong. It also serves to protect the interests of student–athletes, ensure academic excellence, and encourage fair play.

In this case, we provide a brief history of the NCAA and examples of the rules they have regarding college football. We then view how these rules relate to ethics. The next section covers some of the major college football scandals within the past few years, how these scandals were handled by the schools and the NCAA, and the impact of these scandals upon the colleges' communities. It is crucial to note, however, that these scandals are not common to college football as a whole. The majority of football teams receive no NCAA infractions during the year, and those reported are usually minor in nature. Universities have their own set of expectations for student–athletes, including showing up on time to practice and behaving responsibly that go above and beyond NCAA rules. However, when NCAA violations occur, universities have a responsibility to report them in a timely manner. Therefore, the next section covers examples of ways universities addressed unethical behavior in their football programs through self-imposed sanctions, which signifies that they consider compliance to be an important component of their football programs. We conclude by analyzing how effective the NCAA appears to be in curbing misconduct and preventing future unethical behavior from occurring. This case should demonstrate that ethics and compliance is just as important to nonprofit organizations and educational institutions as they are for the business world.

OVERVIEW OF NCAA

The NCAA was formed in 1906 under the premise of protecting student–athletes from being endangered and exploited. The Association was established with a constitution and a set of bylaws with the ability to be amended as issues arise. As the number of competitive college sports grew, the NCAA was divided into three Divisions, I, II, and III, to deal with the rising complexity of the programs. Universities are given the freedom to decide which division they want to belong to based on their desired level of competitiveness in collegiate sports.

Each Division is equipped with the power to establish a group of presidents or other university officials with the authority to write and enact policies, rules, and regulations for their Divisions. Each Division is ultimately governed by the President of the NCAA and the Executive Committee. Under the Executive Committee are groups formed in each Division, such as the Legislative Committee, as well as Cabinets and Boards of Directors.

In the early 1980s, questions began to arise concerning the level of education student–athletes received. Some thought these students were held to a lower academic standard so they could focus on their sport, which could lead to negative consequences for their futures. As a result, the NCAA strengthened the academic requirements of student–athletes to ensure they took academics just as seriously as athletics. It also established the Presidents Commission, composed of presidents of universities in each Division that collaboratively set agendas with the NCAA. Table 2 provides a list of six of the Principles for Conduct of Intercollegiate Athletics that can be found in Article 2 of the Constitution.

Throughout the Constitution, the NCAA emphasizes the responsibility each university has in overseeing its athletics department and being compliant with the terms established by its conferences. The NCAA establishes principles, rules, and enforcement guidelines to both guide the universities in their oversight of the athletics department as well as penalize those failing to regulate their own misconduct. In article ten of the bylaws, a description of ethical and unethical conduct among student–athletes is provided, along with corresponding disciplinary actions taken if any of these conditions are violated. Honesty and sportsmanship are emphasized as the basis of ethical conduct, while wagering, withholding information, and fraud are among the unethical behaviors listed. Article 11 describes the appropriate behavior for athletics personnel. Honesty and sportsmanship is again the basis for ethical behavior, but with an added emphasis on responsibility for NCAA regulations. Article 11 cites the Head Coach as responsible for creating an atmosphere of compliance and monitoring the behavior of his or her subordinates, including assistant coaches and players.

The NCAA takes the enforcement of rules seriously and tries to ensure the penalties fit the violation if misconduct does occur. The organization also makes sure the penalties are handed down in a timely manner, not only to indicate the seriousness of the infraction but also to maintain a credible and effective enforcement program. This method tries to correct or eliminate deviant behavior while maintaining fairness to those members of the Association not involved in violations. Employees (coaches and other administrative

TABLE 2 Principles for Conduct of Intercollegiate Athletics

The Principle of Institutional Control and Responsibility
- Puts the responsibility for the operations and behaviors of staff on the president of the university

The Principle of Student-Athlete Well-Being
- Requires integration of athletics and education, maintaining a culturally diverse and gender equitable environment, protection of student-athlete's health and safety, creating an environment that is conducive to positive coach/student-athlete relationships, coaches and administrative staff show honesty, fairness, and openness in their relationships with student–athletes, and student-athlete involvement in decisions that will affect them

The Principle of Sportsmanship and Ethical Conduct
- Maintains that respect, fairness, civility, honesty, and responsibility are values that need to be adhered to through the establishment of policies for sportsmanship and ethical conduct in the athletics program which must be consistent with the mission and goals of the university. Everyone must be continuously educated about the policies.

The Principle of Sound Academic Standards
- Maintains that student–athletes need to be held to the same academic standards as all other students

The Principle of Rules Compliance
- Requires compliance with NCAA rules. Notes that the NCAA will help institutions in developing their compliance program and explains the penalty for noncompliance

The Principle Governing Recruiting
- Promotes equity among prospective students and protects them from exorbitant pressures

Source: National Collegiate Athletic Association, *2011–2012 NCAA® Division III Manual* (Indianapolis, IN: National Collegiate Athletics Association, 2011).

staff) are exhorted to have high ethical standards since they work among and influence young people. The NCAA makes it a requirement that each employee engage in exemplary conduct so as not to cause harm to the student–athletes in any way. They are also given a responsibility to cooperate with the NCAA.

The NCAA lays out three types of violations and corresponding penalties, depending on the nature and scope of the violation. Secondary violations are the least severe and can result in fines, suspensions for games, and reduction in scholarships. For major violations, some of the penalties are the same as secondary violations, but the scope is far more severe. For example, suspensions will be longer and fines larger. However, some penalties are specific only to major violations, such as a public reprimand, a probationary period for up to five years, and limits on recruiting. The last type involves repeat violations that occur within a five-year period from the start date of the initial violation. The penalties for repeat violations are the most severe, including elimination of all financial aid and recruiting activities and resignation of institutional staff members who serve on boards, committees, or in cabinets. Table 3 lists some of the more prominent unethical practices the NCAA lists specifically concerning college football.

The NCAA incorporates a compliance approach to ethics by developing and enforcing rules to keep the games fair and respectful of student–athletes' rights. The NCAA Committee on Sportsmanship and Ethical Conduct identified respect and integrity as two critical elements in the NCAA 2011 and 2012 Football Rules and Interpretations. The NCAA strives to keep football games fun and entertaining without sacrificing the health and safety of the student–athletes participating. As previously mentioned, the NCAA

TABLE 3 Unethical Practices Prohibited by the NCAA

- Use of the helmet as a weapon.

- Targeting and initiating contact. Players, coaches and officials should emphasize the elimination of targeting and initiating contact against a defenseless opponent and/or with the crown of the helmet.

- Using nontherapeutic drugs in the game of football.

- Unfair use of a starting signal, called "Beating the ball." This involves deliberately stealing an advantage from the opponent. An honest starting signal is needed, but a signal that has for its purpose starting the team a fraction of a second before the ball is put in play, in the hope that it will not be detected by the officials, is illegal.

- Feigning an injury. An injured player must be given full protection under the rules, but feigning injury is dishonest, unsportsmanlike and contrary to the spirit of the rules.

- Talking to an opponent in any manner that is demeaning, vulgar, or abusive, intended to incite a physical response or verbally put an opponent down.

- For a coach to address, or permit anyone on his bench to address, uncomplimentary remarks to any official during the progress of a game, or to indulge in conduct that might incite players or spectators against the officials. , is a violation of the rules of the game and must likewise be considered conduct unworthy of a member of the coaching profession.

Source: Adapted from National Collegiate Athletics Association, *Football 2011 and 2012 Rules and Interpretations* (Indianapolis, IN: National Collegiate Athletics Association, 2011).

places emphasis on the level of education student–athletes receive and encourages athletes to focus on their grades to ensure they have career opportunities post-athletics. The core of the NCAA concerns ethics. This organization takes not only key players into consideration, but also other stakeholders, such as the college community and the sports society as a whole.

Aside from its involvement with student–athlete academics, the NCAA is likewise involved with other off-the-field activities to protect the best interests of student–athletes. According to NCAA guidelines, college football coaches are not permitted to actively begin recruiting prospective players to their school until the prospective player is at least a junior in high school. These coaches have a limit on the number of phone calls and off-campus visits they are permitted to make to prospective students. These rules are in place to ensure student–athletes do not feel pressured by these colleges. Once the student–athletes are in college, a set of rules made between the NCAA and the individual college limit the types of gifts a student–athlete can accept. Parents of student–athletes, for example, are able to give any number and type of gifts to their own children, but must be wary when it comes to other members of the team. Student–athletes generally cannot accept gifts at reduced prices (e.g., a free iPod) and other gifts, such as practice uniforms for the team, must be cleared by the school first.

Despite the NCAA's wide array of rules and regulations, there have been many criticisms of the organization's practices. One of these criticisms has to do with a former investigator of the NCAA, Ameen Najjar, who worked on investigating reports of rule violations from the University of Miami. Najjar was promptly dismissed from the NCAA when it was found he was going outside the NCAA's rules of investigation in order to collect more evidence for the case. Not only was this a major embarrassment for the NCAA, but critics state Najjar followed orders from others within the organization and was put up as a scapegoat when the rule-breaking investigative techniques came to light. The NCAA also faces a lawsuit wherein they are accused of allowing the video game company EA to use the likeness of NCAA basketball players in their video games without giving the players any compensation.

Additionally, misconduct in college sports continues to be a challenge for the NCAA. Often other stakeholders are involved in the misconduct. For instance, college sports games that have been "rigged" (managed fraudulently) have often been traced to wealthy sports boosters with inside knowledge of the sports in which they heavily invest. A majority of the time, this rigging is done to benefit gambling outcomes among these boosters. In addition, as mentioned earlier, college sports often bring in significant amounts of revenue for the university that creates pressure to overlook misconduct. Authority figures in the sports program can be tempted to cheat when recruiting players and cover up misconduct to avoid penalties.

When a college sports program is accused of misconduct that violates NCAA rules, the NCAA conducts an investigation to determine whether the allegations are true. If these schools are found to be in violation, the NCAA levies penalties against the team. However, the NCAA also received criticism from those who disapprove of the severity and effectiveness of the sanctions meant to discourage sports programs from misconduct. On the one hand, some stakeholders believe the NCAA sanctions are too tough. On the other hand, others feel they are not strict enough. They state some of the major college football programs hit by NCAA sanctions were able to recover from these penalties quickly and did not suffer much during the course of the sanctions. This argument implies that avoiding the risks of punishment is less costly to the team than the benefits of bending the rules. Whether NCAA sanctions are too harsh or not harsh enough, pressure to maintain the sports programs provides the opportunity for misconduct in the college sports community, as well as creates significant challenges for the NCAA.

CHALLENGES FOR ETHICS AND COMPLIANCE IN COLLEGE FOOTBALL

College football is far more than just a sport. For many universities, it is a business that brings millions of dollars to colleges all over the United States. Being a business, there are always ethical and compliance issues that take place. The question is whether schools ignore issues taking place because of the amount of money a football program generates for the school. If so, this creates a significant conflict of interest. In the past few years, a number of highly publicized scandals have rocked the college football industry and led to heavy criticism of the schools where the scandals occurred. The actions of the NCAA in response to these scandals received mixed reactions from stakeholders. However, a more serious concern for the NCAA is how to ensure college sports teams comply with ethical policies as well as combating the tendency for colleges to remain complacent because of the success of the sports team. The following examples describe three major college football scandals, how the schools reacted to the scandals, and the sanctions, if any, the NCAA took against the team.

Penn State Scandal

In 2011 accusations arose alleging that a former assistant coach of the Penn State football team sexually assaulted at least eight young boys over the course of many years. It was not long before the school itself was implicated in suspecting or knowing about the crime but not taking adequate steps to stop it. Two university officials turned themselves in to authorities for being accused of covering up the crimes.

According to investigations, the first report of potential misconduct between the former assistant coach Jerry Sandusky and an underage boy came in 1998. The report came to University police and the Senior Vice President for Finance and Business, Gary Schultz. This matter was investigated internally and resulted in no criminal charges based on a lack of evidence. In 2001 a graduate assistant allegedly witnessed the perpetrator sexually assaulting a young boy in the Penn State football team's practice center. The graduate assistant reported the incident to Head Coach Joe Paterno, who staked his reputation on running a program known for ethics and integrity. While Paterno appeared to have notified campus officials, the officials did not report to police, allowing the crime to continue. A later report conducted by former director of the FBI Louis Freeah indicated the coach and school officials covered up the crimes. This led to accusations that the school cared more about its reputation and the success of its football program than it did about the young victims. This case is even more serious as such misconduct does not just constitute an NCAA violation; it is a criminal act that harmed many people. Although Joe Paterno did report the crime to campus officials, some felt it was his responsibility to do more to ensure the crimes were reported to the proper authorities. The assistant coach continued to interact with young boys and be around the college campus after the reports were made.

The negligent behavior of Penn State officials, both within the administration and the football department, might be explained through the strength of the football program and the complacency of the university culture. Head Coach Joe Paterno had been at Penn State's football department for more than 60 years at the time of the scandal. The way he ran the department indicated a reliance on old football standards and an inability or unwillingness to adapt to new ones. Unfortunately, this culture had pitfalls that did not hold up to modern ethical standards. Some reports claim that on different occasions he advocated for football players not to be held to the same standards as regular students, implying football players should be treated differently than other students by the university. When football players got in trouble with the law, Paterno felt the university should not take action but rather let the police deal with it. Although he butted heads with many people when it came to these views, school directors were on his side of the argument. This is likely because of the large amount of revenue the program brought into the school. According to one accusation, Coach Paterno used this revenue as a threat to stop all fund raising if a certain director he disagreed with was not fired. If these allegations are true, then Paterno created a culture within the football department wherein members did not need to be held accountable according to school regulations. This in turn indicates a complacent university culture when it came to the football program.

The NCAA agreed the misconduct was partially the fault of the football program's and Penn State's complacency. In addition to the negative impact on the victims, Penn State suffered reputational damage and received a major blow to its football program. The NCAA imposed sanctions against Penn State costing $60 million in fines, a four-year postseason ban prohibiting the school from being eligible for any post games until 2016, and a four-year reduction in scholarships amounting to ten scholarships per year for the football program. The football team's wins from between 1998 and 2011 were vacated. These penalties drastically hurt the football program's ability to compete against other teams. In total, there were seven penalties placed on the university and athletics program combined. The NCAA is taking steps to make sure the activities that took place at Penn State do not happen again. As an aside, the Paterno family announced they were filing a lawsuit against the

NCAA and its President on behalf of Penn State, citing the investigation conducted by former director of the FBI Louis Freeah—a report the NCAA relied heavily upon in imposing sanctions against Penn State—was seriously flawed in its conclusions of blame.

The NCAA also put ten corrective sanctions on Penn State formulated specifically for them. The main corrective measure was that the university must sign an Athletic Integrity Agreement. In doing so, this allowed the NCAA to require Penn State to take eight corrective steps. These steps include the addition of a compliance officer for the athletics department, the creation of a compliance council and a full disclosure program, adding internal accountability and certifications for this accountability, implementation of an external compliance review/certification process, drafting an athletics code of conduct, conducting training and education, and appointing an independent athletics integrity monitor. All of the steps will be continuously updated to ensure their internal and external controls stay relevant. The NCAA's goal for the corrective sanctions is to find and stop unethical behavior before it becomes a problem.

Ohio State

The Ohio State scandal was a result of rule violations from student–athletes and a subsequent cover-up of the violations by the coach. In December 2010 five players on Ohio State's football team were suspended for using the gear the football team supplied to barter for cash and tattoos. Under the NCAA rules, it is illegal for a Division I football player to receive any benefit from anyone that is not offered to the public. Head Coach Jim Tressel became aware of the violation and failed to report it to the school for a period of nine months. This enabled the team to continue to play in games they otherwise would have been ineligible to play. In addition to the suspensions, the NCAA also banned Ohio State from a bowl game for one year, took five scholarships away for the following three years, and put the team on a one-year probation. When it was discovered Tressel had prior knowledge of the violation, the NCAA issued a five-year show-cause order on him, forcing him to resign and virtually ending his career as a coach in collegiate athletics. A college can hire a coach who has an outstanding show-cause order, but they may be penalized simply for hiring him. In addition, if a coach with a show-cause order does in fact get hired and makes a subsequent violation, the consequences will be far more severe on both the coach and the university. Most colleges will not take the risk of hiring a coach with this kind of label.

This was not the only violation to be found among members of the Ohio State football team. After the bartering scandal, the NCAA suspended three other players for accepting money from a booster. A booster is a fan who has a significant amount of money and invests in the team to build better facilities, contribute to scholarships, and sometimes have a choice in who the coaching staff will be. However, student–athletes are not to take any money or gifts from boosters directly. It is a direct violation of the rules of the NCAA. Additionally, other players were suspended for being overpaid by the same booster for work in a summer job.

The NCAA placed these sanctions on Ohio State for failure to properly oversee their athletics program. Many of the administrators commented if they knew of the football players' conduct, they would have taken corrective action against it. Ohio State took responsibility for its actions and cooperated with the NCAA investigation. Ohio State imposed its own penalties against the football program, including vacating the 2010 season. Yet the NCAA made it a point to show the administrators it is their responsibility to know what is going on within their organization. Additionally, the NCAA also noted Tressel withheld information multiple times from NCAA investigators. In total, the sanctions cost Ohio State an estimated $8 million.

University of Arkansas

Head Coach Bobby Petrino was respected and admired for his coaching abilities by everyone, even those who did not have a high opinion of him personally. Before coaching at University of Arkansas in 2007, Petrino left bitter feelings at the football organizations where he previously worked. For example, he secretly tried to get one of his former bosses fired, he pressured a student to go to practice rather than attend a funeral where he was to be a pallbearer, and he left his job with the Atlanta Falcons by leaving a short note in the lockers of each player before the season ended. Petrino's questionable behavior continued while he coached for the University of Arkansas. He had been with the university since 2007 and transformed the team into championship material. However, a motorcycle accident in early 2012 revealed a latent scandal brewing for several months.

At the time of the accident Petrino claimed he was riding alone, but changed his story as the police report was about to become public. He admitted he rode with Jessica Dorrell, a 25-year-old former student who Petrino hired as the Student Athlete Development Coordinator just a week prior. He further admitted he initially lied about the details of the accident because he and Dorrell were involved in an inappropriate relationship. Petrino hoped to keep this information secret as is evidenced by the fact he filed the report with a state trooper who worked as his personal security after he parted ways with Dorrell.

This incident was a scandal for two reasons. First, Petrino was married with four children, and second, he had hired Dorrell without stating to the university there was a conflict of interest due to their personal relationship. Because she was hired as a state employee, not disclosing the conflict of interest was illegal. Additionally, the position she was given reported directly to Petrino himself. Upon investigation, it was found that Petrino also gave Dorrell gifts amounting to $20,000.

All of these things taken together caused the Athletic Director of the University of Arkansas Jeff Long to fire Petrino. However, the decision was not easy for him to make. Petrino's contributions to the success of the football team were no small matter, and the consequences of letting him go would affect the team's performance. However, keeping Petrino as Head Coach would demonstrate that the university condoned the misconduct. Dorrell resigned a few days after Petrino was fired.

In less than a year after the University of Arkansas scandal, Petrino was hired as Head Coach of the Hilltoppers of Western Kentucky University. Some say this arrangement is good for both of the parties involved. Petrino gets to coach football for a lower ranking football program while waiting for the scandal to blow over, and Western Kentucky University gets to take advantage of Petrino's coaching for a few years. The arrangement drew some criticism to the school. Some say the hiring of a coach recently fired for a scandal speaks to the fact that the school values winning games over ethical behavior.

Fortunately for the University of Arkansas and Bobby Petrino, NCAA rules had not been violated, so sanctions were avoided. Jeff Long showed ethical leadership in the way he handled the Petrino scandal even without pressure from the NCAA. Long refused to be complacent when the misconduct became apparent even when, in the short term, it did not seem like it would benefit the university. The football team suffered from the loss of Coach Petrino, but the university's actions express it expects high ethical standards from its football program and will accept no less. Because it creates a culture of ethics and compliance, schools like the University of Arkansas step up to the plate and make the right decision even when misconduct does not constitute an NCAA violation.

SELF-REPORTING AND MONITORING STUDENT ATHLETES

Minor violations become scandals when they are covered up for long periods of time by the university, the football program authorities, or both. No matter where the cover up begins or ends, the ultimate responsibility lies with the university to monitor the actions of the football program. If the culture of the university fosters misconduct, minor violations will inevitably become scandals. On the other hand, universities that monitor their athletics programs so minor violations are caught immediately and reported to the NCAA are less likely to be involved in major scandals. This act of self-reporting demonstrates a concern with ethical behavior and accountability for their actions. Furthermore, the NCAA takes these measures into account when deciding on the appropriate level of penalties for violations.

In 2011 the NCAA approached Boise State with 22 allegations of misconduct within its athletics department. Becoming aware of this misconduct, the university as well as the head coaches acted immediately and in collaboration with the NCAA. During the university's investigation, they found other violations the NCAA was unaware of and reported them to the Association. Violations included incidents when assistant coaches arranged low-cost housing and transportation for prospective football players. While the monetary value of these accommodations was under $5,000, the duration of time these activities had gone on was five years. Boise State developed and submitted a set of self-imposed sanctions against the athletic department that included three fewer preseason practices for the current and upcoming year and three fewer scholarships for the next two years. After reviewing the incidents and the proposed sanctions, the NCAA eliminated three more scholarships for an additional year and placed the university on probation for three years. The NCAA imposed harsher sanctions due to what it perceived to be a lack of institutional control and the fact that the infractions had gone on for so long. The university admitted it lost control over compliance because of the rate of growth of the football program. It claims it has taken steps to strengthen its compliance department by hiring a new director and adding new language to its student handbook to clarify its expectations.

The University of New Mexico also received sanctions for misconduct in its football program. The case involved academic fraud that occurred in 2004 and was not discovered by the university until 2007. Two former assistant coaches helped three recruits and one currently enrolled student receive academic credit through an online course for which the students did not complete work. Despite the fact the incident occurred three years prior, the university took the matter seriously and imposed heavy sanctions. It reduced the number of scholarship offers by one, the overall number of scholarships by two, the number of coaches allowed to recruit by one for the next two years, and the number of official visits to recruits by four for one year. It also imposed a two-year probation period on the football program and reduced the number of academic non-qualifiers by half for two years. Because of the seriousness of academic fraud, the NCAA accepted most of the self-imposed sanctions offered by the university but reduced the number of scholarships by five rather than two for a period of two years rather than one year.

Many of these issues involve providing college athletes with special favors. For decades a pressing issue has been one of paying college athletes. There are various rules that must be followed to avoid the appearance of paying college athletes or providing them with special treatment. At Ohio State University, student athletes disobeyed the rules by trading athletic equipment for tattoos. The main argument against athletes receiving compensation is that if the players were paid, then college sports would lose its appeal. In 2013-14 the courts will make a decision about whether a lawsuit arguing that players be compensated for use of their likeness goes forward. However, the major issue still remains over whether student athletes be paid a salary or reimbursed for expenses caused by sports-related activities and medical care.

The integrity of the NCAA and collegiate athletics depends on transparency and a level playing field. The NCAA and universities are mindful that most collegiate athletes do not enter professional sports and will have to find a career outside of athletics. Therefore, any attempt to treat collegiate athletics like professional sports could be detrimental. The goal of all stakeholders should be to help young men and women develop the ability to have a career and contribute to society.

CONCLUSION

The NCAA strives to prevent unethical behavior in collegiate athletics by objectively setting and enforcing standards of conduct. They also encourage and help universities establish their own system of compliance and control, since the ultimate responsibility lies with the universities and the cultures they create. Even when colleges impose sanctions on their football programs, the NCAA examines the sanctions objectively and either accepts the sanctions as sufficient or supplements them with more penalties that better match the misconduct. This should not discourage universities from self-reporting, however. While there is no guarantee a football program will not be penalized for reporting misconduct or adopting self-imposed sanctions, the more proactive a football program appears to be, the more consideration it may receive when the NCAA examines the situation. Additionally, a proactive ethical culture creates a reputation for ethics and compliance that may help the program bounce back quicker after a misconduct incident.

The NCAA stands as a compliance-oriented organization. At the same time, it promotes certain values the universities should adopt when developing sports programs. The NCAA rules should not be accepted as totally sufficient but used as a minimum benchmark for ethical conduct. NCAA guidelines serve as a framework for how collegiate sports programs should behave and offers consequences for non-compliance. Universities involved in both minor and major violations have come to realize the importance of emphasizing ethics and compliance in their sports programs.

QUESTIONS

1. How does the NCAA encourage collegiate football programs to develop a culture of ethics and compliance?
2. Is it a valid criticism that the NCAA is based more on compliance than ethical values?
3. How can student athletes, coaches, and university administrators demonstrate a proactive response to ethics and compliance?

SOURCES

Andrea Adelson, "Boise State self-imposes sanctions," *ESPN*, May 5, 2011, http://sports.espn.go.com/ncf/news/story?id=6476963 (accessed May 30, 2013); Zac Al-Khateeb, "Bama fans turn out en masse to celebrate the Tide's championship victory," *The Crimson White*, January 22, 2013, http://cw.ua.edu/2013/01/22/bama-fans-turn-out-en-masse-to-celebrate-the-tides-15th-bcs-national-championship/ (accessed April 23, 2013); Associated Press, "Bobby Petrino to Western Kentucky," *ESPN*, December 11, 2012,http://espn.go.com/college-football/story/_/id/8732857/bobby-petrino-hired-head-coach-western-kentucky-hilltoppers (accessed May 30, 2012); Associated Press, "Lobos begin self-imposed penalties for four possible rules violations," *ESPN*, January 5, 2008, http://sports.espn.go.com/ncf/news/story?id=3182809 (accessed May 30, 2013); Associated Press, "NCAA denies Boise State's appeal," October 10, 2012, *ESPN*, http://espn.go.com/college-football/story/_/id/8486550/ncaa-upholds-ruling-boise-state-broncos-scholarship-sanctions (accessed May 30, 2013); The Associated Press, "NCAA to reconsider Boise St. sanctions," *NCAA*, June 29, 2012, http://www.ncaa.com/news/football/article/2012-06-29/ncaa-reconsider-boise-st-sanctions (accessed May 30, 2013); Associated Press, "Penn State lists 1st director of ethics and compliance," *WITF*, March 8, 2013, http://www.witf.org/news/2013/03/penn-state-names-1st-director-of-ethics-and-compliance.php (accessed May 30, 2013); Rachel Bachman and Matthew Futterman, "College Football's Big-Money, Big-Risk Business Model," *The Wall Street Journal*, http://online.wsj.com/article/SB10001424127887324024004578169472607407806.html (accessed April 23, 2013); Rachel Bachman, Kevin Helliker, and John Miller, "A Discipline Problem Paterno Fought Penn State Official Over Punishment of Players," *The Wall Street Journal*, November 22, 2011, http://online.wsj.com/article/SB10001424052970204443404577052073672561402.html (accessed May 30, 2013); Thomas Bradley, "Breaking it down: 'Tattoo-Gate' scandal costs Ohio State almost $8M," *The Lantern*, June 16, 2012, http://www.thelantern.com/campus/breaking-it-down-tattoo-gate-scandal-costs-ohio-state-almost-8m-1.2875925#.UZqbSUrD77o (accessed May 30, 2013); College Sports Scholarships, "NCAA and NAIA Sports Recruiting," http://www.collegesportsscholarships.com/ncaa-recruiting-rules-contact-visits.htm (accessed April 23, 2013); Abby Davidson, "Why the N.C.A.A.'s Sanctions Against Penn State Are Fair," *The New Yorker*, July 23, 2012, http://www.newyorker.com/online/blogs/closeread/2012/07/punishing-penn-state-sandusky-scandal.html (accessed April 28, 2013); Division III Commissioners Association, "Sportsmanship and Ethical Conduct Committee," http://www.diiicomm.org/committees/sportsmanship/mission (accessed April 23, 2013); "Do college football or basketball teams cheat in recruiting? Does it really happen?" Recruiting-101.com, http://recruiting-101.com/do-college-football-or-basketball-teams-cheat-in-recruiting-%C2%A0does-it-really-happen/ (accessed May 30, 2013); Darren Everson, "What Is Your Team Worth?" *The Wall Street Journal*, January 7, 2013. http://online.wsj.com/article/SB10001424127887324391104578225802183417888.html (accessed March 23, 2013); Mike Fish, "The Most Powerful Boosters," *ESPN*, January 12, 2006, http://sports.espn.go.com/ncf/news/story?id=2285986 (accessed May 30, 2013); Marilee Gallagher, "Penn State Penalties: Did NCAA Give University the 'Death Penalty' in Disguise?" *Bleacher Report*, July 23, 2012, http://bleacherreport.com/articles/1268899-penn-state-penalties-did-ncaa-give-university-the-death-penalty-in-disguise (accessed May 30, 2013); Adam Himmelsbach, "Scandal Involving Petrino Goes Beyond X's and O's," *The New York Times*, April 6, 2012, http://www.nytimes.com/2012/04/07/sports/ncaafootball/bobby-petrino-scandal-goes-beyond-football-acumen.html?pagewanted=all&_r=1& (accessed May 30, 2013); The Ivy League, "NCAA Rules: A Guide for Parents of Student-Athletes," Brown Bears, www.brownbears.com/compliance/files/parentsrules.pdf?dec (accessed April 23, 2013); Jerry Hinnen, "Emails released in O'Bannon suit show 'real concern' at NCAA," *CBS Sports*, April 26, 2013, from http://www.cbssports.com/collegefootball/blog/eye-on-college-football/22144772/emails-released-in-obannon-suit-show-real-concern-at-ncaa (accessed May 30, 2013); Vince Huth, "Column: NCAA sanctions maybe not severe enough," *The Daily Cardinal*, September 7, 2012, http://host.madison.com/daily-cardinal/sports/columnists/column-ncaa-sanctions-maybe-not-severe-enough/article_a7522bb0-f8b7-11e1-9517-001a4bcf887a.html (accessed May 30, 2013); Scott Jaschik, "The Football Dividend," Inside Higher Ed, October 29, 2012, http://www.insidehighered.com/news/2012/10/29/research-finds-financial-impact-colleges-win-football-games (accessed May 30, 2013); Armen Keteyian (correspondent) and Draggan Mihailovich (producer), "Has college football become a campus commodity?" *CBS News*, originally aired as part of "The College Game" on November 18, 2012, http://www.cbsnews.com/8301-18560_162-57551556/has-college-football-become-a-campus-commodity/ (accessed April 23, 2013); Paige Kuznar, "Students pickup post-game garbage, earn cash," *The Battalion Online*, October 3, 2012, http://www.thebatt.com/lifestyles/students-pickup-post-game-garbage-earn-cash-1.2917853#. UVdXg1eMBGM (accessed April 23, 2013); Bill Littlefield, "'Cheating The Spread': Scandals In College Sports," Only A Game, January 26, 2013, http://onlyagame.wbur.org/2013/01/26/cheating-the-spread (accessed May 30, 2013); Stewart Mandel, "Bobby Petrino's hire at WKU shows emphasis on winning above all else," *Sports Illustrated*, December 10, 2012, http://sportsillustrated.cnn.com/2012/writers/stewart_mandel/12/10/bobby-petrino-western-kentucky/index.html (accessed May 30, 2013); Susan Montoya Bryan, "NCAA penalizes New Mexico for football violations," *USA Today*, August 20, 2008, http://usatoday30.usatoday.com/sports/college/football/2008-08-20-1452036409_x.htm?csp=34 (accessed May 30, 2013); National Collegiate Athletic Association Home Page, http://ncaa.org (accessed April 23, 2013); National Collegiate Athletic Association, *2011-2012 NCAA˚ Division I Manual* (Indianapolis, IN: National Collegiate Athletics Association, 2011); National Collegiate Athletic Association, "2012 AND 2013 NCAA Football Rules and Interpretations," NCAA Publications, http://www.ncaapublications.com/p-4292-2012-and-2013-ncaa-football-rules-and-interpretations.aspx (accessed May 30, 2013); National Collegiate Athletic Association, "History," August 13, 2012, http://www.ncaa.org/wps/wcm/connect/public/ncaa/about+the+ncaa/history (April 23, 2013); "NCAA to reconsider penalties imposed on Boise State football," *USA Today*, June 29, 2012, http://usatoday30.usatoday.com/sports/college/football/mwest/story/2012-06-29/boise-state-ncaa-reconsider-sanctions/55921852/1 (accessed May 30, 2013); "Ohio State gets one-year bowl ban," *ESPN*, December 22, 2011, http://espn.go.com/college-football/story/_/id/7372757/ohio-state-buckeyes-football-penalties-include-bowl-ban (accessed May 30, 2013); Chip Patterson, "Joe Paterno's family to sue NCAA on behalf of Penn State," *CBS Sports*, May 30, 2013, http://www.cbssports.com/collegefootball/blog/eye-on-college-football/22327207/joe-paterno-family-to-sue-ncaa (accessed May 30, 2013); Penn State, "Becker named as first director of University ethics and compliance," March 7, 2013, http://news.psu.edu/story/267725/2013/03/07/administration/becker-named-first-director-university-ethics-and-compliance (accessed May 30, 2013); Penn State, "Ethics and Compliance Hotline," Office of Internal Audit, http://www.internalaudit.psu.edu/hotline/ (accessed May 30, 2013); "Penn State Football Coach Sex Abuse Scandal: Officials Step Down," *YouTube*, November 7, 2011, http://www.youtube.com/watch?v=zkfcYHlvYpU (accessed March 23, 2013); "The Penn State Scandal, Piece by Piece," *Pittsburgh Post-Gazette*, http://blogs.post-gazette.com/scandal/timeline.php (accessed May 30, 2013); "Police look at Bobby Petrino Crash," *ESPN*, April 7, 2012, http://espn.go.com/college-football/story/_/id/7784107/arkansas-state-police-looking-closer-football-coach-bobby-petrino-crash (accessed May 30, 2013); Christopher P. Ryan, "Penn State NCAA Sanctions Go Too Far," *Policymic*, http://www.policymic.com/articles/11704/penn-state-ncaa-sanctions-go-too-far (accessed May 30, 2013); "Scandal Brings down Arkansas Football Coach," *Fox News*, April 11, 2012, http://video.foxnews.com/v/1557329306001/scandal-brings-down-arkansas-football-coach/ (accessed March 23, 2013; Mark Schlabach, "NCAA sends message to Ohio State," *ESPN*, December 20, 2011, http://espn.go.com/college-football/story/_/id/7373708/ncaa-sends-message-sanctions-ohio-state-buckeyes (accessed May 30, 2013); Allen St. John, "The Economics of Scandal: A $55, 735 Hiring Cost Arkansas Football Coach Bobby Petrino $18 Million," *Forbes*, April 11, 2012, http://www.forbes.com/sites/allenstjohn/2012/04/11/the-economics-of-scandal-a-55735-hiring-cost-arkansas-football-coach-bobby-petrino-18-million/ (accessed May 30, 2013); Staff Report, "A&M football season, Manziel generate $37 million in media exposure revenue," *The Battalion Online*, January 18, 2013, http://www.thebatt.com/a-m-football-season-manziel-generate-37-million-in-media-exposure-revenue-1.2973571#.UVdYOleMBGM (accessed April 23, 2013); Trevor Stevens and Jennifer Keith, "Funding for Kyle Field Renovation Gains Clarity," *The Battalion Online*, January 17, 2013, http://www.thebatt.com/funding-for-kyle-field-renovation-gains-clarity-1.2972858#. UVdYZFeMBGM (accessed April 23, 2013); John Taylor, "Document release sheds further light on Petrino scandal," *NBC Sports*, April 20, 2012, http://collegefootballtalk.nbcsports.com/2012/04/20/document-release-sheds-further-light-on-petrino-scandal/ (accessed May 30, 2013); John Taylor, "It's official: NCAA accepts Vols' self-imposed sanctions," *NBC Sports*, August 24, 2011, http://collegefootballtalk.nbcsports.com/2011/08/24/its-official-ncaa-accepts-vols-self-imposed-sanctions/ (accessed May 30, 2013); Mark Torrence, "Crimson Tide weight room gets $9 million makeover," *The Crimson White*, February 28, 2013, http://cw.ua.edu/2013/02/28/crimson-tide-weight-room-gets-9-million-makeover/ (accessed April 23, 2013); "University of Miami: Self-imposed sanctions have strengthened our mission," *The Miami Herald*, February 21, 2013, http://www.miamiherald.com/2013/02/21/3246573/university-of-miami-self-imposed.html (accessed May 30, 2013); Steve Wieberg, "Sanctions against Ohio State Just the Latest NCAA Scandal," *USA Today*, December 21, 2011, http://usatoday30.usatoday.com/sports/college/football/bigten/story/2011-12-20/ohio-state-sanctions-ncaa-scandals/52132580/1 (accessed March 23, 2013); Dan Wolken, "NCAA enforcement staff's tasks won't get any easier," *USA Today*, February 18, 2012, http://www.usatoday.com/story/sports/college/2013/02/18/miami-ncaa-enforcement-ameen-najjar-julie-roe-lach-mark-emmert-ken-wainstein/1929011/ (accessed May 30, 2013); Charlie Zegers, "Show Cause," About.com, http://basketball.about.com/od/collegebasketballglossary/g/show-cause.htm (accessed May 30, 2013).

CASE 7

Google: The Quest to Balance Privacy with Profits*

INTRODUCTION

When Sergey Brin and Larry Page created their search engine "BackRub" in 1996, they could not imagine at the time what the future held for their creation. BackRub was unique because it used links to rank web pages. Before this time, search engines tended to use algorithms that only took into account key words, so when a certain item was searched, the user might receive links to webpages that were both legitimate and less legitimate (or irrelevant). Brin and Page's algorithm, dubbed PageRank, accounted for links, roughly equivalent to citations that went into and out of the website. This complex mathematical algorithm worked. Results were ranked according to their relative importance, allowing users to see the most "legitimate" search results first. In 1998, the search engine Google was officially born, named after the term "gogol," a mathematical term for a 1 followed by 100 zeros.

Google's ease of use propelled the search engine to its number one status, ousting competing search engines such as WebCrawler and Infoseek. As Google gained in popularity, it expanded into a number of different ventures, including advertising, book publishing, social networking, and mobile phones. The company also acquired or owns a number of other well-known sites, such as Orkut (a social-networking site popular in Brazil and India), the photo-sharing site Picasa, and YouTube, the most popular video sharing site in the world. In 2011 it launched Google+, a social networking site watched carefully by its competitor Facebook. For four consecutive years, Google was considered to be the most valuable brand in the world (although it was surpassed by Apple in 2011). Approximately two billion searches a day are performed through Google's search engine.

As is common with most large companies, Google has experienced its share of ethical issues. Its mantra "Don't Be Evil" raised questions after it entered China, where it allowed the government to censor some of its sites. Google's wide reach and its plans to publish millions of books online incurred lawsuits from both publishers, who accused the company of violating copyrights, and governments, who feared Google's power violated antitrust laws.

However, the hot topic on many users' minds is Internet privacy. In order to improve its search engine's capability, Google keeps information users input without

*This material was developed by Jennifer Sawayda and Michelle Urban under the direction of O.C. Ferrell and Linda Ferrell. Stephanie Amalfitano and Matthew Moody worked on a previous edition of this case. This case is intended for classroom discussion rather than to illustrate effective or ineffective handling of administrative, ethical, or legal decisions by management. All sources for this case were obtained through publicly available material.

user permission (although their privacy statement informs users about the recordkeeping). This led many people to question whether Google violates users' privacy. In light of the increasing amount of cyber-attacks and the government's determination to crack down on these illegal attacks, consumers worry their private information might be compromised.

This case analyzes Google's efforts to be a good corporate citizen as well as the privacy issues the company has faced. The analysis starts off by providing background on Google, its technology, and its initiatives. Google's core principles will be discussed as well as its efforts to become a socially responsible company. We then discuss the criticisms levied against Google, including its initial attempts to break into the censored Chinese market, its tracking of users, and changes to its privacy policies. We examine how Google has sometimes clashed with government authorities, resulting in an agreement to submit to privacy audits for the next 20 years. Finally, we show ways the government wants to regulate Internet data collection practices and Google's response to the proposed legislation.

COMPANY CULTURE

Google adopted a decentralized approach to empower its employees. Its corporate headquarters in Mountain View, California, is known as the Googleplex and consists of a campus containing an on-site gymnasium, daycare, and laundry service. When Sergey Brin and Larry Page founded the company, they recognized employees had to work hard and put in long hours to make the company not only successful but flexible enough to adapt to the changing environment. Thus, Google employees are provided with benefits to make the complex their second home. In addition to the more common perks of bonuses and health insurance, Google employees receive a massage every other week, free gourmet lunches, an outdoor volleyball court, roller hockey, tuition reimbursement, and discounts on solar panels should employees wish to install them on their residential homes. Google employees also have the option to bring their pets to work. Google strove to make its corporate culture fun and innovative; in fact, two of its core principles, "You can be creative without a suit" and "You don't need to be at your desk to need an answer," demonstrate the company's divergence from a more formal office environment. The company adopted ten core principles that it has strived to maintain since the beginning of its founding. These principles are outlined in Table 1.

At the same time, Google works to ensure it has top talent at the company. While it reinvents the office experience, it has also begun taking different tactics in recruiting to ensure it hires the most creative, talented individuals. For instance, Google recruiters take a bottom-up approach when reading résumés. Recognizing that top items such as education and work experience do not always guarantee the applicant is innovative, some Google recruiters look at the bottom of the résumé where applicants put personal and more creative information. This type of mentality—being more concerned with hiring creative people rather than those who excelled in school—is further emphasized by the fact that Google provides employees with 20 percent of the workweek to pursue their own unique projects. Not only does this make employees feel empowered, but it contributes unique project ideas for Google to pursue. This empowered and innovative company culture is one of the major reasons why Google became successful in different market niches.

TABLE 1: Google's Ten Core Principles

Focus on the user and all else will follow.
It's best to do one thing really, really well.
Fast is better than slow.
Democracy on the web works.
You don't need to be at your desk to need an answer.
You can make money without doing evil.
There's always more information out there.
The need for information crosses all borders.
You can be serious without a suit.
Great just isn't good enough.

Source: "Ten things we know to be true," Google, http://www.google.com/about/company/philosophy/ (accessed April 15, 2013)

PRODUCTS

Although Google started out as a search engine, it has since branched out into a variety of fields, including consumer electronics and productivity tools. The acquisition of Motorola Mobility provides Google with access to a wide range of patents and enables it to expand into the handset industry. While it would be too long to list all of Google's product offerings, some of the more popular offerings are listed below.

Search Engine

According to Larry Page, a good search engine "understands exactly what you mean and gives you back exactly what you want." This philosophy was the founding principle behind the creation of Google and is a top reason why the Google search engine surpassed its competitors.

Google could not have gained such prominence without an in-depth search index of articles, websites, and other content. The company creates this index using programs called "Googlebots," or crawlers that visit websites, copies the content, and follows its links to other webpages. This process is constantly repeated to ensure the most updated material incorporates into the index. Google's index is one of the most extensive in the world at 100 million gigabytes. Google uses technology such as PageRank to organize the results according to their perceived relevancy.

When a user types a search term into Google's search box, Google's index matches the term with what is deemed the most relevant materials and creates a list of these materials for the user. Each item of the list is followed by a few sentences describing the web page (called a "snippet"). To maintain a competitive edge, Google responds quickly to its users' queries. With a response time of approximately one-fourth of a second, Google ensures users get information almost instantaneously.

Web Browser

Google Chrome is an open source web browser that competes with Internet Explorer, Safari, Opera, and Mozilla Firefox. Google Chrome is praised for its speed, support, and security. The browser loads within seconds and maintains a simplistic design to make it easier for users to navigate. Like other browsers, Google Chrome allows users to pin multiple tabs and alert the user if he or she lands on a website considered risky (i.e., websites believed to contain malware). Chrome also regularly updates the browser to ensure it has the latest software to combat new malware attacks. Additionally, Google Chrome connects users to its Chrome web store where users can download apps, extensions, and more.

Email Account

Google's email account service, called Gmail, has approximately 425 million active users. Gmail surpassed Hotmail to become the top email service provider. The top three email service providers account for more than 1 billion users (the other two are Hotmail and Yahoo!). Users like Gmail for many reasons, but especially because of the ability to hold a large amount of data. Gmail has 7,600 megabytes of free storage, contains built-in chat functions, and has filters and labels for users to organize their mail. Gmail is fully integrated with other products, such as Google Voice, YouTube, and Google Reader.

YouTube

In 2006 Google acquired the video sharing site YouTube for $1.65 billion. YouTube is the third most popular site in the world. The site allows users to upload their original videos of up to 15 minutes in length. Both corporations and the average consumer use the video sharing site to post short videos ranging from spoofs to corporate messages to news events. YouTube has enabled Google to make millions in advertising revenues, and videos are often preceded by short advertisements.

Although YouTube opened new opportunities in marketing and entertainment, it has not been without its share of controversy. YouTube was sued by organizations such as Viacom for copyright infringement after finding copyrighted content on YouTube's site. YouTube specifically warns users wanting to upload content with the disclosure: "Do not upload TV shows, music videos or commercials without permission unless they consist entirely of content that you created yourself." However, not all users heed the warning. To detect and eliminate copyrighted material loaded onto YouTube, Google uses a system called Content ID to compare files on the site for similarities. If matches occur, then Google contacts the copyright holder and removes the video if so desired.

Android

In 2005 Google acquired the startup firm Android Inc. Android Inc. worked on mobile phone technology, and Google hoped to use this technology to break into the smartphone market. In 2008 the Android Operating System was released by the Open Handset Alliance, a team of organizations led by Google. The Android operating system is an open source platform; the source code is available for outside users to view (rather than protected under copyright). The Android operating system is most often used in mobile devices and tablet computers but can also be used in smartbooks and other devices.

The Android operating system has been used in HTC, Samsung, Motorola, T-Mobile, and Sony mobile phones. Android phones have become the most popular smartphone, with market share at about 50 percent, making it a strong competitor with the Apple iPhone. The number of Android apps downloaded since Android's release surpassed 10 billion. The Android has come far in its few years on the market and successfully increased Google's reach into electronics.

Advertising

Google's main source of revenue comes from advertising. In 2012 the company earned about $43.7 billion in advertising revenue. The primary form of advertising for Google is Google AdWords, introduced in 2000. Google AdWords differs from traditional advertising in that companies only pay when users click on the link or advertisement. The pay-per-click advertising is beneficial to companies because it offers a targeted way of reaching their audience. After the ads are created, companies choose keywords related to the business. When users type in these words, the company's ad appears along with the search results. Pay-per-click results appear at the right of the screen. By using AdWords, companies increase the effectiveness of their advertising dollars because they only pay for advertising to consumers interested enough to click on the advertisement.

Google also offers display advertising and mobile advertising. Display advertising provides companies with the choice to display their ads through text, videos, images, and interactive displays. Video ads and banner ads on YouTube became a popular advertising venue for businesses, particularly since YouTube is the third most accessed site in the world. Google Display Network gives companies the choice to place ads on related websites to target those consumers more interested in the company's product. Google's Mobile Advertising is also gaining in popularity. Mobile advertisements, or ads that appear on mobile phones, tablet computers, and apps, might soon revolutionize the advertising industry. Hence, mobile advertising has a great opportunity to transform Google's advertising offerings.

Google Wallet

If Google has its way, carrying wallets will become a thing of the past. Google developed a new mobile application called Google Wallet that substitutes for credit cards. First, users of phones with the Google Wallet app register their credit cards. At the checkout counter, users simply wave their phones in front of the payment terminal and enter a four-digit password for the transaction to go through. Many users like the convenience of Google Wallet. However, as of this writing, Google Wallet only works in stores that offer Master-Card PayPass and only about 15,000 merchants currently do so. Yet as paying with mobile technology gains in popularity, more merchants will likely purchase the technology to process mobile payments. Google Wallet may soon become a common sight on smart phones.

Newer Products

Google offers a number of other products to businesses and consumers. Its Google Analytics is a market research tool that helps businesses analyze their website and mobile traffic. Google Analytics is one way to make statistical analysis easier for businesses. Google

Analytics holds 82 percent market share among analytics companies. Google Drive is a site that allows users to store and share documents with other users. Google Drive provides spreadsheets that allow users to compile data and tools to aid in quick data analysis. Google+ is a social networking site allowing friends to communicate with one another and post updates. Although initial enthusiasm for the site was high, Google+ is still below Facebook, with users spending an average of 3–5 minutes on Google+ monthly. Google's free offerings are easily accessible through a user's Google account.

One of Google's newest products is meant to challenge the iPad and Kindle Fire tablet computers. In 2012 Google unveiled the Nexus 7 tablet. The Nexus 7 was built by the computer company Asus but was designed by Google. The tablet undergirds the Apple iPad's price with a selling point of $199. It could be a formidable competitor to Amazon's Kindle Fire, which sells at the same price. The Nexus 7 allows users to read books and magazines or watch movies. Another product that could change the computer industry is Google Glass, a wearable computer in the form of glasses worn on the face. While Google Glass has received positive feedback, it has also created privacy concerns. The glasses are so unassuming that it is relatively easy to record others without their permission. There is also significant concern that Google Glass will enable cheating. Critics speculate that students might use Google Glass during tests without anybody noticing. Concerns over cheating are not limited to the classroom; casinos in New Jersey and Nevada have banned Google Glass from their floors. Google will have to determine whether these concerns will become a hindrance for its newest invention.

GOOGLE'S INITIATIVES

Like all major corporations, Google is expected to act with integrity and give back to the communities where it does business. No longer is it acceptable for major multinationals to pursue profitability without taking into account consumers, employees, communities, and the environment. Google has therefore invested in a number of initiatives that support economic development, environmental awareness, and charitable endeavors.

Google Ventures

In 2009 Google formed Google Ventures as a separate entity to provide funding for startup firms. The company created a $100 million fund to invest in startup companies at the forefront of technological innovation. The company not only invests in firms that market Internet-based technologies or consumer electronics, but also invested in green technology firms, biotechnology companies, and more. Google Ventures' goal is to invest in entrepreneurs that can change the world through technology by having "a healthy disregard for the impossible."

Google Green

Google has recognized the business opportunities from adopting greener operations and technologies. Greener technology not only saves Google money in the long run with decreased energy costs, it also enables the company to create greener products for consumers. According to Google, using its servers for one month uses less energy than leaving a light on for three hours. Google purchases carbon offsets to reduce its emissions to zero. (Purchases of carbon offsets go toward carbon reduction projects. Therefore, a company that cannot reduce its carbon emissions any further can purchase carbon offsets to reduce carbon emissions in other areas.) For employees, Google offers a shuttle system run on bio-diesel, an on-campus car sharing program, and the largest electric vehicle charging station in the country. Google has also invested in alternative energy projects, such as SolarCity's initiatives to place solar panels on residential homes. Other green successses for Google include a solar installation on its campus, energy-efficient data centers, and buildings that are LEED certified.

Google.org

Google.org is the charitable arm of the organization. The purpose of Google.org is to create "technologies to help address global challenges and supports innovative partners through grants, investments and in-kind resources." Google.org contributes grant money, develops tools for nonprofits, and provides disaster relief. The tools Google.org offers include Google for Nonprofits and Google Dengue & Flu Trends. Google for Nonprofits provides resources such as discounts on Google products and free AdWords to nonprofit organizations. Google Dengue & Flu Trends collects updated data on flu and dengue diseases and shows a map of the areas currently active. Google also partnered with the National Center for Missing and Exploited Children to provide tools for the nonprofit's fight against global child exploitation.

Google also encourages employees to get involved in giving back to their communities. For instance, Google matches employee contributions to nonprofits. In June each year Google encourages employees to take a day and donate their time to volunteer in their communities. Google also sponsors the Dollars for Doers Initiative to encourage employees to volunteer at nonprofits. Google pledges to donate $50 to a nonprofit for every five hours a Google employee volunteers.

PRIVACY

Being a large company, Google has many risks and ethical issues it must constantly address. In many ways Google helped advance ethical conduct in the web and technology industry. Google is a recipient of *Ethisphere's* World's Most Ethical Companies for its contributions to the community and the environment. The company consistently ranks among *Fortune* magazine's "100 Best Companies to Work For" because of its fun and innovative work environment.

At the same time, Google has been accused of questionable activity, from antitrust issues to copyright infringement to accepting illegal ads from Canadian pharmaceutical firms. For instance, Google's proposal to digitize books sparked outrage from publishers who still owned the copyrights. Although Google reached a settlement with the publishers, a judge threw out the agreement. Google also faced intense antitrust scrutiny from the European community, which tends to have stricter antitrust laws than the United States. Competitors in Europe claim Google uses its dominant market position to promote its own offerings and demote rival results in search listings. Although Google proposed legally-binding changes in the way it presents search results to Europeans, its competitors rejected Google's proposal. The European Commission must determine whether Google's proposal will be sufficient. Failure to comply with Europe's antitrust laws can result in fines of 10 percent of global revenues. As Google continues to grow and expand into other industries, it will likely face more pressure from those who fear Google might gain too much power. The company must carefully reflect upon these issues when considering new ventures.

For the sake of brevity, this case will analyze one major ethical issue Google has continually wrestled with as it seeks to expand its reach: privacy. The advent of the Internet and mobile technology provides so many opportunities for stakeholders that many do not realize the cost for this information might be privacy. Consumers are shocked to find that web companies such as Google and Facebook track their online activity and often use this information to tailor advertisements or sell to marketers. For Google—which offers so much free content and gets most of its revenue from advertising—this information is valuable to its continued business operations. Some consumers also feel that use of their personal information is a small price to pay in exchange for using Google's superior services. Google's privacy page details what information it collects and how it uses that information. For instance, Google shares information with its partners but claims this information is non-identifiable. According to Google, any information identifying users must have user consent to be shared with outside parties.

Despite Google's attempts to be transparent, there are ethical gray areas regarding the collection and use of data. Because there is so little legislation to regulate how Internet companies gather and employ user information, it is tempting for firms to push the limits on privacy. Going too far, however, creates problems in terms of reputation and legal entanglements. Google has sometimes appeared to take a cavalier attitude toward privacy in the past. For instance, former CEO Eric Schmidt was quoted, "If you don't want anyone to know, don't do it." In 2007 Google was given a "hostile to privacy" rating by Privacy International. Although Google is the most popular search engine, 52 percent of Google users have concerns about their privacy on the site. This could be a potential obstacle for Google since consumer trust plays a big role in how they interact with a company. The following sections discuss some of the major privacy issues Google has experienced.

Google Search Queries

One of the major privacy criticisms levied against Google is the fact that the company keeps track of users' search terms. Consider all of the things you have ever searched for using Google's search engine. Then consider how comfortable you would feel if a company recorded and stored all those search terms…forever. To be fair this practice is not limited to Google—many other Internet firms do the same. However, because Google is the most popular search engine in the world, it is more heavily scrutinized.

The big question users ask is whether their search terms can be traced back to them personally. Google claims that although it stores users' search terms, after 18 months the data becomes "anonymized." Theoretically, it becomes untraceable. However, critics debate this claim because anonymized data from other search engines have been used to locate users. Google claims it treats this information with respect, using it to refine its search engine. Yet under the Third Party Doctrine and the Patriot Act the U.S. government could subpoena this information if it is deemed necessary for national security. Needless to say, Google's storage of users' search terms is an uncomfortable and controversial topic.

Google in China

Google has had a tough time in China. When Google decided to enter the world's most populous country, it faced an ethical dilemma. On the one hand, Google did not want to miss the opportunity to tap into a market consisting of more than 1 billion consumers. On the other hand, entering China required Google to allow the government to censor its users' searches, something that conflicted with Google's mantra "Don't Be Evil." Based on this principle, businesses should not engage in conduct that could benefit the firm at the expense of the interest or welfare of society. Allowing the government to monitor search results—while common in many countries—is considered to be a violation of user rights to privacy in the United States.

Despite criticism, Google applied the principles of utilitarianism to the situation and concluded that the benefits of doing business in China outweighed the costs. It decided it could do more good by providing Chinese citizens with "the greatest amount of information," even if some of that information was censored. Google began self-censoring some of the more controversial search terms to placate Chinese authorities. However, the company encountered problems in China almost from the onset. The government often blocked user access to certain sites, which sometimes caused computer outages. Google claimed the Chinese government interfered with their site. After intense pressure and cyberhacking from Chinese hackers, Google stopped its practice of self-censorship and moved its operations to Hong Kong. Google saw its market share in China plunge, giving its Chinese rival Baidu the upper hand.

In 2012 Google announced it would provide a mechanism to warn users when a search term might encounter censorship. Yet by informing users about which search terms were likely to be restricted, Google once again ran afoul of Chinese authorities. Internet restrictions are not available to consumers or companies, but are government secrets. Calling attention to terms that are clearly restricted went against Chinese government policies. Chinese authorities responded by cutting off services. Google eventually capitulated to the government and discontinued the warning feature. Chinese censorship and privacy will likely remain significant issues Google must regularly address in the oncoming years.

Tracking Users

Tracking users has become a major issue for Google. A storm of criticism was unleashed when government regulators and consumers learned the company's phones tracked users' locations. It was revealed Android phones contained location-logging features that enabled the firm to collect GPS coordinates of its users as well as the coordinates of nearby WiFi networks. Similar tracking features were found on the Apple iPhone. The revelations spurred legislators to write letters to Google asking for clarification on how they track users and use this information.

Privacy advocates claim these tracking features violate users' right to privacy, particularly since most users did not know about the feature. Google defended its phone tracking feature, stating this information was necessary to build Google's location-based network and allow it to effectively compete. It also claims this data is often necessary for certain mobile applications and websites to work.

Google also tracks users on the Internet. Such tracking is not uncommon among Internet search engines. For Google it is often necessary to generate revenue by tailoring ads to users based on the sites they visit. Many privacy advocates do not like this policy, and regulators became concerned over how Google uses the information it collects. Google's privacy policies allow users to opt out of certain tracking functions for advertisement purposes, but users must make the decision to opt out. Google also added a "do not track feature" on its Google Chrome.

On the other hand, supporters of Google tracking maintain that the tracking is necessary to provide the best services to users. These services are often free of cost because Google is able to generate revenue through advertising. Consumers must therefore be proactive in deciding whether they place greater value on their privacy or Google's free services.

Although some people do not appear to mind having their web activity tracked in exchange for Google's free services, Google received heavy backlash for bypassing anti-tracking mechanisms. In 2012 security analysts revealed that Google bypassed default privacy settings on the Safari browser. The Safari browser, developed by Apple, is used by 6 percent of Internet users for desktop browsing and 50 percent for mobile browsing. It is the only major browser to date with a default setting that blocks third-party cookies. Cookies are streams of data installed on a user's computer when he or she visits certain sites. When the person revisits the site, the cookie informs the website about the user's web activity.

Security analysts realized Google used loopholes in the system to track users on the Safari browser. Google offered rationales for bypassing the browser policies but stopped the practice after an article was published in *The Wall Street Journal*. The Federal Trade Commission (FTC) launched an investigation to determine if Google violated its agreement to stop misrepresenting its privacy practices to the public. Google agreed to pay $22.5 million to settle charges by the FTC. U.S. state attorneys general also launched investigations to determine whether to levy fines against Google. Although Google might have legitimate reasons to track user activity, bypassing default mechanisms appeared deceptive and underhanded.

More recently, Google was accused of another privacy violation, this time in the U.K. In 2010 Google made the announcement that it had accidentally scanned data from users' wireless networks. Google uses vans with special detection equipment and cameras to drive around collecting data and photos for its location-based services. Unfortunately, because of software that had inadvertently been uploaded into the company's equipment, its vans also scanned wireless networks of some nearby residences, including their emails. Google promised the Information Commissioner's Office in the U.K. it would destroy the data it collected from U.K. users. A later investigation in 2012 revealed Google still retained some of this user data, placing the company in noncompliance and in breach of their agreement. Although Google apologized and called this retention of data an error, its violations have likely increased its image of being a firm that disregards privacy.

Google was fined $25,000 by the Federal Communications Commission (FCC) in 2012 for deliberately delaying and impeding an investigation into the way they collect information and take photos for their Street View service. While Google employees drove around taking pictures for the service, they also picked up information through unsecured WiFi networks in these neighborhoods. This information included private emails and chat messages that could be traced back to specific people at specific addresses. Google claimed it was not their intention to gather this information, but failed to delete it from their databases within a reasonable amount of time. Further legal action was not taken since the FCC needed more factual evidence that Google claimed not to have. In March 2013, Google agreed to pay a fine of $7 million for Wi-Fi data collection when they took photos for their street-view feature of maps in the United States.

Another privacy related incident for Google involves the Google Play App Store. A developer who started selling his mobile application through Google's app store was shocked to find he was given access to his customers' sensitive information. The privacy policies of the Google Play Store and Google Wallet are hard to understand, and it is alleged that customers do not know the kind of information they give up when making a purchase. Google, again, claims customers are told what kind of information is shared to developers when they purchase an app. However, criticism over its privacy policies continues.

Hacking Attack

In 2011 Google released some disturbing information regarding the privacy of user accounts on Gmail. The company claimed a wide-scale phishing attack had broken into the Gmail accounts of hundreds of users, including politicians, political activists, and military personnel. Google claimed the cyberattack was launched from somewhere inside China. Although government officials are not supposed to send emails containing secret information from their Gmail accounts, many use Gmail for both work and personal purposes. The chance that hackers might gain access to top secret information in emails is a serious concern for the U.S. government. The Chinese government denies it had anything to do with the attack.

After the attack was detected, Google worked to secure user accounts and notify those it suspected were victims of the attack. One security analyst believes the attacks might have occurred for at least a year before discovery. The chances a foreign government entity could use illegally obtained Internet information for harmful purposes became such a concern that the U.S. government stated such a cyberattack could be equivalent to a declaration of war. Although Google was not heavily criticized for the attack, the company should continue to safeguard user information through updated security measures.

Google Privacy Audits

Although Google faced lawsuits from consumers claiming the company violated their privacy rights, a lack of Internet legislation enables Google to continue many of its practices. However, Google found itself in trouble with government authorities after allegedly violating its privacy policies. In 2010 Google launched the failed social networking platform Google Buzz. Users with Gmail accounts received an email that gave them the option of joining or not joining Google Buzz. Those that clicked on Google Buzz were largely unaware the identities of their frequent contacts on Gmail would be made publicly available on the Internet through Google Buzz. Additionally, although users could opt out of having this information released, they claimed the opt out features were difficult to locate. The Federal Trade Commission also alleged that even those users who opted out of joining Google Buzz complained they were still enrolled in certain features of the social network. Also, they claimed those who wanted to leave the network were not fully removed.

Although Google worked to fix these problems after many user complaints, the Federal Trade Commission launched an investigation. It found Google had acted deceptively and violated its privacy policies. Google agreed to settle with the FTC by allowing third parties to conduct biannual privacy audits regarding how the company uses information.

These audits will take place for 20 years. Facebook agreed to a similar deal after allegedly violating users' rights to privacy. If Google is found to be in violation of the agreement, the FTC could impose fines of $16,000 for each violation each day.

These audits are a blow to Google's operations. As one of the first Internet companies to have these kinds of audits imposed on them, the company will have to tread carefully regarding how it collects and uses information. On the other hand, Google might choose to see this as an opportunity to improve its internal controls and privacy policies to ensure users' information is respected. Doing so could gain the trust of users and prevent future legislative action against the company. As the world's largest Internet company the actions Google takes in this area will significantly impact the future activities of other companies.

Changes to Google's Privacy Policy

In early 2012 Google announced new changes to its privacy policies. The company notified users of the change through email. According to the email, Google took all the information it had on its users and combined it. This means instead of having separate privacy policies for each of its offerings (Gmail, Google+, Chrome, etc.), Google created one privacy policy that applies to all of its service offerings equally. Users were initially not happy about the new privacy policy. They feared some of the things they discussed privately, such as through their Gmail accounts or Android phones, might show up in the form of ads on the search engine. Google claimed this simplified the privacy policy process since users only have to read one privacy policy rather than privacy policies for each of its services. Many analysts also state the policy is not new; Google was already doing these things. Users were told that Google's new policy wwould not enable the company to gain any more information than it already collects.

Once again the question comes up as to whether this new privacy policy is invasive. Supporters argue that Google uses this information to create improved services for users. It helps the firm remain competitive with strong rivals such as Apple and Facebook. Critics are concerned that the ease with which Google appears to change its policies could spell trouble for users and their rights to privacy. These concerns become more serious because so many users depend on some aspect of Google, whether it is Gmail, Google+, Android phones, or other services.

The changes in privacy policies concerned government officials in the United States and the European Union (EU). Congressional officials notified Google and asked it to explain the changes to its privacy policies in more detail. Google drafted a 13-page letter to answer government questions. According to Google, users have the ability to turn off certain features that collect data. The company stated the new policy would not impact the amount of data it collects or deletes and it remained highly committed to user privacy.

The EU Justice Commissioner questioned the legality of Google's new policy according to EU law. French data regulators launched an investigation concerning the new policy, believing the policy might not adhere to EU Internet transparency and privacy laws. Google maintains its new policy meets EU regulations. However, in April of 2013, six European countries banded together to take legal action against Google for not complying with the requests of the government. Google could face significant fines and possible restrictions for conducting business in Europe. Because of the multinational nature of Google, it must continually exert caution when making major changes as these changes might conflict with the legal requirements of certain countries. Google has learned time and again that activities which are legal in one country might not necessarily be legal in another.

GOVERNMENT RESPONSE TO PRIVACY ISSUES

Consumer concerns over privacy issues prompted the government to consider new legislation regulating what information Internet companies such as Google can collect and how they can use it. As a result, many firms have instituted "do not track" features that users can click on if they wish to avoid being tracked. Google installed this feature in its Google Chrome. Such self-regulation is an attempt to ward off federal legislation that could seriously limit Google's tracking activities.

Some of the ideas regulators have been discussing include a User's Bill of Rights and a Do Not Track mechanism that would be mandatory for Internet companies to use. The Bill of Rights would make sure companies adhere to certain privacy practices. Its intent would be to make Internet privacy policies easier for users to understand. A Do Not Track mechanism would be similar to Do Not Call legislation. Companies cannot sell to consumers over the telephone if those consumers are on the national Do Not Call registry. Doing so subjects companies to fines. Something similar for the Internet could seriously impact how Internet companies collect information.

Because legislation could be a serious threat to Google, the company spends millions in lobbying and employs lobbyists for its staff. Google hopes to stave off regulation it feels restricts its ability to coordinate targeted advertising or offer customized services to users. The company joined with other Internet firms to protest and defeat two bills being considered, the Stop Online Piracy Act and the Protect IP Act that would restrict how websites use material subject to copyright. However, with privacy issues and Internet breaches becoming a growing concern, chances for increased regulation is likely. Although Google might not be able to forgo legislation restricting some of the activities of Internet firms, it can work with regulators to consider legislation with less of a negative effect on its operations. Google's lobbyists will have a profound impact on the passage of laws safeguarding Internet security.

CONCLUSION

Google's success story is unparalleled among search engine providers. The company started off as a small search engine and ranking system and became one of the most profitable Internet companies in the world. Today the company is the owner or provider of products that go above and beyond its search engine, including Google+, YouTube, Android, Motorola Mobility, the Nexus 7 tablet computer, Google Wallet, and Google Glass. While there might be a risk of Google overextending itself, the company has a talent for making highly profitable acquisitions that increase its global reach.

Google has made itself into the epitome of a "best company to work for." The benefits Google offers its employees are extensive, and Google empowers employees to embark on projects and make decisions to improve the company's operations. The company took a strong stand on green initiatives and supporting technologies to address global challenges.

Google's ten core principles provide a blueprint for how employees should conduct themselves within the company. Its "Don't Be Evil" mantra became a popular phrase to guide Google's actions and determine where it should draw the line.

On the other hand, Google has faced many challenges in privacy, many of which continue to this day. From its controversial move of entering China to tracking users' Internet and smartphone habits, Google has been highly criticized for what many privacy advocates believe are infringements on users' rights. Google has been forced to draw a fine line between using user information to generate revenue and violating user privacy. Because Google is able to generate targeted advertising through its collection of information, the company offers quality Internet services to its users for free. At the same time Google has committed questionable actions that seem to infringe on users' rights, such as bypassing Apple Safari's default no tracking mechanism. Google has also encountered resistance from governments, both in the United States and outside of the country.

The privacy issue Google faces will not be solved anytime soon. With the threat of new regulation, Google took measures such as lobbying to make sure legislation is not passed that proves unfavorable to the company. Because Google depends on tracking and other activities to maintain profitability, it has a large stake in the privacy issue. Yet rather than seeing this solely as a liability, Google might instead choose to improve its privacy practices and increase transparency in its operations. Google has the responsibility to ensure the rights of stakeholders are respected. Although Google made great strides in social responsibility, both the company and society know there is room for improvement. Google is in the unique position to positively impact how companies interact on the Internet.

QUESTIONS

1. How can Google use its power to improve the lives of its stakeholders?
2. Do you feel there is any way Google can respect privacy and yet still maintain its profitability?
3. What are some of the effects government regulation of the Internet might have on Google's operations?

SOURCES

"100 Best Companies to Work For," *Fortune*, http://money.cnn.com/magazines/fortune/bestcompanies/2010/snapshots/4.html (accessed February 18, 2010); "100 Best Companies to Work For," *CNNMoney*, 2012, http://money.cnn.com/magazines/fortune/best-companies/2012/full_list/ (accessed July 6, 2012); "2012 Financial Tables," Google Investor Relations, http://investor.google.com/financial/tables.html (accessed April); "2012 Internet Browser Software Comparisons," *TopTenREVIEWS*, http://internet-browser-review.toptenreviews.com/ (accessed April 2, 2012); Byron Acohido, "Lawmakers request probe of tracking by Apple and Google," *USA Today*, April 25, 2011, 1B; Byron Acohido, "Most Google, Facebook users fret over privacy," *USA Today*, February 9, 2011, 1B; George Anders, "The Rare Find," *Bloomberg Businessweek*, October 17–October 23, 2011, 106–112; Julia Angwin, "Google, FTC Near Privacy Settlement," *The Wall Street Journal*, July 10, 2012, A1; Charles Arthur, "Google faces EC showdown over antitrust regulators," July 1, 2013, http://www.guardian.co.uk/technology/2013/jul/01/google-ec-antitrust-remedies (accessed July 12, 2013); Charles Arthur, "Google Facing Legal Threat from Six European Countries Over Privacy," *The Guardian*, April 2, 2013, http://www.guardian.co.uk/technology/2013/apr/02/google-privacy-policy-legal-threat-europe (accessed April 2, 2013);

Associated Press, "Developments Related to Google's Privacy Concerns," *The Huffington Post*, April 2, 2013, http://www.huffingtonpost.com/huff-wires/20130402/tec-google-privacy-history/?utm_hp_ref=travel&ir=travel (accessed April 2, 2013); Associated Press, "Google buys YouTube for $1.65 billion," *MSNBC*, October 10, 2006, http://www.msnbc.msn.com/id/15196982/ns/business-us_business/t/google-buys-youtube-billion/ (accessed April 2, 2012); Associated Press reporter, "Casinos ban gamblers from wearing Google Glass 'because the device could be used to cheat," *Daily Mail*, June 6, 2013, http://www.dailymail.co.uk/news/article-2337083/Casinos-ban-gamblers-wearing-Google-Glass-device-used-cheat.html (accessed July 12, 2013); John Battelle, "The Birth of Google," *Wired*, August 2005, http://www.wired.com/wired/archive/13.08/battelle.html?pg=2&topic=battelle&topic_set= (accessed October 27, 2011); "Benefits," Google Jobs, http://www.google.com/support/jobs/bin/static.py?page=benefits.html (accessed February 18, 2010); Katherine Boehret, "Google Mobile App Aims To Turn Phones Into Wallets" *The Wall Street Journal*, September 21, 2011, D2; Christina Bonnington, "Google's 10 Billion Android App Downloads: By the Numbers," *Wired*, December 8, 2011, http://www.wired.com/gadgetlab/2011/12/10-billion-apps-detailed/ (accessed April 13, 2012); Bianca Bosker, "Google Privacy Policy Changing For Everyone: So What's Really Going To Happen?" *The Huffington Post*, February 29, 2012, http://www.huffingtonpost.com/2012/02/29/google-privacy-policy-changes_n_1310506.html (accessed June 29, 2012); Mark Brownlow, "Email and Webmail Statistics," *Email Marketing Reports*, January 2012, http://www.email-marketing-reports.com/metrics/email-statistics.htm (accessed April 2, 2012); Thomas Catan, "Google Forks Over Settlement On Rx Ads," *The Wall Street Journal*, August 25, 2011, B1; Loretta Chao, "Google Tips Off Users in China," *The Wall Street Journal*, June 3, 2012, http://online.wsj.com/article/SB10001424052702303552104577439840152584930.html (accessed June 8, 2012); "Company," *Google*, http://www.google.com/corporate/index.html (accessed October 27, 2011); "Display Network," Google Ads, http://www.google.com/ads/displaynetwork/ (accessed June 1, 2012); Morgan Downs (Producer), *Inside the Mind of Google* [DVD], United States: CNBC Originals, 2010; Amir Efrati, "Google Call Data 'Valuable'," *The Wall Street Journal*, May 2, 2011, B3; Ben Elgin, "Google Buys Android for Its Mobile Arsenal," *Bloomberg Businessweek*, August 17, 2005, http://www.webcitation.org/5wk7sIvVb (accessed April 13, 2012); Rip Empson, "Google Biz Chief: Over 10M Websites Now Using Google Analytics," TechCrunch, April 12, 2012, http://techcrunch.com/2012/04/12/google-analytics-officially-at-10m/ (accessed June 1, 2012); Federal Trade Commission, "FTC Charges Deceptive Privacy Practices in Google's Rollout of Its Buzz Social Network," March 30, 2011, http://www.ftc.gov/opa/2011/03/google.shtm (accessed June 28, 2012); Kelly Fiveash, "Google bets biennial privacy audit after Buzz blunder," *The Register*, March 30, 2011, http://www.theregister.co.uk/2011/03/30/google_buzz_ftc_proposed_settlement/ (accessed June 28, 2012); Sara Forden, Eric Engleman, Adam Satariano, and Stephanie Bodoni, "Can the U.S. Get Its Act Together on Privacy?" *Bloomberg Businessweek*, May 16-May 22, 2011, 27–28; FoxNews.com, "Gmail Accounts Compromised by Chinese Hackers, Google Says," June 1, 2011, http://www.foxnews.com/scitech/2011/06/01/gmail-compromised-chinese-hackers-google-says/ (accessed June 28, 2012); Kent German, "A brief history of Android phones," *CNET*, August 2, 2011, http://reviews.cnet.com/8301-19736_7-20016542-251/a-brief-history-of-android-phones/ (accessed April 12, 2012); "Gmail," *Google*, https://accounts.google.com/ServiceLogin?service=mail&passive=true&rm=false&continue=https://mail.google.com/mail/&ss=1&scc=1&ltmpl=default&ltmplcache=2&hl=en (accessed April 2, 2012); David Goldman, "Google unveils $199 'Nexus 7' tablet," *CNNMoney*, June 27, 2012, http://money.cnn.com/2012/06/27/technology/google-nexus-7-tablet/ (accessed June 28, 2012); "Google Ads—Mobile Ads," http://www.google.com/ads/mobile/ (accessed June 1, 2012); "Google AdWords," http://www.google.com/ads/adwords2/ (accessed June 1, 2012); "Google Benefits," http://www.google.com/intl/en/jobs/lifeatgoogle/benefits (accessed November 21, 2011); "Google CEO On Privacy (VIDEO): 'If You Have Something You Don't Want Anyone To Know, Maybe You Shouldn't Be Doing It'," *Huffington Post*, May 25, 2011, http://www.huffingtonpost.com/2009/12/07/google-ceo-on-privacy-if_n_383105.html (accessed June 8, 2012); "Google Green," http://www.google.com/green/ (accessed June 7, 2012); Google, "Human Rights Caucus Briefing," Google Blog, February 1, 2006, http://googleblog.blogspot.com/2006/02/human-rights-caucus-briefing.html#!/2006/02/human-rights-caucus-briefing.html (accessed June 8, 2012); "Google Pay Per Click Marketing," Costa Technologies, Inc., http://www.echicagoweb.com/internet-marketing/pay-per-click-marketing/google-adwords-ppc/ (accessed June 1, 2012); "Google privacy changes 'in breach of EU law'," *BBC*, March 1, 2012, http://www.bbc.com/news/technology-17205754 (accessed June 29, 2012); "Google ranked 'worst' on privacy," *BBC News*, June 11, 2007, http://news.bbc.co.uk/2/hi/technology/6740075.stm (accessed June 8, 2012);

"Google Ventures," http://www.googleventures.com/ (accessed June 1, 2012); "Google.org," http://www.google.org/index.html (accessed June 7, 2012); Josh Halliday, "Google's dropped anti-censorship warning marks quiet defeat in China," *The Guardian*, January 7, 2013, http://www.guardian.co.uk/technology/2013/jan/04/google-defeat-china-censorship-battle (accessed April 15, 2013); Kashmir Hill, "So, What Are These Privacy Audits That Google And Facebook Have To Do For The Next 20 Years?" *Forbes*, November 30, 2011, http://www.forbes.com/sites/kashmirhill/2011/11/30/so-what-are-these-privacy-audits-that-google-and-facebook-have-to-do-for-the-next-20-years/ (accessed June 28, 2012); Andrew Hinton, "2008 World's Most Ethical Companies," *Ethisphere*, 2008, http://ethisphere.com/wme2008/ (accessed June 8, 2012); Tiffany Hsu, "Google creates $280-million solar power fund," *Los Angeles Times,* June 14, 2011, http://articles.latimes.com/2011/jun/14/business/la-fi-google-solar-20110614 (accessed November 9, 2011); Betsy Isaacson, "Google Glass Captures Arrest On Camera, Sparks Controversy," *The Huffington Post*, July 10, 2013, http://www.huffingtonpost.com/2013/07/08/google-glass-arrest_n_3562095.html (accessed July 10, 2013); Don Jeffrey, "Google Argues For Dismissal Of Author's Book-Scan Lawsuit," *Bloomberg*, May 3, 2012, http://www.bloomberg.com/news/2012-05-03/google-argues-for-dismissal-of-authors-book-scan-lawsuit.html (accessed June 8, 2012); Laura June, "Toshiba AC100 Android smartbook hits the United Kingdom," engadget, September 6, 2010, http://www.engadget.com/2010/09/06/toshiba-ac100-android-smartbook-hits-the-united-kingdom/ (accessed April 13, 2012); Tom Krazit, "Google's Chrome browser gets do-not-track feature," *Cnet*, January 14, 2011, http://news.cnet.com/8301-30684_3-20029348-265.html (accessed June 28, 2012); Heather Leonard, "Mobile Advertising Is Google's Next Frontier," *Business Insider*, January 26, 2012, http://articles.businessinsider.com/2012-01-26/tech/30665888_1_iad-platform-mobile-advertising-google-wallet (accessed June 1, 2012); John Letzing, "Google Acknowledges Still Having Contested User Data," *The Wall Street Journal*, July 27, 2012, http://online.wsj.com/article/SB10000872396390443343704577553142360965420.html (accessed August 1, 2012); Sean Ludwig, "Gmail finally blows past Hotmail to become the world's largest email service," *Venture Beat*, June 28, 2012, http://venturebeat.com/2012/06/28/gmail-hotmail-yahoo-email-users/ (accessed April 15, 2013); Mike Luttrell, "Android suffers first-ever market share decline," TG Daily, January 27, 2012, http://www.tgdaily.com/mobility-brief/61070-android-suffers-first-ever-market-share-decline (accessed April 12, 2012); Douglas MacMillan, "Google's Display Ad Sales Should Top $1 Billion," *Bloomberg Businessweek*, February 8, 2010, http://www.businessweek.com/technology/content/feb2010/tc2010027_356976.htm (accessed June 1, 2012); "Rhodri Marsden: Why did my YouTube account get closed down?" *The Independent*, August 12, 2009, http://www.independent.co.uk/life-style/gadgets-and-tech/features/rhodri-marsden-why-did-my-youtube-account-get-closed-down-1770618.html (accessed April 13, 2012); Millward Brown Optimer, *Brandz™ Top 100 Most Valuable Global Brands 2011*, 12–13, http://www.millwardbrown.com/libraries/optimor_brandz_files/2011_brandZ_top100_report.sflb.ashx (accessed October 27, 2011); "More about Content ID," YouTube, http://www.youtube.com/t/contentid_more (accessed April 13, 2012); Jeff Neff, "Apple ends Google's four-year run as the most valuable brand," *Advertising Age*, May 9, 2011, http://www.millwardbrown.com/Libraries/MB_Articles_Downloads/Ad_Age_BrandZ_2011_May.sflb.ashx (accessed October 27, 2011); Dennis O'Reilly, "How to prevent Google from tracking you," *Cnet*, January 30, 2012, http://howto.cnet.com/8301-11310_39-57368016-285/how-to-prevent-google-from-tracking-you/ (accessed June 28, 2012); Alexei Oreskovic and Michael Sin, "Google app store policy raises privacy concerns," *Reuters*, February 14, 2013, http://www.reuters.com/article/2013/02/14/us-google-privacy-idUSBRE91D1LL20130214 (accessed April 4, 2013); Nicole Perlroth, "Under Scrutiny, Google Spends Record Amount on Lobbying," *The New York Times*, April 23, 2012, http://bits.blogs.nytimes.com/2012/04/23/under-scrutiny-google-spends-record-amount-on-lobbying/ (accessed June 29, 2012); "Philosophy and Goals," Open Source Project, http://www.webcitation.org/5wiyo36ap (accessed April 13, 2012); "Privacy Policy," Google: Policies and Principles, http://www.google.com/policies/privacy/ (accessed June 8, 2012); Emil Protalinksi, "Google says it's 'thinking carefully' about Glass design as concerns arise from casinos, regulators over cheating," The Next Web, June 5, 2013, http://thenextweb.com/google/2013/06/05/casinos-in-two-states-have-now-banned-google-glass-over-fear-of-users-cheating-at-card-games/ (accessed July 12, 2013); Kirit Radia, "U.S. to probe alleged Chinese hack of senior officials' Gmail accounts," *ABC News*, June 2, 2011, http://abcnews.go.com/Politics/us-probe-alleged-chinese-hack-senior-officials-gmail/story?id=13744049 (accessed June 28, 2012); Austin Ramzy, "Google Ends Policy of Self-Censorship in China," *TIME*, January 13, 2010, http://www.time.com/time/world/article/0,8599,1953248,00.html (accessed June 8, 2012); Don Reisinger, "Google responds to Congress over policy privacy inquiries," *Cnet*, January 1, 2012, http://news.cnet.com/8301-13506_3-57368788-17/google-responds-to-congress-over-privacy-policy-inquiries/ (accessed June 29, 2012); Reuters, "Google forms $100 million venture fund," March 31, 2009, http://uk.reuters.com/article/2009/03/31/google-fund-idUKN3135783620090331 (accessed June 1, 2012); Shane Richmond, "Google responds to European antitrust investigators," *The Telegraph*, July 2, 2013, http://www.telegraph.co.uk/technology/google/9371092/Google-responds-to-Europe-antitrust-investigators.html (accessed July 12, 2013); Ryan Singel, "Google Busted with Hand in Safari-Browser Cookie Jar," *Wired*, February 17, 2012, http://www.wired.com/threatlevel/2012/02/google-safari-browser-cookie/ (accessed June 29, 2012); "Sources: US decides cyberattack can be 'act of war'," *MSNBC*, May 21, 2011, http://www.msnbc.msn.com/id/43224451/ns/us_news-security/t/sources-us-decides-cyber-attack-can-be-act-war/ (accessed June 28, 2012); David Streitfeld, "Google Is Faulted for Impeding U.S. Inquiry on Data Collection," *New York Times*, April 15, 2012, http://www.nytimes.com/2012/04/15/technology/google-is-fined-for-impeding-us-inquiry-on-data-collection.html?pagewanted=1&ref=davidstreitfeld (accessed April 4, 2013); David Streitfeld and Kevin J. O'Brien, "Google Privacy Inquiries Get Little Cooperation," *New York Times*, May 23, 2012, http://www.nytimes.com/2012/05/23/technology/google-privacy-inquiries-get-little-cooperation.html?pagewanted=all&_r=0 (accessed April 4, 2013); "Top Sites," Alexa, http://www.alexa.com/topsites (accessed April 2, 2012); Jennifer Valentino-DeVries, "What Do Google's Privacy Changes Mean For You?" *The Wall Street Journal*, January 25, 2012, http://blogs.wsj.com/digits/2012/01/25/what-do-googles-privacy-changes-mean-for-you/ (accessed June 29, 2012); Todd Wasserman, "Google Plus users spent just 3.3 minutes there last month," *CNN*, February 28, 2012, http://www.cnn.com/2012/02/28/tech/social-media/google-plus-comscore/index.html (accessed June 1, 2012); "Why Use Google Chrome?" Google, https://www.google.com/chrome/intl/en/more/index.html (accessed April 2, 2012); Christopher Williams, "Google Faces Privacy Investigation Over Merging Search, Gmail, and YouTube Data," *The Telegraph*, April 2, 2013. http://www.telegraph.co.uk/technology/google/9966704/Google-faces-privacy-investigation-over-merging-search-Gmail-and-YouTube-data.html (accessed April 15, 2013); YouTube website, http://www.youtube.com/ (accessed April 2, 2012).

CASE 8

Zappos: Delivering Customer Satisfaction*

Can a company focused on happiness be successful? Zappos, an online retailer, is proving it can. The company's revenue grew from $1.6 million in 2000 to $1.64 billion a decade later. Tony Hsieh, Zappos' CEO says, "It's a brand about happiness, whether to customers or employees or even vendors." Zappos' zany corporate culture and focus on customer satisfaction has made it both successful and a model for other companies.

This case examines how Zappos' focus on stakeholder happiness contributed to its success. First, we examine the history of Zappos, its core values, and unique business model. Next, we analyze the company's corporate culture and how it influences its relationships with employees, customers, the environment, and communities. We then look at some of the challenges the company faced and how it plans to move into the future.

Nick Swinmurn founded Zappos in 1999 after a fruitless day spent shopping for shoes in San Francisco. After looking online, Swinmurn decided to quit his job and start a shoe website that offered the best selection and best service. Originally called ShoeSite.com, the company started as a middleman, transferring orders between customers and suppliers but not holding any inventory (a "drop ship" strategy). The website was soon renamed Zappos, after the Spanish word for shoes (zapatos).

In 2000, entrepreneur Tony Hsieh became the company's CEO. Hsieh, 26 at the time, was an early investor in Zappos, having made $265 million selling his startup company to Microsoft in 1998. Hsieh was not initially sold on the idea of an Internet shoe store, but he could not help but become involved. After becoming CEO, Hsieh made an unconventional decision to keep Zappos going, even selling his San Francisco loft to pay for a new warehouse and once setting his salary at just $24.

Zappos struggled for its first few years, making sales but not generating a profit. The dot-com crash forced Zappos to lay off half its staff, but the company recovered. By the end of 2002, Zappos had sales of $32 million but was still not profitable. In 2003, the company decided in order to offer the best customer service, it had to control the whole value chain—from order to fulfillment to delivery—and began holding its entire inventory. Zappos moved to Las Vegas in 2004 to take advantage of a larger pool of experienced call center employees. The company

---

*This case was developed by Harper Baird, Bernadette Gallegos, and Beau Shelton under the direction of O.C. Ferrell and Linda Ferrell. It is intended for classroom discussion rather than to illustrate effective or ineffective handling of administrative, ethical, or legal decisions by management. All sources used for this case were obtained through publicly available materials.

generated its first profit in 2007 after reaching $840 million in annual sales. Zappos started to be recognized for its unique work environment and approach to customer service.

In 2010, Amazon bought the company for $1.2 billion. Although Hsieh rejected an offer from Amazon in 2005, he believed this buyout would be better for the company than management from the current board of directors or an outside investor. Amazon agreed to let Zappos operate independently and keep Hsieh as CEO (at his current $36,000 annual salary). Hsieh made $214 million from the acquisition, and Amazon set aside $40 million for distribution to Zappos employees. After the acquisition, the company restructured into 10 separate companies organized under the Zappos Family.

CORE VALUES

Zappos has ten core values that guide every activity at the company and form the heart of the company's business model and culture.

- Deliver WOW through service.
- Embrace and drive change.
- Create fun and a little weirdness.
- Be adventurous, creative and open-minded.
- Pursue growth and learning.
- Build open and honest relationships with communication.
- Build a positive team and family spirit.
- Do more with less.
- Be passionate and determined.
- Be humble.[1]

Zappos' core values differ from those of other companies in several ways. In addition to being untraditional, the core values create a framework for the company's actions. This is exemplified in the company's commitment to their customers' and employees' well-being and satisfaction.

ZAPPOS' CUSTOMER-FOCUSED BUSINESS MODEL

The Zappos business model is built around developing long-term customer relationships. Zappos does not compete on price because it believes customers want to buy from the store with the best service and selection. The company strives to create a unique and addicting shopping experience, offering a wide selection of shoes, apparel, accessories, and home products, free shipping to the customer, free shipping and full refunds on returns, and great customer service.

---

[1]Zappos, "Zappos Family Core Values," http://about.zappos.com/our-unique-culture/zappos-core-values (accessed April 2, 2013).

Shopping and Shipping

Zappos strives to make the shopping experience enjoyable. The website is streamlined for an easy shopping experience. Products are grouped in specialized segments, with some (like outdoor products) on their own mini-sites. Customers view each product from multiple angles thanks to photographs taken at the company's studio, and Zappos employees make short videos highlighting the product's features. Zappos analyzes how customers navigate the site to improve features, adapt search results, and plan inventory.

The spirit of simplicity, innovation, and great service extends to Zappos' inventory and distribution systems as well. Zappos has one of the few live inventory systems on the Web. If the Zappos website displays an item, it is in stock. Once the company sells out of an item, the listing is removed from the website. This reduces customer frustration. Its inventory and shipping systems are linked directly to the website via a central database, and all its information systems are developed in-house and customized to the company's needs. Their warehouses operate around the clock, which allows them to get a product to the customer faster. Fast shipping creates an instant gratification similar to shopping in a physical store.

Most companies have a negative view toward returns, but Zappos' mentality is the complete opposite. It sees returns as the ability to maintain customer relationships and to increase its profits. Zappos offers a 100% Satisfaction Guaranteed Return Policy. If customers are not satisfied with a purchase, they can return it within 365 days for a full refund. The customer prints a pre-paid shipping label that allows all domestic customers to return the product for free. This return policy encourages customers to order several styles or different sizes and return the items that do not work out.

While this strategy seems expensive, it actually works to Zappos' advantage. The average industry merchandise return rate is 35 percent, but Zappos' most profitable customers tend to return 50 percent of what they purchase. The customers who have the higher return percentages are the most profitable because they experienced Zappos' customer service and return policy, which create loyalty to the company. These customers are likely to make purchases more often and to spend more on each purchase. Craig Adkins, vice president of services and operations, believes this is exactly what makes Zappos so successful.

Customer Service

What makes the Zappos business model unique is the company's focus on customer service. The company established a method of serving customers and handling their issues distinctive from the rest of the industry. Zappos believes great customer service is an opportunity to make the customer happy.

Customers are encouraged to call Zappos with any questions. The number is displayed on every page of the website. According to Hsieh, Zappos encourages people to call the company because more interaction with customers increases their personal connections with the organization. Customer service representatives actively use social media sites such as Facebook and Twitter to respond to customer issues.

Another key aspect of Zappos' customer service model is that nothing is scripted. Employees have free reign in their decision-making and are expected to spend as much time as they need to "wow" customers. They help customers shop, even on their competitors' websites, encourage them to buy multiple sizes or colors to try (since return shipping is free), and do anything it takes to make the shopping experience memorable.

Zappos' customer service representatives develop relationships with their customers and make them happy. Stories about great customer service include customer support calls that last for hours, sending flowers to customers on their birthdays, and surprise upgrades to faster shipping. Some extreme cases included Zappos hand-delivering shoes to customers who lost luggage and to a groom who forgot the shoes for his wedding. Zappos has even sent pizzas to the homes of customers who tweeted to the company about being hungry.

Zappos believes great customer experiences encourage customers to use the store again. In addition, Zappos' long-term strategy is based on the idea that great customer service will help them expand into other categories. While around 80 percent of Zappos' orders come from shoes, the markets for housewares and apparel are much larger. The company says it will expand into any area it is passionate about and meets their customers' needs.

The company considers word-of-mouth marketing to be the best way to reach new customers. With over 75 percent of purchases made by repeat customers, it is evident Zappos' mission to "provide the best customer service possible" works well for the company.

TRANSPARENCY

Transparency is a critical part of the Zappos model. Employees receive detailed information about the company's performance and are encouraged to share information about the company. Zappos believes employees should develop open and honest relationships with all stakeholders in the hope this will assist in maintaining the company's reputation. Hsieh uses Facebook and Twitter to share information with employees and customers (he has 2.7 million followers on Twitter). When Zappos laid off 124 employees in 2008, Hsieh announced the decision via Twitter and later blogged about it. Although some companies hesitate to open themselves to public criticism, Zappos feels it has nothing to hide. In fact, most of the public posts on Zappos' social media sites are praise from customers.

ZAPPOS INSIGHTS

Zappos' business model is so successful the company offers tours and workshops, which cost $5,000 for two days at the company's headquarters. The company also created Zappos Insights, an online service that allows subscribers to learn more about Zappos' business practices through blogs and videos. These programs have high profit potential for the company because they are built on what Zappos already does best.

CORPORATE CULTURE

The corporate culture at Zappos sets it apart from nearly every other company. It even caught the attention of Amazon CEO Jeff Bezos, who described Zappos' corporate culture as one-of-a-kind. Zappos' unorthodox culture is the work of CEO Tony Hsieh, an innovative and successful entrepreneur. Hsieh built the culture on the idea that if you can attract talented people and employees enjoy their work, great service and brand power naturally develops.

WORK ENVIRONMENT

Zappos is famous for its relaxed and wacky atmosphere. Employee antics include nerf ball wars, office parades, ugly sweater days, and donut-eating contests. The headquarters feature an employee nap room, a wellness center, and an open mic in the cafeteria. Other quirky activities include forcing employees to wear a "reply-all" hat when they accidentally send a company-wide email. This environment isn't just fun; it's also strategic. According to Zappos, "When you combine a little weirdness with making sure everyone is also having fun at work, it ends up being a win-win for everyone: Employees are more engaged in the work that they do, and the company as a whole becomes more innovative."

Hiring and Training

The key to creating a zany work environment lies in hiring the right people. The job application features a crossword puzzle about Zappos and asks employees questions about which superhero they'd like to be and how lucky they are. They may also check how potential employees treat people like their shuttle driver. Zappos is looking for people with a sense of humor who can work hard and play hard. Potential employees go through both cultural and technical interviews to make sure they fit with the company. However, even Hsieh admits finding great employees is tough. He believes pursuing too much growth at once harms the company if the organization starts caring more about the quantity of new employees rather than the quality.

All new employees attend a five-week training program that includes two weeks on the phones providing customer service and a week filling orders in a warehouse. To make sure new employees feel committed to a future with the company, Zappos offers $2,000 to leave the company after the training (less than 1 percent of new employees take the deal).

Even after the initial training is over, employees take 200 hours of classes—with the company, covering everything from the basics of business to advanced Twitter use—and read at least 9 business books a year.

Benefits

Another aspect of Zappos that is unique is the benefits it provides to its employees. The company has an extensive health plan that pays 100 percent of employee's medical benefits and on average 85 percent of medical expenses for employees' dependents. The company provides employees with dental, vision, and life insurance. Other benefits include a flexible spending account, pre-paid legal services, a 40 percent employee discount, free lunches and snacks, paid volunteer time, life coaching, and a car pool program.

Along with the extensive benefits package, Zappos developed a compensation model for its "Customer Loyalty Team" (call center representatives) that incentivizes employee development. All employees are paid $11 per hour for the first 90 days. After 90 days, the employee moves to $13 per hour. To move beyond $13 an hour, employees must demonstrate growth and learning by completing specific skill set courses that allow employees to specialize in certain areas of the call center. Although the reasoning for Zappos' compensation model is to motivate employees and promote personal growth, the $13 base pay is less than the national hourly average of $15.92 earned by call center representatives. However,

Zappos believes its fun and relaxed corporate culture combined with advancement opportunities at the firm create value that extends beyond pay.

Work-Life Integration

One of Zappos' core values is "Build a positive team and family spirit," so the company expects employees to socialize with each other both in and out of the office. In fact, managers spend 10 to 20 percent of their time bonding with team members outside of work. Zappos outings include hiking trips, going to the movies, and hanging out at bars. Hsieh says this increases efficiency by improving communication, building trust, and creating friendships.

Along with creating friendships, employees are encouraged to support each other. Any employee can give another employee a $50 reward for great work. Zappos employees compile an annual "culture book" comprised of essays on the Zappos culture and reviews of the company. The culture book helps employees think about the meaning of their work and is available unedited to the public.

As with its customers, the foundation of Zappos' relationships with its employees is trust and transparency. The company wants its employees, like its customers, to actively discuss any issues or concerns that come up. Hsieh does not have an office; he sits in an open cubicle among the rest of the employees. He believes "the best way to have an open-door policy is not to have a door in the first place." Zappos' management is open with employees by regularly discussing issues on the company blog.

However, this positive work environment comes with the expectation employees will work hard. Employees are evaluated on how well they embody the core values and inspire others; Zappos fires people who do great work if they do not fit with the culture of the company. The organization wants employees to be dedicated to the firm and believes this dedication cannot happen if employees do not share the same values and vision of the organization.

CORPORATE SOCIAL RESPONSIBILITY

Zappos takes an unconventional approach to corporate social responsibility and philanthropy. Many companies have CSR programs dedicated to a certain area or cause such as education, but Zappos prefers to support a variety of programs based on the needs of communities and the interests of employees.

Philanthropy

Zappos is involved in a variety of philanthropic efforts. Programs include donating shoes and gifts as well as giving gift cards to elementary school students. Zappos donates money to organizations such as the Shade Tree, a non-profit that provides shelter to women and children, and the Nevada Childhood Cancer Foundation. Zappos also has a donation request application available on its website.

Sustainability

Zappos started a campaign to improve the company's impact on the environment. A group of employees created the initiative, known as Zappos Leading Environmental Awareness for the Future (L.E.A.F.). The campaign focuses on several environmental efforts, including a new recycling program, community gardens, and getting LEED certification for the company. One recent effort was Zappos Recycles Day, an event to raise awareness on recycling and other ways the company can reduce its carbon footprint. Like the rest of the company, L.E.A.F. is open, with its progress posted on its Twitter account and blog.

Another area on the company's blog is a section on "Eco-friendly Products." Here, the company highlights new products that are organic or manufactured using environmentally friendly procedures. The postings also list ways customers can live more sustainable lifestyles, including tips on how to throw an eco-friendly party and green product recommendations.

Recognition

In addition to being the number one online shoe retailer, Zappos has been recognized for its innovative business practices. The company appeared on several prestigious lists including *Fortune*'s "Best Companies to Work For," *Fast Company*'s "50 Most Innovative Companies," *BusinessWeek*'s "Top 25 Customer Service Champs," and *Ethisphere*'s "World's Most Ethical Companies." The company continues to get recognized for its efforts in creating an environment and business model that encourages transparency and strong relationships among all stakeholders.

ETHICAL CHALLENGES FOR ZAPPOS

Like any company, Zappos faced some challenging business and ethical issues in the past. When these issues occur, Zappos handles situations in a professional and efficient manner. However, the transparency at Zappos makes some business and ethical issues more complex as the company strives to solve problems while keeping its stakeholders informed.

2008 Layoffs

Zappos is known for its commitment to its employees, but the company faced hard economic times that demanded tough decisions. In October 2008, Sequoia Capital, a venture capital firm that was a controlling investor in Zappos, met to discuss the problems presented by the economic downturn and its effect on their portfolio companies. Sequoia Capital instructed Zappos to cut expenses and make the cash flow positive. As a result, Hsieh made the difficult decision to lay off 8 percent of Zappos' employees.

Zappos strived to handle the layoffs in a respectful and kind manner. Hsieh sent an email notifying employees of the layoff and was honest and upfront about the reasons behind the decisions, even discussing the move on Twitter. Employees who were laid off received generous severance packages, including six months of paid COBRA health insurance coverage. Because of the company's honesty and transparency, employees and customers were more understanding of the tough decision Hsieh and Zappos had to make.

Acquisition by Amazon

In 2009 Zappos was acquired by e-commerce giant Amazon.com. Many Zappos customers were confused by the unexpected move and expressed concerns about the future of the company's culture and customer service. Most CEOs would not feel any obligation to address customer concerns over the acquisition, but Tony Hsieh values the support of Zappos' employees and customers.

Shortly after the acquisition, Hsieh issued a statement about why he sold Zappos to Amazon. In the statement, Hsieh discussed the disagreement between Zappos and Sequoia Capital over management styles and company focus. Specifically, Hsieh said, "The board's attitude was that my 'social experiments' might make for good PR but that they didn't move the overall business forward. The board wanted me, or whoever was CEO, to spend less time on worrying about employee happiness and more time selling shoes." Hsieh and Alfred Lin, Zappos CFO and COO, were the only two members on the board committed to preserving Zappos' culture. The board could fire Hsieh and hire a new CEO who focused more on profits.

Hsieh decided the best way to resolve these issues was to buy out the board, but he could not do this on his own. After meeting with Amazon CEO Jeff Bezos, Hsieh committed to a full acquisition, as long as Zappos could operate independently and continue to focus on building its culture and customer service. Many customers were concerned Amazon was not a good fit for Zappos, but Hsieh addressed those concerns, stating Amazon and Zappos have the same goals of creating value for the customer but different ways of how to do it. He also assured customers Zappos would continue to maintain its unique corporate culture. Although consumers were not pleased with the acquisition, they at least understood why it occurred. Moreover, Hsieh's commitment to his beliefs and management style resonated with consumers.

More than Shoes Campaign

To bring awareness to the fact Zappos sells more than just shoes, Zappos created a marketing campaign in 2011 designed to catch people's attention. The company released several advertisements that featured people who appeared to be naked doing daily activities such as running, hailing a cab, and driving a scooter. The creative advertisements had certain parts of models' bodies blocked off with a box that said "more than shoes."

The campaign received criticism from several groups because of their "sexual nature." However, the catch with these ads was that the subjects of the ads were not actually nude; they wore bathing suits or small shorts that were later covered by the box. Because of the negative attention, Zappos pulled the ads and released an apology that explained the production process.

Technical Difficulties

In October 2011, Zappos experienced some technical difficulties that resulted in delays and problems in customers' orders and shipments. Zappos upgraded one of its processing systems, and in the process many orders were deleted or delayed. Some orders had the incorrect shipping information, and products were shipped to the wrong location. Although this upset several customers, Zappos handled the problems and reassured customers that it would get their merchandise as soon as possible. The company also offered different perks, depending on the circumstances of each customer experience.

Another problem Zappos encountered was that every item from 6pm.com, one of its websites, was priced at $49.95 for six hours in 2010. The company shut down the website for a few hours to solve the problem. Zappos honored all the orders from the pricing mistake, which resulted in a $1.6 million loss.

Theft of Customer Information

In January 2012 hackers broke into Zappos' computer system, and the company had to respond to the theft of 24 million customers' critical personal information. The stolen data included customers' names, email addresses, shipping and billing addresses, phone numbers, and the last four digits of their credit cards. Zappos immediately addressed the situation by sending an email to customers notifying them of the security breach. Zappos assured customers the servers containing their full credit card information were not hacked. Zappos' next move was to disconnect its call center, reasoning that the expected amount of calls would overload their system.

While Zappos has a reputation for delivering customer service that is unmatched by any competitor, some customers were unhappy with how Zappos handled the hacking. Many customers were upset by their information being hacked, but the situation was made worse by Zappos' action of disconnecting its call center. Although this situation caused problems for Zappos and blemished its customer service record, the company believes it can restore its reputation.

THE FUTURE OF ZAPPOS

Zappos remains committed to serving its customers and employees. So far, the company has retained its unique culture and continues to expand into new product categories. In a recent interview, Hsieh talked about the growth of Zappos and how he believes expanding into the clothing and merchandise market will help the company to grow. Hsieh says "the sky is the limit" for Zappos, and growing and expanding into many different types of businesses is Zappos' future. Hsieh continues to look for talented and creative individuals. He has pledged $1 million in partnership with Venture for America to bring at least 100 graduates to the Las Vegas area over a 5-year period. As Zappos expands, it will have to work harder to hire the right people, avoid ethical issues, and maintain its quirky culture.

Leadership is a key factor in the success of any company, and for Zappos having Tony Hsieh as a leader is a strong indicator for future success. Hsieh expressed that he will do whatever it takes to make his employees, customers, and vendors happy. The future for any company looks bright when its leadership is committed to such strong values. However, Zappos needs to make sure it continues to focus on its stakeholders and its long-term vision with or without Hsieh.

Ultimately, Zappos intends to continue to deliver happiness to its stakeholders. Hsieh says, "At Zappos, our higher purpose is delivering happiness. Whether it's the happiness our customers receive when they get a new pair of shoes or the perfect piece of clothing, or the happiness they get when dealing with a friendly customer rep over the phone, or the happiness our employees feel about being a part of a culture that celebrates their individuality, these are all ways we bring happiness to people's lives."

QUESTIONS

1. Does Zappos effectively focus on stakeholder happiness, and how does this approach affect the ethical culture?
2. Has Zappos developed long-term relationships with customers and employees that provide a competitive advantage in the purchase of shoes and other products?
3. How has Zappos managed ethical risk, and what are potential ethical risks in the future?

SOURCES

2011 World's Most Ethical Companies," *Ethisphere*, 2011, http://ethisphere.com/2011-worlds-most-ethical-companies (accessed April 14, 2012); Scott Adams, "Refreshing Honesty on Why Zappos Sold to Amazon," *Tech Dirt*, 2010, http://www.techdirt.com/articles/20100607/0014299706.shtml (accessed April 14, 2012); Peter Bernard, "Zappos Hacking Could Cause Consumer Problems Later," *News Channel 8*, 2012, http://www2.tbo.com/news/breaking-news/2012/jan/16/zappos-hacking-could-cause-consumer-problems-later-ar-348177 (accessed April 14, 2012); Diane Brady, "Tony Hsieh: Redefining the Zappos' Business Model," *Bloomberg Business*, May 27, 2005, http://www.businessweek.com/magazine/content/10_23/b4181088591033.htm (accessed April 11, 2012); David Burkus, "The Tale of Two Cultures: Why Culture Trumps Core Values in Building Ethical Organizations," *Value Based Leadership*, 2011, http://www.valuesbasedleadershipjournal.com/issues/vol4issue1/tale_2culture.php (accessed April 14, 2012); Brian Cantor, "How Zappos Escaped Outrage over Customer Service Problems," *Customer Management*, 2011, http://www.customermanagementiq.com/operations/articles/how-zappos-escaped-outrage-over-customer-service-p (accessed April 14, 2012); Max Chafkin, "How I Did It: Tony Hsieh, CEO, Zappos.com," *Inc.*, September 1, 2006, http://www.inc.com/magazine/20060901/hidi-hsieh.html (accessed April 10, 2012); Max Chafkin, "The Zappos Way of Managing," *Inc.*, May 1, 2009, http://www.inc.com/magazine/20090501/the-zappos-way-of-managing.html (accessed April 13, 2012); Andria Cheng, "Zappos, under Amazon, keeps its independent streak," MarketWatch, June 11, 2010, http://www.marketwatch.com/story/zappos-under-amazon-keeps-its-independent-streak-2010-06-11 (accessed April 11, 2012); CNN Money, "Whitewater Rafting? 12 Unusual Perks. Best Companies Rank," 2012, http://money.cnn.com/galleries/2012/pf/jobs/1201/gallery.best-companies-unusual-perks.fortune/3.html (accessed April 14, 2012); Michael Dart and Robin Lewis, "Break the Rules the Way Zappos and Amazon Do," *BusinessWeek.com*, May 2, 2011, 2; Eric Engleman. "Q&A: Zappos CEO Tony Hsieh on Life Under Amazon, Future Plan," *Tech Flash: Seattle's Technology News Source*, 2010, http://www.techflash.com/seattle/2010/09/qa_zappos_ceo_tony_hsieh_on_life_under_amazon_and_moving_beyond_shoes.html (accessed April 14, 2012); Cheryl Fernandez, "Zappos Customer loyalty Team-Pay, Benefits, and Growth Opportunities," October 26, 2010, http://www.youtube.com/watch?v=OB3Qog5Jhq4 (accessed April 29, 2012); Ed Frauenheim, "Jungle survival," *Workforce Management*, September 14, 2009, Vol. 88, Issue 1018–23; Carmine Gallo, "Delivering Happiness the Zappos Way," *BusinessWeek*, May 13, 2009, http://www.businessweek.com/technology/content/may2009/tc20090512_104433.htm (accessed April 10, 2012); "Henderson-Based Zappos Earns Honors for Ethics," *Las Vegas Sun*, 2009, http://www.lasvegassun.com/news/2009/apr/13/henderson-based-zappos-earns-honors-ethics/ (accessed April 14, 2012); Tony Hsieh and Max Chafkin, "Why I Sold Zappos," *Inc.*, June 2010, 100–104; Tony Hsieh, "Zappos: Where Company Culture is #1," Presentation, May 26, 2010, http://www.youtube.com/watch?v=bsLTh9Gity4 (accessed April 13, 2012); John R. Karman III, "Zappos Plans to Add 5, 000 Full-Time Jobs in Bullitt County," *Business First*, 2011, http://www.bizjournals.com/louisville/print-edition/2011/10/28/zappos-plans-to-add-5000-full-time.html (accessed April 14, 2012); Aneel Karnani, "The Case against Corporate Social Responsibility," *MIT Sloan Management Review*, 2010, http://sloanreview.mit.edu/executive-adviser/2010-3/5231/the-case-against-corporate-social-responsibility (accessed April 14, 2012); Elizabeth C. Kitchen, "Zappos.com Hack Affects 24 Million Customers," *Yahoo Voices*,

2012, http://voices.yahoo.com/zapposcom-hack-affects-24-million-customers-10842473.html (accessed April 14, 2012); Sara Lacy, "Amazon-Zappos: Not the Usual Silicon Valley M&A," *BusinessWeek*, July 31, 2009, http://www.businessweek.com/technology/content/jul2009/tc20090730 _169311.htm (accessed April 10, 2012); Greg Lamm, "Zappos Up-Front with Challenges of New Ordering System," *Tech Flash: Seattle's Technology News Source*, 2011, http://www.techflash.com/seattle/2011/10/zappos-up-front-with-challenges.html (accessed April 14, 2012); Jeffrey M. O'Brien, "Zappos Knows How to Kick It," *Fortune*, February 2, 2009, Vol. 159 Issue 2, 54–60; Joyce Routson. "Hsieh of Zappos Takes Happiness Seriously," *Stanford Center for Social Innovation*, 2010, http://csi.gsb.stanford.edu/hsieh-zappos-takes-happiness-seriously (accessed April 14, 2012); Aman Singh, "At Zappos, Getting Fired for not Contributing to Company Culture," *Forbes*, 2010, http://www.forbes.com/sites/csr/2010/11/23/at-zappos-getting-fired-for-not-contributing-to-company-culture (accessed April 14, 2012); United States Bureau of Labor Statistics, May 2011, Occupational Employment and Wages: Customer Service Representatives, http://www.bls.gov/oes/current/oes434051.htm (accessed April 29, 2012); William Wei, "The Future of Zappos: From Shoes to Clothing to a Zappos Airline," *Business Insider*, 2010), http://www.businessinsider.com/zappos-shoes-clothing-airline-2010-10 (accessed April 14, 2012); Samantha Whitehorne, "Cultural Lessons from the Leaders at Zappos.com," *ASAE*, 2009, http://www.asaecenter.org/Resources/ANowDetail.cfm?ItemNumber=43360 (accessed April 14, 2012); Marcie Young and Erin E. Clack, "Zappos Milestone: Focus on Apparel," *Footwear News*, May 4, 2009, http://about.zappos.com/press-center/media-coverage/zappos-milestone-focus-apparel (accessed April 11, 2012);"Zappos CEO Gives $1M to Lure Grads to Las Vegas," *8 News Now KLAS-TV Las Vegas*, December 4, 2012, http://www.8newsnow.com/story/20260504/zappos-ceo-gives-1m-to-lure-grads-to-vegas (accessed July 11, 2013); "Zappos gives up lunch to Give Back to the Community," *Blogs.Zappos.Com*, 2008, http://blogs.zappos.com/blogs/inside-zappos/2008/09/09/zappos-gives-up-lunch-to-give-back-to-community (accessed April 14, 2012); Masha Zager, "Zappos Delivers Service…With Shoes on the Side," *Apparel Magazine*, January 2009, Vol. 50 Issue 5, 10–13.

CASE 9

Enron: Questionable Accounting Leads to Collapse*

Once upon a time, there was a gleaming office tower in Houston, Texas. In front of that gleaming tower was a giant "E," slowly revolving, flashing in the hot Texas sun. But in 2001 the Enron Corporation, which once ranked among the top *Fortune* 500 companies, collapsed under a mountain of debt concealed through a complex scheme of off-balance-sheet partnerships. Forced to declare bankruptcy, the energy firm laid off 4,000 employees; thousands more lost their retirement savings that had been invested in Enron stock. The company's shareholders lost tens of billions of dollars after the stock price plummeted. The scandal surrounding Enron's demise engendered a global loss of confidence in corporate integrity that continues to plague markets today, and eventually it triggered tough new scrutiny of financial reporting practices. In an attempt to explain what went wrong, this case examines the history, culture, and major players in the Enron scandal.

ENRON'S HISTORY

The Enron Corporation was created out of the merger of two major gas pipeline companies in 1985. Through its subsidiaries and numerous affiliates, the company provided products and services related to natural gas, electricity, and communications for its wholesale and retail customers. Enron transported natural gas through pipelines to customers all over the United States. It generated, transmitted, and distributed electricity to the northwestern United States, and marketed natural gas, electricity, and other commodities globally. It was also involved in the development, construction, and operation of power plants, pipelines, and other energy-related projects all over the world, including the delivery and management of energy to retail customers in both the industrial and commercial business sectors.

Throughout the 1990s, Chairman Ken Lay, CEO Jeffrey Skilling, and CFO Andrew Fastow transformed Enron from an old-style electricity and gas company into a $150 billion energy company and Wall Street favorite that traded power contracts in the investment markets. From 1998 to 2000 alone, Enron's revenues grew from about $31 billion to more than $100 billion, making it the seventh-largest company in the *Fortune* 500. Enron's wholesale energy income represented about 93 percent of 2000 revenues, with another 4 percent derived from natural gas and electricity. The remaining 3 percent came from broadband services and exploration. However, a bankruptcy examiner later

---

*This case was prepared by Harper Baird, Jennifer Jackson, and Neil Herndon for and under the direction of O. C. Ferrell and Linda Ferrell. Michelle Urban provided editorial assistance. It was prepared for classroom discussion rather than to illustrate either effective or ineffective handling of an administrative, ethical, or legal decision by management. All sources used for this case were obtained through publicly available material.

reported that although Enron claimed a net income of $979 million in that year, it earned just $42 million. Moreover, the examiner found that despite Enron's claim of $3 billion in cash flow in 2000, the company's actual cash flow was negative $154 million.

ENRON'S CORPORATE CULTURE

When describing the corporate culture of Enron, people like to use the word "arrogant," perhaps justifiably. A large banner in the lobby at corporate headquarters proclaimed Enron "The World's Leading Company," and Enron executives believed competitors had no chance against it. Jeffrey Skilling went so far as to tell utility executives at a conference he was going to "eat their lunch." This overwhelming aura of pride was based on a deep-seated belief that Enron's employees could handle increased risk without danger. Enron's corporate culture reportedly encouraged flouting rules in pursuit of profit. Enron's executive compensation plans seemed less concerned with generating profits for shareholders than enriching officer wealth.

Skilling appears to be the executive who created the system whereby Enron's employees were rated every six months, with those ranked in the bottom 20 percent forced out. This "rank and yank" system created a fierce environment where employees competed against rivals not only outside the company but also at the next desk. Delivering bad news could result in the "death" of the messenger, so problems in the trading operation, for example, were covered up rather than being communicated to management.

Ken Lay once said he felt one of the great successes at Enron was the creation of a corporate culture in which people could reach their full potential. He said he wanted it to be a highly moral and ethical culture and he tried to ensure people honored the values of respect, integrity, and excellence. On his desk was an Enron paperweight with the slogan "Vision and Values." Despite good intentions, however, ethical behavior was not put into practice. Instead, integrity was pushed aside at Enron, particularly by top managers. Some employees at the company believed nearly anything could be turned into a financial product and, with the aid of complex statistical modeling, traded for profit. Short on assets and heavily reliant on intellectual capital, Enron's corporate culture rewarded innovation and punished employees deemed weak.

ENRON'S ACCOUNTING PROBLEMS

Enron's bankruptcy in 2001 was the largest in U.S. corporate history at the time. The bankruptcy filing came after a series of revelations that the giant energy trader had used partnerships, called "special-purpose entities" or SPEs, to conceal losses. In a meeting with Enron's lawyers in August 2001, the company's then-CFO Fastow stated Enron established the SPEs to move assets and debt off its balance sheet and to increase cash flow by showing that funds were flowing through its books when it sold assets. Although these practices produced a favorable financial picture, outside observers believed they constituted fraudulent financial reporting because they did not accurately represent the company's true financial condition. Most of the SPEs were entities in name only, and Enron funded them with its own stock and maintained control over them. When one of these partnerships was unable to meet its obligations, Enron covered the debt with its own stock.

This arrangement worked as long as Enron's stock price was high, but when the stock price fell, cash was needed to meet the shortfall.

After Enron restated its financial statements for fiscal year 2000 and the first nine months of 2001, its cash flow from operations went from a positive $127 million in 2000 to negative $753 million in 2001. With its stock price falling, Enron faced a critical cash shortage. In October 2001, after it was forced to cover some large shortfalls for its partnerships, Enron's stockholder equity fell by $1.2 billion. Already shaken by questions about lack of disclosure in Enron's financial statements and by reports that executives profited personally from the partnership deals, investor confidence collapsed, taking Enron's stock price with it.

For a time, it appeared Dynegy might save the day by providing $1.5 billion in cash, secured by Enron's premier pipeline Northern Natural Gas, and then purchasing Enron for about $10 billion. However, when Standard & Poor's downgraded Enron's debt to below investment grade on November 28, 2001, some $4 billion in off-balance-sheet debt came due, and Enron didn't have the resources to pay. Dynegy terminated the deal. On December 2, 2001, Enron filed for bankruptcy. Enron faced 22,000 claims totaling about $400 billion.

The Whistle-Blower

Assigned to work directly with Andrew Fastow in June 2001, Enron vice president Sherron Watkins, an eight-year Enron veteran, was given the task of finding assets to sell off. With the high-tech bubble bursting and Enron's stock price slipping, Watkins was troubled to find unclear, off-the-books arrangements backed only by Enron's deflating stock. No one seemed able to explain to her what was going on. Knowing she faced difficult consequences if she confronted then-CEO Jeffrey Skilling, she began looking for another job, planning to confront Skilling just as she left for a new position. Skilling, however, suddenly quit on August 14, saying he wanted to spend more time with his family. Chair Ken Lay stepped back in as CEO and began inviting employees to express their concerns and put them into a box for later collection. Watkins prepared an anonymous memo and placed it into the box. When Lay held a companywide meeting shortly thereafter and did not mention her memo, she arranged a personal meeting with him.

On August 22, 2001, Watkins handed Lay a seven-page letter she prepared outlining her concerns. She told him Enron would "implode in a wave of accounting scandals" if nothing was done. Lay arranged to have Enron's law firm, Vinson & Elkins, look into the questionable deals, although Watkins advised against having a party investigate that might be compromised by its own involvement in Enron's scam. Near the end of September, Lay sold $1.5 million of personal stock options, while telling Enron employees the company had never been stronger. By the middle of October, Enron reported a third-quarter loss of $618 million and a $1.2 billion write-off tied to the partnerships that Watkins had warned Lay about.

For her trouble, Watkins had her computer hard drive confiscated, and she was moved from her plush executive office suite on the top floor of the Houston headquarters tower to a sparse office on a lower level. Her new metal desk was no longer filled with the high-level projects that took her all over the world on Enron business. Instead, now a vice president in name only, she faced meaningless "make work" projects. In February 2002 she testified before Congress about Enron's partnerships and resigned from Enron in November of that year.

The Chief Financial Officer

In 2002 the U.S. Justice Department indicted CFO Andrew Fastow on 98 counts for his alleged efforts to inflate Enron's profits. The charges included fraud, money laundering, conspiracy, and one count of obstruction of justice. Fastow faced up to 140 years in jail and millions of dollars in fines if convicted on all counts. Federal officials attempted to recover all of the money Fastow earned illegally, and seized $37 million.

Federal prosecutors argued Enron's case was not about exotic accounting practices but about fraud and theft. They contended Fastow was the brain behind the partnerships used to conceal some $1 billion in Enron debt and that this debt led directly to Enron's bankruptcy. The federal complaints alleged Fastow defrauded Enron and its shareholders through off-balance-sheet partnerships, making Enron appear more profitable than it actually was. They also alleged that Fastow made about $30 million by using these partnerships to get kickbacks disguised as gifts from family members, and taking income himself that should have gone to other entities.

Fastow initially denied any wrongdoing and maintained he was hired to arrange the off-balance-sheet financing and Enron's board of directors, chair, and CEO directed and praised his work. He also claimed lawyers and accountants reviewed his work and approved what was being done, and "at no time did he do anything he believed was a crime." Skilling, COO from 1997 to 2000 before becoming CEO, reportedly championed Fastow's rise at Enron and supported his efforts to keep Enron's stock prices high.

Fastow eventually pleaded guilty to two counts of conspiracy, admitting to orchestrating myriad schemes to hide Enron debt and inflate profits while enriching himself with millions. He surrendered nearly $30 million in cash and property, and agreed to serve up to 10 years in prison once prosecutors no longer needed his cooperation. He was a key government witness against Lay and Skilling. His wife Lea Fastow, former assistant treasurer, quit Enron in 1997 and pleaded guilty to a felony tax crime, admitting to helping hide ill-gotten gains from her husband's schemes from the government. She later withdrew her plea, and then pleaded guilty to a newly filed misdemeanor tax crime. In 2005 she was released from a year-long prison sentence, and then had a year of supervised release.

In the end, Fastow received a lighter sentence than he otherwise might have because of his willingness to cooperate with investigators. In 2006 Fastow gave an eight-and-a-half-day deposition in his role as government witness. He illuminated how Enron managed to get away with what it did, including detailing how many major banks were complicit in helping Enron manipulate its financials so it looked better to investors. In exchange for his deposition, Fastow's sentence was lowered to six years from 10. At the end of 2011, Fastow was released from prison. He works for a Houston law firm and spends time visiting colleges like the University of Colorado–Boulder Leeds School of Business giving presentations on ethics, principles, and insights on what happened at Enron.

The case against Fastow was largely based on information provided by Michael Kopper, the company's managing director and a key player in the establishment and operation of several of the off-balance-sheet partnerships and the first Enron executive to plead guilty to a crime. Kopper, a chief aide to Fastow, pleaded guilty to money laundering and wire fraud. He faced up to 15 years in prison and agreed to surrender $12 million earned from illegal dealings with the partnerships. However, Kopper only served three years and one month of jail time because of the crucial role he played in providing prosecutors with information. After his high-powered days at Enron, Kopper's next job was as a salaried grant writer for Legacy, a Houston-based clinic that provides services to HIV-positive and other chronically ill patients.

Others charged in the Enron affair included Timothy Belden, Enron's former top energy trader, who pleaded guilty to one count of conspiring to commit wire fraud. He was sentenced to two years of court-supervised release and required to pay $2.1 million. Three British bankers, David Bermingham, Giles Darby, and Gary Mulgrew, were indicted in Houston on wire-fraud charges related to a deal at Enron. According to the U.S. Justice Department, they used secret investments to take $7.3 million in income that belonged to their employer. The three men, employees of the finance group Greenwich National Westminster Bank, were arrested in 2004 and extradited to America to face sentencing. They were sentenced to thirty-seven months in prison but were eventually sent back to Britain to serve out the remainder of their time.

The Chief Executive Officer

Former CEO Jeffrey Skilling, generally perceived as Enron's mastermind, was the most difficult to prosecute. At the time of the trial, he was so confident he waived his right to avoid self-incrimination and testified before Congress, saying, "I was not aware of any inappropriate financial arrangements." However, Jeffrey McMahon, who took over as Enron's president and COO in February 2002, told a congressional subcommittee he informed Skilling about the company's off-balance-sheet partnerships in 2000, when he was Enron's treasurer. McMahon said Skilling told him "he would remedy the situation."

Calling Enron's collapse a "run on the bank" and a "liquidity crisis," Skilling said he did not understand how Enron went bankrupt so quickly. He also said the off-balance-sheet partnerships were Fastow's creation. However, the judge dealt a blow to Lay and Skilling when he instructed the jury that it could find the defendants guilty of consciously avoiding knowing about wrongdoing at the company.

Many former Enron employees refused to testify because they were not guaranteed their testimony would not be used against them in future trials, and therefore questions about the company's accounting fraud remain. Skilling was found guilty of honest services fraud and sentenced to 24 years in prison. He is serving his prison time in Colorado. He maintains his innocence and appealed his conviction. After his release from prison Andy Fastow was quoted as saying that the bankruptcy of Enron was not Skillings' fault. In 2008 a panel of judges from the Fifth Circuit Court of Appeals in New Orleans rejected his request to overturn the convictions of fraud, conspiracy, misrepresentation, and insider trading. However, the judges granted Skilling one concession. The three-judge panel determined the original judge applied flawed sentencing guidelines in determining Skilling's sentence. The Court ordered that Skilling be resentenced. The matter was taken to the Supreme Court.

In June 2010 the United States Supreme Court ruled that the honest services law could not be used to convict Skilling because the honest services law applies to bribes and kickbacks, not to conduct that is ambiguous or vague. The Supreme Court decision did not suggest there had been no misconduct, only that Skilling's conduct was not in violation of a criminal fraud law. The court's decision did not overturn the conviction and sent the case back to a lower court for evaluation.

The Chair

Ken Lay became chair and CEO of the company that became Enron in 1986. A decade later, Lay promoted Jeffrey Skilling to president and chief operating officer, and then, as expected, Lay stepped down as CEO in 2001 to make way for Skilling. Lay remained as chair of the board. When Skilling resigned later that year, Lay resumed the role of CEO.

Lay, who held a doctorate in economics from the University of Houston, contended he knew little of what was going on, even though he participated in the board meetings that allowed the off-balance-sheet partnerships to be created. Lay said he believed the transactions were legal because attorneys and accountants approved them. Only months before the bankruptcy in 2001, he reassured employees and investors all was well at Enron, based on strong wholesale sales and physical volume delivered through the marketing channel. He had already been informed there were problems with some of the investments that could eventually cost Enron hundreds of millions of dollars. In 2002, on the advice of his attorney, Lay invoked his Fifth Amendment right not to answer questions that could be incriminating.

Lay was expected to be charged with insider trading, and prosecutors investigated why he began selling $80 million of his own stock beginning in late 2000, even as he encouraged employees to buy more shares of the company. It appears Lay drew down his $4 million Enron credit line repeatedly and then repaid the company with Enron shares. These transactions, unlike usual stock sales, do not have to be reported to investors. Lay says he sold the stock because of margin calls on loans he secured with Enron stock and he had no other source of liquidity. According to Lay, he was largely unaware of the ethical situation within the firm. He relied on lawyers, accountants, and senior executives to inform him of issues such as misconduct. He felt he had been protected from certain knowledge that would have been beneficial and enable him to engage in early correction of the misconduct. Lay claims all decisions he made related to financial transactions were approved by the company's lawyers, and the Enron board of directors. Lynn Brewer, a former Enron executive, states Lay was not informed about alleged misconduct in her division. Additionally, Mike Ramsey, the lead attorney for Lay's defense, claimed he was not aware of most of the items in the indictment. In the end Lay was convicted on 19 counts of fraud, conspiracy, and insider trading. However, the verdict was thrown out in 2005 after he died of heart failure at his home in Colorado. The ruling protected $43.5 million of Lay's estate the prosecution claimed Lay stole from Enron.

The Lawyers

Enron was Houston law firm Vinson & Elkins' top client, accounting for about 7 percent of its $450 million revenue. Enron's general counsel and a number of members of Enron's legal department came from Vinson & Elkins. Vinson & Elkins dismissed Sherron Watkins' allegations of accounting fraud after making inquiries, but this does not appear to leave the firm open to civil or criminal liability. Of greater concern are allegations Vinson & Elkins structured some of Enron's special-purpose partnerships. In her letter to Lay, Watkins indicated the firm wrote opinion letters supporting the legality of the deals. In fact, Enron could not have done many of the transactions without such opinion letters. The firm did not admit liability, but agreed to pay $30 million to Enron to settle claims Vinson & Elkins contributed to the firm's collapse.

Merrill Lynch

The brokerage and investment-banking firm Merrill Lynch also faced scrutiny by federal prosecutors and the SEC for its role in Enron's 1999 sale of Nigerian barges. The sale allowed Enron to improperly record about $12 million in earnings and thereby meet its earnings goals at the end of 1999. Merrill Lynch allegedly bought the barges for $28 million, of which Enron financed $21 million. Fastow gave his word Enron would buy Merrill Lynch's investment out in six months with a 15 percent guaranteed rate of return. Merrill Lynch went ahead with the deal despite an internal document suggesting the transaction might be construed as aiding and abetting Enron's fraudulent manipulation of its income statement. Merrill Lynch denies the transaction was a sham and said it never knowingly helped Enron to falsify its financial reports.

There are also allegations Merrill Lynch replaced a research analyst after his coverage of Enron displeased Enron executives. Enron reportedly threatened to exclude Merrill Lynch from an upcoming $750 million stock offering in retaliation. The replacement analyst is reported to have then upgraded his report on Enron's stock rating. Merrill Lynch maintains it did nothing improper in its dealings with Enron. However, the firm agreed to pay $80 million to settle SEC charges related to the questionable Nigerian barge deal.

Merrill Lynch continued to use risky investment practices that contributed to severe financial losses for the company as the economy entered a recession in 2008. In 2008 Bank of America agreed to purchase the company for $50 billion, possibly after pressure from the federal government.

ARTHUR ANDERSEN LLP

In its role as Enron's auditor, Arthur Andersen was responsible for ensuring the accuracy of Enron's financial statements and internal bookkeeping. Investors used Andersen's reports to judge Enron's financial soundness and future potential, and expected that Andersen's certifications of accuracy and application of proper accounting procedures would be independent and free of any conflict of interest.

However, Andersen's independence was called into question. The accounting firm was one of Enron's major business partners, with more than one hundred employees dedicated to its account, and it sold about $50 million a year in consulting services to Enron. Some Andersen executives accepted jobs with the energy trader. In March 2002 Andersen was found guilty of obstruction of justice for destroying relevant auditing documents during an SEC investigation of Enron. As a result, Andersen was barred from performing audits. The damage to the firm was such that the company no longer operates, although it has not been dissolved formally.

It is still not clear why Andersen auditors failed to ask Enron to better explain its complex partnerships before certifying Enron's financial statements. Some observers believe the large consulting fees Enron paid Andersen unduly influenced the company's decisions. An Andersen spokesperson said the firm looked hard at all available information from Enron at the time. However, shortly after speaking to Lay Vice President Sherron Watkins took her concerns to an Andersen audit partner who reportedly conveyed her questions to senior Andersen management responsible for the Enron account. It is not clear what action, if any, Andersen took.

THE FALLOUT

Although Enron executives obviously engaged in misconduct, some people have questioned the tactics federal investigators used against Enron. Many former Enron employees feel it was almost impossible to obtain a fair trial for Lay and Skilling. The defense was informed that 130 of Enron's top managers, who could have served as witnesses for the defense, were considered unindicted co-conspirators with Lay and Skilling. Therefore, the defense could not obtain witnesses from Enron's top management teams under fear the prosecution would indict the witnesses.

Enron's demise caused tens of billions of dollars of investor losses, triggered a collapse of electricity-trading markets, and ushered in an era of accounting scandals that precipitated a global loss of confidence in corporate integrity. Today companies must defend legitimate but complicated financing arrangements. Legislation like Sarbanes–Oxley, passed in the wake of Enron, placed more restrictions on companies. Four thousand former Enron employees struggled to find jobs, and many retirees lost their entire retirement portfolios. One senior Enron executive committed suicide.

In 2003 Enron announced its intention to restructure and pay off its creditors. It was estimated most creditors would receive between 14.4 cents and 18.3 cents for each dollar they were owed—more than most expected. Under the plan, creditors would receive about two-thirds of the amount in cash and the rest in equity in three new companies, none of which would carry the tainted Enron name. The three companies were Cross-Country Energy Corporation, Prisma Energy International, Inc., and Portland General Electric.

CrossCountry Energy Corporation retained Enron's interests in three North American natural gas pipelines. In 2004 Enron announced an agreement to sell CrossCountry Energy to CCE Holdings LLC for $2.45 billion. The money was to be used for debt repayment, and represented a substantial increase over a previous offer. Similarly, Prisma Energy International, Inc., which took over Enron's nineteen international power and pipeline holdings, was sold to Ashmore Energy International Ltd. The proceeds from the sale were given to creditors through cash distributions. The third company, Portland General Electric (PGE), Oregon's largest utility, emerged from bankruptcy as an independent company through a private stock offering to Enron creditors.

All remaining assets not related to CrossCountry, Prisma, or Portland General were liquidated. Although Enron emerged from Chapter 11 bankruptcy protection in 2004, the company was wound down once the recovery plan was carried out. That year all of Enron's outstanding common stock and preferred stocks were cancelled. Each record holder of Enron Corporation stock on the day it was cancelled was allocated an uncertified, nontransferable interest in one of two trusts that held new shares of the Enron Corporation.

The Enron Creditors Recovery Corporation was formed to help Enron creditors. It states its mission is "to reorganize and liquidate the remaining operations and assets of Enron following one of the largest and most complex bankruptcies in U.S. history." In the unlikely event the value of Enron's assets would exceed the amount of its allowed claims, distributions were to be made to the holders of these trust interests in the same order of priority of the stock they previously held. According to the Enron Creditors Recovery Corporation, the total amount paid to creditors is $21.738 billion.

In addition to repaying its shareholders, Enron paid California for fraudulent activities it committed against the state's citizens. The company was investigated in California for allegedly colluding with at least two other power sellers in 2000 to obtain excess profits by submitting false information to the manager of California's electricity grid. In 2005 Enron agreed to pay California $47 million for taking advantage of California consumers during an energy shortage.

LEARNING FROM ENRON

Enron was the biggest business scandal of its time, and legislation like the Sarbanes–Oxley Act was passed to prevent future business fraud. But did the business world truly learn its lesson from Enron's collapse? Greed and corporate misconduct continued to be a problem throughout the first decade of the twenty-first century, culminating in the 2008–2009 global recession. Corporations praised high performance at any cost, even when employees cut ethical corners. In the mortgage market, companies like Countrywide rewarded their sales force for making risky subprime loans, even going so far as to turn their back on loans they knew contained falsified information in order to make a quick profit. Other companies traded in risky financial instruments like credit default swaps (CDSs) when they knew buyers did not have a clear understanding of the risks of such instruments. Although they promised to insure against default of these instruments, the companies did not have enough funds to cover the losses after the housing bubble burst. The resulting recession affected the entire world, bankrupting such established companies as Lehman Brothers and requiring government intervention in the amount of nearly $1 trillion in TARP (Troubled Asset Referendum Program) funds to salvage numerous financial firms. The economic meltdown inspired a new wave of legislation designed to prevent corporate misconduct, including the Dodd–Frank Wall Street Reform and Consumer Protection Act.

It is unfortunate the Enron scandal did not hinder corporate misconduct. However, Enron still has lessons to teach us. Along with the business scandals of the financial crisis, Enron demonstrates that, first, regulatory agencies must be improved to detect corporate misconduct. Second, companies and regulatory authorities should pay attention to the warnings of concerned employees and "whistle-blowers" like Sherron Watkins. Third, executives should understand the risks and rewards of the financial instruments their companies use and maintain a thorough knowledge of the inner workings of their companies (something Ken Lay claimed he did not have). These conditions are crucial to preventing similar business fraud in the future.

CONCLUSION

The example of Enron shows how an aggressive corporate culture that rewards high performance and gets rid of the "weak links" can backfire. Enron's culture encouraged intense competition, not only among employees from rival firms, but also among Enron employees themselves. Such behavior creates a culture where loyalty and ethics are cast aside in favor of high performance. The arrogant tactics of Jeffrey Skilling and the apparent ignorance of Ken Lay further contributed to an unhealthy corporate culture that encouraged cutting corners and falsifying information to inflate earnings.

The allegations surrounding Merrill Lynch's and Arthur Andersen's involvement in the debacle demonstrate that rarely does any scandal of such magnitude involve only one company. Whether a company or regulatory body participates directly in a scandal or whether it refuses to act by looking the other way, the result can be further perpetuation of fraud. This fact was emphasized during the 2008–2009 financial crisis when the misconduct of several major companies and the failure of monitoring efforts by regulatory bodies contributed to the worst financial crisis since the Great Depression. With the country recovering from widespread corporate corruption, the story of Enron is once again at the forefront of people's minds. Andy Fastow has stated that businesspeople are falling into the same trap as he fell into at Enron and believes fraud is "ten times worse" today than it was during Enron's time.

The Enron scandal became legendary. In 2005, four years after the scandal, a movie was made about the collapse of Enron called *Enron: The Smartest Guys in the Room.* To this day, Jeffrey Skilling continues to maintain his innocence and appeal his case. In April of 2012, however, the Supreme Court denied his appeal, claiming any errors made in the trial were negligible. However, the following year a federal judge reduced Skilling's sentence to 14 years. Enron's auditor, Arthur Andersen, faced over 40 shareholder lawsuits claiming damages of more than $32 billion. In 2009 the defunct company agreed to pay $16 million to Enron creditors. Enron itself faced many civil actions, and a number of Enron executives faced federal investigations, criminal actions, and civil lawsuits. As for the giant tilted "E" logo so proudly displayed outside of corporate headquarters, it was auctioned off for $44,000.

QUESTIONS

1. How did the corporate culture of Enron contribute to its bankruptcy?
2. Did Enron's bankers, auditors, and attorneys contribute to Enron's demise? If so, how?
3. What role did the company's chief financial officer play in creating the problems that led to Enron's financial problems?

SOURCES

Philip Aldrick, "NatWest Three Return to U.K.," *Telegraph.co.uk,* November 7, 2008, http://www.telegraph.co.uk/news/worldnews/northamerica/usa/3394139/NatWest-Three-return-to-UK.html (accessed July 11, 2013); Associated Press, "Merrill Lynch Settles an Enron Lawsuit," *The New York Times,* July 7, 2006, http://www.nytimes.com/2006/07/07/business/07enron.html?scp=3&sq=%22merrill%20lynch%22%20enron&st=cse (accessed July 11, 2013); Associated Press, "Two Enron Traders Avoid Prison Sentences," *The New York Times,* February 15, 2007, http://www.nytimes.com/2007/02/15/business/15enron.html?ex=1329195600&en=0f87e8ca8 3a557ed&ei=50 90&partner=rssuserland&emc=rss (accessed July 11, 2013); Alexei Barrionuevo, "Fastow Gets His Moment in the Sun," *The New York Times,* November 10, 2006, http://www.nytimes.com/2006/11/10/business/10fastow.html (accessed July 11, 2013); Alexei Barrionuevo Jonathan Weil, and John R. Wilke, "Enron's Fastow Charged with Fraud," *The Wall Street Journal,* October 3, 2002, A3–A4; Eric Berger, "Report Details Enron's Deception," *The Houston Chronicle,* March 6, 2003, 1B, 11B; John Carney, "The Truth About Why Jeff Skilling's Jail Sentence Got Downsized," *CNBC,* June 21, 2013, http://www.cnbc.com/id/100835443 (accessed July 11, 2013); CBCNews.ca, "Enron Settles California Price-Gouging Claim," http://www.cbc.ca/money/story/2005/07/15/enron-gouge050715. html, July 15, 2005 (accessed July 11, 2013); Christine Y. Chen, "When Good Firms Get Bad Chi," *Fortune,* November 11, 2002, 56. Kurt Eichenwald, "Enron Founder, Awaiting Prison, Dies in Colorado," *The New York Times,* July 6, 2006, http://www.nytimes.com/2006/07/06/business/06enron. html (accessed September 7, 2009); Scott Cohn, "Fastow: Enron Didn't Have to Go Bankrupt," *CNBC,* June 26, 2013, http://www.cnbc.com/id/100847519 (accessed July 12, 2013); Francesca Di Meglio, "Enron's Andrew Fastow: The Mistakes I Made," *Bloomberg Businessweek,* March 22, 2012, http://www.businessweek.com/articles/2012-03-22/enrons-andrew-fastow-the-mistakes-i-made (accessed July 12, 2013); Peter Elkind and Bethany McLean, "Feds Move up Enron Food Chain," *Fortune,* December 30, 2002, 43–44; Enron Creditors Recovery Co., "Enron Announces Completed

Sale of Prisma Energy International, Inc.," September 7, 2006, http://www.enron.com/index.php?option=com_content& task=view&id=94&Itemid=34 (accessed September 7, 2009); Enron Creditors Recovery Co., "FAQs," http://www.enron.com/index.php?option=com_content&task=view&id=17&Itemid=27 (accessed September 7, 2009); *Enron*, http://www.enron.com/ (accessed July 11, 2013); Associated Press, "Ex-Enron CFO Fastow Indicted on 78 Counts," *The Los Angeles Times*, November 1, 2002, http://articles.latimes.com/2002/nov/01/business/fi-fastow1 (accessed July 11, 2013); Greg Farrell, "Former Enron CFO Charged," *USA Today*, October 3, 2002, B1; Greg Farrell, Edward Iwata, and Thor Valdmanis, "Prosecutors Are Far from Finished," *USA Today*, October 3, 2002, 1–2B; Mark Felsenthal and Lillia Zuill, "AIG Gets $150 Billion Government Bailout;Posts Huge Losses," *Reuters*, November 10, 2008, http://www.reuters.com/article/topNews/idUSTRE4A92FM20081110?feedType=RSS &feedName=topNews (accessed July 11, 2013); O.C. Ferrell, "Ethics." *BizEd*, May/June 2002, 43–45; O.C. Ferrell and Linda Ferrell, "The Responsibility and Accountability of CEOs: The Last Interview with Ken Lay," *Journal of Business Ethics*, November 11, 2010; O.C. Ferrell and Linda Ferrell, *Examining Systemic Issues That Created Enron and the Latest Global Financial Industry Crisis* (2009), White paper; O.C. Ferrell and Linda Ferrell, "Understanding the Importance of Business Ethics in the 2008–2009 Financial Crisis," In Ferrell, Fraedrich, Ferrell, *Business Ethics*, 7th ed. (Boston: Houghton Mifflin, 2009); Jeffrey A. Fick, "Report: Merrill Replaced Enron Analyst," *USA Today*, July 30, 2002, B1; IBD's Washington Bureau, "Finger-Pointing Starts as Congress Examines Enron's Fast Collapse," *Investor's Business Daily*, February 8, 2002, A1; Daren Fonda, "Enron: Picking over the Carcass." *Fortune*, December 30, 2002–January 6, 2003, 56; Mike France, "One Big Client, One Big Hassle," *BusinessWeek*, January 28, 2002, 38–39; Bryan Gruley and Rebecca Smith, "Keys to Success Left Kenneth Lay Open to Disaster," *The Wall Street Journal*, April 26, 2002, A1, A5; Tom Hamburger, "Enron CEO Declines to Testify at Hearing," *The Wall Street Journal*, December 12, 2001, B2; HighBeam Research, "British Bankers Indicted in Enron Case: Three Men Accused of Siphoning Off $7.3 Million Owed to Their Employer," *The Washington Post*, September 13, 2002, http://www.highbeam.com/doc/1P2-369257.html (accessed July 11, 2013); Daniel Kadlec, "Power Failure," *Time*, December 2, 2001, http://www.time.com/time/magazine/article/0,9171,1101011210-186639,00.html#ixzz0updcIQaT (accessed July 11, 2013); Daniel Kadlec, "Enron: Who's Accountable?" *Time*, January 13, 2002, http://www.time.com/time/business/article/0,8599,193520,00.html#ixzz0v0Yku2MF (accessed July 11, 2013); Jeremy Kahn, "The Chief Freaked Out Officer," *Fortune*, December 9, 2002, 197–198, 202; Matthew Karnitschnig, Carrick Mollenkamp, and Dan Fitzpatrick, "Bank of America to Buy Merrill," *The Wall Street Journal*, September 15, 2008, http://online.wsj.com/article/SB122142278543033525.html?mod=special_coverage (accessed July 11, 2013); Kathryn Kranhold and Rebecca Smith, "Two Other Firms in Enron Scheme, Documents Say," *The Wall Street Journal*, May 9, 2002, C1, C12; Scott Lanman and Craig Torres, "Republican Staff Says Fed Overstepped on Merrill Deal (Update 1)," *Bloomberg*, June 10, 2009, http://www.bloomberg.com/apps/news?pid=newsarchive&sid=a5A4F5W_PygQ (accessed July 11, 2013); Juan A. Lozano, "U.S. Court Orders Skilling Resentenced," *The Washington Post*, January 7, 2009, http://www.washingtonpost.com/wp-dyn/content/article/2009/01/06/AR2009010603214.html (accessed July 11, 2013); Bethany McLean, "Why Enron Went Bust," *Fortune*, December 24, 2001, 58, 60–62, 66, 68; Jodie Morse and Amanda Bower, "The Party Crasher," *Fortune*, December 30, 2002–January 6, 2003, 53–56; Belverd E. Needles, Jr. and Marian Powers, "Accounting for Enron," *Houghton Mifflin's Guide to the Enron Crisis* (Boston: Houghton Mifflin, 2003), 3–6; Floyd Norris, "Ruling Could Open Door to New Trial in Enron Case," *The New York Times*, January 6, 2009, http://www.nytimes.com/2009/01/07/business/07enron.html?scp=3&sq=skilling&st=nyt (accessed July 11, 2013); "Playing the Blame Game," *Time*, January 20, 2002, http://www.time.com/time/2002/enron/collapse (accessed July 29, 2010); Brian Ross and Alice Gomstyn, "Lehman Brothers Boss Defends $484 Million in Salary, Bonus," ABC News, October 6, 2008, http://www.abcnews.go.com/Blotter/Story?id=5965360&page=1 (accessed July 11, 2013); Miriam Schulman, "Enron: Whatever Happened to Going Down with the Ship?" Markkula Center for Applied Ethics, www.scu.edu/ethics/publications/ethicalperspectives/schulman0302.html (accessed July 11, 2013); William Sigismond, "The Enron Case from a Legal Perspective," *Houghton Mifflin's Guide to Enron*, 11–13; Rebecca Smith and Kathryn Kranhold, "Enron Knew Portfolio's Value," *The Wall Street Journal*, May 6, 2002, C1, C20; Rebecca Smith and Mitchell Pacelle, "Enron Plans Return to Its Roots," *The Wall Street Journal*, May 2, 2002, A1; Andrew Ross Sorkin,

"Ex-Enron Chief Skilling Appeals to Supreme Court," DealBook Blog, *The New York Times*, March 12, 2009, http://dealbook.blogs.nytimes.com/2009/05/12/former-enron-chiefskilling- appeals-to-supreme-court/?scp=1-b&sq=skilling&st= nyt (accessed September 7, 2009); "Times Topics: Enron," *The New York Times*, http://topics. nytimes.com/top/news/business/companies/enron/index.html?scp=1-spot&sq=Enron&st=cse (accessed July 11, 2013); Jake Ulick, "Enron: A Year Later." CNN Money, December 2, 2002, http://money.cnn.com/2002/11/26/ news/companies/enron_anniversary/index.htm (accessed July 11, 2013); Ungagged.net, "The Other Side of the Enron Story," http://ungagged.net (accessed July 11, 2013); Joseph Weber, "Can Andersen Survive?" *BusinessWeek*, January 28, 2002, 39–40. Thomas Weidlich, "Arthur Andersen Settles Enron Suit for $16 Million," Bloomberg. com, April 28, 2009, http://www.bloomberg.com/apps/news?pid=20601072&sid=avopmnT7eWjs (accessed July 11, 2013); Winthrop Corporation, "Epigraph," *Houghton Mifflin's Guide to Enron*, 1; Wendy Zellner, "A Hero—and a Smoking-Gun Letter," *Business Week*, January 28, 2002, 34–35. James Vicini, "Supreme Court Rejects Jeffrey Skilling's Appeal In Enron Case," *The Huffington Post*, April 16, 2012, http://www.huffingtonpost.com/2012/04/16/ supreme-court-jeffrey-skilling_n_1428432.html (accessed July 11, 2013).

CASE 10

Home Depot Implements Stakeholder Orientation*

When Bernie Marcus and Arthur Blank opened the first Home Depot store in Atlanta in 1979, they forever changed the hardware and home-improvement retailing industry. Marcus and Blank envisioned huge warehouse-style stores stocked with an extensive selection of products offered at the lowest prices. Do-it-yourselfers and building contractors can browse among 40,000 different products for the home and yard, from kitchen and bathroom fixtures to carpeting, lumber, paint, tools, and plant and landscaping items. If a product is not provided in one of the stores, Home Depot offers 250,000 products that can be special ordered. Some Home Depot stores are open twenty-four hours a day, but customers can also order products online. Additionally, the company offers free home-improvement clinics to teach customers how to tackle everyday projects like tiling a bathroom. For those customers who prefer not to "do it yourself," most stores offer installation services. Knowledgeable employees, recognizable by their orange aprons, are on hand to help customers find items or to demonstrate the proper use of a particular tool.

Currently, Home Depot employs more than 300,000 people and operates over 2,250 Home Depot stores in the United States, Mexico, Puerto Rico, China, the Virgin Islands, Guam, and Canada. It also operates five wholly owned subsidiaries: Apex Supply Company, Georgia Lighting, Maintenance Warehouse, National Blinds and Wallpaper, and US Home Systems. The company is the largest home-improvement retailer in the world, with over $74 billion in revenues. Home Depot continues to do things on a grand scale, including putting its corporate muscle behind a tightly focused social responsibility agenda.

MANAGING CUSTOMER RELATIONSHIPS

In 2006 John Costello was the Chief Marketing Officer, or "Chief Customer Officer," as he refers to the position. Costello consolidated marketing and merchandising functions to help consumers achieve their goals in home-improvement projects more effectively and efficiently. According to Costello, "Above all else, a brand is a promise. It says here's what you can expect if you do business with us. Our mission is to empower our customers to

*This case was developed by Jennifer Sawayda, Michelle Urban, and Melanie Drever for and under the direction of O. C. Ferrell and Linda Ferrell. We appreciate the editorial assistance of Danielle Jolley. This case was prepared for classroom discussion rather than to illustrate either effective or ineffective handling of an administrative, ethical, or legal decision by management. All sources used for this case were obtained through publicly available material.

achieve the home or condo of their dreams." When Costello arrived in 2002 Home Depot's reputation was faltering. His plan called for overhauling the Home Depot website as well as integrating mass marketing and direct marketing with in-store experience. The new philosophy was expressed by the new Home Depot mantra: "You can do it. We can help." Teams of people from merchandising, marketing, visual merchandising, and operations attempted to provide the best shopping experience. The idea was simple. Home Depot believed customers should be able to read and understand how one ceiling fan is different from another, and associates (employees) should be able to offer installation and design advice.

In an effort to expand market share, Home Depot developed a new marketing strategy. The company's approach was to emphasize the store's everyday low prices, high product value, and quality energy-saving products. At the same time, the company cut back on special offers like discounts and promotions, in order to combat volatile market conditions and remain competitive within the home improvement segment.

Despite Home Depot's proactive approach to customer issues, the company has had its share of challenges along the way. In the past, the company was forced to deal with negative publicity associated with customer-satisfaction measures published by outside sources. Over the past few years, Home Depot's customer satisfaction scores have significantly improved. However, the University of Michigan's annual American Customer Satisfaction Index in 2013 showed that Home Depot has consistently placed behind competitor Lowe's when it comes to customer satisfaction. The company is down 1 percent from the previous year, whereas Lowe's position has remained unchanged.

Former managers at Home Depot blamed the company's service issues on a culture that operated under principles reminiscent of the military. Under CEO Robert Nardelli, some employees feared being terminated unless they followed directions to a tee. After months of decline in customer satisfaction and other areas, Nardelli was fired and Frank Blake became the newly appointed CEO. Harris Interactive's Reputation Quotient Survey has ranked Home Depot for the past three years, and the company has proven inconsistent with its standing. At one time a number of customers said they appreciated Home Depot's quality services. In 2011 Home Depot ranked 24th on the list. The next year it jumped to 14 but then fell to 17 in 2013. Despite this versatility, Home Depot's customer-satisfaction ratings are still a major improvement from Home Depot's 2007 ranking of 27.

The increase of customer satisfaction was due to several efforts on the part of Frank Blake. The company's Twitter feed was inundated with comments from unsatisfied customers about the customer service they encountered in the stores. Blake quickly admitted to the customer service problems the company faced, apologized for the inconvenience it caused the customers, and encouraged them to continue to leave their feedback so they could make improvements. Each one of the complaints was addressed; some angry followers were appeased by phone calls from store managers and personal emails responding to their specific issues. The responsiveness of Blake and his Senior Manager of Social Media, Sarah Molinari, not only transformed angry protesters into enthusiastic fans but also resulted in a strategic advantage for the company in terms of how it deals with customer feedback.

Inside the stores, self-checkout lanes were installed so customers do not have to spend time waiting in line. However, at peak hours, waiting in line cannot be avoided. In instances such as these, Home Depot associates can scan items in customers' baskets while they are in line and hand them a card that holds all their purchases. When the customer reaches the cashier, they simply scan the card and pay the total they owe. Home Depot was also the first to partner with PayPal, making it easier for customers who do not want to carry their wallet or cash with them to be able to pay more conveniently. Many of the Home Depot associates are given devices called "First Phone," which is a phone/walkie-talkie/scanner. This device allows associates to help customers quickly by calling or paging fellow associates who can answer customers' questions and have immediate access to the price of an item by scanning it right where they stand.

Another way Home Depot practices good customer service and simultaneously acts in a socially responsible manner is through its program designed to teach children basic carpentry skills. Home Depot provides a free program called the Kids Workshop available at all its stores. During the workshops, children learn to create objects used around their homes or neighborhoods. Projects include toolboxes, mail organizers, and window birdhouses and bughouses. Home Depot also offers free workshops especially designed for women and for new homeowners.

ENVIRONMENTAL INITIATIVES

Cofounders Marcus and Blank nurtured a corporate culture that emphasizes social responsibility, especially with regard to the company's impact on the natural environment. Home Depot began its environmental program on the twentieth anniversary of Earth Day in 1990 by adopting a set of Environmental Principles. These principles have since been adopted by the National Retail Hardware Association and Home Center Institute, which represents more than 46,000 retail hardware stores and home centers.

Guided by these principles, Home Depot initiated a number of programs to minimize the firm's—and its customers'—impact on the environment. The retailer began using store and office supplies, advertising, signs, and shopping bags made with recycled content. It also established a process for evaluating the environmental claims made by suppliers. The following year the firm launched a program to recycle wallboard shipping packaging, which became the industry's first "reverse distribution" program. In addition, it was the first retailer in the world to combine a drive-through recycling center with one of its Georgia stores. One year later Home Depot became the first home-improvement retailer to offer wood products from tropical and temperate forests certified as "well-managed" by the Scientific Certification System's Forest Conservation Program. The company also began to replace its hardwood wooden shipping pallets with reusable "slip sheets" to minimize waste and energy usage and decrease pressure on hardwood resources.

In 1999 Home Depot joined the Certified Forests Products Council, a nonprofit organization that promotes responsible forest product buying practices and the sale of wood from Certified Well-Managed Forests. Yet the company continued to sell products made from wood harvested from old growth forests. Protesters led by the Rainforest Action Network, an environmental group, picketed Home Depot and other home center stores for years in an effort to stop the destruction of old growth forests, of which less than 20 percent still survive. Later that year, during Home Depot's twentieth anniversary celebration, Arthur Blank announced Home Depot would stop selling products made from wood harvested in environmentally sensitive areas.

To be certified by the Forest Stewardship Council (FSC), a supplier's wood products must be tracked from the forest, through manufacturing and distribution, to the customer. Harvesting, manufacturing, and distribution practices must ensure a balance of social, economic, and environmental factors. Blank challenged competitors to follow Home Depot's lead, and within two years several met that challenge, including Lowe's, the number-two home-improvement retailer; Wickes, a lumber company; and Andersen Corporation, a window manufacturer. By 2003 Home Depot reported it had reduced its purchases of Indonesian lauan, a tropical rainforest hardwood used in door components, by 70 percent, and continued to increase its purchases of certified sustainable wood products. In an effort to reduce its carbon footprint, Home Depot aimed to decrease not only store operations but also simultaneously reduce transportation emissions emitted by the company. To do this Home Depot installed dual-flush low-flow toilets in stores that reduce water usage by 40 percent. In other efforts, the company switched to high-efficiency T5 fluorescent lighting, which lowered overall wattage and created more energy-efficient lighting in stores. The company then provided new irrigation systems that reduced water usage by 35 percent and only irrigates where and when it is necessary. Also, Home Depot installed LED exterior signs that replaced the fluorescent lighting that was previously in place.

To further its efforts of sustainability, Home Depot installed solar panels on 62 of its retail stores, making it the largest retailer to host solar programs. The company managed to reduce its energy use by 16 percent between 2004 and 2010, and hopes to reach 20 percent by 2015. For its efforts in social responsibility and sustainability, the company was honored with the ranking of one of the top 25 Socially Responsible Dividend Stocks, meaning it is recognized as being a socially responsible investment. Being a responsible investment is determined not only through its environmental initiatives, but also through its social impact. The company also offers a variety of sustainable products through the brand Energy Star, which allows their customers to take part in creating a better tomorrow.

These efforts yielded many rewards in addition to improved relations with environmental stakeholders. Home Depot's environmental programs earned the company an A on the Council on Economic Priorities Corporate Report Card, a Vision of America Award from Keep America Beautiful, and a President's Council for Sustainable Development Award. The company has also been recognized by the U.S. Environmental Protection Agency with its Energy Star Award for Excellence.

EMPLOYEE AND SUPPLIER RELATIONS

Home Depot encourages employees to become involved in the community through volunteer and civic activities. Home Depot strives to apply social responsibility to its employment practices, with the goal of assembling a diverse workforce that reflects the population of the markets it serves. However, in 1997 the company settled a class-action lawsuit brought by female employees who alleged they were paid less than male employees, awarded fewer pay raises, and promoted less often. The $87.5 million settlement represented one of the largest settlements in a gender discrimination lawsuit in U.S. history at the time. In announcing the settlement, the company emphasized it was not admitting to wrongdoing and defended its record, saying it provides equal opportunities for all and has a reputation of supporting women in professional positions.

Since the lawsuit, Home Depot worked to show it appreciates workforce diversity and seeks to give all associates an equal chance to be employed and advance. In 2005 Home Depot formed partnerships with the ASPIRA Association, Inc., the Hispanic Association of Colleges and Universities, and the National Council of La Raza to recruit Hispanic candidates for part-time and full-time positions. Home Depot is a member of the American Association of Retired Persons' (AARP) Featured Retirement Program that helps connect employees 50 years or older with companies that value their experience. Home Depot also has a strong diversity supplier program. As a member of the Women's Business Enterprise National Council and the National Minority Suppliers Development Council, Home Depot came into contact and did business with a diverse range of suppliers, including many minority- and women-owned businesses. In 2005 the company became a founding member of The Resource Institute, whose mission is to help small minority- and women-owned businesses by providing them with resources and training. Home Depot's supplier diversity program won it numerous recognitions. It ranked number 13 for the Top 50 American Organizations for Multicultural Business Opportunities in 2012 and was named the Georgia Minority Supplier Development Council (GMSDC) Buyer of the Year Transportation and Logistics.

NEW TECHNOLOGY INITIATIVES

Home Depot is turning to technology to improve customer service and become more efficient. Compared to its rivals, Home Depot lagged behind technologically. For instance, employees were using computers powered by motorboard batteries and stocking shelves the same way they have for the past 15 years. Unlike its rival Lowe's, Home Depot did not allow customers to order products online and pick them up at the stores. As more consumers choose to complete their transactions on the Web, this represented a weakness for Home Depot. In 2010 Home Depot's online sales constituted only 1.5 percent of overall sales. Although rapid expansion increased its reach, Home Depot was not adapting as quickly to the fast-paced world of technology.

After recognizing its limitations in this field, Home Depot embarked on several technology initiatives. These initiatives are intended to improve both its customer service and Home Depot's daily operations. One small victory Home Depot achieved is beating Lowe's in unleashing a mobile app that enables consumers to order Home Depot products. Additionally, Home Depot invested $64 million to create First Phone, a device that replaces the old computers on associates' carts. Home Depot distributed 30,000 of these devices in over 1,900 of its stores. The device allows associates to communicate with other associates, print labels, process credit and debit card transactions, and manage inventory, among other functions. In 2013 Home Depot rolled out 25,000 new devices called First Phone Junior, a scaled-down version of First Phone that allows employees to manage inventory better, assist customers, and navigate checkout lines efficiently. According to CEO Frank Blake, the purpose of First Phone and the First Phone Junior is to help associates spend less time on routine tasks and more on customer service. Home Depot also redesigned its website to improve navigation and communication channels. The company provided upgrades such as live chat and developed a buy online pickup option. Home Depot managed to reduce response time to customer emails from 24 hours to one hour or less.

In 2011 a special component of the Home Depot website launched for "Pros" (Professional and Contractor Services). This website is intended to decrease the time it takes for professionals and contractors to get in and out of the store, allow them to order online and pick up their goods within a couple of hours, and enable delivery for certain products when ordered in bulk. Home Depot recognizes professionals should spend less time in the store and more on the job. After this website was implemented, the speed to get in and out of the store increased by 27 percent from the previous year. Three percent of the customers identified as Pros make up 30 percent of Home Depot's annual revenue, making this an important market for the retailer. Additionally, Home Depot is improving its logistics. Whereas the company had suppliers send trucks of merchandise directly to the stores, where associates would then unload them, Home Depot created distribution centers to make operations run more smoothly. This change also enables its associates to devote more time to customer service.

These are just a few of the steps Home Depot is taking to adopt a more proactive stance toward technological innovation. By concentrating on innovations that increase customer service, the retailer is attempting to advance its stakeholder orientation into all aspects of its operations. Home Depot invested $1.3 billion in technology over a three-year period.

A STRATEGIC COMMITMENT TO SOCIAL RESPONSIBILITY

In addition to its environmental initiatives, Home Depot focuses corporate social responsibility efforts on affordable housing and disaster relief. For instance, Home Depot believes it has a philanthropic responsibility to improve the communities where it operates. The company partners with Habitat for Humanity to build houses for disadvantaged individuals. In 2002 the company initiated the Home Depot Foundation, which provides additional resources to assist nonprofits in the United States and Canada. The Foundation awards grants to eligible nonprofits and partners with innovative nonprofits across the country working to increase awareness and successfully demonstrate the connection between housing, the urban forest, and the overall health and economic success of their communities. Since its inception, the Foundation invested $300 million in building and renovating affordable, sustainable homes, improving local parks and playgrounds, and repairing community facilities nationwide. In addition, the company invested $80 million in building homes for veterans. More recently, the Home Depot Foundation donated $2.7 million in cash and in-kind donations to fund *Repair Corps,* a partnership with Habitat for Humanity that repairs the homes of disabled veterans.

Additionally, Home Depot addresses the growing needs for relief from disasters such as hurricanes, tornadoes, and earthquakes. Not only is the company one of the first entities on scene to rebuild communities in times of disaster, Home Depot also makes an annual donation of $500,000 to the American Red Cross Annual Disaster Giving Program (ADGP) that enables the organization to respond quickly in times of need. After the 9/11 terrorist attacks, the company set up three command centers with more than 200 associates to coordinate relief supplies such as dust masks, gloves, batteries, and tools to victims and rescue workers. After the 2010 Haitian earthquake, Home Depot Mexico donated $30,000 to Habitat for Humanity to assist in Haiti's recovery efforts in addition to launching a fundraising program for its Mexican associates. Home Depot pledged to double the resources its Mexican associates raised to aid in the relief effort. When Hurricane Sandy hit the American East Coast in 2012, Home Depot responded with $1 million in donations in gift cards, supplies, and contributions to organizations that provided food, clothing, shelter, and volunteer efforts. Members of their own volunteer team, Team Depot, helped with rebuilding efforts.

In 2013 Home Depot responded to the needs of many individuals after tornadoes in Oklahoma and areas of the Southwest greatly impacted their lives. The Home Depot Foundation created a $1 million fund in efforts to provide financial support for the victims of the tragedies. The company donated supplies, workers, and most importantly, time to help alleviate those affected by the tornadoes. More than 250 Home Depot volunteers joined in to assist with disaster relief efforts. Volunteers spent the day sifting through debris and provided any assistance that was needed.

Home Depot strives to secure a socially responsible reputation with stakeholders. Although it received low scores in the past on customer surveys and the American Customer Satisfaction Index, the company is consistently working hard to bring those scores back up. It responded to concerns about its environmental impact by creating new standards and principles to govern its relationship with its suppliers. Despite Home Depot's success, however, the company faces challenges in the future. Still, Home Depot's philanthropic endeavors and its promotion of its products' low prices and high value continue to make it a popular shopping destination.

Knowing stakeholders, especially customers, feel good about a company that actively commits resources to environmental and social issues, Home Depot executives committed to social responsibility as a strategic component of the company's business operations. The company should remain committed to its focused strategy of philanthropy, volunteerism, and environmental initiatives. Customers' concerns over social responsibility and green products have not abated, and Home Depot's sales of green products are strong. Its commitment to social responsibility extends throughout the company, fueled by top-level support from its cofounders and reinforced by a corporate culture that places great value on playing a responsible role within the communities it serves.

CONCLUSION

Over the past 35 years, Home Depot has changed the do-it-yourself home improvement retail environment. Home Depot has even encouraged other retailers to use warehouse-style stores stocked with lower-priced products. The company started with a clear understanding of its various stakeholders and has developed a strong commitment to customers, communities, suppliers, employees, and the environment. As with most large organizations, Home Depot has made some mistakes but seems to be able to recover quickly and respond to ethical issues. The company has become a leader in sustainability, especially in sourcing its products. From the beginning Home Depot has had a strong commitment to communities and has always been ready to respond to disasters such as hurricanes, tornadoes, and floods. Its support of Habitat for Humanity is an ongoing commitment to help those who are less fortunate have their own homes. Encouraging its employees to build houses for Habitat for Humanity has been beneficial in developing strong community relationships.

Home Depot continues to pursue innovation and change to relate to its stakeholders. For instance, it is engaged in a strategic overhaul of its supply chain. The company recognizes that supply chain members need to adhere to strong ethical and sustainability practices to meet consumer standards. The company continues to upgrade and strengthen its competitive position and has earned a strong financial rating because of its effectiveness in implementing strategies targeted toward stakeholders. While Home Depot's economic future depends on recovery in the housing market, the company maintains a solid track record of earnings per share growth. Today the company has 2,257 stores in the United States, Mexico, and Canada. It remains the world's largest home-improvement retailer and is poised for substantial future growth. Its stock reached an all-time high in 2013, increasing 30 percent in value in the first six months of 2013. While the overall stock market was moving in a positive direction, Home Depot significantly outpaced the market.

Research has found that the world's most ethical companies are more profitable than the general stock market index over the long term. Home Depot is a good example of a company that has developed strong relationships with stakeholders and has tried to create an ethical corporate culture. The company recognizes that success is not limited to focusing on only one stakeholder, but that it must take a holistic approach to understand how other stakeholders, including suppliers and employees, can help the firm build trust with communities.

QUESTIONS

1. On the basis of Home Depot's response to environmental issues, describe the attributes of this stakeholder. Assess the company's strategy and performance with environmental and employee stakeholders.
2. As a publicly traded corporation, how can Home Depot justify budgeting so much money for philanthropy? What areas other than the environment, disaster relief, and affordable housing might be appropriate for strategic philanthropy by Home Depot?
3. How is Home Depot working toward reducing its weaknesses to increase its stakeholder orientation?

SOURCES

American Customer Satisfaction Index, "ACSI Commentary February 2012," February 21, 2012, http://www. theacsi.org/acsi-results/acsi-commentary-february-2012, (accessed January 29, 2013); American Customer Satisfaction Index, "ACSI Commentary February 2013," February 2013, http://www.theacsi.org/acsi-results/acsi-commentary-february-2013 (accessed July 15, 2013); Mae Anderson, "Home Depot ups 2010 outlook on strong sales, will hire," USA Today, December 8, 2010, http://www.usatoday.com/money/industries/retail/2010-12-08-home-depot-outlook_N.htm (accessed February 13, 2013); Associated Press, "Home Depot CEO Nardelli Quits," MSNBC, January 3, 2007, http://www.msnbc.msn.com/id/16451112/ (accessed February 13, 2013); Adam Blair, "Home Depot's $64 Million Mobile Investment Rolls Out to 1, 970 Stores." RIS, December 7, 2010, http://risnews. edgl.com/store-systems/Home-Depot-s-$64-Million-Mobile-Investment-Rolls-Out-to-1,600-Stores56966 (accessed February 13, 2013); Tom Brennan, "Home Depot vs. Lowe's," CNBC, August 26, 2008, http://www.cnbc. com/id/26406040/?__source=aol|headline|quote|text|&par=aol (accessed February 13, 2013); Chris Burritt, "Home Depot's Fix-It Lady." Bloomberg BusinessWeek, January 17–23, 2011, 65–67; Miguel Bustillo, "For Lowe's, Landscape Begins to Shift," The Wall Street Journal, February 24, 2011, B3; Jim Carlton, "How Home Depot and Activists Joined to Cut Logging Abuse," The Wall Street Journal, September 26, 2000, A1; Cora Daniels, "To Hire a Lumber Expert, Click Here," Fortune, April 3, 2000, 267–270; Sarah Demaster, "Use proper lumber, demand protesters," BNet, April 5, 1999, http://findarticles.com/p/articles/mi_m0VCW/is_7_25/ai_54373184/ (accessed September 8, 2009); Kirsteny Downey Grimsley, "Home Depot Settles Gender Bias Lawsuit," The Washington Post,

September 20, 1997, D1; Shelly DuBois, "Home Depot Knows When To Call It Quits," *CNN Money*, October 26, 2012, http://management.fortune.cnn.com/2012/10/26/home-depot-knows-when-to-call-it-quits/ (accessed January 31, 2013); Energy Star, *Profiles in Leadership: 2008 ENERGY STAR Award Winners*, http://www.energystar. gov/ia/partners/pt_awards/2008_profiles_in_leadership.pdf (accessed February 13, 2013); "Fortune 500: Home Depot," *CNN Money*, http://money.cnn.com/magazines/fortune/fortune500/2012/snapshots/2968.html (accessed January 24, 2013); Brian Grow, Diane Brady, and Michael Arndt, "Renovating Home Depot," *Businessweek*, March 6, 2006, http://www.businessweek.com/print/magazine/content/06_10/b3974001.htm?chan=gl (accessed September 8, 2009); Habitat for Humanity, "Habitat for Humanity and the Home Depot Foundation Announce National Green Building Effort," March 20, 2008, http://www.habitat.org/newsroom/2008archive/03_21_08_ Home_Depot.aspx (accessed February 13, 2013). Habitat for Humanity, "Habitat for Humanity and The Home Depot Foundation partner to repair homes with veterans and their families," May 31, 2013, http://www. habitatmidohio.org/anniversary_story/habitat-humanity-home-depot-foundation-partner-repair-homes-veterans-families/ (accessed July 15, 2013); Habitat for Humanity, "Habitat for Humanity and The Home Depot Mexico partner to help rebuild Haiti," February 8, 2010, http://www.habitat.org/lac_eng/ newsroom/2010/02_08_2010_homedepot_eng.aspx?tgs=Mi81LzIwMTEgMTI6NDg6NTYgUE0%3d (accessed February 13, 2013); Harris Interactive, "The Annual RQ 2007: The Reputations of the Most Visible Companies," *Marketing Charts*, http://www.marketingcharts.com/direct/corporate-reputation-in-decline-but-top-companies-buck-trend-5129/harris-corporate-reputation-2007-most-visible-companiesjpg/ (accessed February 13, 2013); Harris Interactive, *The Harris Poll 2013 RQ® Summary Report*, 2013, http://www.harrisinteractive.com/ vault/2013%20RQ%20Summary%20Report%20FINAL.pdf (accessed July 15, 2013); Ashley M. Heher, "Home Depot Reports Loss of $54M, but Beats Estimates," *USA Today*, February 24, 2009, http://www.usatoday.com/ money/companies/earnings/2009-02-24-home-depot_N.htm (accessed February 13, 2013); Melissa Hincha-Ownby, "Home Depot Shrinks Energy Bill," *Forbes*, March 11, 2010, http://www.forbes.com/2010/03/10/energy-efficiency-lighting-technology-ecotech-home-depot.html (accessed February 6, 2011); Home Depot, "2008 Annual Report," http://www.homedepot.com/ (accessed September 8, 2009); "Home Depot: A Customer Success Story," *Social Link Media*, August 30, 2011, http://www.socialinkmedia.com/2011/08/the-home-depot-a-customer-service-success-story/ (accessed January 29, 2013); "Home Depot Announces Commitment to Stop Selling Old Growth Wood; Announcement Validates Two-Year Grassroots Environmental Campaign," *Common Dreams Newswire*, http://www.commondreams.org/pressreleases/august99/082699c.htm, August 26, 1999 (accessed February 13, 2013); "Home Depot builds out its online customer service," Internet Retailer, www.internetretailer. com/2010/06/04/home-depot-builds-out-its-online-customer-service, June 4, 2010 (accessed February 13, 2013); Home Depot, "Corporate Financial Review," http://corporate.homedepot.com/en_US/Corporate/Public_ Relations/Online_Press_Kit/Docs/Corp_Financial_Overview.pdf (accessed September 8, 2009); Home Depot, "Disaster Relief," *Home Depot Foundation*, 2012, http://homedepotfoundation.org/page/disaster-relief (accessed January 31, 2013); Home Depot, "Environmental Milestones," 2011, https://corporate.homedepot.com/ CorporateResponsibility/Environment/Pages/Milestones.aspx (accessed January 31, 2013); Home Depot, "The Home Depot Foundation Responds to Superstorm Sandy," *Home Depot Foundation*, 2012, http:// homedepotfoundation.org/page/the-home-depot-foundation-responds-to-superstorm-sandy (accessed January 31, 2013); Home Depot, "Message from the Supplier Diversity Leadership," http://corporate.homedepot.com/wps/ portal/SupplierDiversity (accessed February 13, 2013); Home Depot, "Our History," https://corporate.homedepot. com/Pages/default.aspx (accessed February 13, 2013); Home Depot, "Our Mission and Outreach Efforts," https:// corporate.homedepot.com/Pages/default.aspx (accessed February 13, 2013); "Home Depot Retools Timber Policy," *Memphis Business Journal*, January 2, 2003, www.bizjournals.com/memphis/stories/2002/12/30/daily12.html (accessed February 13, 2013); Home Depot, *Some Actions Last Longer than a Lifetime 2012 Sustainability Report*, https://corporate.homedepot.com/CorporateResponsibility/Environment/Documents/Sustainability__Brochure_ pages.pdf (accessed July 15, 2013); Home Depot, "We Build Community: Team Depot," https://corporate. homedepot.com/Pages/default.aspx (accessed February 13, 2013); The Home Depot Foundation, "Archive for the 'Philanthropy' Category," http://www.homedepotfoundation.org/blog/category/philanthropy/ (accessed July 15,

2013); The Home Depot Foundation, "Our Focus," *Home Depot Foundation*, 2012, http://www. homedepotfoundation.org/page/our-focus/ (accessed January 31, 2013); The Home Depot Foundation, "Who We Are," http://www.homedepotfoundation.org/page/who-we-are (accessed February 13, 2013); Hoovers Inc., "The Home Depot, Inc., Profile," http://www.hoovers.com/company-information/cs/company-profile.The_Home_ Depot_Inc.fbb298e093e95785.html (accessed February 6, 2013); Susan Jackson and Tim Smart, "Mom and Pop Fight Back," *BusinessWeek*, April 14, 1997, 46; Karen Jacobs, "Home Depot Pushes Low Prices, Energy Savings," *Reuters*, September 10, 2008, http://www.reuters.com/article/ousiv/idUSN1051947020080910 (accessed February 13, 2013); Neil Janowitz, "Rolling in the Depot," *Fast Company*, May 2012, 38; Mary Ellen Lloyd, "Home Improvement Spending Remains Tight," *The Wall Street Journal*, May 6, 2009, http://online.wsj.com/article/ SB124162405957992133.html (accessed February 13, 2013); Gene Marcial, "Inside Wall Street: Home Depot is a Home Run," *MSN Money*, October 9, 2012, http://money.msn.com/top-stocks/post.aspx?post=3cc1894a-1bd3- 4fe5-a9a2-876512fd4344 (accessed January 31, 2013); Jena McGregor, "Home Depot Sheds Units," *Businessweek*, January 26, 2009, http://www.businessweek.com/bwdaily/dnflash/content/jan2009/db20090126_454995.htm (accessed February 13, 2013); PR Newswire, "The Home Depot Forms Unprecedented Partnership with Four Leading National Hispanic Organizations," HispanicBusiness.com, February 15, 2005, http://www. hispanicbusiness.com/news/newsbyid.asp?idx=20997&page=1&cat=&more= (accessed February 13, 2013); PR Newswire, "The Home Depot Launches Environmental Wood Purchasing Policy," August 26, 1999, http://www. prnewswire.com/cgi-bin/stories.pl?ACCT=104&STORY=/www/story/08-26-1999/0001010227&EDATE= (accessed September 8, 2009); Reuters, "Home Depot Earnings Q3 2012: Improved Housing Market Boosts Retailer's Sales, Profits," *The Huffington Post*, November 11, 2012, http://www.huffingtonpost.com/2012/11/13/ home-depot-earnings-q3-2012_n_2121025.html (accessed January 31, 2013); Reuters, "Home Depot's Do-It- Yourself Model Fails in China's Do-It-For-Me Market," *Reuters*, September 14, 2012, http://www.reuters.com/ article/2012/09/14/us-homedepot-chinastoreclosure-idUSBRE88D02W20120914 (accessed January 31, 2013); Reuters, "Profile: Home Depot, Inc. (HD.N)," *Reuters*, http://www.reuters.com/finance/stocks/companyProfile? symbol=HD.N (accessed January 24, 2013); Julie Scelfo, "The Meltdown in Home Furnishings," *The New York Times*, January 28, 2009, http://www.nytimes.com/2009/01/29/garden/29industry.html (accessed February 13, 2013); Joel Schectman, "Home Depot Rolls Out New Mobile Devices for Workers," *The Wall Street Journal*, June 21, 2011, http://blogs.wsj.com/cio/2012/06/21/home-depot-rolls-out-new-mobile-devices-for-workers/ (accessed July 15, 2013); Kelsey Swanekamp, "Home Depot Cuts Jobs," *Forbes*, January 26, 2010, http://www.forbes. com/2010/01/26/home-depot-jobs-markets-equities-cuts.html (accessed February 13, 2013); Louis Uchitelle, "Home Depot Girds for Continued Weakness," *The New York Times*, May 18, 2009, http://www.nytimes. com/2009/05/19/business/19depot.html (accessed February 13, 2013); Craig Webb, "Home Depot Exec Reveals New Initiatives to Serve Pros," *ProSales*, August 21, 2012, http://www.prosalesmagazine.com/customer-service/ home-depot-exec-reveals-new-initiatives-to-serve-pros.aspx (accessed January 31, 2013); Marianne Wilson, "Report: Home Depot to Spend $1.3 Billion on Technology and $700 Million on New Stores," *Chain Store Age*, June 20, 2012, http://www.chainstoreage.com/article/report-home-depot-spend-13-billion-technology-and- 700-million-new-stores (accessed January 31, 2013); "World's Most Admired Companies: Home Depot," *CNN Money*, http://money.cnn.com/magazines/fortune/globalmostadmired/2008/snapshots/2968.html (accessed February 13, 2013).

CASE 11

Frauds of the Century*

Before Bernard Madoff, the average consumer likely never heard of a Ponzi scheme. This little-known crime soon became a front-page headline in December 2008 when highly respected securities trader Bernard Madoff admitted to operating a Ponzi scheme for more than a decade. Tom Petters, former CEO and chairman of Petters Worldwide, had already been arrested for an alleged Ponzi scheme in October of that year. A few months later, respected financier R. Allen Stanford was arrested for a Ponzi scheme that cost investors $7 billion. A Ponzi scheme is a type of white-collar crime that occurs when a criminal— often of high repute—takes money from new investors to pay earnings for existing investors. The money is never actually invested and, when the scheme finally collapses, newer investors usually lose their investments.

Ponzi schemes are often mistaken for pyramid schemes. Both types of criminal activities have the same basic structure. Pyramid schemes are illegal but can be hard to detect. They occur when there are no legitimate products or sustainable investments to sell. The difference between a pyramid and a Ponzi scheme is that the perpetrator of the Ponzi scheme asks individuals to invest in something with an above average return. No other action is required. Also, pyramid scheme typically collapse much faster because it requires exponential increases in participants to sustain it. By contrast, Ponzi schemes can survive simply by persuading most existing participants to reinvest their money, with a relatively small number of new participants.

A pyramid scheme offers an opportunity for an individual to make money that requires effort. Usually this is in the form of an investment, business, or product opportunity. The first person recruited then sells or recruits more people, and a type of financial reward is given to those who recruit the next participant. The key aspect of a pyramid scheme is that people pay for getting involved. Each new individual or investor joins in what is believed to be a legitimate opportunity to get a return, which is how the fraudster gets money. However, unlike a legitimate organization, pyramid schemes either do not sell a product, or the investment is almost worthless. All income comes from new people enrolling. Much like Ponzi schemes, when enrollment dries up, the pyramid scheme dissolves. Newer enrollees lose their investments. Both Ponzi schemes and pyramid schemes are highly damaging to consumers and the financial industry at large. In general, it may be difficult to determine if a business opportunity is initially a pyramid scheme.

This case analyzes the detrimental impact Ponzi and pyramid schemes have on society. The first part of this analysis examines the harmful effects of Ponzi schemes as well as some of this century's most infamous Ponzi schemers. We then examine pyramid schemes, their negative impacts, and their confusion with legitimate business models. We conclude this

---

*This case was prepared by Linda Ferrell with editorial assistance and Jennifer Sawayda. It was prepared for classroom discussion rather than to illustrate either effective or ineffective handling of an administrative, ethical, or legal decision by management. All sources used for this case were obtained through publicly available material.

analysis by reemphasizing the unique nature of white-collar criminals and reiterating the need for transparency, internal controls, and compliance standards within an organization.

THE IMPACT OF PONZI SCHEMES ON SOCIETY

Ponzi schemes are highly detrimental to society, not only because of the financial losses they incur but also for the lack of trust consumers feel toward business in general. The financial industry in particular experienced a wide-scale loss of trust because of financial misconduct such as Ponzi schemes. One or two schemers can have a wide ranging impact on the entire industry. Ponzi schemes do not seem to be decreasing: since 2010 there have been approximately 100 actions taken by the SEC against 200 individual Ponzi schemers and 250 companies.

Many people who were victims of Ponzi schemes lost major investments in the fraud. Victims range from low-income to high-income individuals as well as companies and non-profits. Organizations are often impacted the most because of the significant investments they are able to make. For instance, in the Madoff scandal, many nonprofit organizations lost millions after the fraud was revealed. While some investors make money if they invested early enough from fictional profits taken from newer investors, others may lose their entire life savings in the fraud.

Additionally, while Ponzi schemes appear to thrive in the financial industry, they can be present in any industry where investments are made. In India, for instance, farmers were made to believe that there was a significant market for emu meat, feathers, and oil. Farmers who purchased emu chicks received the promise from the con artist that the adult emus would be purchased at double the price originally paid for them. They were also promised monthly payments. However, when the scheme collapsed and the payments stopped, approximately 10,000 farmers were left with about 100,000 birds without any use for them. Albania was also the victim of several Ponzi schemes. In 1996 companies engaging in Ponzi schemes started promising Albanian investors more than 30 percent returns per month. Three million people whose average income was $8,000 per year invested more than $1.2 billion in the schemes. After they lost their investments, the Albanian economy collapsed and a massive uprising resulted in the deaths of 2,000 people.

It is also not uncommon for the victims of Ponzi schemes to unknowingly propagate the scheme through the recruitment of others. Investors with Bernie Madoff often convinced their friends and family members to invest as well and get in on the deal. The community of Lexington, North Carolina, was duped by a $600 million Ponzi scheme from online company ZeekRewards. Many investors were recruited by others in the community, resulting in a massive loss for the town when the scheme collapsed.

Fortunately, there are red flags for Ponzi schemes. These warning signs include high and/or consistent returns with little or no risk, unlicensed sellers, secret methodologies or strategies not divulged to investors, and paperwork problems. The biggest red flag is high and consistent returns. The reason is because the market itself is not consistent, so although an investor may have long-term profitability, short-term profits should vary yearly. Most Ponzi schemers are unlicensed sellers and use what they deem to be "secretive" strategies to confuse investors. Lack of paperwork is another warning signal because Ponzi schemers want to avoid releasing information that could arouse suspicion.

Unfortunately, Ponzi schemers are usually white-collar criminals who, rather than being a stereotypical criminal, are often seen as successful people who inspire trust. The following examples bear this out.

The Original Ponzi Schemer

The Ponzi scheme was named after Charles Ponzi, who in the early twentieth century saw a way to profit from international reply coupons. An international reply coupon was a guarantee of return postage in response to an international letter. Ponzi determined he could make money by swapping out these coupons for more expensive postage stamps in countries where the stamps were of higher value. Ponzi convinced investors to provide him with capital to trade coupons for higher-priced postage stamps. His promise to investors who joined in his scheme was a 50 percent profit in a few days.

Touted as a financial wizard, Ponzi lived a fairly opulent life outside of Boston. He would often bring in as much as $250,000 a day. Part of Ponzi's success came from his personal charisma and ability to con even savvy investors. People trusted Ponzi because he created an image of power, trust, and responsibility—much as Bernard Madoff did a century later. The largest problem with his scheme was that in order to keep giving earlier investors their promised returns, Ponzi had to continually draw new people into the scheme. In July of 1920 the *Boston Post* ran an article exposing the scheme, and soon after regulators raided Ponzi's offices and charged him with mail fraud, knowing his fabricated investment reports were mailed to his clients. Mr. Ponzi's scheme self-destructed in about one year. More recent cases are unusual because the fraudsters were able to continue their fraud for many years.

Tom Petters

It is quite simple to ignore the case of Tom Petters' alleged Ponzi scheme outside his home state of Minnesota. His arrest was eclipsed by that of the more infamous Bernard L. Madoff a few months later. However, Tom Petters has been accused of operating the third largest Ponzi scheme in U.S. history at $3.65 billion. Petters was a highly successful entrepreneur and CEO of Petters Group Worldwide (PGW). The company was involved in a number of different industries, including airlines, direct marketing, Internet auction sites, and retailing. Petters acquired more than 150 companies, including the Polaroid brand and Sun Country Airlines.

However, all was not well at PGW. The company wholesale brokerage firm Petters Company Inc. (PCI) was operating a massive Ponzi scheme. PCI issued promissory notes to investors, who invested money they believed would be used to purchase merchandise for retail stores. As a result of their investment, the company promised investors consistent returns of 15 to 20 percent. Rather than being used to purchase merchandise, the money was used to pay returns to earlier investors and, according to prosecutors, fund Petters' lavish lifestyle and company acquisition spree. Investors were provided with falsified purchase orders to make them believe the purchases took place. The scheme was believed to have gone on for more than a decade.

This changed after a business executive involved in the fraud confessed to authorities and agreed to help investigators gather evidence against Petters in exchange for leniency. Others involved in the fraud also agreed to cooperate. Authorities wire tapped conversations between Petters and his associates that lent evidence to his knowledge and participation in the fraud. Victims of the Ponzi scheme included pastors, hedge funds, missionaries, and more. Petters was arrested in October 2008 and eventually sentenced to 50 years in prison without appeal.

Petters continues to maintain his innocence, stating he did not find out about the fraud until shortly before his arrest. He maintains he trusted his associates, including the woman who blew the whistle on him, to handle the wholesale brokerage firm and had not been involved in the management of PCI since the 1990s. He claimed he was provided with the same falsified documents as everyone else and his biggest mistake was trusting the wrong people. Although he appealed his conviction to the U.S. Court of Appeals for the Eighth Circuit, they upheld his conviction. He appealed to the Supreme Court, but that court refused to hear his case. Petters has been trying to get his conviction thrown out, claiming his lawyer never told him about a deal prosecutors were willing to make that would have lessened his sentence in exchange for a guilty plea.

Bernard L. Madoff

No man has received so much notoriety for conducting a Ponzi scheme as Bernard L. Madoff. Until Madoff's time, the idea of pulling off a Ponzi scheme of such magnitude was not considered feasible. Much of the reason why Madoff's fraud went so long unchecked likely had to do with his respectability and reputation for being a market genius. For instance, he served as chair of the NASDAQ in 1990, 1991, and 1993. Bernard Madoff was a highly successful, legitimate businessperson. He started a legal investment business in 1960 buying and selling over-the-counter stocks not listed on the New York Stock Exchange (NYSE). Eventually, Madoff began using his legitimate success and high visibility to start a second business managing money. He seemed trustworthy and promised consistent returns of 10 to 12 percent, attracting billions of dollars from hundreds of investors. Part of the appeal of investing with Bernie was the appeal of exclusivity. His inaccessibility and "invitation only" approach to new investors created that climate.

Many of his clients were already wealthy and looking for a stable and constant rate of return. To these people, reliable constant returns managed by one of their own seemed like the perfect way to invest. His stated strategy was to buy stocks while also trading options on those stocks as a way to limit the potential losses. His market timing strategy was called the "split-strike conversion." To continuously draw in new clients, Madoff developed relationships with intermediaries, also known as "feeders." Many of the feeders invested money with Madoff. These feeders profited by receiving fees and ensuring Madoff had a stream of money flowing into his operation.

Madoff later admitted he never invested any of his clients' funds. All of the money was deposited in banks, and Madoff simply moved money between Chase Manhattan Bank in New York and Madoff Securities International Ltd., a U.K. Corporation. When the economy collapsed in late 2008, more clients requested their deposits back. Because he knew the game was up, he turned himself in to his sons. Madoff was arrested on December 11, 2008. The official charge was criminal securities fraud. Madoff declared to his sons he had roughly $200–300 million left in the company. The SEC records showed the firm had $17 billion in assets at the beginning of 2008. After his trial, Madoff was sentenced to 150 years in prison for his crime.

Thousands of people submitted claims for restitution in the Madoff case. However, paying back all these investors will be a difficult task. Although Madoff's fraud is billed as a $65 billion Ponzi scheme, Madoff never had anywhere near that amount of money. The figure of $65 billion is the total amount Madoff told people they invested and earned with him. The actual amount may be well below $10 billion.

The Securities and Exchange Commission was highly criticized for not detecting the fraud earlier. Christopher Cox, SEC chair at the start of the fraud investigation, indicated the SEC examiners missed "red flags" in reviewing the Madoff firm. Allegations of wrongdoing started in the early 1990s, and Madoff confirms fraud dating back to that time. Repeated investigations and examinations by the SEC showed no investment fraud. In 2001 Harry Markopolos, a security industry executive, raised concerns about Madoff's activities. Once again the SEC did not find evidence of improper practices. Because many SEC employees ended up working in the investment business on Wall Street, there has been speculation that an overall lack of objectivity clouded these investigations.

R. Allen Stanford

R. Allen Stanford was a highly successful financier who received knighthood from the islands of Antigua and Barbuda. Stanford was the founder and CEO of Stanford Financial Group, a group of financial services firms with its main operations on the island of Antigua. Stanford offered investors certificates of deposits (CDs) with consistent returns of 9.87 percent compounded annual interest. One red flag for investors was this percentage was six percentage points higher than the U.S. average CD rates at the time. While higher returns are not necessarily indicative of fraud, consistently higher returns with few fluctuations should have acted as a warning signal. Another red flag was that employees at Stanford Financial did not appear to be know how the company was able to generate such high returns. When investors inquired, they were told the information was proprietary.

In fact, Stanford allegedly operated a $7 billion Ponzi scheme for two decades. As early as 2003, people began accusing Stanford of a Ponzi scheme. Five years before the scheme was revealed, a former employee alerted the SEC and the National Association of Securities Dealers to what she believed was a Ponzi scheme. Yet nothing came of her claims. In 2006 the SEC began an investigation into Stanford Financial but closed it. One year later the firm paid a fine of $20,000 for violating net capital agreements.

Possibly due to the Madoff scandal shaking the financial world, authorities began to investigate Stanford Financial's consistently higher returns on its CDs. They found evidence Stanford had misused funds and misrepresented and falsified documents to hide the fraud, including providing false information about the bank's investment portfolio. According to SEC allegations, although Stanford Financial told investors their investments were invested in safe, liquid securities, in reality they were invested in real estate and private equity. Approximately 30,000 people are estimated to have been victims of the Ponzi scheme. Stanford was arrested and found guilty on 13 of 14 counts of operating a Ponzi scheme. Although he continues to maintain his innocence, Stanford was sentenced to 110 years in prison. Because claims that Stanford Financial operated a Ponzi scheme had been made years prior to the arrest of Stanford, many stakeholders criticized the SEC for not detecting the fraud earlier.

PYRAMID SCHEMES

As mentioned earlier, pyramid schemes occur when an investment or product of limited value is being offered. Pyramid schemes are illegal because of their intent to defraud. Those who recruit additional participants benefit directly, but a failure to recruit typically means no investment return. A pyramid scheme is an unsustainable business model that involves defrauding investors and customers. Pyramid schemes can be hard to detect, but according to the FTC, two signs that a pyramid scheme might be taking place include inventory loading and a lack of retail sales. Inventory loading occurs when investors must purchase large amounts of inventory when they invest, with automatic purchases at regular intervals. The products usually do not sell because their value is less than their price.

The FTC began to take action against pyramid schemes in the 1970s, and one of its first actions was taken against Koscot Interplanetary, Inc., which recruited people for a fee, charged them for purchasing makeup supplies, and then provided them with fees by recruiting others without encouraging them to sell any product. Sometimes pyramid schemes are associated with direct selling. Direct selling is a legitimate business model, and multilevel marketing is a compensation model.

Multilevel marketing members can make an income through selling the company's legitimate products without signing up new members. The independent contractor (member) can advance beyond the person who recruited him or her. Multilevel marketing is a compensation method that provides commissions for growing the network of sellers. The important distinction between the multilevel marketing compensation method and a pyramid scheme is the revenue is derived from selling products, not paying commissions for joining the network. Internal consumption occurs when people join the network just to buy the product at a discount. Other members join to earn money for a short period of time and then exit the network. Amway was accused of operating a pyramid scheme in the 1970s, but the FTC determined Amway was engaging in multilevel or network marketing.

In 2012 Herbalife, the third largest global direct seller, was accused of being an elaborate pyramid scheme by hedge fund manager William Ackman. Accusations against Herbalife included the following: 1) the majority of distributors for Herbalife lose money, 2) Herbalife pays more for recruiting new distributors than selling actual products, and 3) only the top 1 percent of distributors earns most of the money. Herbalife sells highly respected nutritional products. The product is used in Los Angeles for firefighters and LAPD officers through its fitness center. The product has even been adopted by some Chinese Olympic teams. There is every indication that the Herbalife product is a high-quality nutritional product sold on a global basis. Herbalife vehemently denied Ackman's allegations. Many others support Herbalife's model, stating that if it was a pyramid scheme, it would not be so successful but would have collapsed. Another hedge fund manager Carl Ichan defended Herbalife and invested in the firm. Additionally, because Ackman shorted Herbalife stock (he earns money if the stock goes down), some question whether he has a conflict of interest regarding Herbalife's stock. Most companies that use a multilevel marketing compensation method deal with accusations they are a pyramid scheme because of a misunderstanding that a true pyramid scheme does not have a legitimate product to sell.

The Internet made pyramid schemes even easier to execute due to the ease of networking and recruiting others. In 2003 the FTC charged Arizona Internet company Nex-Gen3000.com and its principals of operating an illegal pyramid scheme involving what the company called Internet "shopping malls." The firm marketed these "malls" to investors as a way to earn substantial income. Principals marketed these "products" through the Nex-Gen site. Investors purchased a "Basic WebSuite" for $185 and a "Power Pack WebSuite" for $555. Investors were told they could earn commissions on each "WebSuite" they sold. In actuality most investors lost money. The FTC found deceptive marketing claims were used to deceive investors as well as convince them to unknowingly deceive others into investing.

This is a complex issue, and investors, distributors, and other stakeholders must exert caution when investing. Perhaps the best advice guarding against pyramid schemes is the same as guarding against a Ponzi scheme: do not put all your eggs in one basket, at least until you thoroughly research the company. In terms of pyramid schemes, investors should carefully examine the business' model and determine if a legitimate product is being sold before investing large sums of money to join the network or buy products.

CONCLUSION

White-collar criminals dupe their victims by establishing themselves as trustworthy and respectable figures. Victims of white-collar crime are trusting clients that believe there are sufficient checks and balances to certify that an operation is legitimate. For instance, Bernard Madoff was an educated and experienced individual in a position of power, trust, respectability, and responsibility who abused his trust for personal gains. Fraudsters of both Ponzi and pyramid schemes use promises and elaborate deception to carry out their scams. While many times these types of fraud collapse fairly quickly due to their unsustainable nature, as this case shows adept white-collar criminals are able to carry on the fraud for many years.

White-collar crime is unique because it is often perpetrated by a rogue individual who knowingly steals, cheats, or manipulates in order to damage others. Often, the only way to prevent white-collar crime is to have internal controls and compliance standards that detect misconduct. In Ponzi and pyramid schemes that continue for a long time, the opportunity exists to deceive others without effective audits, transparency, or understanding of the true nature of the operation. As a result of these more recent cases, individual investors, institutions, and hopefully regulators will exert more diligence in demanding transparency and honesty from those who manage and/or solicit investments.

QUESTIONS

1. How do Ponzi schemes and pyramid schemes differ? How are they similar?
2. Why are white-collar criminals such as Madoff able to carry out their schemes for so long when similar types of fraud often collapse at an early stage?
3. What should be done to ensure large-scale fraud such as Ponzi schemes and pyramid schemes do not happen in the future?

SOURCES

"American Greed: Generous with Other People's Money," http://www.cnbc.com/id/100000111 (accessed May 14, 2013); The Associated Press, "A look at some of the biggest Ponzi schemes," *Bloomberg Businessweek*, July 14, 2012, http://www.businessweek.com/ap/2012-06/D9VD1OU82.htm (accessed May 14, 2013); James Bandler and Nicholas Varchaver with Doris Burke, "How Bernie Did It," *Fortune*, May 11, 2009, 50–71; "Bernard L. Madoff," *The New York Times*, December 18, 2010, http://topics.nytimes.com/top/reference/timestopics/people/m/bernard_l_madoff/index.html (accessed May 13, 2013); Dan Browning, "Petters' cronies plead guilty in fraud scam," *Star Tribune*, October 9, 2008, http://www.startribune.com/business/30631384.html?page=1&c=y (accessed May 14, 2013); Cassel Bryan-Low, "Inside a Swiss Bank, Madoff Warnings," *The Wall Street Journal*, January 14, 2009, 1A; Business Wire via The Motley Fool, "Herbalife Continues to Foster Good Health and Fitness Among Peace Officers in

Los Angeles," May 30, 2013, http://www.dailyfinance.com/2013/05/30/herbalife-continues-to-foster-good-health-and-fitn/ (accessed May 30, 2013); CBS News, "Madoff: Pressure from big clients led to scam," April 9, 2011, http://www.cbsnews.com/stories/2011/04/09/earlyshow/saturday/main20052422.shtml (accessed May 13, 2013); Robert Cookson and Michael Peel, "Whistleblower alleged Stanford 'Ponzi' scheme five years ago," *Financial Times*, February 27, 209, http://www.ft.com/intl/cms/s/0/2cafa90c-0471-11de-845b-000077b07658.html#axzz2THKO4SNe (accessed May 14, 2013); Julie Creswell, "U.S. Agents Scrutinize Texas Firm," *The New York Times*, February 12, 2009, http://www.nytimes.com/2009/02/13/business/13stanford.html?_r=1&ref=business (accessed May 14, 2013); Javier E. David, "Herbalife CEO Casts Doubt on Ackman's motives in selling stock," *CNBC*, January 10, 2013, http://www.cnbc.com/id/100369698 (accessed January 10, 2013); Jean Eaglesham and Jessica Holzer, "Schapiro Defends against GOP Fire," *The Wall Street Journal*, March 10, 2011, C1; Amir Efrati, "Q&A on the Madoff Case," *The Wall Street Journal*, March 12, 2009, http://online.wsj.com/article/SB123005811322430633.html (accessed May 13, 2013); Amir Efrati and Chad Bray, "U.S.: Madoff Had $173 Million in Checks," *The Wall Street Journal*, January 9, 2009, http://online.wsj.com/article/SB123143634250464871.html (accessed May 13, 2013); Tim Elfrink, "The Rise and Fall of the Stanford Financial Group," *Houston Press*, April 8, 2009, http://www.houstonpress.com/2009-04-09/news/the-rise-fall-of-the-stanford-financial-group/full/ (accessed May 14, 2013); Francis Elliott, "Thousands of farmers ruined as emu pyramid scheme collapses," *The Times (United Kingdom)*, August 15, 2012, 28; Robert Frank and Amir Efrati, "Madoff Tried to Stave off Firm's Crash before Arrest," *The Wall Street Journal*, January 7, 2009, http://online.wsj.com/article/SB123129835145559987.html (accessed May 13, 2013); Robert Frank and Tom Lauricella, "Madoff Created Air of Mystery," *The Wall Street Journal*, December 20, 2008, http://online.wsj.com/article/SB122973208705022949.html (accessed May 13, 2013); U.S. Federal Trade Commission, "FTC Charges Internet Mall Is a Pyramid Scam," July 7, 2003, http://www.ftc.gov/opa/2003/07/nexgen.shtm (accessed May 20, 2013); Jamie Heller and Joanna Chung, "Life after Madoff's 'Big Lie'," *The Wall Street Journal*, December 11, 2010, http://online.wsj.com/article/SB10001424052748703727804576011451297639480.html (accessed February 2, 2011); Diana B. Henriques, "Madoff Victims Have Their Day in Appeals Court," *The New York Times*, March 3, 2011, http://www.nytimes.com/2011/03/04/business/04madoff.html (accessed May 13, 2013); Chris Isidore, "Stanford found guilty in Ponzi scheme," *CNNMoney*, March 6, 2012, http://money.cnn.com/2012/03/06/news/companies/stanford_guilty/index.htm (accessed May 14, 2013); Clifford Krauss, Julie Cresswell, and Charlie Savage, "Fraud Case Shakes a Billionaire's Caribbean Realm," *The New York Times*, February 20, 2009, http://www.nytimes.com/2009/02/21/business/21stanford.html?pagewanted=1&ref=robertallenstanford (accessed May 14, 2013); Dale Kurschner, "Tom Petters Interview: Plausible Deniability?" *Twin Cities Business*, May 1, 2012, http://tcbmag.com/News/In-Depth/Tom-Petters-Interview-Plausible-Deniability (accessed May 13, 2013); Dale Kurschner, "Q & A With Tom Petters," *Twin Cities Business*, May 1, 2012, http://tcbmag.com/News/In-Depth/Tom-Petters-Interview-Plausible-Deniability/Q-and-A-with-Tom-Petters-I-believed-it?page=1 (accessed May 14, 2013); Aaron Lucchetti, "Victims Welcome Madoff Imprisonment," *The Wall Street Journal*, March 13, 2009, http://online.wsj.com/article/SB123687992688609801.html (accessed May 13, 2013); Bernard Madoff, "Plea Allocution of Bernard L. Madoff," *The Wall Street Journal*, March 12, 2009, http://online.wsj.com/public/resources/documents/20090315madoffall.pdf (accessed May Calum MacLeod, "China's new rules open door to Amway, Avon, others," *USA Today*, November 30, 2005, http://usatoday30.usatoday.com/money/world/2005-11-30-amway-china-usat_x.htm (accessed May 14, 2013); Pershing Square Capital Management, L.P. *An Executive Summary of Pershing Square Capital Management, L.P.'s Presentation of "Who Wants to be a Millionaire?" A Short Thesis on Herbalife, Ltd (NYSE: HLF)*, December 2012, http://factsaboutherbalife.com/wp-content/uploads/2012/12/Final-Exec-Summary-1.pdf (accessed January 10, 2013); "Petters Wants Sentence Tossed Out," *KNSI*, May 12, 2013, http://knsiradio.com/news/local/petters-wants-sentence-tossed-out/ (accessed May 14, 2013); David Phelps, "Petters aid: Everything was fake," *Star Tribune*, December 11, 2011, http://www.startribune.com/business/134826203.html?refer=y (accessed May 14, 2013); David Phelps, "Petters' Associate Deanna Coleman freed after 11 months in prison," *Star Tribune*, August 25, 2011, http://www.startribune.com/business/128421168.html?refer=y (accessed May 14, 2013); Matthias Rieker, "Victims of Scandal Reflect on Shocking Turnabout," *The Wall Street Journal*, December 23, 2008, http://online.wsj.com/article/SB122972955226822819.html (accessed May 13, 2013); Steven Russolillo, "Herbalife Fights Back Against

Hedge-Fund Claims," *The Wall Street Journal*, January 10, 2013, http://online.wsj.com/article/SB10001424127887324 58150457823381119942712.html (accessed January 10, 2013); Securities and Exchange Commission, "SEC Enforcement Actions," April 2, 2013, http://www.sec.gov/spotlight/enf-actions-ponzi.shtml (accessed May 13, 2013); Erin Skarda, "Albanian Ponzi Schemes," *Time*, March 7, 2002, http://www.time.com/time/specials/packages/article/0,28804,2104982_2104983_2104998,00.html (accessed July 10, 2013); Jenny Strasburg, "Madoff 'Feeders' under Focus," *The Wall Street Journal*, December 27–28, 2008, A1, A8; Christine Stapleton, "Madoff scandal ripples among Palm Beach county foundations," *The Palm Beach Post*, February 8, 2009, http://www.palmbeachpost.com/localnews/content/local_news/epaper/2009/02/08/a1b_foundations_0209.html (accessed September 2, 2009); Ethan Trex, "Who Was Ponzi—What the Heck Was His Scheme?" *CNN.com*, December 23, 2008, http://www.cnn.com/2008/LIVING/wayoflife/12/23/mf.ponzi.scheme/index.html (accessed May 13, 2013); Debra A. Valentine, "Pyramid Schemes," Federal Trade Commission, May 13, 1998, http://www.ftc.gov/speeches/other/dvimf16.shtm (accessed May 14, 2013); "Violent Protests of Pyramid Schemes Spread in Albania," *The New York Times*, January 27, 1997, http://www.nytimes.com/1997/01/27/world/violent-protests-of-pyramid-schemes-spread-in-albania.html (accessed July 10, 2013); Mitch Weiss, "ZeekRewards scam leaves N.C. town millions poorer," *USA Today*, March 30, 2013, http://www.usatoday.com/story/money/business/2013/03/30/authorities-600m-scheme-incubated-nc-town/2037975/ (accessed May 13, 2013).

CASE 12

Insider Trading at the Galleon Group*

The Galleon Group was a privately owned hedge fund firm that provided services and information about investments such as stocks, bonds, and other financial instruments. Galleon made money for itself and others by picking stocks and managing portfolios and hedge funds for investors. At its peak, Galleon was responsible for more than $7 billion in investor income. The company's philosophy was that it was possible to deliver superior returns to investors without employing leverage or timing tactics. Founded in 1997, Galleon attracted employees from firms such as Goldman Sachs, Needham & Co., and ING Barings. Every month, the company held meetings when executives explained the status and strategy of each fund to investors. In addition, Galleon told investors that no employee would be personally trading in any stock or fund the investors held.

In 2009 Raj Rajaratnam, the head of Galleon, was indicted on 14 counts of securities fraud and conspiracy. He and five others were accused of insider trading related to using nonpublic information from company insiders and consultants to make millions in personal profits. Rajaratnam's trial began in 2011, and he pleaded not guilty.

RAJ RAJARATNAM

Rajaratnam, born in Sri Lanka to a middle-class family, received his bachelor's degree in engineering from the University of Sussex in England. In 1983 he earned his MBA from the University of Pennsylvania's Wharton School of Business. With a focus on the computer chip industry, he meticulously developed contacts. He went to manufacturing plants, talked to employees, and connected with executives who would later work with Galleon on their IPOs.

In 1985 the investment banking boutique Needham & Co. hired Rajaratnam as an analyst. The corporate culture at Needham & Co. profoundly influenced Rajaratnam and his business philosophy. George Needham was obsessive about minimizing expenses, making employees stay in budget hotel rooms and take midnight flights to and from meetings. The company also urged analysts to gather as much information as possible. Analysts were encouraged to sift through garbage, question disgruntled employees, and even place people in jobs in the target industries. They went to professional meetings, questioned academics doing research and consulting, and set up clandestine agencies that collected information. At Needham & Co., Rajaratnam developed an aggressive networking and note-taking research strategy that enabled him to make accurate predictions about companies' financial situations.

After a while at Needham, Rajaratnam's personality began to impact the company's culture. Rajaratnam once told a new analyst that Needham's name was on the company, but

*This case was prepared by John Fraedrich, Harper Baird, and Michelle Urban. It was prepared for classroom discussion rather than to illustrate either effective or ineffective handling of an administrative, ethical, or legal decision by management. All sources used for this case were obtained through publicly available material.

he was the boss. He began to push ethical limits when gathering information about companies. For example, concerns about Rajaratnam's activities ended Paine Webber's interest in buying Needham. Soon, similar worries spurred complaints from some inside Needham. By 1996 at least five Needham executives were concerned about Rajaratnam's conduct. Additionally, many of Needham's clients complained. Rajaratnam had potentially conflicting roles in the firm as president, fund manager, and sometime stock analyst. Normally, investment banks keep those areas separate to prevent clients' interests from clashing with the interests of bank-run funds. In 1996, after 11 years at Needham, Rajaratnam left the company and started the Galleon Group, taking several Needham employees with him.

ACCUSATIONS OF INSIDER TRADING AT GALLEON

At Galleon, Rajaratnam developed a flamboyant leadership style. During one meeting, Rajaratnam hired a dwarf to act as an analyst hired to cover "small-cap" stocks. At another meeting, when executives from stun-gun maker Taser International, Inc., came to make an investment pitch, Rajaratnam offered $5,000 to anyone who'd agree to be shocked. One trader, Keryn Limmer, volunteered to be tased and went unconscious. Rajaratnam used his wealth to grow Galleon's business. He held a Super Bowl party in a $250,000-a-week mansion on a man-made island in Biscayne Bay for wealthy investors and executives.

At the same time, Rajaratnam contributed to various causes promoting development in the Indian subcontinent, as well as programs benefiting lower-income South Asian youths in the New York area. He joined the board of the Harlem Children's Zone, an education nonprofit, and later raised about $7.5 million for victims of the South Asian tsunami. He was acknowledged as a celebrity donor and honored with a symphony performance at Lincoln Center.

However, Rajaratnam was already in trouble with the government. In 2005 he paid over $20 million to settle a federal investigation into a fake tax shelter to hide $52 million. Rajaratnam and his business partner then sued their lawyers, claiming they had no idea the shelter was illegal; the pair was awarded $10 million in damages. Galleon also paid $2 million in 2005 to settle an SEC investigation into its stock trading practices. In addition, Intel discovered in 2001 that Roomy Khan, an Intel employee, leaked information about sales and production to Rajaratnam. When Khan left Intel, she took a job with Galleon. Although Intel reported the incidents to the authorities, no one could prove that Rajaratnam actually made trades based on the inside information about Intel.

Analysts live or die on the information they acquire on publicly traded firms. As such, there is a constant struggle to gather key information that can predict changes in stock prices, quarterly reports, and revenue. Rajaratnam had a deep network of acquaintances, including employees at Goldman Sachs Group, Intel Corp., McKinsey & Co., and Applied Materials, Inc. Federal investigators grew more suspicious that the networking and research at Galleon involved illegal activities, however. In 2007 SEC lawyers discovered a new text message from Roomy Khan advising Rajaratnam to "wait for guidance" before buying a stock. The SEC convinced Khan to cooperate in their investigation and allow them to record her conversations with Rajaratnam. This single wiretap eventually led to the discovery of several insider trading rings as investigators persuaded more people to participate in the investigation over the course of two years. Table 1 describes the central players.

TABLE 1 Central Players in the Galleon Information Network

Player and employer	Shared insider information about	Charges/Convictions
Raj Rajaratnam Galleon		At the center of the insider trading network; pled not guilty to 14 charges of insider trading and fraud; sentenced to 11 years in prison and ordered to pay over $66 million in penalties
Danielle Chiesi New Castle/ Bear Stearns	IBM, Sun Microsystems, and AMD	Pled guilty to charges of securities fraud; sentenced to 30 months in prison, two years of supervised release, and 250 hours of community service
Roomy Khan Intel, Galleon	Intel, Hilton, Google, Kronos	Pled guilty to charges of securities fraud, conspiracy to commit securities fraud, obstruction of justice, and agreed to the government's request to use wiretaps; sentenced to one year in prison and ordered to forfeit $1.5 million
Anil Kumar McKinsey & Co.	AMD	Pled guilty to passing inside information to Rajaratnam in exchange for $1.75 million; sentenced to two years probation
Rajiv Goel Intel	Intel	Pled guilty to passing inside information; sentenced to two years probation
Rajat K. Gupta Goldman Sachs	Goldman Sachs, Procter & Gamble, McKinsey	Accused by the SEC of passing insider tips to Rajaratnam; sentenced to two years in prison and a $5 million fine
Adam Smith Galleon	Galleon, ATI, AMD	Pled guilty to giving inside information directly to Rajaratnam over a six-year period; sentenced to two years probation
Michael Cardillo Galleon	Axcan Pharma, Procter & Gamble	Pled guilty to receiving tips indirectly from Rajaratnam; allegedly has evidence about Rajaratnam's trades based on insider information; sentenced to three years probation
Zvi Goffer, a.k.a. the "Octopussy" Schottenfeld Group, Galleon	Hilton, several others	Had a reputation for having multiple sources of inside information; allegedly paid others and gave them prepaid mobile phones to avoid detection; pled not guilty to 14 counts of conspiracy and securities fraud; convicted on all 14 counts and sentenced to 10 years in prison

THE TRIAL

In October 2009 Raj Rajaratnam was arrested on 14 charges of securities and wire fraud and accused of gaining over $63.8 million from insider tips. Rajaratnam was released on a $100 million bond and immediately hired several top defense attorneys and public relations specialists. His trial began in March 2011.

The laws on insider trading are vague and often make it difficult to convict white-collar criminals. Prosecutors had to prove Rajaratnam not only traded on information he knew was confidential but also that the information was important enough to affect the price of a company's stock. The government's main evidence was 45 recorded phone calls between individuals suspected of insider trading, including six witnesses who had already pled guilty and were aiding federal investigators. In many of these phone calls, Raj Rajaratnam discussed confidential information with investors and insiders before the information was released to the public. In one recording, Rajaratnam told employees to cover up evidence of insider trading. Another recording suggests Rajaratnam received a tip from someone on Goldman Sachs' board that the company's stock price would decrease. That information had been talked about during a confidential Goldman Sachs board meeting only a day earlier.

The challenge for the prosecution was to prove Rajaratnam used these tips to make illicit trades. Wiretaps of conversations between Goldman Sachs board member Rajat Gupta and Rajaratnam, along with Rajaratnam's subsequent actions, imply this occurred. For instance, during a board meeting on September 23, 2008, Goldman board members discussed a $5 billion preferred stock investment in Goldman Sachs by Berkshire Hathaway along with a public equity offering. According to the prosecution, a few minutes after the meeting Gupta called Rajaratnam. That same day, right before the market closed, Galleon bought 175,000 shares in Goldman. The announcement about Berkshire Hathaway was announced after the market closed, and the next morning the stock went from $125.05 to $128.44. Galleon liquidated the stock and generated a profit of $900,000.

The government had several key witnesses from the insider trading rings who cooperated with investigators. Before the start of Rajaratnam's trial, 19 members of the Galleon network pled guilty to charges of insider trading, and some agreed to testify against Rajaratnam. Anil Kumar, who pleaded guilty to providing insider information in exchange for over $1.75 million wired to a secret offshore account, told the jury that Rajaratnam offered to hire him as a consultant but told him that he did not want traditional industry research. Rajaratnam also told Kumar his ideas were worth a lot of money.

The prosecution argued that Rajaratnam corrupted his friends and employees in order to make profits for him and Galleon. In his closing argument, Assistant U.S. Attorney Reed Brodsky highlighted that Rajaratnam used his contacts to gain certainty in areas where everyone else had none.

In order to convict Rajaratnam of insider trading, the government had to prove the information he received could only have been acquired via inside sources. Rajaratnam's defense maintained that some of the information Rajaratnam used was publicly available and he was not aware other information had not been publicly disclosed. The defense argued Galleon's public announcements, press releases, investor meetings, government filings, and additional sources showed that the information had appeared days and weeks before Rajaratnam and others had used that information. Good investment advisors are in the business of acquiring, analyzing, and making calculated predictions so their clients' investments increase. The defense attorneys argued that Rajaratnam's access to corporate executives was the reason his investors hired him. The defense also claimed these same executives were aware of the law and of their own duties to their employers and shareholders, and they should have known what they could and could not say about their businesses, whereas Rajaratnam's obligations were to his investors.

Rajaratnam lost money on some of the trades the government said were based on inside information. The defense argued that if he had insider information, the opposite should be true. The defense maintained that Galleon's analysts were right about half of the time, and if they were cheating, they should have been right all of the time.

The defense also questioned the validity of some of the prosecution's witnesses. For example, one witness confessed to the fabrication of a false affidavit, doctor's letter, tax forms, and bank letters, allegedly to protect his original statements to the prosecution. The defense argued that many of the prosecution's witnesses lied to save themselves from heavier prison terms for unrelated misdeeds. Anil Kumar testified that between 2004 and 2009, he gave material nonpublic information about several companies to Rajaratnam. Galleon's records show that Kumar was paid consulting fees for his advice and guidance but he never shared these consulting fees with his McKinsey partners. Instead, he hid them in shell companies in overseas bank accounts and failed to report these consulting fees on his tax returns. Then there is Rajiv Goel, who allegedly gave Rajaratnam material nonpublic information obtained from his employer, Intel. The defense argues Goel filed false tax returns unrelated to Rajaratnam and was therefore facing prison time (he was later sentenced to two years probation). They argued the only way out was to testify against Rajaratnam.

THE VERDICT

After 12 days of deliberation, the jury declared Raj Rajaratnam guilty of all 14 counts of securities fraud and conspiracy. In total, the counts carried a potential sentence of 205 years in prison, although Rajaratnam was actually only sentenced to 11 years in prison. The length of deliberation was because some jurors could not comprehend how such an intelligent person could do something so destructive. Jurors cited the recorded conversations between Rajaratnam and his trading network as some of the most convincing evidence. Rajaratnam and his defense team are appealing the decision. Rajaratnam's lawyers claim prosecutors improperly received permission to wiretap Mr. Rajaratnam's phone calls. In addition to his prison sentence Rajaratnam was ordered to pay $1.45 million to the SEC in a lawsuit related to this matter. It was estimated the total amount of money Rajaratnam profited from the insider tips was $1.29 million, and he agreed to pay back this amount as well as $147,738 for "prejudgment interest." His criminal penalties amounted to a record $63.8 million, the largest imposed against one person in an SEC insider trading case, along with $1.5 million in civil charges. The SEC also sued Rajaratnam that resulted in penalties of more than $92 million in a separate civil insider trading lawsuit.

RAJAT GUPTA

Rajat Gupta, a man of high profile and influence, served as Director of McKinsey & Co., a global management consulting firm, and was on the boards of Goldman Sachs, Procter & Gamble, American Airlines, the Rockefeller, and the Bill and Melinda Gates Foundation. He was well-known, well-respected, and considered to be a man of integrity. This all came to an abrupt halt when he was charged and convicted of insider trading activities.

His conviction was based on the phone call he made to Rajaratnam on September 23, 2008, regarding Berkshire Hathaway's purchase of Goldman Sachs' stock. After this phone call, Galleon made a significant purchase of Goldman stock, made a profit, and quickly liquidated the stock. Because of the sequence of events, Gupta was implicated in insider trading activity.

Rajat Gupta faced an eight to ten year sentence, but only given two years. He and his lawyers immediately began the appeal process, and the judge allowed Gupta to remain free on bail until the results of his appeal are determined. The appeal rests on the use of wiretap evidence some say should have been deemed as hearsay. Gupta's lawyers also maintain there is no evidence Gupta benefited in any way from giving these insider tips, which leads to their conclusion the conviction was based on circumstantial evidence.

There is an additional claim the defense team was prevented from presenting evidence about Gupta's state of mind before the tips that was the basis for the jury's conviction; the possibility of an alternative person giving insider tips; and Gupta's integrity. They claim Gupta was not afforded the opportunity to prove he did not have a motive or the inclination to benefit from giving tips to Rajaratnam. The court allowed the wiretaps but didn't allow evidence to prove Gupta's innocence or lack of motive to give tips to Rajaratnam, which they claim resulted in an unfair trial.

THE IMPACT OF THE GALLEON CASE

The Galleon case is the largest investigation into insider trading within hedge funds. Twenty-six people were charged with fraud and conspiracy. Galleon closed in 2009 after investors quickly withdrew over $4 billion in investments from the company. In addition, over a dozen companies' stocks were traded based on allegedly nonpublic information (see Table 2). These trades could have affected the financial status of the companies, their stock prices, and their shareholders.

TABLE 2 Companies Affected by Galleon's Alleged Insider Information Network

3Com Corp
Advanced Micro Devices
Akamai Technologies
Atheros
Axcan Pharma
Goldman Sachs
Google
Hilton Hotels
IBM
Intel
Kronos
Marvell Technology Group
Polycom
Procter & Gamble
Sun Microsystems

© Cengage Learning

The Galleon insider trading investigation was the first to use wiretaps, which are usually used to convict people of involvement in terrorism, drugs, and organized crime. This set a precedent for insider trading cases, and many suspect this method may be used more frequently in the future. Because investment firms rely on email, phone calls, and other digital information, electronic surveillance will likely become the technique of choice for white-collar crime investigators. Federal authorities also hope the Galleon convictions deter other powerful investment managers from engaging in insider trading. Manhattan U.S. Attorney Preet Bharara said, "Unlawful insider trading should be offensive to everyone who believes in, and relies on, the market. It cheats the ordinary investor.... We will continue to pursue and prosecute those who believe they are both above the law and too smart to get caught."

QUESTIONS

1. Are information gathering techniques like Rajaratnam's common on Wall Street? If so, what could regulators, investors, and executives do to reduce the practice?
2. What are the implications of sharing confidential material information? Is it something that would affect your decision about how to trade a stock if you knew about it?
3. Do you think the secret investigation and conviction of Rajaratnam and other people in the Galleon network will deter other fund managers and investors from sharing non-public information?

SOURCES

Suzanna Andrews, "How Gupta Came Undone." *Bloomberg Businessweek*, May 23–May 29, 2011, 56–63; Alex Berenson, "For Galleon Executive, Swagger in the Spotlight," *The New York Times*, November 1, 2009, http://www.nytimes.com/2009/11/02/business/02insider.html (accessed April 22, 2011); Dealbook, "Timeline of Key Events in the Galleon Case," *The New York Times Dealbook*, March 7, 2011, http://dealbook.nytimes.com/2011/03/07/timeline-of-key-events-in-the-galleon-case (accessed April 22, 2011); "The Defense of Raj Rajaratnam," http://rajdefense.org (accessed April 18, 2011); John Dowd, "Defense Attorney's Opening Statement, *United States of America vs. Raj Rajaratnam*," RajDefense.org, March 9, 2011, http://rajdefense.org/wp-content/uploads/2011.03.09-Opening-Statement-by-John-Dowd.pdf (accessed April 18, 2011); "Galleon's Web," *The Wall Street Journal*, March 10, 2011, http://online.wsj.com/article/SB10001424052748703386704576186592268116056.html (accessed April 18, 2011); David Glovin, Patricia Hurtado, and Bob Van Voris, "Galleon's Rajaratnam Talked on Tape About Goldman Board Source," *Bloomberg Businessweek*, March 31, 2011, http://www.businessweek.com/news/2011-03-31/galleon-s-rajaratnam-talked-on-tape-about-goldman-board-source.html (accessed July 7, 2011); David Glovin, Patricia Hurtado, and Bob Van Voris, "Rajaratnam Sought to 'Conquer' Wall Street, U.S. Tells Jurors," *Bloomberg Businessweek*, April 21, 2011, http://www.businessweek.com/news/2011-04-21/rajaratnam-sought-to-conquer-wall-street-u-s-tells-jurors.html (accessed April 25, 2011); Robert A. Guth and Justin Scheck, "The Man Who Wired Silicon Valley," *The Wall Street Journal*, December 30, 2009, http://online.wsj.com/article/SB126204917965408363.html (accessed April 18, 2011); Zachery Kouwe and Michael J. De la Merced, "Galleon Chief and Associate Indicted in Insider Case," *The New York Times*, December 15, 2009, http://www.nytimes.com/2009/12/16/business/16insider.html?_r=1 (accessed April 15, 2011); Susan Pulliam, "Fund Chief Snared by Taps, Turncoats," *The Wall Street Journal*, December 30, 2009, http://online.wsj.com/article/SB126213287690309579.html (accessed March 20, 2011); Susan Pulliam and Chad Bray, "Galleon Chief Seen Testifying at Trial," *The Wall Street Journal*, March 5, 2011, http://online.wsj.com/article/

SB10001424052748704076804576180803410903550.html (accessed April 18, 2011); Susan Pulliam and Chad Bray, "Jury Hears Galleon Wiretaps," *The Wall Street Journal*, March 11, 2011, A1; Pulliam, Susan, and Chad Bray, "Seasoned Prosecutors Prep for 'War.'" *The Wall Street Journal*, March 9, 2011, http://online.wsj.com/article/SB100014240527487 036628045761889606685479264.html (accessed April 18, 2011); Susan Pulliam and Michael Rothfeld, "Trial Win Adds to Momentum," *The Wall Street Journal*, May 12, 2011, A7; Pulliam, Susan, and Michael Siconolfi, "Wiretapped Voice Spoke Volumes." *The Wall Street Journal*, May 12, 2011, A7; Michael Rothfeld, Susan Pulliam, and Chad Bray, "Fund Titan Found Guilty," *The Wall Street Journal*, May 12, 2011, A1, A6; Adam Shell, "Jury Finds Rajaratnam Guilty," *USA Today*, May 12, 2011, B1, B2; Jenny Strasburg, Jessica Silver-Greenberg, and Jeannette Neumann, "Inside the Galleon Jury Room," *The Wall Street Journal*, May 14, 2011, A1, A2; Bob Van Voris, "Galleon Scandal Scorecard: Hedge Funds, Lawyers and 'Octopussy,'" *Bloomberg*, November 7, 2009, http://www.bloomberg.com/apps/news?pid=newsarchive& sid=aRqWWXio6f4Y (accessed April 18, 2011); Patricia Hurtado and David Glovin, "Rajaratnam Appeal Judges Voice Concern Over U.S. Wiretaps," *Bloomberg*, October 25, 2013, http://www.bloomberg.com/news/2012-10-25/ rajaratnam-appeal-judges-voice-concern-over-u-s-wiretaps.html (accessed January 24, 2013); Sakthi Prasad, "Rajaratnam agrees to pay $1.5 million disgorgement in SEC case," *Reuters*, December 27, 2012, http://www.reuters. com/article/2012/12/27/us-rajaratnam-seclawsuit-idUSBRE8BQ01B20121227 (accessed January 24, 2013); Chad Bray, "Insider Witness Sentenced," *The Wall Street Journal*, February 1, 2013, C3; Chad Bray, "Rajaratnam, SEC Settle Gupta Suit," *The Wall Street Journal*, December 28, 2012, C3; The Economist, "Who's Next?" *The Economist*, June 23, 2012, 74; Walter Pavlo, "Government Witness Rajiv Goel Gets Probation in Galleon Case," *Forbes*, September 24, 2012, http://www.forbes.com/sites/walterpavlo/2012/09/24/government-witness-rajiv-goel-gets-probation-in-galleon-insider-case/ (accessed February 19, 2013); Katherine Burton, "Danielle Chiesi's New Prison Home More Camp Cupcake Than 'Chained Heat'," *Bloomberg*, October 17, 2011, http://www.bloomberg.com/news/2011-10-18/ danielle-chiesi-s-new-prison-home-more-camp-cupcake-than-chained-heat-.html (accessed February 21, 2013); Walter Pavlo, "Danielle Chiesi - 30 Months in Prison and A New Life," *Forbes*, July 21, 2011, http://www.forbes.com/ sites/walterpavlo/2011/07/21/danielle-chiesi-30-months-and-a-new-life/ (accessed February 21, 2013); William Alden, "Roomy Khan, Figure in Galleon Insider Case, Sentenced to One Year in Prison," *New York Times*, January 31, 2013, http://dealbook.nytimes.com/2013/01/31/roomy-khan-figure-in-galleon-insider-case-sentenced-to-one-year-in-prison/ (accessed February 21, 2013); Patricia Hurtado and Bob Van Voris, "Kumar Gets Probation for His Galleon Trial Cooperation," *Bloomberg*, July 19, 2012, http://www.bloomberg.com/news/2012-07-19/anil-kumar-gets-two-years-probation-in-insider-trading-case.html (accessed February 21, 2013); Duff McDonald, "The Humbling of Rajat Gupta: When Uncommon People Commit Common Crimes," *Observer*, October 30, 2012, http:// observer.com/2012/10/the-humbling-of-rajat-gupta-when-uncommon-people-commit-common-crimes/ (accessed February 21, 2013); Nate Raymond, "Rajat Gupta Seeks Insider Trading Conviction Reversal," *Reuters*, January 23, 2013, http://in.reuters.com/article/2013/01/22/goldman-rajat-gupta-appeal-idINDEE90L0EN20130122 (accessed February 21, 2013); Yoshita Singh, "Rajat Gupta Seeks New Trial, Reversal of Conviction," *India West*, January 28, 2013, http://www.indiawest.com/news/8771-rajat-gupta-seeks-new-trial-reversal-of-conviction.html (accessed February 21, 2013); Suzanna Andrews, "How Rajat Gupta Came Undone," *Businessweek*, May 19, 2011, http://www. businessweek.com/magazine/content/11_22/b4230056624680.htm#p1 (accessed February 21, 2013); Peter Lattman, "Galleon Official Is Spared Prison," *The New York Times*, June 26, 2012, http://dealbook.nytimes.com/2012/06/26/ galleon-official-is-spared-prison/ (accessed February 21, 2013); Patricia Hurtado, "Ex-Galleon Fund Manager Cardillo Gets 3 Years Probation," *Bloomberg*, October 25, 2012, http://www.bloomberg.com/news/2012-10-25/ ex-galleon-fund-manager-cardillo-gets-3-years-probation.html (accessed February 26, 2013); Bob Van Voris, "Former Galleon Trader Zvi Goffer Seeks Prison Term of Less Than 10 Years," *Bloomberg*, August 31, 2011, http:// www.bloomberg.com/news/2011-08-31/former-galleon-trader-zvi-goffer-seeks-prison-term-of-less-than-10-years. html (accessed February 26, 2013); Patricia Hurtado, "Galleon Ex-Trader Zvi Goffer, Brother Plead Not Guilty to New Indictment," *Bloomberg*, April 19, 2011. http://www.bloomberg.com/news/2011-04-19/former-galleon-trader-goffer-pleads-not-guilty-to-latest-insider-charges.html (accessed February 26, 2013); Peter Lattman, "2 Defendants Sentenced in Insider Trading Case," *The New York Times*, September 21, 2011, http://dealbook.nytimes. com/2011/09/21/2-defendants-sentenced-in-insider-trading-case/ (accessed February 26, 2013).

CASE 13

Whole Foods Strives to Be an Ethical Corporate Citizen*

INTRODUCTION

In a period of time when green is on everyone's mind, it seems fitting that Whole Foods Markets are popping up with their distinctive green signs in neighborhoods across the country. Beginning with their first expansion in 1984, Whole Foods has consistently grown domestically. In 2007 Whole Foods began opening stores in the United Kingdom. While continually opening new stores, the company fueled its expansion by acquiring other food chains. For instance, it acquired one of its largest competitors, Wild Oats, in 2007. Whole Foods consistently ranks as one of the World's Most Ethical companies for its emphasis on organic food, healthy living, customer satisfaction, quality, and sustainability. The firm has also been elected as one of the top companies to work for. Although customers are considered to be the company's highest valued stakeholder, Whole Foods adopted a stakeholder orientation that focuses on the needs of its stakeholders, including its employees and the community.

Whole Foods spearheaded efforts in the grocery industry to source its food products responsibly and search for innovative solutions to improve its environmental footprint. The company emphasizes healthy living and seeks to contribute to the communities where it does business. However, despite Whole Foods' significant accomplishments in business ethics, it has not been free from criticism. In pursuit of growth, it has been accused of running local stores out of business and received mixed responses from some consumers. Other ethical issues include antitrust investigations and questionable activity by CEO John Mackey.

This case begins by providing brief background information on Whole Foods' history. It then examines Whole Foods' mission and values, followed by how it strives to live out its values to become a good corporate citizen. We also examine ethical issues Whole Foods has faced to demonstrate the complexity companies experience when engaging in ethical decision making.

COMPANY BACKGROUND

In 1978 two entrepreneurs in their twenties used a $45,000 loan to open a small natural foods store in Austin, Texas. John Mackey and his then-girlfriend Rene Lawson Hardy wanted to help people live better. At the time, there were fewer than a dozen natural foods markets in the nation. The couple named their business SaferWay as a spoof on Safeway.

*This material was developed by Casey Caldwell, Erica Lee Turner, and Jennifer Sawayda under the direction of O.C. Ferrell and Linda Ferrell. Danielle Jolley provided editorial assistance. This case is intended for classroom discussion rather than to illustrate effective or ineffective handling of administrative, ethical, or legal decisions by management. All sources for this case were obtained through publicly available material.

The entrepreneurs had a rocky start. At one time they used the store as a residence after being kicked out of their apartment for storing food products. After two years Mackey and Hardy agreed to merge SaferWay with Clarksville Natural Grocery, owned by Craig Weller and Mark Skiles. The newly merged company called themselves Whole Foods Market.

The company continued to face challenges. Less than a year after opening, a devastating flood hit Austin, wiping out Whole Foods' inventory. With no insurance and $400,000 in damages, the company's future looked dire. Yet with the help of the community, the store reopened four weeks after the flood. In 1984 the company expanded into Houston and Dallas. Four years later they acquired a store in New Orleans, followed by one in Palo Alto, California, a year later. The company continued to grow during the 1990s as Whole Foods merged with over a dozen smaller natural groceries across the nation. Whole Foods continued to thrive in the early twenty-first century and today earns more than $10 billion in revenue, owns more than 300 stores, and employs more than 56,000 workers (compared to nineteen workers in 1980). John Mackey continues to lead Whole Foods as the company's CEO.

From the onset, Mackey desired to create a company that incorporated the values of healthy living and conscious capitalism. Conscious capitalists believe "that a new form of capitalism is emerging that holds the potential for enhancing corporate performance while simultaneously trying to advance the quality of life for billions of people."[1] For Mackey, businesses should seek to balance the needs of all stakeholders rather than simply try to earn a profit. As a result, Whole Foods places the customer as first priority. The company adopted criteria such as the Whole Foods Trade Guarantee and the Eco-Scale Rating system to ensure customers receive the highest in quality organic products. Although Whole Foods sells a number of brands, it also sells its own private labels including its 365 Everyday Value, Whole Market, and Whole Kitchen/Whole Pantry. Its 365 Everyday Value private brand is for customers who desire high quality organic food but who also wish to save money. Because organic food usually costs more, the 365 Everyday Value is meant to appeal to more budget-conscious consumers.

However, although Whole Foods recognizes the importance of customers, it also considers the health and well-being of its other stakeholders, including employees and communities. Its mission statement consists of three goals: 1) whole foods; 2) whole people; 3) and whole planet. According to its mission statement, Whole Foods has adopted a stakeholder orientation to guide its activities. This approach, along with a strong adherence to its core values, has been crucial in establishing Whole Food's reputation as a firm committed toward benefiting stakeholders.

MISSION STATEMENT AND CORE VALUES

Whole Foods' core values, described in Table 1, are an outreach of Whole Foods' mission statement. Whereas the mission statement provides a general direction, Whole Foods' values gives additional details about how it is turning its mission into a reality. The core values also provide an idea of how Whole Foods ranks certain stakeholders. Whole Foods calls the company values its Declaration of Interdependence to emphasize how interdependent the company is upon its stakeholders.

---

[1]"What is Conscious Capitalism®?" http://consciouscapitalism.org/learnmore/ (accessed August 24, 2012).

TABLE 1 Whole Foods Market's Core Values

Selling the Highest Quality Natural and Organic Products Available
Satisfying and Delighting Customers
Supporting Team Member Happiness and Excellence
Creating Wealth Through Profits & Growth
Caring about the Community & Environment
Creating ongoing win-win partnerships with suppliers
Promoting the health of all stakeholders through healthy eating education

Source: Whole Foods, "Whole Foods Market's Core Values," http://www.wholefoodsmarket.com/values/corevalues.php#selling (accessed July 13, 2012).

The first two values involve meeting customer needs. Whole Foods describes its commitment toward selling the highest quality natural and organic products available as attempts to be buying agents for customers and not selling agents for manufacturers. Next, Whole Foods turns its attention to the happiness of its employees. Whole Foods believes satisfying customers and employees creates wealth for shareholders. The community, the environment, and suppliers are essential stakeholders for Whole Foods to serve. It is clear from Whole Foods' core values that the company takes a stakeholder orientation in how it does business.

LIVING ITS VALUES

The success of Whole Foods can be credited to the fact it modeled its operations around its key stakeholders. Mackey's vision of a model company was one that earned a profit and yet considered it a responsibility to benefit society. This vision turned Whole Foods into one of the most successful organic grocers in the world. The following section delves further into how Whole Foods meets the needs of its customers, employees, communities, and the environment.

Commitment to Customers

Because customers are the highest priority at Whole Foods, the company adopted a number of strategies to meet the needs of this stakeholder group. For instance, Whole Foods retail stores maintain an inviting environment, complete with eateries and tables both inside and outside the store for visitors to dine. Free sampling is common at Whole Foods locations to allow customers to try the products. Employees are instructed to treat customers like a valued part of the family. Although many consumers consider Whole Foods products to be high-priced, its 365 Everyday Value products appeal to the more price-conscious consumer.

The company also builds customer relationships through the use of social media. Whole Foods maintains Twitter and Facebook accounts that the company actively uses to post information on sales, answering customer concerns, providing articles or tips about healthy eating, and even re-tweeting information from food experts. Each Whole Foods location has pages on social media, as well as some of their departments. This targeted approach allows Whole Foods to connect with customers and address concerns in real-time.

Whole Foods' customer-centered focus has paid off. In the American Customer Satisfaction Survey, Whole Foods was voted the second highest in the supermarket category after Publix. Whole Foods largely differentiates itself from its rivals by emphasizing quality over price. As consumers become more health-conscious and the trend toward organic food continues, Whole Foods has become well suited to attract this target market. To reassure consumers its products are of the highest quality, Whole Foods offers a number of quality standards. Its Whole Trade Guarantee maintains that the company only purchases products that meet the following criteria:

- Meet its quality standards
- Provide more money to producers
- Ensure better wages and working conditions for workers
- Utilize sound environmental practices.[2]

QUALITY STANDARDS Whole Foods compiled a list of standards to guarantee the highest quality for the organic food it sells. The company works to eliminate all genetically modified products in stores whenever possible. It features foods free of artificial preservatives, colors, flavors, sweeteners, and hydrogenated fats. Its private labels are free of high fructose corn syrup, one of the biggest contributors to American obesity. One of the biggest things Whole Foods does that separates it from competitors is its commitment to alerting customers to the presence of genetically modified foods. If the company cannot find a product that is not genetically modified, then the product is labeled to inform customers they are buying something that is not completely "all natural." This labeling is not required by law and demonstrates the company's commitment to reducing genetically modified products. Although using labels might dissuade customers from purchasing a particular product, it also gives Whole Foods a competitive advantage because customers can trust the company to be truthful. Customers tend to do more business with companies they trust, and Whole Foods' second place position on the American Customer Satisfaction Index indicates the firm has indeed reaped the rewards of high customer trust.

ECO-SCALE™ RATING SYSTEM Another set of quality standards Whole Foods has adopted pertains to the cleaning supplies it sells. Whole Foods uses what it terms the Eco-Scale™ Rating System to inform users about the safety and the environmental impact of the cleaning products it features in its stores. According to Whole Foods, the Eco-Scale Rating System is the first such rating system for cleaning supplies for retail stores. To develop these standards, Whole Foods uses a third-party audit system as a way to eliminate bias. Products can be separated into red, orange, yellow, or green categories.

Products in the red category are not sold at Whole Foods; these products do not meet the company's safety and environmental standards. Those in the orange category appear to be "safe" with no significant safety and environmental concerns and no animal testing. Those in the yellow category meet all the standards of the orange category and take further steps to be environmentally-friendly. For instance, products in this category do not have synthetic, petroleum-based thickeners from nonrenewable resources. Yellow products do not contain any ingredients with moderate environmental concerns. Those in the green category are considered to be the safest and most eco-friendly. These products do not have

---

[2]Whole Foods Market IP, L.P.,"Our Whole Trade Guarantee®," 2011, http://www.wholefoodsmarket.com/products/whole-trade.php (accessed July 16, 2012).

any petroleum-based ingredients but are made with plant- and mineral-based ingredients. Products in all of these categories have their ingredients labeled on the packaging and received third-party verification, allowing consumers to make informed decisions about their cleaning purchases. Because Whole Foods' reputation depends upon the organic and green claims of its products, this Eco-Scale Rating System and the company's Quality Standards ensure the authenticity of its products.

Commitment to Employees

If customers are the highest priority stakeholder at Whole Foods, then employees come as a close second. Whole Foods consistently ranks as one of the "Best Companies to Work For" in *Fortune* magazine. Whole Foods is committed to ensuring equality among employees. At a time when executive pay has been highly criticized in proportion to employee salaries, Whole Foods capped the pay of its executives at 19 times the average full-time salary for the firm. CEO John Mackey takes $1 per year in compensation.

Employees receive 20 percent discounts on company products, and Whole Foods members that work at least 30 hours a week are eligible for healthcare coverage. Employees who work between 20 and 30 hours a week can also receive health coverage after working a certain number of service hours. When employees work 6,000 service hours, they are eligible for stock options, providing them with a stake in the company.

While Whole Foods desires its customers to live healthy lives, it also desires the same for its employees. The company began the Team Member Healthy Discount Incentive Program to award employees for living healthy lifestyles. Employees that meet certain benchmarks in cholesterol level, blood pressure, no smoking, and body mass index are eligible for an additional 10 percent discount on Whole Foods purchases.

Additionally, Whole Foods is known for its diversity. Forty-four percent of the Whole Foods workforce consists of minorities, and women also make up 44 percent. Whole Foods offers domestic-partner benefits to same-sex couples. Whole Foods' treatment of its employees results in a low voluntary turnover rate of 9 percent, versus an average turnover rate of about 100 percent for the industry.

While Whole Foods cares for its employees, it also realizes happy employees translate into happier customers—and higher profits. Yet Whole Foods does not seek to empower employees simply through benefits. It also uses the talents of its employees to improve company operations. Self-directed work teams consisting of employees make many of the decisions in the day-to-day operations of the different stores. For instance, teams can hire employees and have control over their scheduling. New team members are elected onto the team by two-thirds of a vote. The company provides its team members with extensive training and resources including an online site called "Whole Foods University" that provides educational information for team members. Courses provided through Whole Foods University range from information on the company's gain sharing program to the company's quality standards. By empowering its employees through teams, perks, and education, Whole Foods has been able to turn its workers into significant contributors of value for the company.

Commitment to other Stakeholders

As Whole Foods demonstrates with its values, consumers and employees are not the only stakeholders the firm considers to be important. Its fourth value includes creating wealth through profits and growth, which is essential for any organization to survive. The more profit Whole Foods is able to generate, the better return for Whole Foods stockholders and investors. Whole Foods believes meeting the needs of consumers and employees helps contribute to wealth for its investors. Such a stakeholder orientation recognizes that each stakeholder is interconnected with another. Whole Foods stock value has grown at approximately 37 percent each year, and its 2011 net income of $343 million jumped 133 percent from its 2009 net income. This growth is important since most grocery stores have seen declining growth in recent years. Whole Foods' profitability demonstrates the company can succeed with a socially responsible focus on organic foods and quality standards.

Whole Foods strongly believes in giving back to the global community, perhaps best emphasized through its Whole Planet Foundation established in October 2005. The Foundation was created with the mission to create economic partnerships with the poor in developing-world communities. Rather than simply providing immediate items such as food or clothing, Whole Foods creates strategic partnerships with microfinance institutions. Microfinance provides small loans, typically $200 or less, to entrepreneurs in developing countries wanting to start their own small businesses. The company's first grant in 2006 helped develop a microfinance program in Costa Rica. Consumers and employees interested in donating can donate on the Foundation's website. Since 2007 employees provided more than $3.25 million to the program.

On a more local level, Whole Foods also established the Whole Kids Foundation. The Whole Kids Foundation was founded with the mission to improve the nutrition of children. The company partners with schools and other organizations to increase the access of children to healthier food. Company partnerships include the LunchBox Project, an online resource providing information for schools that want to increase its offerings of healthy food in their cafeterias, and the Let's Move Salad Bars to Schools Initiative, that provided funds to increase the number of salad bars in schools across the United States. As a grocery store committed to selling healthy and organic foods, Whole Foods has been able to link its philanthropic endeavors to its value of supporting stakeholder health through healthy eating education.

In terms of supplier partnerships, Whole Foods partners with local farmers to offer a variety of produce. Whole Foods is committed to sourcing from local farmers that meet its quality standards, particularly from organic farmers who engage in sustainable agriculture. To qualify as local, food products must have traveled less than seven hours by food or truck to the store. Every one of Whole Foods' eleven regions has guidelines about how to use the term "local" in their stores, and some stores have chosen to adopt stricter criteria for local products by lessening the travel time.

Whole Foods believes sourcing locally grown produce embodies its values of giving back to the community, contributing to sustainability, and offering consumers a variety of high-quality choices from which to choose. For instance, because there is less of a need to package and transport products for long distances, local farmers can make more money, which they in turn can use in their local economies. Additionally, Whole Foods states that support for local farmers encourages them to diversify, which increases Whole Foods' product selection and contributes to biodiversity in the environment. Transporting products shorter distances reduces the greenhouse gases released from vehicles. These win-win relationships with farmers help Whole Foods "give back" to its suppliers and to the environment.

Finally, although not specifically mentioned in its values statement, Whole Foods also considers the concerns of special-interest groups. Whole Foods became the first large supermarket to adopt humane animal treatment standards for the meat products it sells. In developing these standards, Whole Foods discussed ideas with animal rights special-interest groups to decide criteria for sourcing its meat products. Many companies pay little attention to special-interest groups because they are considered secondary stakeholders. In other words, they are not necessarily required for the company's survival. However, Whole Foods realized that collaborating with special-interest groups would not only secure their support but provide it with input on how the company could improve its practices to become a socially responsible company.

Whole Foods representatives met with members from special-interest groups, farmers, and animal experts to determine humane animal-treatment standards species by species. Whole Foods eventually created a supplier certification program in partnership with the Global Animal Partnership to ensure its suppliers were adhering to company standards. The idea behind this program is not only to ensure compliance, however, but also to inform consumers about the meat they are purchasing. For this reason, Whole Foods adopted a ranking system consisting of 5 steps. Step 1 assures consumers that the animal lived outside of a crate or cage. Step 2 indicates that the farm provided some type of enrichment for the animal. Step 3 indicates that the animal had access to the outdoors, and Step 4 means the animal was free to roam or forage when outdoors. Step 5 means the animal lived its entire life with all the body parts it was born with. It is also possible to achieve a Step 5+ ranking, indicating the animal met all these standards and spent its entire life on one farm. This ranking system reiterates Whole Food's concern for the environment as well as consumer choice.

Commitment to Sustainability

Last but not least, Whole Foods is strongly committed to the environment. We have already seen how Whole Foods strives to reduce its environmental impact by selling organic food, sourcing from local farmers, selling eco-friendly products, and reducing transport times for its products. However, Whole Foods also strives to incorporate green practices at an operational level as well. The firm is invested significantly in renewable energy, such as solar, wind power, and biodiesel. This does not necessarily mean Whole Foods powers everything *in its stores* from renewable energy. The company continues to use electricity, and it is difficult for any large firm to use 100 percent renewable energy. Rather, in 2006 Whole Foods made the decision to offset all of its energy use by purchasing wind energy credits. This money goes to fund renewable energy projects in wind farms.

Some of its stores have purchased solar energy installations to power their facilities. A solar energy installation can prevent 1,650 tons of carbon dioxide from being emitted into the atmosphere. The company also began using biodiesel fuel in its trucks and is modifying its trucks to cut back on wind resistance, which in turn saves fuel. Its trucks are equipped with a fuel-saving system that allows them to turn off completely when loading or delivering products and saves the fuel that would have been expended if the trucks were left idling. The firm began to obtain LEED (Leadership in Energy and Environmental Design) certification for some of its stores, meaning they adhere to strict environmental standards and use more eco-friendly building materials such as recycled wood in their construction. Whole Foods' accomplishments in renewable energy earned it a ranking among *Forbes'* "America's Greenest Companies" in 2011.

In the stores themselves, Whole Foods embraces the concept of Reduce, Reuse, and Recycle. The company does not use plastic bags and encourages its customers to use renewable grocery bags when shopping. As part of an incentive, the store provides a nickel refund to those who come with renewable shopping bags. The stores use recycled paper when printing and have begun to use rechargeable batteries to cut down on energy use. To reduce its energy use even further, Whole Foods began to replace its plastic and paper food containers and utensils with all-fiber packaging.

Finally, Whole Foods is continuing to work on selling products that are not only good for consumers but are more beneficial to the environment. The company pledged to support more sustainable sourcing of palm oil, which has traditionally been a strong contributor to deforestation in some countries.

Perhaps one of its biggest landmark commitments, however, is its dedication to seafood sustainability. Whole Foods was the first grocery chain to adopt a sustainability program for seafood caught in the wild. Because overfishing has become such a problem, Whole Foods adopted a three-color labeling system to help consumers make informed decisions. Red labels are a sign the seafood should be avoided because it harms the environment or other marine life. Whole Foods has also developed standards for farmed seafood to make sure the fish are being farmed responsibly.

ETHICAL ISSUES

It is obvious Whole Foods has made great strides in social responsibility. By adopting a stakeholder orientation, Whole Foods has received recognition for ethical business practices, environmental responsibility, and customer satisfaction. However, no company can avoid ethical issues, and even the highest rated in social responsibility can make mistakes. The bigger an organization is, the more ethical risks it assumes. As Whole Foods grew, it encountered several ethical issues that needed to be addressed. Many of these ethical issues are not going away, either. The following section describes some criticisms and even legal issues that Whole Foods has faced, some of which represent risk areas for the company.

Reaction toward Competitors

In its more than 30 years in existence, Whole Foods grew significantly from its humble origins. Some of this growth came from acquiring other stores, and caused criticism from those not wanting their smaller community grocery stores to shut down or be acquired. For instance, in the Jamaica Plain neighborhood of Boston, Whole Foods acquired a local Latin American store called Hi-Lo when it moved into the community. Many local residents objected, considering Whole Foods products to be too expensive. Most large retail chains must exert caution when moving into a new community since their arrival will almost inevitably have an impact on rival, and often smaller, retailers.

While not all its acquisitions go smoothly, Whole Foods had perhaps the most trouble when it wanted to acquire its competitor, organic grocery chain Wild Oats. Wild Oats was the second largest natural grocery chain in the country. In 2007 Whole Foods announced it was acquiring Wild Oats for $565 million. This acquisition would eliminate a key competitor as well as give Whole Foods access into new markets. However, the proposed acquisition generated immediate controversy—this time from regulators. The Federal Trade Commission filed a lawsuit to block the acquisition, claiming it would reduce competition in the industry and thus violate antitrust laws. Cited in the complaint were emails from CEO John Mackey stating a merger between the two companies would help avoid "price wars." (Price wars often happen when two close competitors try to outdo one another and gain market share.) This was another sign that perhaps Whole Foods wanted to gain from less competition.

The FTC also revealed that John Mackey wrote blog posts under a pseudonym between 1999 and 2006 that highly criticized Wild Oats. Mackey wrote several negative postings about Wild Oats' stock prices and its future. While not illegal, many believed these postings were unethical and even manipulative. Whole Foods made sure to distance itself from John Mackey's postings by stating they were done outside of the company. However, as the voice of the company, Mackey's actions brought up serious questions about how Whole Foods approaches competing companies.

Eventually, the FTC and Whole Foods reached a deal. Whole Foods agreed to sell 31 Wild Oats stores and sell the Wild Oats brand. Mackey acknowledged the company would have been better if it had not pursued the merger, particularly as drops in stock prices and the recession caused so much damage. Although the company recovered, it is important for it to approach future acquisitions and relationships with rivals carefully with respect to laws and ethical considerations.

Veering Off-Course

In 2009, in the midst of a recession and a resolution with the FTC over the acquisition of Wild Oats, John Mackey admitted Whole Foods had strayed from one of its core values: healthy eating. In an interview, Mackey admitted, "We sell a bunch of junk." He said Whole Food had "veered off-course" by selling junk food and products unhealthy for consumers. Part of this reason was most likely to court consumers, particularly with the increase in competition. Competition from Trader Joe's and Costco had already led Whole Foods to modify some of its strategies, such as matching Trader Joe's prices on 365 Everyday Value items. However, companies begin to encounter problems when they stray from their corporate values, and Mackey appeared to think Whole Foods was not being a leader in promoting healthy eating habits.

After this admission, Whole Foods re-committed to its value of healthy eating education. The company hired Healthy Eating Specialists and began posting information on its website to educate consumers on healthy eating. The company created incentives for its employees to adopt healthier lifestyles, as described earlier. By proactively engaging in the fight against obesity, Whole Foods began to re-embrace its original core values.

Unions and Health Care

It is no secret that Whole Foods prefers not to have unions. Mackey has cited unions as creating "an adversarial relationship in the workplace." However, he maintains that managers cannot stop employees from unionizing if they so desire. Some disagree and have accused Whole Foods of union-busting by threatening reprisals if they join a union. Whole Foods joined with Starbucks and Costco to oppose the proposed Employee Free Choice Act that give employees the ability to form unions if a majority signed cards suggesting they desired to have a union. The three retailers instead advocated for a secret ballot process for unionization. While it is not necessarily unethical to be against unions, union busting—or purposefully trying to prevent unions by threats or other underhanded tactics—has ethical and legal implications. Whole Foods should remain vigilant to ensure store managers and other officials respect employee rights to organize.

Health care is another debate, not because Whole Foods has a bad health care program for employees. Rather, the controversy stemmed from an op-ed article Mackey wrote against President Obama's universal health care plan. It might be argued that since Mackey wrote the article, Whole Foods should not be dragged into the controversy. However, once again because founders and/or CEOs represent a company, society often associates their actions as speaking for the firm, even if an action was done outside the firm. In this case, Mackey, a strong libertarian, wrote an op-ed article in *The Wall Street Journal* criticizing Obama's health care initiative and proposing alternatives for health care reform, using Whole Foods health care as an example. For instance, Whole Foods provides up to $1,800 of funds per year for employees to use for medical care. Money not spent rolls over into the next year. Afterward, Whole Foods will not cover the insurance costs until the employee meets a $2,500 deductible. According to Mackey, this encourages employees to spend the first $1,800 carefully and provides them with the opportunity to determine what their health care needs are.

Mackey's letter led to anger from supporters of the nationalized health care initiative. Some unions and consumers began to boycott Whole Foods' stores because of Mackey's stance, claiming he sees health care as a privilege and not a right. Others, however, refused to boycott even if they disagreed with Mackey's views. They believed Mackey—and Whole Foods—had the right to express their opinions. This is an interesting ethical issue, not because it had a major impact on Whole Foods' bottom line but because it brings up the issue of businesses' and business representatives' rights to express their viewpoints—particularly in the political process. This ethical issue is not an easy one to settle and continues to be relevant for businesses that have a major stake in a regulatory decision.

CONCLUSION

Whole Foods has strived not only to be a profitable company but to maintain an ethical standpoint when making decisions related to its customers, employees, and all affected stakeholders. While consistently being ranked as one of the World's Most Ethical companies and best companies to work for, Whole Foods has demonstrated its commitment toward selling organic food, satisfying customers, and incorporating quality and sustainability into its products. All products are examined and evaluated to inform customers of every element of their purchase to ensure quality and consumer standards are met.

The company has continually demonstrated its commitment to the environment by implementing the Eco-Scale Rating System, aggressively promoting the use of renewable shopping bags, and beginning to obtain LEED certification for some of its stores. Whole Foods strives to make a beneficial impact within each community where it is located by adopting a stakeholder orientation. These actions contribute to Whole Foods' current status as one of the top natural grocers throughout the United States.

However, as Whole Foods expanded, it faced many ethical challenges, some that will likely continue into the future. As it expands, it must anticipate the reactions from community members and attempt to alleviate any concerns. It should also examine its expansions and acquisitions to ensure pursuing these ventures will not run afoul of regulatory authorities, as it experienced with its unprofitable acquisition of Wild Oats. Finally, Whole Foods must continue to take a stakeholder orientation to all stakeholders—even its competitors. It is important for the firm to realize that just because an action might not be illegal does not mean that it is necessarily ethical.

Although Whole Foods has experienced some negative backlash, overall the company has developed a strong positive reputation among its stakeholders. As a desire for green product options and the concern for corporate social responsibility continue to increase among stakeholders, Whole Foods' careful attention to stakeholder needs and its strong commitment to core values provide it with a significant competitive advantage.

QUESTIONS

1. How has a commitment to corporate values contributed to Whole Foods' success?
2. Describe how Whole Foods' adoption of a stakeholder orientation has influenced the way it operates.
3. What are some ways that Whole Foods might have neglected certain stakeholders in the past?

SOURCES

Whole Foods Market IP, L.P., "Whole Trade Guarantee," http://www.wholefoodsmarket.com/products/whole-trade.php (accessed July 18, 2012); Hadley Freeman, "Over the top and over here: 'Disney World' of food opens first UK store," *The Guardian*, June 6, 2007, http://www.guardian.co.uk/business/2007/jun/07/retail.supermarkets (accessed July 5, 2012); "100 Best Companies to Work For," *CNNMoney*, 2012, http://money.cnn.com/magazines/fortune/best-companies/2012/full_list/ (accessed July 6, 2012); John A. Byrne, "The 12 greatest entrepreneurs of our time," *CNNMoney*, April 9, 2012, http://money.cnn.com/galleries/2012/news/companies/1203/gallery.greatest-entrepreneurs.fortune/9.html (accessed July 13, 2012); Conscious Capitalism®, "What is Conscious Capitalism?" http://www.consciouscapitalism.org/learnmore/ (accessed July 13, 2012); Yahoo! Finance, "Whole Foods Market, Inc. (WFM)," http://finance.yahoo.com/q/is?s=WFM+Income+Statement&annual (accessed July 13, 2012); Maria Halkias, "Container Store, Whole Foods aim for conscious capitalism," *The Dallas Morning News*, August 8, 2010, http://www.dallasnews.com/business/headlines/20100808-Container-Store-Whole-Foods-aim-540.ece (accessed March 7, 2011); Jacqui MacKenzie, "Why I Follow Whole Foods," *Social Media Today*, May 7, 2012, http://socialmediatoday.com/jacqui-mackenzie/503334/why-i-follow-whole-foods (accessed July 16, 2012); Allison Linn, "Whole Foods up, Wal-Mart down in customer satisfaction survey," *MSN*, February 21, 2012, http://lifeinc.today.msnbc.msn.com/_news/2012/02/21/10437549-whole-foods-up-wal-mart-down-in-customer-satisfaction-survey?lite (accessed July 16, 2012); Whole Foods Market IP, L.P., "Declaration of Interdependence," 2012, http://www.wholefoodsmarket.com/company/declaration.php (accessed July 16, 2012); Whole Foods Market IP, L.P., "Our Quality Standards," 2012, http://www.wholefoodsmarket.com/products/quality-standards.php (accessed July 16, 2012); Whole Foods Market IP, L.P., "Whole Foods Market Eco-Scale™ Rating System for Household Cleaning Products," http://www.wholefoodsmarket.com/eco-scale/ratingsystem.php (accessed July 17, 2012); "Whole Foods Market: 100 Best Companies to Work For," *CNNMoney*, http://money.cnn.com/magazines/fortune/best-companies/2012/snapshots/32.html (accessed July 17, 2012); Joseph Brownstein, "Is Whole Foods' Get Healthy Plan Fair?" *ABC News*, January 28, 2010, http://abcnews.go.com/Health/w_DietAndFitnessNews/foods-incentives-make-employees-healthier/story?id=9680047 (accessed July 17, 2012); Melanie J. Martin, "Data on Employee Turnover in the Grocery Industry," *Chron.com*, http://smallbusiness.chron.com/data-employee-turnover-grocery-industry-18817.html (accessed July 17, 2012); Susanna Kim, "7 Companies Offering Health Care Benefits to Part-Time Workers," *ABC News*, October 25, 2011 http://abcnews.go.com/Business/companies-offering-health-care-benefits-perks-part-time/story?id=14805107#4 (accessed July 17, 2012); Donald Luskin, "Whole-Foods-Style Health Care," *SmartMoney*, August 21, 2009, http://www.smartmoney.com/invest/markets/

whole-foods-health-care/ (accessed July 17, 2012); Whole Foods Market IP, L.P., "Training & Development," 2012, http://www.wholefoodsmarket.com/careers/training.php (accessed July 17, 2012); John Mackey and *Grist* staff, "An interview with John Mackey, founder of Whole Foods," *Grist*, December 18, 2004, http://grist.org/article/ little-mackey/ (accessed July 17, 2012); Whole Foods Market, IP, L.P., "Animal Welfare," 2012, http://www. wholefoodsmarket.com/meat/welfare.php (accessed July 18, 2012); Amanda Alix, "Whole Foods Market: A Steady Diet of Growth and Profit," The Motley Fool, Feb. 21, 2012, http://www.fool.com/investing/general/2012/02/21/ whole-foods-market-a-steady-diet-of-growth-and-pro.aspx (accessed July 18, 2012); YAHOO!® Finance, "Whole Foods Market, Inc. (WFM)," http://finance.yahoo.com/q?s=WFM&ql=0 (accessed July 18, 2012); Whole Planet Foundation website, http://www.wholefoodsmarket.com/values/whole-planet-foundation.php (accessed July 18, 2012); Whole Foods Market IP, L.P., "Whole Planet Foundation," 2012, http://www.wholefoodsmarket.com/values/ whole-planet-foundation.php (accessed July 18, 2012); Whole Kids Foundation website, http://www. wholekidsfoundation.org/index.php (accessed July 18, 2012); Whole Foods Market website, http://www. wholefoodsmarket.com/company/ (accessed July 18, 2012); Whole Foods Market IP, L.P., "Locally Grown: The Whole Foods Promise," 2012; http://www.wholefoodsmarket.com/products/locally-grown/ (accessed July 20, 2012); Whole Foods Market IP, L.P., "365 Everyday Value® products," 2012, http://www.wholefoodsmarket.com/ products/365-everyday-value.php (accessed July 20, 2012); Whole Foods Market IP, L.P., "Green Mission." 2012, http://www.wholefoods.com/greenmission (accessed July 20, 2012); Whole Foods Market IP, L.P., "Seafood Sustainability," 2012, http://www.wholefoodsmarket.com/values/seafood.php (accessed July 20, 2012); Whole Foods Market IP, L.P., "How to Make the Best Seafood," 2012, http://www.wholefoodsmarket.com/seafood-ratings/ (accessed July 20, 2012); Kerry A. Dolan "America's Greenest Companies2011," *Forbes*, April 18, 2011, http://www.forbes.com/2011/04/18/americas-greenest-companies.html (accessed November 9, 2011); "Whole Foods' Controversy at Jamaica Plan," *Organic Guide*, January 21, 2011, http://www.organicguide.com/organic/ news/whole-foods-controversy-at-jamaica-plain/ (accessed July 20, 2012); Christopher S. Rugaber, "Whole Foods attacks government case against Wild Oats acquisition," *Denver Post*, July 31, 2007, http://www.denverpost.com/ business/ci_6508028 (accessed July 20, 2012); Associated Press, "Whole Foods CEO's anonymous online life," *CNBC*, July 12, 2007, http://www.msnbc.msn.com/id/19718742/ns/business-us_business/t/whole-foods-ceos-anonymous-online-life/ (accessed July 20, 2012); Timothy W. Martin, "Whole Foods to Sell 31Stores in FTC Deal," *The Wall Street Journal*, March 7, 2009, http://online.wsj.com/article/SB123634938198152983.html?_nocache=1342 806303055&user=welcome&mg=id-wsj (accessed July 20, 2012); "Whole Foods to acquire Wild Oats," *Austin Business Journal*, February 21, 2007, http://www.bizjournals.com/austin/stories/2007/02/19/daily28. html?surround=lfn (accessed July 20, 2012); Katy McLaughlin and Timothy W. Martin, "As Sales Slip, Whole Foods Tries Health Push, *Wall Street Journal*, August 5, 2009, http://online.wsj.com/article/SB124941849645105559. html; Whole Foods Market IP, L.P., "Health Starts Here," 2012, http://www.wholefoodsmarket.com/ healthstartshere/ (accessed July 20, 2012); Holly Rosenkrantz, "Whole Foods, Costco Offer Alternative to Union Bill," *Bloomberg*, March 22, 2009, http://www.bloomberg.com/apps/news?pid=newsarchive&sid=atnjqq9F6._c (accessed July 20, 2012); Josh Harkinson, "Are Starbucks and Whole Foods Union Busters?" *Mother Jones*, April 6, 2009, http://www.motherjones.com/politics/2009/04/are-starbucks-and-whole-foods-union-busting (accessed July 20, 2012); Bruce Watson, "Whole Foods drama continues: Unions join in fight against CEO," *Daily Finance*, August 27, 2009, http://www.dailyfinance.com/2009/08/27/whole-foods-drama-continues-unions-join-in-fight-against-ceo/ (accessed July 20, 2012); Katherine Goldstein, "Whole Foods Backlash: Bloggers Outraged Over CEO's Anti 'Obamacare' Column," *Huffington Post*, May 25, 2011, http://www.huffingtonpost.com/2009/08/18/ the-whole-foods-health-ca_n_262471.html (accessed July 20, 2012); John Mackey, "The Whole Foods Alternative to ObamaCare," *The Wall Street Journal*, August 11, 2009, http://online.wsj.com/article/SB100014240529702042514 0457434217007286507o.html (accessed July 20, 2012).

CASE 14

Apple Inc.'s Ethical Success and Challenges*

Headquartered in Cupertino, California, Apple Inc. experienced many challenges throughout its business history. In 1997 Apple's share price was $3.30. In 2012 its share price rose to $705.07 (although its share price decreased to $425 the following year). For the past five years, Apple earned first place among *Fortune* magazine's World's Most Admired Companies. To millions of consumers, the Apple brand embodies quality, prestige, and innovation.

Although companies tried to copy the Apple business model, none have been able to discover what it is that makes Apple so unique. Many believe Apple's success stems from a combination of several factors, including the remarkable leadership skills of former CEO Steve Jobs, a corporate culture of enthusiasm and innovation, and the high-tech products for which Apple is known. These combining qualities allow Apple to revolutionize the technology and retail industries.

APPLE'S HISTORY

Apple's first product, the Apple I, was vastly different from the Apple products of today. This first handmade computer kit was constructed by Apple co-founder Steve Wozniak. It lacked a graphic user interface (GUI), and buyers had to add their own keyboard and display. Co-founder Steve Jobs convinced Wozniak that it could be sold as a commercial product. In 1976 the Apple I was unveiled at the Home Brew Computer Club and put on sale for $666.66.

Jobs and Wozniak continued to create innovative products. Soon their new company, Apple Computer Inc., surpassed $1 million in sales. However, the mid-1980s saw difficult times for Apple. In 1983 the company introduced the Apple Lisa for $10,000. The product flopped. In 1985 Steve Jobs was ousted after internal conflicts with the Apple CEO. Its computer products the Mac I and the Newton were not successful, and the company underwent several CEO changes. With declining stock prices, the future of Apple was in jeopardy.

Steve Jobs returned to Apple in 1997 to try and save the struggling company. The return of Jobs introduced a new era for Apple. Jobs immediately began to change the company's corporate culture. Before Jobs' return, employees were more open about Apple projects. After he returned, Jobs instituted a "closed door" policy. Today Apple continues to remain vigilant in protecting its technology and ensuring information remains proprietary. Jobs also created a flattened organizational structure; rather than go through layers

*This case was prepared by Jennifer Sawayda, Harper Baird, and Danielle Jolley for and under the direction of O.C. Ferrell and Linda Ferrell. It was prepared for classroom discussion rather than to illustrate either effective or ineffective handling of an administrative, ethical, or legal decision by management. All sources used for this case were obtained through publicly available material on the Apple website.

of management to address employees, he addressed them directly. Perhaps one of the most noticeable changes, however, was Apple's expansion into new product lines within the electronics industry. In 2001 Apple launched the iPod—a portable music player that forever changed the music industry. The company also introduced iTunes, a type of "jukebox" software that allowed users to upload songs from CDs onto their Macs and then organize and manage their personalized song libraries. Two years later Apple introduced the iTunes Store, where users could download millions of their favorite songs for $0.99 each online.

In 2007 Jobs announced Apple Computer, Inc. would be re-named Apple Inc. This signified that Apple was no longer just a computer manufacturer but also a driver in consumer electronics. Some saw this as a shift away from computers toward consumer electronics such as Apple TV, iPods, iTunes, iPhones, and iPads. However, it may be more accurate to say Apple is reinventing computers. With the introduction of tablet computers such as the iPad, Apple began to take market share away from its top competitors in the computer industry. Sales of desktops, laptops, and netbooks began to decline after tablet computers were introduced. Analysts believe tablet computers will continue to grow at a rapid rate.

APPLE'S CORPORATE CULTURE

Apple's transition from a computer to a consumer electronics company is unprecedented—and hard to replicate. Although many can only speculate about why Apple succeeded so well, they tend to credit Steve Jobs' remarkable leadership abilities, Apple's highly skilled employees, and its strong corporate culture.

The concept of evangelism is an important component of Apple's culture. Corporate evangelists refer to people who extensively promote a corporation's products. Apple even had a chief evangelist whose job was to spread the message about Apple and gain support for its products. However, as the name evangelism implies, the role of evangelist takes on greater meaning. Evangelists believe strongly in the company and will spread that belief to others, who in turn convince other people. Therefore, evangelists are not only employees but loyal customers as well. In this way, Apple was able to form what it refers to as a "Mac cult"—customers who are loyal to Apple's Mac computers and who spread a positive message about Macs to their friends and families.

Successful evangelism only occurs with dedicated, enthusiastic employees who are willing to spread the word about Apple. When Jobs returned to Apple, he instituted two cultural changes: he encouraged debate on ideas, and he created a vision employees could believe in. By implementing these two changes, employees felt their input was important and they were a part of something bigger than themselves. Such feelings created a sense of loyalty among many at Apple.

Apple prides itself on its unique corporate culture. On its job site for corporate employees, it ensures potential applicants the organization has a flat structure, lacking the layers of bureaucracy of other corporations. Apple also emphasizes that it does not adhere to the average work day. Instead, Apple markets itself as a fast-paced, innovative, and collaborative environment committed toward doing things "the right way." By offering both challenges and benefits to applicants, Apple hopes to attract those who fit best with its corporate culture.

Apple also looks for retail employees that work well in its culture. Apple wants to ensure that its retail employees make each consumer feel welcome. Inside the Apple retailers are stations where customers can test and experiment with the latest Apple products. Employees are trained to speak with customers within two minutes of entering the store.

To ensure its retailer employees feel motivated, Apple provides extensive training, greater compensation than employees might receive at similar stores, and opportunities to move up to manager, genius (an employee trained to answer the more difficult customer questions), or creative (an employee who trains customers one-on-one or through workshops). Apple also offers young people the chance to intern with Apple or become student representatives at their schools.

Another benefit Apple offers combines employee concerns with those of the environment. In an effort to reduce its overall environmental impact, Apple offers incentives such as transit subsidies for employees who opt to use public transportation. Its Cupertino facility is equipped with shuttles for employees, including free bus service between the Apple headquarters and the train station. Apple's free buses are powered by bio-diesel. These incentives reduce fuel costs for employees while simultaneously lowering emissions released into the environment.

APPLE'S ETHICS

Apple has tried to ensure its employees and those with which they work display appropriate conduct in all situations. It bases its success on "creating innovative, high-quality products and services and on demonstrating integrity in every business interaction." According to Apple, four main principles contribute to integrity: honesty, respect, confidentiality, and compliance. To thoroughly detail these principles, Apple drafted a code of business conduct that applies to all its operations, including those overseas. It also made available on its website specific policies regarding corporate governance, director conflict of interest, and guidelines on reporting questionable conduct. Additionally, Apple provides employees with a Business Conduct Helpline they can use to report misconduct to Apple's Audit and Finance Committee.

Many of Apple's product components are manufactured in countries with low labor costs. The potential for misconduct is high because of differing labor standards and less direct oversight. As a result, Apple makes each of its suppliers sign its "Supplier Code of Conduct" and performs factory audits to ensure compliance. Apple may refuse to do additional business with suppliers who refuse to comply with Apple's standards. To emphasize its commitment toward responsible supplier conduct, Apple releases an annual Apple Supplier Responsibility Report that explains its supplier expectations as well as its audit conclusions and corrective actions the company takes against factories where violations occur.

ETHICAL ISSUES AT APPLE INC.

Although Apple consistently won first place as the World's Most Admired Company, it experienced several ethical issues in recent years. These issues could have a profound effect on the company's future success. Apple's sterling reputation could easily be damaged by serious misconduct or a failure to address risks appropriately.

Privacy

Consumer tracking is a controversial issue. With the increase in social networking, mobile devices, and Internet use, the ability for companies to track customers is greater than ever before. For Apple more customer information can help it better market its products and understand its customers. However, the firm must still show respect for consumer privacy, and a perceived breach in privacy is likely to result in a backlash against the company.

In 2011 Apple experienced just such a backlash. Apple and Google disclosed that certain features on the cell phones they sell collected data on the phones' locations. Consumers and government officials saw this as an infringement on user privacy. The companies announced that users have the option to disable these features on their phones, yet this was not entirely true for Apple. Some of its phones continued to collect location information even after users disabled the feature. Apple attributed this to a glitch it remedied with new software. Both Google and Apple defend their data-collection mechanisms, but many government officials disagree. The government is considering passing legislation on mobile privacy, actions that could have profound effects on Apple and other electronics companies.

Price Fixing

In July of 2013, a judge ruled that Apple had conspired to fix prices on electronic books (e-books) in conjunction with five major book publishers. A federal judge ruled that Apple was part of a deal that required publishers to give Apple's iTunes store the best deals in the marketplace for e-books. According to allegations, Apple allowed publishers to set the e-book prices for the iPad, and Apple received 30 percent of the proceeds (known as the "agency model"). The agency model is thought to be less competitive than the wholesale model, in which retailers and publishers negotiate on the price. However, if a competitor was found to be selling the e-book for less, Apple was to be offered the same lower price. This scheme is more commonly referred to as a most-favored-nation clause and can be used by companies to dominate the market by keeping competitors out. After striking the deal with Apple, publishers then approached Amazon about participating in the contract. Apple denies any wrongdoing and association with this deal and plans to appeal the decision.

Rioting

In early 2012 Apple halted sales of the iPhone 4S at retail stores in China. This result came after massive crowds waiting for 48 hours outside of the flagship store in Beijing began to riot. Tensions grew between prospective buyers waiting overnight who tried to edge themselves closer to the front of the line. The estimated crowd was upwards of 2,000 people, which alarmed police officials. They asked Apple not to open the store for safety precautions. Customers waiting for the iPhone retaliated by throwing eggs at the store and attacking a mall property manager mistaken for an Apple employee. To their dismay, customers were encouraged to purchase the iPhone online or through other authorized sellers. Other stores in Shanghai and one other in Beijing opened as scheduled and quickly sold out of the iPhone 4S. Many questioned Apple's ethics about how they handled this situation and the dangers to customer and employee safety.

Another instance of rioting associated with Apple occurred later in September when more than 2,000 Foxconn plant workers assembling the iPhone 5 broke out into a fight in the plant's dormitories. Authorities sent 5,000 police officials to restore structure to the plant. Workers reportedly broke glass windows of guard shacks and destroyed railings throughout the property. Reasons given for the riot varied, from alleged beatings from factory guards to stress among workers to produce the product in a timely matter to frustration with the work environment itself. This is not the first time Foxconn's environment has been questioned, and as a major supplier of Apple, Apple has the responsibility to ensure workers at the plant are being treated fairly. More on Foxconn will be discussed later in this case.

Sustainability

Apple has taken steps to become a greener company, such as reducing its environmental impact at its facilities. However, the company admits that the majority of its emissions come from its products. In 2011 Apple stated its operations contributed to 23.1 million metric tons of gases being released. While 2 percent came from its facilities, 98 percent came from the life cycle of its products. Since Apple's success hinges on constantly developing and launching new products, the environmental impact of its products is a serious issue.

One practice for which some consumers have criticized Apple is planned obsolescence—pushing people to replace or upgrade their technology whenever Apple comes out with an updated version. Since Apple constantly releases upgraded products, this could result in older technology being tossed aside. Apple undertook different approaches to combat this problem. For one, the company strives to build products with materials suitable for recycling. It also tries to build products that last, along with recycling responsibly. To encourage its customers to recycle, Apple created a recycling program at its stores for old iPods, mobile phones, and Mac computers. Consumers that trade in their old iPods can receive a ten percent discount on a newer version. Consumers recycling old Mac computers that still have value can receive gift cards. Apple partners with regional recyclers that comply with related laws. Despite this recycling program, many consumers feel tossing out their old products is more convenient, particularly if they have no value. E-waste remains a significant issue as long as consumers continue to throw away their old electronics.

Apple made a controversial move by temporarily removing 39 products from the Electronic Product Environmental Assessment Tool (EPEAT) ratings system. The rating system provides green standards for computers and is used by many schools and governments when purchasing computer products. Apple stated that it felt its products adhered to green standards not measured by EPEAT. Many consumers felt Apple might be embracing less eco-friendly products or it was touting itself as being more eco-friendly than it really was. Many large buyers such as the city of San Francisco threatened to drop Apple computers as a result. Apple rejoined the EPEAT rating system after consumer feedback indicated that dropping the system was a mistake. With sustainability becoming a major concern for many buyers, Apple must carefully anticipate consumer reaction before implementing similar changes in the future.

Intellectual Property

Intellectual property theft is a key concern at Apple, an issue the company aggressively pursues. Apple is serious about keeping its proprietary information a secret to prevent other companies from stealing its ideas. This led to many lawsuits between Apple and other technology firms. In 1982 Apple filed a lawsuit against Franklin Computer Corporation that impacted intellectual property laws. Apple alleged Franklin was illegally formatting copies of Apple II's operating system and ROM so they would run on Franklin computers. Franklin's lawyers argued that portions of computer programs were not subject to copyright law. At first the courts sided with Franklin, but the verdict was later overturned. The courts eventually determined that codes and programs are protected under copyright law. This law provided technology companies with more extensive intellectual property protections.

Another notable case was Apple's lawsuit against Microsoft after Apple licensed technology to Microsoft. When Microsoft released Windows 2.0, Apple claimed the licensing agreement was only for Windows 1.0 and that Microsoft's Windows had the "look and feel" of Apple's Macintosh graphic interface system (GUI). The courts ruled in favor of Microsoft, deciding the license did not cover the "look and feel" of Apple's Macintosh GUI. Although there were similarities between the two, the courts ruled that Windows did not violate copyright law or the licensing agreement simply by resembling Macintosh systems.

Two other lawsuits involved more serious ethical issues on Apple's part. One involved Apple's use of the domain name iTunes.co.uk. The domain name had already been registered by Ben Cohen in 2000, who used the name to re-direct users to other sites. Cohen eventually used the domain name to redirect users to the Napster site, a direct competitor of Apple. Apple attempted to purchase the domain name from Cohen, but when negotiations failed the company appealed to UK registry Nominet. Usually, whoever registers the domain name first gets the rights to that name. However, the mediator in the case determined that Cohen abused his registration rights and took unfair advantage of Apple. Apple won the right to use the domain name, which led to complaints that Apple was being favored at the expense of smaller companies.

Apple faced another trademark lawsuit from Cisco Systems in 2007. Cisco claimed Apple infringed on its iPhone trademark. Cisco owned the trademark since 2000. Apple and Cisco negotiated to determine whether to allow Apple to use the trademark. However, Apple walked away from the discussions. According to Cisco, the company then opened up a front organization, Ocean Telecom Services, and filed for the iPhone trademark in the United States. Some stakeholders saw Apple's actions as a deceptive way to get around negotiation procedures. The lawsuit ended with both parties agreeing to use the iPhone name. However, Apple's actions in this situation remain controversial.

The most recent case came in the form of a lawsuit between Samsung and Apple. Apple's claim was that Samsung infringed on multiple intellectual property rights, including patents, trademarks, user interface, style, false designation of origin, unfair competition, and trademark infringement. Specifically, Apple claims Samsung used key features of its iPhone and iPad, including glass screens and rounded corners, along with many performance features and physical similarities. A jury found Samsung guilty of willfully infringing on Apple's design and utility patents. Apple was awarded $1.049 billion in damages, and Samsung's allegations of infringement against Apple were dismissed within the United States.

With the many products Apple releases each year, it makes sense to protect its technology from theft. Apple's aggressiveness regarding patent protection led it to file lawsuits against some powerful companies, including Microsoft and Samsung. It also filed a lawsuit against HTC Corporation, a Taiwanese smartphone manufacturer that makes phones for Google's Android products. Apple accused HTC of replicating a range of cellphone features protected under Apple's patents. Although the lawsuit is directed toward HTC, it also indirectly targets Google since it is a major client. Eventually, the two companies agreed to drop the lawsuits against one another and accepted a 10-year licensing agreement.

The ethical issue is if Apple's claims are legitimate. Is it pursuing companies it honestly believes infringed on its patents, or is it simply trying to cast its competitors in a bad light so it can become the major player in the market? Although it might seem Apple is too aggressive, companies that do not set boundaries and protect their property can easily have it copied by the competition, which can then be used to gain a competitive foothold. It is up to the courts to determine whether Apple's allegations have any validity.

Threats to Other Companies

A recently released document suggests that in 2007 former CEO Steve Jobs allegedly threatened former CEO of Palm Edward Colligan with patent litigation if Palm did not cease and desist poaching valuable Apple employees. Jobs suggested each company should respectively comply with the idea of not taking valuable employees away from other companies. This "unspoken agreement" seems to have also included companies such as Adobe, Google, Intel, Intuit, and Pixar. This document came to light because of lawsuits pursued by former Apple employees. Jobs' firm stance on the matter was made clear to Colligan, who countered with a response that Apple's employees were fair game and this type of collusion was highly unethical. In 2010, the U.S. Department of Justice filed an antitrust lawsuit against the aforementioned companies and required them to dissolve this agreement. Current CEO Tim Cook made it clear Steve Jobs was the only one with knowledge to this agreement and no other Apple employees were involved.

Supply Chain Management Issues

As mentioned earlier, Apple makes each supplier sign its supplier code of conduct and performs factory audits to ensure compliance. In addition, Apple says it has trained over 1 million workers about their rights, increased the number of suppliers it audits by 80 percent, and allows outside organizations to evaluate its labor practices. However, in the last few years serious supply chain issues threaten to undermine Apple's status as a highly admired and ethical company.

To meet the continuous demands of Apple consumers, products from the company must be readily available. For Apple, most of these products are produced throughout Asia, but more specifically within Foxconn factories in China. In the past, multiple accusations pertaining to improper working conditions, underage labor disputes, and worker abuse (that resulted in suicides) have come into question. Apple has been labeled as an unfair sweatshop, and critics launched multiple campaigns against the company. This resulted in negative publicity from protestors, who asked current Apple consumers not to support Apple's unlawful practices by purchasing its products.

Additionally, despite its attempt to audit its factories and enforce strong supplier compliance standards, over 50 percent of the suppliers audited by Apple violated at least one part of its supplier code of conduct every year since 2007. Suppliers claim Apple's manufacturing standards are hard to achieve because suppliers are allowed slim profit margins. In contrast, competitors like Hewlett-Packard allow suppliers to keep more profits if they improve worker conditions. According to suppliers, Apple's focus on the bottom line forces them to find other ways to cut costs, usually by requiring employees to work longer hours and using less expensive but more dangerous chemicals.

In this environment, mistakes and safety issues become more common. According to the company's own audits, 62 percent of Apple's suppliers did not comply with working-hour limits, 35 percent failed to meet Apple's standards to prevent worker injuries, and 32 percent do not follow hazardous-substance management practices. Other problems with Apple's supply chain include underage workers, falsified records, overcrowded worker dormitories, and other labor violations. Apple claims suppliers who violate company policies have 90 days to address the problem, but fewer than 15 suppliers have been dropped for violations since 2007.

Several high-profile events at Apple factories generated even more criticism of its supply chain. In January 2010, over 135 workers fell ill after using a poisonous chemical to clean iPhone screens. In 2011 aluminum dust and improper ventilation caused two explosions that killed 4 people and injured 77. Additionally, over a dozen workers committed suicide at Apple supplier factories. Much of the media attention focused on the conditions at Foxconn, Apple's largest supplier with a background of labor violations. Foxconn continues to assert it is in compliance with all regulations.

Some blame the factory conditions on Apple's culture of innovation and the need to release new or improved products each year, which requires suppliers to work quickly at the expense of safety standards. However, the Foxconn factory is one of only a few facilities in the world with the capacity to build iPods and iPads, and that makes it difficult for Apple to change suppliers. Additionally, inconsistent international labor standards and high competition mean that virtually every major electronics producer faces similar manufacturing issues. As media and consumer scrutiny increase, Apple must continue to address its supply chain management issues. However, as one current Apple executive told the *New York Times*, customer expectations could also be a problem since customers seem to care more about the newest product than the labor conditions of those who made it.

Apple claims it is significantly improving supplier conditions and becoming more transparent about its labor processes. CEO Tim Cook visited Foxconn personally to see about labor conditions. Apple worked with Foxconn to improve worker safety, including testing more equipment and improving workers' hours. The Fair Labor Association (FLA) states that Apple has dramatically improved the accountability of Foxconn and completed 280 of the FLA's recommendations. It appears Apple is improving its supply chain practices. However, continual monitoring of its suppliers and enforcement of ethical standards are necessary to assure stakeholders that Apple takes the well-being of workers in its supply chain seriously.

THE FUTURE OF APPLE INC.

Apple appears optimistic about its future. The company has created a cult following of consumers who are intensely loyal to Apple products. Apple's products are meant to offer superior solutions to those of competitors. In one of Apple's newest offerings, the company is taking its forays in the music industry further. The company reached agreements with record labels to launch iCloud, a service that enables consumers to create and listen to their music collections without having to upload individual songs. While Google and Amazon offer similar music storage services, Apple has more songs at its disposal with iTunes and its record label agreements. Also, in June 2013 Apple filed for a trademark application for an iWatch in Japan, which has fueled speculation that the company is developing a wearable computing device. Many consider wearable computing to be the new direction in innovation. Google has developed the competing Glass eyewear, and it has been reported that Samsung and Microsoft have been developing wearable devices that will sync with other operating systems and platforms. As Apple combats investor speculation that it is no longer innovating, it was reported in July 2013 that Apple has began to test larger screens for smartphones and tablets in response to competition. Apple is designing products to continue expanding its customer base. The company is aiming to refine current products while continuing to develop new ones. Seizing on these opportunities can increase Apple's share of the music and consumer electronics markets.

Apple has its share of threats. It constantly faces lawsuits from various competitors over alleged intellectual property violations. Additionally, although Apple's aggressive stance helped protect its intellectual property, its tight hold over its products and secrets could be disadvantageous as well. Google, for instance, has a more open-source approach. It has shown great support for the open-source movement, which advocates opening software and software codes in order to secure more input from outside sources. Although this openness increases the risks of intellectual property theft, it allows for innovation to occur more rapidly because of additional collaboration. Google's Android phones are beginning to gain market share as a formidable competitor to Apple's iPhones. Apple may eventually need to re-examine whether its closed system is the best way to compete.

The most recognizable threat seen around the world was the death of Steve Jobs. In October 2011 Apple Inc. lost one of the most important aspects to its company. With the passing of Apple founder and CEO, eyes are now turned to CEO Tim Cook. Tim Cook was Apple's corporate operations officer for many years before becoming CEO. Cook takes a more traditional approach in his management style by prioritizing project and supply chain management over creative engineering, attending investor meetings, being accessible to the media, and paying out dividends to stock holders, among other activities. He still maintains the secretive nature of the company but appears to be more approachable than Jobs.

Yet while Cook seems to possess the skills necessary for the CEO position, some fear he lacks the creative skills that made Jobs such a visionary. Jobs was considered to be a "creative builder," able to recognize consumer needs and develop revolutionary products to meet these needs in dynamic ways. A major concern is that Cook does not possess these skills. This prompted many to question whether Cook's leadership might change Apple's culture negatively. On the other hand, others feel Cook could make Apple more competitive with his strong strategic management skills. The change in tone of the company is the big difference between the leadership styles of Cook and Jobs and will likely have a profound impact on the firm.

In the last decade, Apple has excelled at keeping pace with the quickly evolving industry of computers and consumer electronics. Although skeptics have raised questions in the latter half of 2013 on whether Apple is still the driving force behind innovation, many believe new products are on the horizon. Its diversification, collaborative corporate culture, and product evangelism propelled it to heights that could not have been envisioned when Jobs and Wozniak sold their first computer kit in 1976. Although Apple experienced many challenges along the way, the company has clearly showcased its ability to understand consumers and create products that have been implemented and used in customers' everyday lives.

QUESTIONS

1. Explain how Apple's philosophy and organizational culture have impacted how it handles ethical decisions.
2. Why is Apple's industry so competitive and how could this affect the ethical risk in Apple's operations?
3. How do you think Apple has handled the various ethical issues that it has faced in the past?

SOURCES

Jim Aley, "The Beginning," *Bloomberg Businessweek*, Special Issue on Steve Jobs, October 2011, 20–26; Paul Andrews, "Apple-Microsoft Lawsuit Fizzles To A Close -- 'Nothing Left' To Fight About," *The Seattle Times*, June 2, 1993, http://community.seattletimes.nwsource.com/archive/?date=19930602&slug=1704430 (accessed April 16, 2013); Julia Angwin, "Apple, Google Take Heat," *The Wall Street Journal*, May 11, 2011, http://online.wsj.com/article/SB10001424052748703730804576315121174761088.html (accessed April 16, 2013); "Apple and the Environment,"Apple, http://www.apple.com/environment/#recycling (accessed April 16, 2013); "Apple begins counting down to 25 billion App Store downloads," *AppleInsider*, February 17, 2012, http://www.appleinsider.com/articles/12/02/17/apple_begins_counting_down_to_25_billion_app_store_downloads.html (accessed April 16, 2013); "Apple chronology," *CNNMoney*, January 6, 1998, http://money.cnn.com/1998/01/06/technology/apple_chrono/ (accessed April 16, 2013); "Apple, Cisco agree both can use iPhone name," Reuters, February 22, 2007, http://www.reuters.com/article/2007/02/22/us-apple-cisco-idUSWEN460920070222 (accessed April 16, 2013); Apple History, http://www.apple-history.com/ (accessed June 6, 2011); Apple Inc., *Business Conduct: The way we do business worldwide*, 2010, http://files.shareholder.com/downloads/AAPL/1283312876x0x443008/5f38b1e6-2f9c-4518-b691-13a29ac90501/business_conduct_policy.pdf (accessed April 16, 2013); Apple Inc., *Policy on Reporting Questionable Accounting or Auditing Matters*, November 16, 2010, http://files.shareholder.com/downloads/AAPL/1281913948x0x443017/68a6d f9d-b0ef-4870-ba8e-accc695b39e2/reporting_accounting_auditing_matters.pdf (accessed April 16, 2013); Apple, Inc., *Apple Supplier Responsibility 2011 Progress Report*, February 2011; "Apple Introduces iTunes—World's Best and Easiest to Use Jukebox Software," Apple, January 9, 2001, http://www.apple.com/pr/library/2001/jan/09itunes.html (accessed April 16, 2013); "Apple Recycling Program," Apple, http://www.apple.com/recycling/ (accessed April 16, 2013); "Apple's 25% Solution," *Seeking Alpha*, Nov. 7, 2011, http://seekingalpha.com/article/305849-apple-s-25-solution (accessed April 16, 2013); Bloomberg News, "Apple's Tim Cook Visits Foxconn iPhone Plant in China," *Bloomberg News*, March 28, 2012, http://www.bloomberg.com/news/2012-03-29/apple-says-cook-visited-new-foxconn-plant-in-zhengzhou-china.html (accessed April 16, 2013); John Brownlee, "What It's Like To Work At Apple," Cult of Mac, July 7, 2010, http://www.cultofmac.com/what-its-like-to-work-at-apple (accessed April 16, 2013); "Building the Digital Age," BBC News, http://newsvote.bbc.co.uk/mpapps/pagetools/print/news.bbc.co.uk/2/hi/technology/7091190.stm (accessed April 16, 2013); Peter Burrows, "The Wilderness," *Bloomberg Businessweek*, Special Issue on Steve Jobs, October 2011, 28–34; Amanda Cantrell, "Apple's remarkable comeback Story," *CNNMoney*, March 29, 2006, http://money.cnn.com/2006/03/29/technology/apple_anniversary/?cnn=ye (accessed April 16, 2013); Alan Deutschman, "The once and future Steve Jobs," *Salon*, October 11, 2000, http://www.salon.com/technology/books/2000/10/11/jobs_excerpt/ (accessed April 16, 2013); Charles Duhigg, "In China, Human Costs Are Built Into an iPad," *The New York Times*, January 25, 2012, http://www.nytimes.com/2012/01/26/business/ieconomy-apples-ipad-and-the-human-costs-for-workers-in-china.html?pagewanted=all (accessed April 16, 2013); Kit Eaton, "Steve Jobs vs. Tim Cook: Words of Wisdom," *Fast Company*, August 26, 2011, http://www.fastcompany.com/1776013/steve-jobs-vs-tim-cook-words-wisdom (accessed April 16, 2013); Paul Elias, "Samsung Ordered to Pay Apple $1.05B in Patent Case," *Yahoo! Finance*, August 25, 2012, http://finance.yahoo.com/news/samsung-ordered-pay-apple-1-004505800.html (accessed April 16, 2013); "The evangelist's evangelist," Creating Customer Evangelists, http://www.creatingcustomerevangelists.com/resources/evangelists/guy_kawasaki.asp (accessed April 16, 2013); *Facilities Report: 2010 Environmental Update*, http://images.apple.com/environment/reports/docs/Apple_Facilities_Report_2010.pdf (accessed April 16, 2013); "Former Apple evangelist on company's history," CNET News, March 29, 2006, http://news.cnet.com/1606-2_3-6055676.html (accessed April 16, 2013); Bryan Gardiner, "Learning from Failure: Apple's Most Notorious Flops," *Wired*, January 24, 2008, http://www.wired.com/gadgets/mac/multimedia/2008/01/gallery_apple_flops?slide=1&slideView=8 (accessed April 16, 2013); "Governance: Investor Relations," Apple, http://investor.apple.com/governance.cfm (accessed April 16, 2013); Rob Hassett, IMPACT OF APPLE VS. FRANKLIN DECISION, 1983, http://www.internetlegal.com/impactof.htm (accessed April 16, 2013); Miguel Helft, "Will Apple's Culture Hurt the iPhone?," *The New York Times*, October 17,

2010, http://www.nytimes.com/2010/10/18/technology/18apple.html (accessed April 16, 2013); Inside the Minds of Most Hard-Charging CEOs," *Inc.* September 2012, pp. 142-146; Yukari Iwatani Kane and Ethan Smith, "Apple Readies iCloud Service," *The Wall Street Journal*, June 1, 2011, B1; Yukari Iwatani Kane and Ian Sherr, "Apple: Samsung Copied Design," *The Wall Street Journal*, April 19, 2011, http://online.wsj.com/article/SB100014240527487 03916004576271210109389154.html (accessed April 16, 2013); Steve Jobs, "A Greener Apple," Apple, http://www.apple.com/hotnews/agreenerapple/ (accessed April 16, 2013); "Jobs at Apple," Apple, http://www.apple.com/jobs/us/benefits.html (accessed April 16, 2013); Ashby Jones, "So What's Up With this Apple/Google Lawsuit?" *The Wall Street Journal*, March 30, 2010, http://blogs.wsj.com/law/2010/03/03/so-whats-up-with-this-applegoogle-lawsuit/ (accessed April 16, 2013); Dawn Kawamoto, Ben Heskett, and Mike Ricciuti, "Microsoft to invest $150 million in Apple," CNET, August 6, 1997, http://news.cnet.com/MS-to-invest-150-million-in-Apple/2100-1001_3-202143.html (accessed April 16, 2013); Adam Lashinsky, "How Tim Cook Is Changing Apple," *Fortune*, June 11, 2012; Adam Lashinsky, "The Secrets Apple Keeps," *Fortune*, February 6, 2012, pp. 85-94; Lorraine Luk and Ian Sherr, "Apple Tests Larger Screens for iPhones and iPads," *The Wall Street Journal*, July 22, 2013, http://online.wsj.com/article/SB1 0001424127887323829104578620870597r97408176.html?KEYWORDS=Apple (accessed July 23, 2013); Kieren McCarthy "Apple threatens iTunes.co.uk owner," *The Register*, December 6, 2004, http://www.theregister.co.uk/2004/12/06/apple_itunescouk_domain_dispute/ (accessed April 16, 2013); Robert McMillan, "Apple Does About-Face on Green EPEAT Ratings," *Wired*, July 13, 2012, http://www.wired.com/wiredenterprise/2012/07/apple-epeat/ (accessed January 29, 2013); Scott Martin, "Apple invites review of labor practices in overseas factories," *USA Today*, January 16, 2012, 3B; Scott Martin, "How Apple rewrote the rules of retailing," *USA Today*, May 19, 2011, 1B; Nilofer Merchant, "Apple's Startup Culture," *Bloomberg Businessweek*, June 24, 2010, http://www.businessweek.com/innovate/content/jun2010/id20100610_525759.htm (accessed April 16, 2013); Claire Milne, *Nominet UK Dispute Resolution Service Decision of Independent Expert*, March 10, 2005, http://www.nominet.org.uk/digitalAssets/766_itunes.pdf (accessed June 8, 2011); Chris Morrison, "Insanely Great Marketing," *CBS MoneyWatch*, August 10, 2009, http://www.cbsnews.com/8301-505125_162-51330244/insanely-great-marketing (accessed April 16, 2013); "Overview of the Open Source Movement," The University of Texas at Austin Graduate School of Library and Information Science, 2000, http://www.ischool.utexas.edu/~l38613dw/readings/OpenSourceOverview.html (accessed April 16, 2013); Joe Palazzolo, "Apple E-book ruling heaps new doubt on 'MFN' Clauses," Wall Street Journal, July 15, 2013, p. B1; Rocco Pendola, "Amazon vs. Apple: Jeff Bezos Just Squashed Tim Cook," *CNBC*, September 7, 2012, http://www.cnbc.com/id/48945231 (accessed April 16, 2013); Marguerite Reardon and Tom Krazit, "Cisco sues Apple over use of iPhone trademark," CNET News, January 10, 2007, http://news.cnet.com/Cisco-sues-Apple-over-use-of-iPhone-trademark/2100-1047_3-6149285.html (accessed April 16, 2013); Joel Rosenblatt, "Jobs Threatened Suit If Palm Didn't Agree to Hiring Terms," *Bloomberg*, January 22, 2013, http://www.bloomberg.com/news/2013-01-23/jobs-threatened-suit-if-palm-didn-t-agree-to-hiring-terms.html (accessed April 16, 2013); Greg Sandoval, "This is why DOJ accused Apple of fixing e-book prices," *CNET*, April 11, 2013, http://news.cnet.com/8301-13579_3-57412369-37/this-is-why-doj-accused-apple-of-fixing-e-book-prices/ (accessed July 23, 2013); Joanna Stern, "Apple and Foxconn Make Progress on Working Conditions at Factories," *ABC News*, August 21, 2012, http://abcnews.go.com/blogs/technology/2012/08/apple-and-foxconn-make-progress-on-working-conditions-at-factories/ (accessed January 29, 2013); Daisuke Wakabayashi,"Apple Seeks Japan iWatch Trademark," Wall Street Journal, July 2, 2013, p. B5; Martyn Williams, "Timeline: iTunes Store at 10 Billion," ComputerWorld, February 24, 2010, http://www.computerworld.com/s/article/9162018/Timeline_iTunes_Store_at_10_billion (accessed April 16, 2013); "World's Most Admired Companies: Apple," CNNMoney, http://money.cnn.com/magazines/fortune/mostadmired/2011/snapshots/670.html (accessed April 16, 2013); Nick Wingfield, "As Apple's Battle With HTC Ends, Smartphone Patent Fights Continue," *The New York Times*, November 11, 2012, http://www.nytimes.com/2012/11/12/technology/as-apple-and-htc-end-lawsuits-smartphone-patent-battles-continue.html?_r=0 (accessed January 29, 2013); Alberto Zanco, "Apple Inc: A success built on distribution & design," http://www.slideshare.net/Nanor/distribution-policy-apple-presentation (accessed April 16, 2013).

CASE 15

PepsiCo's Journey Toward an Ethical and Socially Responsible Culture*

COMPANY OVERVIEW

PepsiCo is one of the largest food and beverage companies in the world. It manufactures and sells 22 brands of beverages and snack foods that generate over $1 billion each in retail sales. PepsiCo encompasses the Pepsi Cola, Frito-Lay, Tropicana, Quaker, and Gatorade brands and offers products in over 200 countries. The company's headquarters are in New York and employs nearly 300,000 people. In 2007 Indra K. Nooyi became the CEO of PepsiCo. PepsiCo has received many awards and recognitions over the years, including being ranked in the top 25 of the best global brands and earning the Green Award by the Environmental Protection Agency.

COMPANY AND MARKETING HISTORY

The Pepsi recipe was developed by pharmacist Caleb Bradham in the 1890s. Originally marketed under the unassuming name "Brad's Drink," Bradham's creation was renamed Pepsi-Cola in 1898 because of the pepsin and kola nut ingredients used. Awareness of Bradham's new creation spread quickly, and in 1902 he decided to create the Pepsi-Cola Company so people everywhere could enjoy the drink. In 1903 the patent became official, and by 1910 Pepsi-Cola had franchises in 24 states and sold over 100,000 gallons of the syrup annually. However, the Pepsi brand encountered several rocky situations before becoming the success it is today. World War I proved to be an especially turbulent time for Pepsi-Cola. Severe fluctuations in sugar prices caused the company to lose money, and in 1923 Bradham sold the trademark to Craven's Holding Corp., who shortly after sold it to a New York stockbroker named Roy C. Megargel. Megargel fought to revitalize the company but failed. In 1931 the Pepsi-Cola Company underwent its second bankruptcy. Candy manufacturer Charles Guth, president of Loft, Inc., saw Pepsi-Cola as a great investment and decided to purchase the company. Within two years the company was earning over a million dollars and was on its way to making history.

*This material was developed by Danielle Jolley and Jennifer Sawayda under the direction of O.C. Ferrell and Linda Ferrell. It is based on a previous case developed by Kendra Berch and Kimberly Montoya. This case is intended for classroom discussion rather than to illustrate effective or ineffective handling of administrative, ethical, or legal decisions by management. All sources used for this case were obtained through publicly available material.

Building a Brand

Guth had many challenges to overcome in order to save the struggling brand. Through the Great Depression, Pepsi carefully positioned itself as a low cost leader and made advertising history when it released the nation's first jingle "nickel, nickel." With financially-strapped customers reluctant to pay a nickel for a drink, Guth began offering twice the amount of Pepsi for the same price, a tactic that met with resounding success. World War II continued to test Pepsi-Cola's strength with introduced sugar rationing, but Pepsi's marketing campaigns and brand design helped Pepsi make it through the difficult period. For instance, Pepsi changed the colors on the label to be red, white, and blue to show patriotism. Pepsi's success allowed it to begin marketing internationally in 1945.

As more people began earning more disposable income, Pepsi-Cola recognized the marketplace was changing. To maintain a strong brand, its marketing campaigns had to change too. Pepsi therefore said goodbye to the long-running "nickel, nickel" slogan and introduced a more lively "More Bounce to the Ounce" slogan to the after-war population. During the 1950s, Pepsi evolved from the low cost price leader to a more lifestyle drink approach. For example, as Americans became more health conscious, Pepsi introduced slogans such as "The Light Refreshment" and "Refreshing Without Filling."

It was this younger target market and the post-war baby boom generation that set the stage for Pepsi's long-lasting brand image. It all started with Pepsi advertiser Alan Pottasch, who recognized the different nature of the newest generation of consumers. Whereas consumers before the war were more cautious and price-conscious, the post-war baby boomer generation was carefree and hopeful. Pepsi once again capitalized on the changing environment, and under Pottasch launched the "Pepsi Generation" campaign in 1963. The campaign was an advertising breakthrough as it helped set a new standard for advertising in America. The ads portrayed happy Americans living the American dream—with their Pepsis, of course. By associating its brand with youth and excitement, Pepsi-Cola became the forerunner of lifestyle marketing. Future campaigns continued to promote this brand image, with slogans such as "You've Got a Lot to Live. Pepsi's Got a Lot to Give" and "Come Alive. You're in the Pepsi Generation!"

Pepsi successfully adapted its practices and product positioning with the times through its marketing campaigns. The company also pursued a major acquisition strategy as well as an expansion of its product line. In 1964, Pepsi introduced Diet Pepsi in response to the nation's noticeable lifestyle change toward health, along with the Mountain Dew brand. PepsiCo broke into the bottled water industry with its rollout of Aquafina bottled water in 1997. However, the biggest milestone was Pepsi's monumental merger with Frito-Lay, Inc., to become PepsiCo, Inc., the company it is known as today. Pepsi also profited through corporate partnerships, such as a partnership with Starbucks in 1994 to develop coffee drinks.

Celebrity Endorsements

In more recent years, Pepsi used celebrity branding to build upon the Pepsi brand. The 1980s brought in celebrity endorsers like Tina Turner, Michael J. Fox, Gloria Estefan, and David Bowie. By far its biggest celebrity endorser in this time period was Michael Jackson. The singer and PepsiCo struck a $5 million partnership that linked the two together for the rest of the 1980s. With Jackson as its prime celebrity endorser, PepsiCo was able to set itself up as the hip, trendy drink for the new generation. Pepsi's celebrity partnerships enabled the company to gain market share even as Coca-Cola's market share was dropping.

In 2012 PepsiCo celebrated its 25th anniversary of its Michael Jackson partnership by using Jackson's image on special-edition Pepsi cans and featuring his music in advertisements after reaching an agreement with Jackson's estate.

Another notable achievement in marketing history was the inroads Pepsi made into the Soviet market. Perhaps the biggest (indirect) Soviet endorser of the product was the Soviet Premier Nikita Kruschev, who was caught on camera drinking a Pepsi at the 1959 American National Exhibition in Moscow. A favorable relationship developed between the Soviet Union and the company, leading to a trade agreement in 1972 where Pepsi became the first foreign consumer product sold in the Soviet Union. In 1988, Pepsi became the first advertiser to buy time on Soviet television. A Pepsi advertisement aired later that year incorporated Soviet teenage actors to appeal to the younger generation. The Pepsi Generation remained popular in Russia after the Soviet Union's dissolution.

Recent Years

PepsiCo has continued to use celebrity marketing throughout the 1990s and early 2000s, including Ray Charles, Cindy Crawford, and Britney Spears. To appeal to sports fans, PepsiCo tapped into the celebrity status of Shaquille O'Neal and racecar driver Jeff Gordon. In 2006 PepsiCo got a new CEO, Indra Nooyi, who began reorganizing PepsiCo to focus on several initiatives. Under her leadership, PepsiCo's goals included focusing more on countries outside the United States, developing healthier snacks, having a net-zero impact on the environment, and creating a better working environment. PepsiCo began investing heavily in the countries where it does business. For example, PepsiCo created a strategic alliance with Chinese food and beverage company Tingyi Holding Corp. as a way of expanding into the Chinese market. The partners opened up a beverage manufacturing company in Zhengzhou and state their intentions to promote more economic development in the region. The worldwide success of PepsiCo reflects the company's dynamic and adaptable strategy throughout the company's history, leading to its current revenues of over $66.5 billion.

PEPSICO DIVISIONS AND BRANDS

PepsiCo consists of four divisions: PepsiCo Americas Beverages, PepsiCo Americas Foods, PepsiCo Europe, and PepsiCo Middle East, Asia, and Africa. These divisions are further split up into different businesses, including Pepsi Beverages, Frito-Lay, Quaker, Tropicana, and Gatorade. The following are some of PepsiCo's most well-known and profitable businesses.

Pepsi-Cola Brands

Over the years, Pepsi-Cola has gone above and beyond the original Pepsi beverage to incorporate a wide variety of brands. In the United States, some of the most well-known brands include Mountain Dew, Sierra Mist, IZZE, and Aquafina. International brands include Fiesta, Manzanita Sol, and Kas Mas.

However, in the last decade, the growth of soft drinks has lowered due to a new wave of health consciousness sweeping the nation. This is troublesome news for PepsiCo's most popular brand, the Pepsi soft drink. It requires PepsiCo to innovate in order to create or acquire healthier brands that appeal to the more health-conscious consumer. Some of these drinks include Muscle Milk, Honest Tea, and vitamin water. However, PepsiCo began a restructuring of its Beverages division to create better integration between its units. PepsiCo's Americas Beverages merged its two largest bottling companies, the Pepsi Bottling Group and Pepsi Americas, to give it control over 80 percent of its bottling network. In the restructuring process, PepsiCo's Americas Beverages now consists of two businesses, the Pepsi Beverages Company, including the original Pepsi brands, and PepsiCo Beverages Americas, which includes the Tropicana, Gatorade, and Latin American brands.

Frito-Lay

Even before the historic merger between Frito-Lay and Pepsi-Cola, Frito-Lay had a successful business history. It started in 1932 with entrepreneurs C.E. Doolin and Herman W. Lay. During that year, C.E. Doolin sampled corn chips in a Texas café and saw an opportunity for the small chip's future. He purchased the corn chip manufacturing company. Doolin then began selling bags of FRITO corn chips from his Model T Ford.

Also in 1932, a man named Herman W. Lay started selling potato chips. He purchased a manufacturing company and called it the H.W. Lay & Company. In 1961, the two companies joined together to form the Frito-Lay Company. Four years later, it merged with Pepsi-Cola to become the PepsiCo Company. Today, Frito-Lay owns over 50 percent of the snack foods industry in America and includes such well-known brands as Lay's Potato Chips, Frito's Corn Chips, Doritos, Cheetos, Grandma's Cookies, SunChips, and Cracker Jack popcorn. The division contributes $13 billion to PepsiCo.

Frito-Lay has many accomplishments to be proud of that go beyond its products. One of its great prides is its Supplier Diversity Program, first launched in 1983. According to the company, since its founding the Supplier Diversity Program spent over $2.1 billion with minority and women-owned entrepreneurs. Additionally, Frito-Lay made strides in sustainability. Among its many initiatives, Frito-Lay converted its sales cars to hybrid vehicles and partnered with Terracycle to encourage employees and consumers to give used bags to its partner, which then turns the bags into tote bags or other products to sell.

As with all big companies, Frito-Lay experienced its share of controversies. In 1967, Frito-Lay introduced a cartoon character named Frito Bandito, a Mexican bandit with a sombrero who stole other people's corn chips by gunpoint. The Mexican-American population launched a series of protests. They felt the cartoon character was a negative and highly offensive stereotype of Mexicans and Mexican-Americans. Due to the wide popularity of the character, Frito-Lay refused to pull Frito-Bandito, prompting the National Mexican-American Anti-Defamation Committee and other groups to file a $670 million lawsuit against the company. Finally, the cartoon character was removed from the scene in the early 1970s. The controversy emphasized the importance of cultural sensitivity and stakeholder analysis when launching any campaign that might alienate company stakeholders.

Gatorade

Gatorade, the official sports drink of the NBA and major league baseball, dates back to 1965. The formula was developed by a group of scientists after a study revealed players at the University of Florida were losing electrolytes and carbohydrates during games. Gatorade (named after the Florida Gators team) was meant as a solution to that problem by containing a balanced amount of electrolytes and carbohydrates to rejuvenate players. Gatorade was a huge success among sports teams, leading to future innovation with products like the Gatorade Nutrition Shake and the Gatorade Bar. In 1983, Quaker Oats Co. acquired Gatorade, which in turn was acquired by PepsiCo in 2001 when PepsiCo bought the Quaker Oats Co. Gatorade has become the third most popular selling drink under PepsiCo (after Pepsi and Mountain Dew).

Despite Gatorade's success, the brand has seen declining sales and added competition for the sports drink market. One of the problems Gatorade faces is the lack of appeal for the younger generation, who see the beverage as something their parents drank. As a result, PepsiCo created the Gatorade campaign and lineup called the "G Series." The G Series has two major purposes in revitalizing the Gatorade brand: demonstrate that Gatorade can be used for more than hydration and nutrient replacement and target a younger demographic. PepsiCo expanded to include three core product lines: G Series, G Series Fit, and G Series Pro. Consequently, the line has different types of Gatorade meant to be used in a three-step process. The first beverage, "Prime," is filled with carbohydrates and is meant to be used before a game. The second, "Perform," is for during the game. The final, "Recover," is protein-rich and is used after the game (the drinks are in different shaped bottles). With this new system of Gatorade drinks, PepsiCo targets every aspect of the athlete's game time. Gatorade also introduced a low calorie option for athletes engaging in "light activity" titled G2, a G2 powder, and G natural that offers a natural alternative through flavoring and ingredients. G natural is sold primarily through natural grocers and Whole Foods stores across the United States.

CRITICISMS

PepsiCo's success has not come without major challenges or ethical dilemmas. One of the biggest difficulties for any multinational organization is how to successfully enter into other countries, particularly when laws vary from country to country. Although PepsiCo places high emphasis upon researching potential markets, the company encountered several problems that caused tensions with different cultures, in both the United States and abroad. Additionally, PepsiCo still faces heavy criticism for products viewed as largely unhealthy and whose packaging contributes to a large amount of waste. PepsiCo faces the same challenge as other major players in the soda industry: the decline of soda consumption in the United States. This problem is exacerbated by regulatory actions such as the proposed New York City ban on certain soda drink sizes as well as the banning of soda sales within schools.

India

PepsiCo first entered the Indian market in 1989, and since then the company became one of the largest food and beverage companies in the country. Unfortunately for the company, some of the largest and longest running allegations of PepsiCo's wrongdoing are also based in India. The company and other competitors in the industry have been heavily criticized about the quality and the quantity of the water used in their beverages. In 2003, the Centre for Science and Environment (CSE) claimed that the water which PepsiCo and other beverage companies in India were using contained toxins. These toxins included pesticides that contribute to cancer and the overall breakdown of the immune system. According to the

CSE, Pepsi soft drinks had 36 times the level of pesticide residues permitted under European Union Regulations. However, no such law bans the presence of pesticides in India.

Although there is not yet a law in place, PepsiCo found it could still face considerable repercussions for what its stakeholders perceive to be unethical activities. When pesticides were once again reported in the soft drinks a few years later, the Indian state of Kerala temporarily banned the sale of Pepsi and Coca-Cola. Five other Indian states also instituted partial bans. These extreme actions on the part of the local governments reveal the care multinational organizations must take to go above and beyond the national law in social responsibility.

Another major concern in India cited by farmers is that the Pepsi manufacturing plants are polluting the land, making them less fertile for growing crops. A study conducted in 1992 found that PepsiCo India and similar companies created 10,000 metric tons of plastic through their manufacturing and importation processes. About 60–70 percent of this plastic was recyclable, creating a large amount of unnecessary plastic waste. Similar allegations of waste and pollution arose again in 2006, concerning both farmers and government officials alike. The farmers complained that the PepsiCo plant takes the groundwater to run its operations, making it, once again, harder to effectively grow crops.

PepsiCo is attempting to repair its reputation in India. In 2009 it announced that it had replenished more water in India than it removed. PepsiCo also partnered with a number of organizations committed to water conservation, including the Safe Water Network, Water.org, and the Nature Conservancy. Additionally, PepsiCo made water a priority; it set forth a goal to improve its water efficiency by 20 percent per unit of production by 2015, using 2006 as a baseline. A thorough stakeholder orientation is needed to discover ethical courses of action and avoid negative repercussions. In solving these ethical dilemmas, PepsiCo must continue to take different levels of government into account, as well as concerns of NGOs and individual Indians.

Health

The nature of the products manufactured and sold by PepsiCo caused problems for the company regarding health. Although PepsiCo now has numerous products geared toward health, its most popular product is still its signature Pepsi-Cola. At the same time, America is becoming more health-conscious and desires low-calorie, low-fat, and natural items instead of processed sugary and salty foods. Some of the health concerns of drinking soda include the increased caloric intake as well as the possibility of tooth decay due to soda's acidity, caffeine dependence, and weaker bones. Pepsi fought back by creating sodas that have low calorie and sugar content. Unfortunately, this only helps with the weight risk. The acidic nature of the product can still damage the teeth, and the artificial sweeteners used have their own set of health risks. However, PepsiCo has one advantage. Because it diversified into so many different product lines, only about one-quarter of its U.S. revenue is derived from sales of its flagship drink, compared to 60 percent of its main rival Coca-Cola.

PepsiCo has also faced battles from the regulatory area. Some states adopted laws banning the sale of soda in schools. In New York City Mayor Martin Bloomberg attempted to institute a ban on large sugary drinks, approved by the Board of Health, to fight against obesity and diabetes. Under the ban, restaurants, sports stadiums, food carts, movie theaters, and other organizations would be banned from selling sugary drinks in cup sizes of more than 16-ounces (the ban would not extend to grocery stores or diet soda). The ban would have included soda, venti Frappucinos, slurpees, sugar-sweetened dairy drinks with less than 50 percent milk, and drinks with less than 70 percent fruit juice. Restaurants that violate the ban could be faced with $200 fines.

PepsiCo and other soda companies fought back. The ban would result in lost revenue on larger soda sizes (fountain drinks are often marked up 10 to 15 percent), and there were fears other cities might follow New York City's lead. The companies passed around petitions, developed ads on social media sites, radio, and airplane banners, and publicly criticized what they see as the mayor's tolerance of certain "junk" food but not others. Interestingly, PepsiCo had many defenders. A poll revealed that 51 percent of New Yorkers disliked the ban, and the American Beverage Association filed a lawsuit against the Board of Health. The National Association for the Advancement of Colored People and the Hispanic Federation claimed the ban will harm smaller minority-owned businesses. Many were upset with the ban because they believe the city was trying to make decisions for them. A judge responded by blocking the ban.

PepsiCo's traditional snack items met with similar criticism from healthcare professionals. Most of the products are processed and contain a high amount of sodium and sugar as well as being highly caloric and fatty. Frito-Lay Company tried to combat the issue by offering Baked Lays, Baked Cheetos, SunChips, and other healthier alternatives. These alternatives are claimed to be healthier all-around. The health issue is going to be an ongoing battle for the company due to the nature of the industry it is in. Continual research and product development to offer healthier products is important for PepsiCo's future profitability.

Although the battle may be a long one, PepsiCo is making strides to address these concerns. For example, the Frito-Lay website has a special area devoted to health that describes the ingredients of Frito-Lay snacks and encourages consumers to practice moderation in snack food consumption. One of the goals of PepsiCo CEO Indra Nooyi is to invest more in healthier food. Nooyi anticipates further investment will yield $30 billion in the future. Interestingly enough, to tackle this issue, PepsiCo hires people that are potential enemies of the organization: health officials. Formerly employed at institutions like the World Health Organization and the Mayo Clinic, these Pepsi employees are researching healthier ingredients to put in PepsiCo snacks. One success thus far is the introduction of a zero-calorie natural sweetener called stevia into new brands. It is clear that not only are healthier snack foods socially responsible, but they are also good business in an increasingly health-conscious marketplace. PepsiCo has also become an official sponsor of the Academy of Nutrition and Dietetics.

In response to continuous customer concern, in early 2013 PepsiCo announced it would remove the controversial additive, brominated vegetable oil (BVO), used in citrus-flavored Gatorade. This comes after an online petition started by a Mississippi teenager brought attention to the chemical. The chemical possesses the ingredient bromine, which is used in some flame retardants. PepsiCo took customer complaints seriously and began formulating an alternative ingredient to replace BVO. The company settled upon sucrose acetate isobutyrate to take the place of BVO, which is aligned with countries outside of the United States, specifically within the European Union and Japan that have banned BVO. Over time Gatorade has aligned its brand with healthy activities such as athletic individuals and sports events and has evolved many "game day" product extensions. The need to keep this product as healthy as possible is essential for PepsiCo, which is ultimately why the company took necessary precautions by changing ingredients.

Interestingly, while PepsiCo's CEO Indra Nooyi is ready and willing to expand into healthier food products and make major changes when required, she has faced criticism in recent years from a major stakeholder: investors. In 2012 return on capital decreased to about 11.1 percent, the lowest in five years. Even new advertisements did not keep PepsiCo from slipping. It is not unusual for a company to suffer financially in the short-term in the midst of major changes. Yet investors are worried PepsiCo may continue to plunge, and some believe the firm should reduce its size by separating the underperforming beverage business from the snack food business (PepsiCo has so far refused).

While such a conflict seems to be more financial in nature, it has a strong ethical component. Ethical leaders must attempt to balance stakeholder interests, including those of society—who have concerns over the growing issue of obesity and diabetes—and investors who care about profitability and the financial viability of the company. In this case, it is easy to put blame on investors, who have more of a short-term perspective on this issue. While Indra Nooyi describes PepsiCo's changes as "the right thing" to do, investors at first appear to be placing profits over the good of society. However, business ethics is rarely straightforward. A business's first role is to be economically viable; without succeeding financially, a business will fail, and not only drain society of precious resources but also lead to job losses. Hence, investors have a right, and even an ethical duty, to be concerned about the financial performance of a company. PepsiCo must carefully manage this ethical conflict to balance the different interests of various stakeholders.

Aquafina Tap Water

The public's attention was on Aquafina bottled water in 2007 when the watchdog group Corporate Accountability International claimed the company used tap water to fill the water bottles being sold. The water was not regular tap water but came from a public water supply before processing. Aquafina was accused of not being transparent in its business practices. It was not publicly known that the company's procedures included a rigorous seven-step process that removes unwanted substances and is then branded as purified drinking water. Additionally, the label on the Aquafina bottle had snow-capped mountains on it, which seemed to suggest that the water was purified spring water. PepsiCo is now required to put the words "Public Water Source" on the label.

This scenario brings up an ethical situation common in today's marketplace. Many corporations use idyllic scenes on their packages that do not reflect reality. A giant agribusiness, for example, might have a picture of a traditional farm on its package. Some consumers find this to be misleading. Additionally, many consumers do not realize that labeling laws are not as strict in the United States as in other countries. For example, U.S. manufacturers do not have to label when a food product contains genetically-modified ingredients. In these cases, it is often the informed consumer or watchdog group that calls for action, as PepsiCo inevitably discovered.

On top of the tap water dilemma, water bottle companies are dealing with criticisms for the amount of plastic these bottles contribute to land-fills. There are movements around the country like the "Think Outside the Bottle" campaign to challenge people to go back to drinking tap water again in order to stop the amount of waste produced by the bottles. However, the increasing popularity of bottled water does not appear to be diminishing anytime soon. PepsiCo is in the process of developing bottles that use less amounts of plastic per bottle to help the waste issue. Today, the Aquafina bottle weighs 10.9 grams, compared with the 18.5 grams in 2001. This is estimated to have saved 30 million tons of plastic from ending up in landfills since 2008.

More recently PepsiCo paid $9 million to settle a lawsuit alleging that claims about its Naked juices were not truthful. More specifically, Pepsi maintained that its Naked juices were all natural. However, according to the lawsuit, Naked juices contain synthetic vitamins developed by Archer Daniels Midland. This would seem to contradict Pepsi's claim that its Naked juices were all natural. On the other hand, because the term "natural" is ambiguous and not clearly defined, it is questionable whether Pepsi did anything misleading or unethical. The lawsuit also alleged that Naked juices contain genetically-modified ingredients, which Pepsi vehemently denies.

SOCIAL RESPONSIBILITY & SUSTAINABILITY

Despite the many criticisms it has encountered throughout its long history, PepsiCo has recognized the importance of social responsibility to its reputation. As such, PepsiCo continually emphasizes its commitment to sustainable growth and its focus on generating healthy financial returns, while giving back to those communities it serves.

PepsiCo's commitment to its community and toward sustainable growth is outlined in something it calls "Performance with Purpose." PepsiCo gives back to its communities and stakeholders while maintaining high standards, establishing and meeting goals, and producing attainable outcomes. CEO Indra Nooyi claims "Performance with Purpose" consists of three parts: products, the environment, and employees. These areas must be addressed for PepsiCo to be a socially responsible company.

Part of PepsiCo's commitment to this goal includes meeting consumer needs for a spectrum of convenient foods and beverages. PepsiCo has been scrutinized for its unhealthy products and criticized for contributing to obesity. Although PepsiCo made many changes to its product line, incorporating healthier options and reducing fat, sugars, and other unhealthy ingredients, it recognizes the consumers' desire for easy and accessible snack foods and beverages. These food products may not be the healthiest option, but they meet the consumers' needs for easy access. The trick for PepsiCo is to balance the need for convenience with the need for healthier food offerings. Acting in the interests of the consumers, PepsiCo engages in research to develop healthier products and reduce unnecessary editions.

Some ways PepsiCo is trying to increase its responsibility to consumers is partnering with organizations to promote nutrition and avoid certain marketing practices. For instance, PepsiCo partnered with the International Food & Beverage Alliance to develop responsible marketing practices for children under the age of 12. PepsiCo made a commitment that by the end of 2013 it would no longer purchase advertising in programs with an audience consisting of more than 35 percent of children.

PepsiCo also demonstrates social responsibility and dedication to sustainability through several social responsibility efforts like the PepsiCo Guiding Principles, sustainability, commitment to employees, the PepsiCo Foundation, and the Dream Machine. These efforts are described in further detail below.

PepsiCo Guiding Principles

In order to maintain its commitment to its communities and assorted stakeholders, PepsiCo has high standards for quality. By adhering to processes and ensuring proper governance, the company tries to uphold its responsibilities and earn the confidence of stakeholders. To measure its progress and make certain it remains focused, PepsiCo developed the following six guiding principles used to sustain its commitment.

TABLE 1 PepsiCo Guiding Principles

We must always strive to:
1. Care for our customers, our consumers and the world we live in.
2. Sell only products we can be proud of.
3. Speak with truth and candor.
4. Balance short term and long term.
5. Win with diversity and inclusion.
6. Respect others and succeed together.

Source: "PepsiCo Values & Philosophy." PepsiCo. http://www.pepsico.com/Company/PepsiCo-Values-and-Philosophy.html (accessed September 4, 2013).

These guiding principles encompass PepsiCo's overall commitment to its community. Like all companies, PepsiCo's success depends on its stakeholders, so PepsiCo strives to understand consumers' needs and wants. In order to meet stakeholder expectations, product quality, integrity, and honesty are essential to PepsiCo's goals. This requires that the company be transparent and foster communication. By having clear goals and focusing on attainable solutions, PepsiCo is able to grow in a relevant direction and analyze both short and long term consequences. Table 1 describes PepsiCo's Guiding Principles.

Sustainability

PepsiCo views its goal of decreasing its environmental impact not only as socially responsible but also in the best interest of its stakeholders. For PepsiCo, a large part of its sustainability efforts involves reducing the negative effects resulting from the production and consumption of its products. This includes "going green" (for example, through water conservation and the reduction of waste products) and reducing its carbon footprint. PepsiCo reduces its impact on the environment through various water, energy, and packaging initiatives. Because PepsiCo develops products using water, and actually sells bottled water, it is actively implementing programs to reduce waste and conserve resources. This involves water recycling and treatment efforts, where recycled water is treated thoroughly and reused within its products. PepsiCo also invests in clean energy sources, such as its wind turbine project in India that supplies more than two-thirds of the power used in one year by its Mamandur beverage plant. In China PepsiCo developed a green plant in Chongqing that is LEED-certified, incorporates 35 water-and-energy saving designs, and has the ability to reduce carbon emissions by 3,100 tons.

Water conservation has become important to PepsiCo. The company partnered with the Nature Conservancy to embark on a study for sustainable water use and water availability. This study helps PepsiCo understand how the company uses water, ways its use impacts the environment, and strategies for decreasing water usage. For example, in its report on water use, the company studied how several of its facilities throughout the world use water in their operations. It then brainstormed on ideas to restore the watershed. PepsiCo identified the fact that its facilities operate under different conditions in different parts of the world, so its water restoration strategies must be adapted to take advantage of each location's unique characteristics.

In addition to reducing the plastic in its Aquafina bottles, PepsiCo launched other environmental initiatives to reduce the harmful byproducts of its business. In 2010 the company conducted a study termed Abacus II that tracked its 2009 packaging footprint throughout the entire company to pinpoint areas of improvement. This was followed in 2011 by a web-based tool PackTrackPlus to track its packaging footprint based on weight, carbon dioxide emissions, and materials. Understanding the environmental impact of these materials allows PepsiCo to identify ways it can make changes to increase its responsibility to its environmental stakeholders.

PepsiCo adopted a 5R system for improving its environmental impact—Reduce, Recycle, use Renewable resources, Remove environmentally sensitive materials, and promote the Reuse of packaging throughout its operations. PepsiCo has reduced its impact by adopting lighter weight bottles for Aquafina, Propel, and Gatorade products and developing new lighter-weight package designs. The company sells its starch, a waste product from potatoes used in snack foods, for use in paper products, food manufacturing, and more. PepsiCo started using more post-consumer recycled materials in its products. In 2009 its Naked juice began using 100 percent post-consumer recycled plastic. The company is investigating ways to use more renewable materials and began to substitute less eco-friendly materials with renewable resources. Finally, PepsiCo is attempting to increase its reuse of materials. For instance, it began to reuse its shipping cartons, which saves approximately 150,000 tons of paperboard each year.[1]

Employee Commitment

Another aspect of PepsiCo's commitment to social responsibility is reflected in its support of and commitment to employees. It is PepsiCo's goal to encourage a diverse corporate culture along with employee engagement in the workplace and community. This is valuable to PepsiCo because the company sees this as an opportunity to benefit from new perspectives and encourage creativity within the workplace. It understands employees are a key to success. According to the company's philosophy, it is important for PepsiCo to maintain mutual respect, integrity, and safety in the workplace. Because it inspires a collaborative culture, PepsiCo aims to recruit and retain world-class talent through employee satisfaction—what PepsiCo terms "Talent Sustainability." For instance, to encourage employees (associates) to speak out, PepsiCo provides them with a biennial Organizational Health Survey to get their opinions on the organization and the workplace. Additionally, PepsiCo values the talents of its employees and offers management courses at its institution Pepsi University to provide employees with the leadership skills necessary to take on managerial roles within the company.

PepsiCo has also developed a Code of Conduct that addresses various business ethics issues such as bribery and conflicts of interest. The company expects workers to be familiar with its Code of Conduct and employs a chief compliance officer to enforce the Code. PepsiCo provides annual ethics training programs for employees. Training sessions are available online or through workshops. PepsiCo's compliance programs are frequently reviewed by independent third parties to pinpoint key risks. More specific aspects of PepsiCo's compliance program, such as its environmental activities, are audited externally. Finally, the company has what it calls an "Internal Audit

[1]PepsiCo, "Performance with a Purpose: Packaging & Waste," http://www.pepsico.com/Purpose/Environmental-Sustainability/Packaging-and-Waste.html (accessed February 18, 2013).

methodology" and maintains a 24-hour anonymous ethics hotline where employees can report concerns or ethical violations.

PepsiCo Foundation

The PepsiCo Foundation was established in 1962 and provides philanthropic contributions to a variety of nonprofits. Some of the ways the Foundation gives back to the community is through grants, employee programs, and disaster response and relief efforts. PepsiCo's focus is to improve the quality of life for those in the greatest need. Its approach consists of awarding grants to those programs and organizations with proven track records and strives to make an impact expanding beyond its own communities. In 2010, the PepsiCo Foundation gave $29.5 million toward philanthropic endeavors.

PepsiCo encourages employees to engage in its communities through its Matching Gifts Program, where the company matches employee contributions to nonprofit organizations considered eligible. By doing so, PepsiCo creates an ethical and philanthropic climate for its workers. PepsiCo supports the United Way Campaign as well as post-secondary education for employees' children through its ExCEL awards. Additionally, the PepsiCo Foundation contributes to disaster relief through financial assistance, product donations, and human resources. The PepsiCo Foundation contributed to disaster relief for the 2011 Japanese earthquake and tsunami with contributions of $1.5 million and for the 2010 Pakistan floods with an initial donation of $250,000. PepsiCo also partners with water.org and the Safe Water Network to improve access to clean, affordable water in communities worldwide and committed $5 million to Save the Children for improving the lives of children in India and Bangladesh.

Dream Machine

On April 22, 2010 (Earth Day) PepsiCo announced its multi-year partnership with Waste Management, Inc., in support of the Dream Machine recycling initiative. The Dream Machine initiative recognizes that many plastic cans and bottles are needlessly thrown away each year, particularly by busy consumers on the go. The two partners want to see the U.S. beverage container recycling rate increase from a mere 34 percent to 50 percent by 2018. This will be encouraged with PepsiCo's Dream Machine kiosks that act like reverse vending machines. The Dream Machine kiosks are computerized receptacles that give consumers points when they recycle their bottles. The process involves only a few steps. First, the consumer registers on the kiosk. Then he or she scans the can or bottle's barcode and puts it in the appropriate chute. The kiosk then issues the user a receipt that contains reward points redeemable for such things as movie tickets, coupons, or other goods.

Consumers redeem these points at www.greenopolis.com. Greenopolis, LLC is working with PepsiCo to bring these recycling systems to consumers in public areas and stores. Consumers also have another incentive to recycle: the more recycling done, the more PepsiCo will help disabled veterans. PepsiCo is extending its partnership with Entrepreneurship Bootcamp for Veterans with Disabilities (EBV) to offer training in business management to disabled veterans. Thanks to its work promoting careers for veterans, PepsiCo was nominated in 2013 as a Top 100 Military Friendly Employer. The kiosks began with fifty installed around Southern California and now has 4,000 kiosks. The Dream Machines are a way to meet the clear need for greater public access to recycling bins as well as to promote PepsiCo's sustainability efforts.

CONCLUSION

PepsiCo is the classic business success story, starting with one man's invention to becoming a multimillion dollar enterprise with operations across the globe. With success comes controversy, which ultimately the company could not avoid. PepsiCo is moving toward a more balanced stakeholder orientation by identifying stakeholders relevant to the firm and trying to understand and respond to their concerns and needs. The current leadership at PepsiCo understands the importance of stakeholders and the need to develop effective dialogues and other communication to help PepsiCo resolve conflicts. Issues such as nutritional concerns over soft drinks and snack foods create a serious dilemma in balancing the concerns of special-interest groups and the desires of consumers for good tasting food.

While some of the company's past challenges were likely inevitable, some were caused by misunderstanding stakeholder needs or ethical lapses on the part of the company. From a lack of cultural sensitivity to health concerns to environmental degradation, PepsiCo faced its share of ethical dilemmas. However, it has also become a major leader in the sustainability and social responsibility movement. Although it has a long way to go before its snacks can be considered healthy or manufacturing processes truly sustainable, PepsiCo has demonstrated a willingness to invest in innovative solutions for these problems. If PepsiCo can continue to learn from its mistakes, it can make progress in solidifying a reputation as a socially responsible company. The future of PepsiCo depends on continuing to develop an ethical corporate culture built on values that help employees relate to the needs and desires of all stakeholders.

QUESTIONS

1. How does PepsiCo balance those stakeholders such as consumers and shareholders interested in good tasting products and financial performance with special-interest groups and regulators that are more concerned about nutrition?
2. How effective do you think PepsiCo has been in responding to stakeholder concerns about nutrition and sustainability?
3. Do you think it is logical for PepsiCo to partner with nutrition and water conservation nonprofit groups since it received heavy criticism for unhealthy products and wasteful water practices?

SOURCES

PepsiCo, *2009 Annual Report*. http://www.pepsico.com/annual09/talent_sustainability.html (accessed February 19, 2013); Associated Press, "PepsiCo to No Longer Call Naked Juices 'Natural'," *The Wall Street Journal*, July 26, 2013, http://online.wsj.com/article/AP89b2fee0375e41b2bcd2ca6c034ea0bb.html (accessed July 29, 2013); Valerie Bauerlein, "Gatorade, Before and After," *The Wall Street Journal*. April 23, 2010. B8; Valerie Bauerlein, "PepsiCo in Recycling Push," *The Wall Street Journal*. April 22, 2010. B5; Manjyot Bhan, "Environmental Management of Multinational Corporations in India: The Case of PepsiCo," *The Sustainability Review*, March 7, 2010, http://www .thesustainabilityreview.org/2010/03/environmental-management-of-multinational-corporations-in-india-the -case-of-pepsico (accessed February 19, 2013); Nanette Byrnes, "Pepsi Brings in the Health Police," *Bloomberg BusinessWeek*, January 14, 2010. http://www.businessweek.com/magazine/content/10_04/b4164050511214.htm

(accessed February 19, 2013); MarketLine, "Coca Cola and Pepsi Face Criticism in India," *Datamonitor*, July 4, 2006. http://www.datamonitor.com/store/News/coca_cola_and_pepsi_face_criticism_in_india?productid=0E1A0AEE -E4C0-4C4F-B0A1-038A24CF21F0 (accessed February 19, 2013); Ranjit Devraj, "Indian Coke, Pepsi Laced with Pesticide, Says NGO," *India Resource Center*, August, 5 2003, http://www.indiaresource.org/news/2003/4725.html (accessed February 19, 2013); Directors & Boards, "'Go There and Get the Business.' (interview with PepsiCo's Chairman of the Executive Committee Donald M. Kendall on business opp)," *Entrepreneur*, Winter 1991, http:// www.entrepreneur.com/tradejournals/article/10422697_1.html (accessed June 2, 2010); Stuart Elliot, "For a New Brand, Pepsi Starts the Buzz Online: [Business/Financial Desk]," *New York Times*, March 14, 2008, Late Edition (East Coast): New York Times, ProQuest (accessed April 18, 2010); Michael M. Grynbaum, "Judge Blocks New York City's Limits on Big Sugary Drinks," *The New York Times*, March 11, 2013, http://www.nytimes.com/2013/03/12/ nyregion/judge-invalidates-bloombergs-soda-ban.html?pagewanted=all&_r=0 (accessed April 16, 2013); PepsiCo, "Frito-Lay Brands," http://www.pepsico.com/Brands/Frito_Lay-Brands.html (accessed February 19, 2013); PepsiCo, "Gatorade Brands," http://www.pepsico.com/Brands/Gatorade-Brands.html (accessed June 8, 2010); Massachusetts Institute of Technology, "Gatorade: Inventor of the Week Archive," Lemelson-MIT Program, May 2004, http://web .mit.edu/invent/iow/cade.html (accessed February 19, 2013); Hercules Kataveli, "Pepsi announces $1B Russian investment," *Business 2.0 Press*, July 6, 2006, http://business2press.com/2009/07/06/pepsi-announces-1b-russian- investment/ (accessed February 19, 2013); Monica Herrera, "How Michael Jackson, Pepsi Made Marketing History," *BrandWeek*, July 6, 2009, http://www.brandweek.com/bw/content_display/news-and-features/packaged-goods/ e3iba9a089c3eafb2f56a0eb4fe6ab08270 (accessed February 19, 2013); The Pepsi Store, "History of the Birthplace," http://www.pepsistore.com/history.asp (accessed February 19, 2013); Andrew Kaplan, "The Power of One," *Beverage World*, April 15, 2010. http://www.pepsico.com/Download/Beverage_World_Cover_Story_0410_(2).pdf (accessed February 19, 2013); Flora Lewis, "FOREIGN AFFAIRS; Soviets Buy American," *The New York Times*, May 10, 1989, http://www.nytimes.com/1989/05/10/opinion/foreign-affairs-soviets-buy-american.html?pagewanted=1 (accessed February 19, 2013); N. Madison, "What Are the Health Effects of Drinking Soda," *WiseGEEK*, March 30, 2010, http://www.wisegeek.com/what-are-the-health-effects-of-drinking-soda.htm (accessed February 19, 2013); Sanjoy Majumder, "Indian State Bans Pepsi and Coke," *BBC News*. August 9, 2006, http://news.bbc.co.uk/2/hi/south _asia/4776623.stm (accessed February 19, 2013); Betsey McKay, "Creative Father of the 'Pepsi Generation' Turned Lifestyle into a Selling Point," *The Wall Street Journal*, August 4, 2007, http://online.wsj.com/article/ SB118618836469587966-_s1Uy71U3ayaBtosa5tnIqx_PeY_20080803.html (accessed February 19, 2013); Betsey Morris, "The Pepsi challenge," *CNNMoney*, February 19, 2008, http://money.cnn.com/2008/02/18/news/ companies/morris_nooyi.fortune/index.htm (accessed February 19, 2013); Chon A. Noriega, "There May Be a Frito Bandito in Your House," *San Diego Latina Film Festival 2005*, http://www.sdlatinofilm.com/trends12.html (accessed June 8, 2010); PepsiCo India Region, "Our Corporate Profile," http://www.pepsiindia.co.in/Company/ ourcorporateprofile.aspx (accessed June 2, 2010); Frito-Lay "Our History," http://www.fritolay.com/about-us/ history.html (accessed February 19, 2013); PepsiCo, "Our History," http://www.pepsico.com/Company/Our- History.html#block_1967 (accessed February 19, 2013); Yahoo Finance!, "PepsiCo and Waste Management Celebrate Earth Day with Announcement of Multi-year Partnership Designed to Improve On-the-Go Recycling," April 21, 2010. http://finance.yahoo.com/news/PepsiCo-and-Waste-Management-prnews-3203466969.html?x=0& .v=1 (accessed June 9, 2010); PepsiCo, "Pepsi-Cola Brands," http://www.pepsico.com/Brands/Pepsi_Cola-Brands. html (accessed February 19, 2013); PepsiCo, "The PepsiCo Family," http://www.pepsico.com/Company/The -Pepsico-Family.html (accessed February 19, 2013); PepsiCo, "PepsiCo Values & Philosophy," http://www.pepsico .com/Company/PepsiCo-Values-and-Philosophy.html (accessed February 19, 2013); *The Pepsi-Cola Story*, 2005, http://pepsi.com/PepsiLegacy_Book.pdf (accessed June 1, 2010); PepsiCo, *Performance with a Purpose*, http://www .pepsico.com/Download/print-pepsico_human_summ.pdf (accessed June 8, 2010); Reuters, "Aquafina Labels to Spell Out Source-Tap Water," *CNN*, 2007. http://www.cnn.com/2007/HEALTH/07/27/pepsico.aquafina.reut/ (accessed February 19, 2013); Jeff Gordon Online, "Sponsors," http://www.gordonline.com/sponsors.html (accessed February 19, 2013); Frito-Lay, "Steps to a Healthier Planet," http://www.fritolay.com/our-planet/all-steps.html (accessed February 19, 2013); Frito-Lay, "Straight Talk on Snacking," http://www.fritolay.com/your-health/

feature-answers.html (accessed February 19, 2013); Frito-Lay, "Supplier Diversity," http://www.fritolay.com/about-us/supplier-diversity.html (accessed February 19, 2013); Suzanne Vranica, "Pepsi Benches Its Drinks—Beverages Will Snap Long Streak by Sitting Out Super Bowl," *The Wall Street Journal*, December 17, 2009. Eastern edition: Wall Street Journal, ProQuest, April 18, 2010; Mike Esterl and Suzanne Vranica, "Pepsi Brings Back the King of Pop," *The Wall Street Journal*, May 4, 2012, http://online.wsj.com/article/SB10001424052702304746604577381792902984470.html (accessed February 13, 2013); PepsiCo, "Tingyi and PepsiCo Open New Beverage Plant in China," http://www.pepsico.com/PressRelease/Tingyi-and-PepsiCo-Open-New-Beverage-Plant-in-China10252012.html (accessed February 13, 2013); "PepsiCo Inc (PEP: New York)," *Businessweek*, February 13, 2013, http://investing.businessweek.com/research/stocks/earnings/earnings.asp?ticker=PEP (accessed February 13, 2013); Duane Stanford, "Gatorade Goes Back to the Lab," *Businessweek*, November 23, 2011, http://www.businessweek.com/magazine/gatorade-goes-back-to-the-lab-11232011.html (accessed February 13, 2013); Mike Esterl, "Is This the End of the Soft Drink Era?" *The Wall Street Journal*, January 19-20, 2013, B4; Geoff Colvin, "Indra Nooyi's Challenge," *Fortune*, June 11, 2012, 148–156; Mike Esterl, "PepsiCo Slips Despite New Ads," *The Wall Street Journal*, April 27, 2012, B5; Rahim Kanani, "Why PepsiCo Is a Global Leader in Water Stewardship and Sustainable Agriculture," *Forbes*, September 14, 2012, http://www.forbes.com/sites/rahimkanani/2012/09/14/why-pepsico-is-a-global-leader-in-water-stewardship-and-sustainable-agriculture/2/ (accessed February 18, 2013); PepsiCo, "Performance with a Purpose: Packaging & Waste," http://www.pepsico.com/Purpose/Environmental-Sustainability/Packaging-and-Waste.html (accessed February 18, 2013); Julie Deardorff, "Critics Pounce on Coke, Pepsi Health Initiatives," *Chicago Tribune*, February 5, 2012, http://articles.chicagotribune.com/2012-02-05/news/ct-met-coke-pepsi-health-20120205_1_coca-cola-north-america-health-groups-healthy-lifestyle-choices (accessed February 18, 2013); Jason Kessler, "Groups: NYC soda ban unfair to small, minority-owned businesses," *CNN*, January 25, 2013, http://www.cnn.com/2013/01/23/health/new-york-large-drinks (accessed February 18, 2013); Anahad O'Connor, "Soda Bans in Schools Have Limited Impact, *The New York Times*, November 7, 2011, http://well.blogs.nytimes.com/2011/11/07/soda-bans-in-schools-have-limited-benefit/ (accessed February 18, 2013); Laura Petrecca, "Coke, Pepsi, others launch assault against NYC beverage ban," *USA Today*, July 18, 2012, http://usatoday30.usatoday.com/money/industries/food/story/2012-07-09/Coke-Pepsi-fight-soda-ban/56279302/1 (accessed February 18, 2013); Jill Colvin, "New York Soda Ban Approved: Board of Health Oks Limiting Sale of Large-Sized, Sugary Drinks," *New York*, September 13, 2012, http://www.huffingtonpost.com/2012/09/13/new-york-approves-soda-ban-big-sugary-drinks_n_1880868.html (accessed February 18, 2013); PepsiCo, *Performance with Purpose: Sustainability Report PepsiCo Greater China*, 2011, www.pepsico.com/Download/GCR_Sustainability_Report_EN_Final.pdf (accessed February 18, 2013); PepsiCo & the Nature Conservancy, *Striving for Positive Water Impact: Lessons from a Partnership Approach in Five Watersheds*, http://www.pepsico.com/Download/Positive_Water_Impact.pdf (accessed February 18, 2013); PepsiCo, "PepsiCo Foundation," http://www.pepsico.com/Purpose/PepsiCo-Foundation.html (accessed February 18, 2013); PepsiCo, *PepsiCo Policy on Responsible Advertising to Children*. http://www.pepsico.com/Download/PepsiCo_Policy_Responsible.pdf (accessed February 18, 2013); PepsiCo, "PepsiCo Dream Machine Recycling Initiative Donates $500, 000 to the Entrepreneurship Bootcamp for Veterans with Disabilities for Third Consecutive Year," November 12, 2012, http://www.pepsico.com/PressRelease/PepsiCo-Dream-Machine-Recycling-Initiative-Donates-500000-to-the-Entrepreneurshi11122012.html (accessed February 18, 2013); PepsiCo, "Performance with Purpose: Responsible Marketing & Advertising," http://www.pepsico.com/Purpose/Human-Sustainability/Responsible-Marketing.html (accessed February 18, 2013); Candice Choi, "Gatorade to Remove Brominated Vegetable Oil After Consumer Complaints," *The Huffington Post*, January 25, 2013, http://www.huffingtonpost.com/2013/01/25/gatorade-brominated-vegetable-oil_n_2551533.html (accessed February 19, 2013).

CASE 16

Ethical Leadership at Cardinal IG: The Foundation of a Culture of Diversity*

BACKGROUND

Cardinal Glass Industries, Inc., is a corporation that specializes in the design and manufacture of high technology insulating and solar glass. It is organized as a privately held S corporation with 70 shareholders, all of whom are employees. From the corporate offices in Eden Prairie, Minnesota, CEO Roger O'Shaughnessy oversees two research facilities and 29 manufacturing subsidiaries in 16 states. Cardinal Glass is the largest company of its kind in the world. Its 5,500 employees serve customers throughout the United States, Canada, Latin America, Europe, Asia, and the Middle East.

In any organization, ethical leadership is paramount to success, and by all accounts Cardinal Glass Industries is a successful corporation. Although the corporation as a whole has been profitable since inception in 1962, one of its manufacturing plants, Cardinal Insulating Glass (Cardinal IG) in Fargo, North Dakota, consistently outperforms all others in production efficiency and financial performance. Its workforce is the most diverse of any Cardinal subsidiary. The company consists of over 50 percent New American employees (many who speak limited English and recently arrived from unfortunate circumstances in their home country).

This case study explores the main factors contributing to the Fargo plant's success through the stories of plant manager, Dave Pinder, his leadership team, and the Cardinal IG employees.

THE CARDINAL IG STORY

It is an amazing story when you think about it. A diverse group of people, who knew very little about making glass, started up an insulating glass manufacturing plant in Fargo, North Dakota. In a very short period of time, they earned all of the business and

*This case was developed by James Legler, Associate Professor, Offutt School of Business, Concordia College, Moorhead, Minnesota, and Mary Leff, Organizational Development Consultant, Sanford Health System, Fargo, North Dakota © 2012. This case was prepared for classroom discussion rather than to illustrate either effective or ineffective handling of an administrative, ethical, or legal decision by management. All sources used for this case were obtained through publicly available material and interviews with Cardinal IG management.

the respect of one of the biggest window companies in the country and established their
insulating glass plant as the very best in the world.

– Cardinal IG Fargo Leadership Handbook

When Dave Pinder, the newly hired plant manager of Cardinal IG, arrived in Fargo, North Dakota, in 1998, the future plant site was nothing but a flat grain field. He had been hired to start the plant from the ground up—build the new factory, hire and train new employees, and develop relationships with his customers. Along with these responsibilities, CEO Roger O'Shaughnessy gave him complete autonomy to establish the corporate vision of "designing and fabricating the most advanced residential glass products in the industry."

The 33-year-old Pinder brought an unlikely background to the position. A graduate of West Point, a commander in Desert Shield and Desert Storm, his last military assignment had been tactical officer in charge of 200 cadets at the United States Military Academy at West Point. While in the service, he completed a master's degree in leader development and counseling from Long Island University. He spent a brief time with International Paper before being approached by O'Shaughnessy to join the Cardinal leadership team.

Getting started was a daunting task, beginning with building the leadership team. Pinder did not hire glass experts. He couldn't find any. Instead he hired people with leadership potential, a positive attitude, and a passion for learning the business and teaching others. In his words,

> We started with a group of 40 people in a 140,000 square foot building. We knew nothing about making glass. Our first employees jumped into a van and traveled to Iowa for training at another Cardinal IG plant to learn how it was done. We asked those first employees to trust us.

Today, Cardinal IG operates out of a state-of-the-art 500,000 square foot facility in Fargo. The plant runs seven days a week, three shifts per day, supplying the majority of insulating glass found in Marvin Windows. Pella and Anderson Windows are also customers of the company. The Fargo plant became a leadership training center for other Cardinal plants, and Pinder's responsibilities expanded to include troubleshooting and leadership coaching at other manufacturing sites. Cardinal's workforce of 183 people is made up of 55 percent New Americans from 15 different countries, astonishing diversity in a region of the country where U.S.-born Caucasians make up 93 percent of the demographic mix.

Cardinal IG operates in a competitive business environment, and the economic recession and downturn in the building industry added volatility to its challenges. In spite of this, leaders have had to make only incremental changes in operations. The Fargo plant continues to be the best performing plant in the Cardinal manufacturing system.

MISSION AND VISION

Before hiring anyone, Pinder had a good idea of what he wanted to create.

> I had a vision for what I wanted the organization and the culture to look like and a plan to get there to maintain the culture. I wanted a world-class facility—the best of its kind on the planet. The culture must enable you to get the vision. I wanted my employees to love to come to work every day because the work was challenging, meaningful and fun; the

plant was clean and well lit; they felt like they had ownership and a say in the business; they were treated with dignity and respect; and they felt like they were part of a disciplined team … I wrote my leadership philosophy before I hired anyone. I use it to guide all that we do.

Cardinal IG's mission melds the business purpose with Pinder's vision of how that purpose will be achieved. The mission is a constant reference point for all Cardinal IG is working to achieve. It is simple and straightforward:

> **To make money, by thrilling our customers with our product and service, and by taking care of our people.**

The mission influences the hiring process, reward system, leadership, team culture, and work processes. Signs posted throughout the immaculately clean manufacturing floor and training rooms reinforce the mission, report team performance, and emphasize excellence. The company is intentional in keeping all three mission objectives (profitability, customers, and employees) paramount and visible.

VALUES, PRINCIPLES, AND BEHAVIOR

As defined in the *Cardinal IG Leadership Handbook*, company values include loyalty, duty, respect, selfless service, honor, integrity, and personal and moral courage. Values are the foundation of culture but remain abstract unless they are lived in day-to-day actions. Pinder's West Point background and beliefs are reflected in these values and made real in the behaviors he models and expects of his employees. The values are further translated into specific expectations in Cardinal's Guiding Principles, statements that serve as a code of conduct for the way employees do their work and treat one another:

- **Safety**
  Nothing we do is more important than safety. It is our #1 priority.
- **Quality**
  We ensure that every product we ship to our customer is flawless.
- **Service**
  We treat our customers like they are the most important people in the world.
- **Training**
  We develop, implement, and maintain a top-notch training program.
- **Leadership/Teamwork/Communication**
  This organization is led as a team to make Fargo IG the flagship of the company.
- **Cost Awareness**
  We will spend money wisely here—as if the money is our own.
- **Respect for Others**
  We treat others with dignity and fairness while encouraging others to do the same.
- **Care for Families**
  We encourage our people to spend time with their families and balance work accordingly.
- **Integrity**
  When in doubt, do the right thing. Trust is an important part of our relationship.

- **Attitude**
  Remember both positive and negative attitudes are contagious—keep a positive attitude.

- **Keep a Sense of Humor and Have Fun**
  We are serious about our business but have fun working, training, and growing together.

LEADERSHIP THROUGH A MULTI-LEVEL TEAM STRUCTURE

Structure is the process of aligning work through tasks, responsibilities, departments, and divisions. Cardinal IG has a hybrid-type structure that includes a traditional hierarchy—using basic centralized administrative functions that include accounting, sales, and marketing. Yet the heart of the company is an integrated team network embedded in this organizational framework. Teams operate both at the top level and within the many manufacturing divisions within the plant, assuring everyone is working toward the same purpose.

The six manufacturing divisions of the company are responsible for specialized components of production, such as glass cutting/tempering, spacer fabrication, insulating glass production, shipping, and receiving. Each division has a supervisor with broad management responsibility. Division supervisors are salaried workers that previously served as team leaders and are selected for their past performance and leadership potential within the organization. These supervisors meet as a team, and are responsible for upper-level decisions and the recognition program.

Within each of the six divisions, there are three teams, each with its own team leader. Team leaders serve at the front of production, managing the day-to-day operations and maintenance of the plant, and also take on a major part of the human resource functions of the employees. Cardinal IG does not have a human resource department, although it does maintain a centralized function for the technical administration of payroll and benefits to assure compliance with laws and regulations and internal consistency. Duties such as hiring, firing, personnel problems, scheduling, and training are done by the team leaders and department supervisors. "We do not send our problems to the HR department for them to solve. Our team leaders are empowered and taught to solve the problems. They are close to the situation," Pinder says.

This cuts down on bureaucracy, keeps decisions close to those that do the work, and creates ownership of results. The plant runs seven days a week with three weekday shifts and a maintenance team that works on weekends when the plant is not in production. Pinder comments that the team leaders are considered the most crucial part of the organization.

Pinder's philosophy of leadership extends beyond management. All Cardinal IG employees are considered leaders, accountable for their individual behavior and performance as team members. Developing the strong work culture at Cardinal IG Fargo starts when a team member is hired. Pinder meets with all new employees and makes sure it is understood that if they choose to work at Cardinal, they must meet four criteria: *First, be willing to work hard. Second, have a good attitude. Third, be a team player. Fourth, be willing to support the mission.*

The leadership training program established at Cardinal IG is extensive, continual, formal, and informal. It includes quarterly leadership training sessions reinforced by the

Cardinal IG Leadership Handbook. Leadership development is a key part to building confident and competent leaders, and ensures a ready bench of people prepared to lead.

Managers at all levels are trained and expected to serve as mentors and coaches for their employees. Division supervisors, team leaders, and Pinder himself are available to employees at all times. That accessibility is a critical component of teamwork, especially for a company that operates around the clock. Pinder and his entire management team continually reinforce and model teamwork, communication, and accessibility. The Employee Handbook states the following:

> My intention is to run this organization as a team. My role on the team will be like that of a coach. I will provide the vision and direction, while you will run the plant. Together, we will make Fargo IG the flagship plant in the corporation—a world-class performer. To do this, we also must communicate with each other. If you have an idea to make things work better, please let me know about it. Know that I am always available for you—anytime day or night. You are my top priority and you are the organization's most valuable resource.

A leader should always train his or her subordinates to be ready to take over their position at anytime, a philosophy Pinder continually stresses in his leadership training. Recently, Pinder was promoted to president of Cardinal Glass Industries to manage nine IG plants (one of which is Cardinal IG Fargo). Mike Arntson, the production manager who has been with the company since it was started in Fargo, was promoted to plant manager. In a recent interview, Arntson was asked if it was difficult to transition into the new position. "It was not difficult at all. I have been trained for this position, and I have been part of developing the philosophy of the company since I started. It was a natural transition." Leadership is intentionally evolving at Cardinal IG.

A CULTURE OF DISCIPLINE AND RESPECT

In the book *Good to Great* (2001), Jim Collins describes companies that outperformed others as having a "culture of discipline." They have not settled on being just "good" but have characteristics that make them "great." They have a freedom (and responsibility) within a defined framework. They have a fanatical adherence to doing what they do best. These organizations as described by Collins are not autocratic, but caring.

Discipline in this sense is about having a consistent, orderly system of rules that govern conduct and activity. It is about making roles, responsibilities, and expectations clear, and fostering self-regulation. This view of a culture of discipline describes Cardinal IG well, and is influenced by the military background of Pinder. However, discipline is only half of the story. Love is the rest. Pinder describes the balance of love and discipline in an article:

> We hold subordinate leaders accountable and responsible—and the big thing is that you must love—truly love—your subordinates. People might think that sounds strange. "Love? What are you saying Love?" But every employee needs to know that their leaders and I love them and truly care about them, their families, and their futures. If you truly believe that I love you, you're not going to call in, show up late, because you don't want to let me down.
> (Bock, *Open Magazine*, Winter 2007)

Pinder models what it means to balance love and discipline. He has a unique ability to remember names, and he knows the names of all his team members, their family members, and the personal interests of all his employees. He is available 24/7 to all his employees. Pinder has an open door policy and addresses problems immediately. He also emphasizes leadership continually through mentoring and formal training. As he walks around the plant, he stops to visit. Handshakes and hugs are characteristic. Through this constant interaction, he keeps a pulse on the organization, and knows what is happening with individual team members. He requires the same of his leadership team.

Stories are characteristics of Pinder's leadership style, and they contribute to Cardinal's strong culture and identity. He loves sports and brings in many interesting stories. Signs on the walls remind team members of their pursuit of excellence in all they do. The following quote from Vince Lombardi is posted in the plant and emphasized by team leaders:

> *Gentlemen, we are going to relentlessly chase perfection, knowing full well we will not catch it, because nothing is perfect. But we are going to relentlessly chase it because in the process we will catch excellence. I am not remotely interested in just being good.*

ETHICAL EXPECTATIONS

Employees are rarely terminated, but certain actions can result in dismissal. The non-negotiable aspects of behavior are clear, and they are backed by consequences. First, if employees are not living up to the four criteria (work hard, good attitude, team player, support the mission), they can be terminated. There are actually very few of those situations because the hiring and mentoring processes are so strong.

At the same time, Pinder has zero tolerance for racist or sexist comments and jokes, stealing, fighting, drugs, or alcohol in the plant. Pinder is a role model, and his actions match his words. If something is not right, he immediately talks to the team leaders and asks them why they handled the situation the way they did. If it was done incorrectly, he stresses the importance of doing it right. Generally, there is no mystery in knowing what should be done. The balance of discipline and respect/caring of the individual team members is discussed often by the management and the team members.

One story Pinder tells has to do with a Cardinal employee who reported a team leader made a racist joke. Another employee reported a similar incident with the same team leader. "It was honorable that these employees spoke up and alerted us to the situation. We called the team leader in and asked him if it was true. He admitted it and was terminated." Racism is unacceptable and dismissal, if it happens, is non-negotiable. All employees know this.

Although Cardinal's non-negotiable elements are clear, the more difficult part of leadership is dealing with consequences in situations where the solution is less defined. Another example that Pinder gives shows mentoring at a crucial moment.

> *Sometimes we just need to remind people of what is important. We had a team leader who I heard complaining about "all these people and how hard it was to work with them" (referring to New Americans). It was a leadership moment, and I asked him if he was just planted here or did his parents or grandparents come to this area from somewhere else? He*

said they had come from Norway, and I asked him if they spoke English when they came, and he replied "no." He realized that he was just being ignorant. After our talk he changed his attitude.

ALIGNED INCENTIVES, REWARDS, AND RECOGNITION

There are positive consequences for meeting or exceeding performance expectations, too. All employees are part of Cardinal's profit-sharing plan. Cardinal IG pays their employees well but, in addition, they can receive anywhere up to 52 percent additional each month if they meet the target profit goal. The profit-sharing plan is aligned with the culture of performance and teamwork and serves another purpose as well—recruitment. Cardinal IG in general does not advertise or recruit outside of the company for new employees. According to Pinder, "…we have very low turnover. People leave mainly to return to school or to their family. When we want to hire someone new we ask our employees to recommend someone, and the candidates are brothers, sisters, husbands, wives, cousins, and friends. Nobody recommends anyone who would not work hard and contribute to the team."

An important part of the Cardinal IG culture is the award program for recognizing exceptional team members and exceptional teams. Since January 2000, the company has given 140 Employee of the Month awards. The New Americans received 80 of those awards, or 57 percent. Employee of the Month awardees are eligible to compete for the Employee of the Year Award. The Employee of the Year Award is presented at the company's annual employee banquet held at the Ramada Plaza & Suites in Fargo with all employees and spouses present. In the past 11 years, nine of the Employee of the Year awards have been received by New Americans.

SYNERGY THROUGH DIVERSITY

Pinder believes the success of "the Big Story" of Cardinal IG is largely a result of the numerous individual stories of the New Americans who found their way to Cardinal IG. While others viewed this segment of the population as too difficult to communicate with and work with, Pinder applied his trademark formula of discipline and love and built an enormous strength for Cardinal IG.

> *I believe—and many believe—that we've got the best workforce out of 29 factories in 16 states here in Fargo. Why is that? The only thing I can come up with is that we're different. We didn't grow up together and go to school together, go to church together—we don't know everything about each other so we're not all thinking alike. We're from 15 different countries, different cultures, different ways of doing things, and we bring different stuff to the table. And that, synergistic effect, I believe, has enabled us to get to a level that others have not gotten to.* (Bock, Open Magazine, Winter 2007, p 38)

Pinder is often asked if language is a barrier as many of the New Americans come from poor and disrupted countries. He comments, "Heck, no. If someone comes to Cardinal and does not speak English, we put that individual with someone who does (they pair them with someone from their home country). Before long they are speaking English and getting along well. Many of the New Americans speak several languages, including their home country language and English."

The countries represented at Cardinal IG during the past few years include Albania, Algeria, Bosnia, Burundi, Central African Republic, Congo, Eritrea, Ethiopia, Haiti, Iraq, Iran, Kenya, Liberia, Macedonia, Nigeria, Romania, Russia, Rwanda, Somalia, Sudan, Thailand, Togo, Tunisia, Uganda, Vietnam, and the United States. Lutheran Social Services of North Dakota is the primary organization for bringing refugees into the area. It contracts with the U.S. government in relocating and supporting new refugees. Most of these New Americans came to the United States through a long journey consisting of war, violence, poverty, and persecution.

In a recent article for the Lutheran Social Services publication, *The Messenger*, Meg Luther Lindholm describes the New Americans at Cardinal IG. "The stories that people were telling me were so interesting and so strong. A lot of the people that I have met and interviewed for this project could have films made about their lives. They are dramatic. They have been through that kind of experience where they have just had to use their wits to survive from day-to-day. And they have lost so much." Some examples include the following:

> A young Cardinal IG worker from Somalia is a full-time student with a wife and children. He was orphaned at the age of 14 when thugs broke into his family's home. His father didn't have anything for them to steal because they had been robbed earlier in the week. This enraged the thugs, and they killed both of his parents. He fled and eventually made it to the United States and Fargo. Despite all the possible reasons for feeling down and sorry for himself, he has a very positive outlook.
>
> A husband and wife from Sudan fled their homes with only the clothes on their backs when northern Sudanese army troops came into their town and started killing villagers and looting homes. They were separated from their son who had to stay with his grandmother until being reunited with his parents several years later. The husband is now employed at Cardinal IG, and the son is a student at North Dakota State University.
>
> One of Cardinal IG's team leaders is from northwest Bosnia. In 1991, when he was 20 years old, civil war broke out. Serbs put him into slave labor for several years. He was caught in the fighting, was shot in the back, and spent 2½ months in a hospital. He was able to escape by crossing over to Croatia and lived in a refugee camp for several years. He later came to the United States and found his way to Fargo through the refugee program.

Pinder's leadership style breaks through communication and cultural barriers through the universal language of love, respect, and authenticity. By knowing his employees, their families, and their stories, he honors their dignity and makes it a powerful force in the culture and success of "the Big Story."

CONCLUSION

How effective is the Cardinal IG plant in Fargo? It excels at being a great company, not just a good company. From the research collected, success is evident in several areas. It accomplishes its mission well. The financial performance of the company as the top performer within the organization of 29 different plants is evidence of this along with the overall success of the corporation—Cardinal Glass Industries Inc., It is an exceptional plant in taking care of its employees. This is evident in their high retention rate, profit-sharing plan, recognition of excellence, exceptional team members, immaculately clean plant, and the shared values of a diverse workforce.

As we examine the company from a holistic and systems perspective, it is evident many of the elements of the organization are interrelated. They fit together to achieve a shared goal—a great example of an organization "designed" to accomplish its purpose. The elements that make this happen are the strength of its leadership, specific goals and objectives, a team-based structure, strong values and culture, and intentional and disciplined procedures throughout the organization. Cardinal's success cannot be attributed to any one factor but rather the alignment of all its parts in support of its mission.

The Cardinal IG plant also exemplifies ethical leadership. Under Pinder's direction, Cardinal employees are encouraged to pursue the company vision and participate in the firm's ethical corporate culture. The firm developed solid principles that are non-negotiable, such as respect for employees. The firm lives and breathes its values. For instance, 50 percent of the plant's employees are New Americans, demonstrating the firm's strong commitment toward its value of diversity. Additionally, all employees are treated with respect and dignity, reiterating the fact the company values their contributions. Cardinal's strong ethical leadership enables the company to thrive while providing it with the opportunity to become a positive force in its community.

QUESTIONS

1. How has David Pinder embraced ethical leadership to create an ethical culture at Cardinal IG?
2. How has Cardinal's principles and values shaped the ethical behavior of employees?
3. How has Cardinal empowered its employees to practice responsible and accountable leadership?

SOURCES

The above case study was based on information from the Cardinal IG website, www.cardinalcorp.com, retrieved on April 16, 2011; interviews with Dave Pinder, plant manager of Cardinal IG Fargo, on March 10, 2011, and April 7, 2011; interview with Mike Arntson, Cardinal IG Fargo, on April 11, 2012; a presentation by Dave Pinder at the Center for Ethical Leadership, Concordia College, Moorhead, Minnesota, on November 1, 2002; an article from Open Magazine, Issue 3, Winter 2007, by Jodee Bock, titled "From Westpoint to Fargo: A Leaders Journey," Fargo, ND; an article in the Lutheran Social Services publication The Messenger, Winter 2005, titled "Finding common ground"; interviews with Yasmeen Frost and Darci Asche, Lutheran Social Services, New American employment, on May 2, 2011; the book mentioned in the above case was by Jim Collins, "Good To Great: Why Some Companies Make the Leap … and Others Don't" (2001), New York: Harper Collins; the management model used as the framework for the article was by Cavalari and Obloj, "Management Systems" (1993), Belmont, CA: Wadsworth.

CASE 17

Better Business Bureau: Protecting Consumers and Dealing with Organizational Ethics Challenges*

The National Advertising Division was created to ensure the credibility and truthfulness of advertising claims. It is a part of the Better Business Bureau (BBB), one of the best known self-regulatory trade associations in the United States. Self-regulation expresses a commitment on a company's part to adhere to certain rules that demonstrate best practices and social responsibility. Although their standards do not have the force of law, companies that engage in self-regulation agree to go beyond what is legally required. Trade associations such as the Better Business Bureau create self-regulatory programs for their members. The BBB uses its website, newspapers, and the media to inform consumers of businesses who violate these standards. They may also receive low ratings in BBB reliability reports, and accredited members can be expelled from the association. The BBB consists of hundreds of local chapters across the United States and Canada that operate independently but work together through the umbrella organization called the Council of Better Business Bureaus (CBBB).

Because the CBBB recognizes the importance of advertising's influence on consumers, it has established the National Advertising Review Council (NARC) in 1971 in conjunction with the Association of National Advertisers (ANA) and other advertising associations. The NARC establishes policies and procedures for the investigatory arm of the Council, the National Advertising Division (NAD).

The NAD is an important form of self-regulation in developing a transparent marketplace between businesses and consumers. The division has helped many consumers avoid falling prey to advertising scams, and it provides important information on the ethical practices of an organization. Those companies failing to resolve consumer complaints often have their ratings downgraded, a practice that alerts consumers to exert caution in dealing with them. Conversely, accredited members of the BBB or non-accredited members with high ratings are generally perceived to be more honest. Businesses that wish to become members of the BBB agree to comply with eight ethical principles to promote trust in the marketplace. Accredited members must pay a fee to be a member.

The NAD and the BBB are not without their share of critics. Although they claim to rate both members and nonmembers objectively, some argue that the fee structure could

---

*This case was prepared by Danielle Jolley and Jennifer Sawayda for and under the direction of O. C. Ferrell and Linda Ferrell. We appreciate the help of Tayna Freier, Amber Pacheco, and Aubree Roybal on a previous edition of this case. This case was prepared for classroom discussion rather than to illustrate either effective or ineffective handling of an administrative, ethical, or legal decision by management. All sources used for this case were obtained through publicly available material.

taint the perceived objectivity of their ratings. Misconduct committed by certain chapters cast a cloud over the BBB's reputation. BBB chapters collect information and report on businesses within their district, and each chapter must maintain objectivity standards. These standards provide the BBB with its credibility as a trustworthy resource. However, it is difficult for the large organization to monitor every branch for appropriate conduct. Allegations arose that the BBB and the NAD sometimes engaged in questionable conduct. A pay-for-play scheme in one of the BBB's chapters damaged the reputation of this self-regulatory organization. Some also questioned the objectivity and effectiveness of the NAD as well.

This case provides a brief background on the BBB. As we demonstrate, the BBB is not complete without discussing the importance of advertising to the organization that eventually led to the creation of the NAD. We then consider how the BBB became such a noteworthy organization. We examine major cases of business and advertising conflicts the BBB and NAD resolved. We then analyze some ethical challenges the BBB and NAD have faced in their history, particularly in the past few years. We conclude with a description of the actions the BBB and NAD are taking to address these ethical challenges.

HISTORY

The NAD is such a large part of the BBB because the organization owes its existence to self-regulation in the advertising industry. In the nineteenth and the early twentieth centuries, false or exaggerated advertising was the norm. In one particular trial on false advertising involving Coca-Cola, Samuel C. Dobbs, Coca-Cola's sales manager, was moved to the breaking point when the company's lawyer remarked, "Why, all advertising is exaggerated. Nobody really believes it." Dobbs set out to create standards for the advertising industry to ensure the truthfulness of advertising claims and later became president of the Associated Advertising Clubs of America in 1909.

John Irving Romer took Dobbs' idea further, suggesting that Vigilance Committees be set up across the country to monitor the advertising industry and eliminate abuses. These precursors to the BBB culminated in the creation of a National Vigilance Committee in 1912, which is the officially recognized birth date of the BBB. In 1921 the name was changed to the National Better Business Bureau of the Associated Advertising Clubs of the World. Eventually, after several name changes, it was shortened to the Better Business Bureau.

In 1912 the Vigilance Committees first began investigating cases of advertising and selling abuses and helping those involved come to satisfactory resolutions. The committees also worked with the pharmaceutical industry to tackle the industry-wide practice of false advertising. As a result of their efforts, the American Pharmaceutical Association adopted voluntary standards for the industry. Early issues the BBB addressed included deceptive advertising, bait advertising, overcharges for automobile collision insurance, and protection for servicemen against fraudsters. Many of these standards first set forth by the BBB were later adopted by the Federal Trade Commission.

As consumers began to grow in power and importance, the BBB began advising businesses to adopt ethical practices. Over the years the BBB has been praised by a number of presidents for promoting trust and transparency in the marketplace as well as protecting consumers from fraud. The BBB has become a well-known name among consumers.

Research shows that consumers recognize the BBB name over that of the Federal Trade Commission, and one Internet survey revealed that 90 percent of respondents would report a deceptive advertisement to the BBB.

In 1971, the NAD was created as the investigatory arm of the NARC. The NARC establishes policies and procedures for the NAD. The NAD provides services to companies that run national advertising campaigns. These services typically involve advertisement review services usually handled within 60 days, completed by professional counsel, and are low-cost when compared to the cost of legal proceedings. As such, the NAD relies on advertisers' support of the NAD and their willingness to voluntarily abide by its decisions, which helps ensure honesty and openness in advertising. When companies decide to use the NAD's services rather than taking an issue into the court system, they save money that potentially would have been spent on litigation. As such many advertisers voluntarily follow the NAD's rulings.

The NAD's secondary purpose is to aid the Federal Trade Commission (FTC). If the NAD did not investigate the accuracy of advertisements, this responsibility would fall solely upon the FTC. Therefore, the NAD saves resources and time for the FTC so it can focus on more significant issues. As part of its responsibilities, the NAD investigates nationally run advertisements. These ads include a wide variety of media types such as broadcast or cable television, radio, magazines, newspapers, the Internet, and commercial online services. Types of ads investigated include product performance claims, superiority claims against competitive products, and various scientific and technical claims. These claims are either proven or disproven through scientific tests, studies, or alternative forms of investigation such as evidence provided by the advertising company.

The NAD does not investigate locally (state or citywide) run ads. When the NAD finds inaccuracies in an advertisement's claims, it reports the issue to the local BBB office in the area that the ad was run. In addition, the organization does not investigate complaints that address concerns about the good taste of ads, moral questions about products, political, or issue advertising. The mission of the NAD is "to review national advertising for truthfulness and accuracy and foster public confidence in the credibility of advertising." It investigates cases of deceptive ads and inaccurate claims that are reported, while simultaneously completing investigations and screenings of advertisements that make claims without expressly being requested to do so.

STRUCTURE OF THE BBB

Currently there are 113 BBBs independently governed by their own boards of directors. Each local BBB must meet international BBB requirements that the CBBB monitors and enforces. The CBBB is governed by leaders of local BBBs, senior executives from major American corporations, and community leaders. The majority of BBB funding comes from corporate partnerships or membership fees. The National Council of Better Business Bureaus receives franchise fees and funding from corporate partners and sponsors. As a nonprofit organization, the BBB must seek funding from fundraisers, service offerings, and outside sources such as memberships. Although memberships and corporate sponsorships are necessary for the successful operation of the BBB, questions arose whether the BBB (and the NAD) can be truly objective when it depends so heavily upon accreditation fees.

BBB reliability reports are accessed by consumers millions of times each year. Consumers can view these reports online or request paper copies. The BBB website also offers fraud protection along with charity accountability and effectiveness education. Other services include consumer and business education; advertising review services; a BBB Military Line to support military families with questions regarding finances, insurance, and additional topics; a resource library; and recent articles on a wealth of information. The organization has a self-regulation program to enhance consumer confidence in electronic retailing.

The BBB is not limited to businesses; it can be used by nonprofit organizations as well. The BBB Wise Giving Alliance is meant to help donors make informed decisions about charities. Instead of providing reliability reports, the BBB Wise Giving Alliance provides Wise Giving Reports that evaluate organizations on the basis of 20 standards it feels must be met for charity accountability. Some of these standards include proper oversight by charity board members and financial statements that break down how the charity handles expenses.

The BBB provides a BBBOnLine seal for approved businesses to place on their websites. The seal indicates to users that the website belongs to a BBB-accredited business. Internet users on e-commerce sites can feel reassured that the company is approved by the BBB when making purchases online. Businesses who post the BBBOnLine seal on their websites commit to respecting the privacy of users on their site and working with customers and the BBB to resolve disputes.

Through these different outlets, the BBB warns consumers about questionable businesses as well as fraud. Often the different branches post information to alert consumers to be aware of certain scams. For example, local bureaus often publish a list of the top 10 scams to guard against. College students and the elderly are of particular concern to the BBB as they tend to be more likely to fall prey to fraudsters. The organization posts up-to-date news on scams targeting these two demographics to alert vulnerable consumers to current scams.

The mission of the BBB is "to be the leader in advancing marketplace trust" by creating a community of trustworthy businesses, setting standards for marketplace trust, encouraging and supporting best practices, celebrating marketplace roles, and denouncing substandard marketplace behavior. To become an accredited organization under the BBB, members must abide by the BBB Standards of Trust. These standards encompass both organizational performance and integrity. The BBB Standards for Trust are to build trust, advertise honestly, tell the truth, be transparent, honor promises, be responsive, safeguard privacy, and embody integrity.

BBB ACCREDITATION AND RATINGS SYSTEMS

BBB accreditation does not mean the BBB supports or endorses a business's products. In fact, the BBB prides itself on its objectivity toward both accredited and non-accredited businesses. Accreditation means a business promises to commit to the BBB's Code of Business Practices, which incorporates the Standards of Trust, as well as making an effort to resolve customer disputes and complaints.

The process to become accredited starts with applying to the local BBB branch. The BBB reviews the business's practices, and if it decides these meet the organization's high standards, the business can receive accreditation. To become fully accredited, a business must become a member and pay a membership fee to cover accreditation expenses. Accredited businesses can display the BBB logo on their websites and literature.

The BBB rates businesses based on criteria including the number of complaints filed against a business, the severity of the complaints and whether the company takes adequate steps to address the issues, as well as the experience the BBB has had with the organization. Prior to 2009 the BBB used a Satisfactory/Unsatisfactory rating system. Those businesses with few complaints, or which had complaints that were promptly and adequately resolved, tended to be rated as Satisfactory. Those that had many complaints and failed to follow up with consumers might be given an unsatisfactory rating.

After June 1, 2009, the BBB revised its rating system to reflect the different types of businesses in the marketplace. The BBB developed a formula of seventeen different metrics used to arrive at a business' rating. This new system was devised to encourage businesses to improve in any way possible. The ranking system includes A+ to A− (excellent ratings signaling the highest in reliability), B+ to B− (good business rankings for companies that manage their complaints satisfactorily), C+ to C− (average rankings indicating satisfactory customer transactions), D+ to D− (cautionary rankings), and F (reliability is seriously questioned). Other companies remained unranked for certain reasons. Going from a B to an A signifies major improvement overall. The reliability reports expand upon these lettered grades by explaining why a business received the assigned rating.

BBB CASES AND INVESTIGATIONS

While many complaints to the BBB relate to advertising, the BBB is also concerned with making certain companies operate in a fair and equitable manner. For instance, in 2013 a local fitness franchise, Planet Fitness, located in Albuquerque, New Mexico was investigated by the BBB for claims from over 60 customers complaining that the fitness center drafted payments out of their accounts after cancelling memberships. The franchise is known for its low-cost, no contract business model, which appeals to many consumers. The BBB previously gave the local franchise a D−rating. The president of the local BBB addressed the situation and stated that the company placed "hidden" contracts for service and annual fees within documents customers sign upon joining the gym. The local franchise owner combatted accusations, stating consumers inaccurately canceled memberships by not completing all necessary steps. He stated that customers were not reading the fine print of the initial membership papers signed when members join the gym. The franchise owner offered to refund some customers half of the amount previously drafted out of their account. Based on BBB files the company had a previous pattern of complaints and failed to address complaints to correct issues. Thus, investigations by the BBB are important in helping customers make an informed decision about doing business with a certain firm.

In 2012 the BBB of St. Louis found that Griffin Roofing and Construction failed to complete jobs after being contracted after storms. Customers who hired the company found the business appeared to fix damages from hail storms; however, according to allegations, a week later homeowners found the roof in worse shape than it was before the repairs. The BBB investigated the business after receiving numerous complaints and found the company was tied to a Texas-based firm that committed fraud. The BBB suspended Griffin Roofing and Constructions accreditation and told consumers to be aware of potential scams.

NAD CASES AND INVESTIGATIONS

More recently, the NAD ruled on cases involving the new realm of social media advertising. One of the following cases deals with this type of technology-driven advertising. The first two cases are issues reported to the NAD by competitors, and the last was a claim the NAD took upon itself to ensure was accurate. The need for constant examination is important to maintain transparency and ensure accurate communications between businesses and customers. While some NAD investigations result in recommendations to change an advertisement, others are deemed to be truthful and transparent. While not all advertising is necessarily false, some claims could confuse consumers about the message. The NAD is therefore an important organization for consumer protection. After these investigations are complete, companies are given guidance on how to alter inaccurate ads, or they are given approval if all aspects are concise.

Comcast vs. Verizon

The battle between competitors Comcast and Verizon became so intense it required third parties such as the NAD to become involved. Verizon challenged a claim Comcast made stating that its Xfinity Internet service is "the fastest in the nation." Comcast based its decision on a 2011 PC *Magazine* study. However, Comcast did not disclose it actually tied with two other cable companies. In fact, while Comcast was deemed to have the fastest download speeds, it did not have the fastest upload speeds. In addition, in areas where both Comcast Xfinity and Verizon's FiOS were available, the Federal Communications Commission (FCC) determined FiOS was faster. The NAD determined that Comcast's claims were misleading and recommended Comcast modify its advertising.

Months later Comcast filed a complaint against Verizon, challenging Verizon's claims regarding its FiOS. While the NAD did not find issues with Verizon's claims that its FiOS had the fastest Internet speeds, since this was supported by the FCC report, it did believe the way Verizon phrased its claims implied FiOS was significantly faster than cable. The NAD found these implications disparaging and recommended that Verizon modify certain parts of its claims. Both Comcast and Verizon agreed to consider the NAD's recommendations in future advertising.

Pinterest

The NAD recently found itself facing a social media complaint involving the social sharing site Pinterest. The NAD addressed reports about certain pins on Pinterest that advertised for different companies. The division specifically investigated a campaign run by the weight-loss company Nutrisystem. The Nutrisystem campaign touted weight loss of "real customers," posting photos and captions of the results on Pinterest. Some of these customers reportedly lost over 100 pounds each. The NAD ruled that these photos and captions were testimonials. As such, the division stated Nutrisystem needed to make complete disclosure of this information available as well as include disclaimers stating the results in the ads were exceptional cases. This was important to protect consumers from being misled into believing such results were the norm.

Tiffany & Co.

Tiffany & Co. was the subject of an NAD investigation for a claim made by the company that it created a "new alloy metal" called Rubedo. After investigation from the NAD, the claim was supported because the alloy contained gold, silver, copper, zinc, germanium, and silicon. The claim was determined to be a "new" alloy. The division also found there was no danger in confusing consumers with the term "new alloy" because it did not imply Tiffany & Co. created a new element on the periodic table. The NAD was previously uncertain about whether consumers would confuse the "new metal" claim with a new periodic element.

BBB FACES ETHICAL CHALLENGES

One controversy surrounding the BBB has to do with its rating system. Wolfgang Puck is nationally recognized as a great chef with a solid reputation. Ritz-Carlton Hotels are renowned for their superior customer service. Yet some of Puck's restaurants and the Boston branch of the Ritz-Carlton both received "F" ratings from the BBB in the past. Many consumers were left puzzled as to why such prestigious figures and companies known for their service received such poor grades. The answer, according to some (including Puck), was employees of the BBB awarded higher grades to businesses that paid to be accredited BBB members, while punishing those who did not pay with lower ratings (both Puck and the Ritz-Carlton do not pay dues to the BBB). This accusation led critics, including Connecticut Attorney General Richard Blumenthal, to allege the BBB is operating a "pay-for-play" scheme. Pay-for-play is a type of fraud wherein organizations and individuals pay for favorable treatment at the expense of other entities. In the case of the BBB, which claims to award objective ratings despite accreditation, this entails giving favorable "A" ratings to those who pay membership dues while discriminating against those who do not.

Defenders of the BBB claimed some of Puck's restaurants were downgraded because they never addressed customer complaints. Failure to address complaints within a designated time period can downgrade a business's ratings. The reliability report on the Wolfgang Puck restaurant in Beverly Hills gave the restaurant an F grade, signifying the restaurant had not addressed all of its customer complaints or its response was inadequate. Ratings for this restaurant have since been suspended while the BBB investigates potential misconduct in the Los Angeles branch. The Wolfgang Puck Café in Orange, California, however, received an A− ranking, since the BBB received no complaints.

An investigation into the rating system suggested misconduct. Most of the problems occurred within the Los Angeles chapter, the largest branch in the BBB. Business owners within the Los Angeles branch reported the BBB gave their businesses low grades, despite the fact that the number of complaints against their business was low and/or complaints were resolved. They also reported they were told by BBB agents that in order to get a higher grade, they had to become members. Those that chose to do so saw their grades changed the next day. A subsequent investigation by *ABC News* indicated at least some of these claims were true. It was later discovered certain groups subsequently revealed to be businesses masquerading as fictional organizations received high grades from the BBB. One fictional group was dubbed Hamas. The group was registered at a fictional address with the Los Angeles BBB president William Mitchell listed as the leader of the group. After paying accreditation fees of $425, Hamas received an A− rating. In another case, a blogger created a fictional racist skinhead website entitled Stormfront, with the president listed as Aryn Whiting. After paying $425, the website was awarded an A+ rating.

Criticism continued to grow after it was revealed William Mitchell received a salary of $400,000 per year, which many believed was too high for someone in a nonprofit organization. Mitchell was the person who devised the grading system for southern California that replaced the old "satisfactory/unsatisfactory" rating system in 2009. After the BBB was sued, Mitchell admitted the Los Angeles branch employed more than 30 sales representatives to sell memberships to business owners. Those selling memberships to first-year members earned a 45 percent commission. Mitchell resigned following the *ABC News* investigation.

The BBB has also been criticized for being too friendly with businesses. In the past the BBB received fees for performing activities of which consumers were not aware. For instance, in 2005 Cingular paid the BBB $50,000 for information on customer complaints and concerns regarding the company. When consumers came to the BBB with complaints about their cell phone carriers, the BBB requested additional information on their complaint forms. The organization then sold this information to cell phone carriers. The BBB claims this information was being used by cell phone carriers to improve the weak spots in their businesses. When this fact became public, however, many consumers were upset, believing the BBB had not provided adequate disclosure about how their information was being used.

The BBB also launches partnerships with certain businesses that prove profitable for both parties. In 2008 the organization worked with eBay to publish three books; eBay later won the BBB President's Award for "sustained superior performance." The BBB claimed the award had nothing to do with the book deals. Other non-accredited businesses claim the BBB does not work as hard as an intermediary between customers and businesses that refused to pay accreditation dues.

CHALLENGES FOR THE NAD

The NAD is a vehicle for providing a self-regulatory mechanism. Advertisers' willingness to support NAD and voluntarily adhere to its decisions helps to ensure an honest and open playing field in advertising. However, there are also many challenges the NAD faces when promoting truthfulness and accuracy in national advertising campaigns. A few major challenges the NAD faces is voluntary self-regulation among companies, its lack of authority, and the cost associated with doing business with the NAD.

As a non-government agency, the NAD is restricted in the actions it can take. The NAD does not have the authority to issue subpoenas, hold hearings, or levy damages. The NAD cannot pull unsubstantiated advertising and therefore must rely on other governing agencies to enforce their decisions. Failure for a company to comply with a decision from the NAD is referred to the FTC. However, referrals to the FTC do not necessarily guarantee the company will be forced to comply with the NAD's recommendations. The FTC independently examines each case and makes its own decisions. Hence, a company in violation of the NAD's recommendations might not be penalized.

Even though the FTC followed through with some of the NAD decisions presented to it, there has not been a significant number of cases published to support the idea that non-compliance with the NAD results in discipline from the FTC. The FTC publicized five out of 21 cases referred to it involving companies refusing to follow NAD recommendations. Some believe this lack of publicity suggests the FTC recognizes the negative repercussions a disagreement could have on the NAD's credibility, thereby exposing the challenge of the NAD's inability to force firms to modify their advertising claims.

The NAD's lack of authority makes the voluntary self-regulation from companies a challenging issue. The Advertising Self-Regulatory Council (ASRC) was created in order to help companies self-regulate and avoid unnecessary investigations by creating policies and procedures when developing advertisements. The idea is to get all companies to self-regulate their advertisements voluntarily, before the NAD has to step in and provide guidance for an organization. However, there will always be companies unwilling to voluntarily self-regulate. This is why the imminent need for guidelines and procedures are present, to enable competitors to report on these companies. Because the NAD cannot force companies to self-regulate, the NAD sometimes must report unresolved issues to the FTC if it deems a deceptive advertisement could create consumer harm.

Much like issues with the BBB as a whole, there are issues revolving around the cost of doing business with the NAD. First of all, there are costs associated with filing a complaint, and those costs vary depending upon whether the reporting business is a CBBB Corporate Partner. A partner must pay a $5,000 filing fee. A non-partner can pay as much as $20,000 for filing a complaint. The high price is a form of control to keep trivial challenges at bay. Many businesses believe the costs are still less than taking the issue to court. Although it used to be common to get a resolution on an advertising dispute within 60 days, it has been taking longer for complaints to get reviewed. However, the amount of time it takes to settle a major dispute with the NAD is still often less than what it might take in litigation.

CONCLUSION

The BBB implemented changes in an attempt to reestablish its credibility. The BBB recently expelled the Southland branch of the BBB serving the Los Angeles area for its participation in the pay-to-play fraud. It also changed its point system to eliminate the extra points awarded for accreditation, streamlined its processes for receiving complaints, implemented additional procedures for investigating complaints, agreed to review its processes for accrediting businesses, and instituted a procedure requiring an independent third party to help in the review process. While the NAD was not specifically involved in the BBB pay-to-play scandal, its affiliation with the BBB as well as the challenges it faces in regulating advertising has increased the need for the division to ensure the integrity of its objective processes when monitoring advertisements. It is important for the BBB as a whole to consider its own ethics and compliance program to equip bureau leaders to identify misconduct. Furthermore, the Council of Better Business Bureaus could step up the monitoring and auditing of chapters. With so many bureaus, it is unlikely misconduct will be eliminated completely, yet through effective changes, the BBB could greatly reduce its risk of ethical disasters.

QUESTIONS

1. Which is the National Advertising Division's most important stakeholder, businesses or consumers?
2. Do you believe the BBB can be truly impartial given its financial dependence on businesses?
3. What actions would you take to ensure an ethical misconduct disaster such as the pay-for-play scheme does not happen again?

SOURCES

20/20, "Better Business Bureau 20/20 Investigation," *YouTube*, November 13, 2010, http://www.youtube.com/watch?v=Yo8kfV9kONw (accessed May 25, 2013); Katy Bachman, "Comcast Must Back Off Internet Speed Claims," *Adweek*, June 12, 2012, http://www.adweek.com/news/advertising-branding/comcast-must-back-internet-speed-claims-141070 (accessed May 25, 2013); Katy Bachman, "Verizon Advised to Slow Internet Speed Claims," *Adweek*, September 11, 2012, http://www.adweek.com/news/advertising-branding/verizon-advised-slow-internet-speed-claims-143631 (accessed May 25, 2013); Better Business Bureau, "About BBB Accreditation," http://louisville.bbb.org/Business-Accreditation/ (accessed May 25, 2013); Better Business Bureau, "About BBB Wise Giving Alliance," http://www.bbb.org/us/Wise-Giving/ (accessed May 25, 2013); Better Business Bureau, "BBB Accredited Business Seal for the Web," http://www.bbb.org/us/bbb-online-business/ (accessed May 25, 2013); Better Business Bureau, "BBB FAQs and Information," http://www.bbb.org/us/bbb-faqs/ (accessed March 25, 2013); Better Business Bureau, "BBB History and Traditions," http://boston.bbb.org/history-and-traditions/ (accessed May 25, 2013); Better Business Bureau, "BBB Standards for Trust," http://www.bbb.org/us/bbb-standards-for-trust/ (April 16, 2011); Better Business Bureau, "BBB: Maryland Heights-Based Griffin Roofing and Construction Tied to Texas 'Storm Chaser' Godfather Construction," October 26, 2012, http://stlouis.bbb.org/article/bbb-maryland-heights-based-griffin-roofing-and-construction-tied-to-texas-storm-chaser-godfather-construction-37677 (accessed May 25, 2013); Better Business Bureau, *BBB's National Advertising Division*, http://www.bbb.org/us/national-advertising-division/ (accessed April 2013); Better Business Bureau, "Council of Better Business Bureaus," http://www.bbb.org/us/cbbb/ (accessed May 25, 2013); Better Business Bureau, "International Torch Awards Event 2008," http://www.bbb.org/us/torchevent/ (accessed May 25, 2013); Better Business Bureau, "New BBB Ratings System," http://chicago.bbb.org/ratings-info (accessed May 25, 2013); Better Business Bureau, "Rating Explanation," http://www.la.bbb.org/RatingExplanation.aspx?CompanyID=100038852 (accessed May 12, 2011); Better Business Bureau, "Responding to BBB Complaints," http://tucson.bbb.org/SitePage.aspx?site=72&id=2018ff9c-38b7-4c00-a2c5-68342723b0c8 (accessed May 25, 2013); Better Business Bureau, "Standards for Charity Accountability," http://www.bbb.org/us/Charity-Standards/ (accessed May 12, 2011); Better Business Bureau, "Vision, Mission and Values," http://www.bbb.org/us/mission-and-values/ (accessed May 25, 2013); Better Business Bureau, "Wolfgang Puck," http://www.la.bbb.org/Business-Report/Wolfgang-Puck-100048262 (accessed May 12, 2011); Council of Better Business Bureaus, "NAD Finds Tiffany's Claims for Metal Alloy 'Rubedo' Supported," *ASRC*, August 16, 2012, http://www.asrcreviews.org/2012/08/nad-finds-tiffanys-claims-for-metal-alloy-rubedo-supported/ (accessed May 25, 2013); Steve Cox, "A Message from the President of CBBB," BBB Information Center, November 18, 2010, http://www.bbb.org/bbbinformationcenter/ (accessed March 26, 2011); Council of Better Business Bureaus, "Supporting Advertising Industry Self-Regulation," *ASRC*, 2012, http://www.asrcreviews.org/supporting-advertising-industry-self-regulation/ (accessed May 25, 2013); How Stuff Works, "How Better Business Bureaus Work," http://money.howstuffworks.com/better-business-bureau.htm/ (accessed May 25, 2013); Humane Society of the United States, "National Advertising Division of the Better Business Bureau Examines Foie Gras Advertising," January 26, 2009, http://www.humanesociety.org/

news/news/2009/01/better_business_bureau_foie_gras_012609.html (accessed May 25, 2013); D. McPherson, "NAD: Testimonials on Pinterest Need Disclaimers," *Response*, 2012, 10; Neil Parmar, "Is the BBB Too Cozy with the Firms It Monitors?" *Smart Money*, September 24, 2008, http://www.smartmoney.com/investing/economy/Investigating-the-Better-Business-Bureau-23879/?page=all (accessed May 25, 2013); C. Lee Peeler, "Four Decades Later, Ad Industry's Self-Regulation Remains the Gold Standard Yet the Program Does Not Enjoy Broad-Based Financial Support," *Advertising Age*, March 13, 2013, http://adage.com/article/guest-columnists/40-years-adland-s-regulation-remains-gold-standard/240245/ (accessed May 25, 2013); Joseph Rhee, "Better Business Bureau President Apologizes for 'Errors' in Grading System," ABC News, November 16, 2010, http://abcnews.go.com/Blotter/business-bureau-president-apologizes-errors-grading-system/story?id=12153392&page=1 (accessed May 25, 2013); Joseph Rhee, "Controversial Head of L.A. Better Business Bureau Chapter Quits Job," *ABC News*, December 22, 2010, http://abcnews.go.com/Blotter/la-business-bureau-chapter-head-bill-mitchell-quits/story?id=12458713 (accessed May 25, 2013); Joseph Rhee and Brian Ross, "Terror Group Gets 'A' Rating from Better Business Bureau?" *ABC News*, November 12, 2010, http://abcnews.go.com/Blotter/business-bureau-best-ratings-money-buy/story?id=12123843#.UXVBuMp9Dew (accessed May 25, 2013); Chris Ramirez, "4 on Your Side Investigates Planet Fitness," *KOB.com*, February 25, 2013, http://www.kob.com/article/stories/s2943751.shtml (accessed May 25, 2013); Brad Tuttle, "Why the Better Business Bureau Should Give Itself a Bad Grade," *Time*, March 19, 2013, http://business.time.com/2013/03/19/why-the-better-business-bureau-should-give-itself-a-bad-grade/ (accessed May 25, 2013); Claudia M. Vetesi, "Looking for Fast, Reliable, Low-Cost Resolution of Advertising Disputes? Consider Using the National Advertising Division," *Bloomberg Law*, 2013, http://about.bloomberglaw.com/practitioner-contributions/looking-for-fast-reliable-low-cost-resolution-of-advertising-disputes-consider-using-the-national-advertising-division/ (accessed April 18, 2013); John E. VillaFranco and Katherine E. Riley, "So You Want to Self-Regulate? The National Advertising Division as Standard Bearer," *Antitrust* 27(2), 2013, 79–84.

CASE 18

Managing the Risks of Global Bribery in Business*

Bribery is one of the most pervasive forms of corruption in global business. In the United States, the United Kingdom, and many other countries, bribery in business is illegal, particularly when it involves the bribing of foreign officials. Unfortunately, bribery plagues even the most well-respected organizations. Corporations past and present have witnessed or participated in this illegal practice. Multinational organizations face the added challenge of having to monitor their subsidiaries in various countries, some that expect bribes in order to perform business functions. IBM, for instance, paid fines of $10 million to settle claims it paid officials in China and Korea with gifts and other bribes to secure contracts. With fines often reaching into the millions, it is essential for companies to have systems in place to prevent this form of misconduct.

Bribery is defined as the offering of payments or other incentives to gain illicit advantages. In business bribery can be used to influence an organization or individual to provide preferential treatment. Although bribery occurs on a widespread level, it interrupts the competitive process between organizations. Many cultures, including the United States and the United Kingdom, consider bribery to be an unfair way of conducting business. For years corporations have adopted anti-bribery and anti-corruption policies in their organizations. However, these efforts mean little if they are not enforced.

Bribery varies depending on the culture. In some cultures, bribery is a common way of doing business. Many cultures, including the United States, allow companies to provide hospitality or small gifts to those with whom they wish to do business. In fact, in Japan it is often considered rude not to bring a gift. One challenge for many companies is how to determine what constitutes a gift or an act of hospitality and what can be construed as a bribe. Giving a potential client a mug with the company logo on it is likely to be seen as a form of hospitality because it is so small in value it will not likely influence the client's business decision. An all-expenses paid trip to the Bahamas is another question entirely. However, other items are not as easily defined. For instance, is a bottle of wine a gift, or a bribe? What if the wine cost $20? How about if it cost $175? The distinction between gifts and bribes can be a gray area. It is the firm's responsibility to be aware of bribery laws within each country they operate and conduct business accordingly.

Even if the business has operations in a country where bribery is acceptable, laws such as the U.S. Foreign Corrupt Practices Act and the United Kingdom Bribery Act prohibit companies with operations in those countries from bribing foreign officials

*This case was prepared by Danielle Jolley, Julian Mathias, Michelle King, and Jennifer Sawayda for and under the direction of O. C. Ferrell and Linda Ferrell. It was prepared for classroom discussion rather than to illustrate either effective or ineffective handling of an administrative, ethical, or legal decision by management. All sources used for this case were obtained through publicly available material.

anywhere. Another important measure for combating international bribery is the OECD Anti-Bribery Convention, meant to criminalize international bribery of foreign public officials. All 34 member OECD nations are subject to this convention, although some countries are more proactive in enforcing this convention than others. Even countries where bribery is commonplace have passed bribery laws and are prosecuting individuals or companies for acts of bribery. For example, China passed an amendment to its Criminal Law specifying minimum thresholds over which the bribing of foreign government officials can be prosecuted. Companies that offer bribes to foreign officials over $31,640 (RMB 200,000) can be prosecuted under Chinese law. Brazil is contemplating passing its own foreign bribery law.

On the other hand, simply knowing relevant laws on bribery is only one step toward combating this practice. Unfortunately, the distinction between a gift and a bribe continues to remain ambiguous, and even the most wide-sweeping anti-bribery laws are not always clear on this issue. To eliminate this uncertainty for employees, generally accepted practices regarding bribery should be located in the company's code of conduct as well as communicated to all employees. By implementing a code of conduct with clear expectations on bribery versus gifts and entertainment, a company can set a proper example that bribery is not tolerated.

This case analysis examines two of the major laws that impact the use of bribery on a global scale: the Federal Corrupt Practices Act of the United States and the Bribery Act of the United Kingdom. While there are many other global bribery laws, these laws are the most well-recognized anti-bribery laws in the world. We begin by examining the background of these two laws and then discuss the rules and regulations of both. The case explains why these laws were enacted and who is subject to the standards. The analysis provides examples of bribery, along with the consequences. Finally, we offer an overview of how bribery negatively impacts national institutions, including political, social, and economic institutions.

BACKGROUND OF THE UNITED STATES FOREIGN CORRUPT PRACTICES ACT

The development of the Foreign Corrupt Practices Act (FCPA) occurred after a number of scandals shook the nation. The Watergate scandal brought corruption under greater scrutiny. After Watergate, the U.S. Securities and Exchange Commission began investigating more than 400 U.S. companies, including long-term bribery at Lockheed Martin, and discovered many had made questionable and illegal payments to foreign officials in excess of $300 million. Their findings proved the necessity for regulation, which resulted in the creation of the FCPA.

The Foreign Corrupt Practices Act of 1977 made it illegal for individuals or entities to make payments to foreign government officials to assist in securing or retaining business. The FCPA allows for small payments to expedite routine transactions, known as facilitation payments, however. While there is no set amount for facilitation payments, gifts under $100 are generally deemed to be acceptable. These facilitation payments are meant to speed up routine transactions and convince public officials to perform their functions. They are in no way intended to convince government officials to provide preferential treatment to a firm.

Any company with operations in the United States is subject to the FCPA. However, as mentioned earlier, distinguishing between gifts and bribes can be difficult. Under the FCPA, a bribe can be anything of significant value, including money, gifts, travel, or various types of entertainment. Forms of bribery vary from company to company; one organization may view anything less than $100 as acceptable, while another company may see anything more than $10 as a bribe. To avoid discrepancies it is necessary for companies to include their standards on gifts and entertainment in their codes of conduct.

The FCPA always applied to companies listed on the U.S. Stock Exchange. In 1998 the law began applying to foreign companies as well. The FCPA was designed to encourage proper business transactions conducted by companies and individuals. Ultimately, Congress enacted the FCPA to bring a halt to the bribery of foreign officials and attempt to build and restore public confidence in the integrity of the American business system.

With the development of the FCPA, the implications and consequences for bribes changed. Punishment for violating the FCPA varies from case to case. However, penalties generally include up to five years in prison and fines of up to $250,000 for individuals. For business entities, fines can reach $2 million. Also, executives of the company who know about the bribery but do not report it could face prison time.

Bribing government officials comes in many forms. In 2013 Parker Drilling Company was found guilty of authorizing improper payments to entertain Nigerian officials involved in resolving the company's customs disputes. In 2012 Eli Lilly was charged with issuing improper payments to foreign government officials in order to conduct business in Poland, China, Russia, and Brazil. The German-based company Allianz SE was fined $12.3 million to settle charges for making improper payments to public officials in Indonesia. Additionally, in 2012 the Securities and Exchange Commission found Tyco International guilty of arranging improper payments to foreign officials in more than 12 countries. While most of these incidents involve gifts or money, other incidents of bribery under the FCPA include improper travel, money to the public official's favorite charity, and even providing excessive tax breaks. The greatest consideration of whether a gift constitutes a bribe is whether it seeks to sway the public official's opinion to favor the bribing company and whether the bribe was willful and intentional. Intent is essential in establishing liability.

UNITED KINGDOM BRIBERY ACT

The first law dealing with bribery in the United Kingdom was passed in 1889. The law, called the Public Bodies Corrupt Practices Act, illegalized the bribery of any official working under the capacity of a public body. The act was followed by the Prevention of Corruption Acts in 1906 and 1916. However, as the United Kingdom became more globalized, the acts were regarded as unsuitable for complying with international anti-corruption agreements. Pressure increased to reform these laws. In 2008 a working party for the Organisation for Economic Co-operation and Development (OECD) insisted on new regulation. In 2009 a bribery bill was introduced in the Queen's speech. In 2010 the act received royal assent and became the Bribery Act of 2010. It took effect in 2011. While many herald the Bribery Act as taking a strong stance against bribery and corruption, others believe the law may be too harsh. Fears of whether items traditionally seen as gifts could now be perceived as bribes have increased among different companies, prompting many to update their anti-corruption policies and codes of conduct.

The Bribery Act includes provisions against all forms of bribery. The act states the two general offenses include covering the offering, promising, or giving of a bribe to any government official, or the acceptance and request for a bribe by any government official. The Bribery Act places liability on organizations for not detecting bribery in their organizations and failing to adopt adequate procedures to detect bribes. This is known as the strict liability offense. The Bribery Act extends to companies within the United Kingdom operating abroad and for companies present in the United Kingdom. In other words, any company with operations in the United Kingdom is subject to this law. While penalties for violations vary, violating the Bribery Act can carry a maximum of 10 years in prison, unlimited fines, and the possibility of the confiscation of property. While the FCPA and the Bribery Act are similar in many ways, there are significant differences between the two. The Bribery Act is generally believed to be more encompassing than the FCPA. While the FCPA allows for facilitation payments, recognizing it might be hard for businesses to get routine transactions done in a timely manner without them, the Bribery Act initially left no room for these payments. However, after facing pressure from mid- and small-sized businesses, the U.K. government agreed to review and potentially lessen the restrictions against facilitation payments. Because of the new law, global organizations such as Hewlett-Packard began updating their codes of conduct to provide additional guidance on bribery.

Additionally, while the FCPA is concerned with bribing foreign or government officials, the Bribery Act makes it illegal to pay bribes to private and public officials or enterprises. This means a person who offers a bribe could be liable under the Bribery Act even if the bribe was not to a foreign official. Another difference is liability. Under the FCPA a company has strict liability for bribery as it relates to accounting provisions for public companies. However, the Bribery Act applies strict liability to commercial firms that do not appear to have "adequate controls" for preventing bribery.

Some companies worry the Bribery Act will make it too hard to conduct business. The strict liability offense made firms particularly worried they could be held liable for bribery even if the majority of the company was not aware bribery was taking place. However, like the FCPA penalties under the Bribery Act might be reduced if the company is found to have adequate controls against corruption and a proactive corporate culture supporting ethical conduct. The company must report the bribery to the proper authorities the moment the bribery is discovered. While neither law states a firm will *not* be prosecuted because it reported bribery, officials can examine the firm to see if it adopted a proactive approach toward combating bribery. How a prosecution impacts the public's interest is also considered when deciding on potential penalties for bribery violations. Finally, while there are no clear rules distinguishing gifts given as an act of hospitality from bribes, the Serious Fraud Office in the United Kingdom states it will not pursue reasonable gifts of hospitality.

PENALTIES UNDER THE FCPA AND THE U.K. BRIBERY ACT

The following section provides examples of companies or individuals found to be in violation of bribery laws. Table 1 provides a brief summary of additional companies fined under the FCPA. While many firms have been fined under the FCPA, the relative newness of the Bribery Act means that as yet there have been few prosecutions. However, the prosecutions that have occurred demonstrate the Serious Fraud Office in the U.K. takes the topic of bribery seriously.

TABLE 1 Companies Accused of Violating the FCPA

Firm	Accusation
Monsanto	Bribed an environmental official in Indonesia
Avon	Bribed foreign officials in Asia
Johnson & Johnson	Bribed doctors in Europe and offered kickbacks in Iraq
IBM	Bribed officials in South Korea with cash and gifts
Walmart	Bribed Mexican officials to win zoning permits

© Cengage Learning 2015

Pfizer

It is important for companies to carefully monitor their own practices and also those of their subsidiaries. In August 2012, the SEC charged Pfizer Inc. with violating the FCPA when its subsidiaries allegedly bribed doctors and other health care professionals employed by foreign governments to win business. The SEC charges state that employees from Pfizer's subsidiaries in countries including Russia, China, the Czech Republic, and Italy made improper payments to foreign public officials in exchange for regulatory approvals and increased sales. Pfizer was charged with efforts to cover up these bribes through illegal accounting measures by recording these transactions as promotional activities, marketing, and other deceptive entries.

Ultimately, Pfizer was charged with two criminal counts, conspiracy to violate the FCPA, and a violation of the FCPA's anti-bribery provisions. However, the prosecutors agreed to defer prosecution and drop the charges if, after two years, Pfizer continued to take steps to correct and prevent such actions from reoccurring. Such remedial actions include proactively enforcing an anti-corruption program and appointing a senior executive to serve as chief compliance and risk officer. Furthermore, Pfizer must appoint compliance heads for each of its business units as well as develop an executive compliance committee. To settle the case, Pfizer and two subsidiaries agreed to pay $60.2 million. Ultimately, while Pfizer maintains top leadership was unaware of the bribery, the action taken against the company shows they are still responsible.

Siemens: FCPA's Global Reach

In many cases the FCPA resulted in significant penalties for foreign companies. An example of this is the company Siemens Aktiengesellschaft, a German company and global multinational in electronics and electrical engineering. Because Siemens's American Depositary Receipts (ADRs) are traded on the New York Stock Exchange, the company is subject to the FCPA even though it is a foreign firm.

The U.S. Department of Justice alleged Siemens engaged in a global pattern of bribery and made thousands of payments to foreign government officials totaling more than $1.4 billion. The investigation suggested these practices were covered up and supported by inadequate internal controls. Several senior executives were involved in or had knowledge about the bribery. By the time of the ruling these dishonest practices had a strong negative impact on their corporate culture since many employees at different levels of the firm appeared to have knowledge of the bribery.

In 2008 Siemens pleaded guilty to violating both the Anti-Bribery and Company Records and Internal Control Provisions of the FCPA. Siemens agreed to pay a fine of more than $800 million for violating the FCPA, as well as a fine in Munich, Germany for the board's failure to assume its proper supervisory responsibilities in the case. At the time of the judgment, this was an unprecedented case because of the geographic reach and scale of the bribery. Siemens is an example of the global reach of the FCPA. Currently there are several hundred non-U.S. companies with shares traded on the U.S. stock exchange subject to the FCPA.

Bribery is such a routine component of business transactions in some parts of the world that it is often overlooked as a practice capable of causing far-reaching damage. In reality, bribery has the potential to inflict social adversity on a variety of stakeholders. Transparent business transactions deter this deceitful behavior while encouraging fair and ethical market competition. The risks of global bribery are prevalent to everyone in the marketplace where it is used.

Ralph Lauren: Value of Cooperation with the FCPA

While corporations may take steps to avoid corruption and bribery, in a multinational and multi-cultural business environment, corrupt practices can still occur. As a result, the response of those corporations have significant financial and reputational repercussions. This can best be seen in the case of Ralph Lauren Corporation, a designer and marketer of apparel, accessories, home furnishings and fragrances. During an effort to improve its worldwide internal controls and compliance efforts in 2010, Ralph Lauren discovered its Argentine subsidiary paid bribes to government officials to improperly secure the importation of their products in Argentina. These bribes totaled $593,000 paid out over four years. Within two weeks of uncovering the illegal actions, Ralph Lauren reported these findings to the SEC and proved cooperative with the subsequent bribery probe.

In 2013 the SEC entered into a non-prosecution agreement (NPA) with Ralph Lauren, the first NPA the SEC entered into for violations of the FCPA. The SEC stated it did not charge Ralph Lauren with violating the FCPA because of the company's prompt response, thoroughness of its investigation, and cooperation with authorities. Ralph Lauren agreed to pay more than $700,000 in illicit profits and interest earned from the bribes that the subsidiary paid out over the four-year period. However, this amount is minimal in comparison to both the financial, labor, and reputational costs Ralph Lauren would have received if it was prosecuted for bribery.

Ralph Lauren is an exemplary case that will likely be used as a standard for the SEC in hopes that companies will use it as a role model when discovering FCPA violations. George S. Canellos, Acting Director of the SEC's Division of Enforcement, remarked that the SEC wants to send a clear message that responding appropriately to such misconduct when discovered proves beneficial to the company. Furthermore, the Ralph Lauren NPA demonstrates what the SEC views as corporate cooperation with the SEC. While violations of the FCPA may occur despite a corporation's best efforts, Ralph Lauren is an example of the benefits of prompt action and cooperation in light of any such discovery.

Prosecutions under the U.K. Bribery Act

Due to the recent passage of the U.K. Bribery Act in 2010, there have been few instances of prosecution. The first to be prosecuted under the Bribery Act was Clerk Munir Yakub Patel. Patel was convicted of accepting a bribe of £500 ($774) in exchange for not inputting details of a traffic summons into a court database. He was sentenced to four years in prison. The second conviction levied under the Bribery Act was for Mawia Mushtaq, who offered licensing officials £300 ($459) in exchange for passing him on a taxi driver test. A more recent conviction involves a student accused of attempting to bribe his tutor to change his dissertation grade. The student was sentenced to 12 months in prison.

These initial convictions do not pertain to foreign officials, which differs significantly from the intent of the FCPA. While the United States government might prosecute individuals found guilty of bribing non-foreign officials under fraud charges, such bribery would not be considered a violation of the FCPA. These early prosecutions under the Bribery Act emphasize the British government's commitment to combatting bribery in every sphere of life.

While the first three convictions of the Bribery Act dealt with individuals, companies face increased pressure to carefully monitor the ethics and compliance of their operations. Rolls-Royce encountered a situation involving bribery that placed it under the scrutiny of the U.K.'s Serious Fraud Office. Rolls-Royce was investigated for allegedly paying $20 million to the son of the former president of Indonesia, as well as potential bribery in China and other countries. However, because the alleged bribery occurred before July 2011, when the Bribery Act took effect, it cannot be prosecuted under the act. On the other hand, the firm could still be found culpable of bribery, and a civil settlement is a possibility.

Despite the risks of penalties for bribery, an Ernst & Young survey revealed that only about half of British firms adequately check their suppliers to ensure compliance with the Bribery Act. As the actions of the Serious Fraud Office and the penalties under the Bribery Act attest, this ethical failure can result in significant costs to the firm.

NATIONAL INSTITUTIONS AND THE IMPACT OF BRIBERY

To truly understand the impact of bribery on a country's society and economy, the influence of institutions and their tolerance of bribery must be examined. Organizations operate based on taken-for-granted institutional norms and rules. Institutions include political, social, and economic conventions. For example, in the political area, governments develop legislation to regulate business activities, including bribery. In Mexico bribery is not considered as major a concern as in the United States. While the U.S. Department of Justice views the FCPA as its top priority, in Mexico the authorities were unconcerned when Walmart allegedly paid government officials substantial payments to speed up zoning and licensing agreements. Social institutions also provide conventions of acceptable behavior, and in Mexico it is not unusual for individuals to pay bribes to law enforcement officers for traffic violations. Economic systems have embedded conventions as well. Often bribery is more typical in communist countries such as China and is seen as an acceptable way of doing business. Nations with weaker institutions tend to have more incidences of bribery, which indicates corruption in the social, political, and economic sectors. Countries with high-level corruption rates, such as Somalia and North Korea, therefore face political, social, and environmental costs.

The prominent political and social costs of bribery include the people's lack of trust in government. When politicians are corrupt, citizens have no incentive to follow rules and instead engage in the same type of corrupt behavior modeled in the political system. Transparency International reports that citizens who view their leaders as corrupt are more likely to act accordingly. Table 2 provides a list of the countries most likely to use bribery to

TABLE 2 Ten Countries Most Likely to Use Bribery in Business

1. Russia	6. Argentina
2. China	7. Saudi Arabia
3. Mexico	8. Turkey
4. Indonesia	9. India
5. United Arab Emirates	10. Taiwan

Source: Associated Press, "The 10 Countries Most Likely to Use Bribery in Business," *Huffington Post,* November 2, 2011, http://www.huffingtonpost.com/2011/11/02/bribery-business-countries-most-likely_n_1071452.html#slide=449030 (accessed November 30, 2012).

conduct business. Civil unrest that can result from corruption carries the risk of inflicting extreme violence and harm. Thus, the political implications of bribery include a cognitive distancing and lack of trust in government as well as a culture permeating corruption. Governments with a high amount of corruption are likely to be run by despots with little incentive to protect or acknowledge universal human rights.

The economic costs of corruption can be seen throughout the world. Greece ranks 94 in the world for corruption, according to Transparency International. It suffered from economic crises during and after the worldwide financial crisis. Somalia, ranked as the most corrupt country in the world by Transparency International, is associated with piracy. Mexico, rated at 105, also received negative press when Walmex (Wal-Mart de Mexico) paid bribes to government officials in order to accelerate store expansions. It is important to realize the economic costs of bribery fall disproportionately on the bottom half of the population living in poverty. A country perceived as lacking ethical integrity experiences reduced tourism and less regard from the rest of the world. There is an obvious relationship between the level of corruption in a country and its socioeconomic standing.

Countries with high levels of bribery and corruption are also more likely to have greater environmental incidents. In other words, bribes constitute an ethical lapse that overshadows environmental interests. People engaging in bribery are looking to increase wealth and/or gain a competitive advantage in the marketplace. These are the same people that are unlikely to spend extra resources to protect the environment. Furthermore, places with high levels of corruption often have dictatorial and hierarchical types of government where there is little balance of power in government and few consequences for ignoring environmental initiatives. Beyond the natural environment, bribery also hurts businesses and the individuals they deal with. When companies are disadvantaged by unfair competition from bribery, wealth distribution becomes more polarized in the marketplace and companies may be forced to lay off workers. The World Bank's conservative estimate of the annual worldwide cost of bribery is $1 trillion.

Combatting bribery and corruption indicates the need to implement and enforce stiff anti-bribery regulations. Government, industry, and society must take a strong normative stand against the practice of bribery. Complacency toward bribery eventually leads to diffusion of responsibility, where the practice becomes prevalent and acceptable. Instilling descriptive values against bribery is only successful if a normative stance against the practice is followed. A world without bribery would mean a more competitive and ethical marketplace for companies and individuals.

Widespread corruption abroad proves to impose enormous costs on American business and causes damage to business as a whole. It undermines the integrity and effectiveness of governments, while simultaneously creating hardships for small and medium sized enterprises seeking to participate in the global economy. A culture of corruption raises the costs of penetrating foreign markets and undermines predictability and business confidence.

Overall, with the advent of the FCPA and Bribery Act, implications for bribery became more strict and costly. However, there will always be some who attempt to find ways around the law. To support organizational compliance, top government officials must have strong market oversight by championing ethics training programs, enacting effective compliance and reporting mechanisms, and providing competitive structures benefiting entities acting ethically. Unfair advantages in the marketplace that result from bribery inflict harm on a wide range of stakeholders. Reducing bribery strengthens political, economic, and social institutions, perpetuates a higher quality of life, and ensures a sustainable future.

CONCLUSION

It should be obvious that bribery is a major ethical concern throughout the world. While many developed countries such as the United States and the United Kingdom have developed laws to prevent bribery, in many other countries bribery is a part of the culture. This is because basic political, economic, and social institutions provide conventions for what is acceptable. If bribery is seen as an acceptable way to conduct business, then it will be more prevalent within a society. Bribery is considered to be unacceptable because it interferes with fairness in business relationships. It is also seen as stifling free competition and possibly resulting in inflated prices for consumers. Additionally, bribery creates conflicts of interest when an employee takes a bribe to gain a favorable position.

The companies given as examples in this case demonstrate that even highly respected businesses have difficulty fighting against bribery. This is because pressure is placed on many businesses to make payments in order to gain access to markets. An important takeaway is that many areas of bribery are gray areas because minor gifts or entertainment, while generally acceptable, can be questioned by stakeholders.

QUESTIONS

1. What are the differences between the provisions of the United States Foreign Corrupt Practices Act and the United Kingdom Bribery Act?
2. Check for more recent situations where companies have been accused of violating the Foreign Corrupt Practices Act. Why do you think these companies chose to engage in bribery?
3. Why is it so difficult to determine when a minor gift, entertainment, or incentive constitutes a bribe?

SOURCES

David Aaronberg and Nichola Higgins (2010), "The Bribery Act 2010: all bark and no bite..?" *Archbold Review*, No. 5 (London: Sweet & Maxwell, 2010), ISSN 1756–7432; BBC News, "African corruption 'on the wane'." (July 10, 2007, http://news.bbc.co.uk/2/hi/business/6288400.stm (accessed May 13, 2013); Jeffrey Benzing, "Pfizer and Subsidiaries Settle FCPA Charges for $60.2 Million," *Main Justice*, August 7, 2012, August, http://www.mainjustice.com/

justanticorruption/2012/08/07/pfizer-and-subsidiaries-settle-fcpa-charges-for-60-2-million/ (accessed May 13, 2013); Caroline Binham and Carola Hoyos, "SFO weighs deal to end Rolls-Royce probe," *Financial Times*, March 22, 2013, http://www.ft.com/intl/cms/s/0/ff136074-931e-11e2-b3be-00144feabdco.html#axzz2SddrQtHr (accessed May 7, 2013); Caroline Binham and Elizabeth Rigby, "Relaxation of UK bribery law on government agenda," *Financial Times*, May 28, 2013, http://www.ft.com/intl/cms/s/0/cab2111c-c6c8-11e2-a861-00144feab7de.html#axzz2UcadHJe2 (accessed May 29, 2013); *Bloomberg Businessweek*, "I.B.M. to Settle Bribery Charges for $10 Million," *The New York Times*, March 18, 2011, http://www.nytimes.com/2011/03/19/business/global/19blue.html?_r=0 (accessed December 3, 2012); "Bribe conviction for court clerk Munir Patel UK-first," *BBC*, October 14, 2011, http://www.bbc.co.uk/news/uk-england-london-15310150 (accessed March 22, 2013); Siobhain Butterworth, "Government delays Bribery Act – again," *The Guardian*, July 23, 2010, http://www.guardian.co.uk/law/afua-hirsch-law-blog/2010/jul/23/bribery-act-law-bae (accessed May 9, 2013); Eric Carlson, "China's Overseas Bribery Law One Year On," *FCPA Blog*, May 29, 2012, http://www.fcpablog.com/blog/2012/5/29/chinas-overseas-bribery-law-one-year-on.html (accessed May 13, 2013); Corpedia, "The Department of Justice and U.S. Securities and Exchange Commission Release Highly Anticipated Guidance on the Foreign Corrupt Practices Act: What does the Guidance Show and What does This Mean for Your Organization?," Aired on November 28, 2012, Criminal Division of the U.S. Department of Justice and the Enforcement Division of the U.S. Securities and Exchange Commission, A Resource Guide to the *U.S. Foreign Corrupt Practices Act*, November 14, 2012, http://www.justice.gov/criminal/fraud/fcpa/guide.pdf (accessed May 13, 2013); Stella Dawson, "Passage of Brazil anti-bribery bill key to OECD thumbs up," *Thomsen Reuters Foundation*, March 19, 2013, http://www.trust.org/item/?map=passage-of-brazil-anti-bribery-bill-key-to-oecd-thumbs-up/ (accessed May 13, 2013); David Gow, "Record US fine ends Siemens bribery scandal," *The Guardian*, December 15, 2008, http://www.guardian.co.uk/business/2008/dec/16/regulation-siemens-scandal-bribery (accessed May 13, 2013); Mary P. Hansen, "SEC Announces First Non-Prosecution Agreement Involving Foreign Corrupt Practices Act (FCPA) Violations," The National Law Review, April 27, 2013, http://www.natlawreview.com/article/sec-announces-first-non-prosecution-agreement-involving-foreign-corrupt-practices-ac (accessed May 13, 2013); Daniel Kaufmann, "Six Questions on the Cost of Corruption with World Bank Institute Global Governance Director Daniel Kaufmann," *World Bank Group*, http://web.worldbank.org/WBSITE/EXTERNAL/NEWS/0, contentMDK:20190295~menuPK:34457~pagePK:34370~piPK:34424~theSitePK:4607,00.html (accessed May 13, 2013); Roseanne Kay and Kimberley Davies, "A fiery dissertation – the third conviction under the UK Bribery Act of 2010," Association of Corporate Counsel, April 30, 2013, http://www.lexology.com/library/detail.aspx?g=6a6d9625-b9dd-4fd9-bc46-003f1fb13643 (accessed May 7, 2013); Eric Kraeutler, Iain Wright, Benjamin D. Klein, Nicholas Greenwood and David Waldron, "United States: Serious Fraud Office Gets Tough In UK Bribery Act Enforcement Guidelines," *Morgan Lewis*, http://www.morganlewis.com/index.cfm/bnodeID/4409d6fd-1d3d-486a-9485-7ae3082396ba/fuseaction/publication.detail/publicationID/aafc7908-eda0-4377-812b-1c0cf88fd926 (accessed May 9, 2013); Jonath on Marciano, "Only half of British businesses vet their suppliers for UK Bribery Act compliance, according to Ernst & Young," *Ernst & Young*, March 5, 2013, http://www.ey.com/UK/en/Newsroom/News-releases/13-03-05---Only-half-of-British-businesses-vet-their-suppliers-for-UK-Bribery-Act-compliance (accessed May 7, 2013); Daniel Margolis and James Wheaton, "Non-U.S. Companies May Also be Subject to the FCPA," Pillsbury, Winthrop, Shaw Pitman, LLC, August 30, 2009. http://www.pillsburylaw.com/sitefiles/publications/39ab4865beb55357dc2348ac196767cf.pdf (accessed November 30, 2012); Dan Milmo, "Rolls-Royce faces bribery claim inquiry," *The Guardian*, December 9, 2012, http://www.guardian.co.uk/business/2012/dec/09/rolls-royce-faces-bribery-inquiry (accessed May 7, 2013); Nixon Peabody LLP, "Foreign Corrupt Practices Act (FCPA), 2013, http://www.nixonpeabody.com/foreign_corrupt_practices_act_FCPA (accessed May 13, 2013); OECD "OECD Convention on Combating Bribery of Foreign Public Officials in International Business Transactions," http://www.oecd.org/corruption/oecdantibriberyconvention.htm (accessed May 13, 2013); "Public Bodies Corrupt Practices Act 1889," *legislation.gov.uk*, http://www.legislation.gov.uk/ukpga/Vict/52-53/69 (accessed May 9, 2013); Jonathon D. Rockoff and Christopher M. Matthews, "Pfizer Settles Federal Bribery Investigation," *The Wall Street Journal*, August 7, 2012, http://online.wsj.com/article/SB10000872396390444246904577575110723150588.html (accessed May 13, 2013); Securities and Exchange Commission, "SEC Announces Non-Prosecution Agreement with Ralph Lauren Corporation Involving

FCPA Misconduct," April 22, 2013, http://www.sec.gov/news/press/2013/2013-65.htm (accessed May 13, 2013); Securities and Exchange Commission, "SEC Charges Pfizer with FCPA Violations," August 7, 2012, http://www.sec.gov/news/press/2012/2012-152.htm (accessed May 13, 2013); Siemens AG, *Siemens homepage*, http://www.siemens.com/entry/cc/en/ (accessed May 9, 2013); Florian Stamm, (Spring 2006). "The Foreign Corrupt Practices Act: Keeping All Hands on the Table," *Trust the Leaders*, Issue 15 (Spring 2006), 4–7; Valerie Surgenor and David Flint, "United Kingdom: The Bribery Act Strikes Again," *Mondaq*, http://www.mondaq.com/x/211498/White+Collar+Crime+Fraud/The+Bribery+Act+Strikes+Again (accessed May 7, 2013); Transparency International, "Greece: The Cost of a Bribe," March 3, 2012, http://archive.transparency.org/news_room/in_focus/2012/greece_the_cost_of_a_bribe (accessed May 13, 2013); Transparency International UK, "The Bribery Act," http://www.transparency.org.uk/our-work/bribery-act (accessed May 13, 2013); Transparency USA, "U.S. FCPA vs. UK Bribery Act," http://www.transparency-usa.org/documents/FCPAvsBriberyAct.pdf (accessed May 9, 2013); The United States Department of Justice, "Foreign Corrupt Practices Act," http://www.justice.gov/criminal/fraud/fcpa/ (accessed May 13, 2013); Martin Walter, Michelle A. Luebke, and Dmitry Zhdankin, "The Impact of Corruption on the Environment," November 26, 2012. Available at *SSRN*: http://ssrn.com/abstract=2181029; Graeme Wearden, "Queen's speech 2009: bribery bill," *The Guardian*, November 18, 2009, http://www.guardian.co.uk/politics/2009/nov/18/queens-speech-bribery-bill (accessed May 9, 2013); Michael Weinstein, Robert Meyer, and Jeffrey Clark, "The UK Bribery Act vs. the U.S. FCPA," *Ethisphere*, April 22, 2011, http://anticorruption.ethisphere.com/the-uk-bribery-act-vs-the-u-s-fcpa/ (accessed May 9, 2013); Alexandra Wrage and Ann Richardson, "Siemens AG – Violations of the Foreign Corrupt Practices Act," *International Legal Materials* 48(2), 2009, 232–234. doi:10.2307/25691362.

CASE 19

Mattel Responds to Ethical Challenges*

INTRODUCTION

Mattel, Inc. is a global leader in designing and manufacturing toys and family products. Well-known for brands such as Barbie, Fisher-Price, Disney, Hot Wheels, Matchbox, Cabbage Patch Dolls, and board games, the company boasts nearly $6.27 billion in annual revenue. Headquartered in El Segundo, California, with offices across the world, Mattel markets its products in over 150 countries.

It all began in a California garage workshop when Ruth and Elliot Handler and Matt Matson founded Mattel in 1945. The company started out making picture frames, but the founders soon recognized the profitability of the toy industry and changed their emphasis to toys. Mattel became a publicly owned company in 1960, with sales exceeding $100 million by 1965. Over the next forty years, Mattel went on to become the world's largest toy company in terms of revenue.

In spite of its overall success, Mattel had its share of losses over its history. During the mid to late 1990s, Mattel lost millions to declining sales and bad business acquisitions. In January 1997, Jill Barad took over as Mattel's CEO. Barad's management-style was characterized as strict and her tenure at the helm proved challenging for many employees. While Barad was successful in building the Barbie brand to $2 billion by the end of the 20th century, growth slowed in the early 21st. Declining sales at outlets such as Toys "R" Us marked the start of difficulties for the retailer, responsibilities for which Barad accepted and resigned in 2000.

Robert Eckert replaced Barad as CEO. Working to turn things around, Eckert sold unprofitable units and cut hundreds of jobs. In 2000, under Eckert, Mattel was granted the highly sought-after licensing agreement for products related to the *Harry Potter* series of books and movies. The company continued to flourish and build its reputation, earning the Corporate Responsibility Award from UNICEF in 2003. Mattel released its first Annual Corporate Responsibility Report the following year. In 2012 Mattel was recognized as one of *Fortune* magazine's "100 Best Companies to Work For" for the fifth consecutive year. Eckert retired as CEO in 2011 and was replaced by former COO Bryan Stockton.

MATTEL'S CORE PRODUCTS

BARBIE AND AMERICAN GIRL   Among its many lines of popular toy products, Mattel is famous for owning top girls' brands. In 1959, Mattel introduced a product that changed its

---

*This case was prepared by Debbie Thorne, John Fraedrich, OC Ferrell, and Jennifer Jackson, with the editorial assistance of Jennifer Sawayda and Michelle Urban. This case is meant for classroom discussion, and is not meant to illustrate either effective or ineffective handling of an administrative, ethical, or legal decision by management.

future forever: the Barbie doll. One of the founders, Ruth Handler, noticed how her daughter loved playing with paper cutout dolls. She decided to create a doll based on an adult rather than on a baby. Barbie took off to become one of Mattel's critical product lines and the number one girls' brand in the world. Annual sales of Barbie net approximately $2 billion, and one doll is sold approximately every 3 seconds. The Barbie line today includes dolls, accessories, Barbie software, and a broad assortment of licensed products such as books, apparel, food, home furnishings, home electronics, and movies.

The popularity of Barbie allowed Mattel to introduce many different versions of the iconic doll. Barbie has had at least 40 different nationalities, and the company partnered with 75 different fashion designers throughout the years to design Barbie's outfits. Mattel found that while Barbie is popular with children, many adults enjoy collecting special-edition Barbie dolls as a pastime. Mattel often releases limited-edition Barbie dolls at a more expensive price geared toward adult collectors.

Not all of Mattel's Barbie creations were readily accepted by stakeholders. When Mattel released its limited-edition Tokidoki tattoo Barbie, the reaction was mixed. Although Mattel made it clear the doll was for collectors (at $50 per doll), some parents felt the Barbie could cause their impressionable children to desire their own tattoos. Others felt Mattel was simply reflecting societal trends as tattoos become more mainstream in society. On the other hand, Mattel also uses its Barbie doll for philanthropic purposes or to send a social message. For instance, Mattel created a special bald Barbie doll distributed only to hospitals. The doll is meant to help young girls cope with the difficulties of cancer and chemotherapy and is equipped with head scarves, hats, and other accessories. Because of the popularity of Barbie, Mattel learned it can use its dolls to create positive messages for girls.

To supplement the Barbie line, in 1998 Mattel acquired a popular younger type of doll. Mattel announced it would pay $700 million to Pleasant Co. for its high-end American Girl collection. American Girl dolls are sold with books about their lives, which take place during important periods of U.S. history. The American Girls brand includes several book series, accessories, clothing for dolls and girls, and a magazine that ranks in the top ten American children's magazines.

HOT WHEELS   Hot Wheels roared into the toy world in 1968. Co-founder Elliot Handler recognized the potential demand for die-cast cars among boys and decided to create a toy to compete with British company Lesney's Matchbox toys (Lesney was later acquired by Mattel). The original hot wheels were 1:64 scale but in 1970 they were expanded to include cars that were 1:43 scale. More than thirty years later, the brand is hotter than ever and includes high-end collectibles, NASCAR (National Association for Stock Car Auto Racing) and Formula One models for adults, high-performance cars, track sets, and play sets for children of all ages. The brand is connected with racing circuits worldwide. More than 15 million boys aged five to 15 are avid collectors, each owning forty-one cars on average. Two Hot Wheels cars are sold every second of every day, and annual sales total approximately $1 billion. The brand began with cars designed to run on a track and evolved into a "lifestyle" brand with licensed Hot Wheels shirts, caps, lunch boxes, backpacks, and more.

Much like Barbie, there are many adult collectors of hot wheels. These collectors were avid fans of Hot Wheels as children and continue to hold a favorable view of the toys as adults. Adult collectors are estimated to have about 1,550 cars on average. As a result, Mattel created a Hot Wheels website for collectors. The website discusses upcoming Hot Wheel releases, special events, and other Hot Wheels news. Together, Hot Wheels and Barbie generate 45 percent of Mattel's revenue.

CABBAGE PATCH KIDS   Since the introduction of mass-produced Cabbage Patch Kids in 1982, more than 90 million dolls have been sold worldwide. In 1994, Mattel took over selling these beloved dolls after purchasing production rights from Hasbro. In 1996, Mattel created a new line of Cabbage Patch doll, called Snacktime Kids, that was expected to meet with immense success. The Snacktime Kids had moving mouths that enabled children to "feed" them plastic snacks. However, the product backfired. The toy had no on/off switch and reports of children getting their fingers or hair caught in the dolls' mouths surfaced during the 1996 holiday season. Mattel voluntarily pulled the dolls from store shelves by January 1997, and offered consumers a cash refund of $40 on returned dolls. The U.S. Consumer Product Safety Commission applauded Mattel's handling of the Snacktime Kids situation. Mattel effectively managed a situation that could easily have created bad publicity or a crisis situation. Mattel stopped producing Cabbage Patch Kids in 2000.

MATTEL'S COMMITMENT TO ETHICS AND SOCIAL RESPONSIBILITY

Mattel's core products and business environment creates many ethical issues. Because the company's products are designed primarily for children, it must be sensitive to social concerns about children's rights. It must also be aware that the international environment often complicates business transactions. Different legal systems and cultural expectations about business can create ethical conflicts. Finally, the use of technology may present ethical dilemmas, especially regarding consumer privacy. Mattel recognizes these potential issues and takes steps to strengthen its commitment to business ethics. The company also purports to take a stand on social responsibility, encouraging its employees and consumers to do the same.

PRIVACY AND MARKETING TECHNOLOGY   One issue Mattel tries to address repeatedly is privacy and online technology. Advances in technology created special marketing issues for Mattel. The company recognizes that, because it markets to children, it must communicate with parents regarding its corporate marketing strategy. Mattel takes steps to inform both children and adults about its philosophy regarding Internet-based marketing tools. The privacy policy on the Mattel websites describes how Mattel does not collect online information from children under the age of 13 without parental consent. The policy discusses the use of cookies and describes how users can opt out of some of the tracking features. In 2013 Mattel updated its privacy policy on the website to make the site more informative. For instance, the policy discusses mobile applications, pixel tags, social media platforms, and targeted advertising. To increase understanding Mattel developed answers for the most frequently asked Internet privacy questions.[1] By assuring parents their children's privacy is respected, Mattel demonstrates that it takes its responsibility of marketing to children seriously.

EXPECTATIONS OF MATTEL'S BUSINESS PARTNERS   Mattel, Inc. makes a serious commitment to business ethics in its dealings with other industries. In late 1997, the

---

[1]Mattel, Inc., "Mattel, Inc. Online Privacy Statement," 2013, http://corporate.mattel.com/privacy-statement.aspx (accessed February 19, 2013).

company completed its first full ethics audit of each of its manufacturing sites as well as the facilities of its primary contractors. The audit revealed the company was not using any child labor or forced labor, a problem plaguing other overseas manufacturers. However, several contractors were found to be in violation of Mattel's safety and human rights standards and were asked to change their operations or risk losing Mattel's business. The company now conducts an independent monitoring council audit in manufacturing facilities every three years.

In an effort to continue its strong record on human rights and related ethical standards, Mattel instituted a code of conduct titled Global Manufacturing Principles in 1997. One of these principles requires all Mattel-owned and contracted manufacturing facilities to favor business partners committed to ethical standards comparable with those of Mattel. Other principles relate to safety, wages, and adherence to local laws. Mattel's audits and subsequent code of conduct were designed as preventative, not punitive measures. The company is dedicated to creating and encouraging responsible business practices throughout the world.

Mattel also claims to be committed to its workforce. Mattel cares deeply about increasing its employees' skill sets and providing opportunities to excel. This reflects Mattel's concern for relationships between and with employees and business partners. The company's code is a signal to potential partners, customers, and other stakeholders that Mattel made a commitment to fostering and upholding ethical values.

LEGAL AND ETHICAL BUSINESS PRACTICES   Mattel prefers to partner with businesses similarly committed to high ethical standards. At a minimum, partners must comply with the local and national laws of the countries where they operate. In addition, all partners must respect the intellectual property of the company, and support Mattel in the protection of assets such as patents, trademarks, or copyrights. They are responsible for product safety and quality, protecting the environment, customs, evaluation and monitoring, and compliance.

Mattel's business partners must have high standards for product safety and quality, adhering to practices that meet Mattel's safety and quality standards. In recent years, however, safety standards have been seriously violated and will be discussed in more detail later. Because of the global nature of Mattel's business and its history of leadership in this area, the company insists business partners strictly adhere to local and international customs laws. Partners must comply with all import and export regulations. To assist in compliance with standards, Mattel's 1997 Global Manufacturing Principles insists all manufacturing facilities provide the following:

- Full access for on-site inspections by Mattel or parties designated by Mattel
- Full access to those records that enable Mattel to determine compliance with its principles
- An annual statement of compliance with Mattel's Global Manufacturing Principles, signed by an officer of the manufacturer or manufacturing facility[2]

With the creation of the Mattel Independent Monitoring Council (MIMCO), Mattel became the first global consumer products company to apply such a system to facilities and

---

[2]Quoted in S. Prakash Sethi, Emre A. Veral, H. Jack Shapiro, and Olga Emelianova, *Journal of Business Ethics 99* (2011), 483–517.

core contractors worldwide. The company seeks to maintain an independent monitoring system that provides checks and balances to ensure standards are met.

If certain aspects of Mattel's manufacturing principles are not met, Mattel will try to work with them to fix their problems. New partners are not hired unless they meet Mattel's standards. If corrective action is advised but not taken, Mattel terminates its relationship with the partner in question. Overall, Mattel is committed to both business success and ethical standards, and recognizes it is part of a continuous improvement process.

MATTEL CHILDREN'S FOUNDATION   Mattel takes its social responsibilities seriously. Through the Mattel Children's Foundation, established in 1978, the company promotes philanthropy and community involvement among its employees and makes charitable investments to better the lives of children in need. Funding priorities include building a new Mattel Children's Hospital at the University of California, Los Angeles (UCLA), sustaining the Mattel Family Learning Program, and promoting giving among Mattel employees.

In November 1998, Mattel donated a multiyear, $25 million gift to the UCLA Children's Hospital. The gift was meant to support the existing hospital and provide a new state-of-the-art facility. In honor of Mattel's donation, the hospital was renamed Mattel Children's Hospital at UCLA.

The Mattel Family Learning Program uses computer learning labs as a way to advance children's basic skills. Now numbering more than eighty throughout the United States, Hong Kong, Canada, and Mexico, the labs offer software and technology designed to help children with special needs or limited English proficiency.

Mattel employees are encouraged to participate in a wide range of volunteer activities as part of "Mattel Volunteers: Happy to Help." Employees serving on boards of local non-profit organizations or helping with ongoing nonprofit programs are eligible to apply for volunteer grants supporting their organizations. Mattel employees contributing to higher education or nonprofit organizations serving children in need are eligible to have their personal donations matched dollar for dollar up to $5,000 annually.

INTERNATIONAL MANUFACTURING PRINCIPLES   As a U.S.-based multinational company owning and operating facilities and contracting worldwide, Mattel's Global Manufacturing Principles reflect not only its need to conduct manufacturing responsibly, but to respect the cultural, ethical, and philosophical differences of the countries where it operates. These principles set uniform standards across Mattel manufacturers and attempt to benefit both employees and consumers.

Mattel's principles cover issues such as wages, work hours, child labor, forced labor, discrimination, freedom of association, and working conditions. Workers must be paid at least minimum wage or a wage that meets local industry standards (whichever is greater). No one under the age of 16 or the local age limit (whichever is higher) is allowed to work for Mattel facilities. Mattel refuses to work with facilities using forced or prison labor, or use these types of labor itself. Additionally, Mattel does not tolerate discrimination. The company states an individual should be hired and employed based on his or her ability—not on individual characteristics or beliefs. Mattel recognizes all employees' rights to choose to associate with organizations without interference. Regarding working conditions, Mattel facilities and business partners must provide safe working environments for their employees.

OVERSEAS MANUFACTURING

Despite Mattel's best efforts, not all overseas manufacturers faithfully adhere to its high standards. Mattel came under scrutiny over sales of unsafe products. In September 2007, Mattel announced recalls of toys containing lead paint. The problem surfaced when a European retailer discovered lead paint on a toy. An estimated 10 million individual toys produced in China were affected. Mattel quickly stopped production at Lee Der, the company officially producing the recalled toys, after it discovered Lee Der had purchased lead paint used on the toys. Mattel blamed the fiasco on the manufacturers' desires to save money in the face of increasing prices. Mattel CEO Robert Eckert indicated that rising labor and raw material costs and the resulting pressure it created likely caused manufacturers to cut corners in order to save money.

The situation began when Early Light Industrial Co., a subcontractor for Mattel owned by Hong Kong toy tycoon Choi Chee Ming, subcontracted the painting of parts of *Cars* toys to another China-based vendor. The vendor, named Hong Li Da, sourced paint from a non-authorized third-party supplier—a violation of Mattel's requirement to use paint supplied directly by Early Light. The products contained "impermissible levels of lead."

On August 2, 2007, it was announced that another of Early Light's subcontractors, Lee Der Industrial Co., used the same lead paint found on *Cars* products. China immediately suspended the company's export license. Afterward, Mattel pinpointed three paint suppliers working for Lee Der—Dongxin, Zhongxin, and Mingdai. This paint was used by Lee Der to produce Mattel's line of Fisher-Price products. It is said that Lee Der purchased the paint from Mingdai because of an intimate friendship between the two company's owners. On August 11, 2007, Zhang Shuhong, operator of Lee Der, hung himself after paying his 5,000 staff members.

Later that month, Mattel recalled several more toys because of powerful magnets in the toys that could come loose and pose a choking hazard for young children. If more than one magnet is swallowed, the magnets can attract each other inside the child's stomach, causing potentially fatal complications. Over 21 million Mattel toys were recalled, and parents filed several lawsuits claiming these Mattel products harmed their children.

At first, Mattel blamed Chinese subcontractors for the huge toys recalls, but the company later accepted a portion of the blame for its troubles, while maintaining Chinese manufacturers were largely at fault. The Chinese view the situation quite differently. As reported by the state-run Xinhua news agency, the spokesman for China's General Administration of Quality Supervision and Inspection and Quarantine stated the importers were simply doing their jobs and the toys conformed to the necessary regulations when created. The spokesman placed the blame on Mattel's quality control. Mattel also faced criticism from many of its consumers, who believed Mattel denied culpability by placing much of the blame on China. Mattel was later awarded the 2007 "Bad Product" Award by Consumers International.

How did this crisis occur under the watch of a company praised for its ethics and high safety standards? Although Mattel investigated its contractors, it did not audit the entire supply chain, including subcontractors. These oversights left room for violations to occur. Mattel moved to enforce a rule that subcontractors cannot hire suppliers two or three tiers down. In a statement, Mattel says it spent more than 50,000 hours investigating its vendors and testing its toys. Mattel also announced a three-point plan. This plan aims to tighten Mattel's control of production, discover and prevent the unauthorized use of subcontractors, and test the products itself rather than depending on contractors.

THE CHINESE GOVERNMENT'S REACTION

Chinese officials eventually admitted the government's failure to properly protect the public. The Chinese government promised to tighten supervision of exported products, but effective supervision is challenging in such a large country burdened with corruption. In January 2008, the Chinese government launched a four-month-long nationwide product quality campaign, offering intensive training courses to domestic toy manufacturers to help them increase their knowledge of international product standards and safety awareness. As a result of the crackdown, the State Administration for Quality Supervision and Inspection and Quarantine (AQSIQ) announced it revoked the licenses of more than 600 Chinese toy makers. As of 2008, the State Administration for Commerce and Industry (SACI) released a report claiming 87.5 percent of China's newly manufactured toys met quality requirements. While this represents an improvement, the temptation to cut corners remains strong in a country that uses price, not quality, as its main competitive advantage. Where there is demand, there will be people trying to turn a quick profit.

MATTEL VERSUS FORMER EMPLOYEE AND MGA

In 2004, Mattel became embroiled in a bitter intellectual property rights battle with former employee Carter Bryant and MGA Entertainment Inc. over rights to MGA's popular Bratz dolls. Carter Bryant, an on-again/off-again Mattel employee, designed the Bratz dolls and pitched them to MGA. A few months after the pitch, Bryant left Mattel to work at MGA, which began producing Bratz in 2001. In 2002, Mattel launched an investigation into whether Bryant designed the Bratz dolls while employed with Mattel. After two years of investigation, Mattel sued Bryant. A year later MGA fired off a suit of its own, claiming Mattel created Barbies with looks similar to those of Bratz in an effort to eliminate the competition. Mattel answered by expanding its own suit to include MGA and its CEO, Isaac Larian.

For decades, Barbie reigned supreme on the doll market. However, Bratz dolls have given Barbie a run for her money. In 2005, four years after the brand's debut, Bratz sales were at $2 billion. At the same time, Barbie suffered from declining sales. Although still widely popular, many analysts believe Barbie has reached the maturity stage of its product life cycle.

Four years after the initial suit was filed, Bryant settled with Mattel under an undisclosed set of terms. In July 2008, a jury deemed MGA and its CEO liable for what it termed "intentional interference" regarding Bryant's contract with Mattel. In August 2008, Mattel received damages in the range of $100 million. Although Mattel requested damages of $1.8 billion, the company seemed pleased with the principle behind the victory.

In December 2008, Mattel won another victory when a California judge banned MGA from issuing or selling any more Bratz dolls. However, the tide turned on Mattel's victory. In July 2010, the Ninth U.S. Circuit Court of Appeals threw out the ruling. Eventually, the case came down to whether Mattel owned Bryant's ideas under the contract he had with the company. In April 2011, a California federal jury rejected Mattel's claims to ownership.

In another blow to Mattel, the jury ruled the company stole trade secrets from MGA. According to the allegations, Mattel employees used fake business cards to get into MGA showrooms during toy fairs. Mattel was ordered to pay $85 million in liabilities, plus an additional $225 million in damages and legal fees. MGA CEO Isaac Larian also announced he was filing an antitrust case against Mattel. Mattel continues to claim Bryant violated his contract when he worked for the company.

Although the conflict appeared to be settled, the fight between MGA and Mattel continued. The antitrust suit against Mattel was dismissed, and in January 2013 the U.S Court of Appeals overturned MGA's victory over Mattel concerning the theft of trade secrets. However, the court maintains Mattel is responsible for paying MGA's legal fines totaling $137.2 million. MGA CEO Isaac Larian is determined to contest this issue in court again in the near future.

MATTEL LOOKS TOWARD THE FUTURE

Like all major companies, Mattel weathered its share of storms. The company faced a series of difficult and potentially crippling challenges, including the lawsuits with MGA regarding ownership of the Bratz dolls. During the wave of toy recalls, some analysts suggested the company's reputation was battered beyond repair. Mattel, however, refused to go quietly. Although the company admits to poorly handling past affairs, it is attempting to rectify its mistakes and to prevent future mistakes as well. With the economic future of the United States uncertain, Mattel may see slow growth for some time to come. Mattel is hard at work restoring goodwill and faith in its brands, even as it continues to be plagued with residual distrust over the lead paint scandal and its alleged theft of trade secrets. Reputations are hard won and easily lost, but Mattel appears to be steadfast in its commitment to restoring its reputation.

QUESTIONS

1. Do manufacturers of products for children have special obligations to consumers and society? If so, what are these responsibilities?
2. How effective has Mattel been at encouraging ethical and legal conduct by its manufacturers? What changes and additions would you make to the company's Global Manufacturing Principles?
3. To what extent is Mattel responsible for issues related to its production of toys in China? How might Mattel have avoided these issues?

SOURCES

Lisa Bannon and Carlta Vitzhum, "One-Toy-Fits-All: How Industry Learned to Love the Global Kid," *Wall Street Journal*, April 29, 2003, http://online.wsj.com/article/SB105156578439799000.html (accessed February 19, 2013); Adam Bryant, "Mattel CEO Jill Barad and a Toyshop That Doesn't Forget to Play," *New York Times*, October 11, 1998; Bill Duryea, "Barbie-holics: They're Devoted to the Doll," *St. Petersburg Times*, August 7, 1998; Rachel Engers, "Mattel Board Members Buy $30 Million in Stock: Insider Focus," *Bloomberg*, December 22, 2000; Mattel,

Inc., *Hot Wheels* website, www.hotwheels.com/ (accessed February 19, 2013); PR Newswire, "Independent Monitoring Council Completes Audits of Mattel Manufacturing Facilities in Indonesia, Malaysia and Thailand," November 15, 2002, http://www.prnewswire.com/news-releases/independent-monitoring-council-completes-audits-of-mattel-manufacturing-facilities-in-indonesia-malaysia-and-thailand-76850522.html (accessed February 19, 2013); Mattel, Inc., "Investors and Media," http://investor.shareholder.com/mattel/ (accessed February 19, 2013); Mattel, Inc., "Mattel Children's Foundation," http://corporate.mattel.com/about-us/philanthropy/childrenfoundation.aspx (accessed February 19, 2013); Datamonitor, "Independent Monitoring Council Completes Audits of Mattel Plants in China and Mexico," May 7, 2001, http://www.datamonitor.com/store/News/independent_monitoring_council_completes_audits_of_mattel_plants_in_china_and_mexico?productid=ABFDA740-C953-4500-B47C-29916A3C8663 (accessed February 19, 2013); Mattel, Inc., "About Us," *Mattel*, http://corporate.mattel.com/about-us/ (accessed February 19, 2013); "Mattel and U.S. Consumer Product Safety Commission Announce Voluntary Refund Program for Cabbage Patch Kids Snacktime Kids Dolls," U.S. Consumer Product Safety Commission, Office of Information and Public Affairs, Release No. 97–055, January 6, 1997; PR News Wire, "Mattel, Inc., Launches Global Code of Conduct Intended to Improve Workplace, Workers' Standard of Living," Nov. 20, 1997, http://www.prnewswire.com/news-releases/mattel-inc-launches-global-code-of-conduct-intended-to-improve-workplace-workers-standard-of-living-77630507.html (accessed February 19, 2013); Marla Matzer, "Deals on Hot Wheels," *Los Angeles Times*, July 22, 1998; Patricia Sellers, "The 50 Most Powerful Women in American Business," *Fortune*, October 12, 1998; "Toymaker Mattel Bans Child Labor," *Denver Post*, November 21, 1998; Michael White, "Barbie Will Lose Some Curves When Mattel Modernizes Icon," *Detroit News*, November 18, 1997; Laura S. Spark, "Chinese Product Scares Prompt US Fears," *BBC News*, July 10 2007, http://news.bbc.co.uk/2/hi/americas/6275758.stm (accessed February 19, 2013); Benjamin B. Olshin, "China, Culture, and Product Recalls," *S2R*, August 20, 2007, http://www.s2r.biz/s2rpapers/papers-Chinese_Product.pdf (accessed February 19, 2013); U.S. Consumer Products Safety Commission, *Mattel Recalls Batman™ and One Piece™ Magnetic Action Figure Sets*, August 14, 2007, http://service.mattel.com/us/recall/J1944CPSC.pdf (accessed February 19, 2013); Parker Waichman LLP, "Magnetic Toy Sets Defective Project Injury Lawsuits," http://www.yourlawyer.com/topics/overview/magnetic_toy_sets (accessed February 19, 2013); Mattel Customer Service, "Product Recall," April 1, 2008, http://service.mattel.com/us/recall.asp (accessed April 1, 2008); David Barboza and Louise Story, "Toymaking in China, Mattel'S Way," *New York Times*, July 26, 2007, http://www.nytimes.com/2007/07/26/business/26toy.html?pagewanted=1&_r=3&hp (accessed February 19, 2013); Shu-Ching Chen, "A Blow to Hong Kong's Toy King," *Forbes*, August 15, 2007, http://www.forbes.com/2007/08/15/mattel-china-choi-face-markets-cx_jc_0815autofacescan01.html (accessed February 19, 2013); David Barboza, "Scandal and Suicide in China: a Dark Side of Toys," *New York Times*, August 23, 2007, http://www.nytimes.com/2007/08/23/business/worldbusiness/23suicide.html?pagewanted=all (February 19, 2013); United States Government Accountability Office, "The United States Has Not Restricted Imports Under the China Safeguard," September 2005, http://www.gao.gov/new.items/d051056.pdf (accessed February 19, 2013); Jack A. Raisner, "Using the "Ethical Environment" Paradigm to Teach Business Ethics: The Case of the Maquiladoras," *Journal of Business Ethics 16* (1997): 1331–1346; "Mattel awarded $100M in doll lawsuit," *USA Today*, August 27, 2008, B-1; Nicholas Casey, "Mattel Prevails Over MGA in Bratz-Doll Trial," *The Wall Street Journal*, July 18, 2008, B-18–B-19; Nicholas Casey, "Mattel to Get Up to $100 Million in Bratz Case," *The Wall Street Journal*, August 27, 2008, http://online.wsj.com/article/SB121978263398273857-email.html (accessed February 19, 2013); American Girl, www.americangirl.com (accessed February 19, 2013); Mattel, Inc., "Barbie," http://www.barbie.com/ (accessed February 19, 2013); Mattel Inc., *Mattel Annual Report 2008*, 2009, http://files.shareholder.com/downloads/MAT/2328843115x0x283677/D4E18CB7-C8B4-4A28-BCE9-C114B248A26D/MattelAnnualReport2008.pdf (accessed February 19, 2013); Mattel, Inc., "Mattel History," http://www.mattel.com/about_us/history/default.asp?f=true (accessed February 19, 2013); "Learning from Mattel," Tuck School of Business at Dartmouth, http://mba.tuck.dartmouth.edu/pdf/2002-1-0072.pdf (accessed 3 Dec. 2008); Direct Newsline Staff, "Mattel to Sell Learning Company," *Chief Marketer*, October 2, 2000, http://directmag.com/news/marketing_mattel_sell_learning/ (accessed February 19, 2013); Miranda Hitti, "9 Million Mattel Toys Recalled," WebMD, August 14, 2007, http://children.webmd.com/news/20070814/9_million_mattel_toys_recalled (accessed February 19, 2013); Judith Levy, "Third toy recall by Mattel in five weeks," Business Standard, September 5, 2007, http://seekingalpha.com/article/46374-mattel-announces-third-toy-recall (accessed February 19, 2013); Consumers International, *International Bad Product Awards 2007*, http://marketing.by/webroot/delivery/files/InternationalBadProductsAwards-pressbriefing.pdf (accessed February 19, 2013); Gina Keating, "MGA 'still accessing' impact of Bratz ruling: CEO," Yahoo! News, December 4, 2008 http://www.reuters.com/article/2008/12/05/us-mattel-larian-idUSTRE4B405820081205 (accessed February 19, 2013); BBC News, "Bratz loses battle of the dolls," December 5, 2008, http://news.bbc.co.uk/2/hi/business/7767270.stm (accessed February 19, 2013); Andrea Chang, "Mattel must pay MGA $310 million in Bratz case," *Los Angeles Times*, August 5, 2011, http://articles.latimes.com/2011/aug/05/business/la-fi-mattel-bratz-20110805 (accessed February 19, 2013); Ann Zimmerman, "Mattel Loses in Bratz Spat," *The Wall Street Journal*, April22 2011, http://online.wsj.com/article/SB10001424052748703983704576276984087591872.html (accessed February 19, 2–13); Karen Weise, "Briefs: Mattel—Must pay for stealing Bratz secrets," *Bloomberg Businessweek*, August 15–28, 2011, 22; Mattel, "Annual Report 2011," 2011, http://files.shareholder.com/downloads/MAT/2319434112x0x555821/3C654248-30D8-4A8D-A8FC-53A89560A3C3/2011_Mattel_Annual_Report.pdf (accessed February 13, 2013); CNNMoney, "100 Best Companies to Work For," 2012, http://money.cnn.com/magazines/fortune/best-companies/2012/snapshots/79.html (accessed February 13, 2013); Edvard Petterssen and Karen Gullo, "MGA Bratz Win Over Mattel Partly Erased By Appeals Court," *Bloomberg*, January 24, 2013, http://www.bloomberg.com/news/2013-01-24/mga-bratz-win-over-mattel-partly-erased-by-appeals-court.html (accessed February 13, 2013); Frank Shyong and Andrea Chang, "Award is Tossed in Bratz Lawsuit", *Los Angeles Times*, January 25, 2013, http://articles.latimes.com/2013/jan/25/business/la-fi-bratz-mattel-20130125 (accessed February 13, 2013); Brooks Barnes, "Thomas the Tank Engine to Receive a Multimillion Dollar Sheen," *The New York Times*, December 30, 2012, http://www.nytimes.com/2012/12/31/business/media/mattel-to-give-thomas-the-tank-engine-a-multimillion-dollar-sheen.html (accessed February 19, 2013); Kim Carollo and Serena Marshall, "Mattel to Make 'Bald Friend of Barbie'," *ABC News*, March 29, 2012, http://abcnews.go.com/blogs/health/2012/03/29/mattel-to-produce-bald-friend-of-barbie/ (accessed February 19, 2013); Mattel, Inc., "Barbie," http://www.barbiemedia.com/ (accessed February 19, 2013); Christina Cheddar Berk, "Tattooed Barbie Sparks Controversy, Media Frenzy," *CNBC*, October 21, 2011, http://www.cnbc.com/id/44990466/Tattooed_Barbie_Sparks_Controversy_Media_Frenzy (accessed February 19, 2013); CBS News, "Here comes Tattoo Barbie," October 29, 2011, http://www.cbsnews.com/8301-207_162-20127453/here-comes-tattoo-barbie/ (accessed February 19, 2013); Staff Reports, "A history of Hot Wheels," *Albert Lea Tribune*, February 3, 2008, http://www.albertleatribune.com/2008/02/03/a-history-of-hot-wheels/ (accessed February 19, 2013); Mattel Inc., http://www.hotwheelscollectors.com/ (accessed February 19, 2013); Shan Li, "Mattel CEO Robert Eckert to be replaced by COO Bryan Stockton, *Los Angeles Times*, November 21, 2011, http://latimesblogs.latimes.com/money_co/2011/11/mattel-ceo-robert-eckert-steps-down-bryan-stockton.html (accessed February 19, 2013); Edvard Pettersson, "Mattel Wins Dismissal of MGA Entertainment's $1 Billion Antitrust Lawsuit," *Bloomberg*, February 22, 2012, http://www.bloomberg.com/news/2012-02-22/mattel-wins-dismissal-of-mga-entertainment-s-1-billion-antitrust-lawsuit.html (accessed February 19, 2013); S. Prakash Sethi, Emre A. Veral, H. Jack Shapiro, and Olga Emelianova, *Journal of Business Ethics* 99(2011), 483–517; Mattel, Inc., "Mattel, Inc. Online Privacy Statement," 2013, http://corporate.mattel.com/privacy-statement.aspx (accessed February 19, 2013).

CASE 20

Best Buy Fights Against Electronic Waste*

Although Best Buy has not been in business as long as other established brands, the company is a well-known name both within and outside the United States. This consumer electronics retailer is the largest specialty retailer within its sector throughout the United States. To maintain its competitive advantage against rivals in specialty electronics, Best Buy began investigating competitive pricing strategies, international expansion, and the targeting of a younger demographic.

In addition to its discounted and high-quality products, Best Buy became known for its customer-centered approach and sustainable outreach. After realizing the importance of sustainability to its customers, Best Buy implemented an extensive recycling program. In the process, Best Buy earned itself a name as a socially responsible company. The company adopted programs and systems to provide flexibility and aid to its employees. As a result of its corporate and social responsibility initiatives, Best Buy has been awarded numerous honors, including *Ethisphere*'s World's Most Ethical Companies and *Forbes*' America's Most Reputable Companies.

This case provides a brief history of Best Buy, including details on its expansion and the models it implemented to become the success it is today. Next, we discuss Best Buy's vision, along with the actions the company is taking to turn its vision into a reality. We briefly analyze Best Buy's community outreach programs. We look at Best Buy's large-scale environmental initiatives, particularly those regarding energy savings and recycling. Finally, we examine some of the challenges Best Buy is encountering as it struggles to maintain its dominance in the consumer electronics market.

HISTORY

Best Buy has undergone a number of changes over the course of its 40-year history. The company was founded by Richard Schulze, who worked as a representative for a consumer-electronics manufacturer. Schulze recognized that a demand existed among college-age consumers for audio equipment, and in 1966 he opened an audio specialty store called Sound of Music in the Twin Cities (Minnesota) area. A year later, the company acquired the Kencraft Hi-Fi Company. The company continued to grow and flourish over the next few years, hitting $1 million in annual revenue by 1970. Best Buy's equipment was originally targeted to college students who wanted electronic goods at the higher end of the

*This case was developed by Jennifer Sawayda and Danielle Jolley for and under the direction of O. C. Ferrell and Linda Ferrell. Amanda Solosky and Shelby Peters contributed to a previous edition of this case. It was prepared for classroom discussion rather than to illustrate effective or ineffective handling of an administrative, ethical, or legal decision by management. All sources used for this case were obtained through publicly available material.

spectrum. However, because of increasing competition in the consumer electronics industry during the 1970s, Schulze realized his stores had to adapt to compete effectively.

In 1983 Schulze converted his Sound of Music stores into a high-volume discount chain selling electronics, consumer appliances, videocassettes, and records. He renamed this chain Best Buy. Competition remained fierce from companies such as Sears and Wards, and Schulze was once again forced to innovate. He came up with an entirely new model that revolutionized the retail industry as a whole. The changes Schulze implemented included eliminating the backrooms of stores and bringing all merchandise onto the sales floor, paying salespeople hourly wages rather than commissions, and retraining salespeople to be more customer-focused.

Best Buy embarked on partnerships and acquisitions to increase its market share, such as acquiring the computer repair service the Geek Squad. With the downward trend in computer sales in the 2000s, Best Buy embraced what it calls Concept 5 stores—companies that would not only sell products but also teach consumers how to use them. With the acquisition of the Geek Squad, Best Buy furthered this goal and significantly reduced its service turnaround time, leading to higher customer satisfaction and a new chapter in the consumer electronics industry.

Best Buy operates businesses in several countries outside the United States as well, including stores in Canada and Mexico. While attempts to open Best Buy stores in China were unsuccessful, the company's subsidiary Jiangsu Five Star Appliance is thriving. In 2009 the company opened its first stores based in the United Kingdom. Best Buy began opening branded Best Buy stores in the U.K. in 2010. Today, Best Buy is a leading provider of consumer electronics with a presence in U.S., Canadian, British, Chinese, and Mexican markets.

In 2009 the company became the primary online and brick-and-mortar provider for the eastern United States after its rival Circuit City closed its doors. Unlike Best Buy, Circuit City failed to adapt to a fast-paced marketplace; it chose to hire workers at lower wages and encountered severe inventory backlogs that resulted in less loyal employees, greater inefficiencies, and customer dissatisfaction. With 2012's annual revenue of more than $50 billion, Best Buy dominates the marketplace for brick and mortar electronics retailers. The company currently employs about 160,000 people. However, competition from online rivals including Amazon.com has created challenges for Best Buy, resulting in some layoffs.

VISION

"People. Technology. And the pursuit of happiness." This is the corporate vision Best Buy strives to achieve. The company attempts to apply best practices in every facet of its operations. To meet the needs of its customers, employees, vendors, and stockholders, Best Buy adopted a stakeholder orientation that focuses on quality relationships with these various groups. Technology is an inextricable part of this orientation, since the company prides itself on selling quality technological products and services that meet its customers' varied needs. Best Buy wants to create a satisfying work environment and give back to the communities where it operates. The company feels happy employees and communities translate into happy customers. The following sections describe the initiatives Best Buy has implemented to fulfill its vision.

Consumer Engagement

Best Buy views itself as a customer-centered organization and aims to achieve better customer relationships, a greater understanding of customer needs and preferences, and continual engagement in customer dialogue. Best Buy encourages its customers to rate their experiences and products on www.BestBuy.com. The company invited customers to leadership meetings in order to gain a better outlook on their needs. In this way, Best Buy hopes to create a better fit between the company and its customers.

Best Buy takes the concerns of its customers seriously. In 2007 the company published its first Corporate Social Responsibility Report (CSR) in response to consumers' demands to know what Best Buy does in the area of sustainability. Electronic waste has been rapidly accumulating in landfills, and society has become increasingly concerned with how to reduce this waste. Best Buy's surveys revealed its customers want the company to find ways to recycle electronics and use less energy. Best Buy answered this call through implementation of a wide-scale electronics recycling program. Best Buy works to continually improve its customer service. Its subsidiary, the Geek Squad, provides 24-hour service on-site, at home, or through the Internet. The Squad's Agents—wearing their signature white shirts, black ties, black trousers, and sporting Geek Squad logos, complete with black and white cars for at-home services—are often able to make repairs in a matter of hours (versus days or weeks for many other computer repair services). Overall, Best Buy's customer satisfaction ratings display an upward trend in the past few years as the company's customer-centered focus provides it with an advantage in the marketplace and enables it to grab market share.

Employee Engagement

Employees are an integral part of Best Buy's vision. Best Buy requires a talented, dedicated staff to solve technical problems and demonstrate exemplary customer service. As a result, Best Buy invests heavily in training its employees. The company devoted 50,000 hours to employee training to teach employees about the newest features of the Windows 8 product so employees could better assist customers in-store.

Best Buy's corporate culture emphasizes listening to employees as well as customers. Employees are able to post their thoughts on online forums such as the Watercooler and on an internal news site. The company's Chief Ethics Officer Kathleen Edmond demonstrated the importance of communication to the company when she created the Chief Ethics Officer Blog for employees to view. Edmond used cases of unethical events that took place within the company in order to teach employees about ethical conduct. Her actions caused her to be listed in *Ethisphere*'s Most Influential People in Business Ethics.

Best Buy takes a stand on diversity training for its employees. Every year it holds a Cultural Immersion program for its employees at the Lorraine Hotel in Memphis. The hotel was the site where Dr. Martin Luther King, Jr., was assassinated in 1968; in 1991 it was converted into the National Civil Rights Museum. It is Best Buy's goal to encourage employees to practice inclusion and awareness of different cultures.

Finally, Best Buy offers a wide range of benefits for its employees. Employees who work 32 hours at the retailer qualify for family health insurance, tuition assistance, and adoption assistance. In addition to offering flexible programs, Best Buy allows those employees working at least 32 hours a week to reduce his or her hours or engage in job sharing as needed. Due to its flexibility and benefits, Best Buy was awarded first place in *Working Mother*'s 2012 Best Companies for Hourly Workers.

Community Engagement

Best Buy adheres to the belief that being a socially responsible company requires contributing to the communities where it operates. Thus, Best Buy frequently engages stakeholders in these communities, particularly in the areas of education and technology. For instance, Best Buy established the Best Buy Children's Foundation. The Foundation provides grants to eligible nonprofits committed to creating opportunities through technology for increasing education and skills among teenagers. While Best Buy's community programs give back to the communities where it does business, it also provides the company with opportunities to create long-lasting relationships with consumers, employees, and other stakeholders. Best Buy supports corporate philanthropy through programs such as technology access for teams and disaster relief funds.

TECHNOLOGY ACCESS FOR TEENS   In efforts to expand its local community presence, Best Buy began to extend its reach to teens by establishing a new program titled Best Buy Teen Tech Centers. Here, teens go after school and explore the world of current and new technology. The company is developing classes and online tutorials to be used in workshops at the centers. Best Buy seeks to reduce common barriers associated with gaining access to technology, including economic, social, and physical barriers that hinder many from using technology. Because of the growth in technology in recent years, Best Buy understands the role technology plays in education and career field choices. Best Buy employees and their "Geek Squad" are involved to help the program reach as many teens as possible. In 2012 tech centers opened in Chicago, Miami, San Antonio, and St. Paul/ Minneapolis.

DISASTER RELIEF   Best Buy partners with disaster relief organizations to donate money and aid to hard-hit areas around the world. Best Buy donated $200,000 for disaster relief in Haiti after the devastating earthquake in 2010. In late 2012 Best Buy donated 1,000 disaster kits through its partner, The Salvation Army, to provide connectivity in times of crisis. The kits contained batteries, flashlights, and chargers, all to be used when disasters strike unexpectedly.

Best Buy supports employees who live in areas affected by natural disasters. If the Best Buy store in the area is forced to close, employees are paid until the store reopens or are given the opportunity to work at another Best Buy if the store remains closed. Hotlines, counseling services, and employee assistance programs are available for employees impacted by natural disasters.

BECOMING MORE SUSTAINABLE

Becoming more sustainable goes hand in hand with Best Buy's business model and strategy. Best Buy incorporated eco-friendly practices into several facets of its operations, from reduced energy consumption to recycling of electronic waste (e-waste). The company also incorporates innovative eco-friendly inventions into its product line. For instance, Best Buy began selling electric bicycles and providing charging stations for Ford Motor Company's electric cars. To reduce its environmental footprint, Best Buy formed partnerships with other companies such as Energy Star. Best Buy joined with SmartWay Transport to reduce greenhouse gas emissions. SmartWay Transport is a collaboration between the Environmental Protection Agency and the freight industry with the goal of reducing waste and becoming more energy efficient.

Best Buy began to enforce ethical and sustainable practices among its vendors. Suppliers must adhere to the company's Supplier Compliance Standards, and to ensure compliance, Best Buy audits its various suppliers each year. Factories found to have violations are dealt with accordingly; those that do not improve sufficiently in the designated time frame may be dropped. To ensure suppliers are not abusing worker rights, Best Buy conducts ongoing human rights audits.

CONSERVING ENERGY ONE STORE AT A TIME

One area of particular concern to Best Buy is energy consumption. Realizing its stores consume large quantities of energy—some that could be conserved through more sustainable practices—Best Buy joined the Business for Innovative Climate and Energy (BICEP) in February 2010. BICEP is a coalition of companies wanting to advance climate and energy policies within the United States. The focus of BICEP is on embracing innovation in sustainability. According to Best Buy Senior Director of Government Relations, this is one step toward Best Buy's commitment for promoting sustainability both inside the company and among consumers.

As part of Best Buy's energy conservation program, the company set the goal of reducing carbon emissions 20 percent per square foot by 2020. The company's action plan includes improving lighting in its stores through skylights, implementing a "no-idling" policy prohibiting trucks from running their engines outside Best Buy locations, and investigating new energy-saving technologies such as virtual servers and surge protectors/power bars. Additionally, in 2010 Best Buy created an everyday in-store recycling program in U.S. stores with a goal of increasing its recycling rate to 1 billion consumer products in five to six years. That year Best Buy collected more than 75 million pounds of electronic waste for recycling. These changes improved Best Buy's ability to become more sustainable through energy conservation and recycling.

ENVIRONMENTAL SUSTAINABILITY— ENERGY STAR PRODUCTS

In addition to saving energy in its operations, Best Buy sells energy-saving products. Best Buy's extensive partnership with Energy Star saves its customers money on energy costs and helps the environment by selling energy-efficient items. Energy Star–qualified products meet strict efficiency guidelines set by the U.S. Department of Energy and the Environmental Protection Agency. It has been estimated that Energy Star products—including compact fluorescent lights and lighting fixtures—reduce greenhouse gas emissions by 46 million metric tons and saves consumers $6.4 billion in electric bills. During 2008 Best Buy employees underwent Energy Star training so they can provide consumers with detailed information on Energy Star products. In 2009 Best Buy won the Energy Star Excellence in Electronic and Appliance Retailing award for its commitment to saving energy. Best Buy offers everything from refrigerators to laptops to printers that are Energy Star–qualified.

COMBATING E-WASTE

As the world moves toward sustainability, the issue of e-waste takes on an increased importance among consumers. Best Buy surveys revealed that both its employees and consumers are concerned about the growing amount of electronic waste that occurs after an item breaks or, more frequently, becomes obsolete. Without any clear idea of how to recycle these electronic items, consumers were often forced to throw them away—contributing to a greater amount of e-waste in landfills. Stakeholders desired programs that could help them determine how to recycle their used electronics, and Best Buy met that demand with its Best Buy Consumer Electronics Recycling Program. This program brought the recycling of electronic waste to a whole new level. Consumers drop off their used electronics and Best Buy recycles them regardless of their condition or brand. If Best Buy does not recycle a specific product, it helps the customer find a way to recycle it. The tech trade-in service prints out a shipping label so customers can send their unwanted products to places that will recycle the item. The stores take cell phones, DVD players, and most other electronic products. Electronics over 32 inches in size used to cost $10 to recycle, although customers were given a $10 Best Buy gift card to replace the money spent on recycling them. However, in late 2011 Best Buy eliminated this $10 fee. Now consumers can drop off electronics at Best Buy locations free of charge. This is a step toward Best Buy's goal to recycle 1 billion pounds of e-waste by 2014.

Other resources Best Buy uses in its large-scale recycling initiatives are its trade-in program, recycling kiosks, and TV and appliance pickup service. The trade-in program offers consumers two options: trading electronics online or in-store. The online system accepts a wider variety of product trade-ins. After inputting the product information, consumers are provided with a trade-in value and can accept or decline the value offered. If they accept, consumers print a prepaid shipping label and ship the item. They receive a Best Buy gift card or check within 14 days after Best Buy receives the item. The trade-in system allows consumers to exchange an item and use the store credit to buy a newer model of a similar item. The in-store option follows similar steps, although it only allows trade-ins of iPods, mobile phones, and laptops.

Recycling kiosks have become a familiar site at Best Buy stores. Every Best Buy in the United States now has recycling kiosks located near the front entrance. The kiosks are used to recycle small items including rechargeable batteries, cell phones, and ink cartridges. During 2009 Best Buy installed recycling kiosks across its stores in Canada as well.

Best Buy also offers haul-away services for large items. If a customer buys a television from Best Buy and has it delivered, Best Buy offers to haul the old television away and recycle it for free. If consumers want to hire Best Buy to haul a large item off without a purchase, Best Buy charges a $100 fee. This is Best Buy's attempt to gain environmentally conscious customers. The company is dedicated to its mission of recycling unwanted materials and, if possible, giving the products a second life. As part of this mission, since 2003 Best Buy has been a member of the Environmental Protection Agency's Plug Into eCycling program that is committed to increasing consumer awareness about the importance of recycling.

Managing such an extensive recycling program requires that Best Buy collaborate with other organizations committed to the same cause. As a result, Best Buy has partnered with various recycling companies, many that attempt to give used electronics a "second life." Several of Best Buy's recycling partners take the items apart and organize them into plastics, metals, glass, etc. Then they decide whether the products can be repaired before recycling the parts for other uses. To ensure its partners are acting in a socially responsible manner, Best Buy monitors recyclers to make sure they follow safe recycling practices. These partnerships serve to reduce pollution by keeping items out of landfills.

RECYCLING PROGRAM BENEFITS

The environmental benefits of recycling are quite clear—reduction in waste, decreased gas emissions, energy-savings, and more. However, as Best Buy demonstrates, recycling can have positive implications for the business world as well. For example, if a product like a cell phone can be fixed, it can be sent to outlets like eBay who can resell the product. If not, the products are taken apart so the materials can be reused. Best Buy splits the profit made from recycled products with its partners.

Recycling programs encourage manufacturers to take greater responsibility in product design. With the growing demand for sustainability, many manufacturing companies began to embark on new and innovative designs to make their products more recyclable. For example, Dell began using fewer screws in its computers to make them easier to recycle. Best Buy supports this movement toward lighter recyclable electronics, as demonstrated by product offerings like its organic LED (OLED) televisions that are lighter and easier to recycle.

Of course, with the benefits of recycling come costs as well. Televisions are heavy to handle and not as recyclable as other goods. Dealing with them costs companies like Best Buy time and money. However, Best Buy feels the connections developed between Best Buy and the community make the company's effort worth the cost. Best Buy hopes its status as a sustainable and ethical company attracts more loyal customers, aiding both its reputation and its bottom line.

In 2012 Dow Jones announced Best Buy made the Dow Jones Sustainability Index for the second year in a row. The index evaluates 2,500 companies globally, including 600 within the United States and Canada. The index measures and compares companies across 57 industries on environmental, social, and corporate governance standards. To qualify for the index, the companies must score better on sustainability than most of their contemporaries within their industry (best-in-class). The index is used by investors to evaluate sustainability leadership and risk management. Best Buy placed in the 68th percentile and increased their score from the year before by three points.

CHALLENGES FOR BEST BUY

Best Buy faces intense competition from retailers such as Amazon and Apple. Analysts believe the reason for this loss is based on pricing considerations. It is more common for consumers to visit Best Buy stores, find items they want, and shop for those items on Amazon or other e-commerce sites at lower prices (a practice known as showrooming). This trend is causing Best Buy to consider investigating more aggressive pricing strategies as a way to compete. Best Buy has sometimes struggled with delayed delivery services as well. During the 2011 Christmas season, many products ordered at Thanksgiving were delayed and not delivered until after Christmas. Best Buy apologized to thousands of customers and experienced a dip in customer satisfaction ratings. However, overall customer satisfaction rose to its highest score in 2012.

One strategy Best Buy began to implement to combat showrooming started during the holiday season of 2012. Best Buy began a holiday-price matching policy that stated the company would match online prices in hopes to win consumers back. Deducing they could not lose any more market share to online competitors, the company decided to extend the policy indefinitely. In 2013 they implemented the price matching policy, and their stock price increased 95 percent in the next five months. They also reduced their merchandise return policy from 30 days to 15 days. Many retailers are following suit in hopes to win back customers from online competition.

Best Buy faces challenges in global markets. The company's big-box retailers did not perform well in the Chinese market, causing Best Buy to abandon its nine branded stores in that country. Once again, price may have been a primary factor. Chinese consumers indicated that although the environment of Best Buy was much nicer than comparable retailers, the prices were too high. However, Best Buy is not abandoning China entirely. While it is shutting down its branded stores, Best Buy has expanded its Chinese subsidiary Five Star. Currently Five Star has about 200 stores and is looking to add up to 500 more by 2016. The subsidiary took a different approach when targeting China's middle class, specifically by diverging from its initial approach of emulating an American lifestyle. It began to target China's lesser known cities, where 70 percent of consumers are young families. As China's economy progresses, Best Buy is confident these stores will continue to profit.

Along with its China stores, Best Buy looks to close 15 of its big-box stores in Canada, eliminating 900 jobs. This comes after closing 50 U.S. stores in 2012. Continually, sales for Best Buy have slowly declined. New CEO Hubert Joly plans to revive the company by adapting to current and projected market trends and reaching younger demographics through innovative campaigns.

CORPORATE GOVERNANCE CHALLENGES

Perhaps one of the greatest blows to Best Buy came with the ouster of CEO Brian Dunn, who was recognized as an ethical business leader. In April 2012, CEO Brian Dunn resigned after an internal investigation from the audit committee led to accusations he violated company policy by having a 'close personal relationship' with a female employee. The investigation showed Dunn did not misuse any company resources while engaging in inappropriate behavior. However, some of the behavior that occurred included lunch and drinks on multiple occasions along with the distribution of concert and sporting event tickets as gifts. The audit committee spoke with current and former employees, who stated they witnessed evidence of the relationship. A supervisor of the employee informed the committee the employee's workplace behavior was impacted, thereby contributing to a distracting work environment. This violated the company's policy against creating a negative work environment. Brian Dunn was pressured to resign and was provided with a $6.6 million separation package.

Even more distressing for Best Buy came the decision of founder Richard Schulze to step down from his position as Chairman after it was revealed he had knowledge of the relationship. This, along with continual declining sales, may have contributed to the decision. The inappropriate relationship between the CEO and the employee became known by other employees and was reported to Schulze by an executive. Schulze approached CEO Brian Dunn about the incident, but he did not inform the board of the matter. The audit committee found Schulze acted inappropriately by not making other board members aware of the incident. They also stated Schulze did not act according to good governance practices. In confronting the CEO, Schulze divulged the name of the executive who reported the inappropriate relationship. The company believed this could have potentially created a situation of employee retaliation.

The actions of Best Buy's board show that all employees, no matter how high they may be in the organization, must demonstrate appropriate conduct. It also made clear the company makes corporate conduct and employee protection top priorities. However, the scandal still has the potential to damage Best Buy's reputation. The company must continue to reinforce ethical standards and ensure employees and board members understand company expectations for corporate governance.

CONCLUSION

Best Buy occupies an important link in the supply chain of electronic products that reach consumers. In many ways, Best Buy influences producers and suppliers to become more sustainable by encouraging products that reduce waste and are more efficient to use. Its recent initiatives to help consumers recycle old electronic devices provide an incredible opportunity to deal with a significant sustainability problem. Its approach to social responsibility identifies key stakeholders and incorporates important ethical and social concerns in its overall business strategy.

Best Buy's continuous efforts toward sustainability and ethical practices earned it a place among *Ethisphere*'s 2012 list of Most Ethical Companies for four years in a row. While the company will have to overcome obstacles to retain its competitive edge and rebuild its reputation after a corporate governance scandal, Best Buy is a shining example of how a company can use social responsibility, a strong stakeholder orientation, and the enforcement of company values and policies to make a difference. In order to retain this image, Best Buy should continue to maintain high ethical standards regarding its customers, employees, vendors, and the environment.

QUESTIONS

1. Why do you think Best Buy has been able to gain competitive advantages in the retail electronics market while also driving many initiatives to support sustainability?

2. Do you think the resources Best Buy dedicates to help consumers recycle their old electronic devices represent a good investment for Best Buy?
3. How do Best Buy's social responsibility efforts impact key stakeholders such as employees, shareholders, consumers, and suppliers?

SOURCES

Best Buy, *2009 Corporate Social Responsibility (CSR) Report*, http://www.bby.com/cmn/files/BBY_CSR_2009.pdf (accessed March 10, 2011); Zac Bissonenette, "Best Buy Workers Make a Serious Commitment to Diversity," *BloggingStocks*, April 6, 2008, http://www.bloggingstocks.com/2008/04/06/best-buy-workers-makes-a-serious-commitment-to-diversity (accessed July 19, 2013); Best Buy, "Recycle," http://www.bestbuy.com/recycling (accessed February 21, 2013); Best Buy, "From Coast to Coast, More People Recycle Their Electronics With Best Buy Than Any Other Retailer," April 14, 2011, http://www.bby.com/phoenix.zhtml?c=244152&p=irol-newsArticle&ID=1550976&highlight= (accessed July 8, 2011); Best Buy, "Energy Star," http://www.bestbuy.com/site/null/null/pcmcat149900050024.c?id=pcmcat149900050024 (accessed July 19, 2013); Best Buy, "Greener Together," http://www.bestbuy.com/site/null/Best+Buy/pcmcat149900050023.c?id=pcmcat149900050023&DCMP=rdr0001424 (accessed August 13, 2010); Best Buy, "Our Foundation," http://communications.bestbuy.com/communityrelations/our_foundation.asp (accessed August 13, 2010); Best Buy, "Trade-in," http://www.bestbuytradein.com/bb/ (accessed August 16, 2010); Best Buy Career Center, "Culture," http://69.12.100/CareerCenter/Culture.asp (accessed May 9, 2008); Best Buy Career Center, "Diversity," http://69.12.100/CareerCenter/Diversity.asp (accessed May 9, 2008); Environmental Protection Agency, "Best Buy Ramps up Recycling," March 31, 2010, http://www.epa.gov/waste/inforesources/news/2009news/03-bestbuy.htm (accessed August 18, 2010); Environmental Protection Agency, "SmartWay Transport," http://www.epa.gov/smartway/transport/index.htm (accessed July 19, 2013); Ethisphere Institute, "2010's 100 Most Influential People in Business Ethics," *Ethisphere*, http://ethisphere.com/2010s-100-most-influential-people-in-business-ethics/#28(accessed March 10, 2011); *Forbes*, "America's Most Reputable Companies," April 20, 2010, http://www.forbes.com/2010/04/19/kraft-microsoft-google-pepsi-disney-kellogg-cmo-network-america-least-reputable-companies_3.html (accessed July 19, 2013); Marc Gunther, "Best Buy Wants Your Electronic Junk," *Fortune*, December 1, 2009; Anita Hamilton, "Why Circuit City Busted While Best Buy Boomed," *Time*, November 11, 2008, http://www.time.com/time/business/article/0,8599,1858079,00.html (accessed July 19, 2013); Phillip Inman, "Best Buy to battle DSG International with launch of UK stores," *guardian.co.uk*, March 28, 2010, http://www.guardian.co.uk/business/2010/mar/28/best-buy-electronics-retailer-launch-uk-stores (accessed July 19, 2013); John Jannarone, "Forecast for Best Buy: Worst Is Yet to Come," *The Wall Street Journal*, March 4, 2011, C8; Calum MacLeod, "Best Buy, Home Depot find China market a tough sell," *USA Today*, February 23, 2011, 5B; Naureen S. Malik, Naureen, "Best Buy to Sell Ford's Electric Charging Stations," *The Wall Street Journal*, January 7, 2011, http://blogs.wsj.com/digits/2011/01/07/best-buy-to-sell-fords-electric-charging-stations/ (accessed July 19, 2013); Minnesota Council of Foundations, "Responses by Minnesota Foundations & Corporation to 2008 Disasters," http://www.mcf.org/disasters/international08.htm (accessed August 13, 2010); Scott Morris, "Best Buy Joins BICEP Coalition Advocating for Strong Climate and Energy Policy in the United States," Best Buy Sustainability, February 4, 2010. http://www.bby.com/2010/02/24/best-buy-joins-bicep-coalition-advocating-for-strong-climate-and-energy-policy-in-the-united-states/ (accessed August 18, 2010); MSN Money, "Best BUY Company Inc—Company Financial Statements (BBY): Annual Income Statement," http://moneycentral.msn.com/investor/invsub/results/statemnt.aspx?symbol=BBY (accessed March 10, 2011); Jason Norman, "Best Buy to Stock E-Bikes in Select Stores," *Bicycle Retailer*, April 29, 2009, http://www.bicycleretailer.com/news/newsDetail/2648.html (accessed July 19, 2013); *TwinCities Business*, "2003 Minnesota Business Hall of Fame," July 2003, http://www.tcbmag.com/halloffame/minnesotabusinesshalloffame/104304p1.aspx (accessed August 12, 2010); Wolf @ Best Buy, "Haiti Earthquake Relief Efforts," http://www.wolfatbestbuy.com/news/haiti-earthquake-relief-efforts (accessed August 13, 2010); Ethisphere Institute, "Ethisphere Institute

Unveils World's Most Ethical Companies," March 15, 2012, http://ethisphere.com/ethisphere-institute-unveils-2012-worlds-most-ethical-companies/ (accessed February 20, 2013); Laurie Burkitt and Bob Davis, "Chasing China's Shoppers," *The Wall Street Journal*, June 14, 2012, http://online.wsj.com/article/SB10001424052702303444204577460693377819420.html (accessed February 20, 2013); Best Buy, "About Best Buy," http://pr.bby.com/about-best-buy/ (accessed February 20, 2013); Working Mother Media, "2012 Best Companies for Hourly Workers," http://www.workingmother.com/best-companies/best-buy-1 (accessed February 20, 2013); Carmine Gallo, "Best Buy Invests 50, 000 Hours of Employee Training to Attract Windows 8 Customers," *Forbes*, January 9, 2012, http://www.forbes.com/sites/carminegallo/2012/11/09/best-buy-invests-50000-hours-of-employee-training-to-attract-windows-8-customers/ (accessed February 20, 2013); Best Buy, "Recycle," http://www.bestbuy.com/site/Global-Promotions/Recycling-Electronics/pcmcat149900050025.c?id=pcmcat149900050025 (accessed February 20, 2013); "Best Buy donates kits for connectivity," *New Frontier*, http://www.newfrontierpublications.org/nf/best-buy-donates-kits-for-connectivity/ (accessed February 20, 2013); RobecoSam, "Dow Jones Sustainability Indexes," http://www.sustainability-index.com/dow-jones-sustainability-indexes/index.jsp (accessed February 20, 2013); Best Buy, "Best Buy Begins Implementation of New Energy Management System for All U.S. Stores," October 27, 2011, http://pr.bby.com/best-buy-begins-implementation-of-new-energy-management-system-for-all-u-s-stores/ (accessed February 21, 2013); Best Buy, Co., Inc., *Reuters*, Best Buy eliminates $10 fee for its U.S. in-store electronics recycling program, http://www.reuters.com/article/2011/11/10/idUS253022+10-Nov-2011+HUG20111110 (accessed February 21, 2013); *Energy Star® Products: 20 Years of Helping America Save Energy Save Money and Protect the Environment*, http://www.energystar.gov/ia/products/downloads/ES_Anniv_Book_030712_508compliant_v2.pdf (accessed February 21, 2013); American Customer Satisfaction Index, "Benchmarks by Industry," 2013, http://www.theacsi.org/index.php?option=com_content&view=article&id=149&catid=14&Itemid=214&c=Best+Buy+&i=Specialty+Retail+Stores (accessed February 27, 2013); Bill Hudson, "Best Buy among 'Most Hated' for Customer Satisfaction," *CBS Minnesota*, January 18, 2012, http://minnesota.cbslocal.com/2012/01/18/best-buy-among-most-hated-for-customer-satisfaction/ (accessed February 27, 2013); Best Buy, "Focus: Technology Access for Teens," http://pr.bby.com/community-relations/focus-technology-access-for-teens/ (accessed February 27, 2013); Chris Burritt, "Best Buy's Schulze to Step Down as Chairman after Probe," *Bloomberg*, May 14, 2012, http://www.bloomberg.com/news/2012-05-14/best-buy-s-schulze-to-step-down-as-chairman-after-probe.html (accessed February 27, 2013); Ethisphere Institute, "2011 100 Most Influential People in Business Ethics," *Ethisphere*, http://ethisphere.com/2011s-100-most-influential-people-in-business-ethics/ (accessed February 27, 2013); Erin Carlyle, "Best Buy CEO Brian Dunn Gets $6.6 Million Severance Package After 'Friendship' with 29-Year-Old Employee," *Forbes*, May 14, 2012, http://www.forbes.com/sites/erincarlyle/2012/05/14/best-buy-ceo-brian-dunn-gets-6-6-million-severance-package-after-friendship-with-29-year-old-employee/ (accessed February 27, 2013); Miguel Bustillo, "Best Buy CEO Quits in Probe," *The Wall Street Journal*, April 11, 2012, B1; Justin Lahart and Liam Denning, "No Best Option for Best Buy's Shareholders," *The Wall Street Journal*, December 15-16, 2012, B16; Ann Zimmerman, "Best Buy To Close 15 Stores In Canada," *The Wall Street Journal*, February 1, 2013, B3; Laurie Burkitt and Bob Davis, "Chasing China's Shoppers," *The Wall Street Journal*, June 15, 2012, B1; Best Buy, "Find a Lower Price and We'll Match It," http://www.bestbuy.com/site/Global/Low-Price-Guarantee/pcmcat290300050002.c?id=pcmcat290300050002 (accessed March 7, 2013).

INDEX

A

AA1000 framework, 250–251
ABC News investigation, 578–579
Abess, Leonard, 260
Abusive or intimidating behavior, 66–69, 85
Accommodating style of conflict management, 320
Accountability
for board members, 46
defined, 43–44
formal system of, 30
greater demands for, 46–47
Accountants, as gatekeepers, 105–106
Accounting fraud, 77
Acid rain, 350–351
AcountAbility, 250, 262
Act deontologists. 162
Active bribery, 70
Act utilitarians, 160
Acumen, William, 513
Adelphia, 104
Adkins, Craig, 477
Administration law, 97
Advanced Micro Devices (AMD), 292
Adverse opinion, 263
Advertising
to children, 84

deception, social responsibility and, 39–40
false, 78
Google AdWords, 462
greenwashing, 368–369
Mattel, 596
mobile applications for, 293
National Advertising Division, BBB and, 572–581
Advertising Self-Regulatory Council (ASRC), 580
Affiliative leader, 330
Affirmative action programs, 74
Africa, 391
African Agricultural Technology Foundation, 391
African Wildlife Foundation, 399
Age, ethical decision making and, 132
Age Discrimination in Employment Act, 74
Agent Orange, 383
Agricultural Appropriations Bill, of 2013, 385
Agriculture, sustainable, 399
AIG, 77

Air pollution, 350
All-China Federation of Trade Unions (ACFTU), 410
Allianze SE, Germany, 585
Almonte, Linda, 193
Alternative energy sources
about, 363–364
biofuels, 365
geothermal power, 364
hydropower, 365–366
nuclear power, 365
solar power, 364
wind power, 364
Alyeska Pipeline Service Co., 425–426
Amazon.com, 19, 293, 476, 478
Zappos acquisition, 481–482
Amazon rain forests, 355
American Antitrust Institute, 389
American Association for the Advancement of Science, 386
American Association of Retired People (AARP), 32
American Bar Association (ABA), 227
American Customer Satisfaction Index, 410

American Economic Association, 136
American Institute of Certified Public Accountants, 331
American Institute of CPAs Professional Code of Conduct, 219
American International Group, 297
American Lung Association, 361
American Red Cross, 503
Americans with Disabilities Act, 103
America's Greenest Companies, 531
Analyst independence, 108
Andersen, Arthur E., 311
Android, 97, 461–462, 466
Answer, ethical risks, 334
Antitrust activity, global business, 292
Antitrust Improvements Act, 1976, 100 (table)
Anti-trust laws, 99
Google and, 464–465
Apathetic culture, corporate culture, 186–188